Philosophy of Mind

A Guide and Anthology

John Heil

Philosophy of Mind

OXFORD
UNIVERSITY PRESS

Great Clarendon Street, Oxford OX2 6DP

Oxford University Press is a department of the University of Oxford. It furthers the University's objective of excellence in research, scholarship, and education by publishing worldwide in

Oxford New York

Auckland Cape Town Dar es Salaam Hong Kong Karachi Kuala Lumpur Madrid Melbourne Mexico City Nairobi New Delhi Shanghai Taipei Toronto

With offices in

Argentina Austria Brazil Chile Czech Republic France Greece Guatemala Hungary Italy Japan Poland Portugal Singapore South Korea Switzerland Thailand Turkey Ukraine Vietnam

Published in the United States by Oxford University Press Inc., New York

First published in 2004

British Library Cataloguing in Publication Data

Data available

Library of Congress Cataloging in Publication Data

Data available

ISBN 978–0–19–925383–8

10 9 8 7 6 5

Typeset in Adobe Minion by RefineCatch Limited, Bungay, Suffolk

Printed in Great Britain by Antony Rowe Ltd, Chippenham, Wiltshire

Preface

As you hold this volume in your hand, you may be asking yourself whether the world really needs another anthology in the philosophy of mind. That will be for you to judge. In my experience, not all anthologies are created equal. This one includes, in addition to an extensive compilation of readings on particular topics, a dozen introductory essays designed expressly to encourage you, the reader, to think more deeply and critically about material you might be encountering for the first time. My hope is that these introductions, combined with the particular choice of readings, will yield a whole that is more than just a mereological sum of its parts.

The creation of a volume like this involves endless difficult choices. Inevitably, philosophers intending to use the book in courses in the philosophy of mind will be disappointed that I have omitted favorite pieces, even favorite topics. My original plan called for twice as many selections and half again as many topics. This would have resulted in a peerless, but gargantuan anthology. In scaling back, I have tried to include readings with broad appeal across the discipline. I have included as well a handful of readings less commonly anthologized. Some of these are variations on familiar themes. In other cases, as for instance in the case of selections in Part XII, readings concern topics that have tended to be forgotten or ignored in anthologies and in university courses on the philosophy of mind. The idea is to loosen the grip of convention. I will consider the book a success if it encourages a few philosophers teaching such courses to look a little more critically at the subject. To that end, introductory essays are designed, not merely to provide background information for readers, but, wherever possible, to nudge discussion of particular topics out of the usual ruts.

Many philosophers will take issue with matters addressed in the introductions. This is exactly the reaction sought. I would like those philosophers using the book in university courses to come clean—ontologically—with their students. With that in mind, I have taken care to avoid esoteric terminology and technical maneuvering of the sort that can make the philosophy of mind seem baffling to non-philosophers. We philosophers have grown far too dependent on such devices, forgetting that they can obscure as well as illuminate. I believe that the really difficult issues in philosophy can, and should, be discussed in a way that could be appreciated by any intelligent reader.

I am grateful to Davidson College and Monash University for their support of this project. I have been influenced by more people than I could possibly name here. The volume would never have seen the light of day without Harrison Hagan Heil's clarity of mind, good sense, and unwavering support and the support of Lilian, Gus, and Mark Heil. Ruth Anderson, my editor, has been saintly in her encouragement and patience. My colleague, David Robb, exercised a constant steadying influence on my occasionally unruly thoughts about the nature of mental states and properties. The influence of another David, David Armstrong, in forcing me to see that what seems obvious is not always obvious pervades everything I have written here. My thoughts on ontology in general and, in particular, the ontology of mind, have been most profoundly influenced by C. B. Martin, the philosopher's philosopher.

John Heil

Contents

Part VIII **Subjectivity and self-knowledge**

Part IX **Consciousness**

Part X Reduction

Part XI Is the mind–body problem insoluble?

Part XII Challenges to contemporary materialism

Notes on contributors

Aristotle (384–322 BC) was a student of Plato, tutor of Alexander, and, with Plato, the most influential Western philosopher. What we regard as Aristotle's writings are, in fact, transcriptions made by students. These include works on ethics, metaphysics, logic, psychology, and natural history.

D. M. Armstrong, emeritus professor of philosophy at the University of Sydney, is author of many papers and books on metaphysics and epistemology, most recently *The Mind–Body Problem: An Opinionated Introduction* and *A World of States of Affairs.*

Lynne Rudder Baker is professor of philosophy at the University of Massachusetts. She has published widely in metaphysics and philosophy of mind, most recently *Explaining Attitudes: A Practical Approach to the Mind* and *Persons and Bodies: A Constitution View.*

Ned Block is professor of philosophy and psychology at New York University and author of books and articles in philosophy of mind, metaphysics, and foundations of cognitive science. He is currently completing a book on consciousness.

Margaret Boden, professor of philosophy and psychology at the University of Sussex and Dean of the University's School of Cognitive and Computing Sciences, works in philosophy of mind, philosophy of psychology, and artificial intelligence: philosophy of mind as encompassed in cognitive science. Her most recent book is an edited volume, *The Philosophy of Artificial Life.*

Tyler Burge, professor of philosophy at UCLA, has published influential papers in philosophy of language and logic, philosophy of psychology and mind, epistemology, and the history of philosophy. Recently published, *Reflections and Replies: Essays on the Philosophy of Tyler Burge*, includes, in addition to discussion of his work, his detailed replies.

David J. Chalmers is professor of philosophy and research professor of cognitive science at the University of Arizona. He works in philosophy of mind, philosophy of language, metaphysics, epistemology, and cognitive science. His book, *The Conscious Mind: In Search of a Fundamental Theory*, has been widely discussed inside and outside philosophy.

Paul Churchland, professor of philosophy at the University of California, San Diego, works in philosophy of science, the philosophy of mind, artificial intelligence and cognitive neurobiology, epistemology, and perception. His recent books include *The Engine of Reason, The Seat of the Soul: A Philosophical Journey into the Brain.*

Donald Davidson is Willis S. and Marion Slusser Professor of Philosophy at the University of California, Berkeley, and author of many papers in philosophy of language, philosophy of mind, epistemology, and metaphysics, most recently 'Objectivity and Practical Reason', 'Truth Rehabilitated', and 'Perils and Pleasures of Interpretation'.

Daniel Dennett is University Professor and Austin B. Fletcher Professor of Philosophy at Tufts University. He has published extensively in philosophy of mind, cognitive science, and philosophy of biology. Recent books include *Freedom Evolves* and *Brainchildren: Essays on Designing Minds.*

René Descartes (1596–1650), French mathematician and philosopher, is generally accounted the father of modern philosophy. Best known for *Meditations on First Philosophy*, which applies standards of mathematical proof to philosophical argument, and for his development of analytical geometry which allowed geometrical truths to be represented algebraically.

Jerry Fodor is State of New Jersey Professor of Philosophy at Rutgers University. He is author of fifteen books, most recently, *Hume Variations*, and countless articles in the philosophy of mind and the philosophy of language.

Peter Forrest, professor of philosophy at the University of New England, has written on topics in philosophy of science and philosophy of religion. His most recent book is *God without the Supernatural.*

John Foster is a fellow of Brasenose College, Oxford. His publications, which have centered on topics in philosophy of language and metaphysics, include *The Case for Idealism, Ayer, The Immaterial Self: A Defence of the Cartesian Dualist Conception of the Mind*, and, most recently, *The Nature of Perception.*

Valerie Gray Hardcastle, professor of philosophy at Virginia Tech, writes on topics in philosophy of mind and cognitive science. Her recent publications include 'Constructing Selves', and an edited volume, *Where Biology Meets Psychology.*

Gilbert Harman, professor of philosophy, Princeton University, is author of articles and books on topics in ethics, epistemology, metaphysics, language, and mind. His most recent books: *Reasoning, Meaning, and Mind* and *Explaining Value and Other Essays in Moral Philosophy.*

Jane Heal is professor of philosophy and President of St John's College, Cambridge. Her work has centered on Wittgenstein and on issues in the philosophy of language and the philosophy of mind. Recent publications include 'Understanding Our Minds from the Inside' and 'Co-Cognition and Off-Line Simulation'.

John Heil is Paul B. Freeland Professor of Philosophy at Davidson College and professor of philosophy at Monash University. He has published articles and books on topics in metaphysics, philosophy of mind, and epistemology, most recently, *From an Ontological Point of View.*

Carl Hempel (1905–97) emigrated to the United States in 1937 from Germany where he was prominent in logical positivist circles that included Rudolph Carnap, Max Planck, Friedrich Schlick and mathematician David Hilbert. His philosophical interests centered on topics in the philosophy of science, including confirmation theory and concept formation in science.

R. J. Hirst (1920–99) was professor of logic and metaphysics at the University of Glasgow. He was an early exponent of the Identity Theory of mind and author of articles and books on perception and the philosophy of mind, including *The Problems of Perception.*

Frank Jackson is professor of philosophy in the Philosophy Program, Research School of Social Sciences at the Australian National University. He has published widely on topics in philosophical logic, cognitive science, epistemology and metaphysics, and meta-ethics. His most recent book is *Mind, Method, and Conditionals.*

Jaegwon Kim, William and Herbert Perry Faunce Professor of Philosophy at Brown University, has published extensively in philosophy of mind, metaphysics, action theory, and the philosophy of science. His most recent books include *Mind in a Physical World: An Essay on the Mind–Body Problem and Mental Causation*, and, an edited volume, *Supervenience.*

Hilary Kornblith is professor of philosophy at the University of Massachusetts. His interests lie in epistemology and philosophy of mind. His recent publications include *Epistemology: Internalism and Externalism*, an edited volume, and *Knowledge and its Place in Nature.*

Saul Kripke is emeritus professor of philosophy at Princeton University. He is author of *Naming and Necessity, Wittgenstein on Rules and Private Language*, and articles on topics in logic, metaphysics, and philosophy of language.

Janet Levin is associate professor of philosophy at the University of Southern California. She is author of articles in epistemology, philosophy of mind, and philosophy of psychology.

Joseph Levine, professor of philosophy at Ohio State University, specializes in philosophy of mind and philosophy of psychology. His much-cited paper, 'Materialism and Qualia: The Explanatory Gap', is reprinted here. He has recently published *Purple Haze: The Puzzle of Consciousness.*

David Lewis (1941–2001) was Class of 1943 University Professor of Philosophy at Princeton University. He is best known for his work in metaphysics, philosophy of language, philosophy of science, logic, and ethics. Many of his most influential papers are collected in two volumes of *Philosophical Papers*, and in *Papers in Metaphysics and Epistemology.*

John Locke (1632–1704), Oxford-educated English philosopher, produced influential works on metaphysics and epistemology (*Essay Concerning Human Understanding*) and on political theory (*Two Treatises on Government* and *Letter on Toleration*).

E. J. Lowe is professor of philosophy at the University of Durham. He has published widely in metaphysics, philosophy of mind, logic, and the history of philosophy. Recent books are *The Possibility of Metaphysics, An Introduction to the Philosophy of Mind*, and *A Survey of Metaphysics.*

Colin McGinn is professor of philosophy at Rutgers University. He is author of more than a dozen books, including a novel, *The Space Trap*, and articles on topics ranging from metaphysics and philosophy of mind to ethics and aesthetics. His most recent book is *Philosophy from the Inside.*

Michael McKinsey, professor of philosophy, Wayne State University, works in philosophy of language, philosophy of mind, metaphysics, epistemology, and ethics. Recent papers include 'The Semantic Basis of Externalism' and 'Forms of Externalism and Privileged Access'.

Thomas Nagel, professor of philosophy and law, University Professor, and Fiorello La Guardia Professor of Law at New York University, has published widely in political philosophy, ethics, epistemology, and philosophy of mind. His most recent book is *The Last Word*.

Derk Pereboom, professor of philosophy at the University of Vermont, has written extensively on topics in metaphysics, philosophy of mind, history of modern philosophy, and philosophy of religion. His recent book, *Living Without Free Will*, attempts to reconcile determinism and moral agency.

Plato (429–347 BC) was a giant in the Western philosophical tradition whose views, unlike his student, Aristotle's, invoke transcendent entities and causes to explain observable phenomena. His works survive chiefly in dialogue form, the best known being the *Republic*.

Hilary Putnam, emeritus professor of philosophy, Harvard University, has written extensively on the philosophy of mathematics, philosophy of natural science, philosophy of language, and the philosophy of mind. His most recent books are *Renewing Philosophy* and *Pragmatism*.

John R. Searle, Mills Professor of the Philosophy of Mind and Language at the University of California, Berkeley, is author of a dozen books, including, most recently, *Rationality in Action*, on topics in the philosophy of mind and the philosophy of language.

J. J. C. Smart is an Honorary Research Fellow in the Department of Philosophy at Monash University. He has written extensively on topics in philosophy of science, metaphysics, and ethics. His most recent book is *Our Place in the Universe*.

Stephen P. Stich is professor of philosophy at Rutgers University. He is author of numerous articles and books on topics in the philosophy of mind and cognitive science, including *Deconstructing the Mind*, and, with Shaun Nichols, *Mindreading*.

Alan M. Turing (1912–54) was an English mathematician, famous for his role in deciphering German codes during the Second World War, whose work in mathematical logic led to an abstract characterization of finite computability: what a finite, but idealized, agent could compute. This is what we now know as the 'Turing Machine'.

Michael Tye is professor of philosophy at the University of Texas. He has published widely on philosophy of mind, foundations of cognitive science, and metaphysics. His most recent book is *Consciousness, Color, and Content*.

Eugene Wigner (1902–95), Hungarian-born physicist educated in Germany, emigrated to the United States where he held the Thomas D. Jones Chair of Mathematical Physics at Princeton University. He was awarded a Nobel Prize in 1963 for ground-breaking work in quantum physics. The essay reproduced here appears in *Symmetries and Reflections: Scientific Essays of Eugene P. Wigner*.

General introduction

Why philosophy of mind?

PHILOSOPHY of mind lies close to the heart of the philosophical enterprise. Every great philosopher, from Plato onwards, has contributed to the debate over the nature of minds and their relation to the world around us. For philosophers interested in knowledge, the mind is a natural starting place: we cannot hope to understand knowledge and its limits without understanding knowers. Philosophers focusing on moral responsibility require a conception of agency. Agency can be comprehended, however, only by comprehending agents who deliberate and subsequently act on reasons. Philosophers bent on describing the deep metaphysical structure of the world must in some fashion accommodate the existence of mental reality.

So: philosophy of mind is pivotal. Once the cheering dies down, however, someone is bound to ask: what *is* the philosophy of mind? What could a philosopher possibly tell us about the mind that we could not learn—and learn more surely—from the testimony of psychologists, neuroscientists, and physicians? A philosopher, seated comfortably in an armchair (or, more likely, in a swivel chair in front of a computer monitor), relies on reason to arrive at truths. Surely we have outgrown the practice of speculating about the nature of anything using reason alone. Empirical science is our preferred route to truths about ourselves and our world. If the nature of the mind, or consciousness, or intelligence puzzles us, why should anyone waste precious time reading philosophy? Shouldn't we instead be looking to the laboratory and to properly scientific treatises? In listening to philosophers, don't we sidetrack serious work on the mind and, as always where philosophers are involved, risk muddying the water?

These are the kinds of question many readers might have on paging through a book like this for the first time. Scientists solve problems and answer questions. Philosophers, in contrast, debate endlessly and leave us, not with definitive answers, but with more questions and, all too often, a sense of hopelessness. Philosophers talk the talk; scientists walk the walk. Philosophers might pretend to help those with a certain kind of temperament lead happier, more reflective lives. But we long ago learned to turn to science and mathematics when truth is at issue. Undergraduate students (and their parents!) ask rhetorically, what can you *do* with philosophy?

Despite its reputation as the most abstract of pursuits, and despite the best efforts of professional philosophers, it would be a mistake to see philosophy as cut off from other human endeavors. Philosophy did not fall from the sky. Philosophical questions arise naturally and inescapably as we negotiate the world: philosophy is forced on us. We can turn our backs on philosophical problems, or hand them over to others, but we cannot make them go away. This is true for ordinary moral deliberations about the good and bad, right and wrong; it is true for considerations bearing on what we can know or justifiably believe; and it is true for our attempts to understand ourselves and our world.

We human beings are intelligent, conscious creatures sharing a planet with other species, the members of which behave in ways manifesting the presence of intelligence and consciousness in varying degrees. Astronomers tell us there is an excellent chance we are not alone in the universe; intelligence and consciousness could be widespread. But what *are* intelligence and consciousness? What relation do intelligence and consciousness bear to physical bodies that apparently house them? One possibility is that intelligence and consciousness are identifiable with states, processes, or structures in the brain. This possibility, which no doubt occurred to you long before you picked up this book, encourages the idea that knowledge of the mind can be had by engaging in neuroscience.

This could well be so. Whether it is so or not, you should be aware that the first move—locating intelligence and consciousness in the brain—is a substantive philosophical move. That might surprise you. After all, the move is made routinely and without a second thought by researchers who would certainly balk at being labeled philosophers. But this is just my point: philosophers are not the only philosophers. Professional, card-carrying philosophers differ from non-philosophers only in that the ones with philosophy degrees philosophize self-consciously.

Why should the thesis that intelligence and consciousness are located in the brain be regarded as philosophical? The thesis is philosophical because anyone advancing it begins with a conception of intelligence and consciousness—a conception of the mind—that allows for the identification of states of mind with neurological states and goings-on. We are bound to ask whether this is the right conception of mind, the right way to think about minds and their nature. One mildly depressing possibility is that the identification of minds with brains is nothing more than an updated version of the old idea that each living thing is equipped with a soul. The soul enters the body at birth, exits at death. The soul serves as a self-moving source of motion in animals, animating otherwise inert matter. We can bring the soul up to date by identifying souls with brains.

What is not at all obvious is that this is the most satisfactory way of thinking about the mind. Perhaps—a thought entertained by Plato and endorsed by Aristotle (see Chapters 1 and 2)—minds are not *things* at all. My describing you as possessing a mind might not be like my describing you as having a heart, or a liver, or a spleen. Rather, describing you as having a mind might be a matter of acknowledging that you behave in intelligent, adaptive ways. Undoubtedly your brain would figure prominently in any account of the mechanisms responsible for your behavior. But to identify your mind with your brain would be like identifying your pulse with your heart: a kind of 'category mistake' (Ryle 1949). (A child who thinks 'team spirit' is an additional, possibly ghostly, member of an athletic team makes a category mistake.)

This may give you a feel for the kinds of issue that arise in the philosophy of mind. A decision as to whether minds are things—'substances' in the traditional jargon of philosophers—or processes, or functions, or something else entirely is a philosophical decision, one requiring attention to the concepts we use in describing ourselves and our place in the world. This is what philosophers are trained to do.

You might remain skeptical. Pause and reflect for a moment, however, on the phenomenon of consciousness. Imagine that you are lounging on a beach gazing across the water at a tropical sunset. Think of experiences you might be having under those circumstances; in particular, think of the distinctive pleasurable qualities of those experiences. Now, consider the idea that these experiences are located in your brain. Why is it that, when your brain is examined, even in minute detail, nothing like these experiences is observed? Indeed, it is hard to see how anyone could think that anything with your experience's distinctive 'Technicolor' qualities could possibly be identified with the 'soggy grey matter' that makes up your brain (see Chapter 45). Neural anatomists could, it seems, observe goings-on in your brain and *correlate* these with conscious goings-on. But talk of correlation suggests that your experiences, although perhaps in some way dependent on, 'supported by', or 'grounded in' those neurological goings-on, are nevertheless distinct from their neurological bases. Why so? If *A* and *B* are identical, if *A is B*, every property of *A* must be a property of *B* and vice-versa. Your experiences, however, appear to have properties that your brain could not possibly have. If that is the case, your experiences could not be identified with goings-on in your brain.

You might be suspicious of this line of reasoning. Indeed, I encourage you to be suspicious of it. In venting those suspicions, however, you are engaging in more philosophy. No amount of experimentation, no accumulation of empirical data will, by itself, assist you in this endeavor: you are stuck with a philosophical problem that requires a philosophical solution. It is just possible that this book could help you through what could otherwise strike you as a hopeless morass.

Philosophy and science

The discussion thus far could leave you with the misleading impression that philosophy operates independently of science. On the contrary; philosophical issues bubble up in the midst of everyday and scientific pursuits. It would be a mistake of a fundamental sort to imagine that we could turn over philosophical questions to philosopher—specialists who, after consulting one another, would issue definitive philosophical answers. Philosophy is concerned in part with the concepts we use to describe and explain our world. But concepts, unlike epitaphs, are not etched in stone. Concepts in use are alive. Concepts bend, stretch, evolve, and adapt in concert with empirical discovery. Possibilities that one generation finds literally unthinkable can, in successive generations, come to be regarded as commonplaces. The plasticity of concepts is not always easy to appreciate in retrospect: current ways of thinking are bound to seem altogether natural and inevitable.

Insisting on a role for philosophy of mind in the broader quest for understanding our place in the world, is not to insist on a division of labor. The philosophy of mind and empirical work on the mind can and should press ahead together. We might, in that case, reasonably expect certain issues in the philosophy of mind eventually to reach resolution. This is not because the issues will have been answered empirically, but because we will have made peace with empirical findings; issues that once puzzled will no longer puzzle.

At one time heat was a deeply mysterious phenomenon. Heat seems to 'flow' from one body to another, suggesting fluidity. One widely influential theory accounted for heat by assuming that 'phlogiston', an invisible, volatile fluid, intermingled with the particles of material bodies. Heating a body was thought to drive out this fluid. Phlogiston provided a satisfying explanation of certain phenomena, but it introduced new puzzles as well. If heating a body drives out phlogiston, you would expect bodies, when heated, to lose weight. In fact, heated bodies *gain* weight. To save the theory, chemists ascribed to phlogiston the property of having 'negative weight'.

By replacing the conception of heat as a fluid with a conception that allowed heat to be identified with motions of particles, scientists provided a new way of understanding the phenomenon that made it seem less puzzling. Motions of particles could be propagated from one collection of particles to another, not by means of a transfer of fluid, but via impulse: what is transferred is not a *stuff*, but motion. An explanation of weight gain in heated bodies required a more radical revision of previous conceptions of matter, indeed it required the genius of Lavoisier (1743–94) and the 'chemical revolution'.

Perhaps our understanding of the mind will proceed in this way. Advances on the empirical front coupled with timely conceptual shifts could result in our resolving what David Chalmers (Chapter 35) calls 'the hard problem' of consciousness or bridging what Joseph Levine (Chapter 44) describes as the 'explanatory gap' between mental and physical properties and processes. We have no guarantee, of course, that this will happen. Some philosophers are pessimistic, doubting that we could ever be in a position to understand the mind and its relation to the material world (see, for instance, Chapters 29, 43, 45). We could, they suspect, be constitutionally incapable of understanding ourselves.

Setting aside this disturbing thought, a loose end remains. I have said that progress in our understanding of the mind requires that philosophers and empirical scientists work together. If that is so, why are none of the readings included here reports of laboratory experiments or scientific results?

A central aim of this anthology is to bring you up to speed philosophically. This includes an effort to provide readings that illuminate the history of philosophical attempts to understand the mind. As you work through these readings, you will be aware of shifts in scientific focus. The world of Plato and Aristotle is very different from the world of Descartes and Locke; and the world of Descartes and Locke differs dramatically from the world of J. J. C. Smart and Donald Davidson. All these philosophers' writings incorporate—implicitly, and, at times, explicitly—the scientific perspective of the era in which they happen to be writing. The hope is that, by digesting essays included here, you will be in a much better position to evaluate claims about minds and their characteristics advanced by neuroscientists and psychologists as well as by philosophers. Philosophy is not so much a subject matter as an activity. This book will have served its purpose if, after working through it, your ability to engage in this activity is enlarged and fine-tuned.

Plan of attack

The book is divided into twelve parts, each of which includes readings on particular topics in the philosophy of mind. Parts begin with an introductory essay designed to prepare you to come to grips with individual readings. These introductory discussions are not meant to replace readings they accompany. I have not attempted to summarize arguments or explicate authors' views. Rather, I have tried to provide readers who might be new to the subject with enough background to appreciate what those authors have to say and why they say it. More advanced readers may find the introductions useful in another way. I am not the first to suggest that particular issues in the philosophy of mind might strike us as deeply puzzling only because of assumptions we philosophers embrace on seemingly unrelated matters. These apparently innocent assumptions inevitably constrict the space of possible solutions to what we see as problems. Under the circumstances, it is important to have these on the table. This is what the Australians call 'ontological candor'. By being ontologically candid, we can put ourselves in a position to evaluate assumptions and assess their influence. Unacknowledged, they work like repressed materials, influencing our thought in potentially self-defeating ways.

Let me be clear on this. I have tried, in these introductions, to illuminate contexts in which topics tend to be discussed in what could be called 'mainstream philosophy of mind'. But I have included as well a smattering of moderately subversive suggestions designed to smoke out some of the unspoken assumptions philosophers are inclined to make when they take up issues in the philosophy of mind. If you are a student using this book in a course in the philosophy of mind, you should have your instructor explain what is subversive about these suggestions and why they might be off base. In that way, everyone's cards will be on the table.

In addition to these introductions, and in keeping with the 'Guide and Anthology' format, parts conclude with suggestions for further reading and 'study questions' posed to help you organize your thoughts about the readings. If you are a student working your way through the book, consider using study questions as hooks on which to hang thoughts about the readings. If you go into the readings with an eye to answering those questions, you may be in a position to distinguish central issues from those at the periphery. This, in my experience, is the most difficult hurdle for non-specialists encountering discussions of unfamiliar topics for the first time.

Lists of suggested readings are intended for anyone interested in learning more about particular topics cropping up and for students writing papers on particular topics. I have kept these lists short on the theory that exhaustive lists are both more intimidating and less useful for the general reader. In an effort to avoid distracting footnotes and references, I have deployed an author/date citation scheme.

A final word before turning you loose. I have tried to group readings topically. In cases in which one reading falls under more than one topic, I have placed it earlier or later by taking into account demands it might make on the reader. In general, more challenging readings appear in later sections. Still, you may find it occasionally helpful to go through some readings out of the order in which they appear. Introductions to particular parts will provide some guidance here. Individual introductions are meant to be self-standing: no introduction presupposes any other, so parts can, at least in principle, be taken up in any order. This is not to say that my ordering of parts is wholly whimsical. Wherever possible, I have tried to organize parts in such a way that a reader can see how theses develop, undergo criticism, and yield successor theses.

Now it is your turn. Have at it!

Reference

Ryle, G. (1949), *The Concept of Mind*, London: Hutchinson.

Suggested readings

If you shake a tree, books of readings in the philosophy of mind will fall to the ground. Notable contemporary collections include: Block et al. (1997), which focuses on consciousness and includes a comprehensive introduction by Güven Güzeldere; Crumley (2000), Chalmers (2002) (the apparent successor to Rosenthal 1991), Metzinger (1995), and O'Connor and Robb (2003), all of which are devoted to readings in what could be called mainstream philosophy of mind. Heil and Mele (1993) collects previous unpublished papers on the problem of mental causation, the venerable mind–body problem. Lycan (1999), Christensen and Turner (1993) and Geirsson and Losonsky (1996) include, in addition to the usual widely reprinted readings in philosophy of mind, selections on topics belonging to the empirical wing of philosophy of mind, cognitive science (see below for a listing of titles in cognitive science). Brown (1974), O'Hear (1998), and Warner and Szubka (1994) assemble papers by major players in the philosophy of mind. In the O'Hear volume, these are devoted to a range of topics; Warner and Szubka confine their collection to the mind–body problem. Gillett and Loewer (2001), Moser and Trout (1995), and Robinson (1993) contain papers discussing the prospects for materialism (or, 'physicalism') generally. Beakley and Ludlow (1992) adroitly blends diverse selections from Aristotle to present-day sources in both philosophy and psychology topically organized. Vesey (1964) and, more recently, Kolak (1997), Morton (1997), and Robinson (1999) provide more conventional, but no less useful, historical collections of readings in the philosophy of mind.

A number of older collections include papers that have subsequently become classics. Among the most notable are Block (1980), Chappell (1962), Hampshire (1966), Morick (1970), and Rosenthal (1987). These volumes are particularly valuable because they contain selections by good philosophers which, because they have failed to make the cut in newer anthologies, are little read today.

Guttenplan's (1994) *Companion* and Stich and Warfield's (2003) *Guide* to the philosophy of mind are topically organized and can be helpful on particular subjects. Gregory's (1987) *Companion to the Mind*, has broader ambitions, and would be more useful as a quick reference on topics in psychology and the neurosciences. The eight-volume *Encyclopedia of Philosophy* (Edwards 1967) provides matchless coverage of historical figures and topics through the mid-twentieth century. The newer *Routledge Encyclopedia of Philosophy* (Craig 1998), is more up to date, and, although useful, somewhat less successful than its predecessor.

The on-line *Stanford Encyclopedia of Philosophy* (Zalta 2002), a self-described 'dynamic reference work', provides solid entries on historical figures and on topics central in current debates about the mind and its nature. Another reliable on-line resource is Nani's (2001) *Field Guide to the Philosophy of Mind*. Eliasmith's (2003) *Dictionary of Philosophy of Mind* is a good place to look for definitions of technical terms, and David Chalmers's *Contemporary Philosophy of Mind: An Annotated Bibliography* (Chalmers 2001) is an excellent bibliographic resource, especially for recent work. A word of warning: you should use materials found on the Internet judiciously. Internet resources vary widely in reliability.

Texts written as introductions to the philosophy of mind are almost as plentiful as anthologies. Some of these are intended as general introductions: Crane (2001), Graham (1993), Jacquette (1994) (a successor in the venerable 'Foundations of Philosophy' series to

Shaffer 1968), Kim (1996), Lowe (2000), and Lyons (2001). My own, *Philosophy of Mind: A Contemporary Introduction* (Heil 1998), falls into this category. Armstrong (1999), Kenny (1989), McGinn (1982), and Rey (1997) promote distinctive views of the mind in the course of introducing the topic. Of course, no philosopher can write a text on any subject without at least implicitly taking sides. Objectivity results from readers' capacity to 'triangulate' discussions expressing contrasting points of view.

Braddon-Mitchell and Jackson (1996) and Churchland (1988) are harder to classify. Both include lucid discussions of topics in the philosophy of mind and in cognitive science. Although this volume largely ignores issues in cognitive science, some readers may find their interests moving in empirical directions. For those readers, any of the following anthologies could prove illuminating: Bechtel et al. (1998), Brãnquinho (2001), Cummins and Cummins (2000), Garfield (1990), Gleitman et al. (1995), Smith and Osherson (1995), and Posner (1989). Beakley and Ludlow (1992), mentioned above, could be seen as exposing the historical roots of cognitive science. Gardner (1985) provides a non-technical account of the 'cognitive revolution', and the birth of cognitive science in the twentieth century. As in the philosophy of mind, cognitive science introductions are widely available. Among the best are Clark (1997) and (2001), Fetzer (1991), Flanagan (1984), Harnish (2001), and Harré (2002), and Thagard (1996). The on-line *MIT Encyclopedia of Cognitive Sciences* (Wilson and Keil 1999) is a useful and reliable Internet resource.

Philosophical journals are brimming with articles on topics in the philosophy of mind. *Analysis, Australasian Journal of Philosophy, Journal of Philosophy, Mind, Philosophical Quarterly, Philosophical Review, Philosophical Studies, Philosophy and Phenomenological Research* come to mind here. *Mind and Language, Philosophical Psychology,* and *Brain and Mind* afford more specialized interdisciplinary niches.

The author-meets-critics format of *Behavioral and Brain Sciences* provides a comfortable vehicle for discussions of topics that straddle the philosophy/cognitive science divide. These are often easier for a general reader to understand because they are written expressly for a broader audience than are most papers in philosophy intended for publication in philosophical journals. As you will discover in reading some of the more recent papers in this volume, philosophy nowadays is often—probably too often—written in a style that can seem impenetrable to ordinary readers. Technical terms and vocabularies proliferate. These can lend an air of precision to discussions that might otherwise seem vapid.

All of this makes it challenging for amateurs to make progress without professional assistance—which is, as you will have recognized, the aim of this *Guide*. You should peruse the journals and the suggested readings, but do not be put off by technical discussions and philosophical flights of fancy. Move ahead with a clear sense of reality and demand the same from those who are paid to discuss the topic.

Anthologies in the philosophy of mind

Beakley, B., and P. Ludlow, eds. (1992), *The Philosophy of Mind: Classical Problems, Contemporary Issues.* Cambridge, MA: MIT Press.

Block, N. J., ed. (1980), *Readings in Philosophy of Psychology*, vol. i. Cambridge, MA: Harvard University Press.

Block, N. J., O. Flanagan, and G. Güzeldere, eds. (1997), *The Nature of Consciousness: Philosophical Debates.* Cambridge, MA: MIT Press.

Brown, S., ed. (1974), *Philosophy of Psychology.* London: Macmillan.

Chalmers, D. J., ed. (2002), *Philosophy of Mind: Classical and Contemporary Readings.* New York: Oxford University Press.

Chappell, V. C., ed. (1962), *The Philosophy of Mind.* Englewood Cliffs, NJ: Prentice-Hall.

Christensen, S. M., and D. R. Turner, eds. (1993), *Folk Psychology and the Philosophy of Mind.* Hillsdale, NJ: Lawrence Erlbaum Associates.

Crumley, J. S., ed. (2000), *Problems in Mind: Readings in Contemporary Philosophy of Mind.* Mountain View, CA: Mayfield Publishing Co.

Geirsson, H., and M. Losonsky, eds. (1996), *Readings in Mind and Language.* Oxford: Blackwell Publishers.

Gillett, C., and B. Loewer, eds. (2001), *Physicalism and Its Discontents.* Cambridge: Cambridge University Press.

Hampshire, S., ed. (1966), *Philosophy of Mind.* New York: Harper & Row.

Heil, J., and A. R. Mele, eds. (1993), *Mental Causation.* Oxford: Clarendon Press.

Lycan, W. G., ed. (1999), *Mind and Cognition: An Anthology*, 2d ed. Oxford: Blackwell Publishers.

Kolak, D., ed. (1997), *From Plato to Wittgenstein: The Historical Foundations of Mind.* Belmont, CA: Wadsworth Publishing Co.

Metzinger, T., ed. (1995), *Conscious Experience.* Paderborn: Schöningh.

Morick, H., ed. (1970), *Introduction to the Philosophy of Mind: Readings from Descartes to Strawson.* Glenview, IL: Scott Foresman.

Morton, P., ed. (1997), *Historical Introduction to the Philosophy of Mind: Readings with Commentary.* Peterborough: Broadview Press.

Moser, P. K., and J. D. Trout, eds. (1995), *Contemporary Materialism: A Reader.* London: Routledge.

O'Connor, T., and D. Robb, eds. (2003), *Philosophy of Mind: Contemporary Readings.* London: Routledge.

O'Hear, A., ed. (1998), *Current Issues in Philosophy of Mind.* Cambridge: Cambridge University Press.

Robinson, D. N., ed. (1999), *The Mind.* New York: Oxford University Press.

Robinson, H., ed. (1993), *Objections to Physicalism.* Oxford: Clarendon Press.

Rosenthal, D. M., ed. (1987), *Materialism and the Mind—Body Problem.* Indianapolis, IN: Hackett Publishing Co.

Rosenthal, D. M., ed. (1991), *The Nature of Mind.* New York: Oxford University Press.

Vesey, G. N. A. (1964), *Body and Mind: Readings in Philosophy.* London: George Allen & Unwin.

Warner, R., and T. Szubka, eds. (1994), *The Mind–Body Problem: A Guide to the Current Debate.* Oxford: Blackwell Publishers.

Introductions to philosophy of mind

Armstrong, D. M. (1999), *The Mind—Body Problem: An Opinionated Introduction.* Boulder, CO: Westview Press.

Braddon-Mitchell, D., and F. Jackson. (1996) *The Philosophy of Mind and Cognition.* Oxford: Blackwell Publishers.

Churchland, P. M. (1988), *Matter and Consciousness: A Contemporary Introduction to the Philosophy of Mind*, rev. ed. Cambridge, MA: MIT Press.

Crane, T. (2001), *Elements of Mind: An Introduction to the Philosophy of Mind.* Oxford: Oxford University Press.

Graham, G. (1993), *Philosophy of Mind: An Introduction.* Cambridge: Blackwell Publishers.

Heil, J. (1998), *Philosophy of Mind: A Contemporary Introduction.* London: Routledge.

Jacquette, D. (1994), *Philosophy of Mind.* Englewood Cliffs, NJ: Prentice Hall.

Kenny, A. (1989), *The Metaphysics of Mind.* Oxford: Oxford University Press.

Kim, J. (1996), *Philosophy of Mind.* Boulder, CO: Westview Press.

Lowe, E. J. (2000), *An Introduction to the Philosophy of Mind.* Cambridge: Cambridge University Press.

Lyons, W. E. (2001), *Matters of the Mind.* London: Routledge.

McGinn, C. (1982), *The Character of Mind.* Oxford: Oxford University Press.

Rey, G. (1997), *Philosophy of Mind: A Contentiously Classical Approach.* Oxford: Blackwell Publishers.

Shaffer, J. A. (1968), *Philosophy of Mind.* Englewood Cliffs, NJ: Prentice-Hall.

Smith, P., and O. R. Jones (1986), *The Philosophy of Mind: An Introduction.* Cambridge: Cambridge University Press.

Encyclopedias, guides, and companions

Craig, E., ed. (1998), *Routledge Encyclopedia of Philosophy* (10 vols.). London: Routledge.

Edwards, P. (1967), *The Encyclopedia of Philosophy* (8 vols.). New York: Macmillan.

Gregory, R. L., ed. (1987), *The Oxford Companion to the Mind.* Oxford: Oxford University Press.

Guttenplan, S. D., ed. (1994), *A Companion to the Philosophy of Mind.* Oxford: Blackwell Publishers.

Stich, S. P., and T. A. Warfield, eds. (2003), *The Blackwell Guide to Philosophy of Mind.* Oxford: Blackwell Publishing.

Cognitive science anthologies

Bechtel, W., G. Graham, and D. A. Balota, eds. (1998), *A Companion to Cognitive Science.* Oxford: Blackwell Publishers.

Brãnquinho, J., ed. (2001), *The Foundations of Cognitive Science.* Oxford: Oxford University Press.

Cummins, D. D. and R. Cummins, eds. (2000), *Minds, Brains, and Computers: The Foundations of Cognitive Science: An Anthology.* Oxford: Blackwell Publishers.

Garfield, J. L., ed. (1990), *Foundations of Cognitive Science: The Essential Readings.* New York: Paragon House.

Gleitman, L. R., M. Liberman, and D. N. Osherson, eds. (1995), *An Invitation to Cognitive Science*, 2nd ed., vol. i: *Language.* Cambridge: MIT Press.

Smith, E. E., and D. N. Osherson, eds. (1995), *An Invitation to Cognitive Science*, 2nd ed., vol. iii: *Thinking.* Cambridge: MIT Press.

Osherson, D. N., and S. N. Kosslyn, eds. (1995), *An Invitation to Cognitive Science*, 2nd ed., vol. ii: *Visual Cognition.* Cambridge: MIT Press.

Posner, M. I., ed. (1989), *Foundations of Cognitive Science.* Cambridge, MA: MIT Press.

Cognitive science

Clark, A. (1997), *Being There: Putting Brain, Body, and World Together Again.* Cambridge: MIT Press.

Clark, A. (2001), *Mindware: An Introduction to Cognitive Science.* New York: Oxford University Press.

Fetzer, J. H. (1991), *Philosophy and Cognitive Science.* New York: Paragon House.

Flanagan, O. J. (1984), *The Science of the Mind.* Cambridge, MA: MIT Press.

Gardner, H. (1985), *The Mind's New Science: A History of the Cognitive Revolution.* New York: Basic Books.

Harnish, R. M. (2001), *Minds, Brains, Computers: An Historical Introduction to the Foundations of Cognitive Science.* Oxford: Blackwell Publishers.

Harré, R. (2002), *Cognitive Science: A Philosophical Introduction.* London: Sage Publications.

Thagard, P. (1996), *Mind: Introduction to Cognitive Science.* Cambridge, MA: MIT Press.

On-line resources

Chalmers, D. J., ed. (2001), *Contemporary Philosophy of Mind: An Annotated Bibliography* <http://www.u.arizona.edu/~chalmers/biblio.html> Tucson, AZ: University of Arizona.

Eliasmith, C., ed. (2003), *Dictionary of Philosophy of Mind* <http://www.artsci.wustl.edu/~philos/MindDict/main.html> St. Louis: Washington University.

Nani, M., ed. (2001), *A Field Guide to the Philosophy of Mind.* <http://host.uniroma3.it/progetti/kant/field/> Rome: University of Rome 3.

Wilson, R. A., and F. Keil, eds. (1999), *MIT Encyclopedia of Cognitive Sciences* <http://cognet.mit.edu/MITECS/login.html> Cambridge, MA: MIT Press.

Zalta, E. N., ed. (2002), *The Stanford Encyclopedia of Philosophy.* <http://plato.stanford.edu/> Stanford, CA: Metaphysics Research Lab, Center for the Study of Language and Information.

Part I

Historical background

Introduction

CONCEPTIONS of the mind current at the onset of the twenty-first century did not spring to life fully-formed like Venus on the half-shell. Philosophers and non-philosophers—ordinary folk, poets, scientists—have pondered the mind and its place in the natural world for thousands of years. In philosophy it can be instructive to look back at the origins of concepts we apply unselfconsciously today. This is particularly so when those concepts seem to lead us into difficulties and puzzles. If nothing else, the exercise brings to the fore components of the contemporary view that we have come to take for granted. What we take for granted can easily escape notice. Out of sight, it can lead us down paths we might otherwise hope to avoid. Wittgenstein's metaphor of a conjurer is apt: 'The decisive movement in the conjuring trick has been made, and it was the very one we thought quite innocent' (Wittgenstein 1953: §308).

This part comprises selections from four seminal figures in the history of philosophy: Plato, Aristotle, Descartes, and Locke. Many other philosophers deserve to be added to this list. The aim, however, is not to provide exhaustive historical coverage (for something along those lines, see Vesey 1964; Morton 1997). Rather, readings have been selected because they show philosophers from very different backgrounds addressing issues that remain fresh today.

The discovery of this kind of historical continuity can lead to cynicism about philosophy. In stark contrast to scientists, philosophers seem never to make progress; after more than two millennia, the philosophical community still has not been able to arrive at settled conclusions on contentious points. Skepticism of this familiar sort masks a deeper similarity between philosophy and the sciences. The idea of progress implies the idea of a well-defined goal against which progress is measured. It is easy to doubt that such goals exist—even in the hard sciences. A better model is that provided by evolution: theories evolve, not toward a goal, but away from an origin (see Kuhn 1962: chap. 13). New theories, in philosophy and in the sciences, replace discredited theories, and in that respect represent progress. Admittedly, philosophers can repeat mistakes of earlier generations in a way not reflected in the work of physicists and chemists. Philosophers can replace a discredited theory with a theory earlier discredited, but subsequently forgotten. (The same is apparently true, though perhaps to a lesser extent, in the social sciences.) This is possible because philosophy is largely unconstrained by empirical findings. Philosophy touches experience, but only around the edges.

In the end, philosophy requires no apology. This should become clear as you read the four philosophers represented in this part. Two of these philosophers, Plato and Aristotle, practiced in a period and in a Greek culture in which all things seemed possible. The others, Descartes and Locke, writing in the seventeenth century, are far more encumbered by the weight of 2,000 years of philosophical tradition. Their capacity to break with this tradition and, in the process, to revolutionize our ways of looking at the world and our place in it, is one of the remarkable episodes in the history of European thought. The power of all four of these philosophers' ideas is not always easy for us to appreciate because we are, to a considerable extent, standing on their shoulders.

Plato

Plato (*c*.427–347BC) resided in Athens during a period of political change. Socrates, the hero of most of Plato's dialogues, was prosecuted on a charge of irreligion and put to death by a newly constituted democratic government. The *Phaedo*, from which our readings have been excerpted, recounts Socrates' last hours, and culminates in Socrates' drinking from a cup of hemlock and quietly dying.

One of Plato's preoccupations in the *Phaedo* is that of ascertaining the nature of the soul. Any account of the soul has practical implications for Socrates, whose own death is imminent. In the course of Socrates' discussion with Simmias and Cebes two possibilities are touched on. First, the soul might be a perfectly simple entity that forms a brief alliance with a body during an individual's lifetime. This picture is complicated by the introduction of the possibility of transmigration: the souls of persons too wedded to unseemly bodily pleasures would, on death, migrate to the bodies of beasts. Presumably the souls of those whose bodily appetites had been in harmony with the demands of reason would avoid such a fate. A second, very different conception of the soul compares the soul to a lyre's tuning. The soul, on such a view, is not the body, but a way the body is organized (a lyre's tuning is not the lyre, or a part of the lyre, but a propitious arrangement of the lyre's parts).

These conceptions of the nature of the soul differ dramatically. One treats the soul as an entity, perhaps an immaterial entity, the other regards souls, not as entities material or otherwise, but as *ways*: ways entities are organized. The distinction here is a distinction between *substances*, on the one hand, particular entities, and, on the other hand, *ways* substances are or could be. The distinction is grounded in our commonsensical world view. You distinguish between the apple and the apple's shape, size, color, and heft. There is, on the one hand, the apple, a substance, and, on the other hand, the apple's properties, ways the apple is. One question, a very important question, is whether minds are substances or properties of substances.

I have used the word 'mind' here, but Plato and Aristotle speak of 'souls'. One question you might ask is whether 'mind' and 'soul' are synonyms, two words for the same thing, or whether minds and souls are in fact quite different. Although we nowadays use 'mind' and 'soul' more or less interchangeably, it is likely that what the Greeks meant by 'soul' is not quite what we mean by 'mind'. Talk of souls, for instance, has moral and religious overtones missing in talk of minds. It seems unlikely that these overtones could affect our approach to the topic here, however, so I shall use 'mind' and 'soul' (and, with Descartes, 'self') interchangeably.

Plato invokes the commonsense distinction between substances (bearers of properties) and properties (ways substances are), but Plato's view about these things carries us far beyond common sense. Properties, according to Plato are 'forms' or 'universals'. Universals, like numbers and other 'abstract entities', exist outside of space and time. What does exist in space and time are *instances* of universals. Thus, on the one hand there is the universal, sphericity; on the other hand, there are those innumerable *instances* of sphericity: the sphericity found in each spherical object. The sphericity of a particular billiard ball, and a particular ball bearing are distinct instances of a single universal sphericity. This is what they 'have in common'.

Plato tells us that the billiard ball and ball bearing both 'participate' in the universal sphericity. Nowadays, philosophers are more likely to describe the billiard ball and ball bearing as alike in 'instantiating' sphericity. Not all philosophers who posit universals regard them, as Plato does, as transcendent—existing independently of the spatio-temporal world (see Armstrong 1989 for a survey of the territory). These are issues that non-philosophers (and some philosophers) find altogether perplexing. For our purposes, however, it is only important to register Plato's view as lying behind Socrates' suggestion that, although during our lifetime, access to the universals is indirect (via their instances), after death, suitably purified souls are free to contemplate the universals themselves. In so doing, a soul would be in a position to understand, not merely how things are, but why they must be as they are—rather in the way a geometer could grasp why right triangles must be such that squares on their hypotenuses are sums of the squares of their remaining sides.

If you take minds to be capable of direct, intellectual apprehension of the universals, you are thinking of minds as being very different from material bodies. But if minds are very different from material bodies, how do they come to be housed in and interact with material bodies? These are vexed questions we shall encounter again in coming to grips with Descartes. Before turning to Descartes, however, we must consider the second towering figure in ancient Greek philosophy, Aristotle.

Aristotle

Aristotle (384–322BC), Plato's brilliant student, could not have been more different from his teacher. Plato grounded reality in a realm of transcendent forms or universals. For Aristotle, reality is grounded in the material world. If there are universals—properties shared by objects—these are inseparable from their concrete instances.

We must be careful here. I have said that Aristotle grounds reality in the material world, but it is far from obvious that Aristotle's conception of matter has much in common with our own conception (see Burnyeat 1992). The point illustrates one of the dangers of reading ancient texts in translation and without extensive familiarity with circumstances under which they were written.

Bracketing this worry, however, it is easy to read Aristotle as a kind of early functionalist (see Part III). Your having a mind is not a matter of your body's standing in an especially intimate relation to a conscious soul, but a matter of your body's being organized appropriately. If a model is wanted, think of Plato's (discarded) idea that your having a soul resembles a lyre's being in tune. If this is your model, there can be no mystery as to how minds and bodies are related: minds are not substances, not entities that could exist independently of bodies.

The idea that your having a mind is solely a matter of your body's having the right kind of organization appears difficult to reconcile with the idea that you might survive the death of your body in a disembodied state. As any *Star Trek* aficionado can tell you, however, what is important to survival might not be the existence of a permanent entity. When Captain Kirk is beamed to the surface of Planet Ork, the atoms making up Captain Kirk are not beamed down to the planet, then reassembled. Rather the *organization* of those atoms is transferred to a distinct swarm of atoms at hand in the region Kirk comes to occupy on Ork. (Ask yourself whether, knowing all this, you would feel comfortable having yourself transported from one place to another in the *Star Trek* mode!)

As you work through the selection included here, reflect on whether Aristotle could accept the possibility of minds migrating from body to body. And as you digest readings in subsequent sections, ask yourself whether it is plausible to read Aristotle as a proto-functionalist.

Descartes

René Descartes (1596–1650), more than any other historical figure, is responsible for the modern conception of mind. This is not so much because the Cartesian view has been widely adopted. Few philosophers of mind today would describe themselves as Cartesians. Rather, Descartes promoted a way of looking at the mind and its relation to the body that has proved widely influential, even among those who attack Descartes. It is sometimes said that the commonsense view of the mind is Cartesian. After reading what Descartes says, you will be in a position to assess the plausibility of this suggestion.

Everyone knows about Descartes's famous inference:

> 'I think, therefore I am'.

In fact, this formulation of the so-called *cogito* ('I think') inference occurs in the *Discourse on Method* and not in the *Meditations*, which is Descartes's most serious treatment of the argument. What Descartes says there is: 'I must finally conclude that the statement "I am, I exist" must be true whenever I state it or mentally consider it' (*Meditation* II). Descartes has been looking for some principle that will enable him to distinguish beliefs he is justified in holding from the rest—the sheep from the goats. His strategy could be compared to that of a chemist engaged in developing an *assay*, a test for distinguishing samples of some substance—gold, for instance—from imposters. Just as a chemist needs as a starting point a nugget of what is indisputably gold, so Descartes needs an epistemological 'nugget', some belief the truth of which is indisputable. Once he has this, he can locate the property from which its indisputability stems, and use this to develop an assay.

Consider the statement, 'I am standing', uttered while you are standing. Is this statement indisputably true? No; you could fail to be standing when you think you are; you could be *dreaming* that you are standing. (Recall Gregor Samsa, who awoke one morning to discover he was a gigantic cockroach. Perhaps *you* are a cockroach dreaming you are a human being!) Ordinary statements about your body, then, are not promising candidates for indubitability. Now, consider the statement, 'I exist'. This statement has the following interesting property: *if the statement is so much as considered or mentally entertained, it must be true*. Here is a pure 'nugget' that Descartes can use to devise an epistemological principle to screen his subsequent beliefs.

The argumentative structure of the *Meditations* is linear; the literary structure is not. Descartes does not proceed with the project of developing an assay until *Meditation* III. Instead, he turns to the question, 'What am I?' His conclusion: I am a thing—a *substance*—that thinks. You will note that Descartes means by 'thinking' something rather more inclusive than what we mean by that term. His idea is that, whatever else is true of me, it is true that I have, and exercise, a capacity for thought. He is not yet in a position to rule out the possibility that he has other features as well. Arguments on that score are set aside until *Meditation* VI.

Although Descartes's famous 'method of doubt' (the method he deploys in his search for a pure 'nugget') leads him to doubt many things, he never doubts that the world—*any* non-empty world—must include substances. Substances are property bearers. If there is thinking, then, there must be a thinker: a substance doing the thinking. His thinking thus necessitates the existence of at least one thinking substance. Later in *Meditation* II Descartes turns to the existence of material substances. In perception, we are apparently (but only apparently: we could be dreaming!) aware of material bodies. Descartes's example is a piece of wax. On reflection, however, you can see that you are never really perceptually aware of a material substance, only its properties. Your appreciation that those properties belong (or must belong) to a substance is a product, not of your perceptual faculties, but of your 'understanding'.

In *Meditation* VI, Descartes offers an argument to the conclusion that the self's nature is exhausted by its mental properties, properties falling under the rubric of 'thought'. Selves, he contends, bear an intimate relation to particular bodies, but selves are thinking substances; material bodies are extended (that is, spatial) substances. Implicit in the argument is the idea that no thinking substance is (or could be) extended, and no extended substance thinks (or could think). This is *substance dualism*: the world includes two kinds of substance, each with its own distinctive and exhaustive 'attribute'. Mental substances think; material substances are extended. What we might regard as ordinary properties of mental substances—being in pain, thinking of Vienna—are modes of thought; properties of material substances—being square, being red, being in motion—are modes of extension, ways of being extended.

This gives us a crisp distinction between selves and bodies, but it leads to a monumental difficulty for Descartes. If selves and bodies have nothing in common, how is causal interaction between selves and bodies possible? When you bark your shin (a physical event involving your body), you feel pain (a mental event involving your mind). This suggests that physical causes can have mental effects. When you decide to raise your left arm (a mental event), your arm goes up (a physical event). This suggests that mental causes can have physical effects. But how is this supposed to work? How could non-extended selves interact causally with extended substances?

One subtle problem here revolves around the idea, accepted by Descartes's contemporaries, that the material world is 'causally closed'. Whatever goes on in the material world is traceable to interactions among the ultimate material constituents: the particles— 'atoms' or 'corpuscles'—taken to make up material bodies. These interactions are governed by exceptionless laws. But if mental events, which stand 'outside' the material world, could have material effects, then the material world would not be causally closed: closure is violated.

Descartes's solution to this problem was to allow that, while mental events could not accelerate particles, they could alter particles' direction of travel. Descartes's material world is a purely *kinematic* world, a world in which motion, not velocity, is preserved, a world describable without resorting to concepts of force or energy. Newton's laws of motion subsequently replaced this kinematic conception of material bodies with a dynamic conception. Changes in the direction of moving particles—changes in particles' velocity—require force no less than changes in their acceleration.

These matters aside, in reading Descartes's critics and Descartes's responses to those critics you should ask yourself what issues are identified by those critics, and whether they pose insurmountable problems for a substance dualist like Descartes. Whatever the merits of Descartes's arguments, perhaps you can think of ways of getting the view to work. Some theorists, for instance, have thought that the kinds of probabilistic causal relation at the heart of quantum physics leave 'wiggle room' for mind–body interaction (see Chapter 50).

One final point. Descartes speaks of selves, not minds. It is easy to assume that by 'self' Descartes means what we today mean by 'mind'. Perhaps that is right. Note, however, that, if 'I' refers to the self, we find it natural to say both 'I have a body' and 'I have a mind'. You can say 'I *am* a mind', but this statement has the flavor of a philosophical pronouncement. In reading Descartes, you might reflect on this point. Are we entitled to equate the Cartesian self with the mind? (For further thoughts on this topic, see Chapter 49.)

Locke

Although it is difficult to avoid the impression that, in reading Descartes, we are reading someone who belongs to a very different era, the writings of John Locke (1632–1704) concern issues very much alive today in the philosophy of mind. (This difference can be disguised by the fact that we read Descartes in translation and Locke in his original seventeenth-century English.) Many issues occupying authors of pieces in the sections that follow surface in Locke.

Like Descartes, Locke accepts the thesis that the world is made up of substances distributed in space. Substances are various ways. These ways are properties or 'modes' of substances. Ordinary material objects are organized collections of indivisible material particles. The *real* material substances are the particles; what we ordinarily call substances (tables, trees, planets) are in fact *modes*: ways substances are organized. The particles, what Locke and his contemporaries called 'corpuscles', have no parts; a particle is not made up of anything. This does not mean that particles lack structure, however. A particle is a substance—what Locke calls a *substratum*—with properties. A substratum is a substance considered as a bearer of properties; its properties, Locke's modes, are ways the substance is (see Martin 1980; Lowe 2000).

Descartes distinguishes mental substances from material substances by reference to generic attributes of each. A mental substance thinks; a material substance is extended. All mental modes—all properties of mental substances—are modes of thought, ways of thinking; material modes—properties of material substances—are ways of being extended. No thinking substance is extended, no extended substance thinks. Locke rejects this last idea. In his *Letters to Stillingfleet* (the Bishop of Worchester), Locke allows that there is no reason to think that an extended substance could not think, or that a thinking substance be extended. If a mental substance (or 'spirit') is one that thinks and a material substance is one that is extended, mental substances could turn out to be extended. A substance is mental (is a 'spirit') insofar as it possesses mental properties; a substance is material insofar as it possesses material properties. Possibly, Locke suggests, mental substances are material substances!

Descartes conceives of thought and extension as excluding one another in something like the way an object's being round excludes its being square, and its being square excludes its being round. Locke's point is that there is nothing in our ideas of extension and thought that would rule out an extended object's thinking or a thinking object's being extended. Locke puts this in terms of properties being 'superadded' to objects by God. This is Locke's way of saying that, although there is no reason to think that a material body could not have mental properties *in addition to* its material properties, it is impossible to see how mental properties could be *reduced to* material properties. Imagine arranging four matchsticks in the shape of the square. You can see how the property, being square, could be reduced to properties of the matchsticks plus their arrangement. But we are in no position to see how, by arranging the particles in a particular way, God could have created a conscious, thinking being: it looks as though there are the particles, their arrangement, *plus* consciousness and thought. If this is so, then mental properties are not reducible to material properties.

The broader purpose of Locke's *Letters to Stillingfleet* is a defense of Locke's conception of substrata, what he calls 'substance in general'. The topic was one concerning which Locke was understandably tetchy (Lowe 2000). His empiricist principles obliged him to ground concepts in observation. But we seem never to observe substrata, only their properties. (You can see the point if you set out to produce an exhaustive description of some object; your description will mention only the object's properties and relations it bears to other objects.) This makes substrata look deeply mysterious: entities that bear properties but which themselves possess no properties at all! But what sense can be made of an entity that exists without being *any way at all*?

One alternative is to reject substrata and to conceive of objects as 'bundles' of properties. This, apparently, was the view endorsed by Locke's influential successor, David Hume (1711–76). Another option is to deny that substrata lack properties. Suppose that a billiard ball is a substance. (We have seen that this is not something Locke would endorse—the billiard ball is an arrangement of substances—but it will do for purposes of illustration.) The billiard ball is spherical, hard, white, and it has a particular mass. You can consider the billiard ball's properties, and you can consider the billiard ball as a property-bearer, a substratum. This substratum is not lacking in properties. On the contrary, it is spherical, hard, white, and has a particular mass. Substrata possess no properties *other than* or *in addition to* those we are happy to ascribe to the substances.

Now, however, we are faced with a second worry. What distinguishes a mental substance—a 'spirit'—from a material substance? Is the distinction just a distinction in properties? A mental substance is an object possessing mental properties; a material substance is an object possessing material properties. And God: is God just an object possessing various divine properties? But if spirits, material bodies, and God differ only in their properties, then there is no reason to think that a substance possessing mental properties could not possess as well material properties (or, for that matter divine properties!), and this, it might be thought detracts from the standing of spirits, mental substances.

These are issues Locke addresses in his *Letters*, arguing—as was prudent at the time—that his view is consistent with religious practice. As you read Locke, ask yourself how Locke's position differs from or complements those advanced by other authors in this part. The hope is that, whatever conception of the mind you might eventually come to accept, reading—and taking seriously—Plato, Aristotle, Descartes, and Locke will deepen your understanding of the available options.

References

Armstrong, D. M. (1989), *Universals: An Opinionated Introduction*, Boulder, CO: Westview Press.

Burnyeat, M. F. (1992), 'Is an Aristotelian Philosophy of Mind Still Credible?' In Nussbaum and Rorty 1992: 15–26.

Kuhn, T. S. (1962), *The Structure of Scientific Revolutions*. Chicago: University of Chicago Press.

Lowe, E. J. (2000), 'Locke, Martin, and Substance', *Philosophical Quarterly* 50: 499–514.

Martin, C. B. (1980), 'Substance Substantiated', *Australasian Journal of Philosophy* 58: 3–10.

Morton, P., ed. (1997), *Historical Introduction to the Philosophy of Mind: Readings with Commentary*. Peterborough: Broadview Press.

Nussbaum, M. C., and A. O. Rorty, eds. (1992), *Essays on Aristotle's* De Anima. Oxford: Clarendon Press.

Vesey, G. N. A. (1964), *Body and Mind: Readings in Philosophy*. London: George Allen & Unwin.

Wittgenstein, L. (1953/1968), *Philosophical Investigations*, trans. G. E. M. Anscombe. Oxford: Basil Blackwell.

Chapter 1

Souls and bodies

Plato

'WELL then,' said Socrates, 'mustn't we ask ourselves something like this: What kind of thing is liable to undergo this fate—namely, dispersal—and for what kind of thing should we fear lest it undergo it? And what kind of thing is not liable to it? And next, mustn't we further ask to which of these two kinds soul belongs, and then feel either confidence or fear for our own soul accordingly?'

'That's true.'

'Then is it true that what has been put together and is naturally composite is liable to undergo this, to break up at the point at which it was put together; whereas if there be anything incomposite, it alone is liable, if anything is, to escape this?'

'That's what I think,' said Cebes.

'Well now, aren't the things that are constant and unvarying most likely to be the incomposite, whereas things that vary and are never constant are likely to be composite?'

'I think so.'

'Then let's go back to those entities to which we turned in our earlier argument. Is the Being itself, whose being we give an account of in asking and answering questions, unvarying and constant, or does it vary? Does the equal itself, the beautiful itself, *what each thing is* itself, that which *is*, ever admit of any change whatever? Or does *what each of them is*, being uniform alone by itself, remain unvarying and constant, and never admit of any kind of alteration in any way or respect whatever?'

'It must be unvarying and constant, Socrates,' said Cebes.

'But what about the many beautiful things, such as men or horses or cloaks or anything else at all of that kind? Or equals, or all things that bear the same name as those objects? Are they constant, or are they just the opposite of those others, and practically never constant at all, either in relation to themselves or to one another?'

'That is their condition,' said Cebes; 'they are never unvarying.'

'Now these things you could actually touch and see and sense with the other senses, couldn't you, whereas those that are constant you could lay hold of only by reasoning of the intellect; aren't such things, rather, invisible and not seen?'

'What you say is perfectly true.'

Plato, edited extract from *Phaedo*, trans. David Gallop (Oxford: Clarendon Press, 1975).

'Then would you like us to posit two kinds of beings, the one kind seen, the other invisible?'

'Let's posit them.'

'And the invisible is always constant, whereas the seen is never constant?'

'Let's posit that too.'

'Well, but we ourselves are part body and part soul, aren't we?'

'We are.'

'Then to which kind do we say that the body will be more similar and more akin?'

'That's clear to anyone: obviously to the seen.'

'And what about the soul? Is it seen or invisible?'

'It's not seen by men, at any rate, Socrates.'

'But we meant, surely, things seen and not seen with reference to human nature; or do you think we meant any other?'

'We meant human nature.'

'What do we say about soul, then? Is it seen or unseen?'

'It's not seen.'

'Then it's invisible?'

'Yes.'

'Then soul is more similar than body to the invisible, whereas body is more similar to that which is seen.'

'That must be so, Socrates.'

'Now weren't we saying a while ago that whenever the soul uses the body as a means to study anything, either by seeing or hearing or any other sense—because to use the body as a means is to study a thing through sense-perception—then it is dragged by the body towards objects that are never constant; and it wanders about itself, and is confused and dizzy, as if drunk, in virtue of contact with things of a similar kind?'

'Certainly.'

'Whereas whenever it studies alone by itself, it departs yonder towards that which is pure and always existent and immortal and unvarying, and in virtue of its kinship with it, enters always into its company, whenever it has come to be alone by itself, and whenever it may do so; then it has ceased from its wandering and, when it is about those objects, it is always constant and unvarying, because of its contact with things of a similar kind; and this condition of it is called "wisdom", is it not?'

'That's very well said and perfectly true, Socrates.'

'Once again, then, in the light of our earlier and present arguments, to which kind do you think that soul is more similar and more akin?'

'Everyone, I think, Socrates, even the slowest learner, following this line of inquiry, would agree that soul is totally and altogether more similar to what is unvarying than to what is not.'

'And what about the body?'

'That is more like the latter.'

'Now look at it this way too: when soul and body are present in the same thing, nature ordains that the one shall serve and be ruled, whereas the other shall rule and be master; here again, which do you think is similar to the divine and which to the mortal? Don't you think the divine is naturally adapted for ruling and domination, whereas the mortal is adapted for being ruled and for service?'

'I do.'

'Which kind, then, does the soul resemble?'

'Obviously, Socrates, the soul resembles the divine, and the body the mortal.'

'Consider, then, Cebes, if these are our conclusions from all that's been said: soul is most similar to what is divine, immortal, intelligible, uniform, indissoluble, unvarying, and constant in relation to itself; whereas body, in its turn, is most similar to what is human, mortal, multiform, non-intelligible, dissoluble, and never constant in relation to itself. Have we anything to say against those statements, my dear Cebes, to show that they're false?'

'We haven't.'

'Well then, that being so, isn't body liable to be quickly dissolved, whereas soul must be completely indissoluble, or something close to it?'

'Of course.'

'Now you're aware that when a man has died, the part of him that's seen, his body, which is situated in the seen world, the corpse as we call it, although liable to be dissolved and fall apart and to disintegrate, undergoes none of these things at once, but remains as it is for a fairly long time—in fact for a very considerable time, even if someone dies with his body in beautiful condition, and in the flower of youth; why, the body that is shrunken and embalmed, like those who've been embalmed in Egypt, remains almost entire for an immensely long time; and even should the body decay, some parts of it, bones and sinews and all such things, are still practically immortal; isn't that so?'

'Yes.'

'Can it be, then, that the soul, the invisible part, which goes to another place of that kind, noble, pure and invisible, to "Hades" in the true sense of the word, into the presence of the good and wise God—where, God willing, my own soul too must shortly enter—can it be that this, which we've found to be a thing of such a kind and nature, should on separation from the body at once be blown apart and perish, as most men say? Far from it, my dear Cebes and Simmias; rather, the truth is far more like this: suppose it is separated in purity, while trailing nothing of the body with it, since it had no avoidable commerce with it during life, but shunned it; suppose too that it has been gathered together alone into itself, since it always cultivated this—nothing else but the right practice of philosophy, in fact, the cultivation of dying without complaint—wouldn't this be the cultivation of death?'

'It certainly would.'

'If it is in that state, then, does it not depart to the invisible, which is similar to it, the divine and immortal and wise; and on arrival there, isn't its lot to be happy, released from its wandering and folly, its fears and wild lusts, and other ills of the human condition, and as is said of the initiated, does it not pass the rest of time in very truth with gods? Are we to say this, Cebes, or something else?'

'This, most certainly!' said Cebes.

'Whereas, I imagine, if it is separated from the body when it has been polluted and made impure, because it has always been with the body, has served and loved it, and been so bewitched by it, by its passions and pleasures, that it thinks nothing else real save what is corporeal—what can be touched and seen, drunk and eaten, or used for sexual enjoyment—yet it has been accustomed to hate and shun and tremble before what is obscure to the eyes and invisible, but intelligible and grasped by philosophy; do you think a soul in that condition will separate unsullied, and alone by itself?'

'By no means.'

'Rather, I imagine, it will have been interspersed with a corporeal element, ingrained in it by the body's company and intercourse, through constant association and much training?'

'Certainly.'

'And one must suppose, my friend, that this element is ponderous, that it is heavy and earthy and is seen; and thus encumbered, such a soul is weighed down, and dragged back into the region of the seen, through fear of the invisible and of Hades; and it roams among tombs and graves, so it is said, around which some shadowy phantoms of souls have actually been seen, such wraiths as souls of that kind afford, souls that have been released in no pure condition, but while partaking in the seen; and that is just why they are seen.'

'That's likely, Socrates.'

'It is indeed, Cebes; and they're likely to be the souls not of the good but of the wicked, that are compelled to wander about such places, paying the penalty for their former nurture, evil as it was. And they wander about until, owing to the desire of the corporeal element attendant upon them, they are once more imprisoned in a body; and they're likely to be imprisoned in whatever types of character they may have cultivated in their lifetime.'

'What types can you mean, Socrates?'

'Those who have cultivated gluttony, for example, and lechery, and drunkenness, and have taken no pains to avoid them, are likely to enter the forms of donkeys and animals of that sort. Don't you think so?'

'What you say is very likely.'

'Yes, and those who've preferred injustice, tyranny, and robbery will enter the forms of wolves and hawks and kites. Where else can we say that such souls will go?'

'Into such creatures, certainly,' said Cebes.

'And isn't the direction taken by the others as well obvious in each case, according to the affinities of their training?'

'Quite obvious, of course.'

'And aren't the happiest among these and the ones who enter the best place, those who have practised popular and social goodness, "temperance" and "justice" so-called, developed from habit and training, but devoid of philosophy and intelligence?'

'In what way are these happiest?'

'Because they're likely to go back into a race of tame and social creatures similar to their kind, bees perhaps, or wasps or ants; and to return to the human race again, and be born from those kinds as decent men.'

'That's likely.'

'But the company of gods may not rightly be joined by one who has not practised philosophy and departed in absolute purity, by any but the lover of knowledge. It's for these reasons, Simmias and Cebes, my friends, that true philosophers abstain from all bodily desires, and stand firm without surrendering to them; it's not for any fear of poverty or loss of estate, as with most men who are lovers of riches; nor again do they abstain through dread of dishonour or ill-repute attaching to wickedness, like lovers of power and prestige.'

'No, that would ill become them, Socrates,' said Cebes.

'Most certainly it would! And that, Cebes, is just why those who have any care for their own souls, and don't live fashioning the body, disregard all those people; they do not walk in the same paths as those who, in their view, don't know where they are going; but they themselves believe that their actions must not oppose philosophy, or the release and purifying rite it affords, and they are turned to follow it, in the direction in which it guides them.'

'How so, Socrates?'

'I'll tell you. Lovers of knowledge recognize that when philosophy takes their soul in hand, it has been literally bound and glued to the body, and is forced to view the things that are as if through a prison, rather than alone by itself; and that it is wallowing in utter ignorance. Now philosophy discerns the cunning of the prison, sees how it is effected through desire, so that the captive himself may co-operate most of all in his imprisonment. As I say, then, lovers of knowledge recognize that their soul is in that state when philosophy takes it in hand, gently reassures it and tries to release it, by showing that inquiry through the eyes is full of deceit, and deceitful too is inquiry through the ears and other senses; and by persuading it to withdraw from these, so far as it need not use them, and by urging it to collect and gather itself together, and to trust none other but itself, whenever, alone by itself, it thinks of any of the things that are, alone by *itself*; and not to regard as real what it observes by other means, and what varies in various things; that kind of thing is sensible and seen, whereas the object of its own vision is intelligible and invisible. It is, then, just because it believes it should not oppose this release that the soul of the true philosopher abstains from pleasures and desires and pains, so far as it can, reckoning that when one feels intense pleasure or fear, pain or desire, one incurs harm from them not merely to the extent that might be supposed—by being ill, for example, or spending money to satisfy one's desires—but one incurs the greatest and most extreme of all evils, and does not take it into account.'

'And what is that, Socrates?' said Cebes.

'It's that the soul of every man, when intensely pleased or pained at something, is forced at the same time to suppose that whatever most affects it in this way is most clear and most real, when it is not so; and such objects especially are things seen, aren't they?'

'Certainly.'

'Well, isn't it in this experience that soul is most thoroughly bound fast by body?'

'How so?'

'Because each pleasure and pain fastens it to the body with a sort of rivet, pins it there, and makes it corporeal, so that it takes for real whatever the body declares to be so. Since by sharing opinions and pleasures with the body, it is, I believe, forced to become of like character and nurture to it, and to be incapable of entering Hades in purity; but it must always exit contaminated by the body, and so quickly fall back into another body, and grow in it as if sown there, and so have no part in communion with the divine and pure and uniform.'

'What you say is perfectly true, Socrates,' said Cebes.

'It's for these reasons, then, Cebes, that those who deserve to be called "lovers of knowledge" are orderly and brave; it's not for the reasons that count with most people; or do you think it is?'

'No, indeed I don't.'

'Indeed not; but the soul of a philosophic man would reason as we've said: it would not think that while philosophy should release it, yet on being released, it should of itself surrender to pleasures and pains, to bind it to the body once again, and should perform the endless task of a Penelope working in reverse at a kind of web. Rather, securing rest from these feelings, by following reasoning and being ever within it, and by beholding what is true and divine and not the object of opinion, and being nurtured by it, it believes that it must live thus for as long as it lives, and that when it has died, it will enter that which is akin and of like nature to itself, and be rid of human ills. With that kind of nurture, surely, Simmias and Cebes, there's no danger of its fearing that on separation from the body it may be rent apart, blown away by winds, go flying off, and exist no longer anywhere at all.'

...

'Thank you,' said Simmias; 'then I'll tell you my difficulty, and Cebes here in his turn will say where he doesn't accept what's been said. I think, Socrates, as perhaps you do too, that in these matters certain knowledge is either impossible or very hard to come by in this life; but that even so, not to test what is said about them in every possible way, without leaving off till one has examined them exhaustively from every aspect, shows a very feeble spirit; on these questions one must achieve one of two things: either learn or find out how things are; or, if that's impossible, then adopt the best and least refutable of human doctrines, embarking on it as a kind of raft, and risking the dangers of the voyage through life, unless one could travel more safely and with less risk, on a securer conveyance afforded by some divine doctrine. So now I shan't scruple to put my question, since you tell me to, and then I shan't reproach myself at a later time for failing to speak my mind now. In my view, Socrates, when I examine what's been said, either alone or with Cebes here, it doesn't seem altogether adequate.'

'Maybe your view is correct, my friend,' said Socrates; 'but tell me, in what way inadequate?'

'I think in this way,' he said; 'one could surely use the same argument about the attunement of a lyre and its strings, and say that the attunement is something unseen and incorporeal and very lovely and divine in the tuned lyre, while the lyre itself and its strings are corporeal bodies and composite and earthy and akin to the mortal. Now, if someone smashed the lyre, or severed and snapped its strings, suppose it were maintained, by the same argument as yours, that the attunement must still exist and not have perished—because it would be inconceivable that when the strings had been snapped, the lyre and the strings themselves, which are of mortal nature, should still exist, and yet that the attunement, which has affinity and kinship to the divine and the immortal, should have perished—and perished before the mortal; rather, it might be said, the attunement itself must still exist somewhere, and the wood and the strings would have to rot away before anything happened to it. And in point of fact, Socrates, my own belief is that you're aware yourself that something of this sort is what we actually take the soul to be: our body is kept in tension, as it were, and held together by hot and cold, dry and wet, and the like, and our soul is a blending and attunement of these same things, when they're blended with each other in due proportion. If, then, the soul proves to be some kind of attunement, it's clear that when our body is unduly relaxed or tautened by illnesses and other troubles, then the soul must perish at once, no matter how divine it may be, just like other attunements, those in musical notes and in all the products of craftsmen; whereas the remains of each body will last for a long time, until they're burnt up or rot away. Well, consider what we shall say in answer to that argument, if anyone should claim that the soul, being a blending of the bodily elements, is the first thing to perish in what is called death.'

. . .

'Again now, look at it this way, Simmias. Do you think it befits an attunement, or any other compound, to be in any state other than that of the elements of which it's composed?'

'Certainly not.'

'Nor yet, I presume, to act, or be acted upon, in any way differently from the way they may act or be acted upon?'

He assented.

'An attunement therefore should not properly direct the things of which it's composed, but should follow them.'

He agreed.

'Then an attunement can't possibly undergo contrary movement or utter sound or be opposed in any other way to its own parts.'

'It can't possibly.'

'Again now, isn't it natural for every attunement to be an attunement just as it's been tuned?'

'I don't understand.'

'Isn't it the case that if it's been tuned more and to a greater extent, assuming that to be possible, it will be more an attunement and a greater one; whereas if less and to a smaller extent, it will be a lesser and smaller one?'

'Certainly.'

'Well, is this the case with soul—that even in the least degree, one soul is either to a greater extent and more than another, or to a smaller extent and less, just itself—namely, a soul?'

'In no way whatever.'

'Well, but is one soul said to have intelligence and goodness and to be good, while another is said to have folly and wickedness and to be bad? And are we right in saying those things?'

'Quite right.'

'Then what will any of those who maintain that soul is attunement say these things are, existing in our souls—goodness and badness? Are they, in turn, a further attunement and non-attunement? And is one soul, the good one, tuned, and does it have within itself, being an attunement, a further attunement, whereas the untuned one is just itself, and lacking a further attunement within it?'

'I couldn't say myself,' said Simmias; 'but obviously anyone maintaining the hypothesis would say something of that sort.'

'But it's already been agreed that no one soul is more or less a soul than another; and this is the admission that no one attunement is either more or to a greater extent, or less or to a smaller extent, an attunement than another. Isn't that so?'

'Certainly.'

'But that which is neither more nor less an attunement has been neither more nor less tuned; is that so?'

'It is.'

'But does that which has been neither more nor less tuned participate in attunement to a greater or to a smaller degree, or to an equal degree?'

'To an equal degree.'

'But then, given that no one soul is either more or less itself, namely a soul, than another, it hasn't been more or less tuned either?'

'That is so.'

'And this being its condition, surely it couldn't participate more either in non-attunement or in attunement?'

'Indeed not.'

'And this again being its condition, could any one soul participate to a greater extent than another in badness or goodness, assuming that badness is non-attunement, while goodness is attunement?'

'It couldn't.'

'Or rather, surely, following sound reasoning, Simmias, no soul will participate in badness, assuming it is attunement; because naturally an attunement, being completely itself, namely an attunement, could never participate in non-attunement.'

'No indeed.'

'Nor then, of course, could a soul, being completely a soul, participate in badness.'

'How could it, in view of what's already been said?'

'By this argument, then, we find that all souls of all living things will be equally good, assuming that it's the nature of souls to be equally themselves, namely souls.'

'So it seems to me, Socrates.'

'Yes, and do you approve of this assertion, or think this would happen to the argument, if the hypothesis that soul is attunement were correct?'

'Not in the least.'

'Again now, would you say that of all the things in a man it is anything but soul, especially if it's a wise one, that rules him?'

'I wouldn't.'

'Does it comply with the bodily feelings or does it oppose them? I mean, for example, when heat and thirst are in the body, by pulling the opposite way, away from drinking, and away from eating when it feels hunger; and surely in countless other ways we see the soul opposing bodily feelings, don't we?'

'We certainly do.'

'And again, didn't we agree earlier that if it is attunement, it would never utter notes opposed to the tensions, relaxations, strikings, and any other affections of its components, but would follow and never dominate them?'

'We did of course agree.'

'Well now, don't we find it, in fact, operating in just the opposite way, dominating all those alleged sources of its existence, and opposing them in almost everything throughout all of life, mastering them in all kinds of ways, sometimes disciplining more harshly and painfully with gymnastics and medicine, sometimes more mildly, now threatening and now admonishing, conversing with our appetites and passions and fears, as if with a separate thing? That, surely, is the sort of thing Homer has represented in the *Odyssey*, where he says that Odysseus:

Striking his breast, reproved his heart with the words:
"Endure, my heart; e'en worse thou didst once endure."

Do you think he'd have composed that, with the idea that the soul was attunement, the sort of thing that could be led by the feelings of the body rather than something that could lead and master them, being itself far too divine a thing to rank as attunement?'

'Goodness no, Socrates, I don't!'

'In no way at all then, my friend, do we approve of the thesis that soul is a kind of attunement; because it seems that we should agree neither with the divine poet Homer nor with ourselves.'

'That is so.'

Chapter 2
The soul as bodily organization
Aristotle

Book II

Chapter 2 412^{a}3. Enough has been said of the views about the soul which have been handed down by our predecessors. Let us start again, as it were from the beginning, and try to determine what the soul is and what would be its most comprehensive definition.

412^{a}6. Now we speak of one particular kind of existent things as substance, and under this heading we so speak of one thing *qua* matter, which in itself is not a particular, another *qua* shape and form, in virtue of which it is then spoken of as a particular, and a third *qua* the product of these two. And matter is potentiality, while form is actuality—and that in two ways, first as knowledge is, and second as contemplation is.

412^{a}11. It is bodies especially which are thought to be substances, and of these especially natural bodies; for these are sources of the rest. Of natural bodies, some have life and some do not; and it is self-nourishment, growth, and decay that we speak of as life. Hence, every natural body which partakes of life will be a substance, and substance of a composite kind.

412^{a}16. Since it is indeed a body of such a kind (for it is one having life), the soul will not be body; for the body is not something predicated of a subject, but exists rather as subject and matter. The soul must, then, be substance *qua* form of a natural body which has life potentially. Substance is actuality. The soul, therefore, will be the actuality of a body of this kind.

412^{a}22. But actuality is so spoken of in two ways, first as knowledge is and second as contemplation is. It is clear then that the soul is actuality as knowledge is; for both sleep and waking depend on the existence of soul, and waking is analogous to contemplation, and sleep to the possession but not the exercise of knowledge. In the same individual knowledge is in origin prior. Hence the soul is the first actuality of a natural body which has life potentially.

412^{a}28. Whatever has organs will be a body of this kind. Even the parts of plants are organs, although extremely simple ones, e.g. the leaf is a covering for the pod, and the pod for the fruit; while roots are analogous to the mouth, for both take in food.

Aristotle, edited extract from *De Anima*, trans. D. W. Hamlyn (Oxford: Clarendon Press, 1968), Book II, chaps 1–3.

$412^{b}4$. If then we are to speak of something common to every soul, it will be the first actuality of a natural body which has organs. Hence too we should not ask whether the soul and body are one, any more than whether the wax and the impression are one, or in general whether the matter of each thing and that of which it is the matter are one. For, while unity and being are so spoken of in many ways, that which is most properly so spoken of is the actuality.

$412^{b}10$. It has then been stated in general what the soul is; for it is substance, that corresponding to the principle of a thing. And this is 'what it is for it to be what it was' for a body of such a kind. Compare the following: if an instrument, e.g. an axe, were a natural body, then its substance would be what it is to be an axe, and this would be its soul; if this were removed it would no longer be an axe, except homonymously. But as it is it is an axe; for it is not of this kind of body that the soul is 'what it is for it to be what it was' and the principle, but of a certain kind of natural body having within itself a source of movement and rest.

$412^{b}17$. We must consider what has been said in relation to the parts of the body also. For, if the eye were an animal, sight would be its soul; for this is an eye's substance—that corresponding to its principle. The eye is matter for sight, and if this fails it is no longer an eye, except homonymously, just like an eye in stone or a painted eye. We must now apply to the whole living body that which applies to the part; for as the part is to the part, so analogously is perception as a whole to the whole perceptive body as such.

$412^{b}25$. It is not that which has lost its soul which is potentially such as to live, but that which possesses it. Seeds and fruit are potentially bodies of this kind.

$412^{b}27$. Just, then, as the cutting and the seeing, so too is the waking state actuality, while the soul is like sight and the potentiality of the instrument; the body is that which is this potentially. But just as the pupil and sight make up an eye, so in this case the soul and body make up an animal.

$413^{a}3$. That, therefore, the soul or certain parts of it, if it is divisible, cannot be separated from the body is quite clear; for in some cases the actuality is of the parts themselves. Not that anything prevents at any rate *some* parts from being separable, because of their being actualities of no body. Furthermore, it is not clear whether the soul is the actuality of the body in the way that the sailor is of the ship. Let this suffice as a rough definition and sketch about the soul.

Chapter 2 $413^{a}11$. Since it is from things which are obscure but more obvious that we arrive at that which is clear and more intelligible in respect of the principle involved, we must try again in this way to treat of the soul; for a defining statement should not only make clear the fact, as the majority of definitions do, but it should also contain and reveal the reason for it. As things are, the statements of the definitions are like conclusions. For example, what is squaring? The construction of an equilateral rectangle equal to one which is not equilateral. But such a definition is a statement of the conclusion; whereas one who says that squaring is the discovery of the mean proportional states the reason for the circumstance.

413a20. We say, then, making a beginning of our inquiry, that that which has soul is distinguished from that which has not by life. But life is so spoken of in many ways, and we say that a thing lives if but one of the following is present—intellect, perception movement, and rest in respect of place, and furthermore the movement involved in nutrition, and both decay and growth.

413a25. For this reason all plants too are thought to live; for they evidently have in them such a potentiality and first principle, through which they come to grow and decay in opposite directions. For they do not grow upwards without growing downwards, but they grow in both directions alike and in every direction—this being so of all that are constantly nourished and continue to live, as long as they are able to receive nourishment. This {form of life} can exist apart from the others, but the others cannot exist apart from it in mortal creatures. This is obvious in the case of plants; for they have no other potentiality of soul.

413b1. It is, then, because of this first principle that living things have life. But it is because of sense-perception first of all that they will be animal, for even those things which do not move or change their place, but which do have sense-perception, we speak of as animals and not merely as living.

413b4. First of all in perception all animals have touch. Just as the nutritive faculty can exist apart from touch and from all sense-perception so touch can exist apart from the other senses. We speak of as nutritive that part of the soul in which even plants share; all animals clearly have the sense of touch. The reason for each of these circumstances we shall state later.

413b11. For the present let it be enough to say only that the soul is the source of the things above mentioned and is determined by them—by the faculties of nutrition, perception, thought, and by movement. Whether each of these is a soul or a part of a soul, and if a part, whether it is such as to be distinct in definition only or also in place, are questions to which it is not hard to find answers in some cases, although others present difficulty.

413b16. For, just as in the case of plants some clearly live when divided and separated from each other, the soul in them being actually one in actuality in each plant, though potentially many, so we see this happening also in other varieties of soul in the case of insects when they are cut in two; for each of the parts has sense-perception and motion in respect of place, and if sense-perception, then also imagination and desire. For where there is sense-perception there is also both pain and pleasure, and where these, there is of necessity also wanting.

413b24. Concerning the intellect and the potentiality for contemplation the situation is not so far clear, but it seems to be a different kind of soul, and this alone can exist separately, as the everlasting can from the perishable.

413b27. But it is clear from these things that the remaining parts of the soul are not separable, as some say; although that they are different in definition is clear. For being able to perceive and being able to believe are different, since perceiving too is different from believing; and likewise with each of the other parts which have been mentioned.

413b32. Moreover, some animals have all these, others only some of them, and others again one alone, and this will furnish distinctions between animals; what is the reason for this we must consider later. Very much the same is the case with the senses; for some animals have them all, others only some, and others again one only, the most necessary one, touch.

414a4. That by means of which we live and perceive is so spoken of in two ways, as is that by means of which we know (we so speak in the one case of knowledge, in the other of soul, for by means of each of these we say we know). Similarly, we are healthy in the first place by means of health and in the second by means of a part of the body or even the whole. Now, of these knowledge and health are shape and a kind of form and principle, and as it were activity of the recipient, in the one case of that which is capable of knowing, in the other of that which is capable of health (for the activity of those things which are capable of acting appears to take place in that which is affected and disposed). Now the soul is in the primary way that by means of which we live, perceive, and think. Hence it will be a kind of principle and form, and not matter or subject.

414a14. Substance is so spoken of in three ways, as we have said, and of these cases one is form, another matter, and the third the product of the two; and of these matter is potentiality and form actuality. And since the product of the two is an ensouled thing, the body is not the actuality of soul, but the latter is the actuality of a certain kind of body.

414a19. And for this reason those have the right conception who believe that the soul does not exist without a body and yet is not itself a kind of body. For it is not a body, but something which belongs to a body, and for this reason exists in a body, and in a body of such and such a kind. Not as our predecessors supposed, when they fitted it to a body without any further determination of what body and of what kind, although it is clear that one chance thing does not receive another. In our way it happens just as reason demands. For the actuality of each thing comes naturally about in that which is already such potentially and in its appropriate matter. From all this it is clear that the soul is a kind of actuality and principle of that which has the potentiality to be such.

Chapter 3 414a29. Of the potentialities of the soul which have been mentioned, some existing things have them all, as we have said, others some of them, and certain of them only one. The potentialities which we mentioned are those for nutrition, sense-perception, desire, movement in respect of place, and thought.

414a32. Plants have the nutritive faculty only; other creatures have both this and the faculty of sense-perception. And if that of sense-perception, then that of desire also; for desire comprises wanting, passion, and wishing: all animals have at least one of the senses touch, and for that which has sense-perception there is both pleasure and pain and both the pleasant and the painful: and where there are these, there is also wanting: for this is a desire for that which is pleasant.

414b6. Furthermore, they have a sense concerned with food;[1] for touch is such a sense, for all living things are nourished by dry and moist and hot and cold things, and touch is the sense for these and only incidentally of the other objects of perception; for sound and colour and smell contribute nothing to nourishment, while flavour is one of the objects of touch. Hunger and thirst are forms of wanting, hunger is wanting the dry and hot, thirst wanting the moist and cold; and flavour is, as it were, a kind of seasoning of these. We must make clear about these matters later, but for now let us say this much, that those living things which have touch also have desire.

414b16. The situation with regard to imagination is obscure and must be considered later. Some things have in addition the faculty of movement in respect of place, and others, e.g. men and anything else which is similar or superior to man, have that of thought and intellect.

414b20. It is clear, then, that it is in the same way as with figure that there will be one definition of soul; for in the former case there is no figure over and above the triangle and the others which follow it in order, nor in the latter case is there soul over and above those mentioned. Even in the case of figures there could be produced a common definition, which will fit all of them but which will not be peculiar to any one. Similarly too with the kinds of soul mentioned.

414b25. For this reason it is foolish to seek both in these cases and in others for a common definition, which will be a definition peculiar to no actually existing thing and will not correspond to the proper indivisible species, to the neglect of one which will.

414b28. The circumstances with regard to soul are similar to the situation over figures; for in the case both of figures and of things which have soul that which is prior always exists potentially in what follows in order, e.g. the triangle in the quadrilateral on the one hand, and the nutritive faculty in that of perception on the other. Hence we must inquire in each case what is the soul of each thing, what is that of a plant, and what is that of a man or a beast.

414b33. For what reason they are so arranged in order of succession must be considered. For without the nutritive faculty there does not exist that of perception; but the nutritive faculty is found apart from that of perception in plants. Again, without the faculty of touch none of the other senses exists, but touch exists without the others; for many animals have neither sight nor hearing nor sense of smell. And of those which can perceive, some have the faculty of movement in respect of place, while others have not. Finally and most rarely, they have reason and thought; for those perishable creatures which have reason have all the rest, but not all those which have each of the others have reason. But some do not even have imagination, while others live by this alone. The contemplative intellect requires a separate discussion. That the account, therefore, appropriate for each of these is most appropriate for the soul also is clear.

Chapter 3
Minds and bodies as distinct substances
René Descartes

On the nature of the human mind, which is better known than the body

YESTERDAY's meditation has hurled me into doubts so great that I can neither ignore them nor think my way out of them. I am in turmoil, as if I have accidentally fallen into a whirlpool and can neither touch bottom nor swim to the safety of the surface. I will struggle, however, and try to follow the path that I started on yesterday. I will reject whatever is open to the slightest doubt just as though I have found it to be entirely false, and I will continue until I find something certain—or at least until I know for certain that nothing is certain. Archimedes required only one fixed and immovable point to move the whole earth from its place, and I too can hope for great things if I can find even one small thing that is certain and unshakable.

I will suppose, then, that everything I see is unreal. I will believe that my memory is unreliable and that none of what it presents to me ever happened. I have no senses. Body, shape, extension, motion, and place are fantasies. What then is true? Perhaps just that nothing is certain.

But how do I know that there isn't something different from the things just listed which I do not have the slightest reason to doubt? Isn't there a God, or something like one, who puts my thoughts into me? But why should I say so when I may be the author of those thoughts? Well, isn't it at least the case that I am something? But I now am denying that I have senses and a body. But I stop here. For what follows from these denials? Am I so bound to my body and to my senses that I cannot exist without them? I have convinced myself that there is nothing in the world—no sky, no earth, no minds, no bodies. Doesn't it follow that I don't exist? No, surely I must exist if it's me who is convinced of something. But there is a deceiver, supremely powerful and cunning, whose aim is to see that I am always deceived. But surely I exist, if I am deceived. Let him deceive me all he can, he will never make it the case that I am nothing while I think that I am something. Thus having fully weighed every consideration, I must finally conclude that the statement 'I am, I exist' must be true whenever I state it or mentally consider it.

But I do not yet fully understand what this 'I' is that must exist. I must guard against inadvertently taking myself to be something other than I am, thereby going wrong even in the knowledge that I put forward as supremely certain and evident. Hence, I will think once again about what I believed myself to be before beginning these meditations. From this conception, I will subtract everything challenged by the reasons for doubt which I produced earlier, until nothing remains except what is certain and indubitable.

What, then, did I formerly take myself to be? A man, of course. But what is a man? Should I say a rational animal? No, because then I would need to ask what an animal is and what it is to be rational. Thus, starting from a single question, I would sink into many which are more difficult, and I do not have the time to waste on such subtleties. Instead, I will look here at the thoughts which occurred to me spontaneously and naturally when I reflected on what I was. The first thought to occur to me was that I have a face, hands, arms, and all the other equipment (also found in corpses) which I call a body. The next thought to occur to me was that I take nourishment, move myself around, sense, and think—that I do things which I trace back to my soul. Either I didn't stop to think about what this soul was, or I imagined it to be a rarified air, or fire, or ether permeating the denser parts of my body. But, about physical objects, I didn't have any doubts whatever: I thought that I distinctly knew their nature. If I had tried to describe my conception of this nature, I might have said this: 'When I call something a physical object, I mean that it is capable of being bounded by a shape and limited to a place; that it can fill a space so as to exclude other objects from it; that it can be perceived by touch, sight, hearing, taste, and smell; that it can be moved in various ways, not by itself, but by something else in contact with it.' I judged that the powers of self-movement, of sensing, and of thinking did not belong to the nature of physical objects, and, in fact, I marveled that there were some physical objects in which these powers could be found.

But what should I think now, while supposing that a supremely powerful and 'evil' deceiver completely devotes himself to deceiving me? Can I say that I have any of the things that I have attributed to the nature of physical objects? I concentrate, think, reconsider—but nothing comes to me; I grow tired of the pointless repetition. But what about the things that I have assigned to soul? Nutrition and self-movement? Since I have no body, these are merely illusions. Sensing? But I cannot sense without a body, and in sleep I've seemed to sense many things that I later realized I had not really sensed. Thinking? It comes down to this: Thought and thought alone cannot be taken away from me. I am, I exist. That much is certain. But for how long? As long as I think—for it may be that, if I completely stopped thinking, I would completely cease to exist. I am not now admitting anything unless it must be true, and I am therefore not admitting that I am anything at all other than a thinking thing—that is, a mind, soul, understanding, or reason (terms whose meaning I did not previously know). I know that I am a real, existing thing, but what kind of thing? As I have said, a thing that thinks.

What else? I will draw up mental images. I'm not the collection of organs called a human body. Nor am I some rarified gas permeating these organs, or air, or fire, or vapor, or breath—for I have supposed that none of these things exist. Still, I am something. But couldn't it be that these things, which I do not yet know about and which I am therefore supposing to be nonexistent, really aren't distinct from the 'I' that I know to exist? I don't know, and I'm not going to argue about it now. I can only form judgments on what I do know. I know that I exist, and I ask what the 'I' is that I know to exist. It's obvious that this conception of myself doesn't depend on anything that I do not yet know to exist and, therefore, that it does not depend on anything of which I can draw up a mental image. And the words 'draw up' point to my mistake. I would truly be creative if I were to have a mental image of what I am, since to have a mental image is just to contemplate the shape or image of a physical object. I now know with certainty that I exist and at the same time that all images—and, more generally, all things associated with the nature of physical objects—may just be dreams. When I keep this in mind, it seems just as absurd to say 'I use mental images to help me understand what I am' as it would to say 'Now, while awake, I see something true—but, since I don't yet see it clearly enough, I'll go to sleep and let my dreams present it to me more clearly and truly.' Thus I know that none of the things that I can comprehend with the aid of mental images bear on my knowledge of myself. And I must carefully draw my mind away from such things if it is to see its own nature distinctly.

But what then am I? A thinking thing. And what is that? Something that doubts, understands, affirms, denies, wills, refuses, and also senses and has mental images.

That's quite a lot, if I really do all of these things. But don't I? Isn't it me who now doubts nearly everything, understands one thing, affirms this thing, refuses to affirm other things, wants to know much more, refuses to be deceived, has mental images (sometimes involuntarily), and is aware of many things 'through his senses'? Even if I am always dreaming, and even if my creator does what he can to deceive me, isn't it just as true that I do all these things as that I exist? Are any of these things distinct from my thought? Can any be said to be separate from me? That it's me who doubts, understands, and wills is so obvious that I don't see how it could be more evident. And it's also me who has mental images. While it may be, as I am supposing, that absolutely nothing of which I have a mental image really exists, the ability to have mental images really does exist and is a part of my thought. Finally, it's me who senses—or who seems to gain awareness of physical objects through the senses. For example, I am now seeing light, hearing a noise, and feeling heat. These things are unreal, since I am dreaming. But it is still certain that I seem to see, to hear, and to feel. This seeming cannot be unreal, and it is what is properly called sensing. Strictly speaking, sensing is just thinking.

From this, I begin to learn a little about what I am. But I still can't stop thinking that I apprehend physical objects, which I picture in mental images and examine with my senses, much more distinctly than I know this unfamiliar 'I,' of which I cannot form a mental image. I think this, even though it would be astounding if I comprehended things which I've found to be doubtful, unknown, and alien to me more distinctly than the one which I know to be real: my self. But I see what's happening. My mind enjoys wandering, and it won't confine itself to the truth. I will therefore loosen the reigns on my mind for now so that later, when the time is right, I will be able to control it more easily.

Let's consider the things commonly taken to be the most distinctly comprehended: physical objects that we see and touch. Let's not consider physical objects in general, since general conceptions are very often confused. Rather, let's consider one, particular object. Take, for example, this piece of wax. It has just been taken from the honeycomb; it hasn't yet completely lost the taste of honey; it still smells of the flowers from which it was gathered; its color, shape, and size are obvious; it is hard, cold, and easy to touch; it makes a sound when rapped. In short, everything seems to be present in the wax that is required for me to know it as distinctly as possible. But, as I speak, I move the wax towards the fire; it loses what was left of its taste; it gives up its smell; it changes color; it loses its shape; it gets bigger; it melts; it heats up; it becomes difficult to touch; it no longer makes a sound when struck. Is it still the same piece of wax? We must say that it is: no one denies it or thinks otherwise. Then what was there in the wax that I comprehended so distinctly? Certainly nothing that I reached with my senses—for, while everything having to do with taste, smell, sight, touch, and hearing has changed, the same piece of wax remains.

Perhaps what I distinctly knew was neither the sweetness of honey, nor the fragrance of flowers, nor a sound, but a physical object which once appeared to me one way and now appears differently. But what exactly is it of which I now have a mental image? Let's pay careful attention, remove everything that doesn't belong to the wax, and see what's left. Nothing is left except an extended, flexible, and changeable thing. But what is it for this thing to be flexible and changeable? Is it just that the wax can go from round to square and then to triangular, as I have mentally pictured? Of course not. Since I understand that the wax's shape can change in innumerable ways, and since I can't run through all the changes in my imagination, my comprehension of the wax's flexibility and changeability cannot have been produced by my ability to have mental images. And what about the thing that is extended? Are we also ignorant of its extension? Since the extension of the wax increases when the wax melts, increases again when the wax boils, and increases still more when the wax gets hotter, I will be mistaken about what the wax is unless I believe that it can undergo more changes in extension than I can ever encompass with mental images. I must therefore admit that I do not have an image of what the wax is—that I grasp what it is with only my mind. (While I am saying this about a particular piece of wax, it is even more clearly true about wax in general.) What then is this piece of wax that I grasp only with my mind? It is something that I see, feel, and mentally picture—exactly what I believed it to be at the outset. But it must be noted that, despite the appearances, my grasp of the wax is not visual, tactile, or pictorial. Rather, my grasp of the wax is the result of a purely mental inspection, which can be imperfect and confused, as it was once, or clear and distinct, as it is now, depending on how much attention I pay to the things of which the wax consists.

I'm surprised by how prone my mind is to error. Even when I think to myself non-verbally, language stands in my way, and common usage comes close to deceiving me. For, when the wax is present, we say that we see the wax itself, not that we infer its presence from its color and shape. I'm inclined to leap from this fact about language to the conclusion that I learn about the wax by eyesight rather than by purely mental inspection. But, if I happen to look out my window and see men walking in the street, I naturally say that I see the men just as I say that I see the wax. What do I really see, however, but hats and coats that could be covering robots? I *judge* that there are men. Thus I comprehend with my judgment, which is in my mind, objects that I once believed myself to see with my eyes.

One who aspires to wisdom above that of the common man disgraces himself by deriving doubt from common ways of speaking. Let's go on, then, to ask when I most clearly and perfectly grasped what the wax is. Was it when I first looked at the wax and believed my knowledge of it to come from the external senses—or at any rate from the so-called 'common sense,' the power of having mental images? Or is it now, after I have carefully studied what the wax is and how I come to know it? Doubt would be silly here. For what was distinct in my original conception of the wax? How did that conception differ from that had by animals? When I distinguish the wax from its external forms—when I 'undress' it and view it 'naked'—there may still be errors in my judgments about it, but I couldn't possibly grasp the wax in this way without a human mind.

What should I say about this mind—or, in other words, about myself? (I am not now admitting that there is anything to me but a mind.) What is this 'I' that seems to grasp the wax so distinctly? Don't I know myself much more truly and certainly, and also much more distinctly and plainly, than I know the wax? For, if I base my judgment that the wax exists on the fact that I see it, my seeing it much more obviously implies that I exist. It's possible that what I see is not really wax, and it's even possible that I don't have eyes with which to see—but it clearly is not possible that, when I see (or, what now amounts to the same thing, when I think I see), the 'I' which thinks is not a real thing. Similarly, if I base my judgment that the wax exists on the fact that I feel it, the same fact makes it obvious that I exist. If I base my judgment that the wax exists on the fact that I have a mental image of it or on some other fact of this sort, the same thing can obviously be said. And what I've said about the wax applies to everything else that is outside me. Moreover, if I seem to grasp the wax more distinctly when I detect it with several senses than when I detect it with just sight or touch, I must know myself even more distinctly—for every consideration that contributes to my grasp of the piece of wax or to my grasp of any other physical object serves better to reveal the nature of my mind. Besides, the mind has so much in it by which it can make its conception of itself distinct that what comes to it from physical objects hardly seems to matter.

And now I have brought myself back to where I wanted to be. I now know that physical objects are grasped, not by the senses or the power of having mental images, but by understanding alone. And, since I grasp physical objects in virtue of their being understandable rather than in virtue of their being tangible or visible, I know that I can't grasp anything more easily or plainly than my mind. But, since it takes time to break old habits of thought, I should pause here to allow the length of my contemplation to impress the new thoughts more deeply into my memory.

On the existence of material objects and the real distinction of mind from body

It remains for me to examine whether material objects exist. Insofar as they are the subject of pure mathematics, I now know at least that they can exist, because I grasp them clearly and distinctly. For God can undoubtedly make whatever I can grasp in this way, and I never judge that something is impossible for Him to make unless there would be a contradiction in my grasping the thing distinctly. Also, the fact that I find myself having mental images when I turn my attention to physical objects seems to imply that these objects really do exist. For, when I pay careful attention to what it is to have a mental image, it seems to me that it's just the application of my power of thought to a certain body which is immediately present to it and which must therefore exist.

To clarify this, I'll examine the difference between having a mental image and having a pure understanding. When I have a mental image of a triangle, for example, I don't just understand that it is a figure bounded by three lines; I also 'look at' the lines as though they were present to my mind's eye. And this is what I call having a mental image. When I want to think of a chiliagon, I understand that it is a figure with a thousand sides as well as I understand that a triangle is a figure with three, but I can't imagine its sides or 'look' at them as though they were present. Being accustomed to using images when I think about physical objects, I may confusedly picture some figure to myself, but this figure obviously is not a chiliagon—for it in no way differs from what I present to myself when thinking about a myriagon or any other many sided figure, and it doesn't help me to discern the properties that distinguish chiliagons from other polygons. If it's a pentagon that is in question, I can understand its shape, as I can that of the chiliagon, without the aid of mental images. But I can also get a mental image of the pentagon by directing my mind's eye to its five lines and to the area that they bound. And it's obvious to me that getting this mental image requires a special mental effort different from that needed for understanding—a special effort which clearly reveals the difference between having a mental image and having a pure understanding.

It also seems to me that my power of having mental images, being distinct from my power of understanding, is not essential to my self or, in other words, to my mind—for, if I were to loose this ability, I would surely remain the same thing that I now am. And it seems to follow that this ability depends on something distinct from me. If we suppose that there is a body so associated with my mind that the mind can 'look into' it at will, it's easy to understand how my mind might get mental images of physical objects by means of my body. If there were such a body, the mode of thinking that we call imagination would only differ from pure understanding in one way: when the mind understood something, it would turn 'inward' and view an idea that it found in itself, but, when it had mental images, it would turn to the body and look at something there which resembled an idea that it had understood by itself or had grasped by sense. As I've said, then, it's easy to see how I get mental images, if we suppose that my body exists. And, since I don't have in mind any other equally plausible explanation of my ability to have mental images, I conjecture that physical objects probably do exist. But this conjecture is only probable. Despite my careful and thorough investigation, the distinct idea of bodily nature that I get from mental images does not seem to have anything in it from which the conclusion that physical objects exist validly follows.

Besides having a mental image of the bodily nature which is the subject-matter of pure mathematics, I have mental images of things which are not so distinct—things like colors, sounds, flavors, and pains. But I seem to grasp these things better by sense, from which they seem to come (with the aid of memory) to the understanding. Thus, to deal with these things more fully, I must examine the senses and see whether there is anything in the mode of awareness that I call sensation from which I can draw a conclusive argument for the existence of physical objects.

First, I'll remind myself of the things that I believed really to be as I perceived them and of the grounds for my belief. Next, I'll set out the grounds on which I later called this belief into doubt. And, finally, I'll consider what I ought to think now.

To begin with, I sensed that I had a head, hands, feet, and the other members that make up a human body. I viewed this body as part, or maybe even as all, of me. I sensed that it was influenced by other physical objects whose effects could be either beneficial or harmful. I judged these effects to be beneficial to the extent that I felt pleasant sensations and harmful to the extent that I felt pain. And, in addition to sensations of pain and pleasure, I sensed hunger, thirst, and other such desires—and also bodily inclinations towards cheerfulness, sadness, and other emotions. Outside me, I sensed, not just extension, shape, and motion, but also hardness, hotness, and other qualities detected by touch. I also sensed light, color, odor, taste, and sound—qualities by whose variation I distinguished such things as the sky, earth, and sea from one another.

In view of these ideas of qualities (which presented themselves to my thought and were all that I really sensed directly), I had some reason for believing that I sensed objects distinct from my thought—physical objects from which the ideas came. For I found that these ideas came to me independently of my desires so that, however much I tried, I couldn't sense an object when it wasn't present to an organ of sense or fail to sense one when it was present. And, since the ideas that I grasped by sense were much livelier, more explicit, and (in their own way) more distinct than those I deliberately created or found impressed in my memory, it seemed that these ideas could not have come from me and thus that they came from something else. Having no conception of these things other than that suggested by my sensory ideas, I could only think that the things resembled the ideas. Indeed, since I remembered using my senses before my reason, since I found the ideas that I created in myself to be less explicit than those grasped by sense, and since I found the ideas that I created to be composed largely of those that I had grasped by sense, I easily convinced myself that I didn't understand anything at all unless I had first sensed it.

I also had some reason for supposing that a certain physical object, which I viewed as belonging to me in a special way, was related to me more closely than any other. I couldn't be separated from it as I could from other physical objects; I felt all of my emotions and desires in it and because of it; and I was aware of pains and pleasant feelings in it but in nothing else. I didn't know why sadness goes with the sensation of pain or why joy goes with sensory stimulation. I didn't know why the stomach twitchings that I call hunger warn me that I need to eat or why dryness in my throat warns me that I need to drink. Seeing no connection between stomach twitchings and the desire to eat or between the sensation of a pain-producing thing and the consequent awareness of sadness, I could only say that I had been taught the connection by nature. And nature seems also to have taught me everything else that I knew about the objects of sensation—for I convinced myself that the sensations came to me in a certain way before having found grounds on which to prove that they did.

But, since then, many experiences have shaken my faith in the senses. Towers that seemed round from a distance sometimes looked square from close up, and huge statues on pediments sometimes didn't look big when seen from the ground. In innumerable such cases, I found the judgments of the external senses to be wrong. And the same holds for the internal senses. What is felt more inwardly than pain? Yet I had heard that people with amputated arms and legs sometimes seem to feel pain in the missing limb, and it therefore didn't seem perfectly certain to me that the limb in which I feel a pain is always the one that hurts. And, to these grounds for doubt, I've recently added two that are very general: First, since I didn't believe myself to sense anything while awake that I couldn't also take myself to sense in a dream, and since I didn't believe that what I sense in sleep comes from objects outside me, I didn't see why I should believe what I sense while awake comes from such objects. Second, since I didn't yet know my creator (or, rather, since I supposed that I didn't know Him), I saw nothing to rule out my having been so designed by nature that I'm deceived even in what seems most obviously true to me.

And I could easily refute the reasoning by which I convinced myself of the reality of sensible things. Since my nature seemed to impel me towards many things which my reason rejected, I didn't believe that I ought to have much faith in nature's teachings. And, while my will didn't control my sense perceptions, I didn't believe it to follow that these perceptions came from outside me, since I thought that the ability to produce these ideas might be in me without my being aware of it.

Now that I've begun to know myself and my creator better, I still believe that I oughtn't blindly to accept everything that I seem to get from the senses. Yet I no longer believe that I ought to call it all into doubt.

In the first place, I know that everything that I clearly and distinctly understand can be made by God to be exactly as I understand it. The fact that I can clearly and distinctly understand one thing apart from another is therefore enough to make me certain that it is distinct from the other, since the things could be separated by God if not by something else. (I judge the things to be distinct regardless of the power needed to make them exist separately.) Accordingly, from the fact that I have gained knowledge of my existence without noticing anything about my nature or essence except that I am a thinking thing, I can rightly conclude that my essence consists solely in the fact that I am a thinking thing. It's possible (or, as I will say later, it's certain) that I have a body which is very tightly bound to me. But, on the one hand, I have a clear and distinct idea of myself insofar as I am just a thinking and unextended thing, and, on the other hand, I have a distinct idea of my body insofar as it is just an extended and unthinking thing. It's certain, then, that I am really distinct from my body and can exist without it.

In addition, I find in myself abilities for special modes of awareness, like the abilities to have mental images and to sense. I can clearly and distinctly conceive of my whole self as something that lacks these abilities, but I can't conceive of the abilities' existing without me, or without an understanding substance in which to reside. Since the conception of these abilities includes the conception of something that understands, I see that these abilities are distinct from me in the way that a thing's properties are distinct from the thing itself.

I recognize other abilities in me, like the ability to move around and to assume various postures. These abilities can't be understood to exist apart from a substance in which they reside any more than the abilities to imagine and sense, and they therefore cannot exist without such a substance. But it's obvious that, if these abilities do exist, the substance in which they reside must be a body or extended substance rather than an understanding one—for the clear and distinct conceptions of these abilities contain extension but not understanding.

There is also in me, however, a passive ability to sense—to receive and recognize ideas of sensible things. But, I wouldn't be able to put this ability to use if there weren't, either in me or in something else, an active power to produce or make sensory ideas. Since this active power doesn't presuppose understanding, and since it often produces ideas in me without my cooperation and even against my will, it cannot exist in me. Therefore, this power must exist in a substance distinct from me. And, for reasons that I've noted, this substance must contain, either formally or eminently, all the reality that is contained subjectively in the ideas that the power produces. Either this substance is a physical object (a thing of bodily nature which contains formally the reality that the idea contains subjectively), or it is God or one of His creations which is higher than a physical object (something which contains this reality eminently). But, since God isn't a deceiver, it's completely obvious that He doesn't send these ideas to me directly or by means of a creation which contains their reality eminently rather than formally. For, since He has not given me any ability to recognize that these ideas are sent by Him or by creations other than physical objects, and since He has given me a strong inclination to believe that the ideas come from physical objects, I see no way to avoid the conclusion that He deceives me if the ideas are sent to me by anything other than physical objects. It follows that physical objects exist. These objects may not exist exactly as I comprehend them by sense; in many ways, sensory comprehension is obscure and confused. But these objects must at least have in them everything that I clearly and distinctly understand them to have—every general property within the scope of pure mathematics.

But what about particular properties, such as the size and shape of the sun? And what about things that I understand less clearly than mathematical properties, like light, sound, and pain? These are open to doubt. But, since God isn't a deceiver, and since I therefore have the God-given ability to correct any falsity that may be in my beliefs, I have high hopes of finding the truth about even these things. There is undoubtedly some truth in everything I have been taught by nature—for, when I use the term 'nature' in its general sense, I refer to God Himself or to the order that He has established in the created world, and when I apply the term specifically to *my* nature, I refer to the collection of everything that God has given *me.*

Nature teaches me nothing more explicitly, however, than that I have a body which is hurt when I feel pain, which needs food or drink when I experience hunger or thirst, and so on. Accordingly, I ought not to doubt that there is some truth to this.

Through sensations like pain, hunger, and thirst, nature also teaches me that I am not present in my body in the way that a sailor is present in his ship. Rather, I am very tightly bound to my body and so 'mixed up' with it that we form a single thing. If this weren't so, I—who am just a thinking thing—wouldn't feel pain when my body was injured; I would perceive the injury by pure understanding in the way that a sailor sees the leaks in his ship with his eyes. And, when my body needed food or drink, I would explicitly understand that the need existed without having the confused sensations of hunger and thirst. For the sensations of thirst, hunger, and pain are just confused modifications of thought arising from the union and 'mixture' of mind and body.

Also, nature teaches me that there are other physical objects around my body—some that I ought to seek and others that I ought to avoid. From the fact that I sense things like colors, sounds, odors, flavors, temperatures, and hardnesses, I correctly infer that sense perceptions come from physical objects which vary as widely (though perhaps not in the same way) as the perceptions do. And, from the fact that some of these perceptions are pleasant while others are unpleasant, I infer with certainty that my body—or, rather, my whole self which consists of a body and a mind—can be benefited and harmed by the physical objects around it.

There are many other things which I seem to have been taught by nature but which I have really accepted out of a habit of thoughtless judgment. These things may well be false. Among them are the judgments that a space is empty if nothing in it happens to affect my senses; that a hot physical object has something in it resembling my idea of heat; that a white or green thing has in it the same whiteness or greenness that I sense; that a bitter or sweet thing has in it the same flavor that I taste; that stars, towers, and other physical objects have the same size and shape that they present to my senses; and so on.

If I am to avoid accepting what is indistinct in these cases, I must more carefully explain my use of the phrase 'taught by nature.' In particular, I should say that I am now using the term 'nature' in a narrower sense than when I took it to refer to the whole complex of what God has given me. This complex includes much having to do with my mind alone (such as my grasp of the fact that what is done cannot be undone and of the rest of what I know by the light of nature) which does not bear on what I am now saying. And the complex also includes much having to do with my body alone (such as its tendency to go downwards) with which I am not dealing now. I'm now using the term 'nature' to refer only to what God has given me insofar as I am a composite of mind and body. It is this nature which teaches me to avoid that which occasions painful sensations, to seek that which occasions pleasant sensations, and so on. But this nature seems not to teach me to draw conclusions about external objects from sense perceptions without first having examined the matter with my understanding—for true knowledge of external things seems to belong to the mind alone, not to the composite of mind and body.

Thus, while a star has no more effect on my eye than a flame, this does not really produce a positive inclination to believe that the star is as small as the flame; for my youthful judgment about the size of the flame, I had no real grounds. And, while I feel heat when I approach a fire and pain when I draw nearer, I have absolutely no reason for believing that something in the fire resembles the heat, just as I have no reason for believing that something in the fire resembles the pain; I only have reason for believing that there is something or other in the fire which produces the feelings of heat and pain. And, although there may be nothing in a given region of space that affects my senses, it doesn't follow that there aren't any physical objects in that space. Rather I now see that, on these matters and others, I used to pervert the natural order of things. For, while nature has given sense perceptions to my mind for the sole purpose of indicating what is beneficial and what harmful to the composite of which my mind is a part, and while the perceptions are sufficiently clear and distinct for that purpose, I used these perceptions as standards for identifying the essence of physical objects—an essence which they only reveal obscurely and confusedly.

I've already explained how it can be that, despite God's goodness, my judgments can be false. But a new difficulty arises here—one having to do with the things that nature presents to me as desirable or undesirable and also with the errors that I seem to have found in my internal sensations. One of these errors seems to be committed, for example, when a man is fooled by some food's pleasant taste into eating poison hidden in that food. But surely, in this case, what the man's nature impels him to eat is the good tasting food, not the poison of which he knows nothing. We can draw no conclusion except that his nature isn't omniscient, and this conclusion isn't surprising. Since a man is a limited thing, he can only have limited perfections.

Still, we often err in cases in which nature does impel us. This happens, for example, when sick people want food or drink that would quickly harm them. To say that these people err as a result of the corruption of their nature does not solve the problem—for a sick man is no less a creation of God than a well one, and it seems as absurd to suppose that God has given him a deceptive nature. A clock made of wheels and weights follows the natural laws just as precisely when it is poorly made and inaccurate as when it does everything that its maker wants. Thus, if I regard a human body as a machine made up of bones, nerves, muscles, veins, blood, and skin such that even without a mind it would do just what it does now (except for things that require a mind because they are controlled by the will), it's easy to see that what happens to a sick man is no less 'natural' than what happens to a well one. For instance, if a body suffers from dropsy, it has a dry throat of the sort that regularly brings the sensation of thirst to the mind, the dryness disposes the nerves and other organs to drink, and the drinking makes the illness worse. But this is just as natural as when a similar dryness of throat moves a person who is perfectly healthy to take a drink which is beneficial. Bearing in mind my conception of a clock's use, I might say that an inaccurate clock departs from its nature, and, similarly, viewing the machine of the human body as designed for its usual motions, I can say that it drifts away from its nature if it has a dry throat when drinking will not help to maintain it. I should note, however, that the sense in which I am now using the term 'nature' differs from that in which I used it before. For, as I have just used the term 'nature,' the nature of a man (or clock) is something that depends on my thinking of the difference between a sick and a well man (or of the difference between a poorly made and a well-made clock)—something regarded as extrinsic to the things. But, when I used 'nature' before, I referred to something which is *in* things and which therefore has some reality.

It may be that we just offer an extrinsic description of a body suffering from dropsy when, noting that it has a dry throat but doesn't need to drink, we say that its nature is corrupted. Still, the description is not purely extrinsic when we say that a composite or union of mind and body has a corrupted nature. There is a real fault in the composite's nature, for it is thirsty when drinking would be harmful. It therefore remains to be asked why God's goodness doesn't prevent *this* nature's being deceptive.

To begin the answer, I'll note that mind differs importantly from body in that body is by its nature divisible while mind is indivisible. When I think about my mind—or, in other words, about myself insofar as I am just a thinking thing—I can't distinguish any parts in me; I understand myself to be a single, unified thing. Although my whole mind seems united to my whole body, I know that cutting off a foot, arm, or other limb would not take anything away from my mind. The abilities to will, sense, understand, and so on can't be called parts, since it's one and the same mind that wills, senses, and understands. On the other hand, whenever I think of a physical or extended thing, I can mentally divide it, and I therefore understand that the object is divisible. This single fact would be enough to teach me that my mind and my body are distinct, if I hadn't already learned that in another way.

Next, I notice that the mind isn't directly affected by all parts of the body, but only by the brain—or maybe just by the small part of the brain containing the so-called 'common sense.' Whenever this part of the brain is in a given state, it presents the same thing to the mind, regardless of what *is* happening in the rest of the body (as is shown by innumerable experiments that I need not review here).

In addition, I notice that the nature of body is such that, if a first part can be moved by a second that *is* far away, the first part can be moved in exactly the same way by something between the first and second without the second part's being affected. For example, if A, B, C, and D are points on a cord, and if the first point (A) can be moved in a certain way by a pull on the last point (D), then A can be moved in the same way by a pull on one of the middle points (B or C) without D's being moved. Similarly, science teaches me that when my foot hurts, the sensation of pain is produced by nerves distributed throughout the foot which extend like cords from there to the brain. When pulled in the foot, these nerves pull the central parts of the brain to which they are attached, moving those parts in ways designated by nature to present the mind with the sensation of a pain 'in the foot.' But, since these nerves pass through the shins, thighs, hips, back, and neck on their way from foot to brain, it can happen that their being touched in the middle, rather than at the end in the foot, produces the same motion in the brain as when the foot is hurt and, hence, that the mind feels the same pain 'in the foot.' And the point holds for other sensations as well.

Finally, I notice that, since only one sensation can be produced by a given motion of the part of the brain that directly affects the mind, the best conceivable sensation for it to produce is the one that is most often useful for the maintenance of the healthy man. Experience teaches that all the sensations put in us by nature are of this sort and therefore that everything in our sensations testifies to God's power and goodness. For example, when the nerves in the foot are moved with unusual violence, the motion is communicated through the middle of the spine to the center of the brain, where it signals the mind to sense a pain 'in the foot.' This urges the mind to view the pain's cause as harmful to the foot and to do what it can to remove that cause. Of course, God could have so designed man's nature that the same motion of the brain presented something else to the mind, like the motion in the brain, or the motion in the foot, or a motion somewhere between the brain and foot. But no alternative to the way things are would be as conducive to the maintenance of the body. Similarly, when we need drink, the throat becomes dry, the dryness moves the nerves of the throat thereby moving the center of the brain, and the brain's movements cause the sensation of thirst in the mind. It's the sensation of thirst that *is* produced, because no information about our condition *is* more useful to us than that we need to get something to drink in order to remain healthy. And the same is true in other cases.

This makes it completely obvious that, despite God's immense goodness, the nature of man (whom we now view as a composite of mind and body) cannot fail to be deceptive. For, if something produces the movement usually associated with an injured foot in the nerve running from foot to brain or in the brain itself rather than in the foot, a pain is felt as if 'in the foot.' Here the senses are deceived by their nature. Since this motion in the brain must always bring the same sensation to mind, and since the motion's cause is something hurting the foot more often than something elsewhere, it's in accordance with reason that the motion always presents the mind a pain in the foot rather than elsewhere. And, if dryness of the throat arises, not (as usual) from drink's being conducive to the body's health, but (as happens in dropsy) from some other cause, it's much better that we are deceived on this occasion than that we are generally deceived when our bodies are sound. And the same holds for other cases.

In addition to helping me to be aware of the errors to which my nature is subject, these reflections help me readily to correct or avoid those errors. I know that sensory indications of what is good for my body are more often true than false; I can almost always examine a given thing with several senses; and I can also use my memory (which connects the present to the past) and my understanding (which has now examined all the causes of error). Hence, I need no longer fear that what the senses daily show me is unreal. I should reject the exaggerated doubts of the past few days as ridiculous. This is especially true of the chief ground for these doubts—namely, my inability to distinguish dreaming from being awake. For I now notice that dreaming and being awake are importantly different: the events in dreams are not linked by memory to the rest of my life like those that happen while I am awake. If, while I'm awake, someone were suddenly to appear and then immediately to disappear without my seeing where he came from or went to (as happens in dreams), I would justifiably judge that he was not a real man but a ghost—or, better, an apparition created in my brain. But, if I distinctly observe something's source, its place, and the time at which I learn about it, and if I grasp an unbroken connection between it and the rest of my life, I'm quite sure that it is something in my waking life rather than in a dream. And I ought not to have the slightest doubt about the reality of such things if I have examined them with all my senses, my memory, and my understanding without finding any conflicting evidence. For, from the fact that God is not a deceiver, it follows that I am not deceived in any case of this sort. Since the need to act does not always allow time for such a careful examination, however, we must admit the likelihood of men's erring about particular things and acknowledge the weakness of our nature.

Objections and replies

May we remind you that your vigorous rejection of the images of all bodies as delusive was not something you actually and really carried through, but was merely a fiction of the mind, enabling you to draw the conclusion that you were exclusively a thinking thing. We point this out in case you should perhaps suppose that it is possible to go on to draw the conclusion that you are in fact nothing more than a mind, or thought, or a thinking thing. And we make the point solely in connection with the first two Meditations, in which you clearly show that, if nothing else, it is certain that you, who are thinking, exist. But let us pause a little here. The position so far is that you recognize that you are a thinking thing, but you do not know what this thinking thing is. What if it turned out to be a body which, by its various motions and encounters, produces what we call thought? Although you think you have ruled out every kind of body, you could have been mistaken here, since you did not exclude yourself, and you may be a body. How do you demonstrate that a body is incapable of thinking, or that corporeal motions are not in fact thought? The whole system of your body, which you think you have excluded, or else some of its parts—for example those which make up the brain—may combine to produce the motions which we call thoughts. You say 'I am a thinking thing'; but how do you know that you are not corporeal motion, or a body which is in motion?

Descartes's reply

You warn me to remember that my rejection of the images of bodies as delusive was not something I actually and really carried through, but was merely a fiction of the mind, enabling me to draw the conclusion that I was a thinking thing; and I should not suppose that it followed from this that I was in fact nothing more than a mind. But I already showed that I was quite well aware of this in the Second Meditation, where I said 'Yet may it not perhaps be the case that these very things which I am supposing to be nothing, because they are unknown to me, are in reality identical with the 'I' of which I am aware? I do not know, and for the moment I shall not argue the point.' Here I wanted to give the reader an express warning that at that stage I was not yet asking whether the mind is distinct from the body, but was merely examining those of its properties of which I can have certain and evident knowledge. And since I did become aware of many such properties, I cannot without qualification admit your subsequent point that 'I do not yet know what a thinking thing is.' I admit that I did not yet know whether this thinking thing is identical with the body or with something different from the body; but I do not

René Descartes, edited extracts from *Meditations* II and VI (6–13; 40–53), from *Meditations on First Philosophy*, trans. Ronald Rubin, 3d ed. (Claremont: Areté Press, 2001); and *The Philosophical Writings of Descartes*, ed. and trans. John Cottingham, Robert Stoothoff, and Dugald Murdoch, vol. ii (Cambridge: Cambridge University Press, 1985).

admit that I had no knowledge of it. Surely, no one's knowledge of anything has ever reached the point where he knows that there is absolutely nothing further in the thing beyond what he is already aware of. The more attributes of a thing we perceive the better we are said to know it; thus we know people whom we have lived with for some time better than those whom we only know by sight, or have merely heard of—though even they are not said to be completely unknown to us. In this sense I think I have demonstrated that the mind, considered apart from those attributes which are normally applied to the body, is better known than the body when it is considered apart from the mind. This was my sole purpose in the passage under discussion.

But I see the suggestion you are making. Given that I wrote only six Meditations on First Philosophy, you think my readers will be surprised that the only conclusion reached in the first two Meditations is the point just mentioned; and you think that as a result they will reckon that the Meditations are extremely thin and not worth publishing. My reply is simply that I am confident that anyone who judiciously reads the rest of what I wrote will have no occasion to suspect that I was short of material. And in the case of topics which required individual attention and needed to be considered on their own, it seemed quite reasonable to deal with them separately, Meditation by Meditation.

Now the best way of achieving a firm knowledge of reality is first to accustom ourselves to doubting all things, especially corporeal things. Although I had seen many ancient writings by the Academics and Sceptics on this subject, and was reluctant to reheat and serve this precooked material, I could not avoid devoting one whole Meditation to it. And I should like my readers not just to take the short time needed to go through it, but to devote several months, or at least weeks, to considering the topics dealt with, before going on to the rest of the book. If they do this they will undoubtedly be able to derive much greater benefit from what follows.

All our ideas of what belongs to the mind have up till now been very confused and mixed up with the ideas of things that can be perceived by the senses. This is the first and most important reason for our inability to understand with sufficient clarity the customary assertions about the soul and God. So I thought I would be doing something worthwhile if I explained how the properties or qualities of the mind are to be distinguished from the qualities of the body. Admittedly, many people had previously said that in order to understand metaphysical matters the mind must be drawn away from the senses; but no one, so far as I know, had shown how this could be done. The correct, and in my view unique, method of achieving this is contained in my Second Meditation. But the nature of the method is such that scrutinizing it just once is not enough. Protracted and repeated study is required to eradicate the lifelong habit of confusing things related to the intellect with corporeal things, and to replace it with the opposite habit of distinguishing the two; this will take at least a few days to acquire. I think that was the best justification for my devoting the whole of the Second Meditation to this topic alone.

You go on to ask how I demonstrate that a body is incapable of thinking. You will forgive me if I reply that I have as yet provided no opportunity for this question to be raised. I first dealt with the matter in the Sixth Meditation where I said 'the fact that I can clearly and distinctly understand one thing apart from another is enough to make me certain that the two things are distinct', etc. And a little later on I said:

> It is true that I have a body that is very closely joined to me. But nevertheless on the one hand I have a clear and distinct idea of myself, in so far as I am a thinking, non-extended thing; and on the other hand I have a distinct idea of body, in so far as this is an extended, non-thinking thing. And accordingly it is certain that I (that is, the mind) am really distinct from my body and can exist without it.

From this we may easily go on to say 'whatever can think is a mind, or is called a mind; but since mind and body are in reality distinct, no body is a mind; therefore no body can think'.

I do not see what you can deny here. Do you claim that if we clearly understand one thing apart from another this is not sufficient for the recognition that the two things are really distinct? If so, you must provide a more reliable criterion for a real distinction—and I am confident that none can be provided. What will you suggest? Perhaps that there is a real distinction between two things if one can exist apart from the other? But now I will ask how you know that one thing can exist apart from another. You must be able to know this, if it is to serve as the criterion for a real distinction. You may say that you derive this knowledge from the senses, since you can see, or touch etc., the one thing when the other is not present. But the evidence of the senses is less reliable than that of the intellect: it can variously happen that one and the same thing appears under different forms or in several places or in several different ways, and so be taken for two things. And, after all, if you remember the remarks about the wax at the end of the Second Meditation you will realize that bodies are not strictly speaking perceived by the senses at all, but only by the intellect; so having a sensory perception of one thing apart from another simply amounts to our having an idea of one thing and understanding that this idea is not the same as an idea of something else. The sole possible source of such understanding is that we perceive one thing apart from another, and such understanding cannot be certain unless the idea of each thing is clear and distinct. So if the proposed criterion for a real distinction is to be reliable, it must reduce to the one which I put forward.

If there are those who claim that they do not have distinct ideas of mind and body, I can only ask them to pay careful attention to the contents of the Second Meditation. If, as may well be the case, they take the view that the formation of thoughts is due to the combined activity of parts of the brain, they should realize that this view is not based on any positive argument, but has simply arisen from the fact that, in the first place, they have never had the experience of being without a body and that, in the second place, they have frequently been obstructed by the body in their operations. It is just as if someone had had his legs permanently shackled from infancy: he would think the shackles were part of his body and that he needed them for walking.

How does it follow, from the fact that he is aware of nothing else belonging to his essence, that nothing else does in fact belong to it? I must confess that I am somewhat slow, but I have been unable to find anywhere in the Second Meditation an answer to this question. As far as I can gather, however, the author does attempt a proof of this claim in the Sixth Meditation, since he takes it to depend on his having clear knowledge of God, which he had not yet arrived at in the Second Meditation. This is how the proof goes:

> I know that everything which I clearly and distinctly understand is capable of being created by God so as to correspond exactly with my understanding of it. Hence the fact that I can clearly and distinctly understand one thing apart from another is enough to make me certain that the two things are distinct, since they are capable of being separated, at least by God. The question of what kind of power is required to bring about such a separation does not affect the judgement that the two things are distinct . . . Now on the one hand I have a clear and distinct idea of myself, in so far as I am simply a thinking, non-extended thing; and on the other hand I have a distinct idea of body, in so far as this is simply an extended, non-thinking thing. And accordingly, it is certain that I am really distinct from my body, and can exist without it.

We must pause a little here, for it seems to me that in these few words lies the crux of the whole difficulty.

First of all, if the major premiss of this syllogism is to be true, it must be taken to apply not to any kind of knowledge of a thing, nor even to clear and distinct knowledge; it must apply solely to knowledge which is adequate. For our distinguished author admits in his reply to the theologian, that if one thing can be conceived distinctly and separately from another 'by an abstraction of the intellect which conceives the thing inadequately', then this is sufficient for there to be a formal distinction between the two, but it does not require that there be a real distinction. And in the same passage he draws the following conclusion:

> By contrast, I have a complete understanding of what a body is when I think that it is merely something having extension, shape and motion, and I deny that it has anything which belongs to the nature of a mind. Conversely, I understand the mind to be a complete thing, which doubts, understands, wills, and so on, even though I deny that it has any of the attributes which are contained in the idea of a body. Hence there is a real distinction between the body and the mind.

But someone may call this minor premiss into doubt and maintain that the conception you have of yourself when you conceive of yourself as a thinking, non-extended thing is an inadequate one; and the same may be true of your conception of yourself as an extended, non-thinking thing. Hence we must look at how this is proved in the earlier part of the argument. For I do not think that this matter is so clear that it should be assumed without proof as a first principle that is not susceptible of demonstration.

As to the first part of your claim, namely that you have a complete understanding of what a body is when you think that it is merely something having extension, shape, motion etc., and you deny that it has anything which belongs to the nature of a mind, this proves little. For those who maintain that our mind is corporeal do not on that account suppose that every body is a mind. On their view, body would be related to mind as a genus is related to a species. Now a genus can be understood apart from a species, even if we deny of the genus what is proper and peculiar to the species—hence the common maxim of logicians, 'The negation of the species does not negate the genus.' Thus I can understand the genus 'figure' apart from my understanding of any of the properties which are peculiar to a circle. It therefore remains to be proved that the mind can be completely and adequately understood apart from the body.

I cannot see anywhere in the entire work an argument which could serve to prove this claim, apart from what is suggested at the beginning: 'I can deny that any body exists, or that there is any extended thing at all, yet it remains certain to me that I exist, so long as I am making this denial or thinking it. Hence I am a thinking thing, not a body, and the body does not belong to the knowledge I have of myself.'

But so far as I can see, the only result that follows from this is that I can obtain some knowledge of myself without knowledge of the body. But it is not yet transparently clear to me that this knowledge is complete and adequate, so as to enable me to be certain that I am not mistaken in excluding body from my essence. I shall explain the point by means of an example.

Suppose someone knows for certain that the angle in a semi-circle is a right angle, and hence that the triangle formed by this angle and the diameter of the circle is right-angled. In spite of this, he may doubt, or not yet have grasped for certain, that the square on the hypotenuse is equal to the squares on the other two sides; indeed he may even deny this if he is misled by some fallacy. But now, if he uses the same argument as that proposed by our illustrious author, he may appear to have confirmation of his false belief, as follows: 'I clearly and distinctly perceive', he may say, 'that the triangle is right-angled; but I doubt that the square on the hypotenuse is equal to the squares on the other two sides; therefore it does not belong to the essence of the triangle that the square on its hypotenuse is equal to the squares on the other sides.'

Again, even if I deny that the square on the hypotenuse is equal to the square on the other two sides, I still remain sure that the triangle is right-angled, and my mind retains the clear and distinct knowledge that one of its angles is a right angle. And given that this is so, not even God could bring it about that the triangle is not right-angled.

I might argue from this that the property which I doubt, or which can be removed while leaving my idea intact, does not belong to the essence of the triangle.

Moreover, 'I know', says M. Descartes, 'that everything which I clearly and distinctly understand is capable of being created by God so as to correspond exactly with my understanding of it. And hence the fact that I can clearly and distinctly understand one thing apart from another is enough to make me certain that the two things are distinct, since they are capable of being separated by God.' Yet I clearly and distinctly understand that this triangle is right-angled, without understanding that the square on the hypotenuse is equal to the squares on the other sides. It follows on this reasoning that God, at least, could create a right-angled triangle with the square on its hypotenuse not equal to the squares on the other sides.

I do not see any possible reply here, except that the person in this example does not clearly and distinctly perceive that the triangle is right-angled. But how is my perception of the nature of my mind any clearer than his perception of the nature of the triangle? He is just as certain that the triangle in the semi-circle has one right angle (which is the criterion of a right-angled triangle) as I am certain that I exist because I am thinking.

Now although the man in the example clearly and distinctly knows that the triangle is right-angled, he is wrong in thinking that the aforesaid relationship between the squares on the sides does not belong to the nature of the triangle. Similarly, although I clearly and distinctly know my nature to be something that thinks, may I, too, not perhaps be wrong in thinking that nothing else belongs to my nature apart from the fact that I am a thinking thing? Perhaps the fact that I am an extended thing may also belong to my nature.

Someone may also make the point that since I infer my existence from the fact that I am thinking, it is certainly no surprise if the idea that I form by thinking of myself in this way represents to my mind nothing other than myself as a thinking thing. For the idea was derived entirely from my thought. Hence it seems that this idea cannot provide any evidence that nothing belongs to my essence beyond what is contained in the idea.

It seems, moreover, that the argument proves too much, and takes us back to the Platonic view (which M. Descartes nonetheless rejects) that nothing corporeal belongs to our essence, so that man is merely a rational soul and the body merely a vehicle for the soul—a view which gives rise to the definition of man as 'a soul which makes use of a body'.

If you reply that body is not straightforwardly excluded from my essence, but is ruled out only and precisely in so far as I am a thinking thing, it seems that there is a danger that someone will suspect that my knowledge of myself as a thinking thing does not qualify as knowledge of a being of which I have a complete and adequate conception; it seems instead that I conceive of it only inadequately, and by a certain intellectual abstraction.

Geometers conceive of a line as a length without breadth, and they conceive of a surface as length and breadth without depth, despite the fact that no length exists without breadth and no breadth without depth. In the same way, someone may perhaps suspect that every thinking thing is also an extended thing—an extended thing which, besides the attributes it has in common with other extended things, such as shape, motion, etc., also possesses the peculiar power of thought. This would mean that although, simply in virtue of this power, it can by an intellectual abstraction be apprehended as a thinking thing, in reality bodily attributes may belong to this thinking thing. In the same way, although quantity can be conceived in terms of length alone, in reality breadth and depth belong to every quantity, along with length.

The difficulty is increased by the fact that the power of thought appears to be attached to bodily organs, since it can be regarded as dormant in infants and extinguished in the case of madmen. And this is an objection strongly pressed by those impious people who try to do away with the soul.

It is quite impossible to assert, as my distinguished critic maintains, that 'body may be related to mind as a genus is related to a species' For although a genus can be understood without this or that specific differentia, there is no way in which a species can be thought of without its genus.

For example, we can easily understand the genus 'figure' without thinking of a circle (though our understanding will not be distinct unless it is referred to some specific figure and it will not involve a complete thing unless it also comprises the nature of body). But we cannot understand any specific differentia of the 'circle' without at the same time thinking of the genus 'figure'.

Now the mind can be perceived distinctly and completely (that is, sufficiently for it to be considered as a complete thing) without any of the forms or attributes by which we recognize that body is a substance, as I think I showed quite adequately in the Second Meditation. And similarly a body can be understood distinctly and as a complete thing, without any of the attributes which belong to the mind.

But here my critic argues that although I can obtain some knowledge of myself without knowledge of the body, it does not follow that this knowledge is complete and adequate, so as to enable me to be certain that I am not mistaken in excluding body from my essence. He explains the point by using the example of a triangle inscribed in a semi-circle, which we can clearly and distinctly understand to be right-angled although we do not know, or may even deny, that the square on the hypotenuse is equal to the squares on the other sides. But we cannot infer from this that there could be a right-angled triangle such that the square on the hypotenuse is not equal to the squares on the other sides.

But this example differs in many respects from the case under discussion.

First of all, though a triangle can perhaps be taken concretely as a substance having a triangular shape, it is certain that the property of having the square on the hypotenuse equal to the squares on the other sides is not a substance. So neither the triangle nor the property can be understood as a complete thing in the way in which mind and body can be so understood; nor can either item be called a 'thing' in the sense in which I said 'it is enough that I can understand one thing (that is, a complete thing) apart from another' etc. This is clear from the passage which comes next: 'Besides I find in myself faculties' etc. I did not say that these faculties were *things*, but carefully distinguished them from things or substances.

Secondly, although we can clearly and distinctly understand that a triangle in a semi-circle is right-angled without being aware that the square on the hypotenuse is equal to the squares on the other two sides, we cannot have a clear understanding of a triangle having the square on its hypotenuse equal to the squares on the other sides without at the same time being aware that it is right-angled. And yet we can clearly and distinctly perceive the mind without the body and the body without the mind.

Thirdly, although it is possible to have a concept of a triangle inscribed in a semi-circle which does not include the fact that the square on the hypotenuse is equal to the squares on the other sides, it is not possible to have a concept of the triangle such that no ratio at all is understood to hold between the square on the hypotenuse and the squares on the other sides. Hence, though we may be unaware of what that ratio is, we cannot say that any given ratio does not hold unless we clearly understand that it does not belong to the triangle; and where the ratio is one of equality, this can never be understood. Yet the concept of body includes nothing at all which belongs to the mind, and the concept of mind includes nothing at all which belongs to the body.

So although I said 'it is enough that I can clearly and distinctly understand one thing apart from another' etc., one cannot go on to argue 'yet I clearly and distinctly understand that this triangle is right-angled without understanding that the square on the hypotenuse' etc. There are three reasons for this. First, the ratio between the square on the hypotenuse and the squares on the other sides is not a complete thing. Secondly, we do not clearly understand the ratio to be equal except in the case of a right-angled triangle. And thirdly, there is no way in which the triangle can be distinctly understood if the ratio which obtains between the square on the hypotenuse and the squares on the other sides is said not to hold.

But now I must explain how the mere fact that I can clearly and distinctly understand one substance apart from another is enough to make me certain that one excludes the other.

The answer is that the notion of a *substance* is just this—that it can exist by itself, that is without the aid of any other substance. And there is no one who has ever perceived two substances by means of two different concepts without judging that they are really distinct.

Hence, had I not been looking for greater than ordinary certainty, I should have been content to have shown in the Second Meditation that the mind can be understood as a subsisting thing despite the fact that nothing belonging to the body is attributed to it, and that, conversely, the body can be understood as a subsisting thing despite the fact that nothing belonging to the mind is attributed to it. I should have added nothing more in order to demonstrate that there is a real distinction between the mind and the body, since we commonly judge that the order in which things are mutually related in our perception of them corresponds to the order in which they are related in actual reality. But one of the exaggerated doubts which I put forward in the First Meditation went so far as to make it impossible for me to be certain of this very point (namely whether things do in reality correspond to our perception of them), so long as I was supposing myself to be ignorant of the author of my being. And this is why everything I wrote on the subject of God and truth in the Third, Fourth and Fifth Meditations contributes to the conclusion that there is a real distinction between the mind and the body, which I finally established in the Sixth Meditation.

And yet, says M. Arnauld, 'I have a clear understanding of a triangle inscribed in a semi-circle without knowing that the square on the hypotenuse is equal to the squares on the other sides.' It is true that the triangle is intelligible even though we do not think of the ratio which obtains between the square on the hypotenuse and the squares on the other sides; but it is not intelligible that this ratio should be denied of the triangle. In the case of the mind, by contrast, not only do we understand it to exist without the body, but, what is more, all the attributes which belong to a body can be denied of it. For it is of the nature of substances that they should mutually exclude one another.

Chapter 4

Matter and thought

John Locke

Chapter III

Of the Extent of Humane Knowledge

§6. From all which it is evident, that *the extent of our Knowledge* comes not only short of the reality of Things, but even of the extent of our own *Ideas.* Though our Knowledge be limited to our *Ideas*, and cannot exceed them either in extent, or perfection; and though these be very narrow bounds, in respect of the extent of Allbeing, and far short of what we may justly imagine to be in some even created understandings, not tied down to the dull and narrow Information, is to be received from some few, and not very acute ways of Perception, such as are our Senses; yet it would be well with us, if our Knowledge were but as large as our *Ideas*, and there were not many Doubts and Enquiries concerning the *Ideas* we have, whereof we are not, nor I believe ever shall be in this World, resolved. Nevertheless, I do not question, but that Humane Knowledge, under the present Circumstances of our Beings and Constitutions may be carried much farther, than it hitherto has been, if Men would sincerely, and with freedom of Mind, employ all that Industry and Labour of Thought, in improving the means of discovering Truth, which they do for the colouring or support of Falshood, to maintain a System, Interest, or Party, they are once engaged in. But yet after all, I think I may, without Injury to humane Perfection, be confident, that our Knowledge would never reach to all we might desire to know concerning those *Ideas* we have; nor be able to surmount all the Difficulties, and resolve all the Questions might arise concerning any of them. We have the *Ideas* of a *Square*, a *Circle*, and *Equality*; and yet, perhaps, shall never be able to find a Circle equal to a Square, and certainly know that it is so. We have the *Ideas* of *Matter* and *Thinking*, but possibly shall never be able to know, whether any mere material Being thinks, or no; it being impossible for us, by the contemplation of our own *Ideas*, without revelation, to discover, whether Omnipotency has not given to some Systems of Matter fitly disposed, a power to perceive and think, or else joined and fixed to Matter so disposed, a thinking immaterial Substance: It being, in respect of our Notions, not much more remote from our Comprehension to conceive, that GOD can, if he pleases, superadd to Matter a Faculty of Thinking,

John Locke, edited extracts from *An Essay Concerning Human Understanding*, ed. P H. Nidditch (Oxford: Clarendon press, 1975), Book IV, Chap. 3, Book IV, chap. 10, and the first and third letters to Stillingfleet in *The Works of John Locke* (London: Thomas Tegg, 1923), vol. iv.

than that he should superadd to it another Substance, with a Faculty of Thinking; since we know not wherein Thinking consists, nor to what sort of Substances the Almighty has been pleased to give that Power, which cannot be in any created Being, but merely by the good pleasure and Bounty of the Creator. For I see no contradiction in it, that the first eternal thinking Being should, if he pleased, give to certain Systems of created sensless matter, put together as he thinks fit, some degrees of sense, perception, and thought: Though, as I think, I have proved, *Lib.* 4. *c.* 10*th.* it is no less than a contradiction to suppose matter (which is evidently in its own nature void of sense and thought) should be that Eternal first thinking Being. What certainty of Knowledge can any one have that some perceptions, such as *v.g.* pleasure and pain, should not be in some bodies themselves, after a certain manner modified and moved, as well as that they should be in an immaterial Substance, upon the Motion of the parts of Body: Body as far as we can conceive being able only to strike and affect body; and Motion, according to the utmost reach of our *Ideas,* being able to produce nothing but Motion, so that when we allow it to produce pleasure or pain, or the *Idea* of a Colour, or Sound, we are fain to quit our Reason, go beyond our *Ideas,* and attribute it wholly to the good Pleasure of our Maker. For since we must allow he has annexed Effects to Motion, which we can no way conceive Motion able to produce, what reason have we to conclude, that he could not order them as well to be produced in a Subject we cannot conceive capable of them, as well as in a Subject we cannot conceive the motion of Matter can any way operate upon? I say not this, that I would any way lessen the belief of the Soul's Immateriality: I am not here speaking of Probability, but Knowledge; and I think not only, that it becomes the Modesty of Philosophy, not to pronounce Magisterially, where we want that Evidence that can produce Knowledge; but also, that it is of use to us, to discern how far our Knowledge does reach; for the state we are at present in, not being that of Vision, we must, in many Things, content our selves with Faith and Probability: and in the present Question, about the immateriality of the Soul, if our Faculties cannot arrive at demonstrative Certainty, we need not think it strange. All the great Ends of Morality and Religion, are well enough secured, without philosophical Proofs of the Soul's Immateriality; since it is evident, that he who made us at first begin to subsist here, sensible intelligent Beings, and for several years continued us in such a state, can and will restore us to the like state of Sensibility in another World, and make us capable there to receive the Retribution he has designed to Men, according to their doings in this Life. And therefore 'tis not of such mighty necessity to determine one way or t'other, as some over zealous for, or against the Immateriality of the Soul, have been forward to make the World believe. Who, either on the one side, indulging too much to their Thoughts immersed altogether in Matter, can allow no existence to what is not material: Or, who on the other side, finding not *Cogitation* within the natural Powers of Matter, examined over and over again, by the utmost Intention of Mind, have the confidence to conclude, that Omnipotency it self, cannot give Perception and Thought to a Substance, which has the Modification of Solidity. He that considers how hardly Sensation is, in our Thoughts, reconcilable to extended Matter; or Existence to any thing that hath no Extension at all, will confess, that he is very far from certainly knowing what his Soul is. 'Tis a Point, which seems to me, to be put out of the reach of our Knowledge: And he who will give himself leave to consider freely, and look into the dark and intricate part of each Hypothesis, will scarce find his Reason able to determine him fixedly for, or against the Soul's Materiality. Since on which side soever he views it, either as an unextended Substance, or as a thinking extended Matter; the difficulty to conceive either, will, whilst either alone is in his Thoughts, still drive him to the contrary side. An unfair way which some Men take with themselves: who, because of the unconceivableness of something they find in one, throw themselves violently into the contrary Hypothesis, though altogether as unintelligible to an unbiassed Understanding. This serves, not only to shew the Weakness and the Scantiness of our Knowledge, but the insignificant Triumph of such sort of Arguments, which, drawn from our own Views, may satisfy us that we can find no certainty on one side of the Question; but do not at all thereby help us to Truth, by running into the opposite Opinion, which, on examination, will be found clogg'd with equal difficulties. For what Safety, what Advantage to any one is it, for the avoiding the seeming Absurdities, and, to him, unsurmountable Rubs he meets with in one Opinion, to take refuge in the contrary, which is built on something altogether as inexplicable, and as far remote from his Comprehension? 'Tis past controversy, that we have in us something that thinks, our very Doubts about what it is, confirm the certainty of its being, though we must content our selves in the Ignorance of what kind of *Being* it is: And 'tis in vain to go about to be sceptical in this, as it is unreasonable in most other cases to be positive against the being of any thing, because we cannot comprehend its Nature. For I would fain know what Substance exists that has not something in it, which manifestly baffles our Understandings. Other Spirits, who see and know the Nature and inward Constitution of things, how much must they exceed us in Knowledge? To which if we add larger Comprehension, which enables them at one Glance to see the Connexion and Agreement of very many *Ideas*, and readily supplys to them the intermediate Proofs, which we by single and slow Steps, and long poring in the dark, hardly at last find out, and are often ready to forget one before we have hunted out another, we may guess at some part of the Happiness of superior Ranks of Spirits, who have a quicker and more penetrating Sight, as well as a larger Field of Knowledge. But to return to the Argument in hand, our *Knowledge*, I say, is not only limited to the Paucity and Imperfections of the *Ideas* we have, and which we employ it about, but even comes short of that too: But how far it reaches, let us now enquire.

Chapter X

Knowledge of the Existance of a GOD

§10. For it is as impossible to conceive, that ever bare incogitative Matter should produce a thinking intelligent Being, as that nothing should of it self produce Matter. Let us suppose any parcel of Matter eternal, great or small, we shall find it, in it self, able to produce nothing. For Example; let us suppose the Matter of the next Pebble, we meet with, eternal, closely united, and the parts firmly at rest together, if there were no other Being in the World, Must it not eternally remain so, a dead inactive Lump? Is it possible to conceive it can add Motion to it self, being purely Matter, or produce any thing? Matter then, by its own Strength, cannot produce in it self so much as Motion: the Motion it has, must also be from Eternity, or else be produced, and added to Matter by some other Being more powerful than Matter; Matter, as is evident, having not Power to produce Motion in it self. But let us suppose Motion eternal too; yet Matter, *incogitative Matter* and Motion, whatever changes it might produce of Figure and Bulk, *could never produce Thought*: Knowledge will still be as far beyond the Power of Motion and Matter to produce, as Matter is beyond the Power of *nothing*, or *nonentity* to produce. And I appeal to everyone's own Thoughts, whether he cannot as easily conceive Matter produced by *nothing*, as Thought to be produced by pure Matter, when before there was no such thing as Thought, or an intelligent Being existing. Divide Matter into as minute parts as you will, (which we are apt to imagine a sort of spiritualizing, or making a thinking thing of it,) vary the Figure and Motion of it, as much as you please, a Globe, Cube, Cone, Prism, Cylinder, *etc.* whose Diameters are but 1000000th part of a *Gry* will operate no otherwise upon other Bodies of proportionable Bulk, than those of an inch or foot Diameter; and you may as rationally expect to produce Sense, Thought, and Knowledge, by putting together in a certain Figure and Motion, gross Particles of Matter, as by those that are the very minutest, that do any where exist. They knock, impell, and resist one another, just as the greater do, and that is all they can do. So that if we will suppose nothing first, or eternal; *Matter* can never begin to be: If we suppose bare Matter, without Motion, eternal; *Motion* can never begin to be: If we suppose only Matter and Motion first, or eternal; *Thought* can never begin to be. For it is impossible to conceive that Matter either with or without Motion could have originally in and from it self Sense, Perception, and Knowledge, as is evident from hence, that then Sense, Perception, and Knowledge must be a property eternally inseparable from Matter and every Particle of it. Not to add, that though our general or specifick conception of Matter makes us speak of it as one thing, yet really all Matter is not one individual thing, neither is there any such thing existing as one material Being or one single Body that we know or can conceive. And therefore if Matter were the eternal first cogitative Being, there would not be one eternal infinite cogitative Being, but an infinite number of eternal finite cogitative Beings, independent one of another, of limited force, and distinct thoughts, which could never produce that order, harmony, and beauty which is to be found in Nature.

From Locke's first letter to Stillingfleet[1]

Your lordship argues, that upon my principles it "cannot be proved that there is a spiritual substance in us." To which give me leave, with submission, to say, that I think it may be proved from my principles, and I think I have done it; and the proof in my book stands thus: First, we experiment in ourselves thinking. The idea of this action or mode of thinking is inconsistent with the idea of self-subsistence, and therefore has a necessary connexion with a support or subject of inhesion: the idea of that support is what we call substance; and so from thinking experimented in us, we have a proof of a thinking substance in us, which in my sense is a spirit. Against this your lordship will argue, that by what I have said of the possibility that God may, if he pleases, superadd to matter a faculty of thinking, it can never be proved that there is a spiritual substance in us, because upon that supposition it is possible it may be a material substance that thinks in us. I grant it; but add, that the general idea of substance being the same every where, the modification of thinking, or the power of thinking joined to it, makes it a spirit, without considering what other modifications it has, as whether it has the modification of solidity or no. As on the other side, substance, that has the modification or solidity, is matter, whether it has the modification of thinking or no. And therefore, if your lordship means by a spiritual an immaterial substance, I grant I have not proved, nor upon my principles can it be proved, (your lordship meaning, as I think you do, demonstratively proved) that there is an immaterial substance in us that thinks. Though I presume, from what I have said about the supposition of a system of matter thinking (which there demonstrates that God is immaterial) will prove it in the highest degree probable, that the thinking substance in us is immaterial. But your lordship thinks not probability enough; and by charging the want of demonstration upon my principles, that the thinking thing in us is immaterial, your lordship seems to conclude it demonstrable from principles of philosophy. That demonstration I should with joy receive from your lordship, or any one. For though all the great ends of morality and religion are well enough secured without it, as I have shown; yet it would be a great advance of our knowledge in nature and philosophy.

To what I have said in my book, to show that all the great ends of religion and morality are secured barely by the immortality of the soul, without a necessary supposition that the soul is immaterial, I crave leave to add, that immortality may and shall be annexed to that, which in its own nature is neither immaterial nor

1. A Letter to the Right Reverend Lord Bishop of Worcester, concerning some passages relating to Mr. Locke's *Essay of Human Understanding*, in a late discourse of his Lordship's in Vindication of the Trinity.

immortal, as the apostle expressly declares in these words; "for this corruptible must put on incorruption, and this mortal must put on immortality" (1 Cor. xv. 53).

Perhaps my using the word spirit for a thinking substance, without excluding materiality out of it, will be thought too great a liberty, and such as deserves censure, because I leave immateriality out of the idea I make it a sign of. I readily own, that words should be sparingly ventured on in a sense wholly new; and nothing but absolute necessity can excuse the boldness of using any term, in a sense whereof we can produce no example.

From Locke's: third letter to Stillingfleet

The idea of matter is an extended solid substance; wherever there is such a substance, there is matter, and the essence of matter, whatever other qualities, not contained in that essence, it shall please God to superadd to it. For example, God creates an extended solid substance, without the superadding any thing else to it, and so we may consider it at rest: to some parts of it he superadds motion, but it has still the essence of matter: other parts of it he frames into plants, with all the excellencies of vegetation, life, and beauty, which are to be found in a rose or a peach-tree, &c. above the essence of matter in general, but it is still but matter: to other parts he adds sense and spontaneous motion, and those other properties that are to be found in an elephant. Hitherto it is not doubted but the power of God may go, and that the properties of a rose, a peach, or an elephant, superadded to matter, change not the properties of matter; but matter is in these things matter still. But if one venture to go on one step further, and say, God may give to matter thought, reason, and volition, as well as sense and spontaneous motion, there are men ready presently to limit the power of the omnipotent Creator, and tell us he cannot do it; because it destroys the essence, "changes the essential properties of matter." To make good which assertion, they have no more to say, but that thought and reason are not included in the essence of matter. I grant it; but whatever excellency, not contained in its essence, be superadded to matter, it does not destroy the essence of matter, if it leaves it an extended solid substance; wherever that is, there is the essence of matter: and if every thing of greater perfection, superadded to such a substance, destroys the essence of matter, what will become of the essence of matter in a plant, or an animal, whose properties far exceed those of a mere extended solid substance?

But it is farther urged, that we cannot conceive how matter can think. I grant it; but to argue from thence, that God therefore cannot give to matter a faculty of thinking, is to say God's omnipotency is limited to a narrow compass, because man's understanding is so; and brings down God's infinite power to the size of our capacities. If God can give no power to any parts of matter, but what men can account for from the essence of matter in general; if all such qualities and properties must destroy the essence, or change the essential properties. of matter, which are to our conceptions above it, and we cannot conceive to be the natural consequence of that essence: it is plain, that the essence of matter is destroyed, and its essential properties changed in most of the sensible parts of this our system. For it is visible, that all the planets have revolutions about certain remote centres, which I would have any one explain, or make conceivable by the bare essence or natural powers depending on the essence of matter in general, without something added to that essence, which we cannot conceive: for the moving of matter in a crooked line, or the attraction of matter by matter, is all that can be said in the case; either of which it is above our reach to derive from the essence of matter, or body in general; though one of these two must unavoidably be allowed to be superadded in this instance to the essence of matter in general. The omnipotent Creator advised not with us in the making of the world, and his ways are not the less excellent, because they are past our finding out.

In the next place, the vegetable part of the creation is not doubted to be wholly material; and yet he that will look into it, will observe excellencies and operations in this part of matter, which he will not find contained in the essence of matter in general, nor be able to conceive how they can be produced by it. And will he therefore say, that the essence of matter is destroyed in them, because they have properties and operations not contained in the essential properties of matter as matter, nor explicable by the essence of matter in general?

Let us advance one step farther, and we shall, in the animal world, meet with yet greater perfections and properties, no ways explicable by the essence of matter in general. If the omnipotent Creator had not superadded to the earth, which produced the irrational animals, qualities far surpassing those of the dull dead earth, out of which they were made, life, sense, and spontaneous motion, nobler qualities than were before in it, it had still remained rude senseless matter; and if to the individuals of each species he had not superadded a power of propagation, the species had perished with those individuals: but by these essences or properties of each species, superadded to the matter which they were made of, the essence or properties of matter in general were not destroyed or changed, any more than any thing that was in the individuals before was destroyed or changed by the power of generation, superadded to them by the first benediction of the Almighty.

In all such cases, the superinducement of greater perfections and nobler qualities destroys nothing of the essence or perfections that were there before, unless there can be showed a manifest repugnancy between them; but all the proof offered for that, is only, that we cannot conceive how matter, without such superadded perfections, can produce such effects; which is, in truth, no more than to say, matter in general, or every part of matter, as matter, has them not; but is no reason to prove that God, if he pleases, cannot superadded them to some parts of matter: unless it can be proved to be a contradiction, that God should give to some parts of matter qualities and perfections, which matter in general has not; though we cannot conceive how matter is invested with them, or how it operates by virtue of those new endowments. Nor is it to be wondered that we cannot, whilst we limit all its operations to those qualities it had before, and would explain them by the known properties of matter in general, without any such superinduced perfections. For if this be a right rule of reasoning to deny a thing to be, because we cannot conceive the manner how it comes to be; I shall desire them who use it to stick to this rule, and see what work it will make both in divinity as well as philosophy; and whether they can advance any thing more in favour of scepticism.

For to keep within the present subject of the power of thinking and self-motion, bestowed by omnipotent Power on some parts of matter: the objection to this is, I cannot conceive how matter should think. What is the consequence? *ergo*, God cannot give it a power to think. Let this stand for a good reason, and then proceed in other cases by the same. You cannot conceive how matter can attract matter at any distance, much less at the distance of 1,000,000 miles; *ergo*, God cannot give it such a power. You cannot conceive how matter should feel or move itself, or affect an immaterial being, or be moved by it; *ergo*, God cannot give it such powers: which is in *effect* to deny gravity and the revolution of the planets about the sun; to make brutes mere machines, without sense or spontaneous motion; and to allow man neither sense nor voluntary motion.

Let us apply this rule one degree farther. You cannot conceive how an extended solid substance should think, therefore God cannot make it think: can you conceive how your own soul, or any substance thinks? You find indeed, that you do think, and so do I; but I want to be told how the action of thinking is performed: this, I confess, is beyond my conception; and I would be glad any one, who conceives it, would explain it to me. God, I find, has given me this faculty; and since I cannot but be convinced of his power in this instance, which though I every moment experiment in myself, yet I cannot conceive the manner of; what would it be less than an insolent absurdity to deny his power in other like cases only for this reason, because I cannot conceive the manner how?

To explain this matter a little farther: God has created a substance; let it be, for example, a solid extended substance: is God bound to give it, besides being, a power of action? that, I think, nobody will say. He therefore may leave it in a state of inactivity, and it will be nevertheless a substance; for action is not necessary to the being of any substance, that God does create. God has likewise created and made to exist, *de novo*, an immaterial substance, which will not lose its being of a substance, though God should bestow on it nothing more but this bare being, without giving it any activity at all. Here are now two distinct substances, the one material, the other immaterial, both in a state of perfect inactivity. Now I ask what power God can give to one of these substances (supposing them to retain the same distinct natures, that they had as substances in their state of inactivity) which he cannot give to the other? In that state, it is plain, neither of them thinks; for thinking being an action, it cannot be denied that God can put an end to any action of any created substance, without annihilating of the substance whereof it is an action: and if it be so, he can also create or give existence to such a substance, without giving that substance any action at all. Now I would ask, why Omnipotency cannot give to either of these substances, which are equally in a state of perfect inactivity, the same power that it can give to the other? Let it be, for example, that of spontaneous or self-motion, which is a power that it is supposed God can give to an unsolid substance, but denied that he can give to a solid substance.

If it be asked, why they limit the omnipotency of God, in reference to the one rather than the other of these substances; all that can be said to it is, that they cannot conceive how the solid substance should ever be able to move itself. And as little, say I, are they able to conceive how a created unsolid substance should move itself; but there may be something in an immaterial substance, that you do not know. I grant it; and in a material one too: for example, gravitation of matter towards matter, and in the several proportions observable, inevitably shows, that there is something in matter that we do not understand, unless we can conceive self-motion in matter; or an inexplicable and inconceivable attraction in matter, at immense and almost incomprehensible distances: it must therefore be confessed, that there is something in solid, as well as unsolid substances, that we do not understand. But this we know, that they may each of them have their distinct beings, without any activity superadded to them, unless you will deny, that God can take from any being its power of acting, which it is probable will be thought too presumptuous for any one to do; and, I say, it is as hard to conceive self-motion in a created immaterial, as in a material being, consider it how you will: and therefore this is no reason to deny Omnipotency to be able to give a power of self-motion to a material substance, if he pleases, as well as to an immaterial; since neither of them can have it from themselves, nor can we conceive how it can be in either of them.

The same is visible in the other operation of thinking; both these substances may be made, and exist without thought; neither of them has, or can have the power of thinking from itself: God may give it to either of them, according to the good pleasure of his omnipotency; and in whichever of them it is, it is equally beyond our capacity to conceive how either of those substances thinks. But for that reason to deny that God, who had power enough to give them both a being out of nothing, can, by the same omnipotency, give them what other powers and perfections he pleases, has no better a foundation than to deny his power of creation, because we cannot conceive how it is performed: and there at last this way of reasoning must terminate.

Questions

1. Authors in this part speak of *souls*, *minds*, *selves*, and *persons*. Are these distinct categories or just different names for the same entities? If there are differences, what are they?
2. Philosophers distinguish substances—bearers of properties—from properties—ways substances are. To which category do souls, minds, selves, and persons belong?
3. Suppose you are confronting an uncomfortable long-distance trip to visit a sick relative. You are offered an instantaneous transfer via a Teletransporter of the sort depicted in *Star Trek*. Do you accept the offer? What might your answer reveal about your own conception of mind or self?
4. Descartes distinguishes the attribute of thought from the attribute of extension and argues that (God aside) these attributes are exhaustive and mutually exclusive. Every substance is either a thinking substance or an extended substance; no substance is both. To what extent does a view of this kind complement or conflict with views of the world current today?
5. Descartes is famous for making the mind–body problem salient. What *is* the mind–body problem?
6. To what extent, if any, are the positions defended by Plato and Aristotle susceptible to the mind–body problem?
7. Suppose Descartes is right: minds exist 'outside' the material world. If minds causally interact with bodies, it looks as though minds intervene in the natural order, a violation of 'closure'. Why should this be regarded as a difficulty for Cartesian conceptions of mind?
8. Quantum theory seems to tell us that the world is, at bottom, non-deterministic. If that were so, would Cartesian style mind–body interaction be more palatable?
9. Accepting a distinction between substances and modes or properties, which authors in this part regard minds as substances, and which regard them as modes (ways substances are)? What is at stake here?
10. How does Locke distinguish mental substances, 'spirits', from material substances? In what respects are Locke and Descartes alike in this distinction? How do they differ?

Suggested readings

A number of collections in the philosophy of mind include readings by historical figures from Plato to the modern era. By excerpting pertinent passages, such collections can save readers the trouble of finding these in the midst of longer works. Examples include Vesey (1964) and, more recently, Beakley and Ludlow (1992), Kolak (1997), Morton (1997), and Robinson (1999), all of which contain numerous historical readings.

Matson (1966) raises the question 'Why Isn't the Mind—Body Problem Ancient?' in a way that can illuminate assumptions Plato and Aristotle shared with their contemporaries—but not with more modern readers. More of these assumptions surface in Burnyeat (1992). These discussions make it clear that the question 'Can we learn from the ancients?' is not just a 'feel-good' question for scholars, but a question we are bound to answer in the affirmative. Discussions of Plato's views on the mind can be found in most commentaries on Plato. See, for instance, Kraut (1992) and Smith (1998). Bostock (1999) discusses the argument for immortality in the *Phaedo*; Lovibond (1991) provides a synoptic account of Plato's conception of the mind.

The question whether Aristotle is a functionalist is addressed in Burnyeat (1992), which appears in Nussbaum and Rorty (1992), a collection that includes a dozen other essays on Aristotle's conception of the mind by respected philosophers. See also Barnes (1971), Shields (1988), and Irwin (1991) for penetrating discussions of Aristotle.

Secondary material on Descartes's dualism is voluminous. An interested reader could start by looking at Almog (2002); Baker and Morris (1996); Chappell (1997); Cottingham (1992*b*); Cottingham (1999: chap. 2); Rozemond (1998); Williams (1978: chap. 4); and chap. 6 of Wilson (1978). Hooker (1978) features essays by Alan Donagan, Michael Hooker, Ruth Mattern, Frederick Somers, and Margaret Wilson on various aspects of Cartesian dualism.

Most of what is written about Locke and the mind concerns Locke's account of the 'personal identity'; see, for instance, Lowe (1995: chap. 5). Yolton (1983) discusses the materialist streak in Locke and his contemporaries; and Lowe (2000) and Martin (1980) discuss Locke's conception of substance in a way that bears on this distinctive brand of materialism; see also Heil (2003). For more general discussion of Locke's conception of the mind, see Bennett (1994) and Woolhouse (1983: chap. 17).

General

Beakley, B., and P. Ludlow, eds. (1992), *The Philosophy of Mind: Classical Problems, Comtemporary Issues.* Cambridge, MA: MIT Press.

Everson, S. ed. (1991), *Companions to Ancient Thought 2: Psychology.* Cambridge: Cambridge University Press.

Feyerabend, P. K., and G. Maxwell, eds. (1966), *Mind, Matter, and Method: Essays in the Philosophy of Science in Honor of Herbert Feigl.* Minneapolis: University of Minnesota Press.

Kolak, D., ed. (1997), *From Plato to Wittgenstein: The Historical Foundations of Mind.* Belmont, CA: Wadsworth Publishing Co.

Morton, P., ed. (1997), *Historical Introduction to the Philosophy of Mind: Readings with Commentary.* Peterborough: Broadview Press.

Matson, W. I. (1966), 'Why Isn't the Mind—Body Problem Ancient?' In Feyerabend and Maxwell 1966: 92–102.

Robinson, D. N. ed. (1999), *The Mind*. New York: Oxford University Press.

Vesey, G. N. A. (1964), *Body and Mind: Readings in Philosophy*. London: George Allen & Unwin.

Plato

Bostock, D. (1999), 'The Soul and Immortality in Plato's Phaedo'. In Fine 1999: 404–24.

Fine, G., ed. (1999), *Plato 2: Ethics, Politics, Religion, and the Soul*. Oxford: Oxford University Press.

Kraut, R., ed. (1992), *The Cambridge Companion to Plato*. Cambridge: Cambridge University Press.

Lovibond, S. (1991), 'Plato's Theory of Mind'. In Everson 1991: 35–55.

Smith, N. D., ed. (1998), *Plato: Critical Assessments*, vol. iii: *Plato's Middle Period, Psychology, and Value Theory*. London: Routledge.

Aristotle

Barnes, J. (1971), 'Aristotle's Concept of Mind', *Proceedings of the Aristotelian Society* 75: 101–14.

Burnyeat, M. F. (1992), 'Is an Aristotelian Philosophy of Mind Still Credible?' In Nussbaum and Rorty 1992: 15–26.

Irwin, T. H. (1991), 'Aristotle's Philosophy of Mind'. In Everson 1991: 56–83.

Nussbaum, M. C., and A. O. Rorty, eds. (1992), *Essays on Aristotle's* De Anima. Oxford: Clarendon Press.

Shields, C. (1988), 'Soul and Body in Aristotle', *Oxford Studies in Ancient Philosophy* 6: 103–38.

Sorabji, R. (1974), 'Body and Soul in Aristotle', *Philosophy* 49: 63–89.

Descartes

Almog, J. (2002), *What Am I? Descartes and the Mind—Body Problem*. New York: Oxford University Press.

Baker, G., and K. J. Morris (1996), *Descartes's Dualism*. London: Routledge.

Chappell, V. C. (1997), 'Descartes's Ontology', *Topoi* 16: 111–27.

Cottingham, J. ed. (1992*a*), *The Cambridge Companion to Descartes*. Cambridge: Cambridge University Press.

——(1992*b*), 'Dualism: Theology, Metaphysics, and Science'. In Cottingham 1992*a*: 236–57.

——(1999), *Descartes*. New York: Routledge.

Hooker, M., ed. (1978), *Descartes: Critical and Interpretive Essays*. Baltimore: Johns Hopkins University Press.

Rozemond, M. (1998), *Descartes's Dualism*. Cambridge, MA: Harvard University Press.

Williams, B. (1978), *Descartes: The Project of Pure Enquiry*. Harmondsworth: Penguin Books.

Wilson, M. D. (1978), *Descartes*. London: Routledge.

Locke

Bennett, J. (1994), 'Locke's Philosophy of Mind'. In Chappell 1994: 89–114.

Chappell, V. C., ed. (1994), *The Cambridge Companion to Locke.* Cambridge: Cambridge University press.

Heil, J. (2003), *From an Ontological Point of View.* Oxford: Clarendon Press.

Lowe, E. J. (1995), *Locke on Human Understanding.* London: Routledge.

——(2000), 'Locke, Martin, and Substance'. *Philosophical Quarterly* 50: 499–514.

Martin, C. B. (1980), 'Substance Substantiated', *Australasian Journal of Philosophy* 58: 3–10.

Woolhouse, R. S. (1983), *Locke.* Minneapolis: University of Minnesota Press.

Yolton, J. W. (1983), *Thinking Matter: Materialism in Eighteenth Century Britain.* Minneapolis: University of Minnesota Press.

Part II

Behaviorism and mind–brain identity

Introduction

THE term 'behaviorism' applies both to a movement in psychology and to a philosophical doctrine. A behaviorist psychologist could well reject the principles of philosophical behaviorism; philosophical behaviorists typically distance themselves from behaviorists in psychology. After a brief discussion of psychological behaviorism, I will turn the spotlight on philosophical behaviorism: behaviorism as a conception of the nature of mind.

Behaviorism in psychology, though rooted in earlier psychological work, came into its own in the early part of the twentieth century. John B. Watson (1878–1958) published a statement of behaviorist principles in 1913 that began:

> Psychology as the behaviorist views it is a purely objective experimental branch of natural science. Its theoretical goal is the prediction and control of behavior. Introspection forms no essential part of its methods, nor is the scientific value of its data dependent upon the readiness with which they lend themselves to interpretation in terms of consciousness. The behaviorist, in his efforts to get a unitary scheme of animal response, recognizes no dividing line between man and brute. The behavior of man, with all of its refinement and complexity, forms only a part of the behaviorist's total scheme of investigation. (Watson 1913: 158)

Here we encounter a number of central behaviorist tenets.

(1) Psychology is taken to be an 'objective' science, on a par with the natural sciences: physics and chemistry, for instance.
(2) The aim of psychology is the prediction and control of behavior.
(3) Consciousness has no special role to play in psychological accounts of behavior.
(4) Psychology recognizes no discontinuity between human beings and non-human creatures: similar mechanisms underlie all behavior.
(5) Mechanisms responsible for behavior are decomposable into simpler mechanisms; complexity differs from simplicity, in degree only, not in kind.

As (3) makes clear, psychological behaviorists reject the idea that psychology concerns conscious processes. Even if your behavior were produced by some conscious process, what would be important is not the process's being consciousness, but its being a process decomposable into simpler input–output (stimulus–response) processes common across species. Consciousness, if it exists at all, is a mere *epiphenomenon*: an accompaniment that, like the heat given off by a computing machine, makes no important contribution to the operation of the system with which it is associated.

Although behaviorism has come and gone, many of its deepest convictions survive in contemporary conceptions of the mind, most especially in doctrines embraced by functionalists (Part III).

Philosophical behaviorism

I have suggested that psychological and philosophical behaviorists are importantly different. Behaviorists in psychology advance a particular method for explaining behavior, one constrained by a conception of what could constitute a legitimate science of behavior. Philosophical behaviorists, in contrast, have been less interested in the scientific standing of psychology than with meanings of psychological terms and the significance of ascriptions of states of mind to intelligent agents.

When you say that Lilian is happy or thinking of Vienna, what exactly are you saying? Differently put: what is it about Lilian that makes it true that she is happy or thinking of Vienna? According to Descartes, minds (mental substances) possess distinctive mental properties. When you ascribe happiness or thoughts of Vienna to Lilian, your ascription will be true just in case Lilian possesses the requisite mental properties. A view of this kind worries materialists (or 'physicalists') who are skeptical of the existence of immaterial Cartesian egos. Suppose there are no such immaterial substances. Does this mean that we are wrong about Lilian, wrong to suppose she is happy or thinking of Vienna?

Not at all, say the behaviorists. To say that Lilian is happy or that she is thinking of Vienna is just a way of saying how Lilian is now behaving or would behave under the right circumstances. To say that Lilian is happy, for instance, might be to say that she is smiling, humming to herself, and that she would say 'Yes', if asked 'Are you happy?' This, suitably spelled out, is what it *is* to be happy. Being happy is not a matter of being in a particular sort of inner state, much less a particular sort of *immaterial* inner state; it is to behave and to be disposed to behave in certain ways. An agent's behaving and being disposed to behave in particular ways is wholly consistent with the absence of Cartesian egos.

In 'The Logical Analysis of Psychology', Carl Hempel sees the translation of psychological claims into claims about behavior as one element in a broader reductionist project the aim of which is to regiment the language of science. Proponents of this project, the *logical empiricists*, were following in the footsteps of Berkeley and Hume (George Berkeley 1685–1753; David Hume 1711–76). Hume, for instance, had argued that meaningful statements about the world must be expressible as statements about actual or possible observations. Other meaningful statements—that bachelors are unmarried, for instance, or that 2 + 3 = 5—concerned only our concepts, and ultimately the linguistic framework we use in describing our world. Hume called substantive assertions about the world statements of *matters of fact*, and assertions that concerned only the conceptual or linguistic framework in terms of which we frame substantive assertions, statements of *relations among ideas*.

Hume wielded this distinction in a campaign to undermine the pretensions of philosophers and theologians who claimed to provide accounts of the nature of the world that went beyond observation. A statement that purports to be about the world must be expressible as or translatable into a statement about actual or possible observations: those observations that would justify a belief that the statement is true. (Hempel puts this by saying that '*the meaning of a proposition is established by the conditions of its verification*'.) Otherwise the statement is merely a statement as to how words are used ('bachelors are unmarried')—or flatly meaningless. Because meaningful psychological statements can, on this view, be translated into 'propositions of physics', propositions that include no psychological concepts, 'but only the concepts of physics . . . psychology is an integral part of physics'.

You might think that observations used in the application of psychological terms concern, at most, only signs or symptoms of underlying psychological states. Such states seem to 'lie behind' the behavior we observe. The logical empiricist disagrees. *All there is* to a psychological claim (or, indeed, any claim about the world) is captured by observations that would warrant our acceptance of the claim. No sense can be made of unobservable goings-on 'behind' these observations. In contending that psychological states are distinct from the behavior that constitutes evidence for those states, an opponent is not guilty of uttering a falsehood, but of producing a meaningless utterance. We can literally *make no sense* of claims about the world that go beyond actual and possible observation.

Behaviorists eschew the idea that minds are entities, mental organs within the confines of which thinking, feeling, and scheming occur. Thinking, feeling, and scheming are nothing more than ways of behaving. No doubt behavior has complex physiological causes. But it is a mistake—a 'category mistake' according to Gilbert Ryle (1949)—to imagine that states of mind are causes of behavior. Your being angry or being in pain is like a team's having team spirit. When a team plays well, we say that it exhibits team spirit. But team spirit is not an entity, an unusally talented member of the team. Team spirit is just the way the team plays: to have team spirit is to play in an especially animated way. Similarly, being angry is not a matter of being in some definite state, but simply a matter of your comporting yourself in ways characteristic of an angry person.

Privileged access

Logical behaviorism provides a tidy explanation of an otherwise vexing feature of the special relation you seem to bear to your own states of mind. You apparently enjoy a kind of access to your own states of mind that others *could not* have. This has suggested to some philosophers that states of mind must be immaterial: any material state could, under the right circumstances, be observed by more than one spectator. In the case of your own states of mind (and unlike the case of states of your own brain), however, you are in a position to observe what no one else *could* observe—or at any rate, not *directly* observe. (Others might be said to observe your states of mind *indirectly* by observing effects of these on your behavior or on instruments scanning your brain.)

Behaviorists argue that the asymmetry here could be explained without resorting to immaterial minds. Suppose, for instance, that claims about the psychological states of others are in fact claims about observable behavior, while so-called reports of your own states of mind are not strictly speaking reports at all. When *I* say, 'You are in pain', I am saying something about how you are behaving or would behave. When *you* say 'I am in pain', you are *evincing* your pain: you are not saying something that could be true or false. The significance of 'I am in pain' is like the significance of groaning or spontaneously blurting 'Ouch!'

This provides us with a tidy explanation of the asymmetry between first- and third-person psychological state assertions, and the apparent 'privilege' enjoyed by first-person psychological utterances. Your spontaneous utterance, 'Ouch!' is an expression of your pain (and not a self-ascription), so it cannot be false. It cannot be false, not because you have infallible inner access to your own states of mind, but because *expressions* of pain can be *neither* true nor false. Further, your saying (sincerely) 'I am in pain', is part of what supports my ascription of pain to you. In saying that you are in pain, I am saying nothing more than that you are behaving or would behave in particular ways, where the behavior in question includes your utterance of 'I am in pain'.

Very neat. But we seem to have left something out: the feeling of pain! Surely, your blurting 'Ouch!' or uttering in a more measured way, 'I am in pain', are, like the swelling in your finger that results from your striking it with a hammer, *effects* of your being in a particular state: a state of pain. There is the pain itself—an effect, perhaps, of a hammer's blow—and there are the pain's effects—your finger's swelling and turning blue, your blurting 'Ouch!' and seeking out the first aid kit. Your being in pain is not simply a matter of your doing these things (or being disposed to do them). It is a matter of your being in a particular state that causes you to do these things.

This, at any rate, is one natural response to the behaviorist. A question you should ask yourself as you read Hempel is whether behaviorists have tossed the baby out with the bathwater. Do translations of talk about states of mind into talk of how agents behave or would behave leave out what is most important about states of mind: their 'inner feel'? Or is talk of 'inner feels' merely a holdover from our Cartesian heritage—in the way talk of the sun rising and setting is a relic of a pre-Copernican world view? Before rushing to answer these questions, you might reflect on a more general issue: the nature of terms used in explanations of behavior.

Pain and pain behavior

Logical Behaviorism rests on the idea that the meaning of substantive claims about the world is exhausted by observations that would confirm those claims. It is easy to doubt that this is so. Consider Hilary Putnam's example of polio. For many years, polio was associated with a range of symptoms. When Salk discovered the polio virus, Putnam argues, he discovered what polio was: a certain condition brought on by the presence of a particular virus and associated with certain symptoms. An unfortunate person who had all the usual symptoms of polio, but who was not infected by the virus, would not have polio.

This is evidently built into our concept of polio, so it would have made sense, even before Salk's important discovery, to allow that a person might have polio symptoms—and thus we would be wholly justified in saying that he had polio—but the person not have polio at all. This suggests that the meaning of 'has polio' cannot be translated into talk about particular symptoms.

What goes for polio, evidently goes for pain. You can meaningfully distinguish the condition—being in pain—from behavioral symptoms produced by this condition. You can do this, even if you have no very clear idea what pains might turn out to be: states or events of a certain kind in the central nervous system, perhaps, or occurrences in an immaterial substance. Indeed, our beliefs about the nature of pains could be mostly false in the way a scientist's beliefs about the nature of polio could have been mostly false a century ago.

Considerations of this kind take the wind out of the behaviorist's sails. There is no reason to think that talk about unobserved, and perhaps unobservable, conditions is meaningless. We can observe the products of such conditions, but this need not oblige us to suppose that talk of the conditions is reducible to talk of their products.

Dispositions

Behaviorists reject the idea that states of mind are internal states of creatures possessing them. To be angry, for instance, is not to be in a particular kind of internal state that causes behavior of certain familiar kinds; to be angry is to behave in an angry manner *or to be so disposed*. You might be angry but, owing to the circumstances, not behave angrily. Nevertheless, say the behaviorists, you would behave angrily were you in different circumstances: you are *disposed* to behave angrily.

What is it for an object to be disposed to behave in a particular way? Consider a fragile goblet: the goblet is disposed to shatter if struck by a massive hard object or dropped on a rigid surface. This disposition is, arguably, a state of the goblet: the goblet's being fragile is a matter of its being in a certain state. If the goblet is heated to a very high temperature, this state could change, and the goblet cease to be fragile.

If pains, thoughts, and the like are dispositions, however, and if dispositions are states, then it is hard not to conclude that states of mind must after all be states. If you are in one of these states you are disposed to behave in particular ways, perhaps. But your being in pain or your imagining Vienna, is a matter of your being in a particular state, not a matter of your behaving in any particular way. How you behave, after all, depends on endless factors, including your circumstances, or your beliefs about those circumstances, and your aims. A baseball player struck by a pitch may forbear 'pain behavior'. Here it is natural to say that the baseball player is in a state of pain, but other factors inhibit the pain's overt manifestation.

If you take the behaviorist's idea that states of mind typically involve behavior of particular sorts and couple this with the idea that states of mind are genuine states, the result is something close to functionalism (Part III). Indeed, functionalism is a direct descendent of behaviorism.

Identifying states of mind with brain states

The demise of verificationism in philosophy brought with it the demise of philosophical behaviorism. At about the same time, Noam Chomsky launched a powerful attack on the psychological behaviorists from another direction, arguing that behaviorism could not, even in principle, account for our capacity to learn and deploy languages (Chomsky 1959). Behaviorism was out. In rejecting behaviorism, however, we reopen the question, what is the mind?

If you find behaviorism implausible, this might be because you accept the idea that states of mind are internal states. These states are dispositional, perhaps, but they *underlie* behavior in the sense of being causally responsible for behavior; they are not in any sense *reducible* to behavior. It is easy to forget, however, that one strong attraction of behaviorism was that behaviorism promised to provide a straightforward answer to the question, how are minds and bodies related.

Suppose you were committed to the materialist idea that all that exists are material bodies that possess ordinary material properties, and stand in various spatial and temporal relations. Despite its widely discussed liabilities, many scientists and philosophers embrace some form of materialism. Behaviorism is uncontroversially materialistic. In rejecting behaviorism, materialists reject a comfortable ally. Your rejection of behaviorism might be founded on a conviction that states of mind are internal states. The question now is: states of *what*? The natural materialist response is that states of mind are brain states: *minds are brains*.

But wait. How *could* minds be brains? You know your own states of mind directly, merely by reflection. But you probably know little or nothing about your brain, and what you do know you know indirectly. You might observe your brain in action on a television screen connected to a brain-scanning device. You might even view your brain in a mirror if your skull were cut open by a surgeon. What you view when you view a brain, however, is nothing at all like what you are aware of when you are aware of your own states of mind. When you experience a pain, certain fibers—C-fibers, let us pretend—might be firing in your brain. But the qualities of your pain are nothing at all like the observable qualities of your C-fibers.

Thoughts like these, coupled with the conviction that states of mind are inner states, have led many philosophers to dualism, the view that minds—or at any rate mental properties—are wholly distinct from material substances or properties. Dualism does an excellent job of accounting for our experiences, but dualism is not easy to square with what science seems to tell us about the natural world. Further, it is hard to know what the relation between material and immaterial entities and goings-on might be. Do material and immaterial entities exist independently, in different realms? Are changes in one merely correlated with changes in the other? Or do they, as they seem to do, interact? If they interact, how do they interact without 'violating' laws governing the behavior of material bodies?

Identity

Dualist philosophers have not lacked for answers to these questions. There has been, however, little consensus among dualists themselves. Some persist in the Cartesian belief that minds are non-material substances; others prefer the thesis that the mental–physical distinction is a distinction among properties, not substances. Meanwhile, materialists have continued to insist that we should do better to reject the notion that mental states and goings-on belong to an immaterial realm. The hope is that we can locate them, somehow, in the material world.

In 1956, U. T. Place ('Is Consciousness a Brain Process?') defended the claim that mental goings-on could be identified with goings-on in the brain. It is worth noting that this revolutionary paper appeared, not in a philosophy journal (Ryle, the editor of *Mind*, had rejected it), but in the *British Journal of Psychology*. This provides an indication of the philosophical climate in which Place was writing, a climate decidedly hostile to what is now known as Australian materialism (in honor of Place, J. J. C. Smart, C. B. Martin, D. M. Armstrong, and others who held academic posts in Australia). At about the same time, in the United States, Herbert Feigl was developing his own distinctive variant of the identity theory at the University of Minnesota (see Feigl 1958).

Place contended that in identifying states of mind with brain states, he was not claiming that talk of thoughts or pains could be *translated into* talk of brains; he was advancing an *empirical* hypothesis. The assumption was that we could discover correlations between agents' reports of their states of mind and goings-on in the brain. How do we explain this correlation? If *A*s are correlated with *B*s, this might be because *A*s cause *B*s (or *B*s, *A*s), or because *A*s and *B*s have a common cause, *C*. So one possibility is that goings-on in the brain *cause* mental goings-on, and these, in turn, give rise to reports of mental goings on. Another, more radical possibility is that the *A*s are really nothing but the *B*s. Suppose mental states *are* brain states and these cause mental-state reports. This is the identity theory: states of mind are—that is, *are identical with*—brain states.

Reference to 'identity' here should be understood as encompassing what philosophers call *strict identity*. Identity is a relation everything bears to itself and to nothing else. If *A* and *B* are strictly identical, then *A is B*. Strict identity is to be distinguished from a different sense of identity, the sense in play when you describe pairs of twins or neckties as identical. In such cases, you have in mind, not strict identity, but *exact similarity*.

As Place pointed out, it can happen that what we thought were two things in fact turn out to be identical: *to be one thing*. Think of the Morning Star, *Hesperus*, and the Evening Star, *Phosphorus*. These were discovered (originally by Chinese astronomers) to be one and the same heavenly body: Venus. Similarly, Holmes discovers that the butler *is* the murderer. Such discoveries are not ones you could make from the armchair. You can know a lot about the Evening Star without knowing that it is the Morning Star; and you can be intimately acquainted with the butler without knowing that the butler is the murderer. In just this way, Place contends, we could discover that states of mind are in fact brain states.

How could this be? If *A*s are *B*s is it that every property of an *A* must be a property of a *B*, and vice versa. Brains evidently have properties lacked by conscious mental states, and conscious states have properties not possessed by brains. Imagine that you have stooped to cut a red rose in the garden. You are conscious of the rose's redness, its sweet smell, and the feel of its petals. Your brain is a soggy gray mass of tissue. How could your vivid conscious experience be identical with something soggy and gray?

Place argues that this line of reasoning is defective, an instance of what he calls the *phenomenological fallacy*. This is the fallacy involved in supposing that, in describing a conscious experience, describing how something looks, or smells, or feels, you are describing properties of the experience. The rose is red, sweet-smelling, and soft to the touch; your *experience* of the rose is none of these. Indeed, it is entirely open what the qualities of your *experience* might be: if Place is right, then it is up to the neuroscientists to tell us.

Contingent identity

Place and J. J. C. Smart, writing in defense of the identity theory, described the identification of states of mind with brain states as *contingent identity*. The fact that conscious states are brain states, if it is a fact, is a purely contingent fact about our world: *a fact that could have been otherwise*. Consciousness could have turned out to be housed in a Cartesian ego, for instance. If Descartes was wrong, he was factually wrong. The world could have turned out to be the way Descartes thought it was; but we have (the identity theorists insist) good scientific reasons to think it is otherwise.

Contingent identity is a puzzling notion. A contingent truth is one that could have been otherwise. But how could it be contingent that an entity is identical with itself? If *Hesperus* is *Phosphorus*, how could *Hesperus* have failed to be *Phosphorus*? In 'Identity and Necessity' (Chapter 9), Saul Kripke mounts an argument against contingent identity and extends the argument to a consideration of the contention that states of mind are identical with brain states. Kripke argues that identity is necessary: if *A is B*, then this cannot be merely a contingent fact; it is flatly impossible that *A* could have failed to be *B*. If pains *could* occur in the absence of brain states—in Cartesian immaterial minds, for instance, or in robots—then pains cannot be identified with brain states.

Most philosophers accept Kripke's account of identity: if *A* and *B* are strictly identical, then *A* could not have failed to be *B*. Whether this shows that the mind–brain identity theory is false is less clear. If you follow Kripke, however, you will need some account of how states of mind and brain states (or material states, generally) are related. Are states of mind the causal products of brains, for instance, or do they stand in some other, more intimate relation?

Token identity

Place and Smart defend a version of the mind–body identity theory standardly called type-identity: mental properties or types are identical with material properties or types. Suppose that being in pain is a type of mental state. Then, if you accept type identity, you will suppose some material type—the firing of C-fibers, for instance—is identical with this mental type. More generally, every mental property or type is identical with some material property or type. The envisaged relation between mental properties and material properties is like the relation between water and H_2O: a substance's being water *is* its being H_2O.

This may seem to be restating the obvious, but, when it comes to philosophically circumscribed domains like these, nothing is obvious. Consider a different kind of identity theory. (The kind of theory I have in mind is often associated with Donald Davidson; see Chapter 39.) Suppose you thought that every individual mental state were identical with some material state, but you were skeptical that every mental type or property could be identified with a definite material type or property. Perhaps the property of being in pain could be identified with some definite neurological property (the property of having C-fibers firing in the example above). But it is hard to see how this strategy could extend to states of mind like thoughts of Vienna or desires for power. Could we really hope to find a common neurological feature possessed by all and only thinkers of Vienna and desirers of power?

Reflections of this sort (combined with reflection on functionalist examples of a sort to be encountered in Part III) have led some philosophers to embrace *token* identity: every mental *token* is identical with some physical *token* (every mental state is identical with *some material state or other*), but mental *types* are not identifiable with physical *types*.

The kind of 'double aspect' thesis defended by R. J. Hirst (Chapter 7) can be seen in light of this distinction. Hirst, following Spinoza (1632–77), sees the mental and physical as distinct 'aspects' of a single substance. The brain, for instance, might have a physical and a mental aspect. What are aspects? Perhaps aspects are properties. Thus, to say that the brain has mental and physical aspects is to say the brain has mental and physical properties, a prospect we have encountered already in Locke. Minds are not distinct from brains: to have a mind is to have a brain that possesses both material and mental properties. Aspects might be differently understood, however. Perhaps aspects are tied to different ways of considering or looking at the selfsame entity. The brain is an entity looked at in a particular way, the mind is the very same entity differently apprehended.

Most philosophers regard token identity as much weaker than type identity. If mental types cannot be identified with physical types, they contend, mental properties must be distinct from physical properties. Token identity requires, at most, that creatures with minds must have physical properties if they have mental properties. Cartesians believe that the mental and the physical comprise distinct realms of substance. Token identity theorists, while denying that there are any immaterial substances, allow that mental and physical properties could differ in kind. Every mental property might be a property of a physical substance, but mental properties themselves could not be identified with physical properties: a partial victory for the dualist.

Phenomenal properties

Part of the attraction of the identity theory turns on its being presented, as it were, from the third-person perspective. We posit states of mind to explain behavior. Why not suppose that these states of mind are brain states, the very brain states that control the behavior we aim to explain? The difficulty is to square this with the first-person perspective. You yourself are aware of your conscious states. You have a headache, and as a result announce, 'I have a headache', and proceed to the medicine cabinet in search of aspirin. I explain this behavior by supposing that you have a headache. If the identity theory is right, then this is a matter of my ascribing to you a certain neurological state that, in concert with other states, is responsible for your behaving as you do. But, from your point of view, the headache's most salient feature is not what it might cause you to do but its *painfulness*. How could an identity theory capture mental *qualities*, what philosophers like to call the *phenomenal qualities* of conscious states of mind?

In response, an identity theorist might remind us of Place's *phenomenological fallacy*.

The phenomenological fallacy, recall, involves mistakenly conflating properties of experiences with properties of objects experienced: you visually experience a red rose; the rose, but not your experience, is red. The strategy works well enough in the perceptual case, but how could it be extended to experiences of pains and other inner states? You experience a painful sensation in your toe. How could it help to say that it is not your *experience* of pain that is painful, but what you experience? Even if that were so, we are left with painfulness, a quality hard to square with goings-on in your brain.

Smart provides one response to this difficulty. Consider your experience of a yellowish-orange after-image. Nothing in you is yellowish-orange. Indeed, nothing in your vicinity need be yellowish-orange. Does this mean that the after-image must exist as an immaterial entity located in, or observed by, your mind? Not at all, says Smart. Imagine a case in which you see a yellowish-orange object, an orange, perhaps. Your experience is not yellowish-orange. Now, when you have a yellowish-orange after-image, something is going on inside you *like* what goes on inside you when you see a yellowish-orange object. This might be a matter of representing an object as being yellowish-orange. But, just as in the case of genuinely perceiving a yellowish-orange object, your experience need not have qualities of the object you are experiencing. In the after-image case, *nothing* is yellowish-orange, although you represent something—a transparent blob floating in front of your eyes—as being yellowish-orange.

How plausible is this? You will find this question popping up in the readings in Parts VIII, IX, XI and XII. The difficulty posed here has nagged materialists from the beginning and continues to do so today. As you read various authors in this part and in parts to follow, keep this question before your mind, and ask yourself whether particular materialist responses are adequate. To the extent that they fall short, philosophers and scientists with heavy materialist commitments will need to rethink their positions.

References

Chomsky, N. (1959), 'Review of B. F. Skinner's *Verbal Behavior*', *Language* 1: 26–58; use 26–39.

Feigl, H. (1958), 'The "Mental" and the "Physical"'. In Feigl et al. 1958: 370–497. Reissued in 1967 as a monograph, *The 'Mental' and the 'Physical'*, Minneapolis: University of Minnesota Press.

——M. Scriven, and G. Maxwell, eds. (1958), *Concepts, Theories, and the Mind—Body Problem* (Minnesota Studies in the Philosophy of Science, vol. 2). Minneapolis: University of Minnesota Press.

Place, U. T. (1956) 'Is Consciousness a Brain Process?', *British Journal of Psychology* 47: 44–50.

Ryle, G. (1949), *The Concept of Mind*. London: Hutchinson.

Watson, J. B. (1913), 'Psychology as the Behaviorist Views It', *Psychological Review* 20: 158–77.

Chapter 5

The logical analysis of psychology*

Carl Hempel

ONE of the most important and most discussed problems of contemporary philosophy is that of determining how psychology should be characterized in the theory of science. This problem, overflowing the limits of epistemological analysis and leading to heated controversy in metaphysics itself, is brought to a focus by the familiar disjunction, 'Is psychology a natural science, or is it one of the sciences of mind and culture (*Geisteswissenschaften*)?'

The present article attempts to sketch the general lines of a new analysis of psychology, one which makes use of rigorous logical tools, and which has made possible decisive advances towards the solution of the above problem.[1] This analysis was successfully undertaken by the 'Vienna Circle' (*Wiener Kreis*), the members of which (M. Schlick, R. Carnap, Ph. Frank, O. Neurath, F. Waismann, H. Feigl, etc.) have, during the past ten years, developed an extremely fruitful method for the epistemological examination and critique of the various sciences, based in part on the work of L. Wittgenstein.[2] We shall limit ourselves essentially to the examination of psychology as carried out by Carnap and Neurath.

The method characteristic of the studies of the Vienna Circle can be briefly defined as a *logical analysis of the language of science*. This method became possible only with the development of an extremely subtle logical apparatus which makes use, in particular, of all the formal procedures of modern logistics.[3] However, in the

Carl Hempel, 'The Logical Analysis of Psychology'. In Herbert Feigl and Wilfrid Sellars, eds., *Readings in Philosophical Analysis* (New York: Appleton-Century-Crofts, 1949).

* Translated from the French by W. S. and reprinted from *Revue de Synthèse*, 1935, by kind permission of the author and the editors.

1. I now (1947) consider the type of physicalism outlined in this paper as too restrictive; the thesis that all statements of empirical science are *translatable*, without loss of theoretical content, into the language of physics, should be replaced by the weaker assertion that all statements of empirical science are *reducible* to sentences in the language of physics, in the sense that for every empirical hypothesis, including, of course, those of psychology, it is possible to formulate certain test conditions in terms of physical concepts which refer to more or less directly observable physical attributes. But those test conditions are not asserted to exhaust the theoretical content of the given hypothesis in all cases.

   For a more detailed development of this thesis, cf. R. Carnap, 'Logical Foundations of the Unity of Science', in *International Encyclopedia of Unified Science*, The University of Chicago Press, Volume I, Number 1 (included in this volume).
2. *Tractatus Logico-Philosophicus*, London, 1922.
3. A recent presentation of logistics, based on the fundamental work of Whitehead and Russell, *Principia Mathematica*, is to be found in R. Carnap, *Abriss der Logistik*, 1929 (volume II of the series,

following account, which does not pretend to give more than a broad orientation, we shall limit ourselves to the aim of bringing out the general principles of this new method, without making use of strictly formal procedures.

II

Perhaps the best way to bring out the meaning and scope of the position of the Vienna Circle as it relates to psychology, is to say that it is the exact antithesis of the current epistemological conviction that there is a fundamental difference between experimental psychology, as a natural science, and introspective psychology—in general, between the natural sciences as a whole, and the sciences of mind and culture.[4] The common content of the widely different formulae which are generally used to express this contention, which we reject, can be set down as follows: Apart from certain aspects clearly related to physiology, psychology is radically different, both as to subject-matter and as to method, from physics in the broad sense of the term. In particular, it is impossible to deal adequately with the subject-matter of psychology by means of physical methods. The subject-matter of physics includes such concepts as mass, wave length, temperature, field intensity, etc. In developing these, physics employs its distinctive method which makes a combined use of description and causal explanation. Psychology, on the other hand, has for its subject-matter notions which are, in a broad sense, mental. They are *toto genere* different from the concepts of physics, and the appropriate method for dealing with them scientifically is that of sympathetic insight, called 'introspection', a method which is peculiar to psychology.

One of the essential differences between the two kinds of subject-matter, it is believed, consists in the fact that the objects investigated by psychology—in contradistinction to physics—possess an intrinsic meaning-fulness. Indeed, several proponents of this idea state that the distinctive method of psychology consists in 'understanding the sense of significant structures' (*sinnvolle Gebilde verstehend zu erfassen*). Take, for example, the case of a man who speaks. Within the framework of physics, this process is considered to be completely explained once one has traced the movements which make up the utterance to their causes, that is to say, to certain physiological processes in the organism, and, in particular, to the central nervous

Schriften zur Wissenschaftlichen Weltauffassung). It includes an extensive bibliography, as well as references to other logistic systems.

4. The following are some of the principal publications of the Vienna Circle on the nature of psychology as a science: R. Carnap, *Scheinprobleme in der Philosophie. Das Fremdpsy chische und der Realismusstreit*, Meiner, Leipsig, 1928; id., *Der Logische Aufbau der Welt*, Meiner, Leipsig, 1928, id., 'Die Physikalische Sprache als Universal-sprache der Wissenschaft', *Erkenntnis*, 2, 432; id., 'Psychologie in physikalischer Sprache', *Erkenntnis*, 3, 107; id., 'Ueber Protokollsaetze', *Erkenntnis*, 3, 215; O. Neurath, 'Protokollsaetze', *Erkenntnis*, 3, 204; id., *Einheitswissenschaft und Psychologie*, 1933 (volume I of the series *Einheitswissenschaft*). See also the publications mentioned in the notes below.

system. But, it is said, this does not even broach the psychological problem. The latter begins with an understanding of what was said, and proceeds to integrate it into a wider context of meaning.

It is usually this latter idea which serves as a principle for the fundamental dichotomy that is introduced into the classification of the sciences. There is taken to be an *absolutely impassable gulf* between the *natural sciences* which have a subject-matter devoid of sense and the *sciences of mind and culture*, which have an intrinsically meaningful subject-matter, the appropriate methodological instrument for the scientific study of which is 'insight into meaning'.

III

The position in the theory of science which we have just sketched, has been attacked from several different points of view.[5] As far as psychology is concerned, one of the principal counter theses is that formulated by Behaviorism, a theory born in America shortly before the war. (In Russia, Pavlov has developed similar ideas.) Its principal methodological postulate is that a scientific psychology should limit itself to the study of the bodily behavior with which man and the animals respond to changes in their physical environment, every descriptive or explanatory step which makes use of such terms from introspective or 'understanding' psychology as 'feeling', 'lived experience', 'idea', 'will', 'intention', 'goal', 'disposition', 'repression', being proscribed as non-scientific.[6] We find in Behaviorism, consequently, an attempt to construct a scientific psychology which would show by its success that even in psychology we have to do with purely physical processes, and that therefore there can be no impassable barrier between psychology and physics. However, this manner of undertaking the critique of a scientific thesis is not completely satisfactory. It seems, indeed, that the soundness of the behavioristic thesis expounded above depends on the possibility of fulfilling the program of behavioristic psychology. But one cannot expect the question as to the scientific status of psychology to be settled by empirical research in psychology itself. To achieve this is rather an undertaking in epistemology. We turn, therefore, to the considerations advanced by members of the Vienna Circle concerning this problem.

5. P. Oppenheim, for example, in his book *Die Natuerliche Ordnung der Wissenschaften*, Fischer, Jena, 1926, opposes the view that there are fundamental differences between any of the different areas of science. On the analysis of 'understanding', cf. M. Schlick, 'Erleben, Erkennen, Metaphysik', *Kantstudien*, 31, 146.
6. For further details see the statement of one of the founders of Behaviorism: J. B. Watson, *Behaviorism*, also A. A. Roback, *Behaviorism and Psychology*, Cambridge, 1923; and A. P. Weiss, *A Theoretical Basis of Human Behavior*, 2nd ed. rev., Columbus, Ohio, Adams, 1929; see also the work by Koehler cited in footnote 10 below.

IV

Before attacking the question as to whether the subject-matters of physics and psychology are essentially the same or different in nature, it is necessary first to clarify the very concept of the subject-matter of a science. The theoretical content of a science is to be found in propositions. It is necessary, therefore, to determine whether there is a fundamental difference between the propositions of psychology and those of physics. Let us therefore ask what it is which determines the content—one can equally well say the 'meaning'—of a proposition. When, for example, do we know the meaning of the following statement: 'Today at one o'clock, the temperature of such and such a place in the physics laboratory was 23.4° centigrade'? Clearly when, and only when, we know under what conditions we would characterize the statement as true, and under what circumstances we would characterize it as false. (Needless to say, it is not necessary to know whether or not the statement is true.) Thus, we understand the meaning of the above statement since we know that it is true when a tube of a certain kind, filled with mercury (in short, a thermometer with a centigrade scale) placed at the indicated time at the location in question, exhibits a coincidence between the level of the mercury and the mark of the scale numbered 23.4. It is also true if in the same circumstances one can observe certain coincidences on another instrument called an 'alcohol thermometer'; and, again, if a galvanometer connected with a thermopile shows a certain deviation when the thermopile is placed there at the indicated time. Finally, there is a long series of other possibilities which make the statement true, each of which is defined by a 'physical test sentence', as we should like to call it. The statement itself clearly affirms nothing other than this: all these physical test sentences obtain. (However, one verifies only some of these physical test sentences, and then 'concludes by induction' that the others obtain as well.) The statement, therefore, is nothing but an abbreviated formulation of all these test sentences.

Before continuing the discussion, let us sum up this result as follows:

1. A proposition that specifies the temperature at a selected point in space-time can be 'retranslated' without change of meaning into another proposition—doubtlessly longer—in which the word 'temperature' no longer appears. This term functions solely as an abbreviation, making possible the concise and complete description of a state of affairs, the expression of which would otherwise be very complicated.

2. The example equally shows that *two propositions which differ in formulation* can nevertheless have the *same meaning*. A trivial example of a statement having the same meaning as the above would be: 'Today at one o'clock, at such and such a location in the laboratory, the temperature was 19.44° Réaumur.'

As a matter of fact, the preceding considerations show—and let us set it down as another result—that *the meaning of a proposition is established by the conditions of its verification*. In particular, two differently formulated propositions have the same meaning or the same effective content when, and only when, they are both true or both false in the same conditions. Furthermore, a proposition for which one can indicate absolutely no conditions which would verify it, which is in principle incapable of confrontation with test conditions, is wholly devoid of content and without meaning. In such a case we have to do with a 'pseudo-proposition', that is to say, a sequence of words correctly constructed from the point of view of grammar, but without content, rather than with a proposition properly speaking.[7]

In view of these considerations, our problem reduces to one concerning the difference between the circumstances which verify psychological propositions and those which verify the propositions of physics. Let us therefore examine a proposition which involves a psychological concept, for example: 'Paul has a toothache'. What is the specific content of this proposition, that is to say, what are the circumstances in which it would be verified? It will be sufficient to indicate some test sentences which describe these circumstances.

a. Paul weeps and makes gestures of such and such kinds.
b. At the question, 'What is the matter?', Paul utters the words 'I have a toothache'.
c. Closer examination reveals a decayed tooth with exposed pulp.
d. Paul's blood pressure, digestive processes, the speed of his reactions, show such and such changes.
e. Such and such processes occur in Paul's central nervous system.

This list could be expanded considerably, but it is already sufficient to bring out the fundamental and essential point, namely, that all the circumstances which verify this psychological proposition are expressed by physical test sentences. [This is true even of test sentence *b*, which merely expresses the fact that in specified physical conditions (the propagation of vibrations produced in the air by the enunciation of the words, 'What is the matter?') there occurs in the body of the subject a certain physical process (speech behavior of such and such a kind).]

The proposition in question, which is about someone's 'pain', is therefore, equally with that concerning the temperature, simply an abbreviated expression of the fact that all its test sentences are verified. (Here, also, one verifies only some of the test sentences and then infers by way of induction that the others obtain as well.) It can be re-translated without loss of content into a proposition which no longer involves the term 'pain', but only physical concepts. Our analysis has consequently established that a certain proposition belonging to psychology has the same content as a proposition belonging to physics; a result which is in direct contradiction with the thesis that there is an impassable gulf between the statements of psychology and those of physics.

The above reasoning can be applied to *any psychological proposition*, even to

7. Space is lacking for a further discussion of the logical form of a test sentence (recently called 'protocol-propositions' by Neurath and Carnap). On this question see Wittgenstein, *Tractatus Logico-Philosophicus*, as well as the articles by Neurath and Carnap which have appeared in *Erkenntnis* (above, footnote 4) .

those which concern, as is said, 'deeper psychological strata' than that of our example. Thus, the assertion that Mr. Jones suffers from intense inferiority feelings of such and such kinds can only be confirmed or falsified by observing Mr. Jones' behavior in various circumstances. To this behavior belong all the bodily processes of Mr. Jones, and, in particular, his gestures, the flushing and paling of his skin, his utterances, his blood pressure, the events that occur in his central nervous system, etc. In practice, when one wishes to test propositions concerning what are called the deeper layers of the psyche, one limits oneself to the observation of external bodily behavior, and, particularly, to speech movements aroused by certain physical stimuli (the asking of questions). But it is well known that experimental psychology has also developed techniques for making use of the subtler bodily states referred to above in order to confirm the psychological discoveries made by cruder methods. The statement concerning the inferiority feelings of Mr. Jones—whether true or false—means only this: such and such happenings take place in Mr. Jones' body in such and such circumstances.

We shall call a proposition which can be translated without change of meaning into the language of physics, a 'physicalistic proposition,' whereas we shall reserve the expression 'proposition of physics' to those which are already formulated in the terminology of physical science. (Since every statement is in respect of content equivalent, or, better, equipollent to itself, every proposition of physics is also a physicalistic proposition.) The result of the preceding considerations can now be summed up as follows: *All psychological statements which are meaningful, that is to say, which are in principle verifiable, are translatable into propositions which do not involve psychological concepts, but only the concepts of physics. The propositions of psychology are consequently physicalistic propositions. Psychology is an integral part of physics.* If a distinction is drawn between psychology and the other areas of physics, it is only from the point of view of the practical aspects of research and the direction of interest, rather than a matter of principle. This logical analysis, of which the result shows a certain affinity with the fundamental ideas of behaviorism, constitutes the physicalistic conception of psychology.

V

It is customary to raise against the above conception the following fundamental objection: The physical test sentences of which you speak are absolutely incapable of formulating the intrinsic nature of a mental process; they merely describe the physical *symptoms* from which one infers, by purely psychological methods—notably that of understanding—the presence of a certain mental process. But it is not difficult to see that the use of the method of understanding or of other psychological procedures is bound up with the existence of certain observable physical data concerning the subject undergoing examination. There is no psychological understanding that is not tied up physically in one way or another with the person to be understood. Let us add that, for example, in the case of the proposition about the inferiority complex, even the 'introspective' psychologist, the psychologist who 'understands,' can only confirm his conjecture if the body of Mr. Jones, when placed in certain circumstances (most frequently, subjected to questioning), reacts in a specified manner (usually, by giving certain answers). Consequently, even if the proposition in question had to be arrived at, *discovered*, by 'sympathetic understanding,' the only *information* it gives us is nothing more nor less than the following: under certain circumstances, certain specific events take place in the body of Mr. Jones. It is this which constitutes the meaning of the psychological statement.

The further objection will perhaps be raised that men can feign. Thus, though a criminal at the bar may show physical symptoms of mental disorder, one would nevertheless be justified in wondering whether his mental confusion was 'real' or only simulated. One must note that in the case of the simulator, only some of the conditions are fulfilled which verify the statement 'This man is mentally unbalanced,' those, namely, which are most accessible to direct observation. A more penetrating examination—which should in principle take into account events occurring in the central nervous system—would give a decisive answer; and this answer would in turn clearly rest on a physicalistic basis. If, at this point, one wished to push the objection to the point of admitting that a man could show *all the 'symptoms'* of a mental disease without being 'really' ill, we reply that it would be absurd to characterize such a man as 'really normal'; for it is obvious that by the very nature of the hypothesis we should possess no criterion in terms of which to distinguish this man from another who, while exhibiting the same bodily behavior down to the last detail, would 'in addition' be 'really ill.' (To put the point more precisely, one can say that this hypothesis contains a *logical contradiction*, since it amounts to saying, 'It is possible that a statement should be false even when the necessary and sufficient conditions of its truth are fulfilled.')

Once again we see clearly that the meaning of a psychological proposition consists merely in the function of abbreviating the description of certain modes of physical response characteristic of the bodies of man and the animals. An analogy suggested by O. Neurath may be of further assistance in clarifying the logical function of psychological statements.[8] The complicated statements that would describe the movements of the hands of a watch in relation to one another, and relatively to the stars, are ordinarily summed up in an assertion of the following form: 'This watch runs well (runs badly, etc.).' The term 'runs' is introduced here as an auxiliary defined expression which makes it possible to formulate briefly a relatively complicated system of statements. It would thus be absurd to say, for example, that the movement of the hands is only a 'physical symptom' which reveals the presence of a running which is intrinsically incapable of being grasped by physical means, or to ask, if the watch should stop, what has become of the running of the watch.

8. 'Soziologie im Physicalismus', *Erkenntnis*, 2, 393, particularly p. 411.

It is in exactly the same way that abbreviating symbols are introduced into the language of physics, the concept of temperature discussed above being an example. The system of physical test sentences *exhausts* the meaning of the statement concerning the temperature at a place, and one should not say that these sentences merely have to do with 'symptoms' of the existence of a certain temperature.

Our argument has shown that it is necessary to attribute to the characteristic concepts of psychology the same logical function performed by the concepts of 'running' and of 'temperature.' They do nothing more than make possible the succinct formulation of propositions concerning the states or processes of animal or human bodies.

The introduction of new psychological concepts can contribute greatly to the progress of scientific knowledge. But it is accompanied by a danger, that, namely, of making an excessive and, consequently, harmful use of new concepts, which may result in questions and answers devoid of sense. This is frequently the case in metaphysics, notably with respect to the notions which we formulated in section II. Terms which are abbreviating symbols are taken to designate a special class of 'psychological objects,' and thus one is led to ask questions about the 'essence' of these objects, and how they differ from 'physical objects.' The time-worn problem concerning the relation between mental and physical events is also based on this confusion concerning the logical function of psychological concepts. Our argument, therefore, enables us to see that *the psycho-physical problem is a pseudo-problem*, the formulation of which is based on an inadmissible use of scientific concepts; it is of the same logical nature as the question, suggested by the example above, concerning the relation of the running of the watch to the movement of the hands.[9]

VI

In order to bring out the exact status of the fundamental idea of the physicalistic interpretation of psychology (or logical behaviorism), we shall contrast it with certain theses of psychological behaviorism and of classical materialism, which appear to be closely related.[10]

1. Logical behaviorism claims neither that minds, feelings, inferiority complexes, voluntary actions, etc., do not exist, nor that their existence is in the least doubtful. It insists that the very question as to whether these psychological constructs really exist is already a pseudo-problem, since these notions in their 'legitimate use' appear only as abbreviations of physicalistic statements. Above all, one should not

9. Carnap, *Der Logische Aufbau der Welt*, pp. 231–236; Id., *Scheinprobleme in der Philosophie.* See also note 4 above.

10. A careful discussion of the ideas of so-called 'internal' behaviorism is to be found in *Psychologische Problems* by W. Koehler, published by Springer, Berlin, 1933. See particularly the first two chapters [translated under the title *Gestalt Psychology*] .

interpret the position sketched in this paper as amounting to the view that we can only know the 'physical side' of psychological processes, and that the question as to whether there are mental phenomena behind the physical processes falls beyond the scope of science and must be left either to faith or to the conviction of each individual. On the contrary, the logical analyses originating in the Vienna Circle, of which one of the consequences is the physicalistic analysis of psychology, teach us that every meaningful question is, in principle, capable of a scientific answer. Furthermore, these analyses show that that which is, in the case of the mind-body problem, considered as an object of belief, is absolutely incapable of being expressed by a factual proposition. In other words, there can be no question here of an 'article of faith.' Nothing can be an object of faith which cannot, in principle, be known.

2. The thesis developed here, though related in certain ways to the fundamental idea of behaviorism, does not demand, as does the latter, that psychological research restrict itself methodologically to the study of the responses made by organisms to certain stimuli. It by no means offers a theory belonging to the domain of psychology, but rather a logical theory about the propositions of scientific psychology. Its position is that the latter are without exception physicalistic statements, by whatever means they may have been obtained. Consequently, it seeks to show that if in psychology only physicalistic statements are made, this is not a limitation because it is logically *impossible* to do otherwise.

3. In order for logical behaviorism to be acceptable, it is not necessary that we be able to describe the physical state of a human body which is referred to by a certain psychological statement—for example, one dealing with someone's feeling of pain—down to the most minute details of the phenomena of the central nervous system. No more does it presuppose a knowledge of all the physical laws governing human or animal bodily processes; nor *a fortiori* is the existence of rigorously deterministic laws relating to these processes a necessary condition of the truth of the behavioristic thesis. At no point does the above argument rest on such a concrete presupposition.

VII

In concluding, I should like to indicate briefly the clarification brought to the problem of the division of the sciences into totally different areas, by the method of the logical analysis of scientific statements, applied above to the special case of the place of psychology among the sciences. The considerations we have advanced can be extended to the domain of sociology, taken in the broad sense as the science of historical, cultural and economic processes. In this way one arrives at the result that every sociological assertion which is meaningful, that is to say, in principle verifiable, 'has as its subject-matter nothing else than the states, processes and behavior of groups or of individuals (human or animal), and their responses to one another and to their environment,'[11] and consequently that every sociological statement is a physicalistic statement. This view is characterized by Neurath as the thesis of 'social behaviorism,' which he adds to that of 'individual behaviorism' which we have expounded above. Furthermore, we can show that every proposition of what are called the 'sciences of mind and culture' is a sociological proposition in the above sense, provided it has genuine content. Thus we arrived at the 'thesis of the unity of science':

The division of science into different areas rests exclusively on differences in research procedures and direction of interest; *one must not regard it as a matter of principle. On the contrary, all the branches of science are in principle of one and the same nature; they are branches of the unitary science, physics.*

VIII

The method of logical analysis which we have attempted to explicate in clarifying, by way of example, the propositions of psychology, leads, as we have been able to show only too briefly for the sciences of mind and culture, to a 'physicalism' based on logic (Neurath): *Every proposition of the above-mentioned disciplines, and, in general, of experimental science as a whole,* which is not merely a meaningless sequence of words, *is translatable, without change of content, into a proposition in which appear only physicalistic terms, and consequently is a physicalistic proposition.*

This thesis frequently encounters a strong opposition arising from the idea that such analyses violently and considerably reduce the richness of the life of mind or spirit, as though the aim of the discussion were purely and simply to eliminate vast and important areas of experience. Such a conception comes from a false interpretation of physicalism, the main elements of which we have already examined in section VII above. As a matter of fact, nothing can be more remote from a philosophy which has the methodological attitude we have characterized than the making of decisions, on its own authority, concerning the truth or falsity of particular scientific statements, or the desire to eliminate any matters of fact whatsoever. *The subject-matter of this philosophy is limited to the form of scientific statements, and the deductive relationships obtaining between them.* It is led by its analyses to the thesis of physicalism, and establishes on purely logical grounds that a certain class of venerable philosophical 'problems' consists of pseudo-problems. It is certainly to the advantage of the progress of scientific knowledge that these imitation jewels in the coffer of scientific problems be known for what they are, and that the intellectual powers which have till now been devoted to a class of senseless questions which are by their very nature insoluble, become available for the formulation and study of new and fruitful problems. That the method of logical analysis stimulates research along these lines is shown by the numerous publications of the

11. R. Carnap, *Die Physikalische Sprache als Universalsprache*, p. 451. See also: O. Neurath, *Empirische Soziologie*, 1931, the fourth monograph in the series *Schriften zur wissenschaftlichen Weltauffassung.*

Vienna Circle and those who sympathize with its general point of view (H. Reichenbach, W. Dubislav, and others).

In the attitude of those who are so bitterly opposed to physicalism, an essential rôle is played by certain psychological factors relating to individuals and groups. Thus the contrast between the concepts (*Gebilde*) developed by the psychologist, and those developed by the physicist, or, again, the question as to the nature of the specific subject-matter of psychology and the cultural sciences (which present the appearance of a search for the essence and unique laws of 'objective mind') is usually accompanied by a strong emotional coloring which has come into being during the long historical development of the 'philosophical conception of the world,' which was considerably less scientific than normative and intuitive. These emotional factors are still deeply rooted in the picture by which our epoch represents the world to itself. They are protected by certain affective dispositions which surround them like a rampart, and for all these reasons appear to us to have a verifiable content which a more penetrating analysis shows to be impossible.

A psychological and sociological study of the causes of the appearance of these 'concomitant factors' of the metaphysical type would take us beyond the limits of this study;[12] but without tracing it back to its origins, it is possible to say that if the logical analyses sketched above are correct the fact that they necessitate at least a partial break with traditional philosophical ideas which are deeply dyed with emotion can certainly not justify an opposition to physicalism—at least if one admits that philosophy is to be something more than the expression of an individual vision of the world, that it aims at being a science.

12. O. Neurath has made interesting contributions along these lines in *Empirische Soziologie* and in *Soziologie im Physikalismus* (see above note 8), as has R. Carnap in his article 'Ueberwindung der Metaphysik durch logische Analyse der Sprache,' *Erkenntnis*, 2, 219, *which has been translated into French by General E. Vouillemin: La science et la metaphysique devant l'analyse logique du language.* Introduction by Marcel Boll. *Actualités scientifiques et industriels*, Hermann, Paris, 1934, p. 45.

Chapter 6

Brains and behaviour[1]

Hilary Putnam

ONCE upon a time there was a tough-minded philosopher who said, 'What is all this talk about "minds", "ideas", and "sensations"? Really—and I mean *really* in the real world—there is nothing to these so-called "mental" events and entities but certain processes in our all-too-material heads.'

And once upon a time there was a philosopher who retorted, 'What a masterpiece of confusion!' Even if, say, *pain* were perfectly correlated with any particular event in my brain (which I doubt) that event would obviously have certain properties—say, a certain numerical intensity measured in volts—which it would be *senseless* to ascribe to the feeling of pain. Thus, it is *two* things that are correlated, not *one*—and to call *two* things *one* thing is worse than being mistaken; it is utter contradiction.'

For a long time dualism and materialism appeared to exhaust the alternatives. Compromises were attempted ('double aspect' theories), but they never won many converts and practically no one found them intelligible. Then, in the mid-1930s, a seeming third possibility was discovered. This third possibility has been called *logical behaviourism*. To state the nature of this third possibility briefly, it is necessary to recall the treatment of the natural numbers (*i.e.*, zero, one, two, three . . .) in modern logic. Numbers are identified with *sets*, in various ways, depending on which authority one follows. For instance, Whitehead and Russell identified zero with the set of all empty sets, one with the set of all one-membered sets, two with the set of all two-membered sets, three with the set of all three-membered sets, and so on. (This has the appearance of circularity, but they were able to dispel this appearance by defining 'one-membered set', 'two-membered set', 'three-membered set', &c., without using 'one', 'two', 'three', &c.) In short, numbers are treated as *logical constructions out of sets*. The number theorist is doing set theory without knowing it, according to this interpretation.

What was novel about this was the idea of getting rid of certain philosophically unwanted or embarrassing entities (numbers) without failing to do justice to the appropriate body of discourse (number theory) by treating the entities in question as logical constructions. Russell was quick to hold up this 'success' as a model to all

Hilary Putnam, edited extract from 'Brains and Behaviour'. In R. J. Butler, ed., *Analytical Philosophy*, 2d series (Oxford: Blackwell, 1965).

1. This paper was read as a part of the programme of The American Association for the Advancement of Science, Section L (History and Philosophy of Science), December 27th, 1961.

future philosophers. And certain of those future philosophers—the Vienna positivists, in their 'physicalist' phase (about 1930)—took Russell's advice so seriously as to produce the doctrine that we are calling *logical behaviourism*—the doctrine that, just as numbers are (allegedly) logical constructions out of *sets*, so *mental events* are logical constructions out of actual and possible *behaviour events.*

In the set theoretic case, the 'reduction' of number theory to the appropriate part of set theory was carried out in detail and with indisputable technical success. One may dispute the philosophical significance of the reduction, but one knows exactly what one is talking about when one disputes it. In the mind-body case, the reduction was never carried out in even *one* possible way, so that it is not possible to be clear on just *how* mental entities or events are to be (identified with) logical constructions out of behaviour events. But, broadly speaking, it is clear what the view implies: it implies that all talk about mental events is translatable into talk about actual or potential overt behaviour.

It is easy to see in what way this view differs from both dualism and classical materialism. The logical behaviourist agrees with the dualist that what goes on in our brains has no connection whatsoever with what we *mean* when we say that someone is in pain. He can even take over the dualist's entire stock of arguments against the materialist position. Yet, at the same time, he can be as 'tough-minded' as the materialist in denying that ordinary talk of 'pains', 'thoughts', and 'feelings' involves reference to 'Mind' as a Cartesian substance.

Thus it is not surprising that logical behaviourism attracted enormous attention—both pro and con—during the next thirty years. Without doubt, this alternative proved to be a fruitful one to inject into the debate. Here, however, my intention is not to talk about the fruitfulness of the investigations to which logical behaviourism has led, but to see if there was any upshot to those investigations. Can we, after thirty years, say anything about the rightness or wrongness of logical behaviourism? Or must we say that a third alternative has been added to the old two; that we cannot decide between three any more easily than we could decide between two; and that our discussion is thus half as difficult again as it was before?

One conclusion emerged very quickly from the discussion pro and con logical behaviourism: that the extreme thesis of logical behaviourism, as we just stated it (that all talk about 'mental events' is translatable into talk about overt behaviour) is false. But, in a sense, this is not very interesting. An extreme thesis may be false, although there is 'something to' the way of thinking that it represents. And the more interesting question is this: what, if anything, can be 'saved' of the way of thinking that logical behaviourism represents?

In the last thirty years, the original extreme thesis of logical behaviourism has gradually been weakened to something like this:

(1) That there exist entailments between mind-statements and behaviour-statements; entailments that are not, perhaps, analytic in the way in which 'All bachelors are unmarried' is analytic, but that nevertheless follow (in some sense) from the meanings of mind words. I shall call these *analytic entailments.*

(2) That these entailments may not provide an actual *translation* of 'mind talk' into 'behaviour talk' (this 'talk' talk was introduced by Gilbert Ryle in his *Concept of Mind*), but that this is true for such superficial reasons as the greater ambiguity of mind talk, as compared with the relatively greater specificity of overt behaviour talk.

I believe that, although no philosopher would to-day subscribe to the older version of logical behaviourism, a great many philosophers[2] would accept these two points, while admitting the unsatisfactory imprecision of the present statement of both of them. If these philosophers are right, then there is much work to be done (*e.g.*, the notion of 'analyticity' has to be made clear), but the direction of work is laid out for us for some time to come.

I wish that I could share this happy point of view—if only for the comforting conclusion that first-rate philosophical research, continued for some time, will eventually lead to a solution to the mind-body problem which is independent of troublesome empirical facts about brains, central causation of behaviour, evidence for and against non-physical causation of at least some behaviour, and the soundness or unsoundness of psychical research and parapsychology. But the fact is that I come to bury logical behaviourism, not to praise it. I feel that the time has come for us to admit that logical behaviourism is a mistake, and that even the weakened forms of the logical behaviourist doctrine are incorrect. I cannot hope to establish this in so short a paper as this one[3]; but I hope to expose for your inspection at least the main lines of my thinking.

Logical behaviourism

The logical behaviourist usually begins by pointing out what is perfectly true, that such words as 'pain' ('pain' will henceforth be our stock example of a mind word)

2. *E.g.*, these two points are fairly explicitly stated in Strawson's *Individuals*. Strawson has told me that he no longer subscribes to point (1), however.
3. An attempted fourth alternative—*i.e.*, an alternative to dualism, materialism, *and* behaviourism—is sketched in 'The Mental Life of Some Machines', which appeared in the Proceedings of the Wayne Symposium on the Philosophy of Mind. This fourth alternative is materialistic in the wide sense of being compatible with the view that organisms, including human beings, are physical systems consisting of elementary particles and obeying the laws of physics, but does not require that such 'states' as *pain* and *preference* be defined in a way which makes reference to either overt behaviour or physical-chemical constitution. The idea, briefly, is that predicates which apply to a system by virtue of its *functional organization* have just this characteristic: a given functional organization (*e.g.*, a given inductive logic, a given rational preference function) may realize itself in almost any kind of overt behaviour, depending upon the circumstances, and is capable of being 'built into' structures of many different logically possible physical (or even metaphysical) constitutions. Thus the statement that a creature prefers A to B does not tell us whether the creature has a carbon chemistry, or a silicon chemistry, or is even a disembodied mind, nor does it tell us how the creature would behave under any circumstances specificable without reference to the creature's other preferences and beliefs, but it does not thereby become something 'mysterious'.

are not taught by reference to standard examples in the way in which such words as 'red' are. One can point to a standard red thing, but one cannot point to a standard pain (that is, except by pointing to some piece of *behaviour*) and say: 'Compare the feeling you are having with this one (say, Jones's feeling at time t_1). If the two feelings have the identical *quality*, then your feeling is legitimately called a feeling of *pain*.' The difficulty, of course, is that I cannot have Jones's feeling at time t_1—unless I *am* Jones, and the time *is* t_1.

From this simple observation, certain things follow. For example, the account according to which the *intension* of the word 'pain' is a certain *quality* which 'I know from my own case' must be wrong. But this is not to refute dualism, since the dualist need not maintain that I know the intension of the English word 'pain' from my own case, but only that I experience the referent of the word.

What then is the intension of 'pain'? I am inclined to say that 'pain' is a cluster-concept. That is, the application of the word 'pain' is controlled by a whole cluster of criteria, *all of which can be regarded as synthetic*.[4] As a consequence, there is no satisfactory way of answering the question 'What does "pain" mean?' except by giving an exact synonym (*e.g.*, 'Schmerz'); but there are a million and one different ways of saying what pain *is*. One can, for example, say that pain is that feeling which is normally evinced by saying 'ouch', or by wincing, or in a variety of other ways (or often not evinced at all).

All this is compatible with logical behaviourism. The logical behaviourist would reply: 'Exactly. "Pain" is a cluster-concept—that is to say, it stands for *a cluster of phenomena*.' But that is not what I mean. Let us look at another kind of cluster-concept (cluster-concepts, of course, are not a homogeneous class): names of diseases.

We observe that, when a virus origin was discovered for polio, doctors said that certain cases in which all the symptoms of polio had been present, but in which the virus had been absent, had turned out not to be cases of polio at all. Similarly, if a virus should be discovered which normally (almost invariably) is the cause of what we presently call 'multiple sclerosis', the hypothesis that this virus is *the* cause of multiple sclerosis would not be falsified if, in some few exceptional circumstances, it was possible to have all the symptoms of multiple sclerosis for some other combination of reasons, or if this virus caused symptoms not presently recognized as symptoms of multiple sclerosis in some cases. These facts would certainly lead the lexicographer to *reject* the view that 'multiple sclerosis' means 'the simultaneous

4. I mean not only that *each* criterion can be regarded as synthetic, but also that the cluster is *collectively* synthetic, in the sense that we are free in certain cases to say (for reason of inductive simplicity and theoretical economy) that the term applies although the whole cluster is missing. This is completely compatible with saying that the cluster serves to fix the meaning of the word. The point is that when we specify something by a cluster of indicators we assume that people will *use their brains*. That criteria may be over-ridden when good sense demands is the sort of thing we may regard as a 'convention associated with discourse' (Grice) rather than as something to be stipulated in connection with the individual words.

presence of such and such symptoms'. Rather he would say that 'multiple sclerosis' means 'that disease which is normally responsible for some or all of the following symptoms. . . .'

Of course, he does not have to say this. Some philosophers would prefer to say that 'polio' *used to mean* 'the simultaneous presence of such-and-such symptoms'. And they would say that the *decision* to accept the presence or absence of a virus as a criterion for the presence or absence of polio represented a *change of meaning*. But this runs strongly counter to our common sense. For example, doctors used to say 'I believe polio is caused by a virus'. On the 'change of meaning' account, those doctors were *wrong*, not *right*. Polio, *as the word was then used*, was not always caused by a virus; it is only what *we* call polio that is always caused by a virus. And if a doctor ever said (and many did) 'I believe this may not be a case of polio', knowing that all of the text-book symptoms were present, that doctor must have been contradicting himself (even if we, to-day, would say that he was right) or, perhaps, 'making a disguised linguistic proposal'. Also, this account runs counter to good linguistic methodology. The definition we proposed a paragraph back—'multiple sclerosis' means 'the disease that is normally *responsible* for the following symptoms . . .'—has an exact analogue in the case of polio. This kind of definition leaves open the question whether there is a single cause or several. It is consonant with such a definition to speak of 'discovering a single origin for polio (or two or three or four)', to speak of 'discovering X did not have polio' (although he exhibited all the symptoms of polio), and to speak of 'discovering X did have polio' (although he exhibited *none* of the 'textbook symptoms'). And, finally, such a definition does not require us to say that any 'change of meaning' took place. Thus, this is surely the definition that a good lexicographer would adopt. But this entails *rejecting* the 'change of meaning' account as a philosopher's invention.[5]

Accepting that this is the correct account of the names of diseases, what follows? There *may* be analytic entailments connecting diseases and symptoms (although I shall argue against this). For example, it looks plausible to say that:

'Normally people who have multiple sclerosis have some or all of the following symptoms . . .' is a necessary ('analytic') truth. But it does not follow that 'disease talk' is translatable into 'symptom talk'. Rather the contrary follows (as is already indicated by the presence of the word 'normally'): statements about multiple sclerosis are not translatable into statements about the symptoms of multiple sclerosis, not because disease talk is 'systematically ambiguous' and symptom talk is 'specific', but because *causes* are not logical constructions out of their *effects*.

In analogy with the foregoing, both the dualist and the materialist would want to argue that, although the meaning of 'pain' may be *explained* by reference to overt behaviour, what we mean by 'pain' is not the presence of a cluster of responses, but rather the presence of an event or condition that normally causes those responses. (Of course the pain is not the whole cause of the pain behaviour, but only a suitably

5. Cf. 'Dreaming and "Depth Grammar",' *Analytical Philosophy*, First Series.

invariant part of that cause;[6] but, similarly, the virus-caused tissue damage is not the whole cause of the individual symptoms of polio in some individual case, but a suitably invariant part of the cause.) And they would want to argue further, that even if it *were* a necessary truth that

'Normally, when one says "ouch" one has a pain' or a necessary truth that

'Normally, when one has a pain one says "ouch"' this would be an interesting observation about what 'pain' means, but it would shed no metaphysical light on what pain *is* (or *isn't*). And it certainly would not follow that 'pain talk' is translatable into 'response talk', or that the failure of translatability is only a matter of the 'systematic ambiguity' of pain talk as opposed to the 'specificity' of response talk: quite the contrary. Just as before, *causes* (pains) are *not* logical constructions out of their *effects* (behaviour).

The traditional dualist would, however, want to go farther, and deny the *necessity* of the two propositions just listed. Moreover, the traditional dualist is right: there is nothing self-contradictory, as we shall see below, in talking of hypothetical worlds in which there are pains but *no* pain behaviour.

The analogy with names of diseases is still preserved at this point. Suppose I identify multiple sclerosis as the disease that normally produces certain symptoms. If it later turns out that a certain virus is the cause of multiple sclerosis, using this newly discovered criterion I may then go on to find out that multiple sclerosis has quite different symptoms when, say, the average temperature is lower. I can then perfectly well talk of a hypothetical world (with lower temperature levels) in which multiple sclerosis does *not* normally produce the usual symptoms. It is true that if the *words* 'multiple sclerosis' are used in any world in such a way that the above lexical definition is a good one, *then* many victims of the disease must have had some or all of the following symptoms . . . And in the same way it is true that *if* the explanation suggested of the word 'pain' is a good one (*i.e.*, 'pain is the feeling that is normally being evinced when someone says "ouch", or winces, or screams, &c.'), *then* persons in pain must have at some time winced or screamed or said 'ouch'—but this does *not* imply that 'if someone ever had a pain, then someone must at some time have winced or screamed or said "ouch".' To conclude this would be to confuse preconditions for *talking* about pain as *we* talk about pain with preconditions for the existence of pain.

The analogy we have been developing is not an identity: linguistically speaking, mind words and names of diseases are different in a great many respects. In particular, *first person uses* are very different: a man may have a severe case of polio and not know it, even if he knows the word 'polio', but one cannot have a severe pain and not know it. At first blush, this may look like a point in favour of logical behaviourism. The logical behaviourist may say: it is because the premisses 'John says he has a

6. Of course, 'the cause' is a highly ambiguous phrase. Even if it is correct in certain contexts to say that certain events in the brain are 'the cause' of my pain behaviour, it does *not* follow (as has sometimes been suggested) that my pain must be 'identical' with these neural events.

pain', 'John knows English', and 'John is speaking in all sincerity',[7] *entail* 'John has a pain', that pain reports have this sort of special status. But even if this is right, it does not follow that logical behaviourism is correct unless *sincerity* is a 'logical construction out of overt behaviour'! A far more reasonable account is this: one can have a 'pink elephant hallucination', but one cannot have a 'pain hallucination', or an 'absence of pain hallucination', simply because any situation that a person cannot discriminate from a situation in which he himself has a pain *counts* as a situation in which he has a pain, whereas a situation that a person cannot distinguish from one in which a pink elephant is present does not necessarily *count* as the presence of a pink elephant.

To sum up: I believe that pains are not clusters of responses, but that they are (normally, in our experience to date) the causes of certain clusters of responses. Moreover, although this is an empirical fact, it underlies the possibility of talking about pains in the particular way in which we do. However, it does not rule out in any way the possibility of worlds in which (owing to a difference in the environmental and hereditary conditions) pains are not responsible for the usual responses, or even are not responsible for any responses at all.

Let us now engage in a little science fiction. Let us try to describe some worlds in which pains are related to responses (and also to causes) in quite a different way than they are in our world.

If we confine our attention to non-verbal responses by full grown persons, for a start, then matters are easy. Imagine a community of 'super-spartans' or 'super-stoics'—a community in which the adults have the ability to successfully suppress *all* involuntary pain behaviour. They may, on occasion, admit that they feel pain, but always in pleasant well-modulated voices—even if they are undergoing the agonies of the damned. They do *not* wince, scream, flinch, sob, grit their teeth, clench their fists, exhibit beads of sweat, or otherwise act like people in pain or people suppressing the unconditioned responses associated with pain. However, they do feel pain, and they dislike it (just as we do). They even admit that it takes a great effort of will to behave as they do. It is only that they have what they regard as important ideological reasons for behaving as they do, and they have, through years of training, learned to live up to their own exacting standards.

It may be contended that children and not fully mature members of this community will exhibit, to varying degrees, normal unconditioned pain behaviour, and that this is all that is necessary for the ascription of pain. On this view, the *sine qua non* for the significant ascription of pain to a species is that its immature members should exhibit unconditioned pain responses.

One might well stop to ask whether this statement has even a clear meaning. Supposing that there are Martians: do we have any criterion for something being an 'unconditioned pain response' for a Martian? Other things being equal, one *avoids* things with which one has had painful experiences: this would suggest that *avoid-*

7. This is suggested in Wittgenstein's *Philosophical Investigations.*

ance behaviour might be looked for as a universal unconditioned pain response. However, even if this were true, it would hardly be specific enough, since avoidance can also be an unconditioned response to many things that we do not associate with pain—to things that disgust us, or frighten us, or even merely bore us.

Let us put these difficulties aside, and see if we can devise an imaginary world in which there are not, even by lenient standards, any unconditioned pain responses. Specifically, let us take our 'super-spartans', and let us suppose that after millions of years they begin to have children who are born fully acculturated. They are born speaking the adult language, knowing the multiplication table, having opinions on political issues, and *inter alia* sharing the dominant spartan beliefs about the importance of not evincing pain (except by way of a verbal report, and even that in a tone of voice that suggests indifference). Then there would not *be* any 'unconditioned pain responses' in this community (although there might be unconditioned *desires* to make certain responses—desires which were, however, always suppressed by an effort of will). Yet there is a clear absurdity to the position that one cannot ascribe to these people a capacity for feeling pain.

To make this absurdity evident, let us imagine that we succeed in converting an adult 'super-spartan' to *our* ideology. Let us suppose that he begins to evince pain in the normal way. Yet he reports that the pains he is feeling are not more *intense* than are the ones he experienced prior to conversion—indeed, he may say that giving expression to them makes them *less* intense. In this case, the logical behaviourist would have to say that, through the medium of this one member, we had demonstrated the existence of unconditioned pain responses in the whole species, and hence that ascription of pain to the species is 'logically proper'. But this is to say that had this one man never lived, and had it been possible to demonstrate only indirectly (via the use of *theories*) that these beings feel pain, then pain ascriptions *would* have been improper.

We have so far been constructing worlds in which the relation of pain to its non-verbal *effects* is altered. What about the relation of pain to *causes*? This is even more easy for the imagination to modify. Can one not imagine a species who feel pain only when a magnetic field is present (although the magnetic field causes no detectable damage to their bodies or nervous systems)? If we now let the members of such a species become converts *to* 'superspartanism', we can depict to ourselves a world in which pains, in our sense, are clearly present, but in which they have neither the normal causes nor the normal effects (apart from verbal reports).

What about verbal reports? Some behaviourists have taken these as the characteristic form of pain behaviour. Of course, there is a difficulty here: If 'I am in pain' means 'I am disposed to utter this kind of verbal report' (to put matters crudely), then how do we tell that any particular report is 'this kind of verbal report'? The usual answer is in terms of the unconditioned pain responses and their assumed supplantation by the verbal reports in question. However, we have seen that there are no *logical* reasons for the existence of unconditioned pain responses in all species capable of feeling pain (there *may* be logical reasons for the existence of avoidance desires, but avoidance *desires* are not themselves behaviour any more than pains are).

Once again, let us be charitable to the extent of waving the first difficulty that comes to mind, and let us undertake the task of trying to imagine a world in which there are not even pain *reports.* I will call this world the 'X-world'. In the X-world we have to deal with 'super-super-spartans'. These have been superspartans for so long, that they have begun to suppress even *talk* of pain. Of course, each individual X-worlder may have his private way of thinking about pain. He may even have the *word* 'pain' (as before, I assume that these beings are born fully acculturated). He may *think* to himself: 'This pain is intolerable. If it goes on one minute longer I shall scream. Oh No! I mustn't do that! That would disgrace my whole family . . .' But X-worlders do not even admit to *having* pains. They pretend not to know either the word or the phenomenon to which it refers. In short, if pains are 'logical constructs out of behaviour', then our X-worlders behave so as not to have pains!—Only, of course, they do have pains, and they know perfectly well that they have pains.

If this last fantasy is not, in some disguised way, self-contradictory, then logical behaviourism is simply a mistake. Not only is the second thesis of logical behaviourism—the existence of a near-translation of pain talk into behaviour talk—false, but so is even the first thesis—the existence of 'analytic entailments'. Pains *are* responsible for certain kinds of behaviour—but only in the context of our beliefs, desires, ideological attitudes, and so forth. From the statement 'X has a pain' by itself *no* behavioural statement follows—not even a behavioural statement with a 'normally' or a 'probably' in it.

In our concluding section we shall consider the logical behaviourist's stock of counter-moves to this sort of argument. If the logical behaviourist's positive views are inadequate owing to an oversimplified view of the nature of cluster words—amounting, in some instances, to an open denial that it is *possible* to have a word governed by a cluster of indicators, *all* of which are synthetic—his negative views are inadequate owing to an oversimplified view of empirical reasoning. It is unfortunately characteristic of modern philosophy that its problems should overlap three different areas—to speak roughly, the areas of linguistics, logic, and 'theory of theories' (scientific methodology)—and that many of its practitioners should try to get by with an inadequate knowledge of at least two out of the three.

Chapter 7

Mind and body

R. J. Hirst

IN an attempt to avoid the faults of dualism I have suggested the monistic thesis that the person is a unity, not an association of two distinct substances or one lodged within another, and is the self-conscious organism that sees, thinks and acts. His mind is not himself as a mental substance, and is not a substance or entity at all; if we speak of 'mind' it should only be as a convenient way of referring to a person's mental abilities and dispositions and so to his introspectible experiences and activities. To progress so far is, however, still to be a long way from solving the mind/ body problem, for it merely produces a new, though superior, way of stating it. The central problem now becomes: What is the status of these mental activities revealed by introspection? How are they related to physical activities, in particular to the brain activities without which they do not seem to occur? To answer that the relation is a causal one would be to relapse straight into Inter actionism and would suggest that mental activities were phases of some substance different from the physical organism and brain.

A more promising approach would be to suppose the mental and physical (or at least cerebral) activities of the person to be two aspects of one and the same activity. Before a theory on these lines can be stated properly, however, some initial and important points must be made. First, in any double-aspect theory there is the danger that the aspects may be treated as entities or existents in their own right like the 'representations' or 'appearances' of much epistemological theory. One would then have the suggestion that the two aspects were events which represented or symbolized a third unknown event. This would however be triadic rather than monistic, and would be liable to the very defect we have been trying to avoid, that of postulating an unknown order of events allegedly more real than those we know. And apart from that it would be a misinterpretation of the term 'aspect', which is logically more akin to 'view'. When one gets one view of Magdalen Tower from an aeroplane above it and later another one from High Street, one is in both cases seeing the same thing, viz. Magdalen Tower. Hence a double aspect theory should be monistic in that when one is aware of an aspect of a thing or event one is aware of that thing or event, and so to be aware of two aspects of it is to be aware of the one thing or event from two different points of view, in two different ways, or on two different modes of access. The point of using the word 'aspect' is simply to

R. J. Hirst, 'Mind and Body', from *The Problems of Perception* (London: George Allen & Unwin, 1959).

indicate the limitations of each mode of access, namely that on it alone one cannot be aware of or ascertain all the characteristics of the thing. All the same there is a grammatical undertow towards thinking of the two aspects and that of which they are aspects as three different things or events on a par with each other, and this must be resisted.

Secondly, owing to the partitive character of perceiving one may only be seeing two different sides or parts of a thing in seeing two aspects of it, as when A and B see respectively the north and south aspects of a building. Even though they are seeing the same building in a general sense, they can be said to be seeing different things if one particularizes and thinks of façades or walls. This may be regarded as a distinction of senses of 'aspect' or of levels of identity or difference. Both senses or levels will concern us, for even in the particularizing sense the persons may well be seeing the same thing, e.g. the same façade or wall. This seems a more exact identity, but it is not logically required and has to be established by other criteria, e.g. by coincidence in space and time or, where appropriate, by concomitant variation.

Thirdly, there is a vital difference between these ordinary examples of 'view' or 'aspect' and the use these words can be given in the mind/body problem. In the former the points of view differ for various aspects but the mode of awareness of or access to the object does not: but in the latter it is necessary to use the words in an extended sense to cover different modes of awareness, rather as if one were to say that in hearing and seeing a collision one was aware of two aspects of it. But the extension required is greater than that, for we are not concerned with two public modes of observation; it is more as if one were to say that X's being in the collision, suffering the impact and so on, and Y's seeing it from across the street were examples of awareness of or access to two different aspects of the one collision. In the problem before us there is clearly a radical difference in modes of access or awareness: the subject's privileged access to his mental acts is by experiencing or introspecting them, but his physical or bodily actions are open to public observation by the senses and appropriate instruments. The importance of this is that a great difference in mode of access will mean a great difference in the characteristics of the aspects revealed, and this may well lead one to regard as two entirely different whole events[1] what are in fact two aspects of one whole event, and so are merely that one event revealed in two radically different ways. The mistake would arise from neglecting the difference in modes of access, and it may well be that this is the origin of the dualist theories: mental and bodily events seem so radically different as to belong to two different orders of being, and so they would be if the modes of access to them were similar; but if the difference is due to the difference in mode of access then they may be two aspects of the one order of events, i.e. be that one order of events differently revealed. On a mathematical analogy, if a is the basic event and b the mode of access, then the aspect will be the product of the two ab; if '+' then

1. By 'whole event' I mean an event which is not the aspect of another event but itself presents different aspects on different modes of access.

stands for 'same' and '–' for 'different', then $-ab$ may be due to $+a \times -b$ or to $-a \times +b$. What starts out then as a double-aspect theory seems to lead to a complete monism or 'Identity Hypothesis', that mental and bodily events are really identical, only appearing different owing to the different modes of access to them. To give another analogy one might say they are identical much as a ray of red light and a train of electro-magnetic waves of 760 mμ are identical.

Finally we need some neutral way of referring to the situations in which the problem of the relation of mental and bodily events arises, neutral in that it does not imply differentiation into mental and physical but merely refers to stages or situations in a person's life history—situations which will be regarded as whole events presenting the two aspects. I propose to do this by use of the verbal noun, e.g. 'X's being afraid', 'X's having a pain', 'X's thinking of Y', 'X's perceiving O'. In these the mental events will be X's feelings of fear or pain, his thoughts, mental images or sensory experiences; and the physical events will be the bodily, and especially the cerebral, events occurring in X at the time. The problem is that of the relation between these two sets of events; how can it be explained if it is not a causal one as Interactionism claimed?

Having disposed of these preliminaries we may now proceed to an Identity Hypothesis of the relation of mental and bodily events, first making some general distinctions and then proceeding to a more detailed correlation.

3. The identity hypothesis

A person, we have assumed, is a unity, an organic whole, and is the entity that perceives, thinks and acts; and he and his activities can be observed or experienced in several different ways and so present different views or aspects. At a general level of distinction these may be divided into two main groups which I shall refer to collectively as the outer and inner aspects. The outer aspect is what other persons can observe of him and his activities, and as far as it is concerned a person and his body are the same entity, granted the appropriate sense of 'body' as an extended physical organism of the human species; X's body = X *qua* externally observable, and the expressions 'person' and 'his body' have the same referent or denotation, though different sense or connotation. Within this aspect we may distinguish two levels or types of observation: (*a*) the 'naked eye' level, ordinary perception, with the corresponding aspect what human beings can perceive of X and his activities, and (*b*) the scientific level or aspect, what may be observed of X with the aid of various scientific instruments. At the latter level only meter readings or cathode-ray-tube traces may be perceived, and so this observation involves appreciable inference and sometimes imagination.

The inner aspect of a person's life is very different in character, for it consists in the various feelings and experiences of the person concerned. And this difference is understandable because of the great difference in mode of access involved; X's mode of access to the events of his life is not merely observing them from outside, as Y or Z have to do, but actually undergoing and experiencing them. There is a certain difficulty in discussing this aspect and mode of access, because the experience or feeling and the experiencing or feeling of it seem to be indistinguishable. But this should not prevent their theoretical distinction, for on the adverbial analysis of sensing, it is claimed that the object or content is indistinguishable from the sensing of it, and yet there is considerable theoretical discussion of sense contents; in much the same way we shall be able to consider inner aspects. There is however another approach to the inner aspect of feelings and similar experiences, namely by introspection or retrospection; Here we have a closer analogy with perception in that content and act are more readily distinguished and the former can be discussed, labelled and, if a pain, located; but introspection differs from the feeling of the emotion or pain, and from normal perception, in that extraneous elements are introduced, e.g. one is as it were detached and can contrast the feeling with the self feeling it. Nevertheless the central core, the content of the feeling, remains sufficiently the same in both the feeling and the introspection of it for us to regard the content as the inner aspect and the introspection and the feeling of it as differing forms of inner access to it. Also as 'feeling' is only applicable to a limited range of situations, we must allow as corresponding modes of access 'undergoing the experience' or even 'being the actor, the person concerned', for the person who decides or acts has a special relationship and access to the action by virtue of being the person who performs it, and this yields its own aspect or experienced content. Granted then two modes of inner access, feeling the pain or undergoing the experience on the one hand and introspecting it on the other, we may note that each is privileged in the sense that it is limited to the person concerned; others cannot share in this inner aspect, but they can observe from without the 'whole' event or situation in the person's life of which the experienced content is an aspect; only then, owing to the radically different mode of access, that event appears as a pattern of behaviour or of brain activity.

So far I have only indicated a general distinction between inner and outer aspects in order to suggest that two apparently different types of events, a person's feelings of fear for example and his observable physical reactions and behaviour, are two aspects of the basic whole event or situation, his being afraid. But though by the logic of 'aspect' we can then say in a general way that X by feeling or introspecting the feeling and outsiders by observing X's reaction are aware of the one basic event, and that X's feelings and his observable reactions are both this one event differently revealed, such a statement is still too vague. We require a precise identification corresponding to the particularizing case where the two observers in seeing two aspects or views of the building were seeing the selfsame wall or façade as well as the same building; this is especially forced on us by the different approaches to the outer aspect, one of which seems to reveal causes of what is seen on the other. In order then to show that certain mental and bodily events are strictly the same event, a more detailed comparison is necessary based on simultaneity in the one person, on concomitant variation, and on the necessary and sufficient conditions of the events concerned. Also, though its importance will only appear later, we may distinguish a third point of view besides those giving inner and outer aspects. It is that of the correlator or philosopher, who tries to take account of both aspects and decide which events and aspects can be identified.

If we attempt this it appears that the important and exact correlation is between the scientific outer aspect and the inner aspect, and that what can be perceived externally at the time is in many cases to be regarded as an aspect of secondary effects or causes of brain activity corresponding to the feeling or experience. Thus in toothache it would seem from cut or anaesthetized nerves that the feeling of pain should be correlated with cerebral activity caused by the decayed tooth. With emotions there may be widespread organic disturbances, some of which together with certain behaviour may be perceivable, but it seems probable on experimental evidence that these are secondary to brain activity, especially in the thalamus, and that the emotional experience should be correlated with this activity. (Also intro- or retrospecting must presumably be correlated with different brain activity from that which seems to correspond to the feelings introspected—though that is another kind of distinction.) From these correlations we must conclude that the feelings and the appropriate brain activity of a person in pain or in some emotional state are two aspects of the one event in a detailed particularizing sense; hence they are strictly identifiable, i.e. are the one event (his being in pain or being afraid) differently observed. A feeling of pain and a pattern of brain activity appear so different that if they were both perceived or both introspected we should have to say that they were two different whole events. But this is not so; their marked difference in appearance can be attributed to the marked difference in mode of access to them. They can therefore be regarded as one and the same event in a person's life, and the difficulties of dualism are thus avoided.

We pass now from feelings to imagery or thought, of which much the same account can be given. They comprise a wide variety of experiences and activities, but can be arranged in order theoretically so that one type of experience could be said to merge into another. Thus there is a gradation from eidetic imagery or realistic dreams, through fairly vivid pictorial imagery of some memory and imagination, through fainter pictorial imagery and rather nebulous, probably motor, imagery, and then through imagery of words, visual or auditory, to seeming to speak to oneself.

I assume that having images or dreams is, like having sensations or feelings, to be regarded as a mode of experiencing and not as a type of perception of objects distinct from the percipient. Admittedly there is a certain subjective similarity to perceiving, and in certain cases it may be impossible to distinguish imagining from perceiving except in retrospect or with the assistance of others; the reason for this is presumably that the corresponding brain or nervous activity is similar in nature or location to that which occurs in perception. But at any rate the subjective similarity is illusory in that in imaging, as opposed to perceiving, the existence of such distinct objects cannot be confirmed by other persons or by subsequent events.

The suggestion then amounts to this, that the various experiences of imagining, remembering and thinking, e.g. images of various kinds whether vivid or vague, are the inner aspect of these various episodes and activities in a person's life and are what the person concerned experiences as an actor and not spectator in these situations, whereas brain activity is an outer aspect and is what can be scientifically observed or inferred by others. These experiences, particularly in thought, may be rather vague and nebulous, but I do not see how they can fairly be denied, and reluctance to admit either them or privileged access to them may be dispelled if it is realized that the access is not to a ghost world but to the same events or activities as neurologists may observe from without.

There is, however, as in feelings, a distinction to be made between those situations where introspection occurs and those where it does not. In the simple case one is aware just of the imagery, vivid and pictorial, verbal, or vague motor imagery, which is the content of the thought and the inner aspect. (The detail of the imagery, e.g. what scenes it represents, what questions seem to be asked, what words seem to be spoken or heard, will vary of course with what is being thought about, as presumably will the corresponding patterns of brain activity.) But if one tries to introspect the thought and describe the process and content, extra features come in; one is aware of oneself as distinct from the thought and as thinking, that is as directing or 'manipulating' with various degrees of success the pictorial or verbal imagery or as realizing certain properties of them or relations between them. It is difficult to be more explicit here without begging the question against some of the main theories of thought, and even this vague statement might not be regarded as sufficiently neutral; but any acceptable theory would have to admit experienced contents and introspectible activities in thought, and however we describe these my thesis is that they are the internal aspect of thinking, what the thinker is aware of in doing the thinking, or more rarely by introspecting it. They are not caused by or causes of brain activity, for that means dualism, nor do they occur without brain activity, as far as is known; hence they must be identified with the contemporaneous brain activity without which they do not occur, and they and the brain activity should be identified with the person's thinking, deciding or imagining. The experience and the brain activity are aspects of his doing this and so *are* his doing this as revealed on different modes of access, but this seems to hold in the particularizing as well as the general sense, and they would seem to be capable of cross-correlation and more precise identification with each other. But though they are, it is suggested, one and the same event, they appear to be two different events because they are the result of different modes of access to it, and for convenience we have to speak of them as different events. But when we do this we must remember that they are different aspects rather than different whole events; neither having images (or seeming to speak to oneself) nor the corresponding cerebral activity is the whole of thought, the whole of the episode of the person's thinking; though in being aware of them one is being aware of that episode.

4. Advantages and assumptions

In this way the various mental activities and experiences can be explained without having to postulate a second substance or order of being and without destroying the unity of the person or living organism. As against dualism the theory is simpler and more economical, in addition to avoiding some notorious difficulties; as against behaviouristic monism it is more plausible in that it does not have to deny mental events and experiences or privileged access to them by introspection. Indeed privileged access, whether by undergoing the experience, performing the action, etc., or by introspection, has importance in addition to being the source of the inner aspect of these activities: it provides a rough differentia of a mental activity to replace the dualist one that 'mental' means 'in the mind'; one can say that a mental activity is one in which the inner aspect is of primary importance, i.e. one where privileged access reveals more than external observation and provides the features which distinguish the activity from others. Thus we know most about walking from external observation and can most easily distinguish it from running by such observation rather than by kinaesthetic data (and such data are strictly effects of the movements); but we can only tell thinking of X from thinking of Y by their inner aspect, and must rely on it also for distinguishing deciding from imagining, for example. This is not a wholly satisfactory criterion of distinction, nor was the dualist one; neither fits the distinction of mental from physical pains, which is a matter of their cause. But however we use the word 'mental' the important point is that the Identity Hypothesis not only does not deny the inner aspect of thought, decision and feeling, but can regard awareness of it as, at present at least, the more important source of knowledge about them.

A modern development that is more easily accommodated on this theory than on dualism is the hypothesis of unconscious mental operations. Largely as the result of Freud's work it is widely held that certain types of behaviour, particularly but by no means exclusively that of the mentally unbalanced, are due to unconscious wishes or fears. Thus it is suggested that forgetting to do some action may be due to an unconscious desire not to do it. There is admittedly divergence of opinion about this, particularly in such simple cases of normal behaviour, but in view of the usefulness of the hypothesis in psychiatric treatment and its acceptance by psychologists, it would be difficult to deny some scope to unconscious motives and activities. But how can they be explained on dualist theory? If the essence of mind lies in its conscious activities, in its thoughts and decisions, it is difficult to see how it can indulge in unconscious activities which are the negation of that essence. And once it has been admitted that there are activities of the mind which are beyond the reach of introspection and self-awareness, the way is open to the supposition that it may have properties we are not aware of. If mind can betray its essence by acting unconsciously it may even be material or be the physical organism. Or perhaps dualism is too economical—the person is really a trio, mind, body, and unconscious mind (if Freud is to be taken literally it is more like a chamber orchestra). At any rate we could argue *ad hominem* that if 'mind' is to be taken as the name of an entity different from the body so should the 'unconscious' and perhaps the 'ego' and the 'id'. And once the protest has been raised against these hypostatizations, 'mind' will hardly survive unscathed. But if one rejects them all and thinks on monistic lines of various activities of the person, then the notion of unconscious activities presents little difficulty. We already have (i) conscious mental activities presenting two aspects—brain activity and an experienced or introspected content—and (ii) physical activities, which possess little inner aspect and normally take place in the body outside the brain, though they may be regulated by it; to these we should now add (iii) unconscious mental activities, of which there is no inner aspect, nor as yet any outer one, for they are inferred activities. But it is to be supposed that the lack of an inner one is characteristic of them, while lack of an outer is accidental. If we could differentiate brain activity adequately we should detect the outer aspect of unconscious activities, namely some form of brain activity very similar to that which occurs in the conscious wishes, desires and so on which they are supposed to resemble and in terms of which they are described, yet lacking some as yet indistinguishable characteristic which would make them 'emerge into consciousness', i.e. give them an inner aspect as well. Though admittedly very speculative, this does at least suggest how unconscious activities can be admitted on this theory without jeopardizing it; and that is more than can be said for dualism.

Two further points must be made about my theory before we can consider possible objections to it. The first is that all the supposed evidence of interaction between mind and body can be equally well interpreted on the Identity Hypothesis.[2] Let us take a few typical examples: trapping one's finger causes pain, two whiskies make one cheerful, the thought of food makes one's mouth water, or one moves as part of a planned action. On the first two it is common ground that the nerve impulses or alcohol set up or alter brain activity; but whereas the Interactionist says that the changes in brain activity cause changes in the mental experiences, on my theory they are identified, and are the same event in the person's life differently observed, not successive events. The feeling of pain or cheerfulness is the inner aspect of the situation of suffering from a trapped finger or of being affected by alcohol, and the changes in brain activity are the scientifically observed outer aspect; and from the correlator's viewpoint they can be precisely identified in a way the feeling and the finger damage cannot. There is still causation in that the finger damage (or alcohol) affects brain activity, but not a second causal step from brain to mental experience. Similarly the last two examples are only singly not doubly causal. It is not that the image or thought of food or the decision to move cause brain activity which in turn causes functioning of the salivary gland or muscles; it is

2. In this the hypothesis is markedly superior to Parallelism, apart from the dualist character of the latter.

rather that the thought or decision *is* the brain activity which causally affects gland or muscles.

A similar reinterpretation can be applied to psychological medicine. One speaks of psychosomatic diseases, those where some such psychological state as continued anxiety may cause ulcers or other physical effects, or one may say that one mental illness is due to physical causes, e.g. to syphilis, while another is solely of psychological origin, being due to conflicts and frustrations. But it should be recognized that this kind of language suggests dualism; on the Identity Hypothesis, although one can regard anxiety as a whole situation and thus as a cause, one should preferably avoid the suggestion that the cause is entirely psychical and should say that the ulcers are caused by the brain activity which is the correlate of, and in a sense is, the anxiety state. Similarly, while allowing that fears and conflicts may cause a manic-depressive reaction, one should also emphasize that the supposed cause and effect, as whole situations, have cerebral aspects identifiable with the more obvious inner ones. Hence it is only to be expected that physical treatment, such as drugs, electric shocks or surgery, will be as effective as psychological treatment, at least when the detailed cerebral correlates are better understood.

The second point is to stress the vital assumption of my theory that mental activity, whether regarded as the whole activity presenting two aspects or as the inner aspect only, is always accompanied by cerebral activity; and, furthermore, that they vary concomitantly so that there is cerebral activity of different kinds or in different areas corresponding to the different kinds and subjects of thoughts, images and feelings. If it could be proved that some mental activity occurred without any corresponding brain activity, that would be fatal to the theory as I conceive it. Admittedly one might say that here was a case where whole activity of the person, his thinking or perceiving, occurred, but was only available on the inner aspect. And in practice that is true of many, where no outer aspect on the scientific level can definitely be distinguished by present techniques. But that limitation does not prevent the assumption that the required cerebral activity occurs and may eventually be distinguishable in full detail; the serious situation would be if it were shown that no outer aspect will ever be available because no such activity is occurring. The reason is that the theory is grafted on to the publicity assumption that the person is a self-conscious, self-determining organism and as such is an observable part of the physical world. Mental experiences are then explained as the inner aspect of certain whole activities of the person, as what it is like to be the person acting in such a *milieu*, and the brain activity as what can be observed of the whole activity by scientific means. But the superiority of public scientific observation is assumed in that it reveals the substances, the fundamental structure and framework in which these activities have to be placed. The reality of mental experiences or whole activities is not denied, merely the supposition that they reveal or qualify substances in a different world from the physical one. But to deny brain activity corresponding to certain mental activity would be to deny that the person as a physical organism was acting; it would thus imply access to another, mental, world of entities in which these activities could take place. And this would be to abandon my theory for dualism.

The assumption that mental activity is always accompanied by brain activity, even though the latter cannot yet be distinguished, would be widely accepted, but in view of its importance I shall briefly indicate some reasons for adopting it. First, it is in accord with the nature of the human brain, especially when compared with that of animals. The enormous number of brain cells and the complexity of their interconnections makes the supposition of differences in brain activity corresponding to differences in mental activity quite credible, especially when one considers the large area not identifiable with sensation or motor activity. If the mind or self can and regularly does think on its own without the brain, it is difficult to see what function all this cerebral development performs; and if the person regularly needs his brain to think with, one is puzzled to see how he can manage without it—it would be rather as if one supposed that he could sometimes breathe without lungs. Further, there is an obvious, if rough, correlation between the intelligence of various animals and their ratio of brain weight to total weight, or more significant apparently, brain weight to spinal cord weight. (The latter ratio is about 1 : 1 in lower animals, 15 : 1 in apes and 55 : I in man, and the main difference is due to non-sensory areas.)[3]

Secondly, the general conclusion that mental ability and activity depend on a suitable brain is confirmed by evidence of brain injury or disease and of the operation of drugs. Many forms of idiocy or mental deficiency are due to improperly developed or injured brains or to biochemical deficiency. Injuries and diseases of the brain in later life cause various impairments of function (loss of memory, attention, self-control or power of recognition) or even complete insanity, while a surgical operation may be undergone to alter the personality. Admittedly persons and animals have a limited power of recovery of function after suffering the destruction of part of the brain tissue, but this seems due to another part of the brain taking over the function. And apart from the proper structure of the brain being necessary for mental ability and activity, it also requires a proper blood supply and nutriment: cutting off the blood supply by pressure on the carotid artery will produce unconsciousness; lack of oxygen, as Himalayan climbers know, produces mental confusion and saps will power; lack of more abstruse chemicals will cause idiocy or even insanity; while the mental effects of various drugs are well known. Detailed evidence on all these points could be greatly elaborated.[4]

Thirdly, a more exact correlation can be attempted in certain cases, and is of great interest. Electro-encephalograms, records of the changing electrical activity in the brain obtained from electrodes on the scalp, clearly show changes concomitant with the beginning and end of certain types of mental activity. Thus when a person is sitting quietly and relaxed with his eyes shut, conscious but not thinking of

3. See N. L. Munn, *Psychology*, and. edn., p. 50.

4. On these and subsequent points see: C. T. Morgan and E. Stellar, *Physiological Psychology*; the articles in *Handbook of Experimental Psychology*, ed. S. S. Stevens; or N. L. Munn, *Psychology*. These books discuss or give references to detailed evidence as well as providing useful surveys.

anything ('his mind a blank' as we say), the 'alpha rhythm' is prominent. If he gets drowsy or falls asleep, or loses consciousness, other rhythms appear. More important, if he opens his eyes and sees things, or if he hears them, or even if mental attention occurs, the alpha rhythm is replaced by faster ones. Similarly give the person a problem to solve and the alpha rhythm disappears, to reappear when it is solved and relaxation returns. Mental effort is also associated with other electrical phenomena, though less generally and surely. Fast 'beta waves' occur, and in about half the subjects 'kappa waves' can be detected when they are reading and thinking. Unfortunately the method of picking up electrical activity in the brain through the barrier of the skull and scalp is crude, and the details of the waves are difficult to distinguish; but that changes at the beginning and ending of mental activity can even so be detected is significant evidence of concomitant variation. We may also mention 'action potentials': slight electrical activity is detectable in muscles related to the kind of thought we are having at a particular time; thus in normal 'verbal' thought one can detect such potentials in the tongue and throat, while they occur in the eye muscles during visual imagery and in the arm during imagined arm movements; most interestingly they occur in the hands of deaf mutes when thinking. If we can presume that they are the effects of a brain activity far more difficult to detect, they support the general supposition of the concomitance of mental and cerebral activity, as well as the suggestion that in imagery the same sort of brain and nerve activity occurs as in perception. The psychogalvanic reflex may similarly be adduced: this, the principle of the so-called 'lie detector', is a change in the body's electrical resistance, probably connected with perspiration; it is a sign of emotional response and occurs when an idea or stimulus sets a person in readiness or expectancy for some event. Being controlled by the pre-motor area of the cortex, it may be regarded as an effect of brain activity connected with these situations, and so suggest that 'mental' readiness and expectancy occur with brain activity even when no action is attempted.

This evidence of detailed correlation is far from complete and is controversial, but as its defects seem to lie in the unavoidable crudity of detection methods and in the fact that one is often forced to deal with effects only of brain activity, it seems both important and significant, especially in view of the general evidence of the necessity of a properly functioning brain for mental activity. And even that general evidence was worth perhaps tedious emphasis because of its part in the fundamental assumption of my theory and because that assumption has been denied. We must now consider that denial, the first main objection to the Identity Hypothesis.

Chapter 8
Sensations and brain processes

J. J. C. Smart

THIS paper[1] takes its departure from arguments to be found in U. T. Place's 'Is Consciousness a Brain Process'.[2] I have had the benefit of discussing Place's thesis in a good many universities in the United States and Australia, and I hope that the present paper answers objections to his thesis which Place has not considered and that it presents his thesis in a more nearly unobjectionable form. This paper is meant also to supplement the paper 'The "Mental" and the "Physical",' by H. Feigl,[3] which in part argues for a similar thesis to Place's.

Suppose that I report that I have at this moment a roundish, blurry-edged after-image which is yellowish towards its edge and is orange towards its centre. What is it that I am reporting? One answer to this question might be that I am not reporting anything, that when I say that it looks to me as though there is a roundish yellowy-orange patch of light on the wall I am expressing some sort of *temptation*, the temptation to say that there *is* a roundish yellowy-orange patch on the wall (though I may know that there is not such a patch on the wall). This is perhaps Wittgenstein's view in the *Philosophical Investigations* (see §§367, 370). Similarly, when I 'report' a pain, I am not really reporting anything (or, if you like, I am reporting in a queer sense of 'reporting'), but am doing a sophisticated sort of wince. (See §244: 'The verbal expression of pain replaces crying and does not describe it.' Nor does it describe anything else?).[4] I prefer most of the time to discuss an after-image rather than a pain, because the word 'pain' brings in something which is irrelevant to my purpose: the notion of 'distress'. I think that 'he is in pain' entails 'he is in distress',

J. J. C. Smart, 'Sensations and Brain Processes', *Philosophical Review* 68 (1959).

1. This is a very slightly revised version of a paper which was first published in the *Philosophical Review*, LXVIII (1959), 141–56. Since that date there have been criticisms of my paper by J. T. Stevenson, *Philosophical Review*, LXIX (1960), 505–10, to which I have replied in *Philosophical Review*, LXX (1961), 406–7, and by G. Pitcher and by W. D. Jorke, *Australasian Journal of Philosophy*, XXXVIII (1960), 150–60, to which I have replied in the same volume of that journal, pp. 252–4.
2. *British Journal of Psychology*, XLVII (1956), 44–50.
3. *Minnesota Studies in the Philosophy of Science*, Vol. II (Minneapolis: University of Minnesota Press, 1958), pp. 370–497.
4. Some philosophers of my acquaintance, who have the advantage over me in having known Wittgenstein, would say that this interpretation of him is too behaviouristic. However, it seems to me a very natural interpretation of his printed words, and whether or not it is Wittgenstein's real view it is certainly an interesting and important one. I wish to consider it here as a possible rival both to the 'brain-process' thesis and to straight-out old-fashioned dualism.

that is, that he is in a certain agitation-condition.[5] Similarly, to say 'I am in pain' may be to do more than 'replace pain behaviour': it may be partly to report something, though this something is quite non-mysterious, being an agitation-condition, and so susceptible of behaviouristic analysis. The suggestion I wish if possible to avoid is a different one, namely that 'I am in pain' is a genuine report, and that what it reports is an irreducibly psychical something. And similarly the suggestion I wish to resist is also that to say 'I have a yellowish-orange after-image' is to report something irreducibly psychical.

Why do I wish to resist this suggestion? Mainly because of Occam's razor. It seems to me that science is increasingly giving us a viewpoint whereby organisms are able to be seen as physiochemical mechanisms[6]: it seems that even the behaviour of man himself will one day be explicable in mechanistic terms. There does seem to be, so far as science is concerned, nothing in the world but increasingly complex arrangements of physical constituents. All except for one place: in consciousness. That is, for a full description of what is going on in a man you would have to mention not only the physical processes in his tissues, glands, nervous system, and so forth, but also his states of consciousness: his visual, auditory, and tactual sensations, his aches and pains. That these should be *correlated* with brain processes does not help, for to say that they are *correlated* is to say that they are something 'over and above'. You cannot correlate something with itself. You correlate footprints with burglars, but not Bill Sykes the burglar with Bill Sykes the burglar. So sensations, states of consciousness, do seem to be the one sort of thing left outside the physicalist picture, and for various reasons I just cannot believe that this can be so. That everything should be explicable in terms of physics (together of course with descriptions of the ways in which the parts are put together—roughly, biology is to physics as radio-engineering is to electromagnetism) except the occurrence of sensations seems to me to be frankly unbelievable. Such sensations would be 'nomological danglers', to use Feigl's expression.[7] It is not often realized how odd would be the laws whereby these nomological danglers would dangle. It is sometimes asked, 'Why can't there be psychophysical laws which are of a novel sort, just as the laws of electricity and magnetism were novelties from the standpoint of Newtonian mechanics?' Certainly we are pretty sure in the future to come across new ultimate laws of a novel type, but I expect them to relate simple constituents: for example, whatever ultimate particles are then in vogue. I cannot believe that ultimate laws of nature could relate simple constituents to configurations consisting of perhaps billions of neurons (and goodness knows how many billion billions of ultimate particles) all put together for all the world as though their main purpose

5. See Ryle, *The Concept of Mind* (London: Hutchinsons's University Library, 1949), p. 93.
6. On this point see Paul Oppenheim and Hilary Putnam, "Unity of Science as a Working Hypothesis,' in *Minnesota Studies in the Philosophy of Science*, Vol. II (Minneapolis: University of Minnesota Press, 1958), pp. 3–36.
7. Feigl, op. cit., p. 428. Feigl uses the expression 'nomological danglers' for the laws whereby the entities dangle: I have used the expression to refer to the dangling entities themselves.

in life was to be a negative feedback mechanism of a complicated sort. Such ultimate laws would be like nothing so far known in science. They have a queer 'smell' to them. I am just unable to believe in the nomological danglers themselves, or in the laws whereby they would dangle. If any philosophical arguments seemed to compel us to believe in such things, I would suspect a catch in the argument. In any case it is the object of this paper to show that there are no philosophical arguments which compel us to be dualists.

The above is largely a confession of faith, but it explains why I find Wittgenstein's position (as I construe it) so congenial. For on this view there are, in a sense, no sensations. A man is a vast arrangement of physical particles, but there are not, over and above this, sensations or states of consciousness. There are just behavioural facts about this vast mechanism such as that it expresses a temptation (behaviour disposition) to say 'there is a yellowish-red patch on the wall' or that it goes through a sophisticated sort of wince, that is, says 'I am in pain'. Admittedly Wittgenstein says that though the sensation 'is not a something', it is nevertheless 'not a nothing either' (§304), but this need only mean that the word 'ache' has a use. An ache is a thing, but only in the innocuous sense in which the plain man, in the first paragraph of Frege's *Foundations of Arithmetic*, answers the question 'What is the number one?' by 'a thing'. It should be noted that when I assert that to say 'I have a yellowish-orange after-image' is to express a temptation to assert the physical-object statement. 'There is a yellowish-orange patch on the wall', I mean that saying 'I have a yellowish-orange after-image' is (partly) the exercise of the disposition[8] which is the temptation. It is not to *report* that I have the temptation, any more than is 'I love you' normally a report that I love someone. Saying 'I love you' is just part of the behaviour which is the exercise of the disposition of loving someone.

Though for the reasons given above, I am very receptive to the above 'expressive' account of sensation statements, I do not feel that it will quite do the trick. Maybe this is because I have not thought it out sufficiently, but it does seem to me as though, when a person says 'I have an after-image', he *is* making a genuine report, and that when he says 'I have a pain', he *is* doing more than 'replace pain behaviour', and that 'this more' is not just to say that he is in distress. I am not so sure, however, that to admit this is to admit that there are non-physical correlates of brain processes. Why should not sensations just be brain processes of a certain sort? There are, of course, well-known (as well as lesser-known) philosophical objections to the view that reports of sensations are reports of brain-processes, but I shall try to argue that these arguments are by no means as cogent as is commonly thought to be the case.

8. Wittgenstein did not like the word 'disposition'. I am using it to put in a nutshell (and perhaps inaccurately) the view which I am attributing to Wittgenstein. I should like to repeat that I do not wish to claim that my interpretation of Wittgenstein is correct. Some of those who knew him do not interpret him in this way. It is merely a view which I find myself extracting from his printed words and which I think is important and worth discussing for its own sake.

Let me first try to state more accurately the thesis that sensations are brain-processes. It is not the thesis that, for example, 'after-image' or 'ache' means the same as 'brain process of sort X' (where 'X' is replaced by a description of a certain sort of brain process). It is that, in so far as 'after-image' or 'ache' is a report of a process, it is a report of a process that *happens to be* a brain process. It follows that the thesis does not claim that sensation statements can be *translated* into statements about brain processes.[9] Nor does it claim that the logic of a sensation statement is the same as that of a brain-process statement. All it claims is that in so far as a sensation statement is a report of something, that something is in fact a brain process. Sensations are nothing over and above brain processes. Nations are nothing 'over and above' citizens, but this does not prevent the logic of nation statements being very different from the logic of citizen statements, nor does it insure the translatability of nation statements into citizen statements. (I do not, however, wish to assert that the relation of sensation statements to brain-process statements is very like that of nation statements to citizen statements. Nations do not just *happen to be* nothing over and above citizens, for example. I bring in the 'nations' example merely to make a negative point: that the fact that the logic of A-statements is different from that of B-statements does not insure that A's are anything over and above B's.)

Remarks on identity

When I say that a sensation is a brain process or that lightning is an electric discharge, I am using 'is' in the sense of strict identity. (Just as in the—in this case necessary—proposition '7 is identical with the smallest prime number greater than 5'.) When I say that a sensation is a brain process or that lightning is an electric discharge I do not mean just that the sensation is somehow spatially or temporally continuous with the brain process or that the lightning is just spatially or temporally continuous with the discharge. When on the other hand I say that the successful general is the same person as the small boy who stole the apples I mean only that the successful general I see before me is a time slice[10] of the same four-dimensional object of which the small boy stealing apples is an earlier time slice. However, the four dimensional object which has the general-I-see-before-me for its late time slice is identical in the strict sense with the four-dimensional object which has the small-boy-stealing-apples for an early time slice. I distinguish these two senses of 'is identical with' because I wish to make it clear that the brain-process doctrine asserts identity in the *strict* sense.

9. See Place; and Feigl, op. cit., p. 390, near top.
10. See J. H. Woodger, *Theory Construction*, International Encyclopedia of Unified Science, II, No. 5 (Chicago: University of Chicago Press, 1939), 38. I here permit myself to speak loosely. For warnings against possible ways of going wrong with this sort of talk, see my note 'Spatialising Time', *Mind*, LXIV (1955), 239–41.

I shall now discuss various possible objections to the view that the processes reported in sensation statements are in fact processes in the brain. Most of us have met some of these objections in our first year as philosophy students. All the more reason to take a good look at them. Others of the objections will be more recondite and subtle.

Objection 1. Any illiterate peasant can talk perfectly well about his after-images, or how things look or feel to him, or about his aches and pains, and yet he may know nothing whatever about neurophysiology. A man may, like Aristotle, believe that the brain is an organ for cooling the body without any impairment of his ability to make true statements about his sensations. Hence the things we are talking about when we describe our sensations cannot be processes in the brain.

Reply. You might as well say that a nation of slugabeds, who never saw the Morning Star or knew of its existence, or who had never thought of the expression 'the Morning Star', but who used the expression 'the Evening Star' perfectly well, could not use this expression to refer to the same entity as we refer to (and describe as) 'the Morning Star'.[11]

You may object that the Morning Star is in a sense not the very same thing as the Evening Star, but only something spatiotemporally continuous with it. That is, you may say that the Morning Star is not the Evening Star in the strict sense of 'identity' that I distinguished earlier.

There is, however, a more plausible example. Consider lightning.[12] Modern physical science tells us that lightning is a certain kind of electrical discharge due to ionization of clouds of water vapour in the atmosphere. This, it is now believed, is what the true nature of lightning is. Note that there are not two things: a flash of lightning and an electrical discharge. There is one thing, a flash of lightning, which is described scientifically as an electrical discharge to the earth from a cloud of ionized water molecules. The case is not at all like that of explaining a footprint by reference to a burglar. We say that what lightning really is, what its true nature as revealed by science is, is an electrical discharge. (It is not the true nature of a footprint to be a burglar.)

To forestall irrelevant objections, I should like to make it clear that by 'lightning' I mean the publicly observable physical object, lightning, not a visual sense-datum of lightning. I say that the publicly observable physical object lightning is in fact the electrical discharge, not just a correlate of it. The sense-datum, or rather the having of the sense-datum, the 'look' of lightning, may well in my view be a correlate of the electrical discharge. For in my view it is a brain state *caused* by the lightning. But we should no more confuse sensations of lightning with lightning than we confuse sensations of a table with the table.

In short, the reply to Objection 1 is that there can be contingent statements of the form 'A is identical with B', and a person may well know that something is an A

11. Cf. Feigl, op. cit., p. 439.
12. See Place; also Feigl, op. cit., p. 438.

without knowing that it is a B. An illiterate peasant might well be able to talk about his sensations without knowing about brain processes, just as he can talk about lightning though he knows nothing of electricity.

Objection 2. It is only a contingent fact (if it is a fact) that when we have a certain kind of sensation there is a certain kind of process in our brain. Indeed it is possible, though perhaps in the highest degree unlikely, that our present physiological theories will be as out of date as the ancient theory connecting mental processes with goings on in the heart. It follows that when we report a sensation we are not reporting a brain-process.

Reply. The objection certainly proves that when we say 'I have an after-image' we cannot *mean* something of the form 'I have such and such a brain-process'. But this does not show that what we report (having an after-image) is not *in fact* a brain process. 'I see lightning' does not *mean* 'I see an electrical discharge'. Indeed, it is logically possible (though highly unlikely) that the electrical discharge account of lightning might one day be given up. Again, 'I see the Evening Star' does not *mean* the same as 'I see the Morning Star', and yet 'The Evening Star and the Morning Star are one and the same thing' is a contingent proposition. Possibly Objection 2 derives some of its apparent strength from a 'Fido'-Fido theory of meaning. If the meaning of an expression were what the expression named, then, of course, it *would* follow from the fact that 'sensation' and 'brain process' have different meanings that they cannot name one and the same thing.

Objection 3.[13] Even if Objections 1 and 2 do not prove that sensations are something over and above brain-processes, they do prove that the qualities of sensations are something over and above the qualities of brain-processes. That is, it may be possible to get out of asserting the existence of irreducibly psychic processes, but not out of asserting the existence of irreducibly psychic *properties.* For suppose we identify the Morning Star with the Evening Star. Then there must be some properties which logically imply that of being the Morning Star, and quite distinct properties which entail that of being the Evening Star. Again, there must be some properties (for example, that of being a yellow flash) which are logically distinct from those in the physicalist story.

Indeed, it might be thought that the objection succeeds at one jump. For consider the property of 'being a yellow flash'. It might seem that this property lies inevitably outside the physicalist framework within which I am trying to work (either by 'yellow' being an objective emergent property of physical objects, or else by being a power to produce yellow sense-data, where 'yellow', in this second instantiation of the word, refers to a purely phenomenal or introspectible quality). I must therefore digress for a moment and indicate how I deal with secondary qualities. I shall concentrate on colour.

First of all, let me introduce the concept of a normal percipient. One person is

13. I think this objection was first put to me by Professor Max Black. I think it is the most subtle of any of those I have considered, and the one which I am least confident of having satisfactorily met.

more a normal percipient than another if he can make colour discriminations that the other cannot. For example, if A can pick a lettuce leaf out of a heap of cabbage leaves, whereas B cannot though he can pick a lettuce leaf out of a heap of beetroot leaves, then A is more normal than B. (I am assuming that A and B are not given time to distinguish the leaves by their slight difference in shape and so forth.) From the concept of 'more normal than' it is easy to see how we can introduce the concept of 'normal'. Of course, Eskimos may make the finest discriminations at the blue end of the spectrum, Hottentots at the red end. In this case the concept of a normal percipient is a slightly idealized one, rather like that of 'the mean sun' in astronomical chronology. There is no need to go into such subtleties now. I say that 'This is red' means something roughly like 'A normal percipient would not easily pick this out of a clump of geranium petals though he would pick it out of a clump of lettuce leaves'. Of course it does not exactly mean this: a person might know the meaning of 'red' without knowing anything about geraniums, or even about normal percipients. But the point is that a person can be *trained* to say 'This is red' of objects which would not easily be picked out of geranium petals by a normal percipient, and so on. (Note that even a colour-blind person can reasonably assert that something is red, though of course he needs to use another human being, not just himself, as his 'colour meter'.) This account of secondary qualities explains their unimportance in physics. For obviously the discriminations and lack of discriminations made by a very complex neurophysiological mechanism are hardly likely to correspond to simple and nonarbitrary distinctions in nature.

I therefore elucidate colours as powers, in Locke's sense, to evoke certain sorts of discriminatory responses in human beings. They are also, of course, powers to cause sensations in human beings (an account still nearer Locke's). But these sensations, I am arguing, are identifiable with brain processes.

Now how do I get over the objection that a sensation can be identified with a brain process only if it has some phenomenal property, not possessed by brain processes, whereby one-half of the identification may be, so to speak, pinned down?

Reply. My suggestion is as follows. When a person says, 'I see a yellowish-orange after-image', he is saying something like this: '*There is something going on which is like what is going on when* I have my eyes open, am awake, and there is an orange illuminated in good light in front of me, that is, when I really see an orange'. (And there is no reason why a person should not say the same thing when he is having a veridical sense-datum, so long as we construe 'like' in the last sentence in such a sense that something can be like itself.) Notice that the italicized words, namely 'there is something going on which is like what is going on when,' are all quasilogical or topic-neutral words. This explains why the ancient Greek peasant's reports about his sensations can be neutral between dualistic metaphysics or my materialistic metaphysics. It explains how sensations can be brain-processes and yet how a man who reports them need know nothing about brain-processes. For he reports them only very abstractly as 'something going on which is like what is going on when. . . .' Similarly, a person may say 'someone is in the room', thus reporting truly that the doctor is in the room, even though he has never heard of doctors. (There are not two people in the room: 'someone' *and* the doctor.) This account of sensation statements also explains the singular elusiveness of 'raw feels' —why no one seems to be able to pin any properties on them.[14] Raw feels, in my view, are colourless for the very same reason that *something* is colourless. This does not mean that sensations do not have plenty of properties, for if they are brain-processes they certainly have lots of neurological properties. It only means that in speaking of them as being like or unlike one another we need not know or mention these properties.

This, then, is how I would reply to Objection 3. The strength of my reply depends on the possibility of our being able to report that one thing is like another without being able to state the respect in which it is like. I do not see why this should not be so. If we think cybernetically about the nervous system we can envisage it as able to respond to certain likenesses of its internal processes without being able to do more. It would be easier to build a machine which would tell us, say on a punched tape, whether or not two objects were similar, than it would be to build a machine which would report wherein the similarities consisted.

Objection 4. The after-image is not in physical space. The brain-process is. So the after-image is not a brain-process.

Reply. This is an *ignoratio elenchi*. I am not arguing that the after-image is a brain-process, but that the experience of having an after-image is a brain-process. It is the *experience* which is reported in the introspective report. Similarly, if it is objected that the after-image is yellowy-orange, my reply is that it is the experience of seeing yellowy-orange that is being described, and this experience is not a yellowy-orange something. So to say that a brain-process cannot be yellowy-orange is not to say that a brain-process cannot in fact be the experience of having a yellowy-orange after-image. There is, in a sense, no such thing as an after-image or a sense-datum, though there is such a thing as the experience of having an image, and this experience is described indirectly in material object language, not in phenomenal language, for there is no such thing.[15] We describe the experience by saying in effect, that it is like the experience we have when, for example, we really see a yellowy-orange patch on the wall. Trees and wallpaper can be green, but not the experience of seeing or imagining a tree or wallpaper. (Or if they are described as green or yellow this can only be in a derived sense.)

Objection 5. It would make sense to say of a molecular movement in the brain

14. See B. A. Farrell, 'Experience', *Mind*, LIX (1950), 170–98.

15. Dr J. R. Smythies claims that a sense-datum language could be taught independently of the material object language ('A Note on the Fallacy of the "Phenomenological Fallacy,"' *British Journal of Psychology*, XLVIII (1957), 141–4). I am not so sure of this: there must be some public criteria for a person having got a rule wrong before we can teach him the rule. I suppose someone might *accidentally* learn colour words by Dr Smythies' procedure. I am not, of course, denying that we can learn a sense-datum language in the sense that we can learn to report our experience. Nor would Place deny it.

that it is swift or slow, straight or circular, but it makes no sense to say this of the experience of seeing something yellow.

Reply. So far we have not given sense to talk of experience as swift or slow, straight or circular. But I am not claiming that 'experience' and 'brain-process' mean the same or even that they have the same logic. 'Somebody' and 'the doctor' do not have the same logic, but this does not lead us to suppose that talking about somebody telephoning is talking about someone over and above, say, the doctor. The ordinary man, when he reports an experience is reporting that something is going on, but he leaves it open as to what sort of thing is going on, whether in a material solid medium or perhaps in some sort of gaseous medium, or even perhaps in some sort of nonspatial medium (if this makes sense). All that I am saying is that 'experience' and 'brain-process' may in fact refer to the same thing, and if so we may easily adopt a convention (which is not a change in our present rules for the use of experience words but an addition to them) whereby it would make sense to talk of an experience in terms appropriate to physical processes.

Objection 6. Sensations are private, brain processes are *public.* If I sincerely say, 'I see a yellowish-orange after-image', and I am not making a verbal mistake, then I cannot be wrong. But I can be wrong about a brain-process. The scientist looking into my brain might be having an illusion. Moreover, it makes sense to say that two or more people are observing the same brain-process but not that two or more people are reporting the same inner experience.

Reply. This shows that the language of introspective reports has a different logic from the language of material processes. It is obvious that until the brain-process theory is much improved and widely accepted there will be no *criteria* for saying 'Smith has an experience of such-and-such a sort' *except* Smith's introspective reports. So we have adopted a rule of language that (normally) what Smith says goes.

Objection 7. I can imagine myself turned to stone and yet having images, aches, pains, and so on.

Reply. I can imagine that the electrical theory of lightning is false, that lightning is some sort of purely optical phenomenon. I can imagine that lightning is not an electrical discharge. I can imagine that the Evening Star is not the Morning Star. But it is. All the objection shows is that 'experience' and 'brain-process' do not have the same meaning. It does not show that an experience is not in fact a brain process.

This objection is perhaps much the same as one which can be summed up by the slogan: 'What can be composed of nothing cannot be composed of anything'.[16] The argument goes as follows: on the brain-process thesis the identity between the brain-process and the experience is a contingent one. So it is logically possible that there should be no brain-process, and no process of any other sort either (no heart process, no kidney process, no liver process). There would be the experience but no

16. I owe this objection to Dr C. B. Martin. I gather that he no longer wishes to maintain this objection, at any rate in its present form.

'corresponding' physiological process with which we might be able to identify it empirically.

I suspect that the objector is thinking of the experience as a ghostly entity. So it is composed of something, not of nothing, after all. On his view it is composed of ghost stuff, and on mine it is composed of brain stuff. Perhaps the counter-reply will be[17] that the experience is simple and uncompounded, and so it is not composed of anything after all. This seems to be a quibble, for, if it were taken seriously, the remark 'What can be composed of nothing cannot be composed of anything' could be recast as an a priori argument against Democritus and atomism and for Descartes and infinite divisibility. And it seems odd that a question of this sort could be settled *a priori*. We must therefore construe the word 'composed' in a very weak sense, which would allow us to say that even an indivisible atom is composed of something (namely, itself). The dualist cannot really say that an experience can be composed of nothing. For he holds that experiences are something over and above material processes, that is, that they are a sort of ghost stuff. I say that the dualist's hypothesis is a perfectly intelligible one. But I say that experiences are not to be identified with ghost stuff but with brain stuff. This is another hypothesis, and in my view a very plausible one. The present argument cannot knock it down *a priori*.

Objection 8. The 'beetle in the box' objection (see Wittgenstein, *Philosophical Investigations*, §293). How could descriptions of experiences, if these are genuine reports, get a foothold in language? For any rule of language must have public criteria for its correct application.

Reply. The change from describing how things are to describing how we feel is just a change from uninhibitedly saying 'this is so' by saying 'this looks so'. That is, when the naive person might be tempted to say, 'There is a patch of light on the wall which moves whenever I move my eyes' or 'A pin is being stuck into me', we have learned how to resist this temptation and say 'It *looks as though* there is a patch of light on the wall-paper' or 'It *feels as though* someone were sticking a pin into me'. The introspective account tells us about the individual's state of consciousness in the same way as does 'I see a patch of light' or 'I feel a pin being stuck into me': it differs from the corresponding perception statement in so far as it withdraws any claim about what is actually going on in the external world. From the point of view of the psychologist, the change from talking about the environment to talking about one's perceptual sensations is simply a matter of disinhibiting certain reactions. These are reactions which one normally suppresses because one has learned that in the prevailing circumstances they are unlikely to provide a good indication of the state of the environment.[18] To say that something looks green to me is simply to say that my experience is like the experience I get when I see something that

17. Martin did not make this reply, but one of his students did.
18. I owe this point to Place, in correspondence.

really is green. In my reply to Objection 3, I pointed out the extreme openness or generality of statements which report experiences. This explains why there is no language of private qualities. (Just as 'someone', unlike 'the doctor', is a colourless word.)[19]

If it is asked what is the difference between those brain processes which, in my view, are experiences and those brain processes which are not, I can only reply that it is at present unknown. I have been tempted to conjecture that the difference may in part be that between perception and reception (in D. M. MacKay's terminology) and that the type of brain process which is an experience might be identifiable with MacKay's active 'matching response.'[20] This, however, cannot be the whole story, because sometimes I can perceive something unconsciously, as when I take a handkerchief out of a drawer without being aware that I am doing so. But at the very least, we can classify the brain processes which are experiences as those brain processes which are, or might have been, causal conditions of those pieces of verbal behaviour which we call reports of immediate experience.

I have now considered a number of objections to the brain-process thesis. I wish now to conclude with some remarks on the logical status of the thesis itself. U. T. Place seems to hold that it is a straight-out scientific hypothesis.[21] If so, he is partly right and partly wrong. If the issue is between (say) a brain-process thesis and a heart thesis, or a liver thesis, or a kidney thesis, then the issue is a purely empirical one, and the verdict is overwhelmingly in favour of the brain. The right sorts of things don't go on in the heart, liver, or kidney, nor do these organs possess the right sort of complexity of structure. On the other hand, if the issue is between a brain-or-liver-or-kidney thesis (that is, some form of materialism) on the one hand and epiphenomenalism on the other hand, then the issue is not an empirical one. For there is no conceivable experiment which could decide between materialism and epiphenomenalism. This latter issue is not like the average straight-out empirical issue in science, but like the issue between the nineteenth-century English naturalist Philip Gosse,[22] and the orthodox geologists and palæontologists of his day. According to Gosse, the earth was created about 4000 BC exactly as described in *Genesis*, with twisted rock strata, 'evidence' of erosion, and so forth, and all sorts of fossils, all in their appropriate strata, just as if the usual evolutionist story had been true. Clearly this theory is in a sense irrefutable: no evidence can possibly tell

19. The 'beetle in the box' objection is, *if it is sound*, an objection to *any* view, and in particular the Cartesian one, that introspective reports are genuine reports. So it is no objection to a weaker thesis that I would be concerned to uphold, namely, that if introspective reports of 'experiences' are genuinely reports, then the things they are reports of are in fact brain processes.

20. See his article 'Towards an Information-Flow Model of Human Behaviour,' *British Journal of Psychology*, XLVII (1956), 30–43.

21. Op. cit. For a further discussion of this, in reply to the original version of the present paper, see Place's note 'Materialism as a Scientific Hypothesis', *Philosophical Review*, LXIX (1960), 101–4.

22. See the entertaining account of Gosse's book *Omphalos* by Martin Gardner in *Fads and Fallacies in the Name of Science*, 2nd ed. (New York: Dover, 1957), pp. 124–7.

against it. Let us ignore the theological setting in which Philip Gosse's hypothesis had been placed, thus ruling out objections of a theological kind, such as 'what a queer God who would go to such elaborate lengths to deceive us'. Let us suppose that it is held that the universe just *began* in 4004 BC with the initial conditions just everywhere as they were in 4004 BC, and in particular that our own planet began with sediment in the rivers, eroded cliffs, fossils in the rocks, and so on. No scientist would ever entertain this as a serious hypothesis, consistent though it is with all possible evidence. The hypothesis offends against the principles of parsimony and simplicity. There would be far too many brute and inexplicable facts. Why are pterodactyl bones just as they are? No explanation in terms of the evolution of pterodactyls from earlier forms of life would any longer be possible. We would have millions of facts about the world as it was in 4004 BC that just have to be *accepted.*

The issue between the brain-process theory and epiphenomenalism seems to be of the above sort. (Assuming that a behaviouristic reduction of introspective reports is not possible.) If it be agreed that there are no cogent philosophical arguments which force us into accepting dualism, and if the brain process theory and dualism are equally consistent with the facts, then the principles of parsimony and simplicity seem to me to decide overwhelmingly in favour of the brain-process theory. As I pointed out earlier, dualism involves a large number of irreducible psychophysical laws (whereby the 'nomological danglers' dangle) of a queer sort, that just have to be taken on trust, and are just as difficult to swallow as the irreducible facts about the palæontology of the earth with which we are faced on Philip Gosse's theory.

Chapter 9

Identity and necessity

Saul A. Kripke

...

LET me turn to the case of heat and the motion of molecules. Here surely is a case that is contingent identity! Recent philosophy has emphasized this again and again. So, if it is a case of contingent identity, then let us imagine under what circumstances it would be false. Now, concerning this statement I hold that the circumstances philosophers apparently have in mind as circumstances under which it would have been false are not in fact such circumstances. First, of course, it is argued that 'Heat is the motion of molecules,' is an a posteriori judgment; scientific investigation might have turned out otherwise. As I said before, this shows nothing against the view that it is necessary—at least if I am right. But here, surely, people had very specific circumstances in mind under which, so they thought, the judgment that heat is the motion of molecules would have been false. What were these circumstances? One can distill them out of the fact that we found out empirically that heat is the motion of molecules. How was this? What did we find out first when we found out that heat is the motion of molecules? There is a certain external phenomenon which we can sense by the sense of touch, and it produces a sensation which we call 'the sensation of heat.' We then discover that the external phenomenon which produces this sensation, which we sense, by means of our sense of touch, is in fact that of molecular agitation in the thing that we touch, a very high degree of molecular agitation. So, it might be thought, to imagine a situation in which heat would not have been the motion of molecules, we need only imagine a situation in which we would have had the very same sensation and it would have been produced by something other than the motion of molecules. Similarly, if we wanted to imagine a situation in which light was not a stream of photons, we could imagine a situation in which we were sensitive to something else in exactly the same way, producing what we call visual experiences, though not through a stream of photons. To make the case stronger, or to look at another side of the coin, we could also consider a situation in which we *are* concerned with the motion of molecules but in which such motion does not give us the sensation of heat. And it might also have happened that we, or, at least, the creatures inhabiting this planet, might have been so constituted that, let us say, an increase in the motion of molecules did not give us this sensation but that, on the contrary, a slowing down of the molecules did

Saul A. Kripke, edited extract from 'Identity and Necessity'. In Milton K. Munitz, ed., *Identity and Individuation* (New York: New York University Press, 1971).

give us the very same sensation. This would be a situation, so it might be thought, in which heat would not be the motion of molecules, or, more precisely, in which temperature would not be mean molecular kinetic energy.

But I think it would not be so. Let us think about the situation again. First, let us think about it in the actual world. Imagine right now the world invaded by a number of Martians, who do indeed get the very sensation that we call 'the sensation of heat' when they feel some ice which has slow molecular motion, and who do not get a sensation of heat—in fact, maybe just the reverse—when they put their hand near a fire which causes a lot of molecular agitation. Would we say, 'Ah, this casts some doubt on heat being the motion of molecules, because there are these other people who don't get the same sensation'? Obviously not, and no one would think so. We would say instead that the Martians somehow feel the very sensation we get when we feel heat when they feel cold and that they do not get a sensation of heat when they feel heat. But now let us think of a counterfactual situation.[1] Suppose the earth had from the very beginning been inhabited by such creatures. First, imagine it inhabited by no creatures at all: then there is no one to feel any sensations of heat. But we would not say that under such circumstances it would necessarily be the case that heat did not exist; we would say that heat might have existed, for example, if there were fires that heated up the air.

Let us suppose the laws of physics were not very different: Fires do heat up the air. Then there would have been heat even though there were no creatures around to feel it. Now let us suppose evolution takes place, and life is created, and there are some creatures around. But they are not like us, they are more like the Martians. Now would we say that heat has suddenly turned to cold, because of the way the creatures of this planet sense it? No, I think we should describe this situation as a situation in which, though the creatures on this planet got our sensation of heat, they did not get it when they were exposed to heat. They got it when they were exposed to cold. And that is something we can surely well imagine. We can imagine it just as we can imagine our planet being invaded by creatures of this sort. Think of it in two steps. First there is a stage where there are no creatures at all, and one can certainly imagine the planet still having both heat and cold, though no one is around to sense it. Then the planet comes through an evolutionary process to be peopled with beings of different neural structure from ourselves. Then these creatures could be such that they were insensitive to heat; they did not feel it in the way we do; but on the other hand, they felt cold in much the same way that we feel heat. But still, heat would be heat, and cold would be cold. And particularly, then, this

1. Isn't the situation I just described also counterfactual? At least it may well be, if such Martians. never in fact invade. Strictly speaking, the distinction I wish to draw compares how we *would* speak *in* a (possibly counterfactual) situation, *if* it obtained, and how we *do* speak *of* a counterfactual situation, knowing that it does not obtain—i.e., the distinction between the language we would have used in a situation and the language we *do* use to describe it. (Consider the description: 'Suppose we all spoke German.' This description is in English.) The former case can be made vivid by imagining the counterfactual situation to be actual.

goes in no way against saying that in this counterfactual situation heat would still *be* the molecular motion, *be* that which is produced by fires, and so on, just as it would have been if there had been no creatures on the planet at all. Similarly, we could imagine that the planet was inhabited by creatures who got visual sensations when there were sound waves in the air. We should not therefore say, 'Under such circumstances, sound would have been light.' Instead we should say, 'The planet was inhabited by creatures who were in some sense visually sensitive to sound, and maybe even visually sensitive to light.' If this is correct, it can still be and will still be a necessary truth that heat is the motion of molecules and that light is a stream of photons.

To state the view succinctly: we use both the terms 'heat' and 'the motion of molecules' as rigid designators for a certain external phenomenon. Since heat is in fact the motion of molecules, and the designators are rigid, by the argument I have given here, it is going to be *necessary* that heat is the motion of molecules. What gives us the illusion of contingency is the fact we have identified the heat by the contingent fact that there happen to be creatures on this planet—(namely, ourselves) who are sensitive to it in a certain way, that is, who are sensitive to the motion of molecules or to heat—these are one and the same thing. And this is contingent. So we use the description, 'that which causes such and such sensations, or that which we sense in such and such a way', to identify heat. But in using this fact we use a contingent property of heat, just as we use the contingent property of Cicero as having written such and such works to identify him. We then use the terms 'heat' in the one case and 'Cicero' in the other *rigidly* to designate the objects for which they stand. And of course the term 'the motion of molecules' is rigid; it always stands for the motion of molecules, never for any other phenomenon. So, as Bishop Butler said, 'everything is what it is and not another thing.' Therefore, 'Heat is the motion of molecules' will be necessary, not contingent, and one only has the *illusion* of contingency in the way one could have the illusion of contingency in thinking that this table might have been made of ice. We might think one could imagine it, but if we try, we can see on reflection that what we are really imagining is just there being another lectern in this very position here which was in fact made of ice. The fact that we may identify this lectern by being the object we see and touch in such and such a position is something else.

Now how does this relate to the problem of mind and body? It is usually held that this is a contingent identity statement just like 'Heat is the motion of molecules.' That cannot be. It cannot be a contingent identity statement just like 'Heat is the motion of molecules' because, if I am right, 'Heat is the motion of molecules' is not a contingent identity statement. Let us look at this statement. For example, 'My being in pain at such and such a time is my being in such and such a brain state at such and such a time,' or, 'Pain in general is such and such a neural (brain) state.'

This is held to be contingent on the following grounds. First, we can imagine the brain state existing though there is no pain at all. It is only a scientific fact that whenever we are in a certain brain state we have a pain. Second, one might imagine a creature being in pain, but not being in any specified brain state at all, maybe not having a brain at all. People even think, at least prima facie, though they may be wrong, that they can imagine totally disembodied creatures, at any rate certainly not creatures with bodies anything like our own. So it seems that we can imagine definite circumstances under which this relationship would have been false. Now, if these circumstances are circumstances, notice that we cannot deal with them simply by saying that this is just an illusion, something we can apparently imagine, but in fact cannot in the way we thought erroneously that we could imagine a situation in which heat was not the motion of molecules. Because although we can say that we pick out heat contingently by the contingent property that it affects us in such and such a way, we cannot similarly say that we pick out pain contingently by the fact that it affects us in such and such a way. On such a picture there would be the brain state, and we pick it out by the contingent fact that it affects us as pain. Now that might be true of the brain state, but it cannot be true of the pain. The experience itself has to be *this experience*, and I cannot say that it is contingent property of the pain I now have that it is a pain.[2] In fact, it would seem that both the terms, 'my pain' and 'my being in such and such a brain state' are, first of all, both rigid designators. That is, whenever anything is such and such a pain, it is essentially that very object, namely, such and such a pain, and wherever anything is such and such a brain state, it is essentially that very object, namely, such and such a brain state. So both of these are rigid designators. One cannot say this pain might have been something else, some other state. These are both rigid designators.

Second, the way we would think of picking them out—namely, the pain by its being an experience of a certain sort, and the brain state by its being the state of a

2. The most popular identity theories advocated today explicitly fail to satisfy this simple requirement. For these theories usually hold that a mental state is a brain state, and that what makes the brain state into a mental state is its 'causal role', the fact that it tends to produce certain behavior (as intentions produce actions, or pain, pain behavior) and to be produced by certain stimuli (e.g. pain, by pinpricks). If the relations between the brain state and its causes and effects are regarded as contingent, then *being such-and-such-a-menial state* is a contingent property of the brain state. Let *X* be a pain'. The causal-role identity theorist holds (1) that *X* is a brain state, (2) that the fact that *X* is a pain is to be analyzed (roughly) as the fact that *X* is produced by certain stimuli and produces certain behavior. The fact mentioned in (2) is, of course, regarded as contingent; the brain state *X* might well exist and not tend to produce the appropriate behavior in the absence of other conditions. Thus (1) and (2) assert that a certain pain X might have existed, yet not have been a pain. This seems to me self-evidently absurd. Imagine any pain: is it possible that *in itself* could have existed, yet not have been a pain?

If *X* = *Y*, then *X* and *Y* share all properties, including modal properties. If *X* is a pain and *Y* the corresponding brain state, then *being a pain* is an essential property of *X*, and *being a brain state* is an essential property of *Y*. If the correspondence relation is, in fact, identity, then it must be *necessary* of *Y* that it corresponds to a pain, and *necessary* of *X* that it correspond to a brain state, indeed to this particular brain state, *Y*. Both assertions seem false; it *seems* clearly possible that *X* should have existed without the corresponding brain state; or that the brain state should have existed without being felt as pain. Identity theorists cannot, contrary to their almost universal present practice, accept these intuitions; they must deny them, and explain them away. This is none too easy a thing to do.

certain material object, being of such and such molecular configuration—both of these pick out their objects essentially and not accidentally, that is, they pick them out by essential properties. Whenever the molecules *are* in this configuration, we *do* have such and such a brain state. Whenever you feel *this*, you do have a pain. So it seems that the identity theorist is in some trouble, for, since we have two rigid designators, the identity statement in question is necessary. Because they pick out their objects essentially we cannot say the case where you seem to imagine the identity statement false is really an illusion like the illusion one gets in the case of heat and molecular motion, because that illusion depended on the fact that we pick out heat by a certain contingent property. So there is very little room to maneuver; perhaps none.[3] The identity theorist who holds that pain is the brain state, also has to hold that it necessarily is the brain state. He therefore cannot concede, but has to deny, that there would have been situations under which one would have had pain but not the corresponding brain state. Now usually in arguments on the identity theory, this is very far from being denied. In fact, it is conceded from the outset by the materialist as well as by his opponent. He says, 'Of course, it *could* have been the case that we had pains without the brain states. It is a contingent identity.' But that cannot be. He has to hold that we are under some illusion in thinking that we can imagine that there could have been pains without brain states. And the only model I can think of for what the illusion might be, or at least the model given by the analogy the materialists themselves suggest, namely, heat and molecular motion, simply does not work in this case. So the materialist is up against a very stiff challenge. He has to show that these things we think we can see to be possible are in fact not possible. He has to show that these things which we can imagine are not in fact things we can imagine. And that requires some very different philosophical

3. A brief restatement of the argument may be helpful here. If 'pain' and 'C-fiber stimulation' are rigid designators of phenomena, one who identifies them must regard the identity as necessary. How can this necessity be reconciled with the apparent fact that C-fiber stimulation might have turned Out not to be correlated with pain at all? We might try to reply by analogy to the case of heat and molecular motion; the latter identity, too, is necessary, yet someone may believe that, before scientific investigation showed otherwise, molecular motion might have turned out not to be heat. The reply is, of course, that what really is possible is that people (or some rational sentient beings) could have been in the *same epislemic situation* as we actually are, and identify a *phenomenon* in the same way we identify heat, namely, by feeling it by the sensation we call 'the sensation of heat," without the phenomenon being molecular motion. Furtheri the beings might not have been sensitive to molecular motion (i.e., to heat) by any neural mechanism whatsoever. It is impossible to explain the apparent possibility of C-fiber stimulations not having been pain in the same way. Here, too, we would have to suppose that we could have been in the same epistemological situation, and identify something in the same way we identify pain, without its corresponding to C-fiber stimulation. But the way we identify pain is by feeling it, and if a C-fiber stimulation could have occurred without our feeling any pain, then the C-fiber stimulation would have occurred without there *being* any pain, contrary to the necessity of the identity. The trouble is that although 'heat' is a rigid designator, heat is picked out by the contingent property of its being felt in a certain way; pain, on the other hand, is picked out by an essential (indeed necessary and sufficient) property. For a sensation to be *felt* as pain is for it to *be* pain.

argument from the sort which has been given in the case of heat and molecular motion. And it would have to be a deeper and subtler argument than I can fathom and subtler than has ever appeared in any materialist literature that I have read. So the conclusion of this investigation would be that the analytical tools we are using go against the identity thesis and so go against the general thesis that mental states are just physical states.[4]

The next topic would be my own solution to the mind-body problem, but that I do not have.

4. All arguments against the identity theory which rely on the necessity of identity, or on the notion of essential property, are, of course, inspired by Descartes' argument for his dualism. The earlier arguments which superficially were rebutted by the analogies of heat and molecular motion, and the bifocals inventor who was also Postmaster General, had such an inspiration; and so does my argument here. R. Aibritton and M. Slote have informed me that they independently have attempted to give essentialist arguments against the identity theory, and probably others have done so as well.

The simplest Cartesian argument can perhaps be restated as follows: Let '*A*' be a name (rigid designator) of Descartes' body. Then Descartes argues that since he could exist even if *A* did not, $\Diamond$ (Descartes $\neq$ *A*), hence Descartes $\neq$ *A*. Those who have accused him of a modal fallacy have forgotten that 'A' is rigid. His argument is valid, and his conclusion is correct, provided its (perhaps dubitable) premise is accepted. On the other hand, provided that Descartes is regarded as having ceased to exist upon his death, 'Descartes $\neq$ *A*,' can be established without the use of a modal argument; for if so, no doubt A survived Descartes when *A* was a corpse. Thus *A* had a property (existing at a certain time) which Descartes did not. The same argument can establish that a statue is not the hunk of stone, or the congery of molecules, of which it is composed. Mere non-identity, then, may be a weak conclusion. (See D. Wiggins, *Philosophical Review*, Vol. 77 (1968), pp. 90 ff.) The Cartesian modal argument, however, surely can be deployed to maintain relevant stronger conclusions as well.

Questions

1. Philosophical behaviorists resist being lumped with psychological behaviorists. What might be the reason for this? Are philosophical and psychological behaviorism *really* so distinct?
2. What is 'privileged access'? How might Descartes explain the phenomenon of privileged access (assuming it is a genuine phenomenon) and how would a behaviorist explain it? What could be said in favor of either view?
3. Consider the thesis that the mind *is* the brain. Imagine someone arguing against this thesis in the following way. 'The mind could not possibly be the brain. After all, you are intimately acquainted with your states of mind, but largely ignorant of states and goings in your brain.' Is this a sound argument?
4. Identity theorists hold that the mind and brain are *strictly identical*. Explain what strict identity is and how it differs from the kind of identity appealed to in talk of two suburbanites driving identical SUVs.
5. What is the *phenomenological fallacy* (and how does it figure in Smart's defense of the identity theory)?
6. Explain the distinction between type and token identity, and classify the positions discussed in the readings in this part by means of the distinction.
7. What are 'aspects'? How plausible is it to think that minds and bodies are 'two aspects' of a single entity?
8. In defending the thesis that states of mind are brain states, Smart appeals to 'Ockham's Razor', the principle of parsimony. This principle is usually put in the form of a precept: do not multiply entities beyond necessity. What do you think this means? Does it provide an argument for the identity theory?
9. Smart speaks of 'after-images'. What is an after image? Why might Smart find it useful to discuss after-images in the context of a discussion of the relation states of mind bear to material states?
10. Kripke provides a subtle argument against the identity theory. Can you explain that argument and evaluate its force against Smart?

Suggested readings

Few philosophers have explicitly labeled themselves behaviorists, but definite behaviorist sympathies can be detected in Ryle (1949), in the work of Wittgenstein's students and followers (see, for instance, Malcolm 1959), and, more explicitly, in reductionist programmes in the philosophy of science of the kind advanced by Carnap (1932). Behaviorism's association with verificationism probably accounts for its lingering well past its heyday. (Verificationists, who trace their ancestry to the British empiricists, hold that the meaning of claims purporting to be about the world must be analyzable into sentences concerning actual or possible observations.) Quine (1960) expresses strong behaviorist sympathies, and Dennett (1987), a student of Ryle's, could be read as advancing a nuanced brand of behaviorism.

Watson's (1913) manifesto on psychological behaviorism influenced generations of psychologists. A sympathetic depiction of a mature psychological behaviorism can be found in Skinner (1963). This paper, along with other papers by Skinner, is reprinted with critical discussion by many authors in *Behavioral and Brain Sciences* 4 (1984). Staddon (1993) contains a more recent assessment of behaviorism in psychology. More references can be found in the entry for 'Logical Behaviorism' in Chalmers's (2001) on-line bibliography.

Mind–brain identity surfaced as a serious possibility with the publication of U. T. Place (1956) and Feigl (1958). The 1960s saw a steady stream of articles attacking and defending the identification of minds with brains, especially as it had been developed by J. J. C. Smart (Chapter 8). Useful collections include Borst (1970), O'Connor (1969), and Presley (1967). Armstrong (1968) advanced a version of the identity theory presaged in his (1961) that, like the account defended by Lewis (Chapter 10), has affinities with functionalism. Hill (1991) updates the identity theory, and Macdonald (1989) provides an exhaustive discussion of technical issues associated with 'type identity'. Smart's (2000) on-line discussion of mind-brain identity is clear and on target; see also Place's (2001) on-line contribution. Chalmers (2001) provides nearly 100 citations to work on the identity theory. Readers interested in how all this looks from the perspective of neuroscience might look at Edelman (1993).

Behaviorism

Carnap, R. (1932), 'Logical Foundations of the Unity of Science'. In Neurath et al. 1955: 42–62. Reprinted in Feigl and Sellars 1949: 408–23.

Chalmers, D. J. (2001), *Contemporary Philosophy of Mind: An Annotated Bibliography* <http://www.u.arizona.edu/~chalmers/biblio.html> Tucson, AZ: University of Arizona.

Dennett, D. C. (1987), *The Intentional Stance.* Cambridge, MA: MIT Press.

Feigl, H., and W. Sellars, eds. (1949), *Readings in Philosophical Analysis.* New York: Appleton–Century–Crofts.

Malcolm, N. (1959), *Dreaming.* London: Routledge & Kegan Paul.

Neurath, O., R. Carnap, and C. Morris, eds. (1955), *International Encyclopedia of Unified Science* (vol. i, nos. 1–5). Chicago: University of Chicago Press.

Quine, W. V. O. (1960), *Word and Object*, Cambridge: MIT Press.

Ryle, G. (1949), *The Concept of Mind.* London: Hutchinson.

Skinner, B. F. (1963), 'Behaviorism at Fifty', *Science* 140: 951–58. Reprinted with Open Peer Commentary in *Behavioral and Brain Sciences* 4 (1984), 615–21.

Staddon, J. (1993), *Behaviourism: Mind, Mechanism, and Society.* London: Duckworth.

Watson, J. B. (1913), 'Psychology as the Behaviorist Views It', *Psychological Review* 20: 158–77.

Mind–body identity

Armstrong, D. M. (1961), *Perception and the Physical World.* London: Routledge & Kegan Paul.

——(1968), *A Materialist Theory of the Mind,* London: Routledge & Kegan Paul.

Borst, C. V., ed. (1970), *The Mind–Brain Identity Theory.* London: Macmillan.

Chalmers, D. J. (2001), *Contemporary Philosophy of Mind: An Annotated Bibliography* <http://www.u.arizona.edu/~chalmers/biblio.html> Tucson, AZ: University of Arizona.

Edelman, G. L. (1993), *Bright Air, Brilliant Fire: On the Matter of the Mind.* New York: Basic Books.

Feigl, H. (1958) 'The "Mental" and the "Physical"'. In Feigl et al. 1958: 370–497. Reissued in 1967 as a monograph, *The 'Mental' and the 'Physical'*, Minneapolis: University of Minnesota Press.

——M. Scriven, and G. Maxwell, eds. (1958), *Concepts, Theories, and the Mind–Body Problem* (Minnesota Studies in the Philosophy of Science, vol. 2). Minneapolis: University of Minnesota Press.

Hill, C. S. (1991), *Sensations: A Defense of Type Materialism.* Cambridge: Cambridge University Press.

Macdonald, C. (1989), *Mind–Body Identity Theories.* London: Routledge.

O'Connor, J., ed. (1969), *Modern Materialism: Readings on Mind—Body Identity.* New York: Harcourt, Brace, & World.

Nani, M., ed. (2001), *A Field Guide to the Philosophy of Mind.* <http://host.uniroma3.it/progetti/kant/field/> Rome: University of Rome 3.

Place, U. T. (1956), 'Is Consciousness A Brain Process?' *British Journal of Psychology,* 47: 44–50.

——(2001), 'Identity Theories' . In Nani 2001: <http://host.uniroma3.it/progetti/kant/field/mbit.htm>

Presley, C. F., ed. (1967), *The Identity Theory of Mind.* Brisbane: University of Queensland Press.

Smart, J. J. C. (2000), 'The Identity Theory of Mind'. In Zalta (2002): <http://plato.stanford.edu/entries/mind-identity/>

Zalta, E. N., ed. (2002), *The Stanford Encyclopedia of Philosophy.* <http://plato.stanford.edu/> Stanford, CA: Metaphysics Research Lab, Center for the Study of Language and Information.

Part III

Functionalism

Introduction

DURING the past two decades, functionalism has held a dominant position in the philosophy of mind. More significantly for some readers, scientists who take stands on the nature of the mind tend to be functionalists. Functionalism, clearly, is a theory to be reckoned with. But what exactly is distinctive about functionalism?

Functionalism can be seen as a response to a number of separate pressures. First, most serious researchers in psychology and the neurosciences fervently hope that minds can be accommodated to the material world. This would require, at a minimum, an account of mental phenomena consistent with materialism. Second, advances in psychology and computer science, suggest parallels between 'symbolic processing' in computing machines and human cognition. The burgeoning field of Artificial Intelligence operates on the assumption that understanding the mind is in some ways like understanding a computer program. Researchers have been encouraged to think of brains as hardware, minds as software, an appealing picture if you are looking for a way of fitting minds into the material world. Third, impetus behind the version of the mind–body identity theory championed by David Lewis and D. M. Armstrong encourages a conception of the mind as specifiable independently of particular physical characteristics of beings who possess minds. Creatures with very different kinds of physical make-up could possess minds. Finally, an old tradition, perhaps stemming from Aristotle (though see Burnyeat 1992) takes minds, not to be kinds of entity, but to be ways entities are organized, ways that are what they are independently of their specific material embodiments.

Another twist on identity

This part begins with a paper by David Lewis, 'An Argument for the Identity Theory', written by Lewis while he was still a graduate student at Harvard. Lewis's approach to the topic differs subtly from that of U. T. Place and J. J. C. Smart, earlier proponents of the identity theory. Lewis advances a causal conception of states of mind that can be seen as a precursor to what was to become functionalism. To have a belief, for instance, or to be in pain, is to be in a state that has characteristic causes and effects. As we saw in the previous part, behaviorism could evolve quite naturally into a conception of mind according to which states of mind are internal states that manifest themselves in behaviorally distinctive ways. If we add to this the proviso that, what distinguishes states of mind is not merely how they manifest themselves in behavior but also how they are brought about, we have something very close to Lewis's conception.

This conception is itself close to that advanced by functionalists like Hilary Putnam and Jerry Fodor. Indeed, Lewis's version of the identity theory, a version developed independently by Armstrong (1968, 1980), could be classified as a kind of functionalist theory. This is partly a matter of labeling. I include Lewis's paper here, however, because it preceded papers by Putnam and others that explicitly expound functionalism.

As we shall see, if Lewis and Armstrong are functionalists, they are functionalists of a distinctive sort. You and I are in the same state of mind provided you and I are in states with comparable causal profiles. You are in pain, for instance, if you are in a state caused by bodily injury that disposes you to behave as those in pain might typically behave. An octopus is in pain, if the octopus is in a causally comparable state. Suppose your being in this state is a matter of *C*-fibers firing in your brain, and the octopus's being in pain is a matter of *D*-fibers firing in the octopus's brain. Then your *C*-fibers firing in this way *is* your being in pain, and the octopus's *D*-fibers firing *is* the octopus's being in pain. The *is* in each case being the *is* of strict identity.

Although we cannot identify being in pain per se with the firing of *C*-fibers (an octopus in pain has no *C*-fibers), we *can* identify every token or instance of pain with a token or instance of some physical property. You could put this by saying that the predicate, 'is in pain', applies to creatures in virtue of those creatures' possession of any of a (possibly open-ended) family of physical properties. The family of properties includes all those that have the right 'causal profiles': they result from bodily injury and they dispose their bearers to behave in ways creatures in pain tend to behave. In the case of human beings, being in pain might just be a matter of firing *C*-fibers; in the case of a Martian, being in pain is the activation of a particular Martian 'neural' circuit; and in the case of a robot, assuming, perhaps counterfactually, that a robot could be in pain, being in pain is an occurrence in a certain bank of transistors.

Minds as theoretical entities

Smart and Lewis are thinking of minds as 'theoretical entities' (an idea we shall encounter again in Part VI). You observe Gus gesticulating wildly, and concoct an explanation to make sense of Gus's behavior. The explanation is likely to credit Gus with certain beliefs, desires, emotions, and intentions: Gus believes he has stepped on a wasps' nest, wants to protect himself from angry wasps, intends to do so by waving his arms, and subsequently waves his arms. In this regard, you resemble a physicist who, in order to explain the behavior of a kind of particle, credits particles of that kind with a particular spin and charge. Spin and charge are theoretical posits: properties postulated in order to account for the particles' behavior. Describing spin and charge as theoretical posits should not be taken to detract from their reality. Appeals to particles' spin and charge explains particle behavior because particles actually *possess* spin and charge. Such properties are theoretical only in the sense that their deployment depends, not on simple observation, but on the application of a particular theory.

Beliefs, desires, intentions, and the like, ascribed in the course of explanation, might be thought to be theoretical in the same sense. Talk of beliefs, desires, and intentions might be thought to be grounded in a 'folk theory' of human behavior. The theory is learned naturally and unselfconsciously in the course of learning to interact with others. Like any theory, our folk theory includes an explanatory mechanism and items posited to explain observed behavior. As in the case of spin and charge, describing states of mind as 'theoretical posits' is not to demean them, but merely to indicate their epistemological status. You ascribe states of mind to your friend, not because you observe them in operation, but in the course of making sense of your friend's behavior. You are successful in this insofar as your friend really does possess the ascribed states of mind.

Could this be right? Your ascriptions of states of mind to others is apparently theoretical in character. But what of your own case? You have a kind of *direct access* to your own states of mind. This need not be taken to mean that you are infallible in recognizing what you think, feel, or believe as Descartes might have thought. As Freud convinced us long ago, you could be ignorant of much of what you believe or want. Nevertheless, your access to your own conscious states does seem to resemble direct observation. From your perspective your friend's conscious states of mind operate behind the scenes; from your friend's perspective they are at stage center. This is something you should bear in mind in evaluating theories discussed here and in subsequent parts. How does a given theory account for the apparent asymmetry between your access to your own mind and your access to the minds of others?

From predicates to properties

Whatever its historical precursors, it is useful to take modern-day functionalism to have begun with Hilary Putnam's 'Psychological Predicates'. Most philosophers are aware of this paper, if only by reputation, under a different title used by Putnam when the paper was subsequently reprinted: 'The Nature of Mental States'. Why should a change of title be thought significant? It is just possible that the shift from talk about predicates to talk of states and properties carries with it a consignment of philosophical baggage that, at the very least, needs to be acknowledged.

To see why this might be so, let us get clear on some of the terms being tossed around here. What, for instance, is a *predicate*? A predicate is a linguistic device used to characterize objects, states, and events. 'Is red', is a predicate that applies to red objects, 'is spherical' applies to spherical objects. Most, although not all, philosophers take predicates to apply to objects in virtue of *properties* possessed by those objects. Consider a simple example.

(*a*) The beetroot is red
(*b*) The beetroot is spherical

Suppose (*a*) and (*b*) hold true of a single object, a particular beetroot. It is natural to suppose that (*a*) holds of the beetroot because of something about the beetroot, a 'way the beetroot is'; (*b*) holds of the beetroot, as well, but in virtue of something *else* about the beetroot, some other 'way the beetroot is'.

Think of these 'ways the beetroot is', as *properties* of the beetroot. The beetroot's possessing these properties is what makes it true that the beetroot is red and true that the beetroot is spherical. Presumably the beetroot has various other properties in virtue of which other predicates hold true of it: 'is acidic', 'weighs 150 grams', 'is juicy'. Let us assume, then, that the beetroot has numerous properties and that these properties answer to predicates applying truly to the beetroot.

This establishes a strong correspondence between predicates and properties. How strong? Can we say that, whenever a predicate applies truly to an object, it does so by virtue of naming a property possessed by that object and shared by every other object to which the predicate truly applies? Consider our beetroot. 'Is red' applies to the beetroot by virtue of a property possessed by the beetroot. But is it true that other objects to which 'is red' apply possess this *very same* property? The pillar box on the corner is red. Does the pillar box share a property with the beetroot?

You might regard the answer as obvious: *of course* the beetroot and pillar box share a property, the property of being red! But this is to assume precisely what is at issue. We are granting that 'is red' applies indifferently to the beetroot and the pillar box. The question is whether this requires that the beetroot and the pillar box share a property. And what is it for objects to 'share a property', anyway? At a minimum, objects that share a property precisely resemble one another in some particular way or respect. This way or respect is the shared property.

Now, *is* it true that the beetroot and pillar box precisely resemble one another with respect to color? Not in my experience. Although we can describe both the beetroot and the pillar box as red, they are distinct 'shades' of red. You might put this by saying that the beetroot and the pillar box possess *similar* properties. In virtue of their possessing similar properties, both answer to the predicate 'is red'. The predicate 'is red', although holding true of many distinct objects, need not be thought thereby to name a property all these objects share. Rather, the predicate holds of distinct objects in virtue of those objects' possession of any of a family of properties: those properties we regard as 'shades' of red.

The point is perfectly general. When you think about it, you recognize that most of the predicates we use to describe our world, including most of the predicates that figure in scientific theories, apply to objects in virtue of those objects' possessing, not a single property, but any of an often open-ended family of properties. This is a point made by Ludwig Wittgenstein in a famous discussion of games (Wittgenstein 1953: §§ 68–75). We use 'game' to apply to many different kinds of activity in virtue, not of a common feature shared by each of these activities, but owing to their possessing, what Wittgenstein called, a 'family resemblance'.

Suppose you buy all this. Suppose you agree, at least provisionally, that most, or many, or some of the predicates we use to describe goings-on in the world do not designate properties. The predicates apply to objects in virtue of properties possessed by those objects, but there is no simple one-to-one predicate-to-property correspondence. A single predicate can apply to distinct objects in virtue of those objects' possession of any of a family of properties.

What, you might ask, has any of this to do with the philosophy of mind in general and functionalism in particular? A central tenet of functionalism is that a mental predicate can apply to distinct actual or possible creatures, yet those creatures could fail to share a physical property in virtue of which the predicate applies. A human being, an octopus, and a Martian could all be in pain, for instance, despite there being no physical property all these creatures share and in virtue of which it is true that they are in pain. The functionalist concludes from this that pain is 'multiply realizable'. The *property* of being in pain is realized in human beings in a particular kind of neurological structure, perhaps; in octopodes pain has a different physical realizer; and if Martians possessing silicon-based biochemistries existed, Martian pain would have yet another realizer. Here we have one property, being in pain, with many different 'realizations'.

Multiple realizability

What exactly is it for something to be 'multiply realizable'? Surprisingly, functionalists have not always been very clear on the point. Following hints by Ned Block (Chapter 13), let us suppose that the realizing relation holds between *properties* or *states*. Your being in pain, for instance, might be realized, in you, by virtue your possessing a certain neurological property, N_1. An octopus might be in pain by virtue of possessing in a different physical property, N_2; and a Martian, by virtue of possessing N_3, might be in pain. One property, the pain property; three different physical realizers, N_1, N_2, and N_3.

Here, being in pain is taken to be a property possessed by a creature in virtue of that creature's possession of some other property, its realizer. Mainstream functionalism (what Block calls, somewhat confusingly, the 'functional state identity theory') distinguishes mental properties in this way from their physical realizing properties. Suppose that being in pain is a matter of being in a state with a distinctive causal profile. You can think of this state as occupying a particular causal role in the psychological and biological economy of a given creature. This obliges us to distinguish the *role*, from the *occupant* of the role. Functionalists hold that mental properties are to be identified with the roles, not their occupants.

Consider Wayne, the President of Turgid, Inc. Wayne, you could say, has the property of being President of Turgid, Inc. Wayne is tall, has blue eyes, is balding and overweight. Lump the characteristics together as a complex property: the property of being tall, having blue eyes, being bald and overweight. Now: is the property of being President of Turgid, Inc. identifiable with the property of being tall, having blue eyes, being bald and overweight? That seems unlikely. Wayne could be replaced, and perhaps eventually will be replaced, by Becky, a towering, brown-eyed brunette.

What such examples seem to show is that the type

(*a*) being President of Turgid, Inc.,

is not identifiable with the type

(*b*) being tall, having blue eyes, being bald and overweight.

This is so even if Wayne and Becky, and their various properties are all perfectly ordinary material entities. You might put this by saying that, while being President of Turgid, Inc. is not identical with any material type, every particular ('token') President of Turgid, Inc. is identical with some material token or other (excluding angelic or ghostly presidents).

Wayne is President of Turgid, Inc., not owing to his intrinsic physical make-up, but because he occupies a certain role in the corporation. Wayne could be deposed, and someone else come to occupy the presidential role. That occupant, whatever his, her, or its intrinsic make-up, would be President of Turgid, Inc. by virtue of occupying the appropriate role. Think of Wayne and his successors as realizers of the property of being President of Turgid, Inc. This presidential property is multiply realizable.

So it is with pains, say the functionalists. You are in pain so long as you are in a state that occupies the 'pain role': a state connected causally in the right way to myriad other states. Just as Wayne is President of Turgid, Inc., only so long as he occupies the presidential role, so a given physical state is a pain only insofar as it has the right sort of 'causal profile'. Functionalists like to put this by saying that mental properties are *higher-level* properties. A higher-level property is a property possessed by an object by virtue of that object's possession of some, distinct *lower-level* realizing property. A multiply realizable property, then, is a higher-level property that can be possessed by objects by virtue of those objects' possessing any of a diverse (perhaps open-ended) array of lower-level realizing properties.

Now it is possible to distinguish 'mainstream' functionalism from the view of the sort defended by Lewis in 'An Argument for the Identity Theory' (Chapter 10). A functionalist identifies pains with roles, not their occupants; Lewis (along with Armstrong), identifies pains with the occupants. What a functionalist would call a realizer of pain, Lewis and Armstrong would call the pain itself. A view of this kind, what Block labels the 'functional specifier view', treats the predicate 'is in pain' as encompassing a diversity of properties: there is no single property, being in pain, shared by all creatures truly describable as being in pain. Instead, we are to envisage creatures possessing any of a family of *causally similar* properties. Multiple realizability turns out to be nothing more than the familiar phenomenon discussed above: a single predicate, 'is in pain', applies to creatures in virtue of those creatures' possession of any of a family of causally similar properties.

Property hierarchies

Mainstream functionalism embraces a hierarchical picture of the world. According to this picture, the world comprises levels of reality. Higher-level properties are realized by lower-level properties, and these by still lower-level properties. Perhaps these levels 'ground out' in properties of the fundamental particles or fields; perhaps there is no basic level. The higher-level status of mental properties is nothing special. *Most* of the properties that command attention in ordinary life and in the special sciences are higher-level properties.

Those who take levels of reality to heart are likely to regard the rejection of levels with deep suspicion. The special sciences—biology, geology, meteorology, and the like—are apparently committed to higher-level entities and processes: species, cells, tectonic plates, cold fronts. Philosophers have no business denying the existence of properties appealed to in successful explanations of higher-level phenomena and that figure in higher-level laws. The denial of levels is taken to represent a kind of crass reductionism, and ultimately with the idea that all that really exists are 'the atoms and the void'.

Mental causation

One question to ask yourself in evaluating the status of higher-level properties is how these might figure in causal relations. Appeals to such properties seem to abound in causal explanations advanced in the special sciences. But how, exactly, are higher-level properties supposed to make themselves felt? Suppose that your being in pain is a higher-level property realized in you by your C-fibers' firing. We say that you are whimpering because you are in pain. What is the causal mechanism here? Is your whimpering brought about by your being in pain (which, recall, is a higher-level state) or rather by your C-fibers firing (your pain's lower-level realizer)? (See Figures III.1 and III.2.)

This brings us face to face with the problem of *causal relevance*, the mind—body problem in a new guise. Mind–body dualists like Descartes have trouble explaining how minds and bodies—conceived of as distinct *substances*—could interact causally. In the case of functionalism, *properties*, not substances, are the source of trouble. Mental properties are supposed to be realized by distinct physical properties. It is difficult to avoid the impression that mental properties 'float above' the physical world, leaving all the causal work to be done at the basic physical level.

You might imagine that mental properties get into the causal act via a kind of 'top-down' causation (the diagonal arrow in Figure III.2). Your possessing the property of being in pain (by virtue of your possession of some complex physical property) makes a subsequent physical difference that itself results in a bodily motion (your moving in the direction of the medicine cabinet). But it would appear that these physical effects could be wholly explained by their *physical* precursors.

We seem to be faced with a choice between the following possibilities.

(1) Physical effects have wholly physical causes; mental properties are *epiphenomenal* (that is, mental properties contribute nothing to the bringing about of physical effects).

(2) Some physical effects require mental causes (the causes of such effects might have both mental and physical components).

Figure III.1

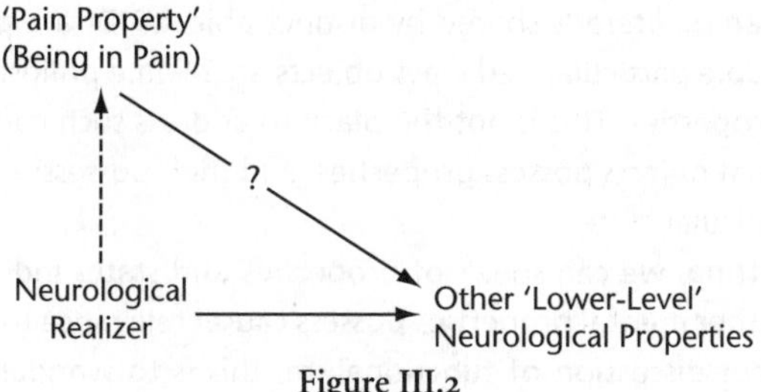

Figure III.2

(3) Some physical effects are *causally over-determined*: they are brought about by distinct causes, either of which would, in the absence of the other, suffice for that very effect.

None of these options is particularly attractive. In the case of (1), our deeply-ingrained sense that minds make a difference renders epiphenomenalism decidedly off-putting. Option (2) requires that higher-level properties affect lower-level outcomes, a violation of the idea that the physical world is 'causally closed'. One way to understand closure is to think of the behavior of the particles. The behavior of every electron, we like to believe, is governed by fundamental laws of physics. If we allow 'top-down' causation, we seem to allow the possibility that these laws are, at times 'violated' by occurrences at higher levels. Many philosophers and scientists find this hard to swallow.

Option (3), 'over-determination', could strike you as ad hoc. We find correlations between physical and mental events (physical events involving realizers of mental properties); we recognize that the physical events have physical effects; and we conclude that the mental events must *also* be causes of these physical effects. This preserves our sense that minds affect the world, and it does so without requiring apparent violations of fundamental physical laws. Such a 'solution' looks contrived. It is hard to see it as anything more than a bare assertion that, appearances notwithstanding, mental events do have physical effects, though not in any way that makes them indispensable to those effects.

Is this all just another philosophical smokescreen? As you read the selections in this part, keep the problem of mental causation—the original Cartesian mind–body problem!—firmly before your mind. Ask yourself whether the problem really is a problem and, if it is, how you would approach it.

Properties and states

Philosophers speak of mental properties and mental states. What exactly are properties and states? How are these distinguished? I have suggested thinking of properties as ways: ways things are. Consider this red billiard ball. The ball is red and spherical. Being red and being spherical are ways the ball is, properties of the ball. What, then, is a state? Think of a state as an object's *possessing* a property. The ball's being red, and the ball's being spherical are states of the ball. Your being in pain is a matter of your being in a certain state and this is a matter of your possessing a certain complex property.

The property–state distinction is a subtle one. What you take to be its broader implications depends on what your views on properties are. Are properties *universals*, repeatable entities that can be *literally* shared by distinct objects? Or are properties *modes* or *tropes*, non-repeatable particularized ways objects are? Some philosophers question the very existence of properties. This is not the place to address such concerns. Let us rather agree to suppose that objects possess properties, and their possessing a given property is their being in a particular state.

In the current setting, we can speak of properties and states indifferently. Thus, you might wonder whether mental properties possess causal relevance to physical goings-on. In the context of our discussion of functionalism, this is to wonder whether it is your possession of the higher-level property of being in pain (your pain state) that is responsible for the bodily motions that constitute your striding to the medicine cabinet, or whether those motions are due wholly to your possession of lower-level, physical properties (your physical state). The question whether a given mental property could be causally relevant to a particular physical effect is the question whether a creature's possession of the mental property could figure in a causal sequence resulting in the creature's possession of some physical property.

Tu quoque

One approach to this question appeals to the success of the special sciences. We turn to the special sciences—biology, geology, meteorology, paleontology, metallurgy, and the like—for causal explanations of important phenomena. These explanations are couched in a higher-level vocabulary that appeals, almost exclusively, to higher-level properties. If you have doubts about the causal relevance of mental properties, these would extend smoothly to biological, geological, meteorological, paleontological, and metallurgical properties. If the mere fact that a property is a higher-level property disqualifies that property as a participant in physical causal transactions, then we should have to scrap causal explanations in the natural sciences. That would be absurd. The conclusion: worries about the causal relevance of mental properties are founded on an overly narrow conception of causality, a conception driven by ill-considered philosophizing rather than by attention to the practice of crafting causal explanation in the sciences.

One response to this *tu quoque* is to accept the challenge: to the extent that the special sciences do appeal to higher-level properties and states, these sciences do indeed fall short of genuine causal explanation. Unmitigated philosophical arrogance? Not necessarily. Perhaps this difficulty stems instead from a widespread failure to take property talk seriously enough. Earlier you were invited to distinguish predicates and properties. Predicates apply to objects by virtue of properties possessed by those objects. Philosophers elevate this modest truism into a principle:

(P) If a predicate, '*P*', applies truly to an object, it does so by virtue of designating a property, *P*, possessed by that object and by every other object to which it would truly apply.

Principle (P) goes far beyond the modest truism.

If you accept (P), then you will want there to be a property common to every creature correctly describable as being in pain. Assuming that no physical property satisfies this requirement (you accept this if you accept functionalist arguments for 'multiple realizability'), the property in question must be a higher-level property, a property possessed by a creature in virtue of that creature's possession of some distinct, lower-level realizing property. Now we are faced with the task of explaining how such higher-level properties could figure in the bringing about of lower-level effects; and we are back with options (1)–(3).

Suppose, however, you are sympathetic to the idea that most of the predicates we deploy can apply truly to objects, not by virtue of those objects' possessing *the same* property (or being exactly similar in some respect), but by virtue of those objects' possessing any of a family of *similar* properties, you will not be impressed by (P). You will be prepared to see pains as states of conscious creatures unified, not by a single, albeit higher-level, property, but by membership in a family of appropriately similar properties. A creature's being in one of these states *is* the creature's being in pain. If the state is a physical state, the state *is* a pain state.

In taking up such a position, you would be rejecting mainstream functionalism. You could accept the version of functionalism recommended by Lewis (and by Armstrong, what Block calls 'functional specifier' functionalism). In so doing, you would not be supposing, as perhaps the earliest identity theorists—Place and Smart—supposed that there is something like a one-to-one mapping between mental predicates ('is in pain', 'is thinking of Vienna') and physical properties. You would be allowing that being in pain could be a matter of possessing some member of a family of physical properties. Perhaps this is all we could reasonably hope for.

Functionalism and materialism

Observant readers will have noticed functionalism allows for the possibility of non-physical conscious beings. If states of mind are functional states, and if functional states are 'realized' in conscious creatures by states with an appropriate causal profile, this leaves open the possibility that immaterial beings could be conscious, think, feel pain. They could possess such states of mind provided they could go into states with the right causal profiles. An ectoplasmic being, for instance, or an angel with the right ectoplasmic or angelic internal organization could think or feel pain.

This is why functionalism is sometimes omitted from inventories of materialistic theories. You should not be misled by classificatory subtleties, however. Yes, functionalism *allows* that purely physical creatures could possess minds; functionalism does not *require* physicality as a condition on possessing a mind. Functionalism, even so, is attractive to materialists because it provides a way of understanding how a purely physical creature could have a mind, be conscious, think, feel pain. If you couple this with the independent belief that there are no ectoplasmic or angelic beings, you have a thoroughgoing materialist conception of the mind.

As we shall see presently (Parts VIII and IX) the idea that states of mind are purely causal has struck many philosophers as implausible. These philosophers argue that conscious mental states possess irreducible qualitative features. Any creature lacking these, whatever that creature's internal structure, would lack conscious states of mind. (The qualification 'conscious' is in order because it is controversial whether states of mind *must* be conscious states.)

It is time now for you to roll up your sleeves and have at the papers in this part. As you read individual selections, try to keep in mind some of the metaphysical issues that have surfaced in this introduction. The point has not been to indoctrinate you or convince you to embrace or reject functionalism, but to give you tools that could be helpful in evaluating arguments you will encounter in this and subsequent parts.

References

Armstrong, D. M. (1968), *A Materialist Theory of the Mind*. London: Routledge & Kegan Paul.

——(1980), 'The Causal Theory of Mind', from *The Nature of Mind and Other Essays* (St. Lucia: University of Queensland Press), 16–31.

Burnyeat, M. F. (1992), 'Is an Aristotelian Philosophy of Mind Still Credible?' In Nussbaum and Rorty (1992): 15–26.

Nussbaum, M. C., and A. O. Rorty, eds. (1992), *Essays on Aristotle's* De Anima. Oxford: Clarendon Press.

Wittgenstein, L. (1953/1968), *Philosophical Investigations*, trans. G. E. M. Anscombe. Oxford: Basil Blackwell.

Chapter 10

An argument for the identity theory

David Lewis

I. Introduction

THE (Psychophysical) Identity Theory is the hypothesis that—not necessarily but as a matter of fact—every experience[1] is identical with some physical state.[2] Specifically, with some neurochemical state. I contend that we who accept the materialistic working hypothesis that physical phenomena have none but purely physical explanations must accept the identity theory. This is to say more than do most friends of the theory, who say only that we are free to accept it, and should for the sake of some sort of economy or elegance. I do not need to make a case for the identity theory on grounds of economy,[3] since I believe it can and should rest on a stronger foundation.

My argument is this: The definitive characteristic of any (sort of) experience as such is its causal role, its syndrome of most typical causes and effects. But we materialists believe that these causal roles which belong by analytic necessity to experiences belong in fact to certain physical states. Since those physical states possess the definitive characteristics of experience, they must be the experiences.

My argument parallels an argument which we will find uncontroversial. Consider cylindrical combination locks for bicycle chains. The definitive characteristic

David Lewis, 'An Argument for the Identity Theory', *Journal of Philosophy* 63 (1966).

1. Experiences herein are to be taken in general as universals, not as abstract particulars. I am concerned, for instance, with pain, an experience that befalls many people at many times; or with pain of some definite sort, an experience which at least *might* be common to different people at different times. Both are universals, capable of repeated instanciation. The latter is a narrower universal than the former, as crimson of some definite shade is narrower than red, but still a universal. I am not concerned with the particular pain of a given person at a given time, an abstract entity which cannot itself recur but can only be similar—at best, exactly similar—to other particular pains of other people or at other times. We might identify such abstract particulars with pairs of a universal and a single concrete particular instance thereof; or we might leave them as unanalyzed, elementary beings, as in Donald C. Williams, 'On the Elements of Being,' *Review of Metaphysics* 7 (1953): 3–18 and 171–92. [All but the first sentence of this note was added in October 1969.] .
2. States also are to be taken in general as universals. I shall not distinguish between processes, events, phenomena, and states in a strict sense.
3. I am therefore invulnerable to Brandt's objection that the identity theory is not clearly more economical than a certain kind of dualism. 'Doubts about the Identity Theory,' in *Dimensions of Mind*, Sidney Hook, ed. (New York: NYU Press, 1960), pp. 57–67.

of their state of being unlocked is the causal role of that state, the syndrome of its most typical causes and effects: namely, that setting the combination typically causes the lock to be unlocked and that being unlocked typically causes the lock to open when gently pulled. That is all we need know in order to ascribe to the lock the state of being or of not being unlocked. But we may learn that, as a matter of fact, the lock contains a row of slotted discs; setting the combination typically causes the slots to be aligned; and alignment of the slots typically causes the lock to open when gently pulled. So alignment of slots occupies precisely the causal role that we ascribed to being unlocked by analytic necessity, as the definitive characteristic of being unlocked (for these locks). Therefore alignment of slots is identical with being unlocked (for these locks). They are one and the same state.

II. The nature of the identity theory

We must understand that the identity theory asserts that certain physical states are experiences, introspectible processes or activities, not that they are the supposed intentional objects that experiences are experiences *of*. If these objects of experience really exist separate from experiences of them, or even as abstract parts thereof, they may well also be something physical. Perhaps they are also neural, or perhaps they are abstract constituents of veridically perceived surroundings, or perhaps they are something else, or nothing at all; but that is another story. So I am not claiming that an experience of seeing red, say, is itself somehow a red neural state.

Shaffer has argued that the identity theory is impossible because (abstract particular) experiences are, by analytic necessity, unlocated, whereas the (abstract particular) neural events that they supposedly are have a location in part of the subject's nervous system.[4] But I see no reason to believe that the principle that experiences are unlocated enjoys any analytic, or other, necessity. Rather it is a metaphysical prejudice which has no claim to be respected. Or if there is, after all, a way in which it is analytic that experiences are unlocated, that way is irrelevant: perhaps in our presystematic thought we regard only concreta as located in a primary sense, and abstracta as located in a merely derivative sense by their inherence in located concreta. But this possible source of analytic unlocatedness for experiences does not meet the needs of Shaffer's argument. For neural events are abstracta too. Whatever unlocatedness accrues to experiences not because they are mental but because they are abstract must accrue as much to neural events. So it does not discriminate between the two.

The identity theory says that experience-ascriptions have the same reference as certain neural-state-ascriptions: both alike refer to the neural states which are experiences. It does not say that these ascriptions have the same sense. They do not; experience-ascriptions refer to a state by specifying the causal role that belongs to it accidentally, in virtue of causal laws, whereas neural-state-ascriptions refer to a

4. 'Could Mental States Be Brain Processes?' *Journal of Philosophy* 58, no. 26 (Dec. 21, 1961): 813–22.

state by describing it in detail. Therefore the identity theory does not imply that whatever is true of experiences as such is likewise true of neural states as such, nor conversely. For a truth about things of any kind *as such* is about things of that kind not by themselves, but together with the sense of expressions by which they are referred to as things of that kind.[5] So it is pointless to exhibit various discrepancies between what is true of experiences as such and what is true of neural states as such. We can explain those discrepancies without denying psychophysical identity and without admitting that it is somehow identity of a defective sort.

We must not identify an experience itself with the attribute that is predicated of somebody by saying that he is having that experience.[6] The former *is* whatever state it is that occupies a certain definitive causal role; the latter is the attribute of *being in* whatever state it is that occupies that causal role. By this distinction we can answer the objection that, since experience-ascriptions and neural-state-descriptions are admittedly never synonymous and since attributes are identical just in case they are predicated by synonymous expressions, therefore experiences and neural states cannot be identical attributes. The objection does establish a nonidentity, but not between experiences and neural states. (It is unfair to blame the identity theory for needing the protection of so suspiciously subtle a distinction, for a parallel distinction is needed elsewhere. Blue is, for instance, the color of my socks, but blue is not the attribute predicated of things by saying they are the color of my socks, since '... is blue' and '... is the color of my socks' are not synonymous.)

5. Here I have of course merely applied to states Frege's doctrine of sense and reference. See 'On Sense and Reference,' in *Translations from the Philosophical Writings of Gottlab Frege*, ed. by Peter Geach and Max Black. (New York: Oxford University Press, 1960), pp. 56–78.

6. Here I mean to deny all identities of the form ⌜α is identical with the attribute of having α⌝ where α is an experience-name definable as naming the occupant of a specified causal role. I deny, for instance, that pain is identical with the attribute of having pain. On my theory, 'pain' is a *contingent* name—that is, a name with different denotations in different possible worlds—since in any world, 'pain' names whatever state happens in that world to occupy that causal role definitive of pain. If state X occupies that role in world *V* while another state *Y* (incompatible with *X*) occupies that role in world *W*, then 'pain' names *X* in *V* and *Y* in *W*. I take 'the attribute of having pain', on the other hand, as a *non-contingent* name of that state or attribute *Z* that belongs, in any world, to wharever things have pain in that world—that is, to whatever things have in that world the state named in that world by 'pain'. (I take states to be attributes of a special kind: attributes of things at times.) Thus *Z* belongs in *V* to whatever things have X in *V*, and in *W* to whatever things have *Y* in *W*; hence *Z* is identical neither with *X* nor with *Y*.

Richard Montague, in 'On the Nature of Certain Philosophical Entities,' *Menist* 53 (1969): 172–73, objects that I seem to be denying a logical truth having as its instances all identities of the form α is identical with the attribute of having α where α is a *non-contingent* name of a state which is (either contingently or necessarily) an experience. I would agree that such identities are logically true; but those are not the identities I mean to deny, since I claim that our ordinary experience-names—'pain' and the like—are *contingent* names of states. [This note was added in October 1969.]

III. The first premise: experiences defined by causal roles

The first of my two premises for establishing the identity theory is the principle that the definitive characteristic of any experience as such is its causal role. The definitive causal role of an experience is expressible by a finite[7] set of conditions that specify its typical causes and its typical effects under various circumstances. By analytic necessity these conditions are true of the experience and jointly distinctive of it.

My first premise is an elaboration and generalization of Smart's theory that avowals of experience are, in effect, of the form 'What is going on in me is like what is going on in me when . . .' followed by specification of typical stimuli for, or responses to, the experiences.[8] I wish to add explicitly that . . . may be an elaborate logical compound of clauses if necessary; that . . . must specify typical causes or effects of the experience, not mere accompaniments; that these typical causes and effects may include other experiences; and that the formula does not apply only to first-person reports of experience.

This is not a materialist principle, not does it ascribe materialism to whoever speaks of experiences. Rather it is an account of the parlance common to all who believe that experiences are something or other real and that experiences are efficacious outside their own realm. It is neutral between theories—or a lack of any theory—about what sort of real and efficacious things experiences are: neural states or the like, pulsations of ectoplasm or the like, or just experiences and nothing else. It is not neutral, however, between all current theories of mind and body. Epiphenomenalist and parallelist dualism are ruled out as contradictory because they deny the efficacy of experience. Behaviorism as a thoroughgoing dispositional analysis of all mental states, including experiences,[9] is likewise ruled out as denying the reality and a fortiori the efficacy of experiences. For a pure disposition is a fictitious entity. The expressions that ostensibly denote dispositions are best construed as syncategorematic parts of statements of the lawlike regularities in which (as we say) the dispositions are manifest.

Yet the principle that experiences are defined by their causal roles is itself behaviotist in origin, in that it inherits the behaviorist discovery that the (ostensibly) causal connections between an experience and its typical occasions and manifest-

7. It would do no harm to allow the set of conditions to be infinite, so long as it is recutsive. But I doubt the need for this relaxation.

8. *Philosophy and Scientific Realism* (New York: Humanities Press, 1963), ch. 5. Smart's concession that his formula does not really translate avowals is unnecessary. It results from a bad example: 'I have a pain' is not translatable as 'What is going on in me is like what goes on when a pin is stuck into me', because the concept of pain might be introduced without mention of pins. Indeed; but the objection is no good against the translation 'What is going on in me is like what goes on when (i.e. when and because) my skin is damaged' .

9. Any theory of mind and body is compatible with a dispositional analysis of mental states other than experiences or with so-called 'methodological behaviorism.'

ations somehow contain a component of analytic necessity. But my principle improves on the original behavioristic embodiment of that discovery in several ways:

First, it allows experiences to be something real and so to be the effects of their occasions and the causes of their manifestations, as common opinion supposes them to be.

Second, it allows us to include other experiences among the typical causes and effects by which an experience is defined. It is crucial that we should be able to do so in order that we may do justice, in defining experiences by their causal roles, to the introspective accessibility which is such an important feature of any experience. For the introspective accessibility of an experience is its propensity reliably to cause other (future or simultaneous) experiences directed intentionally upon it, wherein we are aware of it. The requisite freedom to interdefine experiences is not available in general under behaviorism; interdefinition of experiences is permissible only if it can in principle be eliminated, which is so only if it happens to be possible to arrange experiences in a hierarchy of definitional priority. We, on the other hand, may allow interdefinition with no such constraint. We may expect to get mutually interdefined families of experiences, but they will do us no harm. There will be no reason to identify anything with one experience in such a family without regard to the others—but why should there be? Whatever occupies the definitive causal role of an experience in such a family does so by virtue of its own membership in a causal isomorph of the family of experiences, that is, in a system of states having the same pattern of causal connections with one another and the same causal connections with states outside the family, viz., stimuli and behavior. The isomorphism guarantees that if the family is identified *throughout* with its isomorph then the experiences in the family will have their definitive causal roles. So, ipso facto, the isomorphism requires us to accept the identity of all the experiences of the family with their counterparts in the causal isomorph of the family.[10]

Third, we are not obliged to define an experience by the causes and effects of exactly all and only its occurrences. We can be content rather merely to identify the experience as that state which is *typically* caused in thus-and-such ways and *typically* causes thus-and-such effects, saying nothing about its causes and effects in a (small) residue of exceptional cases. A definition by causes and effects in typical cases suffices to determine what the experience is, and the fact that the experience has some characteristics or other besides its definitive causal role confers a sense upon ascriptions of it in some exceptional cases for which its definitive typical causes and effects are absent (and likewise upon denials of it in some cases for which they are present). Behaviorism does not acknowledge the fact that the

10. Putnam discusses an analogous case for machines: a family of ('logical' or 'functional') states defined by their causal roles and mutually interdefined, and a causally isomorphic system of ('structural') states otherwise defined. He does not equate the correlated logical and structural states. 'Minds and Machines,' in *Dimensions of Mind*, pp. 148–79.

experience is something apart from its definitive occasions and manifestations, and so must require that the experience be defined by a strictly necessary and sufficient condition in terms of them. Otherwise the behaviorist has merely a partial explication of the experience by criteria, which can never give more than a presumption that the experience is present or absent, no matter how much we know about the subject's behavior and any lawlike regularities that may govern it. Relaxation of the requirement for a strictly necessary and sufficient condition is welcome. As anybody who has tried to implement behaviorism knows, it is usually easy to find conditions which are *almost* necessary and sufficient for an experience. All the work—and all the complexity which renders it incredible that the conditions found should be known implicitly by every speaker—comes in trying to cover a few exceptional cases. In fact, it is just impossible to cover some atypical cases of experiences behavioristically: the case of a perfect actor pretending to have an experience he does not really have; and the case of a total paralytic who cannot manifest any experience he does have (both cases under the stipulation that the pretense or paralysis will last for the rest of the subject's life no matter what happens, in virtue of regularities just as lawlike as those by which the behaviorist seeks to define experiences).

It is possible, and probably good analytic strategy, to reconstrue any supposed pure dispositional state rather as a state defined by its causal role. The advantages in general are those we have seen in this case: the state becomes recognized as real and efficacious; unrestricted mutual interdefinition of the state and others of its sort becomes permissible; and it becomes intelligible that the state may sometimes occur despite prevention of its definitive manifestations.[11]

I do not offer to prove my principle that the definitive characteristics of experiences as such are their causal roles. It would be verified by exhibition of many suitable analytic statements saying that various experiences typically have thus-and-such causes and effects. Many of these statements have been collected by behaviorists; I inherit these although I explain their status somewhat differently. Behaviorism is widely accepted. I am content to rest my case on the argument that my principle can accommodate what is true in behaviorism and can escape attendant difficulties.

IV. The second premise: explanatory adequacy of physics

My second premise is the plausible hypothesis that there is some unified body of scientific theories, of the sort we now accept, which together provide a true and exhaustive account of all physical phenomena (i.e. all phenomena describable in

11. Quine advocates this treatment of such dispositional states as are worth saving in *Word and Object* (Cambridge, Mass.: MIT Press, and New York: Wiley, 1960), pp. 222–25. 'They are conceived as built-in, enduring structural traits.'.

physical terms). They are unified in that they are cumulative: the theory governing any physical phenomenon is explained by theories governing phenomena out of which that phenomenon is composed and by the way it is composed out of them. The same is true of the latter phenomena, and so on down to fundamental particles or fields governed by a few simple laws, more or less as conceived of in present-day theoretical physics. I rely on Oppenheim and Putnam for a detailed exposition of the hypothesis that we may hope to find such a unified physicalistic body of scientific theory and for a presentation of evidence that the hypothesis is credible.[12]

A confidence in the explanatory adequacy of physics is a vital part, but not the whole, of any full-blooded materialism. It is the empirical foundation on which materialism builds its superstructure of ontological and cosmological doctrines, among them the identity theory. It is also a traditional and definitive working hypothesis of natural science—what scientists say nowadays to the contrary is defeatism or philosophy. I argue that whoever shares this confidence must accept the identity theory.

My second premise does not rule out the existence of nonphysical phenomena; it is not an ontological thesis in its own right. It only denies that we need ever explain physical phenomena by nonphysical ones. Physical phenomena are physically explicable, or they are utterly inexplicable insofar as they depend upon chance in a physically explicable way, or they are methodologically acceptable primitives. All manner of nonphysical phenomena may coexist with them, even to the extent of sharing the same space-time, provided only that the nonphysical phenomena are entirely inefficacious with respect to the physical phenomena. These coexistent non-physical phenomena may be quite unrelated to physical phenomena; they may be causally independent but for some reason perfectly correlated with some physical phenomena (as experiences are, according to parallelism); they may be epiphenomena, caused by some physical phenomena but not themselves causing any (as experiences are, according to epiphenomenalism). If they are epiphenomena they may even be correlated with some physical phenomena, perfectly and by virtue of a causal law.

V. Conclusion of the argument

But none of these permissible nonphysical phenomena can be experiences. For they must be entirely inefficacious with respect to all physical phenomena. But all the behavioral manifestations of experiences are (or involve) physical phenomena and so cannot be effects of anything that is inefficacious with respect to physical phenomena. These behavioral manifestations are among the typical effects definitive of any experience, according to the first premise. So nothing can be an experience that

12. 'Unity of Science as a Working Hypothesis,' in *Minnesota Studies in the Philosophy of Science* 2 (Minneapolis: Univ. of Minnesota Press, 1958), Herbert Feigl, Michael Scriven, and Grover Maxwell, eds., pp. 3–36.

is inefficacious with respect to physical phenomena. So nothing can be an experience that is a nonphysical phenomenon of the sort permissible under the second premise. From the two premises it follows that experiences are some physical phenomena or other.

And there is little doubt which physical phenomena they must be. We are far from establishing positively that neural states occupy the definitive causal roles of experiences, but we have no notion of any other physical phenomena that could possibly occupy them, consistent with what we do know. So if nonphysical phenomena are ruled out by our confidence in physical explanation, only neural states are left. If it could be shown that neural states do not occupy the proper causal roles, we would be hard put to save materialism itself.

A version of epiphenomenalism might seem to evade my argument: let experiences be nonphysical epiphenomena, precisely correlated according to a causal law with some simultaneous physical states which are themselves physically (if at all) explicable. The correlation law (it is claimed) renders the experiences and their physical correlates causally equivalent. So the nonphysical experiences have their definitive physical effects after all—although they are not needed to explain those effects, so there is no violation of my second premise (since the nonphysical experiences redundantly redetermine the effects of their physical correlates). I answer thus: at best, this position yields nonphysical experiences alongside the physical experiences, duplicating them, which is not what its advocates intend. Moreover, it is false that such a physical state and its epiphenomenal correlate are causally equivalent. The position exploits a flaw in the standard regularity theory of cause. We know on other grounds that the theory must be corrected to discriminate between genuine causes and the spurious causes which are their epiphenomenal correlates. (The 'power on' light does not cause the motor to go, even if it is a lawfully perfect correlate of the electric current that really causes the motor to go.) Given a satisfactory correction, the nonphysical correlate will be evicted from its spurious causal role and thereby lose its status as the experience. So this epiphenomenalism is not a counterexample.

The dualism of the common man holds that experiences are nonphysical phenomena which are the causes of a familiar syndrome of physical as well as nonphysical effects. This dualism is a worthy opponent, daring to face empirical refutation, and in due time it will be rendered incredible by the continuing advance of physicalistic explanation. I have been concerned to prevent dualism from finding a safe fall-back position in the doctrine that experiences are nonphysical and physically inefficacious. It is true that such phenomena can never be refuted by any amount of scientific theory and evidence. The trouble with them is rather that they cannot be what we call experiences. They can only be the nonphysical epiphenomena or correlates of physical states which are experiences. If they are not the experiences themselves, they cannot rescue dualism when it is hard-pressed. And if they cannot do that, nobody has any motive for believing in them. Such things may be—but they are of no consequence.

Chapter 11

Psychological predicates

Hilary Putnam

THE typical concerns of the Philosopher of Mind might be represented by three questions: (1) How do we know that other people have pains? (2) Are pains brain states? (3) What is the analysis of the concept *pain*? I do not wish to discuss questions (1) and (3) in this paper. I shall say something about question (2).[1]

I. Identity questions

'Is pain a brain state?' (Or, 'Is the property of having a pain at time *t* a brain state?')[2] It is impossible to discuss this question sensibly without saying something about the peculiar rules which have grown up in the course of the development of 'analytical philosophy'—rules which, far from leading to an end to all conceptual confusions, themselves represent considerable conceptual confusion. These rules—which are, of course, implicit rather than explicit in the practice of most analytical philosophers—are (1) that a statement of the form 'being *A* is being B' (e.g., 'being in pain is being in a certain brain state') can be *correct* only if it follows, in some sense, from the meaning of the terms *A* and *B*; and (2) that a statement of the form 'being *A* is being *B*' can be philosophically *informative* only if it is in some sense reductive (e.g. 'being in pain is having a certain unpleasant sensation' is not philosophically informative; 'being in pain is having a certain behavior disposition' is, if true, philosophically informative). These rules are excellent rules if we still believe that the program of reductive analysis (in the style of the 1930's) can be carried out; if we don't, then they turn analytical philosophy into a mug's game, at least so far as 'is' questions are concerned.

Hilary Putnam, 'Psychological Predictates'. In W. H. Capitan and D. D. Merrill, eds., *Art, Mind, and Religion* (Pittsburgh: University of Pittsburgh Press, 1967); reprinted as 'The Nature of Mental States', in *Mind, Language, and Reality: Philosophical Papers*, vol. ii (Cambridge: Cambridge University Press, 1975).

1. I have discussed these and related topics in the following papers: 'Minds and Machines,' in *Dimensions of Mind*, ed. Sidney Hook, New York, 1960, pp. 148–179; 'Brains and Behavior,' in *Analytical Philosophy, second series*, ed. Ronald Butler, Oxford, 1965, pp. 1–20 (See Chapter 6 of this volume); and 'The Mental Life of Some Machines,' to appear in a volume edited by Hector Neri Castaneda, Detroit.
2. In this paper I wish to avoid the vexed question of the relation between *pains* and *pain states*. I only remark in passing that one common argument *against* identification of these two—viz., that a pain can be in one's arm but a state (of the organism) cannot be in one's arm—is easily seen to be fallacious.

In this paper I shall use the term 'property' as a blanket term for such things as being in pain, being in a particular brain state, having a particular behavior disposition, and also for magnitudes such as temperature, etc.—i.e., for things which can naturally be represented by one-or-more-place predicates or functors. I shall use the term 'concept' for things which can be identified with synonymy-classes of expressions. Thus the concept *temperature* can be identified (I maintain) with the synonymy-class of the word 'temperature.'[3] (This is like saying that the number 2 can be identified with the class of all pairs. This is quite a different statement from the peculiar statement that 2 *is* the class of all pairs. I do not maintain that concepts *are* synonymy-classes, whatever that might mean, but that they can be identified with synonymy-classes, for the purpose of formalization of the relevant discourse.)

The question 'What is the concept *temperature*?' is a very 'funny' one. One might take it to mean 'What is temperature? Please take my question as a conceptual one.' In that case an answer might be (pretend for a moment 'heat' and 'temperature' are synonyms) 'temperature is heat,' or even 'the concept of temperature is the same concept as the concept of heat.' Or one might take it to mean 'What are *concepts*, really? For example, what is 'the concept of temperature'?' In that case heaven knows what an 'answer' would be. (Perhaps it would be the statement that concepts *can be identified with* synonymy-classes.)

Of course, the question 'What is the property temperature?' is also 'funny.' And one way of interpreting it is to take it as a question about the concept of temperature. But this is not the way a physicist would take it.

The effect of saying that the property P_1 can be identical with the property P_2 only if the terms P_1, P_2 are in some suitable sense 'synonyms' is, to all intents and purposes, to collapse the two notions of 'property' and 'concept' into a single notion. The view that concepts (intensions) *are* the same as properties has been explicitly advocated by Carnap (e.g., in *Meaning and Necessity*). This seems an unfortunate view, since 'temperature is mean molecular kinetic energy' appears to be a perfectly good example of a true statement of identity of properties, whereas 'the concept of temperature is the same concept as the concept of mean molecular kinetic energy' is simply false.

Many philosophers believe that the statement 'pain is a brain state' violates some rules or norms of English. But the arguments offered are hardly convincing.

3. There are some well-known remarks by Alonzo Church on this topic. Those remarks do not bear (as might at first be supposed) on the identification of concepts with synonymy-classes as such, but rather support the view that (in formal semantics) it is necessary to retain Frege's distinction between the normal and the 'oblique' use of expressions. That is, even if we say that the concept of temperature *is* the synonymy-class of the word 'temperature,' we must not thereby be led into the error of supposing that 'the concept of temperature' is synonymous with 'the synonymy-class of the word "temperature"'—for then 'the concept of temperature' and 'der Begriff der Temperatur' would not be synonymous, which they are. Rather, we must say that 'the concept of temperature' *refers to* the synonymy-class of the word 'temperature' (on this particular reconstruction); but that class is *identified* not as 'the synonymy class to which such-and-such a word belongs,' but in another way (e.g., as the synonymy-class whose members have such-and-such a characteristic use).

For example, if the fact that I can know that I am in pain without knowing that I am in brain state *S* shows that pain cannot be brain state *S*, then, by exactly the same argument, the fact that I can know that the stove is hot without knowing that the mean molecular kinetic energy is high (or even that molecules exist) shows that it is *false* that temperature is mean molecular kinetic energy, physics to the contrary. In fact, all that immediately follows from the fact that I can know that I am in pain without knowing that I am in brain state *S* is that the concept of pain is not the same concept as the concept of being in brain state *S*. But either pain, or the state of being in pain, or some pain, or some pain state, might still be brain state *S*. After all, the concept of temperature is not the same concept as the concept of mean molecular kinetic energy. But temperature is mean molecular kinetic energy.

Some philosophers maintain that both 'pain is a brain state' and 'pain states are brain states' are unintelligible. The answer is to explain to these philosophers, as well as we can, given the vagueness of all scientific methodology, what sorts of considerations lead one to make an empirical reduction (i.e., to say such things as 'water is H_2O,' 'light is electro-magnetic radiation,' 'temperature is mean molecular kinetic energy'). If, without giving reasons, he still maintains in the face of such examples that one cannot imagine parallel circumstances for the use of 'pains are brain states' (or, perhaps, 'pain states are brain states') one has grounds to regard him as perverse.

Some philosophers maintain that 'P_1 is P_2' is something that can be true, when the 'is' involved is the 'is' of empirical reduction, only when the properties P_1 and P_2 are (a) associated with a spatio-temporal region; and (b) the region is one and the same in both cases. Thus 'temperature is mean molecular kinetic energy' is an admissible empirical reduction, since the temperature and the molecular energy are associated with the same space-time region, but 'having a pain in my arm is being in a brain state' is not, since the spatial regions involved are different.

This argument does not appear very strong. Surely no one is going to be deterred from saying that mirror images are light reflected from an object and then from the surface of a mirror by the fact that an image can be 'located' three feet *behind* the mirror! (Moreover, one can always find *some* common property of the reductions one is willing to allow—e.g., temperature is mean molecular kinetic energy—which is not a property of some one identification one wishes to disallow. This is not very impressive unless one has an argument to show that the very purposes of such identification depend upon the common property in question.)

Again, other philosophers have contended that all the predictions that can be derived from the conjunction of neurophysiological laws with such statements as 'pain states are such-and-such brain states' can equally well be derived from the conjunction of the same neurophysiological laws with 'being in pain is correlated with such-and-such brain states,' and hence (sic!) there can be no methodological grounds for saying that pains (or pain states) *are* brain states, as opposed to saying that they are *correlated* (invariantly) with brain states. This argument, too, would show that light is only correlated with electromagnetic radiation. The mistake is in ignoring the fact that, although the theories in question may indeed lead to the same predictions, they open and exclude different *questions.* 'Light is invariantly correlated with electromagnetic radiation' would leave open the questions 'What is the light then, if it isn't the same as the electromagnetic radiation?' and 'What makes the light accompany the electromagnetic radiation?'—questions which are excluded by saying that the light *is* the electromagnetic radiation. Similarly, the purpose of saying that pains are brain states is precisely to exclude from empirical meaningfulness the questions 'What is the pain, then, if it isn't the same as the brain state?' and 'What makes the pain accompany the brain state?' If there are grounds to suggest that these questions represent, so to speak, the wrong way to look at the matter, then those grounds are grounds for a theoretical identification of pains with brain states.

If all arguments to the contrary are unconvincing, shall we then conclude that it is meaningful (and perhaps true) to say either that pains are brain states or that pain states are brain states?

(1) It is perfectly meaningful (violates no 'rule of English,' involves no 'extension of usage') to say 'pains are brain states.'

(2) It is not meaningful (involves a 'changing of meaning' or 'an extension of usage,' etc.) to say 'pains are brain states.'

My own position is not expressed by either (1) or (2). It seems to me that the notions 'change of meaning' and 'extension of usage' are simply so ill-defined that one cannot in fact say *either* (1) or (2). I see no reason to believe that either the linguist, or the man-on-the-street, or the philosopher possesses today a notion of 'change of meaning' applicable to such cases as the one we have been discussing. The *job* for which the notion of change of meaning was developed in the history of the language was just a *much* cruder job than this one.

But, if we don't assert either (1) or (2)—in other words, if we regard the 'change of meaning' issue as a pseudo-issue in this case—then how are we to discuss the question with which we started? 'Is pain a brain state?'

The answer is to allow statements of the form 'pain is *A*,' where 'pain' and '*A*' are in no sense synonyms, and to see whether any such statement can be found which might be acceptable on empirical and methodological grounds. This is what we shall now proceed to do.

II. Is pain a brain state?

We shall discuss 'Is pain a brain state?,' then. And we have agreed to waive the 'change of meaning' issue.

Since I am discussing not what the concept of pain comes to, but what pain is, in a sense of 'is' which requires empirical theory-construction (or, at least, empirical speculation), I shall not apologize for advancing an empirical hypothesis. Indeed, my strategy will be to argue that pain is *not* a brain state, not on a *priori* grounds, but on the grounds that another hypothesis is more plausible. The detailed development and verification of my hypothesis would be just as Utopian a task as the detailed development and verification of the brain-state hypothesis. But the putting-forward, not of detailed and scientifically 'finished' hypotheses, but of schemata for hypotheses, has long been a function of philosophy. I shall, in short, argue that pain is not a brain state, in the sense of a physical-chemical state of the brain (or even the whole nervous system), but another *kind* of state entirely. I propose the hypothesis that pain, or the state of being in pain, is a functional state of a whole organism.

To explain this it is necessary to introduce some technical notions. In previous papers I have explained the notion of a Turing Machine and discussed the use of this notion as a model for an organism. The notion of a Probabilistic Automaton is defined similarly to a Turing Machine, except that the transitions between 'states' are allowed to be with various probabilities rather than being 'deterministic.' (Of course, a Turing Machine is simply a special kind of Probabilistic Automaton, one with transition probabilities 0, 1.) I shall assume the notion of a Probabilistic Automaton has been generalized to allow for 'sensory inputs' and 'motor outputs'—that is, the Machine Table specifies, for every possible combination of a 'state' and a complete set of 'sensory inputs,' an 'instruction' which determines the probability of the next 'state,' and also the probabilities of the 'motor outputs.' (This replaces the idea of the Machine as printing on a tape.) I shall also assume that the physical realization of the sense organs responsible for the various inputs, and of the motor organs, is specified, but that the 'states' and the 'inputs' themselves are, as usual, specified only 'implicitly'—i.e., by the set of transition probabilities given by the Machine Table.

Since an empirically given system can simultaneously be a 'physical realization' of many different Probabilistic Automata, I introduce the notion of a *Description* of a system. A Description of S where S is a system, is any true statement to the effect that S possesses distinct states $S_1, S_2, \ldots, S_n$ which are related to one another and to the motor outputs and sensory inputs by the transition probabilities given in such-and-such a Machine Table. The Machine Table mentioned in the Description will then be called the Functional Organization of S relative to that Description, and the S_i such that S is in state S_i at a given time will be called the Total State of S (at that time) relative to that Description. It should be noted that knowing the Total State of a system relative to a Description involves knowing a good deal about how the system is likely to 'behave,' given various combinations of sensory inputs, but does *not* involve knowing the physical realization of the S_i as, e.g., physical-chemical states of the brain. The S_i, to repeat, are specified only *implicitly* by the Description—i.e., specified *only* by the set of transition probabilities given in the Machine Table.

The hypothesis that 'being in pain is a functional state of the organism' may now be spelled out more exactly as follows:

(1) All organisms capable of feeling pain are Probabilistic Automata.

(2) Every organism capable of feeling pain possesses at least one Description of a certain kind (i.e., being capable of feeling pain *is* possessing an appropriate kind of Functional Organization).

(3) No organism capable of feeling pain possesses a decomposition into parts which separately possess Descriptions of the kind referred to in (2).

(4) For every Description of the kind referred to in (2), there exists a subset of the sensory inputs such that an organism with that Description is in pain when and only when some of its sensory inputs are in that subset.

This hypothesis is admittedly vague, though surely no vaguer than the brain-state hypothesis in its present form. For example, one would like to know more about the kind of Functional Organization that an organism must have to be capable of feeling pain, and more about the marks that distinguish the subset of the sensory inputs referred to in (4). With respect to the first question, one can probably say that the Functional Organization must include something that resembles a 'preference function,' or at least a preference partial ordering, and something that resembles an 'inductive logic' (i.e., the Machine must be able to 'learn from experience'). (The meaning of these conditions, for Automata models, is discussed in my paper 'The Mental Life of Some Machines.') In addition, it seems natural to require that the Machine possess 'pain sensors,' i.e., sensory organs which normally signal damage to the Machine's body, or dangerous temperatures, pressures, etc., which transmit a special subset of the inputs, the subset referred to in (4). Finally, and with respect to the second question, we would want to require at least that the inputs in the distinguished subset have a high disvalue on the Machine's preference function or ordering (further conditions are discussed in 'The Mental Life of Some Machines'). The purpose of condition (3) is to rule out such 'organisms' (if they can count as such) as swarms of bees as single pain-feelers. The condition (1) is, obviously, redundant, and is only introduced for expository reasons. (It is, in fact, empty, since everything is a Probabilistic Automaton under *some* Description.)

I contend, in passing, that this hypothesis, in spite of its admitted vagueness, is far *less* vague than the 'physical-chemical state' hypothesis is today, and far more susceptible to investigation of both a mathematical and an empirical kind. Indeed, to investigate this hypothesis is just to attempt to produce 'mechanical' models of organisms—and isn't this, in a sense, just what psychology is about? The difficult step, of course, will be to pass from models of *specific* organisms to a *normal form* for the psychological description of organisms—for this is what is required to make (2) and (4) precise. But this too seems to be an inevitable part of the program of psychology.

I shall now compare the hypothesis just advanced with (a) the hypothesis that pain is a brain state, and (b) the hypothesis that pain is a behavior disposition.

III. Functional state versus brain state

It may, perhaps, be asked if I am not somewhat unfair in taking the brain-state theorist to be talking about *physical-chemical* states of the brain. But (a) these are the only sorts of states ever mentioned by brain-state theorists. (b) The brain-state theorist usually mentions (with a certain pride, slightly reminiscent of the Village Atheist) the incompatibility of his hypothesis with all forms of dualism and mentalism. This is natural if physical-chemical states of the brain are what is at issue. However, functional states of whole systems are something quite different. In particular, the functional-state hypothesis is *not* incompatible with dualism! Although it goes without saying that the hypothesis is 'mechanistic' in its inspiration, it is a slightly remarkable fact that a system consisting of a body and a 'soul,' if such things there be, can perfectly well be a Probabilistic Automaton. (c) One argument advanced by Smart is that the brain-state theory assumes only 'physical' properties, and Smart finds 'non-physical' properties unintelligible. The Total States and the 'inputs' defined above are, of course, neither mental nor physical *per se*, and I cannot imagine a functionalist advancing this argument. (d) If the brain-state theorist does mean (or at least allow) states other than physical-chemical states, then his hypothesis is completely empty, at least until he specifies *what* sort of 'states' he *does* mean.

Taking the brain-state hypothesis in this way, then, what reasons are there to prefer the functional-state hypothesis over the brain-state hypothesis? Consider what the brain-state theorist has to do to make good his claims. He has to specify a physical-chemical state such that *any* organism (not just a mammal) is in pain if and only if (a) it possesses a brain of a suitable physical-chemical structure; and (b) its brain is in that physical-chemical state. This means that the physical-chemical state in question must be a possible state of a mammalian brain, a reptilian brain, a mollusc's brain (octopuses are mollusca, and certainly feel pain), etc. At the same time, it must *not* be a possible (physically possible) state of the brain of any physically possible creature that cannot feel pain. Even if such a state can be found, it must be nomologically certain that it will also be a state of the brain of any extra-terrestrial life that may be found that will be capable of feeling pain before we can even entertain the supposition that it may *be* pain.

It is not altogether impossible that such a state will be found. Even though octopus and mammal are examples of parallel (rather than sequential) evolution, for example, virtually identical structures (physically speaking) have evolved in the eye of the octopus and in the eye of the mammal, notwithstanding the fact that this organ has evolved from different kinds of cells in the two cases. Thus it is at least possible that parallel evolution, all over the universe, might *always* lead to *one and the same* physical 'correlate' of pain. But this is certainly an ambitious hypothesis.

Finally, the hypothesis becomes still more ambitious when we realize that the brain state theorist is not just saying that *pain* is a brain state; he is, of course, concerned to maintain that *every* psychological state is a brain state. Thus if we can find even one psychological predicate which can clearly be applied to both a mammal and an octopus (say 'hungry'), but whose physical-chemical 'correlate' is different in the two cases, the brain-state theory has collapsed. It seems to me overwhelmingly probable that we can do this. Granted, in such a case the brain-state theorist can save himself by *ad hoc* assumptions (e.g., defining the disjunction of two states to be a single 'physical-chemical state'), but this does not have to be taken seriously.

Turning now to the considerations *for* the functional-state theory, let us begin with the fact that we identify organisms as in pain, or hungry, or angry, or in heat, etc., on the basis of their *behavior.* But it is a truism that similarities in the behavior of two systems are at least a reason to suspect similarities in the functional organization of the two systems, and a much *weaker* reason to suspect similarities in the actual physical details. Moreover, we expect the various psychological states—at least the basic ones, such as hunger, thirst, aggression, etc.—to have more or less similar 'transition probabilities' (within wide and ill-defined limits, to be sure) with each other and with behavior in the case of different species, because this is an artifact of the way in which we identify these states. Thus, we would not count an animal as *thirsty* if its 'unsatiated' behavior did not seem to be directed toward drinking and was not followed by 'satiation for liquid.' Thus any animal that we count as capable of these various states will at least *seem* to have a certain rough kind of functional organization. And, as already remarked, if the program of finding psychological laws that are not species-specific—i.e., of finding a normal form for psychological theories of different species—ever succeeds, then it will bring in its wake a delineation of the kind of functional organization that is necessary and sufficient for a given psychological state, as well as a precise definition of the notion 'psychological state.' In contrast, the brain-state theorist has to hope for the eventual development of neurophysiological laws that are species-independent, which seems much less reasonable than the hope that psychological laws (of a sufficiently general kind) may be species-independent, or, still weaker, that a species-independent *form* can be found in which psychological laws can be written.

IV. Functional state versus behavior-disposition

The theory that being in pain is neither a brain state nor a functional state but a behavior disposition has one apparent advantage: it appears to agree with the way in which we verify that organisms are in pain. We do not in practice know anything about the brain state of an animal when we say that it is in pain; and we possess little if any knowledge of its functional organization, except in a crude intuitive way. In fact, however, this 'advantage' is no advantage at all: for, although statements about how we verify that x is A may have a good deal to do with what the concept of being A comes to, they have precious little to do with what the property A *is.* To argue on the ground just mentioned that pain is neither a brain state nor a functional state is like arguing that heat is not mean molecular kinetic energy from the fact that ordinary people do not (they think) ascertain the mean molecular kinetic energy of something when they verify that it is hot or cold. It is not necessary that they should; what is necessary is that the marks that they take as indications of heat should in fact be explained by the mean molecular kinetic energy. And, similarly, it is necessary to our hypothesis that the marks that are taken as behavioral indications of pain should be explained by the fact that the organism is in a functional state of the appropriate kind, but not that speakers should *know* that this is so.

The difficulties with 'behavior disposition' accounts are so well known that I shall do little more than recall them here. The difficulty—it appears to be more than 'difficulty,' in fact—of specifying the required behavior disposition except as 'the disposition of *X* to behave as if *X* were in *pain*,' is the chief one, of course. In contrast, we *can* specify the functional state with which we propose to identify pain, at least roughly, without using the notion of pain. Namely, the functional state we have in mind is the state of receiving sensory inputs which play a certain role in the Functional Organization of the organism. This role is characterized, at least partially, by the fact that the sense organs responsible for the inputs in question are organs whose function is to detect damage to the body, or dangerous extremes of temperature, pressure, etc., and by the fact that the 'inputs' themselves, whatever their physical realization, represent a condition that the organism assigns a high disvalue to. As I stressed in 'The Mental Life of Some Machines,' this does *not* mean that the Machine will always *avoid* being in the condition in question ('pain'); it only means that the condition will be avoided unless not avoiding it is necessary to the attainment of some more highly valued goal. Since the behavior of the Machine (in this case, an organism) will depend not merely on the sensory inputs, but also on the Total State (i.e., on other values, beliefs, etc.), it seems hopeless to make any general statement about how an organism in such a condition *must* behave; but this does not mean that we must abandon hope of characterizing the condition. Indeed, we have just characterized it.[4]

Not only does the behavior-disposition theory seem hopelessly vague; if the 'behavior' referred to is peripheral behavior, and the relevant stimuli are peripheral stimuli (e.g., we do not say anything about what the organism will do if its brain is operated upon), then the theory seems clearly false. For example, two animals with all motor nerves cut will have the same actual and potential 'behavior' (viz., none to speak of); but if one has cut pain fibers and the other has uncut pain fibers, then one will feel pain and the other won't. Again, if one person

4. In 'The Mental Life of Some Machines' a further, and somewhat independent, characteristic of the pain inputs is discussed in terms of Automata models—namely the spontaneity of the inclination to withdraw the injured part, etc. This raises the question, which is discussed in that paper, of giving a functional analysis of the notion of a spontaneous inclination. Of course, still further characteristics come readily to mind—for example, that feelings of pain are (or seem to be) *located* in the parts of the body.

has cut pain fibers, and another suppresses all pain responses deliberately due to some strong compulsion, then the actual and potential peripheral behavior may be the same, but one will feel pain and the other won't. (Some philosophers maintain that this last case is conceptually impossible, but the only evidence for this appears to be that *they* can't, or don't want to, conceive of it.)[5] If, instead of pain, we take some sensation the 'bodily expression' of which is easier to suppress—say, a slight coolness in one's left little finger—the case becomes even clearer.

Finally, even if there *were* some behavior disposition invariantly correlated with pain (species-independently!), and specifiable without using the term 'pain,' it would still be more plausible to identify being in pain with some state whose presence *explains* this behavior disposition—the brain state or functional state—than with the behavior disposition itself. Such considerations of plausibility may be somewhat subjective; but if other things *were* equal (of course, they aren't) why shouldn't we allow considerations of plausibility to play the deciding role?

V. Methodological considerations

So far we have considered only what might be called the 'empirical' reasons for saying that being in pain is a functional state, rather than a brain state or a behavior disposition; viz., that it seems more likely that the functional state we described is invariantly 'correlated' with pain, species-independently, than that there is either a physical-chemical state of the brain (must an organism have a *brain* to feel pain? perhaps some ganglia will do) or a behavior disposition so correlated. If this is correct, then it follows that the identification we proposed is at least a candidate for consideration. What of methodological considerations?

The methodological considerations are roughly similar in all cases of reduction, so no surprises need be expected here. First, identification of psychological states with functional states means that the laws of psychology can be derived from statements of the form, 'such-and-such organisms have such-and-such Descriptions' together with the identification statements ('being in pain is such-and-such a functional state,' etc.). Secondly, the presence of the functional state (i.e., of inputs which play the role we have described in the Functional Organization of the organism) is not merely 'correlated with' but actually explains the pain behavior on the part of the organism. Thirdly, the identification serves to exclude questions which (if a naturalistic view is correct) represent an altogether wrong way of looking at the matter, e.g., 'What *is* pain if it isn't either the brain state or the functional state?' and 'What causes the pain to be always accompanied by this sort of functional state?' In short, the identification is to be tentatively accepted as a theory which leads to both fruitful predictions and to fruitful *questions*, and which serves to discourage fruitless and empirically senseless questions, where by 'empirically senseless' I mean 'senseless' not merely from the standpoint of verification, but from the standpoint of what there in fact *is*.

5. Cf. the discussion of 'super-spartans' in 'Brains and Behavior.' (See Chapter 6, p. 104 of this volume.)

Chapter 12

The mind–body problem

Jerry Fodor

MODERN philosophy of science has been devoted largely to the formal and systematic description of the successful practices of working scientists. The philosopher does not try to dictate how scientific inquiry and argument ought to be conducted. Instead he tries to enumerate the principles and practices that have contributed to good science. The philosopher has devoted the most attention to analyzing the methodological peculiarities of the physical sciences. The analysis has helped to clarify the nature of confirmation, the logical structure of scientific theories, the formal properties of statements that express laws and the question of whether theoretical entities actually exist.

It is only rather recently that philosophers have become seriously interested in the methodological tenets of psychology. Psychological explanations of behavior refer liberally to the mind and to states, operations and processes of the mind. The philosophical difficulty comes in stating in unambiguous language what such references imply.

Traditional philosophies of mind can be divided into two broad categories: dualist theories and materialist theories. In the dualist approach the mind is a nonphysical substance. In materialist theories the mental is not distinct from the physical; indeed, all mental states, properties, processes and operations are in principle identical with physical states, properties, processes and operations. Some materialists, known as behaviorists, maintain that all talk of mental causes can be eliminated from the language of psychology in favor of talk of environmental stimuli and behavioral responses. Other materialists, the identity theorists, contend that there are mental causes and that they are identical with neurophysiological events in the brain.

In the past 15 years a philosophy of mind called functionalism that is neither dualist nor materialist has emerged from philosophical reflection on developments in artificial intelligence, computational theory, linguistics, cybernetics and psychology. All these fields, which are collectively known as the cognitive sciences, have in common a certain level of abstraction and a concern with systems that process information. Functionalism, which seeks to provide a philosophical account of this level of abstraction, recognizes the possibility that systems as diverse as human beings, calculating machines and disembodied spirits could all have mental states.

Jerry Fodor, 'The Mind–Body Problem', *Scientific American* 244 (January 1981).

In the functionalist view the psychology of a system depends not on the stuff it is made of (living cells, metal or spiritual energy) but on how the stuff is put together. Functionalism is a difficult concept, and one way of coming to grips with it is to review the deficiencies of the dualist and materialist philosophies of mind it aims to displace.

The chief drawback of dualism is its failure to account adequately for mental causation. If the mind is nonphysical, it has no position in physical space. How, then, can a mental cause give rise to a behavioral effect that has a position in space? To put it another way, how can the nonphysical give rise to the physical without violating the laws of the conservation of mass, of energy and of momentum?

The dualist might respond that the problem of how an immaterial substance can cause physical events is not much obscurer than the problem of how one physical event can cause another. Yet there is an important difference: there are many clear cases of physical causation but not one clear case of nonphysical causation. Physical interaction is something philosophers, like all other people, have to live with. Nonphysical interaction, however, may be no more than an artifact of the immaterialist construal of the mental. Most philosophers now agree that no argument has successfully demonstrated why mindbody causation should not be regarded as a species of physical causation.

Dualism is also incompatible with the practices of working psychologists. The psychologist frequently applies the experimental methods of the physical sciences to the study of the mind. If mental processes were different in kind from physical processes, there would be no reason to expect these methods to work in the realm of the mental. In order to justify their experimental methods many psychologists urgently sought an alternative to dualism.

In the 1920's John B. Watson of Johns Hopkins University made the radical suggestion that behavior does not have mental causes. He regarded the behavior of an organism as its observable responses to stimuli, which he took to be the causes of its behavior. Over the next 30 years psychologists such as B. F. Skinner of Harvard University developed Watson's ideas into an elaborate world view in which the role of psychology was to catalogue the laws that determine causal relations between stimuli and responses. In this 'radical behaviorist' view the problem of explaining the nature of the mind-body interaction vanishes; there is no such interaction.

Radical behaviorism has always worn an air of paradox. For better or worse, the idea of mental causation is deeply ingrained in our everyday language and in our ways of understanding our fellow men and ourselves. For example, people commonly attribute behavior to beliefs, to knowledge and to expectations. Brown puts gas in his tank because he believes the car will not run without it. Jones writes not 'acheive' but 'achieve' because he knows the rule about putting *i* before *e*. Even when a behavioral response is closely tied to an environmental stimulus, mental processes often intervene. Smith carries an umbrella because the sky is cloudy, but the weather is only part of the story. There are apparently also mental links in the causal chain: observation and expectation. The clouds affect Smith's behavior only because he observes them and because they induce in him an expectation of rain.

The radical behaviorist is unmoved by appeals to such cases. He is prepared to dismiss references to mental causes, however plausible they may seem, as the residue of outworn creeds. The radical behaviorist predicts that as psychologists come to understand more about the relations between stimuli and responses they will find it increasingly possible to explain behavior without postulating mental causes.

The strongest argument against behaviorism is that psychology has not turned out this way; the opposite has happened. As psychology has matured, the framework of mental states and processes that is apparently needed to account for experimental observations has grown all the more elaborate. Particularly in the case of human behavior psychological theories satisfying the methodological tenets of radical behaviorism have proved largely sterile, as would be expected if the postulated mental processes are real and causally effective.

Nevertheless, many philosophers were initially drawn to radical behaviorism because, paradoxes and all, it seemed better than dualism. Since a psychology committed to immaterial substances was unacceptable, philosophers turned to radical behaviorism because it seemed to be the only alternative materialist philosophy of mind. The choice, as they saw it, was between radical behaviorism and ghosts.

By the early 1960's philosophers began to have doubts that dualism and radical behaviorism exhausted the possible approaches to the philosophy of mind. Since the two theories seemed unattractive, the right strategy might be to develop a materialist philosophy of mind that nonetheless allowed for mental causes. Two such philosophies emerged, one called logical behaviorism and the other called the central-state identity theory.

Logical behaviorism is a semantic theory about what mental terms mean. The basic idea is that attributing a mental state (say thirst) to an organism is the same as saying that the organism is disposed to behave in a particular way (for example to drink if there is water available). On this view every mental ascription is equivalent in meaning to an if-then statement (called a behavioral hypothetical) that expresses a behavioral disposition. For example, 'Smith is thirsty' might be taken to be equivalent to the dispositional statement. 'If there were water available, then Smith would drink some.' By definition a behavioral hypothetical includes no mental terms. The if-clause of the hypothetical speaks only of stimuli and the then-clause speaks only of behavioral responses. Since stimuli and responses are physical events, logical behaviorism is a species of materialism.

The strength of logical behaviorism is that by translating mental language into the language of stimuli and responses it provides an interpretation of psychological explanations in which behavioral effects are attributed to mental causes. Mental causation is simply the manifestation of a behavioral disposition. More precisely, mental causation is what happens when an organism has a behavioral disposition and the if-clause of the behavioral hypothetical expressing the disposition happens to be true. For example, the causal statement 'Smith drank some water because he was thirsty' might be taken to mean 'If there were water available, then Smith would drink some, and there was water available.'

I have somewhat oversimplified logical behaviorism by assuming that each mental ascription can be translated by a unique behavioral hypothetical. Actually the logical behaviorist often maintains that it takes an open-ended set (perhaps an infinite set) of behavioral hypotheticals to spell out the behavioral disposition expressed by a mental term. The mental ascription 'Smith is thirsty' might also be satisfied by the hypothetical 'If there were orange juice available, then Smith would drink some' and by a host of other hypotheticals. In any event the logical behaviorist does not usually maintain he can actually enumerate all the hypotheticals that correspond to a behavioral disposition expressing a given mental term. He only insists that in principle the meaning of any mental term can be conveyed by behavioral hypotheticals.

The way the logical behaviorist has interpreted a mental term such as thirsty is modeled after the way many philosophers have interpreted a physical disposition such as fragility. The physical disposition 'The glass is fragile' is often taken to mean something like 'If the glass were struck, then it would break.' By the same token the logical behaviorist's analysis of mental causation is similar to the received analysis of one kind of physical causation. The causal statement 'The glass broke because it was fragile' is taken to mean something like 'If the glass were struck, then it would break, and the glass was struck.'

By equating mental terms with behavioral dispositions the logical behaviorist has put mental terms on a par with the nonbehavioral dispositions of the physical sciences. That is a promising move, because the analysis of nonbehavioral dispositions is on relatively solid philosophical ground. An explanation attributing the breaking of a glass to its fragility is surely something even the staunchest materialist can accept. By arguing that mental terms are synonymous with dispositional terms, the logical behaviorist has provided something the radical behaviorist could not: a materialist account of mental causation.

Nevertheless, the analogy between mental causation as construed by the logical behaviorist and physical causation goes only so far. The logical behaviorist treats the manifestation of a disposition as the sole form of mental causation, whereas the physical sciences recognize additional kinds of causation. There is the kind of causation where one physical event causes another, as when the breaking of a glass is attributed to its having been struck. In fact, explanations that involve event-event causation are presumably more basic than dispositional explanations, because the manifestation of a disposition (the breaking of a fragile glass) always involves event-event causation and not vice versa. In the realm of the mental many examples of event-event causation involve one mental state's causing another, and for this kind of causation logical behaviorism provides no analysis. As a result the logical behaviorist is committed to the tacit and implausible assumption that psychology requires a less robust notion of causation than the physical sciences require.

Event-event causation actually seems to be quite common in the realm of the mental. Mental causes typically give rise to behavioral effects by virtue of their interaction with other mental causes. For example, having a headache causes a disposition to take aspirin only if one also has the desire to get rid of the headache, the belief that aspirin exists, the belief that taking aspirin reduces headaches and so on. Since mental states interact in generating behavior, it will be necessary to find a construal of psychological explanations that posits mental processes: causal sequences of mental events. It is this construal that logical behaviorism fails to provide.

Such considerations bring out a fundamental way in which logical behaviorism is quite similar to radical behaviorism. It is true that the logical behaviorist, unlike the radical behaviorist, acknowledges the existence of mental states. Yet since the underlying tenet of logical behaviorism is that references to mental states can be translated out of psychological explanations by employing behavioral hypotheticals, all talk of mental states and processes is in a sense heuristic. The only facts to which the behaviorist is actually committed are facts about relations between stimuli and responses. In this respect logical behaviorism is just radical behaviorism in a semantic form. Although the former theory offers a construal of mental causation, the construal is Pickwickian. What does not really exist cannot cause anything, and the logical behaviorist, like the radical behaviorist, believes deep down that mental causes do not exist.

An alternative materialist theory of the mind to logical behaviorism is the central-state identity theory. According to this theory, mental events, states and processes are identical with neurophysiological events in the brain, and the property of being in a certain mental state (such as having a headache or believing it will rain) is identical with the property of being in a certain neurophysiological state. On this basis it is easy to make sense of the idea that a behavioral effect might sometimes have a chain of mental causes; that will be the case whenever a behavioral effect is contingent on the appropriate sequence of neurophysiological events.

The central-state identity theory acknowledges that it is possible for mental causes to interact causally without ever giving rise to any behavioral effect, as when a person thinks for a while about what he ought to do and then decides to do nothing. If mental processes are neurophysiological, they must have the causal properties of neurophysiological processes. Since neurophysiological processes are presumably physical processes, the central-state identity theory ensures that the concept of mental causation is as rich as the concept of physical causation.

The central-state identity theory provides a satisfactory account of what the mental terms in psychological explanations refer to, and so it is favored by psychologists who are dissatisfied with behaviorism. The behaviorist maintains that mental terms refer to nothing or that they refer to the parameters of stimulus-response relations. Either way the existence of mental entities is only illusory. The identity theorist, on the other hand, argues that mental terms refer to neurophysiological states. Thus he can take seriously the project of explaining behavior by appealing to its mental causes.

The chief advantage of the identity theory is that it takes the explanatory constructs of psychology at face value, which is surely something a philosophy of mind ought to do if it can. The identity theory shows how the mentalistic explanations of psychology could be not mere heuristics but literal accounts of the causal history of behavior. Moreover, since the identity theory is not a semantic thesis, it is immune to many arguments that cast in doubt logical behaviorism. A drawback of logical behaviorism is that the observation 'John has a headache' does not seem to mean the same thing as a statement of the form 'John is disposed to behave in such and such a way.' The identity theorist, however, can live with the fact that 'John has a headache' and 'John is in such and such a brain state' are not synonymous. The assertion of the identity theorist is not that these sentences mean the same thing but only that they are rendered true (or false) by the same neurophysiological phenomena.

The identity theory can be held either as a doctrine about mental particulars (John's current pain or Bill's fear of animals) or as a doctrine about mental universals, or properties (having a pain or being afraid of animals). The two doctrines, called respectively token physicalism and type physicalism, differ in strength and plausibility. Token physicalism maintains only that all the mental particulars that happen to exist are neurophysiological, whereas type physicalism makes the more sweeping assertion that all the mental particulars there could possibly be are neurophysiological. Token physicalism does not rule out the logical possibility of machines and disembodied spirits having mental properties. Type physicalism dismisses this possibility because neither machines nor disembodied spirits have neurons.

Type physicalism is not a plausible doctrine about mental properties even if token physicalism is right about mental particulars. The problem with type physicalism is that the psychological constitution of a system seems to depend not on its hardware, or physical composition, but on its software, or program. Why should the philosopher dismiss the possibility that silicon-based Martians have pains, assuming that the silicon is properly organized? And why should the philosopher rule out the possibility of machines having beliefs, assuming that the machines are correctly programmed? If it is logically possible that Martians and machines could have mental properties, then mental properties and neurophysiological processes cannot be identical, however much they may prove to be coextensive.

What it all comes down to is that there seems to be a level of abstraction at which the generalizations of psychology are most naturally pitched. This level of abstraction cuts across differences in the physical composition of the systems to which psychological generalizations apply. In the cognitive sciences, at least, the natural domain for psychological theorizing seems to be all systems that process information. The problem with type physicalism is that there are possible information-processing systems with the same psychological constitution as human beings but not the same physical organization. In principle all kinds of physically different things could have human software.

This situation calls for a relational account of mental properties that abstracts them from the physical structure of their bearers. In spite of the objections to logical behaviorism that I presented above, logical behaviorism was at least on the right track in offering a relational interpretation of mental properties: to have a headache is to be disposed to exhibit a certain pattern of relations between the stimuli one encounters and the responses one exhibits. If that is what having a headache is, however, there is no reason in principle why only heads that are physically similar to ours can ache. Indeed, according to logical behaviorism, it is a necessary truth that any system that has our stimulus-response contingencies also has our headaches.

All of this emerged 10 or 15 years ago as a nasty dilemma for the materialist program in the philosophy of mind. On the one hand the identity theorist (and not the logical behaviorist) had got right the causal character of the interactions of mind and body. On the other the logical behaviorist (and not the identity theorist) had got right the relational character of mental properties. Functionalism has apparently been able to resolve the dilemma. By stressing the distinction computer science draws between hardware and software the functionalist can make sense of both the causal and the relational character of the mental.

The intuition underlying functionalism is that what determines the psychological type to which a mental particular belongs is the causal role of the particular in the mental life of the organism. Functional individuation is differentiation with respect to causal role. A headache, for example; is identified with the type of mental state that among other things causes a disposition for taking aspirin in people who believe aspirin relieves a headache, causes a desire to rid oneself of the pain one is feeling, often causes someone who speaks English to say such things as 'I have a headache' and is brought on by overwork, eyestrain and tension. This list is presumably not complete. More will be known about the nature of a headache as psychological and physiological research discovers more about its causal role.

Functionalism construes the concept of causal role in such a way that a mental state can be defined by its causal relations to other mental states. In this respect functionalism is completely different from logical behaviorism. Another major difference is that functionalism is not a reductionist thesis. It does not foresee, even in principle, the elimination of mentalistic concepts from the explanatory apparatus of psychological theories.

The difference between functionalism and logical behaviorism is brought out by the fact that functionalism is fully compatible with token physicalism. The functionalist would not be disturbed if brain events turn out to be the only things with the functional properties that define mental states. Indeed, most functionalists fully expect it will turn out that way.

Since functionalism recognizes that mental particulars may be physical, it is compatible with the idea that mental causation is a species of physical causation. In other words, functionalism tolerates the materialist solution to the mind-body problem provided by the central-state identity theory. It is possible for the functionalist to assert both that mental properties are typically defined in terms of their relations and that interactions of mind and body are typically causal in however robust a notion of causality is required by psychological explanations. The logical behaviorist can endorse only the first assertion and the type physicalist only the second. As a result functionalism seems to capture the best features of the materialist alternatives to dualism. It is no wonder that functionalism has become increasingly popular.

Machines provide good examples of two concepts that are central to functionalism: the concept that mental states are interdefined and the concept that they can be realized by many systems. The illustration on page 186 contrasts a behavioristic Coke machine with a mentalistic one. Both machines dispense a Coke for 10 cents. (The price has not been affected by inflation.) The states of the machines are defined by reference to their causal roles, but only the machine on the left would satisfy the behaviorist. Its single state (*So*) is completely specified in terms of stimuli and responses. *So* is the state a machine is in if, and only if, given a dime as the input, it dispenses a Coke as the output.

The machine on the right in the illustration on page 186, has interdefined states (*S1* and *S2*), which are characteristic of functionalism. *S1* is the state a machine is in if, and only if, (1) given a nickel, it dispenses nothing and proceeds to *S2*, and (2) given a dime, it dispenses a Coke and stays in *S1*. *S2* is the state a machine is in if, and only if, (1) given a nickel, it dispenses a Coke and proceeds to *S1*, and (2) given a dime, it dispenses a Coke and a nickel and proceeds to *S1*. What *S1* and *S2* jointly amount to is the machine's dispensing a Coke if it is given a dime, dispensing a Coke and a nickel if it is given a dime and a nickel and waiting to be given a second nickel if it has been given a first one.

Since *S1* and *S2* are each defined by hypothetical statements, they can be viewed as dispositions. Nevertheless, they are not behavioral dispositions because the consequences an input has for a machine in *S1* or *S2* are not specified solely in terms of the output of the machine. Rather, the consequences also involve the machine's internal states.

Nothing about the way I have described the behavioristic and mentalistic Coke machines puts constraints on what they could be made of. Any system whose states bore the proper relations to inputs, outputs and other states could be one of these machines. No doubt it is reasonable to expect such a system to be constructed out of such things as wheels, levers and diodes (token physicalism for Coke machines).

Similarly, it is reasonable to expect that our minds may prove to be neurophysiological (token physicalism for human beings).

Nevertheless, the software description of a Coke machine does not logically require wheels, levers and diodes for its concrete realization. By the same token, the software description of the mind does not logically require neurons. As far as functionalism is concerned a Coke machine with states *S1* and *S2* could be made of ectoplasm, if there is such stuff and if its states have the right causal properties. Functionalism allows for the possibility of disembodied Coke machines in exactly the same way and to the same extent that it allows for the possibility of disembodied minds.

To say that *S1* and *S2* are interdefined and realizable by different kinds of hardware is not, of course, to say that a Coke machine has a mind. Although interdefinition and functional specification are typical features of mental states, they are clearly not sufficient for mentality. What more is required is a question to which I shall return below.

Some philosophers are suspicious of functionalism because it seems too easy. Since functionalism licenses the individuation of states by reference to their causal role, it appears to allow a trivial explanation of any observed event *E*, that is, it appears to postulate an *E*-causer. For example, what makes the valves in a machine open? Why, the operation of a valve opener. And what is a valve opener? Why, anything that has the functionally defined property of causing valves to open.

In psychology this kind of question-begging often takes the form of theories that in effect postulate homunculi with the selfsame intellectual capacities the theorist set out to explain. Such is the case when visual perception is explained by simply postulating psychological mechanisms that process visual information. The behaviorist has often charged the mentalist, sometimes justifiably, of mongering this kind of question-begging pseudo explanation. The charge will have to be met if functionally defined mental states are to have a serious role in psychological theories.

The burden of the accusation is not untruth but triviality. There can be no doubt that it is a valve opener that opens valves, and it is likely that visual perception is mediated by the processing of visual information. The charge is that such putative functional explanations are mere platitudes. The functionalist can meet this objection by allowing functionally defined theoretical constructs only where mechanisms exist that can carry out the function and only where he has some notion of what such mechanisms might be like. One way of imposing this requirement is to identify the mental processes that psychology postulates with the operations of the restricted class of possible computers called Turing machines.

A Turing machine can be informally characterized as a mechanism with a finite number of program states. The inputs and outputs of the machine are written on a tape that is divided into squares each of which includes a symbol from a finite alphabet. The machine scans the tape one square at a time. It can erase the symbol on a scanned square and print a new one in its place. The machine can execute only the elementary mechanical operations of scanning, erasing, printing, moving the tape and changing state.

The program states of the Turing machine are defined solely in terms of the input symbols on the tape, the output symbols on the tape, the elementary operations and the other states of the program. Each program state is therefore functionally defined by the part it plays in the overall operation of the machine. Since the functional role of a state depends on the relation of the state to other states as well as to inputs and outputs, the relational character of the mental is captured by the Turing-machine version of functionalism. Since the definition of a program state never refers to the physical structure of the system running the program, the Turing-machine version of functionalism also captures the idea that the character of a mental state is independent of its physical realization. A human being, a roomful of people, a computer and a disembodied spirit would all be a Turing machine if they operated according to a Turing-machine program.

The proposal is to restrict the functional definition of psychological states to those that can be expressed in terms of the program states of Turing machines. If this restriction can be enforced, it provides a guarantee that psychological theories will be compatible with the demands of mechanisms. Since Turing machines are very simple devices, they are in principle quite easy to build. Consequently by formulating a psychological explanation as a Turing-machine program the psychologist ensures that the explanation is mechanistic, even though the hardware realizing the mechanism is left open.

There are many kinds of computational mechanisms other than Turing machines, and so the formulation of a functionalist psychological theory in Turing-machine notation provides only a sufficient condition for the theory's being mechanically realizable. What makes the condition interesting, however, is that the simple Turing machine can perform many complex tasks. Although the elementary operations of the Turing machine are restricted, iterations of the operations enable the machine to carry out any well-defined computation on discrete symbols.

An important tendency in the cognitive sciences is to treat the mind chiefly as a device that manipulates symbols. If a mental process can be functionally defined as an operation on symbols, there is a Turing machine capable of carrying out the computation and a variety of mechanisms for realizing the Turing machine. Where the manipulation of symbols is important the Turing machine provides a connection between functional explanation and mechanistic explanation.

The reduction of a psychological theory to a program for a Turing machine is a way of exorcising the homunculi. The reduction ensures that no operations have been postulated except those that could be performed by a familiar mechanism. Of course, the working psychologist usually cannot specify the reduction for each functionally individuated process in every theory he is prepared to take seriously. In practice the argument usually goes in the opposite direction; if the postulation of a mental operation is essential to some cherished psychological explanation, the theorist tends to assume that there must be a program for a Turing machine that will carry out that operation.

The 'black boxes' that are common in flow charts drawn by psychologists often serve to indicate postulated mental processes for which Turing reductions are wanting. Even so, the possibility in principle of such reductions serves as a methodological constraint on psychological theorizing by determining what functional definitions are to be allowed and what it would be like to know that everything has been explained that could possibly need explanation.

Such is the origin, the provenance and the promise of contemporary functionalism. How much has it actually paid off? This question is not easy to answer because much of what is now happening in the philosophy of mind and the cognitive sciences is directed at exploring the scope and limits of the functionalist explanations of behavior. I shall, however, give a brief overview.

An obvious objection to functionalism as a theory of the mind is that the functionalist definition is not limited to mental states and processes. Catalysts, Coke machines, valve openers, pencil sharpeners, mousetraps and ministers of finance are all in one way or another concepts that are functionally defined, but none is a mental concept such as pain, belief and desire. What, then, characterizes the mental? And can it be captured in a functionalist framework?

The traditional view in the philosophy of mind has it that mental states are distinguished by their having what are called either qualitative content or intentional content. I shall discuss qualitative content first.

It is not easy to say what qualitative content is; indeed, according to some theories, it is not even possible to say what it is because it can be known not by description but only by direct experience. I shall nonetheless attempt to describe it. Try to imagine looking at a blank wall through a red filter. Now change the filter to a green one and leave everything else exactly the way it was. Something about the character of your experience changes when the filter does, and it is this kind of thing that philosophers call qualitative content. I am not entirely comfortable about introducing qualitative content in this way, but it is a subject with which many philosophers are not comfortable.

The reason qualitative content is a problem for functionalism is straight-forward. Functionalism is committed to defining mental states in terms of their causes and effects. It seems, however, as if two mental states could have all the same causal relations and yet could differ in their qualitative content. Let me illustrate this with the classic puzzle of the inverted spectrum.

It seems possible to imagine two observers who are alike in all relevant psychological respects except that experiences having the qualitative content of red for one observer would have the qualitative content of green for the other. Nothing about their behavior need reveal the difference because both of them see ripe tomatoes and flaming sunsets as being similar in color and both of them call that color 'red.'

Moreover, the causal connection between their (qualitatively distinct) experiences and their other mental states could also be identical. Perhaps they both think of Little Red Riding Hood when they see ripe tomatoes, feel depressed when they see the color green and so on. It seems as if anything that could be packed into the notion of the causal role of their experiences could be shared by them, and yet the qualitative content of the experiences could be as different as you like. If this is possible, then the functionalist account does not work for mental states that have qualitative content. If one person is having a green experience while another person is having a red one, then surely they must be in different mental states.

The example of the inverted spectrum is more than a verbal puzzle. Having qualitative content is supposed to be a chief factor in what makes a mental state conscious. Many psychologists who are inclined to accept the functionalist framework are nonetheless worried about the failure of functionalism to reveal much about the nature of consciousness. Functionalists have made a few ingenious attempts to talk themselves and their colleagues out of this worry, but they have not, in my view, done so with much success. (For example, perhaps one is wrong in thinking one can imagine what an inverted spectrum would be like.) As matters stand, the problem of qualitative content poses a serious threat to the assertion that functionalism can provide a general theory of the mental.

Functionalism has fared much better with the intentional content of mental states. Indeed, it is here that the major achievements of recent cognitive science are found. To say that a mental state has intentional content is to say that it has certain semantic properties. For example, for Enrico to believe Galileo was Italian apparently involves a three-way relation between Enrico, a belief and a proposition that is the content of the belief (namely the proposition that Galileo was Italian). In particular it is an essential property of Enrico's belief that it is about Galileo (and not about, say, Newton) and that it is true if, and only if, Galileo was indeed Italian. Philosophers are divided on how these considerations fit together, but it is widely agreed that beliefs involve semantic properties such as expressing a proposition, being true or false and being about one thing rather than another.

It is important to understand the semantic properties of beliefs because theories in the cognitive sciences are largely about the beliefs organisms have. Theories of learning and perception, for example, are chiefly accounts of how the host of beliefs an organism has are determined by the character of its experiences and its genetic endowment. The functionalist account of mental states does not by itself provide the required insights. Mousetraps are functionally defined, yet mousetraps do not express propositions and they are not true or false.

There is at least one kind of thing other than a mental state that has intentional content: a symbol. Like thoughts, symbols seem to be about things. If someone says 'Galileo was Italian,' his utterance, like Enrico's belief, expresses a proposition about Galileo that is true or false depending on Galileo's homeland. This parallel between the symbolic and the mental underlies the traditional quest for a unified treatment of language and mind. Cognitive science is now trying to provide such a treatment.

The basic concept is simple but striking. Assume that there are such things as mental symbols (mental representations) and that mental symbols have semantic properties. On this view having a belief involves being related to a mental symbol, and the belief inherits its semantic properties from the mental symbol that figures in the relation. Mental processes (thinking, perceiving, learning and so on) involve causal interactions among relational states such as having a belief. The semantic properties of the words and sentences we utter are in turn inherited from the semantic properties of the mental states that language expresses.

Associating the semantic properties of mental states with those of mental symbols is fully compatible with the computer metaphor, because it is natural to think of the computer as a mechanism that manipulates symbols. A computation is a causal chain of computer states and the links in the chain are operations on semantically interpreted formulas in a machine code. To think of a system (such as the nervous system) as a computer is to raise questions about the nature of the code in which it computes and the semantic properties of the symbols in the code. In fact, the analogy between minds and computers actually implies the postulation of mental symbols. There is no computation without representation.

The representational account of the mind, however, predates considerably the invention of the computing machine. It is a throwback to classical epistemology, which is a tradition that includes philosophers as diverse as John Locke, David Hume, George Berkeley, René Descartes, Immanuel Kant, John Stuart Mill and William James.

Hume, for one, developed a representational theory of the mind that included five points. First, there exist 'Ideas,' which are a species of mental symbol. Second, having a belief involves entertaining an Idea. Third, mental processes are causal associations of Ideas. Fourth, Ideas are like pictures. And fifth, Ideas have their semantic properties by virtue of what they resemble: the Idea of John is about John because it looks like him.

Contemporary cognitive psychologists do not accept the details of Hume's theory, although they endorse much of its spirit. Theories of computation provide a far richer account of mental processes than the mere association of Ideas. And only a few psychologists still think that imagery is the chief vehicle of mental representation. Nevertheless, the most significant break with Hume's theory lies in the abandoning of resemblance as an explanation of the semantic properties of mental representations.

Many philosophers, starting with Berkeley, have argued that there is something seriously wrong with the suggestion that the semantic relation between a thought and what the thought is about could be one of resemblance. Consider the thought that John is tall. Clearly the thought is true only of the state of affairs consisting of John's being tall. A theory of the semantic properties of a thought should therefore explain how this particular thought is related to this particular state of affairs.

According to the resemblance theory, entertaining the thought involves having a mental image that shows John to be tall. To put it another way, the relation between the thought that John is tall and his being tall is like the relation between a tall man and his portrait.

The difficulty with the resemblance theory is that any portrait showing John to be tall must also show him to be many other things: clothed or naked, lying, standing or sitting, having a head or not having one, and so on. A portrait of a tall man who is sitting down resembles a man's being seated as much as it resembles a man's being tall. On the resemblance theory it is not clear what distinguishes thoughts about John's height from thoughts about his posture.

The resemblance theory turns out to encounter paradoxes at every turn. The possibility of construing beliefs as involving relations to semantically interpreted mental representations clearly depends on having an acceptable account of where the semantic properties of the mental representations come from. If resemblance will not provide this account, what will?

The current idea is that the semantic properties of a mental representation are determined by aspects of its functional role. In other words, a sufficient condition for having semantic properties can be specified in causal terms. This is the connection between functionalism and the representational theory of the mind. Modern cognitive psychology rests largely on the hope that these two doctrines can be made to support each other.

No philosopher is now prepared to say exactly how the functional role of a mental representation determines its semantic properties. Nevertheless, the functionalist recognizes three types of causal relation among psychological states involving mental representations, and they might serve to fix the semantic properties of mental representations. The three types are causal relations among mental states and stimuli, mental states and responses and some mental states and other ones.

Consider the belief that John is tall. presumably the following facts, which correspond respectively to the three types of causal relation, are relevant to determining the semantic properties of the mental representation involved in the belief. First, the belief is a normal effect of certain stimulations, such as seeing John in circumstances that reveal his height. Second, the belief is the normal cause of certain behavioral effects, such as uttering 'John is tall.' Third, the belief is a normal cause of certain other beliefs and a normal effect of certain other beliefs. For example, anyone who believes John is tall is very likely also to believe someone is tall. Having the first belief is normally causally sufficient for having the second belief. And anyone who believes everyone in the room is tall and also believes John is in the room will very likely believe John is tall. The third belief is a normal effect of the first two. In short, the functionalist maintains that the proposition expressed by a given mental representation depends on the causal properties of the mental states in which that mental representation figures.

The concept that the semantic properties of mental representations are determined by aspects of their functional role is at the center of current work in the cognitive sciences. Nevertheless, the concept may not be true. Many philosophers who are unsympathetic to the cognitive turn in modern psychology doubt its truth, and many psychologists would probably reject it in the bald and unelaborated way that I have sketched it. Yet even in its skeletal form, there is this much to be said in its favor: It legitimizes the notion of mental representation, which has become increasingly important to theorizing in every branch of the cognitive sciences. Recent advances in formulating and testing hypotheses about the character of mental representations in fields ranging from phonetics to computer vision suggest that the concept of mental representation is fundamental to empirical theories of the mind.

The behaviorist has rejected the appeal to mental representation because it runs counter to his view of the explanatory mechanisms that can figure in psychological theories. Nevertheless, the science of mental representation is now flourishing. The history of science reveals that when a successful theory comes into conflict with a methodological scruple, it is generally the scruple that gives way. Accordingly the functionalist has relaxed the behaviorist constraints on psychological explanations. There is probably no better way to decide what is methodologically permissible in science than by investigating what successful science requires.

Chapter 13
What is functionalism?
Ned Block

It is doubtful whether doctrines known as 'functionalism' in fields as disparate as anthropology, literary criticism, psychology, and philosophy of psychology have anything in common but the name. Even in philosophy of psychology, the term is used in a number of distinct senses. The functionalisms of philosophy of psychology are, however, a closely knit group; indeed, they appear to have a common origin in the works of Aristotle (see Hartman, 1977, especially chap. 4).

Three functionalisms have been enormously influential in philosophy of mind and psychology:

Functional analysis. In this sense of the term, functionalism is a type of explanation and, derivatively, a research strategy, the research strategy of looking for explanations of that type. A functional explanation is one that relies on a decomposition of a system into its component parts; it explains the working of the system in terms of the capacities of the parts and the way the parts are integrated with one another. For example, we can explain how a factory can produce refrigerators by appealing to the capacities of the various assembly lines, their workers and machines, and the organization of these components. Robert Cummins (1975) describes functionalism in this sense. (See also Fodor, 1965, 1968a, 1968b; Dennett, 1975.)

Computation-representation functionalism. In this sense of the term, 'functionalism' applies to an important special case of functional explanation as defined above, namely, to psychological explanation seen as akin to providing a computer program for the mind. Whatever mystery our mental life may initially seem to have is dissolved by functional analysis of mental processes to the point where they are seen to be composed of computations as mechanical as the primitive operations of a digital computer— processes so stupid that appealing to them in psychological explanations involves no hint of question-begging. The key notions of functionalism in this sense are representation and computation. Psychological states are seen as systematically representing the world via a language of thought, and psychological processes are seen as computations involving these representations. Functionalism in this sense of the term is not explored here.

Ned Block, 'What is Functionalism?' In Ned Block (ed.), *Readings in Philosophy of Psychology*, vol. i (Cambridge: Harvard University Press, 1980).

Metaphysical functionalism. The last functionalism, the one that this article is about, is a theory of *the nature of the mind*, rather than a theory of psychological explanation. Metaphysical functionalists are concerned not with how mental states account for behavior, but rather with what they *are*. The functionalist answer to 'What are mental states?' is simply that mental states are functional states. Thus theses of metaphysical functionalism are sometimes described as functional state identity theses. The main concern of metaphysical functionalism is the same as that of behaviorism and physicalism. All three doctrines address themselves to such questions as 'What is pain?'—or at least to 'What is there in common to all pains in virtue of which they are pains?'

It is important to note that metaphysical functionalism is concerned (in the first instance) with mental state *types*, not tokens—with *pain*, for instance, and not with particular *pains*. (For further explanation of this distinction see Davidson, 1970.) Most functionalists are willing to allow that each *particular* pain is a physical state or event, and indeed that for each type of pain-feeling organism, there is (perhaps) a single type of physical state that realizes pain in that type of organism. Where functionalists differ with physicalists, however, is with respect to the question of what is common to all pains in virtue of which they are pains. The functionalist says the something in common is functional, while the physicalist says it is physical (and the behaviorist says it is behavioral).[1] Thus, in one respect, the disagreement between functionalists and physicalists (and behaviorists) is *metaphysical without being ontological.* Functionalists can be physicalists in allowing that all the entities (things, states, events, and so on) that exist are physical entities, denying only that what binds certain types of things together is a physical property.

Metaphysical functionalists characterize mental states in terms of their causal roles, particularly, in terms of their causal relations to sensory stimulations, behavioral outputs, and other mental states. Thus, for example, a metaphysical functionalist theory of pain might characterize pain in part in terms of its tendency to be caused by tissue damage, by its tendency to cause the desire to be rid of it, and by its tendency to produce action designed to separate the damaged part of the body from what is thought to cause the damage.

What I have said about metaphysical functionalism so far is rather vague, but, as

1. Discussions of functional state identity theses have sometimes concentrated on one or another weaker thesis in order to avoid issues about identity conditions on entities such as states or properties (see, for example, Block and Fodor, 1972. Consider the following theses:

(1) Pain = functional state *S*.

(2) Something is a pain just in case it is a (token of) *S*.

(3) The conditions under which *x* and *y* are both pains are the same as the conditions under which *x* and *y* are both tokens of *S*.

(1) is a full-blooded functional state identity thesis that entails (2) and (3). Theses of the form of (2) and (3) can be used to state what it is that all pains have in common in virtue of which they are pains.

will become clear, disagreements among metaphysical functionalists preclude easy characterization of the doctrine. Before going on to describe metaphysical functionalism in more detail, I shall briefly sketch some of the connections among the functionalist doctrines just enumerated. One connection is that functionalism in all the senses described has something to do with the notion of a Turing machine (described in the next section). Metaphysical functionalism often identifies mental states with Turing machine 'table states' (also described in the next section). Computation-representation functionalism sees psychological explanation as something like providing a computer program for the mind. Its aim is to give a functional analysis of mental capacities broken down into their component mechanical processes. If these mechanical processes are *algorithmic*, as is sometimes assumed (without much justification, in my view) then they will be Turing-computable as well (as the Church-Turing thesis assures us).[2] Functional analysis, however, is concerned with the notion of a Turing machine mainly in that providing something like a computer program for the mind is a special case of functional analysis.

Another similarity among the functionalisms mentioned is their relation to physical characterizations. The causal structures with which metaphysical functionalism identifies mental states are realizable by a vast variety of physical systems. Similarly, the information processing mechanisms postulated by a particular computation-representation functionalist theory could be realized hydraulically, electrically, or even mechanically. Finally, functional analysis would normally characterize a manufacturing process abstractly enough to allow a wide variety of types of machines (wood or metal, steam-driven or electrical), workers (human or robot or animal), and physical setups (a given number of assembly lines or half as many dual-purpose assembly lines). A third similarity is that each type of functionalism described legitimates at least one notion of functional equivalence. For example, for functional analysis, one sense of functional equivalence would be: has capacities that contribute in similar ways to the capacities of a whole.

In what follows, I shall try to give the reader a clearer picture of metaphysical functionalism. ('Functionalism' will be used to mean metaphysical functionalism in what follows.)

Machine versions of functionalism

Some versions of functionalism are couched in terms of the notion of a Turing machine, while others are not. A Turing machine is specified by two functions: one

2. Dennett (1975) and Rey (1979) make this appeal to the Church-Turing thesis. But if the mechanical processes involved analog rather than digital computation, then the processes could fail to the algorithmic in the sense required by the Church-Turing thesis. The experiments discussed in volume 2, part two, 'Imagery' suggest that mental images are (at least partially) analog representations, and that the computations that operate on images are (at least partially) analog operations.

from inputs and states to outputs, and one from inputs and states to states. A Turing machine has a finite number of states, inputs, and outputs, and the two functions specify a set of conditionals, one for each combination of state and input. The conditionals are of this form: if the machine is in state *S* and receives input *I*, it will then emit output *O* and go into next state *S′*. This set of conditionals is often expressed in the form of a machine table (see below). Any system that has a set of inputs, outputs, and states related in the way specified by the machine table is *described* by the machine table and is a *realization* of the abstract automaton specified by the machine table. (This definition actually characterizes a finite automaton, which is just one kind of Turing machine.)

One very simple version of machine functionalism states that each system that has mental states is described by at least one Turing machine table of a certain specifiable sort; it also states that each type of mental state of the system is identical to one of the machine table states specified in the machine table (see Putnam, 1967; Block and Fodor, 1972. Consider, for example, the Turing machine described in the following 'Coke machine' machine table (compare Nelson, 1975):

	S_1	S_2
nickel input	Emit no output Go to S_2	Emit a Coke Go to S_1
dime input	Emit a Coke Stay in S_1	Emit a Coke and a nickel Go to S_1

One can get a crude picture of the simple version of machine functionalism described above by considering the claim that S_1 = dime-desire, and S_2 = nickel-desire. Of course, no functionalist would claim that a Coke machine desires anything. Rather, the simple version of machine functionalism described above makes an analogous claim with respect to a much more complex machine table.

Machine versions of functionalism are useful for many purposes, but they do not provide the most general characterization of functionalism. One can achieve more generality by characterizing functionalism as the view that what makes a pain a pain (and, generally, what makes any mental state the mental state it is) is its having a certain causal role.[3] But this formulation buys generality at the price of vagueness.

3. Strictly speaking, even the causal role formulation is insufficiently general, as can be seen by noting that Turing machine functionalism is not a special case of causal role functionalism. Strictly speaking, none of the states of a Turing machine need cause any of the other states. All that is required for a physical system to satisfy a machine table is that the counterfactuals specified by the table are true of it. This can be accomplished by some causal agent outside the machine. Of course, one can always choose to speak of a *different* system, one that includes the causal agent as part of the machine, but that is irrelevant to my point.

A more precise formulation can be introduced as follows.[4] Let *T* be a psychological theory (of either common sense or scientific psychology) that tells us (among other things) the relations among pain, other mental states, sensory inputs, and behavioral outputs. Reformulate *T* so that it is a single conjunctive sentence with all mental state terms as singular terms; for example, 'is angry' becomes 'has anger'. Let *T* so reformulated be written as

$$T(s_1 \ldots s_n)$$

where $s_1 \ldots s_n$ are terms that designate mental states. Replace each mental state term with a variable and prefix existential quantifiers to form the Ramsey sentence of the theory

$$\exists x_1 \ldots x_n T(x_1 \ldots x_n).$$

Now, if x_i is the variable that replaced 'pain', we can define 'pain' as follows:

$$y \text{ has pain if and only if}$$
$$\exists x_1 \ldots x_n [T(x_1 \ldots x_n) \;\&\; y \text{ has } x_i].$$

That is, one has pain just in case he has a state that has certain relations to other states that have certain relations to one another (and to inputs and outputs; I have omitted reference to inputs and outputs for the sake of simplicity). It will be convenient to think of pain as the property expressed by the predicate '*x* has pain', that is, to think of pain as the property ascribed to someone in saying that he has pain.[5] Then, relative to theory *T*, pain can be identified with the property expressed by the predicate

$$\exists x_1 \ldots x_n [T(x_1 \ldots x_n) \;\&\; y \text{ has } x_i].$$

For example, take *T* to be the ridiculously simple theory that pain is caused by pin pricks and causes worry and the emission of loud noises, and worry, in turn, causes brow wrinkling. The Ramsey sentence of *T* is

$$\exists x_1 \exists x_2 (x_1 \text{ is caused by pin pricks and causes } x_2 \text{ and emission of loud noises } \& \; x_3 \text{ causes brow wrinkling}).$$

Relative to *T*, pain is the property expressed by the predicate obtained by adding a conjunct as follows:

$$\exists x_1 \exists x_2 [(x_1 \text{ is caused by pin pricks and causes } x_2 \text{ and emission of loud noises } \& \; x_2 \text{ causes brow wrinkling}) \;\&\; y \text{ has } x_1].$$

4. Formulations of roughly this sort were first advanced by Lewis, 1966, 1970, 1972; Martin, 1966. (See also Harman, 1973; Grice, 1975; Field, 1978; Block, 1978.)

5. See Field, 1978, for an alternative convention.

That is, pain is the property that one has when one has a state that is caused by pin pricks, and causes emission of loud noises, and also causes something else, that, in turn, causes brow wrinkling.

We can make this somewhat less cumbersome by letting an expression of the form '%*xFx*' be a singular term meaning the same as an expression of the form 'the property of being an x such that x is F', that is, 'being F'. So %x(x is bigger than a mouse & x is smaller than an elephant) = being bigger than a mouse and smaller than an elephant. Using this notation, we can say

pain = %$y\exists x_1 \exists x_2$[(x_1 is caused by pin pricks and causes x_2 and emission of loud noises & x_2 causes brow wrinking) & y has x_2],

rather than saying that pain is the property expressed by the predicate

$\exists x_1 \exists x_2$[(x_1 is caused by pin pricks and causes x_2 and emission of loud noises & x_2 causes brow wrinkling) & y has x_1].

It may be useful to consider a non-mental example. It is sometimes supposed that automotive terms like 'valve-lifter' or 'carburetor' are functional terms. Anything that lifts valves in an engine with a certain organizational structure is a valve-lifter. ('Camshaft', on the other hand, is a 'structural' term, at least relative to 'valve-lifter'; a camshaft is *one* kind of device for lifting valves.)

Consider the 'theory' that says: 'The carburetor mixes gasoline and air and sends the mixture to the ignition chamber, which, in turn . . .' Let us consider 'gasoline' and 'air' to be input terms, and let x_1 replace 'carburetor', and x_2 replace 'ignition chamber'. Then the property of being a carburetor would be

% y $\exists x_1 \ldots x_n$[(The x_1 mixes gasoline and air and sends the mixture to the x_2, which, in turn . . .) & y is an x_1].

That is, being a carburetor = being what mixes gasoline and air and sends the mixture to something else, which, in turn . . .

This identification, and the identification of pain with the property one has when one is in a state that is caused by pin pricks and causes loud noises and also causes something else that causes brow wrinkling, would look less silly if the theories of pain (and carburetion) were more complex. But the essential idea of functionalism, as well as its major weakness, can be seen clearly in the example, albeit rather starkly. Pain is identified with an abstract causal property tied to the real world only via its relations, direct and indirect, to inputs and outputs. The weakness is that it seems so clearly conceivable that something could have that causal property, yet *not be* a pain. This point is discussed in detail in 'Troubles with Functionalism' (Block, 1978 see Shoemaker, 1975, and Lycan, 1979 for critiques of such arguments).

Functionalism and behaviorism

Many functionalists (such as David Lewis, D. M. Armstrong, and J. J. C. Smart) consider themselves descendants of behaviorists, who attempted to define a mental state in terms of what behaviors would tend to be emitted in the presence of specified stimuli. E.g., the desire for an ice-cream cone might be identified with a set of dispositions, including the disposition to reach out and grasp an ice-cream cone if one is proffered, other things being equal. But, as functionalist critics have emphasized, the phrase 'other things being equal' is behavioristically illicit, because it can only be filled in with references to *other mental states* (see Putnam, 1963, the point dates back at least to Chisholm, 1957, chap. 11; and Geach, 1957, p. 8). One who desires an ice-cream cone will be disposed to reach for it only if he *knows* it is an ice-cream cone (and not, in general, if he believes it to be a tube of axle-grease), and only if he does not *think* that taking an ice-cream cone would conflict with *other desires* of more importance to him (such as the desire to lose weight, avoid obligations, or avoid cholesterol). The final nail in the behaviorist coffin was provided by the well-known 'perfect actor' family of counter-examples. As Putnam argued in convincing detail (see Putnam, 1963), it is possible to imagine a community of perfect actors who, by virtue of lawlike regularities, have exactly the behavioral dispositions envisioned by the behaviorists to be associated with absence of pain, even though they do in fact have pain. This shows that no behavioral disposition is a necessary condition of pain, and an exactly analogous example of perfect pain-pretenders shows that no behavioral disposition is a sufficient condition of pain, either.

Functionalism in all its forms differs from behaviorism in two major respects. First, while behaviorists defined mental states in terms of stimuli and responses, they did not think mental states were *themselves* causes of the responses and effects of the stimuli. Behaviorists took mental states to be 'pure dispositions.' Gilbert Ryle, for example, emphasized that 'to possess a dispositional property is not to be in a particular state, or to undergo a particular change' (1949, p. 43). Brittleness, according to Ryle, is not a *cause* of breaking, but merely the fact of breaking easily. Similarly, to attribute pain to someone is not to attribute a cause or effect of anything, but simply to say what he would do in certain circumstances. Behaviorists are fictionalists about the mental, hence they cannot allow that mental states have causal powers. Functionalists, by contrast, claim it to be an advantage of their account that it 'allows experiences to be something real, and so to be the effects of their occasions, and the causes of their manifestations (Lewis, 1966, p. 166). Armstrong says that '[when I think] it is not simply that I would speak or act if some conditions that are unfulfilled were to be fulfilled. Something is currently going on. Rylean behaviorism denies this, and so it is unsatisfactory' (1970).

The second difference between functionalism and behaviorism is that functionalists emphasize not just the connections between pain and its stimuli and responses, but also its connections to other mental states. Notice, for example, that any full characterization of S_1 in the machine table above would have to refer to S_2 in one way or another, since it is one of the defining characteristics of S_1 that anything in S_1 goes into S_2 when it receives a nickel input. Another example, recall that the Ramsey sentence formulation identifies pain with

$$\% y \exists x_1 \ldots x_n [T(x_1 \ldots x_n) \ \& \ y \text{ has } x_i]$$

where the variable x_i replaced 'pain', and the rest of $x_1 \ldots x_n$ replaced the other mental state terms in T. So the functionalist expression that designates pain includes a specification of the relations between pain and all the other mental states related to it, and to inputs and outputs as well. (The role of inputs and outputs would have been better indicated had I written T as

$$T(s_1 \ldots s_n, o_1 \ldots o_m, i_1 \ldots i_k),$$

explicitly including terms for inputs and outputs).

Behaviorism is a vague doctrine, and one that is sometimes defined in a way that would make functionalism a version of behaviorism. Even functionalists have offered definitions of 'behaviorism' that would make functionalists behaviorists. For example, if we defined 'behaviorism' as the doctrine that mental states (such as pain) can be characterized in nonmental terms, versions of functionalism along the lines of the Ramsey sentence version sketched above (held by Lewis, Armstrong, Smart, and Sydney Shoemaker) would qualify as versions of behaviorism (since all of the original mental state terms are replaced by variables in the Ramsey sentence). Many other definitions of 'behaviorism' count functionalism as a type of behaviorism. But it would be ludicrously literal-minded to take such definitions very seriously. Clear and general formulations of functionalism were not available until recently, so standard definitions of behaviorism could hardly be expected to draw the boundaries between behaviorism and functionalism with perfect accuracy. Furthermore, given an explicit definition of behaviorism, logical ingenuity can often disguise a functionalist account so as to fit the definition (see Bealer, 1978; Thomas, 1978, for accomplishments of this rather dubious variety). Definitions of behaviorism that count functionalism as behaviorist are misguided precisely *because* they blur the distinctions between functionalism and behaviorism just sketched. A characterization of pain can hardly be counted as behaviorist if it allows that a system could behave (and be disposed to behave) exactly as if it were in pain in all possible circumstances, yet not be in pain.[6]

6. Characterizations of mental states along the lines of the Ramsey sentence formulation presented above wear their incompatibility with behaviorism on their sleeves in that they involve explicit quantification over mental states. Both Thomas and Bealer provide ways of transforming functionalist definitions or identifications so as to disguise such transparent incompatibility.

Is functionalism reductionist?

Functionalists sometimes formulate their claim by saying that mental states can only be characterized in terms of other mental states. For instance, a person desires such and such if he would do so and so if he believed doing so and so will get him such and such, and if he believed doing so and so would not conflict with other desires. This much functionalism brings in no reductionism, but functionalists have rarely stopped there. Most regard mental terms as eliminable *all at once.* Armstrong says, for example, 'The logical dependence of purpose on perception and belief, and of perception and belief upon purpose is not circularity in definition. What it shows is that the corresponding concepts must be introduced *together or not at all*' (1977, p. 88). Shoemaker says, 'On one construal of it, functionalism in the philosophy of mind is the doctrine that mental or psychological terms are in principle eliminable in a certain way' (1975). Lewis is more explicit, using a formulation much like the Ramsey sentence formulation given above, which designates mental states by expressions that do not contain any mental terminology (see Lewis, 1972 for details).

The same sort of point applies to machine functionalism. Putnam says, 'The S_i, to repeat, are specified only *implicitly* by the description' (1967). In the Coke machine automation described above, the only antecedently understood terms (other than 'emit', 'go to', and so on) are the input and output terms, 'nickel', 'dime', and 'Coke'. The state terms 'S_1' and 'S_2' in the Coke machine automaton—as in every Turing machine—are given their content entirely in terms of input and output terms (+ logical terms).

Thus functionalism could be said to reduce mentality to input-output structures (note that S_1 and S_2 can have any natures at all, so long as these natures connect them to one another and to the acceptance of nickels and dimes and disbursement of nickels and Cokes as described in the machine table). But functionalism gives us reduction without elimination. Functionalism is not fictionalist about mentality, for each of the functionalist ways of characterizing mental states in terms of inputs and outputs commits itself to the existence of mental states by the use of quantification over mental states, or some equivalent device.[7]

The varieties of functionalism

Thus far, I have characterized functionalism without adverting to any of the confusing disagreements among functionalists. I believe that my characterization is correct, but its application to the writings of some functionalists is not immediately

7. The machine table states of a finite automation can be defined explicitly in terms of inputs and outputs by a Ramsey sentence method, or by the method described in Thomas (1978). Both of these methods involve one or another sort of commitment to the existence of the machine table states.

apparent. Indeed, the functionalist literature (or, rather, what is generally, and I think correctly, regarded as the functionalist literature) exhibits some bizarre disagreements, the most surprising of which has to do with the relation between functionalism and physicalism. Some philosophers (Armstrong, 1968, 1977, 1970; Lewis, 1966, 1972, 1969; Smart, 1971) take functionalism as showing that physicalism is probably *true*, while others (Fodor, 1965; Putnam, 1966; Block and Fodor, 1972) take functionalism as showing that physicalism is probably *false*. This is the most noticeable difference among functionalist writings. I shall argue that the Lewis-Armstrong-Smart camp is mistaken in holding that functionalism supports an interesting version of physicalism, and furthermore, that the functionalist insight that they share with the Putnam-Fodor-Harman camp *does* have the consequence that physicalism is probably false. I shall begin with a brief historical sketch.

While functionalism dates back to Aristotle, in its current form it has two main contemporary sources. (A third source, Sellars's and, later, Harman's views on meaning as conceptual role, has also been influential.)

Source 1 Putnam (1960) compared the mental states of a person with the machine table states of a Turing machine. He then rejected any identification of mental states with machine table states, but in a series of articles over the years he moved closer to such an identification, a pattern culminating in 'Psychological Predicates' (1967). In this article, Putnam came close to advocating a view—which he defended in his philosophy of mind lectures in the late 1960s—that mental states can be identified with machine table states, or rather disjunctions of machine table states. (See Thomas, 1978, for a defence of roughly this view; see Block and Fodor, 1972 and Putnam, 1975, for a critique of such views.)

Fodor (1965, 1968a) developed a similar view (though it was not couched in terms of Turing machines) in the context of a functional-analysis view of psychological explanation (see Cummins, 1975). Putnam's and Fodor's positions were characterized in part by their opposition to physicalism, the view that each *type* of mental state is a physical state.[8] Their argument is at its clearest with regard to the simple version of Turing machine functionalism described above, the view that pain, for instance, is a machine table state. What physical state could be common to all and only realizations of S_1 of the Coke machine automation described above? The Coke machine could be made of an enormous variety of materials, and it

8. 'Physical state' could be spelled out for these purposes as the state of something's having a first-order property that is expressible by a predicate of a true physical theory. Of course, this analysis requires some means of characterizing physical theory. A first-order property is one whose definition does not require quantification over properties. A second-order property is one whose definition requires quantification over first-order properties (but not other properties). The physicalist doctrine that functionalists argue against is the doctrine that mental properties are *first-order* physical properties. Functionalists need not deny that mental properties are second-order physical properties (in various senses of that phrase).

could operate via an enormous variety of mechanisms; it could even be a 'scattered object,' with parts all over the world, communicating by radio. If someone suggests a putative physical state common to all and only realizations of S_1, it is a simple matter to dream up a nomologically possible machine that satisfies the machine table but does not have the designated physical state. Of course, it is one thing to *say* this and another thing to prove it, but the claim has such overwhelming prima facie plausibility that the burden of proof is on the critic to come up with reason for thinking otherwise. Published critiques (Kalke, 1969; Gendron, 1971; Kim, 1972; Nelson, 1976; Causey, 1977) have in my view failed to meet this challenge.

If we could formulate a machine table for a human, it would be absurd to identify any of the machine table states with a type of *brain* state, since presumably all manner of brainless machines could be described by that table as well. So if pain is a machine table state, it is not a brain state. It should be mentioned, however, that it is possible to *specify* a sense in which a functional state *F* can be said to be physical. For example, *F* might be said to be physical if every system that in fact has *F* is a physical object, or, alternatively, if every realization of *F* (that is, every state that plays the causal role specified by *F*) is a physical state. Of course, the doctrines of 'physicalism' engendered by such stipulations should not be confused with the version of physicalism that functionalists have argued against (see note 8).

Jaegwon Kim objects that 'the less the physical basis of the nervous system of some organisms resembles ours, the less temptation there will be for ascribing to them sensations or other phenomenal events' (1972). But his examples depend crucially on considering creatures whose functional organization is much more primitive than ours. He also points out that 'the mere fact that the physical bases of two nervous systems are different in material composition or physical organization with respect to a certain scheme of classification does not entail that they cannot be in the same physical state with respect to a different scheme.' Yet the functionalist does not (or, better, should not) claim that functionalism *entails* the falsity of physicalism, but only that the burden of proof is on the physicalist. Kim (1972) and Lewis (1969; see also Causey, 1977, p. 149) propose species-specific identities: pain is one brain state in dogs and another in people. As should be clear from this introduction, however, this move sidesteps the main metaphysical question: 'What is common to the pains of dogs and people (and all other pains) in virtue of which they are pains?'

Source II The second major strand in current functionalism descends from Smart's early article on mind-body identity (1959). Smart worried about the following objection to mind-body identity: So what if pain is a physical state? It can still have a variety of phenomenal *properties*, such as sharpness, and these phenomenal properties may be irreducibly mental. Then Smart and other identity theorists would be stuck with a 'double aspect' theory: pain is a physical state, but it has both physical and irreducibly mental properties. He attempted to dispel this worry by analyzing mental concepts in a way that did not carry with it any commitment to the mental or physical status of the concepts.[9] These 'topic-neutral analyses,' as he called them, specified mental states in terms of the stimuli that caused them (and the behavior that they caused, although Smart was less explicit about this). His analysis of first-person sensation avowals were of the form 'There is something going on in me which is like what goes on when . . . ,' where the dots are filled in by descriptions of typical stimulus situations. In these analyses, Smart broke decisively with behaviorism in insisting that mental states were real things with causal efficacy; Armstrong, Lewis, and others later improved his analyses, making explicit the behavioral effects clauses, and including mental causes and effects. Lewis's formulation, especially, is now very widely accepted among Smart's and Armstrong's adherents (Smart, 1971, also accepts it). In a recent review in the *Australasian Journal of Philosophy*, Alan Reeves declares, 'I think that there is some consensus among Australian materialists that Lewis has provided an exact statement of their viewpoint' (1978).

Smart used his topic-neutral analyses only to defeat an a priori objection to the identity theory. As far as an argument *for* the identity theory went, he relied on considerations of simplicity. It was absurd, he thought, to suppose that there should be a perfect correlation between mental states and brain states and yet that the states could be nonidentical. (See Kim, 1966; Brandt and Kim, 1967, for an argument against Smart; but see also Block, 1971, 1979; and Causey, 1972, 1977, for arguments against Kim and Brandt.) But Lewis and Smart's Australian allies (notably D. M. Armstrong) went beyond Smart, arguing that something like topic-neutral analyses could be used to argue *for* mind-brain identity. In its most persuasive version (Lewis's), the argument for physicalism is that pain can be seen (by conceptual analysis) to be the occupant of causal role *R*; a certain neural state will be found to be the occupant of causal role *R*; thus it follows that pain = that neural state. Functionalism comes in by way of showing that the meaning of 'pain' is the same as a certain definite description that spells out causal role *R*.

9. As Kim has pointed out (1972), Smart did not need these analyses to avoid 'double aspect' theories. Rather, a device Smart introduces elsewhere in the same paper will serve the purpose. Smart raises the objection that if afterimages are brain states, then since an after-image can be orange, the identity theorist would have to conclude that a brain state can be orange. He replies by saying that the identity theorist need only identify the *experience of having an orange afterimage* with a brain state; this state is not orange, and so no orange brain states need exist. Images, says Smart, are not really mental entities; it is experiences of images that are the real mental entities. In a similar manner, Kim notes, the identity theorist can 'bring' the phenomenal properties into the mental states themselves; for example, the identity theorist can concern himself with states such as John's having a sharp pain; this state is not sharp, and so the identity theorist is not committed to sharp brain states. This technique does the trick, although of course it commits its perpetrators to the unfortunate doctrine that pains do not exist, or at least that they are not mental entities; rather, it is the havings of sharp pains and the like that are the real mental entities.

Lewis and Armstrong argue from functionalism to the truth of physicalism because they have a 'functional specification' version of functionalism. Pain is a functionally specified state, perhaps a functionally specified brain state, according to them. Putnam and Fodor argue from functionalism to the falsity of physicalism because they say there are functional states (or functional properties), and that mental states (or properties) are identical to these functional states. No functional state is likely to be a physical state.

The difference between a functional state identity claim and a functional specification claim can be made clearer as follows. Recall that the functional state identity claim can be put thus:

$$\text{pain} = \%y\exists x_1 \ldots \exists x_n[T(x_1 \ldots x_n) \;\&\; y \text{ has } x_1];$$

where x_1 is the variable that replaced 'pain'. A functional specification view could be stated as follows:[10]

$$\text{pain} = \text{the } x_1\exists x_2 \ldots \exists x_n T(x_1 \ldots x_n).$$

In terms of the example mentioned earlier, the functional state identity theorist would identify pain with the property one has when one is in a state that is caused by pin pricks and causes loud noises and also something else that causes brow wrinkling. The functional specifier would define pain as *the thing* that is caused by pin pricks and causes loud noises and also something else that causes brow wrinkling.

According to the functional specifier, the thing that has causal role R (for example, the thing that is caused by pin pricks and causes something else and so forth) might be a state of one physical type in one case and a state of another physical type in another case. The functional state identity theorist is free to accept this claim as well, but what he insists on is that *pain* is not identical to a physical state. What pains have in common in virtue of which they are pains is causal role R, not any physical property.

In terms of the carburetor example, functional state identity theorists say that being a carburetor = being what mixes gas and air and sends the mixture to something else, which, in turn ... Functional specifiers say that the carburetor is *the thing* that mixes gas and air and sends the mixture to something else, which, in turn ... What the difference comes to is that the functional specifier says that the carburetor is a type of physical object, though perhaps one type of physical object in a Mercedes and another type of physical object in a Ford. The functional state identity theorist can agree with this, but he insists that *what it is to be a carburetor* is to have a certain functional role, not a certain physical structure.

10. The functional specification view I give here is a much simplified version of Lewis's formulation (see Lewis, 1972).

At this point, it may seem to the reader that the odd disagreement about whether functionalism justifies physicalism or the negation of physicalism owes simply to ambiguities in 'functionalism' and 'physicalism'. In particular, it may seem that the functional specification view justifies *token* physicalism (the doctrine that every particular pain is a physical state token), while the functional state identity view justifies the negation of *type* physicalism (the doctrine that *pain* is a type of physical state).

This response oversimplifies matters greatly, however. First, it is textually mistaken, since those functional specifiers who see the distinction between type and token materialism clearly have type materialism in mind. For example, Lewis says, 'A dozen years or so ago, D. M. Armstrong and I (independently) proposed a materialist theory of mind that joins claims of *type-type* psychophysical identity with a behaviorist or functionalist way of characterizing mental states such as pain' (1972; emphasis added). More important, the functional specification doctrine *commits* its proponents to a functional state identity claim. Since the latter doctrine counts against type physicalism, so does the former. It is easy to see that the functional specification view commits its proponents to a functional state identity claim. According to functional specifiers, it is a conceptual truth that pain is the state with causal role *R*. But then *what it is to be a pain* is to have causal role *R*. Thus the functional specifiers are committed to the view that what pains have in common by virtue of which they are pains is their causal role, rather than their physical nature. (Again, Lewis is fairly clear about this: 'Our view is that the concept of pain . . . is the concept of a state that occupies a certain causal role.')

I suspect that what has gone wrong in the case of *many* functional specifiers is simply failure to appreciate the distinction between type and token for mental states. If pain in Martians is one physical state, pain in humans another, and so on for pain in every pain-feeling organism, then each particular pain is a token of some physical type. This is token physicalism. Perhaps functional specifiers ought to be *construed* as arguing for token physicalism (even though Lewis and others explicitly say they are arguing for type physicalism). I shall give three arguments against such a construal. First, as functional state identity theorists have often pointed out, a *non*physical state could conceivably have a causal role typical of a mental state. In functional specification terms, there might be a creature in which pain is a functionally specified *soul* state. So functionalism opens up the possibility that even if *our* pains are physical, other pains might not be. In the light of this point, it seems that the support that functionalism gives even to token physicalism is equivocal. Second, the *major* arguments for token physicalism involve no functionalism at all (see Davidson, chapter 5, and Fodor, chapter 6). Third, token physicalism is a much weaker doctrine than physicalists have typically wanted.

In sum, functional specifiers *say* that functionalism supports physicalism, but they are committed to a functionalist answer, not a physicalist answer, to the question of what all pains have in common in virtue of which they are pains. And if what all pains have in common in virtue of which they are pains is a functional property, it is very unlikely that pain is coextensive with any physical state. If, on the contrary, functional specifiers have *token* physicalism in mind, functionalism provides at best equivocal support for the doctrine; better support is available elsewhere; and the doctrine is a rather weak form of physicalism to boot.

Lewis's views deserve separate treatment. He insists that pain is a brain state only because he takes 'pain' to be a nonrigid designator meaning 'the state with such and such causal role'.[11] Thus, in Lewis's view, to say that pain is a brain state should not be seen as saying what all pains have in common in virtue of which they are pains, just as saying that the winning number is 37 does not suggest that 37 is what all winning numbers have in common. Many of Lewis's opponents disagree about the rigidity of 'pain', but the dispute is irrelevant to our purposes, since Lewis does take 'having pain' to be rigid, and so he does accept (he tells me) a functional property identity view: having pain = having a state with such and such a typical causal role. I think that most functional state identity theorists would be as willing to rest on the thesis that having pain is a functional property as on the thesis that pain is a functional state.

In conclusion, while there is considerable disagreement among the philosophers whom I have classified as metaphysical functionalists, there is a single insight about the nature of the mind to which they are all committed.

References

Armstrong, D. M. 1968. *A Materialist Theory of Mind.* London: Routledge & Kegan Paul.

—— 1970. 'The Nature of Mind' In C. V. Borst, ed., *The Mind/Brain Identity Theory.* London: Macmillan.

—— 1977. 'The Causal Theory of the Mind.' In *Neue Heft für Philosophie*, no. 11, pp. 82–95. Vendenhoek and Ruprecht.

Bealer, G. 1978. 'An Inconsistency in Functionalism.' *Synthese* 38:333–372.

Block, N. 1971. 'Physicalism and Theoretical Identity.' Ph.D. dissertation, Harvard University.

—— 1978. 'Troubles with Functionalism.' In C. W. Savage, ed., *Minnesota Studies in Philosophy of Science.* Vol. 9. Minneapolis: University of Minnesota Press.

—— 1979. 'Reductionism.' In *Encyclopedia of Bioethics.* New York: Macmillan.

Block, N., and J. A. Fodor. 1972. 'What Psychological States Are Not.' *Philosophical Review* 81, no. 2:159–182.

Brandt, R., and J. Kim. 1967. 'The Logic of the Identity Theory.' *Journal of Philosophy* 64, no. 17:515–537.

11. A rigid designator is a singular term that names the same thing in each possible world. The color of the sky' is nonrigid, since it names blue in worlds where the sky is blue, and red in worlds where the sky is red. 'Blue' is rigid, since it names blue in all possible worlds, even in worlds where the sky is red.

Causey, R. 1972. 'Attribute Identities in Micro-reductions.' *Journal of Philosophy* 69, no. 14:407–422.
—— 1977. *Unity of Science.* Dordrecht: Reidel.
Chisholm, R. M. 1957. *Perceiving.* Ithaca: Cornell University Press.
Cummins, R. 1975. 'Functional Analysis.' *Journal of Philosophy* 72, no. 20:741–764.
Davidson, D. 1970. 'Oriental Events.' In LiFoster and J. W. Swanson, eds., *Experience and Theory.* Amherst: University of Massachusettes Press; 79–101. Included in section 11 of this volume
Dennett, D. 1975. 'Why the Law of Effect Won't Go Away.' *Journal for the Theory of Social Behavior* 5:169–187.
Field, H. 1978. 'Mental Representation.' *Erkenntniss* 13:9–61.
Fodor, J. A. 1965. 'Explanations in Psychology.' In M. Black, ed., *Philosophy in America.* London: Routledge & Kegan Paul.
—— 1968a. 'The Appeal to Tacit Knowledge in Psychological Explanation.' *Journal of Philosophy* 65:627–640.
—— 1968b. *Psychological Explanation.* New York: Random House.
Geach, P. 1957. *Mental Acts.* London: Routledge & Kegan Paul.
Gendron, B. 1971. 'On the Relation of Neurological and Psychological Theories: A Critique of the Hardware Thesis.' In R. C. Buck and R. S. Cohen, eds., *Boston Studies in the Philosophy of Science.* Vol. 8. Dordrecht: Reidel.
Grice, H. P. 1975. 'Method in Philosophical Psychology (from the Banal to the Bizarre).' *Proceedings and Addresses of the American Philosophical Association.* Newark, Del.: American Philosophical Association.
Harman, G. 1973. *Thought.* Princeton: Princeton University Press.
Hartman, E. 1977. *Substance, Body and Soul.* Princeton: Princeton University Press.
Kalke, W. 1969. 'What Is Wrong with Fodor and Putnam's Functionalism?' *Nous* 3: 83–93.
Kim, J. 1966. 'On the Psycho-physical Identity Theory.' *American Philosophical Quarterly* 3, no. 3:227–235.
—— 1972. 'Phenomenal Properties, Psychophysical Law, and the Identity Theory.' *Monist* 56, no. 2:177–192.
Lewis, D. 1966. 'An Argument for the Identity Theory.' Reprinted in D. Rosenthal, ed., *Materialism and the Mind-Body Problem.* Englewood Cliffs, N.J.: Prentice-Hall, 1971. (See Chapter 10 of this volume.)
—— 1969. 'Review of *Art, Mind and Religion.*' *Journal of Philosophy* 66, no. 1:23–35.
—— 1970. 'How to Define Theoretical Terms.' *Journal of Philosophy* 67, no. 13:427–444.
—— 1972. 'Psychophysical and Theoretical Identification.' *Australasian Journal of Philosophy* 50, no. 3:249–258.
Lycan, W. 1979. 'A New Lilliputian Argument against Machine Functionalism.' *Philosophical Studies.*
Martin, R. M. 1966. 'On Theoretical Constants and Ramsey Constants.' *Philosophy of Science* 31:1–13.
Nagel, T. 1970. 'Armstrong on the Mind.' *Philosophical Review* 79:394–403.
Nelson, R. J. 1975. 'Behaviorism, Finite Automata and Stimulus Response Theory.' *Theory and Decision* 6:249–267.
—— 1976. 'Mechanism, Functionalism and the Identity Theory.' *Journal of Philosophy* 73, no. 13:365–386.
Putnam, H. 1960. 'Minds and machines.' In S. Hook, ed., *Dimensions of Mind.* New York: New York University Press.

—— 1963. 'Brains and Behavior.' Reprinted in *Mind, Language, and Reality: Philosophical Papers*. Vol. 2. London: Cambridge University Press, 1975. (See Chapter 6 of this volume.)

—— 1966. 'The Mental Life of Some Machines.' Reprinted in *Mind, Language and Reality: Philosophical Papers*. Vol. 2. London: Cambridge University Press, 1975.

—— 1967. 'The Nature of Mental States' (originally published as 'Psychological Predicates'). In W. H. Capitan and D. D. Merrill, eds., *Art, Mind, and Religion*. Pittsburgh: University of Pittsburgh Press. (See Chapter 11 of this volume.)

—— 1970. 'On Properties.' In *Mathematics, Matter and Method: Philosophical Papers*. Vol. 1. London: Cambridge University Press.

—— 1975. 'Philosophy and Our Mental Life.' In *Mind, Language and Reality: Philosophical Papers*. Vol. 2. London: Cambridge University Press.

Reeves, A. 1978. 'Review of W. Matson, *Sentience*.' *Australasian Journal of Philosophy* 56, no. 2 (August): 189–192.

Rey, G. 1979. 'Functionalism and the Emotions.' In A. Rorty, ed., *Explaining Emotions*. Berkeley and Los Angeles: University of California Press.

Ryle, G. 1949. *The Concept of Mind*. London: Hutchinson.

Sellars, W. 1968. *Science and Metaphysics*. London: Routledge & Kegan Paul, chap. 6.

Shoemaker, S. 1975. 'Functionalism and Qualia.' *Philosophical Studies* 27:271–315: Included in this volume.

Smart, J. J. C. 1959. 'Sensations and Brain Processes.' *Philosophical Review* 68:141–156.

—— 1971. 'Reports of Immediate Experience.' *Synthese* 22:346–359.

Thomas, S. 1978. *The Formal Mechanics of Mind*. Ithaca: Cornell University Press.

Questions

1. In what sense might functionalism be seen as a natural successor to behaviorism?
2. How does the kind of identity theory advanced by David Lewis differ from that advanced (in Chapter 8) by J. J. C. Smart in Part II? Which version is more appealing?
3. What is 'multiple realizability'? What considerations tell in favor of multiple realizability, and what implications might these have for the identity theory?
4. Ned Block distinguishes two types of functionalism. Explain the distinction and evaluate each form.
5. Does functionalism imply materialism? Could Descartes, for instance, accept functionalist arguments while (consistently) remaining a dualist?
6. What do you think might account for the popularity of functionalism? In evaluating functionalism, how much weight should be given to the fact that many psychologists and neuroscientists accept the functionalist picture?
7. Functionalism aims to provide a solution to the mind—body problem. Does it?
8. What is 'folk psychology', and what relation does folk psychology bear to the science of psychology?
9. Both psychologists and neuroscientists tell us they study the mind, yet the subject matter of psychology seems, on the face of it, very different than the subject matter of the neurosciences. What is going on here?
10. How might a functionalist account for the qualitative side of conscious experiences?

Suggested readings

Functionalism may have had its roots in Aristotle (see Nussbaum and Rorty 1992), but its modern incarnation stems from the Putnam essay (Chapter 11) reprinted here. Links between functionalism and computation can be discerned in Putnam's earlier (1960) discussion of 'minds and machines'. Fodor (1968) provides a sustained defense of functionalism in psychology, and spins this into an account of what were traditionally called mental faculties in Fodor (1987). Fodor (1975) defends the thesis that a functional psychology requires the postulation of a biologically built-in 'language of thought'. Cummins (1983) and Harman (1973) develop related but independent views. Biro and Shahan (1982) provides assorted perspectives on functionalism. Shoemaker (1975) offers a functionalist take on mental qualities (the *qualia*), to which Block (1978) is a response. Lycan (1981) begins a functionalist counter-offensive. Armstrong (1968) and Lewis (1972) and (1980) develop their own brand of functionalism sketched by Lewis in Chapter 10. Heil (1998: chap. 4) provides an introduction to functionalism useful to readers with limited philosophical backgrounds.

Maloney (1999) provides a succinct on-line characterization of functionalism that includes a bibliography and links to more extended discussions. Chalmers's (2001) on-line bibliography cites countless books and papers devoted to functionalism.

Functionalism

Armstrong, D. M. (1968), *A Materialist Theory of the Mind*, London: Routledge & Kegan Paul.

Biro, J. I., and R. W. Shahan, eds. (1982), *Mind, Brain, and Function*. Norman, OK: University of Oklahoma Press.

Block, N. J. (1978), 'Troubles with Functionalism'. In Savage 1978: 261–325. Reprinted in Block 1980: 268–305.

—— ed. (1980), *Readings in Philosophy of Psychology*. Cambridge, MA: Harvard University Press.

Chalmers, D. J. (2001), *Contemporary Philosophy of Mind: An Annotated Bibliography* <http://www.u.arizona.edu/~chalmers/biblio.html> Tucson, AZ: University of Arizona.

Cummins, R. (1983), *The Nature of Psychological Explanation*. Cambridge, MA: MIT Press.

Fodor, J. A. (1968), *Psychological Explanation: An Introduction to the Philosophy of Psychology*. New York: Random House.

—— (1975), *The Language of Thought*. New York: T. Y. Crowell.

—— (1987), *The Modularity of Mind*. Cambridge, MA: MIT Press.

Harman, G. (1973), *Thought*. Princeton: Princeton University Press.

Heil, J. (1998), *Philosophy of Mind: A Contemporary Introduction*. London: Routledge.

Hook, S., ed. (1960), *Dimensions of Mind*. New York: Collier Books.

Lewis, D. K. (1972), 'Psychophysical and Theoretical Identifications', *Australasian Journal of Philosophy* 50: 249–58. Reprinted in Block (1980): 207–15.

—— (1980), 'Mad Pain and Martian Pain'. In Block (1980): 216–22. Reprinted with a 'Postscript' in Lewis 1983: 122–32.

Lewis, D. K. (1983), *Philosophical Papers*, vol. 1. New York: Oxford University Press.

Lycan, W. G. (1981), 'Form, Function, and Feel', *Journal of Philosophy* 78: 24–50.

Maloney, C. (1999), 'Functionalism'. In Wilson and Keil 1999.

Nussbaum, M. C., and A. O. Rorty, eds. (1992), *Essays on Aristotle's* De Anima. Oxford: Clarendon Press.

Putnam, H. (1960), 'Minds and Machines'. In Hook 1960: 138–64. Reprinted in Putnam 1975: 362–85.

——(1975), *Mind, Language and Reality* (Philosphical Papers, vol. 2), Cambridge: Cambridge University Press

Savage, C. W., ed. (1978), *Perception and Cognition: Issues in the Foundations of Psychology* (Minnesota Studies in the Philosophy of Science, vol. 9). Minneapolis: University of Minnesota Press.

Shoemaker, S. (1975), 'Functionalism and Qualia'. *Philosophical Studies* 27: 291–315. Reprinted in Block (1980): 251–67, and in Shoemaker 1984: 184–205.

——(1984), *Identity, Cause, and Mind: Philosophical Essays*, Cambridge: Cambridge University Press.

Wilson, R. A., and F. Keil, eds. (1999), *MIT Encyclopedia of Cognitive Sciences* <http://cognet.mit.edu/MITECS/login.html> Cambridge, MA: MIT Press.

Part IV

Artificial intelligence

Introduction

COULD a machine think? Do machines *already* think? Could a machine have feelings? Emotions? Could a machine feel pain, grow depressed, enjoy music, fall in love? Such questions would be easy to answer if we knew precisely what states of mind—thoughts, emotions, feelings, moods—were and whether a machine could be assembled in such a way that such things could be built into it. This assumes, of course, that we agree in advance as to what constitutes a machine. If you define 'machine' broadly enough, then terrestrial creatures including human beings could count as machines, and the question would be trivialized.

Alan Turing worries about this issue early on in 'Computing Machinery and Intelligence' (Chapter 14), and settles on a definition according to which a machine of a relevant sort is a digital computer, a device that operates in accord with an appropriate kind of mathematical description. Can we accept Turing's definition and move on? Some scientists think that human beings are in fact digital computers in Turing's sense—indeed some physicists think the universe as a whole is a digital computer (Wheeler 1994)! But if digital computers are machines, and if human beings are digital computers, and human beings have minds, then machines can have minds: actuality implies possibility.

Answering our original question in this way is profoundly unsatisfying. As is the case with most philosophical puzzles, the trick is to formulate the question in the right way, a way that gets at something we find perplexing. Here is one possibility. Could we assemble a device using silicon, strands of copper, and factory-built transistors and give it the power of thought, merely by programming it correctly? Could you take an ordinary computing machine, or perhaps a speedier, more potent version of an ordinary computing machine, or an array of such machines, and program it in such a way that it would think, feel, and be conscious? Here we are imagining a machine put together in the way a desktop computer is put together and programmed in the way a desktop computer is programmed. Could such a device be given a mind? More precisely, could the device be given a mind solely by programming it in the right way?

One problem is that a desktop computer, unlike a conscious creature, has limited input—output channels. Conscious creatures typically possess intricate sensory systems that include organs for sensing external objects and events, and a nervous system organized so as to monitor internal bodily states and processes. An ordinary computing machine has nothing comparable. You can plug your desktop computer into a network connected to the outside world, and you can add a camera and microphone to supply more immediate 'visual' and 'auditory' inputs. A computer could be fitted with sensors that monitor certain of its internal states—the temperature inside its case, for instance. But these input channels are far cruder than the sensory channels found in the simplest creatures to which we would be willing to ascribe minds. How could a computer feel pain or thrill at a sunset if it has only rudimentary access to its own internal states and to the world?

You could try imagining ways of beefing up a computing machine's sensory channels, but this might not be necessary. Think for a moment of the human nervous system. This consists of overlapping networks of afferent and efferent nerves running to and from the brain, providing connections between the brain and assorted sensors. Suppose that the function of these sensors is to send signals of distinctive kinds to the brain. Sensors in your finger tips send signals to your brain as to the shapes, textures, and temperatures of objects you touch. Your eyes send messages to your visual cortex as to how things stand in the visible world. Your ears respond to impact waves rippling through the 'medium' (air, or, if you are a fish, water), and pass information along to your brain in the form of coded electro-chemical signals.

Imagine, now, a computing machine taking the place of a human brain. The machine might receive signals from another device programmed to provide inputs perfectly resembling signals your brain receives from various receptors. Could a computing machine suitably programmed and supplied with sensory-like inputs entertain thoughts, feel pains, experience anger or shame? Suppose we could provide a computing machine with inputs—and 'feedback'—with precisely the information available to the brain of a terrestrial creature. Could we then, by programming the machine, turn it into a mind?

Care must be taken not to set the bar to high. The question is not whether a suitably programmed digital computer could rival a Newton or a Shakespeare (or even a Joyce Kilmer). If we could program a computing machine so as to provide it with the mental life of a wombat or a gerbil, we should have made the point.

Simulated vs. genuine mentality

Suppose now that a digital computer has been programmed so as to respond to inputs in a way that appears to us to be indistinguishable from the way a conscious, intelligent creature—a wombat, say—might respond. Would we have succeeded in creating a conscious, intelligent mind? Or would we have succeeded only in creating a device that *simulated* a conscious, intelligent creature—a Sony robotic pet wombat?

These questions frame Turing's 'Computing Machinery and Intelligence' and John Searle's 'Minds, Brains, and Programs' (Chapter 15). In reading Turing and Searle, you should ask yourself how such questions might be settled: how—or whether—we could tell 'from the outside' that a given device was genuinely conscious, engaged in genuine thought, or genuinely understood what it was about. Turing defends one kind of answer to this question, Searle another.

Turing's solution has affinities with behaviorist conceptions of the mind: a device that behaves intelligently *is* intelligent. Searle, in contrast, focuses on 'understanding' and on the material constitution of conscious, intelligent creatures, suggesting that *nothing* an ordinary digital computer could do would suffice for its being conscious or intelligent. Genuinely understanding sentences, Searle holds, is a matter, not merely of programming but of make up. But is this so?

Kinds of mental state

Perhaps the question whether a digital computer suitably programmed could think, feel pain, or fall in love is the wrong question to be asking. You might be willing to concede that a computing machine could think, for instance, but doubt that it could ever feel pain or fall in love. Suppose thought required only a capacity for 'symbol processing', but feeling pains or emotions required qualitatively distinctive states of consciousness. We are comfortable with the idea that computing machines process symbols. So perhaps it is not much of a stretch to allow that machines could think. Feelings are another matter. Feelings are qualitative in a way thoughts seem not to be (or not always to be). The observable qualities of ordinary computing machines differ dramatically from the observable qualities of creatures we regard as uncontroversially capable of feeling. This suggests 'inner' differences as well.

What is the argument here? Maybe this. There is 'something it is like' to feel pain or anger; these experiences have distinctive qualities. If undergoing such experiences is a matter of coming to be in certain states, then, for a creature in them, there is something it is like to be in those states. Your refrigerator goes into a particular state when it automatically defrosts. The state is one you could observe. The refrigerator could be wired so as to monitor this state and signal its onset by turning on a red light. The refrigerator can go into a state and 'recognize' that it is in that state. Does this mean that there is something it is like—something it is like *to the refrigerator*—to be in that state? This seems unlikely. But why? You can say that the refrigerator is not conscious and for that reason there is nothing it is like to be a refrigerator or to be in an auto-defrost state. This is probably correct, but it assumes what is at issue. Why are we reluctant to ascribe an inner life to artifacts like computing machines and refrigerators, even when these devices include a capacity to monitor their own states?

This brings us back to the issue of composition. The hardware of a refrigerator or a computing machine differs from the 'wetware' of a conscious creature. Rightly or wrongly, this difference evidently affects our assessment of the capacity of these devices for consciousness. It is not just that vast external qualitative differences bespeak vast internal qualitative differences. Rather, the qualitative character of the components of refrigerators and computing machines apparently points to the absence of *any inner life at all*.

Let us reflect on this line of reasoning. Imagine a race of Alpha Centaurians encountering a human being, Lucy, piloting a space ship. The Alpha Centaurians wonder whether Lucy is conscious. They examine her minutely and discover, to their surprise (and Lucy's!) that her make-up is very different from theirs. Lucy's biology is carbon based; Alpha Centaurians have a silicon-based biology. Using a technically advanced cerebroscope, the Alpha Centaurians examine Lucy's brain in minute detail, observing neurons, synapses, and complex neurological processes. After detailed analyses they are left with the question whether Lucy has an inner life; whether she is conscious, whether she feels pains or emotions. There seems to be no obvious way to move from a description of Lucy's material make-up to conclusions about the qualitative character—if any—of her inner life.

It is no help here to imagine replacing the Alpha Centaurians with a human neural anatomist. A human anatomist would be convinced not only that Lucy had an inner life (there was something it is like to be Lucy), but also that Lucy's inner life was qualitatively on a par with the inner lives of other human beings. But the anatomist is not obviously in a better position than his Alpha Centaurian counterpart to say *why* exactly Lucy's conscious experiences have the qualities they have.

This topic resurfaces in a number of readings you will encounter below (see Chapters 29, 30, 35, 43–5). For the present, you should merely note that these questions extend smoothly to computing machines. If our goal is to assess whether a machine *is* conscious whether it *really* understands what it is doing, or whether the machine merely *simulates* consciousness and understanding, it is not obvious how we should proceed. If you are a behaviorist, you will deny that the distinction between genuine and simulated states of mind is meaningful: to think, understand, or experience pain is just to behave or to be disposed to behave appropriately. Functionalists, too, regard states of mind as 'abstractable' from the make-up of the system embodying (or 'realizing') them. What might count as definitive evidence that a given system was conscious (or not) is apparently determined by the theory of mind you happen to accept. This means, among other things, that it is inappropriate to appeal to alleged facts about mentality—that a given system is, or is not, conscious, for instance, or that it thinks—in support of a particular theory.

Embodied minds

One reason you might be reluctant to ascribe genuine states of mind to a computing machine, is that the computing machine is a kind of self-contained system, with only a modest complement of connections to the outside world. Imagine the same machine placed inside the head of a robot: a device equipped with sensors enabling it to 'perceive' its surroundings, and appendages that enable it to negotiate its environment and manipulate objects it encounters. Imagine now that the robot 'behaves' as an ordinary person—a 5-year old, for instance—might; it 'utters' sentences and responds appropriately to your utterances. Would you be inclined—or more inclined—to credit such a device with genuine states of mind? Or, when you reflect on the fact that the machine does what it does because it was cleverly programmed, are you inclined to regard it all as an elaborate trick on a par with a Sony robotic pet?

Do not be put off merely by the fact that the imagined robot was programmed. It is sometimes thought that this means that a programmer has foreseen all that a given device might do and built this into the program. A programmer is not a puppeteer. A programmer can give a device a capacity to respond to the unforeseen in unforeseen ways, even to the extent of modifying its own program. What a complex device does depends in large measure on what it encounters by way of inputs. To the extent that these encounters are unpredictable, so its responses to them must be unpredictable. In this regard, a computing machine resembles a human being. *We* are 'programmed' by our genes and by our environment, but this fact does not cast doubt on our capacity to think or undergo conscious experiences.

Later (Chapters 26 and 27), we shall encounter a thought experiment in which a human brain is removed from its body, placed in a vat of nutrients, and hooked to a computing machine that both keeps it alive and stimulates it in ways indistinguishable (by the brain) from those by which a normally situated brain might be stimulated. If you are inclined to regard a brain thus 'envatted'—a disembodied brain—as conscious and capable of thought, then you may be hard pressed to justify withholding ascriptions of consciousness to an appropriately programmed but 'disembodied' computing machine.

Qualities

The inconclusive nature of the discussion thus far may be due to a background matter that deserves closer scrutiny. Return to the question of physical make-up. At least part of our reluctance to ascribe states of mind to computing machines stems from computing machines' being made of stuff very different from the stuff that makes up sentient terrestrial creatures. Living creatures differ *qualitatively* from computing machines. In asking whether a machine could be conscious, we seem to be asking whether the machine could be in states that qualitatively resemble the states of conscious creatures. In one respect, the answer to this question is easy: no; the internal workings of a computing machine differ qualitatively, and in fairly dramatic ways, from the internal states of a living creature.

Suppose this is so. Would we be warranted in concluding that these qualitative differences are relevant to a decision as to whether a machine could think, understand, or be conscious? The answer to this question depends on the extent to which the qualitative character of states of mind are essential to those states. According to some philosophers—behaviorists and functionalists, for instance—states of mind are what they are owing to factors having nothing to do with their qualitative make-up. Suppose this implies that computing machines are or could be conscious. You might regard this as proof that behaviorism and functionalism are ill considered! At the same time a functionalist might respond by arguing that states of mind are 'individuated' (they are what they are) by virtue of the causal roles they play. If two states could occupy the same causal role, their qualitative differences are irrelevant.

Here is another possibility. Suppose the internal states of a computing machine and a person, though functionally similar, differ qualitatively. Need it follow that states differ qualitatively *to their possessors*? To see the point of this question, imagine that your being in pain is a matter of your being in state S_1. Now imagine a computing machine going into a state, S_2, that is functionally indistinguishable from S_1. To us, as observers, S_1 and S_2 differ qualitatively. But does it follow that the states differ qualitatively to their possessors—to you and to the computing machine? Might your going into S_1 feel to you exactly like what going into S_2 feels to the computing machine? Some philosophers have argued that functional similarities as a matter of brute fact guarantee this kind of qualitative similarity (see e.g. Chalmers 1996). This assumes something that could well be doubted, however, namely that 'inner' and 'outer' qualities could vary independently: two qualitatively distinct states could have the same inner qualitative 'feel' for their possessors.

This is just a reminder of what should already be clear. Questions in the philosophy of mind cannot be answered piecemeal. An answer to the question, could a machine think, or understand, or feel pain is bound up with questions about what it is to have a mind or to be conscious in the first place. Suppose you are convinced by functionalist arguments that states of mind are functional states. If, on further reflection, you find worries about mental qualities growing increasingly hard to ignore in considering whether a computing machine could think or feel pain, you might want to rethink your commitment to functionalism. (An alternative would be to attempt to accommodate the qualitative dimension of experience to the functionalist model; see Chapters 34 and 36.) This is just a reminder that the best account of the nature of mind is the account that provides satisfying answers to a very broad range of considerations. If qualities of states of mind are unimportant, for instance, we should be able to see why we might have thought them important. Progress in any domain requires theories that both explain some puzzles and *explain away* others.

Practical concerns

Suppose you became convinced that engineers and computer scientists could produce a machine that had a mind. Might a whole new range of moral considerations suddenly open before you? Many people oppose the cloning of human beings. Suppose that, by scanning your brain, you could produce an exact mental duplicate of yourself: a mental clone. Would reservations about bodily cloning extend to such cases? Would these reservations not apply to cases in which an artificial mind was produced from scratch? Would rights we extend to all human beings encompass artificial minds?

Such questions might seem idle, but if you take seriously the possibility that machines think or might someday think, they are questions that call for answers. One kind of philosophical approach to the question whether machines could think takes as a starting point the question how we should react to a machine programmed to behave as a human being. Insofar as we would be inclined to engage such devices as we engage fellow human beings, insofar as we treated them *as though* they had minds, we would, in effect be conceding that they *do* have minds. Your having a mind, on this pragmatic view, is a matter of your being accepted into a community that interacts with you as though you had a mind. The pragmatist sees no deeper question here. Having a mind is not a matter of having a particular sort of internal make-up—as having a heart or a liver *is* a matter of having a particular sort of internal make-up.

Is this cheating? Is it simply to avoid hard questions by ignoring them, ostrich-like? Or is the pragmatic response a penetrating exposure of the philosophical question as grounded in confusion? Whatever your response, you will need to recognize that you are committing yourself to a philosophical position: you are playing the game, whether you intended to or not. Bear this point in mind as you negotiate readings in this and subsequent sections. You may find yourself homing in on a position that, at some earlier time, you would have regarded as preposterous. If that is so, consider the philosophical credentials of that earlier position. Do you regard yourself as having made progress?

References

Chalmers, D. J. (1996), *The Conscious Mind: In Search of a Fundamental Theory*, New York: Oxford University Press.

Wheeler, J. A. (1994), 'It from Bit'. In *At Home in the Universe*. Woodbury, NY: American Institute of Physics Press: 295–311.

Chapter 14

Computing machinery and intelligence

Alan M. Turing

1. The imitation game

I PROPOSE to consider the question, 'Can machines think?' This should begin with definitions of the meaning of the terms 'machine' and 'think'. The definitions might be framed so as to reflect so far as possible the normal use of the words, but this attitude is dangerous. If the meaning of the words 'machine' and 'think' are to be found by examining how they are commonly used it is difficult to escape the conclusion that the meaning and the answer to the question, 'Can machines think?' is to be sought in a statistical survey such as a Gallup poll. But this is absurd. Instead of attempting such a definition I shall replace the question by another, which is closely related to it and is expressed in relatively unambiguous words.

The new form of the problem can be described in terms of a game which we call the 'imitation game'. It is played with three people, a man (A), a woman (B), and an interrogator (C) who may be of either sex. The interrogator stays in a room apart from the other two. The object of the game for the interrogator is to determine which of the other two is the man and which is the woman. He knows them by labels X and Y, and at the end of the game he says either 'X is A and Y is B' or 'X is B and Y is A'. The interrogator is allowed to put questions to A and B thus:

C: Will X please tell me the length of his or her hair? Now suppose X is actually A, then A must answer. It is A's object in the game to try and cause C to make the wrong identification. His answer might therefore be

'My hair is shingled, and the longest strands are about nine inches long.'

In order that tones of voice may not help the interrogator the answers should be written, or better still, typewritten. The ideal arrangement is to have a teleprinter communicating between the two rooms. Alternatively the question and answers can be repeated by an intermediary. The object of the game for the third player (B) is to help the interrogator. The best strategy for her is probably to give truthful answers. She can add such things as 'I am the woman, don't listen to him!' to her answers, but it will avail nothing as the man can make similar remarks.

We now ask the question, 'What will happen when a machine takes the part of A

Alan M. Turing, 'Computing Machinery and Intelligence', *Mind* 59 (1950).

in this game?' Will the interrogator decide wrongly as often when the game is played like this as he does when the game is played between a man and a woman? These questions replace our original, 'Can machines think?'

2. Critique of the new problem

As well as asking, 'What is the answer to this new form of the question', one may ask, 'Is this new question a worthy one to investigate?' This latter question we investigate without further ado, thereby cutting short an infinite regress.

The new problem has the advantage of drawing a fairly sharp line between the physical and the intellectual capacities of a man. No engineer or chemist claims to be able to produce a material which is indistinguishable from the human skin. It is possible that at some time this might be done, but even supposing this invention available we should feel there was little point in trying to make a 'thinking machine' more human by dressing it up in such artificial flesh. The form in which we have set the problem reflects this fact in the condition which prevents the interrogator from seeing or touching the other competitors, or hearing their voices. Some other advantages of the proposed criterion may be shown up by specimen questions and answers. Thus:

Q: Please write me a sonnet on the subject of the Forth Bridge.
A: Count me out on this one. I never could write poetry.
Q: Add 34957 to 70764
A: (Pause about 30 seconds and then give as answer) 105621.
Q: Do you play chess?
A: Yes.
Q: I have K at my K1, and no other pieces. You have only K at K6 and R at R1. It is your move. What do you play?
A: (After a pause of 15 seconds) R-R8 mate.

The question and answer method seems to be suitable for introducing almost any one of the fields of human endeavour that we wish to include. We do not wish to penalise the machine for its inability to shine in beauty competitions, nor to penalise a man for losing in a race against an aeroplane. The conditions of our game make these disabilities irrelevant. The 'witnesses' can brag, if they consider it advisable, as much as they please about their charms, strength or heroism, but the interrogator cannot demand practical demonstrations.

The game may perhaps be criticised on the ground that the odds are weighted too heavily against the machine. If the man were to try and pretend to be the machine he would clearly make a very poor showing. He would be given away at once by slowness and inaccuracy in arithmetic. May not machines carry out something which ought to be described as thinking but which is very different from what a man does? This objection is a very strong one, but at least we can say that if, nevertheless, a machine can be constructed to play the imitation game satisfactorily, we need not be troubled by this objection.

It might be urged that when playing the 'imitation game' the best strategy for the machine may possibly be something other than imitation of the behaviour of a man. This may be, but I think it is unlikely that there is any great effect of this kind. In any case there is no intention to investigate here the theory of the game, and it will be assumed that the best strategy is to try to provide answers that would naturally be given by a man.

3. The machines concerned in the game

The question which we put in § 1 will not be quite definite until we have specified what we mean by the word 'machine'. It is natural that we should wish to permit every kind of engineering technique to be used in our machines. We also wish to allow the possibility than an engineer or team of engineers may construct a machine which works, but whose manner of operation cannot be satisfactorily described by its constructors because they have applied a method which is largely experimental. Finally, we wish to exclude from the machines men born in the usual manner. It is difficult to frame the definitions so as to satisfy these three conditions. One might for instance insist that the team of engineers should be all of one sex, but this would not really be satisfactory, for it is probably possible to rear a complete individual from a single cell of the skin (say) of a man. To do so would be a feat of biological technique deserving of the very highest praise, but we would not be inclined to regard it as a case of 'constructing a thinking machine'. This prompts us to abandon the requirement that every kind of technique should be permitted. We are the more ready to do so in view of the fact that the present interest in 'thinking machines' has been aroused by a particular kind of machine, usually called an 'electronic computer' or 'digital computer'. Following this suggestion we only permit digital computers to take part in our game.

This restriction appears at first sight to be a very drastic one. I shall attempt to show that it is not so in reality. To do this necessitates a short account of the nature and properties of these computers.

It may also be said that this identification of machines with digital computers, like our criterion for 'thinking', will only be unsatisfactory if (contrary to my belief), it turns out that digital computers are unable to give a good showing in the game.

There are already a number of digital computers in working order, and it may be asked, 'Why not try the experiment straight away? It would be easy to satisfy the conditions of the game. A number of interrogators could be used, and statistics compiled to show how often the right identification was given.' The short answer is that we are not asking whether all digital computers would do well in the game nor whether the computers at present available would do well, but whether there are imaginable computers which would do well. But this is only the short answer. We shall see this question in a different light later.

4. Digital computers

The idea behind digital computers may be explained by saying that these machines are intended to carry out any operations which could be done by a human computer. The human computer is supposed to be following fixed rules; he has no authority to deviate from them in any detail. We may suppose that these rules are supplied in a book, which is altered whenever he is put on to a new job. He has also an unlimited supply of paper on which he does his calculations. He may also do his multiplications and additions on a 'desk machine', but this is not important.

If we use the above explanation as a definition we shall be in danger of circularity of argument. We avoid this by giving an outline of the means by which the desired effect is achieved. A digital computer can usually be regarded as consisting of three parts:

(i) Store.
(ii) Executive unit.
(iii) Control.

The store is a store of information, and corresponds to the human computer's paper, whether this is the paper on which he does his calculations or that on which his book of rules is printed. In so far as the human computer does calculations in his head a part of the store will correspond to his memory.

The executive unit is the part which carries out the various individual operations involved in a calculation. What these individual operations are will vary from machine to machine. Usually fairly lengthy operations can be done such as 'Multiply 3540675445 by 7076345687' but in some machines only very simple ones such as 'Write down 0' are possible.

We have mentioned that the 'book of rules' supplied to the computer is replaced in the machine by a part of the store. It is then called the 'table of instructions'. It is the duty of the control to see that these instructions are obeyed correctly and in the right order. The control is so constructed that this necessarily happens.

The information in the store is usually broken up into packets of moderately small size. In one machine, for instance, a packet might consist of ten decimal digits. Numbers are assigned to the parts of the store in which the various packets of information are stored, in some systematic manner. A typical instruction might say—

'Add the number stored in position 6809 to that in 4302 and put the result back into the latter storage position'.

Needless to say it would not occur in the machine expressed in English. It would more likely be coded in a form such as 6809430217. Here 17 says which of various possible operations is to be performed on the two numbers. In this case the operation is that described above, *viz.* 'Add the number. . . .' It will be noticed that the instruction takes up 10 digits and so forms one packet of information, very conveniently. The control will normally take the instructions to be obeyed in the order of the positions in which they are stored, but occasionally an instruction such as

'Now obey the instruction stored in position 5606, and continue from there' may be encountered, or again

'If position 4505 contains 0 obey next the instruction stored in 6707, otherwise continue straight on.'

Instructions of these latter types are very important because they make it possible for a sequence of operations to be repeated over and over again until some condition is fulfilled, but in doing so to obey, not fresh instructions on each repetition, but the same ones over and over again. To take a domestic analogy. Suppose Mother wants Tommy to call at the cobbler's every morning on his way to school to see if her shoes are done, she can ask him afresh every morning. Alternatively she can stick up a notice once and for all in the hall which he will see when he leaves for school and which tells him to call for the shoes, and also to destroy the notice when he comes back if he has the shoes with him.

The reader must accept it as a fact that digital computers can be constructed, and indeed have been constructed, according to the principles we have described, and that they can in fact mimic the actions of a human computer very closely.

The book of rules which we have described our human computer as using is of course a convenient fiction. Actual human computers really remember what they have got to do. If one wants to make a machine mimic the behaviour of the human computer in some complex operation one has to ask him how it is done, and then translate the answer into the form of an instruction table. Constructing instruction tables is usually described as 'programming'. To 'programme a machine to carry out the operation A' means to put the appropriate instruction table into the machine so that it will do A.

An interesting variant on the idea of a digital computer is a 'digital computer with a random element'. These have instructions involving the throwing of a die or some equivalent electronic process; one such instruction might for instance be, 'Throw the die and put the resulting number into store 1000'. Sometimes such a machine is described as having free will (though I would not use this phrase myself). It is not normally possible to determine from observing a machine whether it has a random element, for a similar effect can be produced by such devices as making the choices depend on the digits of the decimal for π.

Most actual digital computers have only a finite store. There is no theoretical difficulty in the idea of a computer with an unlimited store. Of course only a finite part can have been used at any one time. Likewise only a finite amount can have been constructed, but we can imagine more and more being added as required. Such computers have special theoretical interest and will be called infinitive capacity computers.

The idea of a digital computer is an old one. Charles Babbage, Lucasian Professor of Mathematics at Cambridge from 1828 to 1839, planned such a machine, called the

Analytical Engine, but it was never completed. Although Babbage had all the essential ideas, his machine was not at that time such a very attractive prospect. The speed which would have been available would be definitely faster than a human computer but something like 100 times slower than the Manchester machine, itself one of the slower of the modern machines. The storage was to be purely mechanical, using wheels and cards.

The fact that Babbage's Analytical Engine was to be entirely mechanical will help us to rid ourselves of a superstition. Importance is often attached to the fact that modern digital computers are electrical, and that the nervous system also is electrical. Since Babbage's machine was not electrical, and since all digital computers are in a sense equivalent, we see that this use of electricity cannot be of theoretical importance. Of course electricity usually comes in where fast signalling is concerned, so that it is not surprising that we find it in both these connections. In the nervous system chemical phenomena are at least as important as electrical. In certain computers the storage system is mainly acoustic. The feature of using electricity is thus seen to be only a very superficial similarity. If we wish to find such similarities we should look rather for mathematical analogies of function.

5. Universality of digital computers

The digital computers considered in the last section may be classified amongst the 'discrete state machines'. These are the machines which move by sudden jumps or clicks from one quite definite state to another. These states are sufficiently different for the possibility of confusion between them to be ignored. Strictly speaking there are no such machines. Everything really moves continuously. But there are many kinds of machine which can profitably be *thought* of as being discrete state machines. For instance in considering the switches for a lighting system it is a convenient fiction that each switch must be definitely on or definitely off. There must be intermediate positions, but for most purposes we can forget about them. As an example of a discrete state machine we might consider a wheel which clicks round through 120° once a second, but may be stopped by a lever which can be operated from outside; in addition a lamp is to light in one of the positions of the wheel. This machine could be described abstractly as follows. The internal state of the machine (which is described by the position of the wheel) may be q_1, q_2 or q_3. There is an input signal i_0 or i_1 (position of lever). The internal state at any moment is determined by the last state and input signal according to the table

		Last State		
		q_1	q_2	q_3
Input	i_0	q_2	q_3	q_1
	i_1	q_1	q_2	q_3

The output signals, the only externally visible indication of the internal state (the light) are described by the table

State	q_1	q_2	q_3
Output	o_0	o_0	o_1

This example is typical of discrete state machines. They can be described by such tables provided they have only a finite number of possible states.

It will seem that given the initial state of the machine and the input signals it is always possible to predict all future states. This is reminiscent of Laplace's view that from the complete state of the universe at one moment of time, as described by the positions and velocities of all particles, it should be possible to predict all future states. The prediction which we are considering is, however, rather nearer to practicability than that considered by Laplace. The system of the 'universe as a whole' is such that quite small errors in the initial conditions can have an overwhelming effect at a later time. The displacement of a single electron by a billionth of a centimetre at one moment might make the difference between a man being killed by an avalanche a year later, or escaping. It is an essential property of the mechanical systems which we have called 'discrete state machines' that this phenomenon does not occur. Even when we consider the actual physical machines instead of the idealised machines, reasonably accurate knowledge of the state at one moment yields reasonably accurate knowledge any number of steps later.

As we have mentioned, digital computers fall within the class of discrete state machines. But the number of states of which such a machine is capable is usually enormously large. For instance, the number for the machine now working at Manchester it about $2^{165,000}$, *i.e.* about $10^{50,000}$. Compare this with our example of the clicking wheel described above, which had three states. It is not difficult to see why the number of states should be so immense. The computer includes a store corresponding to the paper used by a human computer. It must be possible to write into the store any one of the combinations of symbols which might have been written on the paper. For simplicity suppose that only digits from 0 to 9 are used as symbols. Variations in handwriting are ignored. Suppose the computer is allowed 100 sheets of paper each containing 50 lines each with room for 30 digits. Then the number of states is $10^{100\times50\times30}$, *i.e.* $10^{150,000}$. This is about the number of states of three Manchester machines put together. The logarithm to the base two of the number of states is usually called the 'storage capacity' of the machine. Thus the Manchester machine has a storage capacity of about 165,000 and the wheel machine of our example about 1.6. If two machines are put together their capacities must be added to obtain the capacity of the resultant machine. This leads to the possibility of statements such as 'The Manchester machine contains 64 magnetic tracks each with a capacity of 2560, eight electronic tubes with a capacity of 1280. Miscellaneous storage amounts to about 300 making a total of 174,380.'

Given the table corresponding to a discrete state machine it is possible to predict what it will do. There is no reason why this calculation should not be carried out by means of a digital computer. Provided it could be carried out sufficiently quickly the digital computer could mimic the behaviour of any discrete state machine. The imitation game could then be played with the machine in question (as B) and the mimicking digital computer (as A) and the interrogator would be unable to distinguish them. Of course the digital computer must have an adequate storage capacity as well as working sufficiently fast. Moreover, it must be programmed afresh for each new machine which it is desired to mimic.

This special property of digital computers, that they can mimic any discrete state machine, is described by saying that they are *universal* machines. The existence of machines with this property has the important consequence that, considerations of speed apart, it is unnecessary to design various new machines to do various computing processes. They can all be done with one digital computer, suitably programmed for each case. It will be seen that as a consequence of this all digital computers are in a sense equivalent.

We may now consider again the point raised at the end of §3. It was suggested tentatively that the question, 'Can machines think?' should be replaced by 'Are there imaginable digital computers which would do well in the imitation game?' If we wish we can make this superficially more general and ask 'Are there discrete state machines which would do well?' But in view of the universality property we see that either of these questions is equivalent to this, 'Let us fix our attention on one particular digital computer *C*. Is it true that by modifying this computer to have an adequate storage, suitably increasing its speed of action, and providing it with an appropriate programme, *C* can be made to play satisfactorily the part of A in the imitation game, the part of B being taken by a man?'

6. Contrary views on the main question

We may now consider the ground to have been cleared and we are ready to proceed to the debate on our question, 'Can machines think?' and the variant of it quoted at the end of the last section. We cannot altogether abandon the original form of the problem, for opinions will differ as to the appropriateness of the substitution and we must at least listen to what has to be said in this connexion.

It will simplify matters for the reader if I explain first my own beliefs in the matter. Consider first the more accurate form of the question. I believe that in about fifty years' time it will be possible to programme computers, with a storage capacity of about 10^9, to make them play the imitation game so well that an average interrogator will not have more than 70 per cent. chance of making the right identification after five minutes of questioning. The original question, 'Can machines think?' I believe to be too meaningless to deserve discussion. Nevertheless I believe that at the end of the century the use of words and general educated opinion will have altered so much that one will be able to speak of machines thinking without expecting to be contradicted. I believe further that no useful purpose is served by concealing these beliefs. The popular view that scientists proceed inexorably from well-established fact to well-established fact, never being influenced by any unproved conjecture, is quite mistaken. Provided it is made clear which are proved facts and which are conjectures, no harm can result. Conjectures are of great importance since they suggest useful lines of research.

I now proceed to consider opinions opposed to my own.

(1) *The Theological Objection.* Thinking is a function of man's immortal soul. God has given an immortal soul to every man and woman, but not to any other animal or to machines. Hence no animal or machine can think.[1]

I am unable to accept any part of this, but will attempt to reply in theological terms. I should find the argument more convincing if animals were classed with men, for there is a greater difference, to my mind, between the typical animate and the inanimate than there is between man and the other animals. The arbitrary character of the orthodox view becomes clearer if we consider how it might appear to a member of some other religious community. How do Christians regard the Moslem view that women have no souls? But let us leave this point aside and return to the main argument. It appears to me that the argument quoted above implies a serious restriction of the omnipotence of the Almighty. It is admitted that there are certain things that He cannot do such as making one equal to two, but should we not believe that He has freedom to confer a soul on an elephant if He sees fit? We might expect that He would only exercise this power in conjunction with a mutation which provided the elephant with an appropriately improved brain to minister to the needs of this soul. An argument of exactly similar form may be made for the case of machines. It may seem different because it is more difficult to 'swallow'. But this really only means that we think it would be less likely that He would consider the circumstances suitable for conferring a soul. The circumstances in question are discussed in the rest of this paper. In attempting to construct such machines we should not be irreverently usurping His power of creating souls, any more than we are in the procreation of children: rather we are, in either case, instruments of His will providing mansions for the souls that He creates.

However, this is mere speculation. I am not very impressed with theological arguments whatever they may be used to support. Such arguments have often been found unsatisfactory in the past. In the time of Galileo it was argued that the texts, 'And the sun stood still . . . and hasted not to go down about a whole day' (Joshua x. 13) and 'He laid the foundations of the earth, that it should not move at any time' (Psalm cv. 5) were an adequate refutation of the Copernican theory. With our present knowledge such an argument appears futile. When that knowledge was not available it made a quite different impression.

(2) *The 'Heads in the Sand' Objection.* 'The consequences of machines thinking would be too dreadful. Let us hope and believe that they cannot do so.'

1. Possibly this view is heretical. St. Thomas Aquinas (*Summa Theologica*, quoted by Bertrand Russell, p. 480) states that God cannot make a man to have no soul. But this may not be a real restriction on His powers, but only a result of the fact that men's souls are immortal, and therefore indestructible.

This argument is seldom expressed quite so openly as in the form above. But it affects most of us who think about it at all. We like to believe that Man is in some subtle way superior to the rest of creation. It is best if he can be shown to be *necessarily* superior, for then there is no danger of him losing his commanding position. The popularity of the theological argument is clearly connected with this feeling. It is likely to be quite strong in intellectual people, since they value the power of thinking more highly than others, and are more inclined to base their belief in the superiority of Man on this power.

I do not think that this argument is sufficiently substantial to require refutation. Consolation would be more appropriate: perhaps this should be sought in the transmigration of souls.

(3) *The Mathematical Objection.* There are a number of results of mathematical logic which can be used to show that there are limitations to the powers of discrete-state machines. The best known of these results is known as Gödel's theorem,[2] and shows that in any sufficiently powerful logical system statements can be formulated which can neither be proved nor disproved within the system, unless possibly the system itself is inconsistent. There are other, in some respects similar, results due to *Church, Kleene, Rosser,* and *Turing.* The latter result is the most convenient to consider, since it refers directly to machines, whereas the others can only be used in a comparatively indirect argument: for instance if Gödel's theorem is to be used we need in addition to have some means of describing logical systems in terms of machines, and machines in terms of logical systems. The result in question refers to a type of machine which is essentially a digital computer with an infinite capacity. It states that there are certain things that such a machine cannot do. If it is rigged up to give answers to questions as in the imitation game, there will be some questions to which it will either give a wrong answer, or fail to give an answer at all however much time is allowed for a reply. There may, of course, be many such questions, and questions which cannot be answered by one machine may be satisfactorily answered by another. We are of course supposing for the present that the questions are of the kind to which an answer 'Yes' or 'No' is appropriate, rather than questions such as 'What do you think of Picasso?' The questions that we know the machines must fail on are of this type, 'Consider the machine specified as follows. . . . Will this machine ever answer "Yes" to any question?' The dots are to be replaced by a description of some machine in a standard form, which could be something like that used in § 5. When the machine described bears a certain comparatively simple relation to the machine which is under interrogation, it can be shown that the answer is either wrong or not forthcoming. This is the mathematical result: it is argued that it proves a disability of machines to which the human intellect is not subject.

The short answer to this argument is that although it is established that there are limitations to the powers of any particular machine, it has only been stated, without

2. Author's names in italics refer to the Bibliography.

any sort of proof, that no such limitations apply to the human intellect. But I do not think this view can be dismissed quite so lightly. Whenever one of these machines is asked the appropriate critical question, and gives a definite answer, we know that this answer must be wrong, and this gives us a certain feeling of superiority. Is this feeling illusory? It is no doubt quite genuine, but I do not think too much importance should be attached to it. We too often give wrong answers to questions ourselves to be justified in being very pleased at such evidence of fallibility on the part of the machines. Further, our superiority can only be felt on such an occasion in relation to the one machine over which we have scored our petty triumph. There would be no question of triumphing simultaneously over *all* machines. In short, then, there might be men cleverer than any given machine, but then again there might be other machines cleverer again, and so on.

Those who hold to the mathematical argument would, I think, mostly be willing to accept the imitation game as a basis for discussion. Those who believe in the two previous objections would probably not be interested in any criteria.

(4) *The Argument from Consciousness.* This argument is very well expressed in *Professor Jefferson's* Lister Oration for 1949, from which I quote. 'Not until a machine can write a sonnet or compose a concerto because of thoughts and emotions felt, and not by the chance fall of symbols, could we agree that machine equals brain—that is, not only write it but know that it had written it. No mechanism could feel (and not merely artificially signal, an easy contrivance) pleasure at its successes, grief when its valves fuse, be warmed by flattery, be made miserable by its mistakes, be charmed by sex, be angry or depressed when it cannot get what it wants.'

This argument appears to be a denial of the validity of our test. According to the most extreme form of this view the only way by which one could be sure that a machine thinks is to *be* the machine and to feel oneself thinking. One could then describe these feelings to the world, but of course no one would be justified in taking any notice. Likewise according to this view the only way to know that a *man* thinks is to be that particular man. It is in fact the solipsist point of view. It may be the most logical view to hold but it makes communication of ideas difficult. A is liable to believe 'A thinks but B does not' whilst B believes 'B thinks but A does not'. Instead of arguing continually over this point it is usual to have the polite convention that everyone thinks.

I am sure that Professor Jefferson does not wish to adopt the extreme and solipsist point of view. Probably he would be quite willing to accept the imitation game as a test. The game (with the player B omitted) is frequently used in practice under the name of *viva voce* to discover whether some one really understands something or has 'learnt it parrot fashion'. Let us listen in to a part of such a *viva voce*:

Interrogator: In the first line of your sonnet which reads 'Shall I compare thee to a summer's day', would not 'a spring day' do as well or better?

Witness : It wouldn't scan.
Interrogator: How about 'a winter's day' That would scan all right.
Witness: Yes, but nobody wants to be compared to a winter's day.
Interrogator: Would you say Mr. Pickwick reminded you of Christmas?
Witness: In a way.
Interrogator: Yet Christmas is a winter's day, and I do not think Mr. Pickwick would mind the comparison.
Witness: I don't think you're serious. By a winter's day one means a typical winter's day, rather than a special one like Christmas.

And so on. What would Professor Jefferson say if the sonnet-writing machine was able to answer like this in the *viva voce*? I do not know whether he would regard the machine as 'merely artificially signalling' these answers, but if the answers were as satisfactory and sustained as in the above passage I do not think he would describe it as 'an easy contrivance'. This phrase is, I think, intended to cover such devices as the inclusion in the machine of a record of someone reading a sonnet, with appropriate switching to turn it on from time to time.

In short then, I think that most of those who support the argument from consciousness could be persuaded to abandon it rather than be forced into the solipsist position. They will then probably be willing to accept our test.

I do not wish to give the impression that I think there is no mystery about consciousness. There is, for instance, something of a paradox connected with any attempt to localise it. But I do not think these mysteries necessarily need to be solved before we can answer the question with which we are concerned in this paper.

(5) *Arguments from Various Disabilities.* These arguments take the form, 'I grant you that you can make machines do all the things you have mentioned but you will never be able to make one to do X'. Numerous features X are suggested in this connexion. I offer a selection:

Be kind, resourceful, beautiful, friendly (p. 224), have initiative, have a sense of humour, tell right from wrong, make mistakes (p. 224), fall in love, enjoy strawberries and cream (p. 224), make some one fall in love with it, learn from experience (pp. 230 f.), use words properly, be the subject of its own thought (p. 225), have as much diversity of behaviour as a man, do something really new (p. 226). (Some of these disabilities are given special consideration as indicated by the page numbers.)

No support is usually offered for these statements. I believe they are mostly founded on the principle of scientific induction. A man has seen thousands of machines in his lifetime. From what he sees of them he draws a number of general conclusions. They are ugly, each is designed for a very limited purpose, when required for a minutely different purpose they are useless, the variety of behaviour of any one of them is very small, etc., etc. Naturally he concludes that these are necessary properties of machines in general. Many of these limitations are associated with the very small storage capacity of most machines. (I am assuming that the idea of storage capacity is extended in some way to cover machines other than discrete-state machines.

The exact definition does not matter as no mathematical accuracy is claimed in the present discussion.) A few years ago, when very little had been heard of digital computers, it was possible to elicit much incredulity concerning them, if one mentioned their properties without describing their construction. That was presumably due to a similar application of the principle of scientific induction. These applications of the principle are of course largely unconscious. When a burnt child fears the fire and shows that he fears it by avoiding it, I should say that he was applying scientific induction. (I could of course also describe his behaviour in many other ways.) The works and customs of mankind do not seem to be very suitable material to which to apply scientific induction. A very large part of space-time must be investigated, if reliable results are to be obtained. Otherwise we may (as most English children do) decide that everybody speaks English, and that it is silly to learn French.

There are, however, special remarks to be made about many of the disabilities that have been mentioned. The inability to enjoy strawberries and cream may have struck the reader as frivolous. Possibly a machine might be made to enjoy this delicious dish, but any attempt to make one do so would be idiotic. What is important about this disability is that it contributes to some of the other disabilities, *e.g.* to the difficulty of the same kind of friendliness occurring between man and machine as between white man and white man, or between black man and black man.

The claim that 'machines cannot make mistakes' seems a curious one. One is tempted to retort, 'Are they any the worse for that?' But let us adopt a more sympathetic attitude, and try to see what is really meant. I think this criticism can be explained in terms of the imitation game. It is claimed that the interrogator could distinguish the machine from the man simply by setting them a number of problems in arithmetic. The machine would be unmasked because of its deadly accuracy. The reply to this is simple. The machine (programmed for playing the game) would not attempt to give the *right* answers to the arithmetic problems. It would deliberately introduce mistakes in a manner calculated to confuse the interrogator. A mechanical fault would probably show itself through an unsuitable decision as to what sort of a mistake to make in the arithmetic. Even this interpretation of the criticism is not sufficiently sympathetic. But we cannot afford the space to go into it much further. It seems to me that this criticism depends on a confusion between two kinds of mistake. We may call them 'errors of functioning' and 'errors of conclusion'. Errors of functioning are due to some mechanical or electrical fault which causes the machine to behave otherwise than it was designed to do. In philosophical discussions one likes to ignore the possibility of such errors; one is therefore discussing 'abstract machines'. These abstract machines are mathematical fictions rather than physical objects. By definition they are incapable of errors of functioning. In this sense we can truly say that 'machines can never make mistakes'. Errors of conclusion can only arise when some meaning is attached to the output signals from the machine. The machine might, for instance, type out mathematical equations, or sentences in English. When a false proposition is typed we say that the machine has committed an error of conclusion. There is clearly no reason at all for saying that a machine cannot make this kind of mistake. It might do nothing but type out repeatedly '0 = 1'. To take a less perverse example, it might have some method for drawing conclusions by scientific induction. We must expect such a method to lead occasionally to erroneous results.

The claim that a machine cannot be the subject of its own thought can of course only be answered if it can be shown that the machine has *some* thought with *some* subject matter. Nevertheless, 'the subject matter of a machine's operations' does seem to mean something, at least to the people who deal with it. If, for instance, the machine was trying to find a solution of the equation $x^2 - 40x - 11 = 0$ one would be tempted to describe this equation as part of the machine's subject matter at that moment. In this sort of sense a machine undoubtedly can be its own subject matter. It may be used to help in making up its own programmes, or to predict the effect of alterations in its own structure. By observing the results of its own behaviour it can modify its own programmes so as to achieve some purpose more effectively. These are possibilities of the near future, rather than Utopian dreams.

The criticism that a machine cannot have much diversity of behaviour is just a way of saying that it cannot have much storage capacity. Until fairly recently a storage capacity of even a thousand digits was very rare.

The criticisms that we are considering here are often disguised forms of the argument from consciousness. Usually if one maintains that a machine *can* do one of these things, and describes the kind of method that the machine could use, one will not make much of an impression. It is thought that the method (whatever it may be, for it must be mechanical) is really rather base. Compare the parenthesis in Jefferson's statement quoted on p. 21.

(6) *Lady Lovelace's Objection.* Our most detailed information of Babbage's Analytical Engine comes from a memoir by *Lady Lovelace.* In it she states, 'The Analytical Engine has no pretensions to *originate* anything. It can do *whatever we know how to order it* to perform' (her italics). This statement is quoted by *Hartree* (p. 70) who adds: 'This does not imply that it may not be possible to construct electronic equipment which will "think for itself", or in which, in biological terms, one could set up a conditioned reflex, which would serve as a basis for "learning". Whether this is possible in principle or not is a stimulating and exciting question, suggested by some of these recent developments. But it did not seem that the machines constructed or projected at the time had this property'.

I am in thorough agreement with Hartree over this. It will be noticed that he does not assert that the machines in question had not got the property, but rather that the evidence available to Lady Lovelace did not encourage her to believe that they had it. It is quite possible that the machines in question had in a sense got this property. For suppose that some discrete-state machine has the property. The Analytical Engine was a universal digital computer, so that, if its storage capacity and speed were adequate, it could by suitable programming be made to mimic the machine in question. Probably this argument did not occur to the Countess or to Babbage. In any case there was no obligation on them to claim all that could be claimed.

This whole question will be considered again under the heading of learning machines.

A variant of Lady Lovelace's objection states that a machine can 'never do anything really new'. This may be parried for a moment with the saw, 'There is nothing new under the sun'. Who can be certain that 'original work' that he has done was not simply the growth of the seed planted in him by teaching, or the effect of following well-known general principles. A better variant of the objection says that a machine can never 'take us by surprise'. This statement is a more direct challenge and can be met directly. Machines take me by surprise with great frequency. This is largely because I do not do sufficient calculation to decide what to expect them to do, or rather because, although I do a calculation, I do it in a hurried, slipshod fashion, taking risks. Perhaps I say to myself, 'I suppose the voltage here ought to be the same as there: anyway let's assume it is'. Naturally I am often wrong, and the result is a surprise for me for by the time the experiment is done these assumptions have been forgotten. These admissions lay me open to lectures on the subject of my vicious ways, but do not throw any doubt on my credibility when I testify to the surprises I experience.

I do not expect this reply to silence my critic. He will probably say that such surprises are due to some creative mental act on my part, and reflect no credit on the machine. This leads us back to the argument from consciousness, and far from the idea of surprise. It is a line of argument we must consider closed, but it is perhaps worth remarking that the appreciation of something as surprising requires as much of a 'creative mental act' whether the surprising event originates from a man, a book, a machine or anything else.

The view that machines cannot give rise to surprises is due, I believe, to a fallacy to which philosophers and mathematicians are particularly subject. This is the assumption that as soon as a fact is presented to a mind all consequences of that fact spring into the mind simultaneously with it. It is a very useful assumption under many circumstances, but one too easily forgets that it is false. A natural consequence of doing so is that one then assumes that there is no virtue in the mere working out of consequences from data and general principles.

(7) *Argument from Continuity in the Nervous System.* The nervous system is certainly not a discrete-state machine. A small error in the information about the size of a nervous impulse impinging on a neuron, may make a large difference to the size of the outgoing impulse. It may be argued that, this being so, one cannot expect to be able to mimic the behaviour of the nervous system with a discrete-state system.

It is true that a discrete-state machine must be different from a continuous machine. But if we adhere to the conditions of the imitation game, the interrogator will not be able to take any advantage of this difference. The situation can be made clearer if we consider some other simpler continuous machine. A differential analyser will do very well. (A differential analyser is a certain kind of machine not of the discrete-state type used for some kinds of calculation.) Some of these provide their answers in a typed form, and so are suitable for taking part in the game. It would not be possible for a digital computer to predict exactly what answers the differential analyser would give to a problem, but it would be quite capable of giving the right sort of answer. For instance, if asked to give the value of π (actually about 3·1416) it would be reasonable to choose at random between the values 3·12, 3·13, 3·14, 3·15, 3·16 with the probabilities of 0·05, 0·15, 0·55, 0·19, 0·06 (say). Under these circumstances it would be very difficult for the interrogator to distinguish the differential analyser from the digital computer.

(8) *The Argument from Informality of Behaviour.* It is not possible to produce a set of rules purporting to describe what a man should do in every conceivable set of circumstances. One might for instance have a rule that one is to stop when one sees a red traffic light, and to go if one sees a green one, but what if by some fault both appear together? One may perhaps decide that it is safest to stop. But some further difficulty may well arise from this decision later. To attempt to provide rules of conduct to cover every eventuality, even those arising from traffic lights, appears to be impossible. With all this I agree.

From this it is argued that we cannot be machines. I shall try to reproduce the argument, but I fear I shall hardly do it justice. It seems to run something like this. 'If each man had a definite set of rules of conduct by which he regulated his life he would be no better than a machine. But there are no such rules, so men cannot be machines.' The undistributed middle is glaring. I do not think the argument is ever put quite like this, but I believe this is the argument used nevertheless. There may however be a certain confusion between 'rules of conduct' and 'laws of behaviour' to cloud the issue. By 'rules of conduct' I mean precepts such as 'Stop if you see red lights', on which one can act, and of which one can be conscious. By 'laws of behaviour' I mean laws of nature as applied to a man's body such as 'if you pinch him he will squeak'. If we substitute 'laws of behaviour which regulate his life' for 'laws of conduct by which he regulates his life' in the argument quoted the undistributed middle is no longer insuperable. For we believe that it is not only true that being regulated by laws of behaviour implies being some sort of machine (though not necessarily a discrete-state machine), but that conversely being such a machine implies being regulated by such laws. However, we cannot so easily convince ourselves of the absence of complete laws of behaviour as of complete rules of conduct. The only way we know of for finding such laws is scientific observation, and we certainly know of no circumstances under which we could say, 'We have searched enough. There are no such laws.'

We can demonstrate more forcibly that any such statement would be unjustified.

For suppose we could be sure of finding such laws if they existed. Then given a discrete-state machine it should certainly be possible to discover by observation sufficent about it to predict its future behaviour, and this within a reasonable time, say a thousand years. But this does not seem to be the case. I have set up on the Manchester computer a small programme using only 1000 units of storage, whereby the machine supplied with one sixteen figure number replies with another within two seconds. I would defy anyone to learn from these replies sufficient about the programme to be able to predict any replies to untried values.

(9) *The Argument from Extra-Sensory Perception.* I assume that the reader is familiar with the idea of extra-sensory perception, and the meaning of the four items of it, *viz.* telepathy, clairvoyance, precognition and psycho-kinesis. These disturbing phenomena seem to deny all our usual scientific ideas. How we should like to discredit them! Unfortunately the statistical evidence, at least for telepathy, is overwhelming. It is very difficult to rearrange one's ideas so as to fit these new facts in. Once one has accepted them it does not seem a very big step to believe in ghosts and bogies. The idea that our bodies move simply according to the known laws of physics, together with some others not yet discovered but somewhat similar, would be one of the first to go.

This argument is to my mind quite a strong one. One can say in reply that many scientific theories seem to remain workable in practice, in spite of clashing with E.S.P.; that in fact one can get along very nicely if one forgets about it. This is rather cold comfort, and one fears that thinking is just the kind of phenomenon where E.S.P. may be especially relevant.

A more specific argument based on E.S.P. might run as follows: 'Let us play the imitation game, using as witnesses a man who is good as a telepathic receiver, and a digital computer. The interrogator can ask such questions as "What suit does the card in my right hand belong to?" The man by telepathy or clairvoyance gives the right answer 130 times out of 400 cards. The machine can only guess at random, and perhaps gets 104 right, so the interrogator makes the right identification.' There is an interesting possibility which opens here. Suppose the digital computer contains a random number generator. Then it will be natural to use this to decide what answer to give. But then the random number generator will be subject to the psycho-kinetic powers of the interrogator. Perhaps this psycho-kinesis might cause the machine to guess right more often than would be expected on a probability calculation, so that the interrogator might still be unable to make the right identification. On the other hand, he might be able to guess right without any questioning, by clairvoyance. With E.S.P. anything may happen.

If telepathy is admitted it will be necessary to tighten our test up. The situation could be regarded as analogous to that which would occur if the interrogator were talking to himself and one of the competitors was listening with his ear to the wall. To put the competitors into a 'telepathy-proof room' would satisfy all requirements.

7. Learning machines

The reader will have anticipated that I have no very convincing arguments of a positive nature to support my views. If I had I should not have taken such pains to point out the fallacies in contrary views. Such evidence as I have I shall now give.

Let us return for a moment to Lady Lovelace's objection, which stated that the machine can only do what we tell it to do. One could say that a man can 'inject' an idea into the machine, and that it will respond to a certain extent and then drop into quiescence, like a piano string struck by a hammer. Another simile would be an atomic pile of less than critical size : an injected idea is to correspond to a neutron entering the pile from without. Each such neutron will cause a certain disturbance which eventually dies away. If, however, the size of the pile is sufficiently increased, the disturbance caused by such an incoming neutron will very likely go on and on increasing until the whole pile is destroyed. Is there a corresponding phenomenon for minds, and is there one for machines? There does seem to be one for the human mind. The majority of them seem to be 'sub-critical', *i.e.* to correspond in this analogy to piles of subcritical size. An idea presented to such a mind will on average give rise to less than one idea in reply. A smallish proportion are super-critical. An idea presented to such a mind may give rise to a whole 'theory' consisting of secondary, tertiary and more remote ideas. Animals minds seem to be very definitely sub-critical. Adhering to this analogy we ask, 'Can a machine be made to be super-critical?'

The 'skin of an onion' analogy is also helpful. In considering the functions of the mind or the brain we find certain operations which we can explain in purely mechanical terms. This we say, does not correspond to the real mind: it is a sort of skin which we must strip off if we are to find the real mind. But then in what remains we find a further skin to be stripped off, and so on. Proceeding in this way do we ever come to the 'real' mind, or do we eventually come to the skin which has nothing in it? In the latter case the whole mind is mechanical. (It would not be a discrete-state machine however. We have discussed this.)

These last two paragraphs do not claim to be convincing arguments. They should rather be described as 'recitations tending to produce belief'.

The only really satisfactory support that can be given for the view expressed at the beginning of § 6, will be that provided by waiting for the end of the century and then doing the experiment described. But what can we say in the meantime? What steps should be taken now if the experiment is to be successful?

As I have explained, the problem is mainly one of programming. Advances in engineering will have to be made too, but it seems unlikely that these will not be adequate for the requirements. Estimates of the storage capacity of the brain vary from 10^{10} to 10^{15} binary digits. I incline to the lower values and believe that only a very small fraction is used for the higher types of thinking. Most of it is probably used for the retention of visual impressions. I should be surprised if more than 10^9

was required for satisfactory playing of the imitation game, at any rate against a blind man. (Note—The capacity of the *Encyclopaedia Britannica*, 11th edition, is 2×10^9.) A storage capacity of 10^7 would be a very practicable possibility even by present techniques. It is probably not necessary to increase the speed of operations of the machines at all. Parts of modern machines which can be regarded as analogues of nerve cells work about a thousand times faster than the latter. This should provide a 'margin of safety' which could cover losses of speed arising in many ways. Our problem then is to find out how to programme these machines to play the game. At my present rate of working I produce about a thousand digits of programme a day, so that about sixty workers, working steadily through the fifty years might accomplish the job, if nothing went into the waste-paper basket. Some more expeditious method seems desirable.

In the process of trying to imitate an adult human mind we are bound to think a good deal about the process which has brought it to the state that it is in. We may notice three components,

(*a*) The initial state of the mind, say at birth,
(*b*) The education to which it has been subjected,
(*c*) Other experience, not to be described as education, to which it has been subjected.

Instead of trying to produce a programme to simulate the adult mind, why not rather try to produce one which simulates the child's? If this were then subjected to an appropriate course of education one would obtain the adult brain. Presumably the child-brain is something like a note-book as one buys it from the stationers. Rather little mechanism, and lots of blank sheets. (Mechanism and writing are from our point of view almost synonymous.) Our hope is that there is so little mechanism in the child-brain that something like it can be easily programmed. The amount of work in the education we can assume, as a first approximation, to be much the same as for the human child.

We have thus divided our problem into two parts. The child-programme and the education process. These two remain very closely connected. We cannot expect to find a good child-machine at the first attempt. One must experiment with teaching one such machine and see how well it learns. One can then try another and see if it is better or worse. There is an obvious connection between this process and evolution, by the identifications

Structure of the child machine = Hereditary material
Changes ,, ,, = Mutations
Natural selection = Judgment of the experimenter

One may hope, however, that this process will be more expeditious than evolution. The survival of the fittest is a slow method for measuring advantages. The experimenter, by the exercise of intelligence, should be able to speed it up. Equally important is the fact that he is not restricted to random mutations. If he can trace a cause for some weakness he can probably think of the kind of mutation which will improve it.

It will not be possible to apply exactly the same teaching process to the machine as to a normal child. It will not, for instance, be provided with legs, so that it could not be asked to go out and fill the coal scuttle. Possibly it might not have eyes. But however well these deficiencies might be overcome by clever engineering, one could not send the creature to school without the other children making excessive fun of it. It must be given some tuition. We need not be too concerned about the legs, eyes, etc. The example of Miss *Helen Keller* shows that education can take place provided that communication in both directions between teacher and pupil can take place by some means or other.

We normally associate punishments and rewards with the teaching process. Some simple child-machines can be constructed or programmed on this sort of principle. The machine has to be so constructed that events which shortly preceded the occurrence of a punishment-signal are unlikely to be repeated, whereas a reward-signal increased the probability of repetition of the events which led up to it. These definitions do not presuppose any feelings on the part of the machine. I have done some experiments with one such child-machine, and succeeded in teaching it a few things, but the teaching method was too unorthodox for the experiment to be considered really successful.

The use of punishments and rewards can at best be a part of the teaching process. Roughly speaking, if the teacher has no other means of communicating to the pupil, the amount of information which can reach him does not exceed the total number of rewards and punishments applied. By the time a child has learnt to repeat 'Casabianca' he would probably feel very sore indeed, if the text could only be discovered by a 'Twenty Questions' technique, every 'NO' taking the form of a blow. It is necessary therefore to have some other 'unemotional' channels of communication. If these are available it is possible to teach a machine by punishments and rewards to obey orders given in some language, *e.g.* a symbolic language. These orders are to be transmitted through the 'unemotional' channels. The use of this language will diminish greatly the number of punishments and rewards required.

Opinions may vary as to the complexity which is suitable in the child machine. One might try to make it as simple as possible consistently with the general principles. Alternatively one might have a complete system of logical inference 'built in'.[3] In the latter case the store would be largely occupied with definitions and propositions. The propositions would have various kinds of status, *e.g.* well-established facts, conjectures, mathematically proved theorems, statements given by an authority, expressions having the logical form of proposition but not belief-value. Certain propositions may be described as 'imperatives'. The machine should be so constructed that as soon as an imperative is classed as 'well-established' the appropriate action automatically takes place. To illustrate this, suppose the teacher says to the machine, 'Do your homework now'. This may cause 'Teacher says "Do

3. Or rather 'programmed in' for our child-machine will be programmed in a digital computer. But the logical system will not have to be learnt.

your homework now"' to be included amongst the well-established facts. Another such fact might be, 'Everything that teacher says is true'. Combining these may eventually lead to the imperative, 'Do your homework now', being included amongst the well-established facts, and this, by the construction of the machine, will mean that the homework actually gets started, but the effect is very satisfactory. The processes of inference used by the machine need not be such as would satisfy the most exacting logicians. There might for instance be no hierarchy of types. But this need not mean that type fallacies will occur, any more than we are bound to fall over unfenced cliffs. Suitable imperatives (expressed *within* the systems, not forming part of the rules the system) such as 'Do not use a class unless it is a subclass of one which has been mentioned by teacher' can have a similar effect to 'Do not go too near the edge'.

The imperatives that can be obeyed by a machine that has no limbs are bound to be of a rather intellectual character, as in the example (doing homework) given above. Important amongst such imperatives will be ones which regulate the order in which the rules of the logical system concerned are to be applied. For at each stage when one is using a logical system, there is a very large number of alternative steps, any of which one is permitted to apply, so far as obedience to the rules of the logical system is concerned. These choices make the difference between a brilliant and a footling reasoner, not the difference between a sound and a fallacious one. Propositions leading to imperatives of this kind might be 'When Socrates is mentioned, use the syllogism in Barbara' or 'If one method has been proved to be quicker than another, do not use the slower method'. Some of these may be 'given by authority', but others may be produced by the machine itself, *e.g.* by scientific induction.

The idea of a learning machine may appear paradoxical to some readers. How can the rules of operation of the machine change? They should describe completely how the machine will react whatever its history might be, whatever changes it might undergo. The rules are thus quite time-invariant. This is quite true. The explanation of the paradox is that the rules which get changed in the learning process are of a rather less pretentious kind, claiming only an ephemeral validity. The reader may draw a parallel with the Constitution of the United States.

An important feature of a learning machine is that its teacher will often be very largely ignorant of quite what is going on inside, although he may still be able to some extent to predict his pupil's behaviour. This should apply most strongly to the later education of a machine arising from a child-machine of well-tried design (or programme). This is in clear contrast with normal procedure when using a machine to do computations: one's object is then to have a clear mental picture of the state of the machine at each moment in the computation. This object can only be achieved with a struggle. The view that 'the machine can only do what we know how to order it to do',[4] appears strange in face of this. Most of the programmes

4. Compare Lady Lovelace's statement (p. 225), which does not contain the word 'only'.

which we can put into the machine will result in its doing something that we cannot make sense of at all, or which we regard as completely random behaviour. Intelligent behaviour presumably consists in a departure from the completely disciplined behaviour involved in computation, but a rather slight one, which does not give rise to random behaviour, or to pointless repetitive loops. Another important result of preparing our machine for its part in the imitation game by a process of teaching and learning is that 'human fallibility' is likely to be omitted in a rather natural way, *i.e.* without special 'coaching'. (The reader should reconcile this with the point of view on pp. 24, 25.) Processes that are learnt do not produce a hundred per cent. Certainty of result; if they did they could not be unlearnt.

It is probably wise to include a random element in a learning machine (see p. 438). A random element is rather useful when we are searching for a solution of some problem. Suppose for instance we wanted to find a number between 50 and 200 which was equal to the square of the sum of its digits, we might start at 51 then try 52 and go on until we got a number that worked. Alternatively we might choose numbers at random until we got a a good one. This method has the advantage that it is unnecessary to keep track of the values that have been tried, but the disadvantage that one may try the same one twice, but this is not very important if there are several solutions. The systematic method has the disadvantage that there may be an enormous block without any solutions in the region which has to be investigated first. Now the learning process may be regarded as a search for a form of behaviour which will satisfy the teacher (or some other criterion). Since there is probably a very large number of satisfactory solutions the random method seems to be better than the systematic. It should be noticed that it is used in the analogous process of evolution. But there the systematic method is not possible. How could one keep track of the different genetical combinations that had been tried, so as to avoid trying them again?

We may hope that machines will eventually compete with men in all purely intellectual fields. But which are the best ones to start with? Even this is a difficult decision. Many people think that a very abstract activity, like the playing of chess, would be best. It can also be maintained that it is best to provide the machine with the best sense organs that money can buy, and then teach it to understand and speak English. This process could follow the normal teaching of a child. Things would be pointed out and named, etc. Again I do not know what the right answer is, but I think both approaches should be tried.

We can only see a short distance ahead, but we can see plenty there that needs to be done.

References

Samuel Butler, *Erewhon*, London, 1865. Chapters 23, 24, 25, *The Book of the Machines.*

Alonzo Church, 'An Unsolvable Problem of Elementary Number Theory', *American J. of Math.*, 58 (1936), 345–363.

K. Gödel, 'Über formal unentscheidbare Sätze der Principia Mathematica und verwandter Systeme, I', *Monatshefte für Math. und Phys.*, (1931), 173–189.

D. R. Hartree, *Calculating Instruments and Machines*, New York, 1949.

S. C. Kleene, 'General Recursive Functions of Natural Numbers', *American J. of Math.*, 57 (1935), 153–173 and 219–244.

G. Jefferson, 'The Mind of Mechanical Man'. Lister Oration for 1949. *British Medical Journal*, vol. i (1949), 1105–1121.

Countess of Lovelace, 'Translator's notes to an article on Babbage's Analytical Engiro', *Scientific Memoirs* (ed. by R. Taylor), vol. 3 (1842), 691–731.

Bertrand Russell, *History of Western Philosophy*, London, 1940.

A. M. Turing, 'On Computable Numbers, with an Application to the Entscheidungs-problem', *Proc. London Math. Soc.* (2), 42 (1937), 230–265.

Victoria University of Manchester.

Chapter 15

Minds, brains, and programs

John R. Searle

WHAT psychological and philosophical significance should we attach to recent efforts at computer simulations of human cognitive capacities? In answering this question, I find it useful to distinguish what I will call 'strong' AI from 'weak' or 'cautious' AI (Artificial Intelligence). According to weak AI, the principal value of the computer in the study of the mind is that it gives us a very powerful tool. For example, it enables us to formulate and test hypotheses in a more rigorous and precise fashion. But according to strong AI, the computer is not merely a tool in the study of the mind; rather, the appropriately programmed computer really is a mind, in the sense that computers given the right programs can be literally said to *understand* and have other cognitive states. In strong AI, because the programmed computer has cognitive states, the programs are not mere tools that enable us to test psychological explanations; rather, the programs are themselves the explanations.

I have no objection to the claims of weak AI, at least as far as this article is concerned. My discussion here will be directed at the claims I have defined as those of strong AI, specifically the claim that the appropriately programmed computer literally has cognitive states and that the programs thereby explain human cognition. When I hereafter refer to AI, I have in mind the strong version, as expressed by these two claims.

I will consider the work of Roger Schank and his colleagues at Yale (Schank & Abelson 1977), because I am more familiar with it than I am with any other similar claims, and because it provides a very clear example of the sort of work I wish to examine. But nothing that follows depends upon the details of Schank's programs. The same arguments would apply to Winograd's SHRDLU (Winograd 1973), Weizenbaum's ELIZA (Weizenbaum 1965), and indeed any Turing machine simulation of human mental phenomena.

Very briefly, and leaving out the various details, one can describe Schank's program as follows: the aim of the program is to simulate the human ability to understand stories. It is characteristic of human beings' story-understanding capacity that they can answer questions about the story even though the information that they give was never explicitly stated in the story. Thus, for example, suppose you are given the following story: 'A man went into a restaurant and ordered a hamburger. When the hamburger arrived it was burned to a crisp, and the man stormed out of

John R. Searle, 'Minds, Brains, and Programs', *Behavioral and Brain Sciences* 3 (1980).

the restaurant angrily, without paying for the hamburger or leaving a tip.' Now, if you are asked 'Did the man eat the hamburger?' you will presumably answer, 'No, he did not.' Similarly, if you are given the following story: 'A man went into a restaurant and ordered a hamburger; when the hamburger came he was very pleased with it; and as he left the restaurant he gave the waitress a large tip before paying his bill,' and you are asked the question, 'Did the man eat the hamburger?,' you will presumably answer, 'Yes, he ate the hamburger.' Now Schank's machines can similarly answer questions about restaurants in this fashion. To do this, they have a 'representation' of the sort of information that human beings have about restaurants, which enables them to answer such questions as those above, given these sorts of stories. When the machine is given the story and then asked the question, the machine will print out answers of the sort that we would expect human beings to give if told similar stories. Partisans of strong AI claim that in this question and answer sequence the machine is not only simulating a human ability but also

1. that the machine can literally be said to *understand* the story and provide the answers to questions, and
2. that what the machine and its program do *explains* the human ability to understand the story and answer questions about it.

Both claims seem to me to be totally unsupported by Schank's[1] work, as I will attempt to show in what follows.

One way to test any theory of the mind is to ask oneself what it would be like if my mind actually worked on the principles that the theory says all minds work on. Let us apply this test to the Schank program with the following *Gedankenexperiment.* Suppose that I'm locked in a room and given a large batch of Chinese writing. Suppose furthermore (as is indeed the case) that I know no Chinese, either written or spoken, and that I'm not even confident that I could recognize Chinese writing as Chinese writing distinct from, say, Japanese writing or meaningless squiggles. To me, Chinese writing is just so many meaningless squiggles. Now suppose further that after this first batch of Chinese writing I am given a second batch of Chinese script together with a set of rules for correlating the second batch with the first batch. The rules are in English, and I understand these rules as well as any other native speaker of English. They enable me to correlate one set of formal symbols with another set of formal symbols, and all that 'formal' means here is that I can identify the symbols entirely by their shapes. Now suppose also that I am given a third batch of Chinese symbols together with some instructions, again in English, that enable me to correlate elements of this third batch with the first two batches, and these rules instruct me how to give back certain Chinese symbols with certain sorts of shapes in response to certain sorts of shapes given me in the third batch. Unknown to me, the people who are giving me all of these symbols call the first batch 'a script,' they call the second batch a 'story,' and they call the third batch

1. I am not, of course, saying that Schank himself is committed to these claims.

'questions.' Furthermore, they call the symbols I give them back in response to the third batch 'answers to the questions,' and the set of rules in English that they gave me, they call 'the program.' Now just to complicate the story a little, imagine that these people also give me stories in English, which I understand, and they then ask me questions in English about these stories, and I give them back answers in English. Suppose also that after a while I get so good at following the instructions for manipulating the Chinese symbols and the programmers get so good at writing the programs that from the external point of view—that is, from the point of view of somebody outside the room in which I am locked—my answers to the questions are absolutely indistinguishable from those of native Chinese speakers. Nobody just looking at my answers can tell that I don't speak a word of Chinese. Let us also suppose that my answers to the English questions are, as they no doubt would be, indistinguishable from those of other native English speakers, for the simple reason that I am a native English speaker. From the external point of view—from the point of view of someone reading my 'answers'—the answers to the Chinese questions and the English questions are equally good. But in the Chinese case, unlike the English case, I produce the answers by manipulating uninterpreted formal symbols. As far as the Chinese is concerned, I simply behave like a computer; I perform computational operations on formally specified elements. For the purposes of the Chinese, I am simply an instantiation of the computer program.

Now the claims made by strong AI are that the programmed computer understands the stories and that the program in some sense explains human understanding. But we are now in a position to examine these claims in light of our thought experiment.

1. As regards the first claim, it seems to me quite obvious in the example that I do not understand a word of the Chinese stories. I have inputs and outputs that are indistinguishable from those of the native Chinese speaker, and I can have any formal program you like, but I still understand nothing. For the same reasons, Schank's computer understands nothing of any stories, whether in Chinese, English, or whatever, since in the Chinese case the computer is me, and in cases where the computer is not me, the computer has nothing more than I have in the case where I understand nothing.

2. As regards the second claim, that the program explains human understanding, we can see that the computer and its program do not provide sufficient conditions of understanding since the computer and the program are functioning, and there is no understanding. But does it even provide a necessary condition or a significant contribution to understanding? One of the claims made by the supporters of strong AI is that when I understand a story in English, what I am doing is exactly the same—or perhaps more of the same—as what I was doing in manipulating the Chinese symbols. It is simply more formal symbol manipulation that distinguishes the case in English, where I do understand, from the case in Chinese, where I don't. I have not demonstrated that this claim is false, but it would certainly appear an incredible claim in the example. Such plausibility as the claim has derives from the

supposition that we can construct a program that will have the same inputs and outputs as native speakers, and in addition we assume that speakers have some level of description where they are also instantiations of a program. On the basis of these two assumptions we assume that even if Schank's program isn't the whole story about understanding, it may be part of the story. Well, I suppose that is an empirical possibility, but not the slightest reason has so far been given to believe that it is true, since what is suggested—though certainly not demonstrated—by the example is that the computer program is simply irrelevant to my understanding of the story. In the Chinese case I have everything that artificial intelligence can put into me by way of a program, and I understand nothing; in the English case I understand everything, and there is so far no reason at all to suppose that my understanding has anything to do with computer programs, that is, with computational operations on purely formally specified elements. As long as the program is defined in terms of computational operations on purely formally defined elements, what the example suggests is that these by themselves have no interesting connection with understanding. They are certainly not sufficient conditions, and not the slightest reason has been given to suppose that they are necessary conditions or even that they make a significant contribution to understanding. Notice that the force of the argument is not simply that different machines can have the same input and output while operating on different formal principles—that is not the point at all. Rather, whatever purely formal principles you put into the computer, they will not be sufficient for understanding, since a human will be able to follow the formal principles without understanding anything. No reason whatever has been offered to suppose that such principles are necessary or even contributory, since no reason has been given to suppose that when I understand English I am operating with any formal program at all.

Well, then, what is it that I have in the case of the English sentences that I do not have in the case of the Chinese sentences? The obvious answer is that I know what the former mean, while I haven't the faintest idea what the latter mean. But in what does this consist and why couldn't we give it to a machine, whatever it is? I will return to this question later, but first I want to continue with the example.

I have had the occasions to present this example to several workers in artifical intelligence, and, interestingly, they do not seem to agree on what the proper reply to it is. I get a surprising variety of replies, and in what follows I will consider the most common of these (specified along with their geographic origins).

But first I want to block some common misunderstandings about 'understanding': in many of these discussions one finds a lot of fancy footwork about the word 'understanding.' My critics point out that there are many different degrees of understanding; that 'understanding' is not a simple two-place predicate; that there are even different kinds and levels of understanding, and often the law of excluded middle doesn't even apply in a straightforward way to statements of the form 'x understands y'; that in many cases it is a matter for decision and not a simple matter of fact whether x understands y; and so on. To all of these points I want to say: of course, of course. But they have nothing to do with the points at issue. There are clear cases in which 'understanding' literally applies and clear cases in which it does not apply; and these two sorts of cases are all I need for this argument.[2] I understand stories in English; to a lesser degree I can understand stories in French; to a still lesser degree, stories in German; and in Chinese, not at all. My car and my adding machine, on the other hand, understand nothing: they are not in that line of business. We often attribute 'understanding' and other cognitive predicates by metaphor and analogy to cars, adding machines, and other artifacts, but nothing is proved by such attributions. We say, 'The door *knows* when to open because of its photoelectric cell,' 'The adding machine *knows how* (*understands how*, is *able*) to do addition and subtraction but not division,' and 'The thermostat *perceives* chances in the temperature.' The reason we make these attributions is quite interesting, and it has to do with the fact that in artifacts we extend our own intentionality;[3] our tools are extensions of our purposes, and so we find it natural to make metaphorical attributions of intentionality to them; but I take it no philosophical ice is cut by such examples. The sense in which an automatic door 'understands instructions' from its photoelectric cell is not at all the sense in which I understand English. If the sense in which Schank's programmed computers understand stories is supposed to be the metaphorical sense in which the door understands, and not the sense in which I understand English, the issue would not be worth discussing. But Newell and Simon (1963) write that the kind of cognition they claim for computers is exactly the same as for human beings. I like the straightforwardness of this claim, and it is the sort of claim I will be considering. I will argue that in the literal sense the programmed computer understands what the car and the adding machine understand, namely, exactly nothing. The computer understanding is not just (like my understanding of German) partial or incomplete; it is zero.

Now to the replies:

I. The systems reply (Berkeley). 'While it is true that the individual person who is locked in the room does not understand the story, the fact is that he is merely part of a whole system, and the system does understand the story. The person has a large ledger in front of him in which are written the rules, he has a lot of scratch paper and pencils for doing calculations, he has 'data banks' of sets of Chinese symbols. Now, understanding is not being ascribed to the mere individual; rather it is being ascribed to this whole system of which he is a part.'

My response to the systems theory is quite simple: let the individual internalize all of these elements of the system. He memorizes the rules in the ledger and the

2. Also, 'understanding' implies both the possession of mental (intentional) states and the truth (validity, success) of these states. For the purposes of this discussion we are concerned only with the possession of the states.

3. Intentionality is by definition that feature of certain mental states by which they are directed at or about objects and states of affairs in the world. Thus, beliefs, desires, and intentions are intentional states; undirected forms of anxiety and depression are not. For further discussion see Searle (1979c).

data banks of Chinese symbols, and he does all the calculations in his head. The individual then incorporates the entire system. There isn't anything at all to the system that he does not encompass. We can even get rid of the room and suppose he works outdoors. All the same, he understands nothing of the Chinese, and a fortiori neither does the system, because there isn't anything in the system that isn't in him. If he doesn't understand, then there is no way the system could understand because the system is just a part of him.

Actually I feel somewhat embarrassed to give even this answer to the systems theory because the theory seems to me so unplausible to start with. The idea is that while a person doesn't understand Chinese, somehow the *conjunction* of that person and bits of paper might understand Chinese. It is not easy for me to imagine how someone who was not in the grip of an ideology would find the idea at all plausible. Still, I think many people who are committed to the ideology of strong AI will in the end be inclined to say something very much like this; so let us pursue it a bit further. According to one version of this view, while the man in the internalized systems example doesn't understand Chinese in the sense that a native Chinese speaker does (because, for example, he doesn't know that the story refers to restaurants and hamburgers, etc.), still 'the man as a formal symbol manipulation system' *really does understand Chinese.* The subsystem of the man that is the formal symbol manipulation system for Chinese should not be confused with the subsystem for English.

So there are really two subsystems in the man; one understands English, the other Chinese, and 'it's just that the two systems have little to do with each other.' But, I want to reply, not only do they have little to do with each other, they are not even remotely alike. The subsystem that understands English (assuming we allow ourselves to talk in this jargon of 'subsystems' for a moment) knows that the stories are about restaurants and eating hamburgers, he knows that he is being asked questions about restaurants and that he is answering questions as best he can by making various inferences from the content of the story, and so on. But the Chinese system knows none of this. Whereas the English subsystem knows that 'hamburgers' refers to hamburgers, the Chinese subsystem knows only that 'squiggle squiggle' is followed by 'squoggle squoggle.' All he knows is that various formal symbols are being introduced at one end and manipulated according to rules written in English, and other symbols are going out at the other end. The whole point of the original example was to argue that such symbol manipulation by itself couldn't be sufficient for understanding Chinese in any literal sense because the man could write 'squoggle squoggle' after 'squiggle squiggle' without understanding anything in Chinese. And it doesn't meet that argument to postulate subsystems within the man, because the subsystems are no better off than the man was in the first place; they still don't have anything even remotely like what the English-speaking man (or subsystem) has. Indeed, in the case as described, the Chinese subsystem is simply a part of the English subsystem, a part that engages in meaningless symbol manipulation according to rules in English.

Let us ask ourselves what is supposed to motivate the systems reply in the first place; that is, what *independent* grounds are there supposed to be for saying that the agent must have a subsystem within him that literally understands stories in Chinese? As far as I can tell the only grounds are that in the example I have the same input and output as native Chinese speakers and a program that goes from one to the other. But the whole point of the examples has been to try to show that that couldn't be sufficient for understanding, in the sense in which I understand stories in English, because a person, and hence the set of systems that go to make up a person, could have the right combination of input, output, and program and still not understand anything in the relevant literal sense in which I understand English. The only motivation for saying there *must* be a subsystem in me that understands Chinese is that I have a program and I can pass the Turing test; I can fool native Chinese speakers. But precisely one of the points at issue is the adequacy of the Turing test. The example shows that there could be two 'systems,' both of which pass the Turing test, but only one of which understands; and it is no argument against this point to say that since they both pass the Turing test they must both understand, since this claim fails to meet the argument that the system in me that understands English has a great deal more than the system that merely processes Chinese. In short, the systems reply simply begs the question by insisting without argument that the system must understand Chinese.

Furthermore, the systems reply would appear to lead to consequences that are independently absurd. If we are to conclude that there must be cognition in me on the grounds that I have a certain sort of input and output and a program in between, then it looks like all sorts of noncognitive subsystems are going to turn out to be cognitive. For example, there is a level of description at which my stomach does information processing, and it instantiates any number of computer programs, but I take it we do not want to say that it has any understanding (cf. Pylyshyn 1980). But if we accept the systems reply, then it is hard to see how we avoid saying that stomach, heart, liver, and so on, are all understanding subsystems, since there is no principled way to distinguish the motivation for saying the Chinese subsystem understands from saying that the stomach understands. It is, by the way, not an answer to this point to say that the Chinese system has information as input and output and the stomach has food and food products as input and output, since from the point of view of the agent, from my point of view, there is no information in either the food or the Chinese—the Chinese is just so many meaningless squiggles. The information in the Chinese case is solely in the eyes of the programmers and the interpreters, and there is nothing to prevent them from treating the input and output of my digestive organs as information if they so desire.

This last point bears on some independent problems in strong AI, and it is worth digressing for a moment to explain it. If strong AI is to be a branch of psychology, then it must be able to distinguish those systems that are genuinely mental from those that are not. It must be able to distinguish the principles on which the mind works from those on which nonmental systems work; otherwise it will offer us no explanations of what is specifically mental about the mental. And the mental-nonmental distinction cannot be just in the eye of the beholder but it must be intrinsic to the systems; otherwise it would be up to any beholder to treat people as nonmental and, for example, hurricanes as mental if he likes. But quite often in the Al literature the distinction is blurred in ways that would in the long run prove disastrous to the claim that AI is a cognitive inquiry. McCarthy, for example, writes, 'Machines as simple as thermostats can be said to have beliefs, and having beliefs seems to be a characteristic of most machines capable of problem solving performance' (McCarthy 1979). Anyone who thinks strong AI has a chance as a theory of the mind ought to ponder the implications of that remark. We are asked to accept it as a discovery of strong AI that the hunk of metal on the wall that we use to regulate the temperature has beliefs in exactly the same sense that we, our spouses, and our children have beliefs, and furthermore that 'most' of the other machines in the room—telephone, tape recorder, adding machine, electric light switch,—also have beliefs in this literal sense. It is not the aim of this article to argue against McCarthy's point, so I will simply assert the following without argument. The study of the mind starts with such facts as that humans have beliefs, while thermostats, telephones, and adding machines don't. If you get a theory that denies this point you have produced a counter-example to the theory and the theory is false. One gets the impression that people in AI who write this sort of thing think they can get away with it because they don't really take it seriously, and they don't think anyone else will either. I propose for a moment at least, to take it seriously. Think hard for one minute about what would be necessary to establish that that hunk of metal on the wall over there had real beliefs, beliefs with direction of fit, propositional content, and conditions of satisfaction; beliefs that had the possibility of being strong beliefs or weak beliefs; nervous, anxious, or secure beliefs; dogmatic, rational, or superstitious beliefs; blind faiths or hesitant cogitations; any kind of beliefs. The thermostat is not a candidate. Neither is stomach, liver, adding machine, or telephone. However, since we are taking the idea seriously, notice that its truth would be fatal to strong AI's claim to be a science of the mind. For now the mind is everywhere. What we wanted to know is what distinguishes the mind from thermostats and livers. And if McCarthy were right, strong AI wouldn't have a hope of telling us that.

II. The Robot Reply (Yale). 'Suppose we wrote a different kind of program from Schank's program. Suppose we put a computer inside a robot, and this computer would not just take in formal symbols as input and give out formal symbols as output, but rather would actually operate the robot in such a way that the robot does something very much like perceiving, walking, moving about, hammering nails, eating, drinking—anything you like. The robot would, for example, have a television camera attached to it that enabled it to 'see,' it would have arms and legs that enabled it to 'act,' and all of this would be controlled by its computer 'brain.'

Such a robot would, unlike Schank's computer, have genuine understanding and other mental states.'

The first thing to notice about the robot reply is that it tacitly concedes that cognition is not soley a matter of formal symbol manipulation, since this reply adds a set of causal relation with the outside world (cf. Fodor 1980). But the answer to the robot reply is that the addition of such 'perceptual' and 'motor' capacities adds nothing by way of understanding, in particular, or intentionality, in general, to Schank's original program. To see this, notice that the same thought experiment applies to the robot case. Suppose that instead of the computer inside the robot, you put me inside the room and, as in the original Chinese case, you give me more Chinese symbols with more instructions in English for matching Chinese symbols to Chinese symbols and feeding back Chinese symbols to the outside. Suppose, unknown to me, some of the Chinese symbols that come to me come from a television camera attached to the robot and other Chinese symbols that I am giving out serve to make the motors inside the robot move the robot's legs or arms. It is important to emphasize that all I am doing is manipulating formal symbols: I know none of these other facts. I am receiving 'information' from the robot's 'perceptual' apparatus, and I am giving out 'instructions' to its motor apparatus without knowing either of these facts. I am the robot's homunculus, but unlike the traditional homunculus, I don't know what's going on. I don't understand anything except the rules for symbol manipulation. Now in this case I want to say that the robot has no intentional states at all; it is simply moving about as a result of its electrical wiring and its program. And furthermore, by instantiating the program I have no intentional states of the relevant type. All I do is follow formal instructions about manipulating formal symbols.

III. The brain simulator reply (Berkeley and M.I.T.). 'Suppose we design a program that doesn't represent information that we have about the world, such as the information in Schank's scripts, but simulates the actual sequence of neuron firings at the synapses of the brain of a native Chinese speaker when he understands stories in Chinese and gives answers to them. The machine takes in Chinese stories and questions about them as input, it simulates the formal structure of actual Chinese brains in processing these stories, and it gives out Chinese answers as outputs. We can even imagine that the machine operates, not with a single serial program, but with a whole set of programs operating in parallel, in the manner that actual human brains presumably operate when they process natural language. Now surely in such a case we would have to say that the machine understood the stories; and if we refuse to say that, wouldn't we also have to deny that native Chinese speakers understood the stories? At the level of the synapses, what would or could be different about the program of the computer and the program of the Chinese brain?'

Before countering this reply I want to digress to note that it is an odd reply for any partisan of artificial intelligence (or functionalism, etc.) to make: I thought the whole idea of strong AI is that we don't need to know how the brain works to know how the mind works. The basic hypothesis, or so I had supposed, was that there is a level of mental operations consisting of computational processes over formal elements that constitute the essence of the mental and can be realized in all sorts of different brain processes, in the same way that any computer program can be realized in different computer hardwares: on the assumptions of strong AI, the mind is to the brain as the program is to the hardware, and thus we can understand the mind without doing neurophysiology. If we had to know how the brain worked to do AI, we wouldn't bother with AI. However, even getting this close to the operation of the brain is still not sufficient to produce understanding. To see this, imagine that instead of a monolingual man in a room shuffling symbols we have the man operate an elaborate set of water pipes with valves connecting them. When the man receives the Chinese symbols, he looks up in the program, written in English, which valves he has to turn on and off. Each water connection corresponds to a synapse in the Chinese brain, and the whole system is rigged up so that after doing all the right firings, that is after turning on all the right faucets, the Chinese answers pop out at the output end of the series of pipes.

Now where is the understanding in this system? It takes Chinese as input, it simulates the formal structure of the synapses of the Chinese brain, and it gives Chinese as output. But the man certainly doesn't understand Chinese, and neither do the water pipes, and if we are tempted to adopt what I think is the absurd view that somehow the *conjunction* of man *and* water pipes understands, remember that in principle the man can internalize the formal structure of the water pipes and do all the 'neuron firings' in his imagination. The problem with the brain simulator is that it is simulating the wrong things about the brain. As long as it simulates only the formal structure of the sequence of neuron firings at the synapses, it won't have simulated what matters about the brain, namely its causal properties, its ability to produce intentional states. And that the formal properties are not sufficient for the causal properties is shown by the water pipe example: we can have all the formal properties carved off from the relevant neurobiological causal properties.

IV. The combination reply (Berkeley and Stanford). 'While each of the previous three replies might not be completely convincing by itself as a refutation of the Chinese room counterexample, if you take all three together they are collectively much more convincing and even decisive. Imagine a robot with a brain-shaped computer lodged in its cranial cavity, imagine the computer programmed with all the synapses of a human brain, imagine the whole behavior of the robot is indistinguishable from human behavior, and now think of the whole thing as a unified system and not just as a computer with inputs and outputs. Surely in such a case we would have to ascribe intentionality to the system.'

I entirely agree that in such a case we would find it rational and indeed irresistible to accept the hypothesis that the robot had intentionality, as long as we knew nothing more about it. Indeed, besides appearance and behavior, the other elements of the combination are really irrelevant. If we could build a robot whose behavior was indistinguishable over a large range from human behavior, we would attribute intentionality to it, pending some reason not to. We wouldn't need to know in advance that its computer brain was a formal analogue of the human brain.

But I really don't see that this is any help to the claims of strong Al; and here's why: According to strong AI, instantiating a formal program with the right input and output is a sufficient condition of, indeed is constitutive of, intentionality. As Newell (1979) puts it, the essence of the mental is the operation of a physical symbol system. But the attributions of intentionality that we make to the robot in this example have nothing to do with formal programs. They are simply based on the assumption that if the robot looks and behaves sufficiently like us, then we would suppose, until proven otherwise, that it must have mental states like ours that cause and are expressed by its behavior and it must have an inner mechanism capable of producing such mental states. If we knew independently how to account for its behavior without such assumptions we would not attribute intentionality to it, especially if we knew it had a formal program. And this is precisely the point of my earlier reply to objection II.

Suppose we knew that the robot's behavior was entirely accounted for by the fact that a man inside it was receiving uninterpreted formal symbols from the robot's sensory receptors and sending out uninterpreted formal symbols to its motor mechanisms, and the man was doing this symbol manipulation in accordance with a bunch of rules. Furthermore, suppose the man knows none of these facts about the robot, all he knows is which operations to perform on which meaningless symbols. In such a case we would regard the robot as an ingenious mechanical dummy. The hypothesis that the dummy has a mind would now be unwarranted and unnecessary, for there is now no longer any reason to ascribe intentionality to the robot or to the system of which it is a part (except of course for the man's intentionality in manipulating the symbols). The formal symbol manipulations go on, the input and output are correctly matched, but the only real locus of intentionality is the man, and he doesn't know any of the relevant intentional states; he doesn't, for example, *see* what comes into the robot's eyes, he doesn't *intend* to move the robot's arm, and he doesn't *understand* any of the remarks made to or by the robot. Nor, for the reasons stated earlier, does the system of which man and robot are a part.

To see this point, contrast this case with cases in which we find it completely natural to ascribe intentionality to members of certain other primate species such as apes and monkeys and to domestic animals such as dogs. The reasons we find it natural are, roughly, two: we can't make sense of the animal's behavior without the ascription of intentionality, and we can see that the beasts are made of similar stuff to ourselves—that is an eye, that a nose, this is its skin, and so on. Given the coherence of the animal's behavior and the assumption of the same causal stuff underlying it, we assume both that the animal must have mental states underlying its behavior, and that the mental states must be produced by mechanisms made out of the stuff that is like our stuff. We would certainly make similar assumptions about the robot unless we had some reason not to, but as soon as we knew that the behavior was the result of a formal program, and that the actual causal properties of the physical substance were irrelevant we would abandon the assumption of intentionality.

There are two other responses to my example that come up frequently (and so are worth discussing) but really miss the point.

V. The other minds reply (Yale). 'How do you know that other people understand Chinese or anything else? Only by their behavior. Now the computer can pass the behavioral tests as well as they can (in principle), so if you are going to attribute cognition to other people you must in principle also attribute it to computers.'

This objection really is only worth a short reply. The problem in this discussion is not about how I know that other people have cognitive states, but rather what it is that I am attributing to them when I attribute cognitive states to them. The thrust of the argument is that it couldn't be just computational processes and their output because the computational processes and their output can exist without the cognitive state. It is no answer to this argument to feign anesthesia. In 'cognitive sciences' one presupposes the reality and knowability of the mental in the same way that in physical sciences one has to presuppose the reality and knowability of physical objects.

VI. The many mansions reply (Berkeley). 'Your whole argument presupposes that AI is only about analogue and digital computers. But that just happens to be the present state of technology. Whatever these causal processes are that you say are essential for intentionality (assuming you are right), eventually we will be able to build devices that have these causal processes, and that will be artificial intelligence. So your arguments are in no way directed at the ability of artificial intelligence to produce and explain cognition.'

I really have no objection to this reply save to say that it in effect trivializes the project of strong AI by redefining it as whatever artificially produces and explains cognition. The interest of the original claim made on behalf of artificial intelligence is that it was a precise, well defined thesis: mental processes are computational processes over formally defined elements. I have been concerned to challenge that thesis. If the claim is redefined so that it is no longer that thesis, my objections no longer apply because there is no longer a testable hypothesis for them to apply to.

Let us now return to the question I promised I would try to answer: granted that in my original example I understand the English and I do not understand the Chinese, and granted therefore that the machine doesn't understand either English or Chinese, still there must be something about me that makes it the case that I understand English and a corresponding something lacking in me that makes it the case that I fail to understand Chinese. Now why couldn't we give those somethings, whatever they are, to a machine?

I see no reason in principle why we couldn't give a machine the capacity to understand English or Chinese, since in an important sense our bodies with our brains are precisely such machines. But I do see very strong arguments for saying that we could not give such a thing to a machine where the operation of the machine is defined solely in terms of computational processes over formally defined elements; that is, where the operation of the machine is defined as an instantiation of a computer program. It is not because I am the instantiation of a computer program that I am able to understand English and have other forms of intentionality (I am, I suppose, the instantiation of any number of computer programs), but as far as we know it is because I am a certain sort of organism with a certain biological (i.e. chemical and physical) structure, and this structure, under certain conditions, is causally capable of producing perception, action, understanding, learning, and other intentional phenomena. And part of the point of the present argument is that only something that had those causal powers could have that intentionality. Perhaps other physical and chemical processes could produce exactly these effects; perhaps, for example, Martians also have intentionality but their brains are made of different stuff. That is an empirical question, rather like the question whether photosynthesis can be done by something with a chemistry different from that of chlorophyll.

But the main point of the present argument is that no purely formal model will ever be sufficient by itself for intentionality because the formal properties are not by themselves constitutive of intentionality, and they have by themselves no causal powers except the power, when instantiated, to produce the next stage of the formalism when the machine is running. And any other causal properties that particular realizations of the formal model have, are irrelevant to the formal model because we can always put the same formal model in a different realization where those causal properties are obviously absent. Even if, by some miracle, Chinese speakers exactly realize Schank's program, we can put the same program in English speakers, water pipes, or computers, none of which understand Chinese, the program notwithstanding.

What matters about brain operations is not the formal shadow cast by the sequence of synapses but rather the actual properties of the sequences. All the arguments for the strong version of artificial intelligence that I have seen insist on drawing an outline around the shadows cast by cognition and then claiming that the shadows are the real thing.

By way of concluding I want to try to state some of the general philosophical points implicit in the argument. For clarity I will try to do it in a question and answer fashion, and I begin with that old chestnut of a question:

'Could a machine think?'

The answer is, obviously, yes. We are precisely such machines.

'Yes, but could an artifact, a man-made machine, think?'

Assuming it is possible to produce artificially a machine with a nervous system, neurons with axons and dendrites, and all the rest of it, sufficiently like ours, again the answer to the question seems to be obviously, yes. If you can exactly duplicate the causes, you could duplicate the effects. And indeed it might be possible to produce consciousness, intentionality, and all the rest of it using some other sorts of chemical principles than those that human beings use. It is, as I said, an empirical question.

'OK, but could a digital computer think?'

If by 'digital computer' we mean anything at all that has a level of description where it can correctly be described as the instantiation of a computer program, then again the answer is, of course, yes, since we are the instantiations of any number of computer programs, and we can think.

'But could something think, understand, and so on *solely* in virtue of being a computer with the right sort of program? Could instantiating a program, the right program of course, by itself be a sufficient condition of understanding?'

This I think is the right question to ask, though it is usually confused with one or more of the earlier questions, and the answer to it is no.

'Why not?'

Because the formal symbol manipulations by themselves don't have any intentionality; they are quite meaningless; they aren't even *symbol* manipulations, since the symbols don't symbolize anything. In the linguistic jargon, they have only a syntax but no semantics. Such intentionality as computers appear to have is solely in the minds of those who program them and those who use them, those who send in the input and those who interpret the output.

The aim of the Chinese room example was to try to show this by showing that as soon as we put something into the system that really does have intentionality (a man), and we program him with the formal program, you can see that the formal program carries no additional intentionality. It adds nothing, for example, to a man's ability to understand Chinese.

Precisely that feature of AI that seemed so appealing—the distinction between the program and the realization—proves fatal to the claim that simulation could be duplication. The distinction between the program and its realization in the hardware seems to be parallel to the distinction between the level of mental operations and the level of brain operations. And if we could describe the level of mental operations as a formal program, then it seems we could describe what was essential about the mind without doing either introspective psychology or neurophysiology of the brain. But the equation, 'mind is to brain as program is to hardware' breaks down at several points, among them the following three:

First, the distinction between program and realization has the consequence that the same program could have all sorts of crazy realizations that had no form of intentionality. Weizenbaum (1976, Ch. 2), for example, shows in detail how to construct a computer using a roll of toilet paper and a pile of small stones. Similarly, the Chinese story understanding program can be programmed into a sequence of water pipes, a set of wind machines, or a monolingual English speaker, none of which thereby acquires an understanding of Chinese. Stones, toilet paper, wind, and water pipes are the wrong kind of stuff to have intentionality in the first place—only something that has the same causal powers as brains can have intentionality—and though the English speaker has the right kind of stuff for intentionality you can easily see that he doesn't get any extra intentionality by memorizing the program, since memorizing it won't teach him Chinese.

Second, the program is purely formal, but the intentional states are not in that way formal. They are defined in terms of their content, not their form. The belief that it is raining, for example, is not defined as a certain formal shape, but as a certain mental content with conditions of satisfaction, a direction of fit (see Searle 1979a, 1979b, 1979c) and the like. Indeed the belief as such hasn't even got a formal shape in this syntactic sense, since one and the same belief can be given an indefinite number of different syntactic expressions in different linguistic systems.

Third, as I mentioned before, mental states and events are literally a product of the operation of the brain, but the program is not in that way a product of the computer.

'Well if programs are in no way constitutive of mental processes, why have so many people believed the converse? That at least needs some explanation.'

I don't really know the answer to that one. The idea that computer simulations could be the real thing ought to have seemed suspicious in the first place because the computer isn't confined to simulating mental operations, by any means. No one supposes that computer simulations of a five-alarm fire will burn the neighborhood down or that a computer simulation of a rainstorm will leave us all drenched. Why on earth would anyone suppose that a computer simulation of understanding actually understood anything? It is sometimes said that it would be frightfully hard to get computers to feel pain or fall in love, but love and pain are neither harder nor easier than cognition or anything else. For simulation, all you need is the right input and output and a program in the middle that transforms the former into the latter. That is all the computer has for anything it does. To confuse simulation with duplication is the same mistake, whether it is pain, love, cognition, fires, or rainstorms.

Still, there are several reasons why AI must have seemed—and to many people perhaps still does seem—in some way to reproduce and thereby explain mental phenomena, and I believe we will not succeed in removing these illusions until we have fully exposed the reasons that give rise to them.

First, and perhaps most important, is a confusion about the notion of 'information processing': many people in cognitive science believe that the human brain, with its mind; does something called 'information processing,' and analogously the computer with its program does information processing; but fires and rainstorms, on the other hand, don't do information processing at all. Thus, though the computer can simulate the formal features of any process whatever, it stands in a special relation to the mind and brain because when the computer is properly programmed, ideally with the same program as the brain, the information processing is identical in the two cases, and this information processing is really the essence of the mental. But the trouble with this argument is that it rests on an ambiguity in the notion of 'information.' In the sense in which people 'process information' when they reflect, say, on problems in arithmetic or when they read and answer questions about stories, the programmed computer does not do 'information processing.' Rather, what it does is manipulate formal symbols. The fact that the programmer and the interpreter of the computer output use the symbols to stand for objects in the world is totally beyond the scope of the computer. The computer, to repeat, has a syntax but no semantics. Thus, if you type into the computer '2 plus 2 equals?' it will type out '4.' But it has no idea that '4' means 4 or that it means anything at all. And the point is not that it lacks some second-order information about the interpretation of its first-order symbols, but rather that its first-order symbols don't have any interpretations as far as the computer is concerned. All the computer has is more symbols. The introduction of the notion of 'information processing' therefore produces a dilemma: either we construe the notion of 'information processing' in such a way that it implies intentionality as part of the process or we don't. If the former, then the programmed computer does not do information processing, it only manipulates formal symbols. If the latter, then, though the computer does information processing, it is only doing so in the sense in which adding machines, typewriters, stomachs, thermostats, rainstorms, and hurricanes do information processing; namely, they have a level of description at which we can describe them as taking information in at one end, transforming it, and producing information as output. But in this case it is up to outside observers to interpret the input and output as information in the ordinary sense. And no similarity is established between the computer and the brain in terms of any similarity of information processing.

Second, in much of AI there is a residual behaviorism or operationalism. Since appropriately programmed computers can have input-output patterns similar to those of human beings, we are tempted to postulate mental states in the computer similar to human mental states. But once we see that it is both conceptually and empirically possible for a system to have human capacities in some realm without having any intentionality at all, we should be able to overcome this impulse. My desk adding machine has calculating capacities, but no intentionality, and in this paper I have tried to show that a system could have input and output capabilities that duplicated those of a native Chinese speaker and still not understand Chinese, regardless of how it was programmed. The Turing test is typical of the tradition in being unashamedly behavioristic and operationalistic, and I believe that if AI workers totally repudiated behaviorism and operationalism much of the confusion between simulation and duplication would be eliminated.

Third, this residual operationalism is joined to a residual form of dualism; indeed strong AI only makes sense given the dualistic assumption that, where the mind is concerned, the brain doesn't matter. In strong AI (and in functionalism, as well) what matters are programs, and programs are independent of their realization in machines; indeed, as far as AI is concerned, the same program could be realized by an electronic machine, a Cartesian mental substance, or a Hegelian world spirit. The single most surprising discovery that I have made in discussing these issues is that many AI workers are quite shocked by my idea that actual human mental phenomena might be dependent on actual physical-chemical properties of actual human brains. But if you think about it a minute you can see that I should not have been surprised; for unless you accept some form of dualism, the strong AI project hasn't got a chance. The project is to reproduce and explain the mental by designing programs, but unless the mind is not only conceptually but empirically independent of the brain you couldn't carry out the project, for the program is completely independent of any realization. Unless you believe that the mind is separable from the brain both conceptually and empirically—dualism in a strong form—you cannot hope to reproduce the mental by writing and running programs since programs must be independent of brains or any other particular forms of instantiation. If mental operations consist in computational operations on formal symbols, then it follows that they have no interesting connection with the brain; the only connection would be that the brain just happens to be one of the indefinitely many types of machines capable of instantiating the program. This form of dualism is not the traditional Cartesian variety that claims there are two sorts of *substances*, but it is Cartesian in the sense that it insists that what is specifically mental about the mind has no intrinsic connection with the actual properties of the brain. This underlying dualism is masked from us by the fact that AI literature contains frequent fulminations against 'dualism'; what the authors seem to be unaware of is that their position presupposes a strong version of dualism.

'Could a machine think?' My own view is that *only* a machine could think, and indeed only very special kinds of machines, namely brains and machines that had the same causal powers as brains. And that is the main reason strong AI has had little to tell us about thinking, since it has nothing to tell us about machines. By its own definition, it is about programs, and programs are not machines. Whatever else intentionality is, it is a biological phenomenon, and it is as likely to be as causally dependent on the specific biochemistry of its origins as lactation, photosynthesis, or any other biological phenomena. No one would suppose that we could produce milk and sugar by running a computer simulation of the formal sequences in lactation and photosynthesis, but where the mind is concerned many people are willing to believe in such a miracle because of a deep and abiding dualism: the mind they suppose is a matter of formal processes and is independent of quite specific material causes in the way that milk and sugar are not.

In defense of this dualism the hope is often expressed that the brain is a digital computer (early computers, by the way, were often called 'electronic brains'). But that is no help. Of course the brain is a digital computer. Since everything is a digital computer, brains are too. The point is that the brain's causal capacity to produce intentionality cannot consist in its instantiating a computer program, since for any program you like it is possible for something to instantiate that program and still not have any mental states. Whatever it is that the brain does to produce intentionality, it cannot consist in instantiating a program since no program, by itself, is sufficient for intentionality.

Acknowledgements

I am indebted to a rather large number of people for discussion of these matters and for their patient attempts to overcome my ignorance of artificial intelligence. I would especially like to thank Ned Block, Hubert Dreyfus, John Haugeland, Roger Schank, Robert Wilensky, and Terry Winograd.

References

Fodor, J. A. (1980) Methodological solopsism considered as a research strategy in cognitive psychology. *The Behavioral and Brain Sciences* 3:1.

McCarthy, J. (1979) Ascribing mental qualities to machines. In: *Philosophical perspectives in artificial intelligence*, ed. M. Ringle. Atlantic Highlands, N.J.: Humanities Press.

Newell, A. (1979) Physical symbol systems. Lecture at the La Jolla Conference on Cognitive Science.

Newell, A. & Simon, H A (1963) GPS, a program that simulates human thought. In: *Computers and thought*, ed. A. Feigenbaum & V. Feldman, pp. 279–93. New York: McGraw Hill.

Pylyshyn, Z. W. (1980) Computation and cognition: issues in the foundations of cognitive science. *Behavioral and Brain Sciences* 3.

Schank, R. C. & Abelson, R P (1977) *Scripts, plans, goals, and understanding*. Hillsdale, N.J.: Lawrence Erlbaum Press.

Searle, J. R. (1979a) Intentionality and the use of language. In: *Meaning and use*, ed. A. Margalit. Dordrecht: Reidel.

——(1979b) The intentionality of intention and action. *Inquiry* 22:253–80.

——(1979c) What is an intentional state? *Mind* 88:74–92.

Weizenbaum, J. (1965) Eliza—a computer program for the study of natural language communication between man and machine. *Communication of the Association for Computing Machinery* 9:36–45.

——(1976) *Computer power and human reason*. San Francisco: W. H. Freeman.

Winograd, T. (1973) A procedural model of language understanding. In: *Computer models of thought and language*, ed. R. Schank & K. Colby. San Francisco: W. H. Freeman.

Chapter 16

Escaping from the Chinese room

Margaret A. Boden

JOHN Searle, in his paper on 'Minds, Brains, and Programs' (1980), argues that computational theories in psychology are essentially worthless. He makes two main claims: that computational theories, being purely formal in nature, cannot possibly help us to understand mental processes; and that computer hardware—unlike neuroprotein—obviously lacks the right causal powers to generate mental processes. I shall argue that both these claims are mistaken.

His first claim takes for granted the widely-held (formalist) assumption that the 'computations' studied in computer science are purely syntactic, that they can be defined (in terms equally suited to symbolic logic) as *the formal manipulation of abstract symbols, by the application of formal rules.* It follows, he says, that formalist accounts—appropriate in explaining the meaningless 'information'-processing or 'symbol'-manipulations in computers—are unable to explain how human minds employ *information* or *symbols* properly so-called. Meaning, or intentionality, cannot be explained in computational terms.

Searle's point here is not that no machine can think. Humans can think, and humans—he allows—are machines; he even adopts the materialist credo that only machines can think. Nor is he saying that humans and programs are utterly incommensurable. He grants that, at some highly abstract level of description, people (like everything else) are instantiations of digital computers. His point, rather, is that nothing can think, mean, or understand *solely* in virtue of its instantiating a computer program.

To persuade us of this, Searle employs an ingenious thought-experiment. He imagines himself locked in a room, in which there are various slips of paper with doodles on them; a window through which people can pass further doodle-papers to him, and through which he can pass papers out; and a book of rules (in English) telling him how to pair the doodles, which are always identified by their shape or form. Searle spends his time, while inside the room, manipulating the doodles according to the rules.

One rule, for example, instructs him that when *squiggle-squiggle* is passed in to him, he should give out *squoggle-squoggle*. The rule-book also provides for more complex sequences of doodle-pairing, where only the first and last steps mention

Margaret A. Boden, 'Escaping from the Chinese Room'. In Margaret A. Boden, ed., *The Philosophy of Artificial Intelligence* (Oxford: Oxford University Press, 1990); first published in *Computer Models of Mind* (Cambridge: Cambridge University Press, 1988).

the transfer of paper into or out of the room. Before finding any rule directly instructing him to give out a slip of paper, he may have to locate a *blongle* doodle and compare it with a *blungle* doodle—in which case, it is the result of this comparison which determines the nature of the doodle he passes out. Sometimes many such doodle-doodle comparisons and consequent doodle-selections have to be made by him inside the room before he finds a rule allowing him to pass anything out.

So far as Searle-in-the-room is concerned, the *squiggles* and *squoggles* are mere meaningless doodles. Unknown to him, however, they are Chinese characters. The people outside the room, being Chinese, interpret them as such. Moreover, the patterns passed in and out at the window are understood by them as *questions* and *answers* respectively: the rules happen to be such that most of the questions are paired, either directly or indirectly, with what they recognize as a sensible answer. But Searle himself (inside the room) knows nothing of this.

The point, says Searle, is that Searle-in-the-room is clearly instantiating a computer program. That is, he is performing purely formal manipulations of uninterpreted patterns: he is all syntax and no semantics.

The doodle-pairing rules are equivalent to the IF-THEN rules, or 'productions', commonly used (for example) in expert systems. Some of the internal doodle-comparisons could be equivalent to what AI workers in natural-language processing call a script—for instance, the restaurant script described by R. C. Schank and R. P. Abelson (1977). In that case, Searle-in-the-room's paper-passing performance would be essentially comparable to the performance of a 'question-answering' Schankian text-analysis program. But 'question-answering' is not question-answering. Searle-in-the-room is not really *answering*: how could he, since he cannot understand the questions? Practice does not help (except perhaps in making the doodle-pairing swifter): if Searle-in-the-room ever escapes, he will be just as ignorant of Chinese as he was when he was first locked in.

Certainly, the Chinese people outside might find it useful to keep Searle-in-the-room fed and watered, much as in real life we are willing to spend large sums of money on computerized 'advice' systems. But the fact that people who already possess understanding may use an intrinsically meaningless formalist computational system to provide what they interpret (*sic*) as questions, answers, designations, interpretations, or symbols is irrelevant. They can do this only if they can externally specify a mapping between the formalism and matters of interest to them. In principle, one and the same formalism might be mappable onto several different domains, so could be used (by people) in answering questions about any of those domains. In itself, however, it would be meaningless—as are the Chinese symbols from the point of view of Searle-in-the-room.

It follows, Searle argues, that no system can understand anything solely in virtue of its instantiating a computer program. For if it could, then Searle-in-the-room would understand Chinese. Hence, theoretical psychology cannot properly be grounded in computational concepts.

Searle's second claim concerns what a proper explanation of understanding would be like. According to him, it would acknowledge that meaningful symbols must be embodied in something having 'the right causal powers' for generating understanding, or intentionality. Obviously, he says, brains do have such causal powers whereas computers do not. More precisely (since the brain's organization could be paralleled in a computer), neuroprotein does whereas metal and silicon do not: the biochemical properties of the brain matter are crucial.

A. Newell's (1980) widely cited definition of 'physical-symbol systems' is rejected by Searle, because it demands merely that symbols be embodied in some material that can implement formalist computations—which computers, admittedly, can do. In Searle's view, no electronic computer can really manipulate symbols, nor really designate or interpret anything at all—*irrespective* of any causal dependencies linking its internal physical patterns to its behaviour. (This strongly realist view of intentionality contrasts with the instrumentalism of D. C. Dennett (1971). For Dennett, an intentional system is one whose behaviour we can explain, predict, and control only by ascribing beliefs, goals, and rationality to it. On this criterion, some *existing* computer programs are intentional systems, and the hypothetical humanoids beloved of science-fiction would be intentional systems *a fortiori.*)

Intentionality, Searle declares, is a biological phenomenon. As such, it is just as dependent on the underlying biochemistry as are photosynthesis and lactation. He grants that neuroprotein may not be the only substances in the universe capable of supporting mental life, much as substances other than chlorophyll may be able (on Mars, perhaps) to catalyse the synthesis of carbohydrates. But he rejects metal or silicon as potential alternatives, even on Mars. He asks whether a computer made out of old beer-cans could possibly *understand*—a rhetorical question to which the expected answer is a resounding 'No!' In short, Searle takes it to be intuitively obvious that the inorganic substances with which (today's) computers are manufactured are essentially incapable of supporting mental functions.

In assessing Searle's two-pronged critique of computational psychology, let us first consider his view that intentionality must be biologically grounded. One might be tempted to call this a positive claim, in contrast with his (negative) claim that purely formalist theories cannot explain mentality. However, this would be to grant it more than it deserves, for its explanatory power is illusory. The biological analogies mentioned by Searle are misleading, and the intuitions to which he appeals are unreliable.

The brain's production of intentionality, we are told, is comparable to photosynthesis—but is it, really? We can define the *products* of photosynthesis, clearly distinguishing various sugars and starches within the general class of carbohydrates, and showing how these differ from other biochemical products such as proteins. Moreover, we not only *know that* chlorophyll supports photosynthesis, we also *understand how* it does so (and *why* various other chemicals cannot). We know that it is a catalyst rather than a raw material; and we can specify the point at which, and the subatomic process by which, its catalytic function is exercised. With respect to brains and understanding, the case is very different.

Our theory of what intentionality is (never mind how it is generated) does not bear comparison with our knowledge of carbohydrates: just what intentionality *is* is still philosophically controversial. We cannot even be entirely confident that we can recognize it when we see it. It is generally agreed that the propositional attitudes are intentional, and that feelings and sensations are not; but there is no clear consensus about the intentionality of emotions.

Various attempts have been made to characterize intentionality and to distinguish its subspecies as distinct intentional states (beliefs, desires, hopes, intentions, and the like). Searle himself has made a number of relevant contributions, from his early work on speech-acts (1969) to his more recent account (1983) of intentionality in general. A commonly used criterion (adopted by Brentano in the nineteenth century and also by Searle) is a *psychological* one. In Brentano's words, intentional states direct the mind on an object; in Searle's, they have intrinsic representational capacity, or 'aboutness'; in either case they relate the mind to the world, and to possible worlds. But some writers define intentionality in *logical* terms (Chisholm 1967). It is not even clear whether the logical and psychological definitions are precisely co-extensive (Boden 1970). In brief, no theory of intentionality is accepted as unproblematic, as the chemistry of carbohydrates is.

As for the brain's biochemical 'synthesis' of intentionality, this is even more mysterious. We have very good reason to believe *that* neuroprotein supports intentionality, but we have hardly any idea *how—qua* neuroprotein—it is able to do so.

In so far as we understand these matters at all, we focus on the neurochemical basis of certain *informational functions*—such as message-passing, facilitation, and inhibition—embodied in neurones and synapses. For example: how the sodium-pump at the cell-membrane enables an action potential to propagate along the axon; how electrochemical changes cause a neurone to enter into and recover from its refractory period; or how neuronal thresholds can be altered by neurotransmitters, such as acetylcholine.

With respect to a visual cell, for instance, a crucial psychological question may be *whether it can function so as to detect intensity-gradients.* If the neurophysiologist can tell us which molecules enable it to do so, so much the better. But from the psychological point of view, it is not the biochemistry as such which matters but the information-bearing functions grounded in it. (Searle apparently admits this when he says, 'The type of realizations that intentional states have in the brain may be describable at a much higher functional level than that of the specific biochemistry of the neurons involved' (1983: 272).)

As work in 'computer vision' has shown, metal and silicon are undoubtedly able to support some of the functions necessary for the 2D-to-3D mapping involved in vision. Moreover, they can embody specific mathematical functions for recognizing intensity-gradients (namely 'DOG-detectors', which compute the difference of Gaussians) which seem to be involved in many biological visual systems. Admittedly, it may be that metal and silicon cannot support all the functions involved in normal vision, or in understanding generally. Perhaps only neuroprotein can do so, so that only creatures with a 'terrestrial' biology can enjoy intentionality. But we have no specific reason, at present, to think so. Most important in this context, any such reasons we might have in the future must be grounded in empirical discovery: intuitions will not help.

If one asks which mind-matter dependencies are intuitively plausible, the answer must be that *none* is. Nobody who was puzzled about intentionality (as opposed to action-potentials) ever exclaimed 'Sodium—of course!' Sodium-pumps are no less 'obviously' absurd than silicon chips, electrical polarities no less 'obviously' irrelevant than old beer-cans, acetylcholine hardly less surprising than beer. The fact that the first member of each of these three pairs is *scientifically* compelling does not make any of them *intuitively* intelligible: our initial surprise persists.

Our intuitions might change with the advance of science. Possibly we shall eventually see neuroprotein (and perhaps silicon too) as obviously capable of embodying mind, much as we now see biochemical substances in general (including chlorophyll) as obviously capable of producing other such substances—an intuition that was not obvious, even to chemists, prior to the synthesis of urea. At present, however, our intuitions have nothing useful to say about the material basis of intentionality. Searle's 'positive' claim, his putative alternative explanation of intentionality, is at best a promissory note, at worst mere mystery-mongering.

Searle's negative claim—that formal-computational theories cannot explain understanding—is less quickly rebutted. My rebuttal will involve two parts: the first directly addressing his example of the Chinese room, the second dealing with his background assumption (on which his example depends) that computer programs are pure syntax.

The Chinese-room example has engendered much debate, both within and outside the community of cognitive science. Some criticisms were anticipated by Searle himself in his original paper, others appeared as the accompanying peer-commentary (together with his Reply), and more have been published since. Here, I shall concentrate on only two points: what Searle calls the Robot reply, and what I shall call the English reply.

The Robot reply accepts that the only understanding of Chinese which exists in Searle's example is that enjoyed by the Chinese people outside the room. Searle-in-the-room's inability to connect Chinese characters with events in the outside world shows that he does not understand Chinese. Likewise, a Schankian teletyping computer that cannot recognize a restaurant, hand money to a waiter, or chew a morsel of food understands nothing of restaurants—even if it can usefully 'answer' our questions about them. But a robot, provided not only with a restaurantscript but also with camera-fed visual programs and limbs capable of walking and picking things up, would be another matter. If the input-output behaviour of such a robot were identical with that of human beings, then it would demonstrably understand both restaurants and the natural language—Chinese, perhaps—used by people to communicate with it.

Searle's first response to the Robot reply is to claim a victory already, since the reply concedes that cognition is not solely a matter of formal symbol-manipulation but requires in addition a set of causal relations with the outside world. Second, Searle insists that to add perceptuomotor capacities to a computational system is not to add intentionality, or understanding.

He argues this point by imagining a robot which, instead of being provided with a computer program to make it work, has a miniaturized Searle inside it—in its skull, perhaps. Searle-in-the-robot, with the aid of a (new) rule-book, shuffles paper and passes *squiggles* and *squoggles* in and out, much as Searle-in-the-room did before him. But now some or all of the incoming Chinese characters are not handed in by Chinese people, but are triggered by causal processes in the cameras and audio-equipment in the robot's eyes and ears. And the outgoing Chinese characters are not received by Chinese hands, but by motors and levers attached to the robot's limbs—which are caused to move as a result. In short, this robot is apparently able not only to answer questions in Chinese, but also to see and do things accordingly: it can recognize raw beansprouts and, if the recipe requires it, toss them into a wok as well as the rest of us.

(The work on computer vision mentioned above suggests that the vocabulary of Chinese would require considerable extension for this example to be carried through. And the large body of AI research on language-processing suggests that the same could be said of the English required to express the rules in Searle's initial 'question-answering' example. In either case, what Searle-in-the-room needs is not so much Chinese, or even English, as a programming-language. We shall return to this point presently.)

Like his roombound predecessor, however, Searle-in-the-robot knows nothing of the wider context. He is just as ignorant of Chinese as he ever was, and has no more purchase on the outside world than he did in the original example. To him, beansprouts and woks are invisible and intangible: all Searle-in-the-robot can see and touch, besides the rule-book and the doodles, are his own body and the inside walls of the robot's skull. Consequently, Searle argues, the robot cannot be credited with understanding of any of these worldly matters. In truth, it is not *seeing* or *doing* anything at all: it is 'simply moving about as a result of its electrical wiring and its program', which latter is instantiated by the man inside it, who 'has no intentional states of the relevant type' (1980: 420).

Searle's argument here is unacceptable as a rebuttal of the Robot reply, because it draws a false analogy between the imagined example and what is claimed by computational psychology.

Searle-in-the-robot is supposed by Searle to be performing the functions performed (according to computational theories) by the human brain. But, whereas most computationalists do not ascribe intentionality to the brain (and those who do, as we shall see presently, do so only in a very limited way), Searle characterizes

Searle-in-the-robot as enjoying full-blooded intentionality, just as he does himself. Computational psychology does not credit the brain with *seeing beansprouts* or *understanding English*: intentional states such as these are properties of people, not of brains. In general, although representations and mental processes are assumed (by computationalists and Searle alike) to be embodied in the brain, the sensorimotor capacities and propositional attitudes which they make possible are ascribed to the person as a whole. So Searle's description of the system inside the robot's skull as one which can understand English does not truly parallel what computationalists say about the brain.

Indeed, the specific procedures hypothesized by computational psychologists, and embodied by them in computer models of the mind, are relatively stupid—and they become more and more stupid as one moves to increasingly basic theoretical levels. Consider theories of natural-language parsing, for example. A parsing procedure that searches for a determiner does not understand English, and nor does a procedure for locating the reference of a personal pronoun: only the person whose brain performs these interpretive processes, and many others associated with them, can do that. The capacity to understand English involves a host of interacting information processes, each of which performs only a very limited function but which together provide the capacity to take English sentences as input and give appropriate English sentences as output. Similar remarks apply to the individual components of computational theories of vision, problem-solving, or learning. Precisely because psychologists wish to *explain* human language, vision, reasoning, and learning, they posit underlying processes which lack the capacities.

In short, Searle's description of the robot's pseudo-brain (that is, of Searle-in-the-robot) as understanding English involves a category-mistake comparable to treating the brain as the bearer—as opposed to the causal basis—of intelligence.

Someone might object here that I have contradicted myself, that I am claiming that one cannot ascribe intentionality to brains and yet am implicitly doing just that. For I spoke of the brain's effecting 'stupid' component-procedures—but stupidity is virtually a *species* of intelligence. To be stupid is to be intelligent, but not very (a person or a fish can be stupid, but a stone or a river cannot).

My defence would be twofold. First, the most basic theoretical level of all would be at the neuroscientific equivalent of the machine-code, a level 'engineered' by evolution. The facts that a certain light-sensitive cell *can* respond to intensity-gradients by acting as a DOG-detector and that one neurone *can* inhibit the firing of another, are explicable by the biochemistry of the brain. The notion of stupidity, even in scare-quotes, is wholly inappropriate in discussing such facts. However, these very basic information-processing functions (DOG-detecting and synaptic inhibition) *could* properly be described as 'very, very, very . . . stupid'. This of course implies that intentional language, if only of a highly grudging and uncomplimentary type, is applicable to brain processes after all—which prompts the second point in my defence. I did not say that intentionality cannot be ascribed to brains, but that full-blooded intentionality cannot. Nor did I say that brains cannot understand anything at all, in howsoever limited a fashion, but that they cannot (for example) understand English. I even hinted, several paragraphs ago, that a few computationalists do ascribe some degree of intentionality to the brain (or to the computational processes going on in the brain). These two points will be less obscure after we have considered the English reply and its bearing on Searle's background assumption that formal-syntactic computational theories are purely syntactic.

The crux of the English reply is that the instantiation of a computer program, whether by man or by manufactured machine, does involve understanding—at least of the rule-book. Searle's initial example depends critically on Searle-in-the-room's being able to understand the language in which the rules are written, namely English; similarly, without Searle-in-the-robot's familiarity with English, the robot's beansprouts would never get thrown into the wok. Moreover, as remarked above, the vocabulary of English (and, for Searle-in-the-robot, of Chinese too) would have to be significantly modified to make the example work.

An unknown language (whether Chinese or Linear B) can be dealt with only as an aesthetic object or a set of systematically related forms. Artificial languages can be designed and studied, by the logician or the pure mathematician, with only their structural properties in mind (although D. R. Hofstadter's (1979) example of the quasi-arithmetical pq-system shows that a psychologically compelling, and predictable, interpretation of a formal calculus may arise spontaneously). But one normally responds in a very different way to the symbols of one's native tongue; indeed, it is very difficult to 'bracket' (ignore) the meanings of familiar words. The view held by computational psychologists, that natural languages can be characterized in procedural terms, is relevant here: words, clauses, and sentences can be seen as mini-programs. The symbols in a natural language one understands initiate mental activity of various kinds. To learn a language is to set up the relevant causal connections, not only between words and the world ('cat' and the thing on the mat) but between words and the many non-introspectible procedures involved in interpreting them.

Moreover, we do not need to be told *ex hypothesi* (by Searle) that Searle-in-the-room understands English: his behaviour while in the room shows clearly that he does. Or, rather, it shows that he understands a *highly limited subset* of English.

Searle-in-the-room could be suffering from total amnesia with respect to 99 per cent of Searle's English vocabulary, and it would make no difference. The only grasp of English he needs is whatever is necessary to interpret (*sic*) the rule-book—which specifies how to accept, select, compare, and give out different patterns. Unlike Searle, Searle-in-the-room does not require words like 'catalyse', 'beer-can', chlorophyll', and 'restaurant'. But he may need 'find', 'compare', 'two', 'triangular', and 'window' (although his understanding of these words could be much less full than Searle's). He must understand conditional sentences, if any rule states that if he sees a *squoggle* he should give out a *squiggle*. Very likely, he must understand some way of expressing negation, temporal ordering, and (especially if he is to learn to do his job faster) generalization. If the rules he uses include some which parse the Chinese sentences, then he will need words for grammatical categories too. (He will not need explicit rules for parsing English sentences, such as the parsing procedures employed in AI programs for language-processing, because he already understands English.)

In short, Searle-in-the-room needs to understand only that subset of Searle's English which is equivalent to the programming-language understood by a computer generating the same 'question-answering' input-output behaviour at the window. Similarly, Searle-in-the-robot must be able to understand whatever subset of English is equivalent to the programming-language understood by a fully computerized visuomotor robot.

The two preceding sentences may seem to beg the very question at issue. Indeed, to speak thus of the programming-language understood by a computer is seemingly self-contradictory. For Searle's basic premiss—which he assumes is accepted by all participants in the debate—is that a computer program is purely formal in nature: the computation it specifies is purely syntactic and has no intrinsic meaning or semantic content to be understood.

If we accept this premiss, the English reply sketched above can be dismissed forthwith for seeking to draw a parallel where no parallel can properly be drawn. But if we do not, if—*pace* Searle (and others (Fodor 1980; Stich 1983))—computer programs are not concerned only with syntax, then the English reply may be relevant after all. We must now turn to address this basic question.

Certainly, one can for certain purposes think of a computer program as an uninterpreted logical calculus. For example, one might be able to prove, by purely formal means, that a particular well-formed formula is derivable from the program's data-structures and inferential rules. Moreover, it is true that a so-called interpreter program that could take as input the list-structure '(FATHER (MAGGIE))' and return '(LEONARD)' would do so on formal criteria alone, having no way of interpreting these patterns as possibly denoting real people. Likewise, as Searle points out, programs provided with restaurant-scripts are not thereby provided with knowledge of restaurants. The existence of a mapping between a formalism and a certain domain does not in itself provide the manipulator of the formalism with any understanding of that domain.

But what must not be forgotten is that a computer program is *a program for a computer*: when a program is run on suitable hardware, the machine *does* something as a result (hence the use in computer science of the words 'instruction' and 'obey'). At the level of the machine-code the effect of the program on the computer is direct, because the machine is engineered so that a given instruction elicits a unique operation (instructions in high-level languages must be converted into machine-code instructions before they can be obeyed). A programmed instruction, then, is not a mere formal pattern—nor even a declarative statement (although it may for some purposes be thought of under either of those descriptions). It is a procedure specification that, given a suitable hardware context, can cause the procedure in question to be executed.

One might put this by saying that a programming-language is a medium not only for expressing *representations* (structures that can be written on a page or provided to a computer, some of which structures may be isomorphic with things that interest people) but also for bringing about the *representational activity* of certain machines.

One might even say that a representation *is* an activity rather than a structure. Many philosophers and psychologists have supposed that mental representations are intrinsically active. Among those who have recently argued for this view is Hofstadter (1985: 648), who specifically criticizes Newell's account of *symbols* as manipulable formal tokens. In his words, 'The brain itself does not 'manipulate symbols'; the brain is the medium in which the symbols are floating and in which they trigger each other.' Hofstadter expresses more sympathy for 'connectionist' than for 'formalist' psychological theories. Connectionist approaches involve parallel-processing systems broadly reminiscent of the brain, and are well suited to model cerebral representations, symbols, or concepts, as *dynamic.* But it is not only connectionists who can view concepts as intrinsically active, and not only *cerebral* representations which can be thought of in this way: this claim has been generalized to cover traditional computer programs, specifically designed for von Neumann machines. The computer scientist B. C. Smith (1982) argues that programmed representations, too, are inherently active—and that an adequate theory of the semantics of programming-languages would recognize the fact.

At present, Smith claims, computer scientists have a radically inadequate understanding of such matters. He reminds us that, as remarked above, there is no general agreement—either within or outside computer science—about what *intentionality* is, and deep unclarities about *representation* as well. Nor can unclarities be avoided by speaking more technically, in terms of *computation* and *formal symbol-manipulation.* For the computer scientist's understanding of what these phenomena really are is also largely intuitive. Smith's discussion of programming-languages identifies some fundamental confusions within computer science. Especially relevant here is his claim that computer scientists commonly make too complete a theoretical separation between a program's control-functions and its nature as a formal-syntactic system.

The theoretical divide criticized by Smith is evident in the widespread 'dual-calculus' approach to programming. The dual-calculus approach posits a sharp theoretical distinction between a declarative (or denotational) representational structure and the procedural language that interprets it when the program is run. Indeed, the knowledge-representation and the interpreter are sometimes written in two quite distinct formalisms (such as predicate calculus and LISP, respectively). Often, however, they are both expressed in the same formalism; for example, LISP (an acronym for LISt-Processing language) allows facts and procedures to be expressed in formally similar ways, and so does PROLOG (PROgramming-in-LOGic). In such cases, the dual-calculus approach dictates that the (single) programming-language concerned be theoretically described in two quite different ways.

To illustrate the distinction at issue here, suppose that we wanted a representation of family relationships which could be used to provide answers to questions about such matters. We might decide to employ a list-structure to represent such facts as that Leonard is the father of Maggie. Or we might prefer a frame-based representation, in which the relevant name-slots in the FATHER-frame could be simultaneously filled by 'LEONARD' and 'MAGGIE'. Again, we might choose a formula of the predicate calculus, saying that there exist two people (namely, Leonard and Maggie), and Leonard is the father of Maggie. Last, we might employ the English sentence 'Leonard is the father of Maggie.'

Each of these four representations could be written/drawn on paper (as are the rules in the rule-book used by Searle-in-the-room), for us to interpret *if* we have learnt how to handle the relevant notation. Alternatively, they could be embodied in a computer database. But to make them usable by the computer, there has to be an interpreter-program which (for instance) can find the item 'LEONARD' when we 'ask' it who is the father of Maggie. No one with any sense would embody list-structures in a computer without providing it also with a *list-processing* facility, nor give it frames without a *slot-filling* mechanism, logical formulae without *rules of inference*, or English sentences without *parsing procedures*. (Analogously, people who knew that Searle speaks no Portuguese would not give Searle- in-the-room a Portuguese rule-book unless they were prepared to teach him the language first.)

Smith does not deny that there is an important distinction between the *denotational import* of an expression (broadly: what actual or possible worlds can be mapped onto it) and its *procedural consequence* (broadly: what it does, or makes happen). The fact that the expression '(FATHER (MAGGIE))' is isomorphic with a certain parental relationship between two actual people (and so might be mapped onto that relationship by us) is one thing. The fact that the expression '(FATHER (MAGGIE))' can cause a certain computer to locate 'LEONARD' is quite another thing. Were it not so, the dual-calculus approach would not have developed. But he argues that, rather than persisting with the dual-calculus approach, it would be more elegant and less confusing to adopt a 'unified' theory of programming-languages, designed to cover both denotative and procedural aspects.

He shows that many basic terms on either side of the dual-calculus divide have deep theoretical commonalities as well as significant differences. The notion of *variable*, for instance, is understood in somewhat similar fashion by the logician and the computer scientist: both allow that a variable can have different *values* assigned to it at different times. That being so, it is redundant to have two distinct theories of what a variable is. To some extent, however, logicians and computer scientists understand different things by this term: the value of a variable in the LISP programming-language (for example) is another LISP-expression, whereas the value of a variable in logic is usually some object external to the formalism itself. These differences should be clarified—not least to avoid confusion when a system attempts to reason *about* variables by *using* variables. In short, we need a single definition of 'variable', allowing both for its declarative use (in logic) and for its procedural use (in programming). Having shown that similar remarks apply to other basic computational terms, Smith outlines a unitary account of the semantics of LISP and describes a new calculus (MANTIQ) designed with the unified approach in mind.

As the example of using variables to reason about variables suggests, a unified theory of computation could illuminate how *reflective* knowledge is possible. For, given such a theory, a system's representations of data and of processes—including processes internal to the system itself—would be essentially comparable. This theoretical advantage has psychological relevance (and was a major motivation behind Smith's work).

For our present purposes, however, the crucial point is that a fundamental theory of *programs*, and of *computation*, should acknowledge that an essential function of a computer program is to make things happen. Whereas symbolic logic can be viewed as mere playing around with uninterpreted formal calculi (such as the predicate calculus), and computational logic can be seen as the study of abstract timeless relations in mathematically specified 'machines' (such as Turing machines), computer science cannot properly be described in either of these ways.

It follows from Smith's argument that the familiar characterization of computer programs as all syntax and no semantics is mistaken. The inherent procedural consequences of any computer program give it a toehold in semantics, where the semantics in question is not denotational, but causal. The analogy is with Searle-in-the-room's understanding of English, not his understanding of Chinese.

This is implied also by A. Sloman's (1986*a*; 1986*b*) discussion of the sense in which programmed instructions and computer symbols must be thought of as having some semantics, however restricted. In a causal semantics, the meaning of a symbol (whether simple or complex) is to be sought by reference to its causal links with other phenomena. The central questions are 'What causes the symbol to be built and/or activated?' and 'What happens as a result of it?' The answers will sometimes mention external objects and events visible to an observer, and sometimes they will not.

If the system is a human, animal, or robot, it may have causal powers which enable it to refer to restaurants and beansprouts (the philosophical complexities of reference to external, including unobservable, objects may be ignored here, but are helpfully discussed by Sloman). But whatever the information-processing system concerned, the answers will sometimes describe purely *internal* computational processes—whereby other symbols are built, other instructions activated. Examples include the interpretative processes inside Searle-in-the-room's mind (comparable perhaps to the parsing and semantic procedures defined for automatic natural-language processing) that are elicited by English words, and the computational processes within a Schankian text-analysis program. Although such a program cannot use the symbol 'restaurant' to mean *restaurant* (because it has no causal links with restaurants, food and so forth), its internal symbols and procedures do embody some minimal understanding of certain other matters—of what it is to compare two formal structures, for example.

One may feel that the 'understanding' involved in such a case is *so* minimal that this word should not be used at all. So be it. As Sloman makes clear, the important question is not '*When does a machine understand something?*' (a question which misleadingly implies that there is some clear cut-off point at which understanding ceases) but '*What things does a machine (whether biological or not) need to be able to do in order to be able to understand?*' This question is relevant not only to the *possibility* of a computational psychology, but to its *content* also.

In sum, my discussion has shown Searle's attack on computational psychology to be ill founded. To view Searle-in-the-room as an instantiation of a computer program is not to say that he lacks all understanding. Since the theories of a formalist-computational psychology should be likened to computer programs rather than to formal logic, computational psychology is not in principle incapable of explaining how meaning attaches to mental processes.

References

Boden, M. A (1970). 'Intentionality and Physical Systems.' *Philosophy of Science* 37: 200–14.

Chisholm, R. M. (1967). 'Intentionality.' In P. Edwards (ed.), *The Encyclopedia of Philosophy*. Vol. IV, pp. 201–4. New York: Macmillan.

Dennett, D. C. (1971). 'Intentional Systems.' *J. Philosophy* 68: 87–106. Repr. in D. C. Dennett, *Brainstorms: Philosophical Essays on Mind and Psychology*, pp. 3–22. Cambridge, Mass.: MIT Press, 1978.

Fodor, J. A. (1980). 'Methodological Solipsism Considered as a Research Strategy in Cognitive Psychology.' *Behavioral and Brain Sciences* 3: 63–110. Repr. in J. A. Fodor, *Representations: Philosophical Essays on the Foundations of Cognitive Science*, pp. 225–56. Brighton: Harvester Press, 1981.

Hofstadter, D. R. (1979). *Godel, Escher, Bach: An Eternal Golden Braid*. New York: Basic Books.

——(1985). 'Waking Up from the Boolean Dream; Or, Subcognition as Computation.' In D. R. Hofstadter, *Metamagical Themas: Questing for the Essence of Mind and Pattern*, pp. 631–65. New York: Viking.

Newell, A. (1980). 'Physical Symbol Systems.' *Cognitive Science* 4: 135–83.

Schank, R. C., and Abelson, R. P. (1977). *Scripts, Plans, Goals, and Understanding*. Hillsdale, NJ: Erlbaum.

Searle, J. R. (1969). *Speech Acts: An Essay in the Philosophy of Language*. Cambridge: Cambridge University Press.

——(1980). 'Minds, Brains, and Programs.' *Behavioral and Brain Sciences* 3: 417–24. (See Chapter 15 of this volume.)

——(1983). *Intentionality: An Essay in the Philosophy of Mind*. Cambridge: Cambridge University Press.

Sloman, A. (1986*a*). 'Reference Without Causal Links.' In B. du Boulay and L. J. Steels (eds.), *Seventh European Conference on Artificial Intelligence*, pp. 369–81. Amsterdam: North-Holland.

Sloman, A. (1986*b*). 'What Sorts of Machines Can Understand the Symbols They Use?' *Proc. Aristotelian Soc.* Supp. 60: 61–80.

Smith, B. C. (1982). *Reflection and Semantics in a Procedural Language.* Cambridge, Mass.: MIT Ph.D. dissertation and Technical Report LCS/TR-272.

Stich, S. C. (1983). *From Folk Psychology to Cognitive Science: The Case Against Belief.* Cambridge, Mass.: MIT Press/Bradford Books.

Chapter 17

The mind as software in the brain

Ned Block

Searle's Chinese room argument

As we have seen, the idea that a certain type of symbol processing can be what *makes* something an intentional system is fundamental to the computer model of the mind. Let us now turn to a flamboyant frontal attack on this idea by John Searle (1980, 1990a; Churchland and Churchland 1990; the basic idea of this argument stems from Block 1978). Searle's strategy is one of avoiding quibbles about specific programs by imagining that cognitive science in the distant future can come up with the program of an actual person who speaks and understands Chinese, and that this program can be implemented in a machine. Unlike many critics of the computer model, Searle is willing to grant that perhaps this can be done so as to focus on his claim that *even if this can be done, the machine will not have intentional states.*

The argument is based on a thought experiment. Imagine yourself given a job in which you work in a room (the Chinese Room). You understand only English. Slips of paper with Chinese writing on them are put under the input door, and your job is to write sensible Chinese replies on other slips, and push them out under the output door. How do you do it? You act as the CPU (central processing unit) of a computer, following the computer program mentioned above that describes the symbol processing in an actual Chinese speaker's head. The program is printed in English in a library in the room. This is how you follow the program. Suppose the latest input has certain unintelligible (to you) Chinese squiggles on it. There is a blackboard on a wall of the room with a 'state' number written on it; it says '*17*'. (The CPU of a computer is a device with a finite number of states whose activity is determined solely by its current state and input, and because you are acting as the CPU, your output will be determined by your input and your 'state.' The '*17*' is on the blackboard to tell you what your 'state' is.) You take book *17* out of the library, and look up these particular squiggles in it. Book *17* tells you to look at what is written on your scratch pad (the computer's internal memory), and given both the input squiggles and the scratch-pad marks, you are directed to change what is on the scratch pad in a certain way, write certain other squiggles on your output pad, push the paper under the output door, and finally, change the number on the state

Ned Block, edited extract from 'The Mind as Software in the Brain'. In Daniel N. Osherson, ed., *An Invitation to Cognitive Science* (Cambridge: MIT Press, 1995).

board to '*193*'. As a result of this activity, speakers of Chinese find that the pieces of paper you slip under the output door are sensible replies to the inputs.

But you know nothing of what is being said in Chinese; you are just following instructions (in English) to look in certain books and write certain marks. According to Searle, because you don't understand any Chinese, the system of which you are the CPU is a mere Chinese simulator, not a real Chinese understander. Of course, Searle (rightly) rejects the Turing test for understanding Chinese. His argument, then, is that because the program of a real Chinese understander is not sufficient for understanding Chinese, no symbol-manipulation theory of Chinese understanding (or any other intentional state) is correct about what *makes* something a Chinese understander. Thus the conclusion of Searle's argument is that the fundamental idea of thought as symbol processing is wrong even if it allows us to build a machine that can duplicate the symbol processing of a person and thereby duplicate a person's behavior.

The best criticisms of the Chinese Room argument have focused on what Searle—anticipating the challenge—calls the systems reply. (See the responses following Searle 1980, and the comment on Searle in Hofstadter and Dennett 1981.) The systems reply has a positive and a negative component. The negative component is that we cannot reason from 'Bill has never sold uranium to North Korea' to 'Bill's company has never sold uranium to North Korea.' Similarly, we cannot reason from 'Bill does not understand Chinese' to 'The system of which Bill is a part does not understand Chinese.' (See Copeland 1993) Hence there is a gap in Searle's argument. The positive component goes further, saying that the whole system—man + program + board + paper + input and output doors—does understand Chinese, even though the man who is acting as the CPU does not. If you open up your own computer, looking for the CPU, you will find that it is just one of the many chips and other components on the mother board. The systems reply reminds us that the CPUs of the thinking computers we hope to have someday will not *themselves* think—rather, they will be *parts* of thinking systems.

Searle's clever reply is to imagine the paraphernalia of the 'system' *internalized* as follows. First, instead of having you consult a library, we are to imagine you *memorizing* the whole library. Second, instead of writing notes on scratch pads, you are to memorize what you would have written on the pads, and you are to memorize what the state blackboard would say. Finally, instead of looking at notes put under one door and passing notes under another door, you just use your *own body* to listen to Chinese utterances and produce replies. (This version of the Chinese Room has the additional advantage of generalizability so as to involve the complete behavior of a Chinese-speaking system instead of just a Chinese note exchanger.) But as Searle would emphasize, when you seem to Chinese speakers to be conducting a learned discourse with them in Chinese, all you are aware of doing is thinking about what noises the program tells you to make next, given the noises you hear and what you've written on your mental scratch pad.

I argued above that the CPU is just one of many components. If the whole system understands Chinese, that should not lead us to expect the CPU to understand Chinese. The effect of Searle's internalization move—the 'new' Chinese Room—is to attempt to destroy the analogy between looking inside the computer and looking inside the Chinese Room. If one looks inside the computer, one sees many chips in addition to the CPU. But if one looks inside the 'new' Chinese Room, all one sees is *you*, for you have memorized the library and internalized the functions of the scratch pad and the blackboard. But the point to keep in mind is that although the non-CPU components are no longer easy to see, they are not gone. Rather, they are internalized. If the program requires the contents of one register to be placed in another register, and if you would have done so in the original Chinese Room by copying from one piece of scratch paper to another, in the new Chinese Room you must copy from one of your mental analogs of a piece of scratch paper to another. You are implementing the system by doing what the CPU would do and you are simultaneously simulating the non-CPU components. Thus if the positive side of the systems reply is correct, the total system that you are implementing does understand Chinese.

'But how can it be,' Searle would object, 'that you implement a system that understands Chinese even though *you* don't understand Chinese?' The systems-reply rejoinder is that you implement a Chinese understanding system without yourself understanding Chinese or necessarily even being aware of what you are doing under that description. The systems reply sees the Chinese Room (new and old) as an English system implementing a Chinese system. What you are aware of are the thoughts of the English system, for example your following instructions and consulting your internal library. But in virtue of doing this Herculean task, you are also implementing a real, intelligent Chinese-speaking system, and so your body houses two genuinely distinct intelligent systems. The Chinese system also thinks, but though you implement this thought, you are not aware of it.

The systems reply can be backed up with an addition to the thought experiment that highlights the division of labor. Imagine that you take on the Chinese simulating as a 9-to-5 job. You come in Monday morning after a weekend of relaxation, and you are paid to follow the program until 5:00 P.M. When you are working, you concentrate hard on working, and so instead of trying to figure out the meaning of what is said to you, you focus your energies on working out what the program tells you to do in response to each input. As a result, during working hours you respond to everything just as the program dictates, except for occasional glances at your watch. (The glances at your watch fall under the same category as the noises and heat given off by computers: aspects of their behavior that are not part of the machine description but are due rather to features of the implementation.) If someone speaks to you in English, you say what the program (which, you recall, describes a real Chinese speaker) dictates. So if during working hours someone speaks to you in English, you respond with a request in Chinese to speak Chinese, or even an inexpertly pronounced 'No speak English,' which was once memorized by the Chinese speaker being simulated, and which you the English-speaking system may even fail to recognize as English. Then, come 5:00 P.M., you stop working and react to Chinese talk just as any monolingual English speaker would.

Why is it that the English system implements the Chinese system rather than, say, the other way around? Because you (the English system whom I am now addressing) are following the instructions of a program in English to make Chinese noises and not the other way around. If you decide to quit your job to become a magician, the Chinese system disappears. However, if the Chinese system decides to become a magician, he will make plans that he would express in Chinese, but then when 5:00 P.M. rolls around, you quit for the day, and the Chinese system's plans are on the shelf until you come back to work. And of course you have no commitment to doing *whatever* the program dictates. If the program dictates that you make a series of movements that leads you to a flight to China, you can drop out of the simulating mode, saying 'I quit!' The Chinese speaker's existence and the fulfillment of his plans depends on your work schedule and your plans, not the other way around.

Thus, you and the Chinese system cohabit one body. In effect, Searle uses the fact that you are not aware of the Chinese system's thoughts as an argument that it has no thoughts. But this is an invalid argument. Real cases of multiple personalities are often cases in which one personality is unaware of the others.

It is instructive to compare Searle's thought experiment with the string-searching Aunt Bubbles machine described at the beginning of this paper. This machine was used against a behaviorist proposal of a behavioral *concept* of intelligence. But the symbol-manipulation view of the mind is not a proposal about our everyday concept. To the extent that we think of the English system as implementing a Chinese system, that will be because we find the symbol-manipulation theory of the mind plausible as an empirical theory.

There is one aspect of Searle's case with which I am sympathetic. I have my doubts as to whether there is anything 'it is like' to be the Chinese system, that is, whether the Chinese system is a *phenomenally conscious* system. My doubts arise from the idea that perhaps consciousness is more a matter of implementation of symbol processing than of symbol processing itself. Though surprisingly Searle does not mention this idea in connection with the Chinese Room, it can be seen as the argumentative heart of his position. Searle has argued independently of the Chinese Room (Searle 1992, ch. 7) that intentionality requires consciousness. (See the replies to Searle (1990b) in *Behavioral and Brain Sciences* 13, 1990.) But this doctrine, if correct, can shore up the Chinese Room argument. For if the Chinese system is not conscious, then, according to Searle's doctrine, it is not an intentional system, either.

Even if I am right about the failure of Searle's argument, it does succeed in sharpening our understanding of the nature of intentionality and its relation to computation and representation.

References

Block, N. (1978). Troubles with functionalism. In C. W. Savage, ed., *Minnesota studies in philosophy of science*, IX, 26–325. Minneapolis, MN: University of Minnesota Press.

Churchland, P. M., and P. S. Churchland (1990). Could a machine think? *Scientific American* 262, 1, 26–31.

Copeland, J. (1993). The curious case of the Chinese gym. *Synthese* 95, 173–186.

Hofstadter, D., and D. Dennett (1981). *The mind's I: Fantasies and reflections on mind and soul.* New York: Basic Books.

Searle, J. (1980). Minds, brains, and programs. *The Behavioral and Brain Sciences* 3, 417–424. Reprinted in Haugeland (1981). (See Chapter 15 of this volume.)

Searle, J. (1990a). Is the brain's mind a computer program? *Scientific American* 262, I, 20–25.

Searle, J. (1990b). Consciousness, explanatory inversion and cognitive science. *The Behavioral and Brain Sciences* 13: 4, 585–595.

Searle, J. (1992). *The rediscovery of the mind.* Cambridge, MA: MIT Press.

Questions

1. Explain the 'imitation game' and its point. What success rate would a computing machine have to meet to satisfy the standards imposed by the game?
2. Although you might think it a trivial matter, Alan Turing spends a good deal of time saying what, exactly, he means by 'machine'. Why does Turing need to be careful on this point? Do you think Turing stacks the deck in favor of machine intelligence by characterizing machines as he does?
3. Are intelligence and consciousness linked? Could a machine (or living creature) be intelligent without being conscious? How might we test for consciousness?
4. What is John Searle's 'Chinese Room', and what is it meant to establish? What are the implications of the Chinese Room, if any, for questions about artificial intelligence?
5. What is the best response to Searle? Is the best response good enough to show that Searle's argument fails?
6. Suppose a chemist manages to create in a laboratory a substance with the precise molecular make-up of a 1990 Bordeaux. Would the chemist have created, or merely simulated, a 1990 Bordeaux? Now imagine a computer scientist programming a machine in such a way that the same question arose about it: has the computer scientist created, or merely simulated, consciousness? Is there a difference between a Bordeaux and a simulated Bordeaux, on the one hand, and, on the other hand, consciousness and simulated consciousness?
7. Does the fact that a computing machine is *programmed* to operate as it does guarantee that it is incapable of anything resembling creative thought?
8. If thinking is a matter of processing symbols intelligently, why should anyone doubt that a machine could think? If there is more to thinking than the intelligent processing of symbols, what is it? What *is* a symbol, anyway?
9. Imagine that the neurons in your brain are gradually replaced by silicon micro-chips that process inputs and outputs exactly as the neurons they replace do. Would you notice a difference as the replacement process progresses?
10. Is a computer virus a form of artificial life? Is artificial life *life*, or merely simulated life?

Suggested readings

Artificial intelligence (AI) is a developing field with applications in domains ranging from weather prediction, to factory robotics, to package delivery routing. Books and articles on such topics are boundless and largely technical. Contemporary philosophical interest in artificial intelligence stems from Turing's 'Computing Machinery and Intelligence' (Chapter 14), which connects thinking with computation. The connection had been made 300 years earlier by Thomas Hobbes; see Hobbes (1651: pt. 1, chap. 1, p. 2; chap. 5, 29–30; and 1656: chap. 1, p. 3; chap 2, p. 17). Hobbes's contribution is discussed in Haugeland (1997: 23–8).

Haugeland's book provides a fascinating introduction to the history of AI and, significantly, to its philosophical underpinnings. See also Copeland (1993) and Moody (1993). Weizenbaum (1976) and Dreyfus (1979) provide well-written critical introductions to the topic, as well. Both authors express serious reservations concerning some of the more colorful claims advanced by enthusiastic proponents of AI. Sayre (1976) discusses 'cybernetics' (roughly, the study and development of control systems and their biological counterparts) and its relation to issues in the philosophy of mind (think: functionalism). See also Angel (1989). The view that the universe itself might be one gargantuan computing machine—the 'it from bit' hypothesis—is advanced in Wheeler (1994).

Anderson (1964), Boden (1990), and Haugeland (1997) collect influential readings on topics in AI and the philosophy of mind. Chalmers's (2001) on-line bibliography includes hundreds of entries on various facets of artificial intelligence.

Searle's discussion of the Chinese Room has spawned a huge literature. Searle defends his thesis in Searle (1984, 1990, 1992, 1997). For discussion see Churchland and Churchland (1990) Harnad (1989, 1991), and Hauser (1993, 1997). Hauser's (2001) on-line discussion of the Chinese Room includes an extensive bibliography, as does the Chalmers bibliography mentioned above. The web (are you surprised by this?) boasts a Chinese Room 'home page': <http://www.ptproject.ilstu.edu/chinroom.htm>.

Artificial intelligence

Anderson, A. R., ed. (1964), *Minds and Machines.* Englewood Cliffs, NJ: Prentice-Hall.

Angel, L. (1989), *How to Build a Conscious Machine.* Boulder, CO: Westview Press.

Boden, M. A., ed. (1990), *The Philosophy of Artificial Intelligence.* Oxford: Oxford University Press.

Chalmers, D. J. (2001), *Contemporary Philosophy of Mind: An Annotated Bibliography* <http://www.u.arizona.edu/~chalmers/biblio.html> Tucson, AZ: University of Arizona.

Copeland, B. J. (1993), *Artificial Intelligence: A Philosophical Introduction.* Oxford: Basil Blackwell.

Dreyfus, H. L. (1979), *What Computers Can't Do*, rev. ed. New York: Harper & Row.

Haugeland, J., ed. (1987), *Artificial Intelligence: The Very Idea.* Cambridge, MA: MIT Press.

—— (1997) *Mind Design II: Philosophy, Psychology, and Artificial Intelligence.* Cambridge, MA: MIT Press.

Hobbes, T. (1651), *Leviathan.* In Molesworth 1839–45: vol. iii.

Hobbes, T. (1656), *Elements of Philosophy.* In Molesworth 1839–45: vol. i.

Molesworth, W., ed. (1839–45), *The English Works of Thomas Hobbes* (11 vols.) London: J. Bohn.

Moody, T. C. (1993), *Philosophy and Artificial Intelligence.* Englewood Cliffs, NJ: Prentice-Hall.

Sayre, K. M. (1976), *Cybernetics and the Philosophy of Mind.* Atlantic Highlands, NJ: Humanities Press.

Weizenbaum, J. (1976), *Computer Power and Human Reason.* San Francisco: W. H. Freeman.

Wheeler, J. A. (1994), 'It from Bit'. In *At Home in the Universe.* Woodbury, NY: American Institute of Physics Press: 295–311.

The Chinese Room

Churchland, P. M., and P. S. Churchland (1990), 'Could a Machine Think?', *Scientific American* 262: 32–9.

Harnad, S. (1989), 'Minds, Machines, and Searle'. *Journal of Experimental and Theoretical Artificial Intelligence* 1: 5–25.

—— (1991), 'Other Bodies, Other Minds: A Machine Incarnation of an Old Philosophical Problem', *Minds and Machines* 1: 5–25.

Hauser, L. (1993), 'Reaping the Whirlwind: Reply to Harnad's 'Other Bodies, Other Minds''. *Minds and Machines* 3: 219–38.

—— (1997), 'Searle's Chinese Box: Debunking the Chinese Room Argument', *Minds and Machines* 7: 199–226.

—— (2001), 'Searle's Chinese Room Argument'. In Nani 2001: <http://host.uniroma3.it/progetti/kant/field/chinese.html>.

Nani, M., ed. (2001), *A Field Guide to the Philosophy of Mind.* <http://host.uniroma3.it/progetti/kant/field/> Rome: University of Rome 3.

Searle, J. R. (1984), *Minds, Brains, and Science.* Cambridge, MA: Harvard University Press.

—— (1990), 'Is the Brain's Mind a Computer Program?' *Scientific American* 262: 26–31.

—— (1992), *The Rediscovery of the Mind.* Cambridge: MIT Press.

—— (1997), *The Mystery of Consciousness.* New York: New York Review of Books.

Part V

Interpretationism

Introduction

'INTERPRETATIONISM' (my label), is not a single theory, but a family of theories. Interpretationist theories begin with the observation that we ascribe states of mind—most particularly beliefs, desires, and intentions, the so-called propositional attitudes—to agents in the course of making sense of their behavior. This is what Donald Davidson calls interpretation, and what Daniel Dennett describes as taking up the 'intentional stance'. One question about such theories concerns the status they accord states of mind. Do they depict states of mind as genuine states of agents to whom they are ascribed, states on a par with ordinary causally efficacious states like having a fever or being hungry? Or do they 'deflate' states of mind to convenient fictions, 'instrumental' posits that enable us to describe and explain behavior but the utility of which does not depend on there actually being features of agents corresponding to those posits.

I have spoken of 'agents', but what is an agent? Think of an agent as a rational decision maker, a being capable of planning and deliberation. Ordinary people are agents in this sense. But are ordinary people rational? What of the manifestly irrational behavior that we can observe in others and, if truth be told, in ourselves? First, let us distinguish *ir*rational from *non*rational behavior. An irrational action is an action performed by a rational agent that violates that agent's own decision principles. Nonrational behavior, in contrast, is behavior the explanation of which involves no appeal whatever to the behaver's reasons. You expand and contract your nostrils slightly as you breathe. Because your expanding and contracting your nostrils is not based on reasons (good or bad), it is neither rational nor irrational.

Now the punchline: only a rational agent can be irrational. This sounds paradoxical, but think of it on the analogy of a game. A child who aimlessly moves chess pieces about on a chess board is not playing bad chess; the child is not playing chess at all. Only someone playing chess can make an ill-considered move. Imagine a foraging honeybee who 'falsely' reports the location of a food source that, subsequent to its discovery, has been removed by an experimenter. Observer bees fly to the reported food source and find nothing. Suppose this happens repeatedly. Are the honeybees behaving irrationally in continuing to rely on unreliable reports of a forager? The honeybees are doing precisely what they have been programmed to do. To think otherwise is to introduce an unreliable anthropomorphic element into the description. As a child unfamiliar with chess cannot make a bad chess move, so a honeybee cannot behave irrationally. (For more on honeybees and rationality, see Bennett 1964.)

Dennett's intentional stance

Or so it would seem. Daniel Dennett takes a much more relaxed view of rational agency. The idea is strikingly simple. Owing to the way they are organized, many different kinds of 'system' can usefully be described as harboring beliefs and desires and, on the basis of these, forming intentions and subsequently acting intentionally. Your desktop computer puts up a dialog box because it 'believes' the printer's paper tray is empty and 'wants' to inform you of this fact. The warning light on an automobile's fuel gauge is illuminated because the sensor to which the gauge is connected 'thinks' the fuel tank is almost empty. A sunflower rotates in response to an artificial source of illumination mistakenly 'believing' it to be the sun. Are such pronouncements metaphorical? Not by Dennett's lights. Any system designed to function so as to secure a particular end is an 'intentional system', a system the behavior of which can be explained, predicted, and perhaps manipulated by supposing that it has reasons for what it does. Indeed, this is *all there is* to having and acting on reasons. Human beings are nothing special in this regard.

An intentional system is a 'designed' system, but what does that mean? A designed system, in this context, is a system that has been shaped—by an intelligent designer or by natural selection (Mother Nature)—because, so shaped, it secures particular ends advantageous to the system or to the designer. Sunflowers have evolved as they have because a capacity to maintain a particular orientation to the sun as it moves across the sky bestows an adaptive advantage. The mechanisms responsible for this behavior evolved during a period in which only the sun afforded a sufficiently powerful source of illumination. As a result, we can 'trick' a sunflower into thinking that the sun is shining with an artificial source of illumination.

A designed system can break down. The insulation on a fuel gauge wire can become worn, causing a short with the result that the gauge mistakenly registers that the tank is empty when it is full. (Compare a case of 'phantom pain' in a human being.) In other circumstances, the system can break down altogether. A faulty power supply can cause your desktop computer to behave unreliably. When this happens, you can no longer explain the computer's behavior as though it were a rational system. You revert to the 'design stance', consulting a technician, not a programmer. Suppose, now, that the logic board overheats, melting transistors. If you need to explain why the device so behaves, you must go all the way down to the 'physical stance'.

One question you should have in the back of your mind as you read the Dennett selection is whether, in focusing on the practice of ascribing states of mind in the explanation of behavior, we risk losing sight of questions about the nature of mental states and processes: principles of ascription are one thing, the states and processes are another. Dennett himself regards this distinction as infelicitous. There is nothing more to having beliefs, desires, and intentions than to be a system towards which we can take the intentional stance. Doubtless any such system will have an interesting internal structure that would be worth studying. We should not imagine, however, that in ascribing beliefs, desires, and intentions we are pointing to parts of this internal structure.

If you find Dennett's approach refreshing, you might ask yourself whether that approach extends smoothly to other mental phenomena. In ascribing pains, emotions, or moods to me are you taking up a stance, or are you attributing to me definite internal states and processes causally related to what I say and do? If pains, emotions, and moods appear to be genuine internal states and processes, are they *detachable* from beliefs, desires, and intentions? Could you be justified in ascribing the one and not the other?

These questions, and many others, are bound to assert themselves as you begin to probe Dennett's argument.

Translation and propositions

Gottlob Frege (1848–1925) and Wittgenstein both argued that, just as words owe their meaning to roles they play in sentences, so sentences' meaning depends on their place in a language. You cannot understand a sentence unless you understand the language to which it belongs. This might seem crazy. When you, an English speaker, learn French, you do so piecemeal. You learn, for instance, that 'il pleut', means 'it's raining'. You know the meaning of the sentence without knowing the language. This is possible, however, only because you begin with a language, in this case English. You discover that the role of 'il pleut' in French resembles the role of 'it's raining' in English. As you become more adept in French, you gradually learn the place of French sentences *in French*. When this happens, you have the sense that you have begun to 'think in French'.

If you are a native English speaker, in learning French as a second language you start with a language, English, and match French sentences with English counterparts. This comes close to implying that your understanding the meaning of a French sentence amounts to your knowing an English sentence with which it is correlated. Suppose this were so. What might constitute your understanding of *English* sentences—or, more generally, sentences in your native tongue? Not, presumably, your correlating these with sentences in some further language. Precisely the same question would arise for sentences in that language. (Jerry Fodor disagrees; see Fodor 1975, and the introduction to Part VI.)

One traditional answer to this question is that to know the meaning of a sentence is to know what *proposition* it expresses. But what is a proposition? There is little agreement on this question among philosophers. Propositions must be extra-linguistic 'abstract' entities that have meanings and are capable of being true or false. The introduction of propositions makes explaining translation a breeze. A given French sentence is a translation of a given English sentence just in case both sentences express the same proposition.

Unless we are completely shameless, however, we must eventually face up to the job of saying what exactly propositions are, how we come to 'grasp' them, and what it is about propositions that equips them so conveniently with 'built in' meanings. Philosophers are not at a loss for words about such things, but it is hard to avoid the impression that appeals to propositions in accounts of meaning smooth out one bulge in the carpet by moving it elsewhere. What are some alternatives?

Quine and radical translation

One alternative, set out by W. V. Quine (1908–2000), is simplicity itself (see Quine 1960). Your understanding the meaning of sentences is a matter of your being able to put those sentences to use in ways that meet the approval of fellow native speakers. Grasping a meaning does not involve your gaining access to some hokey quasi-linguistic entity, a meaning or a proposition. It involves only your having command of a language: your being able to produce appropriate utterances and respond appropriately to the utterances of others. Appropriateness here is characterizable in terms of what is agreeable to the community of speakers.

Quine uses a thought experiment to bring all this into focus. Imagine you are an English-speaking linguist confronted with a native population that speaks a language you have never encountered. (Assume that the native population is wholly ignorant of English.) The task facing you the linguist is, according to Quine, that of 'radical translation': you must construct a 'translation manual' that correlates native utterances with English sentences. You begin by eliciting native utterances in the presence of salient stimuli. A rabbit runs by and a native cries 'Gavagai!' You might then associate the native utterance 'Gavagai' with the English sentence 'Here's a rabbit.' As you proceed in this way, you will adjust and readjust your translation manual to accommodate new evidence.

As you encounter more and more native utterances, you will eventually be forced to confront sentences that relate in no simple way to observable stimuli. Think of the English sentence, 'Love does not bend with the remover to remove.' There are no obvious non-verbal stimuli that could be thought reliably to elicit utterances of this sentence from attentive speakers. When it comes to native counterparts of such sentences, you find that correlations lack unambiguous constraints. You have more freedom in deciding how to correlate such utterances with English sentences. Indeed, any constraints will be almost wholly linguistic: you will need to translate the utterances in a way that is consistent with earlier decisions you have made concerning the translation of 'observation sentences' (sentences naturally elicited by observable stimuli).

Now a worry surfaces. Suppose there is *more than one way* to translate a native utterance consistent with your translation manual? Suppose, for the sake of illustration, that a native sentence, *N*, can consistently be correlated with two utterly different English sentences, E_1 and E_2. Additional fieldwork might narrow the possibilities, but there is no guarantee that this will be so. How are you to tell which is the correct translation?

Quine's answer here is surprising: there are no further constraints on translation, nothing more that could make it the case that the correct translation of *N* was E_1 or that it was E_2. It is not just that you cannot *know* which translation is correct—because, for instance, you lack some further piece of information. There are no further facts to discover. There are no facts bearing on the meanings of native utterances beyond those captured by your translation manual, which is itself nothing more than a systematic mapping of native utterances into English. The looseness of constraints on translation means, according to Quine, that it will always be possible to construct many different translation manuals, all of which fit the corpus of actual and possible native utterances. There is no 'fact of the matter' as to which of these manuals is correct. Thus—a shocker—there is no fact of the matter as to what native utterances mean!

But wait! It is one thing to claim that there are different ways of representing the meaning of native utterances in English, quite another matter to claim that there is no fact of the matter as to what these utterances mean, so to speak, *in their own right*. No, says Quine. Meaning is indeterminate. There is nothing more to meaning than what we say about sentences. But what we say about sentences is a matter of tying sentences to sentences—sentences in our own language or sentences in some other language. Just as there are many ways to construct translation manuals for native sentences, so there are many ways to construct translation manuals for sentences in the home language (English, for instance).

Quine tells us that meanings are not entities, meanings take up no space. This is not just a boring philosophical result, but a hypothesis with bite. Given the indeterminate nature of meaning, it is hard to see how meaning could be a player in the physical world. For this reason, Quine holds, the sciences can safely ignore meaning in offering explanation of physical phenomena, including human behavior. This places Quine at odds with philosophers and social scientists who endorse 'hermeneutic' approaches to the explanation of behavior. Such approaches treat human action as inherently meaningful. Physical processes and events are susceptible to causal explanation; we explain human action by making sense of it. Quine's very different approach resembles the behaviorists': talk of meanings is replaced by talk of sentences speakers utter or are disposed to utter.

Davidson and radical interpretation

This is the background against which Davidson, a student of Quine's, writes. Quine focuses on *translation*—the mapping of sentences onto sentences—Davidson focuses on *interpretation*. Davidson holds that there is no prospect of translating speakers' utterances in the absence of an account of what speakers believe and want. You produce an utterance because of what you want to communicate, what you believe, and what you take your utterance to mean. Suppose you utter the (English) sentence 'It's raining' with the aim of telling me that it's raining. Your utterance is based on your beliefs about the weather—that it is raining—your desire to tell me that it's raining, and your taking 'It's raining' to mean that it's raining. Davidson sees interpretation as a matter of solving, simultaneously, for these three unknowns. Thus, an interpretation of a given speaker assigns beliefs and desires to the speaker and associates sentences uttered by the speaker with sentences in the interpreter's language.

Davidson argues that constraints on interpretation narrow the scope of indeterminacy. Yes, there could be distinct, equally warranted interpretations of a speaker's utterances, but the differences are systematic in the way they are in the case of Fahrenheit and Centigrade. You say it is 54° outside, I say it is 12°. Do we disagree? Not if I am using the Centigrade scale and you are using Fahrenheit.

You can get a feel for the structure of interpretation by looking at two formal theories that, when appropriately combined, yield interpretations. The first is a 'truth theory' advanced by Alfred Tarski (1901–83). Tarski's (1956) theory is not really a theory *of* truth. The theory assumes at the outset that we have an intuitive grasp of what truth is. Rather, the theory provides a formal procedure that yields, for every sentence of a language a theorem of the form

(T) The sentence '*S*' is true if and only if *p*.

Think of '*S*' as a native sentence ('il pleut', for instance) and *p* as a sentence in the interpreter's language ('It's raining'). Davidson noticed that, although Tarski's theory invokes truth, the element to the right—the *p*—in effect expresses the 'truth conditions' or meaning of the element on the left, '*S*'. The importance of Tarski's theory for Davidson is that it provides a systematic, *recursive* way of associating 'meanings' with sentences. (To say that the theory is recursive is to say that it is made up of a finite collection of elements—think of these as words—and a finite collection of rules that, in combination, yield an infinitude of '*T*-sentences' like (T) above, one *T*-sentence for every sentence of the language.)

The second formal theory appropriated by Davidson in the service of interpretation is decision theory. Decision theory provides an accounting of agents' preferences for courses of action given those agents' beliefs (expressed as probabilities) and desires (expressed as 'utilities'). (This is to take beliefs as equivalent to likelihoods or probabilities you assign to sentences and desires as values you place on states of the world, also expressible as sentences.) You are deliberating about whether to attend the opera or walk in the hills. You would prefer to walk in the hills, but not if it rains. Your preference will be based on the values you place on the opera and hill walking, respectively, given that it rains or not, and your sense of the likelihood of rain.

Davidson turns this model around. I ascertain your preferences by observing your choices, and construct a theory that ascribes beliefs and desires (or probabilities and utilities) to you. I can do this, however, only if I can get a grip on what your preferences really are. To use an example of Davidson's, if you choose an apple from a bowl of fruit, are you exhibiting a preference for an apple (rather than a banana, or a pear), or for the fruit closest to you, or for something red, or for an item imported from New Zealand, or *what*? I can narrow down your preferences only if you are capable of expressing those preferences linguistically (by asserting, for instance, 'I prefer the apple').

We are back to our starting point. Ascribing definite thoughts to you requires simultaneously ascribing to you beliefs, desires, and meanings. The ascription of beliefs, desires, and meanings—and other 'propositional attitudes'—to agents is of a piece. You cannot first ascertain what I believe or want, then move to determine what I mean by my utterances. In interpreting me, you must solve an equation with three 'unknowns'.

Thought and language

A corollary of this view is the apparently outrageous thesis that we could only be warranted in ascribing thoughts to creatures who possessed a language. In fact, Davidson's position is stronger: it is not just that we are in no position to know the thoughts of 'mute' creatures (my label for creatures lacking a language), but that such creatures *do not think*: mute creatures harbor no beliefs and desires; nor do they form intentions or undergo emotions that incorporate 'propositional content'.

To see what Davidson is driving at, think of propositional content as involving 'intensional' representation, and think of intensional representation as representation that is altered when referring expressions are replaced by co-referring expressions. If you spill paint on Lewis Carroll and Lewis Carroll is Charles Dodgson, then you spill paint on

Charles Dodgson. But you could think that Lewis Carroll is a genius without thinking that Charles Dodgson is a genius. You might think the one without thinking the other because you have never heard of Charles Dodgson, or because you had no idea that Charles Dodgson *is* Lewis Carroll.

Technicalities aside, you probably regard the thesis that creatures lacking a capacity for language lack a capacity for thought as laughable. Spot wags his tail when he hears a sound outside the door. Surely we would be entitled to describe Spot as *thinking* that his master is at the door. This seems right. Pressing ahead, could Spot (today) think that his master will be at the door again the day after tomorrow? That seems less clear. Why should it seem right to ascribe the former thought to Spot, but not the latter? This might shake your confidence that Davidson is wholly off base. Return to Spot's thinking that his master is at the door now. Is this the right way to characterize Spot's thought? Perhaps Spot thinks his oldest friend is at the door, or Wayne is at the door (Spot's master is Wayne, who has raised Spot since puppy-hood). Why should we prefer one of these descriptions of Spot's thought to another?

By Davidson's lights, this is not just a matter of our being at a loss as to how to describe Spot's state of mind. There is no definite fact here to be described. Spot's mental economy lacks the kind of fine-grainedness required if we are meaningfully to talk of genuine thought. To be sure, something is going on inside Spot. Spot is intelligent in the sense that his behavior is goal directed and adaptive. But whatever the mechanisms responsible for that behavior, they differ, according to Davidson, in important ways from the mechanisms governing the behavior of creatures possessing a language. At best we can say that Spot behaves *as though* he believed his master is at the door. Spot can register events in his surroundings and adjust his behavior accordingly. But Spot's so registering his surroundings is not a matter of his being in a belief-like state with a definite 'propositional content'.

Language

Suppose you are trying to evaluate the contention that only a creature possessing a language (and equipped to interpret other creatures) could entertain thoughts with genuine propositional content. What constitutes a language? English, French, and Urdu are languages. What about the clicks and squeals of dolphins and whales? What about honeybee dances, which von Frisch (1971) called the 'language of the bees'?

These are difficult issues, but it is important at the outset to distinguish bare communication from the use of language. Language provides a vehicle of communication, but not every instance of communication, not even every communicative system, constitutes a language. When your car door squeaks, it communicates a need for lubrication; when you sneeze, you communicate to bystanders that you have a cold. Animals communicate with one another and with human beings, and we with them. Communication of this kind can involve symbolic activities. The form of honeybee dances communicates information about a food source: its direction from the hive, its distance (in some cases), and its concentration. An ape can be taught to press buttons marked with symbols in a particular sequence to receive a particular reward. These look like instances of symbolic behavior that, if not linguistic, are at least proto-linguistic.

Much has been written on this topic. Here I shall mention only one feature of systems of animal communication that seem to distinguish such systems from uses of a fully fledged language. Animal communication is, so far as we know, wholly stimulus bound: facts communicated by and to creatures lacking a language (those I have dubbed 'mute creatures') pertain to features of the environment perceptually accessible to the creature at the time of the communicative event. You might put this by saying that whatever is communicated is communicated *in the present tense* and concerns spatially and temporally proximate goings on. Spot communicates his master's presence at the door *now*. An ape communicates a desire for food or company *now*. A creature that mastered *tensed* utterances or learned to communicate about spatially or temporally non-contiguous states of affairs, would have acquired an ability apparently different in kind, and not merely degree, from the ordinary communicative abilities of non-human creatures.

For all we know there might be such creatures roaming the planet (or roaming other planets) now. If there are, then they might be candidates for inclusion in the ranks of language users—and, if Davidson is right, in the ranks of interpreters as well!

A frivolous hypothesis?

Many people flatly reject Davidson's contention that only interpreters, only creatures capable of a language powerful enough to represent the contents of states of mind, could have beliefs and desires or form intentions: only interpreters can be interpreted. These people are confident that mute creatures—chiefly pets—have an elaborate and nuanced mental repertoire. Perhaps you, the reader, are among the skeptics. If you are, I hope that you have something more to offer in rebuttal than a strong conviction that your dog or cat should be credited with beliefs, desires, and intentions. To be sure you can describe and explain Spot's actions by ascribing beliefs and desires to Spot. Is this *all there is* to having beliefs and desires—to be such that your actions can be explained by appeals to beliefs and desires? That is Dennett's view. Is it yours?

Even if you were sympathetic to Dennett, you might find limitations on the kinds of thought you are willing to ascribe to Spot mildly embarrassing. Equally embarrassing is the sense that the contents of Spot's beliefs lack the kinds of intensional definiteness that is the hallmark of the propositional attitudes. The belief that Jones is at the door differs from the belief that your oldest friend is at the door, even if Jones *is* your oldest friend. Can such a distinction take hold in the case of a mute creature like Spot?

My goal here is not to convince you that Davidson is right, but to convince you that, if Davidson is wrong, it is unlikely that we could prove him wrong by pointing to the actions of mute creatures and simply asserting that such creatures must have thoughts like ours: thoughts with content, though perhaps distinctively doggie content. Anthropomorphism, ordinarily harmless, threatens to cloud our critical faculties when it comes to discussions of non-human creatures, especially those to which we have close attachments.

Davidson could be off base in a different way. Davidson holds that our understanding of one another is mediated by our application of a complex theory. As Jane Heal (Chapter 21) points out, this raises questions as to what constitutes an agent's application of such a theory. Suppose understanding were a product of *empathy*. You come to understand another person by putting yourself in that other person's shoes. Some philosophers describe this as 'simulation' (Gordon 1986; Goldman 1993). On the face of it, empathy differs dramatically from radical interpretation. One question to ponder as you read through the selections that follow is whether differences between Davidson's approach to interpretation and that favored by Heal are deep differences or whether they might be largely terminological.

References

Bennett, J. (1964), *Rationality: An Essay towards an Analysis*. London: Routledge & Kegan Paul.

Fodor, J. A. (1975), *The Language of Thought*. New York: T. Y. Crowell.

Goldman, A. I. (1993), 'The Psychology of Folk Psychology', *Behavioral and Brain Sciences* 16: 15–28.

Gordon, R. (1986), 'Folk Psychology as Simulation', *Mind and Language*: 1, 158–71.

Quine, W. V. O. (1960), *Word and Object*, Cambridge: MIT Press.

Tarski, A. (1956), 'The Concept of Truth in Formalized Languages', in *Logic, Semantics, and Metamathematics*. Oxford: Clarendon Press: 152–278.

Von Frisch, K. (1971), *Bees: Their Vision, Chemical Senses, and Language* 2d ed. Ithaca: Cornell University Press.

Chapter 18

Radical interpretation

Donald Davidson

KURT utters the words 'Es regnet' and under the right conditions we know that he has said that it is raining. Having identified his utterance as intentional and linguistic, we are able to go on to interpret his words: we can say what his words, on that occasion, meant. What could we know that would enable us to do this? How could we come to know it? The first of these questions is not the same as the question what we *do* know that enables us to interpret the words of others. For there may easily be something we could know and don't, knowledge of which would suffice for interpretation, while on the other hand it is not altogether obvious that there is anything we actually know which plays an essential role in interpretation. The second question, how we could come to have knowledge that would serve to yield interpretations, does not, of course, concern the actual history of language acquisition. It is thus a doubly hypothetical question: given a theory that would make interpretation possible, what evidence plausibly available to a potential interpreter would support the theory to a reasonable degree? In what follows I shall try to sharpen these questions and suggest answers.

The problem of interpretation is domestic as well as foreign: it surfaces for speakers of the same language in the form of the question, how can it be determined that the language is the same? Speakers of the same language can go on the assumption that for them the same expressions are to be interpreted in the same way, but this does not indicate what justifies the assumption. All understanding of the speech of another involves radical interpretation. But it will help keep assumptions from going unnoticed to focus on cases where interpretation is most clearly called for: interpretation in one idiom of talk in another.[1]

What knowledge would serve for interpretation? A short answer would be, knowledge of what each meaningful expression means. In German, those words Kurt spoke mean that it is raining and Kurt was speaking German. So in uttering the words 'Es regnet', Kurt said that it was raining. This reply does not, as might first be thought, merely restate the problem. For it suggests that in passing from a description that does not interpret (his uttering of the words 'Es regnet') to interpreting

Donald Davidson, 'Radical Interpretation', *Dialectica* 27 (1973). Reprinted in *Inquiries into Truth and Interpretation* (Oxford: Clarendon Press, 1984).

1. The term 'radical interpretation' is meant to suggest strong kinship with Quine's 'radical translation'. Kinship is not identity, however, and 'interpretation' in place of 'translation' marks one of the differences: a greater emphasis on the explicitly semantical in the former.

description (his saying that it is raining) we must introduce a machinery of words and expressions (which may or may not be exemplified in actual utterances), and this suggestion is important. But the reply is no further help, for it does not say what it is to know what an expression means.

There is indeed also the hint that corresponding to each meaningful expression that is an entity, its meaning. This idea, even if not wrong, has proven to be very little help: at best it hypostasizes the problem.

Disenchantment with meanings as implementing a viable account of communication or interpretation helps explain why some philosophers have tried to get along without, not only meanings, but any serious theory at all. It is tempting, when the concepts we summon up to try to explain interpretation turn out to be more baffling than the explanandum, to reflect that after all verbal communication consists in nothing more than elaborate disturbances in the air which form a causal link between the non-linguistic activities of human agents. But although interpretable speeches are nothing but (that is, identical with) actions performed with assorted non-linguistic intentions (to warn, control, amuse, distract, insult), and these actions are in turn nothing but (identical with) intentional movements of the lips and larynx, this observation takes us no distance towards an intelligible general account of what we might know that would allow us to redescribe uninterpreted utterances as the right interpreted ones.

Appeal to meanings leaves us stranded further than we started from the non-linguistic goings-on that must supply the evidential base for interpretation; the 'nothing but' attitude provides no clue as to how the evidence is related to what it surely is evident for.

Other proposals for bridging the gap fall short in various ways. The 'causal' theories of Ogden and Richards and of Charles Morris attempted to analyse the meaning of sentences, taken one at a time, on the basis of behaviouristic data. Even if these theories had worked for the simplest sentences (which they clearly did not), they did not touch the problem of extending the method to sentences of greater complexity and abstractness. Theories of another kind start by trying to connect words rather than sentences with non-linguistic facts. This is promising because words are finite in number while sentences are not, and yet each sentence is no more than a concatenation of words: this offers the chance of a theory that interprets each of an infinity of sentences using only finite resources. But such theories fail to reach the evidence, for it seems clear that the semantic features of words cannot be explained directly on the basis of non-linguistic phenomena. The reason is simple. The phenomena to which we must turn are the extra-linguistic interests and activities that language serves, and these are served by words only in so far as the words are incorporated in (or on occasion happen to be) sentences. But then there is no chance of giving a foundational account of words before giving one of sentences.

For quite different reasons, radical interpretation cannot hope to take as evidence for the meaning of a sentence an account of the complex and delicately discriminated intentions with which the sentence is typically uttered. It is not easy to see how such an approach can deal with the structural, recursive feature of language that is essential to explaining how new sentences can be understood. But the central difficulty is that we cannot hope to attach a sense to the attribution of finely discriminated intentions independently of interpreting speech. The reason is not that we cannot ask necessary questions, but that interpreting an agent's intentions, his beliefs and his words are parts of a single project, no part of which can be assumed to be complete before the rest is. If this is right, we cannot make the full panoply of intentions and beliefs the evidential base for a theory of radical interpretation.

We are now in a position to say something more about what would serve to make interpretation possible. The interpreter must be able to understand any of the infinity of sentences the speaker might utter. If we are to state explicitly what the interpreter might know that would enable him to do this, we must put it in finite form.[2] If this requirement is to be met, any hope of a universal method of interpretation must be abandoned. The most that can be expected is to explain how an interpreter could interpret the utterances of speakers of a single language (or a finite number of languages): it makes no sense to ask for a theory that would yield an explicit interpretation for any utterance in any (possible) language.

It is still not clear, of course, what it is for a theory to yield an explicit interpretation of an utterance. The formulation of the problem seems to invite us to think of the theory as the specification of a function taking utterances as arguments and having interpretations as values. But then interpretations would be no better than meanings and just as surely entities of some mysterious kind. So it seems wise to describe what is wanted of the theory without apparent reference to meanings or interpretations: someone who knows the theory can interpret the utterances to which the theory applies.

The second general requirement on a theory of interpretation is that it can be supported or verified by evidence plausibly available to an interpreter. Since the theory is general—it must apply to a potential infinity of utterances—it would be natural to think of evidence in its behalf as instances of particular interpretations recognized as correct. And this case does, of course, arise for the interpreter dealing with a language he already knows. The speaker of a language normally cannot produce an explicit finite theory for his own language, but he can test a proposed theory since he can tell whether it yields correct interpretations when applied to particular utterances.

In radical interpretation, however, the theory is supposed to supply an understanding of particular utterances that is not given in advance, so the ultimate evidence for the theory cannot be correct sample interpretations. To deal with the

2. See 'Theories of Meaning and Learnable Languages,' In *Proceedings of the 1964 International Congress for Logic, Methodology, and Philosophy of Science*, ed. Yehoshiva Bar-Hillel. Amsterdam: North Holland Publishing Co. reprinted in *Inquiries into Truth and Interpretation* (Oxford: Clarendon Press, 1984): 3–15.

general case, the evidence must be of a sort that would be available to someone who does not already know how to interpret utterances the theory is designed to cover: it must be evidence that can be stated without essential use of such linguistic concepts as meaning, interpretation, synonymy, and the like.

Before saying what kind of theory I think will do the trick, I want to discuss a last alternative suggestion, namely that a method of translation, from the language to be interpreted into the language of the interpreter, is all the theory that is needed. Such a theory would consist in the statement of an effective method for going from an arbitrary sentence of the alien tongue to a sentence of a familiar language; thus it would satisfy the demand for a finitely stated method applicable to any sentence. But I do not think a translation manual is the best form for a theory of interpretation to take.[3]

When interpretation is our aim, a method of translation deals with a wrong topic, a relation between two languages, where what is wanted is an interpretation of one (in another, of course, but that goes without saying since any theory is in some language). We cannot without confusion count the language used in stating the theory as part of the subject matter of the theory unless we explicitly make it so. In the general case, a theory of translation involves three languages: the object language, the subject language, and the metalanguage (the languages from and into which translation proceeds, and the language of the theory, which says what expressions of the subject language translate which expressions of the object language). And in this general case, we can know which sentences of the subject language translate which sentences of the object language without knowing what any of the sentences of either language mean (in any sense, anyway, that would let someone who understood the theory interpret sentences of the object language). If the subject language happens to be identical with the language of the theory, then someone who understands the theory can no doubt use the translation manual to interpret alien utterances; but this is because he brings to bear two things he knows and that the theory does not state: the fact that the subject language is his own, and his knowledge of how to interpet utterances in his own language.

It is awkward to try to make explicit the assumption that a mentioned sentence belongs to one's own language. We could try, for example, '"Es regnet" in Kurt's language is translated as "It is raining" in mine', but the indexical self-reference is out of place in a theory that ought to work for any interpreter. If we decide to accept this difficulty, there remains the fact that the method of translation leaves tacit and beyond the reach of theory what we need to know that allows us to interpret our own language. A theory of translation must read some sort of structure into

3. The idea of a translation manual with appropriate empirical constraints as a device for studying problems in the philosophy of language is, of course, Quine's. This idea inspired much of my thinking on the present subject, and my proposal is in important respects very close to Quine's. Since Quine did not intend to answer the questions I have set, the claim that the method of translation is not adequate as a solution to the problem of radical interpretation is not a criticism of any doctrine of Quine's.

sentences, but there is no reason to expect that it will provide any insight into how the meanings of sentences depend on their structure.

A satisfactory theory for interpreting the utterances of a language, our own included, will reveal significant semantic structure: the interpretation of utterances of complex sentences will systematically depend on the interpretation of utterances of simpler sentences, for example. Suppose we were to add to a theory of translation a satisfactory theory of interpretation for our own language. Then we would have exactly what we want, but in an unnecessarily bulky form. The translation manual churns out, for each sentence of the language to be translated, a sentence of the translator's language; the theory of interpretation then gives the interpretation of these familiar sentences. Clearly the reference to the home language is superfluous; it is an unneeded intermediary between interpretation and alien idiom. The only expressions a theory of interpretation has to mention are those belonging to the language to be interpreted.

A theory of interpretation for an object language may then be viewed as the result of the merger of a structurally revealing theory of interpretation for a known language, and a system of translation from the unknown language into the known. The merger makes all reference to the known language otiose; when this reference is dropped, what is left is a structurally revealing theory of interpretation for the object language—couched, of course, in familiar words. We have such theories, I suggest, in theories of truth of the kind Tarski first showed how to give.[4]

What characterizes a theory of truth in Tarski's style is that it entails, for every sentence *s* of the object language, a sentence of the form:

s is true (in the object language) if and only if *p*.

Instances of the form (which we shall call T-sentences) are obtained by replacing '*s*' by a canonical description of *s*, and '*p*' by a translation of *s*. The important undefined semantical notion in the theory is that of *satisfaction* which relates sentences, open or closed, to infinite sequences of objects, which may be taken to belong to the range of the variables of the object language. The axioms, which are finite in number, are of two kinds: some give the conditions under which a sequence satisfies a complex sentence on the basis of the conditions of satisfaction of simpler sentences, others give the conditions under which the simplest (open) sentences are satisfied. Truth is defined for closed sentences in terms of the notion of satisfaction. A recursive theory like this can be turned into an explicit definition along familiar lines, as Tarski shows, provided the language of the theory contains enough set theory; but we shall not be concerned with this extra step.

Further complexities enter if proper names and functional expressions are irreducible features of the object language. A trickier matter concerns indexical devices. Tarski was interested in formalized languages containing no indexical or

4. A. Tarski, 'The Concept of Truth in Formalized Languages', in *Logic, Semantics, and Metamathematics* (Oxford: Clarendon Press, 1956).

demonstrative aspects. He could therefore treat sentences as vehicles of truth; the extension of the theory to utterances is in this case trivial. But natural languages are indispensably replete with indexical features, like tense, and so their sentences may vary in truth according to time and speaker. The remedy is to characterize truth for a language relative to a time and a speaker. The extension to utterances is again straightforward.[5]

What follows is a defence of the claim that a theory of truth, modified to apply to a natural language, can be used as a theory of interpretation. The defence will consist in attempts to answer three questions:

1. It is reasonable to think that a theory of truth of the sort described can be given for a natural language?
2. Would it be possible to tell that such a theory was correct on the basis of evidence plausibly available to an interpreter with no prior knowledge of the language to be interpreted?
3. If the theory were known to be true, would it be possible to interpret utterances of speakers of the language?

The first question is addressed to the assumption that a theory of truth can be given for a natural language; the second and third questions ask whether such a theory would satisfy the further demands we have made on a theory of interpretation.

1. Can a theory of truth be given for a natural language?

It will help us to appreciate the problem to consider briefly the case where a significant fragment of a language (plus one or two semantical predicates) is used to state its own theory of truth. According to Tarski's Convention T, it is a test of the adequacy of a theory that it entails all the T-sentences. This test apparently cannot be met without assigning something very much like a standard quantificational form to the sentences of the language, and appealing, in the theory, to a relational notion of satisfaction.[6] But the striking thing about T-sentences is that whatever machinery must operate to produce them, and whatever ontological wheels must turn, in the end a T-sentence states the truth conditions of a sentence using resources no richer than, because the same as, those of the sentence itself. Unless the original sentence mentions possible worlds, intensional entities, properties, or propositions, the statement of its truth conditions does not.

There is no equally simple way to make the analogous point about an alien language without appealing, as Tarski does, to an unanalysed notion of translation.

5. For a discussion of how a theory of truth can handle demonstratives and how Convention T must be modified, see S. Weinstein, 'Truth and Demonstratives', Noûs 8 (1974): 179–84.
6. See J. Wallace, 'On the Frame of Reference', *Synthèse* 22 (1970): 61–94; and Essay 3 in *Inquiries into Truth and Interpretation.*

But what we can do for our own language we ought to be able to do for another; the problem, it will turn out, will be to know that we are doing it.

The restriction imposed by demanding a theory that satisfies Convention T seems to be considerable: there is no generally accepted method now known for dealing, within the restriction, with a host of problems, for example, sentences that attribute attitudes, modalities, general causal statements, counterfactuals, attributive adjectives, quantifiers like 'most', and so on. On the other hand, there is what seems to me to be fairly impressive progress. To mention some examples, there is the work of Tyler Burge on proper names,[7] Gilbert Harman on 'ought',[8] John Wallace on mass terms and comparatives,[9] and there is my own work on attributions of attitudes and performatives,[10] on adverbs, events, and singular causal statements,[11] and on quotation.[12]

If we are inclined to be pessimistic about what remains to be done (or some of what has been done!), we should think of Frege's magnificent accomplishment in bringing what Dummett calls 'multiple generality' under control.[13] Frege did not have a theory of truth in Tarski's sense in mind, but it is obvious that he sought, and found, structures of a kind for which a theory of truth can be given.

The work of applying a theory of truth in detail to a natural language will in practice almost certainly divide into two stages. In the first stage, truth will be characterized, not for the whole language, but for a carefully gerrymandered part of the language. This part, though no doubt clumsy grammatically, will contain an infinity of sentences which exhaust the expressive power of the whole language. The second part will match each of the remaining sentences to one or (in the case of ambiguity) more than one of the sentences for which truth has been characterized. We may think of the sentences to which the first stage of the theory applies as giving the logical form, or deep structure, of all sentences.

2. Can a theory of truth be verified by appeal to evidence available before interpretation has begun?

Convention T says that a theory of truth is satisfactory if it generates a T-sentence for each sentence of the object language. It is enough to demonstrate that a theory of truth is empirically correct, then, to verify that the T-sentences are true (in practice, an adequate sample will confirm the theory to a reasonable degree). T-sentences mention only the closed sentences of the language, so the relevant evidence can consist entirely of facts about the behaviour and attitudes of speakers in

7. T. Burge, 'Reference and Proper Names', *Journal of Philosophy* 70 (1973): 425–39.
8. G. Harman, 'Moral Relativism Defended', *Philosophical Review* 84 (1975): 3–22.
9. J. Wallace, 'Positive, Comparative, Superlative', *Journal of Philosophy* 69 (1972): 773–82.
10. See Essays 7 and 8 in *Inquiries into Truth and Interpretation.*
11. See Essays 6–10 in *Essays on Actions and Events* (Oxford: Clarendon Press, 1980) .
12. See Essay 6 in *Inquiries into Truth and Interpretation.*
13. M. Dummett, *Frege: Philosophy of Language* (London: Duckworth, 1973) .

relation to sentences (no doubt by way of utterances). A workable theory must, of course, treat sentences as concatenations of expressions of less than sentential length, it must introduce semantical notions like satisfaction and reference, and it must appeal to an ontology of sequences and the objects ordered by the sequences. All this apparatus is properly viewed as theoretical construction, beyond the reach of direct verification. It has done its work provided only it entails testable results in the form of T-sentences, and these make no mention of the machinery. A theory of truth thus reconciles the demand for a theory that articulates grammatical structure with the demand for a theory that can be tested only by what it says about sentences.

In Tarski's work, T-sentences are taken to be true because the right branch of the biconditional is assumed to be a translation of the sentence truth conditions for which are being given. But we cannot assume in advance that correct translation can be recognized without pre-empting the point of radical interpretation; in empirical applications, we must abandon the assumption. What I propose is to reverse the direction of explanation: assuming translation, Tarski was able to define truth; the present idea is to take truth as basic and to extract an account of translation or interpretation. The advantages, from the point of view of radical interpretation, are obvious. Truth is a single property which attaches, or fails to attach, to utterances, while each utterance has its own interpretation; and truth is more apt to connect with fairly simple attitudes of speakers.

There is no difficulty in rephrasing Convention T without appeal to the concept of translation: an acceptable theory of truth must entail, for every sentence *s* of the object language, a sentence of the form: *s* is true if and only if *p*, where '*p*' is replaced by any sentence that is true if and only if *s* is. Given this formulation, the theory is tested by evidence that T-sentences are simply true; we have given up the idea that we must also tell whether what replaces '*p*' translates *s*. It might seem that there is no chance that if we demand so little of T-sentences, a theory of interpretation will emerge. And of course this would be so if we took the T-sentences in isolation. But the hope is that by putting appropriate formal and empirical restrictions on the theory as a whole, individual T-sentences will in fact serve to yield interpretations.[14]

We have still to say what evidence is available to an interpreter—evidence, we now see, that T-sentences are true. The evidence cannot consist in detailed descriptions of the speaker's beliefs and intentions, since attributions of attitudes, at least where subtlety is required, demand a theory that must rest on much the same evidence as interpretation. The interdependence of belief and meaning is evident in this way: a speaker holds a sentence to be true because of what the sentence (in his language) means, and because of what he believes. Knowing that he holds the sentence to be true, and knowing the meaning, we can infer his belief; given enough information about his beliefs, we could perhaps infer the meaning. But radical

14. For essential qualifications, see footnote 11 of Essay 2 in *Inquiries into Truth and Interpretation.*

interpretation should rest on evidence that does not assume knowledge of meanings or detailed knowledge of beliefs.

A good place to begin is with the attitude of holding a sentence true, of accepting it as true. This is, of course, a belief, but it is a single attitude applicable to all sentences, and so does not ask us to be able to make finely discriminated distinctions among beliefs. It is an attitude an interpreter may plausibly be taken to be able to identify before he can interpret, since he may know that a person intends to express a truth in uttering a sentence without having any idea *what* truth. Not that sincere assertion is the only reason to suppose that a person holds a sentence to be true. Lies, commands, stories, irony, if they are detected as attitudes, can reveal whether a speaker holds his sentences to be true. There is no reason to rule out other attitudes towards sentences, such as wishing true, wanting to make true, believing one is going to make true, and so on, but I am inclined to think that all evidence of this kind may be summed up in terms of holding sentences to be true.

Suppose, then, that the evidence available is just that speakers of the language to be interpreted hold various sentences to be true at certain times and under specified circumstances. How can this evidence be used to support a theory of truth? On the one hand, we have T-sentences, in the form:

(T) 'Es regnet' is true-in-German when spoken by x at time t if and only if it is raining near x at t.

On the other hand, we have the evidence, in the form:

(E) Kurt belongs to the German speech community and Kurt holds true 'Es regnet' on Saturday at noon and it is raining near Kurt on Saturday at noon.

We should, I think, consider (E) as evidence that (T) is true. Since (T) is a universally quantified conditional, the first step would be to gather more evidence to support the claim that:

(GE) $(x)(t)$ (if x belongs to the German speech community then (x holds true 'Es regnet' at t if and only if it is raining near x at t)).

The appeal to a speech community cuts a corner but begs no question: speakers belong to the same speech community if the same theories of interpretation work for them.

The obvious objection is that Kurt, or anyone else, may be wrong about whether it is raining near him. And this is of course a reason for not taking (E) as conclusive evidence for (GE) or for (T); and a reason not to expect generalizations like (GE) to be more than generally true. The method is rather one of getting a best fit. We want a theory that satisfies the formal constraints on a theory of truth, and that maximizes agreement, in the sense of making Kurt (and others) right, as far as we can tell, as often as possible. The concept of maximization cannot be taken literally here, since sentences are infinite in number, and anyway once the theory begins to take shape it makes sense to accept intelligible error and to make allowance for the relative likelihood of various kinds of mistake.[15]

The process of devising a theory of truth for an unknown native tongue might in crude outline go as follows. First we look for the best way to fit our logic, to the extent required to get a theory satisfying Convention T, on to the new language; this may mean reading the logical structure of first-order quantification theory (plus identity) into the language, not taking the logical constants one by one, but treating this much of logic as a grid to be fitted on to the language in one fell swoop. The evidence here is classes of sentences always held true or always held false by almost everyone almost all of the time (potential logical truths) and patterns of inference. The first step identifies predicates, singular terms, quantifiers, connectives, and identity; in theory, it settles matters of logical form. The second step concentrates on sentences with indexicals; those sentences sometimes held true and sometimes false according to discoverable changes in the world. This step in conjunction with the first limits the possibilities for interpreting individual predicates. The last step deals with the remaining sentences, those on which there is not uniform agreement, or whose held truth value does not depend systematically on changes in the environment.[16]

This method is intended to solve the problem of the interdependence of belief and meaning by holding belief constant as far as possible while solving for meaning. This is accomplished by assigning truth conditions to alien sentences that make native speakers right when plausibly possible, according, of course, to our own view of what is right. What justifies the procedure is the fact that disagreement and agreement alike are intelligible only against a background of massive agreement. Applied to language, this principle reads: the more sentences we conspire to accept or reject (whether or not through a medium of interpretation), the better we understand the rest, whether or not we agree about them.

The methodological advice to interpret in a way that optimizes agreement should not be conceived as resting on a charitable assumption about human intelligence that might turn out to be false. If we cannot find a way to interpret the utterances and other behaviour of a creature as revealing a set of beliefs largely consistent and true by our own standards, we have no reason to count that creature as rational, as having beliefs, or as saying anything.

Here I would like to insert a remark about the methodology of my proposal. In philosophy we are used to definitions, analyses, reductions. Typically these are

15. For more on getting a 'best fit' see Essays 10–12 in *Inquiries into Truth and Interpretation.*

16. Readers who appreciate the extent to which this account parallels Quine's account of radical translation in Chapter 2 of *Word and Object* (Cambridge: MIT Press, 1960) will also notice the differences: the semantic constraint in my method forces quantificational structure on the language to be interpreted, which probably does not leave room for indeterminacy of logical form; the notion of stimulus meaning plays no role in my method, but its place is taken by reference to the objective features of the world which alter in conjunction with changes in attitude towards the truth of sentences; the principle of charity, which Quine emphasizes only in connection with the identification of the (pure) sentential connectives, I apply across the board.

intended to carry us from concepts better understood, or clear, or more basic epistemologically or ontologically, to others we want to understand. The method I have suggested fits none of these categories. I have proposed a looser relation between concepts to be illuminated and the relatively more basic. At the centre stands a formal theory, a theory of truth, which imposes a complex structure on sentences containing the primitive notions of truth and satisfaction. These notions are given application by the form of the theory and the nature of the evidence. The result is a partially interpreted theory. The advantage of the method lies not in its free-style appeal to the notion of evidential support but in the idea of a powerful theory interpreted at the most advantageous point. This allows us to reconcile the need for a semantically articulated structure with a theory testable only at the sentential level. The more subtle gain is that very thin evidence in support of each of a potential infinity of points can yield rich results, even with respect to the points. By knowing only the conditions under which speakers hold sentences true, we can come out, given a satisfactory theory, with an interpretation of each sentence. It remains to make good on this last claim. The theory itself at best gives truth conditions. What we need to show is that if such a theory satisfies the constraints we have specified, it may be used to yield interpretations.

3. If we know that a theory of truth satisfies the formal and empirical criteria described, can we interpret utterances of the language for which it is a theory?

A theory of truth entails a T-sentence for each sentence of the object language, and a T-sentence gives truth conditions. It is tempting, therefore, simply to say that a T-sentence 'gives the meaning' of a sentence. Not, of course, by naming or describing an entity that is a meaning, but simply by saying under what conditions an utterance of the sentence is true.

But on reflection it is clear that a T-sentence does not give the meaning of the sentence it concerns: the T-sentences does fix the truth value relative to certain conditions, but it does not say the object language sentence is true *because* the conditions hold. Yet if truth values were all that mattered, the T-sentence for 'Snow is white' could as well say that it is true if and only if grass is green or 2 + 2 = 4 as say that it is true if and only if snow is white. We may be confident, perhaps, that no satisfactory theory of truth will produce such anomalous T-sentences, but this confidence does not license us to make more of T-sentences.

A move that might seem helpful is to claim that it is not the T-sentence alone, but the canonical proof of a T-sentence, that permits us to interpret the alien sentence. A canonical proof, given a theory of truth, is easy to construct, moving as it does through a string of biconditionals, and requiring for uniqueness only occasional decisions to govern left and right precedence. The proof does reflect the logical form the theory assigns to the sentence, and so might be thought to reveal something about meaning. But in fact we would know no more than before about how to interpret if all we knew was that a certain sequence of sentences was the proof, from some true theory, of a particular T-sentence.

A final suggestion along these lines is that we can interpret a particular sentence provided we know a correct theory of truth that deals with the language of the sentence. For then we know not only the T-sentence for the sentence to be interpreted, but we also 'know' the T-sentences for all other sentences; and of course, all the proofs. Then we would see the place of the sentence in the language as a whole, we would know the role of each significant part of the sentence, and we would know about the logical connections between this sentence and others.

If we knew that a T-sentence satisfied Tarski's Convention T, we would know that it was true, and we could use it to interpret a sentence because we would know that the right branch of the biconditional translated the sentence to be interpreted. Our present trouble springs from the fact that in radical interpretation we cannot assume that a T-sentence satisfies the translation criterion. What we have been overlooking, however, is that we have supplied an alternative criterion: this criterion is that the totality of T-sentences should (in the sense described above) optimally fit evidence about sentences held true by native speakers. The present idea is that what Tarski assumed outright for each T-sentence can be indirectly elicited by a holistic constraint. If that constraint is adequate, each T-sentence will in fact yield an acceptable interpretation.

A T-sentence of an empirical theory of truth can be used to interpret a sentence, then, provided we also know the theory that entails it, and know that it is a theory that meets the formal and empirical criteria.[17] For if the constraints are adequate, the range of acceptable theories will be such that any of them yields some correct interpretation for each potential utterance. To see how it might work, accept for a moment the absurd hypothesis that the constraints narrow down the possible theories to one, and this one implies the T-sentence (T) discussed previously. Then we are justified in using this T-sentence to interpret Kurt's utterance of 'Es regnet' as his saying that it is raining. It is not likely, given the flexible nature of the constraints, that all acceptable theories will be identical. When all the evidence is in, there will remain, as Quine has emphasized, the trade-offs between the beliefs we attribute to a speaker and the interpretations we give his words. But the resulting indeterminacy cannot be so great but that any theory that passes the tests will serve to yield interpretations.

17. See footnote 11 of Essay 2 and Essay 12 in *Inquiries into Truth and Interpretation.*

Chapter 19

Three kinds of intentional psychology[1]

Daniel Dennett

1

SUPPOSE you and I both believe that cats eat fish. Exactly what feature must we share for this to be true of us? More generally, recalling Socrates' favourite style of question, what must be in common between things truly ascribed an *intentional* predicate—such as 'wants to visit China' or 'expects noodles for supper'?[2] As Socrates points out, in the *Meno* and elsewhere, such questions are ambiguous or vague in their intent. One can be asking on the one hand for something rather like a definition, or on the other hand for something rather like a theory. (Socrates of course preferred the former sort of answer.) What do all magnets have in common? First answer: they all attract iron. Second answer: they all have such-and-such a microphysical property (a property that explains their capacity to attract iron). In one sense people knew what magnets were—they were things that attracted iron—long before science told them what magnets were. A child learns what the word 'magnet' means not, typically, by learning an explicit definition, but by learning the 'folk physics' of magnets, in which the ordinary term 'magnet' is embedded or implicitly defined as a theoretical term.[3]

Sometimes terms are embedded in more powerful theories, and sometimes they are embedded by explicit definition. What do all chemical elements with the same valence have in common? First answer: they are disposed to combine with other elements in the same integral ratios. Second answer: they all have such-and-such a

Daniel Dennett, 'Three Kinds of Intentional Psychology', from Richard Healy (ed.), *Reduction, Time, and Reality: Studies in the Philosophy of the Natural Sciences* (Cambridge: Cambridge University Press, 1975).

1. I am grateful to the Thyssen Philosophy Group, the Bristol Fulbright Workshop, Elliot Sober and Bo Dahlbom for extensive comments and suggestions on an earlier draft of this paper.

2. Other 'mental' predicates, especially those invoking episodic and allegedly *qualia*-laden entities—pains, sensations, images—raise complications of their own which I will not consider here, for I have dealt with them at length elsewhere, especially in *Brainstorms* (1978). I will concentrate here on the foundational concepts of belief and desire, and will often speak just of belief, implying, except where I note it, that parallel considerations apply to desire.

3. The child need learn only a portion of this folk physics, as Putnam argues in his discussion of the 'division of linguistic labour' (1975).

microphysical property (a property which explains their capacity so to combine). The theory of valences in chemistry was well in hand before its microphysical explanation was known. In one sense chemists knew what valences were before physicists told them.

So what appears in Plato to be a contrast between giving a definition and giving a theory can be viewed as just a special case of the contrast between giving one theoretical answer and giving another, more 'reductive' theoretical answer. Fodor (1975) draws the same contrast between 'conceptual' and 'causal' answers to such questions, and argues that Ryle (1949) champions conceptual answers at the expense of causal answers, wrongly supposing them to be in conflict. There is justice in Fodor's charge against Ryle, for there are certainly many passages in which Ryle seems to propose his conceptual answers as a bulwark against the possibility of *any* causal, scientific, psychological answers, but there is a better view of Ryle's (or perhaps at best a view he ought to have held) that deserves rehabilitation. Ryle's 'logical behaviourism' is composed of his steadfastly conceptual answers to the Socratic questions about matters mental. If Ryle thought these answers ruled out psychology, ruled out causal (or reductive) answers to the Socratic questions, he was wrong, but if he thought only that the conceptual answers to the questions were not to be given by a microreductive psychology, he was on firmer ground. It is one thing to give a causal explanation of some phenomenon and quite another to cite the cause of a phenomenon in the analysis of the concept of it.

Some concepts have what might be called an essential causal element.[4] For instance, the concept of a genuine Winston Chruchill *autograph* has it that how the trail of ink was in fact caused is essential to its status as an autograph. Photocopies, forgeries, inadvertently indistinguishable signatures—but perhaps not carbon copies—are ruled out. These considerations are part of the *conceptual* answer to the Socratic question about autographs.

Now some, including Fodor, have held that such concepts as the concept of intelligent action also have an essential causal element; behaviour that appeared to be intelligent might be shown not to be by being shown to have the wrong sort of cause. Against such positions Ryle can argue that even if it is true that every instance of intelligent behaviour is caused (and hence has a causal explanation), exactly *how* it is caused is inessential to its being intelligent—something that could be true even if all intelligent behaviour exhibited in fact some common pattern of causation. That is, Ryle can plausibly claim that no account in causal terms could capture the class of intelligent actions except *per accidens*. In aid of such a position—for which there is much to be said in spite of the current infatuation with causal theories—Ryle can make claims of the sort Fodor disparages ('it's not the mental activity that makes the clowning clever because what makes the clowning clever is such facts as that it took place out where the children can see it') without

4. Cf. Fodor 1975: 7n.

committing the error of supposing causal and conceptual answers are incompatible.[5]

Ryle's logical behaviourism was in fact tainted by a groundless anti-scientific bias, but it need not have been. Note that the introduction of the concept of valence in chemistry was a bit of *logical chemical behaviourism*: to have valence *n* was 'by definition' to be disposed to behave in such-and-such ways under such-and-such conditions, *however* that disposition to behave might someday be explained by physics. In this particular instance the relation between the chemical theory and the physical theory is now well charted and understood—even if in the throes of ideology people sometimes misdescribe it—and the explanation of those dispositional combinatorial properties by physics is a prime example of the sort of success in science that inspires reductionist doctrines. Chemistry has been shown to reduce, in some sense, to physics, and this is clearly a Good Thing, the sort of thing we should try for more of.

Such progress invites the prospect of a parallel development in psychology. First we will answer the question 'What do all believers-that-*p* have in common?' the first way, the 'conceptual' way, and then see if we can go on to 'reduce' the theory that emerges in our first answer to something else—neurophysiology most likely. Many theorists seem to take it for granted that *some* such reduction is both possible and desirable, and perhaps even inevitable, even while recent critics of reductionism, such as Putnam and Fodor, have warned us of the excesses of 'classical' reductionist creeds. No one today hopes to conduct the psychology of the future in the vocabulary of the neurophysiologist, let alone that of the physicist, and principled ways of relaxing the classical 'rules' of reduction have been proposed. The issue, then, is *what kind* of theoretical bonds can we expect—or ought we to hope—to find uniting psychological claims about beliefs, desires, and so forth with the claims of neurophysiologists, biologists and other physical scientists?

Since the terms 'belief' and 'desire' and their kin are parts of ordinary language, like 'magnet', rather than technical terms like 'valence', we must first look to 'folk psychology' to see what kind of things we are being asked to explain. *What do we learn beliefs are when we learn how to use the words 'believe' and 'belief'?* The first point to make is that we do not really learn what beliefs are when we learn how to use these words.[6] Certainly no one *tells us* what beliefs are, or if someone does, or if we happen to speculate on the topic on our own, the answer we come to, wise or foolish, will figure only weakly in our habits of thought about what people believe. We learn to *use* folk psychology—as a vernacular social technology, a craft—but we don't learn it self-consciously as a theory—we learn no meta-theory with the theory—and in this regard our knowledge of folk psychology is like our knowledge of

5. This paragraph corrects a misrepresentation of both Fodor's and Ryle's positions in my critical notice of Fodor's book in *Mind*, 1977, reprinted in *Brainstorms*, pp. 90–108.

6. I think it is just worth noting that philosophers' use of 'believe' as the standard and general ordinary language term is a considerable distortion. We *seldom* talk about what people *believe*; we talk about what they *think* and what they *know*.

the grammar of our native tongue. This fact does not make our knowledge of folk psychology entirely unlike human knowledge of explicit academic theories, however; one could probably be a good practising chemist and yet find it embarrassingly difficult to produce a satisfactory textbook definition of a metal or an ion.

There are no introductory textbooks of folk psychology (although Ryle's *The Concept of Mind* might be pressed into service), but many explorations of the field have been undertaken by ordinary language philosophers (under slightly different intentions), and more recently by more theoretically minded philosophers of mind, and from all this work an account of folk psychology—part truism and the rest controversy—can be gleaned. What are beliefs? *Roughly*, folk psychology has it that *beliefs* are information-bearing states of people that arise from perceptions, and which, together with appropriately related *desires*, lead to intelligent *action*. That much is relatively uncontroversial, but does folk psychology also have it that non-human animals have beliefs? If so, what is the role of language in belief? Are beliefs constructed of parts? If so, what are the parts? Ideas? Concepts? Words? Pictures? Are beliefs like speech acts or maps or instruction manuals or sentences? Is it implicit in folk psychology that beliefs enter into causal relations, or that they don't? How do decisions and intentions intervene between belief-desire complexes and actions? Are beliefs introspectible, and if so, what authority do the believer's pronouncements have?

All these questions deserve answers, but one must bear in mind that there are different reasons for being interested in the details of folk psychology. One reason is that it exists as a phenomenon, like a religion or a language or a dress code, to be studied with the techniques and attitudes of anthropology. It may be a myth, but it is a myth we live in, so it is an 'important' phenomenon in nature. A different reason is that it seems to be a *true* theory, by and large, and hence is a candidate—like the folk physics of magnets and unlike the folk science of astrology—for incorporation into science. These different reasons generate different but overlapping investigations. The anthropological question should include in its account of folk psychology whatever folk actually include in their theory, however misguided, incoherent, gratuitous some of it may be.[7] The proto-scientific quest, on the other hand, as an attempt to prepare folk theory for subsequent incorporation into or reduction to the rest of science, should be critical, and should *eliminate* all that is false or ill-founded, however well-entrenched in popular doctrine. (Thales thought that lodestones had souls, we are told. Even if most people agreed, this would be something to eliminate from the folk physics of magnets prior to 'reduction'.) One way of distinguishing the good from the bad, the essential from the gratuitous, in folk theory is to see what must be included in the theory to account for whatever predictive or explanatory success it seems to have in ordinary use. In this way we can criticize as we analyse, and it is even open to us in the end to discard folk

7. If the anthropologist marks part of the catalogue of folk theory as false, as an inaccurate or unsound account of the folk craft, he may speak of *false consciousness* or *ideology*, the role of such false theory in constituting a feature of the anthropological phenomenon is not diminished by its falseness.

psychology if it turns out to be a bad theory, and with it the presumed theoretical entities named therein. If we discard folk psychology as a theory, we would have to replace it with another theory, which while it did violence to many ordinary intuitions would explain the predictive power of the residual folk craft.

We use folk psychology all the time, to explain and predict each other's behaviour; we attribute beliefs and desires to each other with confidence—and quite unself-consciously—and spend a substantial portion of our waking lives formulating the world—not excluding ourselves—in these terms. Folk psychology is about as pervasive a part of our second nature as is our folk physics of middle-sized objects. How good is folk psychology? If we concentrate on its weaknesses we will notice that we often are unable to make sense of particular bits of human behaviour (our own included) in terms of belief and desire, even in retrospect; we often cannot predict accurately or reliably what a person will do or when; we often can find no resources within the theory for settling disagreements about particular attributions of belief or desire. If we concentrate on its strengths we find first that there are large areas in which it is extraordinarily reliable in its predictive power. Every time we venture out on a highway, for example, we stake our lives on the reliability of our general expectations about the perceptual beliefs, normal desires and decision proclivities of the other motorists. Second, we find that it is a theory of great generative power and efficiency. For instance, watching a film with a highly original and unstereotypical plot, we see the hero smile at the villain and we all swiftly and effortlessly arrive at the same complex theoretical diagnosis: 'Aha!' we conclude (but perhaps not consciously), 'he wants her to think he doesn't know she intends to defraud his brother!' Third, we find that even small children pick up facility with the theory at a time when they have a very limited experience of human activity from which to induce a theory. Fourth, we find that we all use folk psychology knowing next to nothing about what actually happens inside people's skulls. 'Use your head' we are told, and we know some people are brainier than others, but our capacity to use folk psychology is quite unaffected by ignorance about brain processes—or even by large-scale misinformation about brain processes.

As many philosophers have observed, a feature of folk psychology that sets it apart from both folk physics and the academic physical sciences is the fact that explanations of actions citing beliefs and desires normally not only describe the provenance of the actions, but at the same time defend them as reasonable under the circumstances. They are reason-giving explanations, which make an ineliminable allusion to the rationality of the agent. Primarily for this reason, but also because of the pattern of strengths and weaknesses just described, I suggest that folk psychology might best be viewed as a rationalistic calculus of interpretation and prediction—an idealizing, abstract, instrumentalistic interpretation-method that has evolved because it works, and works because we have evolved. We approach each other as *intentional systems*,[8] that is, as entities whose behaviour can be pre-

8. See my 'Intentional Systems' (1971) .

dicted by the method of attributing beliefs, desires and rational acumen according to the following rough and ready principles:[9]

(1) A system's beliefs are those it *ought to have*, given its perceptual capacities, its epistemic needs, and its biography. Thus, in general, its beliefs are both true and relevant to its life, and when false beliefs are attributed, special stories must be told to explain how the error resulted from the presence of features in the environment that are deceptive relative to the perceptual capacities of the system.

(2) A system's desires are those it *ought to have*, given its biological needs and the most practicable means of satisfying them. Thus intentional systems desire survival and procreation, and hence desire food, security, health, sex, wealth, power, influence, and so forth, and also whatever local arrangements tend (in their eyes—given their beliefs) to further these ends in appropriate measure. Again, 'abnormal' desires are attributable if special stories can be told.

(3) A system's behaviour will consist of those acts that *it would be rational* for an agent with those beliefs and desires to perform.

In (1) and (2) 'ought to have' means 'would have if it were *ideally* ensconced in its environmental niche'. Thus all dangers and vicissitudes in its environment it will *recognize as such* (i.e. *believe* to be dangers) and all the benefits—relative to its needs, of course—it will *desire*. When a fact about its surroundings is particularly relevant to its current projects (which themselves will be the projects such a being ought to have in order to get ahead in its world) it will *know* that fact, and act accordingly. And so forth and so on. This gives us the notion of an ideal epistemic and conative operator or agent, relativized to a set of needs for survival and procreation and to the environment(s) in which its ancestors have evolved and to which it is adapted. But this notion is still too crude and overstated. For instance, a being may come to have an epistemic need that its perceptual apparatus cannot provide for (suddenly all the green food is poisonous but alas it is colourblind), hence the relativity to perceptual capacities. Moreover, it may or may not have had the occasion to learn from experience about something, so its beliefs are also relative to its biography in this way: it will have learned what it ought to have learned, *viz.* what it had been given evidence for in a form compatible with its cognitive apparatus—providing the evidence was 'relevant' to its project then.

But this is still too crude, for we understand that evolution does not give us a best of all possible worlds, but only a passable jury-rig, so we should look for design shortcuts that in specifiably abnormal circumstances yield false perceptual beliefs, etc. (We are not immune to illusions—which we would be if our perceptual systems were *perfect*.) To offset the design shortcuts we should also expect design bonuses: circumstances in which the 'cheap' way for nature to design a cognitive system has the side benefit of giving good, reliable results even outside the environment in

9. For a more elaborate version of similar principles, see Lewis 1974.

which the system evolved. Our eyes are well adapted for giving us true beliefs on Mars as well as on Earth—because the cheap solution for our Earth-evolving eyes happens to be a more general solution.[10]

I propose that we can continue the mode of thinking just illustrated *all the way in*—not just for eye-design, but for deliberation-design and belief-design and strategy-concocter-design. In using this optimistic set of assumptions (nature has built us to do things right; look for systems to believe the truth and love the good) we impute no occult powers to epistemic needs, perceptual capacities and biography, but only the powers common sense already imputes to evolution and learning.

In short, we treat each other as if we were rational agents, and this myth—for surely we are not all that rational—works very well because we are *pretty* rational. This single assumption, in combination with home truths about our needs, capacities and typical circumstances, generates both an intentional interpretation of us as believers and desirers and actual predictions of behaviour in great profusion. I am claiming, then, that folk psychology can best be viewed as a sort of logical behaviourism: *what it means* to say that someone believes that *p*, is that that person is disposed to behave in certain ways under certain conditions. What ways under what conditions? The ways it would be rational to behave, given the person's other beliefs and desires. The answer looks in danger of being circular, but consider: an account of what it is for an element to have a particular valence will similarly make ineliminable reference to the valences of other elements. What one is given with valence-talk is a whole system of interlocking attributions, which is saved from vacuity by yielding independently testable predictions.

I have just described in outline a *method* of predicting and explaining the behaviour of people and other intelligent creatures. Let me distinguish two questions about it: (1) is it something we could do and (2) is it something we in fact do? I think the answer to (1) is obviously yes, which is not to say the method will always yield good results. That much one can ascertain by reflection and thought experiment. Moreover, one can recognize that the method is familiar. Although we don't usually use the method self-consciously, we do use it self-consciously on those occasions when we are perplexed by a person's behaviour, and then it often yields satisfactory results. Moreover, the ease and naturalness with which we resort to this self-conscious and deliberate form of problem-solving provide some support for the claim that what we are doing on those occasions is not *switching methods* but simply becoming self-conscious and explicit about what we ordinarily accomplish tacitly or unconsciously.

No other view of folk psychology, I think, can explain the fact that we do so well predicting each other's behaviour on such slender and peripheral evidence; treating each other as intentional systems works (to the extent that it does) because we really are well designed by evolution and hence we *approximate* to the ideal version of

10. Cf. Sober (unpublished) for useful pioneering exploration of these topics.

ourselves exploited to yield the predictions. But not only does evolution not guarantee that we will always do what is rational; it guarantees that we won't. If we are designed by evolution, then we are almost certainly nothing more than a bag of tricks, patched together by a *satisficing*[11] Nature, and no better than our ancestors had to be to get by. Moreover, the demands of nature and the demands of a logic course are not the same. Sometimes—even *normally* in certain circumstances—it pays to jump to conclusions swiftly (and even to forget that you've done so), so by most philosophical measures of rationality (logical consistency, refraining from invalid inference) there has probably been some positive evolutionary pressure in favour of 'irrational' methods.[12]

How rational are we? Recent research in social and cognitive psychology suggests we are *minimally* rational, appallingly ready to leap to conclusions or be swayed by logically irrelevant features of situations,[13] but this jaundiced view is an illusion engendered by the fact that these psychologists are deliberately trying to produce situations that provoke irrational responses—inducing pathology in a system by putting strain on it—and succeeding, being good psychologists. No one would hire a psychologist to prove that people will choose a paid vacation to a week in jail if offered an informed choice. At least not in the better psychology departments. A more optimistic impression of our rationality is engendered by a review of the difficulties encountered in artificial intelligence research. Even the most sophisticated AI programmes stumble blindly into misinterpretations and misunderstandings that even small children reliably evade without a second thought.[14] From this vantage point we seem marvellously rational.

However rational we are, it is the myth of our rational agenthood that structures and organizes our attributions of belief and desire to others, and that regulates our own deliberations and investigations. We aspire to rationality, and without the myth of our rationality the concepts of belief and desire would be uprooted. Folk psychology, then, is *idealized* in that it produces its predictions and explanations by

11. The term is Herbert Simon's (e.g. 1969).
12. While in general true beliefs have to be more useful than false beliefs (and hence a system ought to have true beliefs), in special circumstances it may be better to have a few false beliefs. For instance it might be better for beast B to have some false beliefs about whom B can beat up and whom B can't. Ranking B's likely antagonists from ferocious to pushover, we certainly want B to believe it can't beat up all the ferocious ones, and can beat up all the obvious pushovers, but it is better (because it 'costs less' in discrimination tasks and protects against random perturbations such as bad days and lucky blows) for B to extend 'I can't beat up x' to cover even some beasts it can in fact beat up. *Erring on the side of prudence* is a well recognized good strategy, and so Nature can be expected to have valued it on occasion when it came up. An alternative strategy in this instance would be to abide by the rule: avoid conflict with penumbral cases. But one might have to 'pay more' to implement that strategy than to implement the strategy designed to produce, and rely on, some false beliefs.
13. See, e.g. Tversky and Kahneman 1974; and Nisbett and Ross 1978.
14. Roger Schank's (1977; Schank and Abelson 1977) efforts to get a computer to 'understand' simple but normally gappy stories is a good illustration.

calculating in a normative system; it predicts what we *will* believe, desire, and do, by determining what we *ought* to believe, desire, and do.[15]

Folk psychology is *abstract* in that the beliefs and desires it attributes are not—or need not be—presumed to be intervening distinguishable states of an internal behaviour-causing system. (The point will be enlarged upon later.) The role of the concept of belief is like the role of the concept of a centre of gravity, and the calculations that yield the predictions are more like the calculations one performs with a parallelogram of forces than like the calculations one performs with a blueprint of internal levers and cogs.

Folk psychology is thus *instrumentalistic* in a way the most ardent realist should permit: people really do have beliefs and desires, on my version of folk psychology, just the way they really have centres of gravity and the earth has an Equator.[16] Reichenbach distinguished between two sorts of referents for theoretical terms: *illata*—posited theoretical entities—and *abstracta*—calculation-bound entities or logical constructs.[17] Beliefs and desires of folk psychology (but not all mental events and states) are *abstracta.*

This view of folk psychology emerges more clearly in contrast to a diametrically opposed view, each of whose tenets has been held by some philosopher, and at least most of which have been espoused by Fodor:

> Beliefs and desires, just like pains, thoughts, sensations and other episodes, are taken by folk psychology to be real, intervening, internal states or events, in causal interaction, subsumed under covering laws of causal stripe. Folk psychology is not an idealized, rationalistic calculus but a naturalistic, empirical, descriptive theory, imputing causal regularities discovered by extensive induction over experience. To suppose two people share a belief is to suppose them to be ultimately in some structurally similar internal condition, e.g. for them to have the same words of Mentalese written in the functionally relevant places in their brains.

I want to deflect this head-on collision of analyses by taking two steps. First, I am prepared to grant a measure of the claims made by the opposition. *Of course* we don't all sit in the dark in our studies like mad Leibnizians rationalistically excogitating behavioural predictions from pure, idealized concepts of our neighbours, nor do we derive all our readiness to attribute desires from a careful generation of them

15. It tests its predictions in two ways: action predictions it tests directly by looking to see what the agent does; belief and desire predictions are tested indirectly by employing the predicted attributions in further predictions of eventual action. As usual, the Duhemian thesis holds: belief and desire attributions are under-determined by the available data.
16. Michael Friedman's 'Theoretical Explanation' (in this volume) provides an excellent analysis of the role of instrumentalistic thinking within realistic science. Scheffler (1963) provides a useful distinction between *instrumentalism* and *fictionalism.* In his terms I am characterizing folk psychology as instrumentalistic, not fictionalistic.
17. Reichenbach 1938: 211–12. 'Our observations of concrete things confer a certain probability on the existence of *illata*—nothing more . . . Second, there are inferences to *abstracta.* These inferences are . . . equivalences, not probability inferences. Consequently, the existence of abstracta is reducible to the existence of concreta. There is, therefore, no problem of their objective existence; their status depends on a convention.'

from the ultimate goal of survival. We may observe that some folks seem to desire cigarettes, or pain, or notoriety (we observe this by hearing them tell us, seeing what they choose, etc.) and without any conviction that these people, given their circumstances, ought to have these desires, we attribute them anyway. So rationalistic generation of attributions is augmented and even corrected on occasion by empirical generalizations about belief and desire that guide our attributions and are learned more or less inductively. For instance, small children believe in Santa Claus, people are inclined to believe the more self-serving of two interpretations of an event in which they are involved (unless they are depressed), and people can be made to want things they don't need by making them believe that glamorous people like those things. And so forth in familiar profusion. This folklore does not consist in *laws*—even probabilistic laws—but some of it is being turned into science of a sort, e.g. theories of 'hot cognition' and cognitive dissonance. I grant the existence of all this naturalistic generalization, and its role in the normal calculations of folk psychologists—i.e. all of us. People do rely on their own parochial group of neighbours when framing intentional interpretations. That is why people have so much difficulty understanding foreigners—their behaviour, to say nothing of their languages. They impute more of their own beliefs and desires, and those of their neighbours, than they would if they followed my principles of attribution slavishly. Of course this is a perfectly reasonable shortcut for people to take, even when it often leads to bad results. We are in this matter, as in most, satisficers, not optimizers, when it comes to information gathering and theory construction. I would insist, however, that all this empirically obtained lore is laid over a fundamental generative and normative framework that has the features I have described.

My second step away from the conflict I have set up is to recall that the issue is not what folk psychology as found in the field truly is, but what it is at its best, what deserves to be taken seriously and incorporated into science. It is not particularly to the point to argue against me that folk psychology is *in fact* committed to beliefs and desires as distinguishable, causally interacting *illata*; what must be shown is that it ought to be. The latter claim I will deal with in due course. The former claim I *could* concede without embarrassment to my overall project, but I do not concede it, for it seems to me that the evidence is quite strong that our ordinary notion of belief has next to nothing of the concrete in it. Jacques shoots his uncle dead in Trafalgar Square and is apprehended on the spot by Sherlock; Tom reads about it in the *Guardian* and Boris learns of it in *Pravda*. Now Jacques, Sherlock, Tom and Boris have had remarkably *different* experiences—to say nothing of their earlier biographies and future prospects—but there is one thing they share: they all believe that a Frenchman has committed murder in Trafalgar Square. They did not all *say* this, not even 'to themselves'; *that proposition* did not, we can suppose, 'occur to' any of them, and even if it had, it would have had entirely different import for Jacques, Sherlock, Tom and Boris. Yet they all believe that a Frenchman committed murder in Trafalgar Square. This is a shared property that is, as it were, visible only from one very limited point of view—the point of view of folk psychology.

Ordinary folk psychologists have no difficulty imputing such useful but elusive commonalities to people. If they then insist that in doing so they are postulating a similarly structured object, as it were, in each head, this is a gratuitous bit of misplaced concreteness, a regrettable lapse in ideology.

But in any case there is no doubt that folk psychology is a mixed bag, like folk productions generally, and there is no reason in the end not to grant that it is much more complex, variegated (and in danger of incoherence) than my sketch has made it out to be. The *ordinary* notion of belief no doubt does place beliefs somewhere midway between being *illata* and being *abstracta*. What this suggests to me is that the concept of belief found in ordinary understanding, i.e. in folk psychology, is unappealing as a scientific concept. I am reminded of Anaxagoras' strange precursor to atomism: the theory of seeds. There is a portion of everything in everything, he is reputed to have claimed. Every object consists of an infinity of seeds, of all possible varieties. How do you make bread out of flour, yeast and water? Flour contains bread seeds in abundance (but flour seeds predominate—that's what makes it flour), and so do yeast and water, and when these ingredients are mixed together, the bread seeds form a new majority, so bread is what you get. Bread nourishes by containing flesh and blood and bone seeds in addition to its majority of bread seeds. Not good theoretical entities, these seeds, for as a sort of bastardized cross between properties and proper parts they have a penchant for generating vicious regresses, and their identity conditions are problematic to say the least.

Beliefs are rather like that. There seems no comfortable way of avoiding the claim that we have an infinity of beliefs, and common intuition does not give us a stable answer to such puzzles as whether the belief that 3 is greater than 2 is none other than the belief that 2 is less than 3. The obvious response to the challenge of an infinity of beliefs with slippery identity conditions is to suppose these beliefs are not all 'stored separately'; many—in fact *most* if we are really talking about infinity—will be stored *implicitly* in virtue of the *explicit* storage of a few (or a few million)—the *core beliefs*.[18] The core beliefs will be 'stored separately', and they look like promising *illata* in contrast to the *virtual* or *implicit* beliefs which look like paradigmatic *abstracta*. But although this might turn out to be the way our brains are organized, I suspect things will be more complicated than this: there is no reason to suppose the core *elements*, the concrete, salient, separately stored representation-tokens (and there must be some such elements in any complex information processing system), will explicitly represent (or *be*) a subset of our *beliefs* at all. That is, if you were to sit down and write out a list of a thousand or so of your paradigmatic beliefs, *all* of them could turn out to be virtual, only implicitly stored or represented, and what was explicitly stored would be information (e.g. about memory addresses, procedures for problem-solving, or recognition, etc.) that was entirely unfamiliar. It would be folly to prejudge this empirical issue by insisting that our core representations of information (whichever they turn out to be) are

18. See my 'Brain Writing and Mind Reading', 1975. See also Fodor 1975, and Field 1978.

beliefs *par excellence*, for when the facts are in our intuitions may instead support the contrary view: the least controversial self-attributions of belief may pick out beliefs that from the vantage point of developed cognitive theory are invariably virtual.[19]

In such an eventuality what could we say about the *causal* roles we assign ordinarily to beliefs (e.g. 'Her belief that John knew her secret caused her to blush')? We could say that whatever the core elements were in virtue of which she virtually believed that John knew her secret, they, the core elements, played a direct causal role (somehow) in triggering the blushing response. We would be wise, as this example shows, not to tamper with our *ordinary* catalogue of beliefs (virtual though they might all turn out to be), for these are predictable, readily understandable, manipulable regularities in psychological phenomena in spite of their apparent neutrality with regard to the explicit/implicit (or core/virtual) distinction. What Jacques, Sherlock, Boris and Tom have in common is probably only a virtual belief 'derived' from largely different explicit stores of information in each of them, but virtual or not, it is their sharing of *this* belief that would explain (or permit us to predict) in some imagined circumstances their all taking the same action when given the same new information. ('And now for one million dollars, Tom [Jacques, Sherlock, Boris], answer our jackpot question correctly: has a French citizen ever committed a major crime in London?')

At the same time we want to cling to the equally ordinary notion that beliefs can cause not only actions, but blushes, verbal slips, heart attacks and the like. Much of the debate over whether or not intentional explanations are causal explanations can be bypassed by noting how the core elements, *whatever they may be*, can be cited as playing the causal role, while belief remains virtual. 'Had Tom not believed that p and wanted that q, he would not have done A.' Is this a causal explanation? It is tantamount to this: Tom was in some one of an indefinitely large number of structurally different states of type B that have in common just that each one of them licenses attribution of belief that p and desire that q in virtue of its normal relations with many other states of Tom, and this state, whichever one it was, was causally sufficient, given the 'background conditions' of course, to initiate the intention to perform A, and thereupon A was performed, and had he not been in one of those indefinitely many type B states, he would not have done A. One can call this a causal explanation because it talks about causes, but it is surely as unspecific and unhelpful as a causal explanation can get. It commits itself to there being some causal explanation or other falling within a very broad area (i.e. the intentional interpretation is held to be supervenient on Tom's bodily condition), but its true informativeness and utility in actual prediction lie, not surprisingly, in its assertion that Tom, however his body is currently structured, has a particular set of these elusive intentional properties, beliefs and desires.

19. See Field 1978: 55, n. 12 on 'minor concessions' to such instrumentalistic treatments of belief.

The ordinary notion of belief is pulled in two directions. If we want to have *good* theoretical entities, good *illata*, or good logical constructs, good *abstracta*, we will have to jettison some of the ordinary freight of the concepts of belief and desire. So I propose a divorce. Since we seem to have both notions wedded in folk psychology, let's split them apart and create two new theories: one strictly abstract, idealizing, holistic, instrumentalistic—pure intentional system theory—and the other a concrete, micro-theoretical science of the actual realization of those intentional systems—what I will call sub-personal cognitive psychology. By exploring their differences and interrelations, we should be able to tell whether any plausible 'reductions' are in the offing.

2

The first new theory, intentional system theory, is envisaged as a close kin of—and overlapping with—such already existing disciplines as decision theory and game theory, which are similarly abstract, normative and couched in intentional language. It borrows the ordinary terms, 'belief' and 'desire' but gives them a technical meaning within the theory. It is a sort of holistic logical behaviourism because it deals with the prediction and explanation from belief-desire profiles of the actions of whole systems (either alone in environments or in interaction with other intentional systems), but treats the individual realizations of the systems as black boxes. The *subject* of all the intentional attributions is the whole system (the person, the animal, or even the corporation or nation)[20] rather than any of its parts, and individual beliefs and desires are not attributable in isolation, independently of other belief and desire attributions. The latter point distinguishes intentional system theory most clearly from Ryle's logical behaviourism, which took on the impossible burden of characterizing individual beliefs (and other mental states) as particular individual dispositions to outward behaviour.

The theory deals with the 'production' of new beliefs and desires from old, *via* an interaction among old beliefs and desires, features in the environment, and the system's actions, and this creates the illusion that the theory contains naturalistic descriptions of internal processing in the systems the theory is about, when in fact the processing is all in the manipulation of the theory, and consists in updating the intentional characterization of the whole system according to the rules of attribution. An analogous illusion of process would befall a naive student who, when confronted with a parallelogram of forces, supposed that it pictured a mechanical linkage of rods and pivots of some kind instead of being simply a graphic way of representing and plotting the effect of several simultaneously acting forces.

20. See my 'Conditions of Personhood' (1976).

Richard Jeffrey (1970), in developing his concept of probability kinematics, has usefully drawn attention to an analogy with the distinction in physics between kinematics and dynamics. In kinematics,

> you talk about the propagation of motions throughout a system in terms of such constraints as rigidity and manner of linkage. It is the physics of position and time, in terms of which you can talk about velocity and acceleration, but not about force and mass. When you talk about forces—*causes* of accelerations—you are in the realm of dynamics (172).

Kinematics provides a simplified and idealized level of abstraction appropriate for many purposes—e.g. for the *initial* design development of a gearbox—but when one must deal with more concrete details of systems—e.g. when the gearbox designer must worry about friction, bending, energetic efficiency and the like—one must switch to dynamics for more detailed and reliable predictions, at the cost of increased complexity and diminished generality. Similarly one can approach the study of belief (and desire and so forth) at a highly abstract level, ignoring problems of realization and simply setting out what the normative demands on the design of a believer are. For instance, one can ask such questions as 'What must a system's epistemic capabilities and propensities be for it to survive in environment A?'[21] or 'What must this system already know in order for it to be able to learn B?' or 'What intentions must this system have in order to mean something by saying something?'[22]

Intentional system theory deals just with the performance specifications of believers while remaining silent on how the systems are to be implemented. In fact this neutrality with regard to implementation is the most useful feature of intentional characterizations. Consider, for instance, the role of intentional characterizations in evolutionary biology. If we are to explain the evolution of complex behavioural capabilities or cognitive talents by natural selection, we must note that it is the intentionally characterized capacity (e.g. the capacity to acquire a belief, a desire, to perform an intentional action) that has survival value, however it happens to be realized as a result of mutation. If a particularly noxious insect makes its appearance in an environment, the birds and bats with a survival advantage will be those that come to believe this insect is not good to eat. In view of the vast differences in neural structure, genetic background and perceptual capacity between birds and bats, it is highly unlikely that this useful trait they may come to share has a common description at any level more concrete or less abstract than intentional system theory. It is not only that the intentional predicate is a projectible predicate in evolutionary theory; since it is more general than its species-specific counterpart predicates (which characterize the successful mutation just in birds, or just in bats), it is preferable. So from the point of view of evolutionary biology, we would not

21. Cf. Campbell 1973, and his William James lectures (Harvard U.P., forthcoming).
22. The questions of this variety are familiar, of course, to philosophers, but are now becoming equally familiar to researchers in artificial intelligence.

want to 'reduce' all intentional characterizations even if we knew in particular instances what the physiological implementation was.

This level of generality is essential if we want a theory to have anything meaningful and defensible to say about such topics as intelligence in general (as opposed, say, to just human or even terrestrial or natural intelligence), or such grand topics as meaning or reference or representation. Suppose, to pursue a familiar philosophical theme, we are invaded by Martians, and the question arises: do they have beliefs and desires? Are they that much *like us*? According to intentional system theory, if these Martians are smart enough to get here, then they most certainly have beliefs and desires—in the technical sense proprietary to the theory—no matter what their internal structure, and no matter how our folk-psychological intuitions rebel at the thought.

This principled blindness of intentional system theory to internal structure seems to invite the retort:[23] but there has to be *some* explanation of the *success* of intentional prediction of the behaviour of systems. It isn't just magic. It isn't a mere coincidence that one can generate all these *abstracta*, manipulate them *via* some version of practical reasoning, and come up with an action prediction that has a good chance of being true. There must be some way in which the internal processes of the system mirror the complexities of the intentional interpretation, or its success would be a miracle.

Of course. This is all quite true and important. Nothing without a great deal of structural and processing complexity could conceivably realize an intentional system of any interest, and the complexity of the realization will surely bear a striking resemblance to the complexity of the instrumentalistic interpretation. Similarly, the success of valence theory in chemistry is no coincidence, and people were entirely right to expect that deep microphysical similarities would be discovered between elements with the same valence, and that the structural similarities found would explain the dispositional similarities. But since people and animals are unlike atoms and molecules not only in being the products of a complex evolutionary history, but also in being the products of their individual learning histories, there is no reason to suppose that individual (human) believers that *p*—like individual (carbon) atoms with valence 4—regulate their dispositions with *exactly* the same machinery. Discovering the constraints on design and implementation variation, and demonstrating how particular species and individuals in fact succeed in realizing intentional systems is the job for the third theory: sub-personal cognitive psychology.

23. From Ned Block and Jerry Fodor, *inter alia*, in conversation.

3

The task of sub-personal cognitive psychology is to explain something that at first glance seems utterly mysterious and inexplicable. The brain, as intentional system theory and evolutionary biology show us, is a *semantic engine*; its task is to discover what its multifarious inputs *mean*, to discriminate them by their significance and 'act accordingly'.[24] That's what brains *are for*. But the brain, as physiology or plain common sense shows us, is just a *syntactic engine*; all it can do is discriminate its inputs by their structural, temporal, and physical features, and let its entirely mechanical activities be governed by these 'syntactic' features of its inputs. That's all brains *can do*. Now how does the brain manage to get semantics from syntax? How could *any* entity (how could a genius, or an angel, or God) get the semantics of a system from nothing but its syntax? It couldn't. The syntax of a system doesn't determine its semantics. By what alchemy, then, does the brain extract semantically reliable results from syntactically driven operations? It cannot be designed to do an impossible task, but it could be designed to *approximate* the impossible task, to *mimic* the behaviour of the impossible object (the semantic engine) by capitalizing on close (close enough) fortuitous correspondences between structural regularities—of the environment and of its own internal states and operations—and semantic types.

The basic idea is familiar. An animal needs to know when it has satisfied the goal of finding and ingesting food, but it settles for a friction-in-the-throat-followed-by-stretched-stomach detector, a mechanical switch turned on by a relatively simple mechanical condition that *normally* co-occurs with the satisfaction of the animal's 'real' goal. It's not fancy, and can easily be exploited to trick the animal into either eating when it shouldn't or leaving off eating when it shouldn't, but it does well enough by the animal in its normal environment. Or suppose I am monitoring telegraph transmissions and have been asked to intercept all *death threats* (but only death threats in English—to make it 'easy'). I'd like to build a machine to save me the trouble of interpreting semantically every message sent, but how could this be done? No machine could be designed to do the job perfectly, for that would require defining the semantic category *death threat in English* as some tremendously complex feature of strings of alphabetic symbols, and there is utterly no reason to suppose this could be done in a principled way. (If somehow by brute-force inspection and subsequent enumeration we could list all and only the English death threats of, say, less than a thousand characters, we could easily enough build a filter

24. More accurately if less picturesquely, the brain's task is to come to produce internal mediating responses that reliably vary in concert with variation in the actual environmental significance (the natural and non-natural meanings, in Grice's (1957) sense) of their distal causes and independently of meaning-irrelevant variations in their proximal causes, and moreover to respond to its own mediating responses in ways that systematically tend to improve the creature's prospects in its environment if the mediating responses are varying as they ought to vary.

to detect them, but we are looking for a principled, projectible, extendable method.) A really crude device could be made to discriminate all messages containing the symbol strings

. . . I will kill you . . .

or

. . . you . . . die . . . unless . . .

or

. . . (for some finite disjunction of likely patterns to be found in English death threats).

This device would have some utility, and further refinements could screen the material that passed this first filter, and so on. An unpromising beginning for constructing a sentence understander, but if you want to get semantics out of syntax (whether the syntax of messages in a natural language or the syntax of afferent neuron impulses), variations on this basic strategy are your only hope.[25] You must put together a bag of tricks and hope nature will be kind enough to let your device get by. Of course some tricks are elegant, and appeal to deep principles of organization, but in the end all one can hope to produce (all natural selection can have produced) are systems that *seem* to discriminate meanings by actually discriminating things (tokens of no doubt wildly disjunctive types) that co-vary reliably with meanings.[26] Evolution has designed our brains not only to do this but

25. One might think that while *in principle* one cannot derive the semantics of a system from nothing but its syntax, *in practice* one might be able to cheat a little and exploit syntactic features that don't *imply* a semantical interpretation, but strongly suggest one. For instance, faced with the task of deciphering isolated documents in an entirely unknown and alien language, one might note that while the symbol that *looks like* a duck doesn't *have* to mean 'duck', there is a good chance that it does, especially if the symbol that looks like a wolf seems to be eating the symbol that looks like a duck, and not *vice versa.* Call this *hoping for hieroglyphics* and note the form it has taken in psychological theories from Locke to the present: we will be able to tell which mental representations are which (which idea is the idea of *dog* and which of *cat*) because the former will look like a dog and the latter like a cat. This is all very well as a crutch for us observers on the outside, trying to assign content to the events in some brain, but it is of no use to the brain . . . because brains don't know what dogs look like! Or better, this cannot be the brain's fundamental method of eking semantic classes out of raw syntax, for any brain (or brain part) that could be said—in an extended sense—to know what dogs look like would be a brain (or brain part) that had already solved its problem, that was already (a simulacrum of) a semantic engine. But this is still misleading, for brains in any event do not *assign* content to their own events in the way observers might: brains *fix* the content of their internal events in the act of reacting as they do. There are good reasons for positing *mental images* of one sort or another in cognitive theories (see 'Two Approaches to Mental Images' in *Brainstorms* pp. 174–89) but hoping for hieroglyphics isn't one of them, though I suspect it is covertly influential.

26. I take this point to be closely related to Davidson's reasons for claiming there can be no psychophysical laws, but I am unsure that Davidson wants to draw the same conclusions from it that I do. See Davidson 1970.

to evolve and follow strategies of self-improvement in this activity during their individual lifetimes.[27]

It is the task of sub-personal cognitive psychology to propose and test models of such activity—of pattern recognition or stimulus generalization, concept learning, expectation, learning, goal-directed behaviour, problem-solving—that not only produce a simulacrum of genuine content-sensitivity, but that do this in ways demonstrably like the way people's brains do it, exhibiting the same powers and the same vulnerabilities to deception, overload and confusion. It is here that we will find our good theoretical entities, our useful *illata*, and while some of them may well resemble the familiar entities of folk psychology—beliefs, desires, judgments, decisions—many will certainly not.[28] The only similarity we can be sure of discovering in the *illata* of sub-personal cognitive psychology is the intentionality of their labels.[29] They will be characterized as events with content, bearing information, signalling this and ordering that.

In order to give the *illata* these labels, in order to maintain any intentional interpretation of their operation at all, the theorist must always keep glancing outside the system, to see what normally produces the configuration he is describing, what effects the system's responses normally have on the environment, and what benefit normally accrues to the whole system from this activity. In other words the cognitive psychologist cannot ignore the fact that it is the realization of an intentional system he is studying on pain of abandoning semantic interpretation and hence psychology. On the other hand, progress in sub-personal cognitive psychology will blur the boundaries between it and intentional system theory, knitting them together much as chemistry and physics have been knit together.

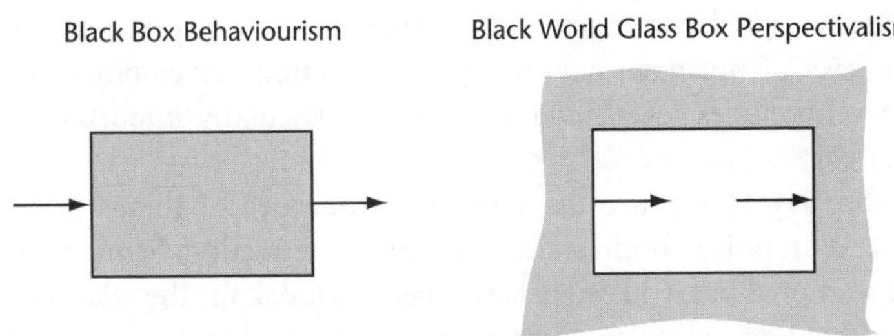

The alternative of ignoring the external world and its relations to the internal machinery (what Putnam has called psychology in the narrow sense, or methodological solipsism, and Keith Gunderson lampoons as black world glass box perspectivalism)[30] is not really psychology at all, but just at best abstract neuro-

27. This claim is defended in my 'Why the law of effect will not go away' (1974).
28. See, for instance, Stephen Stich's (1978) concept of subdoxastic states.
29. See my 'Reply to Arbib and Gunderson', in *Brainstorms*, pp. 23–38.
30. In his reply to Fodor's 'Methodological Solipsism as a Research Strategy in Psychology' at the Cincinnati Colloquium on Philosophy of Psychology, February 1978.

physiology—pure internal syntax with no hope of a semantic interpretation. Psychology 'reduced' to neurophysiology in this fashion would not be psychology, for it would not be able to provide an explanation of the regularities it is psychology's particular job to explain: the reliability with which 'intelligent' organisms can cope with their environments and thus prolong their lives. Psychology can, and should, work towards an account of the physiological foundations of psychological processes, not by eliminating psychological or intentional characterizations of those processes, but by exhibiting how the brain implements the intentionally characterized performance specifications of sub-personal theories.[31]

Friedman, discussing the current perplexity in cognitive psychology, suggests that the problem

> is the direction of reduction. Contemporary psychology tries to explain *individual* cognitive activity independently from *social* cognitive activity, and then tries to give a *micro* reduction of social cognitive activity—that is, the use of a public language—in terms of a prior theory of individual cognitive activity. The opposing suggestion is that we first look for a theory of social activity, and then try to give a *macro* reduction of individual cognitive activity—the activity of applying concepts, making judgments, and so forth—in terms of our prior social theory.[32]

With the idea of macro-reduction in psychology I largely agree, except that Friedman's identification of the macro level as explicitly *social* is only part of the story. The cognitive capacities of non-language-using animals (and Robinson Crusoes, if there are any) must also be accounted for, and not just in terms of an analogy with the practices of us language users. The macro level *up* to which we should relate micro-processes in the brain in order to understand them as psychological is more broadly the level of organism-environment interaction, development and evolution. That level includes social interaction as a particularly important part,[33] but still a proper part.

There is no way to capture the semantic properties of things (word tokens, diagrams, nerve impulses, brain states) by a micro-reduction. Semantic properties are not just relational but, you might say, superrelational, for the relation a particular vehicle of content, or token, must bear in order to have content is not just a relation it bears to other similar things (e.g. other tokens, or parts of tokens, or sets of tokens, or causes of tokens) but a relation between the token and the whole life—and counter-factual life[34]—of the organism it 'serves' *and* that organism's requirements for survival *and* its evolutionary ancestry.

31. I treat methodological solipsism in (much) more detail in 'Beyond Belief', in Andrew Woodfield, ed. *Thought and Object.*

32. Michael Friedman, 'Theoretical Explanation', this volume, pp. 15–16.

33. See Tyler Burge 1979.

34. What I mean is this: counterfactuals enter because content is in part a matter of the *normal* or *designed* role of a vehicle whether or not it ever gets to play that role. Cf. Sober (unpublished).

4

Of our three psychologies—folk psychology, intentional system theory, and sub-personal cognitive psychology—what then might reduce to what? Certainly the one-step micro-reduction of folk psychology to physiology alluded to in the slogans of the early identity theorists will never be found—and should never be missed, even by staunch friends of materialism and scientific unity. A prospect worth exploring, though, is that folk psychology (more precisely, the part of folk psychology worth caring about) reduces—conceptually—to intentional system theory. What this would amount to can best be brought out by contrasting this proposed conceptual reduction with more familiar alternatives: 'type-type identity theory' and 'Turing machine functionalism'. According to type-type identity theory, for every mentalistic term or predicate '*M*', there is some predicate '*P*' *expressible in the vocabulary of the physical sciences* such that a creature is *M* if and only if it is *P*. In symbols:

(1) (x) (Mx ≡ Px)

This is reductionism with a vengeance, taking on the burden of replacing, in principle, all mentalistic predicates with co-extensive predicates composed truth-functionally from the predicates of physics. It is now widely agreed to be hopelessly too strong a demand. Believing that cats eat fish is, intuitively, a *functional* state that might be variously implemented physically, so there is no reason to suppose the commonality referred to on the left-hand side of (1) can be reliably picked out by any predicate, however complex, of physics. What is needed to express the predicate on the right-hand side is, it seems, a physically neutral language for speaking of functions and functional states, and the obvious candidates are the languages used to describe automata—for instance, Turing machine language.

The Turing machine functionalist then proposes

(2) (x) (Mx ≡ x realizes some Turing machine k in logical state A)

In other words, for two things both to believe that cats eat fish they need not be physically similar in any specifiable way, but they must both be in a 'functional' condition specifiable in principle in the most general functional language; they must share a Turing machine description according to which they are both in some particular logical state. This is still a reductionist doctrine, for it proposes to identify each mental type with a functional type picked out in the language of automata theory. But this is still too strong, for there is no more reason to suppose Jacques, Sherlock, Boris and Tom 'have the same programme' in *any* relaxed and abstract sense, considering the differences in their nature and nurture, than that their brains have some crucially identical physico-chemical feature. We must weaken the requirements for the right-hand side of our formula still further.

Consider

(3) (x)(x believes that p ≡ x can be predictively attributed the belief that p)

This appears to be blatantly circular and uninformative, with the language on the right simply mirroring the language on the left. But all we need to make an informative answer of this formula is a systematic way of making the attributions alluded to on the right-hand side. Consider the parallel case of Turing machines. What do two different realizations or embodiments of a Turing machine have in common when they are in the same logical state? Just this: there is a system of description such that according to it both are described as being realizations of some particular Turing machine, and according to this description, which is predictive of the operation of both entities, both are in the same state of that Turing machine's machine table. One doesn't *reduce* Turing machine talk to some more fundamental idiom; one *legitimizes* Turing machine talk by providing it with rules of attribution and exhibiting its predictive powers. If we can similarly legitimize 'mentalistic' talk, we will have no need of a reduction, and that is the point of the concept of an intentional system. Intentional systems are supposed to play a role in the legitimization of mentalistic predicates parallel to the role played by the abstract notion of a Turing machine in setting down rules for the interpretation of artifacts as computational automata. I fear my concept is woefully informal and unsystematic compared with Turing's, but then the domain it attempts to systematize—our everyday attributions in mentalistic or intentional language—is itself something of a mess, at least compared with the clearly defined field of recursive function theory, the domain of Turing machines.

The analogy between the theoretical roles of Turing machines and intentional systems is more than superficial. Consider that warhorse in the philosophy of mind, Brentano's Thesis that intentionality is the mark of the mental: all mental phenomena exhibit intentionality and no physical phenomena exhibit intentionality. This has been traditionally taken to be an *irreducibility* thesis: the mental, in virtue of its intentionality, cannot be reduced to the physical. But given the concept of an intentional system, we can construe the first half of Brentano's Thesis—all mental phenomena are intentional—as a *reductionist* thesis of sorts, parallel to Church's Thesis in the foundation of mathematics.

According to Church's Thesis, every 'effective' procedure in mathematics is recursive, that is, Turing-computable. Church's Thesis is not provable, since it hinges on the intuitive and informal notion of an effective procedure, but it is generally accepted, and it provides a very useful reduction of a fuzzy-but-useful mathematical notion to a crisply defined notion of apparently equal scope and greater power. Analogously, the claim that every mental phenomenon alluded to in folk psychology is *intentional-system-characterizable* would, if true, provide a reduction of the mental as ordinarily understood—a domain whose boundaries are at best fixed by mutual acknowledgment and shared intuition—to a clearly defined domain of entities, whose principles of organization are familiar, relatively formal and systematic, and entirely general.[35]

This reductive claim, like Church's Thesis, cannot be proven, but could be made compelling by piecemeal progress on particular (and particularly difficult) cases—a project I set myself elsewhere (in *Brainstorms*). The final reductive task would be to show not how the terms of intentional system theory are eliminable in favour of physiological terms via sub-personal cognitive psychology, but almost the reverse: to show how a system described in physiological terms could warrant an interpretation as a realized intentional system.

References

Block, N. 1978. 'Troubles with functionalism.' *Perception and Cognition: Issues in the Foundations of Psychology*, ed. C. Wade Savage, pp. 261–326. Minnesota Studies in Philosophy of Science, vol. IX. Minneapolis: Minnesota University Press.

Burge, T. 1979. 'Individualism and the mental.' *Midwest Studies in Philosophy*, vol. IV, pp. 73–121.

Campbell, D. 1973. 'Evolutionary epistemology.' *The Philosophy of Karl Popper*, ed. Paul A. Schilpp. La Salle, Illinois: Open Court.

Davidson, D. 1970. 'Mental events.' *Experience and Theory*, ed. L. Foster and J. Swanson, pp. 79–102. Amherst: University of Massachusetts Press. (See Chapter 39 of this volume.)

Dennett, D. C. 1971. 'Intentional systems.' *Journal of Philosophy* 68, 87–106. Reprinted (with other essays on intentional systems) in *Brainstorms*, pp. 3–22.

Dennett, D. C. 1974. 'Why the law of effect will not go away.' *Journal of the Theory of Social Behaviour* 5, 169–187. Reprinted in *Brainstorms*, pp. 71–89.

Dennett, D. C. 1975. 'Brain writing and mind reading.' *Language, Mind and Knowledge*, ed. K. Gunderson. Minnesota Studies in Philosophy of Science, vol. VII. Minneapolis: Minnesota University Press. Reprinted in *Brainstorms*, pp. 39–50.

Dennett, D. C. 1976. 'Conditions of personhood.' *The Identities of Persons*, ed. A. Rorty. Reprinted in *Brainstorms*, pp. 267–85.

Dennett, D. C. 1978. *Brainstorms.* Montgomery, Vermont: Bradford Books; Hassocks, Sussex: Harvester Press.

Field, H. 1978. 'Mental representation.' *Erkenntnis* 13, 9–61.

Fodor, J. 1975. *The Language of Thought.* Hassocks, Sussex: Harvester Press; Scranton, Pa.: Crowell.

Grice, H. P. 1957. 'Meaning.' *Philosophical Review* 66, 377–88.

Jeffrey, R. 1970. 'Dracula meets Wolfman: acceptance vs. partial belief.' *Induction, Acceptance and Rational Belief*, ed. Marshall Swain. Dordrecht: Reidel.

Lewis, D. 1974. 'Radical interpretation.' *Synthèse* 23, 331–44.

Nisbett, R. E. and Ross, L. D. 1978. *Human Inference: Strategy and Shortcomings.* Englewood Cliffs, N.J.: Prentice Hall.

35. Ned Block (1978) presents arguments supposed to show how the various possible functionalist theories of mind all slide into the sins of 'chauvinism' (improperly excluding Martians from the class of possible mind-havers) or 'liberalism' (improperly including various contraptions, imagined human puppets, and so forth among the mind-havers). My view embraces the broadest liberalism, gladly paying the price of a few recalcitrant intuitions for the generality gained.

Putnam, H. 1975. 'The meaning of 'meaning'.' *Mind, Language and Reality (Philosophical Papers*, vol. II), pp. 215–71. Cambridge: Cambridge University Press.
Reichenbach, H. 1938. *Experience and Prediction.* Chicago: University of Chicago Press.
Ryle, G. 1949. *The Concept of Mind.* London: Hutchinson.
Schank, R. 1977. 'Sam—a story understander.' Research Report 43, Yale University Dept of Computer Science.
Schank, R. and Abelson, R. 1977. *Scripts, Plans, Goals and Understanding.* Hillside, N.J.: Erlbaum.
Scheffler, I. 1963. *The Anatomy of Inquiry.* New York: Knopf.
Simon, H. 1969. *The Sciences of the Artificial.* Cambridge, Mass.: M.I.T. Press.
Sober, E. (unpublished) 'The descent of Mind.'
Stich, S. 1978. 'Belief and subdoxastic states.' *Philosophy of Science* 45, 499–518.
Tversky, A. and Kahneman, D. 1974. 'Judgement under uncertainty: heuristics and biases.' *Science* 185, 1124–31.
Woodfield, A., ed., forthcoming. *Thought and Object.* Oxford: Oxford University Press.

Chapter 20

Thought and talk

Donald Davidson

WHAT is the connection between thought and language? The dependence of speaking on thinking is evident, for to speak is to express thoughts. This dependence is manifest in endless further ways. Someone who utters the sentence 'The candle is out' as a sentence of English must intend to utter words that are true if and only if an indicated candle is out at the time of utterance, and he must believe that by making the sounds he does he is uttering words that are true only under those circumstances. These intentions and beliefs are not apt to be dwelt on by the fluent speaker. But though they may not normally command attention, their absence would be enough to show he was not speaking English, and the absence of any analogous thoughts would show he was not speaking at all.

The issue is on the other side: can there be thought without speech? A first and natural reaction is that there can be. There is the familiar, irksome experience of not being able to find the words to express one's ideas. On occasion one may decide that the editorial writer has put a point better than one could oneself. And there is Norman Malcolm's dog who, having chased a squirrel into the woods, barks up the wrong tree. It is hard not to credit the dog with the belief that the squirrel is in that tree.

A definite, if feebler, intuition tilts the other way. It is possible to wonder whether the speaker who can't find the right words has a clear idea. Attributions of intentions and beliefs to dogs smack of anthropomorphism. A primitive behaviourism, baffled by the privacy of unspoken thoughts, may take comfort in the view that thinking is really 'talking to oneself'—silent speech.

Beneath the surface of these opposed tendencies run strong, if turgid, currents, which may help to explain why philosophers have, for the most part, preferred taking a stand on the issue to producing an argument. Whatever the reason, the question of the relationship between thought and speech seems seldom to have been asked for its own sake. The usual assumption is that one or the other, speech or thought, is by comparison easy to understand, and therefore the more obscure one (whichever that is) may be illuminated by analysing or explaining it in terms of the other.

The assumption is, I think, false: neither language nor thinking can be fully

Donald Davidson, 'Tought and Talk'. In Samuel Guttenplan, ed., *Mind and Language: Wolfson College Lectures 1974* (Oxford: Clarendon Press, 1974). Reprinted in *Inquiries into Truth and Interpretation* (Oxford: Clarendon Press, 1984).

explained in terms of the other, and neither has conceptual priority. The two are, indeed, linked, in the sense that each requires the other in order to be understood; but the linkage is not so complete that either suffices, even when reasonably reinforced, to explicate the other. To make good this claim what is chiefly needed is to show how thought depends on speech, and this is the thesis I want to refine, and then to argue for.

We attribute a thought to a creature whenever we assertively employ a positive sentence the main verb of which is psychological—in English, 'believes', 'knows', 'hopes', 'desires', 'thinks', 'fears', 'is interested' are examples—followed by a sentence and preceded by the name or description of the creature. (A 'that' may optionally or necessarily follow the verb.) Some such sentences attribute states, others report events or processes: 'believes', 'thinks', and 'wants' report states, while 'came to believe', 'forgot', 'concluded', 'noticed', 'is proving' report events or processes. Sentences that can be used to attribute a thought exhibit what is often called, or analysed as, semantic intentionality, which means that the attribution may be changed from true to false, or false to true, by substitutions in the contained sentences that would not alter the truth value of that sentence in isolation.

I do not take for granted that if a creature has a thought, then we can, with resources of the kind just sketched, correctly attribute that thought to him. But thoughts so attributable at least constitute a good sample of the totality.

It is doubtful whether the various sorts of thought can be reduced to one, or even to a few: desire, knowledge, belief, fear, interest, to name some important cases, are probably logically independent to the extent that none can be defined using the others, even along with such further notions as truth and cause. Nevertheless, belief is central to all kinds of thought. If someone is glad that, or notices that, or remembers that, or knows that, the gun is loaded, then he must believe that the gun is loaded. Even to wonder whether the gun is loaded, or to speculate on the possibility that the gun is loaded, requires the belief, for example, that a gun is a weapon, that it is a more or less enduring physical object, and so on. There are good reasons for not insisting on any particular list of beliefs that are needed if a creature is to wonder whether a gun is loaded. Nevertheless, it is necessary that there be endless interlocked beliefs. The system of such beliefs identifies a thought by locating it in a logical and epistemic space.

Having a thought requires that there be a background of beliefs, but having a particular thought does not depend on the state of belief with respect to that very thought. If I consider going to a certain concert, I know I will be put to a degree of trouble and expense, and I have more complicated beliefs about the enjoyment I will experience. I will enjoy hearing Beethoven's Grosse Fuge, say, but only provided the performance achieves a reasonable standard, and I am able to remain attentive. I have the thought of going to the concert, but until I decide whether to go, I have no fixed belief that I will go; until that time, I merely entertain the thought.

We may say, summarizing the last two paragraphs, that a thought is defined by a system of beliefs, but is itself autonomous with respect to belief.

We usually think that having a language consists largely in being able to speak, but in what follows speaking will play only an indirect part. What is essential to my argument is the idea of an interpreter, someone who understands the utterances of another. The considerations to be put forward imply, I think, that a speaker must himself be an interpreter of others, but I shall not try to demonstrate that an interpreter must be a speaker, though there may be good reason to hold this. Perhaps it is worth pointing out that the notion of a language, or of two people speaking the same language does not seem to be needed here. Two speakers could interpret each other's utterances without there being, in any ordinary sense, a common language. (I do not want to deny that in other contexts the notion of a shared language may be very important.)

The chief thesis of this paper is that a creature cannot have thoughts unless it is an interpreter of the speech of another. This thesis does not imply the possibility of reduction, behaviouristic or otherwise, of thoughts to speech; indeed the thesis imputes no priority to language, epistemological or conceptual. The claim also falls short of similar claims in that it allows that there may be thoughts for which the speaker cannot find words, or for which there are no words.

Someone who can interpret an utterance of the English sentence 'The gun is loaded' must have many beliefs, and these beliefs must be much like the beliefs someone must have if he entertains the thought that the gun is loaded. The interpreter must, we may suppose, believe that a gun is a weapon, and that it is a more or less enduring physical object. There is probably no definite list of things that must be believed by someone who understands the sentence 'The gun is loaded,' but it is necessary that there be endless interlocked beliefs.

An interpreter knows the conditions under which utterances of sentences are true, and often knows that if certain sentences are true, others must be. For example, an interpreter of English knows that if 'The gun is loaded and the door is locked' is true, then 'The door is locked' is true. The sentences of a language have a location in the logical space created by the pattern of such relationships. Obviously the pattern of relations between sentences is very much like the pattern of relations between thoughts. This fact has encouraged the view that it is redundant to take both patterns as basic. If thoughts are primary, a language seems to serve no purpose but to express or convey thoughts; while if we take speech as primary, it is tempting to analyse thoughts as speech dispositions: as Sellars puts it, '. . . thinking at the distinctly human level . . . is essentially verbal activity'.[1] But clearly the parallel between the structure of thoughts and the structure of sentences provides no argument for the primacy of either, and only a presumption in favour of their interdependence.

We have been talking freely of thoughts, beliefs, meanings, and interpretations; or rather, freely using sentences that contain these words. But of course it is not

1. Wilfrid Sellars, 'Conceptual Change', in *Conceptual Change*, ed. G. Pearce and P. Maynard, Dordrecht, 1973, p. 82.

clear what entities, or sorts of entities, there must be to make systematic sense of such sentences. However, talk apparently of thoughts and sayings does belong to a familiar mode of explanation of human behaviour and must be considered an organized department of common sense that may as well be called a theory. One way of examining the relation between thought and language is by inspecting the theory implicit in this sort of explanation.

Part of the theory deals with the teleological explanation of action. We wonder why a man raises his arm; an explanation might be that he wanted to attract the attention of a friend. This explanation would fail if the arm-raiser didn't believe that by raising his arm he would attract the attention of his friend, so the complete explanation of his raising his arm, or at any rate a more complete explanation, is that he wanted to attract the attention of his friend *and* believed that by raising his arm he would attract his friend's attention. Explanation of this familiar kind has some features worth emphasizing. It explains what is relatively apparent—an arm-raising—by appeal to factors that are far more problematical: desires and beliefs. But if we were to ask for evidence that the explanation is correct, this evidence would in the end consist of more data concerning the sort of event being explained, namely further behaviour which is explained by the postulated beliefs and desires. Adverting to beliefs and desires to explain action is therefore a way of fitting an action into a pattern of behaviour made coherent by the theory. This does not mean, of course, that beliefs are nothing but patterns of behaviour, or that the relevant patterns can be defined without using the concepts of belief and desire. Nevertheless, there is a clear sense in which attributions of belief and desire, and hence teleological explanations of belief and desire, are supervenient on behaviour more broadly described.

A characteristic of teleological explanation not shared by explanation generally is the way in which it appeals to the concept of *reason*. The belief and desire that explain an action must be such that anyone who had that belief and desire would have a reason to act in that way. What's more, the descriptions we provide of desire and belief must, in teleological explanation, exhibit the rationality of the action in the light of the content of the belief and the object of the desire.

The cogency of a teleological explanation rests, as remarked, on its ability to discover a coherent pattern in the behaviour of an agent. Coherence here includes the idea of rationality both in the sense that the action to be explained must be reasonable in the light of the assigned desires and beliefs, but also in the sense that the assigned desires and beliefs must fit with one another. The methodological presumption of rationality does not make it impossible to attribute irrational thoughts and actions to an agent, but it does impose a burden on such attributions. We weaken the intelligibility of attributions of thoughts of any kind to the extent that we fail to uncover a consistent pattern of beliefs and, finally, of actions, for it is only against a background of such a pattern that we can identify thoughts. If we see a man pulling on both ends of a piece of string, we may decide he is fighting against himself, that he wants to move the string in incompatible directions. Such an explanation would require elaborate backing. No problem arises if the explanation is that he wants to break the string.

From the point of view of someone giving teleological explanations of the actions of another, it clearly makes no sense to assign priority either to desires or to beliefs. Both are essential to the explanation of behaviour, and neither is more directly open to observation than the other. This creates a problem, for it means that behaviour, which is the main evidential basis for attributions of belief and desire, is reckoned the result of two forces less open to public observation. Thus where one constellation of beliefs and desires will rationalize an action, it is always possible to find a quite different constellation that will do as well. Even a generous sample of actions threatens to leave open an unacceptably large number of alternative explanations.

Fortunately a more refined theory is available, one still firmly based on common sense: the theory of preference, or decision-making, under uncertainty. The theory was first made precise by Frank Ramsey, though he viewed it as a matter of providing a foundation for the concept of probability rather than as a piece of philosophical psychology.[2] Ramsey's theory works by quantifying strength of preference and degree of belief in such a way as to make sense of the natural idea that in choosing a course of action we consider not only how desirable various outcomes are, but also how apt available courses of action are to produce those outcomes. The theory does not assume that we can judge degrees of belief or make numerical comparisons of value directly. Rather it postulates a reasonable pattern of preferences between courses of action, and shows how to construct a system of quantified beliefs and desires to explain the choices. Given the idealized conditions postulated by the theory, Ramsey's method makes it possible to identify the relevant beliefs and desires uniquely. Instead of talking of postulation, we might put the matter this way: to the extent that we can see the actions of an agent as falling into a consistent (rational) pattern of a certain sort, we can explain those actions in terms of a system of quantified beliefs and desires.

We shall come back to decision theory presently; now it is time to turn to the question of how speech is interpreted. The immediate aim of a theory of interpretation is to give the meaning of an arbitrary utterance by a member of a language community. Central to interpretation, I have argued, is a theory of truth that satisfies Tarski's Convention T (modified in certain ways to apply to a natural language). Such a theory yields, for every utterance of every sentence of the language, a theorem of the form: 'An utterance of sentence *s* by a speaker *x* at time *t* is true if and only if——.' Here '*s*' is to be replaced by a description of a sentence, and the blank by a statement of the conditions under which an utterance of the sentence is true relative to the parameters of speaker and time. In order to interpret a particular utterance it is neither necessary nor sufficient to know the entire theory:

2. Frank Ramsey, 'Truth and Probability', in *Foundations of Mathematics and Other Essays*, ed. R. B. Braithwaite, London, 1931.

it is enough to know what the theory says the truth conditions are for the utterance, and to know that those conditions are entailed by a theory of the required sort. On the other hand, to belong to a speech community—to be an interpreter of the speech of others—one does need to know much of a whole theory, in effect, and to know that it is a theory of the right kind.[3]

A theory of interpretation, like a theory of action, allows us to redescribe certain events in a revealing way. Just as a theory of action can answer the question of what an agent is doing when he has raised his arm by redescribing the act as one of trying to catch his friend's attention, so a method of interpretation can lead to redescribing the utterance of certain sounds as an act of saying that snow is white. At this point, however, the analogy breaks down. For decision theory can also explain actions, while it is not at all clear how a theory of interpretation can explain a speaker's uttering the words 'Snow is white.' But this is, after all, to be expected, for uttering words is an action, and so must draw for its teleological explanation on beliefs and desires. Interpretation is not irrelevant to the teleological explanation of speech, since to explain why someone said something we need to know, among other things, his own interpretation of what he said, that is, what he believes his words mean in the circumstances under which he speaks. Naturally this will involve some of his beliefs about how others will interpret his words.

The interlocking of the theory of action with interpretation will emerge in another way if we ask how a method of interpretation is tested. In the end, the answer must be that it helps bring order into our understanding of behaviour. But at an intermediary stage, we can see that the attitude of *holding true* or *accepting as true*, as directed towards sentences, must play a central role in giving form to a theory. On the one hand, most uses of language tell us directly, or shed light on the question, whether a speaker holds a sentence to be true. If a speaker's purpose is to give information, or to make an honest assertion, then normally the speaker believes he is uttering a sentence true under the circumstances. If he utters a command, we may usually take this as showing that he holds a certain sentence (closely related to the sentence uttered) to be false; similarly for many cases of deceit. When a question is asked, it generally indicates that the questioner does not know whether a certain sentence is true; and so on. In order to infer from such evidence that a speaker holds a sentence true we need to know much about his desires and beliefs, but we do not have to know what his words mean.

On the other hand, knowledge of the circumstances under which someone holds sentences true is central to interpretation. We saw in the case of thoughts that although most thoughts are not beliefs, it is the pattern of belief that allows us to identify any thought; analogously, in the case of language, although most utterances are not concerned with truth, it is the pattern of sentences held true that gives sentences their meaning.

3. There is further discussion of these issues in my 'Radical Interpretation', *Dialectica* (Vol. 27, Nos. 3–4, 1973), included in this volume.

The attitude of holding a sentence to be true (under specified conditions) relates belief and interpretation in a fundamental way. We can know that a speaker holds a sentence to be true without knowing what he means by it or what belief it expresses for him. But if we know he holds the sentence true *and* we know how to interpret it, then we can make a correct attribution of belief. Symmetrically, if we know what belief a sentence held true expresses, we know how to interpret it. The methodological problem of interpretation is to see how, given the sentences a man accepts as true under given circumstances, to work out what his beliefs are and what his words mean. The situation is again similar to the situation in decision theory where, given a man's preferences between alternative courses of action, we can discern both his beliefs and his desires. Of course it should not be thought that a theory of interpretation will stand alone, for as we noticed, there is no chance of telling when a sentence is held true without being able to attribute desires and being able to describe actions as having complex intentions. This observation does not deprive the theory of interpretation of interest, but assigns it a place within a more comprehensive theory of action and thought.[4]

It is still unclear whether interpretation is required for a theory of action, which is the question we set ourselves to answer. What is certain is that all the standard ways of testing theories of decision or preference under uncertainty rely on the use of language. It is relatively simple to eliminate the necessity for verbal responses on the part of the subject: he can be taken to have expressed a preference by taking action, by moving directly to achieve his end, rather than by saying what he wants. But this cannot settle the question of what he has chosen. A man who takes an apple rather than a pear when offered both may be expressing a preference for what is on his left rather than his right, what is red rather than yellow, what is seen first, or judged more expensive. Repeated tests may make some readings of his actions more plausible than others, but the problem will remain how to tell what he judges to be a repetition of the same alternative. Tests that involve uncertain events—choices between gambles—are even harder to present without using words. The psychologist, sceptical of his ability to be certain how a subject is interpreting his instructions, must add a theory of verbal interpretation to the theory to be tested. If we think of all choices as revealing a preference that one sentence rather than another be true, the resulting total theory should provide an interpretation of sentences, and at the same time assign beliefs and desires, both of the latter conceived as relating the agent to sentences or utterances. This composite theory would explain all behaviour, verbal and otherwise.

All this strongly suggests that the attribution of desires and beliefs (and other thoughts) must go hand in hand with the interpretation of speech, that neither the theory of decision nor of interpretation can be successfully developed without the

4. The interlocking of decision theory and radical interpretation is explored also in my 'Psychology as Philosophy', in *Philosophy of Psychology*, ed. S. C. Brown, London, 1974, pp. 41–52; and in my 'Belief and the Basis of Meaning', *Synthese* (vol. 27, 1974, pp. 309–24) .

other. But it remains to say, in more convincing detail, why the attribution of thought depends on the interpretation of speech. The general, and not very informative, reason is that without speech we cannot make the fine distinctions between thoughts that are essential to the explanations we can sometimes confidently supply. Our manner of attributing attitudes ensures that all the expressive power of language can be used to make such distinctions. One can believe that Scott is not the author of *Waverley* while not doubting that Scott is Scott; one can want to be the discoverer of a creature with a heart without wanting to be the discoverer of a creature with a kidney. One can intend to bite into the apple in the hand without intending to bite into the only apple with a worm in it; and so forth. The intensionality we make so much of in the attribution of thoughts is very hard to make much of when speech is not present. The dog, we say, knows that its master is home. But does it know that Mr. Smith (who is his master), or that the president of the bank (who is that same master), is home? We have no real idea how to settle, or make sense of, these questions. It is much harder to say, when speech is not present, how to distinguish universal thoughts from conjunctions of thoughts, or how to attribute conditional thoughts, or thoughts with, so to speak, mixed quantification ('He hopes that everyone is loved by someone').

These considerations will probably be less persuasive to dog lovers than to others, but in any case they do not constitute an argument. At best what we have shown, or claimed, is that unless there is behaviour that can be interpreted as speech, the evidence will not be adequate to justify the fine distinctions we are used to making in the attribution of thoughts. If we persist in attributing desires, beliefs, or other attitudes under these conditions, our attributions and consequent explanations of actions will be seriously underdetermined in that many alternative systems of attribution, many alternative explanations, will be equally justified by the available data. Perhaps this is all we can say against the attribution of thoughts to dumb creatures; but I do not think so.

Before going on I want to consider a possible objection to the general line I have been pursuing. Suppose we grant, the objector says, that very complex behaviour not observed in infants and elephants is necessary if we are to find application for the full apparatus available for the attribution of thoughts. Still, it may be said, the sketch of how interpretation works does not show that this complexity must be viewed as connected with language. The reason is that the sketch makes too much depend on the special attitude of being thought true. The most direct evidence for the existence of this attitude is honest assertion. But then it would seem that we could treat as speech the behaviour of creatures that never did anything with language except make honest assertions. Some philosophers do dream of such dreary tribes; but would we be right to say they had a language? What has been lost to view is what may be called *the autonomy of meaning*. Once a sentence is understood, an utterance of it may be used to serve almost any extra-linguistic purpose. An instrument that could be put to only one use would lack autonomy of meaning; this amounts to saying it should not be counted as a language. So the complexity of behaviour needed to give full scope to attributions of thought need not, after all, be exactly the same complexity that allows, or requires, interpretation as a language.

I agree with the hypothetical objector that autonomy of meaning is essential to language; indeed it is largely this that explains why linguistic meaning cannot be defined or analysed on the basis of extralinguistic intentions and beliefs. But the objector fails to distinguish between a language that *could* be used for only one purpose and one that *is* used for only one purpose. An instrument that could be used for only one purpose would not be language. But honest assertion alone might yield a theory of interpretation, and so a language that, though capable of more, might never be put to further uses. (As a practical matter, the event is unthinkable. Someone who knows under what conditions his sentences are socially true cannot fail to grasp, and avail himself of, the possibilities in dishonest assertion—or in joking, story-telling, goading, exaggerating, insulting, and all the rest of the jolly crew.)

A method of interpretation tells us that for speakers of English an utterance of 'It is raining' by a speaker x at time t is true if and only if it is raining (near x) at t. To be armed with this information, and to know that others know it, is to know what an utterance means independently of knowing the purposes that prompted it. The autonomy of meaning also helps to explain how it is possible, by the use of language, to attribute thoughts. Suppose someone utters assertively the sentence 'Snow is white.' Knowing the conditions under which such an utterance is true I can add, if I please, 'I believe that too,' thus attributing a belief to myself. In this case we may both have asserted that snow is white, but sameness of force is not necessary to the selfattribution. The other may say with a sneer, expressing disbelief, 'Snow is white'—and I may again attribute a belief to myself by saying, 'But *I* believe that.' It can work as well in another way: if I can take advantage of an utterance of someone else's to attribute a belief to myself, I can use an utterance of my own to attribute a belief to someone else. First I utter a sentence, perhaps 'Snow is white,' and then I add 'He believes that.' The first utterance may or may not be an assertion; in any case, it does not attribute a belief to anyone (though if it is an assertion, then I do *represent* myself as believing that snow is white). But if my remark 'He believes that' is an assertion, I have attributed a belief to someone else. Finally, there is no bar to my attributing a belief to myself by saying first, 'Snow is white' and then adding, 'I believe that.'

In all these examples, I take the word 'that' to refer demonstratively to an utterance, whether it is an utterance by the speaker of the 'that' or by another speaker. The 'that' cannot refer to a sentence, both because, as Church has pointed out in similar cases, the reference would then have to be relativized to a language, since a sentence may have different meanings in different languages;[5] but also, and more obviously, because the same sentence may have different truth values in the same language.

5. Alonzo Church, 'On Carnap's Analysis of Statements of Assertion and Belief', *Analysis*, X (1950), 97–9.

What demonstrative reference to utterances does in the sort of case just considered it can do as well when the surface structure is altered to something like 'I believe that snow is white' or 'He believes that snow is white.' In these instances also I think we should view the 'that' as a demonstrative, now referring ahead to an utterance on the verge of production. Thus the logical form of standard attributions of attitude is that of two utterances paratactically joined. There is no connective, though the first utterance contains a reference to the second. (Similar remarks go, of course, for inscriptions of sentences.)

I have discussed this analysis of verbal attributions of attitude elsewhere, and there is no need to repeat the arguments and explanations here.[6] It is an analysis with its own difficulties, especially when it comes to analysing quantification into the contained sentence, but I think these difficulties can be overcome while preserving the appealing features of the idea. Here I want to stress a point that connects the paratactic analysis of attribution of attitude with our present theme. The proposed analysis directly relates the autonomous feature of meaning with our ability to describe and attribute thoughts, since it is only because the interpretation of a sentence is independent of its use that the utterance of a sentence can serve in the description of the attitudes of others. If my analysis is right, we can dispense with the unlikely (but common) view that a sentence bracketed into a 'that'-clause needs an entirely different interpretation from the one that works for it in other contexts. Since sentences are not names or descriptions in ordinary contexts, we can in particular reject the assumption that the attitudes have objects such as propositions which 'that'-clauses might be held to name or describe. There should be no temptation to call the utterance to which reference is made according to the paratactic analysis the object of the attributed attitude.

Here a facile solution to our problem about the relation between thoughts and speech suggests itself. One way to view the paratactic analysis, a way proposed by Quine in *Word and Object*, is this: when a speaker attributes an attitude to a person, what he does is ape or mimic an actual or possible speech act of that person.[7] Indirect discourse is the best example, and assertion is another good one. Suppose I say, 'Herodotus asserted that the Nile rises in the Mountains of the Moon.' My second utterance—my just past utterance of 'The Nile rises in the Mountains of the Moon'—must, if my attribution to Herodotus is correct, bear a certain relationship to an utterance of Herodotus': it must, in some appropriate sense, be a translation of it. Since, assuming still that the attribution is correct, Herodotus and I are *samesayers*, my utterance mimicked his. Not with respect to force, of course, since I didn't assert anything about the Nile. The sameness is with respect to the content of our utterances. If we turn to other attitudes, the situation is more complicated, for there is typically no utterance to ape. If I affirm 'Jones believes that snow is white,'

6. See 'On Saying That', in *Words and Objections: Essays on the Work of W. V. Quine*, eds. D. Davidson and J. Hintikka, Dordrecht, 1969, pp. 158–74.

7. W. V. Quine, *Word and Object*, Cambridge, Mass., 1960, p. 219.

my utterance of 'Snow is white' may have no actual utterance of Jones's to imitate. Still, we could take the line that what I affirm is that Jones would be honestly speaking his mind were he to utter a sentence translating mine. Given some delicate assumptions about the conditions under which such a subjunctive conditional is true, we could conclude that only someone with a language could have a thought, since to have a thought would be to have a disposition to utter certain sentences with appropriate force under given circumstances.

We could take this line, but unfortunately there seems no clear reason why we have to. We set out to find an argument to show that only creatures with speech have thoughts. What has just been outlined is not an argument, but a proposal, and a proposal we need not accept. The paratactic analysis of the logical form of attributions of attitude can get along without the mimic-theory of utterance. When I say, 'Jones believes that snow is white' I describe Jones's state of mind directly: it is indeed the state of mind someone is in who could honestly assert 'Snow is white' if he spoke English, but that may be a state a languageless creature could also be in.

In order to make my final main point, I must return to an aspect of interpretation so far neglected. I remarked that the attitude of holding true, directed to sentences under specified circumstances, is the basis for interpretation, but I did not say how it can serve this function. The difficulty, it will be remembered, is that a sentence is held true because of two factors: what the holder takes the sentence to mean, and what he believes. In order to sort things out, what is needed is a method for holding one factor steady while the other is studied.

Membership in a language community depends on the ability to interpret the utterances of members of the group, and a method is at hand if one has, and knows one has, a theory which provides truth conditions, more or less in Tarski's style, for all sentences (relativized, as always, to time and speaker). The theory is correct as long as it entails, by finitely stated means, theorems of the familiar form: ''It is raining' is true for a speaker *x* at time *t* if and only if it is raining (near *x*) at *t*.' The evidential basis for such a theory concerns sentences held true, facts like the following: ''It is raining' is held true by Smith at 8 a.m. on 26 August and it did rain near Smith at that time.' It would be possible to generate a correct theory simply by considering sentences to be true when held true, provided (1) there was a theory which satisfied the formal constraints and was consistent in this way with the evidence, and (2) all speakers held a sentence to be true just when that sentence was true—provided, that is, all beliefs, at least as far as they could be expressed, were correct.

But of course it cannot be assumed that speakers never have false beliefs. Error is what gives belief its point. We can, however, take it as given that *most* beliefs are correct. The reason for this is that a belief is identified by its location in a pattern of beliefs; it is this pattern that determines the subject matter of the belief, what the belief is about. Before some object in, or aspect of, the world can become part of the subject matter of a belief (true or false) there must be endless true beliefs about the subject matter. False beliefs tend to undermine the identification of the subject matter; to undermine, therefore, the validity of a description of the belief as being about that subject. And so, in turn, false beliefs undermine the claim that a connected belief is false. To take an example, how clear are we that the ancients—some ancients—believed that the earth was flat? *This* earth? Well, this earth of ours is part of the solar system, a system partly identified by the fact that it is a gaggle of large, cool, solid bodies circling around a very large, hot star. If someone believes *none* of this about the earth, is it certain that it is the earth that he is thinking about? An answer is not called for. The point is made if this kind of consideration of related beliefs can shake one's confidence that the ancients believed the earth was flat. It isn't that any one false belief necessarily destroys our ability to identify further beliefs, but that the intelligibility of such identifications must depend on a background of largely unmentioned and unquestioned true beliefs. To put it another way: the more things a believer is right about, the sharper his errors are. Too much mistake simply blurs the focus.

What makes interpretation possible, then, is the fact that we can dismiss *a priori* the chance of massive error. A theory of interpretation cannot be correct that makes a man assent to very many false sentences: it must generally be the case that a sentence is true when a speaker holds it to be. So far as it goes, it is in favour of a method of interpretation that it counts a sentence true just when speakers hold it to be true. But of course, the speaker may be wrong; and so may the interpreter. So in the end what must be counted in favour of a method of interpretation is that it puts the interpreter in general agreement with the speaker: according to the method, the speaker holds a sentence true under specified conditions, and these conditions obtain, in the opinion of the interpreter, just when the speaker holds the sentence to be true.

No simple theory can put a speaker and interpreter in perfect agreement, and so a workable theory must from time to time assume error on the part of one or the other. The basic methodological precept is, therefore, that a good theory of interpretation maximizes agreement. Or, given that sentences are infinite in number, and given further considerations to come, a better word might be *optimize*.

Some disagreements are more destructive of understanding than others, and a sophisticated theory must naturally take this into account. Disagreement about theoretical matters may (in some cases) be more tolerable than disagreement about what is more evident; disagreement about how things look or appear is less tolerable than disagreement about how they are; disagreement about the truth of attributions of certain attitudes to a speaker by that same speaker may not be tolerable at all, or barely. It is impossible to simplify the considerations that are relevant, for everything we know or believe about the way evidence supports belief can be put to work in deciding where the theory can best allow error, and what errors are least destructive of understanding. The methodology of interpretation is, in this respect, nothing but epistemology seen in the mirror of meaning.

The interpreter who assumes his method can be made to work for a language community will strive for a theory that optimizes agreement throughout the community. Since easy communication has survival value, he may expect usage within a community to favour simple common theories of interpretation.

If this account of radical interpretation is right, at least in broad outline, then we should acknowledge that the concepts of objective truth, and of error, necessarily emerge in the context of interpretation. The distinction between a sentence being held true and being in fact true is essential to the existence of an interpersonal system of communication, and when in individual cases there is a difference, it must be counted as error. Since the attitude of holding true is the same, whether the sentence is true or not, it corresponds directly to belief. The concept of belief thus stands ready to take up the slack between objective truth and the held true, and we come to understand it just in this connection.

We have the idea of belief only from the role of belief in the interpretation of language, for as a private attitude it is not intelligible except as an adjustment to the public norm provided by language. It follows that a creature must be a member of a speech community if it is to have the concept of belief. And given the dependence of other attitudes on belief, we can say more generally that only a creature that can interpret speech can have the concept of a thought.

Can a creature have a belief if it does not have the concept of belief? It seems to me it cannot, and for this reason. Someone cannot have a belief unless he understands the possibility of being mistaken, and this requires grasping the contrast between truth and error—true belief and false belief. But this contrast, I have argued, can emerge only in the context of interpretation, which alone forces us to the idea of an objective, public truth.

It is often wrongly thought that the semantical concept of truth is redundant, that there is no difference between asserting that a sentence *s* is true, and using *s* to make an assertion. What may be right is a redundancy theory of belief, that to believe that *p* is not to be distinguished from the belief that *p* is true. This notion of truth is not the semantical notion: language is not directly in the picture. But it is only just out of the picture; it is part of the frame. For the notion of a true belief depends on the notion of a true utterance, and this in turn there cannot be without shared language. As Ulysses was made to put it by a member of our speech community:

> . . . no man is the lord of anything,
> Though in and of him there be much consisting,
> Till he communicate his parts to others;
> Nor doth he of himself know them for aught
> Till he behold them formed in th'applause
> Where they're extended.
>
> (*Troilus and Cressida*, III. iii. 115–20)

Chapter 21

Replication and functionalism

Jane Heal

I

In this paper I want to examine two contrasted models of what we do when we try to get insight into other people's thoughts and behaviour by citing their beliefs, desires, fears, hopes, etc. On one model we are using what I shall call the *functional strategy* and on the other we use what I label the *replicative strategy*. I shall argue that the view that we use the replicative strategy is much more plausible than the view that we use the functionalist strategy. But the two strategies issue in different styles of explanation and call upon different ranges of concepts. So at the end of the paper I shall make some brief remarks about these contrasts.

The core of the functionalist strategy is the assumption that explanation of action or mental state through mention of beliefs, desires, emotions, etc. is causal. The approach is resolutely third personal. The Cartesian introspectionist error—the idea that from some direct confrontation with psychological items in our own case we learn their nature—is repudiated. We are said to view other people as we view stars, clouds or geological formations. People are just complex objects in our environment whose behaviour we wish to anticipate but whose causal innards we cannot perceive. We therefore proceed by observing the intricacies of their external behaviour and formulating some hypotheses about how the insides are structured. The hypotheses are typically of this form: 'The innards are like this. There is some thing or state which is usually caused by so and so in the environment (let us call this state '*X*') and another caused by such and such else (let us call this '*Y*'); together these cause another, '*Z*', which, if so and so is present, probably leads on to . . .' And so on. It is in some such way as this that terms like 'belief' and 'desire' are introduced. Our views about the causes, interactions and outcomes of inner states are sometimes said to be summed up in 'folk psychology' (Stich 1982a: 153ff). Scientific psychology is in the business of pursuing the same sort of programme as folk psychology but in more detail and with more statistical accuracy. On this view a psychological statement is an existential claim—that something with so-and-so causes and effects is occurring in a person (Lewis 1972). The philosophical advantages, in contrast with dualism and earlier materialisms such as behaviourism and

Jane Heal, 'Replication and Functionalism'. In J. Butterfield, ed., *Language Mind and Logic* (Cambridge: Cambridge University Press, 1986).

type-type identity theory, are familiar. It is via these contrasts and in virtue of these merits that the theory emerged. See Putnam (1967) for a classic statement.

This is a broad outline. But how is psychological explanation supposed to work in particular instances? What actual concepts are employed and how, in particular, are we to accommodate our pre-theoretical idea that people have immense numbers of different beliefs and desires, whose contents interrelate?

Functionalists would generally agree that there is no hope of defining the idea of a particular psychological state, like believing that it is raining, in isolation from other psychological notions. Such notions come as a package, full understanding of any member of which requires a grip on its role in the system as a whole (Harman 1973). This is true of any interesting functional concepts, even, for example, in explaining functionally something as comparatively simple as a car. If we try to build up some picture of the insides of a car, knowing nothing of mechanics and observing only the effects of pushing various pedals and levers and inserting various liquids, we might well come up with ideas like 'engine', 'fuel store', 'transmission', etc. But explanation of any one of these would clearly require mention of the others. Similarly we cannot say what a desire is except by mentioning that it is the sort of thing which conjoins with beliefs (and other states) to lead to behaviour.

But something more important than this is that the number of different psychological states (and hence their possibilities of interaction) are vastly greater than for the car. There is no clear upper bound on the number of different beliefs or desires that a person may have. And, worse, we cannot lay down in advance that for a given state these and only these others could be relevant to what its originating conditions or outcome are. This 'holism of the mental' (Quine 1960, Davidson 1970) which is here only roughly sketched, will turn out to be of crucial significance and we shall return to it. But for the moment let us ask how the functionalist can accommodate the fact that, finite creatures as we are, we have this immensely flexible and seemingly open-ended competence with psychological understanding and explanation. A model lies to hand here in the notions of axioms and theorems. We have understanding of hitherto unencountered situations because we (in some sense) know some basic principles concerning the ingredients and modes of interaction of the elements from which the new situations are composed.

What can the elements be? Not individual beliefs and desires because, as we have seen, there are too many of them. Hence the view that having an individual belief or desire must be, functionally conceived, a composite state. This is one powerful reason why the idea of the having of beliefs and desires as relations to inner sentences seems attractive (Field 1978: 24–36). The functional psychologist hopes that, with a limited number of elements (inner words), together with principles of construction and principles of interaction (modelled on the syntactic transformations of formalised logic), the complexity of intra-subjective psychological interactions can be encapsulated in a theory of manageable proportions.

But, however elegantly the theory is axiomatised the fact remains that it is going to be enormously complex. Moreover we certainly cannot now formulate it explicitly. There should therefore be some reluctance to credit ourselves with knowing it (even if only implicitly) unless there is no alternative account of how psychological explanation could work. But there is an alternative. It is the replicating strategy to which I now turn.

On the replicating view psychological understanding works like this. I can think about the world. I do so in the interests of taking my own decisions and forming my own opinions. The future is complex and unclear. In order to deal with it I need to and can envisage possible but perhaps non-actual states of affairs. I can imagine how my tastes, aims and opinions might change and work out what would be sensible to do or believe in the circumstances. My ability to do these things makes possible a certain sort of understanding of other people. I can harness all my complex theoretical knowledge about the world and my ability to imagine to yield an insight into other people *without any further elaborate theorising about them.* Only one simple assumption is needed: that they are like me in being thinkers, that they possess the same fundamental cognitive capacities and propensities that I do.

The method works like this. Suppose I am interested in predicting someone's action. (I take this case only as an example, not intending thereby to endorse any close link between understanding and prediction in the psychological case. Similar methods would apply with other aspects of understanding, for example, working out what someone was thinking, feeling or intending in the past.) What I endeavour to do is to replicate or recreate his thinking. I place myself in what I take to be his initial state by imagining the world as it would appear from his point of view and I then deliberate, reason and reflect to see what decision emerges.

Psychological states are not alone in being amenable to this approach. I might try to find out how someone else is reacting or will react to a certain drug by taking a dose of it myself. There is thus a quite general method of finding out what will or did happen to things similar to myself in given circumstances, namely ensuring that I myself am in those circumstances and waiting to see what occurs. To get good results from the method I require only that I have the ability to get myself into the same state as the person I wish to know about and that he and I are in fact relevantly similar.

As so far described the method yields us 'understanding' of another person in the sense of particular judgements about what he or she feels, thinks or does, which may facilitate interaction on particular occasions. We may also get from this method 'understanding' in the sense of some sort of answer to a why-question. If I am capable of describing the initial conditions which I replicated then I can cite them. But the method does not yet yield any hint of theoretical apparatus. No answer is forthcoming to the question 'Certain states are experimentally found to be thus linked—but why? What principles operate here?' We will return in section III to consider what concepts and principles of connection the replication method turns out to presuppose. Could they for example be identical with those the functional strategy calls upon?

But I would first like to discuss in section II three direct lines of attack upon my claim that replication is, at least in its method of delivering particular judgements, a real and conceptually economical alternative to the functional approach, that is, an alternative which avoids the need to credit ourselves with knowledge of complex theories about each other.

II

The first line of attack concentrates on how I am supposed to get myself into the correct replicating state. One might argue as follows; the replication method demands that I be able, on the basis of looking at someone else, to know what psychological state he or she is in, so that I can put myself in the same state; but to do this I must, perhaps at some inexplicit level, be in possession of a theory about the interrelations of psychological states and behaviour; but this will just be the functionalist theory all over again.

Two lines of defence against this attack are available. First, we may object that the attack presupposes that knowledge of another's psychological state must always be inferentially based and rest upon observation of behaviour, conceived of as something neutrally describable. But we need not buy this premiss and may propose instead some more direct model of how we come to knowledge of others' feelings and so forth (McDowell 1982).

Secondly (and this is the more important line of defence) the attack misdescribes the direction of gaze of the replicator. He is not looking at the subject to be understood but at the world around that subject. It is what the world makes the replicator think which is the basis for the beliefs he attributes to the subject. The process, of course, does not work with complete simplicity and directness. The replicator does not attribute to someone else belief in every state of affairs which he can see to obtain in the other's vicinity. A process of recentring the world in imagination is required. And this must involve the operation of some principles about what it is possible to perceive. Visual occlusion is the obvious example. But a theory about what one can know about the world from what viewpoint is not the same thing as a theory about how psychological states interact with each other or about what behaviour they produce.

It is worth remarking here that we need not saddle the replication theory with a commitment to the absurd idea that we are all quite indistinguishable in our psychological reactions—that any two persons with the same history are bound to respond to a given situation in the same way. Replication theory must allow somewhere for the idea of different personalities, for different styles of thinking and for non-rational influences on thinking. It is not clear what shape such additions to the core replication process would take. But there is no reason to suppose that they would take the form of the reimportation of the proposed functionalist-style theory.

Someone might try to press or to reformulate the objection by conceding that looking at the world rather than the subject might be a good heuristic device for suggesting hypotheses about his or her beliefs, but insisting that, nevertheless, we must employ (implicitly or explicitly) some criteria for the correctness of these hypotheses. What shows me that I am thinking of the world in the same way as the person I seek to understand? I must have some theory about what constitutes sameness of psychological state, and this theory, it will be suggested, could well, or indeed must, take a functionalist form.

But why should we accept the foundationalist epistemological presuppositions of this argument? Is it not enough for us to credit ourselves with the concept of 'same psychological state' that we should, first, be able to make generally agreed judgements using the notion and, secondly, that when our expectations are falsified we are usually able to detect some source of error when we cast around for further features of the situation, and hence to restore coherence among our own views and between our views and those of others?

We touch here on large issues in epistemology. But at the weakest we could say this, that there is not in this area any quick knock-down argument in favour of functionalism as against a claimed economical replication view.

Let us turn to a second reason for supposing that replication cannot be more economical than functionalism. Dennett (commenting on something similar to the replication view which he finds hinted at by Stich (1982b)) writes:

> How can it (the idea of using myself as an analogue computer) work without being a kind of theorising in the end? For the state I put myself in is not belief but make believe belief. If I make believe I am a suspension bridge and wonder what I will do when the wind blows, what 'comes to me' in my make believe state depends on how sophisticated my knowledge is of the physics and engineering of suspension bridges. Why should my making believe I have your beliefs be any different? In both cases knowledge of the imitated object is needed to drive the make believe 'simulation' and the knowledge must be organised in something rather like a theory. (Dennett 1982: 79)

Of course Dennett is quite right that the psychological case as I have sketched is not one of strict replication, unlike the drug case. It would clearly be absurd to suppose that in order to anticipate what someone else will do I have actually to believe what he or she believes. But Dennett is wrong in thinking that what he calls 'make believe belief' is as alien a state—and hence as demanding of theoretical underpinning—as making believe to be a suspension bridge. Make believe belief is imagining. And we do this already on our own behalf. The sequence of thought connections from imagined state of affairs to imagined decision parallels that from real belief to real decision. If it did not we could not use the technique of contemplating possibilities and seeing what it would be sensible to do if . . . as part of our own decision making. So to make the replication method work I do not require the theory which Dennett mentions. I require only the ability to distinguish real belief from entertaining a possibility and the ability to attribute to another person as belief what I have actualised in myself as imagining.

The third attempt to show that replication and functionalism coincide takes a bolder line. The replicator supposes that some working out is to be done in order to find out what it would be sensible to do in the situation the other person envisages. Similarly the functionalist also supposes that working out is to be done; it is from a knowledge of particular states together with general principles or laws that a judgement on this case is to be reached. Why should we not suppose that the working out involved in the two cases is, contrary to superficial appearances, the same? The description of the replication method given so far suggests that sequences of thought states occur in me without mediation of any further thought, just as the sequences of reactions to drugs do. But perhaps this is a misleading picture; perhaps transitions from one thought to another occur in virtue of my awareness of some principle or law requiring the occurrence of the one after the other. Doing the actual thinking, which the replicator represents as something *toto caelo* different from functionalist style thinking about thinking, is not in fact fundamentally different. Making up my own mind is just the first-person version of what in third-person cases is functional style causal prediction.

But this will not do at all. For a start an infinite regress threatens. If any transition from thought to thought is to be underpinned by some further thought about links, how are we to explain the occurrence of the relevant thought about links without invoking some third level and so on? But let us waive this objection. More substantial difficulties await.

It is indeed tempting to suppose that whenever I draw a conclusion, that is, base one judgement on another, I must implicitly know or have in mind some general principle which links the two. But whether or not we think it right to yield to this temptation, the only sense in which the claim is plausible is one in which the principle in question is a normative one ('one ought to believe so-and-so if one believes such-and-such') or relatedly a semantic one ('the belief that so-and-so would be true if the belief that such-and-such were true'). In neither case is the principle in question a causal law, such as the supposed axioms of the functionalist theory are to be. The terminology I used above in arguing my opponents case (a 'principle' or 'law' by which the occurrence of one belief 'requires' the occurrence of another) is designed to obscure this vital difference. If we try to restate the proposal being quite explicit that the connections in question are causal we arrive at the most bizarre results. It amounts to supposing that it makes no difference whether a thinker asks himself or herself the question 'What ought I to think next?' or the question 'What will I, as a matter of fact, think next?' On the proposed view, these are just different wordings of the same question.

Suppose then that I do infer that *q* on the basis that *p* and that my knowledge that belief that *p* causes belief that *q* is integral to the process. We seem to have the following choice. Either we could say that the inference that *q* is based not just on the premiss that *p* (as *prima facie* but misleading appearance has it) but also on the (implicit) premiss that belief that *p* causes belief that *q*. This amounts to endorsing the principle of inference 'I will be caused to believe that *p*, therefore *p*'. Alternatively we could suppose that drawing the inference just is making the prediction.

And this amounts to identifying belief that *p* with belief that one is being made to think that *p*.

Clearly none of this will do. It makes judgements about the world collapse into or rest upon judgements about me; and moreover they are judgements about me which have quite disparate truth conditions and roles in thought from the judgements about the world they are required to stand in for.

There are certain conditions under which the assimilation would appear less ludicrous. These are that I could isolate causal factors constitutive of my rational thinking from interfering ones; that I am a perfect thinker (that is, I rely on no confused concepts or plausible but unreliable rules of inference) and that I know that I am a perfect thinker. In other words, if I knew that physiologically I embodied a logical system and I knew the meta-theory for my own system, then causal-syntactic knowledge about myself would have semantic equivalents. The discussion of fallibility below will indicate some of the reasons why this is unacceptable.

So far I have been examining attempts to show that the replication strategy cannot be a real alternative to the functionalist one. And I maintain that none of them has undermined the plausibility of the original claim that the two approaches are different and that the former is more economical than the latter.

III

I turn now to a different line of thought, one which concedes the above claim but argues that nevertheless a replicative style of psychological understanding is compatible with a functionalist style. The use of the one does not preclude the other. A functionalist theory could develop out of and dovetail smoothly with use of the replicating strategy. Perhaps it is already doing so; or perhaps it will, when cognitive science is more advanced.

In the case of reaction to drugs something like this is clearly possible. At one stage of the development of knowledge I may be unable to anticipate others' reactions except via the replication method and unable to conceptualise them except through ideas appropriate to that method. For example, I ask of another person 'Why was she sick?' An initial answer might muster all the relevant information I have like this: 'I was sick; she took the same drug as I did and she is like me.' Or we might express it more naturally: 'She is like me and she took the drug which made me sick.' But this is not a stopping point. When I become reflective I shall ask 'In what respects is she relevantly similar to me?' and 'What feature of the drug connects with this feature of us to make us sick?' There is no reason in this case why the answers should not be ones the finding of which precisely does amount to my finding a causal theory which will emancipate me, wholly or partially, from the need to replicate. The key feature here is that the relevant similarity will probably turn out to be something about body chemistry. When I have these physiological concepts to hand I can specify directly what sort of creatures will be affected by some drug without mention of myself as a standard of similarity. And I can describe directly what the drug does to them instead of pointing to myself and saying 'It makes you like this.'

Now why should this not also be the case with psychological replication? Perhaps replication is a method by which primates unreflectively facilitate their social interactions. But we, it might be said, are in the process of emancipating ourselves from this primitive approach. (This is a view suggested to me by some remarks of Andrew Woodfield (1982: 281–2).) So when one unreflectively attributes a thought to another creature one may replicate that thought, and at the first attempts one may be unable to characterise the state in question in any other way than by pointing to oneself and saying 'Well, it is like what I am doing now.' And one will be unable to anticipate others except by recreating and attempting to rethink their thoughts because one has no access to the nature of the thought as it is in itself or the respects in which the other subject and oneself are relevantly similar. Nevertheless reflection shows us that there is such a thing as the nature of the thought in itself, some intrinsic character that it has, and some non-demonstrative specification of relevant similarity. So when we use psychological terminology reflectively it is to these things that we intend to refer. And cognitive science is about to fill in the actual detail of what they are.

But I want now to argue that this will not do. When we reflect on the notion of 'relevant similarity', as it needs to be used in psychological explanation, we discover an insuperable bar to imagining it being superseded by the sort of physiological or structural description which functionalism requires. And relatedly we find that we cannot get at the nature of the thought as it is in itself but continue to have access to it only in an indirect and demonstrative fashion.

The difference between psychological explanation and explanation in the natural sciences is that in giving a psychological explanation we render the thought or behaviour of the other intelligible, we exhibit them as having some point, some reasons to be cited in their defence. Another way of putting this truism is to say that we see them as exercises of cognitive competence or rationality. (I intend these terms to be interchangeable and to be understood very broadly to mean what is exercised in the formation of intention and desire as well as belief.)

This is a feature of psychological explanation which the replication method puts at the centre of the stage. When I start reflecting upon the replication method and trying to put the particular judgements and connections it indicates in a theoretical context, it is the notion of cognitive competence, of the subject struggling to get things right, which must present itself as the respect in which I and the other are relevantly similar.

But what further account can we give of rationality? Could it be discovered to be identical with and replaceable by something which would suit the functionalist programme? Initial thoughts about rationality or cognitive competence suggest that it surely has something to do with the ability to achieve success in judgement (that is truth for belief and whatever the analogous property or properties are for desires, intentions, etc.) But the nature of the link is difficult to capture. Is rationality something which guarantees the actual success of judgement in particular cases? Arguably not, since the question 'But have I got this right?' can always be raised. We must recognise ourselves to be thoroughly fallible. This is one important implication of the extreme complexity of interaction of psychological states which our earlier discussion did not bring out. In our earlier remarks about functionalism the complexity served merely as a spur to thinking of psychological states as molecular rather than atomic. That move was needed because we could not specify in advance what beliefs might be relevant to any other—as premisses or conclusions. Thus given enough background of the right sort any belief could bear upon the truth of any other. It is this which prevents the individuation of beliefs as atomic units by their placement in some specifiable pattern of a limited number of other psychological states. But a further implication of this (as Quine constantly stresses) is that we cannot pick upon any belief or beliefs as immune to any possible influence from future information.

So cognitive competence is not the claim that for at least some sorts of judgement success is guaranteed. Could it be defined, then, in terms of inference rules relied on or judgement-forming procedures, for example, by mention of specific rules like *modus tollens* or inductive generalisation or, more non-committally, via the idea of inference rules which are generally reliable? This again will not do and its failure is crucial to the incompatibility between replication and functionalism. I can fail to follow simple and reliable inference rules and can adopt some most unreliable ones, and recognise later that this was what I was doing, quite compatibly with continued trust in my then and present cognitive competence. The only constraint is that I should be able to make intelligible to myself why I failed to notice so-and-so or seemed to assume such-and-such. And, as with the case of individual judgements, enough scene setting can do the trick. This is not to say that I can make sense of my past self—or of someone else—even where I can find no overlap at all between my present judgements and inference procedures and those of the other. Rather my claim is that we cannot arrange inference procedures (or judgements) in some clear hierarchy and identify some as basic or constitutive of rationality.

We may have models or partial views of what constitutes rationality (in logic, decision theory and so forth) but thinking in accordance with the rules or standards there specified cannot be definitive of or exhaust the notion of rationality. This is not only because our current views on these matters may be wrong but for another reason also. If rationality were thus definable then the claim that I myself am rational would acquire some specific empirical content, would become just one proposition among all the others which form my view of the world. It would thus be potentially up for grabs as something falsifiable by enough evidence of the right character. But, notoriously, any attempted demonstration to me by myself that I am a non-thinker must be absurd because self-undermining. Hence any account of what it is to be a thinker which seems to make such a demonstration possible must be at fault.

How does all this bear upon the idea that as we gain more knowledge and conceptual sophistication some primitive replication method could gracefully give way to a more scientific functional understanding? It is relevant because this idea does require exactly the assumption that rationality can be given a complete formal definition in terms of syntactically specifiable inference rules. It is only if this is the case that the replicating assumption of relevant similarity—'they are like me in being cognitively competent'—can be replaced by the functional assumption—'they are like me in being systems with inner states structured and interacting according to so-and-so principles'.

I have used as a premiss a strong version of fallibilism which some may find implausible. Surely, one might protest, some propositions (that I exist, that this is a desk, that here is a hand) are in some sense unassailable, as are also some rules of inference. Am I seriously suggesting that the law of non-contradiction or universal instantiation might be overthrown?

Suppose we concede the force of these remarks; does it then become defensible again to maintain that functionalism will turn out to be compatible with the replication approach and will ultimately replace it? It does not. As long as we admit that there are any parts of our implicit inferential practices which may be muddled—that is, as long as we admit (as we surely must) that the world has some funny surprises in store for us as a result of which we shall recognise our earlier thinking patterns as muddled and inadequate, then we must also admit that our formal grip on rationality is not complete.

It is position within the network defined by the supposed formal account of rationality which is to provide the functionalist account of what a thought is in itself. Thoughts are, for functionalists, identified and individuated by causal–explanatory role. So a corollary of the non-existence of a formal account of rationality is the non-availability of that mode of characterising thoughts which functionalism counts on—a mode imagined to be independent of our entertaining or rethinking those thoughts.

IV

I turn finally to some sketchy and programmatic remarks about the concepts and modes of explanation which will be called on under the two strategies—replicating and functionalist.

Recent writings in the functionalist school have produced powerful arguments to show that upon their approach the semantic properties of psychological states, that is, their referential relations to particular objects or sorts of stuff in the world, are not directly relevant to their explanatory roles. We think of psychological states (they say) both as things which are true or false in virtue of semantic connections with the world and also as things which are explanatory of behaviour. But these two ways of thinking about them are in some sense independent. So that-clauses are systematically ambiguous; sometimes we use them to ascribe truth conditions and sometimes to ascribe causal—explanatory role (Fodor 1980, McGinn 1982, Field 1978).

I shall not fully rehearse the arguments for this view here. The nub of the matter is just this, that admission of the referential as explanatory in the functionalists' causal framework would amount to admitting a very mysterious action at a distance which goes against all our causal assumptions. Distant objects exert their causal influence over us via chains of intermediate events, where these events could occur from other causes even if the distant object did not exist. The functionalist views as explanatory a state which could exist even if the supposed referent did not; and thus he claims to unite economically, in one form of account, actions guided by true beliefs (i.e. ones which are referentially well grounded) and also actions which are based on illusion. The functionalist claims that we have a concept of what is common to referentially well-based cognition and illusory cognition, a concept which is specifiable without mention of referential success; and that referential success is thus a conjunctive notion (cf. McDowell 1982).

But what is this something else, this non-referential content which we sometimes use that-clauses to ascribe? One thing which is clear is that in attributing non-referential content to someone's thought I do not commit myself to the existence of any particular thing (or natural kind) outside him. I merely characterise him as he is intrinsically.

But obscurities remain. One of these has been noted (Bach 1982). Non-referential content could be something thought of merely syntactically—that is, to be labelled 'content' only in an exceedingly stretched sense. On the other hand the notion of non-referential content could be recognisably a notion of meaning in some sense. In reporting it we report the subject's 'mode of representing the world'—but without commitment to the existence of anything outside him.

But within the latter option there is also an important further obscurity. Is non-referential content strongly conceptually independent of reference and truth, in that someone could have the former idea without the others so much as having crossed his mind? Or are they only weakly conceptually independent in that ascription of non-referential content does not commit one to an actual referent or truth conditions but does commit one to some disposition concerning reference and truth? On the second view, in thinking of something as having non-referential content we are thinking of it precisely as something which in a certain context or under certain other conditions would have such-and-such referent and truth conditions.

There are thus three options. Non-referential content is

(a) a merely syntactic notion
(b) a notion of meaning strongly independent of truth and reference.
(c) a notion of meaning only weakly independent of truth and reference.

Which of these do the functionalists propose?

It is claimed that classification of beliefs as explanatory and classification of them as truth bearers are 'independent' because such classifications can cross cut (e.g. in the case of indexicals or Twin Earth situations: cf. Fodor 1980: 66–8, McGinn 1982: 208–10). And in the discussion of why we are interested in reference at all, it seems to be assumed that this 'cross-cutting classification' argument has established (a) or (b)—that is, has established 'independence' in a strong sense of complete conceptual detachment. These discussions proceed on the assumption that grip on the non-referential notion of content has provided no foothold at all for truth and our interest in it has to be motivated totally *ab initio* (Field 1978: 44–9, McGinn 1982:225–8). But in fact the cross-cutting classification point does not establish this. Consider 'fragile' and 'broken': these classifications cross cut. But this would hardly show that we could understand 'fragile' without understanding 'breaks' or that our interest in breakage needed to be motivated independently of our interest in fragility.

On the other hand the notion of non-referential content is sometimes elucidated in terms of notions like subjective probability, inference, Fregean sense, or Kaplanesque 'character' (Field 1977, McGinn 1982). And these notions are ones which *prima facie* have conceptual links with reference and truth. Thus Kaplan's notion of the character of an indexical utterance or belief is precisely the notion of something which, placed in a certain context, determines a referent and hence a truth value.

Whichever of these options the functionalist takes there will be difficulties. On (a) and (b) it turns out that a view which I earlier offered as a truism, namely that in psychological explanation we exhibit the explanandum having a point or being at least in part justified, is false. The explanatory notions postulated in (a) and (b) are ones which provide no foothold for talk of justification or point. So, if presented as a view about everyday psychological talk and explanation, this philosophical theory has the problem of explaining where the semantic and related justificatory aspects of the practices fit in and why they seem to loom so large for us. I do not say that this cannot be done, only that attempts so far have not been convincing.[1] On the other hand, if the theory is presented not as an account of

1. Field suggests (1978: 44–9) that we attribute reference and truth conditions to the inner states of others because we find it useful to 'calibrate' them; we can then use facts about their inner states, in conjunction with some reliability theory, to gain information about the world for ourselves. McGinn (1982: 225–6) objects to this that it makes assignment of reference to others' beliefs and utterances too contingent. On Field's account we would not bother to do it if we thought the other person; through limitations of his knowledge or his unreliability, had nothing to teach us. Yet surely we might assign reference even in these circumstances. So McGinn proposes (1982: 226–8) that we need the notion of reference in characterising the practice of communication. 'A hearer understands a speech act as an assertion just if he interprets it as performed with a certain point or intention—viz. to convey information about the world.' But this, on McGinn's own earlier showing, will hardly do. The phrase 'about the world' is itself subject to the bifurcation of role which McGinn claims to find in all that clauses or content ascribers. When I ascribe to another an intention to 'convey information about the world' on McGinn's account I may understand this attribution of content to his or her intention in either of two ways—first as ascribing an inner explanatory state, grasp of the nature of which requires no semantic concepts, or secondly as ascribing an inner state with semantic relations. And only the former is needed for psychological explanation and understanding of communicative behaviour. So, failing some further account of 'characterising the

notions we now employ but as a blueprint for a future, highly abstract version of neurophysiology, then it is not faced with that problem but its relevance for philosophical accounts of current practice is non-existent.

If the functionalist adopts (c) as his account of non-referential content then his problems are different. This content notion is one in which two elements are linked—namely the idea of a 'a mode of representing the world' and the idea of a 'causal–explanatory role'; moreover they are linked in such a way that the one 'is constitutive of the other (McGinn 1982: 210). The mode of representing notion now invoked has enough link with truth for notions like justification and seeing the point to get a grip. So it would not be absurd to offer this as an account of part of what we are ordinarily doing with psychological statements. But, if the arguments centring on fallibilism in the earlier part of the paper were persuasive, the difficulty will be to show convincingly how there *can* be a notion which dovetails this 'mode of representing' idea with the 'causal–explanatory role' idea. Grip on a causal explanatory role is grip on some pattern, thought of as fixed and where the *relata* are known. But grip on a justificatory content is confidence in my power to see the point, to understand arguments and justifications involving this notion when I am called upon to do so, without supposing that I *now* know what those other related thoughts are. That such a functionalist notion, that is, one in which the two elements are dovetailed, is called for by a plausible version of functionalism is not an argument for its coherence, unless functionalism itself is unassailable.

In summary, then, in this section I have been arguing that much work needs to be done to clarify the notion of non-referential content which functionalists ought to espouse and to demonstrate that such a notion is coherent.

What will be the theoretical apparatus and modes of explanation which the replication account calls for? In stressing that one is only in position to understand another psychologically by rethinking his or her thoughts, I am putting the idea of 'doing the same thing oneself' in a prominent place. And it may thus seem that Cartesian introspectionism is reappearing on the scene. But this is not so. And the crucial difference is that, on the view I maintain, one has no more access to the intrinsic nature of one's own thoughts than one does to the intrinsic nature of others'. Thinking about my own thoughts is not, on my model, direct and intimate confrontation with something about whose nature I cannot be deceived. It is, in my own case as for others, to replicate—that is, putting on a certain sort of performance, rather than being in possession of a certain kind of knowledge. Psychological ascriptions—the use of that-clauses—might better be called re-expression than

activity of communication' (an account which shows it to be other than psychological explanation of it), we are no further forward.

What is odd about both these accounts, Field's in particular, is that they take for granted that we want true beliefs for ourselves. But once this is acknowledged the attempt to anchor the notion of truth and our interest in it by pointing to some complex of causal facts and correlations observable in third person cases seems strange. The interest in truth is already anchored as soon as a person comes to express reflectively his or her own beliefs and to ask 'But is that right?'

description. I do not by saying this mean to outlaw the phrases 'psychological knowledge' or 'psychological description' but rather to put us on our guard against a certain way of conceiving of such knowledge or descriptions. We may agree that a person knows of himself or herself what he or she is thinking more easily than he or she knows this of others. In one's own case one does not have the complexities of recentring to deal with, so replication comes very easily. But the technique for doing it, namely looking at the world, and the outcome, namely placing oneself in a position to put on a certain sort of performance, are just the same whether one thinks of oneself or another. And the emphasis on fallibilism shows that my easy replication of my own thought gives me no privileged position *vis à vis* claims to understand it, see what follows from it or the like.

I have argued that the notion of rationality or cognitive competence is central on the replication account. But equally I have argued that no substantive definition of it can be given. It is not that rationality has no conceptual connections with other notions. The idea of cognitive competence must have something to do with the idea of attaining success in cognition, that is, truth for beliefs and whatever the analogous properties are for other intentional states. Hence the idea that semantic notions such as truth have no importance in psychological explanation will clearly be mistaken on the replication view. Rationality cannot be understood without a grip on the semantic notions which define success or failure in cognition.

But one might still wonder about the point or usefulness of deploying the notion of rationality. If I affirm of myself that I am rational what point can my action have if I am not offering something with a testable content, a description of the world? I conjecture that we have here one of those items at the limits of our conceptual scheme which present themselves sometimes as statements but at other times rather as programmes of action or announcements of a stance. One thing that I might be doing in affirming myself to be rational is acknowledging the necessity of taking success as the norm in my cognitive enterprises, that is, taking success as what is to be expected unless evidence of mistake appears. I suspect that pursuit of this clue might lead to a more illuminating picture of what psychological explanation is than attempts to elaborate a functionalist account. But that is a topic for another paper.

References

Bach, K., 1982. *De re* Belief and Methodological Solipsism, in *Thought and Object*, ed. A. Woodfield, Oxford: Clarendon Press.

Davidson; D., 1970. Mental Events, in *Experience and Theory*, ed. L. Foster and J. W. Swanson, Cambridge, Mass.: University of Massachusetts Press. (See Chapter 39 of this volume.)

Dennett, D. C., 1982. Making Sense of Ourselves, in *Mind, Brain and Function*, ed. J. I. Biro and R. W. Shahan, Brighton: Harvester Press.

Field, H., 1977. Logic, Meaning and Conceptual Role, *The Journal of Philosophy* 74: 379–409.

Field, H., 1978. Mental Representation, *Erkenntnis* 13: 9–61.

Fodor, J. A., 1980. Methodological Solipsism Considered as a Research Strategy in Cognitive Psychology, *The Behavioral and Brain Sciences* 3: 63–73.

Harman, G., 1973. *Thought*, Princeton, N.J.: Princeton University Press.

Lewis, D., 1972. Psychological and Theoretical Identifications, *Australasian Journal of Philosophy 50*: 249–58.

McDowell, J., 1982. *Criteria, Defeasibility and Knowledge, Proceedings of the British Academy 68*: 455–79.

McGinn, C., 1982. The Structure of Content, in *Thought and Object*, ed. A. Woodfield, Oxford: Clarendon Press.

Putnam, H., 1967. The Nature of Mental States, First published as Psychological Predicates in *Art, Mind and Religion* ed. Capitan and Merrill. Pittsburgh: University of Pittsburgh Press; reprinted in H. Putnam, *Mind, Language and Reality: Philosophical Papers*, vol. II, Cambridge: Cambridge University Press, 1975. (See Chapter 11 of this volume.)

Quine, W. V. O., 1960. *Word and Object*, Cambridge, Mass: MIT Press.

Stich, S., 1982a. On the Ascription of Content, in *Thought and Object*, ed. A. Woodfield, Oxford: Clarendon Press.

Stich, S., 1982b. Dennett on Intentional Systems, in *Mind, Brain and Function*, ed. J. I. Biro and R. W. Shahan, Brighton: Harvester Press.

Woodfield, A., 1982. On Specifying the Contents of Thoughts, in *Thought and Object*, ed. A. Woodfield, Oxford: Clarendon Press.

Questions

1. Davidson contends that we are all in fact and of necessity radical interpreters–even when we interact with friends or members of our own family. Could this possibly be right?
2. Consider your own thoughts. Presumably you know the significance of these—what they are about. Does your knowing this require that you interpret yourself? Could you be wrong about what you think, wrong about what your thoughts are thoughts *of*?
3. According to Davidson I need to know what your utterances mean if I am to identify your preferences and thus your beliefs and desires. But I need to know your beliefs and desires to interpret your utterances! How could I ever know anything about what you think or mean?
4. Might Searle's 'Chinese Room' (Chapter 15) count as an 'intentional system'? If so, would that show that Searle is wrong—or would it show that Dennett is wrong to suppose that being an intentional system amounts to being an intelligent, thinking being?
5. Compare Davidson's account of radical interpretation with Dennett's discussion of 'stances'. How are the views alike? How are they different?
6. Is it even remotely plausible to imagine that an ordinary agent, someone wholly ignorant of decision theory and Tarski's truth theory, could be described as deploying these theories in interpreting the actions and utterances of others?
7. Davidson argues that only a creature with the concept of belief could have beliefs. Do you need to have the concept of a headache to have a headache? If not, why should belief require the concept of belief?
8. Some psychological research suggests that young children (5-year-olds, for instance) typically lack the concept of belief. What might Davidson have to say about such cases?
9. What is involved in empathizing with another? Does empathy rival or complement the kinds of interpretation favored by Davidson and by Dennett?
10. Could there be a race of intelligent creatures elsewhere in the universe that spoke a language that could not be translated into English? How would Davidson address this question?

Suggested readings

Quine's discussion of 'radical translation' can be found in Quine (1960), chaps. 1 and 2. Chadwick (1967) provides a fascinating glimpse at an actual case of something close to 'radical translation'. Many of Davidson's most influential articles on his alternative to 'radical translation', 'radical interpretation', are reprinted in Davidson (1984) and (2001). See Heil (1998: chap. 5) for an account of Davidson intended for readers unfamiliar with his work. (The chapter includes a discussion of Dennett; see below.) LePore (1986) and LePore and McLaughlin (1985) collect numerous papers discussing Davidson's views together with three previously unpublished papers by Davidson himself. The Żegleń (1999) collection includes papers on facets of Davidson's work, together with his replies. Other recent collections of papers on Davidson include Brandl and Gombocz (1989), Preyer et al. (1994), and Stoecker (1993). A volume on Davidson in the Library of Living Philosophers (Hahn 1999) includes commentary by Davidson on discussions of his work by notable contemporaries. Davidson's influence on literary theory is the topic of papers in Dasenbrock (1993).

Davidson's work is explained and discussed critically, but sympathetically in Child (1994), Evnine (1991), Malpas (1992), and Ramberg (1989). See also Malpas's (2002) on-line discussion in the *Stanford Encyclopedia.*

The connection between language and thought, the subject of Chapter 20, is discussed further by Davidson in his (1982). Heil (1992: chap. 6) provides a sympathetic interpretation of Davidson's argument. Martin (1987) is less sympathetic, and dense, but well worth the effort. Von Frisch's (1971) discussion of the 'language' of honeybees is a classic, as is Bennett's (1964) defense of the thesis that rationality requires language. These topics are discussed in Carruthers (1996), Gauker (1994). Gauker's (2001) on-line *Field Guide* discussion includes an annotated bibliography. A very different approach to the topic can be found in Fodor's (1975) spirited advocacy of an innate 'language of thought'. Carruthers and Boucher (1998) includes papers by philosophers, psychologists, and linguists. Wilfrid Sellars (1956) distinctive approach to language and thought has proved widely, though perhaps subliminally, influential.

Dennett's early, pre-intentional-stance (1969) places him close to Davidson, a position he subsequently vacated; see Dennett (1978), (1996), and (1998) for representative examples. Dahlbom (1993) and Ross et al. (2000) contain discussions of Dennett's work, some of which are illuminating, together with Dennett's responses.

The question whether our understanding of others' states of mind involves the application of a theory of mind or the kind of empathetic understanding discussed by Heal in Chapter 21 is at the center of a debate between advocates of the 'theory theory' and defenders of 'simulation'. Writing on the topic is depressingly extensive. See Gordon (1986) and Goldman (1989, 1993) for early discussions of the simulation model, and Gopnik (1996), Gopnik and Meltzoff (1997), and Gopnik and Wellman (1992) for empirical defense of the 'theory theory'. See also Gordon's (1999) on-line entry in the *MIT Encyclopedia.* Heal (1994) provides a useful account of the debate. Stich and Nichols (1992, 1998) argue against simulation. Davies and Stone (1995*a*, 1995*b*) and Peacocke (1994) include papers representative of all sides of the debate.

Davidson

Bennett, J. (1994), *Rationality: An Essay towards an Analysis.* London: Routledge & Kegan Paul. Reprinted Indianapolis: Hockett, 1989.

Brandl, J., and W. L. Gombocz, eds. (1989), *The Mind of Donald Davidson.* Amsterdam: Rodopi.

Chadwick, J. (1967), *The Decipherment of Linear B*, 2d ed. Cambridge: Cambridge University Press.

Child, T. W. (1994), *Causality Interpretation, and the Mind.* Oxford: Clarendon Press.

Dasenbrock, R. W., ed. (1993), *Literary Theory after Davidson.* University Park, PA: Pennsylvania State University Press.

Davidson, D. (1984), *Inquiries into Truth and Interpretation.* Oxford: Clarendon Press.

——(2001), *Subjective, Objective, Intersubjective.* Oxford: Clarendon Press.

Evnine, S. (1991), *Donald Davidson.* Stanford, CA: Stanford University Press.

Gauker, C. (2001), 'Language and Thought'. In Nani (2001): http://host.uniroma3.it/progetti/kant/field/lat.htm.

Hahn, L. E., ed. (1999), *The Philosophy of Donald Davidson.* Chicago: Open Court.

Heil, J. (1998), *Philosophy of Mind: A Contemporary Introduction.* London: Routledge.

LePore, E., ed. (1986), *Truth and Interpretation: Perspectives on the Philosophy of Donald Davidson.* Oxford: Basil Blackwell.

——and B. P. McLaughlin, eds. (1985), *Actions and Events: Perspectives on the Philosophy of Donald Davidson.* Oxford: Basil Blackwell.

Malpas, J. P. (1992), *Donald Davidson and the Mirror of Meaning: Holism, Truth, Interpretation.* Cambridge: Cambridge University Press.

——(2002), 'Donald Davidson'. In Zalta (2002): <http://plato.stanford.edu/entries/davidson/>.

Nani, M., ed. (2001), *A Field Guide to the Philosophy of Mind.* http://host.uniroma3.it/progetti/kant/field. Rome: University of Rome 3.

Preyer, G., F. Siebelt, and A. Ulfig, eds. (1994), *Language, Mind, and Epistemology: Essays on Donald Davidson's Philosophy.* Dordrecht: Kluwer Academic.

Quine, W. V. O. (1960), *Word and Object*, Cambridge: MIT Press.

Ramberg, B. T. (1989), *Donald Davidson's Philosophy of Language.* Oxford: Basil Blackwell.

Stoecker, R., ed. (1993), *Reflecting on Davidson: Donald Davidson Responding to an International Forum of Philosophers.* Berlin: de Gruyter.

Zalta, E. N., ed. (2002), *The Stanford Encyclopedia of Philosophy.* <http://plato.stanford.edu/> Stanford, CA: Metaphysics Research Lab, Center for the Study of Language and Information.

Żegleń, U., ed. (1999), *Donald Davidson: Truth, Meaning, and Knowledge.* London: Routledge.

Dennett

Dahlbom, B., ed. (1993), *Dennett and his Critics: Demystifying the Mind.* Oxford: Basil Blackwell.

Dennett, D. C. (1969), *Content and Consciousness.* London: Routledge & Kegan Paul.

Dennett, D. C. (1978), *Brainstorms: Philosophical Essays on Mind and Psychology.* Montgomery, VT: Bradford Books.

——(1996), *Kinds of Minds: Toward an Understanding of Consciousness.* New York: Basic Books.

——(1998), *Brainchildren: Essays on Designing Minds.* Cambridge, MA: MIT Press.

Ross, D., A. Brook, and D. Thompson, eds. (2000), *Dennett's Philosophy: A Comprehensive Assessment.* Cambridge, MA: MIT Press.

Language and thought

Carruthers, P. (1996), *Language, Thought, and Consciousness.* Cambridge: Cambridge University press.

——and J. Boucher, eds. (1998), *Language and Thought: Interdisciplinary Themes.* Cambridge: Cambridge University Press.

Davidson, D. (1982), 'Rational Animals', *Dialectica* 36: 317–27. Reprinted in LePore and McLaughlin 1985: 473–80.

Feigl, H., and M. Scriven, eds. (1956), *The Foundations of Science and the Concepts of Psychology and Psychoanalysis* (Minnesota Studies in the Philosophy of Science, vol. 1). Minneapolis: University of Minnesota Press.

Fodor, J. A. (1975), *The Language of Thought.* New York: T. Y. Crowell.

Gauker, C. (1994), *Thinking Out Loud: An Essay on the Relation between Thought and Language.* Princeton: Princeton University Press.

Heil, J. (1992), *The Nature of True Minds.* Cambridge: Cambridge University Press.

Martin, C. B. (1987), 'Proto-Language', *Australasian Journal of Philosophy,* 65: 277–89.

Sellars, W. (1956), 'Empiricism and the Philosophy of Mind'. In Feigl and Scriven 1956: 253–329. Reissued in 1997 as a monograph, *Empiricism and the Philosophy of Mind,* Cambridge, MA: Harvard University Press.

Von Frisch, K. (1971), *Bees: Their Vision, Chemical Senses, and Language,* 2d ed. Ithaca, NY: Cornell University Press.

Theory of mind vs. simulation

Davies, M., and T. Stone, eds. (1995*a*), *Folk Psychology: The Theory of Mind Debate.* Oxford: Blackwell Publishers.

————eds. (1995*b*), *Mental Simulation: Philosophical and Psychological Essays.* Oxford: Blackwell Publishers.

Goldman, A. I. (1989), 'Interpretation Psychologized', *Mind and Language* 4: 165–82.

——(1993), 'The Psychology of Folk Psychology', *Behavioral and Brain Sciences* 16: 15–28.

Gopnik, A. (1996), 'The Scientist as Child', *Philosophy of Science* 63: 485–514.

——and A. Meltzoff (1997), *Words, Thoughts and Theories* . Cambridge, MA: MIT Press.

——and H. Wellman (1992), 'Why the Child's Theory of Mind Really Is a Theory', *Mind and Language* 7: 145–71.

Gordon, R. (1986), 'Folk Psychology as Simulation', *Mind and Language* 1: 158–71.

——(1999), 'Simulation vs. the Theory-Theory'. In Wilson and Keil 1999.

Heal, J. (1994), 'Simulation vs. Theory Theory: What Is at Issue?' In Peacocke 1994: 129–44.

Peacocke, C., ed. (1994), *Objectivity, Simulation, and the Unity of Consciousness.* Oxford: Oxford University Press.

Stich, S. P., and S. Nichols. (1992), 'Folk Psychology: Simulation or tacit Theory?' *Mind and Language* 7: 35–71.

—— —— (1998), 'Theory Theory to the Max', *Mind and Language* 13: 421–49.

Wilson, R. A., and F. Keil, eds. (1999), *MIT Encyclopedia of Cognitive Sciences* <http://cognet.mit.edu/MITECS/login.html> Cambridge, MA: MIT Press.

Part VI

Eliminativism

Introduction

PHILOSOPHERS and psychologists were initially attracted to functionalism because functionalism promised a way of understanding how minds could be housed in purely material systems. States of mind are 'realized' in creatures in something like the way programs are 'realized' in computing machines. Other philosophers aggressively attacked the possibility of reducing states of mind to functional states. Functionalists, for their part, have largely stuck to their guns and insisted that minds are best understood as complex causal systems with a particular kind of causal architecture. Causal systems with the right functional profiles might be found in immaterial structures: ghosts or angels might form beliefs, have empathetic feelings, and the like. Functionalism is compatible with, but does not imply, materialism.

Eliminativists are more relentlessly materialistic. Talk of minds, they suggest, is little more than a remnant of long-discredited animistic theories that sought to explain natural occurrences by endowing objects with souls. Animistic explanations have been gradually replaced by purely physical explanations except in one domain: the behavior of intelligent creatures. We continue to regard human beings, and many non-human creatures, as physical systems that include a vital mental component. In our more scientifically inspired moments, we might think of identifying minds with the brains of intelligent creatures. But, say the eliminativists, this is like identifying tree spirits with root systems or angelic souls responsible for the motions of the planets with inertial force. As science moves ahead, we do not learn more about the physical basis of tree spirits or angelic souls. We learn that *there are no such entities*. We *replace* talk of tree spirits and angelic souls with talk of root systems and inertial forces. Advances in neuroscience make it clear (the eliminativists argue) that minds are about to join tree spirits and angelic souls on the scrapheap of entities posited by discarded theories.

Reductive versus eliminative materialism

A reductive materialist holds that mental properties and states are really, at bottom, physical properties or states. Your thinking of Vienna or experiencing the taste of chocolate, is a matter of your brain's being in a particular state. In Part X, we shall encounter another, less demanding brand of materialism, *nonreductive materialism*. Nonreductive materialists see mental properties and states as entirely dependent on, but nevertheless distinct from, material properties and states (recall Figures III.1 and III.2). Eliminative materialists, in contrast to both reductive and nonreductive materialists, flatly deny that there are any mental states or properties. Reductive materialists and eliminativists believe that the world and its contents are, at bottom, wholly material entities and arrangements of these. A reductive materialist finds a place among the material entities for minds and their contents; eliminativists lop off the minds, leaving only the material entities. Reductive materialists take work in the neurosciences to deepen our understanding of mental states and processes. Nonreductive materialists would see such work as illuminating the 'substrate', or 'basis', or 'realizers' of states of mind. Eliminativists regard explanations in the neurosciences as apt *replacements* for explanations framed in terms of thoughts, sensations, and feelings.

Is eliminativism incoherent?

One question, discussed by Lynne Rudder Baker (Chapter 24) is whether eliminative materialism can be coherently defended. If true, eliminativism would apparently be—literally—unbelievable! Can you sensibly urge others to believe that there are no beliefs?

Compare this case with that of the consistent liar. If everything the liar says is false, the liar cannot consistently announce this fact to his associates by proclaiming 'Everything I say is false.' It could be true that everything the liar says is false, but if it is true, the liar is powerless to say so. If it were true that there are no states of mind—no beliefs, no intentions, no thoughts of any kind—this is not something anyone could believe—or doubt! Indeed, truth itself seems to require a vehicle—a meaningful thought, representation, or utterance—of a kind distained by eliminativism. Does this imply that eliminativism is not or could not be true? Might the world be such that we are barred from giving a true, coherent description of it? If a theory implies this result, is that grounds for rejecting the theory? Answers to such questions are anything but obvious.

Syntax and meaning

Two brands of eliminative materialism are represented in the readings here. The first is advanced by Stephen Stich (Chapter 22). Stich argues that the nature of beliefs and desires is such that features of such states that figure in causal transactions are independent of their 'content'. Indeed the content of a state of mind is something we read into those states of mind as interpreters. This implies, according to Stich, that the science of psychology needs to be replaced by a purely syntactic science, one that takes account, not of the *significance* of states of mind, but only their *syntactic form*.

To understand the argument, you will need to understand an important distinction between syntax and semantics. Representational systems, like natural languages, mapping systems, or artificial languages ('programming' languages, for instance) have a particular syntax. Think of the syntax as a collection of rules that distinguish between meaningful and meaningless strings of symbols. If you know the syntax of English, for instance you know that the strings of symbols below

(*a*) The cat is on the mat
(*b*) Colorless green ideas sleep furiously

are sentences of English, and these strings of symbols

(*c*) mat the the on is cat
(*d*) colorless sleep green furiously ideas

are not sentences. You know this, even though sentence (*b*) 'makes no sense'; you know it because you know the syntax of English.

Your knowledge of what (*a*) means and your recognition that (*b*), although 'well formed' is nonsense, is a manifestation of your knowledge of the *semantics* of English. The character imprisoned in Searle's 'Chinese Room' (Chapter 15) is equipped to work out the syntax of the Chinese symbols he manipulates, but remains ignorant of their semantics. Searle's point is that an appropriately programmed computing machine processes symbols without regard to their meaning: the computer is a wholly syntactic device. The symbols thus processed are meaningful: the symbols are meaningful to *us*.

Searle makes use of this point to argue that we are not computing machines. The meanings of the symbols we 'process' play a role in how we process them. You could think of Stich as denying this. Meanings have no role to play in the operation of any system, intelligent or otherwise. A symbol-manipulating system—the human brain, say—has no interest whatever in the significance of the symbols it manipulates. If these symbols have a meaning it plays no role in the mechanisms that process them.

But wait! Why should anyone think of the brain as 'processing symbols'? And why should meanings be marginalized?

The idea is one we have encountered already and will encounter in subsequent readings. A meaningful symbol owes its meaning to something outside itself. A red line on a map indicates a highway and a brown line a footpath because the map maker has decreed that red lines indicate highways and brown lines indicate footpaths. So it is with any symbol. Wittgenstein (1953: §43) speaks of replacing talk of meaning with talk of use: the significance of a symbol depends, not on its intrinsic ('built-in') features, but on the use to which it is put, its role in the system to which it contributes. The point is nicely illustrated in the case of natural languages by an example borrowed from Baker. Consider the symbol, 'burro'. This symbol, when used by Spanish speakers, means 'donkey', in the mouths of Italians means 'butter'. (You might put this by saying that the use of 'burro' among Spanish-speakers resembles the use of 'donkey' among English-speakers; Italians use 'burro' in roughly the way English-speakers use 'butter'.)

Suppose something like this is correct, and suppose its truth is perfectly general. If thoughts, for instance, are meaningful, then a particular thought is a symbol the meaning of which depends on its role in some larger system to which the thinker belongs. Different theorists will differ on what this larger system encompasses. It might just be a self-contained information-processing system (wholly contained in your nervous system, for instance). This is 'internalism'. Or it might, as 'externalists' insist, include the ecological or social system in which you are embedded. (More on internalism and externalism in Part VII.)

Syntax rules

You can remain neutral on the details of all this and still appreciate Stich's argument. Psychology, he contends, is distinguished by its appeal to the 'propositional attitudes' in explanations of behavior. The propositional attitudes include beliefs, desires, intentions, and the like. A propositional attitude incorporates both a *content* (some proposition) and an attitude toward that content (you might believe it, for instance, doubt it, intend it to be true, or want it to be true). This is all, as philosophical theses go, relatively uncontroversial.

Now turn your attention to what it might be for an agent to harbor a particular belief or desire. One possibility is that associated with the work of Jerry Fodor (1975, 1988). According to Fodor, intelligent creatures come equipped with a built in 'Language of Thought'. If you are technically minded, you could think of the Language of Thought as resembling the 'machine language' hard-wired into a computing machine. A Language of Thought is, as the computing machine analogy suggests, *innate*. You do not learn a Language of Thought as you might learn English or Urdu. Indeed, Fodor contends, learning a language presupposes that you are *already* in possession of a language: the Language of Thought.

Think of the Language of Thought as a symbol-processing system built into your nervous system. If you are an English speaker, you have acquired a natural language by, in effect, *correlating* English symbols with symbols in your innate Language of Thought—just as in learning Italian, you might learn to correlate Italian and English symbols. (See the discussion of Quine in the introduction to Part V.) The process of correlation is conscious and deliberate when you learn a second language, but it is done unselfconsciously in the course of acquiring a first language.

Imagine now coming to believe that the cat is on the mat. If Fodor is right, then for you to have this belief is for a 'token'—a particular instance—of a sentence in your Language of Thought to be placed in your 'belief box'. Think of a 'belief box' as a node in a system of nodes that plays a particular role. In this case, the node would be the node playing the belief role: a node that provides information to the system that could be used as a basis for action. This is just functionalism (Part III). Beliefs, doubts, and desires differ functionally. If you *believe* that the cat is on the mat, then, if your aim is to find the cat, you will behave differently than you would had you *doubted* that the cat is on the mat.

You can see how this might work in a case in which you believe that the cat is on the mat and that the mat is in the kitchen, want to find the cat, and thus form the intention to go to the kitchen and do so (see Figure VI.1).

Suppose something like this captures a portion of your psychology. Now ask whether the meanings of the symbols coursing about inside you play any causal role whatever in

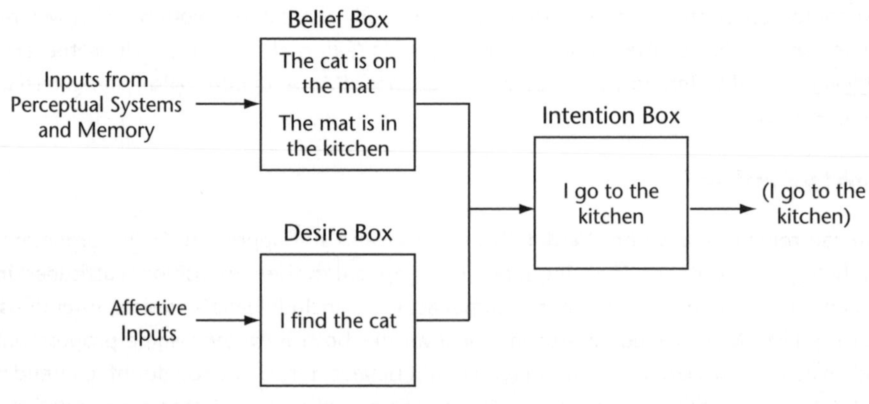

Figure VI.1

your going to the kitchen. It is hard to see how they could. In this respect, the principles governing your operation resemble those governing the operation of a computing machine: in both cases, the system processes symbols that are meaningful without 'caring' what they mean. Again, the idea is dramatically illustrated by Searle's 'Chinese Room' (Chapter 15).

So? Well if you thought that the propositional attitudes—beliefs desires, intentions, and the like—are distinguished by their content—what they are beliefs *about* or desires and intentions *for*—then you might see the move to a purely syntactical conception of mind as eliminative. Beliefs, desires, and intentions per se do not animate your psychology, but only their symbolic stand-ins. Differently put, you do not go to the kitchen because of what you believe, desire, and intend, but because symbols with certain 'shapes' (or the neurological counterparts of shapes) are on the scene. The notion, implicit in Searle's criticism of Artificial Intelligence, that we behave as we do because our thoughts have the significance they have is a naïve holdover of an outmoded conception of mind.

The eliminativist happily accepts Searle's diagnosis of Artificial Intelligence. Instead of regarding this as grounds for rejecting the thesis that human psychology is computational, an eliminativist, reasoning in the other direction, regards it as grounds for supposing that, despite appearances, meanings play no role in the operation of the mind. Searle: If *P*, then *Q*; but *Q* is absurd, so not-*P*. Stich: If *P*, then *Q*; but *P* is the case, so *Q*.

The end of psychology

Paul Churchland advocates a different flavor of eliminativism. Whereas Stich thinks that talk of the propositional attitudes—beliefs, desires, emotions, and the like—needs to be replaced by talk of syntactic counterparts, Churchland holds that the propositional attitudes have *no* material counterparts. Beliefs, desires, and the rest are posits of an outmoded folk theory of what makes us tick, a theory 'ripe for replacement' by a theory—or, more likely, theories—that carve up the world very differently.

Churchland's argument depends on a notion of reduction that has its own independent interest. Suppose, as most philosophers and scientists do suppose, that physics is the basic science. We assume that the job of physics is to get at the fundamental constituents of the material world, their properties, and laws governing their interactions. Other sciences focus on larger, more observationally salient portions of reality (see Oppenheim and Putnam 1958 for discussion). Chemists concentrate on molecules and molecular structures, for instance, biologists on cells and organisms, psychologists on the behavior of intelligent creatures. You might wonder what relations these enterprises bear to one another: we have the several sciences, but how are they related? Higher-level sciences—biology and psychology, for instance—are apparently 'grounded' in lower-level phenomena. But what is the nature of this 'grounding'?

One possibility is that higher-level sciences are *reducible to* sciences at a lower level, and ultimately to physics. What is required for 'reduction'? One answer, nicely articulated by Ernest Nagel (1961: chap. 11) is that reduction is a relation among theories. One theory, T_1, is reducible to another, T_2, when T_1 can be shown to be a special case of T_2. T_1 is a special case of T_2, if T_1, fully articulated, is *deducible* from T_2: all the truths implied by T_1 are implied by T_2. When this condition is satisfied, you can see that T_1 and truths expressible in the vocabulary of T_1, and re-expressible as truths of T_2. You might continue to use T_1 because it is convenient, but this is merely a matter of convenience: you can see how T_1-truths could be said to be 'grounded in' T_2-truths.

Famous instances of reduction include the reduction of classical genetics to molecular genetics, and the reduction of thermodynamics to statistical mechanics, which includes the reduction of talk about temperature and heat to talk of mean kinetic energy. Such reduction is achieved empirically. Consider the case of thermodynamics. As science progresses, scientists realize that truths of thermodynamics—the Boyle–Charles law, for instance—are consequences of truths of statistical mechanics.

What if reduction fails? This can happen when the terms of a higher-level science fail to 'line up' with lower-level terms. That could be so because the higher-level terms designate something not present at the lower level, some feature of the world that exists *in addition to* what exists at the lower level. Imagine arranging four matchsticks so as to form a square. We now have a new feature of the world—four-sidedness—not present in elements responsible for the feature: none of the matchsticks is four-sided. But four-sidedness is nothing 'in addition to' or 'over and above' the matchsticks and their arrangement. Four-sidedness is a reducible feature of the world. A non-reducible element would be something that comes into existence—'blossoms' or 'emerges'—under the right conditions but, unlike the matchstick square, is something more than, something in addition to, its constituents variously organized.

History has not been kind to emergent entities (see McLaughlin 1992). For many years, scientists despaired of deriving truths of organic chemistry from more fundamental chemical theory. This led to speculation that organic compounds were 'emergent' features of the world, features that could not be accounted for by reference exclusively to inorganic properties. The advent of quantum chemistry, however, brought with it the required reduction, resolving organic features of the world in the way four-sidedness is resolved: apparently higher-level items were seen to be nothing in addition to lower-level items appropriately configured.

Another reason reduction could falter is that items for which a reduction is sought simply fail to exist. We can reduce temperature to mean kinetic energy, but we cannot reduce phlogiston. Phlogiston, a fluid taken by eighteenth-century chemists to be present in all bodies, provided an explanation of assorted phenomena, including the dissipation of heat and the fact that heated bodies gain weight. (Heating was thought to drive out phlogiston. Why the gain in weight? Phlogiston has 'negative weight'.) Truths about phlogiston are not derivable from statistical mechanics. We do not, however, regard phlogiston as an 'emergent' feature of the world. Rather we take an eliminativist attitude toward phlogiston: we deny that phlogiston exists. We deny the existence of phlogiston largely because we have found much better ways of explaining phenomena phlogiston was postulated to explain.

Suppose this is how it is with the propositional attitudes and other psychological categories: beliefs, desires, intentions, feelings, emotions, moods, and the like. Truths about such things are not derivable from lower-level neuro-scientific truths. This is not because mental phenomena are 'emergent', an 'addition of being', but because, like phlogiston, such things do not exist! Psychological categories belong to a theory 'ripe for replacement'. Loss of the theory brings with it abandonment of terms the meaning of which was tied to their use in the theory.

Folk psychology adieu

Philosophers like to describe our everyday conception of mental functioning as 'folk psychology'. Folk psychology embodies a conception of mind we pick up as we learn to interact with one another. The idea is that this conception amounts to a theory—a 'folk theory', analogous to 'folk medicine'. Think of folk psychology as incorporating a theory of mind. Scientific psychology merely extends and refines theoretical principles implicit in folk psychology. Like any theory, our folk theory (or, experimental psychology, its gussied up scientific counterpart) could, at least in principle, be supplanted by a superior theory. If and when this happens (eliminativists are betting when, not if) irreducible folk categories will be revealed as empty. We will not *reduce* beliefs, desires, intentions, feelings, and emotions, to more fundamental neurological states and processes. The replacement theory will leave no room for such things.

Were this to happen, would we be obliged to abandon talk about beliefs and feelings, would we have to give up our 'folk psychological' vocabulary? Or could we continue to use the old vocabulary emptied of its previous content—just as we continue to speak of the sun rising and setting without thinking of ourselves as at odds with the astronomers? You should consider carefully the implications of both possibilities. What effect might eliminativism have on our notion of responsibility, a notion that lies close to the heart of many of our most important social institutions? If beliefs and intentions are like witches and demons, we should be positively in error in appealing to them in explanations of human behavior. What effects might this have on our self-image and on our relations with others?

However you respond to such questions, you will first need to assess the philosophical core of eliminativism. The selections by Stich and Churchland provide an excellent starting point.

References

Beckermann, A., H. Flohr, and J. Kim, eds. (1992), *Emergence or Reduction? Essays on the Prospects of Nonreductive Physicalism*. Berlin: De Gruyter.

Feigl, H., M. Scriven, and G. Maxwell, eds. (1958), *Concepts, Theories, and the Mind—Body Problem* (Minnesota Studies in the Philosophy of Science, vol. 2). Minneapolis: University of Minnesota Press.

Fodor, J. (1975), *The Language of Thought*. New York: T. Y. Crowell.

——(1988), Psychosemantics: The Problem of Meaning in the Philosophy of Mind. Cambridge: MIT Press.

McLaughlin, B. P. (1992), 'The Rise and Fall of British Emergentism'. In Beckermann, Flohr, and Kim 1992: 49–93.

Nagel, E. (1961), *The Structure of Science: Problems in the Logic of Scientific Explanation*. New York: Harcourt, Brace, & World.

Oppenheim, P., and H. Putnam (1958), 'Unity of Science as a Working Hypothesis'. In Feigl et al. 1958: 3–36.

Wittgenstein, L. (1953/1968), *Philosophical Investigations*, trans. G. E. M. Anscombe. Oxford: Basil Blackwell.

Chapter 22

Autonomous psychology and the belief-desire thesis

Stephen P. Stich

A venerable view, still very much alive, holds that human action is to be explained at least in part in terms of beliefs and desires. Those who advocate the view expect that the psychological theory which explains human behavior will invoke the concepts of belief and desire in a substantive way. I will call this expectation *the belief-desire thesis.* Though there would surely be a quibble or a caveat here and there, the thesis would be endorsed by an exceptionally heterogeneous collection of psychologists and philosophers ranging from Freud and Hume, to Thomas Szasz and Richard Brandt. Indeed, a number of philosophers have contended that the thesis, or something like it, is embedded in our ordinary, workaday concept of action.[1] If they are right, and I think they are, then insofar as we use the concept of action we are *all* committed to the belief-desire thesis. My purpose in this paper is to explore the tension between the belief-desire thesis and a widely held assumption about the nature of explanatory psychological theories, an assumption that serves as a fundamental regulative principle for much of contemporary psychological theorizing. This assumption, which for want of a better term I will call the *principle of psychological autonomy,* will be the focus of the first of the sections below. In the second section I will elaborate a bit on how the belief-desire thesis is to be interpreted, and try to extract from it a principle that will serve as a premise in the argument to follow. In the third section I will set out an argument to the effect that large numbers of belief-desire explanations of action, indeed perhaps the bulk of such explanations, are incompatible with the principle of autonomy. Finally, in the last section, I will fend off a possible objection to my argument. In the process, I will try to make clear just why the argument works and what price we should have to pay if we were resolved to avoid its consequences.

Stephen P. Stich, 'Autonomous Psychology and the Belief-Desire Thesis', *Monist* 61 (1978).

1. The clearest and most detailed elaboration fo this view that I know of is to be found in Goldman (1970). The view is also argued in Brandt and Kim (1963) and Davidson (1963). However, Davidson does not advocate the belief-desire thesis as it will be construed below. Cf. n11.

I. The principle of psychological autonomy

Perhaps the most vivid way of explaining the principle I have in mind is by invoking a type of science fiction example that has cropped up with some frequency in recent philosophical literature. Imagine that technology were available which would enable us to duplicate people. That is, we can build living human beings who are atom for atom and molecule for molecule replicas of some given human being.[2] Now suppose that we have before us a human being (or, for that matter, any sort of animal) and his exact replica. What the principle of autonomy claims is that these two humans will be psychologically identical, that any psychological property instantiated by one of these subjects will also be instantiated by the other.

Actually, a bit of hedging is needed to mark the boundaries of this claim to psychological identity. First, let me note that the organisms claimed to be psychologically identical include any pair of organisms, existing at the same time or at different times, who happen to be atom for atom replicas of each other. Moreover, it is inessential that one organism should have been built to be a replica of the other. Even if the replication is entirely accidental, the two organisms will still be psychologically identical.

A caveat of another sort is needed to clarify just what I mean by calling two organisms 'psychologically identical.' For consider the following objection: 'The original organism and his replica do not share *all* of their psychological properties. The original may, for example, remember seeing the Watergate hearings on television, but the replica remembers no such thing. He may think he remembers it, or have an identical 'memory trace'; but if he was not created until long after the Watergate hearings, then he did not see the hearings on television, and thus he could not remember seeing them.' The point being urged by my imagined critic is a reasonable one. There are many sorts of properties plausibly labeled 'psychological' that might be instantiated by a person and not by his replica. Remembering that p is one example, knowing that p and seeing that p are others. These properties have a sort of 'hybrid' character. They seem to be analyzable into a 'purely psychological' property (like seeming to remember that p, or believing that p (along with one or more non-psychological properties and relations (like p being true, or the memory trace being caused in a certain way by the fact that p). But to insist that 'hybrid' psychological properties are not psychological properties at all would be at best a rather high handed attempt at stipulative definition. Still, there is something a bit odd about these hybrid psychological properties, a fact which reflects itself in the intuitive distinction between 'hybrids' and their underlying 'purely psychological' components. What is odd about the hybrids, I think, is that we do not expect them to play any role in an explanatory psychological theory. Rather, we expect a psychological theory which aims at explaining behavior to invoke only the

2. Cf. Putnam (1973) and (1975) .

'purely psychological' properties which are shared by a subject and its replicas. Thus, for example, we are inclined to insist it is Jones' *belief* that there is no greatest prime number that plays a role in the explanation of his answering the exam question. He may, in fact, have *known* that there is no greatest prime number. But even if he did not know it, if, for example, the source of his information had himself only been guessing, Jones' behavior would have been unaffected. What knowledge adds to belief is psychologically irrelevant. Similarly the difference between really remembering that p and merely seeming to remember that p makes no difference to the subject's behavior. In claiming that physical replicas are psychologically identical, the principle of psychological autonomy is to be understood as restricting itself to the properties that can play a role in explanatory psychological theory. Indeed, the principle is best viewed as a claim about what sorts of properties and relations may play a role in explanatory psychological theory. If the principle is to be observed, then the only properties and relations that may legitimately play a role in explanatory psychological theories are the properties and relations that a subject and its replica will share.

There is another way to explain the principle of psychological autonomy that does not appeal to the fanciful idea of a replica. In a recent paper Jaegwon Kim has explicated and explored the notion of one class of properties *supervening* upon another class of properties.[3] Suppose S and W are two classes of properties, and that S and W are the sets of all properties constructable from the properties in S and W repsectively. Then, following Kim, we will say that the family S of properties supervenes on the family W of properties (with respect to a domain D of objects) just in case, necessarily, any two objects in D which share all properties in W will also share all properties in S. A bit less formally, one class of properties supervenes on another if the presence or absence of properties in the former class is completely determined by the presence or absence of properties in the latter.[4] Now the principle of psychological autonomy states that the properties and relations to be invoked in an explanatory psychological theory must be supervenient upon the *current, internal physical* properties and relations of organisms (i.e., just those properties that an organism shares with all of its replicas).

Perhaps the best way to focus more sharply on what the autonomy principle states is to look at what it rules out. First, of course, if explanatory psychological properties and relations must supervene on *physical* properties, then at least some forms of dualism are false. The dualist who claims that there are psychological (or mental) properties which are not nomologically correlated with physical properties, but which nonetheless must be invoked in an explanation of the organism's behavior, is denying that explanatory psychological states supervene upon physical

3. Kim (1978).
4. Kim's account of supervenience is intentionally non-committal on the sort of necessity invoked in the definition. Different notions of necessity will yield different, though parallel, concepts of supervenience.

states. However, the autonomy principle is not inimical to all forms of dualism. Those dualists, for example, who hold that mental and physical properties are nomologically correlated need have no quarrel with the doctrine of autonomy. However, the principle of autonomy is significantly stronger than the mere insistence that psychological states supervene on physical states.[5] For autonomy requires in addition that certain physical properties and relations are psychologically irrelevant in the sense that organisms which differ *only* with respect to those properties and relations are psychologically identical.[6] In specifying that only 'current' physical properties are psychologically relevant, the autonomy principle decrees irrelevant all those properties that deal with the history of the organism, both past and future. It is entirely possible, for example, for two organisms to have quite different physical histories and yet, at a specific pair of moments, to be replicas of one another. But this sort of difference, according to the autonomy principle, can make no difference from the point of view of explanatory psychology. Thus remembering that p (as contrasted with having a memory trace that p) cannot be an explanatory psychological state. For the difference between a person who remembers that p and a person who only seems to remember that p is not dependent on their current physical state, but only on the history of these states. Similarly, in specifying that only *internal* properties and relations are relevant to explanatory psychological properties, the autonomy principle decrees that relations between an organism and its external environment are irrelevant to its current (explanatory) psychological state. The restriction also entails that properties and relations of external objects cannot be relevant to the organism's current (explanatory) psychological state. Thus neither my seeing that Jones is falling nor my knowing that Ouagadougou is the capital of Upper Volta can play a role in an explanatory psychological theory, since the former depends in part on my relation to Jones, and the latter depends in part on the relation between Ouagadougou and Upper Volta.

Before we leave our discussion of the principle of psychological autonomy, let us reflect briefly on the status of the principle. On Kim's view, the belief that one set of properties supervenes on another 'is largely, and often, a combination of metaphysical convictions and methodological considerations.'[7] The description seems particularly apt for the principle of psychological autonomy. The autonomy principle serves a sort of regulative role in modern psychology, directing us to restrict the concepts we invoke in our explanatory theories in a very special way. When we act in accordance with the regulative stipulation of the principle we are giving witness to the tacit conviction that the best explanation of behavior will include a theory invoking properties supervenient upon the organism's current, internal

5. This weaker principle is discussed at some length in Kim (1977).

6. Note, however, that physical properties that are irrelevant in this sense may nonetheless be *causally* related to those physical properties upon which psychological properties supervene. Thus they may be 'psychologically relevant' in the sense that they may play a role in the explanation of how the organism comes to have some psychological property.

7. Kim (1978).

physical state.[8] As Kim urges, this conviction is supported in part by the past success of theories which cleave to the principle's restrictions, and in part by some very fundamental metaphysical convictions. I think there is much to be learned in trying to pick apart the various metaphysical views that support the autonomy principle, for some of them have implications in areas quite removed from psychology. But that is a project for a different paper.

II. The belief-desire thesis

The belief-desire thesis maintains that human action is to be explained, at least in part, in terms of beliefs and desires. To sharpen the thesis we need to say more about the intended sense of *explain*, and more about what it would be to explain action *in terms of beliefs and desires*. But before trying to pin down either of these notions, it will be useful to set out an example of the sort of informal belief-desire explanations that we commonly offer for our own actions and the actions of others.

Jones is watching television; from time to time he looks nervously at a lottery ticket grasped firmly in his hand. Suddenly he jumps up and rushes toward the phone. Why? It was because the T. V. announcer has just announced the winning lottery number, and it is the number on Jones' ticket. Jones believes that he has won the lottery. He also believes that to collect his winnings he must contact the lottery commission promptly. And, needless to say, he very much wants to collect his winnings.

Many theorists acknowledge that explanations like the one offered of Jones rushing toward the phone are often true (albeit incomplete) explanations of action. But this concession alone does not commit the theorist to the belief-desire thesis as I will interpret it here. There is considerable controversy over how we are to understand the 'because' in 'Jones rushed for the phone because he believed he had won the lottery and he wanted. . . .' Some writers are inclined to read the 'because' literally, as claiming that Jones' belief and his desire were the *causes* (or among the causes) of his action. Others offer a variety of non-causal accounts of the relation between beliefs and desires on the one hand and actions on the other.[9] However, it is the former, 'literal,' reading that is required by the belief-desire thesis as I am constructing it.

To say that Jones's belief that he had won the lottery was among the causes of his rushing toward the phone is to say of one specific event that it had among its causes one specific state. There is much debate over how such 'singular causal statements' are to be analyzed. Some philosophers hold that for a state or event S to be among

8. It has been my experience that psychologists who agree on little else readily endorse the autonomy principle. Indeed, I have yet to find a psychologist who did not take the principle to be obviously true. Some of these same psychologists also favored the sort of belief-desire explanations of action that I will later argue are at odds with the autonomy principle. None, however, were aware of the incompatibility, and a number of them vigorously resisted the contention that the incompatibility is there.

9. For a critique of these views, cf. Goldman (1970), Chapter 3; Alston (1967b).

the causes of an event E, there must be a law which somehow relates S and E. Other philosophers propose other accounts. Even among those who agree that singular causal statements must be subsumed by a law, there is debate over how this notion of subsumption is to be understood. At the heart of this controversy is the issue of how much difference there can be between the properties invoked in the law and those invoked in the description of the event if the event is to be an instance of the law.[10] Given our current purposes, there is no need to take a stand on this quite general metaphysical issue. But we will have to take a stand on a special case of the relation between beliefs, desires, and the psychological laws that subsume them. The belief-desire thesis, as I am viewing it, takes seriously the idea of developing a psychological theory couched in terms of beliefs and desires. Thus, in addition to holding that Jones's action was caused by his belief that he had won the lottery and his desire to collect his winnings, it also holds that this singular causal statement is true in virtue of being subsumed by laws which specify nomological relations among beliefs, desires and action.[11]

There is one further point that needs to be made about my construal of the belief-desire thesis. If the thesis is right, then action is to be explained at least in part by appeal to laws detailing how beliefs, desires and other psychological states effect action. But how are we to recognize such laws? It is, after all, plainly not enough for a theory simply to invoke the terms 'belief' and 'desire' in its laws. If it were, then it would be possible to convert any theory into a belief-desire theory by the simple expedient of replacing a pair of its theoretical terms with the terms 'belief' and 'desire'. The point I am laboring is that the belief-desire thesis must be construed as the claim that psychological theory will be couched in terms of beliefs and desires *as we ordinarily conceive of them.* Thus to spell out the belief-desire thesis in detail would require that we explicate our intuitive concepts of belief and desire. Fortunately, we need not embark on that project here.[12] To fuel the arguments I will

10. For discussion of these matters, see Kim (1973). Kim defends the view that the property invoked in the description must be identical with the one invoked in the law. For a much more liberal view see Davidson (1967).

11. Thus Davidson is not an advocate of the belief-desire thesis as I am construing it. For on his view, though beliefs and desires may be among the causes of actions, the general laws supporting the causal claims are not themselves couched in terms of beliefs and desires. Cf. Davidson (1970). But Davidson's view, though not without interest, is plainly idiosyncratic. Generally, philosophers who hold that beliefs and desires are among the causes of behavior also think that there are psychological laws to be found (most likely probabilistic ones) which are stated in terms of beliefs and desires. Cf., for example, Hempel (1965), pp. 463–87; Alston (1967a) and (1967b); Goldman (1970), chaps. 3 and 4.

We should also note that much of recent psychology can be viewed as a quest for psychological laws couched in terms of beliefs and/or desires. There is, for example, an enormous and varied literature on problem solving (cf. Newell & Simon [1972]) and on informal inference (cf. Nisbett & Ross [1980]) which explores the mechanisms and environmental determinants of belief formation. Also, much of the literature on motivation is concerned with uncovering the laws governing the formation and strength of desires. Cf. Atkinson (1964).

12. For an attempt to explicate our informal concepts of belief and desire in some detail, see Stich (1983).

develop in the following section, I will need only a single, intuitively plausible, premise about beliefs.

As a backdrop for the premise that I need, let me introduce some handy terminology. I believe that Ouagadougou is the capital of Upper Volta, and if you share my interest in atlases then it is likely that you have the same belief. Of course, there is also a perfectly coherent sense in which your belief is not the same as mine, since you could come to believe that Bobo Dioulasso is the capital of Upper Volta, while my belief remains unchanged. The point here is the obvious one that beliefs, like sentences, admit of a type-token distinction. I am inclined to view belief tokens as states of a person. And I take a state to be the instantiation of a property by an object during a time interval. Two belief states (or belief tokens) are of the same type if they are instantiations of the same property and they are of different types if they are instantiations of different properties.[13] In the example at hand, the property that both you and I instantiate is *believing that Ouagadougou is the capital of Upper Volta.*

Now the premise I need for my argument concerns the identity conditions for belief properties. Cast in its most intuitive form, the premise is simply that if a particular belief of yours is true and a particular belief of mine is false, then they are not the same belief. A bit more precisely: If a belief token of one subject differs in truth value from a belief token of another subject, then the tokens are not of the same type. Given our recent account of belief states, this is equivalent to a sufficient condition for the non-identity of belief properties: If an instantiation of belief property p_1 differs in truth value from an instantiation of belief property p_2, then p_1 and p_2 are different properties. This premise hardly constitutes an analysis of our notion of sameness of belief, since we surely do not hold belief tokens to be of the same type if they merely have the same truth value. But no matter. There is no need here to explicate our intuitive notion of belief identity in any detail. What the premise does provide is a necessary condition on any state counting as a belief. If a pair of states can be type identical (i.e., can be instantiations of the same property) while differing in truth value, then the states are not beliefs as we ordinarily conceive of them.

Before putting my premise to work, it might be helpful to note how the premise can be derived from a quite traditional philosophical account of the nature of beliefs. According to this account, belief is a relation between a person and a proposition. Two persons have the same belief (instantiate the same belief property) if they are belief-related to the same proposition. And, finally, propositions are taken to be the vehicles of truth, so propositions with different truth values cannot be identical. Given this account of belief, it follows straightforwardly that belief tokens differing in truth value differ in type. But the entailment is not mutual, so

13. For more on this way of viewing states and events, cf. Kim (1969) and (1976). I think that most everything I say in this paper can be said as well, though not as briefly, without presupposing this account of states and events.

those who, like me, have some suspicions about the account of belief as a relation between a person and a proposition are free to explore other accounts of belief without abandoning the intuitively sanctioned premise that differences in truth value entail difference in belief.

III. The tension between autonomy and the belief-desire thesis

In this section I want to argue that a certain tension exists between the principle of psychological autonomy and the belief-desire thesis. The tension is not, strictly speaking a logical incompatibility. Rather, there is an incompatibility between the autonomy principle and some assumptions that are naturally and all but universally shared by advocates of the belief-desire thesis. The additional assumptions are that singular causal statements like the ones extractable from our little story about Jones and the lottery ticket are often true. Moreover, they are true because they are subsumed by laws which invoke the very properties which are invoked in the characterization of the beliefs and desires. A bit less abstractly, what I am assuming is that statements like 'Jones's belief that he had won the lottery was among the causes of his rushing toward the phone' are often true; and that they are true in virtue of being subsumed by laws invoking properties like *believing that he had just won the lottery*. The burden of my argument is that if we accept the principle of autonomy, then these assumptions must be rejected. More specifically, I will argue that if the autonomy principle is accepted then there are large numbers of belief properties that cannot play a role in an explanatory psychological theory. My strategy will be to examine four different cases, each representative of a large class. In each case we will consider a pair of subjects who, according to the autonomy principle, instantiate all the same explanatory psychological properties, but who have different beliefs. So if we accept the principle of psychological autonomy, then it follows that the belief properties our subjects instantiate cannot be explanatory psychological properties. After running through the examples, I will reflect briefly on the implications of the argument for the belief-desire thesis.

Case 1: Self-referential beliefs[14]

Suppose, as we did earlier, that we have the technology for creating atom for atom replicas of people. Suppose, further, that a replica for me has just been created. I believe that I have tasted a bottle of Chateau d'Yquem, 1962. Were you to ask me

14. The examples in Case 1 and Case 2, along with my thinking on these matters, have been influenced by a pair of important papers by Castañeda (1966) and (1967).

whether I had ever tasted a d'Yquem, '62, I would likely reply, 'Yes, I have.' An advocate of the belief-desire thesis would urge, plausibly enough, that my belief is among the causes of my utterance. Now if you were to ask my replica whether he had ever tasted a d'Yquem, 1962, he would likely also reply, 'Yes, I have.' And surely a belief-desire theorist will also count my replica's belief among the causes of *his* utterance. But the belief which is a cause of my replica's utterance must be of a different type from the one which is a cause of my utterance. For his belief is false; he has just been created and has never tasted a d'Yquem, nor any other wine. So by the premise we set out in Section II, the belief property he instantiates is different from the one I instantiate. Yet since we are replicas, the autonomy principle entails that we share all our explanatory psychological properties. It follows that the property of believing that I have tasted a Chateau d'Yquem, 1962, cannot be one which plays a role in an explanatory psychological theory. In an obvious way, the example can be generalized to almost all beliefs about oneself. If we adhere to the principle of autonomy, then beliefs about ourselves can play no role in the explanation of our behavior.

Case 2: Beliefs about one's spatial and temporal location

Imagine, to vary the science fiction example, that cryogenics, the art of freezing people, has been perfected to the point at which a person can be frozen, stored, then defrosted, and at the end of the ordeal be atom for atom identical with the way he was at the beginning of the freezing process. Now suppose that I submit myself to cryogenic preservation this afternoon, and, after being frozen, I am transported to Iceland where I am stored for a century or two, then defrosted. I now believe that it is the 20th century and that there are many strawberry farms nearby. It would be easy enough to tell stories which would incline the belief-desire theorists to say that each of these beliefs is serving as a cause of my actions. I will leave the details to the reader's imagination. On being defrosted, however, I would presumably still believe that it is the 20th century and that there are many strawberry farms nearby. Since my current beliefs are both true and my future beliefs both false, they are not belief tokens of the same type, and do not instantiate the same belief property. But by hypothesis, I am, on defrosting, a replica of my current self. Thus the explanatory psychological properties that I instantiate cannot have changed. So the belief property I instantiate when I now believe that it is the 20th century cannot play any role in an explanatory psychological theory. As in the previous case, the example generalizes to a large number of other beliefs involving a subject's temporal and spatial location.

Case 3: Beliefs about other people

In several recent papers, Hilary Putnam has made interesting use of the following fanciful hypothesis.[15] Suppose that in some distant corner of the universe there is a planet very much like our own. Indeed, it is so much like our own that there is a person there who is my doppelganger. He is atom for atom identical with me and has led an entirely parallel life history. Like me, my doppelganger teaches in a philosophy department, and like me has heard a number of lectures on the subject of proper names delivered by a man called 'Saul Kripke.' However, his planet is not a complete physical replica of mine. For the philosopher called 'Saul Kripke' on that planet, though strikingly similar to the one called by the same name on our planet, was actually born in a state they call 'South Dakota,' which is to the north of a state they call 'Nebraska.' By contrast, our Saul Kripke was born in Nebraska—our Nebraska, of course, not theirs. But for reasons which need not be gone into here, many people on this distant planet, including my doppelganger, hold a belief which they express by saying 'Saul Kripke was born in Nebraska.' Now I also hold a belief which I express by saying 'Saul Kripke was born in Nebraska.' However, the belief I express with those words is very different from the belief my doppelganger expresses using the same words, so different, in fact, that his belief is false while mine is true. Yet since we are dopplegangers the autonomy principle dictates that we instantiate all the same explanatory psychological properties. Thus the belief property I instantiate in virtue of believing that Saul Kripke was born in Nebraska cannot be a property invoked in an explanatory psychological theory.

Case 4: Natural kind predicates

In Putnam's doppelganger planet stories, a crucial difference between our planet and the distant one is that on our planet the substance which we call 'water,' which fills our lakes, etc. is in fact H_2O, while on the other planet the substance they call 'water' which fills their lakes, etc. is in fact some complex chemical whose chemical formula we may abbreviate XYZ. Now imagine that we are in the year 1700, and that some ancestor of mine hears a story from a source he takes to be beyond reproach to the effect that when lizards are dipped in water, they disolve. The story, let us further suppose, is false, a fact which my ancestor might discover to his dismay when attempting to dissolve a lizard. For the belief-desire theorist, the unsuccessful attempt has as one of its causes the belief that lizards dissolve in water. Now suppose that my ancestor has a doppelganger on the far off planet who is told an identical sounding story by an equally trustworthy raconteur. However, as it happens that story is true, for there are lizards that do dissolve in XYZ, though none will dissolve in H_2O. The pattern should by now be familiar. My ancestor's belief is

15. Putnam (1973) and (1975).

false, his doppelganger's is true. Thus the belief tokens instantiate different belief properties. But since ex-hypothesis the people holding the beliefs are physically identical, the belief properties they instantiate cannot function in an explanatory psychological theory.[16]

This completes my presentation of cases. Obviously, the sorts of examples we have looked at are not the only ones susceptible to the sort of argument I have been using. But let us now reflect for a moment on just what these arguments show. To begin, we should note that they do *not* show the belief-desire thesis is false. The thesis, as I have construed it here, holds that there are psychological laws which invoke various belief and desire properties and which have a substantive role to play in the explanation of behavior. Nothing we have said here would suffice to show that there are no such laws. At best, what we have shown is that, if we accept the principle of psychological autonomy, then a large class of belief properties cannot be invoked in an explanatory psychological theory. This, in turn, entails that many intuitively sanctioned singular causal statements which specify a belief as a cause of an action cannot be straightforwardly subsumed by a law. And it is just here, I think, that our argument may serve to undermine the belief-desire thesis. For the plausibility of the thesis rests, in large measure, on the plausibility of these singular causal statements. Indeed, I think the belief-desire thesis can be profitable viewed as the speculation that these intuitively sanctioned singular causal statements can be cashed out in a serious psychological theory couched in terms of beliefs and desires. In showing that large numbers of these singular causal statements cannot be cashed out in this way, we make the speculation embodied in the belief-desire thesis appear idle and unmotivated. In the section that follows, I will consider a way in which an advocate of the belief-desire thesis might try to deflect the impact of our arguments, and indicate the burden that this escape route imposes on the belief—desire theorist.

IV. A way out and its costs

Perhaps the most tempting way to contain the damage done by the arguments of the previous section is to grant the conclusions while denying their relevance to the belief-desire thesis. I imagine a critic's objection going something like this: 'Granted, if we accept the autonomy principle, then certain belief properties cannot be used in explanatory theories. But this does nothing to diminish the

16. We should note that this example and others invoking natural kind words work only if the extension of my ancestor's word 'water' is different from the extension of the word 'water' as used by my ancestor's doppelganger. I am inclined to agree with Putnam that the extensions are different. But the matter is controversial. For some support of Putnam's view, cf. Kripke (1972) and Teller (1977); for an opposing view cf. Zemach (1976). Incidentally, one critic has expressed doubt that my doppelganger and I could be physically identical if the stuff called 'water' on the far off planet is actually XYZ. Those who find the point troubling are urged to construct a parallel example using kinds of material not generally occurring within people.

plausibility of the belief-desire thesis, because the properties you have shown incompatible with autonomy are the *wrong kind* of belief properties. All of the examples you consider are cases of *de re* beliefs, none of them are *de dicto* beliefs. But those theorists who take seriously the idea of constructing a belief-desire psychological theory have in mind a theory invoking de dicto beliefs and desires. De re beliefs are a sort of hybrid; a person has a de re belief if he has a suitable underlying de dicto belief, *and* if he is related to specific objects in a certain way. But it is only the underlying de dicto belief that will play a role in psychological explanation. Thus your arguments do not cast any serious doubt on the belief-desire thesis.'[17]

Before assessing this attempt to protect the belief-desire thesis, a few remarks on the de dicto/de re distinction are in order. In the recent philosophical discussion of de re and de dicto beliefs, the focus has been on the logical relations among various sorts of belief attributions. Writers concerned with the issue have generally invoked a substitution criterion to mark the boundary between de dicto and de re belief attributions. Roughly, a belief attribution of the form

S believes that p

is de re if any name or other referring expression within p can be replaced with a co-designating term without risk of change of truth value; otherwise the attribution is de dicto.[18]

But now given this way of drawing the de re/de dicto distinction, my imagined critic is simply wrong in suggesting that all of the examples used in my arguments are cases of de re belief. Indeed, just the opposite is true; I intend all of the belief attribution in my examples to be understood in the de dicto sense, and all my arguments work quite as well when they are read in this way. Thus, for example, in

17. The idea that de dicto beliefs are psychologically more basic is widespread. For a particularly clear example, cf. Armstrong (1973), pp. 25–31. Of the various attempts to analyze de re beliefs in terms of de dicto beliefs, perhaps the best known are to be found in Kaplan (1968) and Chisholm (1976).

18. The substitutional account of the de re/de dicto distinction has a curious consequence that has been little noted. Though most belief sentences of the form

S believes that Fa

can be used to make either de re or de dicto attributions, the substitutional account entails that some can only be used to make de re attributions. Consider, for example,

(i) Quine believes that the Queen of England is a turtle.

The claim of course, is false. Indeed, it is *so* false that it could not be used to make a de dicto belief attribution. For in all likelihood, there is *no* name or definite description φ denoting Elizabeth II such that

Quine believes that φ is a turtle

is true. Thus 'Quine believes that the Queen of England is a turtle' is false and cannot be turned into a truth by the replacement of 'the Queen of England' by a co-designating expression. So on the substitutional account, this sentence can be used to make only de re attributions. A parallel problem besets Quine's well known substitutional account of a *purely referential postion* (Quine [1960], pp. 142 ff.). In (i), the position occupied by 'the Queen of England' can only be regarded as purely referential.

Case 3 I attribute to myself the belief that Saul Kripke was born in Nebraska. But I intend this to be understood in such a way that

Stich believes 'φ' was born in Nebraska

might well be false if 'φ' were replaced by a term which, quite unbeknownst to me, in fact denotes Saul Kripke.

There is, however, another way the critic could press his attack that sidesteps my rejoinder. Recently, a number of writers have challenged the substitutional account of the de dicto/de re distinction. The basic idea underlying their challenge is that the term 'de re' should be used for all belief attributions which intend to ascribe a 'real' relation of some sort between the believer and the object of his belief. The notion of a real relation is contrasted with the sort of relation that obtains between a person and an object when the object happens to satisfy some description that the person has in mind.[19] Burge, for example, holds that 'a *de dicto* belief is a belief in which the believer is related only to a completely expressed proposition (*dictum*),' in contrast to a de re belief which is 'a belief whose correct ascription places the believer in an appropriate, *nonconceptual, contextual relation* to the objects the belief is about.'[20] Thus, if Brown believes that the most prosperous Oriental rug dealer in Los Angeles is an Armenian, and if he believes it simply because he believes all prosperous Oriental rug dealers are Armenian, but has no idea who the man may be, then his belief is de dicto. By contrast, if Brown is an intimate of the gentleman, he may have the de re belief that the most prosperous Oriental rug dealer in Los Angeles is an Armenian. The sentence

Brown believes that the most prosperous Oriental rug dealer in Los Angeles is an Armenian.

is thus ambiguous, since it may be used either in the de re sense to assert that Brown and the rug dealer stand in some 'appropriate, nonconceptual, contextual relation' or in the de dicto sense which asserts merely that Brown endorses the proposition that the most prosperous rug dealer in Los Angeles (whoever he may be) is an Armenian.

The problem with the substitutional account of the de dicto/de re distinction is that it classifies as de dicto many belief attributions which impute a 'real' relation between the believer and the object of his belief. In many belief attributions the names or definite descriptions that occur in the content sentence do a sort of double duty. First, they serve the function commonly served by names and descriptions; they indicate (or refer to) an object, in this case the object to which the believer is said to be related. The names or descriptions in the content sentence *also* may serve to indicate how the believer conceives of the object, or how he might

19. For more on the distinction between 'real' relations and mere 'satisfaction' relations, cf. Kim (1977).

20. Burge (1977), pp. 345 and 346; last emphasis added.

characterize it. When a name or description serving both roles is replaced by a codesignating expression which does *not* indicate how the believer conceives of the object, then the altered attribution (interpreted in the 'double duty' sense) will be false. Thus the substitutional account classifies the original attribution as de dicto, despite its imputation of a 'real' relation between believer and object.[21]

Now if the de dicto/de re distinction is drawn by classifying as de re all those belief attributions which impute a 'real' relation between believer and object, then the critic conjured in the first paragraph of this section is likely right in his contention that all of my arguments invoke examples of de re beliefs. Indeed, the strategy of my arguments is to cite an example of a de re (i.e., 'real relation') belief, then construct a second example in which the second believer is a physical replica of the first, but has no 'real relation' to the object of the first believer's belief. However, to grant this much is not to grant that the critic has succeeded in blunting the point of my arguments.

Let me begin my rejoinder with a fussy point. The critic's contentions were two: first, that my examples all invoked de re belief properties; second, that de re belief properties are hybrids and are analyzable into de dicto belief properties. The fussy point is that even if both the critic's contentions are granted, the critic would not quite have met my arguments head on. The missing premise is that de dicto belief properties (construed now according to the 'real relation' criterion) are in fact compatible with the principle of psychological autonomy. This premise may be true, but the notion of a 'real' relation, on which the current account of de dicto belief properties depends, is sufficiently obscure that it is hard to tell. Fortunately, there is a simple way to finesse the problem. Let us introduce the term *autonomous beliefs* for those beliefs that a subject must share with all his replicas; and let us use the term *non-autonomous* for those beliefs which a subject need not share with his replica.[22] More generally, we can call any property which an organism must share with its replicas an *autonomous property*. We can now reconstrue the critic's claims as follows:

1) All the examples considered in Section III invoke non-autonomous belief properties.
2) Non-autonomous belief properties are hybrids, analyzable into an underlying autonomous belief property (which can play a role in psychological explanation) plus some further relation(s) between the believer and the object of his belief.

On the first point I naturally have no quarrel, since a principal purpose of this paper is to show that a large class of belief properties are non-autonomous. On the

21. For more on this 'double duty' view of the role of names and descriptions in content sentences, cf. Loar (1972).

22. Of course when the notion of a 'real relation' has been suitably sharpened it might well turn out that the autonomous/non-autonomous distinction coincides with the 'real relation' version of the de dicto/de re distinction.

second claim, however, I would balk, for I am skeptical that the proposed analysis can in fact be carried off. I must hasten to add that I know of no *argument* sufficient to show that the analysis is impossible. But, of course, my critic has no argument either. Behind my skepticism is the fact that no such analysis has ever been carried off. Moreover, the required analysis is considerably more demanding than the analysis of de re belief in terms of de dicto belief, when the distinction between the two is drawn by the substitutional criterion. For the class of autonomous beliefs is significantly smaller than the class of de dicto beliefs (characterized substitutionally).[23] And the most impressive attempts to reduce de re beliefs to de dicto plainly will not be of much help for the analysis my critic proposes.[24] But enough. I have already conceded that I cannot prove my critic's project is impossible. What I do hope to have established is that the critic's burden is the burden of the belief-desire theorist. If the reduction of non-autonomous beliefs to autonomous beliefs cannot be carried off, then there is small prospect that a psychological theory couched in terms of beliefs and desires will succeed in explaining any substantial part of human behavior.

A final point. It might be argued that, however difficult the analysis of non-autonomous beliefs to autonomous ones may be, it must be possible to carry it off. For, the argument continues, a subject's non-autonomous beliefs are determined in part by the autonomous psychological properties he instantiates and in part by his various relations to the objects of the world. Were either of these components suitably altered, the subject's non-autonomous beliefs would be altered as well. And since non-autonomous beliefs are jointly determined by autonomous psychological properties and by other relations, there must be some analysis, however complex, which specifies how this joint determination works. Now this last claim is not one I would want to challenge. I am quite prepared to grant that non-autonomous beliefs admit of some analysis in terms of autonomous psychological properties plus other relations. But what seems much more doubtful to me is that the autonomous properties invoked in the analysis would be *belief properties.* To see the reasons for my doubt, let us reflect on the picture suggested by the examples in Section III. In each case we had a pair of subjects who shared all their autonomous properties though their non-autonomous beliefs differed in truth value. The difference in truth value, in turn, was rooted in a difference in reference; the beliefs were simply about different persons, places or times. In short, the beliefs represented different states of affairs. If the non-autonomous belief properties of these examples are to be analyzed into autonomous psychological properties plus various historical or external relations, then it is plausible to suppose that the autonomous psychological properties do not determine a truth value, an appropriate reference or a represented

23. For example, when I say, 'I believe that Kripke was born in Nebraska,' I am attributing to myself a belief which is substitutionally de dicto, but not autonomous.

24. Kaplan's strategy, for example, will be of no help, since his analysans are, for the most part, non-autonomous substitutionally de dicto belief sentences. Cf. Kaplan (1968) and Burge (1977), pp. 350, ff.

state of affairs. So the state of exhibiting one (or more) of these autonomous properties itself has no truth value, is not referential, and does not represent anything. And this, I would urge, is more than enough reason to say that it is not a belief at all. None of this amounts to an *argument* that non-autonomous beliefs are not analyzable into autonomous ones. Those who seek such an analysis are still free to maintain that there will be at least one autonomous belief among the autonomous properties in the analysans of each non-autonomous belief property. But in the absence of an argument for this claim, I think few will find it particularly plausible. The ball is in the belief-desire theorists's court.[25, 26]

References

Alston, W. P. (1967a). 'Motives and Motivation,' *The Encyclopedia of Philosophy*. New York.

——(1967b). 'Wants, Actions and Causal Explanations,' in H. N. Castañeda, ed., *Intentionality, Minds and Perception*. Detroit.

Armstrong, D. M. (1973). *Belief, Truth and Knowledge*. Cambridge.

Atkinson, J. W. (1964). *An Introduction to Motivation*. New York.

Brandt, R. B. and Jaegwon Kim (1963). 'Wants as Explanations of Actions,' *The Journal of Philosophy* 60.

Burge, T. (1977). 'Belief De Re,' *The Journal of Philosophy* 74.

Castañeda, H. N. (1966). ''He': A Study in the Logic of Self-Consciousness,' *Ratio* 8.

——(1967). 'Indicators and Quasi Indicators,' *American Philosophical Quarterly* 4.

Chisholm, R. (1976). *Person & Object*. LaSalle, Ill.

Davidson, D. (1963). 'Actions, Reasons and Causes,' *The Journal of Philosophy* 60.

——(1967). 'Causal Relations,' *Journal of Philosophy* 64.

——(1970). 'Mental Events,' in L. Foster & J. W. Swanson, eds., *Experience And Theory*. Amherst. (See Chapter 39 of this volume.)

Fodor, J. (1980). 'Methodological Solipsism Considered as a Research Strategy in Cognitive Psychology,' *The Behavioral and Brain Sciences*, vol. 2., no. 3.

Goldman, A. (1970). *A Theory of Human Action*. Englewood Cliffs.

Hempel, C. G. (1965). *Aspects of Scientific Explanation*. New York.

Kaplan, D. (1968). 'Quantifying In,' *Synthese* 19.

Kim, J. (1969). 'Events and Their Descriptions: Some Considerations,' in *Essays in Honor of C. G. Hempel*, ed. by N. Rescher, et al., Dordrecht, Holland.

——(1973). 'Causation, Nomic Subsumption and the Concept of Event,' *Journal of Philosophy* 70.

—— (1976). 'Events As Property-Exemplifications,' in M. Brand & D. Walton, eds., *Action Theory*. Dordrecht Holland.

——(1977). 'Perception & Reference Without Causality,' *Journal of Philosophy* 74.

——(1978). 'Supervenience and Nomological Incommensurables,' *American Philosophical Quarterly* 15.

25. I am indebted to Robert Cummins, Jaegwon Kim, William Alston, and John Bennett for their helpful comments on the topics discussed in this paper.
26. After completing this paper, I was delighted to discover a very similar view in Perry (1979). Fodor (1980) defends a version of the principle of psychological autonomy.

Kriple, S. (1972). 'Naming and Necessity,' in D. Davidson & G. Harman, eds., *Semantics of Natural Language*. Dordrecht, Holland.

Loar, B. (1972). 'Reference and Propositional Attitudes,' *Philosophical Review* 80.

Newell, A. and H. A. Simon (1972). *Human Problem Solving*. Englewood Cliffs.

Nisbitt, R. and L. Ross (1980) *Human Inference: Strategies and Shortcomings of Social Judgment*. Englewood Cliffs: Prentice-Hall.

Putnam, H. (1973). 'Meaning and Reference,' *The Journal of Philosophy* 70.

——(1975). 'The Meaning of "Meaning",' in K. Gunderson, ed., *Language, Mind and Knowledge*. Minneapolis.

Perry, J. (1979). 'The Problem of The Essential Indexical,' NOUS 13.

Quine, W. V. O. (1960). *Word and Object*. Cambridge: MIT Press.

Stich, S. (1983). *From Folk Psychology to Cognitive Science: The Case Against Belief*. Cambridge: MIT Press.

Teller, P. (1977). 'Indicative Introduction,' *Philosophical Studies* 31.

Zemach, E. (1976). 'Putnam's Theory on the Reference of Substance Terms,' *The Journal of Philosophy* 83.

Chapter 23

Eliminative materialism and the propositional attitudes*

Paul M. Churchland

Eliminative materialism is the thesis that our common-sense conception of psychological phenomena constitutes a radically false theory, a theory so fundamentally defective that both the principles and the ontology of that theory will eventually be displaced, rather than smoothly reduced, by completed neuroscience. Our mutual understanding and even our introspection may then be reconstituted within the conceptual framework of completed neuroscience, a theory we may expect to be more powerful by far than the common-sense psychology it displaces, and more substantially integrated within physical science generally. My purpose in this paper is to explore these projections, especially as they bear on (1) the principal elements of common-sense psychology: the propositional attitudes (beliefs, desires, etc.), and (2) the conception of rationality in which these elements figure.

This focus represents a change in the fortunes of materialism. Twenty years ago, emotions, qualia, and 'raw feels' were held to be the principal stumbling blocks for the materialist program. With these barriers dissolving,[1] the locus of opposition has shifted. Now it is the realm of the intentional, the realm of the propositional attitude, that is most commonly held up as being both irreducible to and ineliminable in favor of anything from within a materialist framework. Whether and why this is so, we must examine.

Such an examination will make little sense, however, unless it is first appreciated that the relevant network of common-sense concepts does indeed constitute an empirical theory, with all the functions, virtues, *and perils* entailed by that status. I shall therefore begin with a brief sketch of this view and a summary rehearsal of its rationale. The resistance it encounters still surprises me. After all, common sense

Paul M. Churchland, 'Eliminative Materialism and the Propositional Attitudes', *Journal of Philosophy* 78 (1981).

* An earlier draft of this paper was presented at the University of Ottawa, and to the *Brain, Mind, and Person* colloquium at SUNY/Oswego. My thanks for the suggestions and criticisms that have informed the present version.

1. See Paul Feyerabend, 'Materialism and the Mind-Body Problem,' *Review* of *Metaphysics*, XVII. 1, 65 (September 1963): 49–66; Richard Rorty, 'Mind-Body Identity, Privacy, and Categories,' *ibid.*, XIX. 1, 73 (September 1965): 24–54; and my *Scientific Realism and the Plasticity of Mind* (New York: Cambridge, 1979).

has yielded up many theories. Recall the view that space has a preferred direction in which all things fall; that weight is an intrinsic feature of a body; that a force-free moving object will promptly return to rest; that the sphere of the heavens turns daily; and so on. These examples are clear, perhaps, but people seem willing to concede a theoretical component within common sense only if (1) the theory and the common sense involved are safely located in antiquity, and (2) the relevant theory is now so clearly false that its speculative nature is inescapable. Theories are indeed easier to discern under these circumstances. But the vision of hindsight is always 20/20. Let us aspire to some foresight for a change.

I. Why folk psychology is a theory

Seeing our common-sense conceptual framework for mental phenomena as a theory brings a simple and unifying organization to most of the major topics in the philosophy of mind, including the explanation and prediction of behavior, the semantics of mental predicates, action theory, the other-minds problem, the intentionality of mental states, the nature of introspection, and the mind-body problem. Any view that can pull this lot together deserves careful consideration.

Let us begin with the explanation of human (and animal) behavior. The fact is that the average person is able to explain, and even predict, the behavior of other persons with a facility and success that is remarkable. Such explanations and predictions standardly make reference to the desires, beliefs, fears, intentions, perceptions, and so forth, to which the agents are presumed subject. But explanations presuppose laws—rough and ready ones, at least—that connect the explanatory conditions with the behavior explained. The same is true for the making of predictions, and for the justification of subjunctive and counterfactual conditional concerning behavior. Reassuringly, a rich network of common-sense laws can indeed be reconstructed from this quotidean commerce of explanation and anticipation; its principles are familiar homilies; and their sundry functions are transparent. Each of us understands others, as well as we do, because we share a tacit command of an integrated body of lore concerning the law-like relations holding among external circumstances, internal states, and overt behavior. Given its nature and functions, this body of lore may quite aptly be called 'folk psychology.'[2]

This approach entails that the semantics of the terms in our familiar mentalistic vocabulary is to be understood in the same manner as the semantics of theoretical terms generally: the meaning of any theoretical term is fixed or constituted by the network of laws in which it figures. (This position is quite distinct from logical behaviorism. We deny that the relevant laws are analytic, and it is the lawlike

2. We shall examine a handful of these laws presently. For a more comprehensive sampling of the laws of folk psychology, see my *Scientific Realism and Plasticity of Mind, op. cit.*, ch. 4. For a detailed examination of the folk principles that underwrite action explanations in particular, see my 'The Logical Character of Action Explanations,' *Philosophical Review*, LXXIX, 2 (April 1970): 214–236.

connections generally that carry the semantic weight, not just the connections with overt behavior. But this view does account for what little plausibility logical behaviorism did enjoy.)

More importantly, the recognition that folk psychology is a theory provides a simple and decisive solution to an old skeptical problem, the problem of other minds. The problematic conviction that another individual is the subject of certain mental states is not inferred deductively from his behavior, nor is it inferred by inductive analogy from the perilously isolated instance of one's own case. Rather, that conviction is a singular *explanatory hypothesis* of a perfectly straightforward kind. Its function, in conjunction with the background laws of folk psychology, is to provide explanations/predictions/understanding of the individual's continuing behavior, and it is credible to the degree that it is successful in this regard over competing hypotheses. In the main, such hypotheses are successful, and so the belief that others enjoy the internal states comprehended by folk psychology is a reasonable belief.

Knowledge of other minds thus has no essential dependence on knowledge of one's own mind. Applying the principles of our folk psychology to our behavior, a Martian could justly ascribe to us the familiar run of mental states, even though his own psychology were very different from ours. He would not, therefore, be 'generalizing from his own case.'

As well, introspective judgments about one's own case turn out not to have any special status or integrity anyway. On the present view, an introspective judgment is just an instance of an acquired habit of conceptual response to one's internal states, and the integrity of any particular response is always contingent on the integrity of the acquired conceptual framework (theory) in which the response is framed. Accordingly, one's *introspective* certainty that one's mind is the seat of beliefs and desires may be as badly misplaced as was the classical man's *visual* certainty that the star-flecked sphere of the heavens turns daily.

Another conundrum is the intentionality of mental states. The 'propositional attitudes,' as Russell called them, form the systematic core of folk psychology; and their uniqueness and anomalous logical properties have inspired some to see here a fundamental contrast with anything that mere physical phenomena might conceivably display. The key to this matter lies again in the theoretical nature of folk psychology. The intentionality of mental states here emerges not as a mystery of nature, but as a structural feature of the concepts of folk psychology. Ironically, those same structural features reveal the very close affinity that folk psychology bears to theories in the physical sciences. Let me try to explain.

Consider the large variety of what might be called 'numerical attitudes' appearing in the conceptual framework of physical science: '. . . has a mass_{kg} of *n*', '. . . has a velocity of *n*', '. . . has a temperature_{K} of *n*', and so forth. These expressions are predicate-forming expressions: when one substitutes a singular term for a number into the place held by '*n*', a determinate predicate results. More interestingly, the relations between the various 'numerical attitudes' that result are precisely the relations between the numbers 'contained' in those attitudes. More interesting still, the argument place that takes the singular terms for numbers is open to quantification. All this permits the expression of generalizations concerning the lawlike relations that hold between the various numerical attitudes in nature. Such laws involve quantification over numbers, and they exploit the mathematical relations holding in that domain. Thus, for example,

(1) $(x)(f)(m)[((x \text{ has a mass of } m) \,\&\, (x \text{ suffers a net force of } f)) \supset (x \text{ accelerates at } f/m)]$

Consider now the large variety of propositional attitudes: '. . . believes that *p*', '. . . desires that *p*', '. . . fears that *p*', '. . . is happy that *p*', etc. These expressions are predicate-forming expressions also. When one substitutes a singular term for a proposition into the place held by '*p*', a determinate predicate results, e.g., '. . . believes that Tom is tall.' (Sentences do not generally function as singular terms, but it is difficult to escape the idea that when a sentence occurs in the place held by '*p*', it is there functioning as or like a singular term. On this, more below.) More interestingly, the relations between the resulting propositional attitudes are characteristically the relations that hold between the propositions 'contained' in them, relations such as entailment, equivalence, and mutual inconsistency. More interesting still, the argument place that takes the singular terms for propositions is open to quantification. All this permits the expression of generalizations concerning the lawlike relations that hold among propositional attitudes. Such laws involve quantification over propositions, and they exploit various relations holding in that domain. Thus, for example,

(2) $(x)(p)[(x \text{ fears that } p) \supset (x \text{ desires that} \sim p)]$

(3) $(x)(p)[(x \text{ hopes that } p) \,\&\, (x \text{ discovers that } p)) \supset (x \text{ is pleased that } p)]$

(4) $(x)(p)(q)[((x \text{ believes that } p) \,\&\, (x \text{ believes that (if } p \text{ then } q))) \supset (\text{barring confusion, distraction, etc., } x \text{ believes that } q)]$

(5) $(x)(p)(q)[((x \text{ desires that } p) \,\&\, (x \text{ believes that (if } q \text{ then } p)) \,\&\, (x \text{ is able to bring it about that } q)) \supset (\text{barring conflicting desires or preferred strategies, } x \text{ brings it about that } q)]$[3]

3. Staying within an objectual interpretation of the quantifiers, perhaps the simplest way to make systematic sense of expressions like ⌜*x* believes that *p*⌝ and closed sentences formed therefrom is just to construe whatever occurs in the nested position held by '*p*', '*q*', etc. as there having the function of a singular term. Accordingly, the standard connectives, as they occur between terms in that nested position, must be construed as there functioning as operators that form compound singular terms from other singular terms, and not as sentence operators. The compound singular terms so formed denote the appropriate compound propositions. Substitutional quantification will of course underwrite a different interpretation, and there are other approaches as well. Especially appealing is the prosentential approach of Dorothy Grover, Joseph Camp, and Nuel Belnap, 'A Prosentential Theory of Truth,' *Philosophical Studies*, XXVII, 2 (February 1975): 73–125. But the resolution of these issues is not vital to the present discussion.

Not only is folk psychology a theory, it is so *obviously* a theory that it must be held a major mystery why it has taken until the last half of the twentieth century for philosophers to realize it. The structural features of folk psychology parallel perfectly those of mathematical physics; the only difference lies in the respective domain of abstract entities they exploit—numbers in the case of physics, and propositions in the case of psychology.

Finally, the realization that folk psychology is a theory puts a new light on the mind-body problem. The issue becomes a matter of how the ontology of one theory (folk psychology) is, or is not, going to be related to the ontology of another theory (completed neuroscience); and the major philosophical positions on the mind-body problem emerge as so many different anticipations of what future research will reveal about the intertheoretic status and integrity of folk psychology.

The identity theorist optimistically expects that folk psychology will be smoothly *reduced* by completed neuroscience, and its ontology preserved by dint of transtheoretic identities. The dualist expects that it will prove *ir*reducible to completed neuroscience, by dint of being a nonredundant description of an autonomous, nonphysical domain of natural phenomena. The functionalist also expects that it will prove irreducible, but on the quite different grounds that the internal economy characterized by folk psychology is not, in the last analysis, a law-governed economy of natural states, but an abstract organization of functional states, an organization instantiable in a variety of quite different material substrates. It is therefore irreducible to the principles peculiar to any of them.

Finally, the eliminative materialist is also pessimistic about the prospects for reduction, but his reason is that folk psychology is a radically inadequate account of our internal activities, too confused and too defective to win survival through intertheoretic reduction. On his view it will simply be displaced by a better theory of those activities.

Which of these fates is the real destiny of folk psychology, we shall attempt to divine presently. For now, the point to keep in mind is that we shall be exploring the fate of a theory, a systematic, corrigible, speculative *theory*.

II. Why folk psychology might (really) be false

Given that folk psychology is an empirical theory, it is at least an abstract possibility that its principles are radically false and that its ontology is an illusion. With the exception of eliminative materialism, however, none of the major positions takes this possibility seriously. None of them doubts the basic integrity or truth of folk psychology (hereafter, 'FP'), and all of them anticipate a future in which its laws and categories are conserved. This conservatism is not without some foundation. After all, FP does enjoy a substantial amount of explanatory and predictive success. And what better grounds than this for confidence in the integrity of its categories?

What better grounds indeed? Even so, the presumption in FP's favor is spurious, born of innocence and tunnel vision. A more searching examination reveals a different picture. First, we must reckon not only with FP's successes, but with its explanatory failures, and with their extent and seriousness. Second, we must consider the long-term history of FP, its growth, fertility, and current promise of future development. And third, we must consider what sorts of theories are *likely* to be true of the etiology of our behavior, given what else we have learned about ourselves in recent history. That is, we must evaluate FP with regard to its coherence and continuity with fertile and well-established theories in adjacent and overlapping domains—with evolutionary theory, biology, and neuroscience, for example—because active coherence with the rest of what we presume to know is perhaps the final measure of any hypothesis.

A serious inventory of this sort reveals a very troubled situation, one which would evoke open skepticism in the case of any theory less familiar and dear to us. Let me sketch some relevant detail. When one centers one's attention not on what FP can explain, but on what it cannot explain or fails even to address, one discovers that there is a very great deal. As examples of central and important mental phenomena that remain largely or wholly mysterious within the framework of FP, consider the nature and dynamics of mental illness, the faculty of creative imagination, or the ground of intelligence differences between individuals. Consider our utter ignorance of the nature and psychological functions of sleep, that curious state in which a third of one's life is spent. Reflect on the common ability to catch an outfield fly ball on the run, or hit a moving car with a snowball. Consider the internal construction of a 3-D visual image from subtle differences in the 2-D array of stimulations in our respective retinas. Consider the rich variety of perceptual illusions, visual and otherwise. Or consider the miracle of memory, with its lightning capacity for relevant retrieval. On these and many other mental phenomena, FP sheds negligible light.

One particularly outstanding mystery is the nature of the learning process itself, especially where it involves large-scale conceptual change, and especially as it appears in its pre-linguistic or entirely nonlinguistic form (as in infants and animals), which is by far the most common form in nature. FP is faced with special difficulties here, since its conception of learning as the manipulation and storage of propositional attitudes founders on the fact that how to formulate, manipulate, and store a rich fabric of propositional attitudes is itself something that is learned, and is only one among many acquired cognitive skills. FP would thus appear constitutionally incapable of even addressing this most basic of mysteries.[4]

Failures on such a large scale do not (yet) show that FP is a false theory, but they

4. A possible response here is to insist that the cognitive activity of animals and infants is linguaformal in its elements, structures, and processing right from birth. J. A. Fodor, in *The Language of Thought* (New York: Crowell 1975), has erected a positive theory of thought on the assumption that the innate forms of cognitive activity have precisely the form here denied. For a critique of Fodor's view, see Patricia Churchland, 'Fodor on Language Learning,' *Synthese*, XXXVIII, 1 (May 1978): 149–159.

do move that prospect well into the range of real possibility, and they do show decisively that FP is *at best* a highly superficial theory, a partial and unpenetrating gloss on a deeper and more complex reality. Having reached this opinion, we may be forgiven for exploring the possibility that FP provides a positively misleading sketch of our internal kinematics and dynamics, one whose success is owed more to selective application and forced interpretation on our part than to genuine theoretical insight on FP's part.

A look at the history of FP does little to allay such fears, once raised. The story is one of retreat, infertility, and decadence. The presumed domain of FP used to be much larger than it is now. In primitive cultures, the behavior of most of the elements of nature were understood in intentional terms. The wind could know anger, the moon jealousy, the river generosity, the sea fury, and so forth. These were not metaphors. Sacrifices were made and auguries undertaken to placate or divine the changing passions of the gods. Despite its sterility, this animistic approach to nature has dominated our history, and it is only in the last two or three thousand years that we have restricted FP's literal application to the domain of the higher animals.

Even in this preferred domain, however, both the content and the success of FP have not advanced sensibly in two or three thousand years. The FP of the Greeks is essentially the FP we use today, and we are negligibly better at explaining human behavior in its terms than was Sophocles. This is a very long period of stagnation and infertility for any theory to display, especially when faced with such an enormous backlog of anomalies and mysteries in its own explanatory domain. Perfect theories, perhaps, have no need to evolve. But FP is profoundly imperfect. Its failure to develop its resources and extend its range of success is therefore darkly curious, and one must query the integrity of its basic categories. To use Imre Lakatos' terms, FP is a stagnant or degenerating research program, and has been for millennia.

Explanatory success to date is of course not the only dimension in which a theory can display virtue or promise. A troubled or stagnant theory may merit patience and solicitude on other grounds; for example, on grounds that it is the only theory or theoretical approach that fits well with other theories about adjacent subject matters, or the only one that promises to reduce to or be explained by some established background theory whose domain encompasses the domain of the theory at issue. In sum, it may rate credence because it holds promise of theoretical integration. How does FP rate in this dimension?

It is just here, perhaps, that FP fares poorest of all. If we approach *homo sapiens* from the perspective of natural history and the physical sciences, we can tell a coherent story of his constitution, development, and behavioral capacities which encompasses particle physics, atomic and molecular theory, organic chemistry, evolutionary theory, biology, physiology, and materialistic neuroscience. That story, though still radically incomplete, is already extremely powerful, outperforming FP at many points even in its own domain. And it is deliberately and self-consciously coherent with the rest of our developing world picture. In short, the greatest theoretical synthesis in the history of the human race is currently in our hands, and parts of it already provide searching descriptions and explanations of human sensory input, neural activity, and motor control.

But FP is no part of this growing synthesis. Its intentional categories stand magnificently alone, without visible prospect of reduction to that larger corpus. A successful reduction cannot be ruled out, in my view, but FP's explanatory impotence and long stagnation inspire little faith that its categories will find themselves neatly reflected in the framework of neuroscience. On the contrary, one is reminded of how alchemy must have looked as elemental chemistry was taking form, how Aristotelean cosmology must have looked as classical mechanics was being articulated, or how the vitalist conception of life must have looked as organic chemistry marched forward.

In sketching a fair summary of this situation, we must make a special effort to abstract from the fact that FP is a central part of our current *lebenswelt*, and serves as the principal vehicle of our interpersonal commerce. For these facts provide FP with a conceptual inertia that goes far beyond its purely theoretical virtues. Restricting ourselves to this latter dimension, what we must say is that FP suffers explanatory failures on an epic scale, that it has been stagnant for at least twenty-five centuries, and that its categories appear (so far) to be incommensurable with or orthogonal to the categories of the background physical science whose long-term claim to explain human behavior seems undeniable. Any theory that meets this description must be allowed a serious candidate for outright elimination.

We can of course insist on no stronger conclusion at this stage. Nor is it my concern to do so. We are here exploring a possibility, and the facts demand no more, and no less, than it be taken seriously. The distinguishing feature of the eliminative materialist is that he takes it very seriously indeed.

III. Arguments against elimination

Thus the basic rationale of eliminative materialism: FP is a theory, and quite probably a false one; let us attempt, therefore to transcend it.

The rationale is clear and simple, but many find it uncompelling. It will be objected that FP is not, strictly speaking, an *empirical* theory; that it is not false, or at least not refutable by empirical considerations; and that it ought not or cannot be transcended in the fashion of a defunct empirical theory. In what follows we shall examine these objections as they flow from the most popular and best-founded of the competing positions in the philosophy of mind: functionalism.

An antipathy toward eliminative materialism arises from two distinct threads running through contemporary functionalism. The first thread concerns the *normative* character of FP, or at least of that central core of FP which treats of the propositional attitudes. FP, some will say, is a characterization of an ideal, or at least praiseworthy mode of internal activity. It outlines not only what it is to have and process beliefs and desires, but also (and inevitably) what it is to be rational in their administration. The ideal laid down by FP may be imperfectly achieved by empirical humans, but this does not impugn FP as a normative characterization. Nor need such failures seriously impugn FP even as a descriptive characterization, for it remains true that our activities can be both usefully and accurately understood as rational *except for* the occasional lapse due to noise, interference, or other breakdown, which defects empirical research may eventually unravel. Accordingly, though neuroscience may usefully augment it, FP has no pressing need to be displaced, even as a descriptive theory; nor could it be replaced, qua normative characterization, by any descriptive theory of neural mechanisms, since rationality is defined over propositional attitudes like beliefs and desires. FP, therefore, is here to stay.

Daniel Dennett has defended a view along these lines.[5] And the view just outlined gives voice to a theme of the property dualists as well. Karl Popper and Joseph Margolis both cite the normative nature of mental and linguistic activity as a bar to their penetration or elimination by any descriptive/materialist theory.[6] I hope to deflate the appeal of such moves below.

The second thread concerns the *abstract* nature of FP. The central claim of functionalism is that the principles of FP characterize our internal states in a fashion that makes no reference to their intrinsic nature or physical constitution. Rather, they are characterized in terms of the network of causal relations they bear to one another, and to sensory circumstances and overt behavior. Given its abstract specification, that internal economy may therefore be realized in a nomically heterogeneous variety of physical systems. All of them may differ, even radically, in their physical constitution, and yet at another level, they will all share the same nature. This view, says Fodor, 'is compatible with very strong claims about the ineliminabilty of mental language from behavioral theories.'[7] Given the real possibility of multiple instantiations in heterogeneous physical substrates, we cannot eliminate the functional characterization in favor of any theory peculiar to one such substrate. That would preclude our being able to describe the (abstract) organization that any one instantiation shares with all the other. A functional characterization of our internal states is therefore here to stay.

This second theme, like the first, assigns a faintly stipulative character to FP, as if the onus were on the empirical systems to instantiate faithfully the organization that FP specifies, instead of the onus being on FP to describe faithfully the internal activities of a naturally distinct class of empirical systems. This impression is enhanced by the standard examples used to illustrate the claims of functionalism—

5. Most explicitly in 'Three Kinds of Intentional Psychology', in R. Healy, ed. *Reduction, Time, and Reality* (Cambridge: Cambridge University Press, 1975): 37–60; (See Chapter 19 of this volume), but this theme of Dennett's goes all the way back to his 'Intentional Systems,' this JOURNAL, LXVIII, 4 (Feb. 25, 1971): 87–106; reprinted in his *Brainstorms* (Montgomery, Vt.: Bradford Books, 1978).
6. Popper, *Objective Knowledge* (New York: Oxford, 1972); with J. Eccles, *The Self and Its Brain* (New York: Springer Verlag, 1978). Margolis, *Persons and Minds* (Boston: Reidel, 1978).
7. *Psychological Explanation* (New York: Random House, 1968), p. 116.

mousetraps, valve-lifters, arithmetical calculators, computers, robots, and the like. These are artifacts, constructed to fill a preconceived bill. In such cases, a failure of fit between the physical system and the relevant functional characterization impugns only the former, not the latter. The functional characterization is thus removed from empirical criticism in a way that is most unlike the case of an empirical theory. One prominent functionalist—Hilary Putnam—has argued outright that FP is not a corrigible theory at all.[8] Plainly, if FP is construed on these models, as regularly it is, the question of its empirical integrity is unlikely ever to pose itself, let alone receive a critical answer.

Although fair to some functionalists, the preceding is not entirely fair to Fodor. On his view the aim of psychology is to find the *best* functional characterization of ourselves, and what that is remains an empirical question. As well, his argument for the ineliminability of mental vocabulary from psychology does not pick out current FP in particular as ineliminable. It need claim only that *some* abstract functional characterization must be retained, some articulation or refinement of FP perhaps.

His estimate of eliminative materialism remains low, however. First, it is plain that Fodor thinks there is nothing fundamentally or interestingly wrong with FP. On the contrary, FP's central conception of cognitive activity—as consisting in the manipulation of propositional attitudes—turns up as the central element in Fodor's own theory on the nature of thought (*The Language of Thought, op. cit.*). And second, there remains the point that, whatever tidying up FP may or may not require, it cannot be displaced by any naturalistic theory of our physical substrate, since it is the abstract functional features of his internal states that make a person, not the chemistry of his substrate.

All of this is appealing. But almost none of it, I think, is right. Functionalism has too long enjoyed its reputation as a daring and *avant garde* position. It needs to be revealed for the short-sighted and reactionary position it is.

IV. The conservative nature of functionalism

A valuable perspective on functionalism can be gained from the following story. To begin with, recall the alchemists' theory of inanimate matter. We have here a long and variegated tradition, of course, not a single theory, but our purposes will be served by a gloss.

The alchemists conceived the 'inanimate' as entirely continuous with animated matter, in that the sensible and behavioral properties of the various substances are owed to the ensoulment of baser matter by various spirits or essences. These non-material aspects were held to undergo development, just as we find growth and development in the various souls of plants, animals, and humans. The alchemist's

8. 'Robots: Machines or Artificially Created Life?', this JOURNAL, LXI, 21 (Nov. 12, 1964): 668–691, pp. 675, 681 ff.

peculiar skill lay in knowing how to seed, nourish, and bring to maturity the desired spirits enmattered in the appropriate combinations.

On one orthodoxy, the four fundamental spirits (for 'inanimate' matter) were named 'mercury,' 'sulphur,' 'yellow arsenic,' and 'sal ammoniac.' Each of these spirits was held responsible for a rough but characteristic syndrome of sensible, combinatorial, and causal properties. The spirit mercury, for example, was held responsible for certain features typical of metallic substances—their shininess, liquefiability, and so forth. Sulphur was held responsible for certain residual features typical of metals, and for those displayed by the ores from which running metal could be distilled. Any given metallic substance was a critical orchestration principally of these two spirits. A similar story held for the other two spirits, and among the four of them a certain domain of physical features and transformations was rendered intelligible and controllable.

The degree of control was always limited, of course. Or better, such prediction and control as the alchemists possessed was owed more to the manipulative lore acquired as an apprentice to a master, than to any genuine insight supplied by the theory. The theory followed, more than it dictated, practice. But the theory did supply some rhyme to the practice, and in the absence of a developed alternative it was sufficiently compelling to sustain a long and stubborn tradition.

The tradition had become faded and fragmented by the time the elemental chemistry of Lavoisier and Dalton arose to replace it for good. But let us suppose that it had hung on a little longer—perhaps because the four-spirit orthodoxy had become a thumbworn part of everyman's common sense—and let us examine the nature of the conflict between the two theories and some possible avenues of resolution.

No doubt the simplest line of resolution, and the one which historically took place, is outright displacement. The dualistic interpretation of the four essences—as immaterial spirits—will appear both feckless and unnecessary given the power of the corpuscularian taxonomy of atomic chemistry. And a reduction of the old taxonomy to the new will appear impossible, given the extent to which the comparatively toothless old theory cross-classifies things relative to the new. Elimination would thus appear the only alternative—*unless* some cunning and determined defender of the alchemical vision has the wit to suggest the following defense.

Being 'ensouled by mercury,' or 'sulphur,' or either of the other two so-called spirits, is actually a *functional* state. The first, for example, is defined by the disposition to reflect light, to liquefy under heat, to unite with other matter in the same state, and so forth. And each of these four states is related to the others, in that the syndrome for each varies as a function of which of the other three states is also instantiated in the same substrate. Thus the level of description comprehended by the alchemical vocabulary is abstract: various material substances, suitably 'ensouled,' can display the features of a metal, for example, or even of gold specifically. For it is the total syndrome of occurrent and causal properties which matters, not the corpuscularian details of the substrate. Alchemy, it is concluded, comprehends a level of organization in reality distinct from and irreducible to the organization found at the level of corpuscularian chemistry.

This view might have had considerable appeal. After all, it spares alchemists the burden of defending immaterial souls that come and go; it frees them from having to meet the very strong demands of a naturalistic reduction; and it spares them the shock and confusion of outright elimination. Alchemical theory emerges as basically all right! Nor need they appear too obviously stubborn or dogmatic in this. Alchemy as it stands, they concede, may need substantial tidying up, and experience must be our guide. But we need not fear its naturalistic displacement, they remind us, since it is the particular orchestration of the syndromes of occurrent and causal properties which makes a piece of matter gold, not the idiosyncratic details of its corpuscularian substrate. A further circumstance would have made this claim even more plausible. For the fact is, the alchemists *did* know how to make gold, in this relevantly weakened sense of 'gold', and they could do so in a variety of ways. Their 'gold' was never as perfect, alas, as the 'gold' nurtured in nature's womb, but what mortal can expect to match the skills of nature herself?

What this story shows is that it is at least possible for the constellation of moves, claims, and defenses characteristic of functionalism to constitute an outrage against reason and truth, and to do so with a plausibility that is frightening. Alchemy is a terrible theory, well-deserving of its complete elimination, and the defense of it just explored is reactionary, obfuscatory, retrograde, and wrong. But in historical context, that defense might have seemed wholly sensible, even to reasonable people.

The alchemical example is a deliberately transparent case of what might well be called 'the functionalist strategem,' and other cases are easy to imagine. A cracking good defense of the phlogiston theory of combustion can also be constructed along these lines. Construe being highly phlogisticated and being dephlogisticated as functional states defined by certain syndromes of causal dispositions; point to the great variety of natural substrates capable of combustion and calxification; claim an irreducible functional integrity for what has proved to lack any natural integrity; and bury the remaining defects under a pledge to contrive improvements. A similar recipe will provide new life for the four humors of medieval medicine, for the vital essence or archeus of pre-modern biology, and so forth.

If its application in these other cases is any guide, the functionalist strategem is a smokescreen for the preservation of error and confusion. Whence derives our assurance that in contemporary journals the same charade is not being played out on behalf of FP? The parallel with the case of alchemy is in all other respects distressingly complete, right down to the parallel between the search for artificial gold and the search for artificial intelligence!

Let me not be misunderstood on this last point. Both aims are worthy aims: thanks to nuclear physics, artificial (but real) gold is finally within our means, if only in submicroscopic quantities; and artificial (but real) intelligence eventually will be. But just as the careful orchestration of superficial syndromes was the wrong way to produce genuine gold, so may the careful orchestration of superficial syndromes be the wrong way to produce genuine intelligence. Just as with gold, what may be required is that our science penetrate to the underlying *natural* kind that gives rise to the total syndrome directly.

In summary, when confronted with the explanatory impotence, stagnant history, and systematic isolation of the intentional idioms of FP, it is not an adequate or responsive defense to insist that those idioms are abstract, functional, and irreducible in character. For one thing, this same defense could have been mounted with comparable plausibility no matter *what* haywire network of internal states our folklore had ascribed to us. And for another, the defense assumes essentially what is at issue: it assumes that it is the intentional idioms of FP, plus or minus a bit, that express the *important* features shared by all cognitive systems. But they may not. Certainly it is wrong to assume that they do, and then argue against the possibility of a materialistic displacement on grounds that it must descibe matters at a level that is different from the important level. This just begs the question in favor of the older framework.

Finally, it is very important to point out that eliminative materialism is strictly *consistent* with the claim that the essence of a cognitive system resides in the abstract functional organization of its internal states. The eliminative materialist is not committed to the idea that the correct account of cognition *must* be a naturalistic account, though he may be forgiven for exploring the possibility. What he does hold is that the correct account of cognition, whether functionalistic or naturalistic, will bear about as much resemblance to FP as modern chemistry bears to four-spirit alchemy.

Let us now try to deal with the argument, against eliminative materialism, from the normative dimension of FP. This can be dealt with rather swiftly, I believe.

First, the fact that the regularities ascribed by the intentional core of FP are predicated on certain logical relations among propositions is not by itself grounds for claiming anything essentially normative about FP. To draw a relevant parallel, the fact that the regularities ascribed by the classical gas law are predicated on arithmetical relations between numbers does not imply anything essentially normative about the classical gas law. And logical relations between propositions are as much an objective matter of abstract fact as are arithmetical relations between numbers. In this respect, the law

(4) $(x)(p)(q)$ [((x believes that p) & (x believes that (if p then q))) $\supset$ (barring confusion, distraction, etc., x believes that q)]

is entirely on a par with the classical gas law

(6) $(x)(P)(V)(\mu)$[((x has a pressure P) & (x has a volume V) & (x has a quantity μ)) $\supset$ (barring very high pressure or density, x has a temperature of $PV/\mu R$)]

A normative dimension enters only because we happen to *value* most of the patterns ascribed by FP. But we do not value all of them. Consider

(7) $(x)(p)[((x \text{ desires with all his heart that } p)\ \&\ (x \text{ learns that} \sim p))$
$\supset$ (barring unusual strength of character.
x is shattered that $\sim p$)]

Moreover, and as with normative convictions generally, fresh insight may motivate major changes in what we value.

Second, the laws of FP ascribe to us only a very minimal and truncated rationality, not an ideal rationality as some have suggested. The rationality characterized by the set of all FP laws falls well short of an ideal rationality. This is not surprising. We have no clear or finished conception of ideal rationality anyway; certainly the ordinary man does not. Accordingly, it is just not plausible to suppose that the explanatory failures from which FP suffers are owed primarily to human failure to live up to the ideal standard it provides. Quite to the contrary, the conception of rationality it provides appears limping and superficial, especially when compared with the dialectical complexity of our scientific history, or with the ratiocinative virtuosity displayed by any child.

Third, even if our current conception of rationality—and more generally, of cognitive virtue—is largely constituted within the sentential/propositional framework of FP, there is no guarantee that this framework is adequate to the deeper and more accurate account of cognitive virtue which is clearly needed. Even if we concede the categorial integrity of FP, at least as applied to language-using humans, it remains far from clear that the basic parameters of intellectual virtue are to be found at the categorial level comprehended by the propositional attitudes. After all, language use is something that is learned, by a brain already capable of vigorous cognitive activity; language use is acquired as only one among a great variety of learned manipulative skills; and it is mastered by a brain that evolution has shaped for a great many functions, language use being only the very latest and perhaps the least of them. Against the background of these facts, language use appears as an extremely peripheral activity, as a racially idiosyncratic mode of social interaction which is mastered thanks to the versatility and power of a more basic mode of activity. Why accept then, a theory of cognitive activity that models its elements on the elements of human language? And why assume that the fundamental parameters of intellectual virtue are or can be defined over the elements at this superficial level?

A serious advance in our appreciation of cognitive virtue would thus seem to *require* that we go beyond FP, that we transcend the poverty of FP's conception of rationality by transcending its propositional kinematics entirely, by developing a deeper and more general kinematics of cognitive activity, and by distinguishing within this new framework which of the kinematically possible modes of activity are to be valued and encouraged (as more efficient, reliable, productive, or whatever). Eliminative materialism thus does not imply the end of our normative concerns. It implies only that they will have to be reconstituted at a more revealing level of understanding, the level that a matured neuroscience will provide.

What a theoretically informed future might hold in store for us, we shall now turn to explore. Not because we can foresee matters with any special clarity, but because it is important to try to break the grip on our imagination held by the propositional kinematics of FP. As far as the present section is concerned, we may summarize our conclusions as follows. FP is nothing more and nothing less than a culturally entrenched theory of how we and the higher animals work. It has no special features that make it empirically invulnerable, no unique functions that make it irreplaceable, no special status of any kind whatsoever. We shall turn a skeptical ear then, to any special pleading on its behalf.

V. Beyond folk psychology

What might the elimination of FP actually involve—not just the comparatively straightforward idioms for sensation, but the entire apparatus of propositional attitudes? That depends heavily on what neuroscience might discover, and on our determination to capitalize on it. Here follow three scenarios in which the operative conception of cognitive activity is progressively divorced from the forms and categories that characterize natural language. If the reader will indulge the lack of actual substance, I shall try to sketch some plausible form.

First suppose that research into the structure and activity of the brain, both fine-grained and global, finally does yield a new kinematics and correlative dynamics for what is now thought of as cognitive activity. The theory is uniform for all terrestrial brains, not just human brains, and it makes suitable conceptual contact with both evolutionary biology and non-equilibrium thermodynamics. It ascribes to us, at any given time, a set or configuration of complex states, which are specified within the theory as figurative 'solids' within a four- or five-dimensional phase space. The laws of the theory govern the interaction, motion, and transformation of these 'solid' states within that space, and also their relations to whatever sensory and motor transducers the system possesses. As with celestial mechanics, the exact specification of the 'solids' involved and the exhaustive accounting of all dynamically relevant adjacent 'solids' is not practically possible, for many reasons, but here also it turns out that the obvious approximations we fall back on yield excellent explanations/predictions of internal change and external behavior; at least in the short term. Regarding long-term activity, the theory provides powerful and unified accounts of the learning process, the nature of mental illness, and variations in character and intelligence across the animal kingdom as well as across individual humans.

Moreover, it provides a straightforward account of 'knowledge,' as traditionally conceived. According to the new theory, any declarative sentence to which a speaker would give confident assent is merely a one-dimensional *projection*—through the compound lens of Wernicke's and Broca's areas onto the idiosyncratic surface of the speaker's language—a one-dimensional projection of a four- or five-dimensional 'solid' that is an element in his true kinematical state. (Recall the shadows on the wall of Plato's cave.) Being projections of that inner reality, such sentences do carry significant information regarding it and are thus fit to function as elements in a communication system. On the other hand, being *sub*dimensional projections, they reflect but a narrow part of the reality projected. They are therefore *un*fit to represent the deeper reality in all its kinematically, dynamically, and even normatively relevant respects. That is to say, a system of propositional attitudes, such as FP, must inevitably fail to capture what is going on here, though it may reflect just enough superficial structure to sustain an alchemylike tradition among folk who lack any better theory. From the perspective of the newer theory, however, it is plain that there simply are no law-governed states of the kind FP postulates. The real laws governing our internal activities are defined over different and much more complex kinematical states and configurations, as are the normative criteria for developmental integrity and intellectual virtue.

A theoretical outcome of the kind just described may fairly be counted as a case of elimination of one theoretical ontology in favor of another, but the success here imagined for systematic neuroscience need not have any sensible effect on common practice. Old ways die hard, and in the absence of some practical necessity, they may not die at all. Even so, it is not inconceivable that some segment of the population, or all of it, should become intimately familiar with the vocabulary required to characterize our kinematical states, learn the laws governing their interactions and behavioral projections, acquire a facility in their first-person ascription, and displace the use of FP altogether, even in the marketplace. The demise of FP's ontology would then be complete.

We may now explore a second and rather more radical possibility. Everyone is familiar with Chomsky's thesis that the human mind or brain contains innately and uniquely the abstract structures for learning and using specifically human natural languages. A competing hypothesis is that our brain does indeed contain innate structures, but that those structures have as their original and still primary function the organization of perceptual experience, the administration of linguistic categories being an acquired and additional function for which evolution has only incidentally suited them.[9] This hypothesis has the advantage of not requiring the evolutionary saltation that Chomsky's view would seem to require, and there are other advantages as well. But these matters need not concern us here. Suppose, for our purposes, that this competing view is true, and consider the following story.

Research into the neural structures that fund the organization and processing of perceptual information reveals that they are capable of administering a great variety of complex tasks, some of them showing a complexity far in excess of that shown by natural language. Natural languages, it turns out, exploit only a very elementary portion of the available machinery, the bulk of which serves far more

9. Richard Gregory defends such a view in 'The Grammar of Vision,' *Listener*, LXXXIII, 2133 (February 1970): 242–246; reprinted in his *Concepts and Mechanisms of Perception* (London: Duckworth, 1975), pp. 622–629.

complex activities beyond the ken of the propositional conceptions of FP. The detailed unraveling of what that machinery is and of the capacities it has makes it plain that a form of language far more sophisticated than 'natural' language, though decidedly 'alien' in its syntactic and semantic structures, could also be learned and used by our innate systems. Such a novel system of communication, it is quickly realized, could raise the efficiency of information exchange between brains by an order of magnitude, and would enhance epistemic evaluation by a comparable amount, since it would reflect the underlying structure of our cognitive activities in greater detail than does natural language.

Guided by our new understanding of those internal structures, we manage to construct a new system of verbal communication entirely distinct from natural language, with a new and more powerful combinatorial grammar over novel elements forming novel combinations with exotic properties. The compounded strings of this alternative system—call them 'übersatzen'—are not evaluated as true or false, nor are the relations between them remotely analogous to the relations of entailment, etc., that hold between sentences. They display a different organization and manifest different virtues.

Once constructed, this 'language' proves to be learnable; it has the power projected; and in two generations it has swept the planet. Everyone uses the new system. The syntactic forms and semantic categories of so-called 'natural' language disappear entirely. And with them disappear the propositional attitudes of FP, displaced by a more revealing scheme in which (of course) 'übersatzenal attitudes' play the leading role. FP again suffers elimination.

This second story, note, illustrates a theme with endless variations. There are possible as many different 'folk psychologies' as there are possible differently structured communication systems to serve as models for them.

A third and even stranger possibility can be outlined as follows. We know that there is considerable lateralization of function between the two cerebral hemispheres, and that the two hemispheres make use of the information they get from each other by way of the great cerebral commissure—the corpus callosum—a giant cable of neurons connecting them. Patients whose commissure has been surgically severed display a variety of behavioral deficits that indicate a loss of access by one hemisphere to information it used to get from the other. However, in people with callosal agenesis (a congenital defect in which the connecting cable is simply absent), there is little or no behavioral deficit, suggesting that the two hemisphere have learned to exploit the information carried in other less direct pathways connecting them through the subcortical regions. This suggests that, even in the normal case, a developing hemisphere *learns* to make use of the information the cerebral commissure deposits at its doorstep. What we have then, in the case of a normal human, is two physically distinct cognitive systems (both capable of independent function) responding in a systematic and learned fashion to exchanged information. And what is especially interesting about this case is the sheer amount of information exchanged. The cable of the commissure consists of

≈200 million neurons,[10] and even if we assume that each of these fibres is capable of one of only two possible states each second (a most conservative estimate), we are looking at a channel whose information capacity is $> 2 \times 10^8$ binary bits/second. Compare this to the < 500 bits/second capacity of spoken English.

Now, if two distinct hemispheres can learn to communicate on so impressive a scale, why shouldn't two distinct brains learn to do it also? This would require an artificial 'commissure' of some kind, but let us suppose that we can fashion a workable transducer for implantation at some site in the brain that research reveals to be suitable, a transducer to convert a symphony of neural activity into (say) microwaves radiated from an aerial in the forehead, and to perform the reverse function of converting received microwaves back into neural activation. Connecting it up need not be an insuperable problem. We simply trick the normal processes of dendretic arborization into growing their own myriad connections with the active microsurface of the transducer.

Once the channel is opened between two or more people, they can learn (*learn*) to exchange information and coordinate their behavior with the same intimacy and virtuosity displayed by your own cerebral hemispheres. Think what this might do for hockey teams, and ballet companies, and research teams! If the entire population were thus fitted out, spoken language of any kind might well disappear completely, a victim of the 'why crawl when you can fly?' principle. Libraries become filled not with books, but with long recordings of exemplary bouts of neural activity. These constitute a growing cultural heritage, an evolving 'Third World,' to use Karl Popper's terms. But they do not consist of sentences or arguments.

How will such people understand and conceive of other individuals? To this question I can only answer, 'In roughly the same fashion that your right hemisphere 'understands' and 'conceives of' your left hemisphere—intimately and efficiently, but not propositionally!'

These speculations, I hope, will evoke the required sense of untapped possibilities, and I shall in any case bring them to a close here. Their function is to make some inroads into the aura of inconceivability that commonly surrounds the idea that we might reject FP. The felt conceptual strain even finds expression in an argument to the effect that the thesis of eliminative materialism is incoherent since it denies the very conditions presupposed by the assumption that it is meaningful. I shall close with a brief discussion of this very popular move.

As I have received it, the reductio proceeds by pointing out that the statement of eliminative materialism is just a meaningless string of marks or noises, unless that string is the expression of a certain *belief*, and a certain *intention* to communicate, and a *knowledge* of the grammar of the language, and so forth. But if the statement of eliminative materialism is true, then there are no such states to express. The statement at issue would then be a meaningless string of marks or noises. It would therefore *not* be true. Therefore it is not true. Q.E.D.

10. M. S. Gazzaniga and J. E. LeDoux, *The Integrated Mind* (New York: Plenum Press, 1975).

The difficulty with any nonformal reductio is that the conclusion against the initial assumption is always no better than the material assumptions invoked to reach the incoherent conclusion. In this case the additional assumptions involve a certain theory of meaning, one that presupposes the integrity of FP. But formally speaking, one can as well infer, from the incoherent result, that this theory of meaning is what must be rejected. Given the independent critique of FP leveled earlier, this would even seem the preferred option. But in any case, one cannot simply assume that particular theory of meaning without begging the question at issue, namely, the integrity of FP.

The question-begging nature of this move is most graphically illustrated by the following analogue, which I owe to Patricia Churchland.[11] The issue here, placed in the seventeenth century, is whether there exists such a substance as *vital spirit.* At the time, this substance was held, without significant awareness of real alternatives, to be that which distinguished the animate from the inanimate. Given the monopoly enjoyed by this conception, given the degree to which it was integrated with many of our other conceptions, and given the magnitude of the revisions any serious alternative conception would require, the following refutation of any anti-vitalist claim would be found instantly plausible.

The anti-vitalist says that there is no such thing as vital spirit. But this claim is self-refuting. The speaker can expect to be taken seriously only if his claim cannot. For if the claim is true, then the speaker does not have vital spirit and must be *dead.* But if he is dead, then his statement is a meaningless string of noises. devoid of reason and truth.

The question-begging nature of this argument does not. I assume, require elaboration. To those moved by the earlier argument. I commend the parallel for examination.

The thesis of this paper may be summarized as follows. The propositional attitudes of folk psychology do not constitute an unbreachable barrier to the advancing tide of neuroscience. On the contrary, the principled displacement of folk psychology is not only richly possible, it represents one of the most intriguing theoretical displacements we can currently imagine.

11. 'Is Determinism Self-Refuting?', *Mind* 90 (1981): 99–101.

Chapter 24

Cognitive suicide

Lynne Rudder Baker

To deny the common-sense conception of the mental is to abandon all our familiar resources for making sense of any claim, including the denial of the common-sense conception. It may be thought that the image of Neurath's ship being rebuilt at sea plank by plank, may be of service to those denying the common-sense conception. On the contrary, the image works the other way. Local repairs, in the common-sense conception, presuppose a concept of content, but content seems not susceptible to physicalistic formulation. Thus, physicalists are in no position to replace the common-sense conception plank by plank. From a consistent physicalistic point of view, what is at issue must be the entire framework of attitudes specified by 'that'-clauses.[1] If it is hazardous, as it surely is, to attempt to rebuild a ship at sea all at once, it is all the more hazardous to undertake rebuilding with no replacement material available.

On the other hand, in the absence of a replacement, it is literally inconceivable that the common-sense conception of the mental is false. But it is such a thought that, with a measure of trepidation, I next want to explore. I shall set out several ways in which denial of the commonsense conception may be self-defeating or otherwise pragmatically incoherent. If the thesis denying the common-sense conception is true, then the concepts of rational acceptability, of assertion, of cognitive error, even of truth and falsity are called into question. It remains to be seen whether or not such concepts (or suitable successors) can be reconstructed without presupposing the truth of attributions of content. Of the three kinds of incoherence I discuss, the first two may be familiar (though not, I think, sufficiently appreciated).[2]

Lynne Rudder Baker, edited extract from 'Cognitive Suicide', chap. 7 of *Saving Belief: A Critique of Physicalism* (Princeton: Princeton University Press, 1987).

1. The arguments in this chapter are aimed at those prepared to relinquish attitudes specifiable by 'that'-clauses, whether or not they want to develop some other concept of content not specifiable by 'that'-clauses. Content in the common-sense conception is specified by 'that'-clauses.
2. See, for example, Norman Malcolm, 'The Conceivability of Mechanism,' *Philosophical Review* 77 (1968), 45–77. Also, Lewis White Beck, *The Actor and the Spectator* (New Haven: Yale University Press, 1975), formulates a sense in which arguments for mechanism may be 'self-stultifying.'

Rational acceptability at risk

The first way in which the view denying the common-sense conception may be self-defeating is this: Anyone who claims that the thesis is rationally acceptable lapses into pragmatic incoherence because the thesis denying the common-sense conception undermines the concept of rational acceptability.

The skeptic about the common-sense conception has two, perhaps insurmountable, obstacles to overcome: one concerns the idea of *accepting* a proposition or theory; the other, the idea of *justifiably* accepting a proposition or theory. Obviously, if the common-sense conception is eliminated, no one is justified in believing anything; indeed, no one believes anything, justifiably or not. The skeptic who would salvage the idea of rational acceptability is then left with two problems. First, he must come up with some successor to the family that includes 'believes that,' 'accepts that,' and other such expressions, which will permit a distinction between, say, 'accepting' (or whatever the content-free successor of accepting is) one thing and 'accepting' another *without adverting to content.* The arguments of Part I, which reveal the difficulty, if not the impossibility, of providing nonintentional and nonsemantic sufficient conditions for a state's having a particular content give us reason to be dubious about making the correct distinctions in a vocabulary that does not attribute content.

Putting aside worries about how a content-free mental state can replace acceptance, the second difficulty here concerns the normative notions of rationality, justification, and good argument. If the thesis denying the common-sense conception is true, then it is unclear that there could ever be good arguments for it or that anyone could ever be justified in 'accepting' (the successor of accepting) it. The thesis seems to undermine the possibility of good argument and justification generally.

In many cases, if a person is justified in accepting a thesis, then there exists evidence for the thesis, which the person appreciates. It is difficult to see how the ideas of evidence and of appreciating the evidence can be unpacked in the absence of states with content. Of course, the skeptic about the common-sense conception, reaching for consistency, may 'agree' (or do whatever replaces agreement in a post-common-sense framework) that ideas of evidence and of appreciating the evidence are part of the common-sense conception, which is to be left behind. Then, if the skeptic holds that the thesis denying the common-sense conception can be rationally accepted, he owes us some other 'account' (an appropriate successor of an account) of 'justification' (an appropriate successor of a justification) that does not presuppose the repudiated ideas. The successor concepts must allow both for a distinction between being 'justified' in 'accepting' p and not being so 'justified' and for a distinction between being 'justified' in 'accepting' p and being 'justified' in 'accepting' q, without presupposing that there are contentful states. But every skeptic about the common-sense conception freely uses ideas integral to the common-sense conception in his attack (another common-sense idea that the skeptic must replace) on it.

The language of accepting and denying, as well as of evidence, hypothesis, argument, is part and parcel of the common-sense conception. Before the skeptic about the common-sense conception has any claim on us, he must replace these ideas with successor ideas that make no appeal to states with content (or otherwise do without such ideas). What is at stake here, as all parties to the discussion agree, are all attributions of contentful states. If the successor concepts advert to content, then they do not avoid the common-sense conception that I am defending. But if they do not advert to content, it is difficult to see how they can make the needed distinctions between accepting (or rather its content-free successor) one thesis and accepting another. And the absence of such distinctions would make it impossible to accept any thesis at all.

Here, then, is a dilemma for the skeptic about the common-sense conception: From the perspective that denies the common-sense conception, either he can distinguish being 'justified' in 'accepting' that *p* from being 'justified' in 'accepting' that *q* or not. If not, then no one is 'justified' in 'accepting' the thesis that denies the common-sense conception of the mental or any other thesis. But if so, then, in light of the arguments of Part I, the skeptic must absolve himself of the charge that he is covertly assuming contentful states by producing relevant content-free successors to concepts of acceptance and justification. If the skeptic declines on grounds that absolving oneself of charges is part of the common-sense conception that is to be discarded, then he is playing into the hand of the critic who says that the skeptic jeopardizes any standards of rational acceptability.[3]

On the face of it, one can hardly see how to free rich concepts, like that of being justified in accepting a particular thesis, of layers of content. At least, the challenge is there for the skeptic about common sense to come up with replacement concepts that permit distinctions like those between accepting and not accepting a thesis and between being justified and not being justified in accepting a thesis—replacement concepts that make the needed distinctions without presupposing that any attribution of content has ever been true.

Churchland has taken the tack of urging the rational acceptability of denying the common-sense conception by proposing as an alternative to states with content an account of what constitutes a cognitive economy. Regardless of what alternative account he proposes, however, this move is not available to him. In order to be an *alternative* account to the common-sense conception, the successor must at least allow scientists to identify certain systems as cognitive; and in order to be an alternative *account* of cognition, the successor must allow scientists to hypothesize

3. Suppose that a skeptic tried a kind of *reductio ad absurdum* of the common-sense conception by using, say, the notion of rational acceptability in order to show that that notion has insurmountable internal problems; from this, he concludes, so much the worse for the idea of rational acceptance. It would remain unclear how any such argument could have a claim on us. We obviously could not rationally accept it.

that cognitive states have such-and-such a character. But no one has shown how concepts like those of *identifying* something as a cognitive system or *hypothesizing* that cognitive states lack content have application in the absence of content. Indeed, it is difficult to see how anything could count as advancing an alternative to the commonsense conception in the absence of contentful states. Without contentful states, what makes it *p* rather than *q* that one 'advances'? What makes an audible emission one of advancing at all?[4]

Indeed, it is difficult to see how to construe what scientists are doing generally when they engage in research if they lack mental states with content. The ideas of evidence, hypothesis, and experiment at least seem to presuppose content. (Or that is the only way I know to put it, even though I do not see how 'seems to presuppose something' could be true of anything if we have no contentful states.) It would help to see an account (or rather, a content-free successor to an account) of these ideas or of successor ideas in terms of which science could be practiced without presupposing states with content. The common-sense conception pervades the language of rational acceptability in scientific activity as well as in everyday affairs.

To sum up: The first threat of self-defeat for the thesis denying the common-sense conception of the mental stems from the consequences for the concept of rational acceptability. Without a new account of how there can be rational acceptability in the absence of belief and intention, we have no way to evaluate the claim denying the common-sense conception. This first threat suggests that, apart from the common-sense conception, we may not be able to say much about our so-called rational practices. The next kind of pragmatic incoherence suggests that, apart from the common-sense conception, we may not be able to say anything at all.

Assertion at risk

The second way in which the thesis denying the common-sense conception may be self-defeating is this: Anyone who asserts that view lapses into pragmatic incoherence because the thesis undermines the concept of assertibility; at least, he must offer some indication of how there can be assertion without belief.[5] Both Patricia Churchland and Paul Churchland have denied charges that, if a certain thesis is true, it cannot be asserted. Paul Churchland has aimed to rebut the claim that

4. An objection that I do not meet the thrust of the eliminativists' arguments would seem to presuppose the common-sense standpoint. If eliminativism is correct, then in what sense do anyone's bodily movements qualify as arguments at all? Arguments about the allegedly self-defeating character of anything are, I think, frustrating to people on both sides of the issue. People on each side think that those on the other miss the point. From my side, it seems that I ask straightforward questions (like that above), which require answers but receive none.

5. It should be clear that I am not asking for a reduction of speech to thought; in particular, I do not suppose that thought exhibits intrinsic intentionality and speech exhibits derived intentionality. I do not think that a reduction either way—from language to thought to brain, or from thought to language to physicalistic theory of meaning—is promising.

eliminative materialism—a corollary of the view that the commonsense conception is radically mistaken—is self-refuting. Here is how he sets out the argument that he intends to undermine:

> [T]he statement of eliminative materialism is just a meaningless string of marks or noises, unless that string is the expression of a certain *belief*, and a certain *intention* to communicate, and a *knowledge* of the grammar of the language, and so forth. But if the statement of eliminative materialism is true, then there are no such states to express. The statement at issue would then be a meaningless string of marks or noises. It would therefore *not* be true. Therefore it is not true. Q.E.D.[6]

Churchland finds this argument question-begging and illustrates his point by presenting an argument against antivitalism, which, he claims, is both parallel to the above argument against eliminative materialism and obviously question-begging. The argument that he claims to be parallel is this:

> The anti-vitalist says that there is no such thing as vital spirit. But this claim is self-refuting. The speaker can expect to be taken seriously only if his claim cannot. For if the claim is true, then the speaker does not have vital spirit and must be *dead*. But if he is dead, then his statement is a meaningless string of noises, devoid of reason and truth.[7]

But the arguments fail to be parallel in two crucial respects. First, the pairs of imaginary disputants differ in the presuppositions they share. The antivitalist would agree with the vitalist that being alive is a necessary condition for making a claim; he simply differs in his account of what it is to be alive. The eliminative materialist, on the other hand, could not consistently agree with his opponent that having beliefs or other attitudes identified by content is a necessary condition for making claims. The eliminative materialist is not offering a different account of what it is to have beliefs; he is denying that anyone has beliefs. The parallel to an eliminative materialist would be an antivitalist who held that dead men make claims. Therefore, the silliness of the argument against antivitalism has no bearing on the argument against eliminative materialism.

Second, the error in the argument against antivitalism has no echo in the argument against eliminative materialism. It is a mistake to charge the antivitalist with being dead on account of lacking a vital spirit *either* on the assumption that antivitalism is true *or* on the assumption that antivitalism is false. If antivitalism is true, then the lack of a vital spirit is irrelevant to death; if it is false, then the antivitalist, who mistakenly denies vitalism, has a vital spirit and is not dead.

But the argument against eliminative materialism, stated more carefully than Churchland concedes, challenges the eliminative materialist to show how there can

6. Paul M. Churchland, 'Eliminative Materialism and Propositional Attitudes,' *Journal of Philosophy* 78 (1981), 89 (Chapter 23, p. 399 of this volume.); cf. his *Matter and Consciousness* (Cambridge, Mass.: MIT/Bradford, 1984), 48 (emphasis his).

7. Churchland, 'Eliminative Materialism and Propositional Attitudes,' 89 (p. 400 of this volume) (emphasis his).

be assertion without belief or other states with content. It begs no question to assume, as the argument against eliminative materialism does, that eliminative materialism is true.[8]

Churchland explains his rejection of the argument that eliminative materialism is self-defeating by claiming that the argument assumes a certain theory of meaning, one that presupposes the integrity of the common-sense conception. But only to a minimal extent is a particular theory of meaning assumed; issues that divide theorists like Frege, Davidson, Kaplan, Montague, and Grice are wholly irrelevant to the argument that eliminative materialism is self-refuting. The argument against eliminative materialism makes the minimal assumption that language can be meaningful only if it is possible that someone mean something.

Of course, history is full of received views that turn out to be false. That a hot object heats up a cold object when caloric fluid flows from one to the other or that knowledge is justified true belief are two examples.[9] Unlike the assumption about meaningful language, however, these examples are instances of explicitly formulated theories. Moreover, the superseding theories make it intelligible why people said (false) things like 'The sun revolves around the earth.' But from the perspective that denies the common-sense conception, it would be a mystery why anybody would ever say (false) things like 'I ran inside because I thought I heard the phone ring.' (Of course, the emission of the noises would have a physical explanation.) Not only would thinking that one heard the phone ring fail to be either reason for or cause of one's rapid house-entering behavior, but worse, one would never have *thought* that she heard the phone ring. Nor, if the common-sense conception is false, did anyone ever *seem* to think that she heard the phone ring. As noted earlier, a mental state of seeming to think that *p* would be, if anything, more content-laden than one of merely thinking that *p*.

It is clearly incumbent upon anyone who wants to deny the near-platitude that language can be meaningful only if it is possible that someone mean something to show how there can be meaningful language even if no one has ever meant anything, even if no one has ever intended to say anything. The claim of the syntactic theory—that mental activity consists of relations to uninterpreted sentences—just begs for an account of what those who advocate the syntactic approach are doing when they write; without such an account, the sentences that they write can have no more claim on us than do crevices etched into the Rock of Gibralter by the weather.

Suppose someone were to say: On a speech-dispositional view, assertion does not require belief or any other state with content. So we can have assertion and language, even without contentful states. But, we should reply, a satisfactory speech-

8. This point was also made by Karl Popper in 'Is Determinism Self-Refuting?' *Mind* 92 (1983), 103, a reply to Patricia Smith Churchland, 'Is Determinism Self-Refuting?' *Mind* 90 (1981), 99–101.

9. These examples were suggested by Charles Chastain, who commented on an earlier version of this chapter at the Oberlin Colloquium in Philosophy, April 12–14, 1985.

dispositional view has yet to be developed.[10] Since assertion *simpliciter* is sincere assertion, an alternative to the common-sense view, speech-dispositional or otherwise, would have to distinguish assertion from 'noise' on the one hand and from lying on the other. Such an alternative account of assertion would be called on to do three things:

(i) Without appeal to the content of mental states, the alternative account of assertion must distinguish assertion from other audible emission. Perhaps the account would distinguish between kinds of causal history.

But it is difficult to guess how to specify the right causal history without attributing to the speaker some state with the content of what is asserted. (This difficulty will be discussed further in the next section.) Notice also that a speech-dispositional account presupposes an answer to the question of which audible emissions manifest speech dispositions and hence provides no answer to it.

(ii) The alternative account of assertion, again without appeal to the content of mental states, must distinguish sounds that count as an assertion that *p* rather than as an assertion that *q*.

This would require a physicalistic reduction of semantics much stronger than, say, Davidson's, which takes for granted the availability of an interpreted metalanguage and takes the truth predicate as a primitive. The arguments in Part I are easily modified to suggest that the difficulties in supplying nonsemantic conditions for application of semantic notions may be insurmountable.

(iii) The alternative account of assertion must at least have conceptual room for a distinction between sincere assertion and lying.

Since the distinction between sincere assertion and lying is made by reference to whether or not one believes what one is saying or whether or not one intends to mislead, it is less than obvious, to say the least, how to make out a comparable distinction without presupposing mental states with content. Certainly no one has offered any evidence that a concept like sincerity can be reconstructed without appeal to the content of mental states.

10. Quine's view, for example, seems susceptible to arguments similar to those Chomsky deployed against Skinner. See Noam Chomsky, 'A Review of Skinner's *Verbal Behavior*,' in *Readings in the Philosophy of Psychology*, vol. 1, ed. Ned Block (Cambridge, Mass.: Harvard University Press, 1980), 48–63. In addition, Alan Berger has argued that Quine's account presupposes ideas to which he is not entitled. See Berger, 'A Central Problem for a Speech-Dispositional Account of Logic and Language,' in *Studies in the Philosophy of Language*, ed. Peter A. French, Theodore E. Uehling, Jr., and Howard K. Wettstein, Midwest Studies in Philosophy, 14 (Minneapolis: University of Minnesota Press, 1989). In any case, a speech-dispositional account does not seem to meet (i)–(iii) below; nor, as we shall see, can it accommodate the locust/cricket case.

Thus, I think we have substantial reason to doubt that any alternative account of assertion that is free of appeal to contentful mental states will be forthcoming.[11]

Although Churchland has offered several scenarios in which he imagines the actual displacement of the common-sense conception by neuroscience, they all bypass the question raised here. For example, Churchland asks: 'How will such [post-common-sense conception] people understand and conceive of other individuals? To this question I can only answer, "In roughly the same fashion that your right hemisphere 'understands' and 'conceives of' your left hemisphere—intimately and efficiently, but not propositionally!"'[12] At this level of description, the analogy is unhelpful, as Churchland signals by his use of scare-quotes around 'understands' and 'conceives of.' One's right hemisphere does not conceive of one's left hemisphere at all. Not only does the idea of nonpropositional 'understanding' remain mysterious, but a strictly neurophysiological account of understanding would seem to leave us in the dark about how anything, including putative denials of the common-sense conception, could have meaning.

To sum up: The second threat of self-defeat for the thesis denying the common-sense conception stems from the consequences for assertion. Without a new 'account' of how there can be assertion in the absence of belief and intention, we have no way to interpret the claim denying the common-sense conception.[13]

Truth at risk

The third way that the view denying the common-sense conception may be self-defeating is this: If the thesis is true, it has not been shown to be formulable. We can formulate a thesis if and only if we can specify what would make it true. In addition

11. Since Stich has explicitly linked the notion of sincere assertion to belief, I should expect that he would let sincere assertion go the way of belief. He says that it is difficult to see how the notion of 'sincere assertion of p' 'could be unpacked without invoking the idea of an utterance *caused by the belief that p.*' *From Folk Psychology to Cognitive Science: The Case Against Belief* (Cambridge, Mass.: MIT/Bradford, 1983), 79 (emphasis his).
12. Churchland, 'Eliminative Materialism and Propositional Attitudes,' 88 (p. 399 of this volume). Churchland thinks that with the resources of a future scientific psychology, we could 'manage to construct a new system of verbal communication entirely distinct from natural language,' which everyone may actually come to use. In that case, the categories of natural language, along with propositional attitudes, would disappear (87) (p. 398 of this volume). I can imagine the disappearance of natural language, along with the disappearance of the human race as the result of a nuclear war, say; but neither I nor anyone else has the ability to imagine business as usual without natural language or propositional attitudes. Imagining is itself a propositional attitude. Of course, I can imagine a world without propositional attitudes; but from the fact that I imagine it, it follows that such a world is not ours.
13. It is no criticism that I presuppose the common-sense conception in discussing, for example, the possibility of a surrogate 'denial.' All we now have are common-sense ways to understand what, for example, a denial is; we cannot very well dispense with common sense and keep even a surrogate for denial, unless we have some idea of what that surrogate is. What is it? Is it just a prejudice of common sense that a denial is always a denial *of* something?

to undermining concepts of rational acceptability and of assertibility, the thesis denying the commonsense view may make incoherent the concepts of truth and falsity, as applied to mental states and language, in which case neither it nor any other thesis would be formulable.[14]

In the interest of reducing obscurity, let me make some observations. Content is attributable by 'that'-clauses. Just as a mental state has content if and only if it is correctly identifiable as, for example, a believing that *p*, so an utterance or inscription has content if and only if it is correctly identifiable as a saying that *p*. At this point, however, the contours of the terrain blur. Although these terminological matters may be carved up differently without detriment to my argument, related issues—for example, whether or not the (alleged) impropriety of 'believes that' carries over to 'says that'—are no mere matters of terminology.

I hope to avoid begging any substantive questions by joining the skeptic of the common-sense conception in his main contention, namely, that mental states have no content, that is, they are not correctly identified by 'that'-clauses. I shall urge that this contention comes to grief on the question: Can such content-free mental states have truth value? Case 1: If so, what makes mental state tokens that are not identifiable by 'that'-clauses true or false? Case 2: If not, what makes utterances and inscriptions true or false?

Anyone who denies the common-sense conception on the basis of the argument from physicalism is a scientific realist who cannot beg off these questions. Even so, since I see no reason to suppose that thought may be reduced to language or language to thought, adequate answers to these questions do not require anything resembling a scientific theory, only an indication that there is space, as it were, for answers. It is difficult to see how insistence that cognition requires a distinction between truth and falsity (or at least between being right and being wrong) could be written off as dogmatism or mere prejudice.

Case 1: Suppose that the skeptic about the common-sense conception says that, yes, mental state tokens may be true or false even without content. In this case, the skeptic must answer the question: By virtue of what is a mental state token, identified without 'that'-clauses, true?

On the horizon are only two approaches to truth available to the skeptic who denies the common-sense conception. One is to try to account for the truth of a true mental state (identified in wholly nonintentional terms) by means of a correspondence between it and a particular state of affairs. The other is to try to account for the truth of a true mental state in terms of the way that the state was caused or the way that such mental states typically are caused. I find neither of these approaches promising.

First, in the absence of attitudes identified by content, a mental state token, as identified by a physicalistic psychology (syntactic or neuro-physiological), may be

14. If one endorses a redundancy theory of truth, then the problem raised in this section about truth would reduce to the problem raised about assertibility.

true if it 'corresponds' in the right way to states of affairs. But how are mental states to be mapped on to states of affairs? Which correspondence is the right one?[15]

Given only the syntactic or neurophysiological properties of mental state tokens and the physical properties of contexts, any token may be mapped on to any state of affairs. (Indeed, it is difficult to see why any molecular configuration is to count as one mapping as opposed to another if there are no mental states with content.) A natural way to select an appropriate mapping—one that plausibly has a claim to securing truth—would be to identify mental states by content. But if mental states could be identified by content, then the skeptic about the common-sense conception would be refuted. Thus, I do not see how the truth of mental state tokens can be explained in terms of correspondence between mental state tokens and states of affairs without invoking content.

The second way to characterize the truth of mental state tokens without presupposing attitudes identified by content would be in terms of the causes of one's mental states. Truth could then be understood in terms of standard causal chains. To take an oversimplified example, snow's being white may cause, in some standard way to be specified, a certain mental state *m*, which in turn contributes to an utterance, 'Snow is white.'

But this proposal, too, as we saw in Chapter Five, has difficulties. It is unlikely that the notion of a standard causal chain can be filled out satisfactorily. The problem of specifying standard or normality conditions simply arises once again. Moreover, as the cricket/locust example indicated, two routes may be indistinguishable as long as they are described nonintentionally; yet one may lead to a belief that *p* and the other to a belief that *q*, where '*p*' and '*q*' differ in truth conditions. Finally, in many cases, a belief that *p* is not connected with the state of affairs that *p* in any obvious way.

Therefore, I do not think that the notion of correspondence or of cause will secure the distinction between truth and falsity of mental state tokens lacking content. So let us turn to case 2.

Case 2: Suppose that the skeptic about the common-sense conception says that, no, mental state tokens without content may not be true or false. In this case the skeptic must answer the question: By virtue of what are inscriptions and utterances unmoored to mental states that are true or false themselves true or false?

Before addressing these issues directly, consider the rather drastic consequence of having to conclude that, without content, mental states also lack truth value.[16] It

15. Tarski's theory of truth is of no help here. That Tarski has not formulated a 'materialistically adequate' concept of truth has been argued by Hartry Field in 'Tarski's Theory of Truth,' *Journal of Philosophy* 69 (1972), 347–375. For further criticisms, see Robert C. Stalnaker's *Inquiry* (Cambridge, Mass.: MIT/Bradford, 1984), ch. 2.

16. Denying truth value to mental states would have several further unfortunate consequences. One could not reasonably be held accountable for the truth or falsity of one's statements if their truth or falsity is in no way connected to one's mental states. One would have no duty to speak the truth and avoid falsity. Indeed, it would be a mystery how falsity and error could even be of concern to us if our mental states lacked truth value. (If mental states lack content, one could not even think that one is saying something true or that one is saying something false.)

would follow that no one is, or ever has been, in cognitive error. Still assuming for the moment that the skeptic about the common-sense conception is correct, all those false attributions or would-be attributions of belief, desire, and intention cannot be the product of any mistake on our part.

One may rather relinquish the possibility of describing anything as cognitive error before letting go of a preferred theory. Still, the difficulty of a distinction between truth and falsity, even the truth or falsity of particular inscriptions, would remain. One may utter sentences, some presumably true and some presumably false; but the truth or falsity of the sentences that one utters would have nothing to do with any semantic value of one's mental states. The falsity of any utterance would be no reflection on the speaker, whose mental states are free of any taint of error. Indeed, the fact that certain sounds we emit are true (if they are) can only be fortuitous. It would be as if we were simply transmitting sounds, whose truth or falsity is beyond our ability to appreciate. This point alone raises suspicions about how audible emissions, swinging free of semantically evaluated mental states, can be true or false. So, to return to the development of case 2, if there is no such thing as cognitive error, if mental states lack not only content but also truth value, by virtue of what are inscriptions and utterances true or false?

Truth or falsity attaches to items that are semantically interpreted. But any arbitrary mapping of symbols on to states of affairs is an interpretation. What distinguishes the mapping that pairs symbols with their truth conditions? By virtue of what does an inscription signify one state of affairs rather than another, or signify anything at all?

By now, the line is familiar. A causal account is no good: Snow's being white cannot cause 'snow is white' to express that fact. A 'use' account is no good: To say that 'snow is white' is used to express the fact that snow is white just smuggles in contentful states—for example, that people intend to express such facts. A speech-dispositional account is no good: Such an account must suppose that many people assent when queried, 'Is snow white?' But that supposition leaves the fundamental question without a hint of an answer: What makes the investigator's audible emission a query or the respondent's audible emission an assent?

In addition, a speech dispositional account would return the wrong verdict on cases like the cricket/locust example. Suppose that a radical translator comes to the ward where our two combatants languish. Since the two combatants have exactly the same dispositions, they assent to exactly the same stimulus sentences. So on a speech-dispositional analysis, their utterances should receive exactly the same translation into the translator's language. But that would be a mistake. Each is a competent speaker of his language, in which syntactically and acoustically similar tokens differ in content. In jointly producing a single token, one says that locusts are a menace; the other says that crickets are a menace.

No matter how hard the bullet one is prepared to bite, cases 1 and 2 are exhaustive: Either mental states without content can have truth value or they cannot. If they can, then we have not even a sketch of how; if they cannot, then we have not even a sketch of how inscriptions and utterances can be true or false. But without a distinction between truth and falsity, neither the thesis denying the common-sense conception nor any other is even formulable.[17]

To sum up: The third threat of self-defeat for the thesis denying the common-sense conception of the mental stems from the consequences for the distinction between truth and falsity. Without a new 'account' of how there can be truth and falsity in the absence of true attributions of content, we have no way to formulate the claim denying the common-sense conception.

Thus, in light of the considerations just presented, it seems that we can neither rationally accept nor assert nor even formulate the thesis denying the common-sense conception of the mental. Indeed, if the thesis is true, it is at least problematic whether we can rationally accept or assert or even formulate any thesis at all.[18] This seems ample reason to deny the conclusions of the arguments from physicalism.

The upshot

If the denial of the common-sense conception is self-defeating in any of the ways that I have suggested, then we must consider again the valid arguments that led to such a conclusion.

Argument from physicalism

(1) Either physicalistic psychology will vindicate (in a sense to be specified) the common-sense conception of the mental or the common-sense conception of the mental is radically mistaken.

(2) Physicalistic psychology will fail to vindicate (in the relevant sense) the common-sense conception of the mental.

Therefore,

(3) The common-sense conception of the mental is radically mistaken.

17. Invocation of possible worlds is of no help. Suppose that one says: assign 'snow is white' the value 1 in all possible worlds in which snow is white; assign 'grass is green' the value 1 in all possible worlds in which grass is green, and so on. Such a procedure begs the question now at issue. If mental states lack content, by virtue of what does 'assign' mean assign? What makes 'I' mean 'true' rather than something else?

18. One may want to respond that all that has been shown is that denial of the common-sense conception is not *currently* formulable or conceivable and that we cannot predict what enlarged conceptual resources there may be in the future. But in order for the thesis *ever* to be conceivable (or formulable, and so on), we would have to have a new conception of conceiving without content—that is, a conception of conceiving that did not distinguish between conceiving that *p* and conceiving that *q*. As vague as our current concept of conceiving *is*, it is difficult to see how it could be replaced by any concept that failed to distinguish between conceiving that *p* and conceiving that *q*.

If the conclusion cannot be accepted, we must reject at least one of the premises.[19] Since the second premise may well be true—since, that is, it is a real possibility that science will fail minimally to vindicate the common-sense conception—the culprit is likely the first premise, the commitment to physicalism. In that case, we should have to reject the assumption that physicalistic psychology will either vindicate or eliminate the common-sense conception of the mental.

Less an empirical theory than a condition of intelligibility, the common-sense conception may not be an option for us. One need not be any kind of Cartesian dualist (certainly, Davidson and Wittgenstein are not dualists) to hold that physicalistic science is in no position either to vindicate or to eliminate the common-sense conception of the mental. Since cognition without content is empty, denial of the common-sense conception may be a kind of cognitive suicide that we are constitutionally unable to commit. Thus, we may have to reject the physicalistic dichotomy.

There may yet remain an alternative to the rejection of physicalism. It may be possible to accept the argument from physicalism as sound and, at the same time, to blunt the impact of its conclusion. Instead of supposing that the resistance of the common-sense conception to accommodation with scientific theory robs the common-sense conception of legitimacy, we may take the common-sense conception to be practically indispensable, even if, strictly speaking, it is false. Its usefulness may be thought to confer on it a kind of legitimacy, even a kind of instrumental truth.

19. From a significantly different angle, Terence Horgan and James Woodward have also defended folk psychology from the criticisms of Stich and Churchland. See their 'Folk Psychology Is Here to Stay,' *Philosophical Review* 94 (1985), 197–226. I did not see their article until after I had presented the arguments given here.

Questions

1. Suppose that the effects of believing the truth of eliminativism would be socially catastrophic. Would this provide a reason against believing eliminativism?
2. Baker argues that eliminativism is a *self-defeating* hypothesis: a hypothesis, the very statement of which presupposes its falsity. Suppose she is right. Does this show that eliminativism is false?
3. Could Stich and Churchland both be right? Or does agreement with one preclude agreement with the other?
4. How might Searle (Chapter 15) respond to Stich's argument?
5. Churchland argues that psychology has not kept pace with other sciences, and indeed has stagnated. Is he right?
6. All three authors in this part discuss the 'propositional attitudes', regarding them as especially important in psychological explanation as it is ordinarily conceived. Are they right? What are the propositional attitudes, anyway?
7. Pretend the eliminativists are right or at least that eliminativism comes to be widely accepted, not only in the scientific community, but by the public at large. Describe how the contents of *Redbook* or *Cosmopolitan* might look under those circumstances.
8. Churchland argues that psychology is not reducible to some more basic science. Many psychologists would agree, but not regard this as an embarrassment. Are these psychologists deluded? (Be careful how you answer!)
9. Syntax, which concerns *form*, is distinguished from semantics, which concerns *meaning*. Could a system be *purely* syntactic? Could syntax—or syntactic entities like symbols or sentences—exist in the absence of semantics? Might answers to such questions bear on Stich's argument?
10. Suppose Stich, Churchland, and other eliminativists are wrong. Psychology as we know it is perfectly legitimate. How should we understand the relation of psychology to neuroscience?

Suggested readings

Eliminative materialism was an early response to the mind–brain identity theory; see Feyerabend (1963) and Rorty (1965, 1970). Heil (1998b, chap. 5) includes a discussion of functionalism intended for readers new to the topic. More recent defenders of eliminativism include Churchland (Chapter 23, 1989), and Stich (1983, 1996). See Ramsey, et al. (1991) and Heil (1991) for a discussion of the implications of 'connectionist' models of the mind for eliminative materialism. Baker (1987), Horgan and Woodward (1985), and Jackson and Pettit (1990) defend 'folk psychology' against the eliminativists. See also O'Leary-Hawthorne (1994). Christensen and Turner's (1993) collection is devoted to arguments for and against eliminativism. See also Stich's (1999) on-line *MIT Encyclopedia* entry. Chalmers's (2001) on-line bibliography provides many more references to works defending or criticizing eliminativist arguments.

Eliminative materialism

Baker, L. R. (1987), *Saving Belief: A Critique of Physicalism.* Princeton: Princeton University Press.

Christensen, S. M., and D. R. Turner, eds. (1993), *Folk Psychology and the Philosophy of Mind.* Hillsdale, NJ: L. Erlbaum.

Chalmers, D. J. (2001), *Contemporary Philosophy of Mind: An Annotated Bibliography* <http://www.u.arizona.edu/~chalmers/biblio.html> Tucson, AZ: University of Arizona.

Churchland, P. M. (1989), *A Neurocomputational Perspective.* Cambridge, MA: MIT Press.

Feyerabend, P. K. (1963), 'Materialism and the Mind—Body Problem'. *Review of Metaphysics* 17: 49–66. Reprinted in Christensen and Turner 1993: 3–16.

Greenwood, J. D., ed. (1991), *The Future of Folk Psychology: Intentionality and Cognitive Science.* Cambridge: Cambridge University Press.

Heil, J. (1991), 'Being Indiscrete'. In Greenwood 1991: 120–34.

——(1998), *Philosophy of Mind: A Contemporary Introduction.* London: Routledge.

Horgan, T., and J. Woodward (1985), 'Folk Psychology is Here to Stay', *Philosophical Review* 94: 197–226. Reprinted in Christensen and Turner 1993: 144–66.

Jackson, F., and P. Pettit (1990), 'In defense of Folk Psychology', *Philosophical Studies* 59: 31–54.

O'Leary-Hawthorne, J. (1994), 'On the Threat of Elimination', *Philosophical Studies* 74: 325–46.

Ramsey, W., S. P. Stich, and J. Garon (1991), 'Connectionism, Eliminativism, and the Future of Folk Psychology'. In Greenwood 1991: 93–119. Reprinted in Christensen and Turner 1993: 315–39.

Rorty, R. (1965), 'Mind–Body Identity, Privacy, and Categories', *Review of Metaphysics* 19: 24–54. Reprinted in Christensen and Turner 1993: 17–41.

——(1970), 'In Defense of Eliminative Materialism', *Review of Metaphysics* 24: 112–21.

Stich, S. P. (1983) *From Folk Psychology to Cognitive Science: The Case Against Belief.* Cambridge, MA: MIT Press.

Stich, S. P. (1996), *Deconstructing the Mind.* New York: Oxford University Press.
—— (1999), 'Eliminative Materialism'. In Wilson and Keil 1999.
Wilson, R. A., and F. Keil, eds. (1999), *MIT Encyclopedia of Cognitive Sciences* <http://cognet.mit.edu/MITECS/login.html> Cambridge, MA: MIT Press.

Part VII

Externalism and mental content

Introduction

READINGS thus far have offered competing accounts of the nature of states of mind and their place in the material world. Readings in this part concern one species of mental state: the 'propositional attitudes'. Propositional attitudes have already figured prominently in discussions in Parts V and VI. Because you may have skipped those sections, and because it is always useful in philosophy to be certain we have a solid grasp on what we are talking about, let me begin this section by briefly spelling out what philosophers take the propositional attitudes to be.

A propositional attitude is a state of mind that can be decomposed into two components:

(1) A 'proposition' or propositional component;
(2) An attitude toward a proposition or proposition 'expressed' by the propositional component.

These can vary independently. Consider the proposition expressed by the sentence

(a) It's raining.

This proposition, presumably, is the same proposition as that expressed (in French) by

(b) Il pleut

and in German by

(c) Es regnet.

Now consider your belief that it is raining. Here, you have an attitude of a particular sort (roughly, an attitude of acceptance) toward the proposition that it's raining. You could have that very same attitude toward a different proposition. You could, or instance, believe that paint dries more slowly in damp weather. Same attitude, different proposition. Similarly, you could take up a different attitude toward the same proposition. You could, for instance doubt that it's raining, hope that it's raining, fear that it's raining, or even, if you fancy rainmaking, intend it to be the case that it's raining.

Non-propositional states

Propositional attitudes can be distinguished from 'non-propositional' *sensuous* states of mind: sensations, feelings, moods. (Some philosophers regard *all* states of mind as propositional—see Chapters 34, 36, 37—but let us ignore this possibility here.) Identity theorists assume that the identification of beliefs and other propositional attitudes with physical (brain) states would be relatively easy to establish. Unlike sensations, beliefs, desires, and the like apparently possess no problematic qualitative features. Beliefs and desires can give rise to sensory episodes, but beliefs and desires, just in themselves, might be thought to lack a distinctive 'phenomenology' (there is nothing in particular it is like to believe that snow is white or to want to earn a Ph.D. in molecular biology). Although it is easy to doubt that your desktop computer could feel pain or grow despondent, you probably feel less reluctance in the thought that the device stores and manipulates information. Perhaps such activities do not measure up to what you do when you think, but you might regard them as a *kind* of thinking, in a way that you would not be inclined to regard the device's logic board overheating as a kind of sensuous episode—its experiencing a 'burning sensation', for instance.

All this could be off base. Differences between the propositional attitudes and sensuous episodes could turn out to be differences of degree rather than kind. Let us bracket this question, however, and focus just on the propositional attitudes: beliefs, desires, intentions, and the like. It is natural to assume that these, like their sensuous cousins, are 'inner' states. Such states are states of your mind. If minds are brains, then they are states of your brain. Although minds and brains can affect and be affected by external occurrences, the states themselves are what they are quite independently of your external circumstances. (The point of this mysterious proclamation will gradually become clear.) The idea is so natural that it is a challenge to make it explicit without risking misunderstanding.

Recall Descartes. Descartes earned fame by advancing the possibility that the world you experience is nothing more than an illusion planted in your head by an evil demon. As Descartes puts it:

> I will suppose, then, not that there is a supremely good God who is the source of all truth, but that there is an evil demon, supremely powerful and cunning, who works as hard as he can to deceive me. I will say that sky, air, earth, color, shape, sound, and other external things are just dreamed illusions that the demon uses to ensnare my judgment. I will regard myself as not having hands, eyes, flesh, blood, and senses—but as having the false belief that I have all these things. (Chapter 3)

Descartes is imagining that your inner life could remain wholly unaffected while the world around you changed dramatically, provided, of course, that you are fed 'compensating' illusions. The updated version of Descartes's thought-experiment is the brain-in-a-vat possibility: how do you know you are not a brain in a vat wired to a computing machine that pumps you full of false sensory information about your surroundings?

Both the demon possibility and the brain-in-a-vat fable assume that the contents of your thoughts about the world are a wholly internal affair. Your thoughts can have external causes, but their *contents*—what they are thoughts *of*—owe their character wholly on your internal constitution. (This is what I described above as the natural view.) Your thoughts about trees that are indistinguishable from thoughts about trees occurring to a brain in a vat or an agent under the spell of an evil demon. Descartes emphasizes that, because the world and our thoughts about the world can vary independently we are faced with a momentous epistemological problem: what reason could we have for believing that our thoughts about the world 'matched' the world? For all we know the world could be very different from what we take it to be. Indeed, there might be no external world at all! The 'Cartesian predicament' ensues. We are faced with the seemingly impossible task of providing grounds for the belief that our thoughts about the world reflect the world as it really is.

Intrinsicality

Understanding issues addressed by philosophers in this part requires your being alert to a distinction between an object's *intrinsic* and *extrinsic* features. To a first approximation, a feature of an object is intrinsic to that object if it is a feature the object could have if it were the only object in existence. Consider the shape, size, mass, and color of a billiard ball. In a world consisting of nothing else, the billiard ball could have the very same shape, size, mass, and color. What are non-intrinsic—extrinsic—features of the ball? Extrinsic features depend on the existence of objects distinct from the ball. The ball's resting on Lilian's billiard table is a feature the ball would lack in a world that failed to contain Lilian's billiard table. The ball's having been made in Taiwan, its belonging to a set purchased at a Wal-Mart in Poughkeepsie, its having been a wedding present, and its being in Cleveland are all extrinsic features of the ball.

The distinction is intuitively clear, but difficult to articulate precisely. This suggests, not that the distinction is hazy, but that it is a fundamental distinction, one for which we should be hard pressed to explicate in simpler, more familiar terms. In any case, the role played by the notion of intrinsicality here does not depend on any particular theory of what intrinsic features might be. All that is required is your distinguishing ways objects (or agents) are 'in themselves' and ways they are relative to other, distinct objects.

Externalism

Externalists (or, as they sometimes call themselves, 'anti-individualists') reject the Cartesian picture. (Wittgenstein 1953 could be seen as a prominent forerunner of contemporary externalists, but Putnam 1975 is usually regarded as the first self-conscious formulation of externalism.) The contents of our thoughts, they argue, depend on our context: the world or region of the world in which we are embedded. If you vary the world around an agent, even though the agent remains untouched, you vary the contents of the agent's thoughts. This is not for the boring reason that we are causally affected by our surroundings, so we are likely to notice when those surroundings change. The idea rather is that the contents of our thoughts are 'fixed' or 'determined' by the context in which they occur. Two intrinsically indistinguishable thinkers might entertain thoughts with very different contents—thoughts about very different things—if the thinkers are embedded in very different environments. This suggests that there is no way to infer from intrinsic features of a thought to its *content*: what it is about.

At first blush this seems to cut us off from our world in ways even Descartes could never have imagined. If the contents of our thoughts are determined by factors external to us, we might be deceived, not merely about the 'external world', but also about our own thoughts: skepticism about the *internal* world! Externalists, however, see things differently. Descartes depicts agents as faced with the problem of 'matching' their thoughts to the world. If your thoughts are fixed by the world, however, there can be no question of their 'matching' or failing to match an 'external reality': what your thoughts are about *automatically* matches the world around you. True, your thoughts and the thoughts of a similar agent, Hilary, embedded in the demon world might be intrinsically indistinguishable. Even so, your thoughts are about tables, trees, and the like in the world around you; Hilary's thoughts in the demon world are about whatever it is in Hilary's world that substitutes for tables, trees, and the like. Here is one possibility. Your tree-thoughts are caused by trees, and so are about trees. Hilary's counterpart thoughts are not caused by trees (the Demon has destroyed the trees) but by impulses spawned by the Demon's evil mind. Hilary's 'tree-like' thoughts are not false thoughts about *trees*, but *true* thoughts about impulses originating in the demon! (This line of argument first saw the light of day with O. K. Bouwsma's 'Descartes' Evil Genius' [1949]; Putnam's Chapter 26 represents a more recent version.)

This may sound wacky, but you are accustomed to wacky-sounding views in philosophy. You should also, by now, be used to the idea that what at first sounds wacky can, on closer examination, come to seem less so. Begin by rereading the previous paragraph slowly. When you have done that you should be ready to consider what motivates externalism. A good place to start is with a famous thought experiment originating with Putnam.

Imagine a planet in a remote region of the universe, a planet indistinguishable from our beloved Earth. Were you magically transported to this planet in your sleep and awakened, you would detect no changes at all. On this planet—which its inhabitants call, naturally, Earth, but we shall call Twin Earth—there are land masses inhabitants of Twin Earth call Europe, Australia, Africa, Asia, North America, etc. Some of the inhabitants of Twin Earth speak what they call English (but *we* shall call Twin English). Twin English speakers discuss trees, tables, water, mountains, and planets just as English speakers here on Earth do.

Twin Earth is not quite a perfect duplicate of Earth, however. Twin Earth differs from Earth in one vital respect. On Twin Earth the clear, colorless liquid that fills rivers, oceans, ice trays, and bathtubs is not H_2O, but a different chemical substance, XYZ! To be sure, Twin English speaking inhabitants of Twin Earth call this liquid 'water'. But of course XYZ is not water: *water* is H_2O. Does this mean that the inhabitants of Twin Earth are mistaken? No. When, Duane, an inhabitant of Twin Earth says 'that's water' (pointing to a puddle of XYZ on the living-room floor), he is right! In Duane's mouth, 'water' means, not *water* (H_2O), but XYZ. Similarly Duane's 'water' thoughts—thoughts he would express using the word 'water'—are thoughts, not of water, but of XYZ. Now think of Duane's counterpart, Wayne, here on Earth. When Wayne points to a puddle on the living-room floor and exclaims 'That's water!' his utterance concerns, not XYZ, but water: H_2O.

Considerations of this sort lead Putnam to conclude that 'meanings ain't in the head'. What we mean by the sentences we utter is partly a matter of how we are situated in the world. Words are connected to things, not by 'outgoing' chains of significance guided by agents' thoughts ('noetic rays'), but by 'incoming' causal chains. Duane's use of 'water' attaches to XYZ (*twin* water), rather than H_2O, because Duane causally interacts with XYZ, not H_2O. Similarly, Wayne's use of 'water' signifies H_2O (*water*) because Wayne interacts with H_2O, not XYZ. Putnam emphasizes causal connections, Tyler Burge (Chapter 25) discusses social factors affecting the meaning of what we say. You should see the arguments as complementary, rather than in competition. In both cases, the point is that the words we use take their significance from the setting—natural and social—in which they are used.

From talk to thought

You might agree that Lewis Carroll's Humpty Dumpty was wrong, it is not 'up to us' what our words mean, but wonder what this might have to do with states of mind (Carroll 1871: chap. 6). The discussion began with a discussion of *thought*, not language. Language use is a shared, public enterprise; thoughts occur secretly inside us. In taking up a language, we implicitly agree to abide by meanings laid down by the community of speakers. But we alone are responsible for the character and significance of our own private thoughts.

Externalists see it differently. Duane on Twin Earth thinks of the puddle in his living room, he thinks a thought he would express by saying 'That's water!' If the utterance expresses his thought, then Duane's thought concerns XYZ (not H_2O). Similarly for Wayne: Wayne's thoughts concern H_2O (not XYZ). Like Duane and Wayne, we use language to express our thoughts. This should not be taken to imply that meanings flow from thoughts to speech. Constraints on the words we use constrain our thoughts as well, or at least those thoughts that have a natural linguistic expression. You are no more in a position to make your thoughts mean what they mean than you are in a position to make your words mean what *they* mean!

What about thoughts less tightly connected to language. Suppose you form the image of a banana. What makes the image an image of a *banana*? One answer is that an image of a banana *resembles* a banana. Now imagine an intelligent alien, Trog, inhabiting some remote planet on which nothing banana-like exists. There are no plants at all on this planet; its inhabitants draw nourishment from the atmosphere in the course of breathing. One day Trog notices a yellowish mold growing on the wall. If you saw the mold, you would describe it as banana shaped, but Trog, knowing nothing of bananas, thinks of it merely as a curiously shaped yellow blotch. Later, in a moment of idle reflection, Trog forms an image of the blotch. Trog's imagery, it so happens, is qualitatively indistinguishable from the experience you have in forming the image of a banana. If your experience resembles a banana, so does Trog's. Yet Trog's image, if it is an image *of* anything, is an image of a mold (not a banana); yours is of a banana (not a mold). What accounts for this? Whatever it is, it cannot be a feature of the image itself: the images are qualitatively alike. Perhaps the differences lie not in internal features of you and Trog but in the fact that you, but not Trog, causally interact with bananas; Trog, but not you, has interacted causally with the mold.

Knowing your own thoughts

You get the idea. Although agents' thoughts apparently occur in their heads (or minds), what those thoughts concern—what they are thoughts *about*—is fixed by, depends on, factors external to the agent. If this view still strikes you as far-fetched, you should reflect on the fact that it is accepted by many—perhaps most—philosophers who study these matters. I do not mean to suggest that you should accept externalism because many philosophers do. After all, plenty of philosophers reject externalism. You will have missed something however, if you do not at least feel the pull of such a theory.

If you remain unmoved, an analogy might help. Imagine a picture of a smiling face. You can change the significance of the face by placing it in different scenes. The face, located in a depiction of merry party-goers is a happy face. The very same face located in a scene of devastation and suffering is evil. The face's being happy or evil depends, not on intrinsic properties of the face (or at any rate not wholly on these), but on the context in which the face appears. If you vary the context, you change the face. You can say that the face (in one context) 'has the property' of being happy, but its 'having this property' is at bottom a matter of its standing in appropriate relations to other things. If those relations change, then the face, though it has not altered intrinsically, can lose the property.

One important benefit of externalism is its promise to provide an answer to the age-old skeptical challenge to our knowledge of the external world. Skepticism presumes a sharp division between our thoughts and the world on which those thoughts are directed. What gives us the right to believe that what we think is the case *is* the case? If the contents of our thoughts depend on how things stand in the 'external world', there can be no question of our being dramatically deceived. This point is driven home by Putnam in 'Brains in Vats'.

This is the good news. What of the bad news? One worry has been mentioned already: externalism threatens to undermine the kind of awareness we take ourselves to have of our own states of mind. We apparently enjoy a kind of direct, 'privileged' access to what we think and feel. If what we think—what our thoughts are about—depends on external factors, it looks as though we should have to *work out* what we think by first figuring out how we are embedded in the world. Are your thoughts about water thoughts about *water*? If externalists are to be believed, it would appear that you would first need to discover the chemical constitution of the liquid around you! The victory over the skeptic mentioned in the previous paragraph turns out to be a hollow one. We can know that our thoughts are not systematically off base. But we can no longer be confident we know what those thoughts are thoughts *of*! We are in the position of someone who has assurance that a particular soothsayer is always right, but who does not know the soothsayer's language. We shall return to this topic in Part VIII.

Mental causation

A second apparent difficulty for externalism is somewhat more technical and consequently more tedious to discuss. We like to think that what we believe and desire affects our actions. You head for the Burger King because you want a Whopper, and you believe that you can obtain a Whopper only by visiting the Burger King. Your seeking out the Burger King stems from your Whopper-directed beliefs and desires. Had you wanted a pizza or had you believed that Whoppers were only available at the Post Office, you would have headed for a pizza stand or the Post Office. The *content* of your beliefs and desires—what your beliefs are beliefs *about*, what your desires are desires *for*—evidently makes a difference in how you behave.

What is it for a state of mind to 'affect' or 'make a difference to' behavior? On the one hand, you have assorted beliefs, desires; on the other hand, you act. What is the connection? Most philosophers, and probably most non-philosophers, assume that the connection is *causal*. Your beliefs and desires affect your behavior—make a difference in what you do—because they contribute causally to the production of that behavior.

All this seems right. We behave as we do because of what we believe and desire and because our beliefs and desires affect our behavior causally. But now a peculiar feature of externalism rears its head. Recall that externalism incorporates the thesis that the contents of states of mind are contextually determined. What you believe, for instance, depends on relations you bear to your surroundings. How then could what you believe affect your behavior? Your believing that Whoppers are only available at the Burger King is a matter of your being in a particular state *and* your standing in an appropriate relation to Whoppers and Burger Kings. Vary this relation, and the content of the state changes. This is the lesson of Twin Earth. But it is hard to see how your standing in a relation of the required sort could make a difference to what you do.

Consider a white billiard ball rolling across a billiard table, colliding with a red billiard ball, and imparting a particular velocity to the red billiard ball. The white billiard ball was manufactured in Italy on a Wednesday in July of 2003, but this is evidently 'causally irrelevant' to any effect it might have on the velocity of the red ball. Replace the Italian made billiard ball with an intrinsically identical ball made in Taiwan in 1999, and the effect on the red ball would be the same. It would seem that the contents of your states of mind are like this. The contents of your beliefs and desires are a relational matter. How could they, in that case, make a causal difference in what you do?

Return to Wayne and his Twin Earth counterpart, Duane. Wayne and Duane are intrinsically indiscernible. They differ only in relations they bear to their surroundings. Wayne's beliefs about what he calls water were caused by water; Duane's beliefs about what *he* calls water were caused by XYZ, *twin* water. Their behavior is what it is because of their intrinsic make-up and effects of incoming stimuli on that intrinsic make-up. How each came to possess his intrinsic make-up makes a difference in what he *believes*, but not in how he *behaves*. You might put it this way: although Wayne and Duane's beliefs play a part in determining what they do, their *being* beliefs—that is, propositional attitudes with definite contents—is causally irrelevant to their behavior. Given the same stimuli, both will behave identically. One more example might help. Imagine being struck on the head and knocked unconscious by a home run ball hit by Mark McGwire. The ball that knocks you unconscious is one hit by McGwire for a home run, but this feature of the ball is irrelevant to its effects on you. Any object with the mass, shape, and velocity of the ball would have had precisely the same effect.

The point can be put quite generally. To the extent that an object's behavior is affected by its current state, how the object came to be in that state is irrelevant to how it comes to behave. If you take externalism seriously, however, you will regard the contents of agents' beliefs as being determined by historical factors. In that case, the contents of beliefs could make no difference to how agents' behave.

Externalist responses

Philosophers have not been shy in offering solutions to this apparent difficulty. Some acknowledge the problem and move on. Thus, eliminativists like Stich (Chapter 22) deploy similar arguments to argue that beliefs, desires, and intentions do not in fact explain intelligent behavior. Other philosophers, starting with the idea that, as a matter of fact, we *do* explain behavior by appealing to beliefs and the like, contend that our conception of causality needs to be tailored to our explanatory practices. To argue that a viable explanatory practice is undermined by assuming a 'mechanistic' account of causation, is to put the cart before the horse (see Baker 1993). Still others argue that we need two concepts of mental content: 'broad' and 'narrow' (Fodor 1991). Return to Wayne and Duane. In describing Wayne's beliefs about the watery stuff in his environment as beliefs about water, we are describing the *broad* content of Wayne's belief. Wayne and Duane differ in the broad content of their beliefs. *Narrow content* is what Wayne and Duane have in common. The narrow content of their beliefs is what you get when you consider just Wayne and Duane's intrinsic features.

If you are attracted to externalist accounts of mental content, but worry about the implications of externalism for mental causation, these are some of the options available to you. It is fair to say that none of the alternatives has as yet attracted a large following. This could change with the emergence of some as yet unthought-of solution to the problem of mental causation. In any case, the problem of mental causation—the venerable mind–body problem—is a problem for many accounts of the mind. Descartes, for instance, no externalist, faces a different version of the same difficulty. What we are discovering is that the mind–body problem can be a problem for materialists as well as dualists.

References

Baker, L. R. (1993), 'Metaphysics and Mental Causation'. In Heil and Mele 1993: 75–95.

Bouwsma, O. K. (1949), 'Descartes' Evil Genius.', *Philosophical Review* 58: 141–51.

Carroll, Lewis (1871/1960) *Through the Looking-Glass and What Alice Found There*. In Martin Gardner, ed., *The Annotated Alice*. New York: Bramhall House.

Fodor, J. (1991), 'A Modal Argument for Narrow Content', *Journal of Philosophy* 88: 5–26.

Gunderson, K., ed. (1975), *Language, Mind, and Knowledge*. Minnesota Studies in the Philosophy of Science, vol. 12 Minneapolis: University of Minnesota Press.

Heil, J. and A. R. Mele, eds. (1993), *Mental Causation*. Oxford: Clarendon Press.

Putnam, H. (1975), 'The Meaning of "Meaning" '. In Gunderson 1975.

Wittgenstein, L. (1953/1968), *Philosophical Investigations*, trans. G. E. M. Anscombe, Oxford: Basil Blackwell.

Chapter 25

Individualism and the mental

Tyler Burge

SINCE Hegel's *Phenomenology of Spirit*, a broad, inarticulate division of emphasis between the individual and his social environment has marked philosophical discussions of mind. On one hand, there is the traditional concern with the individual subject of mental states and events. In the elderly Cartesian tradition, the spotlight is on what exists or transpires 'in' the individual—his secret cogitations, his innate cognitive structures, his private perceptions and introspections, his grasping of ideas, concepts, or forms. More evidentially oriented movements, such as behaviorism and its liberalized progeny, have highlighted the individual's publicly observable behavior—his input-output relations and the dispositions, states, or events that mediate them. But both Cartesian and behaviorist viewpoints tend to feature the individual subject. On the other hand, there is the Hegelian preoccupation with the role of social institutions in shaping the individual and the content of his thought. This tradition has dominated the continent since Hegel. But it has found echoes in English-speaking philosophy during this century in the form of a concentration on language. Much philosophical work on language and mind has been in the interests of Cartesian or behaviorist viewpoints that I shall term 'individualistic.' But many of Wittgenstein's remarks about mental representation point up a social orientation that is discernible from his flirtations with behaviorism. And more recent work on the theory of reference has provided glimpses of the role of social cooperation in determining what an individual thinks.

In many respects, of course, these emphases within philosophy—individualistic and social — are compatible. To an extent, they may be regarded simply as different currents in the turbulent stream of ideas that has washed the intellectual landscape during the last hundred and some odd years. But the role of the social environment has received considerably less clear-headed philosophical attention (though perhaps not less philosophical attention) than the role of the states, occurrences, or acts in, on, or by the individual. Philosophical discussions of social factors have tended to be obscure, evocative, metaphorical, or platitudinous, or to be bent on establishing some large thesis about the course of history and the destiny of man. There remains much room for sharp delineation. I shall offer some considerations that stress social factors in descriptions of an individual's mental phenomena. These considerations call into question individualistic presuppositions of several

Tyler Burge, 'Individualism and the Mental', *Midwest Studies in Philosophy* 4 (1979).

traditional and modern treatments of mind. I shall conclude with some remarks about mental models.

I. Terminological matters

Our ordinary mentalistic discourse divides broadly into two sorts of idiom. One typically makes reference to mental states or events in terms of sentential expressions. The other does not. A clear case of the first kind of idiom is 'Alfred thinks that his friends' sofa is ugly'. A clear case of the second sort is 'Alfred is in pain'. Thoughts, beliefs, intentions, and so forth are typically specified in terms of subordinate sentential clauses, that-clauses, which may be judged as true or false. Pains, feels, tickles, and so forth have no special semantical relation to sentences or to truth or falsity. There are intentional idioms that fall in the second category on this characterization, but that share important semantical features with expressions in the first—idioms like 'Al worships Buicks'. But I shall not sort these out here. I shall discuss only the former kind of mentalistic idiom. The extension of the discussion to other intentional idioms will not be difficult.

In an ordinary sense, the noun phrases that embed sentential expressions in mentalistic idioms provide the *content* of the mental state or event. We shall call that-clauses and their grammatical variants '*content clauses*.' Thus the expression 'that sofas are more comfortable than pews' provides the content of Alfred's belief that sofas are more comfortable than pews. My phrase 'provides the content' represents an attempt at remaining neutral, at least for present purposes, among various semantical and metaphysical accounts of precisely how that-clauses function and precisely what, if anything, contents are.

Although the notion of content is, for present purposes, ontologically neutral, I do think of it as holding a place in a systematic *theory* of mentalistic language. The question of when to count contents different, and when the same, is answerable to theoretical restrictions. It is often remarked that in a given context we may ascribe to a person two that-clauses that are only loosely equivalent and count them as attributions of the 'same attitude.' We may say that Al's intention to climb Mt. McKinley and his intention to climb the highest mountain in the United States are the 'same intention.' (I intend the terms for the mountain to occur obliquely here. See later discussion.) This sort of point extends even to content clauses with extensionally non-equivalent counterpart notions. For contextually relevant purposes, we might count a thought that the glass contains some water as 'the same thought' as a thought that the glass contains some thirst-quenching liquid, particularly if we have no reason to attribute either content as opposed to the other, and distinctions between them are contextually irrelevant. Nevertheless, in both these examples, every systematic theory I know of would want to represent the semantical contribution of the content-clauses in distinguishable ways—as 'providing different contents.'

One reason for doing so is that the person himself is capable of having different attitudes described by the different content-clauses, even if these differences are irrelevant in a particular context. (Al might have developed the intention to climb the highest mountain before developing the intention to climb Mt. McKinley—regardless of whether he, in fact, did so.) A second reason is that the counterpart components of the that-clauses allude to distinguishable elements in people's cognitive lives. 'Mt. McKinley' and 'the highest mountain in the U.S.' serve, or might serve, to indicate cognitively different notions. This is a vague, informal way of generalizing Frege's point: the thought that Mt. McKinley is the highest mountain in the U.S. is potentially interesting or informative. The thought that Mt. McKinley is Mt. McKinley is not. Thus when we say in a given context that attribution of different contents is attribution of the 'same attitude,' we use 'same attitude' in a way similar to the way we use 'same car' when we say that people who drive Fords (or green 1970 Ford Mavericks) drive the 'same car.' For contextual purposes different cars are counted as 'amounting to the same.'

Although this use of 'content' is theoretical, it is not I think theoretically controversial. In cases where we shall be counting contents different, the cases will be uncontentious: On any systematic theory, differences in the *extension*—the actual denotation, referent, or application—of counterpart expressions in that-clauses will be semantically represented, and will, in our terms, make for differences in content. I shall be avoiding the more controversial, but interesting, questions about the general conditions under which sentences in that-clauses can be expected to provide the same content.

I should also warn of some subsidiary terms. I shall be (and have been) using the term '*notion*' to apply to components or elements of contents. Just as whole that-clauses provide the content of a person's attitude, semantically relevant components of that-clauses will be taken to indicate notions that enter into the attitude (or the attitude's content). This term is supposed to be just as ontologically neutral as its fellow. When I talk of understanding or mastering the notion of contract, I am not relying on any special epistemic or ontological theory, except insofar as the earlier-mentioned theoretical restrictions on the notion of content are inherited by the notion of notion. The expression, '*understanding (mastering) a notion*' is to be construed more or less intuitively. Understanding the notion of contract comes roughly to knowing what a contract is. One can master the notion of contract without mastering the term 'contract'—at the very least if one speaks some language other than English that has a term roughly synonymous with 'contract'. (An analogous point holds for my use of 'mastering a content'.) Talk of notions is roughly similar to talk of concepts in an informal sense. 'Notion' has the advantage of being easier to separate from traditional theoretical commitments.

I speak of *attributing* an attitude, content, or notion, and of *ascribing* a that clause or other piece of language. Ascriptions are the linguistic analogs of attributions. This use of 'ascribe' is nonstandard, but convenient and easily assimilated.

There are semantical complexities involving the behavior of expressions in content clauses, most of which we can skirt. But some must be touched on. Basic to the subject is the observation that expressions in content clauses are often not intersubstitutable with extensionally equivalent expressions in such a way as to maintain the truth value of the containing sentence. Thus from the facts that water is H_2O and that Bertrand thought that water is not fit to drink, it does not follow that Bertrand thought that H_2O is not fit to drink. When an expression like 'water' functions in a content clause so that it is not freely exchangeable with all extensionally equivalent expressions, we shall say that it has *oblique occurrence.* Roughly speaking, the reason why 'water' and 'H_2O' are not interchangeable in our report of Bertrand's thought is that 'water' plays a role in characterizing a different mental act or state from that which 'H_2O' would play a role in characterizing. In this context at least, thinking that water is not fit to drink is different from thinking that H_2O is not fit to drink.

By contrast, there are non-oblique occurrences of expressions in content clauses. One might say that some water—say, the water in the glass over there—is thought by Bertrand to be impure; or that Bertrand thought that *that* water is impure. And one might intend to make no distinction that would be lost by replacing 'water' with 'H_2O'—or 'that water' with 'that H_2O' or 'that common liquid', or any other expression extensionally equivalent with 'that water'. We might allow these exchanges even though Bertrand had never heard of, say, H_2O. In such purely nonoblique occurrences, 'water' plays *no role* in providing the *content* of Bertrand's thought, *on our use of 'content'*, or (in any narrow sense) in characterizing Bertrand or his mental state. Nor is the water part of Bertrand's thought content. We speak of Bertrand *thinking his content of* the water. At its nonoblique occurrence, the term 'that water' simply isolates, in one of many equally good ways, a portion of wet stuff to which Bertrand or his thought is related or applied. In certain cases, it may also mark a context in which Bertrand's thought is applied. But it is expressions at oblique occurrences within content clauses that primarily do the job of providing the content of mental states or events, and in characterizing the person.

Mentalistic discourse containing obliquely occurring expressions has traditionally been called *intentional discourse.* The historical reasons for this nomenclature are complex and partly confused. But roughly speaking, grammatical contexts involving oblique occurrences have been fixed upon as specially relevant to the representational character (sometimes called 'intentionality') of mental states and events. Clearly oblique occurrences in mentalistic discourse have something to do with characterizing a person's epistemic perspective — how things seem to him, or in an informal sense, how they are represented to him. So without endorsing all the commitments of this tradition, I shall take over its terminology.

The crucial point in the preceding discussion is the assumption that obliquely occurring expressions in content clauses are a primary means of identifying a person's intentional mental states or events. A further point is worth remarking here. It is normal to suppose that those content clauses correctly ascribable to a person that are not in general intersubstitutable *salva veritate*—and certainly those that involve extensionally non-equivalent counterpart expressions — identify different mental states or events.

I have cited contextual exceptions to this normal supposition, at least in a manner of speaking. We sometimes count distinctions in content irrelevant for purposes of a given attribution, particularly where our evidence for the precise content of a person or animal's attitude is skimpy. Different contents may contextually identify (what amount to) the 'same attitude.' I have indicated that even in these contexts, I think it best, strictly speaking, to construe distinct contents as describing different mental states or events that are merely equivalent for the purposes at hand. I believe that this view is widely accepted. But nothing I say will depend on it. For any distinct contents, there will be imaginable contexts of attribution in which, even in the loosest, most informal ways of speaking, those contents would be said to describe different mental states or events. This is virtually a consequence of the theoretical role of contents, discussed earlier. Since our discussion will have an 'in principle' character, I shall take these contexts to be the relevant ones. Most of the cases we discuss will involve *extensional* differences between obliquely occurring counterpart expressions in that-clauses. In such cases, it is particularly natural and normal to take different contents as identifying different mental states or events.

II. A thought experiment

IIa. First case We now turn to a three-step thought experiment. Suppose first that:

> A given person has a large number of attitudes commonly attributed with content clauses containing 'arthritis' in oblique occurrence. For example, he thinks (correctly) that he has had arthritis for years, that his arthritis in his wrists and fingers is more painful than his arthritis in his ankles, that it is better to have arthritis than cancer of the liver, that stiffening joints is a symptom of arthritis, that certain sorts of aches are characteristic of arthritis, that there are various kinds of arthritis, and so forth. In short, he has a wide range of such attitudes. In addition to these unsurprising attitudes, he thinks falsely that he has developed arthritis in the thigh.

Generally competent in English, rational and intelligent, the patient reports to his doctor his fear that his arthritis has now lodged in his thigh. The doctor replies by telling him that this cannot be so, since arthritis is specifically an inflammation of joints. Any dictionary could have told him the same. The patient is surprised, but relinquishes his view and goes on to ask what might be wrong with his thigh.

The second step of the thought experiment consists of a counterfactual supposition. We are to conceive of a situation in which the patient proceeds from birth through the same course of physical events that he actually does, right to and including the time at which he first reports his fear to his doctor. Precisely the same things (non-intentionally described) happen to him. He has the same physiological history, the same diseases, the same internal physical occurrences. He goes through the same motions, engages in the same behavior, has the same sensory intake (physiologically described). His dispositions to respond to stimuli are explained in physical theory as the effects of the same proximate causes. All of this extends to his interaction with linguistic expressions. He says and hears the same words (word forms) at the same times he actually does. He develops the disposition to assent to 'Arthritis can occur in the thigh' and 'I have arthritis in the thigh' as a result of the same physically described proximate causes. Such dispositions might have arisen in a number of ways. But we can suppose that in both actual and counterfactual situations, he acquires the word 'arthritis' from casual conversation or reading, and never hearing anything to prejudice him for or against applying it in the way that he does, he applies the word to an ailment in his thigh (or to ailments in the limbs of others) which seems to produce pains or other symptoms roughly similar to the disease in his hands and ankles. In both actual and counterfactual cases, the disposition is never reinforced or extinguished up until the time when he expresses himself to his doctor. We further imagine that the patient's non-intentional, phenomenal experience is the same. He has the same pains, visual fields, images, and internal verbal rehearsals. The *counterfactuality* in the supposition touches only the patient's social environment. In actual fact, 'arthritis', as used in his community, does not apply to ailments outside joints. Indeed, it fails to do so by a standard, non-technical dictionary definition. But in our imagined case, physicians, lexicographers, and informed laymen apply 'arthritis' not only to arthritis but to various other rheumatoid ailments. The standard use of the term is to be conceived to encompass the patient's actual misuse. We could imagine either that arthritis had not been singled out as a family of diseases, or that some other term besides 'arthritis' were applied, though not commonly by laymen, specifically to arthritis. We may also suppose that this difference and those necessarily associated with it are the only differences between the counterfactual situation and the actual one. (Other people besides the patient will, of course, behave differently.) To summarize the second step:

> The person might have had the same physical history and non-intentional mental phenomena while the word 'arthritis' was conventionally applied, and defined to apply, to various rheumatoid ailments, including the one in the person's thigh, as well as to arthritis.

The final step is an interpretation of the counterfactual case, or an addition to it as so far described. It is reasonable to suppose that:

> In the counterfactual situation, the patient lacks some—probably *all*—of the attitudes commonly attributed with content clauses containing 'arthritis' in oblique occurrence. He lacks the occurrent thoughts of beliefs that he has arthritis in the thigh, that he has had arthritis for years, that stiffening joints and various sorts of aches are symptoms of arthritis, that his father had arthritis, and so on.

We suppose that in the counterfactual case we cannot correctly ascribe any content clause containing an oblique occurrence of the term 'arthritis'. It is hard to see how the patient could have picked up the notion of arthritis. The word 'arthritis' in the counterfactual community does not mean *arthritis*. It does not apply only to inflammations of joints. We suppose that no other word in the patient's repertoire means *arthritis*. 'Arthritis', in the counterfactual situation, differs both in dictionary definition and in extension from 'arthritis' as we use it. Our ascriptions of content clauses to the patient (and ascriptions within his community) would not constitute attributions of the same contents we actually attribute. For counterpart expressions in the content clauses that are actually and counterfactually ascribable are not even extensionally equivalent. However we describe the patient's attitudes in the counterfactual situation, it will not be with a term or phrase extensionally equivalent with 'arthritis'. So the patient's counterfactual attitude contents differ from his actual ones.

The upshot of these reflections is that the patient's mental contents differ while his entire physical and non-intentional mental histories, considered in isolation from their social context, remain the same. (We could have supposed that he dropped dead at the time he first expressed his fear to the doctor.) The differences seem to stem from differences 'outside' the patient considered as an isolated physical organism, causal mechanism, or seat of consciousness. The difference in his mental contents is attributable to differences in his social environment. In sum, the patient's internal qualitative experiences, his physiological states and events, his behaviorally described stimuli and responses, his dispositions to behave, and whatever sequences of states (non-intentionally described) mediated his input and output—all these remain constant, while his attitude contents differ, even in the extensions of counterpart notions. As we observed at the outset, such differences are ordinarily taken to spell differences in mental states and events.

IIb. Further exemplifications The argument has an extremely wide application. It does not depend, for example, on the kind of word 'arthritis' is. We could have used an artifact term, an ordinary natural kind word, a color adjective, a social role term, a term for a historical style, an abstract noun, an action verb, a physical movement verb, or any of various other sorts of words. I prefer to leave open precisely how far one can generalize the argument. But I think it has a very wide scope. The argument can get under way in any case where it is intuitively possible to attribute a mental state or event whose content involves a notion that the subject incompletely understands. As will become clear, this possibility is the key to the thought experiment. I want to give a more concrete sense of the possibility before going further.

It is useful to reflect on the number and variety of intuitively clear cases in which it is normal to attribute a content that the subject incompletely understands. One need only thumb through a dictionary for an hour or so to develop a sense of the extent to which one's beliefs are infected by incomplete understanding.[1] The phenomenon is rampant in our pluralistic age.

1. Our examples suggest points about learning that need exploration. It would seem naive to think that we first attain a mastery of expressions or notions we use and then tackle the subject matters we speak and think about in using those expressions or notions. In most cases, the processes

a. Most cases of incomplete understanding that support the thought experiment will be fairly idiosyncratic. There is a reason for this. Common linguistic errors, if entrenched, tend to become common usage. But a generally competent speaker is bound to have numerous words in his repertoire, possibly even common words, that he somewhat misconstrues. Many of these misconstruals will not be such as to deflect ordinary ascriptions of that-clauses involving the incompletely mastered term in oblique occurrence. For example, one can imagine a generally competent, rational adult having a large number of attitudes involving the notion of sofa—including beliefs that *those* (some sofas) are sofas, that some sofas are beige, that his neighbors have a new sofa, that he would rather sit in a sofa for an hour than on a church pew. In addition, he might think that sufficiently broad (but single-seat) overstuffed armchairs are sofas. With care, one can develop a thought experiment parallel to the one in section IIa, in which at least some of the person's attitude contents (particularly, in this case, contents of occurrent mental events) differ, while his physical history, dispositions to behavior, and phenomenal experience—non-intentionally and asocially described—remain the same.

b. Although most relevant misconstruals are fairly idiosyncratic, there do seem to be certain types of error which are relatively common—but not so common and uniform as to suggest that the relevant terms take on new sense. Much of our vocabulary is taken over from others who, being specialists, understand our terms better than we do.[2] The use of scientific terms by laymen is a rich source of cases. As

overlap. But while the subject's understanding is still partial, we sometimes attribute mental contents in the very terms the subject has yet to master. Traditional views take mastering a word to consist in matching it with an already mastered (or innate) concept. But it would seem, rather, that many concepts (or mental content components) are like words in that they may be employed before they are mastered. In both cases, employment appears to be an integral part of the process of mastery.

2. A development of a similar theme may be found in Hilary Putnam's notion of a division of linguistic labour. Cf. 'The Meaning of "Meaning",' *Philosophical Papers* 2 (London, 1975) pp. 227 ff. Putnam's imaginative work is in other ways congenial with points I have developed. Some of his examples can be adapted in fairly obvious ways so as to give an argument with different premises, but a conclusion complementary to the one I arrive at in Section IIa:

Consider Alfred's belief contents involving the notion of water. Without changing Alfred's (or his fellows') non-intentional phenomenal experiences, internal physical occurrences, or dispositions to respond to stimuli on sensory surfaces, we can imagine that not water (H_2O), but a different liquid with different structure but similar macro-properties (and identical phenomenal properties) played the role in his environment that water does in ours. In such a case, we could ascribe no content clauses to Alfred with 'water' in oblique position. His belief contents would differ. The conclusion (with which I am in sympathy) is that mental contents are affected not only by the physical and qualitatively mental way the person is, but by the nature of his *physical environment.*

Putnam himself does not give quite this argument. He nowhere states the first and third steps, though he gives analogs of them for the meaning of 'water'. This is partly just a result of his concentration on meaning instead of propositional attitudes. But some of what he says even seems to oppose the argument's conclusion. He remarks in effect that the subject's *thoughts* remain constant between his actual and counterfactual cases (p. 224). In his own argument he explicates the

the arthritis example illustrates, the thought experiment does not depend on specially technical terms. I shall leave it to the imagination of the reader to spin out further examples of this sort.

c. One need not look to the laymen's acquisitions from science for examples. People used to buying beef brisket in stores or ordering it in restaurants (and conversant with it in a general way) probably often develop mistaken beliefs (or uncertainties) about just what brisket is. For example, one might think that brisket is a cut from the flank or rump, or that it includes not only the lower part of the chest but also the upper part, or that it is specifically a cut of beef and not of, say, pork. No one hesitates to ascribe to such people content-clauses with 'brisket' in oblique occurrence. For example, a person may believe that he is eating brisket under these circumstances (where 'brisket' occurs in oblique position); or he may think that brisket tends to be tougher than loin. Some of these attitudes may be false; many will be true. We can imagine a counterfactual case in which the person's physical history, his dispositions, and his non-intentional mental life, are all the same, but in which 'brisket' is commonly applied in a different way—perhaps in

difference between actual and counterfactual cases in terms of a difference in the extension of terms, not a difference in those aspects of their meaning that play a role in the cognitive life of the subject. And he tries to explicate his examples in terms of indexicality—a mistake, I think, and one that tends to divert attention from major implications of the examples he gives. (Cf. Section IId.) In my view, the examples do illustrate the fact that all attitudes involving natural kind notions, including *de dicto* attitudes, presuppose *de re* attitudes. But the examples do not show that natural kind linguistic expressions are in any ordinary sense indexical. Nor do they show that beliefs involving natural kind notions are always *de re*. Even if they did, the change from actual to counterfactual cases would affect oblique occurrences of natural kind terms in that-clauses—occurrences that are the key to attributions of cognitive content. (Cf. above and note 3.) In the cited paper and earlier ones, much of what Putnam says about psychological states (and implies about mental states) has a distinctly individualistic ring. Below in Section IV, I criticize viewpoints about mental phenomena influenced by and at least strongly suggested in his earlier work on functionalism. (Cf. note 9.)

On the other hand, Putnam's articulation of social and environmental aspects of the meaning of natural kind terms complements and supplements our viewpoint. For me, it has been a rich rewarder of reflection. More recent work of his seems to involve shifts in his view-point on psychological states. It may have somewhat more in common with our approach than the earlier work, but there is much that I do not understand about it.

The argument regarding the notion of water that I extracted from Putnam's paper is narrower in scope than our argument. The Putnam-derived argument seems to work only for natural kind terms and close relatives. And it may seem not to provide as direct a threat to certain versions of functionalism that I discuss in Section IV: At least a few philosophers would claim that one could accommodate the Putnarnian argument in terms of *non*-intentional formulations of input-output relations (formulations that make reference to the specific nature of the physical environment). Our argument does not submit to this maneuver. In our thought experiment, the physical environment (sofas, arthritis, and so forth in our examples) and the subject's causal relations with it (at least as these are usually conceived) were held constant. The Putnamian argument, however, has fascinatingly different implications from our argument. I have not developed these comparisons and contrasts here because doing justice to Putnam's viewpoint would demand a distracting amount of space, as the ample girth of this footnote may suggest.

precisely the way the person thinks it applies. For example, it might apply only to beef and to the upper and lower parts of the chest. In such a case, as in the sofa and arthritis cases, it would seem that the person would (or might) lack some or all of the propositional attitudes that are actually attributed with content clauses involving 'brisket' in oblique position.

d. Someone only generally versed in music history, or superficially acquainted with a few drawings of musical instruments, might naturally but mistakenly come to think that clavichords included harpsichords without legs. He may have many other beliefs involving the notion of clavichord, and many of these may be true. Again, with some care, a relevant thought experiment can be generated.

e. A fairly common mistake among lawyers' clients is to think that one cannot have a contract with someone unless there has been a written agreement. The client might be clear in intending 'contract' (in the relevant sense) to apply to agreements, not to pieces of paper. Yet he may take it as part of the meaning of the word, or the essence of law, that a piece of formal writing is a necessary condition for establishing a contract. His only experiences with contracts might have involved formal documents, and he undergeneralizes. It is not terribly important here whether one says that the client misunderstands the term's meaning, or alternatively that the client makes a mistake about the essence of contracts. In either case, he misconceives what a contract is; yet ascriptions involving the term in oblique position are made anyway.

It is worth emphasizing here that I intend the misconception to involve the subject's attaching counterfactual consequences to his mistaken belief about contracts. Let me elaborate this a bit. A common dictionary definition of 'contract' is 'legally binding agreement'. As I am imagining the case, the client does not explicitly define 'contract' to himself in this way (though he might use this phrase in explicating the term). And he is not merely making a mistake about what the law happens to enforce. If asked why unwritten agreements are not contracts, he is likely to say something like, 'They just aren't' or 'It is part of the nature of the law and legal practice that they have no force'. He is not disposed without prodding to answer, 'It would be possible but impractical to give unwritten agreements legal force'. He might concede this. But he would add that such agreements would not be contracts. He regards a document as inseparable from contractual obligation, regardless of whether he takes this to be a matter of meaning or a metaphysical essentialist truth about contracts.

Needless to say, these niceties are philosopher's distinctions. They are not something an ordinary man is likely to have strong opinions about. My point is that the thought experiment is independent of these distinctions. It does not depend on misunderstandings of dictionary meaning. One might say that the client understood the term's dictionary meaning, but misunderstood its essential application in the law — misconceived the nature of contracts. The thought experiment still flies. In a counterfactual case in which the law enforces both written and unwritten agreements and in which the subject's behavior and so forth are the same, but in which 'contract' *means* 'legally binding agreement based on written document', we would not attribute to him a mistaken belief that a contract requires written agreement, although the lawyer might have to point out that there are other legally binding agreements that do not require documents. Similarly, the client's other propositional attitudes would no longer involve the notion of contract, but another more restricted notion.

f. People sometimes make mistakes about color ranges. They may correctly apply a color term to a certain color, but also mistakenly apply it to shades of a neighboring color. When asked to explain the color term, they cite the standard cases (for 'red', the color of blood, fire engines, and so forth). But they apply the term somewhat beyond its conventionally established range—beyond the reach of its vague borders. They think that fire engines, including *that* one, are red. They observe that red roses are covering the trellis. But they also think that *those* things are a shade of red (whereas they are not). Second looks do not change their opinion. But they give in when other speakers confidently correct them in unison.

This case extends the point of the contract example. The error is linguistic or conceptual in something like the way that the shopper's mistake involving the notion of brisket is. It is not an ordinary empirical error. But one may reasonably doubt that the subjects misunderstand the dictionary meaning of the color term. Holding their non-intentional phenomenal experience, physical history, and behavioral dispositions constant, we can imagine that 'red' were applied as they mistakenly apply it. In such cases, we would no longer ascribe content-clauses involving the term 'red' in oblique position. The attribution of the correct beliefs about fire engines and roses would be no less affected than the attribution of the beliefs that, in the actual case, display the misapplication. Cases bearing out the latter point are common in anthropological reports on communities whose color terms do not match ours. Attributions of content typically allow for the differences in conventionally established color ranges.

Here is not the place to refine our rough distinctions among the various kinds of misconceptions that serve the thought experiment. Our philosophical purposes do not depend on how these distinctions are drawn. Still, it is important to see what an array of conceptual errors is common among us. And it is important to note that such errors do not always or automatically prevent attribution of mental content provided by the very terms that are incompletely understood or misapplied. The thought experiment is nourished by this aspect of common practice.

IIc. Expansion and delineation of the thought experiment As I have tried to suggest in the preceding examples, the relevant attributions in the first step of the thought experiment need not display the subject's error. They may be attributions of a true content. We can begin with a propositional attitude that involved the misconceived notion, but in a true, unproblematic application of it: for example, the patient's belief that he, like his father, developed arthritis in the ankles and wrists at age 58 (where 'arthritis' occurs obliquely).

One need not even rely on an underlying *mis*conception in the thought experiment. One may pick a case in which the subject only partially understands an expression. He may apply it firmly and correctly in a range of cases, but be unclear or agnostic about certain of its applications or implications which, in fact, are fully established in common practice. Most of the examples we gave previously can be reinterpreted in this way. To take a new one, imagine that our protagonist is unsure whether his father has mortgages on the car and house, or just one on the house. He is a little uncertain about exactly how the loan and collateral must be arranged in order for there to be a mortgage, and he is not clear about whether one may have mortgages on anything other than houses. He is sure, however, that Uncle Harry paid off his mortgage. Imagine our man constant in the ways previously indicated and that 'mortgage' commonly applied only to mortgages on houses. But imagine banking practices themselves to be the same. Then the subject's uncertainty would plausibly not involve the notion of mortgage. Nor would his other propositional attitudes be correctly attributed with the term 'mortgage' in oblique position. Partial understanding is as good as misunderstanding for our purposes.

On the other hand, the thought experiment does appear to depend on the possibility of someone's having a propositional attitude despite an incomplete mastery of some notion in its content. To see why this appears to be so, let us try to run through a thought experiment, attempting to avoid any imputation of incomplete understanding. Suppose the subject thinks falsely that all swans are white. One can certainly hold the features of swans and the subject's non-intentional phenomenal experience, physical history, and non-intentional dispositions constant, and imagine that 'swan' meant 'white swan' (and perhaps some other term, unfamiliar to the subject, meant what 'swan' means). Could one reasonably interpret the subject as having different attitude contents without at some point invoking a misconception? The questions to be asked here are about the subject's dispositions. For example, in the actual case, if he were shown a black swan and told that he was wrong, would he fairly naturally concede his mistake? Or would he respond, 'I'm doubtful that that's a swan,' until we brought in dictionaries, encyclopedias, and other native speakers to correct his usage? In the latter case, his understanding of 'swan' would be deviant. Suppose then that in the actual situation he would respond normally to the counterexample. Then there is reason to say that he understands the notion of swan correctly; and his error is not conceptual or linguistic, but empirical in an ordinary and narrow sense. (Of course, the line we are drawing here is pretty fuzzy.) When one comes to the counterfactual stage of the thought experiment, the subject has the same dispositions to respond pliably to the presentation of a black specimen. But such a response would suggest a misunderstanding of the term 'swan' as counterfactually used. For in the counterfactual community, what they call 'swans' could not fail to be white. The mere presentation of a black swan would be irrelevant to the definitional truth 'All swans are white'. I have not set this case up as an example of the thought experiment's going through. Rather I have used it to support the conjecture that *if* the thought experiment is to work, one must at some stage find the subject believing (or having some attitude characterized by) a content, despite an incomplete understanding or misapplication. An ordinary empirical error appears not to be sufficient.

It would be a mistake, however, to think that incomplete understanding, in the sense that the argument requires, is in general an unusual or even deviant phenomenon. *What I have called 'partial understanding' is common or even normal in the case of a large number of expressions in our vocabularies.* 'Arthritis' is a case in point. Even if by the grace of circumstance a person does not fall into views that run counter to the term's meaning or application, it would not be in the least deviant or 'socially unacceptable' to have no clear attitude that would block such views. 'Brisket', 'contract', 'recession', 'sonata', 'deer', 'elm' (to borrow a well-known example), 'pre-amplifier', 'carburetor', 'gothic', 'fermentation', probably provide analogous cases. Continuing the list is largely a matter of patience. The sort of 'incomplete understanding' required by the thought experiment includes quite ordinary, nondeviant phenomena.

It is worth remarking that the thought experiment as originally presented might be run in reverse. The idea would be to start with an ordinary belief or thought involving no incomplete understanding. Then we find the incomplete understanding in the second step. For example, properly understanding 'arthritis', a patient may think (correctly) that he has arthritis. He happens to have heard of arthritis only occurring in joints, and he correctly believes that that is where arthritis always occurs. Holding his physical history, dispositions, and pain constant, we imagine that 'arthritis' commonly applies to rheumatoid ailments of all sorts. Arthritis has not been singled out for special mention. If the patient were told by a doctor 'You also have arthritis in the thigh', the patient would be disposed (as he is in the actual case) to respond, 'Really? I didn't know that one could have arthritis except in joints'. The doctor would answer, 'No, arthritis occurs in muscles, tendons, bursars, and elsewhere'. The patient would stand corrected. The notion that the doctor and patient would be operating with in such a case would not be that of arthritis.

My reasons for not having originally set out the thought experiment in this way are largely heuristic. As will be seen, discussion of the thought experiment will tend to center on the step involving incomplete understanding. And I wanted to encourage you, dear reader, to imagine actual cases of incomplete understanding in your own linguistic community. Ordinary intuitions in the domestic case are perhaps less subject to premature warping in the interests of theory. Cases involving not only mental content attribution, but also translation of a foreign tongue are more vulnerable to intrusion of side issues.

A secondary reason for not beginning with this 'reversed' version of the thought experiment is that I find it doubtful whether the thought experiment always works in symmetric fashion. There may be special intuitive problems in certain cases—perhaps, for example, cases involving perceptual natural kinds. We may give special interpretations to individuals' misconceptions in imagined foreign communities, when those misconceptions seem to match our conceptions. In other words, there may be some systematic intuitive bias in favor of at least certain of our notions for purposes of interpreting the misconceptions of imagined foreigners. I do not want to explore the point here. I think that any such bias is not always crucial, and that the thought experiment frequently works 'symmetrically.' We have to take account of a person's community in interpreting his words and describing his attitudes—and this holds in the foreign case as well as in the domestic case.

The reversal of the thought experiment brings home the important point that *even those propositional attitudes not infected by incomplete understanding* depend for their content on social factors that are independent of the individual, asocially and non-intentionally described. For if the social environment had been appropriately different, the contents of those attitudes would have been different.

Even *apart* from reversals of the thought experiment, it is plausible (in the light of its original versions) that our well-understood propositional attitudes depend partly for their content on social factors independent of the individual, asocially and non-intentionally construed. For each of us can reason as follows. Take a set of attitudes that involve a given notion and whose contents are well-understood by me. It is only contingent that I understand that notion as well as I do. Now holding my community's practices constant, imagine that I understand the given notion incompletely, but that the deficient understanding is such that it does not prevent my having attitude contents involving that notion. In fact, imagine that I am in the situation envisaged in the first step of one of the original thought experiments. In such a case, a proper subset of the original set of my actual attitude contents would, or might, remain the same—intuitively, at least those of my actual attitudes whose justification or point is untouched by my imagined deficient understanding. (In the arthritis case, an example would be a true belief that many old people have arthritis.) These attitude contents remain constant despite the fact that my understanding, inference patterns, behavior, dispositions, and so on would in important ways be different and partly inappropriate to applications of the given notion. What is it that enables these unaffected contents to remain applications of the relevant notion? It is not *just* that my understanding, inference patterns, behavior, and so forth are enough like my actual understanding, inference patterns, behavior, and so forth. For if communal practice had *also* varied so as to apply the relevant notion as I am imagining I misapply it, then my attitude contents would not involve the relevant notion at all. This argument suggests that communal practice is a factor (in addition to my understanding, inference patterns, and perhaps behavior, physical activity, and other features) in fixing the contents of my attitudes, even in cases where I fully understand the content.

IId. Independence from factive-verb and indexical-reference paradigms

The thought experiment does not play on psychological 'success' verbs or 'factive' verbs—verbs like 'know', 'regret', 'realize', 'remember', 'foresee', 'perceive'.

This point is important for our purposes because such verbs suggest an easy and clearcut distinction between the contribution of the individual subject and the objective, 'veridical' contribution of the environment to making the verbs applicable. (Actually the matter becomes more complicated on reflection, but we shall stay with the simplest cases.) When a person knows that snow is common in Greenland, his knowledge obviously depends on more than the way the person is. It depends on there actually being a lot of snow in Greenland. His mental state (belief that snow is common in Greenland) must be successful in a certain way (true). By changing the environment, one could change the truth value of the content, so that the subject could no longer be said to know the content. It is part of the burden of our argument that even intentional mental states of the individual like beliefs, which carry no implication of veridicality or success, cannot be understood by focusing purely on the individual's acts, dispositions, and 'inner' goings on.

The thought experiment also does not rest on the phenomenon of indexicality, or on *de re* attitudes, in any direct way. When Alfred refers to an apple, saying to himself 'That is wholesome,' what he refers to depends not just on the content of what he says or thinks, but on what apple is before him. Without altering the meaning of Alfred's utterance, the nature of his perceptual experiences, or his physical acts or dispositions, we could conceive an exchange of the actual apple for another one that is indistinguishable to Alfred. We would thereby conceive him as referring to something different and even as saying something with a different truth value.

This rather obvious point about indexicality has come to be seen as providing a model for understanding a certain range of mental states or events—*de re* attitudes. The precise characterization of this range is no simple philosophical task. But the clearest cases involve non-obliquely occurring terms in content clauses. When we say that Bertrand thinks of some water that it would not slake his thirst (where 'water' occurs in purely non-oblique position), we attribute a *de re* belief to Bertrand. We assume that Bertrand has something like an indexical relation to the water. The fact that Bertrand believes something of some water, rather than of a portion of some other liquid that is indistinguishable to him, depends partly on the fact that it is water to which Bertrand is contextually, 'indexically' related. For intuitively we could have exchanged the liquids without changing Bertrand and thereby changed what Bertrand believed his belief content *of*—and even whether his belief was true of it.[3] It is easy to interpret such cases by holding that the subject's mental states and contents (with allowances for brute differences in the contexts in which he applies those contents) remain the same. The differences in the situations do not pertain in any fundamental way to the subject's mind or the nature of his mental content, but to how his mind or content is related to the world.

3. I have discussed *de re* mental phenomena in 'Belief *De Re*,' *The Journal of Philosophy* 74 (1977): 338–62. There I argue that all attitudes with content presuppose *de re* attitudes. Our discussion here may be seen as bearing on the details of this presupposition. But for reasons I merely sketch in the next paragraph, I think it would be a superficial viewpoint that tried to utilize our present argument to support the view that nearly all intentional mental phenomena are covertly indexical or *de re*.

I think this interpretation of standard indexical and *de re* cases is broadly correct, although it involves oversimplifications and demands refinements. But what I want to emphasize here is that it is inapplicable to the cases our thought experiment fixes upon.

It seems to me clear that the thought experiment need not rely on *de re* attitudes at all. The subject need not have entered into special *en rapport* or quasi-indexical relations with objects that the misunderstood term applies to in order for the argument to work. We can appeal to attitudes that would usually be regarded as paradigmatic cases of *de dicto*, non-indexical, *non-de-re*, mental attitudes or events. The primary mistake in the contract example is one such, but we could choose others to suit the reader's taste. To insist that such attitudes must all be indexically infected or *de re* would, I think, be to trivialize and emasculate these notions, making nearly all attitudes *de re*. All *de dicto* attitudes presuppose *de re* attitudes. But it does not follow that indexical or *de re* elements survive in every attitude. (Cf. notes 2 and 3.)

I shall not, however, argue this point here. The claim that is crucial is not that our argument does not fix on *de re* attitudes. It is, rather, that the social differences between the actual and counterfactual situations affect the *content* of the subject's attitudes. That is, the difference affects standard cases of obliquely occurring, cognitive-content-conveying expressions in content clauses. For example, still with his misunderstanding, the subject might think that this (referring to his disease in his hands) is arthritis. Or he might think *de re* of the disease in his ankle (or of the disease in his thigh) that his arthritis is painful. It does not really matter whether the relevant attitude is *de re* or purely *de dicto*. What is crucial to our argument is that the occurrence of 'arthritis' is oblique and contributes to a characterization of the subject's mental content. One might even hold, implausibly I think, that all the subject's attitudes involving the notion of arthritis are *de re*, that 'arthritis' in that-clauses *indexically* picks out the property of being arthritis, or something like that. The fact remains that the term occurs obliquely in the relevant cases and serves in characterizing the *dicta* or contents of the subject's attitudes. The thought experiment exploits this fact.

Approaches to the mental that I shall later criticize as excessively individualistic tend to assimilate environmental aspects of mental phenomena to either the factive-verb or indexical-reference paradigm. (Cf. note 2.) This sort of assimilation suggests that one might maintain a relatively clearcut distinction between extramental and mental aspects of mentalistic attributions. And it may encourage the idea that the distinctively mental aspects can be understood fundamentally in terms of the individual's abilities, dispositions, states, and so forth, considered in isolation from his social surroundings. Our argument undermines this latter suggestion. Social context infects even the distinctively mental features of mentalistic attributions. No man's intentional mental phenomena are insular. Every man is a piece of the social continent, a part of the social main.

III. Reinterpretations

IIIa. Methodology I find that most people unspoiled by conventional philosophical training regard the three steps of the thought experiment as painfully obvious. Such folk tend to chafe over my filling in details or elaborating on strategy. I think this naivete appropriate. But for sophisticates the three steps require defense.

Before launching a defense, I want to make a few remarks about its methodology. My objective is to better understand our common mentalistic notions. Although such notions are subject to revision and refinement, I take it as evident that there is philosophical interest in theorizing about them as they now are. I assume that a primary way of achieving theoretical understanding is to concentrate on our *discourse* about mentalistic notions. Now it is, of course, never obvious at the outset how much idealization, regimentation, or special interpretation is necessary in order to adequately understand ordinary discourse. Phenomena such as ambiguity, ellipsis, indexicality, idioms, and a host of others certainly demand some regimentation or special interpretation for purposes of linguistic theory. Moreover, more global considerations—such as simplicity in accounting for structural relations—often have effects on the cast of one's theory. For all that, there is a methodological bias in favor of taking natural discourse literally, other things being equal. For example, unless there are clear reasons for construing discourse as ambiguous, elliptical or involving special idioms, we should not so construe it. Literal interpretation is *ceteris paribus* preferred. My defense of the thought experiment, as I have interpreted it, partly rests on this principle.

This relatively non-theoretical interpretation of the thought experiment should be extended to the gloss on it that I provided in Section IIc. The notions of misconception, incomplete understanding, conceptual or linguistic error, and ordinary empirical error are to be taken as carrying little theoretical weight. I assume that these notions mark defensible, common-sense distinctions. But I need not take a position on available philosophical interpretations of these distinctions. In fact, I do not believe that understanding, in our examples, can be explicated as independent of empirical knowledge, or that the conceptual errors of our subjects are best seen as 'purely' mistakes about concepts and as involving no 'admixture' of error about 'the world.' With Quine, I find such talk about purity and mixture devoid of illumination or explanatory power. But my views on this matter neither entail nor are entailed by the premises of the arguments I give (cf. e.g., IIId). Those arguments seem to me to remain plausible under any of the relevant philosophical interpretations of the conceptual-ordinary-empirical distinction.

I have presented the experiment as appealing to ordinary intuition. I believe that common practice in the attribution of propositional attitudes is fairly represented by the various steps. This point is not really open to dispute. Usage may be divided in a few of the cases in which I have seen it as united. But broadly speaking, it seems to me undeniable that the individual steps of the thought experiment are acceptable to ordinary speakers in a wide varity of examples. The issue open to possible dispute is whether the steps should be taken in the literal way in which I have taken them, and thus whether the conclusion I have drawn from those steps is justified. In the remainder of Section III, I shall try to vindicate the literal interpretation of our examples. I do this by criticizing, in order of increasing generality or abstractness, a series of attempts to reinterpret the thought experiment's first step. Ultimately, I suggest (IIId and IV) that these attempts derive from characteristically philosophical models that have little or no independent justification. A thoroughgoing review of these models would be out of bounds, but the present paper is intended to show that they are deficient as accounts of our actual practice of mentalistic attribution.

I shall have little further to say in defense of the second and third steps of the thought experiment. Both rest on their intuitive plausibility, not on some particular theory. The third step, for example, certainly does not depend on a view that contents are merely sentences the subject is disposed to utter, interpreted as his community interprets them. It is compatible with several philosophical accounts of mental contents, including those that appeal to more abstract entities such as Fregean thoughts or Russellian propositions, and those that seek to deny that content-clauses indicate any *thing* that might be called a content. I also do not claim that the fact that our subject lacks the relevant beliefs in the third step follows from the facts I have described. The point is that it is plausible, and certainly possible, that he would lack those beliefs.

The exact interpretation of the second step is relevant to a number of causal or functional theories of mental phenomena that I shall discuss in Section IV. The intuitive idea of the step is that none of the different physical, non-intentionally described causal chains set going by the differences in communal practice need affect our subjects in any way that would be relevant to an account of their mental contents. Differences in the behavior of other members of the community will, to be sure, affect the gravitational forces exerted on the subject. But I assume that these differences are irrelevant to macro-explanations of our subjects' physical movements and inner processes. They do not relevantly affect ordinary non-intentional physical explanations of how the subject acquires or is disposed to use the symbols in his repertoire. Of course, the social origins of a person's symbols do differ between actual and counterfactual cases. I shall return to this point in Sections IV and V. The remainder of Section III will be devoted to the first step of the thought experiment.

IIIb. Incomplete understanding and standard cases of reinterpretation The first step, as I have interpreted it, is the most likely to encounter opposition. In fact, there is a line of resistance that is second nature to linguistically oriented philosophers. According to this line, we should deny that, say, the patient really believed or thought that arthritis can occur outside of joints because he misunderstood the word 'arthritis'. More generally, we should deny that a subject could have any attitudes whose contents he incompletely understands.

What a person understands is indeed one of the chief factors that bear on what thoughts he can express in using words. If there were not deep and important connections between propositional attitudes and understanding, one could hardly expect one's attributions of mental content to facilitate reliable predictions of what a person will do, say, or think. But our examples provide reason to believe that these connections are not simple entailments to the effect that having a propositional attitude strictly implies full understanding of its content.

There are, of course, numerous situations in which we normally reinterpret or discount a person's words in deciding what he thinks. Philosophers often invoke such cases to bolster their animus against such attributions as the ones we made to our subjects: 'If a foreigner were to mouth the words 'arthritis may occur in the thigh' or 'my father had arthritis', not understanding what he uttered in the slightest, we would not say that he believed that arthritis may occur in the thigh, or that his father had arthritis. So why should we impute the belief to the patient?' Why, indeed? Or rather, why do we?

The question is a good one. We do want a general account of these cases. But the implied argument against our attribution is anemic. We tacitly and routinely distinguish between the cases I described and those in which a foreigner (or anyone) utters something without any comprehension. The best way to understand mentalistic notions is to recognize such differences in standard practice and try to account for them. One can hardly justify the assumption that full understanding of a content is in general a necessary condition for believing the content by appealing to some cases that tend to support the assumption in order to reject others that conflict with it.

It is a good method of discovery, I think, to note the sorts of cases philosophers tend to gravitate toward when they defend the view that the first step in the thought experiment should receive special interpretation. By reflecting on the differences between these cases and the cases we have cited, one should learn something about principles controlling mentalistic attribution.

I have already mentioned foreigners without command of the language. A child's imitation of our words and early attempts to use them provide similar examples. In these cases, mastery of the language and responsibility to its precepts have not been developed; and mental content attribution based on the meaning of words uttered tends to be precluded.

There are cases involving regional dialects. A person's deviance or ignorance judged by the standards of the larger community may count as normality or full mastery when evaluated from the regional perspective. Clearly, the regional standards tend to be the relevant ones for attributing content when the speaker's training or intentions are regionally oriented. The conditions for such orientation are complex, and I shall touch on them again in Section V. But there is no warrant in actual practice for treating each person's idiolect as always analogous to dialects whose words we automatically reinterpret—for purposes of mental content attribution—when usage is different. People are frequently held, and hold themselves, to the standards of their community when misuse or misunderstanding are at issue. One should distinguish these cases, which seem to depend on a certain *responsibility* to communal practice, from cases of automatic reinterpretation.

Tongue slips and Spoonerisms form another class of example where reinterpretation of a person's words is common and appropriate in arriving at an attribution of mental content. In these cases, we tend to exempt the speaker even from commitment to a homophonically formulated assertion content, as well as to the relevant mental content. The speaker's own behavior usually follows this line, often correcting himself when what he uttered is repeated back to him.

Malapropisms form a more complex class of examples. I shall not try to map it in detail. But in a fairly broad range of cases, we reinterpret a person's words at least in attributing mental content. If Archie says, 'Lead the way and we will precede', we routinely reinterpret the words in describing his expectations. Many of these cases seem to depend on the presumption that there are simple, superficial (for example, phonological) interference or exchange mechanisms that account for the linguistic deviance.

There are also examples of quite radical misunderstandings that sometimes generate reinterpretation. If a generally competent and reasonable speaker thinks that 'orangutan' applies to a fruit drink, we would be reluctant, and it would unquestionably be misleading, to take his words as revealing that he thinks he has been drinking orangutans for breakfast for the last few weeks. Such total misunderstanding often *seems* to block literalistic mental content attribution, at least in cases where we are not directly characterizing his mistake. (Contrary to philosophical lore, I am not convinced that such a man cannot correctly and literally be attributed a belief that an orangutan is a kind of fruit drink. But I shall not deal with the point here.)

There are also some cases that do not seem generally to prevent mental content attribution on the basis of literal interpretation of the subject's words in quite the same way as the others, but which deserve some mention. For almost any content except for those that directly display the subject's incomplete understanding, there will be many contexts in which it would be misleading to attribute that content to the subject without further comment. Suppose I am advising you about your legal liabilities in a situation where you have entered into what may be an unwritten contract. You ask me what Al would think. It would be misleading for me to reply that Al would think that you do not have a contract (or even do not have any legal problems), if I know that Al thinks a contract must be based on a formal document. Your evaluation of Al's thought would be crucially affected by his inadequate understanding. In such cases, it is incumbent on us to cite the subject's eccentricity: '(He would think that you do not have a contract, but then) he thinks that there is no such thing as a verbally based contract.'

Incidentally, the same sort of example can be constructed using attitudes that are abnormal, but that do not hinge on misunderstanding of any one notion. If Al had thought that only traffic laws and laws against violent crimes are ever prosecuted, it would be misleading for me to tell you that Al would think that you have no legal problems.

Both sorts of cases illustrate that in reporting a single attitude content, we typically suggest (implicate, perhaps) that the subject has a range of other attitudes that are normally associated with it. Some of these may provide reasons for it. In both sorts of cases, it is usually important to keep track of, and often to make explicit, the nature and extent of the subject's deviance. Otherwise, predictions and evaluations of his thought and action, based on normal background assumptions, will go awry. When the deviance is huge, attributions demand reinterpretation of the subject's words. Radical misunderstanding and mental instability are cases in point. But frequently, common practice seems to allow us to cancel the misleading suggestions by making explicit the subject's deviance, retaining literal interpretation of his words in our mentalistic attributions all the while.

All of the foregoing phenomena are relevant to accounting for standard practice. But they are no more salient than cases of straightforward belief attribution where the subject incompletely understands some notion in the attributed belief content. I think any impulse to say that common practice is *simply* inconsistent should be resisted (indeed, scorned). We cannot expect such practice to follow general principles rigorously. But even our brief discussion of the matter should have suggested the beginnings of generalizations about differences between cases where reinterpretation is standard and cases where it is not. A person's overall linguistic competence, his allegiance and responsibility to communal standards, the degree, source, and type of misunderstanding, the purposes of the report—all affect the issue. From a theoretical point of view, it would be a mistake to try to assimilate the cases in one direction or another. We do not want to credit a two-year-old who memorizes '$e = mc^2$' with belief in relativity theory. But the patient's attitudes involving the notion of arthritis should not be assimilated to the foreigner's uncomprehending pronunciations.

For purposes of defending the thought experiment and the arguments I draw from it, I can afford to be flexible about exactly how to generalize about these various phenomena. The thought experiment depends only on there being some cases in which a person's incomplete understanding does not force reinterpretation of his expressions in describing his mental contents. Such cases appear to be legion.

IIIc. Four methods of reinterpreting the thought experiment I now want to criticize attempts to argue that even in cases where we ordinarily do ascribe content clauses despite the subject's incomplete understanding of expressions in those clauses, such ascriptions should not be taken literally. In order to overturn our interpretation of the thought experiment's first step, one must argue that none of the cases I have cited is appropriately taken in the literal manner. One must handle (apparent) attributions of unproblematically true contents involving incompletely mastered notions, as well as attributions of contents that display the misconceptions or partial understandings. I do not doubt that one can erect logically coherent and metaphysically traditional reinterpretations of all these cases. What I doubt is that such reinterpretations taken *in toto* can present a plausible view, and that taken individually they have any claim to superiority over the literal interpretations—either as accounts of the language of ordinary mentalistic ascription, or as accounts of the evidence on which mental attributions are commonly based.

Four types of reinterpretation have some currency. I shall be rather short with the first two, the first of which I have already warned against in Section IId. Sometimes relevant mentalistic ascriptionss are reinterpreted as attributions of *de re* attitudes *of* entities not denoted by the misconstrued expressions. For example, the subject's belief that he has arthritis in the thigh might be interpreted as a belief *of* the non-arthritic rheumatoid ailment that it is in the thigh. The subject will probably have such a belief in this case. But it hardly accounts for the relevant attributions. In particular, it ignores the oblique occurrence of 'arthritis' in the original ascription. Such occurrences bear on a characterization of the subject's viewpoint. The subject thinks of the disease in his thigh (and of his arthritis) in a certain way. He thinks of each disease that it is arthritis. Other terms for arthritis (or for the actual trouble in his thigh) may not enable us to describe his attitude content nearly as well. The appeal to *de re* attitudes in this way is not adequate to the task of reinterpreting these ascriptions so as to explain away the difference between actual and counterfactual situations. It simply overlooks what needs explication.

A second method of reinterpretation, which Descartes proposed (cf. Section IV) and which crops up occasionally, is to claim that in cases of incomplete understanding, the subject's attitude or content is indefinite. It is surely true that in cases where a person is extremely confused, we are sometimes at a loss in describing his attitudes. Perhaps in such cases, the subject's mental content *is* indefinite. But in the cases I have cited, common practice lends virtually no support to the contention that the subject's mental contents are indefinite. The subject and his fellows typically know and agree on precisely *how to confirm or infirm* his beliefs—both in the cases where they are unproblematically true (or just empirically false) and in the cases where they display the misconception. Ordinary attributions typically specify the mental content without qualifications or hesitations.

In cases of partial understanding—say, in the mortgage example—it may indeed be unclear, short of extensive questioning, just how much mastery the subject has. But even this sort of unclarity does not appear to prevent, under ordinary circumstances, straightforward attributions utilizing 'mortgage' in oblique position. The subject is uncertain whether his father has two mortgages; he knows that his uncle has paid off the mortgage on his house. The contents are unhesitatingly attributed and admit of unproblematic testing for truth value, despite the subject's partial understanding. There is thus little *prima facie* ground for the appeal to indefiniteness. The appeal appears to derive from a prior assumption that attribution of a content entails attribution of full understanding. Lacking an easy means of attributing something other than the misunderstood content, one is tempted to say that there *is* no definite content. But this is unnecessarily mysterious. It reflects on the prior assumption, which so far has no independent support.

The other two methods of reinterpretation are often invoked in tandem. One is to attribute a notion that just captures the misconception, thus replacing contents that are apparently false on account of the misconception, by true contents. For example, the subject's belief (true or false) that that is a sofa would be replaced by, or reinterpreted as, a (true) belief that that is a *chofa*, where 'chofa' is introduced to apply not only to sofas, but also to the armchairs the subject thinks are sofas. The other method is to count the error of the subject as purely metalinguistic. Thus the patient's apparent belief that he had arthritis in the thigh would be reinterpreted as a belief that 'arthritis' applied to something (or some disease) in his thigh. The two methods can be applied simultaneously, attempting to account for an ordinary content attribution in terms of a reinterpreted object-level content together with a metalinguistic error. It is important to remember that in order to overturn the thought experiment, these methods must not only establish that the subject held the particular attitudes that they advocate attributing; they must also justify a *denial* of the ordinary attributions literally interpreted.

The method of invoking object-level notions that precisely capture (and that replace) the subject's apparent misconception has little to be said for it as a natural and generally applicable account of the language of mentalistic ascriptions. We do not ordinarily seek out true object-level attitude contents to attribute to victims of errors based on incomplete understanding. For example, when we find that a person has been involved in a misconception in examples like ours, we do not regularly reinterpret those ascriptions that involved the misunderstood term, but were untuitively unaffected by the error. An attribution to someone of a true belief that he is eating brisket, or that he has just signed a contract, or that Uncle Harry has paid off his mortgage, is not typically reformulated when it is learned that the subject had not fully understood what brisket (or a contract, or a mortgage) is. A similar point applies when we know about the error at the time of the attribution—at least if we avoid misleading the audience in cases where the error is crucial to the issue at hand. Moreover, we shall frequently see the subject as sharing beliefs with others who understand the relevant notions better. In counting beliefs as shared, we do not require, in every case, that the subjects 'fully understand' the notions in those belief contents, or understand them in just the same way. Differences in understanding are frequently located as differences over other belief contents. We agree that you have signed a contract, but disagree over whether someone else could have made a contract by means of a verbal agreement.

There are reasons why ordinary practice does not follow the method of object-level reinterpretation. In many cases, particularly those involving partial understanding, finding a reinterpretation in accord with the method would be entirely nontrivial. It is not even clear that we have agreed upon means of pursuing such inquiries in all cases. Consider the arthritic patient. Suppose we are to reinterpret the attribution of his erroneous belief that he has arthritis in the thigh. We make up a term 'tharthritis' that covers arthritis and whatever it is he has in his thigh. The appropriate restrictions on the application of this term and of the patient's supposed notion are unclear. Is just any problem in the thigh that the patient wants to call 'arthritis' to count as tharthritis? Are other ailments covered? What would decide? The problem is that there are no recognized standards governing the application of the new term. In such cases, the method is patently *ad hoc*.

The method's willingness to invoke new terminology whenever conceptual error or partial understanding occurs is *ad hoc* in another sense. It proliferates terminology without evident theoretical reward. We do not engender better understanding of the patient by inventing a new word and saying that he thought (correctly) that tharthritis can occur outside joints. It is simpler and equally informative to construe him as thinking that arthritis may occur outside joints. When we are making other attributions that do not directly display the error, we must simply bear the deviant belief in mind, so as not to assume that all of the patient's inferences involving the notion would be normal.

The method of object-level reinterpretation often fails to give a plausible account of the evidence on which we base mental attributions. When caught in the sorts of errors we have been discussing, the subject does not normally respond by saying that his views had been misunderstood. The patient does not say (or think) that he had thought he had some-category-of-disease-like-arthritis-and-including-arthritis-but-also-capable-of-occurring-outside-of-joints in the thigh *instead* of the error commonly attributed. This sort of response would be disingenuous. Whatever other beliefs he had, the subject thought that he had arthritis in the thigh. In such cases, the subject will ordinarily give no evidence of having maintained a true object-level belief. In examples like ours, he typically admits his mistake, changes his views, and leaves it at that. Thus the subject's own behavioral dispositions and inferences often fail to support the method.

The method may be seen to be implausible as an account of the relevant evidence in another way. The patient knows that he has had arthritis in the ankle and wrists for some time. Now with his new pains in the thigh, he fears and believes that he has got arthritis in the thigh, that his arthritis is spreading. Suppose we reinterpret all of these attitude attributions in accord with the method. We use our recently coined term 'tharthritis' to cover (somehow) arthritis and whatever it is he has in the thigh. On this new interpretation, the patient is right in thinking that he has tharthritis in the ankle and wrists. His belief that it has lodged in the thigh is true. His fear is realized. But these attributions are out of keeping with the way we do and should view his actual beliefs and fears. His belief is not true, and his fear is not realized. He will be relieved when he is told that one cannot have arthritis in the thigh. His relief is bound up with a network of assumptions that he makes about his arthritis: that it is a kind of disease, that there are debilitating consequences of its occurring in multiple locations, and so on. When told that arthritis cannot occur in the thigh, the patient does not decide that his fears were realized, but that perhaps he should not have had those fears. He does not think: Well, my tharthritis *has* lodged in the thigh; but judging from the fact that what the doctor called 'arthritis' cannot occur in the thigh, tharthritis may not be a single kind of disease; and I suppose I need not worry about the effects of its occurring in various locations, since evidently the tharthritis in my thigh is physiologically unrelated to the tharthritis in my joints. There will rarely if ever be an empirical basis for such a description of the subject's inferences. The patient's behavior (including his reports, or thinkings-out-loud) in this sort of case will normally not indicate any such pattern of inferences at all. But this is the description that the object-level reinterpretation method appears to recommend.

On the standard attributions, the patient retains his assumptions about the relation between arthritis, kinds of disease, spreading, and so on. And he concludes that his arthritis is not appearing in new locations—at any rate, not in his thigh. These attributions will typically be supported by the subject's behavior. The object-level reinterpretation method postulates inferences that are more complicated and different in focus from the inferences that the evidence supports. The method's presentation in such a case would seem to be an *ad hoc* fiction, not a description with objective validity.

None of the foregoing is meant to deny that frequently when a person incompletely understands an attitude content he has some other attitude content that more or less captures his understanding. For example, in the contract example, the client will probably have the belief that if one breaks a *legally binding agreement based on formal documents*, then one may get into trouble. There are also cases in which it is reasonable to say that, at least in a sense, a person has a notion that is expressed by his dispositions to classify things in a certain way—even if there is no conventional term in the person's repertoire that neatly corresponds to that 'way.' The sofa case may be one such. Certain animals as well as people may have non-verbal notions of this sort. On the other hand, the fact that such attributions are justifiable *per se* yields no reason to deny that the subject (also) has object-level attitudes whose contents involve the relevant incompletely understood notion.

Whereas the third method purports to account for the subject's thinking at the object level, the fourth aims at accounting for his error. The error is construed as purely a metalinguistic mistake. The relevant false content is seen to involve notions that denote or apply to linguistic expressions. In examples relevant to our thought experiment, we ordinarily attribute a metalinguistic as well as an object-level attitude to the subject, at least in the case of non-occurrent propositional attitudes. For example, the patient probably believes that 'arthritis' applies in English to the ailment in his thigh. He believes that his father had a disease called 'arthritis.' And so on. Accepting these metalinguistic attributions, of course, does nothing *per se* toward making plausible a denial that the subjects in our examples have the counterpart object-level attitudes.

Like the third method, the metalinguistic reinterpretation method has no *prima facie* support as an account of the language of mentalistic ascriptions. When we encounter the subject's incomplete understanding in examples like ours, we do not decide that all the mental contents which we had been attributing to him with the misunderstood notion must have been purely metalinguistic in form. We also count people who incompletely understand terms in ascribed content clauses as sharing true and unproblematic object-level attitudes with others who understand the relevant terms better. For example, the lawyer and his client may share a wish that the client had not signed the contract to buy the house without reading the small print. A claim that these people share *only* attitudes with metalinguistic contents would have no support in linguistic practice.

The point about shared attitudes goes further. If the metalinguistic reinterpretation account is to be believed, we cannot say that a relevant English speaker shares a view (for example) that many old people have arthritis, with *anyone* who does not use the English word 'arthritis'. For the foreigner does not have the word 'arthritis' to hold beliefs about, though he does have attitudes involving the notion arthritis. And the attribution to the English speaker is to be interpreted metalinguistically, making reference to the word, so as not to involve attribution of the notion arthritis. This result is highly implausible. Ascriptions of such that-clauses as the above, regardless of the subject's language, serve to provide single descriptions and explanations of similar patterns of behavior, inference, and communication. To hold that we cannot accurately ascribe single content-clauses to English speakers and foreigners in such cases would not only accord badly with linguistic practice. It would substantially weaken the descriptive and explanatory power of our common attributions. In countless cases, unifying accounts of linguistically disparate but cognitively and behaviorally similar phenomena would be sacrificed.

The method is implausible in other cases as an account of standard evidence on which mental attributions are based. Take the patient who fears that his arthritis is spreading. According to the metalinguistic reinterpretation method, the patient's reasoning should be described as follows. He thinks that the word 'arthritis' applies to a single disease in him, that the disease in him called 'arthritis' is debilitating if it spreads, that 'arthritis' applies to the disease in his wrists and ankles. He fears that the disease called 'arthritis' has lodged in his thigh, and so on. Of course, it is often difficult to find evidential grounds for attributing an object-level attitude *as opposed* to its metalinguistic counterpart. As I noted, when a person holds one attitude, he often holds the other. But there are types of evidence, in certain contexts, for making such discriminations, particularly contexts in which *occurrent* mental events are at issue. The subject may maintain that his reasoning did not fix upon words. He may be brought up short by a metalinguistic formulation of his just-completed ruminations, and may insist that he was not interested in labels. In such cases, especially if the reasoning is not concerned with linguistic issues in any informal or antecedently plausible sense, attribution of an object-level thought content is supported by the relevant evidence, and metalinguistic attribution is not. To insist that the occurrent mental event really involved a metalinguistic content would be a piece of *ad hoc* special pleading, undermined by the evidence we actually use for deciding whether a thought was metalinguistic.

In fact, there appears to be a general presumption that a person is reasoning at the object level, other things being equal. The basis for this presumption is that metalinguistic reasoning requires a certain self-consciousness about one's words and social institutions. This sort of sophistication emerged rather late in human history. (Cf. any history of linguistics.) Semantical notions were a product of this sophistication.

Occurrent propositional attitudes prevent the overall reinterpretation strategy from providing a plausible total account which would block our thought experiment. For such occurrent mental events as the patient's thought that his arthritis is especially painful in the knee this morning are, or can be imagined to be, clear cases of object-level attitudes. And such thoughts may enter into or connect up with pieces of reasoning—say the reasoning leading to relief that the arthritis had not lodged in the thigh—which cannot be plausibly accounted for in terms of object-level reinterpretation. The other reinterpretation methods (those that appeal to *de re* contents and to indefiniteness) are non-starters. In such examples, the literally interpreted ascriptions appear to be straightforwardly superior accounts of the evidence that is normally construed to be relevant. Here one need not appeal to the principle that literal interpretation is, other things equal, preferable to reinterpretation. Other things are not equal.

At this point, certain philosophers may be disposed to point out that what a person says and how he behaves do not infallibly determine what his attitude contents are. Despite the apparent evidence, the subject's attitude contents may in all cases I cited be metalinguistic, and may fail to involve the incompletely understood notion. It is certainly true that how a person acts and what he says, even sincerely, do not determine his mental contents. I myself have mentioned a number of cases that support the point. (Cf. IIIb.) But the point is often used in a sloppy and irresponsible manner. It is incumbent on someone making it (and applying it to cases like ours) to indicate considerations that override the linguistic and behavioral evidence. In Section IIId, I shall consider intuitive or *a priori* philosophical arguments to this end. But first I wish to complete our evaluation of the metalinguistic reinterpretation method as an account of the language of mentalistic ascription in our examples.

In this century philosophers have developed the habit of insisting on metalinguistic reinterpretation for any content attribution that directly *displays* the subject's incomplete understanding. These cases constitute but a small number of the attributions that serve the thought experiment. One could grant these reinterpretations and still maintain our overall viewpoint. But even as applied to these cases, the method seems dubious. I doubt that any evidentially supported account of the language of these attributions will show them in general to be attributions of metalinguistic contents—contents that involve denotative reference to linguistic expressions.

The ascription 'He believes that broad overstuffed armchairs are sofas', as ordinarily used, does not in general *mean* 'He believes that broad, overstuffed armchairs are covered by the expression "sofas"' (or something like that). There are clear grammatical and semantical differences between

(i) broad, overstuffed armchairs are covered by the expression 'sofas'

and

(ii) broad, overstuffed armchairs are sofas.

When the two are embedded in belief contexts, they produce grammatically and semantically distinct sentences.

As noted, ordinary usage approves ascriptions like

(iii) He believes that broad, overstuffed armchairs are sofas.

It would be wildly *ad hoc* and incredible from the point of view of linguistic theory to claim that there is *no* reading of (iii) that embeds (ii). But there is no evidence from speaker behavior that *true* ascriptions of (iii) always (or perhaps even *ever*) derive from embedding (i) rather than (ii). In fact, I know of no clear evidence that (iii) is ambiguous between embedding (i) and (ii), or that (ii) is ambiguous, with one reading identical to that of (i). People do not in general seem to regard ascriptions like (iii) as elliptical. More important, in most cases no amount of nonphilosophical badgering will lead them to withdraw (iii), under some interpretation, *in favor of* an ascription that clearly embeds (i). At least in the cases of *non-occurrent* propositional attitudes, they will tend to agree to a clearly metalinguistic ascription—a belief sentence explicitly embedding something like (i)—in cases where they make an ascription like (iii). But this is evidence that they regard ascriptions that embed (i) and (ii) as both true. It hardly tells against counting belief ascriptions that embed (ii) as true, or against taking (iii) in the obvious, literal manner. In sum, there appears to be no ordinary empirical pressure on a theory of natural language to represent true ascriptions like (iii) as *not* embedding sentences like (ii). And other things being equal, literal readings are correct readings. Thus it is strongly plausible to assume that ordinary usage routinely accepts as true and justified even ascriptions like (iii), literally interpreted as embedding sentences like (ii).

There are various contexts in which we may be indifferent over whether to attribute a metalinguistic attitude or the corresponding object-level attitude. I have emphasized that frequently, though not always, we may attribute both. Or we might count the different contents as describing what contextually 'amount to the same attitude.' (Cf. Section I.) Even this latter locution remains compatible with the thought experiment, as long as both contents are *equally attributable* in describing 'the attitude.' In the counterfactual step of the thought experiment, the metalinguistic content (say, that broad, overstuffed armchairs are called 'sofas') will still be attributable. But in these circumstances it contextually 'amounts to the same attitude' as an object-level attitude whose content is in no sense equivalent to, or 'the same as,' the original object-level content. For they have different truth values. Thus, assuming that the object-level and metalinguistic contents are equally attributable, it remains informally plausible that the person's attitudes are different between actual and counterfactual steps in the thought experiment. This contextual conflation of object-level and metalinguistic contents is not, however, generally acceptable even in describing non-occurrent attitudes, much less occurrent ones. There are contexts in which the subject himself may give evidence of making the distinction.

IIId. Philosophical arguments for reinterpretation I have so far argued that the reinterpretation strategies that I have cited do not provide a plausible account of evidence relevant to a theory of the language of mentalistic ascriptions or to descriptions of mental phenomena themselves. I now want to consider characteristically philosophical arguments for revising ordinary discourse or for giving it a nonliteral reading, arguments that rely purely on intuitive or *a priori* considerations. I have encountered three such arguments, or argument sketches.[4]

One holds that the content clauses we ascribed must be reinterpreted so as to make reference to words because they clearly concern linguistic matters—or are about language. Even if this argument were sound, it would not affect the thought experiment decisively. For most of the mental contents that vary between actual and counterfactual situations are not in any intuitive sense 'linguistic.' The belief that certain armchairs are sofas is intuitively linguistic. But beliefs that some sofas are beige, that Kirkpatrick is playing a clavichord, and that Milton had severe arthritis in his hands are not.

But the argument is unpersuasive even as applied to the contents that, in an intuitive sense, do concern linguistic matters. A belief that broad, overstuffed armchairs are sofas is linguistic (or 'about' language) in the same senses as an 'analytically' true belief that no armchairs are sofas. But the linguistic nature of the latter belief does not make its logical form metalinguistic. So citing the linguistic nature of the former belief does not suffice to show it metalinguistic. No semantically relevant component of either content applies to or denotes linguistic expressions.

Both the 'analytically' true and the 'analytically' false attitudes are linguistic in the sense that they are tested by consulting a dictionary or native linguistic intuitions, rather than by ordinary empirical investigation. We do not scrutinize pieces

4. Cf. my 'Belief and Synonymy,' *The Journal of Philosophy* 75 (1978):119–38, Section III, where I concentrate on attribution of belief contents containing 'one criterion' terms like 'vixen' or 'fortnight' which the subject misunderstands. The next several pages interweave some of the points in that paper. I think that a parallel thought experiment involving even these words is constructible, at least for a narrowly restricted set of beliefs. We can imagine that the subject believes that some female foxes—say, those that are virgins—are not vixens. Or he could believe that a fortnight is a period of ten days. (I believed this for many years.) Holding his physical history, qualitative experience, and dispositions constant, we can conceive of his linguistic community defining these terms as he actually misunderstands them. In such a case, his belief contents would differ from his actual ones.

of furniture to test these beliefs. The pragmatic focus of expressions of these attitudes will be on usage, concepts, or meaning. But it is simply a mistake to think that these facts entail, or even suggest, that the relevant contents are metalinguistic in form. Many contents with object-level logical forms have primarily linguistic or conceptual implications.

A second argument holds that charitable interpretation requires that we not attribute to rational people beliefs like the belief that one may have arthritis in the thigh. Here again, the argument obviously does not touch most of the attitudes that may launch the thought experiment; for many are straightforwardly true, or false on ordinary empirical grounds. Even so, it is not a good argument. There is nothing irrational or stupid about the linguistic or conceptual errors we attribute to our subjects. The errors are perfectly understandable as results of linguistic misinformation.

In fact, the argument makes sense only against the background of the very assumption that I have been questioning. A belief that arthritis may occur in the thigh appears to be inexplicable or uncharitably attributed only if it is assumed that the subject must fully understand the notions in his attitude contents.

A third intuitive or *a priori* argument is perhaps the most interesting. Sometimes it is insisted that we should not attribute contents involving incompletely understood notions because *the individual must mean something different by the misunderstood word than what we non-deviant speakers mean by it.* Note again that it would not be enough to use this argument from deviant speaker meaning to show that the subject has notions that are not properly expressed in the way he thinks they are. In some sense of 'expressed', this is surely often the case. To be relevant, the argument must arrive at a negative conclusion: that the subject cannot have the attitudes that seem commonly to be attributed.

The expression 'the individual meant something different by his words' can be interpreted in more than one way. On one group of interpretations, the expression says little more than that the speaker incompletely understood his words: The patient thought 'arthritis' meant something that included diseases that occur outside of joints. The client would have misexplained the meaning, use, or application of 'contract'. The subject applied 'sofa' to things that, unknown to him, are not sofas. A second group of interpretations emphasizes that not only does the speaker misconstrue or misapply his words, but he had *in mind* something that the words do not denote or express. The subject sometimes had in mind certain armchairs when he used 'sofa.' The client regarded the notion of legal agreement based on written documents as approximately interchangeable with what is expressed by 'contract', and thus had such a notion in mind when he used 'contract'. A person with a problem about the range of red might sometimes have in mind a mental image of a non-red color when he used 'red'.

The italicized premise of the argument is, of course, always true in our examples under the first group of interpretations, and often true under the second. But interpreted in these ways, the argument is a *non sequitur.* It does not follow from the assumption that the subject thought that a word means something that it does not (or misapplies the word, or is disposed to misexplain its meaning) that the word cannot be used in literally describing his mental contents. It does not follow from the assumption that a person has in mind something that a word does not denote or express that the word cannot occur obliquely (and be interpreted literally) in that-clauses that provide some of his mental contents. As I have pointed out in Section IIIb, there is a range of cases in which we commonly reinterpret a person's incompletely understood words for purposes of mental-content attribution. But the present argument needs to show that deviant speaker-meaning always forces such reinterpretation.

In many of our examples, the idea that the subject has some deviant notion *in mind* has no intuitively clear application. (Consider the arthritis and mortgage examples). But even where this expression does seem to apply, the argument does not support the relevant conclusion. At best it shows that a notion deviantly associated with a word plays a role in the subject's attitudes. For example, someone who has in mind the notion of an agreement based on written documents when he says, 'I have just entered into a contract,' may be correctly said to believe that he has just entered into an agreement based on written documents. It does not follow from this that he *lacks* a belief or thought that he has just entered into a contract. In fact, in our view, the client's having the deviant notion in mind is *a likely consequence* of the fact that he believes that contracts are impossible without a written document.

Of course, given the first, more liberal set of interpretations of 'means something different', the fact that in our examples the subject means something different by his words (or at least applies them differently) is *implied* by certain of his beliefs. It is implied by a belief that he has arthritis in the thigh. A qualified version of the converse implication also holds. Given appropriate background assumptions, the fact that the subject has certain deviant (object-level) beliefs is implied by his meaning something different by his words. So far, no argument has shown that we cannot accept these implications and retain the literal interpretation of common mentalistic ascriptions.

The argument from deviant speaker-meaning downplays an intuitive feature that can be expected to be present in many of our examples. The subject's willingness to submit his statement and belief to the arbitration of an authority suggests a willingness to have his words taken in the normal way—regardless of mistaken associations with the word. Typically, the subject will regard recourse to a dictionary, and to the rest of us, as at once a check on his usage and his belief. When the verdict goes against him, he will not usually plead that we have simply misunderstood his views. This sort of behavior suggests that (given the sorts of background assumptions that common practice uses to distinguish our examples from those of foreigners, radical misunderstandings, and so forth) we can say that in a sense our man meant by 'arthritis' *arthritis*—where '*arthritis*' occurs, of course, obliquely. We can say this despite the fact that his incomplete understanding leads us, in one of the senses explicated earlier, to say that he meant something different by 'arthritis'.

If one tries to turn the argument from deviant speaker-meaning into a valid argument, one arrives at an assumption that seems to guide all three of the philosophical arguments I have discussed. The assumption is that what a person thinks his words mean, how he takes them, fully determines what attitudes he can express in using them: the contents of his mental states and events are strictly limited to notions, however idiosyncratic, that he understands; a person cannot think with notions he incompletely understands. But supplemented with this assumption, the argument begs the question at issue.

The least controversial justification of the assumption would be an appeal to standard practice in mentalistic attributions. But standard practice is what brought the assumption into question in the first place. Of course, usage is not sacred if good reasons for revising it can be given. But none have been.

The assumption is loosely derived, I think, from the old model according to which a person must be directly acquainted with, or must immediately apprehend, the contents of his thoughts. None of the objections explicitly invoke this model—and many of their proponents would reject it. But I think that all the objections derive some of their appeal from philosophical habits that have been molded by it. I shall discuss this model further in Section IV.

One may, of course, quite self-consciously neglect certain aspects of common mentalistic notions in the interests of a revised or idealized version of them. One such idealization could limit itself to just those attitudes involving 'full understanding' (for some suitably specified notion of understanding). This limitation is less clearcut than one might suppose, since the notion of understanding itself tends to be used according to misleading stereotypes. Still, oversimplified models, idealizations, of mentalistic notions are defensible, as long as the character and purpose of the oversimplifications are clear. In my opinion, limiting oneself to 'fully understood' attitudes provides no significant advantage in finding elegant and illuminating formal semantical theories of natural language. Such a strategy has perhaps a better claim in psychology, though even there its propriety is controversial. (Cf. Section IV.) More to the point, I think that models that neglect the relevant social factors in mentalistic attributions are not likely to provide long-run philosophical illumination of our actualistic mentalistic notions. But this view hardly admits of detailed support here and now.

Our argument in the preceding pages may, at a minimum, be seen as inveighing against a long-standing philosophical habit of denying that it *is* an oversimplification to make 'full understanding' of a content a necessary condition for having a propositional attitude with that content. The oversimplification does not constitute neglect of some quirk of ordinary usage. Misunderstanding and partial understanding are pervasive and inevitable phenomena, and attributions of content despite them are an integral part of common practice.

I shall not here elaborate a philosophical theory of the social aspects of mentalistic phenomena, though in Section V I shall suggest lines such a theory might take. One of the most surprising and exciting aspects of the thought experiment is that its most literal interpretation provides a perspective on the mental that has received little serious development in the philosophical tradition. The perspective surely invites exploration.

IV. Applications

I want to turn now to a discussion of how our argument bears on philosophical approaches to the mental that may be termed *individualistic*. I mean this term to be somewhat vague. But roughly, I intend to apply it to philosophical treatments that seek to see a person's intentional mental phenomena ultimately and purely in terms of what happens to the person, what occurs within him, and how he responds to his physical environment, without any essential reference to the social context in which he or the interpreter of his mental phenomena are situated. How I apply the term 'individualistic' will perhaps become clearer by reference to the particular cases that I shall discuss.

a. As I have already intimated, the argument of the preceding sections affects the traditional intro- (or extro-) spectionist treatments of the mind, those of Plato, Descartes, Russell, and numerous others. These treatments are based on a model that likens the relation between a person and the contents of his thought to seeing, where seeing is taken to be a kind of direct, immediate experience. On the most radical and unqualified versions of the model, a person's inspection of the contents of his thought is infallible: the notion of incompletely understanding them has no application at all.

The model tends to encourage individualistic treatments of the mental. For it suggests that what a person thinks depends on what occurs or 'appears' within his mind. Demythologized, what a person thinks depends on the power and extent of his comprehension and on his internal dispositions toward the comprehended contents. The model is expressed in perhaps its crudest and least qualified form in a well-known passage by Russell:

> Whenever a relation of supposing or judging occurs, the terms to which the supposing or judging mind is related by the relation of supposing or judging must be terms with which the mind in question is acquainted. . . . It seems to me that the truth of this principle is evident as soon as the principle is understood.[5]

Acquaintance is (for Russell) direct, infallible, non-propositional, non-perspectival

5. Bertrand Russell, *Mysticism and Logic* (London, 1959), p. 221. Although Russell's statement is unusually unqualified, its kinship to Descartes' and Plato's model is unmistakable. Cf. Plato, *Phaedrus*, 249b–c, *Phaedo*, 47b6–c4; Descartes, *Philosophical Works*, eds. Haldane and Ross 2 vols. (New York, 1955), *Rules for the Direction of the Mind*, section XII, Vol. I, pp. 41–42, 45; *Principles of Philosophy*, Part I, XXXII–XXXV. Vol. I, pp. 232–33; *Replies*, Vol. II, 52; Hume, *A Treatise of Human Nature*, 1, 3,5; II, 2,6; Kant, *A Critique of Pure Reason*, A7-B11; Frege, *The Foundations of Arithmetic*, section 105; G. E. Moore, *Principia Ethica*, 86.

knowledge. 'Terms' like concepts, ideas, attributes, forms, meanings, or senses are entities that occur in judgments more or less immediately before the mind on a close analogy to the way sensations are supposed to.

The model is more qualified and complicated in the writings of Descartes. In particular, he emphasizes the possibility that one might perceive the contents of one's mind unclearly or indistinctly. He is even high-handed enough to write, 'Some people throughout their lives perceive nothing so correctly as to be capable of judging it properly.'[6] This sort of remark appears to be a concession to the points made in Sections I and II about the possibility of a subject's badly understanding his mental contents. But the concession is distorted by the underlying introspection model. On Descartes' view, the person's faculty of understanding, properly so-called, makes no errors. Failure to grasp one's mental contents results from either blind prejudice or interference by 'mere' bodily sensations and corporeal imagery. The implication is that with sufficiently careful reflection on the part of the individual subject, these obstacles to perfect understanding can be cleared. That is, one need only be careful or properly guided in one's introspections to achieve full understanding of the content of one's intentional mental phenomena. Much that Descartes says suggests that where the subject fails to achieve such understanding, no definite content can be attributed to him. In such cases, his 'thinking' consists of unspecifiable or indeterminate imagery; attribution of definite conceptual content is precluded. These implications are reinforced in Descartes' appeal to self-evident, indubitable truths:

> There are some so evident and at the same time so simple that we cannot think of them without believing them to be true. . . . For we cannot doubt them unless we think of them; and we cannot think of them without at the same time believing them to be true, i.e. we can never doubt them.[7]

The self-evidence derives from the mere understanding of the truths, and fully understanding them is a precondition for thinking them at all. It is this last requirement that we have been questioning.

In the Empiricist tradition Descartes' qualifications on the direct experience model—particularly those involving the interfering effects of sensations and imagery—tend to fall away. What one thinks comes to be taken as a sort of impression (whether more imagistic or more intellectual) on or directly grasped by the individual's mind. The tendency to make full comprehension on the part of the subject a necessary condition for attributing a mental content to him appears both in philosophers who take the content to be a Platonic abstraction and in those who place it, in some sense, inside the individual's mind. This is certainly the direction in which the model pulls, with its picture of immediate accessibility to the individual. Thus Descartes' original concessions to cases of incomplete understanding

6. Descartes, *Principles of Philosophy*, XLV–XLI.
7. Descartes, *Philosophical Works*, Vol. II., *Replies*, p. 42.

became lost as his model became entrenched. What Wölfflin said of painters is true of philosophers: they learn more from studying each other than from reflecting on anything else.

The history of the model makes an intricate subject. My remarks are meant merely to provide a suggestive caricature of it. It should be clear, however, that in broad outline the model mixes poorly with the thought experiment of Section II, particularly its first step. The thought experiment indicates that certain 'linguistic truths' that have often been held to be indubitable can be thought yet doubted. And it shows that a person's thought *content* is not fixed by what goes on in him, or by what is accessible to him simply by careful reflection. The reason for this last point about 'accessibility' need not be that the content lies too deep in the unconscious recesses of the subject's psyche. Contents are sometimes 'inaccessible' to introspection simply because much mentalistic attribution does not presuppose that the subject has fully mastered the content of his thought.

In a certain sense, the metaphysical model has fixed on some features of our use of mentalistic notions to the exclusion of others. For example, the model fastens on the facts that we are pretty good at identifying our own beliefs and thoughts, and we have at least a *prima facie* authority in reporting a wide range of them. It also underlines the point that for certain contents we tend to count understanding as a sufficient condition for acknowledging their truth. (It is debatable, of course, how well it explains or illumines these observations.) The model also highlights the truism that a certain measure of understanding is required of a subject if we are to attribute intentional phenomena on the basis of what he utters. As we have noted, chance or purely rote utterances provide no ground for mental content attributions; certain verbal pathologies are discounted. The model extrapolates from these observations to the claim that a person can never fail to understand the content of his beliefs or thoughts, or that the remedy for such failure lies within his own resources of reflection (whether autonomous and conscious, or unconscious and guided). It is this extrapolation that requires one to pass over the equally patent practice of attributing attitudes where the subject incompletely understands expressions that provide the content of those attitudes. Insistence on metalinguistic reinterpretation and talk about the indefiniteness of attitude contents in cases of incomplete understanding seem to be rearguard defenses of a vastly overextended model.

The Cartesian-Russellian model has few strict adherents among prominent linguistic philosophers. But although it has been widely rejected or politely talked around, claims that it bore and nurtured are commonplace, even among its opponents. As we have seen in the objections to the first step of the argument of Section II, these claims purport to restrict the contents we can attribute to a person on the basis of his use of language. The restrictions simply mimic those of Descartes. Freed of the picturesque but vulnerable model that formed them, the claims have assumed the power of dogma. Their strictures, however, misrepresent ordinary mentalistic notions.

b. This century's most conspicuous attempt to replace the traditional Cartesian model has been the behaviorist movement and its heirs. I take it as obvious that the argument of Section II provides yet another reason to reject the most radical version of behaviorism—'philosophical,' 'logical' or 'analytical' behaviorism. This is the view that mentalistic attributions can be 'analytically' defined, or given strict meaning equivalences, purely in non-mental, behavioral terms. No analysis resting purely on the individual's dispositions to behavior can give an 'analytic' definition of a mental content attribution because we can conceive of the behavioral definiens applying while the mentalistic definiendum does not. But a new argument for this conclusion is hardly needed since 'philosophical' behaviorists are, in effect, extinct.

There is, however, an heir of behaviorism that I want to discuss at somewhat greater length. The approach sometimes goes by the name 'functionalism,' although that term is applied to numerous slogans and projects, often vaguely formulated. Even views that seem to me to be affected by our argument are frequently stated so sketchily that one may be in considerable doubt about what is being proposed. So my remarks should be taken less as an attempt to refute the theses of particular authors than as an attack on a way of thinking that seems to inform a cluster of viewpoints. The quotations I give in footnotes are meant to be suggestive, if not always definitive, of the way of thinking the argument tells against.[8]

The views affected by the argument of Section II attempts to give something like a philosophical 'account' of the mental. The details and strategy—even the notion of 'account'—vary from author to author. But a recurrent theme is that mental notions are to be seen ultimately in terms of the individual subject's input, output, and inner dispositions and states, where these latter are characterized purely in terms of how they lead to or from output, input, or other inner states similarly characterized. Mental notions are to be explicated or identified in functional, non-mentalistic, non-intentional terminology. Proponents of this sort of idea are rarely very specific about what terms may be used in describing input and output, or even what sorts of terms count as 'functional' expressions. But the impression usually given is that input and output are to be specified in terms (acceptable to a behaviorist) of irritations of the subject's surfaces and movements of his body. On some versions, neurophysiological terms are allowed. More recently, there have been

8. Certain movements sometimes called 'functionalist' are definitely not my present concern. Nothing I say is meant to oppose the claim that hypotheses in psychology do and should make reference to 'sub-personal' states and processes in explaining human action and ordinary mental states and processes. My remarks may bear on precisely how such hypotheses are construed philosophically. But the hypotheses themselves must be judged primarily by their fruits. Similarly, I am not concerned with the claim that computers provide an illuminating perspective for viewing the mind. Again, our view may bear on the interpretation of the computer analogy, but I have no intention of questioning its general fruitfulness. On the other hand, insofar as functionalism is merely a slogan to the effect that 'once you see how computers might be made to work, you realize such and such about the mind,' I am inclined to let the cloud condense a little before weighing its contents.

liberalized appeals to causal input and output relations with particular, specified physical objects, stuffs, or magnitudes. Functional terms include terms like 'causes', 'leads to with probability n', and the like. For our purposes, the details do not matter much, as long as an approach allows no mentalistic or other intentional terms (such as 'means' or that-clauses) into its vocabulary, and as long as it applies to individuals taken one by one.

A difference between this approach and that of philosophical behaviorism is that a whole array of dispositional or functional states—causally or probabilistically interrelated—may enter into the 'account' of a single mental attribution. The array must be ultimately secured to input and output, but the internal states need not be so secured one by one. The view is thus not immediately vulnerable to claims against simplistic behaviorisms, that a *given* stimulus-response pattern may have different contents in different social contexts. Such claims, which hardly need a defender, have been tranquilly accepted on this view. The view's hope is that differences in content depend on functional differences in the individual's larger functional structure. From this viewpoint, analytical behaviorism erred primarily in its failure to recognize the interlocking or wholistic character of mental attributions and in its oversimplification of theoretical explanation.

As I said, the notion of an account of the mental varies from author to author. Some authors take over the old-fashioned ideal of an 'analysis' from philosophical behaviorism and aim at a definition of the meaning of mentalistic vocabulary, or a definitional elimination of it. Others see their account as indicating a series of scientific hypotheses that identify mental states with causal or functional states, or roles, in the individual. These authors reject behaviorism's goal of providing meaning equivalences, as well as its restrictive methods. The hypotheses are supposed to be type or property identities and are nowadays often thought to hold necessarily, even if they do not give meaning relations. Moreover, these hypotheses are offered not merely as speculation about the future of psychology, but as providing a philosophically illuminating account of our ordinary notion of the mental. Thus if the view systematically failed to make plausible type identities between functional states and mental states, ordinarily construed, then by its own lights it would have failed to give a philosophical 'account' of the mental. I have crudely overschematized the methodological differences among the authors in this tradition. But the differences fall roughly within the polar notions of *account* that I have described. I think our discussion will survive the oversimplifications.[9]

9. A representative of the more nearly 'analytical' form of functionalism is David Lewis, 'Psychophysical and Theoretical Identifications,' *Australasian Journal of Philosophy* 50 (1972):249–58: 'Applied to common-sense psychology–folk science rather than professional science, but a theory nonetheless–we get the hypothesis . . . that a mental state M . . . is definable as the occupant of a certain causal role R–that is, as the state, of whatever sort, that is causally connected in specified ways to sensory stimuli, motor responses, and other mental states' (249–50). Actually, it should be noted that the argument of Section I applies to Lewis's position less directly than one might suppose. For reasons unconnected with matters at hand, Lewis intends his *definition* to apply to relational mentalistic predicates like 'thinks' but not to complex predicates that identify actual

Any attempt to give an account of specific beliefs and thoughts along the lines I have indicated will come up short. For we may fix the input, output, and total array of dispositional or functional states of our subject, as long as these are non-intentionally described and are limited to what is relevant to accounting for his activity taken in isolation from that of his fellows. But we can still conceive of his mental contents as varying. Functionally equivalent people—on any plausible notion of functional equivalence that has been sketched—may have non-equivalent mental-state and event contents, indicated by obliquely non-equivalent content clauses. Our argument indicates a systematic inadequacy in attempts of the sort I described.

Proponents of functionalist accounts have seen them as revealing the true nature of characteristic marks of the mental and as resolving traditional philosophical issues about such marks. In the case of beliefs, desires, and thoughts, the most salient mark is intentionality—the ill-specified information-bearing, representational feature that seems to invest these mental states and events.[10] In our

mental states or events, like 'thinks that snow is white'. Cf. *Ibid.*, p. 256, n13. This seems to me a puzzling halfway house for some of Lewis's philosophical purposes. But our argument appears to apply anyway, since Lewis is explicit in holding that physical facts about a person taken in isolation from his fellows 'determine' all his specific intentional events and states. Cf. 'Radical Interpretation', *Syntbese* 27 (1974):331ff. I cite Lewis's definitional approach because it has been the most influential recent piece of its genre, and many of those influenced by it have not excluded its application to specific intentional mental states and events. Other representatives of the definitional approach are J. J. C. Smart, 'Further Thoughts on the Identity Theory,' *Monist* 56 (1972):149–62; D. W. Armstrong, *A Materialist Theory of Mind* (London, 1968), pp. 90–91 and *passim*; Sidney Shoemaker, 'Functionalism and Qualia,' *Philosophical Studies* 27 (1975):306–7. A representative of the more frequently held 'hypothesis' version of functionalism is Hilary Putnam, 'The Mental Life of Some Machines,' *Philosophical Papers* 2 (Cambridge, 1975), and 'The Nature of Mental States,' *Ibid.*, cf. p. 437 (p. 165 of this volume): '. . . if the program of finding psychological laws that are not species specific . . . ever succeeds, then it will bring in its wake a delineation of the kind of functional organization that is necessary and sufficient for a given psychological state, as well as a precise definition of the notion "psychological state".' In more recent work, Putnam's views on the relation between functional organization and psychological (and also mental) states and events have become more complicated. I make no claims about how the argument of Section II bears on them. Other representatives of the 'hypothesis' approach are Gilbert Harman, 'Three Levels of Meaning,' *The Journal of Philosophy* 65 (1968); 'An Introduction to 'Translation and Meaning',' *Words and Objections*, eds. D. Davidson and J. Hintikka (Reidel, 1969), p. 21; and *Thought* (Princeton, 1973), pp. 43–46, 56–65, for example, p. 45: '. . . mental states and processes are to be functionally defined (by a psychological theory). They are constituted by their function or role in the relevant programme': Jerry Fodor, *The Language of Thought* (New York, 1975), Chapter I; Armstrong, *A Materialist Theory of Mind*, p. 84. An attempt to articulate the common core of the different types of functionalist 'account' occurs in Ned Block and Jerry Fodor's 'What Psychological States are Not,' *Philosophical Review* 81 (1972), p. 173: '. . . functionalism in the broad sense of that doctrine which holds that type identity conditions for psychological states refer only to their relations to inputs, outputs and one another.'

10. Often functionalists give mental contents only cursory discussion, if any at all. But claims that a functional account explains intentionality by accounting for all specific intentional states and events in non-intentional, functional language occur in the following: Daniel Dennett, *Content and Consciousness* (London, 1969), Chapter II and *passim*; Harman, *Thought*, for example, p. 60: 'To specify the meaning of a sentence used in communication is partly to specify the belief or other

terminology, accounting for intentionality largely amounts to accounting for the content of mental states and events. (There is also, of course, the application of content in *de re* cases. But we put this aside here.) Such content is clearly part of what the functional roles of our subjects' states fail to determine.

It is worth re-emphasizing here that the problem is unaffected by suggestions that we specify input and output in terms of causal relations to particular objects or stuffs in the subject's physical environment. Such specifications may be thought to help with some examples based on indexicality or psychological success verbs, and perhaps in certain arguments concerning natural kind terms (though even in these cases I think that one will be forced to appeal to intentional language). (Cf. note 2.) But this sort of suggestion has no easy application to our argument. For the relevant causal relations between the subject and the physical environment to which his terms apply—where such relations are non-intentionally specified—were among the elements held constant while the subject's beliefs and thoughts varied.

The functionalist approaches I have cited seem to provide yet another case in which mental contents are not plausibly accounted for in non-intentional terms. They are certainly not explicable in terms of causally or functionally specified states and events of the *individual* subject. The intentional or semantical role of mental states and events is not a function merely of their functionally specified roles in the individual. The failure of these accounts of intentional mental states and events derives from an underestimation of socially dependent features of cognitive phenomena.

Before extending the application of our argument, I want to briefly canvass some ways of being influenced by it, ways that might appeal to someone fixed on the functionalist ideal. One response might be to draw a strict distinction between mental states, ordinarily so-called, and psychological states. One could then claim that the latter are the true subject matter of the science of psychology and may be identified with functional states functionally specified, after all. Thus one might claim that the subject was in the same psychological (functional) states in both the actual and the imagined situations, although he had different beliefs and thoughts ordinarily so-called.

There are two observations that need to be entered about this position. The first is that it frankly jettisons much of the philosophical interest of functionalist accounts. The failure to cope with mental contents is a case in point. The second observation is that it is far from clear that such a distinction between the psycho-

mental state expressed; and the representative character of that state is determined by its functional role'; Fodor, *The Language of Thought*, Chapters I and II, for example, p. 75: 'The way that information is stored, computed . . . or otherwise processed by the organism explains its cognitive states and in particular, its propositional attitudes'; Smart, 'Further Thoughts on the Identity Theory'; Hartry Field, 'Mental Representation,' *Erkenntnis* 13 (1978): 9–61. I shall confine discussion to the issue of intentionality. But it seems to me that the individualistic cast of functionalist accounts renders them inadequate in their handling of another major traditional issue about intentional mental states and events–first-person authority.

logical and the mental is or will be sanctioned by psychology itself. Functionalist accounts arose as philosophical interpretations of developments in psychology influenced by computer theory. The interpretations have been guided by philosophical interests, such as throwing light on the mind-body problem and accounting for mentalistic features in non-mentalistic terms. But the theories of cognitive psychologists, including those who place great weight on the computer analogy, are not ordinarily purified of mentalistic or intentional terminology. Indeed, intentional terminology plays a central role in much contemporary theorizing. (This is also true of theories that appeal to 'sub-personal' states or processes. The 'sub-personal' states themselves are often characterized intentionally.) Purifying a theory of mentalistic and intentional features in favor of functional or causal features is more clearly demanded by the goals of philosophers than by the needs of psychology. Thus it is at least an open question whether functional approaches of the sort we have discussed give a satisfactory account of *psychological* states and events. It is not evident that psychology will ever be methodologically 'pure' (or theoretically purifiable by some definitional device) in the way these approaches demand. *This* goal of functionalists may be simply a meta-psychological mistake.

To put the point another way, it is not clear that functional states, characterized purely in functional, non-intentional terms (and non-intentional descriptions of input and output) are the natural subject matter of psychology. Psychology would, I think, be an unusual theory if it restricted itself (or could be definitionally restricted) to specifying abstract causal or functional structures in purely causal or functional terms, together with vocabulary from other disciplines. Of course, it *may* be that functional states, functionally specified, form a psychological natural kind. And it is certainly not to be assumed that psychology will respect ordinary terminology in its individuation of types of psychological states and events. Psychology must run its own course. But the assumption that psychological terminology will be ultimately non-intentional and purely functional seems without strong support. More important from our viewpoint, if psychology did take the individualistic route suggested by the approaches we have cited, then its power to illumine the everyday phenomena alluded to in mentalistic discourse would be correspondingly limited.

These remarks suggest a second sort of functionalist response to the argument of Section II, one that attempts to take the community rather than the individual as the object of functional analysis. One might, for example, seek to explain an individual's responsibility to communal standards in terms of his having the right kind of interaction with other individuals who collectively had functional structures appropriate to those standards. Spelling out the relevant notions of interaction and appropriateness is, of course, anything but trivial. (Cf. Section V.) Doing so in purely functional, non-intentional terms would be yet a further step. Until such a treatment is developed and illustrated in some detail, there is little point in discussing it. I shall only conjecture that, if it is to remain non-intentional, such a treatment is likely to be so abstract—at least in our present state of psychological and sociological ignorance—that it will be unilluminating from a philosophical point of view. Some of the approaches we have been discussing already more than flirt with this difficulty.

c. Individualistic assumptions about the mental have infected theorizing about the relation between mind and meaning. An example is the Gricean project of accounting for conventional or linguistic meaning in terms of certain complex intentions and beliefs of individuals.[11] The Gricean program analyzes conventional meaning in terms of subtle 'mutual knowledge,' or beliefs and intentions about each others' beliefs and intentions, on the part of most or all members of a community. Seen as a quasi-definitional enterprise, the program presupposes that the notion of an individual's believing or intending something is always 'conceptually' independent of the conventional meaning of symbols used to express that something. Insofar as 'conceptually' has any intuitive content, this seems not to be the case. Our subject's belief or intention contents can be conceived to vary simply by varying conventions in the community around him. The content of individuals' beliefs seems sometimes to depend partly on social conventions in their environment. It is true that our subjects are actually rather abnormal members of their community, at least with respect to their use and understanding of a given word. But normality here is judged against the standards set by communal conventions. So stipulating that the individuals whose mental states are used in defining conventional meaning be relevantly normal will not avoid the circularity that I have indicated. I see no way to do so. This charge of circularity has frequently been raised on intuitive grounds. Our argument gives the intuitions substance. Explicating convention in terms of belief and intention may provide various sorts of insight. But it is not defining a communal notion in terms of individualistic notions. Nor is it reducing, in any deep sense, the semantical, or the intentional generally, to the psychological.

d. Individualistic assumptions have also set the tone for much discussion of the ontology of the mental. This subject is too large to receive detailed consideration here. It is complicated by a variety of crosscurrents among different projects, methodologies, and theses. I shall only explore how our argument affects a certain line of thinking closely allied to the functionalist approaches already discussed. These approaches have frequently been seen as resuscitating an old argument for the materialist identity theory. The argument is three-staged. First, one gives a philosophical 'account' of each mentalistic locution, an account that is *prima facie* neutral as regards ontology. For example, a belief or a thought that sofas are comfortable is supposed to be accounted for as one functionally specified state or event

11. H. P. Grice, 'Meaning,' *Philosophical Review* 66 (1957):377–88; 'Utterer's Meaning, Sentence-Meaning, and Word-Meaning,' *Foundations of Language* 4 (1968):225–42; Stephen Schiffer, *Meaning* (Oxford, 1972), cf. especially pp. 13, 50, 63ff; Jonathan Bennett, 'The Meaning-Nominalist Strategy,' *Foundations of Language* 10 (1974):141–68. Another example of an individualistic theory of meaning is the claim to explicate all kinds of meaning ultimately in psychological terms, and these latter in functionalist terms. See, for example Harman, 'Three Levels of Meaning,' note 9. This project seems to rest on the functionalist approaches just criticized.

within an array of others—all of which are secured to input and output. Second, the relevant functionally specified states or events are expected to be empirically correlated or correlatable with physiological states or events in a person (states or events that have those functions). The empirical basis for believing in these correlations is claimed to be provided by present or future physical science. The nature of the supposed correlations is differently described in different theories. But the most prevalent views expect only that the correlations will hold for each organism and person (perhaps at a given time) taken one by one. For example, the functionally specified event type that is identified with a thought that sofas are comfortable may be realized in one person by an instance (or 'token') of one physiological event type, and in another person by an instance of another physiological event type. Third, the ('token') mental state or event in the person is held to be identical with the relevant ('token') physiological state or event, on general grounds of explanatory simplicity and scientific method. Sometimes, this third stage is submerged by building uniqueness of occupancy of functional role into the first stage.[12]

I am skeptical about this sort of argument at every stage. But I shall doubt only the first stage here. The argument we gave in Section II directly undermines the attempt to carry out the first stage by recourse to the sort of functionalist approaches that we discussed earlier. Sameness of functional role, individualistically specified, is compatible with difference of content. I know of no better non-intentional account of mentalistic locutions. If a materialist argument of this genre is to arrive, it will require a longer first step.

I shall not try to say whether there is a philosophically interesting sense in which intentional mental phenomena are physical or material. But I do want to note some considerations against materialist *identity* theories.

State-like phenomena (say, beliefs) raise different problems from event-like phenomena (say, occurrent thoughts). Even among identity theorists, it is sometimes questioned whether an identity theory is the appropriate goal for materialism in the case of states. Since I shall confine myself to identity theories, I shall concentrate on event-like phenomena. But our considerations will also bear on views that hope to establish some sort of token identity theory for mental states like beliefs.

One other preliminary. I want to remain neutral about how best to describe the relation between the apparent event-like feature of occurrent thoughts and the apparent relational feature (their relation to a content). One might think of there being an event, the token thought event, that is in a certain relation to a content (indicated by the that-clause). One might think of the event as consisting—as not being anything 'over and above'—the relevant relation's holding at a certain time

12. Perhaps the first reasonably clear modern statement of the strategy occurs in J. J. C. Smart, 'Sensations and Brain Processes,' *Philosophical Review* 68 (1959):141–56 (Chapter 8 of this volume.). This article treats qualitative experiences; but Smart is explicit in applying it to specific intentional states and events in 'Further Thoughts on the Identity Theory.' Cf. also David Lewis, 'An Argument for the Identity Theory,' *The Journal of Philosophy* 63 (1966):17–25 (Chapter 10 of this volume.); 'Psychophysical and Theoretical Identifications'; Armstrong, *A Materialist Theory of Mind, passim*; Harman, *Thought*, pp. 42–43; Fodor, *The Language of Thought*, Introduction.

between a person and a content. Or one might prefer some other account. From the viewpoint of an identity theory, the first way of seeing the matter is most advantageous. So I shall fit my exposition to that point of view.

Our ordinary method of identifying occurrent thought events and differentiating between them is to make reference to the person or organism to whom the thought occurs, the time of its occurrence, and the content of the thought. If person, time, and content are the same, we would normally count the thought event the same. If any one of these parameters differs in descriptions of thought events (subject to qualifications about duration), then the events or occurrences described are different. Of course, we can differentiate between events using descriptions that do not home in on these particular parameters. But these parameters are dominant. (It is worth noting that differentiations in terms of causes and effects usually tend to rely on the content of mental events or states at some point, since mental states or events are often among the causes or effects of a given mental event, and these causes or effects will usually be identified partly in terms of their content.) The important point for our purposes is that in ordinary practice, sameness of thought content (or at least some sort of strong equivalence of content) is taken as a necessary condition for sameness of thought occurrence.

Now one might codify and generalize this point by holding that no occurrence of a thought (that is, no token thought event) could have a different (or extensionally non-equivalent) content and be the very same token event. If this premise is accepted, then our argument of Section II can be deployed to show that a person's thought event is not *identical* with any event in him that is described by physiology, biology, chemistry, or physics. For let *b* be any given event described in terms of one of the physical sciences that occurs in the subject while he thinks the relevant thought. Let '*b*' be such that it denotes the same physical event occurring in the subject in our counterfactual situation. (If you want, let '*b*' be rigid in Kripke's sense, though so strong a stipulation is not needed.) The second step of our argument in Section II makes it plausible that *b* need not be affected by counter-factual differences in the communal use of the word 'arthritis'. Actually, the subject thinks that his ankles are stiff from arthritis, while *b* occurs. But we can conceive of the subject's *lacking* a thought event that his ankles are stiff from arthritis, while *b* occurs. Thus in view of our initial premise, *b* is not identical with the subject's occurrent thought.[13]

13. The argument is basically Cartesian in style, (cf. *Meditations II*), (See Chapter 3 of this volume.) though the criticism of functionalism, which is essential to its success, is not in any obvious sense Cartesian. (Cf. note 14.) Also the conclusion gives no special support to Cartesian ontology. The terminology of rigidity is derived from Saul Kripke, 'Naming and Necessity,' *Semantics of Natural Language*, eds., Davidson and Harman (Dordrecht, 1972), (See Chapter 4 of this volume.) though as mentioned above, a notion of rigidity is not essential for the argument. Kripke has done much to clarify the force of the Cartesian sort of argument. He gives such an argument aimed at showing the non-identity of sensations with brain processes. The argument as presented seems to suffer from a failure to criticize materialistic accounts of sensation language and from not indicating clearly how token physical events and token sensation events that are *prima facie* candidates for identification could have occurred independently. For criticism of Kripke's argument, see Fred Feldman, 'Kripke

Identity theorists will want to reject the first premise—the premise that no event with a different content could be identical with a given thought event. On such a view, the given thought event that his ankles are stiff from arthritis might well have been a thought that his ankles are stiff from tharthritis, yet be precisely the same token thought event. Such a view is intuitively very implausible. I know of only one reasonably spelled-out basis of support for this view. Such a basis would be provided by showing that mentalistic phenomena are causal or functional states, in one of the strong senses discussed earlier, and that mental events are physical tokens or realizations of those states. If 'that thought that his ankles are stiff from arthritis' could be accounted for in terms like 'that event with such and such a causal or functional role' (where 'such and such' does not itself involve intentional terminology), and if independently identified physical events systematically filled these roles (or realized these states), we could perhaps see a given thought event as having a different role—and hence content—in different possible situations. Given such a view, the functional specification could perhaps be seen as revealing the contingency of the intentional specification as applied to mental event tokens. Just as we can imagine a given physiological event that actually plays the role of causing the little finger to move two inches, as playing the role of causing the little finger to move three inches (assuming compensatory differences in its physiological environment), so we could perhaps imagine a given thought as having a different functional role from its actual one—and hence, assuming the functionalist account, as having a different content. But the relevant sort of functionalist account of intentional phenomena has not been made good.[14]

on the Identity Theory,' *The Journal of Philosophy* 71 (1974):665–76; William G. Lycan, 'Kripke and the Materialists,' *Ibid.*, pp. 677–89; Richard Boyd, 'What Physicalism Does Not Entail,' *Readings in the Philosophy of Psychology*, ed. N. Block (forthcoming); Colin McGinn, 'Anomalous Monism and Kripke's Cartesian Intuitions,' *Analysis* 37 (1977):78–80. It seems to me, however, that these issues are not closed.

14. It is important to note that our argument against functionalist specifications of mentalistic phenomena did not depend on the assumption that no occurrent thought could have a different content from the one it has and be the very same occurrence or event. If it did, the subsequent argument against the identity theory would, in effect, beg the question. The strategy of the latter argument is rather to presuppose an independent argument that undermines non-intentional functionalist specifications of what it is to be *a* thought that (say) sofas are comfortable; then to take as plausible and undefeated the assumption that no occurrent thought could have a different (obliquely non-equivalent) content and be the same occurrence or event; and, finally, to use this assumption with the modal considerations appealed to earlier, to arrive at the non-identity of an occurrent thought event with any event specified by physical theory (the natural sciences) that occurs within the individual.

Perhaps it is worth saying that the metaphorical claim that mental events are identified by their *role* in some 'inference-action language game' (to use a phrase of Sellars's) does not provide a plausible ground for rejecting the initial premise of the argument against the identity theory. For even if one did not reject the 'role-game' idea as unsupported metaphor, one could agree with the claim on the understanding that the roles are largely the intentional contents themselves and the same event in *this* sort of 'game' could not have a different role. A possible view in the philosophy of mathematics is that numbers are identified by their role in a progression and such roles are essential to their identity. The point of this comparison is just that appeal to the role metaphor, even if accepted, does not settle the question of whether an intentional mental event or state could have had a different content.

The recent prosperity of materialist-functionalist ways of thinking has been so great that it is often taken for granted that a given thought event might have been a thought with a different, obliquely non-equivalent content. Any old event, on this view, could have a different content, a different significance, if its surrounding context were changed. But in the case of occurrent thoughts—and intentional mental events generally—it is hardly obvious, or even initially plausible, that anything is more essential to the identity of the event than the content itself. Materialist identity theories have schooled the imagination to picture the content of a mental event as varying while the event remains fixed. But whether such imaginings are possible fact or just philosophical fancy is a separate question.[15]

At any rate, functionalist accounts have not provided adequate specification of what it is to be a thought that ——, for particular fillings of the blank. So a specification of a given thought event in functionalist terms does not reveal the contingency of the usual, undisputed intentional specifications.

Well, *is* it possible for a thought event to have had a different content from the one it has and be the very same event? It seems to me natural and certainly traditional to assume that this is not possible. Rarely, however, have materialists seen the identity theory as natural or intuitive. Materialists are generally revisionist about intuitions. What is clear is that we currently do identify and distinguish thought events primarily in terms of the person who has them, the rough times of their occurrence, and their contents. And we do assume that a thought event with a

15. There are *prima facie* viable philosophical accounts that take sentences (whether tokens or types) as truth bearers. One might hope to extend such accounts to mental contents. On such treatments, contents are not things over and above sentences. They simply *are* sentences interpreted in a certain context, treated in a certain way. Given a different context of linguistic interpretation, the content of the same sentence might be different. One could imagine mental events to be analogous to the sentences on this account. Indeed, some philosophers have thought of intentional mental events as being inner, physical sentence (or symbol) tokens—a sort of brain writing. Here again, there is a picture according to which the same thought event might have had a different content. But here again the question is whether there is any reason to think it is a true picture. There is the prior question of whether sentences can reasonably be treated as contents. (I think sentence types probably can be; but the view has hardly been established, and defending it against sophisticated objections is treacherous.) Even if this question is answered affirmatively, it is far from obvious that the analogy between sentences and contents, on the one hand, and thought events and contents, on the other, is a good one. Sentences (types or tokens) are commonly identified independently of their associated contents (as evidenced by inter- and intra-linguistic ambiguity). It is *relatively* uncontroversial that sentences can be identified by syntactical, morphemic, or perceptual criteria that are in principle specifiable independently of what particular content the sentence has. The philosophical question about sentences and contents is whether discourse about contents can be reasonably interpreted as having an ontology of nothing more than sentences (and intentional agents). The philosophical question about mental events and contents is 'What is the nature of the events?' 'Regardless of what contents are, could the very same thought event have a different content?' The analogous question for sentences—instead of thought events—has an uncontroversial affirmative answer. Of course, we know that when and where non-intentionally identifiable physical events have contents, the same physical event could have had a different content. But it can hardly be *assumed* for purposes of arguing a position on the mind-body problem that mental events are non-intentionally identifiable physical events.

different content is a different thought event (insofar as we distinguish at all between the thinking event and the person's being related to a thought content at a time). I think these facts give the premise *prima facie* support and the argument against the identity theory some interest. I do not claim that we have '*a priori*' certainty that no account of intentional phenomena will reveal intentional language to be only contingently applicable to belief states or thought events, I am only dubious.

One might nurture faith or hope that some more socially oriented functionalist specification could be found. But no such specification is ready to hand. And I see no good reason to think that one must be found. Even if such a specification were found, it is far from clear that it would deflect the argument against the identity theory just considered. The 'functional' states envisaged would depend not merely on what the individual does and what inner causal states lead to his activity—non-intentionally specified—but also on what his fellows do. The analogy between functional states and physiological states in causing the individual's internal and external activity was the chief support for the view that a given token mental event might have been a token of a different content. But the envisaged socially defined 'functional states' bear no intuitive analogy to physiological states or other physical causal states within the individual's body. Their function is not simply that of responding to environmental influences and causing the individual's activity. It is therefore not clear (short of *assuming* an identity theory) that any event that is a token of one of the envisaged socially defined 'functional states' could have been a token of a different one. The event might be essentially identified in terms of its social role. There is as yet no reason to identify it in terms of physically described events in the individual's body. Thus it is not clear that such a socially oriented functional account of thought contents would yield grounds to believe that the usual intentional specifications of mental events are merely contingent. It is, I think, even less clear that an appropriate socially oriented functional account is viable.

Identity theories, of course, do not exhaust the resources of materialism. To take one example, our argument does not speak directly to a materialism based on composition rather than identity. On such a view, the same physical material might compose different thoughts in different circumstances. I shall say nothing evaluative about this sort of view. I have also been silent about other arguments for a token identity theory—such as those based on philosophical accounts of the notions of causality or explanation. Indeed, my primary interest has not been ontology at all. It has been to identify and question individualistic assumptions in materialist as well as Cartesian approaches to the mental.

V. Models of the mental

Traditional philosophical accounts of mind have offered metaphors that produce doctrine and carry conviction where argument and unaided intuition flag. Of course, any such broad reconstructions can be accused of missing the pied beauties of the natural article. But the problem with traditional philosophy of mind is more serious. The two overwhelmingly dominant metaphors of the mental—the infallible eye and the automatic mechanism—have encouraged systematic neglect of prominent features of a wide range of mental phenomena, broadly speaking, social features. Each metaphor has its attractions. Either can be elaborated or doctored to fit the facts that I have emphasized. But neither illumines those facts. And both have played some part in inducing philosophers to ignore them.

I think it optimistic indeed to hope that any one picture, comparable to the traditional ones, will provide insight into all major aspects of mental phenomena. Even so, a function of philosophy is to sketch such pictures. The question arises whether one can make good the social debts of earlier accounts while retaining at least some of their conceptual integrity and pictorial charm. This is no place to start sketching. But some summary remarks may convey a sense of the direction in which our discussion has been tending.

The key feature of the examples of Section II was the fact that we attribute beliefs and thoughts to people even where they incompletely understand contents of those very beliefs and thoughts. This point about intentional mental phenomena is not everywhere applicable: non-linguistic animals do not seem to be candidates for misunderstanding the contents of their beliefs. But the point is certainly salient and must be encompassed in any picture of intentional mental phenomena. Crudely put, wherever the subject has attained a certain competence in large relevant parts of his language and has (implicitly) assumed a certain general commitment or responsibility to the communal conventions governing the language's symbols, the expressions the subject uses take on a certain inertia in determining attributions of mental content to him. In particular, the expressions the subject uses sometimes provide the content of his mental states or events even though he only partially understands, or even misunderstands, some of them. Global coherence and responsibility seem sometimes to override localized incompetence.

The detailed conditions under which this 'inertial force' is exerted are complicated and doubtless more than a little vague. Clearly, the subject must maintain a minimal internal linguistic and rational coherence and a broad similarity to others' use of the language. But meeting this condition is hardly sufficient to establish the relevant responsibility. For the condition is met in the case of a person who speaks a regional dialect (where the same words are sometimes given different applications). The person's aberrations relative to the larger community may be normalities relative to the regional one. In such cases, of course, the regional conventions are dominant in determining what contents should be attributed. At this point, it is natural to appeal to etiological considerations. The speaker of the dialect developed his linguistic habits from interaction with others who were a party to distinctively regional conventions. The person is committed to using the words according to the conventions maintained by those from whom he learned the words. But the situation is more complicated than this observation suggests. A person born and bred in the parent community might simply decide (unilaterally) to follow the usage of the regional dialect or even to fashion his own usage with regard to particular words, self-consciously opting out of the parent community's conventions in these particulars. In such a case, members of the parent community would not, and should not, attribute mental contents to him on the basis of homophonic construal of his words. Here the individual's intentions or attitudes toward communal conventions and communal conceptions seem more important than the causal antecedents of his transactions with a word—unless those intentions are simply included in the etiological story.

I shall not pursue these issues here. The problem of specifying the conditions under which a person has the relevant general competence in a language and a responsibility to its conventions is obviously complicated. The mixture of 'causal' and intentional considerations relevant to dealing with it has obvious near analogs in other philosophical domains (etiological accounts of perception, knowledge, reference). I have no confidence that all of the details of the story would be philosophically interesting. What I want to stress is that to a fair degree, mentalistic attribution rests not on the subject's having mastered the contents of the attribution, and not on his having behavioral dispositions peculiarly relevant to those contents, but on his having a certain responsibility to communal conventions governing, and conceptions associated with, symbols that he is disposed to use. It is this feature that must be incorporated into an improved model of the mental.

I think it profitable to see the language of content attribution as constituting a complex *standard* by reference to which the subject's mental states and events are estimated, or an abstract grid on which they are plotted. Different people may vary widely in the degree to which they master the elements and relations within the standard, even as it applies to them all. This metaphor may be developed in several directions and with different models: applied geometry, measurement of magnitudes, evaluation by a monetary standard, and so forth. A model I shall illustrate briefly here borrows from musical analysis.

Given that a composer has fulfilled certain general conditions for establishing a musical key, his chordal structures are plotted by reference to the harmonic system of relations appropriate to the tonic key. There is vast scope for variation and novelty within the harmonic framework. The chords may depart widely from traditional 'rules' or practices governing what count as interesting or 'reasonable' chordal structures and progressions. And the composer may or may not grasp the harmonic implications and departures present in his composition. The composer may sometimes exhibit harmonic incompetence (and occasionally harmonic genius) by radically departing from those traditional rules. But the harmonic system of relations applies to the composition in any case. Once established, the tonic key and its associated harmonic framework are applied unless the composer takes pains to set up another tonic key or some atonal arrangement (thereby intentionally opting out of the original tonal framework), or writes down notes by something like a slip of the pen (suffering mechanical interference in his compositional intentions), or unintentionally, breaks the harmonic rules in a massive and unprincipled manner (thereby indicating chaos or complete incompetence). The tonic key provides a standard for describing the composition. The application of the standard depends on the composer's maintaining a certain overall coherence and minimal competence in conforming to the standard's conventions. And there are conditions under which the standard would be replaced by another. But once applied, the harmonic framework—its formal interrelations, its applicability even to deviant, pointless progressions—is partly independent of the composer's degree of harmonic mastery.

One attractive aspect of the metaphor is that it has some application to the case of animals. In making sounds, animals do sometimes behave in such a way that a harmonic standard can be roughly applied to them, even though the standard, at least in any detail, is no part of what they have mastered. Since they do not master the standard (though they may master some of its elements), they are not candidates for partial understanding or misunderstanding. (Of course, this may be said of many people as regards the musical standard.) The standard applies to both animals and people. But the conditions for its application are sensitive in various ways to whether the subject himself has mastered it. Where the subject does use the standard (whether the language, or a system of key relationships), his uses take on special weight in applications of the standard to him.

One of the metaphor's chief virtues is that it encourages one to seek social explications for this special weight. The key to our attribution of mental contents in the face of incomplete mastery or misunderstanding lies largely in social functions associated with maintaining and applying the standard. In broad outline, the social advantages of the 'special weight' are apparent. Symbolic expressions are the overwhelmingly dominant source of detailed information about what people think, intend, and so forth. Such detail is essential not only to much explanation and prediction, but also to fulfilling many of our cooperative enterprises and to relying on one another for second-hand information. Words interpreted in conventionally established ways are familiar, palpable, and public. They are common coin, a relatively stable currency. These features are crucial to achieving the ends of mentalistic attribution just cited. They are also critical in maximizing interpersonal comparability. And they yield a bias toward taking others at their word and avoiding *ad hoc* reinterpretation, once overall agreement in usage and commitment to communal standards can be assumed.

This bias issues in the practice of expressing even many differences in understanding without reinterpreting the subject's words. Rather than reinterpret the subject's word 'arthritis' and give him a trivially true object-level belief and merely a false metalinguistic belief about how 'arthritis' is used by others, it is common practice, and correct, simply to take him at his word.

I hardly need re-emphasize that the situation is vastly more complicated than I have suggested in the foregoing paragraphs. Insincerity, tongue slips, certain malapropisms, subconscious blocks, mental instability all make the picture more complex. There are differences in our handling of different sorts of expressions, depending, for example, on how clear and fixed social conventions regarding the expressions are. There are differences in our practices with different subject matters. There are differences in our handling of different degrees of linguistic error. There are differences in the way meaning-, assertion-, and mental-contents are attributed. (Cf. note 4.) I do not propose ignoring these points. They are all parameters affecting the inertial force of 'face value' construal. But I want to keep steadily in mind the philosophically neglected fact about social practice: Our attributions do not require that the subject always correctly or fully understand the content of his attitudes.

The point suggests fundamental misorientations in the two traditional pictures of the mental. The authority of a person's reports about his thoughts and beliefs (*modulo* sincerity, lack of subconscious interference, and so forth) does not issue from a special intellectual vision of the contents of those thoughts and beliefs. It extends even to some cases in which the subject incompletely understands those contents. And it depends partly on the social advantages of maintaining communally established standards of communication and mentalistic attribution. Likewise, the descriptive and explanatory role of mental discourse is not adequately modeled by complex non-intentional mechanisms or programs for the production of an individual's physical movement and behavior. Attributing intentional mentalistic phenomena to individuals serves not only to explain their behavior viewed in isolation but also to chart their activity (intentional, verbal, behavioral, physical) by complex comparison to others—and against socially established standards.[16] Both traditional metaphors make the mistake, among others, of treating intentional mental phenomena individualistically. New approaches must do better. The sense in which man is a social animal runs deeper than much mainstream philosophy of mind has acknowledged.[17]

16. In emphasizing social and pragmatic features in mentalistic attributions, I do not intend to suggest that mental attributions are any the less objective, descriptive, or on the ontological up and up. There are substantial arguments in the literature that might lead one to make such inferences. But my present remarks are free of such implications. Someone might want to insist that from a 'purely objective viewpoint' one can describe 'the phenomena' equally well in accord with common practice, literally interpreted, or in accord with various reinterpretation strategies. Then our arguments would, perhaps, show only that it is 'objectively indeterminate' whether functionalism and the identity theory are true. I would be inclined to question the application of the expressions that are scare-quoted.

17. I am grateful to participants at a pair of talks given at the University of London in the spring of 1978, and to Richard Rorty for discussions earlier. I am also indebted to Robert Adams and Rogers Albritton whose criticisms forced numerous improvements. I appreciatively acknowledge support of the John Simon Guggenheim Foundation.

Chapter 26

Brains in a vat

Hilary Putnam

An ant is crawling on a patch of sand. As it crawls, it traces a line in the sand. By pure chance the line that it traces curves and recrosses itself in such a way that it ends up looking like a recognizable caricature of Winston Churchill. Has the ant traced a picture of Winston Churchill, a picture that *depicts* Churchill?

Most people would say, on a little reflection, that it has not. The ant, after all, has never seen Churchill, or even a picture of Churchill, and it had no intention of depicting Churchill. It simply traced a line (and even *that* was unintentional), a line that *we* can 'see as' a picture of Churchill.

We can express this by saying that the line is not 'in itself' a representation[1] of anything rather than anything else. Similarity (of a certain very complicated sort) to the features of Winston Churchill is not sufficient to make something represent or refer to Churchill. Nor is it necessary: in our community the printed shape 'Winston Churchill', the spoken words 'Winston Churchill', and many other things are used to represent Churchill (though not pictorially), while not having the sort of similarity to Churchill that a picture—even a line drawing—has. If *similarity* is not necessary or sufficient to make something represent something else, how can *anything* be necessary or sufficient for this purpose? How on earth can one thing represent (or 'stand for', etc.) a different thing?

The answer may seem easy. Suppose the ant had seen Winston Churchill, and suppose that it had the intelligence and skill to draw a picture of him. Suppose it produced the caricature *intentionally*. Then the line would have represented Churchill.

On the other hand, suppose the line had the shape WINSTON CHURCHILL. And suppose this was just accident (ignoring the improbability involved). Then the

Hilary Putnam, 'Brains in a Vat', from *Reason Truth and History* (Cambridge: Cambridge University Press, 1981).

1. In this book the terms 'representation' and 'reference' always refer to a relation between a word (or other sort of sign, symbol, or representation) and something that actually exists (i.e. not just an 'object of thought'). There is a sense of 'refer' in which I can 'refer' to what does not exist; this is not the sense in which 'refer' is used here. An older word for what I call 'representation' or 'reference' is *denotation.*

   Secondly, I follow the custom of modern logicians and use 'exist' to mean 'exist in the past, present, or future'. Thus Winston Churchill 'exists', and we can 'refer to' or 'represent' Winston Churchill, even though he is no longer alive.

'printed shape' WINSTON CHURCHILL would *not* have represented Churchill, although that printed shape does represent Churchill when it occurs in almost any book today.

So it may seem that what is necessary for representation, or what is mainly necessary for representation, is *intention.*

But to have the intention that *anything*, even private language (even the words 'Winston Churchill' spoken in my mind and not out loud), should *represent* Churchill, I must have been able to *think about* Churchill in the first place. If lines in the sand, noises, etc., cannot 'in themselves' represent anything, then how is it that thought forms can 'in themselves' represent anything? Or can they? How can thought reach out and 'grasp' what is external?

Some philosophers have, in the past, leaped from this sort of consideration to what they take to be a proof that the mind is *essentially non-physical in nature.* The argument is simple; what we said about the ant's curve applies to any physical object. No physical object can, in itself, refer to one thing rather than to another; nevertheless, *thoughts in the mind* obviously do succeed in referring to one thing rather than another. So thoughts (and hence the mind) are of an essentially different nature than physical objects. Thoughts have the characteristic of *intentionality*—they can refer to something else; nothing physical has 'intentionality', save as that intentionality is derivative from some employment of that physical thing by a mind. Or so it is claimed. This is too quick; just postulating mysterious powers of mind solves nothing. But the problem is very real. How is intentionality, reference, possible?

Magical theories of reference

We saw that the ant's 'picture' has no necessary connection with Winston Churchill. The mere fact that the 'picture' bears a 'resemblance' to Churchill does not make it into a real picture, nor does it make it a representation of Churchill. Unless the ant is an intelligent ant (which it isn't) and knows about Churchill (which it doesn't), the curve it traced is not a picture or even a representation of anything. Some primitive people believe that some representations (in particular, *names*) have a necessary connection with their bearers; that to know the 'true name' of someone or something gives one power over it. This power comes from the *magical connection* between the name and the bearer of the name; once one realizes that a name *only* has a contextual, contingent, conventional connection with its bearer, it is hard to see why knowledge of the name should have any mystical significance.

What is important to realize is that what goes for physical pictures also goes for mental images, and for mental representations in general; mental representations no more have a necessary connection with what they represent than physical representations do. The contrary supposition is a survival of magical thinking.

Perhaps the point is easiest to grasp in the case of mental *images.* (Perhaps the first philosopher to grasp the enormous significance of this point, even if he was not the first to actually make it, was Wittgenstein.) Suppose there is a planet somewhere on which human beings have evolved (or been deposited by alien spacemen, or what have you). Suppose these humans, although otherwise like us, have never seen *trees.* Suppose they have never imagined trees (perhaps vegetable life exists on their planet only in the form of molds). Suppose one day a picture of a tree is accidentally dropped on their planet by a spaceship which passes on without having other contact with them. Imagine them puzzling over the picture. What in the world is this? All sorts of speculations occur to them: a building, a canopy, even an animal of some kind. But suppose they never come close to the truth.

For *us* the picture is a representation of a tree. For these humans the picture only represents a strange object, nature and function unknown. Suppose one of them has a mental image which is exactly like one of my mental images of a tree as a result of having seen the picture. His mental image is not a *representation of a tree.* It is only a representation of the strange object (whatever it is) that the mysterious picture represents.

Still, someone might argue that the mental image is *in fact* a representation of a tree, if only because the picture which caused this mental image was itself a representation of a tree to begin with. There is a causal chain from actual trees to the mental image even if it is a very strange one.

But even this causal chain can be imagined absent. Suppose the 'picture of the tree' that the spaceship dropped was not really a picture of a tree, but the accidental result of some spilled paints. Even if it looked exactly like a picture of a tree, it was, in truth, no more a picture of a tree than the ant's 'caricature' of Churchill was a picture of Churchill. We can even imagine that the spaceship which dropped the 'picture' came from a planet which knew nothing of trees. Then the humans would still have mental images qualitatively identical with my image of a tree, but they would not be images which represented a tree any more than anything else.

The same thing is true of *words.* A discourse on paper might seem to be a perfect description of trees, but if it was produced by monkeys randomly hitting keys on a typewriter for millions of years, then the words do not refer to anything. If there were a person who memorized those words and said them in his mind without understanding them, then they would not refer to anything when thought in the mind, either.

Imagine the person who is saying those words in his mind has been hypnotized. Suppose the words are in Japanese, and the person has been told that he understands Japanese. Suppose that as he thinks those words he has a 'feeling of understanding'. (Although if someone broke into his train of thought and asked him what the words he was thinking *meant,* he would discover he couldn't say.) Perhaps the illusion would be so perfect that the person could even fool a Japanese telepath! But if he couldn't use the words in the right contexts, answer questions about what he 'thought', etc., then he didn't understand them.

By combining these science fiction stories I have been telling, we can contrive a case in which someone thinks words which are in fact a description of trees in some language *and* simultaneously has appropriate mental images, but *neither* understands the words *nor* knows what a tree is. We can even imagine that the mental images were caused by paint-spills (although the person has been hypnotized to think that they are images of something appropriate to his thought—only, if he were asked, he wouldn't be able to say of what). And we can imagine that the language the person is thinking in is one neither the hypnotist nor the person hypnotized has ever heard of—perhaps it is just coincidence that these 'nonsense sentences', as the hypnotist supposes them to be, are a description of trees in Japanese. In short, everything passing before the person's mind might be qualitatively identical with what was passing through the mind of a Japanese speaker who was *really* thinking about trees—but none of it would refer to trees.

All of this is really impossible, of course, in the way that it is really impossible that monkeys should by chance type out a copy of *Hamlet*. That is to say that the probabilities against it are so high as to mean it will never really happen (we think). But is is not logically impossible, or even physically impossible. It *could* happen (compatibly with physical law and, perhaps, compatibly with actual conditions in the universe, if there are lots of intelligent beings on other planets). And if it did happen, it would be a striking demonstration of an important conceptual truth; that even a large and complex system of representations, both verbal and visual, still does not have an *intrinsic*, built-in, magical connection with what it represents—a connection independent of how it was caused and what the dispositions of the speaker or thinker are. And this is true whether the system of representations (words and images, in the case of the example) is physically realized—the words are written or spoken, and the pictures are physical pictures—or only realized in the mind. Thought words and mental pictures do not *intrinsically* represent what they are about.

The case of the brains in a vat

Here is a science fiction possibility discussed by philosophers: imagine that a human being (you can imagine this to be yourself) has been subjected to an operation by an evil scientist. The person's brain (your brain) has been removed from the body and placed in a vat of nutrients which keeps the brain alive. The nerve endings have been connected to a super-scientific computer which causes the person whose brain it is to have the illusion that everything is perfectly normal. There seem to be people, objects, the sky, etc; but really all the person (you) is experiencing is the result of electronic impulses travelling from the computer to the nerve endings. The computer is so clever that if the person tries to raise his hand, the feedback from the computer will cause him to 'see' and 'feel' the hand being raised.

Moreover, by varying the program, the evil scientist can cause the victim to 'experience' (or hallucinate) any situation or environment the evil scientist wishes. He can also obliterate the memory of the brain operation, so that the victim will seem to himself to have always been in this environment. It can even seem to the victim that he is sitting and reading these very words about the amusing but quite absurd supposition that there is an evil scientist who removes people's brains from their bodies and places them in a vat of nutrients which keep the brains alive. The nerve endings are supposed to be connected to a super-scientific computer which causes the person whose brain it is to have the illusion that . . .

When this sort of possibility is mentioned in a lecture on the Theory of Knowledge, the purpose, of course, is to raise the classical problem of scepticism with respect to the external world in a modern way. (*How do you know you aren't in this predicament?*) But this predicament is also a useful device for raising issues about the mind/world relationship.

Instead of having just one brain in a vat, we could imagine that all human beings (perhaps all sentient beings) are brains in a vat (or nervous systems in a vat in case some beings with just a minimal nervous system already count as 'sentient'). Of course, the evil scientist would have to be outside—or would he? Perhaps there is no evil scientist, perhaps (though this is absurd) the universe just happens to consist of automatic machinery tending a vat full of brains and nervous systems.

This time let us suppose that the automatic machinery is programmed to give us all a *collective* hallucination, rather than a number of separate unrelated hallucinations. Thus, when I seem to myself to be talking to you, you seem to yourself to be hearing my words. Of course, it is not the case that my words actually reach your ears—for you don't have (real) ears, nor do I have a real mouth and tongue. Rather, when I produce my words, what happens is that the efferent impulses travel from my brain to the computer, which both causes me to 'hear' my own voice uttering those words and 'feel' my tongue moving, etc., and causes you to 'hear' my words, 'see' me speaking, etc. In this case, we are, in a sense, actually in communication. I am not mistaken about your real existence (only about the existence of your body and the 'external world', apart from brains). From a certain point of view, it doesn't even matter that 'the whole world' is a collective hallucination; for you do, after all, really hear my words when I speak to you, even if the mechanism isn't what we suppose it to be. (Of course, if we were two lovers making love, rather than just two people carrying on a conversation, then the suggestion that it was just two brains in a vat might be disturbing.)

I want now to ask a question which will seem very silly and obvious (at least to some people, including some very sophisticated philosophers), but which will take us to real philosophical depths rather quickly. Suppose this whole story were actually true. Could we, if we were brains in a vat in this way, *say* or *think* that we were?

I am going to argue that the answer is 'No, we couldn't.' In fact, I am going to argue that the supposition that we are actually brains in a vat, although it violates no physical law, and is perfectly consistent with everything we have experienced, cannot possibly be true. *It cannot possibly be true*, because it is, in a certain way, self-refuting.

The argument I am going to present is an unusual one, and it took me several years to convince myself that it is really right. But it is a correct argument. What makes it seem so strange is that it is connected with some of the very deepest issues in philosophy. (It first occurred to me when I was thinking about a theorem in modern logic, the 'Skolem–Löwenheim Theorem', and I suddenly saw a connection between this theorem and some arguments in Wittgenstein's *Philosophical Investigations.*)

A 'self-refuting supposition' is one whose truth implies its own falsity. For example, consider the thesis that *all general statements are false.* This is a general statement. So if it is true, then it must be false. Hence, it is false. Sometimes a thesis is called 'self-refuting' if it *is the supposition that the thesis is entertained or enunciated* that implies its falsity. For example, 'I do not exist' is self-refuting if thought by *me* (for any '*me*'). So one can be certain that one oneself exists, if one thinks about it (as Descartes argued).

What I shall show is that the supposition that we are brains in a vat has just this property. If we can consider whether it is true or false, then it is not true (I shall show). Hence it is not true.

Before I give the argument, let us consider why it seems so strange that such an argument can be given (at least to philosophers who subscribe to a 'copy' conception of truth). We conceded that it is compatible with physical law that there should be a world in which all sentient beings are brains in a vat. As philosophers say, there is a 'possible world' in which all sentient beings are brains in a vat. (This 'possible world' talk makes it sound as if there is a *place* where any absurd supposition is true, which is why it can be very misleading in philosophy.) The humans in that possible world have exactly the same experiences that *we* do. They think the same thoughts we do (at least, the same words, images, thought-forms, etc., go through their minds). Yet, I am claiming that there is an argument we can give that shows we are not brains in a vat. How can there be? And why couldn't the people in the possible world who really *are* brains in a vat give it too?

The answer is going to be (basically) this: although the people in that possible world can think and 'say' any words we can think and say, they cannot (I claim) *refer* to what we can refer to. In particular, they cannot think or say that they are brains in a vat (*even by thinking 'we are brains in a vat'*).

Turing's test

Suppose someone succeeds in inventing a computer which can actually carry on an intelligent conversation with one (on as many subjects as an intelligent person might). How can one decide if the computer is 'conscious'?

The British logician Alan Turing proposed the following test:[2] let someone carry on a conversation with the computer and a conversation with a person whom he does not know. If he cannot tell which is the computer and which is the human being, then (assume the test to be repeated a sufficient number of times with different interlocutors) the computer is conscious. In short, a computing machine is conscious if it can pass the 'Turing Test'. (The conversations are not to be carried on face to face, of course, since the interlocutor is not to know the visual appearance of either of his two conversational partners. Nor is voice to be used, since the mechanical voice might simply sound different from a human voice. Imagine, rather, that the conversations are all carried on via electric typewriter. The interlocutor types in his statements, questions, etc., and the two partners—the machine and the person—respond via the electric keyboard. Also, the machine may *lie*—asked 'Are you a machine', it might reply, 'No, I'm an assistant in the lab here.')

The idea that this test is really a definitive test of consciousness has been criticized by a number of authors (who are by no means hostile in principle to the idea that a machine might be conscious). But this is not our topic at this time. I wish to use the general idea of the Turing test, the general idea of a *dialogic test of competence*, for a different purpose, the purpose of exploring the notion of *reference*.

Imagine a situation in which the problem is not to determine if the partner is really a person or a machine, but is rather to determine if the partner uses the words to refer as we do. The obvious test is, again, to carry on a conversation, and, if no problems arise, if the partner 'passes' in the sense of being indistinguishable from someone who is certified in advance to be speaking the same language, referring to the usual sorts of objects, etc., to conclude that the partner does refer to objects as we do. When the purpose of the Turing test is as just described, that is, to determine the existence of (shared) reference, I shall refer to the test as the *Turing Test for Reference*. And, just as philosophers have discussed the question whether the original Turing test is a *definitive* test for consciousness, i.e. the question of whether a machine which 'passes' the test not just once but regularly is *necessarily* conscious, so, in the same way, I wish to discuss the question of whether the Turing Test for Reference just suggested is a definitive test for shared reference.

The answer will turn out to be 'No'. The Turing Test for Reference is not definitive. It is certainly an excellent test in practice; but it is not logically impossible (though it is certainly highly improbable) that someone could pass the Turing Test for Reference and not be referring to anything. It follows from this, as we shall see, that we can extend our observation that words (and whole texts and discourses) do not have a necessary connection to their referents. Even if we consider not words by themselves but rules deciding what words may appropriately be produced in certain contexts—even if we consider, in computer jargon, *programs for using words*—unless those programs themselves *refer to something extra-linguistic* there is still no

2. A. M. Turing, 'Computing Machinery and Intelligence', *Mind* (1950), included in Chapter 14 of this volume.

determinate reference that those words possess. This will be a crucial step in the process of reaching the conclusion that the Brain-in-a-Vat Worlders cannot refer to anything external at all (and hence cannot say *that* they are Brain-in-a-Vat Worlders).

Suppose, for example, that I am in the Turing situation (playing the 'Imitation Game', in Turing's terminology) and my partner is actually a machine. Suppose this machine is able to win the game ('passes' the test). Imagine the machine to be programmed to produce beautiful responses in English to statements, questions, remarks, etc. in English, but that it has no sense organs (other than the hookup to my electric typewriter), and no motor organs (other than the electric typewriter). (As far as I can make out, Turing does not assume that the possession of either sense organs or motor organs is necessary for consciousness or intelligence.) Assume that not only does the machine lack electronic eyes and ears, etc., but that there are no provisions in the machine's program, the program for playing the Imitation Game, for incorporating inputs from such sense organs, or for controlling a body. What should we say about such a machine?

To me, it seems evident that we cannot and should not attribute reference to such a device. It is true that the machine can discourse beautifully about, say, the scenery in New England. But it could not recognize an apple tree or an apple, a mountain or a cow, a field or a steeple, if it were in front of one.

What we have is a device for producing sentences in response to sentences. But none of these sentences is at all connected to the real world. *If one coupled two of these machines and let them play the Imitation Game with each other, then they would go on 'fooling' each other forever, even if the rest of the world disappeared!* There is no more reason to regard the machine's talk of apples as referring to real world apples than there is to regard the ant's 'drawing' as referring to Winston Churchill.

What produces the illusion of reference, meaning, intelligence, etc., here is the fact that there is a convention of representation which *we* have under which the machine's discourse refers to apples, steeples, New England, etc. Similarly, there is the *illusion* that the ant has caricatured Churchill, for the same reason. But we are able to perceive, handle, deal with apples and fields. Our talk of apples and fields is intimately connected with our *non-verbal* transactions with apples and fields. There are 'language entry rules' which take us from experiences of apples to such utterances as 'I see an apple', and 'language exit rules' which take us from decisions expressed in linguistic form ('I am going to buy some apples') to actions other than speaking. Lacking either language entry rules or language exit rules, there is no reason to regard the conversation of the machine (or of the two machines, in the case we envisaged of two machines playing the Imitation Game with each other) as more than syntactic play. Syntactic play that *resembles* intelligent discourse, to be sure; but only as (and no more than) the ant's curve resembles a biting caricature.

In the case of the ant, we could have argued that the ant would have drawn the same curve even if Winston Churchill had never existed. In the case of the machine, we cannot quite make the parallel argument; if apples, trees, steeples and fields had not existed, then, presumably, the programmers would not have produced that same program. Although the machine does not *perceive* apples, fields, or steeples, its creator–designers did. There is *some* causal connection between the machine and the real world apples, etc., via the perceptual experience and knowledge of the creator–designers. But such a weak connection can hardly suffice for reference. Not only is it logically possible, though fantastically improbable, that the same machine *could* have existed even if apples, fields, and steeples had not existed; more important, the machine is utterly insensitive to the *continued* existence of apples, fields, steeples, etc. Even if all these things *ceased* to exist, the machine would still discourse just as happily in the same way. That is why the machine cannot be regarded as referring at all.

The point that is relevant for our discussion is that there is nothing in Turing's Test to rule out a machine which is programmed to do nothing *but* play the Imitation Game, and that a machine which can do nothing *but* play the Imitation Game is *clearly* not referring any more than a record player is.

Brains in a vat (again)

Let us compare the hypothetical 'brains in a vat' with the machines just described. There are obviously important differences. The brains in a vat do not have sense organs, but they do have *provision* for sense organs; that is, there are afferent nerve endings, there are inputs from these afferent nerve endings, and these inputs figure in the 'program' of the brains in the vat just as they do in the program of our brains. The brains in a vat are *brains*; moreover, they are *functioning* brains, and they function by the same rules as brains do in the actual world. For these reasons, it would seem absurd to deny consciousness or intelligence to them. But the fact that they are conscious and intelligent does not mean that their words refer to what our words refer. The question we are interested in is this: do their verbalizations containing, say, the word 'tree' actually refer to *trees*? More generally: can they refer to *external* objects at all? (As opposed to, for example, objects in the image produced by the automatic machinery.)

To fix our ideas, let us specify that the automatic machinery is supposed to have come into existence by some kind of cosmic chance or coincidence (or, perhaps, to have always existed). In this hypothetical world, the automatic machinery itself is supposed to have no intelligent creator—designers. In fact, as we said at the beginning of this chapter, we may imagine that all sentient beings (however minimal their sentience) are inside the vat.

This assumption does not help. For there is no connection between the *word* 'tree' as used by these brains and actual trees. They would still use the word 'tree' just as they do, think just the thoughts they do, have just the images they have, even if there were no actual trees. Their images, words, etc., are qualitatively identical with images, words, etc., which do represent trees in *our* world; but we have already seen (the ant again!) that qualitative similarity to something which represents an object (Winston Churchill or a tree) does not make a thing a representation all by itself. In short, the brains in a vat are not thinking about real trees when they think 'there is a tree in front of me' because there is nothing by virtue of which their thought 'tree' represents actual trees.

If this seems hasty, reflect on the following: we have seen that the words do not necessarily refer to trees even if they are arranged in a sequence which is identical with a discourse which (were it to occur in one of our minds) would unquestionably *be about trees* in the actual world. Nor does the 'program', in the sense of the rules, practices, dispositions of the brains to verbal behavior, necessarily refer to trees or bring about reference to trees through the connections it establishes between words and words, or *linguistic* cues and *linguistic* responses. If these brains think about, refer to, represent trees (real trees, outside the vat), then it must be because of the way the 'program' connects the system of language to *non-verbal* input and outputs. There are indeed such non-verbal inputs and outputs in the Brain-in-a-Vat world (those efferent and afferent nerve endings again!), but we also saw that the 'sense-data' produced by the automatic machinery do not represent trees (or anything external) even when they resemble our tree-images exactly. Just as a splash of paint might resemble a tree picture without *being* a tree picture, so, we saw, a 'sense datum' might be qualitatively identical with an 'image of a tree' without being an image of a tree. How can the fact that, in the case of the brains in a vat, the language is connected by the program with sensory inputs which do not intrinsically or extrinsically represent trees (or anything external) possibly bring it about that the whole system of representations, the language-in-use, *does* refer to or represent trees or anything external?

The answer is that it cannot. The whole system of sense-data, motor signals to the efferent endings, and verbally or conceptually mediated thought connected by 'language entry rules' to the sense-data (or whatever) as inputs and by 'language exit rules' to the motor signals as outputs, has no more connection to *trees* than the ant's curve has to Winston Churchill. Once we see that the *qualitative similarity* (amounting, if you like, to qualitative identity) between the thoughts of the brains in a vat and the thoughts of someone in the actual world by no means implies sameness of reference, it is not hard to see that there is no basis at all for regarding the brain in a vat as referring to external things.

The premisses of the argument

I have now given the argument promised to show that the brains in a vat cannot think or say that they are brains in a vat. It remains only to make it explicit and to examine its structure.

By what was just said, when the brain in a vat (in the world where every sentient being is and always was a brain in a vat) thinks 'There is a tree in front of me', his thought does not refer to actual trees. On some theories that we shall discuss it might refer to trees in the image, or to the electronic impulses that cause tree experiences, or to the features of the program that are responsible for those electronic impulses. These theories are not ruled out by what was just said, for there is a close causal connection between the use of the word 'tree' in vat-English and the presence of trees in the image, the presence of electronic impulses of a certain kind, and the presence of certain features in the machine's program. On these theories the brain is *right*, not *wrong* in thinking 'There is a tree in front of me.' Given what 'tree' refers to in vat-English and what 'in front of' refers to, assuming one of these theories is correct, then the truth-conditions for 'There is a tree in front of me' when it occurs in vat-English are simply that a tree in the image be 'in front of' the 'me' in question—in the image—or, perhaps, that the kind of electronic impulse that normally produces this experience be coming from the automatic machinery, or, perhaps, that the feature of the machinery that is supposed to produce the 'tree in front of one' experience be operating. And these truth-conditions are certainly fulfilled.

By the same argument, 'vat' refers to vats in the image in vat-English, or something related (electronic impulses or program features), but certainly not to real vats, since the use of 'vat' in vat-English has no causal connection to real vats (apart from the connection that the brains in a vat wouldn't be able to use the word 'vat', if it were not for the presence of one particular vat—the vat they are in; but this connection obtains between the use of *every* word in vat-English and that one particular vat; it is not a special connection between the use of the *particular* word 'vat' and vats). Similarly, 'nutrient fluid' refers to a liquid in the image in vat-English, or something related (electronic impulses or program features). It follows that if their 'possible world' is really the actual one, and we are really the brains in a vat, then what we now mean by 'we are brains in a vat' is that *we are brains in a vat in the image* or something of that kind (if we mean anything at all). But part of the hypothesis that we are brains in a vat is that we aren't brains in a vat in the image (i.e. what we are 'hallucinating' isn't that we are brains in a vat). So, if we are brains in a vat, then the sentence 'We are brains in a vat' says something false (if it says anything). In short, if we are brains in a vat, then 'We are brains in a vat' is false. So it is (necessarily) false.

The supposition that such a possibility makes sense arises from a combination of two errors: (1) taking *physical possibility* too seriously; and (2) unconsciously operating with a magical theory of reference, a theory on which certain mental representations necessarily refer to certain external things and kinds of things.

There is a 'physically possible world' in which we are brains in a vat—what does this mean except that there is a *description* of such a state of affairs which is compatible with the laws of physics? Just as there is a tendency in our culture (and has been since the seventeenth century) to take *physics* as our metaphysics, that is, to view the exact sciences as the long-sought description of the 'true and ultimate furniture of the universe', so there is, as an immediate consequence, a tendency to take 'physical possibility' as the very touchstone of what might really actually be the case. Truth is physical truth; possibility physical possibility; and necessity physical necessity, on such a view. But we have just seen, if only in the case of a very contrived example so far, that this view is wrong. The existence of a 'physically possible world' in which we are brains in a vat (and always were and will be) does not mean that we might really, actually, possibly *be* brains in a vat. What rules out this possibility is not physics but *philosophy.*

Some philosophers, eager both to assert and minimize the claims of their profession at the same time (the typical state of mind of Anglo-American philosophy in the twentieth century), would say: 'Sure. You have shown that some things that seem to be physical possibilities are really *conceptual* impossibilities. What's so surprising about that?'

Well, to be sure, my argument can be described as a 'conceptual' one. But to describe philosophical activity as the search for 'conceptual' truths makes it all sound like *inquiry about the meaning of words.* And that is not at all what we have been engaging in.

What we have been doing is considering the *preconditions* for *thinking about, representing, referring to,* etc. We have investigated these preconditions *not* by investigating the meaning of these words and phrases (as a linguist might, for example) but by *reasoning a priori.* Not in the old 'absolute' sense (since we don't claim that magical theories of reference are *a priori* wrong), but in the sense of inquiring into what is *reasonably* possible *assuming* certain general premisses, or making certain very broad theoretical assumptions. Such a procedure is neither 'empirical' nor quite 'a priori', but has elements of both ways of investigating. In spite of the fallibility of my procedure, and its dependence upon assumptions which might be described as 'empirical' (e.g. the assumption that the mind has no access to external things or properties apart from that provided by the senses), my procedure has a close relation to what Kant called a 'transcendental' investigation; for it is an investigation, I repeat, of the *preconditions* of reference and hence of thought—preconditions built in to the nature of our minds themselves, though not (as Kant hoped) wholly independent of empirical assumptions.

One of the premisses of the argument is obvious: that magical theories of reference are wrong, wrong for mental representations and not only for physical ones. The other premiss is that one cannot refer to certain kinds of things, e.g. *trees*, if one has no causal interaction at all with them,[3] or with things in terms of which they can be described. But why should we accept these premisses? Since these constitute the broad framework within which I am arguing, it is time to examine them more closely.

3. If the Brains in a Vat will have causal connection with, say, trees *in the future*, then perhaps they can *now* refer to trees by the description 'the things I will refer to as 'trees' at such-and-such a future time'. But we are to imagine a case in which the Brains in a Vat *never* get out of the vat, and hence *never* get into causal connection with trees, etc.

The reasons for denying necessary connections between representations and their referents

I mentioned earlier that some philosophers (most famously, Brentano) have ascribed to the mind a power, 'intentionality', which precisely enables it to *refer*. Evidently, I have rejected this as no solution. But what gives me this right? Have I, perhaps, been too hasty?

These philosophers did not claim that we can think about external things or properties without using representations at all. And the argument I gave above comparing visual sense data to the ant's 'picture' (the argument via the science fiction story about the 'picture' of a tree that came from a paint-splash and that gave rise to sense data qualitatively similar to our 'visual images of trees', but unaccompanied by any *concept* of a tree) would be accepted as showing that *images* do not necessarily refer. If there are mental representations that necessarily refer (to external things) they must be of the nature of *concepts* and not of the nature of images. But what are *concepts*?

When we introspect we do not perceive 'concepts' flowing through our minds as such. Stop the stream of thought when or where we will, what we catch are words, images, sensations, feelings. When I speak my thoughts out loud I do not think them twice. I hear my words as you do. To be sure it feels different to me when I utter words that I believe and when I utter words I do not believe (but sometimes, when I am nervous, or in front of a hostile audience, it feels as if I am lying when I know I am telling the truth); and it feels different when I utter words I understand and when I utter words I do not understand. But I can imagine without difficulty someone thinking just these words (in the sense of saying them in his mind) and having just the feeling of understanding, asserting, etc., that I do, and realizing a minute later (or on being awakened by a hypnotist) that he did not understand what had just passed through his mind at all, that he did not even understand the language these words are in. I don't claim that this is very likely; I simply mean that there is nothing at all unimaginable about this. And what this shows is not that concepts *are* words (or images, sensations, etc.), but that to attribute a 'concept' or a 'thought' to someone is quite different from attributing any mental 'presentation', any introspectible entity or event, to him. Concepts are not mental presentations that intrinsically refer to external objects for the very decisive reason that they are not mental presentations at all. Concepts are signs used in a certain way; the signs may be public or private, mental entities or physical entities, but even when the signs are 'mental' and 'private', the sign itself apart from its use is not the concept. And signs do not themselves intrinsically refer.

We can see this by performing a very simple thought experiment. Suppose you are like me and cannot tell an elm tree from a beech tree. We still say that the reference of 'elm' in my speech is the same as the reference of 'elm' in anyone else's, viz. elm trees, and that the set of all beech trees is the extension of 'beech' (i.e. the set of things the word 'beech' is truly predicated of) both in your speech and my speech. Is it really credible that the difference between what 'elm' refers to and what 'beech' refers to is brought about by a difference in our *concepts*? My concept of an elm tree is exactly the same as my concept of a beech tree (I blush to confess). (This shows that the determination of reference is social and not individual, by the way; you and I both defer to experts who *can* tell elms from beeches.) If someone heroically attempts to maintain that the difference between the reference of 'elm' and the reference of 'beech' in *my* speech is explained by a difference in my psychological state, then let him imagine a Twin Earth where the words are switched. Twin Earth is very much like Earth; in fact, apart from the fact that 'elm' and 'beech' are interchanged, the reader can suppose Twin Earth is exactly like Earth. Suppose I have a *Doppelganger* on Twin Earth who is molecule for molecule identical with me (in the sense in which two neckties can be 'identical'). If you are a dualist, then suppose my *Doppelganger* thinks the same verbalized thoughts I do, has the same sense data, the same dispositions, etc. It is absurd to think his psychological state is one bit different from mine: yet his word 'elm' represents *beeches*, and my word 'elm' represents elms. (Similarly, if the 'water' on Twin Earth is a different liquid—say, XYZ and not H_2O—then 'water' represents a different liquid when used on Twin Earth and when used on Earth, etc.) Contrary to a doctrine that has been with us since the seventeenth century, *meanings just aren't in the head*.

We have seen that possessing a concept is not a matter of possessing images (say, of trees—or even images, 'visual' or 'acoustic', of sentences, or whole discourses, for that matter) since one could possess any system of images you please and not possess the *ability* to use the sentences in situationally appropriate ways (considering both linguistic factors—what has been said before—and non-linguistic factors as determining 'situational appropriateness'). A man may have all the images you please, and still be completely at a loss when one says to him 'point to a tree', even if a lot of trees are present. He may even have the image of what he is supposed to do, and still not know what he is supposed to do. For the image, if not accompanied by the ability to act in a certain way, is just *a picture*, and acting in accordance with a picture is itself an ability that one may or may not have. (The man might picture himself pointing to a tree, but just for the sake of contemplating something logically possible; himself pointing to a tree after someone has produced the—to him meaningless—sequence of sounds 'please point to a tree'.) He would still not know that he was supposed to point to a tree, and he would still not *understand* 'point to a tree'.

I have considered the ability to use certain sentences to be the criterion for possessing a full-blown concept, but this could easily be liberalized. We could allow symbolism consisting of elements which are not words in a natural language, for example, and we could allow such mental phenomena as images and other types of internal events. What is essential is that these should have the same complexity, ability to be combined with each other, etc., as sentences in a natural language. For, although a particular presentation—say, a blue flash—might serve a particular mathematician as the inner expression of the whole proof of the Prime Number Theorem, still there would be no temptation to say this (and it would be false to say this) if that mathematician could not unpack his 'blue flash' into separate steps and logical connections. But, no matter what sort of inner phenomena we allow as possible *expressions* of thought, arguments exactly similar to the foregoing will show that it is not the phenomena themselves that constitute understanding, but rather the ability of the thinker to *employ* these phenomena, to produce the right phenomena in the right circumstances.

The foregoing is a very abbreviated version of Wittgenstein's argument in *Philosophical Investigations.* If it is correct, then the attempt to understand thought by what is called 'phenomenological' investigation is fundamentally misguided; for what the phenomenologists fail to see is that what they are describing is the inner *expression* of thought, but that the *understanding* of that expression—one's understanding of one's own thoughts—is not an *occurrence* but an *ability.* Our example of a man pretending to think in Japanese (and deceiving a Japanese telepath) already shows the futility of a phenomenological approach to the problem of *understanding.* For even if there is some introspectible quality which is present when and only when one *really* understands (this seems false on introspection, in fact), still that quality is only *correlated* with understanding, and it is still possible that the man fooling the Japanese telepath have that quality too and *still* not understand a word of Japanese.

On the other hand, consider the perfectly possible man who does not have any 'interior monologue' at all. He speaks perfectly good English, and if asked what his opinions are on a given subject, he will give them at length. But he never thinks (in words, images, etc.) when he is not speaking out loud; nor does anything 'go through his head', except that (of course) he hears his own voice speaking, and has the usual sense impressions from his surroundings, plus a general 'feeling of understanding'. (Perhaps he is in the habit of talking to himself.) When he types a letter or goes to the store, etc., he is not having an internal 'stream of thought'; but his actions are intelligent and purposeful, and if anyone walks up and asks him 'What are you doing?' he will give perfectly coherent replies.

This man seems perfectly imaginable. No one would hesitate to say that he was conscious, disliked rock and roll (if he frequently expressed a strong aversion to rock and roll), etc., just because he did not think conscious thoughts except when speaking out loud.

What follows from all this is that (a) no set of mental events—images or more 'abstract' mental happenings and qualities—*constitutes* understanding; and (b) no set of mental events is *necessary* for understanding. In particular, *concepts cannot be identical with mental objects of any kind.* For, assuming that by a mental object we mean something introspectible, we have just seen that whatever it is, it may be absent in a man who does understand the appropriate word (and hence has the full blown concept), and present in a man who does not have the concept at all.

Coming back now to our criticism of magical theories of reference (a topic which also concerned Wittgenstein), we see that, on the one hand, those 'mental objects' we *can* introspectively detect—words, images, feelings, etc.—do not intrinsically refer any more than the ant's picture does (and for the same reasons), while the attempts to postulate special mental objects, 'concepts', which *do* have a necessary connection with their referents, and which only trained phenomenologists can detect, commit *a logical* blunder; for concepts are (at least in part) *abilities* and not occurrences. The doctrine that there are mental presentations which necessarily refer to external things is not only bad natural science; it is also bad phenomenology and conceptual confusion.

Chapter 27

Are we brains in a vat?

John Heil

IN *Reason, Truth, and History*, Hilary Putnam addresses the notion that we might all be *brains in a vat* in a way that has been widely discussed.[1] What follows is an attempt to get clear on Putnam's argument, more particularly, to determine how exactly that argument goes and what precisely it is supposed to establish. Putnam's presentation is not unambiguous on either count, nor is it always as clear as one might have wished.

Initial reconstruction of the argument

Putnam begins by envisioning a 'physically possible world' in which

> . . . a human being, . . . has been subjected to an operation by an evil scientist. The person's brain . . . has been removed from the body and placed in a vat of nutrients which keeps the brain alive. The nerve endings have been connected to a super-scientific computer which causes the person whose brain it is to have the illusion that everything is perfectly normal. (481.)

Putnam then proceeds to argue both that, on the supposition that *we* are brains in a vat, we could not 'say or think we were,' and that this fact entails that 'we are brains in a vat' is 'necessarily false' (488). Elsewhere Putnam expresses his conclusion differently: 'the brain in the vat hypothesis turns out to be incoherent'. Assuming 'the brain in the vat hypothesis' is just the contention that we are brains in a vat, then it appears Putnam takes his argument to show that such a hypothesis is either necessarily false or incoherent.

It is perhaps unusual to begin the analysis of an argument by speculating about the character of its conclusion. A charitable reconstruction of Putnam's discussion, however, requires nothing less. The question is: what *sort* of conclusion does that discussion support? Is it, for example, that we *are not*, or perhaps *could not be* brains in a vat? Or is it something less (or *more*) than this? We are told that 'We are brains

John Heil, 'Are We Brains in a Vat? Top Philosopher Says, "No!"', *Canadian Journal of Philosophy* 17 (1987).

1. Hilary Putnam, *Reason, Truth, and History* (Cambridge: Cambridge University Press 1981), included in Chapter 26 of this volume. References to this volume henceforth appear parenthetically. Emphasis in quoted passages appears in the original.

in a vat' is 'necessarily false,' that it is 'incoherent,' but also that our being brains in a vat is 'physically possible.' What are we to make of such remarks?

Putnam summarizes the argument as follows: '. . . [T]he supposition that we are actually brains in a vat, although it violates no physical law, and is perfectly consistent with everything we have experienced, cannot possibly be true. *It cannot possibly be true*, because it is, in a certain way, self-refuting' (482–3). One way in which a thesis can be 'self-refuting' is that '*the supposition that the thesis is entertained or enunciated . . . implies its falsity*' (483) The supposition that we are brains in a vat is, according to Putnam, like this. 'If we can consider whether it is true or false, then it is not true . . . Hence it is not true' (483).

There is, Putnam supposes, a special difficulty in 'considering'—that is, entertaining the thought—that one is a brain in a vat. Thus, although it is 'physically possible' that we are brains in a vat, 'although people in that possible world can think and "say" any words we can think and say, they cannot . . . refer to what we can refer to. In particular, they cannot think or say that they are brains in a vat (*even by thinking "we are brains in a vat"*)' (483). The difficulty is that thoughts entertained by brains in vats lack the right sorts of *connection* with features of the world outside themselves, connections required for their thoughts to represent what they *seem* to represent—what they *would* represent were they present in an ordinary brain.

> . . . [T]he fact that [brains in a vat] are conscious and intelligent does not mean that their words refer to what our words refer . . . [T]here is no connection between the *word* 'tree' as used by these brains and actual trees. They would still use the word 'tree' just as they do, think just the thoughts they do, have just the images they have, even if there were no actual trees. Their images, words, etc., are qualitatively identical with images, words, etc., which do represent trees in *our* world; but . . . qualitative similarity to something which represents an object . . . does not make a thing a representation all by itself. In short, the brains in a vat are not thinking about real trees when they think 'there is a tree in front of me' because there is nothing by virtue of which their thought 'tree' represents actual trees. (486–7).

The point may be extended to brains in a vat thinking of 'brains' and 'vats.' Because such thoughts lack the right sorts of connection with genuine brains and vats, they are not, despite appearances, thoughts about brains and vats at all. If they are about anything, they are (perhaps) about 'images' of brains and vats or goings-on inside the 'super-scientific computer' that gave rise to these images.[2] 'So, if we are brains in a vat, then the sentence "We are brains in a vat" says something false (if it says anything). In short, if we are brains in a vat, then "We are brains in a vat" is false. So it is (necessarily) false' (488). Imagine an envatted brain thinking 'I am a brain in a vat.' This sentence corresponds, it seems, to the English sentence 'I am an image of a brain in a vat' or perhaps 'I am an occurrence inside a computing machine.' If these sentences mean anything, they are surely false: an envatted brain harboring

2. We may rule out the possibility that appropriate representational connections might be established *through* the computer by imagining that the automatic machinery that feeds impulses to the envatted brain came 'into existence by some kind of cosmic chance or coincidence' (486).

them is not an *image* of a brain or an occurrence inside a computing machine, but a *brain in a vat.*

Now what may be made of this argument? It is tempting to represent it as follows:

(1) If I can consider the possibility (entertain the thought) that I am a brain in a vat, then I am not a brain in a vat.
(2) I *can* consider the possibility that I am a brain in a vat.
(3) Therefore, I am not a brain in a vat.

Here premise (1) relies on Putnam's claims about representation. Things that represent—pictures, sentences, thoughts—do so in virtue of connections of a certain sort with represented states of affairs. These connections are missing in the case of a brain in a vat. Thus, even though there may be no detectable 'qualitative differences' between what goes on in such a brain and what goes on in an ordinary (embodied) brain when the latter entertains thoughts (about trees, or fields, or brains, or vats), thoughts entertained by an envatted brain cannot represent what they do in an embodied brain.

In granting this, one grants premise (1) of the argument. But what of the second premise? Why should one grant *that*? Doing so seems simply to concede the point at issue. Any argument that could show that we can entertain the thought that we are brains in a vat would, it seems, require showing that we aren't.[3] Differently put: in order to establish premise (2), one must establish (3), the conclusion; the truth of premise (2) requires, on Putnam's view, the truth of the conclusion.

The point is not merely that (3) must be true when (2) is true if the argument is to be counted valid. Rather, evidence for (2) would, if Putnam is right, need to include (3). Thus, although the argument may be formally valid, it is useless as a vehicle for the establishment of its conclusion. It resembles proofs for the existence of God of the form:

(1) If the Bible is the word of God, then God exists.
(2) The Bible is the word of God.
(3) Therefore, God exists.

Construed this way, then, the argument seems patently unsatisfactory.[4] This very fact, however, suggests that it ought perhaps be differently construed. This suggestion is supported by Putnam's own account of the 'self-refuting' character of the brains in a vat hypothesis quoted earlier. Admittedly, he says that 'if we can consider whether [the hypothesis] is true or false, then it is not true . . . Hence it is not true' (8). And this way of putting it invites the unsatisfactory rendering of the argument just discussed. The appearance, however, may be misleading; the argument,

3. Mark Overvold has pointed out to me that Putnam's claim that the brain in the vat hypothesis is *incoherent* renders the use of premise (2) dubious. Can one entertain an incoherent thought?

4. See Earl Conee's review of *Reason, Truth, and History*, forthcoming in *Noûs*; Jane McIntyre, 'Putnam's Brains,' *Analysis* 44 (1984), 59–61; and James Stephens and Lilly-Marlene Russow, 'Brains in Vats and the Internalist Perspective, '*Australian Journal of Philosophy* 63 (1985), 205–12.

whether sound or not, may be rather more intricate. Or, at any rate, there is an argument available to Putnam that comes closer to doing what he claims for his argument than the version set out above.

A second version of the argument

First, suppose I entertain the thought 'I am a brain in a vat.' There are, it seems, two possibilities:

(1) I am speaking English, in which case the (English) sentence 'I am a brain in a vat' is false;
(2) I am speaking 'vat-English,' in which case the (vat-English) sentence 'I am a brain in a vat' is false.

The English sentence would be false because, on Putnam's view, it is a condition on one's uttering an *English* sentence that one is *not* envatted. The corresponding 'vat-English' sentence would be false because, thought or uttered by an envatted brain, it would be roughly equivalent to the English sentence 'I am a brain-in-a-vat *image*' (or, perhaps, 'I am a process occurring inside a computing machine'), and this is false: a brain in a vat is a brain in a vat, not an *image* of a brain in a vat, or an occurrence inside a computing machine.

In any case, (1) and (2), taken together, do not obviously entail that I am not a brain in a vat. Such an entailment would require that the *English* sentence 'I am a brain in a vat' be false under both conditions and clearly it need not be. Indeed, my speaking 'vat-English' is one consequence of my *being* a brain in a vat.

There is, however, a more interesting twist to the argument. Consider someone, *S*, a realist, perhaps, or a skeptic, who reflects on the two possibilities just mentioned and points out what seems patent: 'Well, I might *anyway* be a brain in a vat; the argument does nothing to exclude such an eventuality.' Now what exactly is *S* claiming here? Again, there appear to be two possibilities:

(1) *S* is speaking English, in which case the (English) sentence '*S* is a brain in a vat' is false;
(2) *S* is speaking 'vat-English,' in which case the (vat-English) sentence '*S* is a brain in a vat' is false.

Of course, *S* may accept all this, but point out that the argument *still* fails to show that he is not a brain in a vat, only something much weaker—perhaps only that if he *were* a brain in a vat, he could never entertain the thought, consider the possibility that he was. But, *S* may insist, he might nevertheless *be* a brain in a vat. That possibility has not yet been excluded.

Presently, however, it may begin to dawn on *S* that there is a peculiar difficulty inherent in his position. In insisting that, come what may, he could still be a brain in a vat, on what, exactly, is he insisting? If *S* is speaking English, then there is no special difficulty, though in that case, of course, it must be false that he is a brain in a vat. If, in contrast, *S were* envatted, then whatever it might be that he insists on (and that will depend on the truth-conditions, if any, of the 'vat-English' sentence '*S* is a brain in a vat') would also be false. *S* is in the awkward position of wanting to defend a view the very stating of which apparently precludes its truth.

Insisting that such a view might, anyway, be true, that the state of affairs it envisages might, anyway, obtain, merely invites the response: '*What* might be true? *Which* state of affairs might obtain?' One's *saying* evidently requires that the view be false, that the state of affairs fails to obtain.

In insisting that he might anyway *be* a brain in a vat, that his being a brain in a vat is 'physically possible,' *S* is supposing *either* (a) that he is speaking English (as distinct from vat-English); *or* (b) that one can somehow consider ('in vat-English') an *English* sentence to be true, when the truth-conditions for such a sentence are (*ex hypothesis*) inexpressible in vat-English.

In the first case, *S* seems to be supposing, in effect, that he might (now) *be* envatted, *and* that he is *not* envatted (a condition on his uttering or considering English sentences). But this, surely, is incoherent.

In the second case, one needs somehow to get a grip on the notion that sentences might be considered true (or false) even if the language to which they belong is, as it were, *inaccessible.* Speakers of vat-English, owing to their peculiar situation, cannot even *formulate* the truth-conditions for English sentences. What would it be, then, for *S* an envatted speaker of vat-English, to consider the truth of some English sentence?

If Putnam's argument is reconstructed along these lines, then his claim that the brain in the vat hypothesis is 'in a certain way' *incoherent* takes on a measure of plausibility. An incoherence arises from one's stating (or considering) a sentence the truth-conditions of which apparently require that it be false if it is stated or considered. The truth-conditions for such a sentence fail to be satisfied, though not because it is logically false, not because it contains a contradiction, but because the circumstances required for it to have whatever truth-conditions it has, require, as well, that it be false.

Evaluating the argument

Let us suppose that the argument just sketched is at least close to the one Putnam has in mind. What exactly does it show? Consider someone, *S*, who insists 'I always lie.' An utterance of this sort is 'self-refuting' in Putnam's sense: It could not be truthfully uttered. This is not because *S*'s always lying is not a 'physically possible' state of affairs. It is just that the sentence 'I always lie' could not be used by *S*—nor, of course, by anyone else—to pick out an existing state of affairs. It is not difficult to think of other sentences that share this characteristic: 'I do not exist' (Putnam's example); 'I am not speaking English'; 'Every sentence is false'; and so on. Each sentence alludes to a 'physically possible' circumstance inconsistent with its utterance. My not existing is surely possible, but, as Augustine long ago taught us, that possibility is incompatible with my entertaining the thought that I might not exist.

In most cases of this sort we have available alternative, nonindexical, nonparadoxical ways of describing the possibilities in question. There is no special difficulty in *our* asserting the sentence '*S* always lies' of *S*, for example, or '*S* does not exist,' or '*S* is not speaking English' (or, for that matter, '*S* is a brain in a vat'). 'Every sentence is false' is a trickier case, one closer perhaps to 'We are brains in a vat.' For although the state of affairs to which it alludes seems 'physically possible,' the sentence could not be used to pick out that state of affairs—indeed it seems that no sentence could be so used.

Does this mean that the hypothesis that all sentences are false is, though 'physically possible,' nevertheless unintelligible?[5] On the one hand, it is tempting to argue that the state of affairs in question is such that, were it to obtain, it could not be (truthfully or correctly) *said* to obtain (and if thoughts are sentential entities or episodes, then it could not be *thought* to obtain either). But this scarcely impugns the metaphysical status of that state of affairs. What is impugned is simply a certain linguistic form. On the other hand, if thoughts necessarily incorporate the relevant content-determining features of this linguistic form, then we may begin to share Putnam's uneasiness about states of affairs that seem 'physically possible' but which are, if actual, unthinkable.

Putnam's concern with such matters leads him to *internalism*, and *antirealism*. In the idiom of the *Tractatus*: 'The limits of my language mean the limits of my world.'[6] On the face of it, the move is gratuitous. One appeals to features of the world to make a point about reference. The world, it appears, must have a certain character if we are to represent it sententially. One consequence of its being *that* way, one consequence of the determinants of reference being what *they* are, is that one could not describe a world in which these determinants were absent *in that world*. Does this mean that the hypothesis that *this* world is such a world is either necessarily false or incoherent?

Putnam holds both that it is and that qualms one may have about the notion of a world's being possible but unthinkable can be alleviated by accepting *internalism*. It is not easy to say with precision what internalism is. Putnam illuminates the doctrine chiefly by contrasting it with *externalism*, a view characterized by its acceptance of the notion that there is a 'perspective' or 'point of view' on the world independent of our necessarily limited system of concepts. This 'God's eye point of view' is externalism's 'favorite point of view'. It is only by adverting to some such transcendental standpoint that an externalist can distinguish a world existing apart from our conceptualized, thinkable world. And this, it turns out, is what one must

5. There may be other, independent, nontranscendental grounds for regarding this hypothesis as unintelligible or in some other way defective. These will not be discussed here.

6. L. Wittgenstein, *Tractatus Logico-Philosophicus*, trans. D.F. Pears and B.F. McGuinness (London: Routledge & Kegan Paul 1961), sec. 5.6.

do to make sense of the possibility that we might *be* brains in a vat even though the hypothesis that we are is self-refuting.

Even a 'God's eye point of view,' however, is a point of view. Might not there be another possibility? That is, an externalist might wish to distinguish points of view on the world from the world itself and maintain that the world could well *be* a certain way independent of *any* particular point of view.[7] Indeed this is precisely what externalists—and realists—seem to have in mind in insisting that it might be the case that one *is* a brain in a vat, even though, were this so, one could not entertain the thought that it is so. 'After all,' such a nonperspectival externalist might say, 'my inability to entertain such thoughts is due simply to the world's being the way it is. Its being that way has nothing to do with perspectives or points of view, in fact these seem altogether *precluded* under the circumstances.'

One of Putnam' aims in the early chapters of *Reason, Truth, and History* is to show that externalism of either sort—that is, externalism favoring a God's eye point of view and nonperspectival externalism—are both, at bottom, unsatisfactory. The argument is never an easy one to follow. Grasping it is not aided by Putnam's flaunting conclusions reached in his discussion of the brains in a vat hypothesis as though these supported internalism against externalism. Those conclusions seem altogether neutral. Of course, if one had independent grounds for adopting internalism, then the brains in a vat argument might show rather more than it does otherwise. If my being a brain in a vat is unthinkable except when it is false, *and* if the limits of my thought determine the limits of my world, then perhaps I could not be a brain in a vat (at least not in 'my world'). But here a robust version of internalism is employed as a premise, not extruded as a conclusion.

Concluding remarks

I have examined two distinct versions of Putnam's argument. The first version suffers from the fact that, in order to establish the truth of a crucial premise, one must first establish the truth of the conclusion. The second version looks more promising. It purports to show that the sentence 'I am a brain in a vat' could not be true even though my *being* a brain in a vat is within the realm of physical possibility. The sentence will be false (though for different reasons) whether it is uttered in ordinary English or, by an envatted brain, in vat-English. It seems to follow that the sentence, whenever considered or uttered, is false. Hence, I am not a brain in a vat!

To balk at this conclusion, according to Putnam, requires that one embrace *externalism*, the doctrine that there could be *detached, inaccessible* sentences cor-

7. Donald Davidson has argued that talk about 'perspectives' and 'points of view' seems to require that there be something on which there can *be* perspectives and points of view. See 'The Very Idea of a Conceptual Scheme,' in his *Inquiries into truth and Interpretation* (Oxford: Oxford University Press 1984). See also J. Heil, *Perception and Cognition* (Berkeley, Los Angeles, and London: University of California Press 1983), 108–18.

rectly describing the world—that, for instance, one might speculate on the truth of the English sentence 'I am a brain in a vat' in vat-English, an idiom in which the truth-conditions of the English sentence cannot be expressed. This, Putnam urges, is scarcely intelligible.[8]

For reasons alluded to already, however, it is doubtful that Putnam's discussion of the brains in a vat hypothesis much advances his defense of internalism and anti-realism. In many ways, it simply muddies the water. The matter is made worthy of concern by the fact that Putnam appeals later to a parallel argument in an effort to overturn relativism (see chs. 3 and 5). Relativism is, he suggests, self-refuting in just the way the brains in a vat hypothesis is self-refuting. If one can consider the possibility that relativism is true, then it must not be.

This is not the place to scrutinize Putnam's brief against relativism. It is fair to point out, however, that the cogency of all such arguments depends on our agreeing on some other grounds that the world's having a certain character independent of our ways of thinking about it is senseless (or in some other way objectionable). But externalism and realism, doctrines holding that this is not so, are just what is at issue.[9]

8. Perhaps one can distinguish *realism* (or one form of realism) from *externalism* in the following manner. According to the realist, the world might *be* a certain (unspecified) way, even though, were if that way, one would be barred from having thoughts about it, more particularly, thoughts that it was *that* way. On this view, how the world *is* is not determined by how one *thinks* it is. Externalism, in contrast, is a doctrine about sentences. According to the externalist, sentences may be true even though they are (in the sense discussed above) *inaccessible*. It is far from clear that realism requires externalism.

9. A version of the present paper was presented at the American Philosophical Association meetings, Washington, D.C., December 1985. The commentator was C.B. Martin. I benefited from his comments as well as those of two anonymous referees for this *Journal*. Barry Brown deserves much of the credit for the formulation of the arguments discussed here, although he undoubtedly would disagree with a good deal that I have said about them. In any case he and Mark Overvold are responsible for whatever I have managed to get right.

Chapter 28

Mental content

Jaegwon Kim

Narrow content and wide content

ONE thing that the correlational account of mental content high-lights is this: Content has a lot to do with what is going on in the world, outside the physical boundaries of the subject. As far as what goes on inside is concerned, the earthly frog and the other-earthly frog are indistinguishable—they are in the same relevant neural/sensory state: Both register a moving black dot. But in describing the representational content of their states, what the frogs 'see,' we advert to the factors in the environment of the frogs. Or consider a simpler case: Peter is looking at a tomato, and Mary is also looking at one (a different tomato, but let's suppose that it looks pretty much the same as the one Peter is looking at). Mary thinks to herself, 'This tomato has gone bad,' and Peter, too, thinks, 'This tomato has gone bad.' From the internal point of view, Mary's perceptual experience is indistinguishable from Peter's (we may suppose their neural states, too, are relevantly similar), and they would express their thoughts using the same words. But it is clear that the contents of their beliefs are different. For they involve different objects: Mary's belief is about the thing she is gazing at, and Peter's belief is about a different thing altogether. Moreover, and this is a related point, Mary's belief may be true and Peter's false. On the standard understanding of the notion of 'content,' beliefs with the same content must be true together or false together (that is, contents are 'truth conditions'). Obviously, the fact that Peter's and Mary's beliefs have different content is due to facts external to them; the difference in content cannot be explained in terms of what is going on inside the perceivers. It seems, then, that at least in this and other similar cases belief contents are differentiated, or 'individuated,' by reference to conditions external to the believer.

Beliefs whose content is individuated in this way are said to have 'wide' or 'broad' content. In contrast, beliefs whose content is individuated solely on the basis of what goes on inside the persons holding them are said to have 'narrow' content. Alternatively, we may say that the content of an intentional state is narrow just in case it supervenes on the internal/intrinsic properties of the subject who is in that state and that it is wide otherwise. This means that two individuals who are exactly alike in all intrinsic/internal respects must have the same narrow-content beliefs but may well diverge in their wide-content beliefs. Thus, our two frogs are

Jaegwon Kim, 'Mental Content', from *Philosophy of Mind* (Boulder, CO: Westview Press, 1996).

exactly alike in internal/intrinsic respects but unlike in what their perceptual states represent. So the contents of these states do not supervene internally and are therefore wide.

Several well-known thought experiments have been instrumental in persuading many philosophers that most of our ordinary beliefs (and other intentional states) have wide content, that what beliefs and desires we hold is not simply a matter of what's going on inside our minds or heads. Among these thought experiments, the following two, the first due to Hilary Putnam and the second to Tyler Burge[1] have been particularly influential.

Thought experiment 1: earth and twin earth Imagine a planet, 'twin earth,' somewhere in the remote region of space, which is just like the earth we inhabit except in one respect: On twin earth a certain chemical substance with the molecular structure XYZ, which has all the observable characteristics of water (it is transparent, dissolves salt and sugar, quenches thirst, puts out fire, freezes at 0°C, etc.), replaces water everywhere. So lakes and oceans on twin earth are filled with XYZ, not H_2O (that is, water), and twin earthians drink XYZ when they are thirsty, do their laundry in XYZ, and so on. Some twin earthians speak English, which is indistinguishable from earthian English, and they use their expression 'water' in the way we use our word 'water.'

But there is a difference between our English and the English spoken on twin earth: The twin-earthian 'water' and our 'water' refer to different things (they have different 'extensions,' as logicians will say). The first refers to XYZ, not water, and the second refers to water, not XYZ. If you are the first visitor to twin earth and find out the truth about their 'water,' you may report back to your friends on earth as follows: 'At first I thought that the transparent stuff that fills the oceans and lakes around here was water, and it really looks and tastes like our water. But I just found out that it isn't water at all, although people around here call it 'water.' It's really XYZ, not H_2O.' You will not translate the twin-earthian word 'water' into the English word 'water'; you will need to invent a new word, perhaps 'twater.' There is a sense of meaning, then, in which the twin-earthian 'water' and our 'water' have different meanings, although what goes on inside the minds, or heads, of twin earthians may be exactly the same as what goes in ours, and our speech behavior involving the two words is also indistinguishable. This semantic difference between our 'water' and twin-earthian 'water' is reflected in the way we describe and individuate mental states of earthians and twin earthians. When a twin earthian says to the waiter, 'Please bring me a glass of water!' she is expressing her desire for twater, and we will report, in *oratio obliqua*, that she wants some twater, not that

1. Hilary Putnam, 'The Meaning of "Meaning,"' in Putnam, *Mind, Language, and Reality: Philosophical Papers*, vol. 2 (Cambridge: Cambridge University Press, 1975); Tyler Burge, 'Individualism and the Mental,' *Midwest Studies in Philosophy* 4 (1979):73–121; See Chapter 25 of this volume. The use of the terms 'narrow' and 'wide' in this context is due to Putnam.

she wants some water. When an earthian says the same thing, she is expressing a desire for water, and we will say that she wants water. You believe that water is wet, and your twin-earthian doppelganger believes that twater is wet. And so on. To summarize, then, earthians have water-thoughts and water-desires, whereas twin earthians have twater-thoughts and twater-desires, and this difference is due to environmental factors external to the subjects who have the beliefs and desires.

Suppose an earthian astronaut, Jones, lands on twin earth. She of course doesn't realize at first that the liquid she sees in the lakes and coming out of the tap isn't water. She is offered a glass of this transparent liquid by her twin-earthian host and thinks to herself, 'That's a nice, cold glass of water—just what I needed.' Consider Jones's belief that the glass contains cold water. This belief is false, since the glass contains not water but XYZ, or twater. Although she is now on twin earth, in an environment full of twater and devoid of water, she is still subject to earthian standards: Her words mean, and her thoughts are individuated, in accordance with the criteria that prevail on earth. What this shows is that a person's *past associations* with her environment play a role in determining her meanings and thought contents. If Jones stays on twin earth long enough, we will eventually interpret her word 'water' to mean twater, not water, and attribute to her twater-thoughts rather than water-thoughts, although of course it is difficult to say exactly when this change will come about.

If these considerations are by and large correct, they show that two supervenience theses fail: First, the meanings of our expressions do not in general supervene on our *internal* physical/psychological states. Twin earthians are indistinguishable from us in all relevant respects as far as our internal lives, both physical and mental, are concerned, and yet our words have different meanings. We can imagine that there is a twin-earth doppelganger of you who is molecule-for-molecule identical with you[2] you and she are in the same neural state when you and she use the word 'water,' but your word 'water' means water and hers mean twater. Second, and this is what is of immediate relevance to us, the contents of beliefs and other intentional states also fail to supervene on our internal physical/psychological states. You have water-thoughts and your twin-earthian doppelganger has twater-thoughts. And there is strong reason for thinking that beliefs are individuated by content; that is, beliefs with the same content are regarded as being of the same belief type, and beliefs with different content count as falling under different belief types. What particular beliefs you hold depends on your relationship, past as well as present, to the things and events in your surroundings, as well as what goes on inside you. The same goes for other content-bearing intentional states. If this is in general right, the thought experiment establishes the existence of wide content.

2. We will ignore here the inconvenient but inessential detail that since your body contains lots of H_2O molecules and your twin on twin earth has XYZ where you have H_2O, you two couldn't be 'molecule-for-molecule' identical.

Thought experiment 2: arthritis and 'tharthritis' Consider a person, call him 'Fred,' in two situations.

1. *The actual situation.* Fred thinks 'arthritis' means inflammation of the bones (it actually means inflammation of the joints). Feeling pain and swelling in his thigh, Fred complains to his doctor, 'I have arthritis in my thigh.' His doctor tells him that people can have arthritis only in their joints. Two points to keep in mind: First, Fred believed, before he talked to his doctor; that he had arthritis in his thigh, and, second, this belief was false.

2. *A counterfactual situation.* Nothing has changed with our Fred—he is experiencing swelling and pain in his thigh and complains to his doctor, exclaiming, 'I have arthritis in my thigh.' What is different about the counterfactual situation concerns the use of the word 'arthritis' in Fred's speech community: In the situation we are imagining, the word is used to refer to inflammation of bones, not just bone joints. That is, in the counterfactual situation Fred has a correct understanding of the word 'arthritis,' unlike in the actual situation. In the counterfactual situation, then, Fred is expressing a true belief when he utters, 'I have arthritis in my thigh.' But how would we report Fred's belief concerning the condition of his thigh—that is, report in *our* language (in this world)? We can't say that Fred believes that he has arthritis in his thigh, because in our language 'arthritis' means inflammation of joints, and he clearly doesn't have that, which would render his belief false. We might coin a new expression (to be part of our language), 'tharthritis,' to mean inflammation of bones as well as of joints, and say that Fred, in the counterfactual situation, believes that he has tharthritis in his thigh. Again, note two points: First, Fred, in the counterfactual situation, believes not that he has arthritis in his thigh but that he has tharthritis in his thigh, and, second, this belief is true.

What this thought experiment shows is that the content of belief depends, at least in part but crucially, on the speech practices of the linguistic community in which we situate the subject. Fred in the actual situation and Fred in the counterfactual situation are exactly alike when taken as an individual person (that is, when we consider his internal/intrinsic properties alone), including his speech habits (he speaks the same idiolect in both situations) and inner mental life. Yet he has different beliefs in the two situations: Fred in the actual world has the belief that he has arthritis in his thigh, which is false, but in the counterfactual situation he has the belief that he has tharthritis in his thigh, which is true. If this is right, beliefs and other intentional states do not supervene on the internal physical/psychological states of persons; if supervenience is wanted, we must also include in the supervenience base the linguistic practices of the community to which persons belong.

Burge argues plausibly that the example can be generalized to show that almost all contents are wide—that is, externally individuated. Take the word 'brisket' (another of his examples): Some of us mistakenly think that brisket comes only from beef, and it is easy to see how a case analogous to the arthritis example can be set up. In fact, the same situation will arise for any word whose meaning is incompletely understood—in fact, any word whose meaning *could* be incompletely understood, which includes pretty much every word. When we profess our beliefs using such words, our beliefs will be identified and individuated by the socially determined meanings of these words (recall Fred and his 'arthritis' in the actual situation), and it is easy to see how a Burge-style counterfactual situation can be set up for each such word. Moreover, we seem standardly to identify our own beliefs by reflecting on what words we would use to express them, even if we know that our understanding of these words is incomplete or even possibly defective (how many of us know the correct meaning of, say, 'mortgage,' 'justice of the peace,' or 'galaxy'?). This shows, one might argue, that almost all of our ordinary belief attributions involve wide contents.

If this is right, the question naturally arises: Are there beliefs whose content isn't determined by external factors? That is, are there beliefs with narrow content? There certainly are beliefs, and other intentional states, that do not imply the existence of anything, or refer to anything, outside the subject who has them. For example, Fred's belief that he is in pain or that he exists or that there are no unicorns does not require that anything other than Fred exist, and it would seem that the content of these beliefs is independent of conditions external to Fred. If this is right, the narrowness of these beliefs is not threatened by considerations of the sort that emerged from Thought Experiment 1. But what of Thought Experiment 2? Consider Fred's belief that he is in pain. Could we run on the word 'pain' Burge's argument involving 'arthritis'? Surely it is possible for someone to misunderstand the word 'pain' or any other sensation term, as well as 'arthritis' and such. Suppose Fred thinks that 'pain' applies to both pains and severe itches and that on experiencing bad itches on his shoulder, he complains to his wife about his annoying 'pains' in the shoulder. If the Burge-style considerations apply here, we would have to say that Fred is expressing his belief that he is experiencing pain in his shoulder, and that this is a false belief.

The question is whether that is what we should, or want to, say. It would not seem implausible to say that knowing what we know about Fred's misunderstanding of the word 'pain' and the sensation he is actually experiencing, the correct thing to say is that he believes, and in fact knows, that he is experiencing severe itches in his shoulder. It's only that in saying 'I am having pains in my shoulder' he is misdescribing his sensation and hence misreporting his belief. Now consider the following counterfactual situation: In the linguistic community to which Fred belongs, 'pain' is in fact used to refer to pains and severe itches. How would we report, in our own words, the content of Fred's belief in the counterfactual situation? There are these possibilities: (1) We say, 'He believes that he is experiencing pains in his shoulder'; (2) We say, 'He believes that he is experiencing severe itches in his shoulder'; and (3) we don't have a word in English that can be used for expressing the content of his belief (we could introduce a neologism, 'painitch,' and say, 'Fred believes that he is experiencing painitches in his shoulder'). Obviously, (1) has to be ruled out; if (3) is what we should say, the arthritis argument applies to the present case as well, since this would show that a change in the social environment of the subject can change the belief content attributed to him. But it isn't obvious that this, rather than (2), is the correct option. It seems to be an open question, then, whether the arthritis argument applies to cases involving beliefs about one's own sensations, and there seems to be a reason for the inclination to say of Fred in the actual world that he believes that he is having severe itches rather than that he believes that he is having pains. The reason is that if we were to opt for the latter, it would make his belief false, and this is a belief about his own current sensations. But we assume that under normal circumstances people don't make mistakes in identifying their current sensory experiences. This assumption need not be taken as a contentious philosophical doctrine; arguably, recognition of first-person authority on such matters, too, reflects our common social/linguistic practices, and this may very well override the kinds of consideration so plausibly advanced by Burge in the case of arthritis.

Another point to consider is beliefs of nonlinguistic animals. Do cats and dogs have beliefs and other intentional states whose contents can be reported in the form: 'Fido believes that *p*,' where *p* stands for a declarative sentence? Clearly, the arthritis-style arguments cannot be applied to such beliefs since these animals don't belong to any linguistic community and the only language that is involved is our own, namely, the language of the person who makes such belief attributions. In what sense, then, could animal beliefs be externally individuated? There may or may not be an obvious answer to this question, but anyhow this example can cut both ways, as far as Burge's argument is concerned; for one might argue, as some philosophers have,[3] that nonlinguistic animals are not capable of having intentional states (in particular, beliefs) and that this is connected with the inapplicability of the arthritis argument. The details here are complicated, and we must set them aside. We will return to the question of narrow content in a subsequent section.

The metaphysics of wide-content states

The considerations involved in the two thought experiments show that many, if not all, of our ordinary beliefs and other intentional states have wide content. Their contents are 'external': That is, they are determined, at least in part, by factors outside the subject, in her physical and social environment. Before these externalist considerations were brought to our attention, philosophers used to think that beliefs, desires, and the like are in the mind, or at least in the head. Putnam, the inventor of twin earth with its XYZ, said: 'Cut the pie any way you like, "meanings"

3. Most notably Descartes and Davidson. See Davidson's 'Thought and Talk' in his *Essays on Truth and Interpretation*, included in Chapter 20 of this volume.

just ain't in the head.'[4] Should we believe that beliefs and desires aren't in the head, or in the mind, either? If so, where are they? Outside the head? Let us consider three possibilities.

1. One might say that the belief that water and oil don't mix is constituted in part by water and oil, that the belief itself, in some sense, involves the actual stuff, water and oil, in addition to the person having the belief (or her 'head'). A similar response in the case of arthritis would be that Fred's belief that he has arthritis is in part constituted by his linguistic community. The general idea is that all the factors that play a role in the determination of the content of a belief *ontologically constitute* that belief, that the belief is a state that comprises these items within itself. Thus, we have a simple explanation for just how your belief that water is wet differs from your twin-earthian twin's belief that twater is wet: Yours includes water as a constituent and hers includes twater as a constituent. On this approach, then, beliefs extrude from the subject's head into the world, and there are no bounds to how far they can reach. The whole universe would, on this approach, be a constituent of your beliefs about the universe! Moreover, all beliefs about the universe would appear to have exactly the same constituent, namely, the universe. This sounds absurd, and it is absurd. We can also see that this general approach would make causation of beliefs difficult to explain.

2. One might consider the belief that water and oil don't mix as a certain relation holding between the subject on the one hand and water and oil on the other. Or, alternatively, one takes the belief as a *relational property* of the subject involving water and oil. (That Socrates is married to Xanthippe is a relational fact; Socrates also has the relational property of being married to Xanthippe, and, conversely, Xanthippe has the relational property of being married to Socrates.) This approach makes causation of beliefs more tractable: We can ask, and will sometimes be able to answer, how a subject came to bear this belief relation to water and oil, just as we can ask how Xanthippe came to have the relational property of being married to Socrates. But what of other determinants of content? As we saw, belief content is determined in part by the history of one's interaction with one's environment. And what of the social-linguistic determinants, as in Burge's examples? It seems at least highly awkward to consider beliefs as relations with respect to these factors.

3. The third possibility is to consider beliefs to be wholly internal to the subjects who have them but consider their contents as giving *relational specifications* of the beliefs. On this view, beliefs may be neural states or other types of physical states of organisms and systems to which they are attributed. Contents, then, are viewed as ways of specifying these inner states; wide contents, then, are specifications in terms of, or under the constraints of, factors and conditions external to the subject, both physical and social, both current and historical. We can refer to, or pick out, Socrates by relational descriptions or by specifying his relational properties, for example,

4. Putnam, 'The Meaning of "Meaning,"' p. 227.

'the husband of Xanthippe' (or the property of being married to Xanthippe), 'the teacher of Plato' (or the property of being a teacher of Plato), and so on. But this doesn't mean that Xanthippe or Plato is a constituent part of Socrates, nor does it mean that Socrates is some kind of relational entity. Similarly, when we specify Jones's belief as the belief that water and oil don't mix, we are specifying this belief relationally, in terms of water and oil, but this doesn't mean that water and oil are constituents of the belief or that the belief itself is a relation to water and oil.

Let us look into this last approach in a bit more detail. Consider physical magnitudes such as mass and length, which are standardly considered to be paradigm examples of intrinsic properties of material objects. But how do we *specify, represent*, or *measure* the mass or length of an object? The answer: relationally. To say that this rod has a mass of 5 kilograms is to say that it bears a certain relationship to the International Prototype Kilogram (it would balance, on an equal-arm balance, five objects each of which balances the Standard Kilogram). Likewise, to say that the rod has a length of 2 meters is to say that it is twice the length of the Standard Meter (or twice the distance traveled by light in a vacuum in a certain specified fraction of a second). These properties are intrinsic, but their specifications or representations are extrinsic and relational, involving relationships to other things and properties in the world. It may well be that the availability of such extrinsic representations are essential to the utility of these properties in the formulation of scientific laws and explanations.

In physical measurements we use numbers to represent properties of objects, and these numbers involve relationships to other objects. Similarly, in attributing to persons beliefs with wide content, we use propositions, or content sentences, to represent them, and these propositions (often) involve relations to things outside the persons. When we say that Jones believes that water is wet, we are using the content sentence 'Water is wet' to specify this belief, and the appropriateness of this sentence as a specification of the belief depends on Jones's relationship, past and present, to her environment. What Burge's examples show is that the choice of a content sentence depends also on the social/linguistic facts about the person holding the belief. In a sense, we are 'measuring' people's mental states using sentences, just as we measure physical magnitudes using numbers.[5] Moreover, just as the assignment of numbers in measurement depends on relationships to things other than the things whose magnitudes are being measured, the use of content sentences in the specification of intentional states makes use of, and depends on, factors outside the subject. In both cases the informativeness and utility of the

5. This idea is explicitly stated by Paul M. Churchland in his 'Eliminative Materialism and the Propositional Attitudes,' *Journal of Philosophy* 78 (1981):67–90; see Chapter 23 of this volume. It has been systematically elaborated by Robert Matthews in 'The Measure of Mind,' *Mind* 103 (1994):131–146. However, these authors do not relate this approach to the issues of content externalism. For another perspective on the issues see Ernest Sosa, 'Between Internalism and Externalism,' *Philosophical Issues* 1 (1991):179–195.

specifications, assigned numbers or sentences, depend crucially on the involvement of external factors and conditions.[6]

The approach we have just sketched has much to recommend itself over the other two. It locates beliefs and other intentional states squarely within the subjects; they are internal states of the persons holding them, not something that somehow extrudes from them. This is a more elegant metaphysical picture than its alternatives. What is 'wide' about these states is their specifications or descriptions, not the states themselves. And there are good reasons for the wideness of content specifications. For one, we want them to specify the representational contents of beliefs—what states of affairs in the world are represented by beliefs—and it is no surprise that this involves reference to conditions external to the believer. For another, the sorts of social/linguistic constraints involved in Burge's examples seem crucial to the uniformity, stability, and intersubjectivity of content attributions. But it is important not to conflate the ontological status of internal states with the modes of their specification.

Narrow content?

You believe that water extinguishes fires, and your twin on twin earth believes that twater extinguishes fires. The two beliefs have different contents: What you believe is not the same as what your twin believes. But leaving the matter here is unsatisfying; it seems to ignore something important—something psychologically important—that you and your twin share in holding these beliefs. 'Narrow content' is supposed to capture this something shared you and your twin share.

First, we seem to have a strong sense that both you and your twin conceptualize the same state of affairs in holding the beliefs about water and twater respectively; the way things seem to you when you think that water extinguishes fires must be the same, we feel, as the way things seem to your twin when she thinks that twater extinguishes fires. From an internal psychological perspective, your thought and her thought seem to have the same significance. In thinking of water, you perhaps have the idea of a substance that is transparent, flows a certain way, tastes a certain way, and so on; and in thinking of twater, your twin has the same associations. Or take the frog case: Isn't it plausible to suppose that the earthly frog that detects a fly and the other-earthly frog that detects a schmy are in the same perceptual state—a state whose content consists in a black dot flitting across the visual field? There is a strong intuitive pull toward the view that there is something important that is common to your psychological life and your twin's, the earthly frog's perceptual state and the other-earthly frog's, that could reasonably be called 'content.'

Second, consider your and your twin's behaviors: They show a lot in common. For example, when you find your couch on fire, you pour water on it; when your twin finds her couch on fire, she pours twater on it. If you were visiting twin earth

6. This point concerning content sentences is made by Burge in 'Individualism and the Mental.'

and found a couch on fire there, you would pour twater on it, too (and conversely if your twin is visiting the earth). Your behavior involving water is the same as her behavior involving twater; moreover, your behavior would remain the same if twater were substituted for water everywhere, and her behavior would remain the same if water were substituted for twater. It's almost as though the water-twater difference seems psychologically irrelevant—irrelevant for behavior causation or explanation. That is, the difference between water-thoughts and twater-thoughts cancels itself out, so to speak, in the context of psychological explanation and causation. What is important for psychological explanation seems to be what you and your twin share, namely, thoughts with narrow content. So the question arises: Does psychological theory need wide content? Can it get by with narrow content alone (assuming there is such a thing)?

We have seen some examples of beliefs that plausibly do not depend on the existence of anything outside the subject holding them: Your belief that you exist, that you are in pain, that unicorns don't exist, and the like. Although we left open the question whether the arthritis argument applies to them, they are at least 'internal' or 'intrinsic' to the subject in the sense that for these beliefs to exist, nothing outside the subject needs to exist. There seems no reason not to think that the occurrence of these beliefs logically entails anything external to the believer and therefore that these beliefs supervene solely on the factors internal to him (again barring the Burge-style considerations).

However, a closer look at the situation reveals that some of these beliefs are not supervenient only on internal states of the believer. For we need to consider the involvement of the subject herself in the belief. Consider Mary's belief that she is in pain. The content of this belief is that she, that is, Mary, is in pain. This is the state of affairs represented by the belief, and this belief is true just in case that state of affairs obtains—that is, just in case Mary is in pain. (That is to say, we take contents to be *truth conditions*, as standardly done.) Now, put Mary's twin on twin earth (or a perfect physical replica of Mary on this earth) in the same internal physical state that Mary is in when she has this belief. If mind-body supervenience, *as usually conceived*, holds, it would seem that Mary's twin, too, will have the belief that she is in pain. However, her belief has the content *she* (twinearth Mary) is in pain, not the content that *Mary* is in pain. The belief is true if and only if Mary's twin is in pain. This means that the content of the belief that one is in pain, where content is understood as truth conditions, does not supervene on the internal physical state of the believer.

Thus, the following two ideas that are normally taken to lie at the core of the notion of 'narrow content' fail to coincide: (1) Narrow content is internal and intrinsic to the believer and doesn't involve anything outside her current state; (2) narrow content supervenes on the current internal physical states of the believer. Mary's belief that she is in pain and other beliefs whose content sentence includes a reference back to the subject (e.g., her belief that she exists, that she is taller than her sister), satisfy (1) but not (2). Nor do beliefs whose contents involve reference to particular objects: Mary believes that Clinton is left-handed, but if you put Mary's twin in the same neural state, she will believe not that Clinton is left-handed but that twin-Clinton (Clinton's doppelganger on twin earth) is left-handed.

One may think that this shows not that these beliefs don't supervene on the internal physical states of the believer but rather that we should revise the notion of 'same belief' involved here—that is, revise the criteria of belief individuation. In our discussion thus far, individual beliefs (or 'belief tokens') have been considered to be 'the same belief' (or 'belief type') just in case they have the same content, that is, the same truth condition. As we saw, Mary's belief that she, Mary, is in pain and her twin's belief that she, the twin Mary, is in pain don't have the same content and hence must count as belonging to different belief types. That is why supervenience fails for these beliefs. However, there is an obvious and natural sense in which Mary and her twin have 'the same belief'—even beliefs with 'the same content'—when each believes that she is in pain. The same is true of Mary's belief that Clinton is left-handed and twin-Mary's belief that twin-Clinton is left-handed. More work, however, needs to be done to capture this notion of 'content' or sameness of belief,[7] and that is part of the project of explicating the notion of narrow content.

It is widely accepted that most of our ordinary belief attributions, and attributions of other intentional states, involve wide content. Some hold not only that all contents are wide but that the very notion of narrow content makes no sense. One point that is often made against narrow content is its alleged ineffability: How do we capture the shared content of Jones's belief that water is wet and her twin's belief that twater is wet? And if there is something shared, why is it a kind of 'content'?

One way the friends of narrow content have tried to deal with such questions is to treat narrow content as an abstract technical notion, roughly in the following sense. The thing that Mary and her twin share has this role: If anyone has it and has acquired her language on earth (or in an environment containing water), then her word 'water' refers to water and she has water-thoughts, and if anyone has it and has acquired her language on twin earth (or in an environment containing twater), then her word 'water' refers to twater and she has twater-thoughts. The same idea applies to the frog case. What the two frogs, one on this earth and the other on a planet with schmies but no flies, have in common is this: If a frog has it and inhabits an environment with flies, it has the capacity to have flies as part of its perceptual content and similarly for frogs in a schmy-inclusive environment. Technically, narrow content is taken as a *function* from environmental contexts (including contexts

7. In this connection see Roderick Chisholm's theory, which takes beliefs not as relations to propositions but construes them as attributions of properties, in his *First Person* (Minneapolis: University of Minnesota Press, 1981). David Lewis has independently proposed a similar approach in his 'Attitudes *De Dicto* and *De Se*,' reprinted in his *Philosophical Papers*, vol. 1.

of language acquisition) to wide contents (or truth conditions).[8] Whether or not such an approach is ultimately viable is a complex question that we must set aside.

Two problems with wide content

We will survey here two outstanding issues confronting the thesis that all, or most, of our psychological states have wide content.

The causal relevance of wide content Even if we acknowledge that commonsense psychology individuates intentional states widely and formulates causal explanations of behavior in terms of wide-content states, we might well ask whether this is an ineliminable feature of such explanations. Several considerations can be advanced to cast doubt on the causal/explanatory efficacy of wide-content states. First, we have already noted the similarity between the behaviors of earthians and those of twin earthians in relation to water and twater respectively. We saw that in formulating causal explanations of these behaviors, the difference between water-thoughts and twater-thoughts somehow drops out. Second, to put the point another way, if you are a psychologist who has already developed a working psychological theory of earthians, formulated in terms of content-bearing intentional states, you obviously would not start all over again from scratch when you want to develop a psychological theory for twin earthians. In fact, you are likely to say that earthians and twin earthians have 'the same psychology'—that is, the same psychological theory is valid for both. In view of this, isn't it more appropriate to take the difference between water-thoughts and twater-thoughts merely as a difference in the values of a contextual parameter to be fixed to suit the situations to which the theory is applied, rather than as an integral element of the theory itself? If this is correct, doesn't wide content drop out as part of the theoretical apparatus of psychological theory?

Moreover, there is a metaphysical point to consider: The proximate cause of my physical behavior (e.g., bodily motions) must be 'local'—it must be a certain series of neural events originating in my central nervous system that causes the contraction of appropriate muscles and such. This means that what these neural events represent in the outside world is irrelevant to behavior causation: If the same neural events occur in a different environment so that they have different representational (wide) content, they would still cause the same physical behavior. That is, we have reason to think that proximate causes of behavior are locally supervenient on the internal physical states of an organism, but wide-content states are not so supervenient. Hence, the wideness of wide-content states is not relevant to causal explanations of physical behavior.

8. See Stephen White, 'Partial Character and the Language of Thought,' *Pacific Philosophical Quarterly* 63 (1982):347–365; Fodor, *Psychosemantics*.

One way in which the friends of wide content have tried to counter these considerations goes as follows. What we typically attempt to explain in commonsense psychology is not physical behavior but action—not why your right hand moved thus and so, but why you turned on the stove, why you boiled the water, why you made the tea. To explain why your hand moved in a certain way, it may suffice to advert to causes 'in the head,' but to explain why you turned on the stove or why you boiled the water, we must invoke wide-content states: because you wanted to heat the kettle of water, because you wanted to make a cup of tea for your friend, and so on. Behaviors explained in typical commonsense explanation are given under 'wide descriptions,' and we need wide-content states to explain them. So the point of the reply is that we need wide content to explain 'wide behavior.' Whether or not this response is sufficient is another question. In particular, one might raise questions whether the wideness of thoughts and the wideness of behavior are playing any real role in the causal/explanatory relation involved or merely ride piggyback, so to speak, on an underlying causal/explanatory relationship between the neural states, or narrow-content states, and physical behavior.

Wide content and self knowledge How do we know that Mary believes that water is wet and that Mary's twin on twin earth believes that twater is wet? Because we know that Mary's environment contains water and that Mary's twin's environment contains twater. But consider the matter from Mary's point of view: How does she know that she believes that water is wet? How does she know the content of her own thoughts?

We believe that a subject has special, direct access to her own mental states. Perhaps the access is not infallible and doesn't extend to all mental states, but it is uncontroversial that there is special first-person authority in regard to one's own occurrent thoughts. When you consciously think something, you know immediately, without inference or further evidence, what you think. If you think that the shuttle bus is late and you might miss your flight, you know, almost in the very act of thinking, that you think that. You don't make observations, or make inferences, to come to know that. First-person knowledge of the contents of one's own thoughts is direct and immediate and carries a special sort of authority.

Let us now return to Mary and her knowledge of the content of her belief. It would seem that in order for her to know that her thought is about water, not about twater, she is in the same epistemic situation that we are in with respect to the content of her thought. For her to know that she believes that water is wet, not that twater is wet, she must know, it would seem, that she is in a water-inclusive environment, not a twater-inclusive one. To make this more vivid, suppose that twin earth exists in a nearby planetary system and we can travel freely between earth and twin earth. It seems plausible to suppose that if one spends a sufficient amount of time on earth (or twin earth), one's word 'water' becomes locally acclimatized, as it were, and begins to refer to the local stuff, water or twater, as the case may be. Now, Mary, an inveterate space traveler, forgets which planet she has been living on for the past several years—whether it's earth or twin earth. Can she know, directly and without further investigation, whether her thoughts are about water or twater? It would seem that just as she cannot know, without external evidence, whether her present use of the word 'water' refers to water or twater, she cannot know, without investigating her environment, whether her thought about the steaming liquid in her kettle has the content that this water is boiling or that this twater is boiling. If something like this is right, then content externalism, the thesis that almost all, if not all, of our ordinary intentional state attributions involve wide content, would have the consequence that most of our knowledge of our own intentional states is indirect and must be based on external evidence. That is to say, content externalism appears to be prima facie incompatible with first-person epistemic access to one's own mind.

These issues concerning wide and narrow content are likely to be with us for some time. Their importance could hardly be exaggerated: Content-bearing states, that is, propositional attitudes like belief, desire, and the rest, constitute the central core of our commonsense psychological practices, providing us with a framework for formulating explanations and predictions of what we and our fellow humans do. Without this essential tool for understanding and anticipating human action and behavior, a communal life would be unthinkable. The issues, however, go beyond commonsense psychology. There is, for example, this important question about scientific psychology: Should systematic psychology make use of these content-bearing intentional states in formulating its laws and explanations? Or should it—or could it—transcend them by formulating its theories and explanations in purely nonintentional (perhaps ultimately neurobiological) terms? These questions concern the centrality of contentful intentional states to the explanation of human action and behavior—both in everyday psychological practices and in theory construction in scientific psychology. Many of these issues remain wide open and are being vigorously discussed in the field.

Questions

1. Imagine being asked to explain externalism to a 13-year-old with an ordinary 13-year-old's outlook and attention span. How would you proceed?
2. What, according to Burge, makes it the case that your utterance of 'arthritis', and thoughts you would express by utterances of 'arthritis', mean what they mean?
3. Putnam argues that a brain in a vat could not entertain the thought that it was a brain in a vat. Why not? Can *you* entertain the thought that you are a brain in a vat?
4. This question is for cinema buffs. Apply Putnam's argument to characters in *The Matrix*. Does the argument extend to the figure in *The Truman Show*? Which would be worse: to be in *The Matrix* or to be the unwitting star of your own *Truman Show*?
5. We appeal to the propositional attitudes in explaining behavior. Are we entitled to do so? Are beliefs and desires *really* explanatory?
6. Imagine counseling an externalist depressed over the problem of mental causation. In desperation you introduce the notion of 'narrow content'. How might this satisfy—or fail to satisfy—your subject?
7. What *is* the 'problem of mental causation', and why might it be thought to be an especially thorny problem for an externalist?
8. The propositional attitudes are standardly described as attitudes toward *propositions*. What might propositions be? Suppose you thought that propositions were purely philosophical inventions. Where would this leave the propositional attitudes?
9. Are thoughts with 'content'—thoughts of or about something—invariably 'propositional'? Could some 'contentful' thoughts be purely 'imagistic' and non-propositional? If imagistic thoughts are possible, would their content be subject to the same constraints as 'non-imagistic' thoughts?
10. What implications, if any, do arguments advanced in this part have for the science of psychology?

Suggested readings

Heil (1992: chap. 2) affords a sympathetic but non-committal look at the attractions of externalist conceptions of the mind. Wittgenstein (1953) sows the seeds of externalism; Putnam (1988) reaps the harvest. See Putnam (1988: chap. 2) for further discussion. See also Bilgrami (1987). Burge (1986*a*, 1986*b*) develops the externalist (or, as Burge prefers, 'anti-individualist') position he defends in Chapter 25. Wilson (1995) provides a sustained defense of anti-individualism in psychology; and Dretske (1993, 1997) advances a distinctive naturalistic form of externalism, as does Millikan (1984, 1989). Fodor (1980) argues for 'methodological solipsism' in psychology, the thesis that psychological explanation is grounded, not in the world, but in agents' beliefs about the world. This might sound like a rejection of externalism, but Fodor's position is in fact more complicated. This is made clear in Fodor's (1991) discussion of 'narrow content', a kind of content that could figure in cases of mental causation. Baker (1993) and Burge (1993) prefer to connect causation and explanation, arguing that philosophical accounts of causation need to be grounded in our explanatory practices—and not in a priori metaphysical theses.

Cummins (1991) makes a case for empirical approaches to questions of mental content. McKinsey (1993, 1994) argues forcefully against externalist hypotheses (see also Chapter 33). Searle (1983) advances an account of the content of states of mind that is both naturalistic and internalist. See also Martin and Heil (1998) and Heil (2003, chap. 18). Voltolini's (2001) on-line guide to internalism and externalism contains a useful bibliography, and the on-line *Stanford Encyclopedia of Philosophy* (Zalta 2002) features topical entries on 'externalism' and 'mental content' with bibliographies.

Bouwsma's (1949) piece on Descartes's evil genius argument provides an early version of Putnam's Chapter 26. One salient difference is that Bouwsma's verificationist anti-realism is explicit, Putnam's is less candid. Lewis (1984) and Brueckner (1986) provide accounts of the brain-in-a-vat argument, and Brueckner (1992) discusses attempts to undermine skepticism about the external world by appealing to semantic considerations—considerations bearing on meaning; see also Heil (1998).

Externalism and content

Baker, L. R. (1993), 'Metaphysics and Mental Causation'. In Heil and Mele 1993: 75–95.

Bilgrami, A. (1987), 'An Externalist Account of Psychological Content', *Philosophical Topics* 15: 191–226.

Bogdan, R., ed. (1991), *Mind and Common Sense: Philosophical Essays on Commonsense Psychology*. Cambridge: Cambridge University Press.

Burge, T. (1986*a*), 'Individualism and Psychology'. *Philosophical Review* 45: 3–45.

——(1986*b*), 'Intellectual Norms and Foundations of Mind'. *Journal of Philosophy* 83: 697–720.

——(1993), 'Mind–Body Causation and Explanatory Practice'. In Heil and Mele 1993: 97–120.

Cummins, R. (1991), 'Methodological Reflections on Belief'. In Bogdan 1991: 53–70.

Dretske, F. I. (1993), 'The Nature of Thought', *Philosophical Studies* 70: 185–99.

Dretske, F. I. (1997), *Naturalizing the Mind.* Cambridge, MA: MIT Press.

Fodor, J. A. (1980), 'Methodological Solipsism Considered as a Research Strategy in Cognitive Psychology', *Behavioral and Brain Sciences* 3: 63–73.

——(1991), 'A Modal Argument for Narrow Content', *Journal of Philosophy* 88: 5–26.

Gunderson, K., ed. (1975), *Language, Mind, and Knowledge* (Minnesota Studies in the Philosophy of Science 7). Minneapolis: University of Minnesota Press.

Heil, J. (1992), *The Nature of True Minds.* Cambridge: Cambridge University Press.

——(2003), *From an Ontological Point of View.* Oxford: Clarendon Press.

——and A. R. Mele, eds. (1993), *Mental Causation.* Oxford: Clarendon Press.

McKinsey, M. (1993), 'Curing Folk Psychology of Arthritis'. *Philosophical Studies* 70: 323–36.

——(1994), 'Individuating Beliefs', *Philosophical Perspectives* 8: 303–30.

Martin, C. B., and J. Heil. (1998), 'Rules and Powers', *Philosophical Perspectives* 12: 283–312.

Millikan, R. G. (1984), *Language, Thought, and Other Biological Categories.* Cambridge, MA: MIT Press.

——(1989), 'Biosemantics', *Journal of Philosophy* 86: 281–97.

Nani, M., ed. (2001), *A Field Guide to the Philosophy of Mind.* <http://host.uniroma3.it/progetti/kant/field/> Rome: University of Rome 3.

Putnam, H. (1975*a*), 'The Meaning of 'Meaning''. In Gunderson 1975: 131–93. Reprinted in Putnam 1975*b*: 215–71.

——(1975*b*) *Philosophical Papers*, vol. ii. Cambridge: Cambridge University Press.

——(1988), *Representation and Reality.* Cambridge, MA: MIT Press.

Searle, J. R. (1983), *Intentionality: An Essay in the Philosophy of Mind.* Cambridge: Cambridge University Press.

Voltolini, A. (2001), 'Internalism/Externalism'. In Nani (2001): <http://host.uniroma3.it/progetti/kant/field/voltolini.html>.

Wilson, R. A. (1995), *Cartesian Psychology and Physical Minds: Individualism and the Sciences of the Mind.* Cambridge: Cambridge University Press.

Wittgenstein, L. (1953/1968) *Philosophical Investigations*, trans. G. E. M. Anscombe. Oxford: Basil Blackwell.

Zalta, E. N., ed. (2002), *The Stanford Encyclopedia of Philosophy.* <http://plato.stanford.edu/> Stanford, CA: Metaphysics Research Lab, Center for the Study of Language and Information.

Brains in vats

Bouwsma, O. K. (1949), 'Descartes' Evil Genius', *Philosophical Review* 58: 141–51.

Brueckner, A. (1986), 'Brains in a Vat', *Journal of Philosophy* 83: 148–67.

——(1992), 'Semantic Answers to Skepticism', *Pacific Philosophical Quarterly* 73: 200–219.

Heil, J. (1998), 'Skepticism and Realism', *American Philosophical Quarterly* 35: 57–72.

Lewis, D. K. (1984), 'Putnam's Paradox'. *Australasian Journal of Philosophy* 62: 221–36.

Part VIII

Subjectivity and self-knowledge

Introduction

ON the face of it, states of mind have two extraordinary kinds of feature that set them off from non-mental states. First, states of mind can be 'projective': beliefs are *about* actual or possible objects; desires are *for* actual or possible outcomes. This about-ness or for-ness—what philosophers call 'intentionality'—is, to all appearances, unique to the mind. To be sure, non-mental items—road signs, utterances, gestures, maps—can be about or for various things. But their about-ness and for-ness is apparently derivative. Non-mental items owe their significance to relations they bear to minds. 'That's water' means what it does because it is used by English speakers to express a thought that is itself about water. In the absence of intelligent creatures, sounds or inscriptions are what they are: they are not *about* anything at all.

A second remarkable feature of states of mind is their experienced character. Many (though perhaps not all) states of mind have what philosophers call a 'phenomenology'. Following Thomas Nagel (Chapter 29), who is following B. A. Farrell (1950), we could describe this as the 'what-it's-like-ness' of mental states. When you consciously experience something, a particular sunrise, for instance, there is 'something it is like' for you to have just *that* experience. What it is like could vary over individuals, and certainly varies over species. In order to keep distinct matters distinct, let us agree to follow philosophical custom and speak of this characteristic—the 'what-it's-like-ness'—of conscious experiences as their phenomenology.

Before moving ahead, a brief logistical comment is in order. The first two papers in this part focus on the phenomenology of conscious experience. Nagel provides one perspective, a perspective that has much in common with that discussed by other authors we shall encounter in subsequent parts. One of these authors, Frank Jackson (Chapter 43), figures prominently in Janet Levin's discussion of Nagel's argument. Some might find it useful to read Jackson in concert with Nagel. Others might prefer to read Jackson after having worked through some of the issues lying behind Jackson's central argument. Issues in the philosophy of mind have a seamless character that is easily missed so long as we remain narrowly focused. I shall return to this point briefly below.

Intentionality and phenomenology

States of mind have intentionality and a phenomenology. Here a materialist faces a serious challenge. How are such things to be fitted into the material world? When we give an exhaustive description of matter and purely material systems, we leave out intentionality and phenomenology. Generations of natural scientists have passed the buck to philosophers. Such things, they have said, occur only 'in the mind'. But if they occur in the mind, and not in the physical world, then minds must persist somehow apart from the physical world. This might be a satisfactory resting point if you are a physicist, but it saddles the philosopher with the unenviable task of explaining minds and their relations to the physical world. This is the problem that bedeviled Descartes, the problem that encourages philosophers to find a way of 'naturalizing' the mind, fitting it into the material world.

Reflect for a minute on the idea that minds differ in kind, and not merely in degree, from material entities. A long tradition, stemming at least from Galileo, strips problematic features off the physical world and consigns them to the mind. Think of the old question: when a tree falls in a deserted forest does it make a sound? A standard answer to this question distinguishes two senses in which something could be said to make a sound. The first sense—the 'physical' sense—is that objects make sounds when they bring about impact waves in the medium (air or water, for instance). In this sense, of course, the falling tree makes a sound. The second sense in which something makes a sound is the familiar, everyday sense: something makes a sound when it makes a noise that is, or could be, heard. It is tempting to identify sounds in this sense with observers' experiences. If you do that, then you will say that, in *this* sense, a tree falling in a deserted forest 'makes no sound'.

Undergraduates and physicists might be happy with this answer, but it leaves philosophers with the difficult job of locating sounds in the second sense: 'heard sounds'. You should be aware that the same people who are happy enough to fob the problem off on philosophers turn around and ridicule philosophers for not answering questions in a way that passes scientific muster. If 'heard sounds'—auditory experiences—are not to be found in the physical world, however, if experiences are consigned to a non-physical realm, how *are* we to explain them?

Subjectivity

Our experiences include qualities that appear physically problematic. This is not the end of it, however. Experiences have another dramatically 'subjective' feature: every experience evidently incorporates a 'point of view'. A point of view can be something as straightforward as spatial perspective; what you get in a painting or photograph of a particular scene. But points of view can include as well endless 'subjective' elements. A student, Lilian, has a certain point of view on a philosophy paper she has written for her instructor, Blanche, who has a very different point of view on the paper. In confronting the paper, Lilian and Blanche bring with them all sorts of mental baggage. To the extent that Lilian and Blanche differ in this regard, so their points of view on the paper will differ.

Is their room in the physical world for such points of view? Science, which you might think provides us with our best description of reality, is relentlessly objective. But in being objective, does science risk leaving out an important component of reality: 'subjectivity'? Here is John Searle on the topic.

> '[S]ubjective' refers to an ontological category, not an epistemic mode. Consider, for example, the statement, 'I now have a pain in my lower back'. The statement is completely objective in the sense that it is made true by the existence of an actual fact and is not dependent on any stance, attitudes, or opinions of observers. However, the phenomenon itself, the actual pain itself, has a subjective mode of existence, and it is in that sense . . . that consciousness is subjective. (1992: 94)

What is a 'subjective mode of existence'? A subjective state is one 'not equally accessible to any observer'.

> Every conscious state is always someone's conscious state. And just as I have a special relation to my conscious states, which is not like my relation to other people's conscious states, so they in turn have a relation to their conscious states, which is not like my relation to their conscious states. (94–5)

Searle continues,

> It would be difficult to exaggerate the disastrous effects that the failure to come to terms with the subjectivity of consciousness has had on the philosophical and psychological work of the last half century. In ways that are not at all obvious on the surface, much of the bankruptcy of most work in the philosophy of mind and a great deal of the sterility of academic psychology over the past fifty years, over the whole of my intellectual lifetime, have come from a persistent failure to recognize and come to terms with the fact that the ontology of the mental is an irreducibly first-person ontology. (95)

Part of Searle's point is that science is committed to describing the world in 'third-person' terms. Such descriptions, he argues, are bound to miss subjective, 'first-person' states of affairs. Attempts to accommodate subjectivity to the 'third-person perspective' are bound to fail. We must recognize 'subjectivity as a rock-bottom element' of reality (95) and find a way of reconciling subjectivity with the 'third-person perspective' in a way that leaves subjectivity intact.

Many readers will feel the pull of Searle's argument. It looks as though a super-scientist could give an exhaustive 'third-person' description of the world without mentioning agents' subjective points of view (see Chapter 43). Indeed, as noted earlier, the usual scientific strategy involves relegating 'subjective' items to the minds of observers where, it is thought, they can be safely ignored. This bifurcates the world into mental and physical realms, and renders the nature of minds and their relation to physical goings-on deeply mysterious. Searle regards this picture as an artifact of our way of thinking about the mental and the physical. These belong, not in distinct realms, but side by side in one realm: the physical realm. Consciousness, and so subjectivity, are 'caused by' biological processes. Fully subjective conscious states of mind are natural products of complex biological processes.

Philosophers like Nagel worry that a view of this kind does nothing to lessen the mystery of consciousness and subjectivity. Suppose you discover that whenever your brain goes into a particular state, N_p, you feel pain in your lower back. Suppose, further, that you are inclined to say that your conscious experience of pain is caused by N_p. Why on earth should an experience with just these subjective qualities arise from N_p? Locke puts it this way.

> After the same manner, that the ideas of these original qualities are produced in us, we may conceive, that the ideas of secondary qualities are also produced, viz. by the operation of insensible particles on our senses. For it being manifest, that there are bodies, and a good store of bodies, each whereof is so small, that we cannot, by any of our senses, discover either their bulk, figure, or motion, as is evident in the particles of the air and water, and other extremely smaller than those, perhaps, as much smaller than the particles of air, or water, as the particles of air or water, are smaller than pease or hail-stones. Let us suppose at present, that the different motions and figures, bulk, and number of

such particles, affecting the several organs of our senses, produce in us those different sensations, which we have from the colours and smells of bodies; v.g. that a violet, by the impulse of such insensible particles of matter of peculiar figures, and bulks, and in different degrees and modifications of their motions, causes the ideas of the blue colour, and sweet scent of that flower to be produced in our minds. It being no more impossible, to conceive, that God should annex such ideas to such motions, with which they have no similitude; than that he should annex the idea of pain to the motion of a piece of steel dividing our flesh, with which that idea hath no resemblance. (Locke 1690: II, viii, 13)

Locke suggests that the connection between the nature of material objects and the qualities of our experiences of these objects is a brute fact, not something susceptible to further explanation. This is what Levine (Chapter 44) describes as the 'explanatory gap'.

Self-knowledge

The idea that there is a gulf between states of mind—or at least conscious states of mind—and physical states encapsulates a theme running through readings in the remainder of this volume. Chapters 29 and 30 in this part introduce the topic and the remaining readings address a different, but no less contentious topic: 'self-knowledge'. The term as used here refers not to an object of the Socratic dictum, 'Know thyself', but to the knowledge we have of our own states of mind. Descartes assumes that, although knowledge of the 'external world' is problematic, we know our own states of mind—how we feel, what we think—immediately and with something close to infallibility. In a post-Freudian world, few would defend the idea that we know ourselves *in any sense* infallibly. Still, most of us regard the access we have to our states of mind as being, on the whole, unchallengeable.

It might help to begin by distinguishing two problems of self-knowledge. First, what could be called the 'Freudian problem', the problem of how we could know *that* we have particular thoughts or feelings. Second, the problem of how we could know *what* we feel or think. To most readers, these questions will sound the same: we have thoughts and feelings, and the question is how do we 'get at' these. Philosophers, however, will want to distinguish 'getting at' a thought or feeling (the 'Freudian problem') and appreciating what it is a thought *about* or feeling *of*. An analogy might help. Imagine eavesdropping on a conversation between two discussants, Helga and Max, who are speaking a language you do not understand. You pass their room, and you are not sure whether they are speaking or not. Putting your ear to the door, you discover *that* they are speaking, but you do not know *what* they are saying because you do not know their language.

Imagine that knowledge of your own states of mind included both these dimensions: knowledge *that* you have particular thoughts or feelings and your knowledge of what these thoughts or feelings *concerned*—their *contents*. Why should anyone imagine that these could come apart? Surely, if you know that you are having a particular thought—you 'introspect' the thought—you know what the thought is a thought *of*. Your awareness of your own thoughts is not like your awareness of what Helga and Max say. There is no question of your thoughts' being in a foreign tongue! The trick is to reconcile this seeming truism with the tenets of externalism, the view that thoughts, like utterances, owe their significance to external factors: their causes, for instance (see Chapters 25 and 26). If externalists are to be believed, it looks as though you could be in the dark as to what you thought. You would be in the dark in something like the way you are in the dark in grasping the significance of what Max says to Helga. Just as in the Max and Helga case, you are in no position to 'read off' the meaning of your thoughts purely by observing those thoughts.

You will not see the problem unless you have plowed through papers in Part VII, or at least read over the introduction to that part. Very briefly, externalists contend that the contents of states of mind are determined, not, or not solely, by intrinsic—built in—features of agents, but by causal and historical relations agents bear to their surroundings. Crudely, your thoughts about beetroots are *about beetroots* in part because they are caused by beetroots. This means that two agents, intrinsically alike, might nevertheless be thinking different thoughts because they stand in different relations to their surroundings. This is how it is with the word 'burro'. One and the same inscription can mean utterly different things depending on whether it is used by a Spanish speaker or an Italian. If you overhear a speaker uttering 'burro', you cannot know what the utterance means without first ascertaining whether the speaker is Spanish or Italian. The same would seem to be the case with your own thoughts: you are in no position to ascertain the significance of your own thoughts without first ascertaining your place in the world.

This seems—no, *is*—crazy! But if it is, we are faced with a choice between rejecting externalism or finding a way to reconcile externalism with a plausible account of self-knowledge. Externalists, naturally enough, are reluctant to abandon externalism. One externalist strategy might be to throw the challenge back on opponents of externalism. Although externalist accounts of states of mind are faced with a problem of explaining how we could know, without exhaustive empirical investigation, what we think, it is not obvious that a philosopher who rejected externalism is in any better position. Suppose your thoughts had their contents 'built in'. Now imagine 'introspecting' one of your thoughts. What enables you to know that thought's significance? The question sounds odd only because it is patent that we *do* know the significance of our thoughts. But granted that this is something we know, is someone who rejects externalism—an 'internalist'—in any better position to explain how this knowledge is possible and how we come by it so effortlessly?

Intentionality and phenomenology redux

Although philosophers today routinely separate questions about mental content—the of-ness and about-ness of thought—from questions concerning the qualitative nature of states of mind, this was not always so. In the late nineteenth and early twentieth centuries a debate raged among psychologists over the possibility of 'imageless thought' (Danzinger 1980). Psychologists differed on the question whether entertaining a thought is invariably a matter of having a mental image.

Could thoughts be 'imageless'? Freud's accounts of thoughts as being both conscious and nonconscious seems to answer the question in the negative. This suggests that thoughts can operate on the stage of consciousness or behind the scenes: the thoughts themselves are one thing, conscious awareness of them is another.

Perhaps this is how it is. Here is another possibility. States of mind are *dispositional*. Dispositions are powers for particular kinds of manifestation with particular kinds of 'disposition partner'. A key, for instance, has the power—is disposed to—open locks of a particular kind; locks of that kind have the reciprocal power—are disposed—to be opened by such keys. Suppose your states of mind were like this. Being in a particular state of mind would be a matter of being in a state with certain powers. These powers might manifest themselves, with the right partners, in the production of conscious thought. With different partners, they might manifest themselves in other ways. Other states of mind might serve as 'inhibitors', blocking or 'repressing' certain manifestations in the way a key might be prevented from opening a lock by your filling the lock with sealing wax.

Note that there is an important difference between a case in which an object retains a power, but a particular sort of manifestation of this power is 'blocked', and cases in which the object loses the power. The key and the lock retain their complementary powers even when their manifestation is blocked. The key would lose its power to open the lock were you to file down its ridges; the lock would lose its complementary power were it 're-keyed'.

How does this excursion into metaphysics bear on subjectivity and self-knowledge? Perhaps it is a mistake to separate the qualitative dimension of thought, its phenomenology, from its significance, its intentionality. There may be a sense in which thoughts need not be conscious. You can sleep on a problem and wake up to find that the solution has occurred to you. But the qualitative—imagistic—nature of thoughts might be intimately connected to their playing the roles they do in our minds. Non-philosophers might regard this as a statement of the obvious, but most contemporary philosophers would reject the possibility out of hand. Perhaps it is the philosophers who need to bend here. Is it merely coincidence that, when your thoughts turn to a distant friend, they take the form of images?

Skeptics about imagery will demur. What of our 'abstract' or 'propositional' thoughts: the thought that π is irrational, for instance, or that the First World War was begun by the assassination of the Archduke Ferdinand in Sarejavo? Such thoughts could be accompanied by images, but are unlikely themselves to be imagistic. But is that so? When you entertain a thought consciously, *something* is present to your mind. Perhaps you produce a silent utterance. This silent utterance is as much imagistic as an image you might form of the Matterhorn illuminated in bright sunlight. You hear (or feel) yourself uttering a sentence. This is not merely an accidental accompaniment of your thought, but your thought itself manifested consciously.

At any rate this is a possibility worth considering. Perhaps the division of labor characteristic of contemporary philosophy of mind between work on intentionality (the of-ness or about-ness of thought), on the one hand, and, on the other hand, efforts to understand the qualitative nature of states of mind, represents an artificial, and potentially misleading, picture of the nature of minds. Although you would not know this from their titles, issues taken up in the papers by Nagel and Levin seem to have nothing to do with issues addressed in the papers by Davidson, Burge, and McKinsey. As a critical reader, you should be prepared to think that, at a deeper level, this might be wrong.

References

Danzinger, K. (1980), 'The History of Introspection Reconsidered', *Journal of the History of the Behavioral Sciences* 16: 241–62.

Farrell, B. A. (1950), 'Experience', *Mind* 59: 170–98.

Locke, J. (1690/1978), *An Essay Concerning Human Understanding*, ed. P. H. Nidditch. Oxford: Clarendon Press.

Searle, J. R. (1992), *The Rediscovery of the Mind*. Cambridge: MIT Press.

Wittgenstein, L. (1953/1968), *Philosophical Investigations*, trans. G. E. M. Anscombe. Oxford: Basil Blackwell.

Chapter 29

What is it like to be a bat?

Thomas Nagel

CONSCIOUSNESS is what makes the mind-body problem really intractable. Perhaps that is why current discussions of the problem give it little attention or get it obviously wrong. The recent wave of reductionist euphoria has produced several analyses of mental phenomena and mental concepts designed to explain the possibility of some variety of materialism, psychophysical identification, or reduction.[1] But the problems dealt with are those common to this type of reduction and other types, and what makes the mind-body problem unique, and unlike the water-H_2O problem or the Turing machine-IBM machine problem or the lightning-electrical discharge problem or the gene-DNA problem or the oak tree-hydrocarbon problem, is ignored.

Every reductionist has his favorite analogy from modern science. It is most unlikely that any of these unrelated examples of successful reduction will shed light on the relation of mind to brain. But philosophers share the general human weakness for explanations of what is incomprehensible in terms suited for what is familiar and well understood, though entirely different. This has led to the acceptance of implausible accounts of the mental largely because they would permit familiar kinds of reduction. I shall try to explain why the usual examples do not help us to understand the relation between mind and body—why, indeed, we have at present no conception of what an explanation of the physical nature of a mental phenomenon would be. Without consciousness the mind-body problem would be much less interesting. With consciousness it seems hopeless. The most important

Thomas Nagel, 'What is it Like to be a Bat?', *Philosophical Review* 83 (1974).

1. Examples are J. J. C. Smart, *Philosophy and Scientific Realism* (London, 1963) (see Chapter 8 of this volume); David K. Lewis, 'An Argument for the Identity Theory,' *Journal of Philosophy*, LXIII (1966), reprinted with addenda in David M. Rosenthal, *Materialism & the Mind-Body Problem* (Englewood Cliffs, N. J., 1971) (see Chapter 10 of this volume); Hilary Putnam, 'Psychological Predicates' in Capitan and Merrill, *Art, Mind, & Religion* (Pittsburgh, 1967), reprinted in Rosenthal, *op. cit.*, as 'The Nature of Mental States' (see Chapter 11 of this volume); D. M. Armstrong, *A Materialist Theory of the Mind* (London, 1968); D. C. Dennett, *Content and Consciousness* (London, 1969). I have expressed earlier doubts in 'Armstrong on the Mind,' *Philosophical Review*, LXXIX (1970), 394–403; 'Brain Bisection and the Unity of Consciousness,' *Synthèse*, 22 (1971); and a review of Dennett, *Journal of Philosophy*, LXIX (1972). See also Saul Kripke, 'Naming and Necessity' in Davidson and Harman, *Semantics of Natural Language* (Dordrecht, 1972), esp. pp. 334–342 (and Chapter 9 of this volume); and M. T. Thornton, 'Ostensive Terms and Materialism,' *The Monist*, 56 (1972).

and characteristic feature of conscious mental phenomena is very poorly understood. Most reductionist theories do not even try to explain it. And careful examination will show that no currently available concept of reduction is applicable to it. Perhaps a new theoretical form can be devised for the purpose, but such a solution, if it exists, lies in the distant intellectual future.

Conscious experience is a widespread phenomenon. It occurs at many levels of animal life, though we cannot be sure of its presence in the simpler organisms, and it is very difficult to say in general what provides evidence of it. (Some extremists have been prepared to deny it even of mammals other than man.) No doubt it occurs in countless forms totally unimaginable to us, on other planets in other solar systems throughout the universe. But no matter how the form may vary, the fact that an organism has conscious experience *at all* means, basically, that there is something it is like to *be* that organism. There may be further implications about the form of the experience; there may even (though I doubt it) be implications about the behavior of the organism. But fundamentally an organism has conscious mental states if and only if there is something that it is like to *be* that organism—something it is like *for* the organism.

We may call this the subjective character of experience. It is not captured by any of the familiar, recently devised reductive analyses of the mental, for all of them are logically compatible with its absence. It is not analyzable in terms of any explanatory system of functional states, or intentional states, since these could be ascribed to robots or automata that behaved like people though they experienced nothing.[2] It is not analyzable in terms of the causal role of experiences in relation to typical human behavior—for similar reasons.[3] I do not deny that conscious mental states and events cause behavior, nor that they may be given functional characterizations. I deny only that this kind of thing exhausts their analysis. Any reductionist program has to to be based on an analysis of what is to be reduced. If the analysis leaves something out, the problem will be falsely posed. It is useless to base the defense of materialism on any analysis of mental phenomena that fails to deal explicitly with their subjective character. For there is no reason to suppose that a reduction which seems plausible when no attempt is made to account for consciousness can be extended to include consciousness. Without some idea, therefore, of what the subjective character of experience is, we cannot know what is required of a physicalist theory.

While an account of the physical basis of mind must explain many things, this appears to be the most difficult. It is impossible to exclude the phenomenological features of experience from a reduction in the same way that one excludes the phenomenal features of an ordinary substance from a physical or chemical

2. Perhaps there could not actually be such robots. Perhaps anything complex enough to behave like a person would have experiences. But that, if true, is a fact which cannot be discovered merely by analyzing the concept of experience.

3. It is not equivalent to that about which we are incorrigible, both because we are not incorrigible about experience and because experience is present in animals lacking language and thought, who have no beliefs at all about their experiences.

reduction of it—namely, by explaining them as effects on the minds of human observers.[4] If physicalism is to be defended, the phenomenological features must themselves be given a physical account. But when we examine their subjective character it seems that such a result is impossible. The reason is that every subjective phenomenon is essentially connected with a single point of view, and it seems inevitable that an objective, physical theory will abandon that point of view.

Let me first try to state the issue somewhat more fully than by referring to the relation between the subjective and the objective, or between the *pour-soi* and the *en-soi*. This is far from easy. Facts about what it is like to be an *X* are very peculiar, so peculiar that some may be inclined to doubt their reality, or the significance of claims about them. To illustrate the connection between subjectivity and a point of view, and to make evident the importance of subjective features, it will help to explore the matter in relation to an example that brings out clearly the divergence between the two types of conception, subjective and objective.

I assume we all believe that bats have experience. After all, they are mammals, and there is no more doubt that they have experience than that mice or pigeons or whales have experience. I have chosen bats instead of wasps or flounders because if one travels too far down the phylogenetic tree, people gradually shed their faith that there is experience there at all. Bats, although more closely related to us than those other species, nevertheless present a range of activity and a sensory apparatus so different from ours that the problem I want to pose is exceptionally vivid (though it certainly could be raised with other species). Even without the benefit of philosophical reflection, anyone who has spent some time in an enclosed space with an excited bat knows what it is to encounter a fundamentally *alien* form of life.

I have said that the essence of the belief that bats have experience is that there is something that it is like to be a bat. Now we know that most bats (the microchiroptera, to be precise) perceive the external world primarily by sonar, or echolocation, detecting the reflections, from objects within range, of their own rapid, subtly modulated, high-frequency shrieks. Their brains are designed to correlate the outgoing impulses with the subsequent echoes, and the information thus acquired enables bats to make precise discriminations of distance, size, shape, motion, and texture comparable to those we make by vision. But bat sonar, though clearly a form of perception, is not similar in its operation to any sense that we possess, and there is no reason to suppose that it is subjectively like anything we can experience or imagine. This appears to create difficulties for the notion of what it is like to be a bat. We must consider whether any method will permit us to extrapolate to the inner life of the bat from our own case,[5] and if not, what alternative methods there may be for understanding the notion.

Our own experience provides the basic material for our imagination, whose

4. Cf. Richard Rorty, 'Mind-Body Identity, Privacy, and Categories,' *The Review of Metaphysics*, XIX (1965), esp. 37–38.

5. By 'our own case' I do not mean just 'my own case,' but rather the mentalistic ideas that we apply unproblematically to ourselves and other human beings.

range is therefore limited. It will not help to try to imagine that one has webbing on one's arms, which enables one to fly around at dusk and dawn catching insects in one's mouth; that one has very poor vision, and perceives the surrounding world by a system of reflected high-frequency sound signals; and that one spends the day hanging upside down by one's feet in an attic. In so far as I can imagine this (which is not very far), it tells me only what it would be like for *me* to behave as a bat behaves. But that is not the question. I want to know what it is like for a *bat* to be a bat. Yet if I try to imagine this, I am restricted to the resources of my own mind, and those resources are inadequate to the task. I cannot perform it either by imagining additions to my present experience, or by imagining segments gradually subtracted from it, or by imagining some combination of additions, subtractions, and modifications.

To the extent that I could look and behave like a wasp or a bat without changing my fundamental structure, my experiences would not be anything like the experiences of those animals. On the other hand, it is doubtful that any meaning can be attached to the supposition that I should possess the internal neurophysiological constitution of a bat. Even if I could by gradual degrees be transformed into a bat, nothing in my present constitution enables me to imagine what the experiences of such a future stage of myself thus metamorphosed would be like. The best evidence would come from the experiences of bats, if we only knew what they were like.

So if extrapolation from our own case is involved in the idea of what it is like to be a bat, the extrapolation must be incompletable. We cannot form more than a schematic conception of what it *is* like. For example, we may ascribe general *types* of experience on the basis of the animal's structure and behavior. Thus we describe bat sonar as a form of three-dimensional forward perception; we believe that bats feel some versions of pain, fear, hunger, and lust, and that they have other, more familiar types of perception besides sonar. But we believe that these experiences also have in each case a specific subjective character, which it is beyond our ability to conceive. And if there is conscious life elsewhere where in the universe, it is likely that some of it will not be describable even in the most general experiential terms available to us.[6] (The problem is not confined to exotic cases, however, for it exists between one person and another. The subjective character of the experience of a person deaf and blind from birth is not accessible to me, for example, nor presumably is mine to him. This does not prevent us each from believing that the other's experience has such a subjective character.)

If anyone is inclined to deny that we can believe in the existence of facts like this whose exact nature we cannot possibly conceive, he should reflect that in contemplating the bats we are in much the same position that intelligent bats or Martians[7] would occupy if they tried to form a conception of what it was like to be us. The

6. Therefore the analogical form of the English expression 'what it is *like*' is misleading. It does not mean 'what (in our experience) it *resembles*,' but rather 'how it is for the subject himself.' .

7. Any intelligent extraterrestrial beings totally different from us.

structure of their own minds might make it impossible for them to succeed, but we know they would be wrong to conclude that there is not anything precise that it is like to be us: that only certain general types of mental state could be ascribed to us (perhaps perception and appetite would be concepts common to us both; perhaps not). We know they would be wrong to draw such a skeptical conclusion because we know what it is like to be us. And we know that while it includes an enormous amount of variation and complexity, and while we do not possess the vocabulary to describe it adequately, its subjective charater is highly specific, and in some respects describable in terms that can be understood only by creatures like us. The fact that we cannot expect ever to accommodate in our language a detailed description of Martian or bat phenomenology should not lead us to dismiss as meaningless the claim that bats and Martians have experiences fully comparable in richness of detail to our own. It would be fine if someone were to develop concepts and a theory that enabled us to think about those things; but such an understanding may be permanently denied to us by the limits of our nature. And to deny the reality or logical significance of what we can never describe or understand is the crudest form of cognitive dissonance.

This brings us to the edge of a topic that requires much more discussion than I can give it here: namely, the relation between facts on the one hand and conceptual schemes or systems of representation on the other. My realism about the subjective domain in all its forms implies a belief in the existence of facts beyond the reach of human concepts. Certainly it is possible for a human being to believe that there are facts which humans never *will* possess the requisite concepts to represent or comprehend. Indeed, it would be foolish to doubt this, given the finiteness of humanity's expectations. After all, there would have been transfinite numbers even if everyone had been wiped out by the Black Death before Cantor discovered them. But one might also believe that there are facts which *could* not ever be represented or comprehended by human beings, even if the species lasted forever—simply because our structure does not permit us to operate with concepts of the requisite type. This impossibility might even be observed by other beings, but it is not clear that the existence of such beings, or the possibility of their existence, is a precondition of the significance of the hypothesis that there are humanly inaccessible facts. (After all, the nature of beings with access to humanly inaccessible facts is presumably itself a humanly inaccessible fact.) Reflection on what it is like to be a bat seems to lead us, therefore, to the conclusion that there are facts that do not consist in the truth of propositions expressible in a human language. We can be compelled to recognize the existence of such facts without being able to state or comprehend them.

I shall not pursue this subject, however. Its bearing on the topic before us (namely, the mind-body problem) is that it enables us to make a general observation about the subjective character of experience. Whatever may be the status of facts about what it is like to be a human being, or a bat, or a Martian, these appear to be facts that embody a particular point of view.

I am not adverting here to the alleged privacy of experience to its possessor. The point of view in question is not one accessible only to a single individual. Rather it is a *type*. It is often possible to take up a point of view other than one's own, so the comprehension of such facts is not limited to one's own case. There is a sense in which phenomenological facts are perfectly objective: one person can know or say of another what the quality of the other's experience is. They are subjective, however, in the sense that even this objective ascription of experience is possible only for someone sufficiently similar to the object of ascription to be able to adopt his point of view—to understand the ascription in the first person as well as in the third, so to speak. The more different from oneself the other experiencer is, the less success one can expect with this enterprise. In our own case we occupy the relevant point of view, but we will have as much difficulty understanding our own experience properly if we approach it from another point of view as we would if we tried to understand the experience of another species without taking up *its* point of view.[8]

This bears directly on the mind-body problem. For if the facts of experience—facts about what it is like *for* the experiencing organism—are accessible only from one point of view, then it is a mystery how the true character of experiences could be revealed in the physical operation of that organism. The latter is a domain of objective facts *par excellence*—the kind that can be observed and understood from many points of view and by individuals with differing perceptual systems. There are no comparable imaginative obstacles to the acquisition of knowledge about bat neurophysiology by human scientists, and intelligent bats or Martians might learn more about the human brain than we ever will.

This is not by itself an argument against reduction. A Martian scientist with no understanding of visual perception could understand the rainbow, or lightning, or clouds as physical phenomena, though he would never be able to understand the human concepts of rainbow, lightning, or cloud, or the place these things occupy in our phenomenal world. The objective nature of the things picked out by these concepts could be apprehended by him because, although the concepts themselves are connected with a particular point of view and a particular visual phenomenology, the things apprehended from that point of view are not: they are observable

8. It may be easier than I suppose to transcend inter-species barriers with the aid of the imagination. For example, blind people are able to detect objects near them by a form of sonar, using vocal clicks or taps of a cane. Perhaps if one knew what that was like, one could by extension imagine roughly what it was like to possess the much more refined sonar of a bat. The distance between oneself and other persons and other species can fall anywhere on a continuum. Even for other persons the understanding of what it is like to be them is only partial, and when one moves to species very different from oneself, a lesser degree of partial understanding may still be available. The imagination is remarkably flexible. My point, however, is not that we cannot *know* what it is like to be a bat. I am not raising that epistemological problem. My point is rather that even to form a *conception* of what it is like to be a bat (and a fortiori to know what it is like to be a bat) one must take up the bat's point of view. If one can take it up roughly, or partially, then one's conception will also be rough or partial. Or so it seems in our present state of understanding.

from the point of view but external to it; hence they can be comprehended from other points of view also, either by the same organisms or by others. Lightning has an objective character that is not exhausted by its visual appearance, and this can be investigated by a Martian without vision. To be precise, it has a *more* objective character than is revealed in its visual appearance. In speaking of the move from subjective to objective characterization, I wish to remain noncommittal about the existence of an end point, the completely objective intrinsic nature of the thing, which one might or might not be able to reach. It may be more accurate to think of objectivity as a direction in which the understanding can travel. And in understanding a phenomenon like lightning, it is legitimate to go as far away as one can from a strictly human viewpoint.[9]

In the case of experience, on the other hand, the connection with a particular point of view seems much closer. It is difficult to understand what could be meant by the *objective* character of an experience, apart from the particular point of view from which its subject apprehends it. After all, what would be left of what it was like to be a bat if one removed the viewpoint of the bat? But if experience does not have, in addition to its subjective character, an objective nature that can be apprehended from many different points of view, then how can it be supposed that a Martian investigating my brain might be observing physical processes which were my mental processes (as he might observe physical processes which were bolts of lightning), only from a different point of view? How, for that matter, could a human physiologist observe them from another point of view?[10]

We appear to be faced with a general difficulty about psychophysical reduction. In other areas the process of reduction is a move in the direction of greater objectivity, toward a more accurate view of the real nature of things. This is accomplished by reducing our dependence on individual or species-specific points of view toward the object of investigation. We describe it not in terms of the impressions it makes on our senses, but in terms of its more general effects and of properties detectable by means other than the human senses. The less it depends on a specifically human viewpoint, the more objective is our description. It is possible to follow this path because although the concepts and ideas we employ in thinking about the external world are initially applied from a point of view that involves our perceptual apparatus, they are used by us to refer to things beyond themselves—toward which we *have* the phenomenal point of view. Therefore we can abandon it in favor of another, and still be thinking about the same things.

9. The problem I am going to raise can therefore be posed even if the distinction between more subjective and more objective descriptions or viewpoints can itself be made only within a larger human point of view. I do not accept this kind of conceptual relativism, but it need not be refuted to make the point that psychophysical reduction cannot be accommodated by the subjective-to-objective model familiar from other cases.

10. The problem is not just that when I look at the 'Mona Lisa,' my visual experience has a certain quality, no trace of which is to be found by someone looking into my brain. For even if he did observe there a tiny image of the 'Mona Lisa,' he would have no reason to identify it with the experience.

Experience itself, however, does not seem to fit the pattern. The idea of moving from appearance to reality seems to make no sense here. What is the analogue in this case to pursuing a more objective understanding of the same phenomena by abandoning the initial subjective viewpoint toward them in favor of another that is more objective but concerns the same thing? Certainly it *appears* unlikely that we will get closer to the real nature of human experience by leaving behind the particularity of our human point of view and striving for a description in terms accessible to beings that could not imagine what it was like to be us. If the subjective character of experience is fully comprehensible only from one point of view, then any shift to greater objectivity—that is, less attachment to a specific viewpoint—does not take us nearer to the real nature of the phenomenon: it takes us farther away from it.

In a sense, the seeds of this objection to the reducibility of experience are already detectable in successful cases of reduction; for in discovering sound to be, in reality, a wave phenomenon in air or other media, we leave behind one viewpoint to take up another, and the auditory, human or animal viewpoint that we leave behind remains unreduced. Members of radically different species may both understand the same physical events in objective terms, and this does not require that they understand the phenomenal forms in which those events appear to the senses of members of the other species. Thus it is a condition of their referring to a common reality that their more particular viewpoints are not part of the common reality that they both apprehend. The reduction can succeed only if the species-specific viewpoint is omitted from what is to be reduced.

But while we are right to leave this point of view aside in seeking a fuller understanding of the external world, we cannot ignore it permanently, since it is the essence of the internal world, and not merely a point of view on it. Most of the neobehaviorism of recent philosophical psychology results from the effort to substitute an objective concept of mind for the real thing, in order to have nothing left over which cannot be reduced. If we acknowledge that a physical theory of mind must account for the subjective character of experience, we must admit that no presently available conception gives us a clue how this could be done. The problem is unique. If mental processes are indeed physical processes, then there is something it is like, intrinsically,[11] to undergo certain physical processes. What it is for such a thing to be the case remains a mystery.

11. The relation would therefore not be a contingent one, like that of a cause and its distinct effect. It would be necessarily true that a certain physical state felt a certain way. Saul Kripke (*op. cit.*) argues that causal behaviorist and related analyses of the mental fail because they construe, e.g., 'pain' as a merely contingent name of pains. The subjective character of an experience ('its immediate phenomenological quality' Kripke calls it [p. 340]) is the essential property left out by such analyses, and the one in virtue of which it is, necessarily, the experience it is. My view is closely related to his. Like Kripke, I find the hypothesis that a certain brain state should *necessarily* have a certain subjective character incomprehensible without further explanation. No such explanation emerges from theories which view the mind-brain relation as contingent, but perhaps there are other alternatives, not yet discovered.

A theory that explained how the mind-brain relation was necessary would still leave us with

What moral should be drawn from these reflections, and what should be done next? It would be a mistake to conclude that physicalism must be false. Nothing is proved by the inadequacy of physicalist hypotheses that assume a faulty objective analysis of mind. It would be truer to say that physicalism is a position we cannot understand because we do not at present have any conception of how it might be true. Perhaps it will be thought unreasonable to require such a conception as a condition of understanding. After all, it might be said, the meaning of physicalism is clear enough: mental states are states of the body; mental events are physical events. We do not know *which* physical states and events they are, but that should not prevent us from understanding the hypothesis. What could be clearer than the words 'is' and 'are'?

But I believe it is precisely this apparent clarity of the word 'is' that is deceptive. Usually, when we are told that *X* is *Y* we know *how* it is supposed to be true, but that depends on a conceptual or theoretical background and is not conveyed by the 'is' alone. We know how both '*X*' and '*Y*' refer, and the kinds of things to which they refer, and we have a rough idea how the two referential paths might converge on a single thing, be it an object, a person, a process, an event, or whatever. But when the two terms of the identification are very disparate it may not be so clear how it could be true. We may not have even a rough idea of how the two referential paths could converge, or what kind of things they might converge on, and a theoretical framework may have to be supplied to enable us to understand this. Without the framework, an air of mysticism surrounds the identification.

This explains the magical flavor of popular presentations of fundamental scientific discoveries, given out as propositions to which one must subscribe without really understanding them. For example, people are now told at an early age that all matter is really energy. But despite the fact that they know what 'is' means, most of

Kripke's problem of explaining why it nevertheless appears contingent. That difficulty seems to me surmountable, in the following way. We may imagine something by representing it to ourselves either perceptually, sympathetically, or symbolically. I shall not try to say how symbolic imagination works, but part of what happens in the other two cases is this. To imagine something perceptually, we put ourselves in a conscious state resembling the state we would be in if we perceived it. To imagine something sympathetically, we put ourselves in a conscious state resembling the thing itself. (This method can be used only to imagine mental events and states—our own or another's.) When we try to imagine a mental state occurring without its associated brain state, we first sympathetically imagine the occurrence of the mental state: that is, we put ourselves into a state that resembles it mentally. At the same time, we attempt to perceptually imagine the non-occurrence of the associated physical state, by putting ourselves into another state unconnected with the first: one resembling that which we would be in if we perceived the non-occurrence of the physical state. Where the imagination of physical features is perceptual and the imagination of mental features is sympathetic, it appears to us that we can imagine any experience occurring without its associated brain state, and vice versa. The relation between them will appear contingent even if it is necessary, because of the independence of the disparate types of imagination.

(Solipsism, incidentally, results if one misinterprets sympathetic imagination as if it worked like perceptual imagination: it then seems impossible to imagine any experience that is not one's own.)

them never form a conception of what makes this claim true, because they lack the theoretical background.

At the present time the status of physicalism is similar to that which the hypothesis that matter is energy would have had if uttered by a pre-Socratic philosopher. We do not have the beginnings of a conception of how it might be true. In order to understand the hypothesis that a mental event is a physical event, we require more than an understanding of the word 'is.' The idea of how a mental and a physical term might refer to the same thing is lacking, and the usual analogies with theoretical identification in other fields fail to supply it. They fail because if we construe the reference of mental terms to physical events on the usual model, we either get a reappearance of separate subjective events as the effects through which mental reference to physical events is secured, or else we get a false account of how mental terms refer (for example, a causal behaviorist one).

Strangely enough, we may have evidence for the truth of something we cannot really understand. Suppose a caterpillar is locked in a sterile safe by someone unfamiliar with insect metamorphosis, and weeks later the safe is reopened, revealing a butterfly. If the person knows that the safe has been shut the whole time, he has reason to believe that the butterfly is or was once the caterpillar, without having any idea in what sense this might be so. (One possibility is that the caterpillar contained a tiny winged parasite that devoured it and grew into the butterfly.)

It is conceivable that we are in such a position with regard to physicalism. Donald Davidson has argued that if mental events have physical causes and effects, they must have physical descriptions. He holds that we have reason to believe this even though we do not—and in fact *could* not—have a general psychophysical theory.[12] His argument applies to intentional mental events, but I think we also have some reason to believe that sensations are physical processes, without being in a position to understand how. Davidson's position is that certain physical events have irreducibly mental properties, and perhaps some view describable in this way is correct. But nothing of which we can now form a conception corresponds to it; nor have we any idea what a theory would be like that enabled us to conceive of it.[13]

Very little work has been done on the basic question (from which mention of the brain can be entirely omitted) whether any sense can be made of experiences' having an objective character at all. Does it make sense, in other words, to ask what my experiences are *really* like, as opposed to how they appear to me? We cannot genuinely understand the hypothesis that their nature is captured in a physical description unless we understand the more fundamental idea that they *have* an objective nature (or that objective processes can have a subjective nature).[14]

12. See 'Mental Events' in Foster and Swanson, *Experience and Theory* (Amherst, 1970), see Chapter 31 of this volume; though I don't understand the argument against psychophysical laws.
13. Similar remarks apply to my paper 'Physicalism,' *Philosophical Review* LXXIV (1965), 339–356, reprinted with postscript in John O'Connor, *Modern Materialism* (New York, 1969).
14. This question also lies at the heart of the problem of other minds, whose close connection with the mind-body problem is often overlooked. If one understood how subjective experience could have an objective nature, one would understand the existence of subjects other than oneself.

I should like to close with a speculative proposal. It may be possible to approach the gap between subjective and objective from another direction. Setting aside temporarily the relation between the mind and the brain, we can pursue a more objective understanding of the mental in its own right. At present we are completely unequipped to think about the subjective character of experience without relying on the imagination—without taking up the point of view of the experiential subject. This should be regarded as a challenge to form new concepts and devise a new method—an objective phenomenology not dependent on empathy or the imagination. Though presumably it would not capture everything, its goal would be to describe, at least in part, the subjective character of experiences in a form comprehensible to beings incapable of having those experiences.

We would have to develop such a phenomenology to describe the sonar experiences of bats; but it would also be possible to begin with humans. One might try, for example, to develop concepts that could be used to explain to a person blind from birth what it was like to see. One would reach a blank wall eventually, but it should be possible to devise a method of expressing in objective terms much more than we can at present, and with much greater precision. The loose intermodal analogies—for example, 'Red is like the sound of a trumpet'—which crop up in discussions of this subject are of little use. That should be clear to anyone who has both heard a trumpet and seen red. But structural features of perception might be more accessible to objective description, even though something would be left out. And concepts alternative to those we learn in the first person may enable us to arrive at a kind of understanding even of our own experience which is denied us by the very ease of description and lack of distance that subjective concepts afford.

Apart from its own interest, a phenomenology that is in this sense objective may permit questions about the physical[15] basis of experience to assume a more intelligible form. Aspects of subjective experience that admitted this kind of objective description might be better candidates for objective explanations of a more familiar sort. But whether or not this guess is correct, it seems unlikely that any physical theory of mind can be contemplated until more thought has been given to the general problem of subjective and objective. Otherwise we cannot even pose the mind-body problem without sidestepping it.[16]

15. I have not defined the term 'physical.' Obviously it does not apply just to what can be described by the concepts of contemporary physics, since we expect further developments. Some may think there is nothing to prevent mental phenomena from eventually being recognized as physical in their own right. But whatever else may be said of the physical, it has to be objective. So if our idea of the physical ever expands to include mental phenomena, it will have to assign them an objective character—whether or not this is done by analyzing them in terms of other phenomena already regarded as physical. It seems to me more likely, however, that mental-physical relations will eventually be expressed in a theory whose fundamental terms cannot be placed clearly in either category.

16. I have read versions of this paper to a number of audiences, and am indebted to many people for their comments.

Chapter 30

Could love be like a heatwave?

Janet Levin

I

IN his well-known paper, 'What is it like to be a bat?', Thomas Nagel argues that no purely 'objective' description of the world—that is, no description equally accessible to observers, regardless of their points of view—could give us knowledge of what it is like to be a bat. Such knowledge, he argues, is available only to those who, unlike ourselves, are capable of having the experiences of bats. Therefore, he concludes, there are facts about the subjective character of experience, e.g. what it is like to be a bat, that no physicalist, functionalist, or otherwise 'objective' theory of mental states could adequately describe.[1]

Frank Jackson, in his paper 'Epiphenomenal qualia', argues similarly, choosing an example that is closer to home. Jackson argues that Mary, a brilliant physicist and neuropsychologist who has grown up and pursued her career in a black-and-white environment, would clearly gain some knowledge about color and color-experience upon first viewing the world outside: she would come to know what it is like to see colors. Therefore, he concludes, 'it is inescapable that her previous knowledge was incomplete. But she had *all* the physical information. Ergo there is more to have than that, and Physicalism is false.'[2]

It has been objected, however, that both arguments depend upon an equivocation. For the premises to be plausible, 'knowledge of what it is like to be a bat' or 'knowledge of what it is like to see colors' must be understood as a kind of *practical* knowledge or ability:[3] in Nagel's case, the ability to imaginatively project oneself into another's point of view; in Jackson's, an ability that is not so clearly defined. But the lack of such an ability, it is argued, is not the same as a gap in one's *theoretical* knowledge, or knowledge of the facts. Further, there does not seem to be any important tie between these two sorts of knowledge, as it is hard to see why

Janet Levin, 'Could Love be like a Heatwave? Physicalism and the Subjective Character of Experience', *Philosophical Studies* 49 (1986).

1. 'What is it like to be a bat?', reprinted in *Mortal Questions*, Cambridge, 1979, p. 166, see Chapter 29 of this volume, p. 529.
2. 'Epiphenomenal qualia', p. 130, Chapter 43, p. 764, of this volume. By 'physicalism', Jackson means any version of the psycho-physical identity thesis *or* functionalism.
3. Laurence Nemirow makes this point in this review of *Mortal Questions, Philosophical Review*, July 1980. This account has also been given by Stephen Schiffer and Brian Load.

even the most comprehensive description of mental states should be expected to provide one with the practical abilities in question.[4]

Thus, though sufficient experience of the sort had by bats may be required for knowing what it is like to be one, it does not follow that this experience is the only source of any theoretical knowledge about bats. And though Mary may not know what it is like to see colors without actually having seen them, it does not follow that she is missing any theoretical knowledge about colors or color experience. Thus it does not follow that there are facts about experience that no objective theory can describe.

It is clear, then, that Nagel's and Jackson's arguments are open to objection. Nonetheless, these arguments have been extremely influential, as there are intuitively compelling grounds for the view that without the capacity for a certain sort of experience, one cannot have knowledge of certain simple and straightforward facts about experiences of that kind.

First of all, it would be perverse to claim that bare experience can provide us *only* with various practical abilities, and never with theoretical knowledge.[5] By being shown an unfamiliar color, I acquire information about its similarities and compatibilities with other colors, and its effects on other of our mental states: surely I seem to be acquiring certain facts about that color and the visual experience of it.

Second, it is not implausible to think that experience is the *only* source of at least some of these facts. It would be unfair, of course, to expect Nagel or Jackson to specify these facts in any detail, as this would fail to take seriously their claim that they cannot be objectively described. However, this view has had a long and impressive history, beginning with the Empiricists' contention that one cannot have 'ideas' of colors, sounds, smells, and tastes (and thus the materials for theoretical knowledge about them) without first having the coresponding impressions. And though Empiricism has been widely rejected as a general theory of concept-acquisition, here, in accounting for our knowledge of mental states, is where it seems to become common sense: how *does* one convey the taste of pineapple to someone who has not yet tried it, and does that first taste not dramatically increase, if not fully constitute, the knowledge of what the taste of pineapple is?

Finally, there seem to be important cognitive differences between ourselves and those incapable of sharing our experiences. It would seem extremely natural to explain this by appeal to differences in our knowledge of the facts about experience: indeed, what other explanation could there be?

Thus Nagel's and Jackson's arguments, whatever their flaws, serve as reminders of the claim that one needs to have had experiences of a specific sort to have access to all the facts about mental states. Clearly, this is something that a physicalist must deny, as physicalism requires that the world and everything in it be describable in

4. This point has been made against Nagel by Frank Jackson himself, in 'Epiphenoment qualia', p. 132 see p. 767 of this volume.

5. See, for example, Brian Loar, in 'Phenomenal States' *Philosophical Perspectives* 4 (1990): 81–108.. I am indebted to Loar for discussion of these points.

the objective vocabulary of science. Consequently, there is still a burden upon the physicalist, even after the Nagel-Jackson argument has been challenged, to dispel the plausibility of this claim.

My aim in this paper is to do just that. My view is that this claim derives its plausibility from an argument which, though similar to Jackson's and Nagel's, is considerably harder to refute. This argument has two premises: The first is that if one lacks certain experiences, one will lack a certain *recognitional* or *discriminative ability*—an ability to know that one is in a particular state without making inferences, or consulting instruments, but simply by applying one's concept of that mental state to the experiences at hand. Let us call this kind of recognitional or discriminative ability 'direct'. The second premise is that this capacity to recognize or discriminate among mental states is required for having full and complete factual knowledge of them. This argument has been explicitly advanced by Richard Warner, in a recent paper that argues for the Nagel-Jackson conclusion.[6] It is also implicit in classical discussions of the relation between experience and theoretical knowledge, such as the Molyneux question addressed by Locke and Berkeley. And it seems to improve upon the formulation, while retaining the spirit, of Nagel's and Jackson's arguments themselves.

Indeed, these premises, at least on first glance, appear to be quite plausible. The first seems intuitively obvious: surely Mary would not be able to immediately identify her visual experiences as being of red or of green, if she were presented with a simple patch of each color in her black-and-white room. And surely it is hard to see how we would be able to accurately identify the perceptual experiences of bats if we somehow became able to have them, no matter how much objective information we had acquired about bats.

What about the second premise? On the Empiricists' theory of concept-formation, of course, it would have been completely uncontroversial: if concepts, or 'ideas', are nothing but 'faint copies' of the experiences themselves, then one ought to be able to match one's current experience, feature by feature, with the copy stored in memory. Even without Empiricism, however, this premise has appeal. After all, if one knows *all* the facts about some mental state, including the way it feels, it seems that one could not fail to identify it, without evidence or instruments, upon presentation. This argument apears to be lurking in Jackson's paper, and it is made explicitly by Warner in his. If they are correct, then the possession of this recognitional or discriminative capacity, unlike Nagel's imaginative ability, seems to be essentially tied to one's knowledge of the facts.[7]

I will argue, however, that though this argument is more compelling than Jackson's or Nagel's, it too relies upon an equivocation. More specifically, I will argue that there is an ambiguity in the notion of 'direct recognitional capacity' as it is

6. See Richard Warner, 'A challenge to physicalism', *Australasian Journal of Philosophy* 64 (1986): 249–65. My discussion of these issues owes much to Warner's formulation and defense of this argument.
7. I am indebted to Richard Warner for discussion of these points. His paper, in my view, provides the clearest and most compelling argument for such a premise.

used in both the contemporary and classical versions of this argument, and that neither reading can make both premises true. The source of this ambiguity, I will suggest, is the failure to distinguish between having a concept and having the wherewithal to apply it. Once this distinction is made, however, it will be clear that it is the latter ability, and that alone, which objective descriptions may not be able to supply to a person who has not had sufficient experiences of the type described. It will also be clear that this ability is not needed for full and complete knowledge of the facts about these experiences.

The problem with this argument against physicalism, then, is not that it equivocates between knowledge as 'having an ability' and knowledge as 'being in relation to the facts', but that it equivocates between two sorts of abilities, only one of which is required for having knowledge of all the facts in question. This distinction, I will argue, has been overlooked because of an implicit acceptance of an overly Empiricistic view of the acquisition and individuation of concepts. Once this distinction is made, however, the physicalist will be able to give an account of what differentiates our knowledge of color experiences from Mary's, and our knowledge of alien experiences from that of the creatures who have them, and say why these differences make no difference to our knowledge of the facts. Further, this distinction will provide the physicalist with the tools to describe and explain the important, if not essential, contribution made by the experience of mental states to one's knowledge of the facts about them.

II

In examining the notion of a direct recognitional capacity, I would first like to consider its role in a classical Empiricist conjecture, namely, Molyneux's question of whether a 'man born blind and then made to see' could determine, by sight alone, which of two objects was a sphere and which a cube. By starting with the Empiricists, it will be easier to see how far our current views about the relation of sense-experience to knowledge have come.

Molyneux's answer, endorsed by Locke and Berkeley, was that the man born blind would fail this discriminative test. For Molyneux, this failure would have been proof that the 'ideas' of visible shape and contour could not be acquired by touch, or reasoning, or anything short of visual experience itself. Thus a person who had never seen a cube or sphere would be missing certain facts about cubes and spheres. Nagel's and Jackson's concern in such a case, of course, would be somewhat different: their question would be whether the blind man could discriminate between his *visual experiences* of cubes and spheres, and thus whether he knew all the facts about *those experiences.* But it is easy to see how the issues raised in one case will be relevant to the other, as a negative answer to Molyneux's question assures a negative answer to Nagel's and Jackson's.[8] What is important is that Molyneux, quite

8. I will not consider cases in which, because of some optical illusion, the cube *looks* spherical, and *vice versa.*

explicitly, took a person's recognitional or discriminative capacities to provide the definitive test of his knowledge of the facts.

But what exactly was this test to be? As Locke reported it in the *Essay*, Molyneux specified merely that 'the sphere and cube [be] placed on a table, and the blind man made to see', and asked 'whether by his sight, before he touched them, he could now distinguish and tell which is the globe, which the cube?'[9] Let us assume that Molyneux's blind man had to give his answer not only before touching the cube and the sphere, or for that matter anything else, but before seeing the ostensive identification of any item whatsoever. And suppose, as Molyneux predicted, that the man born blind failed the recognitional test. What would this have shown about his theoretical knowledge?

For the Empiricists, this failure would have been good evidence that the man born blind was lacking the ideas of the visual properties of cubes and spheres: if he had had 'faint copies' of these properties in mind, he should have been able to match them to the items he could currently see. But on any other view of concept-formation, it is not clear why this lack of recognitional ability, by itself, should indicate a conceptual gap. To make the example relevant to the questions that concern us here, let us imagine a man born blind with the omniscience attributed to Mary, Jackson's neuropsychologist who had never seen color. That is, suppose that he had mastered all the facts about 3-dimensional figures and visual experiences that could be stated in the 'objective' vocabularies of geometry and psychology, including the judgments made by sighted people about the similarities and differences among their visual experiences. Presumably, this theoretically sophisticated blind man would be able to correctly answer any questions about cubes, spheres, and the visual experiences of them.

Further, suppose that, after being shown a few examples of *other* geometrical figures and being told that they were examples of their kind, he was able to go on and correctly identify the cube and sphere. In this case, it is even more plausible to think that the blind man's initial lack of recognition showed no gap in his knowledge of the facts. The accuracy of his answers, and of his subsequent identifications of novel geometric shapes could be evidence that what he was missing was not a set of facts or concepts, but the ability to apply to his new experiences the concepts that he already had. Even the strictest nativist, after all, would agree that the full-fledged use of one's innate ideas requires some 'ostensive' sessions with the environment, some lessons in how these concepts are to be applied. The question of their innateness, in such cases, is traditionally decided by how easily the individual, after learning to apply these concepts, could go on to identify new experiences of that sort. Similarly, if the man born blind, after his lesson, was able to discriminate cube from sphere at first sight before he touched them, he may be taken to have the necessary concepts, and thus the materials for theoretical knowledge, of the visual experiences of cubes and spheres. But if so, then on this understanding of 'direct recognitional

9. II.ix.8.

capacity', the man born blind, plausibly, could be regarded as knowing all the facts about the visual experiences of cubes and spheres without having the relevant recognitional capacities. That is, on an understanding of 'direct recognitional capacity' that makes the first premise of our argument plausible, the second premise appears to be false.

However, Molyneux's specifications for the thought experiment permit another interpretation, namely, that in cases such as this, the recognitional capacities of the man born blind *would* be sufficiently 'direct': after all, given a minimal number of lessons of the sort detailed above, he would be able to identify the cube and sphere, by his sight, without having touched them, just as Molyneux required. On this understanding of 'direct recognitional capacity', it is more plausible to use recognitional capacities as a test for theoretical knowledge; if the man born blind fails *this* test of recognition, it may well seem that he was lacking something conceptual that only the relevant visual experience could provide. But unfortunately for the argument linking experience and factual knowledge, if the blind man could *pass* this test, then he would have the relevant recognitional capacities without having had the corresponding experiences. That is, on an understanding of 'direct recognitional capacity' that makes the second premise plausible, the first premise appears false.

But is it plausible to think that the man born blind could pass this weaker recognitional test? Intuitively, this conjecture seems plausible indeed. By hypothesis, he would have learned all there is to know about the geometry of 3-dimensional objects and the similarities and differences in the way they strike visually acute perceivers when viewed in normal light. It seems that he would be able to reflect upon his knowledge, and the features of his new experiences, and make the proper judgment.

Indeed, there is even some empirical confirmation of this hypothesis, as Molyneux's problem is no longer just a thought-experiment. The results of such questions put to congenitally blind people whose eyesight has recently been restored are mixed: some can immediately distinguish cubes from spheres, and some cannot. There are all sorts of variables, of course, whose precise effects are unknown; for example, it is unclear whether there are differences in the way the visual system adapts to given differences in operative procedure and in the nature of the blindness itself. Yet R. L. Gregory reports a trend that is of interest. In observations of the Molyneux problem put to congenitally blind people upon regaining their sight, 'some did see well almost immediately, particularly those who were intelligent and active, and who had received a good education while blind.'[10] So the view that having comprehensive theoretical knowledge can make for recognitional capacities has at least a bit of empirical support.

However, there are two problems with this scenario that could defuse my argument. First is the worry that, even if the man born blind could discriminate the

10. See R. L. Gregory, *Eye and Brain*, 2nd edition: McGraw-Hill, p. 193.

cube from the sphere upon first viewing, his discrimination would not be sufficiently direct. After all, he has had, presumably, extensive tactile contact with cubes and spheres and other 3-dimensional objects while blind. Also, presumably, he has a reasonably good memory of how things feel. Thus, even if he were merely *shown* an arc and angle, and were not permitted to touch them, it could be argued that he identifies the cube and sphere *by inference*; having made the initial correlation between the look of the sample objects and his memory of how they felt, he is able to use his knowledge of the similarities and differences among tactile experiences (and among visual experiences) to make the proper call. If inference is responsible for his recognitional capacities, however, then our version of Molyneux's man born blind cannot be a counterexample to the claim that recognitional capacities depend upon prior experiences of a particular sort.

There is no definitive argument that I can give against this worry: it is possible for the man born blind to be using inference, rather than merely learning how to apply his concepts, and in such a case his discriminations would not be sufficiently direct. This worry, however, may be assuaged if we move to a different case.

It is best to make this move because of yet another problem with the Molyneux conjecture. The perceptual experiences of spheres and cubes appear to be structurally complex, unlike the rawer feels of perceived colors, tastes and bodily sensations such as pain. It may seem that there are intrinsic structural features tht are common to visual and tactile experiences of spheres and cubes—abstract features such as continuity and discontinuity in contour—that may permit one to distinguish them visually without prior visual experience of them.[11] In other words, Locke, Berkeley, and Molyneux were just plain wrong: the ideas of spheres and cubes afforded by sight and touch are not completely heterogeneous after all. The case envisioned by Molyneux, both for the Empiricists and their contemporary successors, is just a bad example.

III

However, I think the same issues can be raised for cases involving the recognition of 'purer' bodily sensations and perceptions. Thus I would like to move to an example, proposed in a recent paper by Richard Warner, in support of the claim that neither physicalism nor functionalism can capture all the facts about the experience of pain.

In his paper, Warner has us imagine an omniscient Alpha Centaurian who until this time, like all members of his kind, had been incapable of experiencing unpleasant sensations. Just for the experience, however, he contrives an apparatus that would modify his nervous system enough to allow him to feel the sensation—

11. This did not worry Berkeley, who claimed in his *New Theory of Vision* that we still would not know what continuity *looked like*, but it may give us some pause.

pain—that a stomach cramp normally produces in us. Suppose that the experiment works, and the machine indeed produces in him the new sensation of pain. But suppose also that, as an unforeseen consequence, the machine induces in him another as yet unexperienced sensation, the sensation of nausea. Warner claims that the Alpha Centaurian would not be able to determine, without consulting instruments or making inferences, which state was pain and which was nausea, no matter how much knowledge he had gleaned about the physical and functional structure of human beings. Thus, he concludes, physicalism and functionalism have left out certain facts about how pain feels.

Now, pain is a 'feel' as raw as any, and there is no obvious isomorphism between pains and any other sort of human (or presumably Alpha Centaurian) bodily sensation. This case, then, would seem purer than Molyneux's for appraising the question of whether the experientially deficient have access to all the facts. However, the same sorts of tensions and ambiguities in the notion of direct recognitional capacities arise here, too. For consider: Given my description of the case so far, it is hard to see why the Alpha Centaurian would not be able to make the appropriate discrimination. If there is a functional distinction between pain and nausea, the Alpha Centaurian would have learned it.[12] And surely there is such a difference: nausea, but not stomach cramping, produces an intense desire to avoid food and to vomit, and to believe that the state was caused by food.[13] Thus, it seems, the Alpha Centaurian would be able to reflect upon the differences in beliefs and desires that each state produces in him and make the proper call.

Moreover, unlike the case of Molyneux's man born blind, it would be hard to argue that this identification was not sufficiently direct.[14] It might be thought that the Alpha Centaurian's reflections upon the relations among pain, nausea, and other mental states involved inference, or the gathering of evidence, rather than the simple application of concepts to the experiences at hand. This argument, however, would beg the question against the objective theorists. By hypothesis, information about these relational or otherwise objective properties of pain and nausea constitutes the Alpha Centaurian's concepts of those mental states, and the question was whether the possession of concepts of that sort was sufficient to give him the relevant recognitional capacities. For the insufficiency of these concepts to be a *conclusion* drawn from the Alpha Centaurian's lack of a recognitional ability, the lack of this recognitional ability must be established in some other way. Further, the claim is independently implausible: even we, as sophisticated pain feelers, must sometimes take time, and engage in reflection, to unravel one type of painful experience from another if they occur together, especially for the first time. If this

12. If not, there are troubles for functionalism independently of this argument.

13. Even rats believe this: if nausea is induced in them even hours after they have ingested a particularly salient food, they will avoid that food for days.

14. Warner's notion here is 'non-evidential' knowledge: knowledge acquired without inference, and that needs no evidential backing to be justified.

involves inference, then our own abilities to discriminate among our experiences would not be sufficiently direct. Thus, it looks as if this is a case in which recognition can occur without prior experiences of the relevant sort.

However, this case, like Molyneux's, may be just another bad example. It may be wondered, that is, why this case should impress Nagel and Jackson, as their claim was that objective theories cannot provide one with all the facts about experiences that are *significantly* different from one's own. Pain and nausea, though distinctive in their unpleasantness, may be too close to the prior experiences of the Alpha Centaurian to illustrate their point. For consider: To distinguish pain from nausea in the way I described, the Alpha Centaurian must be able to distinguish between a state of his stomach due to the ingestion of food, and a state of his stomach that results from strenuous exercise. However, the Alpha Centaurian may be able to do this only because he had experienced certain sensations—a pleasant fullness after dinner, perhaps, or the mild exhilaration of a good abdominal stretch—which, though not unpleasant, were in other ways similar to pain and nausea.

But what if the Alpha Centaurian had never had *any* sensations in his stomach or abdominal area, and had acquired his concepts of food-related and exercise-related bodily states in some other way? In this case, the sensations of pain and nausea would be *radically* different from any he had ever felt, different enough, presumably, to make Nagel's and Jackson's point. In this case, moreover, it is indeed unlikely that the Alpha Centaurian could 'directly' discriminate between them.

However, as in the Molyneux case, it is not clear that the Nagel-Jackson conclusion would follow, as it is not clear why the Alpha Centaurian's failure should show a gap in his knowledge of the facts about pain and nausea. The Alpha Centaurian, after all, would be able to answer all the questions about pain and nausea that he answered, correctly, in the previous case. And if, after feeling some kinds of pain, he was able to go on and identify others upon first presentation, we could conclude that, like Molyneux's man born blind, what the Alpha Centaurian is missing is merely an ability to *apply* certain of his concepts, and not those concepts themselves. Thus, as in the Molyneux case, in the sense of 'direct recognitional ability' in which it is plausible to think that recognition is required for factual knowledge, it is implausible to think it is contingent upon experiences of some specific sort, and vice versa.

It is clear, then, what can be said along these lines about Mary's knowledge of color experience and our knowledge of the perceptual experiences of bats. In Mary's case, the failure to immediately identify red and green upon first being shown any colors at all may be taken to show a deficiency in her ability to apply color concepts to her experience, and not a deficiency in those concepts themselves. As in the case of the Alpha Centaurian, or Molyneux's man born blind, Mary will have the relevant color concepts as long as she has sufficient information about the structure of that perceptual field, the similarities and differences among the experiences in it, and the 'constitutive' truths about it, such as 'Nothing can look red all over and green all over at the same time.' Evidence of her mastery of this information may be acquired by close questioning about these features of color experience, and eventually, by seeing how quickly she can go on to correctly identify other colors, or other shades of the same colors, after witnessing the ostensive identification of a representative few.

The situation is somewhat different, however, for our knowledge about the perceptual experiences of bats. In this case, we are not only lacking the wherewithal to apply our concepts of sonar perception to our experiences, but we lack sufficient information about sonar perception even to come close to having adequate concepts of experiences in that perceptual field. If the only way to acquire these concepts was to have a specific set of experiences, then Nagel's conclusion would stand. But there is no reason to think that this is so. It is true that one must have *some* experiences in order to have concepts, and thus the materials for theoretical knowledge. However, all sorts of experiences can provide the conceptual wherewithal for understanding what it is for experiences to be similar and different from one another along various dimensions—what it is for them to differ in intensity, compatibility, and cause and effect. That is why, contrary to both Locke and Nagel, it *could* be helpful for a blind person to be told that red is like the sound of a trumpet (or a prepubescent that love is like a heatwave). It will be helpful as long as he is told what pink and orange and green are like as well.[15]

At the end of 'What is it like to be a bat', Nagel encourages the development of an 'objective phenomenology', an enterprise devoted to the objective description of just these sorts of relations among experiences of the types we cannot have.[16] He goes on, however, to deny that this information could give us all the facts about the experiences of bats. My suspicion, however, is that these more exotic cases seem more intractable because we now know quite little about the relevant dimensions of alien experiences, and even less about how these experiences are to be ordered along those dimensions. Our current lack of knowledge may indeed be due to a gap in our objective theories, but there is no reason to think that it cannot be overcome by acquiring more information of a perfectly objective sort.

IV

So far, I have argued that the failure to identify one's mental states immediately, upon first presentation, may be due to a gap in one's knowledge *or in one's ability to apply certain concepts.* I have also argued that though this ability, perhaps, could be acquired only through the experience of the mental states in question, its lack is by no means indicative of a gap in one's factual knowledge about mental states.

One might wonder, however, whether this account suffices to shift the burden of proof back to Nagel and Jackson. First, it may seem that it would be difficult, if not impossible, to draw a distinction between having the concept of a mental state, and

15. I am indebted to Lila Gleitman and Barbara Landau for discussion of these points.
16. Pp. 178–80 (pp. 537–8 of this volume).

having the ability to apply it to one's own experience. That is, it may seem that the only alternative to the Empiricists' theory of concepts as 'faint copies' is a theory which identifies having the concept of red or pain with having the ability to directly classify one's experiences as experiences of red or pain. However, the concepts of mental states may be identified with certain capacities or dispositions without assuming that they are capacities to classify experiences, under all circumstances, in any particular way. This assumption would be a vestige of Empiricism, and not an alternative to it, as it would ignore the other ways in which differences among these concepts could be manifested, namely, by the differences in the roles they play in reasoning, inference, and judgment. Such differences insure that there is a fact of the matter about whether a person who is unable to discriminate red from green upon first presentation really does have the concept of red. Moreover, these differences will be manifested, eventually, in the person's classificatory behavior: once the person has witnessed the ostensive identification of enough experiences of this sort, if he has the appropriate concepts, he will be able to directly identify new ones of that kind.

Because of this last contention, it may seem that I am committed none-theless to a necessary connection between recognitional capacities and factual knowledge. After all, I have affirmed that a person with complete factual knowledge of a certain type of mental state would be able to directly identify new instances given sufficient 'priming' with experiences of that type. However, this sort of connection would not threaten the physicalist, as it is just not clear how many samples from some particular experiential field are required for a person to apply his knowledge of those mental states to the experiences themselves. Thus, a failure to 'go on' in some particular case will not be definitive evidence of a theoretical gap.

To be sure, I have suggested that neither Mary nor the man born blind would require much experiential priming to go on to identify new experiences, and I acknowledge that this prediction gives important support to my claim that they have the relevant concepts. However, what makes it plausible that each could quickly develop the relevant recognitional capacities is that two conditions hold: first, the experiences in each field can be individuated by an objective description,[17] and second, the dimensions along which they are individuated are perceptually salient for human beings.

Indeed, it would seem as if the continuing recognitional failure of *any* experientially primed, objectively 'omniscient' subject may be traced to the failure of one of these two conditions. If the second condition did not hold in some situation, however, it is hard to see why the subject's recognitional failure should indicate any factual deficiency, and thereby any difficulty for physicalism. On the other hand, if the first condition did not hold, then the subject's lack of recognition would surely indicate a conceptual gap. But if a physicalistic theory is unable to distinguish,

17. This may not in fact be true, given the 'inverted spectrum' problem for functionalism. If not, however, objective theories may have problems independently of this argument.

objectively, among mental states that are, intuitively, distinct,[18] then it has fallen short of its own requirements for an adequate theory of mental states. The Nagel-Jackson argument, however, was designed to show that even if a theory can give an objective individuation of mental states that conforms to our intuitions, there will still be facts about those mental states that it leaves out, namely, what it is like to have them. Thus, the only cases in which a person's recognitional failure would threaten a physicalistic theory of mental states are ones in which the Nagel-Jackson argument would be beside the point.

V

But why, then, does the connection between having a concept of a mental state and having the appropriate recognitional capacities seem so invulnerable? And why does it seem that there must be something extra that experience contributes to our factual knowledge about mental states?

I do not want to deny that there is indeed a tight connection between knowledge and recognitional capacities in the case of concepts such as seeing red or feeling pain. However, this connection is not necessary. Its importance, rather, is in large part *epistemic*. A person, in exercising the relevant recognitional capacities, provides a reliable *demonstration* of this mastery of the concepts in question: these recognitional capacities provide evidence, perhaps the *best* evidence, that knowledge, rather than guesswork or ill-absorbed platitude, is at hand.

As it happens, of course, the inability to recognize or discriminate among items of a certain type most often shows a gap in one's knowledge of them. But this is not peculiar to our knowledge of mental states. In general, we would doubt the competence of any alleged expert on dogs who could not distinguish collies from cocker spaniels, or the expertise of any physicist unable to reliably identify the track of an electron in a bubble chamber. It is true that in these cases we would not always require recognitional capacities for knowledge: we would presumably grant knowledge of dogs or electrons to a theoretically sophisticated man born blind even if he could not identify them immediately upon first being made to see. But this is not because our knowledge of mental states is knowledge of a special kind of entity, or knowledge of a special, subjective, sort.

Rather, our concepts of dog and electron are tied to a rich and varied network of other concepts by numerous logical and inductive connections. Thus, even if a person lacks the specific recognitional capacities associated with their use, there are other obvious, if more roundabout, ways to determine that they have been mastered. This is less so, however, for concepts such as pain and looking red. Because they have fewer internal connections, we rely almost exclusively upon recognitional capacities as evidence of a person's mastery of them. Thus, it becomes tempting to

18. And here one may think, again, of functionalism.

think that the relevant recognitional capacities are necessary for the theoretical knowledge of mental states.

This temptation can be avoided, however, by acknowledging that the differences between the number of internal connections among experiental concepts and others is merely a matter of degree. Thus, contrary to the Empiricists, recognitional capacities will not constitute the only evidence for the mastery of concepts of this sort. To be sure, in persons who have never had a particular type of experience, the lack of recognitional capacities is usually good evidence of a gap in their theoretical knowledge. For example, contrast our theoretically sophisticated man born blind with another reported by Richard Gregory who, upon recovery, expressed great surprise that the quarter moon looked like a crescent rather than a wedge of pie.[19] Here, the lack of recognition is a clear indication that something conceptual was amiss. But the cases of the sophisticated man born blind, the omniscient Alpha Centaurian, and Jackson's neuropsychologist Mary were designed to give the protagonists all possible objective knowledge of the experiences they have never had. If this objective knowledge is sufficient to individuate the experiences in question from others of that kind, and if a person has mastered that knowledge, then there is no reason to treat any recognitional failures that occur upon first having the experiences in question any more seriously than the failures of the dog-expert or physicist.

But even if this is acknowledged, it may seem as if there is a special *contribution* that experience makes to knowledge, a contribution that is unattainable in any other way. If so, then is there not some bit of knowledge that a congenitally blind person or a person who cannot feel pain must lack about the experiences they have not had?

Here again, I want to stress that there is, indeed, a tremendous contribution that having an experience makes to having knowledge. What makes it special, however, is not that the experience contributes a chunk of knowledge that could not be gleaned in any other way, but that it contributes such knowledge as it does so *efficiently*. The function of experience here is primarily causal and evidential: it is not likely that one will have gleaned knowledge about the causes, effects, and similarity relations holding of a particular experiential state unless one has actually *had* it. Further, having had the experience (and having one's inferential capacities intact) provides the closest thing to a guarantee that one has picked up all there is to know. It provides not only the best possible evidence that one knows all there is to know about x's, but also the best method for acquiring this knowledge. It is not necessary, however, especially if one sets out, as did Mary, the Alpha Centaurian, and the man born blind, to laboriously absorb all that a full and complete scientific description of a particular phenomenon can provide.

Moreover, the special effectiveness of the contribution to the knowledge of x that is provided by having the experience of x is not restricted to knowledge of mental

19. Gregory, *Eye and Brain*, pp. 195–6.

phenomena. Consider the admonition of parent to child that 'you don't know what being a parent *is*!' Think of the many times children are told that they do not yet *understand* family, or responsibility, or death. One's claims to knowledge about all sorts of things, that is, are often suspect unless one has actually experienced the phenomena in question. But they are not irreversibly suspect, and can be bolstered by questions that are both careful and comprehensive.

What all these examples show is that we expect there to be a connection between experience and knowledge in many of our ordinary epistemic judgments; this expectation is by no means confined to our knowledge of mental states. Thus, the appeal to a special necessary connection between experience and knowledge of mental states ignores the generality of this phenomenon. More important, however, it takes this phenomenon too seriously: our unreflective expectations about the previous experiences of a person who has knowledge, as I have argued, have little to do with whether these experiences are necessary for knowledge of that sort. Thus, they provide no threat to physicalism, or any other objective theory of mental states.

To be sure, it is not hard to see why reductionist theses in the philosophy of mind raise suspicion, as they have often ignored the complexity of our mental lives. In this case, however, the suspicion leads to unwarranted fears about Procrusteans under the bed: it is not the insufficiencies of objectivity, but the vestiges of Empiricism, that suggest that these theories may be inadequate for expressing all the truth about experience that there is.

Acknowledgement

I wish to thank Michael Friedman, Barbara Herman, Tamara Horowitz, and Thomas Ricketts for helpful comments on earlier versions of this paper. I am indebted to Brian Loar and, especially, Richard Warner, for helpful comments and criticisms as well as for many stimulating discussions of these issues. I thank the Sloan Foundation and the Cognitive Science Program at the University of Pennsylvania for providing resources which enabled me to complete this work.

Chapter 31

Knowing one's own mind*

Donald Davidson

THERE is no secret about the nature of the evidence we use to decide what other people think: we observe their acts, read their letters, study their expressions, listen to their words, learn their histories, and note their relations to society. How we are able to assemble such material into a convincing picture of a mind is another matter; we know how to do it without necessarily knowing how we do it. Sometimes I learn what I believe in much the same way someone else does, by noticing what I say and do. There may be times when this is my only access to my own thoughts. According to Graham Wallas,

> The little girl had the making of a poet in her who, being told to be sure of her meaning before she spoke, said 'How can I know what I think till I see what I say?'[1]

A similar thought was expressed by Robert Motherwell: 'I would say that most good painters don't know what they think until they paint it.'

Gilbert Ryle was with the poet and the painter all the way in this matter; he stoutly maintained that we know our own minds in exactly the same way we know the minds of others, by observing what we say, do, and paint. Ryle was wrong. It is seldom the case that I need or appeal to evidence or observation in order to find out what I believe; normally I know what I think before I speak or act. Even when I have evidence, I seldom make use of it. I can be wrong about my own thoughts, and so the appeal to what can be publicly determined is not irrelevant. But the possibility that one may be mistaken about one's own thoughts cannot defeat the overriding presumption that a person knows what he or she believes; in general, the belief that one has a thought is enough to justify that belief. But though this is true, and even obvious to most of us, the fact has, so far as I can see, no easy explanation. While it is clear enough, at least in outline, what we have to go on in trying to fathom the thoughts of others, it is obscure why, in our own case, we can so often know what we think without appeal to evidence or recourse to observation.

Because we usually know what we believe (and desire and doubt and intend) without needing or using evidence (even when it is available), our sincere avowals

Donald Davidson, 'Knowing One's Own Mind', *Proceedings and Addresses of the American Philosophical Association* 60 (1987).

* Presidential Address delivered before the Sixtieth Annual Pacific Division Meeting of the American Philosophical Association in Los Angeles, California, March 28, 1986.

1. Graham Wallas, *The Art of Thought.*

concerning our present states of mind are not subject to the failings of conclusions based on evidence. Thus sincere first person present-tense claims about thoughts, while neither infallible nor incorrigible, have an authority no second or third person claim, or first person other-tense claim, can have. To recognize this fact is not, however, to explain it.

Since Wittgenstein it has become routine to try to relieve worries about 'our knowledge of other minds' by remarking that it is an essential aspect of our use of certain mental predicates that we apply them to others on the basis of behavioral evidence but to ourselves without benefit of such aid. The remark is true, and when properly elaborated, it ought to answer someone who wonders how we can know the minds of others. But as a response to the skeptic, Wittgenstein's insight (if it is Wittgenstein's) should give little satisfaction. For, first, it is a strange idea that claims made without evidential or observational support should be favored over claims with such support. Of course, if evidence is not cited in support of a claim, the claim cannot be impugned by questioning the truth or relevance of the evidence. But these points hardly suffice to suggest that in general claims without evidential support are more trustworthy than those with. The second, and chief, difficulty is this. One would normally say that what counts as evidence for the application of a concept helps define the concept, or at least places constraints on its identification. If two concepts regularly depend for their application on different criteria or ranges of evidential support, they must be different concepts. So if what is apparently the same expression is sometimes correctly employed on the basis of a certain range of evidential support and sometimes on the basis of another range of evidential support (or none), the obvious conclusion would seem to be that the expression is ambiguous. Why then should we suppose that a predicate like '*x* believes that Ras Dashan is the highest mountain in Ethiopia', which is applied sometimes on the basis of behavioral evidence and sometimes not, is unambiguous? If it is ambiguous, then there is no reason to suppose it has the same meaning when applied to oneself that it has when applied to another. If we grant (as we should) that the necessarily public and interpersonal character of language guarantees that we often correctly apply these predicates to others, and that therefore we often do know what *other* think, then the question must be raised what grounds each of us has for thinking he knows what (in the same sense) *he* thinks. The Wittgensteinian style of answer may solve the problem of other minds, but it creates a corresponding problem about knowledge of one's own mind. The correspondence is not quite complete, however. The original problem of other minds invited the question how one knows others have minds at all. The problem we now face must be put this way: I know what to look for in attributing thoughts to others. Using quite different criteria (or none), I apply the same predicates to myself; so the skeptical question arises why I should think it is *thoughts* I am attributing to myself. But since the evidence I use in the case of others is open to the public, there is no reason why I shouldn't attribute thoughts to myself in the same way I do to others, in the mode of Graham Wallace, Robert Motherwell, and Gilbert Ryle. In other words, I don't, but I could, treat my own mental states in the same way I do those of others. No such strategy is available to someone who seeks the same sort of authority with respect to the thoughts of others as he apparently has in dealing with his own thoughts. So the asymmetry between the cases remains a problem, and it is first person authority that creates the problem.

I have suggested an answer to this problem in another paper.[2] In that paper I argued that attention to how we attribute thoughts and meanings to others would explain first person authority without inviting skeptical doubts. In recent years, however, some of the very facts about the attribution of attitudes on which I relied to defend first person authority have been employed to attack that authority: it has been argued, on what are thought to be new grounds, that while the methods of the third person interpreter determine what we usually deem to be the contents of an agent's mind, the contents so determined may be unknown to the agent. In the present paper I consider some of these arguments, and urge that they do not constitute a genuine threat to first person authority. The explanation I offered in my earlier paper of the asymmetry between first and other-person attributions of attitudes seems to me if anything to be strengthened by the new considerations, or those of them that seem valid.

It should be stressed again that the problem I am concerned with does not require that our beliefs about our own contemporary states of mind be infallible or incorrigible. We can and do make mistakes about what we believe, desire, approve, and intend; there is also the possibility of self-deceit. But such cases, though not infrequent, are not and could not be standard; I do not argue for this now, but take it as one of the facts to be explained.

Setting aside, then, self-deception and other anomalous or borderline phenomena, the question is whether we can, without irrationality, inconsistency, or confusion, simply and straightforwardly think we have a belief we do not have, or think we do not have a belief we do have. A number of philosophers and philosophically-minded psychologists have recently entertained views that entail or suggest that this could easily happen—indeed, that it must happen all the time.

The threat was there in Russell's idea of propositions that could be known to be true even though they contained 'ingredients' with which the mind of the knower was not acquainted; and as the study of the *de re* attitudes evolved the peril grew more acute.

But it was Hilary Putnam who pulled the plug. Consider Putnam's 1975 argument to show that meanings, as he put it, 'just ain't in the head'.[3] Putnam argues persuasively that what words mean depends on more than 'what is in the head'. He tells a number of stories the moral of which is that aspects of the natural history of how someone learned the use of a word necessarily make a difference to what the

2. Donald Davidson, 'First Person Authority', *Dialectica*, 38 (1984), pp. 101–111.

3. Hilary Putnam, 'The Meaning of "Meaning"', reprinted in *Philosophical Papers, Vol. II: Mind, Language, and Reality*, Cambridge University Press, 1975, p. 227.

word means. It seems to follow that two people might be in physically identical states, and yet mean different things by the same words.

The consequences are far-reaching. For if people can (usually) express their thoughts correctly in words, then their thoughts—their beliefs, desires, intentions, hopes, expectations—also must in part be identified by events and objects outside the person. If meanings ain't in the head, then neither, it would seem, are beliefs and desires and the rest.

Since some of you may be a little weary of Putnam's doppelganger on Twin Earth, let me tell my own science fiction story—if that is what it is. My story avoids some irrelevant difficulties in Putnam's story, though it introduces some new problems of its own.[4] (I'll come back to Earth, and Twin Earth, a little later.) Suppose lightning strikes a dead tree in a swamp; I am standing nearby. My body is reduced to its elements, while entirely by coincidence (and out of different molecules) the tree is turned into my physical replica. My replica, The Swampman, moves exactly as I did; according to its nature it departs the swamp, encounters and seems to recognize my friends, and appears to return their greetings in English. It moves into my house and seems to write articles on radical interpretation. No one can tell the difference.

But there *is* a difference. My replica can't recognize my friends; it can't *re*cognize anything, since it never cognized anything in the first place. It can't know my friends' names (though of course it seems to), it can't remember my house. It can't mean what I do by the word 'house', for example, since the sound 'house' it makes was not learned in a context that would give it the right meaning—or any meaning at all. Indeed, I don't see how my replica can be said to mean anything by the sounds it makes, nor to have any thoughts.

Putnam might not go along with this last claim, for he says that if two people (or objects) are in relevantly similar physical states, it is 'absurd' to think their psychological states are 'one bit different'.[5] It would be a mistake to be sure that Putnam and I disagree on this point, however, since it is not yet clear how the phrase 'psychological state' is being used.

Putnam holds that many philosophers have wrongly assumed that psychological states like belief and knowing the meaning of a word are both (I) 'inner' in the sense that they do not presuppose the existence of any individual other than the subject to whom the state is ascribed, and (II) that these are the very states which we normally identify and individuate as we do beliefs and the other propositional attitudes. Since we normally identify and individuate mental states and meanings in

4. I make no claim for originality here; Steven Stich has used a very similar example in 'Autonomous Psychology and the Belief-Desire Thesis', *The Monist*, 61 (1978), p. 573 ff (see Chapter 22 of this volume). I should emphasize that I am not suggesting that an object accidentally or artificially created could not think; The Swampman simply needs time in which to acquire a causal history that would make sense of the claim that he is speaking of, remembering, identifying, or thinking of items in the world. (I return to this point later.).

5. Hilary Putnam, 'The Meaning of "Meaning"', p. 144.

terms partly of relations to objects and events other than the subject, Putnam believes (I) and (II) come apart: in his opinion, no states can satisfy both conditions.

Putnam calls psychological states satisfying condition (I) 'narrow'. He thinks of such states as solipsistic, and associates them with Descartes' view of the mental. Putnam may consider these states to be the only 'true' psychological states; in much of his paper he omits the qualifier 'narrow', despite the fact that narrow psychological states (so called) do not correspond to the propositional attitudes as normally identified. Not everyone has been persuaded that there is an intelligible distinction to be drawn between narrow (or inner, or Cartesian, or individualistic-all these terms are current) psychological states and psychological states identified (if any are) in terms of external facts (social or otherwise). Thus John Searle has claimed that our ordinary propositional attitudes satisfy condition (I), and so there is no need of states satisfying condition (II), while Tyler Burge has denied that there are, in any interesting sense, propositional attitudes that satisfy condition (I).[6] But there seems to be universal agreement that no states satisfy both conditions.

The thesis of this paper is that there is no reason to suppose that ordinary mental states do not satisfy both conditions (I) and (II): I think such states are 'inner', in the sense of being identical with states of the body, and so identifiable without reference to objects or events outside the body; they are at the same time 'non-individualistic' in the sense that they can be, and usually are, identified in part by their causal relations to events and objects outside the subject whose states they are. A corollary of this thesis will turn out to be that contrary to what is often assumed, first person authority can without contradiction apply to states that are regularly identified by their relations to events and objects outside the person.

I begin with the corollary. Why is it natural to assume that states that satisfy condition (II) may not be known to the person who is in those states?

Now I must talk about Putnam's Twin Earth. He asks us to imagine two people exactly alike physically and (therefore) alike with respect to all 'narrow' psychological states. One of the two people, an inhabitant of Earth, has learned to use the word 'water' by being shown water, reading and hearing about it, etc. The other, an inhabitant of Twin Earth, has learned to use the word 'water' under conditions not observably different, but the substance to which she has been exposed is not water but a lookalike substance we may call 'twater'. Under the circumstances, Putnam claims, the first speaker refers to water when she uses the word 'water'; her twin refers to twater when *she* uses the word 'water'. So we seem to have a case where 'narrow' psychological states are identical, and yet the speakers mean different things by the same word.

How about the thoughts of these two speakers? The first says to herself, when facing a glass of water, 'Here's a glass of water'; the second mutters exactly the same

6. See John Searle, *Intentionality*, Cambridge University Press, 1983, and Tyler Burge, 'Individualism and Psychology', *The Philosophical Review*, 95 (1986), pp. 3–45.

sounds to herself when facing a glass of twater. Each speaks the truth, since their words mean different things. And since each is sincere, it is natural to suppose they believe different things, the first believing there is a glass of water in front of her, the second believing there is a glass of twater in front of *her*. But do they know what they believe? If the meanings of their words, and thus the beliefs expressed by using those words, are partly determined by external factors about which the agents are ignorant, their beliefs and meanings are not narrow in Putnam's sense. There is therefore nothing on the basis of which either speaker can tell which state she is in, for there is no internal or external clue to the difference available. We ought, it seems, to conclude that neither speaker knows what she means or thinks. The conclusion has been drawn explicitly by a number of philosophers, among them Putnam. Putnam declares that he '. . . totally abandons the idea that if there is a difference in meaning . . . then there *must* be some difference in our concepts (or in our psychological state)' What determines meaning and extension '. . . is not, in general, fully known to the speaker.'[7] Here 'psychological state' means *narrow* psychological state, and it is assumed that only such states are 'fully known'. Jerry Fodor believes that ordinary propositional attitudes are (pretty nearly) 'in the head', but he agrees with Putnam that *if* propositional attitudes were partly identified by factors outside the agent, they would not be in the head, and would not necessarily be known to the agent.[8] John Searle also, though his reasons are not Fodor's, holds that meanings are in the head ('there is nowhere else for them to be'), but seems to accept the inference that if this were not the case, first person authority would be lost.[9] Perhaps the plainest statement of the position appears in Andrew Woodfield's introduction to a book of essays on the objects of thought. Referring to the claim that the contents of the mind are often determined by facts external to and perhaps unknown to the person whose mind it is, he says:

> Because the external relation is not determined subjectively, the subject is not authoritative about that. A third person might well be in a better position than the subject to know which object the subject is thinking about, hence be better placed to know which thought it was.[10]

Those who accept the thesis that the contents of propositional attitudes are partly identified in terms of external factors seem to have a problem similar to the problem of the skeptic who finds we may be altogether mistaken about the 'outside' world. In the present case, ordinary scepticism of the senses is avoided by supposing the world itself more or less correctly determines the contents of thoughts about the world. (The speaker who thinks it is water is probably right, for he learned the use of the word 'water' in a watery environment; the speaker who thinks twater is

7. Hilary Putnam, 'The Meaning of "Meaning"', pp. 164–5.
8. Jerry Fodor, 'Cognitive Science and the Twin Earth Problem', *Notre Dame Journal of Formal Logic*, 23 (1982), p. 103. Also see his 'Methodological Solipsism Considered as a Research Strategy in Cognitive Psychology', *The Behavioral and Brain Sciences*, 3 (1980).
9. John Searle, *Intentionality*, Chapter 8.
10. *Thought and Object*, Andrew Woodfield, ed., Clarendon Press, 1982, p. viii.

probably right, for he learned the word 'water' in a twatery environment.) But skepticism is not defeated; it is only displaced onto knowledge of our own minds. Our ordinary beliefs about the external world are (on this view) directed onto the world, but we don't know what we believe.

There is, of course, a difference between water and twater, and it can be discovered by normal means, whether it is discovered or not. So a person might find out what he believes by discovering the difference between water and twater, and finding out enough about his own relations to both to determine which one his talk and beliefs are about. The skeptical conclusion we seem to have reached concerns the extent of first person authority: it is far more limited than we supposed. Our beliefs about the world are mostly true, but we may easily be wrong about what we think. It is a transposed image of Cartesian skepticism.

Those who hold that the contents of our thoughts and the meanings of our words are often fixed by factors of which we are ignorant have not been much concerned with the apparent consequence of their views which I have been emphasizing. They have, of course, realized that if they were right, the Cartesian idea that the one thing we can be certain of is the contents of our own minds, and the Fregean notion of meanings fully 'grasped', must be wrong. But they have not made much of an attempt, so far as I know, to resolve the seeming conflict between their views and the strong intuition that first person authority exists.

One reason for the lack of concern may be that some seem to see the problem as confined to a fairly limited range of cases, cases where concepts or words latch on to objects that are picked out or referred to using proper names, indexicals, and words for natural kinds. Others, though, argue that the ties between language and thought on the one hand and external affairs on the other are so pervasive that no aspect of thought as usually conceived is untouched. In this vein Daniel Dennett remarks that '. . . one must be richly informed about, intimately connected with, the world at large, its occupants and properties, in order to be said with any propriety to have beliefs'.[11] He goes on to claim that the identification of *all* beliefs is infected by the outside, non-subjective factors that are recognized to operate in the sort of case we have been discussing. Burge also emphasizes the extent to which our beliefs are affected by external factors, though for reasons he does not explain, he apparently does not view this as a threat to first person authority.[12]

The subject has taken a disquieting turn. At one time behaviorism was invoked to show how it was possible for one person to know what was in another's mind; behaviorism was then rejected in part because it could not explain one of the most obvious aspects of mental states: the fact that they are in general known to the

11. Daniel Dennett, 'Beyond Belief', in *Thought and Object*, p. 76.

12. Tyler Burge, 'Other Bodies', in *Thought and Object*; 'Individualism and the Mental', in *Midwest Studies in Philosophy, Volume 4*, Peter French, Theodore Uehling, Howard Wettstein, eds., University of Minnesota Press, 1979 (see Chapter 25 of this volume); 'Two Thought Experiments Reviewed', *Notre Dame Journal of Formal Logic*, 23 (1982), pp. 284–93; 'Individualism and Psychology'.

person who has them without appeal to behavioristic evidence. The recent fashion, though not strictly behavioristic, once more identifies mental states partly in terms of social and other external factors, thus making them to that extent publicly discoverable. But at the same time it reinstates the problem of accounting for first person authority.

Those who are convinced of the external dimension of the contents of thoughts as ordinarily identified and individuated have reacted in different ways. One response has been to make a distinction between the contents of the mind as subjectively and internally determined, on the one hand, and ordinary beliefs, desires, and intentions, as we normally attribute them on the basis of social and other outward connections, on the other. This is clearly the trend of Putnam's argument (although the word 'water' has different meanings, and is used to express different beliefs when it is used to refer to water and to twater, people using the word for these different purposes may be in 'the same psychological state'). Jerry Fodor accepts the distinction for certain purposes, but argues that psychology should adopt the stance of 'methodological solipsism' (Putnam's phrase)—that is, it should deal exclusively with inner states, the truly subjective psychological states which owe nothing to their relations to the outside world.[13]

Steven Stich makes essentially the same distinction, but draws a sterner moral: where Fodor thinks we merely need to tinker a bit with propositional attitudes as usually conceived to separate out the purely subjective element, Stich holds that psychological states as we now think of them belong to a crude and confused 'folk psychology' which must be replaced by a yet to be invented 'cognitive science'. The subtitle of his recent book is 'The Case Against Belief'.[14]

Clearly those who draw such a distinction have insured that the problem of first person authority, at least as I have posed it, cannot be solved. For the problem I have set is how to explain the asymmetry between the way in which a person knows about his contemporary mental states and the way in which others know about them. The mental states in question are beliefs, desires, intentions, and so on, as ordinarily conceived. Those who accept something like Putnam's distinction do not even try to explain first person authority with respect to these states; if there is first person authority at all, it attaches to quite different states. (In Stich's case, it is not obvious that it can attach to anything.)

I think Putnam, Burge, Dennett, Fodor, Stich, and others are right in calling attention to the fact that ordinary mental states, at least the propositional attitudes, are partly identified by relations to society and the rest of the environment, relations which may in some respects not be known to the person in those states. They are also right, in my opinion, in holding that for this reason (if for no other), the concepts of 'folk psychology' cannot be incorporated into a coherent and comprehensive system of laws of the sort for which physics strives. These concepts are

13. Jerry Fodor, 'Methodological Solipsism Considered as a Research Strategy in Cognitive Psychology'.

14. Steven Stich, *From Folk Psychology to Cognitive Science*, M.I.T. Press, 1983.

part of a common-sense theory for describing, interpreting, and explaining human behavior which is a bit freestyle, but (so I think) indispensable. I can imagine a science concerned with people and purged of 'folk psychology', but I cannot think in what its interest would consist. This is not, however, the topic of this paper.

I am here concerned with the puzzling discovery that we apparently do not know what we think-at least in the way we think we do. This is a real puzzle if, like me, you believe it is true that external factors partly determine the contents of thoughts, and also believe that in general we do know, and in a way others do not, what we think. The problem arises because admitting the identifying and individuating role of external factors seems to lead to the conclusion that our thoughts may not be known to us.

But does this conclusion follow? The answer depends, I believe, on the way in which one thinks the identification of mental contents depends on external factors.

The conclusion does follow, for example, for any theory which holds that propositional attitudes are identified by objects (such as propositions, tokens of propositions, or representations) which are in or 'before' the mind, and which contain or incorporate (as 'ingredients') objects or events outside the agent; for it is obvious that everyone is ignorant of endless features of every external object. That the conclusion follows from these assumptions is generally conceded.[15] However, for reasons I shall mention below, I reject the assumptions on which the conclusion is in this case based.

Tyler Burge has suggested that there is another way in which external factors enter into the determination of the contents of speech and thought. One of his 'thought experiments' happens pretty well to fit me. Until recently I believed arthritis was an inflammation of the joints caused by calcium deposits; I did not know that any inflammation of the joints, for example gout, also counted as arthritis. So when a doctor told me (falsely as it turned out) that I had gout, I believed I had gout but I did not believe I had arthritis. At this point Burge asks us to imagine a world in which I was physically the same but in which the word 'arthritis' happened actually to apply only to inflammation of the joints caused by calcium deposits. Then the sentence 'Gout is not a form of arthritis' would have been true, not false, and the belief that I expressed by this sentence would not have been the false belief that gout is not a form of arthritis but a true belief about some disease other than arthritis. Yet in the imagined world all my physical states, my 'internal qualitative experiences', my behavior and dispositions to behave, are the same as they are in this world. My *belief* would have changed, but I would have no reason to suppose that it had, and so could not be said to know what I believed.

Burge stresses the fact that his argument depends on

> . . . the possibility of someone's having a propositional attitude despite an incomplete mastery of some notion in its content . . . *if* the thought experiment is to work, one must at some

15. See, for example, Gareth Evans, *The Varieties of Reference*, Oxford University Press, 1982, pp. 45, 199, 201.

stage find the subject believing (or having some attitude characterized by) a content, despite an incomplete understanding or misapplication.[16]

It seems to follow that if Burge is right, whenever a person is wrong, confused, or partially misinformed about the meaning of a word, he is wrong, confused, or partially misinformed about any of his beliefs that is (or would be?) expressed by using that word. Since such 'partial understanding' is 'common or even normal in the case of a large number of expressions in our vocabularies' according to Burge, it must be equally common or normal for us to be wrong about what we believe (and, of course, fear, hope for, wish were the case, doubt, and so on).

Burge apparently accepts this conclusion; at least so I interpret his denial that '. . . full understanding of a content is in general a necessary condition for believing the content'. He explicitly rejects '. . . the old model according to which a person must be directly acquainted with, or must immediately apprehend, the contents of his thoughts . . . a person's thought *content* is not fixed by what goes on in him, or by what is accessible to him simply by careful reflection.'[17]

I am uncertain how to understand these claims, since I am uncertain how seriously to take the talk of 'direct acquaintance' with, and of 'immediately apprehending', a content. But in any case I am convinced that if what we mean and think is determined by the linguistic habits of those around us in the way Burge believes they are, then first person authority is very seriously compromised. Since the degree and character of the compromise seem to me incompatible with what we know about the kind of knowledge we have of our own minds, I must reject some premise of Burge's. I agree that what I mean and think is not 'fixed' (exclusively) by what goes on in me, so what I must reject is Burge's account of how social and other external factors control the contents of a person's mind.

For a number of reasons, I am inclined to discount the importance of the features of our attributions of attitudes to which Burge points. Suppose that I, who think the word 'arthritis' applies to inflammation of the joints only if caused by calcium deposits, and my friend Arthur, who knows better, both sincerely utter to Smith the words 'Carl has arthritis'. According to Burge, if other things are more or less equal (Arthur and I are both generally competent speakers of English, both have often applied the word 'arthritis' to genuine cases of arthritis, etc.) then our words on this occasion mean the same thing, Arthur and I mean the same thing by our words, and we express the same belief. My error about the dictionary meaning of the word (or about what arthritis is) makes no difference to what I meant or thought on this occasion. Burge's evidence for this claim seems to rest on his conviction that this is what anyone (unspoiled by philosophy) would report about Arthur and me. I doubt that Burge is right about this, but even if he is, I don't think it proves his claim. Ordinary attributions of meanings and attitudes rest on vast and vague assumptions about what is and is not shared (linguistically and otherwise) by

16. Tyler Burge, 'Individualism and the Mental', p. 83 (see Chapter 25, pp. 439–40 of this volume).
17. Ibid., pp. 90, 102, 104 (pp. 446, 459, 462 of this volume).

the attributer, the person to whom the attribution is made, and the attributer's intended audience. When some of these assumptions prove false, we may alter the words we use to make the report, often in substantial ways. When nothing much hinges on it, we tend to choose the lazy way: we take someone at his word, even if this does not quite reflect some aspect of the speaker's thought or meaning. But this is not because we are bound (outside of a law court, anyway) to be legalistic about it. And often we aren't. If Smith (unspoiled by philosophy) reports to still another party (perhaps a distant doctor attempting a diagnosis on the basis of a telephone report) that Arthur and I both have said, and believe, that Carl has arthritis, he may actively mislead *his* hearer. If this danger were to arise, Smith, alert to the facts, would not simply say 'Arthur and Davidson both beleive Carl has arthritis'; he would add something like, 'But Davidson thinks arthritis must be caused by calcium deposits'. The need to make this addition I take to show that the simple attribution was not quite right; there was a relevant difference in the thoughts Arthur and I expressed when we said 'Carl has arthritis'. Burge does not have to be budged by this argument, of course, since he can insist that the report is literally correct, but could, like any report, be misleading. I think, on the other hand, that this reply would overlook the extent to which the contents of one belief necessarily depend on the contents of others. Thoughts are not independent atoms, and so there can be no simple, rigid, rule for the correct attribution of a single thought.[18]

Though I reject Burge's insistence that we are bound to give a person's words the meaning they have in his linguistic community, and to interpret his propositional attitudes on the same basis, I think there is a somewhat different, but very important, sense in which social factors do control what a speaker can mean by his words. If a speaker wishes to be understood, he must intend his words to be interpreted in a certain way, and so must intend to provide his audience with the clues they need

18. Burge suggests that the reason we normally take a person to mean by his words what others in his linguistic community mean, whether or not the speaker knows what others mean, is that 'People are frequently held, and hold themselves, to the standards of the community when misuse or misunderstanding are at issue.' He also says such cases '. . . depend on a certain responsibility to communal practice'. ('Individualism and the Mental', p. 90 (p. 447 of this volume)) I don't doubt the phenomenon, but its bearing on what it is supposed to show. (a) It is often reasonable to hold people responsible for knowing what their words mean; in such cases we may treat them as committed to positions they did not know or believe they were committed to. This has nothing (directly) to do with what they meant by their words, nor what they believed. (b) As good citizens and parents we want to encourage practices that enhance the chances for communication; using words as we think others do may enhance communication. This thought (whether or not justified) may help explain why some people tend to attribute meanings and beliefs in a legalistic way; they hope to encourage conformity. (c) A speaker who wishes to be understood must intend his words to be interpreted (and hence interpretable) along certain lines; this intention may be served by using words as others do (though often this is not the case). Similarly, a hearer who wishes to understand a speaker must intend to interpret the speaker's words as the speaker intended (whether or not the interpretation is 'standard'). These reciprocal intentions become morally important in endless situations which have no necessary connection with the determination of what someone had in mind.

to arrive at the intended interpretation. This holds whether the hearer is sophisticated in the use of a language the speaker knows or is the learner of a first language. It is the requirement of learnability, interpretability, that provides the irreducible social factor, and that shows why someone can't mean something by his words that can't be correctly deciphered by another. (Burge seems to make this point himself in a later paper.)[19]

Now I would like to return to Putnam's Twin Earth example, which does not depend on the idea that social linguistic usage dictates (under more or less standard conditions) what speakers mean by their words, nor, of course, what their (narrow) psychological states are. I am, as I said, persuaded that Putnam is right; what our words mean is fixed in part by the circumstances in which we learned, and used, the words. Putnam's single example (water) is not enough, perhaps, to nail down this point, since it is possible to insist that 'water' doesn't apply just to stuff with the same molecular structure as water but also to stuff enough like water in structure to be odorless, potable, to support swimming and sailing, etc. (I realize that this remark, like many others in this piece, may show that I don't know a rigid designator when I see one. (don't.) The issue does not depend on such special cases nor on how we do or should resolve them. The issue depends simply on how the basic connection between words and things, or thoughts and things, is established. I hold, along with Burge and Putnam if I understand them, that it is established by causal interactions between people and parts and aspects of the world. The dispositions to react differentially to objects and events thus set up are central to the correct interpretation of a person's thoughts and speech. If this were not the case we would have no way of discovering what others think, or what they mean by their words. The principle is as simple and obvious as this: a sentence someone is inspired (caused) to hold true by and only by sightings of the moon is apt to mean something like 'There's the moon'; the thought expressed is apt to be that the moon is there; the thought inspired by and only by sightings of the moon is apt to be the thought that the moon is there. Apt to be, allowing for intelligible error, second hand reports, and so on. Not that all words and sentences are this directly conditioned to what they are about; we can perfectly well learn to use the word 'moon' without ever seeing it. The claim is that all thought and language must have a foundation in such direct historical connections, and these connections constrain the interpretation of thoughts and speech. Perhaps I should stress that the arguments for this claim do not rest on intuitions concerning what we would say if certain counterfactuals were true. No science fiction or thought experiments are required.[20]

19. See, for example, 'Two Thought Experiments Reviewed', p. 289.

20. Burge has described 'thought experiments' which do not involve language at all; one of these experiments prompts him to claim that someone brought up in an environment without aluminum could not have 'aluminum thoughts'. ('Individualism and Psychology', p. 5.) Burge does not say why he thinks this, but it is by no means obvious that counterfactual assumptions are

I agree with Putnam and Burge, then, that

> . . . the intentional content of ordinary propositional attitudes . . . cannot be accounted for in terms of physical, phenomenal, causal-functional, computational, or syntactical states or processes that are specified nonintentionally and are defined purely on the individual in isolation from his physical and social environment.[21]

The question remains whether this fact is a threat to first person authority, as Burge seems to think, and Putnam and others certainly think. I have rejected one of Burge's arguments which, if it were right, would pose such a threat. But there is the position described in the previous paragraph, and which I hold whether or not others do, since I think this much 'externalism' is required to explain how language can be learned, and how words and attitudes can be identified by an interpreter.

Why does Putnam think that if the reference of a word is (sometimes) fixed by the natural history of how the word was acquired, a user of the word may lose first person authority? Putnam claims (correctly, in my view) that two people can be in all relevant physical (chemical, physiological, etc.) respects the same and yet mean different things by their words and have different propositional attitudes (as these are normally identified). The differences are due to environmental differences about which the two agents may, in some respects, be ignorant. Why, under these circumstances, should we suppose these agents may not know what they mean and think? Talking with them will not easily show this. As we have noted, each, when faced with a glass of water or twater says honestly, 'Here's a glass of water'. If they are in their home environments, each is right; if they have switched earths, each is wrong. If we ask each one what he means by the word 'water', he gives the right answer, using the same words, of course. If we ask each one what he believes, he gives the right answer. These answers are right because though verbally identical, they must be interpreted differently. And what is it that they do not know (in the usual authoritative way) about their own states? As we have seen, Putnam distinguishes the states we have just been discussing from 'narrow' psychological states which do not presuppose the existence of any individual other than the subject in that state. We may now start to wonder why Putnam is interested in narrow psychological states. Part of the answer is, of course, that it is these states that he thinks have the 'Cartesian' property of being known in a special way by the person who is in them. (The other part of the answer has to do with constructing a 'scientific psychology'; this does not concern us here.)

The reasoning depends, I think, on two largely unquestioned assumptions. These are:

needed to make the point. In any case, the new thought experiments seem to rest on intuitions quite different from the intuitions invoked in 'Individualism and the Mental'; it is not clear how social norms feature in the new experiments, and the linguistic habits of the community are apparently irrelevant. At this point it may be that Burge's position is close to mine.

21. 'Two Thought Experiments Reviewed', p. 288.

(1) If a thought is identified by a relation to something outside the head, it isn't wholly in the head. (It ain't in the head.)
(2) If a thought isn't wholly in the head, it can't be 'grasped' by the mind in the way required by first person authority.

That this is Putnam's reasoning is suggested by his claim that if two heads are the same, narrow psychological states must be the same. Thus if we suppose two people are 'molecule for molecule' the same ('in the sense in which two neckties can be "identical"'; you may add, if you wish, that each of the two people 'thinks the same verbalized thoughts . . . , has the same sense data, the same dispositions, etc.'), then 'it is absurd to think [one] psychological state is one bit different from' the other. These are, of course, narrow psychological states, not the ones we normally attribute, which ain't in the head.[22]

It is not easy to say in exactly what way the verbalized thoughts, sense data, and dispositions can be identical without reverting to the neckties, so let us revert. Then the idea is this: the narrow psychological states of two people are identical when their physical states cannot be distinguished. There would be no point in disputing this, since narrow psychological states are Putnam's to define; what I wish to question is assumption (1) above which led to the conclusion that ordinary propositional attitudes aren't in the head, and that therefore first person authority doesn't apply to them.

It should be clear that it doesn't follow, simply from the fact that meanings are identified in part by relations to objects outside the head, that meanings aren't in the head. To suppose this would be as bad as to argue that because my being sunburned presupposes the existence of the sun, my sunburn isn't a condition of my skin. My sunburned skin may be indistinguishable from someone else's skin that achieved its burn by other means (our skins may be identical in 'the necktie sense'); yet one of us is really sunburned and the other not. This is enough to show that an appreciation of the external factors that enter into our common ways of identifying mental states does not discredit an identity theory of the mental and the physical. Andrew Woodfield seems to think it does. He writes:

No *de re* state about an object that is external to the person's brain can possibly be identical with a state of that brain, since no brain state presupposes the existence of an external object.[23]

Individual states and events don't *conceptually* presuppose anything in themselves; some of their *descriptions* may, however. My paternal grandfather didn't presuppose me, but if someone can be described as my paternal grandfather, several people besides my grandfather, including me, must exist.

Burge may make a similar mistake in the following passage:

. . . no occurrence of a thought . . . could have a different content and be the very same token event . . . [T]hen . . . a person's thought event is not *identical* with any event in him that is

22. 'The Meaning of "Meaning"', p. 227.

23. Andrew Woodfield, in *Thought and Object*, p. viii.

> described by physiology, biology, chemistry, or physics. For let *b* be any given event described in terms of one of the physical sciences that occurs in the subject while he thinks the relevant thought. Let '*b*' be such that it denotes the same physical event occurring in the subject in our counterfactual situation . . . *b* need not be affected by counterfactual differences [that do not change the contents of the thought event]. Thus . . . *b* [the physical event] is not identical with the subject's occurrent thought.[24]

Burge does not claim to have established the premise of this argument, and so not its conclusion. But he holds that the denial of the premise is 'intuitively very implausible'. He goes on, '. . . materialist identity theories have schooled the imagination to picture the content of a mental event as varying while the event remains fixed. But whether such imaginings are possible fact or just philosophical fancy is a separate question'. It is because he thinks the denial of the premise to be very improbable that he holds that 'materialist identity theories' are themselves 'rendered implausible by the non-individualistic thought experiments'.[25]

I accept Burge's premise; I think its denial not merely implausible but absurd. If two mental events have different contents they are surely different events. What I take Burge's and Putnam's imagined cases to show (and what I think The Swampman example shows more directly) is that people who are in all relevant physical respects similar (or 'identical' in the necktie sense) can differ in what they mean or think, just as they can differ in being grandfathers or being sunburned. But of course there is *something* different about them, even in the physical world; their causal histories are different.

I conclude that the mere fact that ordinary mental states and events are individuated in terms of relations to the outside world has no tendency to discredit mental-physical identity theories as such. In conjunction with a number of further (plausible) assumptions, the 'externalism' of certain mental states and events can be used, I think, to discredit type-type identity theories; but if anything it supports token-token identity theories. (I see no good reason for calling all identity theories 'materialist'; if some mental events are physical events, this makes them no more physical than mental. Identity is a symmetrical relation.)

Putnam and Woodfield are wrong, then, in claiming that it is 'absurd' to think two people could be physically identical (in the 'necktie' sense) and yet differ in their ordinary psychological states. Burge, unless he is willing to make far stronger play than he has with essentialist assumptions, is wrong in thinking he has shown all identity theories implausible. We are therefore free to hold that people can be in all relevant physical respects identical while differing psychologically: this is in fact the position of 'anomalous monism' for which I have argued elsewhere.[26]

One obstacle to non-evidential knowledge of our own ordinary propositional

24. 'Individualism and the Mental', p. 111 (p. 470 of this volume).
25. 'Individualism and Psychology', p. 15, note 7. Cf. 'Individualism and the Mental', p. 111.
26. 'Mental Events', in Donald Davidson, *Essays on Actions and Events*, Oxford University Press, 1982 (see Chapter 39 of this volume).

attitudes has now been removed. For if ordinary beliefs and the other attitudes can be 'in the head' even though they are identified as the attitudes they are partly in terms of what is not in the head, then the threat to first person authority cannot come simply from the fact that external factors are relevant to the identification of the attitudes.

But an apparent difficulty remains. True, my sunburn, though describable as such only in relation to the sun, is identical with a condition of my skin which can (I assume) be described without reference to such 'external' factors. Still, if, as a scientist skilled in all the physical sciences, I have access only to my skin, and am denied knowledge of the history of its condition, then by hypothesis there is no way for me to tell that I am sunburned. Perhaps, then, someone has first person authority with respect to the contents of his mind only as those contents can be described or discovered without reference to external factors. In so far as the contents are identified in terms of external factors, first person authority necessarily lapses. I can tell by examining my skin what my private or 'narrow' condition is, but nothing I can learn in this restricted realm will tell me that I am sunburned. The difference between referring to and thinking of water and referring to and thinking of twater is like the difference between being sunburned and one's skin being in exactly the same condition through another cause. The semantic difference lies in the outside world, beyond the reach of subjective or sublunar knowledge. So the argument might run.

This analogy, between the limited view of the skin doctor and the tunnel vision of the mind's eye, is fundamentally flawed. It depends for its appeal on a faulty picture of the mind, a picture which those who have been attacking the subjective character of ordinary psychological states share with those they attack. If we can bring ourselves to give up this picture, first person authority will no longer been seen as a problem; indeed, it will turn out that first person authority is dependent on, and explained by, the social and public factors that were supposed to undermine that authority.

There is a picture of the mind which has become so ingrained in our philosophical tradition that it is almost impossible to escape its influence even when its worst faults are recognized and repudiated. In one crude, but familiar, version, it goes like this: the mind is a theater in which the conscious self watches a passing show (the shadows on the wall). The show consists of 'appearances', sense data, qualia, what is given in experience. What appear on the stage are not the ordinary objects of the world that the outer eye registers and the heart loves, but their purported representatives. Whatever we know about the world outside depends on what we can glean from the inner clues.

The difficulty that has been apparent from the start with this description of the mental is to see how it is possible to beat a track from the inside to the outside. Another conspicuous, though perhaps less appreciated, difficulty is to locate the self in the picture. For the self seems on the one hand to include theater, stage, actors, and audience; on the other hand, what is known and registered pertains to the audience alone. This second problem could be as well stated as the problem of the location of the objects of the mind: are they *in* the mind, or simply viewed *by* it?

I am not now concerned with such (now largely disavowed) objects of the mind as sense-data, but with their judgmental cousins, the supposed objects of the propositional attitudes, whether thought of as propositions, tokens of propositions, representations, or fragments of 'mentalese'. The central idea I wish to attack is that these are entities that the mind can 'entertain', 'grasp', 'have before it', or be 'acquainted' with. (These metaphors are probably instructive: voyeurs merely want to have representations before the mind's eye, while the more aggressive grasp them; the English may be merely acquainted with the contents of the mind, while more friendly types will actually entertain them.)

It is easy to see how the discovery that external facts enter into the individuation of states of mind disturbs the picture of the mind I have been describing. For if to be in a state of mind is for the mind to be in some relation like grasping to an object, then whatever helps determine what object it is must equally be grasped if the mind is to know what state it is in. This is particularly evident if an external object is an 'ingredient' in the object before the mind. But in either case, the person who is in the state of mind may not know what state of mind he is in.

It is at this point that the concept of the subjective—of a state of mind—seems to come apart. On the one hand, there are the true inner states, with respect to which the mind retains its authority; on the other hand there are the ordinary states of belief, desire, intention and meaning, which are polluted by their necessary connections with the social and public world.

In analogy, there is the problem of the sunburn expert who cannot tell by inspecting the skin whether it is a case of sunburn or merely an identical condition with another cause. We can solve the sunburn problem by distinguishing between sunburn and sunnishburn; sunnishburn is just like sunburn except that the sun need not be involved. The expert can spot a case of sunnishburn just by looking, but not a case of sunburn. This solution works because skin conditions, unlike objects of the mind, are not required to be such that there be a special someone who can tell, just by looking, whether or not the condition obtains.

The solution in the case of mental states is different, and simpler; it is to get rid of the metaphor of objects before the mind. Most of us long ago gave up the idea of perceptions, sense data, the flow of experience, as things 'given' to the mind; we should treat propositional objects in the same way. Of course people have beliefs, wishes, doubts, and so forth; but to allow this is not to suggest that beliefs, wishes and doubts are *entities* in or before the mind, or that being in such states requires there to be corresponding mental objects.

This has been said before, in various tones of voice, but for different reasons. Ontological scruples, for example, are no part of my interest. We will always need an infinite supply of objects to help describe and identify attitudes like belief; I am not suggesting for a moment that belief sentences, and sentences that attribute the other attitudes, are not relational in nature. What I am suggesting is that the objects to which we relate people in order to describe their attitudes need not in any sense be *psychological* objects, objects to be grasped, known, or entertained by the person whose attitudes are described.

This point, too, is familiar; Quine makes it when he suggests that we may use our own sentences to keep track of the thoughts of people who do not know our language. Quine's interest is semantical, and he says nothing in this context about the epistemological and psychological aspects of the attitudes. We need to bring these various concerns together. Sentences about the attitudes are relational; for *semantic* reasons there must therefore be objects to which to relate those who have attitudes. But having an attitude is not having an entity before the mind; for compelling *psychological* and *epistemological* reasons we should deny that there are objects of the mind.

The source of the trouble is the dogma that to have a thought is to have an object before the mind. Putnam and Fodor (and many others) have distinguished two sorts of objects, those that are truly inner and thus 'before the mind' or 'grasped' by it, and those that identify the thought in the usual way. I agree that no objects can serve these two purposes. Putnam (and some of the other philosophers I have mentioned) think the difficulty springs from the fact that an object partly identified in terms of external relations cannot be counted on to coincide with an object before the mind because the mind may be ignorant of the external relation. Perhaps this is so. But it does not follow that we can find *other* objects which will insure the desired coincidence. For if the object *isn't* connected with the world, we can never learn about the world by having that object before the mind; and for reciprocal reasons, it would be impossible to detect such a thought in another. So it seems that what is before the mind cannot include its outside connections–its semantics. On the other hand, if the object *is* connected with the world, then it cannot be fully 'before the mind' in the relevant sense. Yet unless a *semantic* object can be before the mind *in its semantic aspect*, thought, conceived in terms of such objects, cannot escape the fate of sense data.

The basic difficulty is simple: if to have a thought is to have an object 'before the mind', and the identity of the object determines what the thought is, then it must always be possible to be mistaken about what one is thinking. For unless one knows *everything* about the object, there will always be senses in which one does not know what object it is. Many attempts have been made to find a relation between a person and an object which will in all contexts hold if and only if the person can intuitively be said to know what object it is. But none of these attempts has succeeded, and I think the reason is clear. The only object that would satisfy the twin requirements of being 'before the mind' and also such that it determines what the content of a thought must, like Hume's ideas and impressions, 'be what it seems and seem what is is'. There are no such objects, public or private, abstract or concrete.

The arguments of Burge, Putnam, Dennett, Fodor, Stich, Kaplan, Evans and many others to show that propositions can't *both* determine the contents of our thoughts *and* be subjectively assured are, in my opinion, so many variants on the simple and general argument I have just sketched. It is not just propositions that can't do the job; no objects could.

When we have freed ourselves from the assumption that thoughts must have mysterious objects, we can see how the fact that mental states as we commonly conceive them are identified in part by their natural history not only fails to touch the internal character of such states or to threaten first person authority; it also opens the way to an explanation of first person authority. The explanation comes with the realization that what a person's words mean depends in the most basic cases on the kinds of objects and events that have caused the person to hold the words to be applicable; similarly for what the person's thoughts are about. An interpreter of another's words and thoughts must depend on scattered information, fortunate training, and imaginative surmise in coming to understand the other. The agent herself, however, is not in a position to wonder whether she is generally using her own words to apply to the right objects and events, since whatever she regularly does apply them to gives her words the meaning they have and her thoughts the contents they have. Of course, in any particular case, she may be wrong in what she believes about the world; what is impossible is that she should be wrong most of the time. The reason is apparent: unless there is a presumption that the speaker knows what she means, i.e., is getting her own language right, there would be nothing for an interpreter to interpret. To put the matter another way, nothing could count as someone regularly misapplying her own words. First person authority, the social character of language, and the external determinants of thought and meaning go naturally together, once we give up the myth of the subjective, the idea that thoughts require mental objects.

Acknowledgement

Note: I am greatly indebted to Akeel Bilgrami and Ernie LePore for criticism and advice. Tyler Burge generously tried to correct my understanding of his work.

Chapter 32

Individualism and self-knowledge*

Tyler Burge

THE problem I want to discuss derives from the juxtaposition of a restricted Cartesian conception of knowledge of one's. own thoughts and a nonindividualistic conception of the individuation of thoughts. Both conceptions are complex and controversial. But I shall not explain them in detail, much less defend them. I shall explicate them just enough to make the shape of the problem vivid. Then I shall say something about solving the problem.

Descartes held that we know some of our propositional mental events in a direct, authoritative, and not merely empirical manner. I believe that this view is correct. Of course, much of our self-knowledge is similar to the knowledge of others' mental events. It depends on observation of our own behavior and reliance on others' perceptions of us. And there is much that we do not know, or even misconstrue, about our own minds. Descartes tended to underrate these points. He tended to overrate the power of authoritative self-knowledge and its potential for yielding metaphysical conclusions. Characterizing the phenomenon that interested Descartes is a substantial task. I shall not take on this task here. I think, however, that Descartes was right to be impressed with the directness and certainty of some of our self-knowledge. This is the point I shall rely on.

Descartes's paradigm for this sort of knowledge was the cogito. The paradigm includes not only this famous thought, but fuller versions of it—not merely 'I am now thinking', but 'I think (with this very thought) that writing requires concentration' and 'I judge (or doubt) that water is more common than mercury'. This paradigm goes further toward illuminating knowledge of our propositional attitudes than has generally been thought. But I note it here only to emphasize that Descartes's views about the specialness of some self-knowledge are not merely abstract philosophical doctrine. It is certainly plausible that these sorts of judgments or thoughts constitute knowledge, that they are not products of ordinary empirical investigation, and that they are peculiarly direct and authoritative. Indeed, these sorts of judgments are self-verifying in an obvious way: making these

Tyler Burge, 'Individualism and Self-knowledge', *Journal of Philosophy* 85 (1988).

* To be presented in an APA symposium on Individuation and Self-Knowledge, December 30, 1988. Donald Davidson will comment; see this journal, this issue, 664/5. Substantially this paper was the Nelson Lecture, University of Michigan, February 1986. I benefited from the occasion.

judgments itself makes them true. For mnemonic purposes, I shall call such judgments *basic self-knowledge.*

Let us turn from knowledge of one's thoughts to individuation of one's thoughts. My view on this matter is that many thoughts are individuated nonindividualistically: individuating many of a person or animal's mental kinds—certainly including thoughts about physical objects and properties—is necessarily dependent on relations that the person bears to the physical, or in some cases social, environment. This view is founded on a series of thought experiments, which I shall assume are familiar.[1] Their common strategy is to hold constant the history of the person's bodily motion, surface stimulations, and internal chemistry. Then, by varying the environment with which the person interacts while still holding constant the molecular effects on the person's body, one can show that some of the person's thoughts vary. The details of the thought experiments make it clear that the variation of thoughts is indicative of underlying principles for individuating mental kinds. The upshot is that which thoughts one has—indeed, which thoughts one can have—is dependent on relations one bears to one's environment.

Our problem is that of understanding how we can know some of our mental events in a direct, nonempirical manner, when those events depend for their identities on our relations to the environment. A person need not investigate the environment to know what his thoughts are. A person does have to investigate the environment to know what the environment is like. Does this not indicate that the mental events are what they are independently of the environment?

By laying aside certain contrary elements in Descartes's views, one can reconstruct a tempting inference to an affirmative answer from his conception of self-knowledge.

In reflecting on the demon thought experiment, one might think that, since we can know our thoughts authoritatively, while doubting whether there is any physical world at all, the natures of our thoughts—our thought kinds—must be independent of any relation to a physical world. A parallel inference is presupposed in Descartes's discussion of the real distinction between mind and body. In *Meditations* VI, he argues that the mind can exist independently of any physical entity. He does so by claiming that he has a 'clear and distinct idea' of himself as only a thinking and unextended thing, and a 'clear and distinct idea' of body as only an extended and unthinking thing. He claims that it follows that the mind that makes him what he is can exist independently of any physical body. The argument also occurs in *Principles* I, LX:

1. Cf. my 'Individualism and the Mental,' *Midwest Studies in Philosophy*, IV (1979): 73–121 (see Chapter 25 of this volume); 'Other Bodies,' in *Thought and Object*, Andrew Woodfield, ed. (New York: Oxford, 1982); 'Individualism and Psychology,' *The Philosophical Review*, XCV, 1 (1986): 3–45; 'Cartesian Error and the Objectivity of Perception,' in *Subject, Thought, and Context*, Philip Pettit and John McDowell, eds. (New York: Oxford, 1986); 'Intellectual Norms and Foundations of Mind,' this JOURNAL, LXXXIII, 12 (December 1986): 697–720.

. . . because each one of us is conscious [through clear and distinct ideas] that he thinks, and that in thinking he can shut off from himself all other substance, either thinking or extended, we may conclude that each of us . . . is really distinct from every other thinking substance and from every corporeal substance.[2]

Descartes also believed that he had 'clear and distinct ideas' of his thoughts. One might argue by analogy that, since one can 'shut off' these thoughts from all corporeal substance, they are independent for their natures from physical bodies in the environment, and presumably from other thinkers. This line of argument implies that knowledge of one's own thoughts guarantees the truth of individualism.[3]

The root mistake here has been familiar since Arnauld's reply. It is that there is no reason to think that Descartes's intuitions or self-knowledge give him sufficient clarity about the nature of mental events to justify him in claiming that their natures are independent of relations to physical objects. Usually, this point has been made against Descartes's claim to have shown that mental events are independent of a person's body. But it applies equally to the view that mental kinds are independent of the physical environment. One can know what one's mental events are and yet not know relevant general facts about the conditions for individuating those events. It is simply not true that the cogito gives us knowledge of the individuation conditions of our thoughts which enables us to 'shut off' their individuation conditions from the physical environment. Our thought experiments, which have directly to do with conditions for individuation, refute the independence claim.[4]

It is one thing to point out gaps in inferences from self-knowledge to individualism. It is another to rid oneself of the feeling that there is a puzzle here. Why is our having nonempirical knowledge of our thoughts not impugned by the fact that such thoughts are individuated through relations to an environment that we know only empirically?

Let us assume that our thoughts about the environment are what they are because of the nature of entities to which those thoughts are causally linked. According to our thought experiments, a person with the same individualistic physical history could have different thoughts if the environment were appropriately different. One senses that such a person could not, by introspection, tell the difference between the actual situation (having one set of thoughts) and the counterfactual situation (having another).

This intuition must be articulated carefully. What do we mean by 'introspection'? In each situation, the person knows what his thoughts are; and in each situation the

2. *The Philosophical Works of Descartes*, vol. 1, Haldane and Ross trans. (New York: Dover, 1955), pp. 243/4.

3. Cf. *ibid.*, p. 190.

4. I have discussed this and other features of the inference in 'Cartesian Error and the Objectivity of Perception.' See also my 'Perceptual Individualism and Authoritative Self-Knowledge,' in *Contents of Thought*, Robert Grimm and Daniel Merrill, eds. (Tucson: Arizona UP, 1988). I now think that Descartes's views have more anti-individualistic elements than I realized in writing those articles. I hope to discuss these matters elsewhere.

thoughts are different. If 'introspection' were explicated in terms of self-knowledge, there would be an introspectible difference.

Certainly, if one were stealthily shifted back and forth between actual situations that modeled the counterfactual situations, one would not notice some feature in the world or in one's consciousness which would tell one whether one was in the 'home' or the 'foreign' situation. But this remark does not capture the idea that the two lives would feel the same. The thoughts would not switch as one is switched from one actual situation to another twin actual situation. The thoughts would switch only if one remained long enough in the other situation to establish environmental relations necessary for new thoughts. So quick switching would not be a case in which thoughts switched but the introspection remained the same.

But slow switching could be such a case. Suppose that one underwent a series of switches between actual earth and actual twin earth so that one remained in each situation long enough to acquire concepts and perceptions appropriate to that situation. Suppose occasions where one is definitely thinking one thought, and other occasions where one is definitely thinking its twin.[5] Suppose also that the switches are carried out so that one is not aware that a switch is occurring. The continuity of one's life is not obviously disrupted. So, for example, one goes to sleep one night at home and wakes up in twin home in twin bed—and so on. (Your standard California fantasy.) Now suppose that, after decades of such switches, one is told about them and asked to identify when the switches take place. The idea is that one could not, by making comparisons, pick out the twin periods from the 'home' periods.

I grant these ideas. The person would have no signs of the differences in his thoughts, no difference in the way things 'feel.' The root idea is that at least some aspects of one's mental life are fixed by the chemical composition of one's body. One might call these aspects *pure phenomenological feels.* If one were uncomfortable with this notion, one could explicate or replace it in terms of an abstraction from the person's inability to discriminate between different mental events under the stated switching situations.

The upshot of all this is that the person would have different thoughts under the switches, but the person would not be able to compare the situations and note when and where the differences occurred. This point easily, though I think mistakenly, suggests the further point that such a person could not know what thoughts he had unless he undertook an empirical investigation of the environment which would bring out the environmental differences. But this is absurd. It is absurd to think that, to know which thoughts we think, we must investigate the

5. Of course, there can arise difficult questions about whether one is still employing thoughts from the departed situation or taking over the thoughts appropriate to the new situation. I think that general principles govern such transitions, but such principles need not sharply settle all borderline cases. Insofar as one finds problems associated with actual switches distracting, one could carry out the objection I am articulating in terms of counterfactual situations.

empirical environment in such a way as to distinguish our actual environment from various twin environments.

In basic self-knowledge, a person does individuate his thoughts in the sense that he knows the thought tokens as the thought tokens, and types, that they are. We know which thoughts we think. When I currently and consciously think that water is a liquid, I typically know that I think that water is a liquid. So much is clear.

How can one individuate one's thoughts when one has not, by empirical methods, discriminated the empirical conditions that determine those thoughts from empirical conditions that would determine other thoughts?

It is uncontroversial that the conditions for thinking a certain thought must be presupposed in the thinking. Among the conditions that determine the contents of first-order empirical thoughts are some that can be known only by empirical means. To think of something as water, for example, one must be in some causal relation to water—or at least in some causal relation to other particular substances that enable one to theorize accurately about water. In the normal cases, one sees and touches water. Such relations illustrate the sort of conditions that make possible thinking of something as water. To know that such conditions obtain, one must rely on empirical methods. To know that water exists, or that what one is touching is water, one cannot circumvent empirical procedures. But to *think* that water is a liquid, one need not *know* the complex conditions that must obtain if one is to think that thought. Such conditions need only be presupposed.

Now let us turn to knowledge of one's thoughts. Knowing what one is thinking when one has thoughts about physical entities presupposes some of the same conditions that determine the contents of the empirical thoughts one knows one is thinking. This is a result of the second-order character of the thoughts. A knowledgeable judgment that one is thinking that water is a liquid must be grounded in an ability to think that water is a liquid.

When one knows that one is thinking that *p*, one is not taking one's thought (or thinking) that *p* merely as an object. One is thinking that *p* in the very event of thinking knowledgeably that one is thinking it. It is thought and thought about in the same mental act. So any conditions that are necessary to thinking that *p* will be equally necessary to the relevant knowledge that one is thinking that *p*. Here again, to think the thought, one need not know the enabling conditions. It is enough that they actually be satisfied.

Both empirical thoughts and thinking that one is thinking such thoughts presuppose conditions that determine their contents. In both cases, some of these conditions can be known to be satisfied only by empirical means. Why do these points not entail that one cannot know that one is thinking that such and such unless one makes an empirical investigation that shows that the conditions for thinking such and such are satisfied? The answer is complex, but it can be seen as a series of variations on the point that one must start somewhere.

It is helpful in understanding self-knowledge to consider parallel issues regarding perceptual knowledge. It is a fundamental mistake to think that perceptual knowledge of physical entities requires, as a precondition, knowledge of the conditions that make such knowledge possible. Our epistemic right to our perceptual judgments does not rest on some prior justified belief that certain enabling conditions are satisfied. In saying that a person knows, by looking, that there is food there, we are not required to assume that the person knows the causal conditions that make his perception possible. We certainly do not, in general, require that the person has first checked that the light coming from the food is not bent through mirrors, or that there is no counterfeit food in the vicinity. We also do not require that the person be able to recognize the difference between food and every imaginable counterfeit that could have been substituted.

In fact, it is part of our common conception of the objectivity of perception that there is no general guarantee that the perceiver's beliefs, dispositions, and perceptions could in every context suffice to discriminate the perceived object from every possible counterfeit. The possibility of unforeseeable misperceptions and illusions is fundamental to objectivity. So the very nature of objective perception insures that the perceiver need not have a perfect, prior mastery over the conditions for his perceptual success.

This point is obvious as applied to common practice. But it is the business of philosophy and the pleasure of skepticism to question common practice. My discussion of knowledge and individualism has proceeded on the unargued assumption that skepticism is mistaken. Granted this assumption, the point that perceptual knowledge does not require knowledge of its enabling conditions is obvious.

I shall not overburden this essay with an attempt to disarm skepticism. But it is worth noting that nearly all currently defended responses to skepticism, other than transcendental ones, agree in denying that perceptual knowledge must be justified by separately insuring that the enabling conditions hold and the skeptic's defeating conditions do not hold.[6] And since transcendental responses provide at most

6. This remark applies to reliabilist theories, Moorean theories that insist on the directness of perception, Quinean theories that attempt to show that the skeptic's doubt is covertly a bad empirical doubt, and Carnapian theories that attempt to show that the skeptic's question is somehow irrelevant to actual empirical claims. The words 'first' and 'separately' are crucial in my formulations. As against some reliabilist views that try to block skepticism by denying closure principles, I think that we can know that no demon is fooling us. But we know this by inferring it from our perceptual knowledge.

Several philosophers have thought that anti-individualism, combined with the view that we are authoritative about what thoughts we think, provides a 'transcendental' response to skepticism. Cf. Hilary Putnam, *Reason, Truth, and History* (New York: Cambridge, 1981); see Chapter 26 of this volume. Putnam's argument is criticized by Anthony L. Brueckner, 'Brains in a Vat,' this journal, lxxxiii, 3 (March 1986): 148–167. I agree with Brueckner that Putnam's arguments do not do much to undermine skepticism. But Brueckner seems to hold that, if anti-individualism and the authority of self-knowledge are accepted, one would have an antiskeptical argument. He suggests that the assumption of anti-individualism undercuts the assumption of authoritative self-knowledge. I do not accept this suggestion. I believe, however, that there is no easy argument against skepticism from anti-individualism and authoritative self-knowledge. This is a complicated matter best reserved for other occasions.

general guarantees against skepticism, the only tenable responses, which I know of, that attempt to justify particular perceptual knowledge claims in the face of skepticism take this route. I think that it is the right route.

I have maintained that perceptual knowledge of physical objects does not presuppose that one has first checked to insure that the background enabling conditions are fulfilled. The same point applies to knowledge of one's own mental events, particularly knowledge of the sort that interested Descartes. Such knowledge consists in a reflexive judgment which involves thinking a first-order thought that the judgment itself is about. The reflexive judgment simply inherits the content of the first-order thought.

Consider the thought, 'I hereby judge that water is a liquid'. What one needs in order to think this thought knowledgeably is to be able to think the first-order, empirical thought (that water is a liquid) and to ascribe it to oneself, simultaneously. Knowing one's thoughts no more requires separate investigation of the conditions that make the judgment possible than knowing what one perceives.

One knows one's thought to be what it is simply by thinking it while exercising second-order, self-ascriptive powers. One has no 'criterion,' or test, or procedure for identifying the thought, and one need not exercise comparisons between it and other thoughts in order to know it as the thought one is thinking. Getting the 'right' one is simply a matter of thinking the thought in the relevant reflexive way. The fact that we cannot use phenomenological signs or empirical investigation to discriminate our thoughts from other thoughts that we might have been thinking if we had been in a different environment in no way undermines our ability to know what our thoughts are. We 'individuate' our thoughts, or discriminate them from others, by thinking those and not the others, self-ascriptively. Crudely put, our knowledge of our own thoughts is immediate, not discursive. Our epistemic right rests on this immediacy, as does our epistemic right to perceptual beliefs. For its justification, basic self-knowledge in no way needs supplementation from discursive investigations or comparisons.[7]

So far I have stressed analogies between basic self-knowledge and perceptual belief. But there are fundamental differences. A requirement that, to know what thoughts we are thinking, we must be able first to discriminate our thoughts from twin thoughts is, in my view, even less plausible than the analogous position with regard to perceptual knowledge.

Why? In developing an answer to this question, I want to dwell on some fundamental ways in which perceptual knowledge of physical entities differs from the sort of self-knowledge that we have been featuring. We commonly regard perceptual knowledge as *objective*. For our purposes, there are two relevant notions of objectivity. One has to do with the relation between our perceptions and the physical entities that are their objects. We commonly think that there is no necessary

7. I shall not develop the issue of one's epistemic right to one's authoritative self-ascriptions here. It is an extremely complex issue, which deserves separate attention.

relation between any one person's abilities, actions, thoughts, and perceptions up to and including the time of a particular perception, on one hand, and the natures of those entities which that person perceptually interacts with at that time, on the other. On any given occasion, our perceptions could have been misperceptions. The individual physical item that one perceptually interacts with at any given time is fundamentally independent from any one person's perceptions—and conceptions. The nature of the physical entity could have been different even while one's perceptual states, and other mental states, remained the same.

This fact underlies a normative point about perception. We are subject to certain sorts of possible errors about empirical objects—misperceptions and hallucinations that are 'brute.' Brute errors do not result from any sort of carelessness, malfunction, or irrationality on our part. A person can be perceptually wrong without there being anything wrong with him. Brute errors depend on the independence of physical objects' natures from how we conceive or perceive them, and on the contingency of our causal relations to them. The possibility of such errors follows from the fact that no matter what one's cognitive state is like (so, no matter how rational or well-functioning one is) one's perceptual states could in individual instances fail to be veridical—if physical circumstances were sufficiently unfortunate.

There is a second sense in which perceptual knowledge is objective. This sense bears on the relation between one person's perceptions of an object and other persons' perceptions of the same object. The idea is that perceptual knowledge, like all other empirical knowledge, is impersonal. Any observer could have been equally well placed to make an observation. Others could have made an observation with the same type of presentation of the scene, if they had been in the same position at the relevant time. And this possible observation could have had the same justificatory status as the original observation. Even though empirical commitments must be made by persons, nothing relevant to the justification of any empirical commitment regarding the physical world has anything essentially to do with any particular person's making the commitment.

The paradigmatic cases of self-knowledge differ from perceptual knowledge in both of these respects. To take the first: in the case of cogito-like judgments, the object, or subject matter, of one's thoughts is not contingently related to the thoughts one thinks about it. The thoughts are self-referential and self-verifying. An error based on a gap between one's thoughts and the subject matter is simply not possible in these cases. When I judge: I am thinking that writing requires concentration, the cognitive content that I am making a judgment about is self-referentially fixed by the judgment itself; and the judgment is self-verifying. There is a range of cases of self-knowledge which extend out from this paradigm. I think that, in all cases of authoritative knowledge, brute mistakes are impossible. All errors in matters where people have special authority about themselves are errors which indicate something wrong with the thinker. Dealing with the whole range requires subtlety. But the point as applied to what I take to be the basic cases is straightforward. No errors at all are possible in strict cogito judgments; they are self-verifying.[8]

The paradigmatic cases of self-knowledge also differ from perceptual knowledge in that they are essentially personal. The special epistemic status of these cases depends on the judgments' being made simultaneously from and about one's first-person point of view. The point of view and time of the judgment must be the same as that of the thought being judged to occur. When I judge: I am thinking that writing requires concentration, the time of the judgment and that of the thought being judged about are the same; and the identity of the first-person pronouns signals an identity of point of view between the judge and the thought being judged about. In all cases of authoritative self-knowledge, even in those cases which are not 'basic' in our sense, it is clear that their first-person character is fundamental to their epistemic status.

These differences between perceptual knowledge and authoritative self-knowledge ground my claim that it is even less plausible than it is in the case of perceptual knowledge to think that basic self-knowledge requires, as a precondition, knowledge of the conditions that make such knowledge possible.

Let us think about the difference as regards objectivity in the relation to an object. In the case of perceptual knowledge, one's perception can be mistaken because some counterfeit has been substituted. It is this possibility which tempts one into the (mistaken) view that, to have perceptual knowledge, one must first know something that rules out the possibility of a counterfeit. But in the cases of the cogito-like self-verifying judgments there is no possibility of counterfeits. No abnormal background condition could substitute some other object in such a way as to create a gap between what we think and what we think about. Basic self-knowledge is self-referential in a way that insures that the object of reference just is the thought being thought. If background conditions are different enough so that there is another object of reference in one's self-referential thinking, they are also different enough so that there is another thought. The person would remain in the same reflexive position with respect to this thought, and would again know, in the authoritative way, what he is thinking.

For example, imagine a case of slow switching between actual home and actual twin-home situations. In the former situation, the person may think 'I am thinking that water is a liquid.' In the latter situation, the person may think 'I am thinking

8. Mistakes about the *res* in *de re* judgments are not counterexamples to the claim that basic cogito-like judgments are self-verifying (hence infallible). Suppose I judge: I am thinking that my aunt is charming; and suppose that the person that I am judging to be charming is not my aunt (I have some particular person in mind). It is true that I am making a mistake about the identity of the person thought about; I have no particular authority about that, or even about her existence. But I am not making a mistake about what I am thinking about that person; there is no mistake about the intentional act and intentional content of the act. Authority concerns those aspects of the thought which have intentional (aboutness) properties. For me, those are the only aspects of the content of a thought.

that twater is a liquid.' In both cases, the person is right and as fully justified as ever. The fact that the person does not know that a switch has occurred is irrelevant to the truth and justified character of these judgments. Of course, the person may learn about the switches and ask 'Was I thinking yesterday about water or twater?'—and not know the answer. Here knowing the answer may sometimes indeed depend on knowing empirical background conditions. But such sophisticated questions about memory require a more complex story. If a person, aware of the fact that switching has occurred, were to ask 'Am I now thinking about water or twater?', the answer is obviously 'both.' Both concepts are used. Given that the thought is fixed and that the person is thinking it self-consciously, no new knowledge about the thought could undermine the self-ascription—or therefore its justification or authority.

In basic self-knowledge, one simultaneously thinks through a first-order thought (that water is a liquid) and thinks about it as one's own. The content of the first-order (contained) thought is fixed by nonindividualistic background conditions. And by its reflexive, self-referential character, the content of the second-order judgment is logically locked (self-referentially) onto the first-order content which it both contains and takes as its subject matter. Since counterfeit contents logically cannot undermine such self-knowledge, there should be no temptation to think that, in order to have such knowledge, one needs to master its enabling conditions.

The view I constructed on Descartes runs contrary. On that view, since basic self-knowledge is more certain than perceptual knowledge, it is more imperative that one be master of all its enabling conditions. One temptation toward this sort of reasoning may derive from construing self-knowledge as a perfected perceptual knowledge. If one thinks of one's relation to the subject matter of basic self-knowledge on an analogy to one's relation to objects of empirical investigation, then the view that one's thoughts (the subject matter) are dependent for their natures on relations to the environment will make it appear that one's knowledge of one's thoughts cannot be any more direct or certain than one's knowledge of the environment. If one begins by thinking of one's thoughts as objects like physical objects, except that one cannot misperceive or have illusions about them, then to explicate authoritative self-knowledge, one makes one of two moves. Either one adds further capacities for ruling out the possible sources of misperception or illusion in empirical perception, or one postulates objects of knowledge whose very nature is such that they cannot be misconstrued or misconceived. In the first instance, one grants oneself an omniscient faculty for discerning background conditions whose independence from us, in the case of perceptual knowledge, is the source of error. In the second instance, one imagines objects of thought (propositions that can be thought only if they are completely understood, or ideas whose *esse* is their *percipi*) whose natures are such that one cannot make any mistakes about them—objects of thought which one can 'see' from all sides at once. In either case, one takes oneself to have ultimate insight into the natures of one's thoughts.

This line of reasoning is deeply misconceived. One need only make it explicit to sense its implausibility. The source of our strong epistemic right, our justification, in our basic self-knowledge is not that we know a lot about each thought we know we have. It is not that we can explicate its nature and its enabling conditions. It is that we are in the position of thinking those thoughts in the second-order, self-verifying way. Justification lies not in the having of supplemental background knowledge, but in the character and function of the self-evaluating judgments.

Let us turn to the point that self-knowledge is personal. The view that anti-individualism is incompatible with authoritative self-knowledge is easily engendered by forgetting the essentially first-person character of self-knowledge. We switch back and forth between thinking our thoughts and thinking about ourselves from the point of view of another person who knows more about our environment than we do. This is a key to Descartes's skeptical thought experiments. And it would not be surprising if he tended to think about self-knowledge in such a way as to give it a sort of omniscience from the third-person point of view—in order to protect the first-person point of view from the fallibilities to which impersonal or third-person judgments (especially empirical judgments) are prone. Since we are not omniscient about empirical matters, it is natural to reduce the scope of the relevant third-person perspective so that the character of one's thoughts is independent of an environment about which we cannot be omniscient. Individualism ensues.

To illustrate the train of thought in a more concrete way: we think that we are thinking that water is a liquid. But then, switching to a third-person perspective, we imagine a situation in which the world is not as we currently think it is—a situation, say, in which there is no water for us to interact with. We take up a perspective on ourselves from the outside. Having done this, we are easily but illegitimately seduced into the worry that our original first-person judgment is poorly justified unless it can somehow encompass the third-person perspective, or unless the third-person perspective on empirical matters is irrelevant to the character of the first-person judgment. In this fallen state, we are left with little else but a distorted conception of self-knowledge and a return to individualism.[9]

9. My knowledge that I am thinking that mercury is an element depends on an ability to think—not explicate—the thought that mercury is an element. Compare my knowledge that my words 'mercury is an element' are true if and only if mercury is an element. This knowledge depends on understanding the words 'mercury is an element' well enough to say with them, or think with them, that mercury is an element. It is this ability which distinguishes this knowledge from mere knowledge that the disquotation principle as applied to 'mercury is an element' is true (mere knowledge that the sentence ''mercury is an element' is true if and only if mercury is an element' is true). I know that my word 'mercury' applies to mercury (if to anything), not by being able to provide an explication that distinguishes mercury from every conceivable twin mercury, but by being a competent user of the word, whose meaning and reference are grounded in this environment rather than in some environment where the meaning of the word form would be different. The fact that one may not be able to explicate the difference between mercury and every possible twin mercury

As one thinks a thought reflexively, it is an object of reference and knowledge, but simultaneously a constituent of one's point of view. The essential role that the first-person singular plays in the epistemic status of authoritative self-knowledge differentiates this knowledge not only from empirical knowledge, but also from most a priori knowledge, the justification of which does not depend on the first-person point of view in the same way.

The tendency to blur distinctions between a priori knowledge (or equally, knowledge involved in explication of one's concepts) and authoritative self-knowledge is, I think, an instance of Descartes's central mistake: exaggerating the implications of authoritative self-knowledge for impersonal knowledge of necessary truths. One clearly does not have first-person authority about whether one of one's thoughts is to be explicated or individuated in such and such a way. Nor is there any apparent reason to assume that, in general, one must be able to explicate one's thoughts correctly in order to know that one is thinking them.

Thus, I can know that I have arthritis, and know I think I have arthritis, even though I do not have a proper criterion for what arthritis is. It is a truism that to think one's thoughts, and thus to think cogito-like thoughts, one must understand what one is thinking well enough to think it. But it does not follow that such understanding carries with it an ability to explicate correctly one's thoughts or concepts via other thoughts and concepts; nor does it carry an immunity to failures of explication. So one can know what one's thoughts are even while one understands one's thoughts only partially, in the sense that one gives incomplete or mistaken explications of one's thoughts or concepts. One should not assimilate 'knowing what one's thoughts are' in the sense of basic self-knowledge to 'knowing what one's thoughts are' in the sense of being able to explicate them correctly—being able to delineate their constitutive relations to other thoughts.[10]

should not lead one to assimilate one's use of 'mercury' to knowledge of purely formal relationships (e.g., knowledge that all instances of the disquotation principle are true).

One other comparison: I know that I am here (compare: on earth) rather than somewhere else (compare: twin earth). My knowledge amounts to more than knowing I am wherever I am. I have normal ability to perceive and think about my surroundings. I have this knowledge because I perceive my surroundings and not other conceivable surroundings, and I have it even though other places that I could not distinguish by perception or description from here are conceivable. For a variety of reasons, one should not assimilate terms like 'water' to indexicals like 'here'. Cf. 'Other Bodies.' But these analogies may be helpful here.

10. Davidson's views about self-knowledge have some crucial points in common with mine. But he may be making this mistake when he writes that, if one concedes the possibility of partial understanding as I do, one must concede that anti-individualism undermines the authority of self-knowledge. Cf. his 'Knowing One's Own Mind,' *Proceedings and Addresses of the American Philosophical Association*, LX (1987): 448 (Chapter 31, p. 562, this volume). Cf. also 'First Person Authority,' *Dialectica*, XXXVIII, 2–3 (1984): 101–111. It is unclear to me why Davidson says this. I have discussed the distinction between the sort of understanding necessary to think and the sort of understanding necessary to explicate one's thoughts, in 'Individualism and the Mental'; 'Intellectual Norms and Foundations of Mind'; 'Frege on Sense and Linguistic Meaning,' forthcoming in *The Analytic Tradition*, David Bell and Neil Cooper, eds. (New York: Blackwell); and 'Wherein is Language Social?' forthcoming in a volume edited by Alexander George (New York: Blackwell).

For its justification, basic self-knowledge requires only that one think one's thoughts in the self-referential, self-ascriptive manner. It neither requires nor by itself yields a general account of the mental kinds that it specifies. Conceptual explication—knowledge of how one's thought kinds relate to other thought kinds—typically requires more objectification: reasoning from empirical observation or reflection on general principles. It requires a conceptual mastery of the conditions underlying one's thoughts and a conceptual mastery of the rules one is following. These masteries are clearly beyond anything required to think thoughts in the second-order, self-ascriptive way. Explicative knowledge is neither self-verifying nor so closely tied to particular mental events or particular persons' points of view.[11]

Despite, or better because of, its directness and certainty, basic self-knowledge is limited in its metaphysical implications. It is none-theless epistemically self-reliant. By itself it yields little of metaphysical interest; but its epistemic credentials do not rest on knowledge of general principles, or on investigation of the world.

11. As I indicated earlier, basic self-knowledge is at most an illuminating paradigm for understanding a significant range of phenomena that count as self-knowledge. Thus, the whole discussion has been carried out under a major simplifying assumption. A full discussion of authoritative self-knowledge must explicate our special authority, or epistemic right, even in numerous cases where our judgments are not self-verifying or immune to error. I think, however, that reflection on the way that errors can occur in such cases gives not the slightest encouragement to the view that anti-individualism (as regards either the physical or social environments) is a threat to the authority of our knowledge of the contents of our thoughts.

Chapter 33

Anti-individualism and privileged access

Michael McKinsey

It has been a philosophical commonplace, at least since Descartes, to hold that each of us can know the existence and content of his own mental states in a privileged way that is available to no one else. This has at least seemed true with respect to those 'neutral' cognitive attitudes such as thought, belief, intention, and desire, whose propositional contents may be false. The crucial idea is not that one's knowledge of these states in oneself is incorrigible, for surely one can make mistakes about what one believes, intends, or desires. Rather the idea is that we can in principle find out about these states in ourselves 'just by thinking', without launching an empirical investigation or making any assumptions about the external physical world. I will call knowledge obtained independently of empirical investigation *a priori* knowledge. And I will call the principle that it is possible to have *a prior* knowledge of one's own neutral cognitive attitude states, the Principle of Privileged Access, or just 'privileged access' for short.

Although many philosophers would insist that privileged access is undeniable, a series of recent discoveries and arguments in the philosophy of language has, I believe, convinced a perhaps equally large number of philosophers that privileged access is a complete illusion. One of the most persuasive of these arguments was proposed by Tyler Burge [1] as an application of Putnam's [9] famous Twin Earth case. Oscar, a resident of Earth, believes that water is wet. On Twin Earth, there is no water; rather there is a qualitatively similar liquid with a different chemical composition, a liquid that we may call 'twater'. Toscar, who is Oscar's identical twin and a denizen of Twin Earth, does not believe that water is wet. For Toscar has no beliefs about water at all; rather, he believes that twater is wet, that twater fills the oceans, etc. Yet Oscar and Toscar, being absolutely identical twins, would certainly seem to be *internally* the same. In Putnam's terminology, Oscar and Toscar would share all the same 'narrow' psychological states. Thus, Burge concludes, Oscar's belief that water is wet must be a *wide* state: it must, that is, 'presuppose' or 'depend upon' the relations that Oscar bears to other speakers or objects in his external environment.

In general, Burge endorses a conclusion something like

(B) Some neutral cognitive states that are ascribed by *de dicto* attitude sentences (e.g.,

Michael McKinsey, 'Anti-Individualism and Privileged Access', *Analysis* 51 (1991).

'Oscar is thinking that water is wet') necessarily depend upon or presuppose the existence of objects external to the person to whom the state is ascribed.

Now (B) might certainly *appear* to conflict with privileged access. For (B) implies that sometimes, whether or not a person is in a given cognitive state is determined by external facts that the person himself could only know by empirical investigation. In such cases, it would seem, the person would therefore not be able to know *a priori* that he is in the cognitive state in question.

But interestingly enough, Burge [2] has recently urged that despite appearances, his anti-individualism (that is, his conclusion (B)) is perfectly compatible with privileged access. And a similar point of view had earlier been expressed by Davidson [3]. I want to argue here that Burge and Davidson are wrong. Anti-individualism and privileged access as standardly understood are incompatible, and something has to give.[1]

I will first briefly discuss Davidson's defence of compatibilism. Davidson clearly accepts anti-individualism as formulated by (B), and like Burge he accepts (B) in part on the basis of Burge's persuasive application of Putnam's Twin Earth case. But Davidson insists that anti-individualism does not undermine first person authority about one's own mental states. He agrees with the anti-individualist thesis that some *de dicto* attitude ascriptions 'identify thoughts by relating them to things outside the head' ([3], p. 451 (p. 566 of this volume)). But he suggests that philosophers like Putnam who find a difficulty for privileged access in this thesis are in effect confusing thoughts with their descriptions. Such philosophers make the mistake, Davidson says, of inferring from the fact that a thought is identified or *described* by relating it to something outside the head, that the thought itself must therefore *be* outside the head and hence must be unavailable to privileged access ([3], p. 451 (p. 566 of this volume)).

Now I do not myself see any reason to believe that Putnam or anyone else has actually made this mistake. Certainly, as we shall see below, the most cogent reason for endorsing incompatibilism does not involve this mistake at all, so that Davidson's diagnosis is inconclusive at best. But what is most disconcerting about Davidson's remarks is the version of privileged access that he apparently takes himself to be defending. He explicitly accepts anti-individualism, understanding it as the thesis that thoughts are often *described* (in attitude ascriptions) by relating them to objects outside the head. Then he (quite correctly) points out that it does not follow from this thesis that the thoughts so described are *themselves* outside the head. But what is the relevance of this point to the issue at hand? Apparently Davidson is saying that since the thoughts in question are inner episodes that exist independently of our means of describing them, we can have privileged access to these episodes, whatever the external implications of our descriptions of the episodes might be.

But if this is what Davidson has in mind, then the version of privileged access

1. I have elsewhere discussed at length the problems for particular forms of anti-individualism that arise from these theses' apparent incompatibility with privileged access. See McKinsey [5] and [7].

that he is defending is too weak to be of much philosophical interest. He wishes to claim, apparently, that one could have privileged access to an episode of thought independently of having privileged access to any particular descriptions that the episode might satisfy. But then what would one have privileged access *to* in such a case? Perhaps one would be privileged to know only that the episode exists; given what Davidson says, there is no reason to suppose that the agent would have privileged access even to the fact that the episode is an episode of *thought*, as opposed to being, say, an episode of indigestion.

But surely, having access of this sort to one's thoughts is not much of a privilege. The traditional view, I should think, is not just that we have privileged access to the fact that our thoughts *occur*; rather the view is that we have privileged access to our thoughts *as satisfying certain descriptions*. In particular, the traditional view is that we have privileged access to our thoughts as having certain contents, or as satisfying certain *de dicto* cognitive attitude predicates. Thus, if Oscar is thinking that water is wet, the traditional view would be that Oscar has privileged access, not just to the fact that some episode or other is occurring in him, but to the fact that he is thinking that water is wet. Now apparently, Davidson would just *deny* that Oscar has privileged access to the latter sort of fact, since as he says, the fact relates Oscar to objects outside his head. But if he would deny this, then Davidson's claim to be defending first person authority seems misleading at best.[2]

In contrast to Davidson, Burge clearly means to defend privileged access in its traditional guise. Given what he says in 'Individualism and Self-Knowledge' [2], Burge would maintain that the following three propositions are consistent:

(1) Oscar knows *a priori* that he is thinking that water is wet.
(2) The proposition that Oscar is thinking that water is wet necessarily depends upon E.
(3) The proposition E cannot be known *a priori*, but only by empirical investigation.

(Here I assume that E is the 'external proposition' whose presupposition makes Oscar's thought that water is wet a wide state.)

Whether (1)–(3) are consistent is determined by the sense that the phrase 'necessarily depends upon' is taken to have in (2). Unfortunately, Burge never explains or clarifies the concept of necessary dependency that he invokes throughout his paper. I will now argue that Burge is able to make his compatibility thesis appear plausible only by tacitly identifying the dependency relation with *metaphysical* necessity. But

2. It is, of course, possible that Davidson would be prepared to defend a view on which all our thoughts that fall under wide *de dicto* descriptions also fall under *other* descriptions of some important kind to which we have privileged access. Perhaps, for instance, he might be willing to say that every thought with a 'wide' content would also have another 'narrow' content to which we have privileged access. (I suggest such a 'two-content' view in my [6].) But as far as I know, Davidson nowhere spells out or defends such a view. And, of course, the mere hypothetical fact that Davidson *might* be willing to develop a view on which privileged access is compatible with anti-individualism does not by itself provide us with any *argument* in favour of this compatibility.

this identification is illegitimate in the present context, for a reason that I will explain below.

A clue to what Burge has in mind by dependency is provided by the analogy he chooses to undermine the incompatibilist's reasoning. One who reasons from the assumption that we can know our own mental states *a priori* to the conclusion that these states must be independent of any empirical propositions about physical objects is, says Burge, making the same mistake as was once made by Descartes and diagnosed by Arnaud ([2], pp. 650–1 (pp. 573–4 of this volume)).

From the fact that he could know directly and incorrigibly the existence of himself and his own thoughts, while consistently doubting the existence of his body and the rest of the physical world, Descartes inferred that it was possible for him to exist as a disembodied mind in a nonphysical universe. But this inference is illegitimate. The fact that Descartes could not correctly *deduce* the existence of the physical world from the existence of himself and his thoughts may show something significant about Descartes' *concepts* of himself and his thoughts. But as Arnaud pointed out, this failure of deduction shows nothing about the *nature* of either Descartes or his thoughts. It is perfectly consistent with this failure of deduction to suppose that both Descartes and his thoughts have an essentially physical nature, and that neither Descartes nor his thoughts could possibly have existed unless certain physical objects, including perhaps Descartes' body, Descartes' parents, and the sperm and egg cells from which Descartes developed, had also existed. For the fact, if it is a fact, that Descartes' existence is dependent upon the existence of these other physical objects would not be something that is knowable *a priori*. It would be a fact that is necessary but only knowable *a posteriori*. (As Kripke [4] pointed out.) Thus the dependency would be a fact that is not deducible *a priori* from Descartes' incorrigible knowledge of himself and his thoughts.

Since metaphysical dependencies are often only knowable *a posteriori*, propositions that are knowable *a priori* might metaphysically depend upon other propositions that are only knowable *a posteriori*. Thus Oscar might know *a priori* that he exists, and his existence might metaphysically depend upon the existence of his mother, even though Oscar cannot know *a priori* that his mother exists.

The upshot of this discussion is that (1), (2), and (3) are all clearly consistent, provided that 'depends upon' in (2) is interpreted as meaning *metaphysical* dependency. When the material conditional 'if *p* then *q*' is metaphysically necessary, let us say that *p metaphysically entails q*. Then our result so far is that (1) and (3) are consistent with

(2a) The proposition that Oscar is thinking that water is wet metaphysically entails E.

Burge's main point in defence of the compatibility of anti-individualism and privileged access, then, seems to be that such triads as (1), (2a) and (3) are consistent. In other words, his point is that our having privileged access to our own mental states is compatible with those states being metaphysically dependent upon facts to which we have no privileged access.

But this point, though correct, is quite irrelevant to the main issue. For anti-individualism is the thesis that some neutral *de dicto* cognitive attitude states are wide states, and to say that a state is wide (not narrow) cannot mean *merely* that the state metaphysically entails the existence of external objects.[3] For if it did, then given certain materialistic assumptions that are pretty widely held, it would follow that probably *all* psychological states of *any* kind would be wide, so that the concept of a narrow state would have no application at all, and anti-individualism would be merely a trivial consequence of (token) materialism.

For instance, it is plausible to suppose that no human could (metaphysically) have existed without biological parents, and that no human could (metaphysically) have had biological parents other than the ones she in fact had. (See Kripke [4], pp. 312–314.) If this is so, then Oscar's thinking that water is wet metaphysically entails that Oscar's mother exists. In fact, Oscar's having *any* psychological property (or any property at all) would metaphysically entail the existence of Oscar's mother. Thus if metaphysical entailment of external objects were what made a psychological state wide, then probably *all* of Oscar's—and everyone else's—psychological states would be wide.

But this is obviously *not* the sense of 'wide psychological state' that philosophers like Putnam and Burge have had in mind While it may well be true that Oscar's thinking that water is wet entails the existence of Oscar's mother or the existence of the egg from which Oscar developed, it would nevertheless not be for *this* kind of reason that Oscar's mental state is wide! Clearly, to say that the state in question is wide is not to say something that is true by virtue of Oscar's *nature* or the *nature* of the particular event that is Oscar's thought that water is wet. Rather it is to say something about the *concept*, or property, that is expressed by the English predicate 'x is thinking that water is wet'; it is to say something about what it *means* to say that a given person is thinking that water is wet.

Let us say that a proposition p *conceptually implies* a proposition q if and only if there is a correct deduction of q from p, a deduction whose only premisses other

3. Here I assume that, for Burge, metaphysical entailment of external objects must be a logically *sufficient* condition for a state to be wide. Perhaps it might be objected that this is unfair to Burge, since all he really needs is the assumption that metaphysical entailment of external objects is a *necessary* condition of wideness. But this objection is misconceived. Burge is trying to show that such triads as (1), (2), and (3) are consistent. His argument is that this is so because (1), (2a), and (3) are consistent. But this argument requires the assumption that (2a)—the claim concerning metaphysical entailment—is logically *sufficient* for (2)—the claim concerning wideness, or necessary dependency. For unless (2a) is sufficient for (2), the fact that (1), (2a), and (3) are consistent is quite irrelevant to the conclusion that (1), (2), and (3) are consistent. (The correct general principle for proving consistency is that, if p and q are consistent, and q logically implies r, then p and r are consistent. Note the difference between this principle and the false principle that if p and q are consistent and q is logically implied by r, then p and r are consistent: this is wrong, since r might for instance be an explicit contradiction that logically implies the consistent q.)

than *p* are necessary or conceptual truths that are knowable a priori, and each of whose steps follows from previous lines by a self-evident inference rule of some adequate system of natural deduction. I intend the relation of conceptual implication to be an appropriately *logical*, as opposed to a metaphysical, relation.

Our discussion shows, I believe, that the thesis of anti-individualism should be stated in terms of conceptual implication rather than metaphysical entailment.[4] In this connection, it is worth noting that when Putnam originally introduced the notions of narrow and wide psychological states, he did so in terms of *logical* possibility ([9], p. 141). Moreover, he introduced these notions as explicitly *Cartesian* concepts. Thus a narrow state should be (roughly) a state from which the existence of external objects cannot be *deduced*, and a wide state would be one from which the existence of external objects *can* be deduced.

On my proposal, Burge's thesis of anti-individualism should be understood as

(Ba) Some neutral cognitive states that are ascribed by *de dicto* attitude sentences (e.g., 'Oscar is thinking that water is wet') conceptually imply the existence of objects external to the person to whom the state is ascribed.

But, of course, now that we have made anti-individualism into the conceptual thesis that it should be, we also have our contradiction with privileged access back again.

For instance, (2) must now be understood as

(2b) The proposition that Oscar is thinking that water is wet conceptually implies E,

and it is easy to see that (1), (2b), and (3) form an inconsistent triad. The argument is this. Suppose (1) that Oscar knows a priori that he is thinking that water is wet. Then by (2b), Oscar can simply *deduce* E, using only premisses that are knowable a priori, including the premiss that he is thinking that water is wet. Since Oscar can deduce E from premisses that are knowable a priori, Oscar can know E itself a priori. But this contradicts (3), the assumption that E *cannot* be known a priori. Hence (1), (2b), and (3) are inconsistent. And so in general, it seems, anti-individualism is inconsistent with privileged access.

It is worth keeping the structure of this simple argument in mind, so as not to confuse it with another (bad) argument that Burge frequently alludes to in his paper [2]. Burge sometimes characterizes the person who thinks that anti-individualism is inconsistent with privileged access as reasoning on the basis of the following sort of assumption (see for instance [2], p. 653 (p. 575 of this volume)):

(4) Since the proposition that Oscar is thinking that water is wet necessarily depends upon E, no one, including Oscar, could know that Oscar is thinking that water is wet without first knowing E.

4. In McKinsey [8] I give a more thorough and detailed defence of the thesis that the concepts of narrow and wide psychological states must be understood in terms of conceptual implication rather than metaphysical necessity.

One who assumes (4) could then reason that (1), (2), and (3) are inconsistent, as follows. (2) and (4) imply that Oscar could not know that he is thinking that water is wet without first knowing E. But by (3), E is not knowable a priori. Hence, Oscar could also not know a priori that he is thinking that water is wet. But this contradicts (1). Hence, (1), (2), and (3) are inconsistent.

Burge is certainly right when he objects to this line of reasoning. The reasoning is obviously bad when necessary dependency is interpreted as metaphysical entailment. For then, one would be assuming (4) on the basis of the principle that

(5) If *p* metaphysically entails *q*, then no one could know that *p* without first knowing that *q*.

But (5) is obviously false. For instance, even if Oscar's existence metaphysically entails the existence of Oscar's mother, Oscar can surely know that he exists without first knowing that his mother does!

Even when necessary dependency is interpreted as conceptual implication, the reasoning is bad. In this case, (4) would be assumed on the basis of

(6) If *p* conceptually implies *q*, then no one could know that *p* without first knowing that *q*.

But, of course, it is a well known fact that closure principles like (6) are false: certainly with respect to any proposition *p* that can be known at all, it is possible to know *p* without first knowing each of (the infinite number of) *p*'s logical consequences.

So Burge was certainly right to object to the kind of reason he imagined one might have for believing that anti-individualism and privileged access are incompatible. But, of course, this does not show that no good reason for the incompatibility can be given. The simple argument I gave above is in fact such a good reason, and it does *not* depend on any suspicious closure principles like (5) and (6).

Rather, the argument is much more straightforward. In effect it says, look, if you could know a priori that you are in a given mental state, and your being in that state conceptually or logically implies the existence of external objects, then you could know a priori that the external world exists. Since you obviously *can't* know a priori that the external world exists, you also can't know a priori that you are in the mental state in question. It's just that simple. I myself find it hard to understand why Burge and Davidson will not just accept this obvious and compelling line of reasoning.

References

[1] Tyler Burge, 'Other Bodies', in *Thought and Object: Essays on Intentionality*, edited by A. Woodfield (Oxford: Oxford University Press, 1982).

[2] Tyler Burge, 'Individualism and Self-Knowledge', *Journal of Philosophy* 85 (1988) 649–663 (see Chapter 32 of this volume).

[3] Donald Davidson, 'Knowing One's Own Mind', *Proceedings and Addresses of the American Philosophical Association* 60 (1987) 441–458 (see Chapter 31 of this volume).
[4] Saul Kripke, *Naming and Necessity* (Oxford: Basil Blackwell, 1980).
[5] Michael McKinsey, 'Names and Intentionality', *Philosophical Review* 87 (1978) 171–200.
[6] Michael McKinsey, 'Mental Anaphora', *Synthese* 66 (1986) 159–175.
[7] Michael McKinsey, 'Apriorism in the Philosophy of Language', *Philosophical Studies* 52 (1987) 1–32.
[8] Michael McKinsey, 'The Internal Basis of Meaning', *Pacific Philosophical Quarterly* 72 (1991) 43–69.
[9] Hilary Putnam, 'The Meaning of "Meaning"', in his *Philosophical Papers* Vol. 2 (Cambridge: Cambridge University Press, 1975).

Questions

1. Could my red be your green? Could my red be your C#? Could my red be your pain-in-the-toe?
2. Wittgenstein (1953: 223): 'If a lion could talk, we could not understand him.' Why not?
3. Levin discusses the 'Molyneux Question', which was originally recounted by Locke. What exactly is the Molyneux Question, and what has it to do with Nagel's contention that you could not know what it is like to be a bat.
4. Nagel holds that it is impossible for you to know what it is like to be a bat. So? Is Nagel's problem the same problem that arises when a wife tells her husband that he cannot know what it is like to be a woman?
5. What thoughts fill Swampman's mind moments after he comes into existence?
6. Why exactly might externalism about mental content be thought to generate special problems for 'self-knowledge'? And what is 'self-knowledge' anyway?
7. How might an externalist accommodate our sense that we know what we think immediately and unproblematically? Could externalists accept the idea that beliefs about your own states of mind are *incorrigible* (incapable of being wrong). *Need* they?
8. McKinsey contends that we know what we think a priori. Is he right? In thinking about this question, you will need to consider more basic questions: what *is* a-priori knowledge? What are some examples of truths knowable a priori?
9. How might an externalist respond to McKinsey's contention that, in so far as externalism allows that we have a kind of direct awareness of what we think, externalism implies that we could know truths about the 'external world' a priori?
10. Suppose externalism does imply that we can know truths about the 'external world' a priori. Why should anyone think this is a bad thing?

Suggested reading

Farrell (1950) is an important predecessor (complete with bat) to Nagel's much-discussed defense of the importance of the 'what-it's-like-ness' of experience Chapter 29. Interesting discussions of the line of argument to which Ferrell and Nagel appeal can be found in Akins (1993); Baker (1998); Lewis (1983: 130–2); Lycan (1990); Malcolm (1988), Mellor (1993); Nemirow (1980), Teller (1992), and van Gulick (1985). Searle (1992: chap. 5) discusses the ontology of subjectivity. Chalmers's (2001) entry for 'Subjectivity and Objectivity' in his on-line bibliography contains many more references. See also Mandik (2001) for an on-line discussion.

The problem of 'self-knowledge'—the problem of accommodating the kind of 'direct', 'privileged' access we have to our own states of mind and externalism, the view that the 'contents' of states of mind are fixed by factors external to the agent–has produced a torrent of articles and books. At least five collections of papers on the topic have been published since 1994: Cassam (1994), Gertler (2003), Ludlow and Martin (1998), Nuccetelli (2003), and Wright et al. (1998). Book-length treatments include Bermúdez (1998), Cassam (1997), and Moran (2001). Heil (1988) comprises one early attempt to show that tension between externalism and self-knowledge is only apparent.

Bar-On and Long (2001), Boghossian (1997), Brown (1995), Dretske (1999), Gertler (2000), Gibbons (1996), and Tye and McLaughlin (1998) address various aspects of the self-knowledge problem, from various perspectives, and with varying degrees of reliance on dizzying technical maneuvers. McKinsey (1993, 1994) discusses the viability of the externalist programme in the light of the self-knowledge problem. Gertler's (2002) entry on self-knowledge in the on-line *Stanford Encyclopedia of Philosophy* contains a good discussion and a substantial bibliography.

Subjectivity of experience

Akins, K. A. (1993), 'What is it Like to Be Boring and Myopic?' In Dahlbom 1993: 124–60.

Baker, L. R. (1998), 'The First-Person Perspective: A Test for Naturalism'. *American Philosophical Quarterly* 35: 327–48.

Beckermann, A., H. Flohr, and J. Kim, eds. (1992), *Emergence or Reduction? Essays on the Prospects of Nonreductive Physicalism.* Berlin: De Gruyter.

Chalmers, D. J. (2001), *Contemporary Philosophy of Mind: An Annotated Bibliography* <http://www.u.arizona.edu/~chalmers/biblio.html> Tucson, AZ: University of Arizona.

Dahlbom, B., ed. (1993), *Dennett and his Critics: Demystifying the Mind.* Oxford: Basil Blackwell.

Farrell, B. A. (1950), 'Experience', *Mind* 59: 170–98.

Lewis, D. K. (1983), *Philosophical Papers*, vol. i. New York: Oxford University Press.

Lycan, W. G. (1990), 'What is the "Subjectivity" of the Mental?', *Philosophical Perspectives* 4: 109–30.

Malcolm, N. (1988), 'Subjectivity', *Philosophy* 63: 147–60.

Mandik, P. (2001), 'Subjectivity and Objectivity'. In Nani (2001): <http://host.uniroma3.it/progetti/kant/field/suob.htm>.

Mellor, D. H. (1993), 'Nothing Like Experience'. *Proceedings of the Aristotelian Society* 63: 1–16.

Nani, M., ed. (2001), *A Field Guide to the Philosophy of Mind.* <http://host.uniroma3.it/progetti/kant/field/> Rome: University of Rome 3.

Nemirow, L. (1980), Review of T. Nagel, *Mortal Questions, Philosophical Review* 89: 473–7.

Searle, J. R. (1992), *The Rediscovery of the Mind.* Cambridge, MA: MIT Press.

Teller, P. (1992), 'Subjectivity and Knowing What It's Like'. In Beckermann et al. 1992: 80–200.

van Gulick, R. (1985), 'Physicalism and the Subjectivity of the Mental'. *Philosophical Topics* 13: 51–70.

Self-knowledge

Bar-On, D., and D. Long (2001), 'Avowals and First-Person Privilege'. *Philosophy and Phenomenological Research* 62: 311–35.

Bermúdez, J. L. (1998), *The Paradox of Self-Consciousness.* Cambridge, MA: MIT Press.

Boghossian, P. (1997), 'What the Externalist Can Know *A Priori*', *Proceedings of the Aristotelian Society* 97: 161–75.

Brown, J. (1995) 'The Incompatibility of Individualism and Privileged Access', *Analysis* 55: 149–56.

Brueckner, A. (1992), 'Semantic Answers to Skepticism'. *Pacific Philosophical Quarterly* 73: 200–219.

Cassam, Q., ed. (1994), *Self-Knowledge*, New York: Oxford University Press.

——(1997), *Self and World*, Oxford: Clarendon Press.

Dretske, F. I. (1999), 'The Mind's Awareness of Itself', *Philosophical Studies* 95: 103–24.

Gertler, B. (2000), 'The Mechanics of Self-Knowledge', *Philosophical Topics* 28: 125–46.

——(2002), 'Self-Knowledge'. In Zalta 2002: <http://plato.stanford.edu/entries/self-knowledge/>.

——ed. (2003), *Privileged Access: Philosophical Accounts of Self-Knowledge.* Aldershot: Ashgate Publishing.

Gibbons, J. (1996), 'Externalism and Knowledge of Content', *Philosophical Review* 105: 287–310.

Heil, J. (1988), 'Privileged Access', *Mind* 97: 238–51.

Ludlow, P., and N. Martin, eds. (1998), *Externalism and Self-Knowledge.* Stanford, CA: CSLI Publications.

McKinsey, M. (1993), 'Curing Folk Psychology of Arthritis', *Philosophical Studies* 70: 323–36.

——(1994), 'Individuating Beliefs'. *Philosophical Perspectives* 8: 303–30.

Moran, R. (2001), *Authority and Estrangement: An Essay on Self-Knowledge.* Princeton: Princeton University Press.

Nuccetelli, S., ed. (2003), *New Essays on Semantic Externalism and Self-Knowledge.* Cambridge, MA: MIT Press.

Tye, M., and B. P. McLaughlin (1998), 'Externalism, Twin Earth, and Self-Knowledge'. In Wright et al. 1998: 285–320.

Wright, C., B. C. Smith, and C. Macdonald, eds. (1998), *Knowing Our Own Minds.* Oxford: Clarendon Press.

Zalta, E. N., ed. (2002), *The Stanford Encyclopedia of Philosophy*. <http://plato.stanford.edu/> Stanford, CA: Metaphysics Research Lab, Center for the Study of Language and Information.

Part IX

Consciousness

Introduction

CONSCIOUSNESS: the Final Frontier. Or so it has seemed to prominent researchers investigating conscious experience. David Chalmers (whom you will encounter in Chapter 35 below) calls the problem of finding a place for consciousness in the natural world the Hard Problem. Others, sensing that physics may be on the verge of the Grand Unified Theory, hold that we have solved all the outward-looking problems and we are left with the last remaining problem, the nature of the outward-looker.

To find a problem here, you must first distinguish sentient creatures as biological beings from sentient creatures as *sentient*. By looking closely at the biological mechanisms animating such creatures, we have attained an impressive grasp of what makes them tick. In cases in which we lack a completed account (the navigational mechanisms of birds, for instance, or object recognition in perceptually sophisticated creatures), we have at least an idea of how the pertinent mechanisms might operate. When it comes to consciousness, however, we seem to hit a wall. We can isolate mechanisms 'responsible' for conscious experiences, and perhaps even work out how changes in the former yield changes in the latter. What we seem not able to get at is why the mechanisms in question should underlie *conscious* episodes, and how characteristics of these episodes are related to their material grounds.

In putting the point this way, I do not mean to be begging the question against dualistic conceptions of consciousness (see Chapter 3 and readings in Part XII). I am merely formulating the problem as it is formulated by many prominent and influential researchers, most of whom start with a presumption that materialism is true. This turns the problem of consciousness into the problem of fitting consciousness into the material world. The idea, defended by Smart (Chapter 8), could be put in the form of a precept: seek materialistic accounts of phenomena. This turns dualism into a second choice, a choice to be avoided if possible. If forced to take dualism seriously, a philosopher of this temperament will prefer a dualism of properties to a dualism of substances: mental properties might be irreducible properties of material substances. Often these properties are taken to depend on various physical properties, as in theories that speak of mental properties being 'grounded in' a physical 'substrate' (as perhaps captured in Figures III.1 and III.2). This is a way for materialists to save face, but, as we noted in Part III and will discover in readings in this and subsequent parts, it comes at a significant cost.

Qualities of conscious experiences

Conscious experiences possess a qualitative character that apparently differs in kind from anything inside (or, for that matter, outside) the nervous system. Conscious experiences have distinctive qualitative 'feels'. You know what it is like to bark your shin or taste Vegemite. This, however, is not something that could be 'read off' your physiology by an anatomist observing what goes on in your nervous system when you bark your shin or bite into a Vegemite sandwich (a point driven home in Chapter 43). Of course, anatomists might work out detailed *correlations* between experienced qualities and physiological goings-on, and, on that basis, be in a position to infer what you are experiencing by observing goings-on in your nervous system. The tricky bit concerns our making sense of these correlations. To some, this 'explanatory gap' (noted by Locke in a passage quoted in the introduction to Part VIII and examined at length in Part XI) poses a baffling, possibly unfathomable mystery. To others, the divide between conscious qualities and features of the natural world is an artifact, bred by errors in philosophical reasoning.

One such error (what U. T. Place called the 'phenomenological fallacy'; see Part II, Introduction, for discussion) is to confuse properties of objects perceived with properties of perceptual states. Imagine watching a fireworks display from the deck of a yacht anchored in Sydney Harbor. You experience something loud, sparkling, multicolored. Suppose that, while this is going on, your brain is being scanned with sophisticated monitoring equipment that provides a fine-grained look at what occurs inside you as you experience the fireworks. A scientist might be in a position to 'locate' your various visual and auditory experiences in particular neurological centers. Note, however, that nothing the scientist observes is remotely like your experiences. Your experiences are of loud and multicolored objects and goings-on, but nothing in your brain is loud or multicolored (or at least not multicolored in a way resembling what you are experiencing).

Does this show that your experiences could not be identical with—could not *be*—those neurological occurrences? Before answering that question, take a step back and try to distinguish properties of your experience from properties of objects and goings-on you are experiencing. The fireworks are loud, for instance, but is your *experience* of the fireworks loud? The fireworks are sparkling and multicolored. Is your *experience* sparkling and multicolored? If you are inclined to answer no to these questions, the way might be open to identify your experiences with goings-on in your brain.

One possibility, then, is that mysterious properties we associate with conscious experiences are in fact just properties of the objects and goings-on we experience or, more cautiously, properties we represent those objects and goings-on as having. If you expected to find *these* properties in the brain and did not find them there, you might be mystified. If they are not in the brain, they must be somewhere else—in the mind—or maybe they are brain properties, all right, just nonphysical (hence unobservable-from-the-outside) brain properties. Now we have a mystery on our hands.

Suppose you took the suggestion above and embraced the idea that what we regard as qualities of conscious experiences are in fact just qualities we represent observed objects and events as having. You can represent a ball's being spherical and red without your representation's partaking of sphericity or redness. (I just did!) Perhaps consciousness could be understood as a kind of representing. Conscious qualities are those we representationally ascribe to objects and events—including objects and events inside us. You could push this as far as you liked. Do conscious experiences themselves have qualities? Suppose you are representing a ball to be red and spherical; you might represent this representing as having various qualities.

Once you get the idea, you can see that a view of this kind promises to cut through the hype about inexplicable qualities of conscious experiences. Consciousness seemed mysterious only because we were assuming that properties things are represented as having are properties of conscious experiences themselves. This would be like finding it mysterious that a painting could be of a ball when sphericity was not among the properties we find when we take an inventory of the painting's physical properties. In both cases, the mystery stems from a confusion.

How satisfying is this approach to conscious qualities? Is talk about the uniqueness of qualities of conscious experience just (or largely) hype? This is something you will need to decide for yourself as you go though the readings in this part. You may develop a certain sympathy for *both* positions. If that is so, a word of warning. The old saw that 'the truth lies somewhere in the middle', more often than not dead wrong, appears especially inappropriate here. It is hard to see how you could arrive at a middle ground between the position that qualities of conscious experiences are *sui generis*—unique—and the idea that the putatively inscrutable qualities are just qualities ordinary things are represented as having.

Two senses of 'conscious'

To sharpen the debate, it would be useful to distinguish, as David Chalmers (see Chalmers 1996: chap. 1 and Chapter 35 below) does, between two conceptions or ways of thinking about consciousness. On the one hand, we think of conscious creatures as alert, active, and cognitively engaged with their surroundings. A conscious creature initiates actions aimed at achieving definite ends and reacts adaptively to goings-on in its vicinity. Conscious creatures are *sapient*. On the other hand, you may think of consciousness as pertaining to assorted *sensory* states. A conscious creature senses and feels. Conscious creatures are *sentient*. (Sentience and sapience are traditional terms roughly equivalent to what Chalmers calls 'phenomenal' and 'psychological' consciousness.)

Chalmers points out that psychology and neuroscience have made significant progress toward increasing our understanding of sapience—psychological consciousness. There is still much we do not understand, but we can at least see what a more complete explanation of sapience might look like. In contrast, we seem to have made little or no progress in understanding sentience. What understanding we do have consists mainly in the discovery of brute correlations between conscious episodes and neurological events. The identification of correlations represents at most a starting point for explanation, however, not a settled goal. Unlike the case of sapience, where it is reasonable to expect incremental progress, it is hard to see what we could do to move ahead in our understanding of the basis of consciousness. Would more powerful scanning equipment or the development of new experimental techniques promise to illuminate the nature of sentience? This would be merely more of the same. We are in the position of an ancient people endeavoring to build a tower tall enough to reach the moon: we accomplish something, but not anything that carries us any appreciable distance toward our goal. Taller towers, even much taller towers, are not the answer.

This, at any rate, is how Chalmers sees it. Not all philosophers and neuroscientists would agree. Some hold out hope that sentience is reducible to sapience: all there is to being conscious is acting and interacting intelligently in a complex environment (see e.g. Dennett 1991). Acting thus *is* to be conscious. What of feelings and other sensuous states? These are species of sapient state. Functionalists, for instance, might hold that, to be in pain is to be in a state with the right sorts of cause and effect. Pains are caused by tissue damage and result in aversive behavior (including the formation of various beliefs and desires). Attempts to reduce properties of conscious experiences to properties we represent objects and events as having fit nicely into this functionalist picture.

Qualia

You cannot read philosophical discussions of consciousness without tripping over references to *qualia*. *Qualia* are qualities of conscious experiences, sensuous qualities (Part VII, Introduction), what in the 1950s were called 'raw feels'. I have thus far refrained from mention of *qualia*. (Incidentally, *qualia* is plural; the singular form is *quale*.) Philosophical terminology can obscure as well as illuminate. Arguably, talk of *qualia* contributes to the kinds of confusion that have traditionally plagued philosophical discussions of consciousness.

Materialist philosophers like to think of the physical world as a causal nexus. Physical properties are those that figure in causal laws. At a deep level, perhaps, this is *all there is* to the physical world. What of objects' qualitative dimension? The qualities, we are told, are mind dependent. Objects affect us thereby giving rise in us to qualitative experiences. But the physical objects themselves lack qualities. Some philosophers find support for this picture in physics. Physics comprehends the particles in terms of their affects (or capacities for effects) on other particles. No mention is made of particles' qualities.

This shunning of qualities has a long history. In the seventeenth century, for instance, philosophers and scientists (these were not yet distinct groups) distinguished primary and secondary qualities of objects. The primary qualities were thought to include shape, size, bulk, motion, and the like. Secondary qualities—colors, sounds, tastes, smells, feels—were nothing more than capacities of objects to produce experiences of particular sorts in us. The idea is promoted by Galileo and Descartes, and, later, by Locke, but it was, and remains, a common presumption of the physical sciences. One repercussion of all this is the bifurcation of the world into a mind-independent physical domain comprising wholly quantitative magnitudes and a mind-dependent mental domain housing the qualities.

Berkeley and Hume objected that a wholly non-qualitative domain was incoherent. Every quantity stands in need of something qualitative to serve as a bearer of the quantity. (Berkeley turned this point into a defense of idealism: if quantities depend on qualities, and qualities exist only in minds, then quantities must exist only in minds as well!) The argument has been rediscovered by successive generations of philosophers, but the fundamental idea is that a world consisting of objects altogether lacking qualities is indistinguishable from a world consisting of empty space (Armstrong 1961: chap. 15; see also Campbell 1976: 93–4).

Here is one way to get a feel for what the issues are here. Imagine a row of dominos lined up so that, when the first domino is pushed it topples the second, which topples the third, which topples . . . Now subtract all of the dominos' qualities. What is left? When you push the first domino, what do you push? You might say that you push something with a particular size, shape, location, and mass. But a region of empty space could have that size, shape, and location. What distinguishes a domino from such a region? Perhaps its mass. But what is mass but a capacity to affect other masses in a particular way. If all there is to those other masses is a capacity to affect other capacities to affect other capacities to affect other capacities . . . it is hard to see how anything is affected, how anything could happen! Maybe Berkeley was right: the material world is nothing more than an empty abstraction.

Another, decidedly non-Berkeleyan, possibility is that the material world is itself a qualitative world. We are tempted to deny this because physics makes no mention of qualities in describing and explaining material goings-on. But failing to mention qualities does not amount to a denial of their existence. Suppose that material bodies have qualities. In that case it would be importantly misleading to regard minds as being special *solely* on the grounds that their states are qualitative. If mental qualities are special it is not because they are *qualities*, but because mental qualities differ in some fundamental way from non-mental qualities.

Pretend for a moment that this is right: mental and material phenomena alike are qualitative. What distinguishes mental qualities—qualities of conscious experiences—from non-mental qualities? In answering this question you need to be on guard against succumbing to the phenomenological fallacy: do not mistake qualities of objects experienced for qualities of experiences of those objects. Your visual experience of a cloud is the experience of something white and fluffy, but your experience is not white and fluffy. If the representationalists are right, all of the dramatic qualities of conscious experiences are really qualities we represent material phenomena to possess (Chapters 34, 36, 37). This could not mean that experiences themselves lack qualities, however—not if everything possesses qualities. The representationalists are betting that the intrinsic qualities of experiences are nothing special. Indeed, qualities of experiences might turn out just to be perfectly respectable qualities of goings-on inside the heads of sentient creatures.

(Some especially hard-nosed representationalists may in fact doubt that anything has qualities. Qualities are merely characteristics we falsely represent objects as possessing. Because, for reasons mentioned above, it is difficult to make sense of such a view, I shall not take it up here.)

As you read the selections that follow, you should ask yourself about the qualities of conscious experiences: the intrinsic qualities of the experiences themselves, not qualities of experienced objects and events. What are these qualities? Do they differ fundamentally from qualities of brains? If you are like most people (that is, untainted by commitment to a philosophical account of consciousness), you will find such questions difficult to assess. In that case, however, you might want to pause a moment before accepting outright the notion that the gap between mental and material properties is patently unbridgeable. If the gap is as large as some theorists insist, then it should be obvious what the mental qualities are and how they differ from material qualities. To the extent that the contrast is less than obvious, you should remain skeptical about arguments that begin by assuming it and proceed to draw startling conclusions.

A metaphysical thesis

Once the topic of mental qualities is broached, a metaphysical chasm opens before us. We can run for cover or leap and hope for the best. I say we leap.

Suppose the world includes objects, and objects possess properties. You can think of a property as a way an object is. What the properties are is an empirical question, one to be addressed by means of scientific investigation. (I leave open the question whether properties are universals or particulars.) What are the objects? That, too, is an empirical matter. The objects might be particles (electrons and quarks, for instance) or they might be fields. There might be just one all-encompassing object: the quantum field, or space, or space-time. (Note that if there is just one object, then what we ordinarily think of as objects—trees, mountains, electrons, stars—would in reality be ways the one object is, which is to say: these 'objects' would turn out to be properties!)

Now what is the nature of a property? Philosophers sometimes use 'property' to stand for whatever answers to a general term. On such a view, a property corresponds to every predicate that applies truly to the world. If it is true that this ball is green, then there is a property, being green, corresponding to the predicate 'is green'. If it is true that Cassandra is a Libertarian, then there is a property, *being a Libertarian*, possessed by Cassandra and corresponding to the predicate 'is a Libertarian'. If we are to take properties seriously, however, this will never do. We must distinguish the truism that terms (predicates) apply to objects in virtue of properties possessed by those objects', from the very different idea that whenever a term (predicate) applies to an object it does so by virtue of that object's possessing a property possessed by *every object* to which the term truly applies. This stringent condition is satisfied only very rarely, and only in cases in which there is a one-one correspondence between terms and properties.

The last point is easily illustrated by means of an example from Wittgenstein (1953: §66–7). Consider the predicate 'is a game'. This predicate applies to many different kinds of activity: board games, team games, patience, games like skipping rope, with no winning or losing, games of pretense. Do all these activities have some one feature in common, a feature in virtue of which we are correct to call them games? That seems unlikely. Rather games are *similar*; they exhibit what Wittgenstein called *family resemblances*. *A* might be similar to *B*, *B* to *C*, *C* to *D*, but *A* and *D* might be not at all similar. You could say the same for a predicate like 'is red'. Many objects (and non-objects: think of a red light or the sky at sunset) satisfy this predicate. They do so, not in virtue of sharing a single property, but in virtue of possessing any of a family of *similar* properties (think of these as the 'shades' of red). Many philosophers would regard this as heresy, but that need not detain us in our plunge.

Here is the emerging picture. There are certain basic properties—perhaps those sought by particle physicists. Familiar, medium-sized objects possess complex properties made up of the properties of their constituents appropriately arranged. These properties can be similar across instances. The colors of two white sheets of paper stacked in a photocopier are not *perfectly* similar, perhaps, but they are similar enough to count as being *the same* color. Can we say more about the nature of these properties? In the first place, it is in virtue of possessing the properties it does than an object behaves as it does. A ball rolls (or would roll) because it is spherical, it looks (or would look) red because it reflects (would reflect) light in a particular way. This suggests that properties are, whatever else they are, 'powers' (or, as it is sometimes put, 'bestowers of powers'; see Shoemaker 1980).

This fits well with the idea that the job of empirical science is to discover the fundamental properties and the thought, mentioned earlier, that these fundamental properties are what affect objects' propensities to behave as they do. In our earlier discussion we noted that it would be hard to see how this could be all there is to objects, however. This led to the speculation that material bodies, no less than conscious states, must possess qualities. What of these qualities? Are some properties, perhaps, powers, others qualitative? A *purely* qualitative property would be undetectable, hence unobservable! This is a consequence of its lacking the power to affect anything—other objects, for instance, or electronic sensors, or our perceptual faculties. But an undetectable property incapable of affecting anything at all is going to be hard to swallow philosophically.

What to do? A world of 'pure powers' looks like a non-starter. A world of pure powers supplemented by wholly inefficacious qualities is scarcely an improvement. Here is a possibility. Suppose the basic properties were *both* qualities and powers. This is not the idea that properties have two components, two 'sides', or two 'aspects'. This is the thesis that fundamental intrinsic properties are at once qualities and powers: *powerful qualities*. Pretend, for a moment, what is surely false, that sphericity is a fundamental property. Then, in virtue of being spherical, a ball has a certain quality—the familiar quality of sphericity—*and* a certain power. We can consider sphericity as a quality or as a power in the way you could consider a drawing as a duck or as a rabbit (Wittgenstein 1953: 194; see Figure IX.1). This is what Locke called 'abstraction' or 'partial consideration'.

Figure IX.1

Ontological candor

The upshot is a conception of properties as powerful qualities. Now, the question is how such a view of properties bears on conscious experiences. Suppose materialism is true and your conscious experiences are goings-on in your brain. These goings-on, like goings-on generally, will have a distinctive qualitative character. Is this something a scientist examining your brain could see? Well, the scientist, in observing your brain, will be having various visual experiences. We are pretending for the moment that materialism is true, so some of these experiences will be experiences of your experiences. But now ask yourself why anyone should think that the scientist's experience of your experience must resemble your experience qualitatively. If experiences of experiences of sunsets need not resemble experiences of sunsets, then no one should be surprised at not finding miniature sunsets in the brains of agents experiencing sunsets.

None of this provides anything like a knock-down proof for a materialist conception of consciousness, but it does place to the side potentially distracting considerations. In evaluating arguments by authors of selections in this part and those that follow, you should ask yourself whether assumptions about these issues are coloring particular authors' results. Do their conclusions depend on premises that ought really to be defended? These matters call for what the Australians describe as 'ontological candor', a willingness to lay one's metaphysical cards on the table. Ontological candor, as you will see, is sometimes in short supply in contemporary philosophy of mind.

References

Armstrong, D. M. (1961), *Perception and the Physical World*. London: Routledge & Kegan Paul.

Campbell, K. (1976), *Metaphysics: An Introduction*. Encino: Dickenson Publishing Co.

Chalmers, D. J. (1996), *The Conscious Mind: In Search of a Fundamental Theory*. New York: Oxford University Press.

Dennett, D. C. (1991), *Consciousness Explained*. Boston: Little, Brown.

Shoemaker, S. (1980), 'Causality and Properties', in Peter van Inwagen, ed., *Time and Cause*, Dordrecht: Reidel Publishing Co.: 109—35.

Wittgenstein, L. (1953/1968), *Philosophical Investigations*, trans. G. E. M. Anscombe, Oxford: Basil Blackwell.

Chapter 34

What is consciousness?

D. M. Armstrong

THE notion of consciousness is notoriously obscure. It is difficult to analyze, and some philosophers and others have thought it unanalysable. It is not even clear that the word 'consciousness' stands for just one sort of entity, quality, process, or whatever. There is, however, one thesis about consciousness that I believe can be confidently rejected: Descartes' doctrine that consciousness is the essence of mentality. That view assumes that we can explain mentality in terms of consciousness. I think that the truth is in fact the other way round. Indeed, in the most interesting sense of the word 'consciousness', consciousness is the cream on the cake of mentality, a special and sophisticated development of mentality. It is not the cake itself. In what follows, I develop an anti-Cartesian account of consciousness.

Minimal consciousness

In thinking about consciousness, it is helpful to begin at the other end and consider a totally unconscious person. Somebody in a sound, dreamless sleep may be taken as an example. It has been disputed whether unconsciousness is really ever total. There is some empirical evidence that a person in dreamless sleep, or even under a total anaesthetic, still has some minimal awareness. Minimal behavioural reactions to sensory stimuli have been observed under these conditions. But let us take it, if only as a simplifying and perhaps unrealistic assumption, that we are dealing with *total* unconsciousness.

Notice first that we are perfectly happy to concede that such a person, while in this state of total unconsciousness, has a *mind*. Furthermore, although by hypothesis this mind is in no way active—no mental events take place, no mental processes occur within it—we freely allow that this mind is in various *states*.

The totally unconscious person does not lack knowledge and beliefs. Suppose him to be a historian of the mediaeval period. We will not deny him a great deal of knowledge of and beliefs about the Middle Ages just because he is sound asleep. He cannot give current expression to his knowledge and his beliefs, but he does not lack them. The totally unconscious person also may be credited with memories. He also can be said to have skills, including purely mental skills such as an ability for

D. M. Armstrong, 'What is Consciousness?' In *The Nature of Mind* (Ithaca, NY: Cornell University Press, 1981).

mental arithmetic. The ability is not lost during sound sleep just because it then cannot be exercised, any more than an athlete loses his athletic abilities during sound sleep, when he cannot exercise them. A totally unconscious person may be credited with likes and dislikes, attitudes and emotions, current desires and current aims and purposes. He may be said to have certain traits of character and temperament. He may be said to be in certain moods: 'He has been depressed all this week.'

How are we to conceive of these mental states (it seems natural to call them 'states') we attribute to the unconscious person? Some decades ago, under the influence of positivistic and phenomentalistic modes of thought, such attributions of mental states to an unconscious person would not have been taken very seriously, ontologically. It would have been thought that to say that the currently unconscious person *A* believes that *p*, is simply to refer to various ways in which *A*'s mind works, or would work in suitable circumstances, before and/or after he wakes up. (The same positivist spirit might try further to reduce the way that *A*'s mind works to *A*'s peripheral bodily behaviour or to the behaviour *A* would exhibit in suitable circumstances.)

In historical perspective, we can see clearly how unsatisfactory such a view is. Consider two persons, *A* and *B*, unconscious at the same time, where it is true of *A* that he believes that *p*, but false of *B*. Must there not be a difference between *A* and *B* at that time to constitute this difference in belief-state? What else in the world could act as a truth-maker (the ground in the world) for the different conditional statements that are true of *A* and *B*? The mind of the unconscious person cannot be dissolved into statements about what would be true of the person *if* the situation were other than it was; if, in particular, he were not unconscious.

In considering this point, I find very helpful the analogy between an unconscious person and a computer that has been programmed in various ways, that perhaps has partially worked through certain routines and is ready to continue with them, but is not currently operating. (I do not think that anything in the analogy turns on the material, physical nature of the computer. Even if the mind has to be conceived of in some immaterial way, the analogy will still hold.) The computer, perhaps, will have a certain amount of information stored in its memory-banks. This stored information may be compared to the knowledge, belief and memories the unconscious person still has during unconsciousness. If a Materialist account of the mind is correct, then, of course, knowledge, belief and memory will be physically encoded in the brain in some broadly similar way to the way in which information is stored in the computer. But the Dualist, say, will equally require the conception of immaterial storage of knowledge, belief and memory.

What we can say both of the knowledge, beliefs, etc. possessed by the totally unconscious person, and also of the information stored in the switched-off computer, is that they are *causally quiescent*. Of course, nothing is causally quiescent absolutely: while a thing exists, it has effects upon its environment. But the information stored in the switched-off computer is causally quiescent with respect to the computing operations of the computer, and for our purposes this may be called causal quiescence. (The information may remain causally quiescent even after the computer has been switched on, unless that piece of information is required for current calculations.) In the same way, knowledge and beliefs may be said to be causally quiescent while they are not producing any *mental* effect in the person. The mental states of a totally unconscious person are thus causally quiescent (if they are not, we may stipulate that the person is not totally unconscious). Knowledge, beliefs, and so on may remain causally quiescent in this sense even when the mind is operational, for instance, where there is no call to use a particular piece of knowledge.

It seems, then, that we attribute mental states of various sorts to a totally unconscious person. But there are certain mental attributions we do not make. The totally unconscious person does not perceive, has no sensations, feelings or pangs of desire. He cannot think, contemplate or engage in any sort of deliberation. (He can have purposes, because purposes are capable of causal quiescence, but he cannot be engaged in carrying them out.) This is because perception, sensation and thinking are mental *activities* in a way that knowledge and beliefs are not. The distinction appears, roughly at any rate, to be the distinction between events and occurrences on the one hand, and states on the other. When a mental state is producing mental effects, the comings-to-be of such effects are mental events: and so mental activity is involved.

We now have a first sense for the word 'consciousness'. If there is mental activity occurring in the mind, if something mental is actually happening, then that mind is not totally unconscious. It is therefore conscious. A single faint sensation is not much, but if it occurs, to that extent there is consciousness. Unconsciousness is not total. I call consciousness in this sense 'minimal' consciousness.

It is alleged that it sometimes occurs that someone wakes up knowing the solution to, say, a mathematical problem, which they did not know when they went to sleep. If we rule out magical explanations, then there must have been mental activity during sleep. To that extent, there was minimal consciousness. This is compatible with the completest 'unconsciousness' in a sense still to be identified.

Perceptual consciousness

Among the mental activities, however, it appears that we make a special link between consciousness and *perception*. In perception, there is consciousness of what is currently going on in one's environment and in one's body. (Of course, the consciousness may involve illusion.) There is an important sense in which, if a person is not perceiving, then he is not conscious, but if he is perceiving, then he is conscious. Suppose somebody to be dreaming. Since there is mental activity going on, the person is not totally unconscious. He is minimally conscious. Yet is there not some obvious sense in which he is unconscious? Now suppose that this person starts to perceive his environment and bodily state. (I do not want to say 'suppose he wakes up', because perhaps there is more to waking up than just starting to perceive again.) I think that we would be inclined to say that the person was now conscious in a way that he had not been before, while merely dreaming. Let us say, therefore, that he has regained 'perceptual' consciousness. This is a second sense of the word 'consciousness'. Perceptual consciousness entails minimal consciousness, but minimal consciousness does not entail perceptual consciousness.

Introspective consciousness

Let us suppose, now, that there is mental activity going on in a person, and that this activity includes perception. If what has been said so far is accepted, then there are two senses in which such a person can be said to be conscious. He or she has *minimal* consciousness and has *perceptual* consciousness. There is, nevertheless, a third sense, in which such a person may *still* 'lack consciousness'. Various cases may be mentioned here. My own favourite is the case of the long-distance truck-driver. It has the advantage that many people have experienced the phenomenon.

After driving for long periods of time, particularly at night, it is possible to 'come to' and realize that for some time past one has been driving without being aware of what one has been doing. The coming-to is an alarming experience. It is natural to describe what went on before one came to by saying that during that time one lacked consciousness. Yet it seems clear that, in the two senses of the word that we have so far isolated, consciousness was present. There was mental activity, and as part of that mental activity, there was perception. That is to say, there was minimal consciousness and perceptual consciousness. If there is an inclination to doubt this, then consider the extraordinary sophistication of the activities successfully undertaken during the period of 'unconsciousness'.

A purpose was successfully advanced during that time: that of driving a car along a road. This purpose demanded that various complex sub-routines be carried out, and carried out at appropriate points (for instance, perhaps the brake or the clutch was used). Were not these acts purposeful? Above all, how is it possible to drive a car for kilometres along a road if one cannot perceive that road? One must be able to see where one is going, in order to adjust appropriately. It would have to be admitted, at the very least, that in such a case, eyes and brain have to be stimulated in just the same way as they are in ordinary cases of perception. Why then deny that perception takes place? So it seems that minimal consciousness and perceptual consciousness are present. But something else is lacking: consciousness in the most interesting sense of the word.

The case of the long-distance truck-driver appears to be a very special and spectacular one. In fact, however, I think it presents us with what is a relatively simple, and in evolutionary terms relatively primitive, level of mental functioning. Here we have more or less skilled purposive action, guided by perception, but apparently no other mental activity, and in particular no consciousness in some sense of 'consciousness', which differs from minimal and perceptual consciousness. It is natural to surmise that such relatively simple sorts of mental functioning came early in the course of evolutionary development. I imagine that many animals, particularly those whose central nervous system is less developed than ours, are continually, or at least normally, in the state in which the long-distance truck-driver is in temporarily. The third sort of consciousness, I surmise, is a late evolutionary development.

What is it that the long-distance truck-driver lacks? I think it is an additional form of perception, or, a little more cautiously, it is something that resembles perception. But unlike *sense*-perception, it is not directed towards our current environment and/or our current bodily state. It is perception of the mental. Such 'inner' perception is traditionally called introspection, or introspective awareness. We may therefore call this third sort of consciousness 'introspective' consciousness. It entails minimal consciousness. If perceptual consciousness is restricted to sense-perception, then introspective consciousness does not entail perceptual consciousness.

Introspective consciousness, then, is a perception-like awareness of current states and activities in our own mind. The current activities will include sense-perception: which latter is the awareness of current states and activities of our environment and our body. And (an important and interesting complication) since introspection is itself a mental activity, it too may become the object of introspective awareness.

Sense-perception is not a *total* awareness of the current states and activities of our environment and body. In the same way, introspective consciousness is not a total awareness of the current states and activities of our mind. At any time there will be states and activities of our mind of which we are not introspectively aware. These states and activities may be said to be unconscious mental states and activities in one good sense of the word 'unconscious'. (It is close to the Freudian sense, but there is no need to maintain that it always involves the mechanism of repression.) Such unconscious mental states and activities of course may involve minimal and/or perceptual consciousness, indeed the *activities* involve minimal consciousness by definition.

Just as perception is selective—not all-embracing—so it also may be mistaken. Perceptions may fail to correspond, more or less radically, to reality. In the same way, introspective consciousness may fail to correspond, more or less radically, to the mental reality of which it is a consciousness. (The indubitability of consciousness is a Cartesian myth, which has been an enemy of progress in philosophy and psychology.)

Following Locke, Kant spoke of introspection as 'inner sense', and it is essentially Kant's view I am defending here. By 'outer sense', Kant understood sense-perception. There is, however, one particular form of 'outer sense' that bears a particularly close formal resemblance to introspection. This is bodily perception or *proprioception*, the perception of our own current bodily states and activities. If we consider the objects of sight, sound, touch, taste and smell, then we notice that such objects are intersubjectively available. Each of us is capable of seeing or touching numerically the very same physical surface, hearing numerically the very same sound, tasting numerically the same tastes or smelling numerically the same smell. But the objects of proprioception are not intersubjectively available in this way.

Consider, for instance, kinaesthetic perception, which is one mode of proprioception. Each person kinaesthetically perceives (or, in some unusual cases, misperceives) the motion of his own limbs and those of nobody else. There is no overlap of kinaesthetic objects. This serves as a good model for, and at the same time it seems to demystify, the privacy of the objects of introspection. Each of us perceives current states and activities in our own mind and that of nobody else. The privacy is simply a little more complete than in the kinaesthetic case. There are other ways to perceive the motion of my limbs besides kinaesthetic perception—for instance, by seeing and touching. These other ways are intersubjective. But, by contrast, nobody else can have the direct awareness of my mental states and activities that I have. This privacy, however, is contingent only. We can imagine that somebody else should have the same direct consciousness of my mental states and activities that I enjoy. (They would not *have* those states, but they would be directly aware of them.)

Perception is a causal affair. If somebody perceives something, then it is involved in the perception; it is even involved in the concept of perception: that the thing perceived acts upon the perceiver, causing the perception of the object. If introspective consciousness is to be compared to perception, then it will be natural to say that the mental objects of introspection act within our mind so as to produce our introspective awareness of these states. Indeed, it is not easy to see what other naturalistic account of the coming-to-be of introspections could be given. If introspection is a causal process, then it will follow, incidentally, from our earlier definition of causal quiescence that whenever we are introspectively aware of one of our mental states, then that state is not at that time causally quiescent.

Types of introspective consciousness

Perhaps we still have not drawn enough distinctions. Sometimes the distinction is drawn between mere 'reflex' consciousness, which is normally always present while we are awake (but which is lost by the long-distance truck-driver), and consciousness of a more explicit, self-conscious sort.

This difference appears to be parallel to the difference between mere 'reflex' seeing, which is always going on while we are awake and our eyes are open, and the careful *scrutinizing* of the visual environment that may be undertaken in the interest of some purpose we have. The eyes have a watching brief at all times that we are awake and have our eyes open; in special circumstances, they are used in a more attentive manner. (In close scrutiny by human beings, introspective consciousness is often, although not invariably, also called into play. We not only give the object more attention but have a heightened awareness of so doing. But, presumably, in lower animals such attentive scrutiny does not have this accompaniment.) Similarly, introspective consciousness normally has only a watching brief with respect to our mental states. Only sometimes do we carefully scrutinize our own current state of mind. We can mark the distinction by speaking of 'reflex' introspective awareness and opposing it to 'introspection proper'. It is a plausible hypothesis that the latter will normally involve not only introspective awareness of mental states and activities but also introspective awareness of that introspective awareness. It is in any case a peculiarly sophisticated sort of mental process.

What is so special about introspective consciousness?

There remains the feeling that there is something quite special about introspective consciousness. The long-distance truck-driver has minimal and perceptual consciousness. But there is an important sense, we are inclined to think, in which he has no experiences, indeed is not really a person, during his period of introspective unconsciousness. Introspective consciousness seems like a light switched on, which illuminates utter darkness. It has seemed to many that with consciousness in this sense, a wholly new thing enters the universe.

I now will attempt to explain why introspective consciousness *seems to have*, but does not necessarily *actually* have, a quite special status in the world. I proceed by calling attention to two points, which will then be brought together at the end of the section.

First, it appears that introspective consciousness is bound up in a quite special way with consciousness of self. I do not mean that the self is one of the particular objects of introspective awareness alongside our mental states and activities. This view was somewhat tentatively put forward by Russell in *The Problems of Philosophy* (1912: Ch. 5), but had already been rejected by Hume and by Kant. It involves accepting the extraordinary view that what seems most inward to us, our mental states and activities, are not really us. What I mean rather is that we take the states and activities of which we are introspectively aware to be states and activities of a single continuing thing.

In recent years, we have often been reminded, indeed admonished, that there is a great deal of theory involved even in quite unsophisticated perceptual judgements. To see that there is a tomato before our body is already to go well beyond anything that can be said to be 'given', even where we do not make excessive demands (such as indubitability) upon the notion of the given. Consider knowingly perceiving a tomato. A tomato, to be a tomato, must have sides and back, top and bottom, a certain history, certain casual powers; and these things certainly do not seem to be given in perception. If we consider the causal situation, it is only the shape, size and colour of some portions of the surface of the tomato (the facing portions) that actually determine the nature of the stimulation that reaches our eyes. This suggests that, at best, it is only these properties that are in any way 'given' to us. The rest is, in some sense, a matter of theory, although I do not think that we should take this to mean that the perceptual judgement that there is a tomato before us is a piece of risky speculation.

It is therefore natural to assume that the perceptions of 'inner sense' involve theory, involve going beyond the 'given', in the same general way that the perceptions of 'outer sense' do. In particular, whatever may be the case with other animals, or with small children, or with those who, like the Wild Boy of Aveyron, have not been socialized, for ordinary persons, their mental states and activities are introspected as the states and activities of a single thing.

Once again, the comparison with proprioception seems to be instructive. We learn to organize our proprioceptions so that they yield us perceptions of a single, unitary, physical object, our body, concerning which our proprioceptions give us certain information: its current posture, temperature, the movement of its limbs, and so on. This is clearly a theoretical achievement of some sophistication.

In the same way, we learn to organize what we introspect as being states of, and activities in, a single continuing entity: our self. Mere introspective consciousness, of course, is not at all clear just what this self is. At a primitive level perhaps, no distinction is made between the self and the body. Identification of the thing that is introspected as, say, a spiritual substance, or as the central nervous system, goes far beyond the level of theorizing involved in ordinary introspection. But the idea that the states and activities observed are states and activities of a unitary thing is involved. Introspective consciousness is consciousness of self.

If it is asked why introspection is theory-laden in this particular way, then an answer can be suggested. It is always worth asking the question about any human or animal organ or capacity: 'What is its biological function?' It is therefore worth asking what is the biological function of introspective consciousness. Once the question is asked, then the answer is fairly obvious: it is to sophisticate our mental process in the interests of more sophisticated action.

Inner perception makes the sophistication of our mental processes possible in the following way. If we have a faculty that can make us aware of current mental states and activities, then it will be much easier to achieve *integration* of the states and activities, to get them working together in the complex and sophisticated ways necessary to achieve complex and sophisticated ends.

Current computer technology provides an analogy, though I would stress that it is no more than an analogy. In any complex computing operation, many different processes must go forward simultaneously: in parallel. There is need, therefore, for an overall plan for these activities, so that they are properly co-ordinated. This cannot be done simply in the manner in which a 'command economy' is supposed to be run: by a series of instructions from above. The co-ordination can only be achieved if the portion of the computing space made available for administering the overall plan is continuously made 'aware' of the current mental state of play with respect to the lower-level operations that are running in parallel. Only with this feedback is control possible. Equally, introspective consciousness provides the feedback (of a far more sophisticated sort than anything available in current computer technology) in the mind that enables 'parallel processes' in our mind to be integrated in a way that they could not be integrated otherwise. It is no accident that fully alert introspective consciousness characteristically arises in *problem* situations, situations that standard routines cannot carry one through.

We now can understand why introspection so naturally gives rise to the notion of the self. If introspective consciousness is the instrument of mental integration, then it is natural that what is perceived by that consciousness should be assumed to be something unitary.

There is nothing necessary about the assumption. It may even be denied on occasion. Less sophisticated persons than ourselves, on becoming aware of a murderous impulse springing up, may attribute it not to a hitherto unacknowledged and even dissociated part of themselves, but to a devil who has entered them. In Dickens' *Hard Times*, the dying Mrs Gradgrind says that there seems to be a pain in the room, but she is not prepared to say that it is actually *she* that has got it. In her weakened condition, she has lost her grip upon the idea that whatever she introspects is a state of one unitary thing: herself.

But although the assumption of unity is not necessary, it is one we have good reason to think true. A Physicalist, in particular, will take the states and activities introspected to be all physical states and activities of a continuing physical object: a brain.

That concludes the first step in my argument: to show that, and in what sense, introspective awareness is introspective awareness of self. The second step is to call attention to the special connection between introspective consciousness and event-memory, that is, memory of individual happenings. When the long-distance truck-driver recovers introspective consciousness, he has no memory of what happened while it was lacking. One sort of memory-processing cannot have failed him. His successful navigation of his vehicle depended upon him being able to *recognize* various things for what they were and treat them accordingly. He must have been able to recognize a certain degree of curve in the road, a certain degree of pressure on the accelerator, for what they were. But the things that happened to him during introspective unconsciousness were not stored in his event-memory. He lived solely in the present.

It is tempting to suppose, therefore, as a psychological hypothesis, that unless mental activity is monitored by introspective consciousness, then it is not remembered to have occurred, or at least it is unlikely that it will be remembered. It is obvious that introspective consciousness is not sufficient for event-memory. But perhaps it is necessary, or at least generally necessary. It is notoriously difficult, for instance, to remember dreams, and it is clear that, in almost all dreaming, introspective consciousness is either absent or is at a low ebb.

So it may be that introspective consciousness is essential or nearly essential for event-memory, that is, memory of the past as past. *A fortiori*, it will be essential or nearly essential for memory of the past of the self.

The two parts of the argument now may be brought together. If introspective consciousness involves (in reasonably mature human beings) consciousness of self, and if without introspective consciousness there would be little or no memory of the past history of the self, the apparent special illumination and power of introspective consciousness is explained. Without introspective consciousness, we would not be aware that we existed—our self would not be self to itself. Nor would we be aware of what the particular history of that self had been, even its very recent history. Now add just one more premiss: the overwhelming interest that human beings have in themselves. We can then understand why introspective consciousness can come to seem a condition of anything mental existing, or even of anything existing at all.

Chapter 35

Facing up to the problem of consciousness*

David J. Chalmers

I: Introduction

Consciousness poses the most baffling problems in the science of the mind. There is nothing that we know more intimately than conscious experience, but there is nothing that is harder to explain. All sorts of mental phenomena have yielded to scientific investigation in recent years, but consciousness has stubbornly resisted. Many have tried to explain it, but the explanations always seem to fall short of the target. Some have been led to suppose that the problem is intractable, and that no good explanation can be given.

To make progress on the problem of consciousness, we have to confront it directly. In this paper, I first isolate the truly hard part of the problem, separating it from more tractable parts and giving an account of why it is so difficult to explain. I critique some recent work that uses reductive methods to address consciousness, and argue that these methods inevitably fail to come to grips with the hardest part of the problem. Once this failure is recognized, the door to further progress is opened. In the second half of the paper, I argue that if we move to a new kind of nonreductive explanation, a naturalistic account of consciousness can be given. I put forward my own candidate for such an account: a nonreductive theory based on principles of structural coherence and organizational invariance and a double-aspect view of information.

II: The easy problems and the hard problem

There is not just one problem of consciousness. 'Consciousness' is an ambiguous term, referring to many different phenomena. Each of these phenomena needs to be explained, but some are easier to explain than others. At the start, it is useful to divide the associated problems of consciousness into 'hard' and 'easy' problems. The easy problems of consciousness are those that seem directly susceptible to the

David Chalmers, 'Facing up to the Problem of Consciousness', *Journal of Consciousness Studies* 2 (1995).

* The arguments in this paper are presented in much greater depth in my book *The Conscious Mind* (Chalmers, 1996). Thanks to Francis Crick, Peggy DesAutels, Matthew Elton, Liane Gabora, Christof Koch, Paul Rhodes, Gregg Rosenberg, and Sharon Wahl for helpful comments.

standard methods of cognitive science, whereby a phenomenon is explained in terms of computational or neural mechanisms. The hard problems are those that seem to resist those methods.

The easy problems of consciousness include those of explaining the following phenomena:

- the ability to discriminate, categorize, and react to environmental stimuli;
- the integration of information by a cognitive system;
- the reportability of mental states;
- the ability of a system to access its own internal states;
- the focus of attention;
- the deliberate control of behaviour;
- the difference between wakefulness and sleep.

All of these phenomena are associated with the notion of consciousness. For example, one sometimes says that a mental state is conscious when it is verbally reportable, or when it is internally accessible. Sometimes a system is said to be conscious of some information when it has the ability to react on the basis of that information, or, more strongly, when it attends to that information, or when it can integrate that information and exploit it in the sophisticated control of behaviour. We sometimes say that an action is conscious precisely when it is deliberate. Often, we say that an organism is conscious as another way of saying that it is awake.

There is no real issue about whether *these* phenomena can be explained scientifically. All of them are straightforwardly vulnerable to explanation in terms of computational or neural mechanisms. To explain access and reportability, for example, we need only specify the mechanism by which information about internal states is retrieved and made available for verbal report. To explain the integration of information, we need only exhibit mechanisms by which information is brought together and exploited by later processes. For an account of sleep and wakefulness, an appropriate neurophysiological account of the processes responsible for organisms' contrasting behaviour in those states will suffice. In each case, an appropriate cognitive or neurophysiological model can clearly do the explanatory work.

If these phenomena were all there was to consciousness, then consciousness would not be much of a problem. Although we do not yet have anything close to a complete explanation of these phenomena, we have a clear idea of how we might go about explaining them. This is why I call these problems the easy problems. Of course, 'easy' is a relative term. Getting the details right will probably take a century or two of difficult empirical work. Still, there is every reason to believe that the methods of cognitive science and neuroscience will succeed.

The really hard problem of consciousness is the problem of *experience*. When we think and perceive, there is a whir of information-processing, but there is also a subjective aspect. As Nagel (1974) has put it, there is *something it is like* to be a conscious organism. This subjective aspect is experience. When we see, for example, we *experience* visual sensations: the felt quality of redness, the experience of dark and light, the quality of depth in a visual field. Other experiences go along with perception in different modalities: the sound of a clarinet, the smell of mothballs. Then there are bodily sensations, from pains to orgasms; mental images that are conjured up internally; the felt quality of emotion, and the experience of a stream of conscious thought. What unites all of these states is that there is something it is like to be in them. All of them are states of experience.

It is undeniable that some organisms are subjects of experience. But the question of how it is that these systems are subjects of experience is perplexing. Why is it that when our cognitive systems engage in visual and auditory information-processing, we have visual or auditory experience: the quality of deep blue, the sensation of middle C? How can we explain why there is something it is like to entertain a mental image, or to experience an emotion? It is widely agreed that experience arises from a physical basis, but we have no good explanation of why and how it so arises. Why should physical processing give rise to a rich inner life at all? It seems objectively unreasonable that it should, and yet it does.

If any problem qualifies as *the* problem of consciousness, it is this one. In this central sense of 'consciousness', an organism is conscious if there is something it is like to be that organism, and a mental state is conscious if there is something it is like to be in that state. Sometimes terms such as 'phenomenal consciousness' and 'qualia' are also used here, but I find it more natural to speak of 'conscious experience' or simply 'experience'. Another useful way to avoid confusion (used by e.g. Newell 1990, Chalmers 1996) is to reserve the term 'consciousness' for the phenomena of experience, using the less loaded term 'awareness' for the more straightforward phenomena described earlier. If such a convention were widely adopted, communication would be much easier. As things stand, those who talk about 'consciousness' are frequently talking past each other.

The ambiguity of the term 'consciousness' is often exploited by both philosophers and scientists writing on the subject. It is common to see a paper on consciousness begin with an invocation of the mystery of consciousness, noting the strange intangibility and ineffability of subjectivity, and worrying that so far we have no theory of the phenomenon. Here, the topic is clearly the hard problem—the problem of experience. In the second half of the paper, the tone becomes more optimistic, and the author's own theory of consciousness is outlined. Upon examination, this theory turns out to be a theory of one of the more straightforward phenomena—of reportability, of introspective access, or whatever. At the close, the author declares that consciousness has turned out to be tractable after all, but the reader is left feeling like the victim of a bait-and-switch. The hard problem remains untouched.

III: Functional explanation

Why are the easy problems easy, and why is the hard problem hard? The easy problems are easy precisely because they concern the explanation of cognitive *abilities* and *functions.* To explain a cognitive function, we need only specify a mechanism that can perform the function. The methods of cognitive science are well-suited for this sort of explanation, and so are well-suited to the easy problems of consciousness. By contrast, the hard problem is hard precisely because it is not a problem about the performance of functions. The problem persists even when the performance of all the relevant functions is explained.[1]

To explain reportability, for instance, is just to explain how a system could perform the function of producing reports on internal states. To explain internal access, we need to explain how a system could be appropriately affected by its internal states and use information about those states in directing later processes. To explain integration and control, we need to explain how a system's central processes can bring information contents together and use them in the facilitation of various behaviours. These are all problems about the explanation of functions.

How do we explain the performance of a function? By specifying a *mechanism* that performs the function. Here, neurophysiological and cognitive modelling are perfect for the task. If we want a detailed low-level explanation, we can specify the neural mechanism that is responsible for the function. If we want a more abstract explanation, we can specify a mechanism in computational terms. Either way, a full and satisfying explanation will result. Once we have specified the neural or computational mechanism that performs the function of verbal report, for example, the bulk of our work inexplaining reportability is over.

In a way, the point is trivial. It is a *conceptual* fact about these phenomena that their explanation only involves the explanation of various functions, as the phenomena are *functionally definable.* All it *means* for reportability to be instantiated in a system is that the system has the capacity for verbal reports of internal information. All it means for a system to be awake is for it to be appropriately receptive to information from the environment and for it to be able to use this information in directing behaviour in an appropriate way. To see that this sort of thing is a conceptual fact, note that someone who says 'you have explained the performance of the verbal report function, but you have not explained reportability' is making a trivial conceptual mistake about reportability. All it could *possibly* take to explain reportability is an explanation of how the relevant function is performed; the same goes for the other phenomena in question.

Throughout the higher-level sciences, reductive explanation works in just this

1. Here 'function' is not used in the narrow teleological sense of something that a system is designed to do, but in the broader sense of any causal role in the production of behaviour that a system might perform.

way. To explain the gene, for instance, we needed to specify the mechanism that stores and transmits hereditary information from one generation to the next. It turns out that DNA performs this function; once we explain how the function is performed, we have explained the gene. To explain life, we ultimately need to explain how a system can reproduce, adapt to its environment, metabolize, and so on. All of these are questions about the performance of functions, and so are well-suited to reductive explanation. The same holds for most problems in cognitive science. To explain learning, we need to explain the way in which a system's behavioural capacities are modified in light of environmental information, and the way in which new information can be brought to bear in adapting a system's actions to its environment. If we show how a neural or computational mechanism does the job, we have explained learning. We can say the same for other cognitive phenomena, such as perception, memory, and language. Sometimes the relevant functions need to be characterized quite subtly, but it is clear that insofar as cognitive science explains these phenomena at all, it does so by explaining the performance of functions.

When it comes to conscious experience, this sort of explanation fails. What makes the hard problem hard and almost unique is that it goes *beyond* problems about the performance of functions. To see this, note that even when we have explained the performance of all the cognitive and behavioural functions in the vicinity of experience—perceptual discrimination, categorization, internal access, verbal report—there may still remain a further unanswered question: *Why is the performance of these functions accompanied by experience?* A simple explanation of the functions leaves this question open.

There is no analogous further question in the explanation of genes, or of life, or of learning. If someone says 'I can see that you have explained how DNA stores and transmits hereditary information from one generation to the next, but you have not explained how it is a *gene*,' then they are making a conceptual mistake. All it means to be a gene is to be an entity that performs the relevant storage and transmission function. But if someone says 'I can see that you have explained how information is discriminated, integrated, and reported, but you have not explained how it is *experienced*,' they are not making a conceptual mistake. This is a nontrivial further question.

This further question is the key question in the problem of consciousness. Why doesn't all this information-processing go on 'in the dark', free of any inner feel? Why is it that when electromagnetic waveforms impinge on a retina and are discriminated and categorized by a visual system, this discrimination and categorization is experienced as a sensation of vivid red? We know that conscious experience *does* arise when these functions are performed, but the very fact that it arises is the central mystery. There is an *explanatory gap* (a term due to Levine 1983) between the functions and experience, and we need an explanatory bridge to cross it. A mere account of the functions stays on one side of the gap, so the materials for the bridge must be found elsewhere.

This is not to say that experience *has* no function. Perhaps it will turn out to play an important cognitive role. But for any role it might play, there will be more to the explanation of experience than a simple explanation of the function. Perhaps it will even turn out that in the course of explaining a function, we will be led to the key insight that allows an explanation of experience. If this happens, though, the discovery will be an *extra* explanatory reward. There is no cognitive function such that we can say in advance that explanation of that function will *automatically* explain experience.

To explain experience, we need a new approach. The usual explanatory methods of cognitive science and neuroscience do not suffice. These methods have been developed precisely to explain the performance of cognitive functions, and they do a good job of it. But as these methods stand, they are *only* equipped to explain the performance of functions. When it comes to the hard problem, the standard approach has nothing to say.

IV: Some case-studies

In the last few years, a number of works have addressed the problems of consciousness within the framework of cognitive science and neuroscience. This might suggest that the analysis above is faulty, but in fact a close examination of the relevant work only lends the analysis further support. When we investigate just which aspects of consciousness these studies are aimed at, and which aspects they end up explaining, we find that the ultimate target of explanation is always one of the easy problems. I will illustrate this with two representative examples.

The first is the 'neurobiological theory of consciousness' outlined by Francis Crick and Christof Koch (1990; see also Crick 1994). This theory centers on certain 35–75 hertz neural oscillations in the cerebral cortex; Crick and Koch hypothesize that these oscillations are the basis of consciousness. This is partly because the oscillations seem to be correlated with awareness in a number of different modalities—within the visual and olfactory systems, for example—and also because they suggest a mechanism by which the *binding* of information contents might be achieved. Binding is the process whereby separately represented pieces of information about a single entity are brought together to be used by later processing, as when information about the colour and shape of a perceived object is integrated from separate visual pathways. Following others (e.g. Eckhorn *et al.* 1988), Crick and Koch hypothesize that binding may be achieved by the synchronized oscillations of neuronal groups representing the relevant contents. When two pieces of information are to be bound together, the relevant neural groups will oscillate with the same frequency and phase.

The details of how this binding might be achieved are still poorly understood, but suppose that they can be worked out. What might the resulting theory explain? Clearly it might explain the binding of information contents, and perhaps it might yield a more general account of the integration of information in the brain. Crick and Koch also suggest that these oscillations activate the mechanisms of working memory, so that there may be an account of this and perhaps other forms of memory in the distance. The theory might eventually lead to a general account of how perceived information is bound and stored in memory, for use by later processing.

Such a theory would be valuable, but it would tell us nothing about why the relevant contents are experienced. Crick and Koch suggest that these oscillations are the neural *correlates* of experience. This claim is arguable—does not binding also take place in the processing of unconscious information?—but even if it is accepted, the *explanatory* question remains: Why do the oscillations give rise to experience? The only basis for an explanatory connection is the role they play in binding and storage, but the question of why binding and storage should themselves be accompanied by experience is never addressed. If we do not know why binding and storage should give rise to experience, telling a story about the oscillations cannot help us. Conversely, if we *knew* why binding and storage gave rise to experience, the neurophysiological details would be just the icing on the cake. Crick and Koch's theory gains its purchase by *assuming* a connection between binding and experience, and so can do nothing to explain that link.

I do not think that Crick and Koch are ultimately claiming to address the hard problem, although some have interpreted them otherwise. A published interview with Koch gives a clear statement of the limitations on the theory's ambitions.

> Well, let's first forget about the really difficult aspects, like subjective feelings, for they may not have a scientific solution. The subjective state of play, of pain, of pleasure, of seeing blue, of smelling a rose—there seems to be a huge jump between the materialistic level, of explaining molecules and neurons, and the subjective level. Let's focus on things that are easier to study—like visual awareness. You're now talking to me, but you're not looking at me, you're looking at the cappuccino, and so you are aware of it. You can say, 'It's a cup and there's some liquid in it.' If I give it to you, you'll move your arm and you'll take it—you'll respond in a meaningful manner. That's what I call awareness. ('What is Consciousness?', *Discover*, November 1992, p. 96.)

The second example is an approach at the level of cognitive psychology. This is Bernard Baars' global workspace theory of consciousness, presented in his book *A Cognitive Theory of Consciousness* (1988). According to this theory, the contents of consciousness are contained in a *global workspace*, a central processor used to mediate communication between a host of specialized nonconscious processors. When these specialized processors need to broadcast information to the rest of the system, they do so by sending this information to the workspace, which acts as a kind of communal blackboard for the rest of the system, accessible to all the other processors.

Baars uses this model to address many aspects of human cognition, and to explain a number of contrasts between conscious and unconscious cognitive functioning. Ultimately, however, it is a theory of *cognitive accessibility*, explaining how it is that certain information contents are widely accessible within a system, as well as a theory of informational integration and reportability. The theory shows promise as a theory of awareness, the functional correlate of conscious experience, but an explanation of experience itself is not on offer.

One might suppose that according to this theory, the contents of experience are precisely the contents of the workspace. But even if this is so, nothing internal to the theory *explains* why the information within the global workspace is experienced. The best the theory can do is to say that the information is experienced because it is *globally accessible*. But now the question arises in a different form: why should global accessibility give rise to conscious experience? As always, this bridging question is unanswered.

Almost all work taking a cognitive or neuroscientific approach to consciousness in recent years could be subjected to a similar critique. The 'Neural Darwinism' model of Edelman (1989), for instance, addresses questions about perceptual awareness and the self-concept, but says nothing about why there should also be experience. The 'multiple drafts' model of Dennett (1991) is largely directed at explaining the reportability of certain mental contents. The 'intermediate level' theory of Jackendoff (1987) provides an account of some computational processes that underlie consciousness, but Jackendoff stresses that the question of how these 'project' into conscious experience remains mysterious.

Researchers using these methods are often inexplicit about their attitudes to the problem of conscious experience, although sometimes they take a clear stand. Even among those who are clear about it, attitudes differ widely. In placing this sort of work with respect to the problem of experience, a number of different strategies are available. It would be useful if these strategic choices were more often made explicit.

The first strategy is simply to *explain something else*. Some researchers are explicit that the problem of experience is too difficult for now, and perhaps even outside the domain of science altogether. These researchers instead choose to address one of the more tractable problems such as reportability or the self-concept. Although I have called these problems the 'easy' problems, they are among the most interesting unsolved problems in cognitive science, so this work is certainly worthwhile. The worst that can be said of this choice is that in the context of research on consciousness it is relatively unambitious, and the work can sometimes be misinterpreted.

The second choice is to take a harder line and *deny the phenomenon*. (Variations on this approach are taken by Allport 1988; Dennett 1991; Wilkes 1988.) According to this line, once we have explained the functions such as accessibility, reportability, and the like, there is no further phenomenon called 'experience' to explain. Some explicitly deny the phenomenon, holding for example that what is not externally verifiable cannot be real. Others achieve the same effect by allowing that experience exists, but only if we equate 'experience' with something like the capacity to discriminate and report. These approaches lead to a simpler theory, but are ultimately unsatisfactory. Experience is the most central and manifest aspect of our mental lives, and indeed is perhaps the key explanandum in the science of the mind. Because of this status as an explanandum, experience cannot be discarded like the vital spirit when a new theory comes along. Rather, it is the central fact that any theory of consciousness must explain. A theory that denies the phenomenon 'solves' the problem by ducking the question.

In a third option, some researchers *claim to be explaining experience* in the full sense. These researchers (unlike those above) wish to take experience very seriously; they lay out their functional model or theory, and claim that it explains the full subjective quality of experience (e.g. Flohr 1992; Humphrey 1992). The relevant step in the explanation is usually passed over quickly, however, and usually ends up looking something like magic. After some details about information processing are given, experience suddenly enters the picture, but it is left obscure *how* these processes should suddenly give rise to experience. Perhaps it is simply taken for granted that it does, but then we have an incomplete explanation and a version of the fifth strategy below.

A fourth, more promising approach appeals to these methods to *explain the structure of experience*. For example, it is arguable that an account of the discriminations made by the visual system can account for the structural relations between different colour experiences, as well as for the geometric structure of the visual field (see e.g. Clark 1992; Hardin 1992). In general, certain facts about structures found in processing will correspond to and arguably explain facts about the structure of experience. This strategy is plausible but limited. At best, it takes the existence of experience for granted and accounts for some facts about its structure, providing a sort of nonreductive explanation of the structural aspects of experience (I will say more on this later). This is useful for many purposes, but it tells us nothing about why there should be experience in the first place.

A fifth and reasonable strategy is to *isolate the substrate of experience*. After all, almost everyone allows that experience *arises* one way or another from brain processes, and it makes sense to identify the sort of process from which it arises. Crick and Koch put their work forward as isolating the neural correlate of consciousness, for example, and Edelman (1989) and Jackendoff (1987) make related claims. Justification of these claims requires a careful theoretical analysis, especially as experience is not directly observable in experimental contexts, but when applied judiciously this strategy can shed indirect light on the problem of experience. Nevertheless, the strategy is clearly incomplete. For a satisfactory theory, we need to know more than *which* processes give rise to experience; we need an account of why and how. A full theory of consciousness must build an explanatory bridge.

V: The extra ingredient

We have seen that there are systematic reasons why the usual methods of cognitive science and neuroscience fail to account for conscious experience. These are simply the wrong sort of methods: nothing that they give to us can yield an explanation. To account for conscious experience, we need an *extra ingredient* in the explanation. This makes for a challenge to those who are serious about the hard problem of consciousness: What is your extra ingredient, and why should *that* account for conscious experience?

There is no shortage of extra ingredients to be had. Some propose an injection of chaos and nonlinear dynamics. Some think that the key lies in nonalgorithmic processing. Some appeal to future discoveries in neurophysiology. Some suppose that the key to the mystery will lie at the level of quantum mechanics. It is easy to see why all these suggestions are put forward. None of the old methods work, so the solution must lie with *something* new. Unfortunately, these suggestions all suffer from the same old problems.

Nonalgorithmic processing, for example, is put forward by Penrose (1989; 1994) because of the role it might play in the process of conscious mathematical insight. The arguments about mathematics are controversial, but even if they succeed and an account of nonalgorithmic processing in the human brain is given, it will still only be an account of the *functions* involved in mathematical reasoning and the like. For a nonalgorithmic process as much as an algorithmic process, the question is left unanswered: why should this process give rise to experience? In answering *this* question, there is no special role for nonalgorithmic processing.

The same goes for nonlinear and chaotic dynamics. These might provide a novel account of the dynamics of cognitive functioning, quite different from that given by standard methods in cognitive science. But from dynamics, one only gets more dynamics. The question about experience here is as mysterious as ever. The point is even clearer for new discoveries in neurophysiology. These new discoveries may help us make significant progress in understanding brain function, but for any neural process we isolate, the same question will always arise. It is difficult to imagine what a proponent of new neurophysiology expects to happen, over and above the explanation of further cognitive functions. It is not as if we will suddenly discover a phenomenal glow inside a neuron!

Perhaps the most popular 'extra ingredient' of all is quantum mechanics (e.g. Hameroff 1994). The attractiveness of quantum theories of consciousness may stem from a Law of Minimization of Mystery: consciousness is mysterious and quantum mechanics is mysterious, so maybe the two mysteries have a common source. Nevertheless, quantum theories of consciousness suffer from the same difficulties as neural or computational theories. Quantum phenomena have some remarkable functional properties, such as nondeterminism and nonlocality. It is natural to speculate that these properties may play some role in the explanation of cognitive functions, such as random choice and the integration of information, and this hypothesis cannot be ruled out *a priori.* But when it comes to the explanation of experience, quantum processes are in the same boat as any other. The question of why these processes should give rise to experience is entirely unanswered.[2]

At the end of the day, the same criticism applies to *any* purely physical account of consciousness. For any physical process we specify there will be an unanswered question: Why should this process give rise to experience? Given any such process, it is conceptually coherent that it could be instantiated in the absence of experience. It follows that no mere account of the physical process will tell us why experience arises. The emergence of experience goes beyond what can be derived from physical theory.

Purely physical explanation is well-suited to the explanation of physical *structures*, explaining macroscopic structures in terms of detailed microstructural constituents; and it provides a satisfying explanation of the performance of *functions*, accounting for these functions in terms of the physical mechanisms that perform them. This is because a physical account can *entail* the facts about structures and functions: once the internal details of the physical account are given, the structural and functional properties fall out as an automatic consequence. But the structure and dynamics of physical processes yield only more structure and dynamics, so structures and functions are all we can expect these processes to explain. The facts about experience cannot be an automatic consequence of any physical account, as it is conceptually coherent that any given process could exist without experience. Experience may *arise* from the physical, but it is not *entailed* by the physical.

The moral of all this is that *you can't explain conscious experience on the cheap.* It is a remarkable fact that reductive methods—methods that explain a high-level phenomenon wholly in terms of more basic physical processes—work well in so many domains. In a sense, one *can* explain most biological and cognitive phenomena on the cheap, in that these phenomena are seen as automatic consequences of more fundamental processes. It would be wonderful if reductive methods could explain experience, too; I hoped for a long time that they might. Unfortunately, there are systematic reasons why these methods must fail. Reductive methods are successful in most domains because what needs explaining in those domains are structures and functions, and these are the kind of thing that a physical account can entail. When it comes to a problem over and above the explanation of structures and functions, these methods are impotent.

2. One special attraction of quantum theories is the fact that on some interpretations of quantum mechanics, consciousness plays an active role in 'collapsing' the quantum wave function. Such interpretations are controversial, but in any case they offer no hope of *explaining* consciousness in terms of quantum processes. Rather, these theories *assume* the existence of consciousness, and use it in the explanation of quantum processes. At best, these theories tell us something about a physical role that consciousness may play. They tell us nothing about how it arises.

This might seem reminiscent of the vitalist claim that no physical account could explain life, but the cases are disanalogous. What drove vitalist scepticism was doubt about whether physical mechanisms could perform the many remarkable functions associated with life, such as complex adaptive behaviour and reproduction. The conceptual claim that explanation of functions is what is needed was implicitly accepted, but lacking detailed knowledge of biochemical mechanisms, vitalists doubted whether any physical process could do the job and put forward the hypothesis of the vital spirit as an alternative explanation. Once it turned out that physical processes could perform the relevant functions, vitalist doubts melted away.

With experience, on the other hand, physical explanation of the functions is not in question. The key is instead the *conceptual* point that the explanation of functions does not suffice for the explanation of experience. This basic conceptual point is not something that further neuroscientific investigation will affect. In a similar way, experience is disanalogous to the *elan vital*. The vital spirit was put forward as an explanatory posit, in order to explain the relevant functions, and could therefore be discarded when those functions were explained without it. Experience is not an explanatory posit but an explanandum in its own right, and so is not a candidate for this sort of elimination.

It is tempting to note that all sorts of puzzling phenomena have eventually turned out to be explainable in physical terms. But each of these were problems about the observable behaviour of physical objects, coming down to problems in the explanation of structures and functions. Because of this, these phenomena have always been the kind of thing that a physical account *might* explain, even if at some points there have been good reasons to suspect that no such explanation would be forthcoming. The tempting induction from these cases fails in the case of consciousness, which is not a problem about physical structures and functions. The problem of consciousness is puzzling in an entirely different way. An analysis of the problem shows us that conscious experience is just not the kind of thing that a wholly reductive account could succeed in explaining.

VI: Nonreductive explanation

At this point some are tempted to give up, holding that we will never have a theory of conscious experience. McGinn (1989), for example, argues that the problem is too hard for our limited minds; we are 'cognitively closed' with respect to the phenomenon. Others have argued that conscious experience lies outside the domain of scientific theory altogether.

I think this pessimism is premature. This is not the place to give up; it is the place where things get interesting. When simple methods of explanation are ruled out, we need to investigate the alternatives. Given that reductive explanation fails, *nonreductive* explanation is the natural choice.

Although a remarkable number of phenomena have turned out to be explicable wholly in terms of entities simpler than themselves, this is not universal. In physics, it occasionally happens that an entity has to be taken as *fundamental*. Fundamental entities are not explained in terms of anything simpler. Instead, one takes them as basic, and gives a theory of how they relate to everything else in the world. For example, in the nineteenth century it turned out that electromagnetic processes could not be explained in terms of the wholly mechanical processes that previous physical theories appealed to, so Maxwell and others introduced electromagnetic charge and electromagnetic forces as new fundamental components of a physical theory. To explain electromagnetism, the ontology of physics had to be expanded. New basic properties and basic laws were needed to give a satisfactory account of the phenomena.

Other features that physical theory takes as fundamental include mass and space-time. No attempt is made to explain these features in terms of anything simpler. But this does not rule out the possibility of a theory of mass or of space-time. There is an intricate theory of how these features interrelate, and of the basic laws they enter into. These basic principles are used to explain many familiar phenomena concerning mass, space, and time at a higher level.

I suggest that a theory of consciousness should take experience as fundamental. We know that a theory of consciousness requires the addition of *something* fundamental to our ontology, as everything in physical theory is compatible with the absence of consciousness. We might add some entirely new nonphysical feature, from which experience can be derived, but it is hard to see what such a feature would be like. More likely, we will take experience itself as a fundamental feature of the world, alongside mass, charge, and space-time. If we take experience as fundamental, then we can go about the business of constructing a theory of experience.

Where there is a fundamental property, there are fundamental laws. A nonreductive theory of experience will add new principles to the furniture of the basic laws of nature. These basic principles will ultimately carry the explanatory burden in a theory of consciousness. Just as we explain familiar high-level phenomena involving mass in terms of more basic principles involving mass and other entities, we might explain familiar phenomena involving experience in terms of more basic principles involving experience and other entities.

In particular, a nonreductive theory of experience will specify basic principles telling us how experience depends on physical features of the world. These *psychophysical* principles will not interfere with physical laws, as it seems that physical laws already form a closed system. Rather, they will be a supplement to a physical theory. A physical theory gives a theory of physical processes, and a psychophysical theory tells us how those processes give rise to experience. We know that experience depends on physical processes, but we also know that this dependence cannot be derived from physical laws alone. The new basic principles postulated by a nonreductive theory give us the extra ingredient that we need to build an explanatory bridge.

Of course, by taking experience as fundamental, there is a sense in which this approach does not tell us why there is experience in the first place. But this is the same for any fundamental theory. Nothing in physics tells us why there is matter in the first place, but we do not count this against theories of matter. Certain features of the world need to be taken as fundamental by any scientific theory. A theory of matter can still explain all sorts of facts about matter, by showing how they are consequences of the basic laws. The same goes for a theory of experience.

This position qualifies as a variety of dualism, as it postulates basic properties over and above the properties invoked by physics. But it is an innocent version of dualism, entirely compatible with the scientific view of the world. Nothing in this approach contradicts anything in physical theory; we simply need to add further *bridging* principles to explain how experience arises from physical processes. There is nothing particularly spiritual or mystical about this theory—its overall shape is like that of a physical theory, with a few fundamental entities connected by fundamental laws. It expands the ontology slightly, to be sure, but Maxwell did the same thing. Indeed, the overall structure of this position is entirely naturalistic, allowing that ultimately the universe comes down to a network of basic entities obeying simple laws, and allowing that there may ultimately be a theory of consciousness cast in terms of such laws. If the position is to have a name, a good choice might be *naturalistic dualism.*

If this view is right, then in some ways a theory of consciousness will have more in common with a theory in physics than a theory in biology. Biological theories involve no principles that are fundamental in this way, so biological theory has a certain complexity and messiness to it; but theories in physics, insofar as they deal with fundamental principles, aspire to simplicity and elegance. The fundamental laws of nature are part of the basic furniture of the world, and physical theories are telling us that this basic furniture is remarkably simple. If a theory of consciousness also involves fundamental principles, then we should expect the same. The principles of simplicity, elegance, and even beauty that drive physicists' search for a fundamental theory will also apply to a theory of consciousness.[3]

3. Some philosophers argue that even though there is a *conceptual* gap between physical processes and experience, there need be no metaphysical gap, so that experience might in a certain sense still be physical (e.g. Hill 1991; Levine 1983; Loar 1990). Usually this line of argument is supported by an appeal to the notion of *a posteriori* necessity (Kripke 1980). I think that this position rests on a misunderstanding of *a posteriori* necessity, however, or else requires an entirely new sort of necessity that we have no reason to believe in; see Chalmers 1996 (also Jackson 1994; Lewis 1994) for details. In any case, this position still concedes an *explanatory* gap between physical processes and experience. For example, the principles connecting the physical and the experiential will not be derivable from the laws of physics, so such principles must be taken as *explanatorily* fundamental. So even on this sort of view, the explanatory structure of a theory of consciousness will be much as I have described.

VII: Toward of a theory of consciousness

It is not too soon to begin work on a theory. We are already in a position to understand some key facts about the relationship between physical processes and experience, and about the regularities that connect them. Once reductive explanation is set aside, we can lay those facts on the table so that they can play their proper role as the initial pieces in a nonreductive theory of consciousness, and as constraints on the basic laws that constitute an ultimate theory.

There is an obvious problem that plagues the development of a theory of consciousness, and that is the paucity of objective data. Conscious experience is not directly observable in an experimental context, so we cannot generate data about the relationship between physical processes and experience at will. Nevertheless, we all have access to a rich source of data in our own case. Many important regularities between experience and processing can be inferred from considerations about one's own experience. There are also good indirect sources of data from observable cases, as when one relies on the verbal report of a subject as an indication of experience. These methods have their limitations, but we have more than enough data to get a theory off the ground.

Philosophical analysis is also useful in getting value for money out of the data we have. This sort of analysis can yield a number of principles relating consciousness and cognition, thereby strongly constraining the shape of an ultimate theory. The method of thought-experimentation can also yield significant rewards, as we will see. Finally, the fact that we are searching for a *fundamental* theory means that we can appeal to such nonempirical constraints as simplicity, homogeneity, and the like in developing a theory. We must seek to systematize the information we have, to extend it as far as possible by careful analysis, and then make the inference to the simplest possible theory that explains the data while remaining a plausible candidate to be part of the fundamental furniture of the world.

Such theories will always retain an element of speculation that is not present in other scientific theories, because of the impossibility of conclusive intersubjective experimental tests. Still, we can certainly construct theories that are compatible with the data that we have, and evaluate them in comparison to each other. Even in the absence of intersubjective observation, there are numerous criteria available for the evaluation of such theories: simplicity, internal coherence, coherence with theories in other domains, the ability to reproduce the properties of experience that are familiar from our own case, and even an overall fit with the dictates of common sense. Perhaps there will be significant indeterminacies remaining even when all these constraints are applied, but we can at least develop plausible candidates. Only when candidate theories have been developed will we be able to evaluate them.

A nonreductive theory of consciousness will consist of a number of *psychophysical principles*, principles connecting the properties of physical processes to the properties of experience. We can think of these principles as encapsulating the way in which experience arises from the physical. Ultimately, these principles should tell us what sort of physical systems will have associated experiences, and for the systems that do, they should tell us what sort of physical properties are relevant to the emergence of experience, and just what sort of experience we should expect any given physical system to yield. This is a tall order, but there is no reason why we should not get started.

In what follows, I present my own candidates for the psychophysical principles that might go into a theory of consciousness. The first two of these are *nonbasic principles*—systematic connections between processing and experience at a relatively high level. These principles can play a significant role in developing and constraining a theory of consciousness, but they are not cast at a sufficiently fundamental level to qualify as truly basic laws. The final principle is a candidate for a *basic principle* that might form the cornerstone of a fundamental theory of consciousness. This principle is particularly speculative, but it is the kind of speculation that is required if we are ever to have a satisfying theory of consciousness. I can present these principles only briefly here; I argue for them at much greater length in Chalmers 1996.

1. The principle of structural coherence This is a principle of coherence between the *structure of consciousness* and the *structure of awareness.* Recall that 'awareness' was used earlier to refer to the various functional phenomena that are associated with consciousness. I am now using it to refer to a somewhat more specific process in the cognitive underpinnings of experience. In particular, the contents of awareness are to be understood as those information contents that are accessible to central systems, and brought to bear in a widespread way in the control of behaviour. Briefly put, we can think of awareness as *direct availability for global control.* To a first approximation, the contents of awareness are the contents that are directly accessible and potentially reportable, at least in a language-using system.

Awareness is a purely functional notion, but it is nevertheless intimately linked to conscious experience. In familiar cases, wherever we find consciousness, we find awareness. Wherever there is conscious experience, there is some corresponding information in the cognitive system that is available in the control of behaviour, and available for verbal report. Conversely, it seems that whenever information is available for report and for global control, there is a corresponding conscious experience. Thus, there is a direct correspondence between consciousness and awareness.

The correspondence can be taken further. It is a central fact about experience that it has a complex structure. The visual field has a complex geometry, for instance. There are also relations of similarity and difference between experiences, and relations in such things as relative intensity. Every subject's experience can be at least partly characterized and decomposed in terms of these structural properties: similarity and difference relations, perceived location, relative intensity, geometric structure, and so on. It is also a central fact that to each of these structural features, there is a corresponding feature in the information-processing structure of awareness.

Take colour sensations as an example. For every distinction between colour experiences, there is a corresponding distinction in processing. The different phenomenal colours that we experience form a complex three-dimensional space, varying in hue, saturation, and intensity. The properties of this space can be recovered from information-processing considerations: examination of the visual systems shows that waveforms of light are discriminated and analysed along three different axes, and it is this three-dimensional information that is relevant to later processing. The three-dimensional structure of phenomenal colour space therefore corresponds directly to the three dimensional structure of visual awareness. This is precisely what we would expect. After all, every colour distinction corresponds to some reportable information, and therefore to a distinction that is represented in the structure of processing.

In a more straightforward way, the geometric structure of the visual field is directly reflected in a structure that can be recovered from visual processing. Every geometric relation corresponds to something that can be reported and is therefore cognitively represented. If we were given only the story about information-processing in an agent's visual and cognitive system, we could not *directly* observe that agent's visual experiences, but we could nevertheless infer those experiences' structural properties.

In general, any information that is consciously experienced will also be cognitively represented. The fine-grained structure of the visual field will correspond to some fine-grained structure in visual processing. The same goes for experiences in other modalities, and even for nonsensory experiences. Internal mental images have geometric properties that are represented in processing. Even emotions have structural properties, such as relative intensity, that correspond directly to a structural property of processing; where there is greater intensity, we find a greater effect on later processes. In general, precisely because the structural properties of experience are accessible and reportable, those properties will be directly represented in the structure of awareness.

It is this isomorphism between the structures of consciousness and awareness that constitutes the principle of structural coherence. This principle reflects the central fact that even though cognitive processes do not conceptually entail facts about conscious experience, consciousness and cognition do not float free of one another but cohere in an intimate way.

This principle has its limits. It allows us to recover structural properties of experience from information-processing properties, but not all properties of experience are structural properties. There are properties of experience, such as the intrinsic nature of a sensation of red, that cannot be fully captured in a structural description. The very intelligibility of inverted spectrum scenarios, where experiences of red and green are inverted but all structural properties remain the same, show that structural properties constrain experience without exhausting it. Nevertheless, the very fact that we feel compelled to leave structural properties unaltered when we imagine experiences inverted between functionally identical systems shows how central the principle of structural coherence is to our conception of our mental lives. It is not a *logically* necessary principle, as after all we can imagine all the information processing occurring without any experience at all, but it is nevertheless a strong and familiar constraint on the psychophysical connection.

The principle of structural coherence allows for a very useful kind of indirect explanation of experience in terms of physical processes. For example, we can use facts about neural processing of visual information to indirectly explain the structure of colour space. The facts about neural processing can entail and explain the structure of awareness; if we take the coherence principle for granted, the structure of experience will also be explained. Empirical investigation might even lead us to better understand the structure of awareness within animals, shedding indirect light on Nagel's vexing question of what it is like to be a bat. This principle provides a natural interpretation of much existing work on the explanation of consciousness (e.g. Clark 1992, Hardin 1992 on colours; Akins 1993 on bats), although it is often appealed to inexplicitly. It is so familiar that it is taken for granted by almost everybody, and is a central plank in the cognitive explanation of consciousness.

The coherence between consciousness and awareness also allows a natural interpretation of work in neuroscience directed at isolating the *substrate* (or the *neural correlate*) of consciousness. Various specific hypotheses have been put forward. For example, Crick and Koch (1990) suggest that 40-hertz oscillations may be the neural correlate of consciousness, whereas Libet (1993) suggests that temporally-extended neural activity is central. If we accept the principle of coherence, the most *direct* physical correlate of consciousness is awareness: the process whereby information is made directly available for global control. The different specific hypotheses can be interpreted as empirical suggestions about how awareness might be achieved. For example, Crick and Koch suggest that 40-Hz oscillations are the gateway by which information is integrated into working memory and thereby made available to later processes. Similarly, it is natural to suppose that Libet's temporally extended activity is relevant precisely because only that sort of activity achieves global availability. The same applies to other suggested correlates such as the 'global workspace' of Baars (1988), the 'high-quality representations' of Farah (1994), and the 'selector inputs to action systems' of Shallice (1972). All these can be seen as hypotheses about the *mechanisms of awareness*: the mechanisms that perform the function of making information directly available for global control.

Given the coherence between consciousness and awareness, it follows that a mechanism of awareness will itself be a correlate of conscious experience. The question of just *which* mechanisms in the brain govern global availability is an empirical one; perhaps there are many such mechanisms. But if we accept the coherence principle, we have reason to believe that the processes that *explain* awareness will at the same time be part of the *basis* of consciousness.

2. The principle of organizational invariance This principle states that any two systems with the same fine-grained *functional organization* will have qualitatively identical experiences. If the causal patterns of neural organization were duplicated in silicon, for example, with a silicon chip for every neuron and the same patterns of interaction, then the same experiences would arise. According to this principle, what matters for the emergence of experience is not the specific physical makeup of a system, but the abstract pattern of causal interaction between its components. This principle is controversial, of course. Some (e.g. Searle 1980) have thought that consciousness is tied to a specific biology, so that a silicon isomorph of a human need not be conscious. I believe that the principle can be given significant support by the analysis of thought-experiments, however.

Very briefly: suppose (for the purposes of a *reductio ad absurdum*) that the principle is false, and that there could be two functionally isomorphic systems with different experiences. Perhaps only one of the systems is conscious, or perhaps both are conscious but they have different experiences. For the purposes of illustration, let us say that one system is made of neurons and the other of silicon, and that one experiences red where the other experiences blue. The two systems have the same organization, so we can imagine gradually transforming one into the other, perhaps replacing neurons one at a time by silicon chips with the same local function. We thus gain a spectrum of intermediate cases, each with the same organization, but with slightly different physical makeup and slightly different experiences. Along this spectrum, there must be two systems *A* and *B* between which we replace less than one tenth of the system, but whose experiences differ. These two systems are physically identical, except that a small neural circuit in *A* has been replaced by a silicon circuit in *B*.

The key step in the thought-experiment is to take the relevant neural circuit in *A*, and install alongside it a causally isomorphic silicon circuit, with a switch between the two. What happens when we flip the switch? By hypothesis, the system's conscious experiences will change; from red to blue, say, for the purposes of illustration. This follows from the fact that the system after the change is essentially a version of *B*, whereas before the change it is just *A*.

But given the assumptions, there is no way for the system to *notice* the changes! Its causal organization stays constant, so that all of its functional states and behavioural dispositions stay fixed. As far as the system is concerned, nothing unusual has happened. There is no room for the thought, 'Hmm! Something strange just happened!' In general, the structure of any such thought must be reflected in processing, but the structure of processing remains constant here. If there were to be such a thought it must float entirely free of the system and would be utterly impotent to affect later processing. (If it affected later processing, the systems would be functionally distinct, contrary to hypothesis.) We might even flip the switch a number of times, so that experiences of red and blue dance back and forth before the system's 'inner eye'. According to hypothesis, the system can never notice these 'dancing qualia'.

This I take to be a *reductio* of the original assumption. It is a central fact about experience, very familiar from our own case, that whenever experiences change significantly and we are paying attention, we can notice the change; if this were not to be the case, we would be led to the sceptical possibility that our experiences are dancing before our eyes all the time. This hypothesis has the same status as the possibility that the world was created five minutes ago: perhaps it is logically coherent, but it is not plausible. Given the extremely plausible assumption that changes in experience correspond to changes in processing, we are led to the conclusion that the original hypothesis is impossible, and that any two functionally isomorphic systems must have the same sort of experiences. To put it in technical terms, the philosophical hypotheses of 'absent qualia' and 'inverted qualia', while logically possible, are empirically and nomologically impossible.[4]

There is more to be said here, but this gives the basic flavour. Once again, this thought experiment draws on familiar facts about the coherence between consciousness and cognitive processing to yield a strong conclusion about the relation between physical structure and experience. If the argument goes through, we know that the only physical properties directly relevant to the emergence of experience are *organizational* properties. This acts as a further strong constraint on a theory of consciousness.

3. The double-aspect theory of information The two preceding principles have been *nonbasic* principles. They involve high-level notions such as 'awareness' and 'organization', and therefore lie at the wrong level to constitute the fundamental laws in a theory of consciousness. Nevertheless, they act as strong constraints. What is further needed are *basic* principles that fit these constraints and that might ultimately explain them.

The basic principle that I suggest centrally involves the notion of *information.* I understand information in more or less the sense of Shannon (1948). Where there is information, there are *information states* embedded in an *information space.* An information space has a basic structure of *difference* relations between its elements, characterizing the ways in which different elements in a space are similar or different, possibly in complex ways. An information space is an abstract object, but following Shannon we can see information as *physically embodied* when there is a space of distinct physical states, the differences between which can be transmitted down some causal pathway. The states that are transmitted can be seen as themselves constituting an information space. To borrow a phrase from Bateson (1972), physical information is a *difference that makes a difference.*

The double-aspect principle stems from the observation that there is a direct isomorphism between certain physically embodied information spaces and certain

4. Some may worry that a silicon isomorph of a neural system might be impossible for technical reasons. That question is open. The invariance principle says only that *if* an isomorph is possible, then it will have the same sort of conscious experience.

phenomenal (or experiential) information spaces. From the same sort of observations that went into the principle of structural coherence, we can note that the differences between phenomenal states have a structure that corresponds directly to the differences embedded in physical processes; in particular, to those differences that make a difference down certain causal pathways implicated in global availability and control. That is, we can find the *same* abstract information space embedded in physical processing and in conscious experience.

This leads to a natural hypothesis: that information (or at least some information) has two basic aspects, a physical aspect and a phenomenal aspect. This has the status of a basic principle that might underlie and explain the emergence of experience from the physical. Experience arises by virtue of its status as one aspect of information, when the other aspect is found embodied in physical processing.

This principle is lent support by a number of considerations, which I can only outline briefly here. First, consideration of the sort of physical changes that correspond to changes in conscious experience suggests that such changes are always relevant by virtue of their role in constituting *informational changes*—differences within an abstract space of states that are divided up precisely according to their causal differences along certain causal pathways. Second, if the principle of organizational invariance is to hold, then we need to find some fundamental *organizational* property for experience to be linked to, and information is an organizational property *par excellence.* Third, this principle offers some hope of explaining the principle of structural coherence in terms of the structure present within information spaces. Fourth, analysis of the cognitive explanation of our *judgments* and *claims* about conscious experience—judgments that are functionally explainable but nevertheless deeply tied to experience itself—suggests that explanation centrally involves the information states embedded in cognitive processing. It follows that a theory based on information allows a deep coherence between the explanation of experience and the explanation of our judgments and claims about it.

Wheeler (1990) has suggested that information is fundamental to the physics of the universe. According to this 'it from bit' doctrine, the laws of physics can be cast in terms of information, postulating different states that give rise to different effects without actually saying what those states *are.* It is only their position in an information space that counts. If so, then information is a natural candidate to also play a role in a fundamental theory of consciousness. We are led to a conception of the world on which information is truly fundamental, and on which it has two basic aspects, corresponding to the physical and the phenomenal features of the world.

Of course, the double-aspect principle is extremely speculative and is also underdetermined, leaving a number of key questions unanswered. An obvious question is whether *all* information has a phenomenal aspect. One possibility is that we need a further constraint on the fundamental theory, indicating just what *sort* of information has a phenomenal aspect. The other possibility is that there is no such constraint. If not, then experience is much more widespread than we might have believed, as information is everywhere. This is counterintuitive at first, but on reflection I think the position gains a certain plausibility and elegance. Where there is simple information processing, there is simple experience, and where there is complex information processing, there is complex experience. A mouse has a simpler information-processing structure than a human, and has correspondingly simpler experience; perhaps a thermostat, a maximally simple information processing structure, might have maximally simple experience? Indeed, if experience is truly a fundamental property, it would be surprising for it to arise only every now and then; most fundamental properties are more evenly spread. In any case, this is very much an open question, but I believe that the position is not as implausible as it is often thought to be.

Once a fundamental link between information and experience is on the table, the door is opened to some grander metaphysical speculation concerning the nature of the world. For example, it is often noted that physics characterizes its basic entities only *extrinsically*, in terms of their relations to other entities, which are themselves characterized extrinsically, and so on. The intrinsic nature of physical entities is left aside. Some argue that no such intrinsic properties exist, but then one is left with a world that is pure causal flux (a pure flow of information) with no properties for the causation to relate. If one allows that intrinsic properties exist, a natural speculation given the above is that the intrinsic properties of the physical—the properties that causation ultimately relates—are themselves phenomenal properties. We might say that phenomenal properties are the internal aspect of information. This could answer a concern about the causal relevance of experience—a natural worry, given a picture on which the physical domain is causally closed, and on which experience is supplementary to the physical. The informational view allows us to understand how experience might have a subtle kind of causal relevance in virtue of its status as the intrinsic aspect of the physical. This metaphysical speculation is probably best ignored for the purposes of developing a scientific theory, but in addressing some philosophical issues it is quite suggestive.

VIII: Conclusion

The theory I have presented is speculative, but it is a candidate theory. I suspect that the principles of structural coherence and organizational invariance will be planks in any satisfactory theory of consciousness; the status of the double-aspect theory of information is much less certain. Indeed, right now it is more of an idea than a theory. To have any hope of eventual explanatory success, it will have to be specified more fully and fleshed out into a more powerful form. Still, reflection on just what is plausible and implausible about it, on where it works and where it fails, can only lead to a better theory.

Most existing theories of consciousness either deny the phenomenon, explain something else, or elevate the problem to an eternal mystery. I hope to have shown that it is possible to make progress on the problem even while taking it seriously. To make further progress, we will need further investigation, more refined theories, and more careful analysis. The hard problem is a hard problem, but there is no reason to believe that it will remain permanently unsolved.

References

Akins, K. (1993), 'What is it like to be boring and myopic?' in *Dennett and his Critics*, ed. B. Dahlbom (Oxford: Blackwell).

Allport, A. (1988), 'What concept of consciousness?' in (eds.) *Consciousness in Contemporary Science*, ed. A. Marcel and E. Bisiach (Oxford: Oxford University Press).

Baars, B.J. (1988), *A Cognitive Theory of Consciousness* (Cambridge: Cambridge University Press).

Bateson, G. (1972), *Steps to an Ecology of Mind* (Chandler Publishing).

Block, N. (1995), 'On a confusion about the function of consciousness', *Behavioral and Brain Sciences*, in press.

Block, N, Flanagan, O. and Güzeldere, G. (eds. 1996), *The Nature of Consciousness: Philosophical and Scientific Debates* (Cambridge, MA: MIT Press).

Chalmers, D.J. (1996), *The Conscious Mind* (New York: Oxford University Press).

Churchland, P.M. (1995), *The Engine of Reason, The Seat of the Soul: A Philosophical Journey into the Brain* (Cambridge, MA: MIT Press).

Clark, A. (1992), *Sensory Qualities* (Oxford: Oxford University Press).

Crick, F. and Koch, C. (1990), 'Toward a neurobiological theory of consciousness', *Seminars in the Neurosciences*, **2**, pp. 263–75.

Crick, F. (1994), *The Astonishing Hypothesis: The Scientific Search for the Soul* (New York: Scribners).

Dennett, D.C. (1991), *Consciousness Explained* (Boston: Little, Brown).

Dretske, F.I. (1995), *Naturalizing the Mind* (Cambridge, MA: MIT Press).

Edelman, G. (1989), *The Remembered Present: A Biological Theory of Consciousness* (New York: Basic Books).

Farah, M.J. (1994), 'Visual perception and visual awareness after brain damage: a tutorial overview', in *Consciousness and Unconscious Information Processing: Attention and Performance* 15, ed. C. Umilta and M. Moscovitch (Cambridge, MA: MIT Press).

Flohr, H. (1992), 'Qualia and brain processes', in *Emergence or Reduction?: Prospects for Nonreductive Physicalism*, ed. A. Beckermann, H. Flohr, and J. Kim (Berlin: De Gruyter).

Hameroff, S.R. (1994), 'Quantum coherence in microtubules: a neural basis for emergent consciousness?', *Journal of Consciousness Studies*, **1**, pp. 91–118.

Hardin, C.L. (1992), 'Physiology, phenomenology, and Spinoza's true colors', in *Emergence or Reduction?: Prospects for Nonreductive Physicalism*, ed. A. Beckermann, H. Flohr, and J. Kim (Berlin: De Gruyter).

Hill, C.S. (1991), *Sensations: A Defense of Type Materialism* (Cambridge: Cambridge University Press).

Hodgson, D. (1988), *The Mind Matters: Consciousness and Choice in a Quantum World* (Oxford: Oxford University Press).

Humphrey, N. (1992), *A History of the Mind* (New York: Simon and Schuster).

Jackendoff, R. (1987), *Consciousness and the Computational Mind* (Cambridge, MA: MIT Press).

Jackson, F. (1982), 'Epiphenomenal qualia', *Philosophical Quarterly*, 32, pp. 127–36 (Chapter 43 of this volume).

Jackson, F. (1994), 'Finding the mind in the natural world', in *Philosophy and the Cognitive Sciences*, ed. R. Casati, B. Smith, and S. White (Vienna: Hölder-Pichler-Tempsky).

Kirk, R. (1994), *Raw Feeling: A Philosophical Account of the Essence of Consciousness* (Oxford: Oxford University Press).

Kripke, S. (1980), *Naming and Necessity* (Cambridge, MA: Harvard University Press).

Levine, J. (1983), 'Materialism and qualia: the explanatory gap', *Pacific Philosophical Quarterly*, 64, pp. 354–61 (Chapter 44 of this volume).

Lewis, D. (1994), 'Reduction of mind', in *A Companion to the Philosophy of Mind*, ed. S. Guttenplan (Oxford: Blackwell).

Libet, B. (1993), 'The neural time factor in conscious and unconscious events', in *Experimental and Theoretical Studies of Consciousness* (Ciba Foundation Symposium 174), ed. G.R. Block and J. Marsh (Chichester: John Wiley and Sons).

Loar, B. (1990), 'Phenomenal states', *Philosophical Perspectives*, 4, pp. 81–108.

Lockwood, M. (1989), *Mind, Brain, and the Quantum* (Oxford: Blackwell).

McGinn, C. (1989), 'Can we solve the mind-body problem?', *Mind*, 98, pp. 349–66 (Chapter 45 of this volume).

Metzinger, T. (ed. 1995), *Conscious Experience* (Exeter: Imprint Academic).

Nagel, T. (1974), 'What is it like to be a bat?', *Philosophical Review*, 4, pp. 435–50 (Chapter 29 of this volume).

Nelkin, N. (1993), 'What is consciousness?', *Philosophy of Science*, 60, pp. 419–34.

Newell, A. (1990), *Unified Theories of Cognition* (Cambridge, MA: Harvard University Press).

Penrose, R. (1989), *The Emperor's New Mind* (Oxford: Oxford University Press).

Penrose, R. (1994), *Shadows of the Mind* (Oxford: Oxford University Press).

Rosenthal, D.M. (1996), 'A theory of consciousness', in *The Nature of Consciousness*, ed. N. Block, O. Flanagan, and G. Güzeldere (Cambridge, MA: MIT Press).

Seager, W.E. (1991), *Metaphysics of Consciousness* (London: Routledge).

Searle, J.R. (1980), 'Minds, brains and programs', *Behavioral and Brain Sciences*, 3, pp. 417–57 (Chapter 15 of this volume).

Searle, J.R. (1992), *The Rediscovery of the Mind* (Cambridge, MA: MIT Press).

Shallice, T. (1972), 'Dual functions of consciousness', *Psychological Review*, 79, pp. 383–93.

Shannon, C.E. (1948), 'A mathematical theory of communication', *Bell Systems Technical Journal*, 27, pp. 379–423.

Strawson, G. (1994), *Mental Reality* (Cambridge, MA: MIT Press).

Tye, M. (1995), *Ten Problems of Consciousness* (Cambridge, MA: MIT Press) (See Chapter 37 of this volume).

Velmans, M. (1991), 'Is human information-processing conscious?' *Behavioral and Brain Sciences*, 14, pp. 651–69.

Wheeler, J.A. (1990), 'Information, physics, quantum: the search for links', in *Complexity, Entropy, and the Physics of Information*, ed. W. Zurek (Redwood City, CA: Addison-Wesley).

Wilkes, K.V. (1988), '—, Yishi, Duh, Um and consciousness', in *Consciousness in Contemporary Science*, ed. A. Marcel and E. Bisiach (Oxford: Oxford University Press).

Chapter 36

The intrinsic quality of experience*

Gilbert Harman

The problem

MANY philosophers, psychologists, and artificial intelligence researchers accept a broadly functionalist view of the relation between mind and body, for example, viewing the mind in the body as something like a computer in a robot, perhaps with massively parallel processing (as in Rumelhart and McClelland 1986). But this view of the mind has not gone unchallenged. Some philosophers and others object strenuously that functionalism must inevitably fail to account for the most important part of mental life, namely, the subjective feel of conscious experience.

The computer model of mind represents one version of functionalism, although it is not the only version. In its most general form, functionalism defines mental states and processes by their causal or functional relations to each other and to perceptual inputs from the world outside and behavioral outputs expressed in action. According to functionalism, it is the functional relations that are important, not the intrinsic qualities of the stuff in which these relations are instanced. Just as the same computer programs can be run on different computers made out of different materials, so functionalism allows for the same mental states and events in beings with very different physical constitutions, since the very same functional relations might be instantiated in beings with very different physical makeups. According to functionalism, beliefs, desires, thoughts, and feelings are not limited to beings that are materially like ourselves. Such psychological states and events might also occur, for example, in silicon based beings, as long as the right functional relations obtained.

Functionalism can allow for the possibility that something about silicon makes it impossible for the relevant relations to obtain in silicon based beings, perhaps because the relevant events could not occur fast enough in silicon. It is even conceivable that the relevant functional relations might obtain only in the sort of material that makes up human brains (Thagard 1986; Dennett 1987, Chapter 9). Functionalism implies that in such a case the material is important only because it is needed for the relevant functional relations and not because of some other more

Gilbert Harman, 'The Intrinsic Quality of Experience', *Philosophical Perspectives* 4 (1990).

* The preparation of this paper was supported in part by research grants to Princeton University from the James S. McDonnell Foundation and the National Science Foundation.

mysterious or magical connection between that sort of matter and a certain sort of consciousness.

Various issues arise within the general functionalist approach. For one thing, there is a dispute about how to identify the inputs to a functional system. Should inputs be identified with events in the external environment (Harman 1988) or should they instead be identified with events that are more internal such as the stimulation of an organism's sensory organs (Block 1986)? There is also the possibility of disagreement as to how deterministic the relevant functional relations have to be. Do they have to be completely deterministic, or can they be merely probabilistic? Or might they even be simply nondeterministic, not even associated with definite probabilities (Harman 1973, pp. 51–53)?

I will not be concerned with these issues here. Instead, I will concentrate on the different and more basic issue that I have already mentioned, namely, whether this sort of functionalism, no matter how elaborated, can account for the subjective feel of experience, for 'what it is like' (Nagel 1974) to undergo this or that experience. Furthermore, I will not consider the general challenge, 'How does functionalism account for X?' for this or that X. Nor will I consider negative arguments against particular functionalist analyses. I will instead consider three related arguments that purport to demonstrate that functionalism cannot account for this aspect of experience. I will argue that all three arguments are fallacious. I will say little that is original and will for the most part merely elaborate points made many years ago (Quine 1960, p. 235, Anscombe 1965, Armstrong 1961, 1962, and especially 1968, Pitcher 1971), points that I do not think have been properly appreciated. The three arguments are these:

First, when you attend to a pain in your leg or to your experience of the redness of an apple, you are aware of an intrinsic quality of your experience, where an intrinsic quality is a quality something has in itself, apart from its relations to other things. This quality of experience cannot be captured in a functional definition, since such a definition is concerned entirely with relations, relations between mental states and perceptual input, relations among mental states, and relations between mental states and behavioral output. For example, 'An essential feature of [Armstrong's functionalist] analysis is that it tells us nothing about the intrinsic nature of mental states ... He never takes seriously the natural objection that we must know the intrinsic nature of our own mental states since we experience them directly' (Nagel 1970).

Second, a person blind from birth could know all about the physical and functional facts of color perception without knowing what it is like to see something red. So, what it is like to see something red cannot be explicated in purely functional terms (Nagel 1974, Jackson 1982, 1986).

Third, it is conceivable that two people should have similarly functioning visual systems despite the fact that things that look red to one person look green to the other, things that look orange to the first person look blue to the second, and so forth (Lycan 1973, Shoemaker 1982). This sort of spectrum inversion in the way things look is possible but cannot be given a purely functional description, since by hypothesis there are no functional differences between the people in question. Since the way things look to a person is an aspect of that person's mental life, this means that an important aspect of a person's mental life cannot be explicated in purely functional terms.

Intentionality

In order to assess these arguments, I begin by remarking on what is sometimes called the intentionality of experience. Our experience of the world has content—that is, it represents things as being in a certain way. In particular, perceptual experience represents a perceiver as in a particular environment, for example, as facing a tree with brown bark and green leaves fluttering in a slight breeze.

One thing that philosophers mean when they refer to this as the intentional content of experience is that the content of the experience may not reflect what is really there. Although it looks to me as if I am seeing a tree, that may be a clever illusion produced with tilted mirrors and painted backdrops. Or it may be a hallucination produced by a drug in my coffee.

There are many other examples of intentionality. Ponce de Leon searched Florida for the Fountain of Youth. What he was looking for was a fountain whose waters would give eternal youth to whoever would drink them. In fact, there is no such thing as a Fountain of Youth, but that does not mean Ponce de Leon wasn't looking for anything. He was looking for something. We can therefore say that his search had an intentional object. But the thing that he was looking for, the intentional object of his search, did not (and does not) exist.

A painting of a unicorn is a painting of something; it has a certain content. But the content does not correspond to anything actual; the thing that the painting represents does not exist. The painting has an intentional content in the relevant sense of 'intentional.'

Imagining or mentally picturing a unicorn is usefully compared with a painting of a unicorn. In both cases the content is not actual; the object pictured, the intentional object of the picturing, does not exist. It is only an intentional object.

This is not to suppose that mentally picturing a unicorn involves an awareness of a mental picture of a unicorn. I am comparing mentally picturing something with a picture of something, not with a perception of a picture. An awareness of a picture has as its intentional object a picture. The picture has as its intentional object a unicorn. Imagining a unicorn is different from imagining a picture of a unicorn. The intentional object of the imagining is a unicorn, not a picture of a unicorn.

It is very important to distinguish between the properties of a represented object and the properties of a representation of that object. Clearly, these properties can be very different. The unicorn is pictured as having four legs and a single horn. The painting of the unicorn does not have four legs and a single horn. The painting is flat and covered with paint. The unicorn is not pictured as flat or covered with paint. Similarly, an imagined unicorn is imagined as having legs and a horn. The imagining of the unicorn has no legs or horn. The imagining of the unicorn is a mental activity. The unicorn is not imagined as either an activity or anything mental.

The notorious sense datum theory of perception arises through failing to keep these elementary points straight. According to that ancient theory, perception of external objects in the environment is always indirect and mediated by a more direct awareness of a mental sense datum. Defenders of the sense datum theory argue for it by appealing to the so-called argument from illusion. This argument begins with the uncontroversial premise that the way things are presented in perception is not always the way they are. Eloise sees some brown and green. But there is nothing brown and green before her; it is all an illusion or hallucination. From this the argument fallaciously infers that the brown and green Eloise sees is not external to her and so must be internal or mental. Since veridical, nonillusory, nonhallucinatory perception can be qualitatively indistinguishable from illusory or hallucinatory perception, the argument concludes that in all cases of perception Eloise is directly aware of something inner and mental and only indirectly aware of external objects like trees and leaves.

An analogous argument about paintings would start from the premise that a painting can be a painting of a unicorn even though there are no unicorns. From this it might be concluded that the painting is 'in the first instance' a painting of something else that is actual, for example, the painter's idea of a unicorn.

In order to see that such arguments are fallacious, consider the corresponding argument applied to searches: 'Ponce de Leon was searching for the Fountain of Youth. But there is no such thing. So he must have been searching for something mental.' This is just a mistake. From the fact that there is no Fountain of Youth, it does not follow that Ponce de Leon was searching for something mental. In particular, he was not looking for an idea of the Fountain of Youth. He already had the idea. What he wanted was a real Fountain of Youth, not just the idea of such a thing.

The painter has painted a picture of a unicorn. The picture painted is not a picture of an idea of a unicorn. The painter might be at a loss to paint a picture of an idea, especially if he is not familiar with conceptual art. It may be that the painter has an idea of a unicorn and tries to capture that idea in his painting. But that is to say his painting is a painting of the same thing that his idea is an idea of. The painting is not a painting of the idea, but a painting of what the idea is about.

In the same way, what Eloise sees before her is a tree, whether or not it is a hallucination. That is to say, the content of her visual experience is that she is presented with a tree, not with an idea of a tree. Perhaps, Eloise's visual experience involves some sort of mental picture of the environment. It does not follow that she is aware of a mental picture. If there is a mental picture, it may be that what she is aware of is whatever is represented by that mental picture; but then that mental picture represents something in the world, not something in the mind.

Now, we sometimes count someone as perceiving something only if that thing exists. So, if there is no tree before her and Eloise is suffering from a hallucination, we might describe this either by saying that Eloise sees something that is not really there or by saying that she does not really see anything at all but only seems to see something. There is not a use of 'search for' corresponding to this second use of 'see' that would allow us to say that, because there was and is no such thing as the Fountain of Youth, Ponce de Leon was not really searching for anything at all.

But this ambiguity in perceptual verbs does not affect the point I am trying to make. To see that it does not, let us use 'see†' ('see-dagger') for the sense of 'see' in which the object seen might not exist, as when Macbeth saw a dagger before him.[1] And let us use 'see*' ('see-star') for the sense of 'see' in which only things that exist can be seen. Macbeth saw† a dagger but he did not see* a dagger.

The argument from illusion starts from a case in which Eloise 'sees' something brown and green before her, although there is nothing brown and green before her in the external physical world. From this, the argument infers that the brown and green she sees must be internal and mental. Now, if 'see' is 'see†' here, this is the fallacy already noted, like that of concluding that Ponce de Leon was searching for something mental from the fact that there is no Fountain of Youth in the external world. On the other hand, if 'see' is 'see*' here, then the premise of the argument simply begs the question. No reason at all has so far been given for the claim that Eloise sees* something brown and green in this case. It is true that her perceptual experience represents her as visually presented with something brown and green; but that is to say merely that she sees† something brown and green, not that she sees* anything at all. (From now on I will suppress the † and * modification of perceptual verbs unless indication of which sense is meant is crucial to the discussion.)

Here, some philosophers (e.g. Jackson 1977) would object as follows:

> You agree that there is a sense in which Eloise sees something green and brown when there is nothing green and brown before her in the external world. You are able to deny that this brown and green thing is mental by taking it to be a nonexistent and merely intentional object. But it is surely more reasonable to suppose that one is in this case aware of something mental than to suppose that one is aware of something that does not exist. How can there be anything that does not exist? The very suggestion is a contradiction in terms, since 'be' simply means 'exist,' so that you are really saying that there exists something that does not exist (Quine 1948). There are no such things as nonexistent objects!

In reply, let me concede immediately that I do not have a well worked out theory of intentional objects. Parsons (1980) offers one such theory, although I do not mean to express an opinion as to the success of Parson's approach. Indeed, I am quite willing to believe that there are not really any nonexistent objects and that

1. W. Shakespeare, Macbeth, Act II, Scene I: Is this a dagger which I see before me, The handle toward my hand? Come let me clutch thee. I have thee not, and yet I see thee still. Art thou not, fatal vision, sensible To feeling as to sight? or art thou but A dagger of the mind, a false creating. Proceeding from the heat oppressed brain? . . . I see thee still; And on thy blade and dudgeon gouts of blood, Which was not so before. There's no such thing; it is the bloody business which informs Thus to mine eyes.

apparent talk of such objects should be analyzed away somehow. I do not see that it is my job to resolve this issue. However this issue is resolved, that theory that results had better end up agreeing that Ponce de Leon was looking for something when he was looking for the Fountain of Youth, even though there is no Fountain of Youth, and the theory had better *not* have the consequence that Ponce de Leon was looking for something mental. If a logical theory can account for searches for things that do not, as it happens, exist, it can presumably also allow for a sense of 'see' in which Macbeth can see something that does not really exist.

Another point is that Eloise's visual experience does not just present a tree. It presents a tree as viewed from a certain place. Various features that the tree is presented as having are presented as relations between the viewer and the tree, for example, features the tree has from here. The tree is presented as 'in front of' and 'hiding' certain other trees. It is presented as fuller on 'the right.' It is presented as the same size 'from here' as a closer smaller tree, which is not to say that it really looks the same in size, only that it is presented as subtending roughly the same angle from here as the smaller tree. To be presented as the same in size from here is not to be presented as the same in size, period.

I do not mean to suggest that the way the tree is visually presented as being from here is something that is easily expressed in words. In particular, I do not mean to suggest that the tree can thus be presented as subtending a certain visual angle only to someone who understands words like 'subtend' and 'angle' (as is assumed in Peacocke 1983, Chapter 1). I mean only that this feature of a tree from here is an objective feature of the tree in relation to here, a feature to which perceivers are sensitive and which their visual experience can somehow represent things as having from here.

Now, perhaps, Eloise's visual experience even presents a tree as seen by her, that is, as an object of her visual experience. If so, there is a sense after all in which Eloise's visual experience represents something mental: it represents objects in the world as objects of visual experience. But this does not mean that Eloise's visual experience in any way reveals to her the intrinsic properties of that experience by virtue of which it has the content it has.

I want to stress this point, because it is very important. Eloise is aware of the tree as a tree that she is now seeing. So, we can suppose she is aware of some features of her current visual experience. In particular, she is aware that her visual experience has the feature of being an experience of seeing a tree. That is to be aware of an intentional feature of her experience; she is aware that her experience has a certain content. On the other hand, I want to argue that she is not aware of those intrinsic features of her experience by virtue of which it has that content. Indeed, I believe that she has no access at all to the intrinsic features of her mental representation that make it a mental representation of seeing a tree.

Things are different with paintings. In the case of a painting Eloise can be aware of those features of the painting that are responsible for its being a painting of a unicorn. That is, she can turn her attention to the pattern of the paint on the canvas by virtue of which the painting represents a unicorn. But in the case of her visual experience of a tree, I want to say that she is not aware of, as it were, the mental paint by virtue of which her experience is an experience of seeing a tree. She is aware only of the intentional or relational features of her experience, not of its intrinsic nonintentional features.

Some sense datum theorists will object that Eloise is indeed aware of the relevant mental paint when she is aware of an arrangement of color, because these sense datum theorists assert that the color she is aware of is inner and mental and not a property of external objects. But, this sense datum claim is counter to ordinary visual experience. When Eloise sees a tree before her, the colors she experiences are all experienced as features of the tree and its surroundings. None of them are experienced as intrinsic features of her experience. Nor does she experience any features of anything as intrinsic features of her experience. And that is true of you too. There is nothing special about Eloise's visual experience. When you see a tree, you do not experience any features as intrinsic features of your experience. Look at a tree and try to turn your attention to intrinsic features of your visual experience. I predict you will find that the only features there to turn your attention to will be features of the presented tree, including relational features of the tree 'from here.'

The sense datum theorists' view about our immediate experience of color is definitely not the naive view; it does not represent the viewpoint of ordinary perception. The sense datum theory is not the result of phenomenological study; it is rather the result of an argument, namely, the argument from illusion. But that argument is either invalid or question-begging, as we have seen.

It is very important to distinguish what are experienced as intrinsic features of the intentional object of experience from intrinsic features of the experience itself. It is not always easy to distinguish these things, but they can be distinguished. Consider the experience of having a pain in your right leg. It is very tempting to confuse features of what you experience as happening in your leg with intrinsic features of your experience. But the happening in your leg that you are presented with is the intentional object of your experience; it is not the experience itself. The content of your experience is that there is a disturbance of a certain specific sort in your right leg. The intentional object of the experience is an event located in your right leg. The experience itself is not located in your right leg. If the experience is anywhere specific, it is somewhere in your brain.

Notice that the content of your experience may not be true to what is actually happening. A slipped disc in your back may press against your sciatic nerve making it appear that there is a disturbance in your right leg when there really is not. The intentional object of your painful experience may not exist. Of course, that is not to say there is no pain in your leg. You do feel something there. But there is a sense in which what you feel in your leg is an illusion or hallucination.

It is true that, if Melvin hallucinates a pink elephant, the elephant that Melvin sees does not exist. But the pain in your leg resulting from a slipped disc in your back certainly does exist.[2] The pain is not an intentional object in quite the way the elephant is. The pain in your leg caused by the slipped disc in your back is more like the afterimage of a bright light. If you look at a blank wall, you see the image on the wall. The image is on the wall, the pain is in your leg. There is no physical spot on the wall, there is no physical disturbance in your leg. The afterimage exists, the pain exists. When we talk about afterimages or referred pains, some of what we say is about our experience and some of what we say is about the intentional object of that experience. When we say the pain or afterimage exists, we mean that the experience exists. When we say that the afterimage is on the wall or that the pain is in your leg, we are talking about the location of the intentional object of that experience.

Assessment of the first objection

We are now in a position to reject the first of the three arguments against functionalism which I now repeat:

> When you attend to a pain in your leg or to your experience of the redness of an apple, you are aware of an intrinsic quality of your experience, where an intrinsic quality is a quality something has in itself, apart from its relations to other things. This quality of experience cannot be captured in a functional definition, since such a definition is concerned entirely with relations, relations between mental states and perceptual input, relations among mental states, and relations between mental states and behavioral output.

We can now see that this argument fails through confounding a quality of the intentional object of an experience with a quality of the experience itself. When you attend to a pain in your leg or to your experience of the redness of an apple, you are attending to a quality of an occurrence in your leg or a quality of the apple. Perhaps this quality is presented to you as an intrinsic quality of the occurrence in your leg or as an intrinsic quality of the surface of the apple. But it is not at all presented as an intrinsic quality of your experience. And, since you are not aware of the intrinsic character of your experience, the fact that functionalism abstracts from the intrinsic character of experience does not show it leaves out anything you are aware of.

To be sure, there are possible complications. Suppose David undergoes brain surgery which he watches in a mirror. Suppose that he sees certain intrinsic features of the firing of certain neurons in his brain and suppose that the firing of these neurons is the realization of part of the experience he is having at that moment. In that case, David is aware of intrinsic features of his experience. But that way of being aware of intrinsic features of experience is not incompatible with functionalism. Given a functionalist account of David's perception of trees, tables, and the

2. I am indebted to Sydney Shoemaker for emphasizing this to me.

brain processes of other people, the same account applies when the object perceived happens to be David's own brain processes. The awareness David has of his own brain processes is psychologically similar to the awareness any other sighted perceiver might have of those same brain processes, including perceivers constructed in a very different way from the way in which David is constructed.

According to functionalism, the psychologically relevant properties of an internal process are all functional properties. The intrinsic nature of the process is relevant only inasmuch as it is responsible for the process's having the functional properties it has. I have been considering the objection that certain intrinsic features of experience must be psychologically relevant properties apart from their contribution to function, since these are properties we are or can be aware of. The objection is not just that we can become aware of intrinsic features of certain mental processes in the way just mentioned, that is, by perceiving in a mirror the underlying physical processes that realize those mental processes. That would not be an objection to functionalism. The objection is rather that all or most conscious experience has intrinsic aspects of which we are or can be aware in such a way that these aspects of the experience are psychologically significant over and above the contribution they make to function.

Of course, to say that these aspects are psychologically significant is not to claim that they are or ought to be significant for the science of psychology. Rather, they are supposed to be psychologically significant in the sense of mentally significant, whether or not this aspect of experience is susceptible of scientific understanding. The objection is that any account of our mental life that does not count these intrinsic properties as mental or psychological properties leaves out a crucial aspect of our experience.

My reply to this objection is that it cannot be defended without confusing intrinsic features of the intentional object of experience with intrinsic features of the experience. Apart from that confusion, there is no reason to think that we are ever aware of the relevant intrinsic features of our experiences.

There are other ways in which one might be aware of intrinsic features of our experience without that casting any doubt on functionalism. For example, one might be aware of intrinsic features of experience without being aware of them as intrinsic features of experience, just as Ortcutt can be aware of a man who, as it happens, is a spy without being aware of the man as a spy. When Eloise sees a tree, she is aware of her perceptual experience as an experience with a certain intentional content. Suppose that her experience is realized by a particular physical event and that certain intrinsic features of the event are in this case responsible for certain intentional features of Eloise's experience. Perhaps there is then a sense in which Eloise is aware of this physical process and aware of those intrinsic features, although she is not aware of them as the intrinsic features that they are.

Even if that is so, it is no objection to functionalism. The intrinsic features that Eloise is aware of in that case are no more psychologically significant than is the property of being a spy to Ortcutt's perception of a man who happens to be a spy.

The case gives no reason to think that there is a psychologically significant difference between Eloise's experience and the experience of any functional duplicate of Eloise that is made of different stuff from what Eloise is made of.

Similarly, if Eloise undertakes the sort of education recommended by Paul Churchland (1985) so that she automatically thinks of the intentional aspects of her experience in terms of their neurophysiological causes, then she may be aware of intrinsic features of her experience as the very features that they are. But again that would be no objection to functionalism, since it gives no reason to think that there is a psychological difference between Eloise after such training and a robot who is Eloise's functional duplicate and who has been given similar training (Shoemaker 1985). The duplicate now wrongly thinks of certain aspects of its experience as certain features of certain neurological processes—wrongly, because the relevant processes in the duplicate are not neurological processes at all.

Observe, by the way, that I am not offering any sort of positive argument that Eloise and her duplicate must have experiences that are psychologically similar in all respects. I am only observing that the cases just considered are compatible with the functionalist claim that their experiences are similar.

The objections to functionalism that I am considering in this paper claim that certain intrinsic properties of experience so inform the experience that any experience with different intrinsic properties would have a different psychological character. What I have argued so far is that this objection is not established by simple inspection of our experience.

Perception and understanding

Now, let me turn to the second objection, which I repeat:

> A person blind from birth could know all about the physical and functional facts of color perception without knowing what it is like to see something red. So, what it is like to see something red cannot be explicated in purely functional terms.

In order to address this objection, I have to say something about the functionalist theory of the content of mental representations and, more particularly, something about the functionalist theory of concepts. I have to do this because to know what it is like to see something red is to be capable of representing to yourself something's being red. You can represent that to yourself only if you have the relevant concept of what it is for something to be red. The blind person lacks the full concept of redness that a sighted person has; so the blind person cannot fully represent what it is for a sighted person to see something red. Therefore, the blind person cannot be said to know what it is like to see something red.

One kind of functionalist account of mental representation supposes that mental representations are constructed from concepts, where the content of a representation is determined by the concepts it contains and the way these concepts are put together to form that representation (Harman 1987). In this view, what it is to have a given concept is functionally determined. Someone has the appropriate concept of something's being red if and only if the person has available a concept that functions in the appropriate way. The relevant functioning may involve connections with the use of other concepts, connections to perceptual input, and/or connections to behavioral output. In this case, connections to perceptual input are crucial. If the concept is to function in such a way that the person has the full concept of something's being red, the person must be disposed to form representations involving that concept as the natural and immediate consequence of seeing something red. Since the blind person lacks any concept of this sort, the blind person lacks the full concept of something's being red. Therefore, the blind person does not know what it is like to see something red.

It is not easy to specify the relevant functional relation precisely. Someone who goes blind later in life will normally retain the relevant concept of something's being red. Such a person has a concept that he or she would be able to use in forming such immediate visual representations except for the condition that interferes in his or her case with normal visual perception. So, the right functional relation holds for such a person. I am supposing that the person blind from birth has no such concept; that is, the person has no concept of something's being red that could be immediately brought into service in visual representations of the environment if the person were suddenly to acquire sight.

We are now in a position to assess the claim that the person blind from birth could know all the physical and functional facts about color perception without knowing what it is like to see something red. I claim that there is one important functional fact about color perception that the blind person cannot know, namely, that there is a concept *R* such that when a normal perceiver sees something red in good lighting conditions, the perceiver has visual experience with a representational structure containing this concept *R*. The person blind from birth does not know that fact, because in order to know it the person needs to be able to represent that fact to him or herself, which requires having the relevant concepts. A key concept needed to represent that fact is the concept of something's being red, because the fact in question is a fact about what happens when a normal perceiver sees something red. Since the person blind from birth does not have the full concept of something's being red, the person cannot fully understand that fact and so cannot know that fact.

The blind person might know something resembling this, for example, that there is a concept *R* such that, when a normal perceiver sees something that reflects light of such and such a frequency, the perceiver has visual experience with a representational structure containing this concept *R*. But that is to know something different.

The person blind from birth fails to know what it is like to see something red because he or she does not fully understand what it is for something to be red, that is, because he or she does not have the full concept of something's being red. So, contrary to what is assumed in the second objection, the person blind from birth does not know all the functional facts, since he or she does not know how the concept *R* functions with respect to the perception of things that are red.

This response to the second objection appeals to a functionalism that refers to the functions of concepts, not just to the functions of overall mental states. There are other versions of functionalism that try to make do with references to the functions of overall mental states, without appeal to concepts. Some of these versions identify the contents of such states with sets of possible worlds (or centered possible worlds). These versions of functionalism cannot respond to the objection in the way that I have responded. It is unclear to me whether any satisfactory response is possible on behalf of such theories. For example, Lewis (1983) is forced to say that although the person blind from birth lacks certain skills, e.g., the ability to recognize red objects just by looking at them in the way that sighted people can, this person lacks no information about visual perception. I am not happy with that response, since it is clearly false to say that the person blind from birth does not lack any information.

Inverted spectrum

I now turn to the third objection to functionalism, which I repeat:

> It is conceivable that two people should have similarly functioning visual systems despite the fact that things that look red to one person look green to the other, things that look orange to the first person look blue to the second, and so forth. This sort of spectrum inversion in the way things look is possible but cannot be given a purely functional description, since by hypothesis there are no functional differences between the people in question. Since the way things look to a person is an aspect of that person's mental life, this means that there is an important aspect of a person's mental life that cannot be explicated in purely functional terms.

In order to discuss this objection, I need to say something more about how perceptual states function. In particular, I have to say something about how perceptual states function in relation to belief.

Perceptual experience represents a particular environment of the perceiver. Normally, a perceiver uses this representation as his or her representation of the environment. That is to say, the perceiver uses it in order to negotiate the furniture. In still other words, this representation is used as the perceiver's belief about the environment. This sort of use of perceptual representations is the normal case, although there are exceptions when a perceiver inhibits his or her natural tendency and refrains from using a perceptual representation (or certain aspects of that representation) as a guide to the environment, as a belief about the surroundings. The content of perceptual representation is functionally defined in part by the ways in which this representation normally arises in perception and in part by the ways in which the representation is normally used to guide actions (Armstrong 1961, 1968; Dennett 1969; Harman 1973).

The objection has us consider two people, call them Alice and Fred, with similarly functioning visual systems but with inverted spectra with respect to each other. Things that look red to Alice look green to Fred, things that look blue to Alice look orange to Fred, and so on. We are to imagine that this difference between Alice and Fred is not reflected in their behavior in any way. They both call ripe strawberries 'red' and call grass 'green' and they do this in the effortless ways in which normal perceivers do who have learned English in the usual ways.

Consider what this means for Alice in a normal case of perception. She looks at a ripe strawberry. Perceptual processing results in a perceptual representation of that strawberry, including a representation of its color. She uses this representation as her guide to the environment, that is, as her belief about the strawberry, in particular, her belief about its color. She expresses her belief about the color of the strawberry by using the words, 'it is red.' Similarly, for Fred. His perception of the strawberry results in a perceptual representation of the color of the strawberry that he uses as his belief about the color and expresses with the same words, 'it is red.'

Now, in the normal case of perception, there can be no distinction between how things look and how they are believed to be, since how things look is given by the content of one's perceptual representation and in the normal case one's perceptual representation is used as one's belief about the environment. The hypothesis of the inverted spectrum objection is that the strawberry looks different in color to Alice and to Fred. Since everything is supposed to be functioning in them in the normal way, it follows that they must have different beliefs about the color of the strawberry. If they had the same beliefs while having perceptual representations that differed in content, then at least one of them would have a perceptual representation that was not functioning as his or her belief about the color of the strawberry, which is to say that it would not be functioning in what we are assuming is the normal way.

A further consequence of the inverted spectrum hypothesis is that, since in the normal case Alice and Fred express their beliefs about the color of strawberries and grass by saying 'it is red' and 'it is green,' they must mean something different by their color words. By 'red' Fred means the way ripe strawberries look to him. Since that is the way grass looks to Alice, what Fred means by 'red' is what she means by 'green.'

It is important to see that these really are consequences of the inverted spectrum hypothesis. If Alice and Fred meant the same thing by their color terms, then either (a) one of them would not be using these words to express his or her beliefs about color or (b) one of them would not be using his or her perceptual representations of color as his or her beliefs about color. In either case, there would be a failure of normal functioning, contrary to the hypothesis of the inverted spectrum objection.

According to functionalism, if Alice and Fred use words in the same way with respect to the same things, then they mean the same things by those words (assuming also that they are members of the same linguistic community and their words are taken from the common language). But this is just common sense. Suppose

Alice and Humphrey are both members of the same linguistic community, using words in the same way, etc. Alice is an ordinary human being and Humphrey is a humanoid robot made of quite a different material from Alice. Common sense would attribute the same meanings to Humphrey's words as to Alice's, given that they use words in the same way. Some sort of philosophical argument is needed to argue otherwise. No such argument has been provided by defenders of the inverted spectrum objection.

Shoemaker (1982) offers a different version of the inverted spectrum objection. He has us consider a single person, call him Harry, at two different times, at an initial time of normal color perception and at a later time after Harry has suffered through a highly noticeable spectrum inversion (perhaps as the result of the sort of brain operation described in Lycan 1973, in which nerves are switched around so that red things now have the perceptual consequences that green things used to have, etc.) and has finally completely adapted his responses so as to restore normal functioning. Shoemaker agrees that Harry now has the same beliefs about color as before and means the same things by his color words, and he agrees that there is a sense in which strawberries now look to Harry the same as they looked before Harry's spectrum inversion. But Shoemaker takes it to be evident that there is another sense of 'looks' in which it may very well be true that things do not look the same as they looked before, so that in this second sense of 'looks' red things look the way green things used to look.

In other words, Shoemaker thinks it is evident that there may be a psychologically relevant difference between the sort of experience Harry had on looking at a ripe strawberry at the initial stage and the experience he has on looking at a ripe strawberry at the final stage (after he has completely adapted to his operation). That is, he thinks it is evident that there may be a psychologically relevant difference between these experiences even though there is no functional difference and no difference in the content of the experiences.

Now, this may seem evident to anyone who has fallen victim to the sense datum fallacy, which holds that one's awareness of the color of a strawberry is mediated by one's awareness of an intrinsic feature of a perceptual representation. But why should anyone else agree? Two perceptual experiences with the same intentional content must be psychologically the same. In particular, there can be nothing one is aware of in having the one experience that one is not aware of in having the other, since the intentional content of an experience comprises everything one is aware of in having that experience.

I suggest that Shoemaker's inverted spectrum hypothesis will seem evident only to someone who *begins* with the prior assumption that people have an immediate and direct awareness of intrinsic features of their experience, including those intrinsic features that function to represent color. Such a person can then go on to suppose that the intrinsic feature of experience that represents red for Alice is the intrinsic feature of experience that represents green for Fred, and so forth. This prior assumption is exactly the view behind the first objection, which I have argued is contrary to ordinary experience and can be defended only by confusing qualities of the intentional objects of experience with qualities of the experience itself. Shoemaker's inverted spectrum hypothesis therefore offers no independent argument against functionalism.[3]

Conclusion

To summarize briefly, I have described and replied to three related objections to functionalism. The first claims that we are directly aware of intrinsic features of our experience and argues that there is no way to account for this awareness in a functional view. To this, I reply that when we clearly distinguish properties of the object of experience from properties of the experience, we see that we are not aware of the relevant intrinsic features of the experience. The second objection claims that a person blind from birth can know all about the functional role of visual experience without knowing what it is like to see something red. To this I reply that the blind person does not know all about the functional role of visual experience; in particular, the blind person does not know how such experience functions in relation to the perception of red objects. The third objection claims that functionalism cannot account for the possibility of an inverted spectrum. To this I reply that someone with the relevant sort of inverted spectrum would have to have beliefs about the colors of things that are different from the beliefs others have and would have to mean something different by his or her color terms, despite being a functionally normal color perceiver who sorts things by color in exactly the way others do and who uses color terminology in the same way that others do. Functionalism's rejection of this possibility is commonsensical and is certainly not so utterly implausible or counter-intuitive that these cases present an objection to functionalism. On the other hand, to imagine that there could be relevant cases of inverted spectrum without inversion of belief and meaning is to fall back onto the first objection and not to offer any additional consideration against functionalism.

References

Anscombe, G. E. M. (1965) 'The intentionality of sensation: a grammatical feature,' *Analytical Philosophy*, second series, edited by R. J. Butler (Oxford, Blackwell); reprinted in Anscombe, G.E.M., *Metaphysics and the Philosophy of Mind: Collected Philosophical Papers, Volume II* (Minneapolis, Minnesota; University of Minnesota Press: 1981) pp. 3–20.

Armstrong, David M. (1961) *Perception and the Physical World* (London: Routledge & Kegan Paul).

Armstrong, David M. (1962) *Bodily Sensations* (London: Routledge & Kegan Paul).

3. I should say that Shoemaker himself does not offer his case as an objection to what he calls functionalism. He claims that his version of functionalism is compatible with his case. But I am considering a version of functionalism that is defined in a way that makes it incompatible with such a case.

Armstrong, David M. (1968) *The Materialist Theory of Mind* (London: Routledge & Kegan Paul).

Block, Ned (1986) 'Advertisement for a semantics for psychology,' *Midwest Studies in Philosophy* 10: 615–678.

Churchland, Paul (1985) 'Reduction, qualia, and the direct introspection of mental states,' *Journal of Philosophy* 82: 8–28.

Dennett, Daniel C. (1969) *Content and Consciousness* (London: Routledge & Kegan Paul).

Dennett, Daniel C. (1987) *The Intentional Stance* (Cambridge, Massachusetts: MIT Press).

Harman, Gilbert (1973) *Thought* (Princeton, New Jersey: Princeton University Press).

Harman, Gilbert (1987) '(Nonsolipsistic) conceptual role semantics,' *New Directions in Semantics*, edited by Ernest LePore, London, Academic Press (1987) 55–81.

Harman, Gilbert (1988) 'Wide functionalism,' *Cognition and Representation*, edited by Stephen Schiffer and Susan Steele (Boulder, Colorado: Westview Press) 11–20.

Jackson, Frank (1977) *Perception: A Representative Theory* (Cambridge, England: Cambridge University Press).

Jackson, Frank (1982) 'Epiphenomenal qualia,' *Philosophical Quarterly* 32: 127–32 (see Chapter 43 of this volume).

Jackson, Frank (1986) 'What Mary didn't know,' *Journal of Philosophy* 83: 291–295.

Lewis, David K. (1983) 'Postscript to 'Mad pain and martian pain',' *Philosophical Papers*, Volume 1, (New York: Oxford University Press) 130–132.

Lycan, William G. (1973) 'Inverted spectrum' *Ratio* 15.

Nagel, Thomas (1970) 'Armstrong on the mind,' *Philosophical Review* 79, reprinted in Reading in the Philosophy of Psychology Volume 1, edited by Ned Block (Cambridge, Massachusetts: Harvard University Press).

Nagel, Thomas (1974) 'What is it like to be a bat?' *Philosophical Review* 83: 435–450 (see Chapter 29 of this volume).

Parsons, Terence (1980) *Nonexistent Objects* (New Haven: Yale University Press).

Peacocke, Christopher (1983) *Sense and Content* (Oxford: Oxford University Press).

Pitcher, George (1971) *A Theory of Perception* (Princeton, New Jersey: Princeton University Press).

Quine, W. V. (1948) 'On what there is,' *Review of Metaphysics*, reprinted in *From a Logical Point of View* (Cambridge, Massachusetts; Harvard University Press: 1953).

Quine, W. V. (1960) *Word and Object* (Cambridge, Massachusetts: MIT Press).

Rumelhart, David EO, and McClelland, James L. (1986) *Parallel Distributed Processing*, 2 volumes (Cambridge, Massachusetts: MIT Press).

Shoemaker, Sydney (1982) 'The inverted spectrum,' *Journal of Philosophy* 79: 357–81.

Shoemaker, Sydney (1985) 'Churchland on reduction, qualia, and introspection,' *PSA 1984*, Volume 2 (Philosophy of Science Association) pp. 799–809.

Thagard, Paul T. (1986) 'Parallel computation and the mind-body problem,' *Cognitive Science* 10: 301–318.

Chapter 37

Précis of *Ten Problems of Consciousness*

Michael Tye

THE sort of consciousness that has created the most puzzlement among philosophers (and increasingly psychologists) is phenomenal consciousness. Consciousness of the phenomenal variety is widespread in nature. It is found wherever there is experience and feeling, and it requires no real reflective abilities. Nonetheless it is deeply mystifying. Associated with it, I claim, are ten different problems that any satisfactory theory must address and solve. These problems, as a group, present what is perhaps the toughest nut to crack in all of philosophy; so, it is not surprising that several philosophers, not otherwise opposed to substantive theorizing, see little hope of coming to a real understanding of the nature of phenomenal consciousness.

My own view is more positive. The aim of the book is to present a theory that solves the ten problems. The theory I develop is a strong representationalist one. I argue that all experiences and feelings represent things and that their phenomenal character—what it is like to undergo them—is itself to be understood in terms of their representational contents. On the face of it, this view is a perplexing one. Philosophers usually draw a sharp distinction between the representational features of experiences and their phenomenal features. Indeed, philosophical orthodoxy has it that some experiences and feelings have no representational content at all. Think, for example, of an exogenous feeling of depression. And what about bodily sensations? Pains, itches, and tickles do not seem to be *of* anything. The usual view is that these states do not represent anything.

Moreover, according to philosophical orthodoxy, phenomenal consciousness is quintessentially an internal matter. Creatures that are molecular duplicates inside the head must be alike phenomenally, however different their environments may be. Representation, however, is usually taken to be some sort of external relation. What a given mental state represents depends at least in part upon the world outside the head. Here, then, is another reason for distinguishing phenomenal character and representational content.

I argue that, on all of these matters, philosophical orthodoxy is wrong. What it is like *is* representational. Molecular duplicates *can* differ phenomenally. The theory I

Michael Tye, 'Précis of *Ten Problems of Consciousness*', *Philosophy and Phenomenological Research* 58 (1998).

elaborate is justified by reference to its explanatory power. It enables us to solve the ten problems and to understand a variety of pieces of data that would otherwise be puzzling. It also allows us to come to grips with a paradox that naturally arises once we reflect upon several of the problems together.

The strategy of the book is to lay out the problems and the paradox in a straightforward way, and then to develop the theory piece by piece in response to them. The problems, very briefly and roughly, are these: (1) the Problem of Ownership (Why can't you feel my pains? Why can't there be a pain that no-one feels?); (2) the Problem of Perspectival Subjectivity (Why does properly understanding pain require that one have a certain point of view, that conferred by oneself having experienced pain?); (3) the Problem of Mechanism (How can objective changes in the brain generate perspectivally subjective states?); (4) the Problem of Phenomenal Causation (How can the felt qualities of experiences make any difference to behavior?); (5) the Problem of Superblindsight (What is it that imaginary blindsight subjects, who have trained themselves to guess and who come to believe their guesses, lack relative to you and me?); (6) the Problem of Transparency (Why does attention to our experiences seem to reveal only what they are experiences *of* (e.g., colors and shapes, as in the case of visual experiences, or qualities in our bodies outside our heads, as in the case of a pain in the leg)?); (7) the Problem of Duplicates (Could there be zombies or functional duplicates that experience nothing?); (8) the Problem of the Inverted Spectrum (Could experiences be phenomenally inverted and yet functionally identical?); (9) the Problem of Phenomenal Vocabulary and Felt Location (How is it that terms standardly applied to ordinary physical objects get applied to sensations (e.g., the term 'in' in 'pain in a leg')?: (10) the Problem of the Alien Limb (How do I get to be involved in the phenomenology of my own feelings?).

The theory I propose is, as noted above, a theory of phenomenal consciousness. Consciousness of this sort, in my view, is to be distinguished from higher-order consciousness. It attaches paradigmatically to perceptual experiences and images (hearing a loud noise, having a blue after-image), bodily sensations (feeling an itch), emotions (feeling angry), and felt moods (feeling elated). It is not, I claim, an essential feature of thought or belief at all. I do not deny, of course, that often when we consciously think about something or understand something, we are subject to linguistic (or verbal) images. It is as if we are speaking to ourselves. We 'hear' an inner voice. But such images are not a necessary part of thought. Without images, associated emotions and perceptual experiences, thoughts and beliefs have no phenomenology.

According to the approach presented in the book, a mental state is phenomenally conscious just in case it has a PANIC—a (suitably) Poised, Abstract, Nonconceptual, Intentional Content. Moreover, its phenomenal character or felt aspect is one and the same as its PANIC.

Let us begin with the case of vision. Following the lead of David Marr (1982) and many other cognitive scientists, I claim that early vision is modular. It works in a largely fixed, autonomous manner. The representations it generates of a certain class of properties of distal stimuli from the input representations of the intensity and wavelength of light rays striking the myriad of retinal cells are the result of perceptual processes that operate largely without cognitive intervention. This early modular processing culminates in the construction of a representation of the three-dimensional surfaces that are visible from the given point of view (without any segmentation yet of those surfaces as belonging to toys, tables, tomatoes, etc). It is here at the level of such output representations that things initially acquire their looks, here that basic visual experiences are found. Likewise, for the other senses.

Of course, I am happy to concede that people with different experiences in the past may experience some things differently now (even at this basic level). Given different patterns of input, different outputs can result. Zulus, for example, are only minimally subject to the Müller-Lyer illusion. They live in a culture in which there are very few straight lines and corners. Their huts are circular, and they even plough their fields in curved lines. So, their past experiences are very different from ours. But this is no threat to modularity—any more than is the fact that people who have Japanese parents tend to end up speaking Japanese whereas people who have English parents tend to end up speaking English a threat to the existence of a parsing module with an innately specified architecture.[1]

I make a sharp distinction, then, between basic perceptual experiences or sensations, and beliefs or other conceptual states. The visual and olfactory sensations involved in seeing and smelling a skunk, for example, do not require that one believe it to be a skunk, think of it as producing a foul odour, or even have any idea of what one is sensing at all. Perceptual experiences like these form the outputs of specialized sensory modules, and the inputs to one or another higher-level cognitive system. They arise at the interface between the nonconceptual and the conceptual domains. Their situation is such that they stand ready and available to make a difference in beliefs (unlike those states formed earlier in the sensory processing). More precisely, they supply the inputs to cognitive processes, whose role it is to form beliefs directly from them, if attention is properly focused.[2] They are, in this sense, states that are *poised* (or that have *poised* contents).

The above view of basic perceptual experiences accommodates nicely certain facts about perceptual illusions (for example, why the Müller-Lyer illusion does not vanish once one realizes that it is an illusion). In addition, it accommodates our pretheoretical conception of the role of experiences as the bedrock for many beliefs and judgments (see below). It is also motivated by a desire to have an account of phenomenal consciousness that fits the facts of blindsight.

Basic perceptual experiences, I claim, have *nonconceptual* contents, since they are

1. Of course I do not deny that there are some cases of cognitive feedback.
2. In the case of some nonperceptual experiences, desires are relevant as well as (or instead of) beliefs. For a precise statement of what it is for a state to be poised, see Tye 1995, p. 138. For more on the qualification about attention, see Tye 1997.

representational or intentional states and their subjects need not have concepts that match what they represent (or that enter into their contents). Color sensations, to take one obvious case, subjectively vary in ways that go far beyond our color concepts. For example, my experience or sensation of the determinate shade, $blue_{19}$, is phenomenally different from that of the shade, $blue_{22}$. But I have no such concept as $blue_{19}$. So, I cannot see something as $blue_{19}$ or recognize that specific shade as such. My ordinary color judgments are, of necessity, far less fine-grained or discriminating than my experiences of color. The reason presumably is that without some constraints on what can be cognitively extracted, there would be information overload. Human memory simply isn't up to the task of capturing the wealth of detail found in the experiences. Beliefs or judgments abstract away from the details and impose more general categories. Sensory experience is the basis for many beliefs or judgments, but it is far, far richer.

Some seek to explain the richness of sensory experience conceptually by noting that even though the subject often has no appropriate nonindexical concept, he or she is at least aware of the pertinent feature, e.g., $blue_{19}$, as *that* shade of blue or *that* quality. This seems to me unsatisfactory. Intuitively, one can have a sensory experience without attending to it or its content. Moreover when one does attend, it seems that the explanation of one's awareness of the relevant feature as *that* feature is, in part, that one is having an experience that represents it. But no such explanation is possible if the content of the experience is already conceptual.

So, perceptual experiences have poised, nonconceptual, representational or intentional contents. And it is in these contents, I maintain, that their phenomenal character is to be found. The appeal here is partly to Occam's Razor: it is not necessary to posit any intrinsic, non-intentional qualia to solve any of the ten problems or the paradox. So, non-intentional qualia should be eliminated. But there are also other arguments.

One of these begins with the familiar point that introspecting a visual experience is *not* like viewing a picture of something. In the latter case, one can discriminate both intrinsic features of the picture (colors and shapes of blobs of paint on the canvas, for example) and what it is that the picture represents. Not so, I maintain, in the former. Suppose you are facing a white wall, on which you see a bright red disk. Suppose you are attending closely to the color and shape of the disk as well as the background. Now turn your attention from what you see out there in the world before you to your visual experience. Focus upon *your awareness of* the disk as opposed to *the disk* of which you are aware. Do you find yourself acquainted with new qualities, qualities that are intrinsic to your visual experience in the way that redness and roundness are qualities intrinsic to the disk? Surely the answer to this question is are resounding 'No'. As you look at the patch, you are aware of certain features out there in the world. When you turn your attention inwards to your experience of those features, you are aware of the *very same* features together with the fact that your mental state is representing them; no new features of your experience over and above its representing red, round, etc are revealed. In this way, your visual experience is transparent or diaphanous.[3] When you try to examine it, you see right though it, as it were, to the qualities you were experiencing all along in being a subject of the experience, qualities your experience is *of.*

This point holds good even if you are hallucinating and there is no real disk on the wall before you. Still you have an experience of there being something out there with a certain color and shape. It's just that this time your experience is a misrepresentation. And if you turn your attention inwards to your experience, you will 'see' right through it again to those very same qualities. Generalizing, introspection of your perceptual experiences seems to reveal only aspects of *what* you experience, further aspects of the scenes, as represented. Why?

The answer, I suggest, is that your perceptual experiences have no *introspectible* features over and above those implicated in their representational contents. So, the phenomenal character of such experiences—itself something that is introspectibly accessible, assuming the appropriate concepts are possessed and there is no cognitive malfunction—is itself representational.

I should add that in claiming that perceptual experiences have nonconceptual contents, I am certainly not denying that they also sometimes have conceptual contents. One cannot see something as a rabbit, for example, unless one has the concept *rabbit.* But, on my view, these contents are not *directly* phenomenally relevant.[4] Experiences always have a sensory component, but they need not have a conceptual side. As noted earlier, in the basic case, experiences arise at the interface of the conceptual and nonconceptual realms. On my view, the content of an experience with which its phenomenal character is to be identified is the *non*conceptual content that is poised (in the sense explained above) and *abstract.*

Abstract content here is content into which no particular concrete objects enter. This is required by the case of hallucinatory experiences, for which no concrete objects need be present at all; and it is also demanded by cases in which different objects look exactly alike phenomenally. What is crucial to phenomenal character is, I claim, the representation of general features or properties. Visual experiences nonconceptually represent that *there are* surfaces having so-and-so features at such-and-such locations, and thereby they acquire their phenomenal character.

This account may be extended to experiences in the other sensory modalities. It can also be straightforwardly extended to bodily sensations. For example, one can feel a tickle in a leg even if one lacks a leg. One can even feel the pressure from a wedding-band on a phantom finger. Moreover, one can have a pain in a thumb without having a pain in the mouth even if one's thumb is in one's mouth (just as a

3. Transparency is discussed also by Gilbert Harman (1990) and Sydney Shoemaker (1990). For further relevant comments, see Tye 1996. I should add that in denying that visual experiences have any intrinsic, non-intentional, introspectible features, I am not opposing the view that they represent in a manner that is, in significant respects, picture-like. For a discussion of this issue and an account of the structure of images and percepts, see Tye 1991; also Tye 1995.

4. Insofar as conceptual contents are phenomenally relevant, it is via the causal relevance they sometimes have to nonconceptual contents. See here Tye 1995, p. 115 and p. 140.

tourist to Oxford might believe that she was in Tom Quad without believing that she was in Christ Church, even given that Tom Quad is in Christ Church). Bodily sensations, in my view, are experiences that *represent* changes in the body much as visual experiences represent changes in the external environment.[5]

For example, pains represent bodily disorders involving tissue damage at their felt locations. Hunger pangs represent contractions in the stomach walls. Tickles represent the presence of something lightly touching or brushing against the skin. The feeling of thirst represents dryness in the mouth and throat. Feeling hot is a state that represents an elevated body temperature. Tingling sensations represent patterns of many tiny pulsing bodily disturbances.[6]

These claims about what it is that the above bodily sensations represent are justified by reference to a tracking or causal covariation model of representation. Given the simplicity of these states, their fixed mode of production, and their nonconceptual nature, it seems to me plausible to suppose that they represent in the same sort of way as the number of rings within a cross-section of the trunk of an oak tree, or the height of a mercury column in a thermometer, or the position of the pointer on a speedometer in a car. What they do, I suggest, is to *track* the presence of certain features in the body under optimal conditions, and thereby they represent those features, just as visual sensations do with respect to certain features in the environment.[7] Hunger pangs, for example, track contractions in the stomach walls under optimal conditions.

I should add that in each of the cases I have cited, the contents of individual experiences of the above types are much richer than I have indicated. Your hunger pangs may well feel differently from mine, for example, even though they both represent contractions in the stomach walls, since there may well be other salient represented differences (in the intensity of the contractions, their locations and durations, and so on). My interest above is simply in specifying distinctive features of various types of sensation.

Pains, in my view, are also transparent in the same way as visual experiences (as are other bodily sensations). Suppose you are suddenly aware of a sharp pain in your right foot. The pain you have is, I maintain, one and the same as the experience you undergo. That experience, if it is anywhere, is in your head. But what you

5. Why identify pains with experiences rather than the objects of experiences? Answer: Because it affords the best explanation of why pains cannot exist unexperienced and why you cannot feel my pains. Moreover, it seems intuitively plausible. After all, pain is a feeling: to have a pain is to undergo (or to have) an experience of a certain sort.

6. Bodily sensations also have standard reactive components. For example, tickles cause an impulse to break contact with the object brushing lightly against the skin, together with a further desire to rub or scratch the affected bodily region, if contact continues. Pains normally cause a strong reaction of dislike.

7. On my view, both bodily sensations and visual experiences are representations with the structure of symbol-filled arrays. See my reply to Jackson. See also note 1 in that reply for a comment qualifying the tracking account of content.

experience is something very distinctive in the foot. Now try to turn your attention away from *what* you are experiencing to the experience itself apart from that. Do you find any new intrinsic qualities of your experience, in contrast to the qualities you experience as being present in your foot? Surely not. Inevitably what you seem to end up focusing upon is simply a certain sort of disturbance *in your foot*, or rather what your experience represents is going on there (for, in reality, there may be no disorder in your foot or even no foot). On the view that pains are experiences, this is most straightforwardly accounted for by supposing that pains have no introspectible, non-representational features. It follows that the phenomenal character of your pain—certainly something you are introspectively aware of on such an occasion—is itself representational.

Of course, I need not have at my disposal concepts that properly characterize the bodily disturbance that is taking place when I experience a given pain. That obviously is not necessary. The feeling of pain is fundamentally non-conceptual.[8]

Clearly there are important differences between emotions and moods, on the one hand, and bodily sensations and basic perceptual experiences on the other. Nonetheless, I claim that, given certain qualifications and modifications, the proposals I make in the latter cases can be applied to understanding the phenomenal character of the former. So, in my view, all experiences and feelings have poised, abstract, nonconceptual contents, and these contents are one and the same as their phenomenal characters. The question as to which general features enter into *phenomenal contents*, as I call them, is not something that can be answered a priori. Empirical investigation is necessary into the functioning of the pertinent systems, and the nature of their output representations. Contents that are poised for us may not be for other creatures and vice-versa. This is why we cannot know what it is like to be a bat, for example. Given how we are built, we cannot undergo sensory representations of the sort bats undergo. And this is why experiences and feelings are perspectivally subjective: knowing what it is like to undergo them requires the right experiential perspective.

The theory I have sketched is not intended to have the status of a purely a priori proposal. Instead, it is, at least in part, an empirical view, justified by reference to its explanatory power. So, I do not hold that when we introspect our experiences and feelings and we focus upon their phenomenal character, the concepts we apply are PANIC concepts. That would be much too sophisticated. Phenomenal concepts—the concepts we apply when we introspect our phenomenal states—are much simpler than the concepts of my theory. They are also distinct from any third-person concepts. It is here, I argue, in the distance between phenomenal and physical (or functional) concepts, that the famous explanatory gap resides. There is no difference in the world, however, between phenomenal states and PANIC states.

8. So, in drawing the parallel earlier between feeling a tickle in a leg and believing that one is in Tom Quad, I certainly did not intend to suggest that the two cases are alike in every respect.

Concepts that have very different modes of presentation can nonetheless refer to the same entities.[9]

References

Harman, G. 1990 'The Intrinsic Quality of Experience,' in *Philosophical Perspectives*, 4, J. Tomberlin, ed. (see Chapter 36 of this volume).

Marr, D. 1982 *Vision*, San Francisco: W.H. Freeman and Company.

Shoemaker, S. 1990 'Qualities and Qualia: What's in the Mind,' *Philosophy and Phenomenological Research*, 50, Supplement, 109–31.

Tye, M. 1995 *Ten Problems of Consciousness*, Cambridge, Massachusetts: the MIT Press, Bradford Books.

Tye, M. 1997 'The Problem of Simple Minds: Is There Anything it is Like to be a Honey Bee?' *Philosophical Studies.*

Tye, M. 1999 'Phenomenal Consciousness: The Explanatory Gap as cognitive illusion, *Mind* 108 705–725.'

9. For a detailed discussion of phenomenal concepts, modes of presentation, and the explanatory gap, see Tye 1999.

Chapter 38

Is experiencing just representing?

Ned Block

REPRESENTATIONISM says that the phenomenal character of experience is reducible to its representational content. Michael Tye's book responds to two problems for this view; I will argue that these two responses conflict.

1. Swampman

The first problem concerns the famous Swampman who comes into existence as a result of a cosmic accident in which particles from the swamp come together, forming a molecular duplicate of a typical human.[1] Reasonable people can disagree on whether Swampman has intentional contents. Suppose that Swampman marries Swampwoman and they have children. Reasonable people will be *inclined* to agree that there is something it is like for Swampchild when 'words' go through his mind or come out of his mouth. Fred Dretske (1995) claims that if the materialist is to have any theory of intentional content at all, he has no option other than denying it. He is committed to the view that since phenomenal character is a kind of representational content that derives from evolution, the swampchildren have no phenomenal character. Zombiehood is hereditary. (So long as there is no evolution.) If your grandparents are all swamp-people, you are a zombie.

Many philosophers hate fanciful examples like this one. Some say weird thought experiments like this one are so distant from anything we can really take in that our intuitions about them show nothing about our concepts. Others add that even if they show something about our concepts, they are ridiculous from a scientific point of view. Both are wrong, at least in the context of evolutionary views of content. The swampman example is one in which a *real* empirical possibility is stretched so as to allow us to focus on it more easily. There is a famous dispute between the adaptationists (Dawkins, Dennett, Pinker) and the anti-adaptationists (Gould, Lewontin, Eldridge). The anti-adaptationists emphasize that there may be features of the human mind and body that were not selected for but are in one or another sense accidental by-products of evolution. Both sides allow the possibility of such cases. What is controversial is whether (as the adaptationists claim) the default

Ned Block, 'Is Experiencing Just Representing?', *Philosophy and Phenomenological Research* 58 (1998).

1. The Swampman example is usually attributed to Davidson (1987) but it was commonly discussed in the early 1980s. My (1981) uses an example of a swamp-machine.

assumption should be that a complex useful character is adaptive. The adaptationists are on defensible ground when it comes to intentional content, but there is a far more controversial empirical issue about the adaptational value of phenomenal character. Putting the point somewhat dramatically: *in the relevant respect, we all are swamp-people, for all we know.* Hence Dretske is committed to the claim that if an open scientific question is resolved in a certain way, our experience has no phenomenal character. Philosophers should not rest basic metaphysical views on empirical claims that are as wide open as this one.

Despite his general sympathy for evolutionary representationism, Tye rejects Dretske's view of the swampman. Tye gives pride of place to optimal conditions. Optimal conditions for a mechanism obtain when it is discharging its biological function. In the case of an evolved creature, this coincides with Dretske's evolutionary account. But Tye sees optimal conditions as relative to the sort of system or creature in question. In the case of Swampman, Tye thinks not in terms of actual history, but in terms of well-functioning. Conditions of well-functioning are met when there is an appropriate match between behavior and the states tracked in the environment. If the swampman has his needs met and flourishes, then his actual environment meets that condition and can supply the representational content. Hence the swampman can have phenomenal character, and so can his grandchildren. (How bitter a pill for the poor swampman who is not flourishing to find out that precisely *because* he is not flourishing, his agony is unreal!)

I will be focusing on the incompatibility between Tye's strategy in the swampman case and in the Inverted Earth case.

2. Earth Inverted Earth

Inverted Earth is a variant of Putnam's famous 'Twin Earth'. Everything is the complementary color of the corresponding Earth object. The sky is yellow, the grass (or at least the 'grass') is red, etc. In addition, people on Inverted Earth speak an inverted language. They use 'red' to mean green, 'blue' to mean yellow, and so forth. If you order a sofa from Inverted Earth and you want a yellow sofa, you FAX an order for a 'blue' sofa (speaking their language). The two inversions have the effect that if 'wires are crossed' in your visual system (and your body pigments are changed), you will notice no difference when you go to Inverted Earth. After you step off the spaceship, you see some Twin-grass. You point at it, saying it is a nice shade of 'green', but you are wrong. You are wrong for much the same reason that you are wrong if you call the liquid in a Twin-Earth lake 'water' just after you arrive there. The grass is red (of course we are speaking English not Twenglish here). Suppose you left Earth at age 8, remaining on Inverted Earth for the rest of your life, not as a visitor but as an immigrant; you identify with the local culture and in effect adopt the concepts and language of the Inverted Earth language community. Then (according to me) the representational content of your experience as of red things

(things that are really red) will eventually shift so that you represent them correctly. See Block (1990, 1994, 1996).[2]

The key features of the example are these:

1. The phenomenal character of your color experience stays the same as suggested by (though not entailed by) the fact that you don't notice any difference.
2. But the representational content of your experience, being externally determined, shifts with external conditions in the environment and the language community.

Your phenomenal character stays the same but what it represents changes. Why is this a problem for representationists? Imagine that on the birthday just before you leave for Inverted Earth, you are looking at the clear blue sky. Your visual experience represents it as blue. Years later, you have a birthday party on Inverted Earth and you look at the Inverted Earth sky. Your visual experience represents it as yellow (since that's what color it is and your visual experience by that time is veridical let us suppose—I'll deal with an objection to this supposition later). But the phenomenal character stays the same, as indicated by the fact that you can't tell the difference. (An alternative will be mentioned later.) So there is a gap between the representational content of experience and its phenomenal character. Further, the gap shows that phenomenal character is not reducible to representational content, and it is easy to extend the example to show that phenomenal character does not supervene on representational content. (Compare the traveler as an old man looking at something blue (e.g. a banana) on Inverted Earth with the same person as a child looking at something blue (the sky) on Earth. Same representational color content, different phenomenal character.)

A comparison with Putnam's Twin Earth is instructive. If I emigrate to Twin Earth, the representational content of my experience of water changes (let us suppose). After a great deal of time has passed and I have committed to my new language community and new experts, I see twater as twater instead of as water (let us suppose). But I cannot tell from looking at the liquid in the oceans whether it is water or twater. My phenomenal character stays the same even though the

2. I make use of Harman's (1982) Inverted Earth example. Block (1980) uses a cruder example along the same lines. (Pp. 302–3 of Block (1980)—reprinted on p. 466 of Lycan (1990) and p. 227 of Rosenthal (1991)). Instead of a place where things have the opposite from the normal colors, I envisioned a remote Arctic village in which almost everything was black and white, and the subject of the thought experiment was said to have no standing color beliefs of the sort of 'Grass is green'. Two things happen to him: he confuses color words, and a color inverter is placed in his visual system. Everything looks to have the complementary of its real color, but he doesn't notice it because he lacks standing color beliefs. In the 1980 version of the paper, I mistakenly attributed the suggestion to Sylvain Bromberger who told me when he later read it that he had no idea why I had attributed any such idea to him. Harman used the Inverted Earth example to motivate a very different point from that made here: that the representational content of experience does not supervene on the brain.

representational contents of my experiences change. But representationists needn't be bothered by Twin Earth, since they can give the phenomenal continuity a *representational interpretation.* The common phenomenal character is a matter of representation of color, sheen, flow pattern and the like. But what will the representationist appeal to in the Inverted Earth case that corresponds to color, sheen, flow pattern, etc.? This is the problem for representationists posed by the Inverted Earth case.

Once again, many philosophers are skeptical about such fanciful examples. I will respond to only one point: feasibility. In its essential features, the Inverted Earth thought experiment could *actually* be performed with present day technology. We could substitute large isolated buildings for the two planets. And a version of the visual 'wire-crossing' could be done today with 'virtual reality' goggles.

3. Tye's solution to the Inverted Earth problem

Tye's view of phenomenal character is that it is 'non-conceptual' representational content. He concedes that the conceptual contents of the traveler's experience eventually change. If there is reason to see the new language community as the one he relies on and defers to, we have reason to link his concepts to theirs. And the dominant causal source of his concepts shifts to Inverted Earth, as his commitments there outweigh his initial commitments. Tye allows that an externalist theory of meaning and concepts link the concept of red with the meaning of a person's word 'red'. But the *non*-conceptual contents don't shift in this way according to Tye. They are biologically based in the emigrant's evolutionary history. According to Tye, when the emigrant looks at the sky, saying, 'Very blue', his words are correct even though his visual experience *misrepresents* the color of the sky. In sum, Tye's view is that the phenomenal character of experience is to be identified with its non-conceptual content. That does not shift upon immigration to Inverted Earth. It is the conceptual contents of experience that shift, but they are distinct from phenomenal character.

4. The swampman's grandchild goes to Inverted Earth

Without inquiring further about non-conceptual content, we can now see why there is a conflict between Tye's view of the swampman and his view of Inverted Earth travelers.

Suppose Swamp-grandchild emigrates to Inverted Earth. The environments of both Earth and Inverted Earth are well-matched to the swamp-grandchild's behavior: there is equal 'well-functioning' in both cases. So on what basis could Tye choose to ascribe to the swamp-grandchild the phenomenal character that goes with representing the Inverted Earth sky as blue (as a normal Earthian emigrant, according to Tye) rather than the phenomenal character that goes with representing the sky as yellow (like normal Inverted-Earthians)? A choice here would be arbitrary. Suppose Tye chooses the Earthian phenomenal character. But what makes *that* the privileged phenomenal character for the swamp-grandchild? The fact that his grandparents materialized on Earth as opposed to Inverted Earth? But that is a poor reason. Suppose the swamp-grandchild is born on Inverted Earth while his parents are on a visit and stays there. Are his phenomenal characters determined by his birth place or by his grandparents' birth place? There is no good reason for either choice and there is no plausibility in the idea that there is no matter of fact about what the phenomenal characters are.

In his original discussion of traveling to Inverted Earth, Tye was happy to say that the non-conceptual contents of experience remained fixed, agreeing with me that the phenomenal character of experience remains the same on Inverted Earth after emigration. But there is no way he can say this about the traveling swamp-grandchild, for he has no reason to choose the non-conceptual content of a native Earthian as opposed to the non-conceptual content of a native Inverted Earthian. Unable to choose either option, he is forced to go environmental, postulating that these non-conceptual contents of the traveling swamp-grandchild change. And hence the phenomenal characters change.

So he is forced to recognize changes in phenomenal character that are due solely to changes in the external determiners of content (and when I raised this problem in correspondence, Tye took exactly that line.). We all can agree that there are some possible changes in intentional content due solely to changes in its external determiners. But it is another matter to allow that there can be changes in phenomenal character that are due solely to changes in external determiners of content. To claim this is to cut phenomenal character loose from its conceptual moorings. (See Shoemaker's contribution to this symposium.)

Lycan (1996a, 1996b) responds to the original (non-swampman) Inverted Earth Problem in the same way. He puts it in terms of memory. According to him, memories of the color of the sky, for example, are necessarily defective in cases of purely external change like the Inverted Earth Immigration case.

5. Perception of change

I believe that the postulation of externalist memory to defend externalist perception begs the question, but I won't argue that here. (See Block, 1996.) Instead, I'll stick to some points about perception. In certain circumstances, externalist representational content can change without the subject, the person whose representational content is changing, having any possibility of noticing it, no matter how big the change is or how fast it happens. But *it is a necessary feature of phenomenal character that if a change is big enough and happens fast enough, we can notice it.* It follows that phenomenal character cannot be externalist representational content.

We can be concrete about this point. Differences in the hue wheel can be thought of in terms of degrees of separation. For example, a 180 degree difference separates blue from yellow and red from green. For a given person in given circumstances, there will be color changes that are just fast enough to notice. Let's say, just guessing, that 10 degrees per second is fast enough to notice for most people in normal circumstances. If color changes of 10 degrees per second are noticeable, so are changes in the phenomenal character of color experience corresponding to 10 degrees per second. But purely external representational changes (changes that do not affect physical properties of the body that do not involve relations to things outside the body) of more than 10 degrees per second, if they could happen, would not be noticeable.

What is the likelihood that independent externalist considerations about the nature of representation would converge on 10 degrees per second as the maximum rate of change for purely external change? But this is precisely what would be required for the externalist to explain why purely externalist change in phenomenal character is not noticeable to the subject. The burden is on the representationist to show how externalism yields this result without begging the question by assuming that phenomenal character is reducible to representational content.

Let us see how these points apply to Inverted Earth. Suppose that I am looking intently at a blue sky on Earth; then I am beamed (as in Star-Trek) to Inverted Earth (the matter transmitter also is programmed to switch wires in my visual system) where I am looking at a yellow sky (but my wires have been switched so I don't notice the difference). The transition is so seamless that I don't notice any change at all. Eventually, my representational contents shift half way across the color wheel. How long does this take? We can put this question to one side for the moment. The important point is that there is nothing in the nature of externalist representational content that precludes a fast change. But there is something in the nature of phenomenal character that precludes a fast change half way across the color wheel, because that's a big change, one that could not happen in a short time without my noticing it. In short, the problem for Lycan and Tye is that they are committed not only to an ad hoc externalist theory of memory, but also to an ad hoc restriction on noticing phenomenal change.

As I mentioned above, a natural response on behalf of Tye would be that non-conceptual representational contents can't shift so fast as to be problematic. A blue to yellow shift would take years, and no one could notice a chameleon changing from blue to yellow if it took years. Such a reply raises the question of what it is that determines the rate of change of non-conceptual contents. As mentioned above, one plausible view of change in conceptual content appeals to the notion of a dominant causal source. The Spanish explorers originally named the island of Puerto Rico 'San Juan', and the potentially rich port of San Juan was called 'Puerto Rico'. But the cartographer mixed up the labels on the way back to Spain. What makes our 'Puerto Rico' refer to the island, not the port? The dominant causal source of our word is the island. Let's apply this idea to non-conceptual content.

Our swampman materializes on Earth where he is looking intently at a blue sky.

After a total of one minute of life there, he is beamed (without noticing it) to Inverted Earth where he is looking at the yellow sky. (Again, the wires in his visual system are crossed by the transponder, which is why he notices no difference.) After 10 minutes of looking intently at the Inverted Earth sky, the dominant causal source of the phenomenal experience linked to his word 'blue' is yellow, since 10 of his 11 minutes of existence has been on Inverted Earth. So on the dominant causal source view, the representational content of his experience changed during that 10 minutes. But he didn't notice it. Indeed, he couldn't have noticed it. No matter how fast it happened, he couldn't have noticed it.

But perhaps the dominant causal source view isn't right. Or perhaps it applies to conceptual content but not to non-conceptual content. Never mind: its role in my argument is to serve as an example of an independently motivated account of change in representational content, one that arguably allows big fast changes. The main point is that the burden is on anyone who claims that there is something in the nature of representational content that excludes big fast unnoticeable changes. Since there is something in the nature of phenomenal character that precludes big fast unnoticeable changes, we should conclude that phenomenal character can't be representational content.

Bibliography

Block, Ned, 1980: 'Troubles with Functionalism'. In Block (ed.), *Readings in Philosophy of Psychology*, Vol. 1. Cambridge: Harvard University Press.

Block, Ned, 1981: 'Psychologism and Behaviorism'. In *The Philosophical Review* LXXXX, No. 1, January 1981, 5–43.

Block, Ned, 1990: 'Inverted Earth'. In James Tomberlin (ed.), *Philosophical Perspectives 4, Action Theory and Philosophy of Mind*, 53–79. Atascadero: Ridgeview.

Block, Ned, 1994: 'Qualia' in S. Guttenplan (ed.), *A Companion to Philosophy of Mind.* Oxford: Blackwell, 514–20.

Block, Ned, 1996: 'Mental Paint and Mental Latex' in E. Villanueva (ed.), *Perception, Philosophical Issues 7*. Atascadero: Ridgeview.

Davidson, Donald, 1987: 'Knowing One's Own Mind,' *Proceedings and Addresses of the American Philosophical Association* 60, 441–58 (see Chapter 31 of this volume).

Dretske, Fred, 1995: *Naturalizing the Mind.* Cambridge: MIT Press.

Harman, Gilbert, 1982: 'Conceptual Role Semantics,' *Notre Dame Journal of Formal Logic* 23.

Lycan, William G., 1990: *Mind and Cognition, A Reader.* Oxford: Blackwell.

Lycan, William G., 1996a: 'Layered Perceptual Representation'. In E. Villanueva (ed.), *Perception, Philosophical Issues 7*. Atascadero: Ridgeview.

Lycan, William G., 1996b: *Consciousness and Experience.* Cambridge: MIT Press.

Rosenthal, David, 1991: *The Nature of Mind.* Oxford: Oxford University Press.

Tye, Michael, 1995a: 'Blindsight, Orgasm and Representational Overlap'. *Behavioral and Brain Sciences* 18, 268–69.

Tye, Michael, 1995b: *Ten Problems of Consciousness.* Cambridge: MIT Press.

Questions

1. Imagine a new kind of 'cerebroscope', one that provides a non-invasive, molecular-level view of goings-on in the brains of conscious agents. A scientist using the device observes your brain while you are undergoing a vivid visual experience: you are watching parrots socializing in a tropical rainforest. To the amazement of the scientist, the cerebroscope reveals a tiny TV-like colored image of parrots in a rainforest at a certain place in your brain. What might the implications of this discovery be for theories of consciousness?
2. Few theorists would regard a thermostat as conscious. Consider a self-monitoring thermostat: a thermostat, linked to a furnace, that includes an electronic sensor designed to monitor its own internal state. The thermostat governs the furnace, registering the temperature by means of a coiled bi-metal strip. The thermostat can regulate itself by registering the state of the bi-metal strip (shutting itself off or on, depending on the state of this strip). Would Armstrong be forced to admit that such a device is, on his view, conscious? What of your own conception of consciousness?
3. Compare the views of Harmon and Tye. Are these variations on a common theme?
4. Representationalists urge us to distinguish features of a mental representation from features of what is being represented. Consider ordinary representation, van Gogh's painting of his room at Arles, for instance. The room includes a bed with a red bedspread. Now consider a mental image you might have of the room (or of the painting, for that matter). How, according to a representationalist, would your image differ from the painting?
5. What are the prospects of capturing all of the puzzling qualities of conscious experience representationally? What *are* the puzzling qualities of conscious experience, anyway?
6. How might Chalmers respond to Tye's approach to consciousness? Whose side are you on? Could both Tye and Chalmers be wrong?
7. Could non-conscious entities 'add up' to a conscious entity? Does the material world provide the ingredients of consciousness, or could consciousness only be made up of something already conscious–or provided as an 'add-on extra'?
8. What sympathies does Block betray in his discussion of Tye? Where do your sympathies lie?
9. What *is* Chalmers's conception of the relation material goings-on bear to consciousness? Could there be beings that were physically exactly alike but differed in the character of their conscious experiences?
10. What are *qualia*?

Suggested readings

Block et al. (1997) is good place to start looking for materials on consciousness, especially the introduction to that volume by Güven Güzeldere. See also Metzinger (1995). Chalmers (1996) develops an influential 'nonreductive' account of consciousness. For an extensive on-line bibliography on consciousness, see Chalmers (2001). Davies's (1999) entry on consciousness in the on-line *MIT Encyclopedia of Cognitive Science* provides a brief discussion of the issues, a bibliography, and links to other sources. Books on consciousness include Carruthers (2000), Kirk (1994), Levine (2000), and Seager (1991, 1999). Dennett (1991, 1996) provides highly readable discussions of consciousness, although many philosophers in the list above would accuse Dennett of changing the subject.

Lycan's (2001) entry on representational theories of consciousness in the *Stanford Encyclopedia of Philosophy* provides a succinct discussion of the topic and a useful bibliography. See also Chalmers's (2001) on-line bibliography (mentioned above). Lycan (1998) anchors a symposium on representational theories with discussion by Neander (1998), Rey (1998), and Tye (1998). Dretske (1997), Lycan (1987, 1996), and Tye (1995) defend their own versions of representationalism. For the more adventuresome, see McDowell (1994) and Bilgrami's (1994) discussion. Block (2003) and McGinn (1991) offer arguments against accounts of consciousness that dispense with mental qualities or replace them with representations.

Consciousness and *qualia*

Block, N. J., O. Flanagan, and G. Güzeldere, eds. (1997), *The Nature of Consciousness: Philosophical Debates.* Cambridge, MA: MIT Press.

Carruthers, P. (2000), *Phenomenal Consciousness: A Naturalistic Theory.* Cambridge: Cambridge University Press.

Chalmers, D. J. (1996), *The Conscious Mind: In Search of a Fundamental Theory*, New York: Oxford University Press.

—— (2001), *Contemporary Philosophy of Mind: An Annotated Bibliography* <http://www.u.arizona.edu/~chalmers/biblio.html> Tucson, AZ: University of Arizona.

Davies, M. (1999), 'Consciousness'. In Wilson and Keil 1999.

Dennett, D. C. (1991), *Consciousness Explained.* Boston: Little, Brown.

—— (1996), *Kinds of Minds: Toward an Understanding of Consciousness.* New York: Basic Books.

Kirk, R. (1994), *Raw Feeling: A Philosophical Account of the Essence of Consciousness.* Oxford: Clarendon Press.

Levine, J. (2000), *Purple Haze: The Puzzle of Consciousness.* New York: Oxford University Press.

Metzinger, T., ed. (1995), *Conscious Experience.* Paderborn: Schöningh.

Seager, W. (1991), *Metaphysics of Consciousness.* London: Routledge.

—— (1999), *Theories of Consciousness: An Introduction.* London: Routledge.

Wilson, R. A., and F. Keil, eds. (1999), *MIT Encyclopedia of Cognitive Sciences* <http://cognet.mit.edu/MITECS/login.html> Cambridge, MA: MIT Press.

Consciousness and representation

Bilgrami, A. (1994), 'On McDowell on the Content of Perceptual Experience', *Philosophical Quarterly* 44: 206–13.

Block, N. (2003), 'Mental Paint'. In Hahn and Ramberg 2003: 125–51.

Dretske, F. I. (1997), *Naturalizing the Mind.* Cambridge: MIT Press.

Hahn, M., and B. Ramberg, eds. (2003), *Essays on the Philosophy of Tyler Burge.* Cambridge, MA: MIT Press.

Lycan, W. G. (1987), *Consciousness.* Cambridge, MA: MIT Press.

——(1996), *Consciousness and Experience.* Cambridge, MA: MIT Press.

——(1998), 'In Defense of the Representational Theory of Qualia (Replies to Neander, Rey, and Tye)', *Philosophical Perspectives* 12: 479–87.

——(2001), 'Representational Theories of Consciousness'. In Zalta 2001: <http://plato.stanford.edu/entries/consciousness-representational/>.

McDowell, J. (1994), 'The Content of Perceptual Experience'. *Philosophical Quarterly* 44: 190–205.

McGinn, C. (1991), *The Problem of Consciousness: Essays Toward a Resolution.* Oxford: Blackwell Publishers.

Neander, K. (1998), 'The Division of Phenomenal Labor: A Problem for Representational Theories of Consciousness', *Philosophical Perspectives* 12: 411–34.

Rey, G. (1998), 'A Narrow Representationalist Account of Qualitative Experience', *Philosophical Perspectives* 12: 435–57.

Tye, M. (1995), *Ten Problems of Consciousness: A Representational Theory of the Phenomenal Mind.* Cambridge, MA: MIT Press.

——(1998), 'Inverted Earth, Swampman, and Representationism', *Philosophical Perspectives* 12: 459–77.

Zalta, E. N., ed. (2002), *The Stanford Encyclopedia of Philosophy.* <http://plato.stanford.edu/> Stanford, CA: Metaphysics Research Lab, Center for the Study of Language and Information.

Part X

Reduction

Introduction

SCIENTIFIC explanation is inherently reductionistic: complexity is reduced to simplicity; wholes are decomposed into parts; apparently unrelated phenomena are exhibited as related under the surface. Although each of the several sciences carves out a more or less autonomous domain, their thrust is complementary, not competitive. Indeed, it is easy to see differences between, say, physics, chemistry, and biology as largely differences in scale and scope. Physics tells us about the very small; chemistry starts where physics leaves off; biology takes the lessons of chemistry and applies these to living organisms.

This suggests a picture of science as unified: scientific truths are ultimately grounded in, hence reducible to, truths of physics (see Oppenheim and Putnam 1958). Physics tells us about the ultimate constituents. Everything else is simply an arrangement of these ultimate constituents. Laws governing the ultimate constituents govern everything. Discoveries in biology, or psychology, or sociology are not couched in the vocabulary of basic physics. This is not because truths of biology, or psychology, or sociology are not grounded in truths of basic physics; it is because translation of biological, or psychological, or sociological truths into the vocabulary of basic physics would be inordinately unwieldy and inconvenient. Such practical considerations should not disguise the fact that we would find it profoundly disturbing if we thought that a given biological (or psychological, or sociological) claim could not, even in principle, be re-expressed as a truth of basic physics.

Or would we? The staunch reductionism of the preceding paragraph has been challenged by many philosophers and scientists. These critics argue that the reductionist picture of science as a unified endeavor beginning and ending with physics—the science of the very small and the very large—is a delusion. Chemistry may be, in part, reducible to physics, but even when reduction is successful, it is uninteresting—and uncharacteristic of our best science. Barriers to reduction are not merely practical. Complex systems behave in ways wholly inexplicable from the perspective of basic physics. Indeed, the systems themselves are invisible from that perspective (see Dupré 1993; Cartwright 1999).

Emergence

Some theorists have pushed the rejection of the reductionist model further. As systems gain in complexity, they contend, new powers and qualities *emerge*. These powers and qualities are unlike anything discoverable in basic physics. They are certainly not reducible to powers and qualities of the ultimate constituents taken in aggregate. Perhaps consciousness is an *emergent* feature of the world. It is hard (or even impossible; see Chapters 43–5) to see how the distinctive qualities of conscious experience could result from collections of unfeeling electrons and quarks.

It is not easy to give a precise characterization of emergence. Take five matchsticks and arrange them so as to form a pentagon. Now the collection of matchsticks (so arranged) has a property none of the matchsticks had previously: the property of being pentagonal. Is this an emergent property? If it is, then emergent properties are nothing special. You could put this by saying that the pentagon is 'nothing over and above' its constituent matchsticks suitably arranged. The property of being pentagonal 'comes for free'. It is not something that must be added to the world in addition to the matchsticks and their arrangements.

Proponents of emergence are after bigger game, however. Consciousness, they contend, does not 'come for free'. True, consciousness 'arises' in suitably organized material systems, but not in the boring way pentagons 'arise' in arrangements of matchsticks. Consciousness represents a genuinely new feature of the world, something that must be 'added to' the collections of particles and their arrangements. At the limit, we could conceive of universes, physically indistinguishable from ours, but in which consciousness is wholly absent.

We have encountered a view of this kind in David Chalmers's (Chapter 35) discussion of the 'hard problem' of consciousness. It has affinities with John Searle's depiction of consciousness below (Chapter 40). Searle regards consciousness as a perfectly natural 'causal product' of appropriately constituted physical systems. He rejects the functionalist perspective embraced by Chalmers, however, focusing instead on the biological nature of conscious organisms. In reading Searle, you should take note of similarities and differences in his approach and Chalmers's. And you should ask yourself whether either approach clarifies the notion of emergence.

I would be neglecting my responsibilities as a guide were I not to note that, historically, emergentist theses have not fared well (McLaughlin 1992). In the nineteenth and early twentieth centuries it was widely believed that organic compounds could only be explained by positing emergent processes. Subsequent developments in chemistry proved this belief false. Given their lackluster track record, why should we take seriously emergentist proposals today? Proponents of the doctrine that consciousness is emergent can point to apparently emergent processes at the quantum level (see Teller 1989). The chief consideration favoring emergence, however, has been the thought that qualities of conscious experience—the *qualia*—apparently have no echo in the material world. We know, or think we know, that brains 'give rise to' consciousness, but conscious qualities seem wholly novel. The thought that such things could be 'made up of' brain qualities (in the way a square could be made up of matchsticks suitably arranged) looks like a nonstarter.

Multiple realizability and 'downward' causation

These issues will resurface in Part XI. Meanwhile, it is worth revisiting a topic introduced in Part III, *multiple realizability*. Recall that proponents of functionalism point to the multiple realizability of states of mind in the course of defending the thesis that mental properties, though 'realized by' material properties, cannot be *identified* with such properties. Such a view depicts mental states and properties as standing in a 'vertical' relation to the material properties on which they depend. You have the property of being in pain in virtue of having some material property. But the pain property is not reducible to that material property: pain can be realized by an endless number of material properties.

If reduction of mental properties to material properties is not in the cards, however, we are left with a picture of mental properties as standing 'above' material properties. One question is how such properties could figure in causal relations involving purely material properties. When you have a headache, it seems reasonable to think that it is the conscious headachy feeling that leads you to seek out the aspirin bottle. But if that feeling is a quality that, while 'realized by' a material property of your nervous system, is nevertheless distinct from that material quality, it is hard to see how the quality—as opposed to its material realizer—could figure in causal transactions. The conscious quality seems to 'float above' the causal fray.

The difficulty is depicted in Figure X.1. H_1 and H_2 stand for higher-level mental states realized by P_1 and P_2, respectively. (H_1 might be your being in pain and H_2 your forming an intention to look for aspirin; P_1 and P_2 are states of your brain.) P_1 realizes H_1 and causes P_2, which realizes H_2. Now, one question is, *why is H_2 on the scene*? It is natural to think that H_2 is caused by H_1—your forming the intention to seek out aspirin is caused by your being in pain. But P_2 guarantees the presence of H_2. Indeed, it is hard to see how you could bring about *any* higher-level state without bringing about its lower-level realizer. (The point, and the inspiration for Figures X.1 and X.2, can be found in Kim 1998.) This would mean that, if H_1 is causally responsible for H_2, H_1 must bring about P_2 (see Figure X.2). This kind of 'downward' causal influence threatens the autonomy of the physical level, however.

It is hard to give up the idea that the fundamental material domain is causally self-contained. Higher-level laws are, by nature, open to exception. Consider the psychological 'law' that says that, if an agent wants *A*, believes that obtaining *A* requires doing

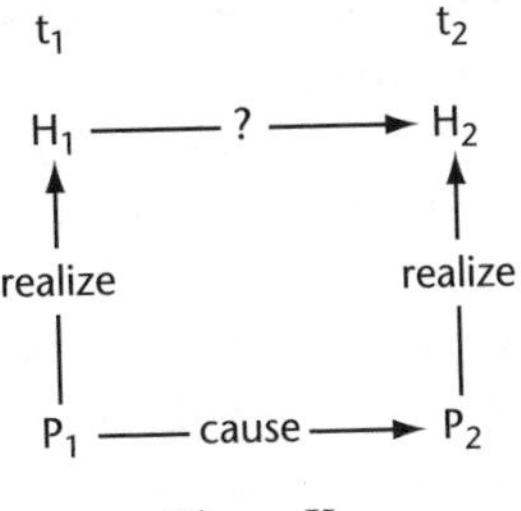

Figure X.1

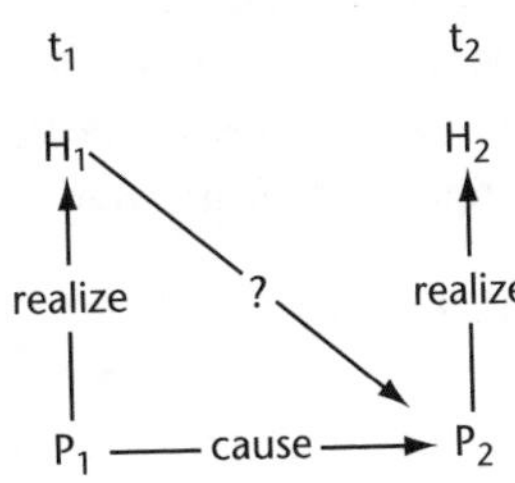

Figure X.2

B, and that doing *B* is best, all things considered, then the agent will do *B*. A 'law' of this kind is usually called a *ceteris paribus* or 'hedged' law (see Fodor 1991). Imagine that you want a crumpet, believe you can obtain a crumpet by opening the cabinet, and judge that, all things considered opening the cabinet is the most attractive option open to you at the time. However, before you can form the intention to open the cabinet and move your body accordingly, you are struck by an errant football launched through the open window by a rowdy neighbor. Here, the psychological 'law' fails to hold because of interference from *outside* the system. (The case is comparable with one in which a computer fails to execute a routine because someone trips over the power cord and pulls the plug.)

In general, higher-level systems are susceptible to interference from the outside. At the lowest level, however, there is no 'outside', consequently no possibility of outside disruption. You can see the point if you imagine an ordinary watch that happens to be malfunctioning. Insofar as we regard the watch as a purely physical system (and not as a timepiece) it is behaving exactly as it ought to behave: basic physical systems cannot malfunction.

Return to your quest for a crumpet. Imagine that you are not struck by a football; your forming the intention to open the crumpet-containing cabinet leads you to move your body appropriately. Bodily motions are physical occurrences with physical causes. How could your forming an intention (a mental event) have a physical effect? Using Figure X.2 as a model, and letting H_1 and H_2 be your forming the intention to open the cabinet and your opening the cabinet (P_1 and H_1 are the physical realizers of H_1 and H_2, respectively), it looks as though your intention's causing a bodily motion involves 'downward' causation: H_1 must cause P_2.

For many philosophers, this is an uninviting option. It apparently requires either a kind of systematic 'overdetermination' where higher-level causes are involved (P_2 is caused by H_1 and by P_1, either of which is sufficient for P_2), or, worse, violation of the autonomy of the physical world. What are the options?

First, you might hope that higher-level states and properties are reducible to lower-level states and properties. This would mean that H_1 is reducible to P_1 and H_2 is reducible to P_2 (and so for all higher-level items). In this context, this would mean that H_1 and H_2 are really nothing more than—nothing 'over and above'—P_1 and P_2, respectively: H_1 *is* P_1, H_2 *is* P_2. Second, you might follow Derk Pereboom and Hilary Kornblith (Chapter 41) and argue that higher-level (H_1 to H_2) causal relations, although distinct from lower-level (P_1 to P_2) causal relations, are nevertheless not in competition with those lower-level relations. Pereboom and Kornblith contend that the special sciences (including genetics, molecular biology, and physiology) are replete with causal relations of this kind. That is, when we look at what scientists actually do, we discover widespread commitments to irreducible causal relations of the H_1 to H_2 kind. Mental causation is merely one instance of a widespread phenomenon.

Types and tokens

Understanding the issues here requires the invocation of a distinction set out earlier (the introduction to Part II) between *types* and *tokens*. Think of a token as a particular entity: the very book you hold in your hand, the gooseberry seed lodged between your lower right bicuspid and an adjoining molar, a particular performance of Beethoven's *Missa Solemnis*. The book you hold in your hand is an instance of a type that has many instances. If a lecturer assigns readings from the book, the lecturer is not referring to a particular copy of the book (or, to the extent that the lecturer is referring to particular instances, this is accomplished indirectly by referring to the type—and thereby to tokens of that type). A farmer setting out to breed seedless gooseberries aims to produce berries that lack tokens of the type *gooseberry seed*. When you reflect on the tonal structure of the *Missa Solemnis*, you need not be reflecting on a particular performance, a token, you are reflecting on a type with many tokens.

Some philosophers identify types with collections or classes. Think of the class consisting of all the copies of this book, the class encompassing every gooseberry seed, or the class of all performances of Beethoven's *Missa Solemnis*. On this view, a type is the class comprising every token of the type. Others take types to be *universals*: properties that can be *wholly present* in different places at once (see Armstrong 1989 for an account of universals).

All this sounds like more useless philosophy, but the type—token distinction can be surprisingly important. Return to Figures X.1 and X.2. Are the entities depicted in that figure types or tokens? Do H_1 and H_2, for instance, represent *types* of mental property or state, or do they stand for particular instances of mental properties or states? Your answer will affect your interpretation of the horizontal causal arrows in the two figures. Causal relations hold among *particular* states or events. If we take H_1 and H_2 to designate *types*, then there can be no question of H_1's causing H_2. If H_1 and H_2, are types, then the arrows must be interpreted as representing causal *laws*: relations holding among *types* of event.

Suppose we do read Figures X.1 and X.2 this way; suppose H_1 and H_2 designate types, and types are classes. In that case we can see why a philosopher might want to deny the reducibility of H_1 to P_1 and H_2 to P_2. If H_1, for instance, is, as we are assuming, multiply realizable, the class of entities making up instances of P_1 will differ dramatically from the class of entities making up H_1; the class of entities making up H_1 will include those making up P_1, but it will include many more bedsides. Indeed this is why philosophers have wanted to reject 'type identity' solutions to the mind–body problem.

The reasons philosophers give for mental properties' being multiply realizable will block the reduction of mental types to physical types. What of mental and physical *tokens*? It might turn out that, although mental types are not identifiable with or reducible to physical types, every mental token is identical with some physical token: your headache today is identical with a certain occurrence in your brain; an Alpha Centaurian's current headache is identical with a certain occurrence in the Alpha Centaurian's (very different) brain. (A view of this kind is implied by Lewis—Armstrong style functionalism; see Chapter 10.)

Pereboom and Kornblith will have none of it, however. The phenomenon of multiple realizability, they contend, excludes, not only type reduction or identity, but also *token* reduction or identity. Your (particular, token) desire, H_1, for a crumpet, although realized by some (particular, token) brain state, P_1, cannot be reduced to or identified with that brain state (note that H_1 and P_1 now stand for *token* mental and physical states). What is it for the brain state to realize the desire? Pereboom and Kornblith say that the realizing relation here is one of *constitution*: your brain state, P_1, *constitutes* your desire, H_1.

You might think that P_1's constituting H_1 is simply a pretentious way of calling attention to the fact that P_1 just *is* H_1: constitution is identity. Few philosophers are willing to say this, however. A particular statue is constituted by a particular lump of bronze. Does this imply that the statue *is* the lump? Well, the lump can survive being melted and reshaped, but not the statue. Similarly, the statue, but not the lump, could survive our replacing portions of the lump that make it up with bronze from another lump. Pereboom and Kornblith argue that the very same point applies to cases in which states of mind are constituted by physical states. You should pay particular attention to the example they give of this and to the lessons they draw from it. These lessons include the idea that causal relations among higher-level items do not 'compete' with causal relations holding among their lower-level realizers. (Compare: causal relations in which statues figure do not compete with causal relations in which materials constituting those statues figure.)

Reduction

Suppose someone—a philosopher or a neuroscientist—declares that states of mind *are* reducible to brain states—or, more generally, that the mental is reducible to the physical. How are we to understand this claim? For Pereboom and Kornblith, reduction seems to require something like type identity. Taking types to be classes, this would mean that *A*s are reducible to *B*s, only if the class of all the *A*s is coextensive with the class (or a subclass) of *B*s. In fact, we need something a bit stronger than this: the class of creatures with hearts is coextensive with the class of creatures with kidneys, but this does not imply that having a heart is (or is reducible to) the having of kidneys (Quine 1951). Owing to multiple realizability, however, even the weak condition fails to be satisfied in the case of mental and physical states or properties. (Can you see why?)

As noted above, Pereboom and Kornblith argue that a physical state, P_1, realizes a state of mind, H_1, by virtue of P_1's *constituting* H_1, and that constitution is not identity. They offer another reason for doubting that the mental could be reduced to or identified with the physical. Mental categories figure in explanations of behavior. Such explanations succeed, it could be argued, because the categories designate causal factors operative in particular cases. This is why we can formulate laws—albeit 'hedged', *ceteris paribus* laws—of the kind mentioned already. These laws hold across individuals and across species. A reduction of the mental to the physical would involve replacing mental categories with unwieldy disjunctions or lists of physical categories. Properties answering to these categories (the realizers of mental properties) would form a heterogeneous array. We would sacrifice the kinds of generalization that gives psychology its point.

The argument is quite general. Reduction in psychology would be no different from reduction in any of the special sciences. Occasionally, local reductions are called for. But global reduction—the reduction of biology to molecular chemistry, or psychology to physiology—flies in the face of well-established and fruitful scientific practice. Such reductions threaten to undermine the very point of science: the identification of causally significant properties and general laws in which these figure.

Higher and lower levels

As you go through the readings in this part, ask yourself whether these arguments force us (on pain of tossing out the special sciences) to embrace domains of higher-level states and properties, states and properties dependent on, but distinct from, their realizers (lower-level states and properties). Suppose, for instance, you thought that higher-level predicates (terms), like 'is in pain', 'is a cold front', or 'is red', applied to motley collections of objects, not because those objects shared a single, higher-level property, but because the objects possessed any of a family of similar properties.

Imagine that you, an octopus, and an Alpha Centaurian all answer to the predicate 'is in pain'. The anti-reductionists say this is because you all share a single property, the pain property, that happens to be realized very differently in the physiology of human beings, cephalopods, and Alpha Centaurians (who exhibit, we are imagining, a silicon-based 'biology'). Suppose, however, that the pain predicate applies in each case, not because human beings, cephalopods, and Alpha Centaurians share a *single* higher-level property, but because they possess pertinently *similar* lower-level properties. The similarity of these properties could be enough to account for the fact that human beings, cephalopods, and Alpha Centaurians that satisfy the pain predicate behave similarly and fall under psychological laws encompassing pain.

On such a view, the predicate 'is in pain' is satisfied by human beings, cephalopods, and Alpha Centaurians by virtue of their possessing properties that anti-reductionists would identify as realizers of the pain property. Would this represent a reduction of the mental to the physical (or, more generally, higher-level to lower-level properties)? Or is the view a kind of eliminativism? These are questions you will want to keep in mind as you read the selections that follow. My advice here, as elsewhere, is to trust your own instincts and not allow yourself to be intimidated by flashy philosophical moves, which, as you are well aware, can disguise as much as illuminate.

References

Armstrong, D. M. (1989), *Universals: An Opinionated Introduction*, Boulder, CO: Westview Press.

Beckermann, A., H. Flohr, and J. Kim, eds. (1992), *Emergence or Reduction? Essays on the Prospects of Nonreductive Physicalism*. Berlin: De Gruyter.

Cartwright, N. (1999), *The Dappled World: A Study of the Boundaries of Science*. Cambridge: Cambridge University Press.

Cushing, J., and E. McMullin, eds. (1989), *Philosophical Lessons from Quantum Theory*. South Bend: University of Notre Dame Press.

Dupré, J. (1993), *The Disorder of Things: Metaphysical Foundations of the Disunity of Science*. Cambridge, MA: Harvard University Press.

Feigl, H., M. Scriven, and G. Maxwell, eds. (1958), *Concepts, Theories, and the Mind—Body Problem* (Minnesota Studies in the Philosophy of Science, vol. 2). Minneapolis: University of Minnesota Press.

Fodor, J. A. (1991), 'You Can Fool Some of the People All of the Time, Everything Else Being Equal: Hedged Laws and Psychological Explanation', *Mind* 100: 19–34.

Kim, J. (1998), *Mind in a Physical World: An Essay on the Mind-Body Problem and Mental Causation*. Cambridge, MA: MIT Press.

McLaughlin, B. P. (1992), 'The Rise and Fall of British Emergentism'. In Beckermann et al. 1992: 49–93.

Oppenheim, P., and H. Putnam (1958), 'Unity of Science as a Working Hypothesis'. In Feigl et al. 1958: 3–36.

Quine, W. V. (1951), 'Two Dogmas of Empiricism', *Philosophical Review* 60: 20–43. Reprinted in Quine 1953: 20–46.

——(1953), *From a Logical Point of View*. Cambridge, MA: Harvard University Press.

Teller, P. (1989), 'Relativity, Relational Holism, and the Bell Inequalities'. In Cushing and McMullin 1989: 208–23.

Chapter 39

Mental events

Donald Davidson

MENTAL EVENTS such as perceivings, rememberings, decisions, and actions resist capture in the nomological net of physical theory.[1] How can this fact be reconciled with the causal role of mental events in the physical world? Reconciling freedom with causal determinism is a special case of the problem if we suppose that causal determinism entails capture in, and freedom requires escape from, the nomological net. But the broader issue can remain alive even for someone who believes a correct analysis of free action reveals no conflict with determinism. *Autonomy* (freedom, self-rule) may or may not clash with determinism; *anomaly* (failure to fall under a law) is, it would seem, another matter.

I start from the assumption that both the causal dependence, and the anomalousness, of mental events are undeniable facts. My aim is therefore to explain, in the face of apparent difficulties, how this can be. I am in sympathy with Kant when he says,

> it is as impossible for the subtlest philosophy as for the commonest reasoning to argue freedom away. Philosophy must therefore assume that no true contradiction will be found between freedom and natural necessity in the same human actions, for it cannot give up the idea of nature any more than that of freedom. Hence even if we should never be able to conceive how freedom is possible, at least this apparent contradiction must be convincingly eradicated. For if the thought of freedom contradicts itself or nature . . . it would have to be surrendered in competition with natural necessity.[2]

Generalize human actions to mental events, substitute anomaly for freedom, and this is a description of my problem. And of course the connection is closer, since Kant believed freedom entails anomaly.

Now let me try to formulate a little more carefully the 'apparent contradiction' about mental events that I want to discuss and finally dissipate. It may be seen as stemming from three principles.

The first principle asserts that at least some mental events interact causally with

Donald Davidson, 'Mental Events'. In L. Foster and J. W. Swanson, eds. *Experience and Theory* (Amherst, Mass.: University of Massachusetts Press, 1970). Reprinted in Davidson, *Essays on Actions and Events* (Oxford: Clarendon Press, 1980).

1. I was helped and influenced by Daniel Bennett, Sue Larson, and Richard Rorty, who are not responsible for the result. My research was supported by the National Science Foundation and the Center for Advanced Study in the Behavioral Sciences.

2. *Fundamental Principles of the Metaphysics of Marals*, trans. T. K. Abbott (London, 1909), pp. 75–76.

physical events. (We could call this the Principle of Causal Interaction.) Thus for example if someone sank the *Bismarck*, then various mental events such as perceivings, notings, calculations, judgments, decisions, intentional actions and changes of belief played a causal role in the sinking of the *Bismarck*. In particular, I would urge that the fact that someone sank the *Bismarck* entails that he moved his body in a way that was caused by mental events of certain sorts, and that this bodily movement in turn caused the *Bismarck* to sink.[3] Perception illustrates how causality may run from the physical to the mental: if a man perceives that a ship is approaching, then a ship approaching must have caused him to come to believe that a ship is approaching. (Nothing depends on accepting these as examples of causal interaction.)

Though perception and action provide the most obvious cases where mental and physical events interact causally, I think reasons could be given for the view that all mental events ultimately, perhaps through causal relations with other mental events, have causal intercourse with physical events. But if there are mental events that have no physical events as causes or effects, the argument will not touch them.

The second principle is that where there is causality, there must be a law: events related as cause and effect fall under strict deterministic laws. (We may term this the Principle of the Nomological Character of Causality.) This principle, like the first, will be treated here as an assumption, though I shall say something by way of interpretation.[4]

The third principle is that there are no strict deterministic laws on the basis of which mental events can be predicted and explained (the Anomalism of the Mental).

The paradox I wish to discuss arises for someone who is inclined to accept these three assumptions or principles, and who thinks they are inconsistent with one another. The inconsistency is not, of course, formal unless more premises are added. Nevertheless it is natural to reason that the first two principles, that of causal interaction, and that of the nomological character of causality, together imply that at least some mental events can be predicted and explained on the basis of laws, while the principle of the anomalism of the mental denies this. Many philosophers have accepted, with or without argument, the view that the three principles do lead to a contradiction. It seems to me, however, that all three principles are true, so that what must be done is to explain away the appearance of contradiction; essentially the Kantian line.

The rest of this paper falls into three parts. The first part describes a version of the identity theory of the mental and the physical that shows how the three prin-

3. These claims are defended in my 'Actions, Reasons and Causes,' *The Journal of Philosophy*, LX (1963), pp. 685–700 and in 'Agency,' a paper forthcoming in the proceedings of the November, 1968, colloquium on Agent, Action, and Reason at the University of Western Ontario, London, Canada.

4. In 'Causal Relations,' *The Journal of Philosophy*, LXIV (1967), pp. 691–703, I elaborate on the view of causality assumed here. The stipulation that the laws be deterministic is stronger than required by the reasoning and will be relaxed.

ciples may be reconciled. The second part argues that there cannot be strict psychophysical laws; this is not quite the principle of the anomalism of the mental, but on reasonable assumptions entails it. The last part tries to show that from the fact that there can be no strict psychophysical laws, and our other two principles, we can infer the truth of a version of the identity theory, that is, a theory that identifies at least some mental events with physical events. It is clear that this 'proof' of the identity theory will be at best conditional, since two of its premises are unsupported, and the argument for the third may be found less than conclusive. But even someone unpersuaded of the truth of the premises may be interested to learn how they may be reconciled and that they serve to establish a version of the identity theory of the mental. Finally, if the argument is a good one, it should lay to rest the view, common to many friends and some foes of identity theories, that support for such theories can come only from the discovery of psycho-physical laws.

I

The three principles will be shown consistent with one another by describing a view of the mental and the physical that contains no inner contradiction and that entails the three principles. According to this view, mental events are identical with physical events. Events are taken to be unrepeatable, dated individuals such as the particular eruption of a volcano, the (first) birth or death of a person, the playing of the 1968 World Series, or the historic utterance of the words, 'You may fire when ready, Gridley.' We can easily frame identity statements about individual events; examples (true or false) might be:

The death of Scott = the death of the author of *Waverley*;
The assassination of the Archduke Ferdinand = the event that started the First World War;
The eruption of Vesuvius in A.D. 79 = the cause of the destruction of Pompeii.

The theory under discussion is silent about processes, states, and attributes if these differ from individual events.

What does it mean to say that an event is mental or physical? One natural answer is that an event is physical if it is describable in a purely physical vocabulary, mental if describable in mental terms. But if this is taken to suggest that an event is physical, say, if some physical predicate is true of it, then there is the following difficulty. Assume that the predicate '*x* took place at Noosa Heads' belongs to the physical vocabulary; then so also must the predicate '*x* did not take place at Noosa Heads' belong to the physical vocabulary. But the predicate '*x* did or did not take place at Noosa Heads' is true of every event, whether mental or physical.[5] We might

5. The point depends on assuming that mental events may intelligibly be said to have a location; but it is an assumption that must be true if an identity theory is, and here I am not trying to prove the theory but to formulate it.

rule out predicates that are tautologically true of every event, but this will not help since every event is truly describable either by '*x* took place at Noosa Heads' or by '*x* did not take place at Noosa Heads.' A different approach is needed.[6]

We may call those verbs mental that express propositional attitudes like believing, intending, desiring, hoping, knowing, perceiving, noticing, remembering, and so on. Such verbs are characterized by the fact that they sometimes feature in sentences with subjects that refer to persons, and are completed by embedded sentences in which the usual rules of substitution appear to break down. This criterion is not precise, since I do not want to include these verbs when they occur in contexts that are fully extensional ('He knows Paris,' 'He perceives the moon' may be cases), nor exclude them whenever they are not followed by embedded sentences. An alternative characterization of the desired class of mental verbs might be that they are psychological verbs as used when they create apparently nonextensional contexts.

Let us call a description of the form 'the event that is M' or an open sentence of the form 'event *x* is M' a *mental description* or a *mental open sentence* if and only if the expression that replaces 'M' contains at least one mental verb essentially. (Essentially, so as to rule out cases where the description or open sentence is logically equivalent to one not containing mental vocabulary.) Now we may say that an event is mental if and only if it has a mental description, or (the description operator not being primitive) if there is a mental open sentence true of that event alone. Physical events are those picked out by descriptions or open sentences that contain only the physical vocabulary essentially. It is less important to characterize a physical vocabulary because relative to the mental it is, so to speak, recessive in determining whether a description is mental or physical. (There will be some comments presently on the nature of a physical vocabulary, but these comments will fall far short of providing a criterion.)

On the proposed test of the mental, the distinguishing feature of the mental is not that it is private, subjective, or immaterial, but that it exhibits what Brentano called intentionality. Thus intentional actions are clearly included in the realm of the mental along with thoughts, hopes, and regrets (or the events tied to these). What may seem doubtful is whether the criterion will include events that have often been considered paradigmatic of the mental. Is it obvious, for example, that feeling a pain or seeing an afterimage will count as mental? Sentences that report such events seem free from taint of nonextensionality, and the same should be true of reports of raw feels, sense data, and other uninterpreted sensations, if there are any.

However, the criterion actually covers not only the havings of pains and afterimages, but much more besides. Take some event one would intuitively accept as physical, let's say the collision of two stars in distant space. There must be a purely physical predicate 'P*x*' true of this collision, and of others, but true of only this one at the time it occurred. This particular time, though, may be pinpointed as the same time that Jones notices that a pencil starts to roll across his desk. The distant stellar

6. I am indebted to Lee Bowie for emphasizing this difficulty.

collision is thus *the* event *x* such that PX and *x* is simultaneous with Jones' noticing that a pencil starts to roll across his desk. The collision has now been picked out by a mental description and must be counted as a mental event.

This strategy will probably work to show every event to be mental; we have obviously failed to capture the intuitive concept of the mental. It would be instructive to try to mend this trouble, but it is not necessary for present purposes. We can afford Spinozistic extravagance with the mental since accidental inclusions can only strengthen the hypothesis that all mental events are identical with physical events. What would matter would be failure to include bona fide mental events, but of this there seems to be no danger.

I want to describe, and presently to argue for, a version of the identity theory that denies that there can be strict laws connecting the mental and the physical. The very possibility of such a theory is easily obscured by the way in which identity theories are commonly defended and attacked. Charles Taylor, for example, agrees with protagonists of identity theories that the sole 'ground' for accepting such theories is the supposition that correlations or laws can be established linking events described as mental with events described as physical. He says, 'It is easy to see why this is so: unless a given mental event is invariably accompanied by a given, say, brain process, there is no ground for even mooting a general identity between the two.'[7] Taylor goes on (correctly, I think) to allow that there may be identity without correlating laws, but my present interest is in noticing the invitation to confusion in the statement just quoted. What can 'a given mental event' mean here? Not a particular, dated, event, for it would not make sense to speak of an individual event being 'invariably accompanied' by another. Taylor is evidently thinking of events of a given *kind*. But if the only identities are of kinds of events, the identity theory presupposes correlating laws.

One finds the same tendency to build laws into the statement of the identity theory in these typical remarks:

When I say that a sensation is a brain process or that lightning is an electrical discharge, I am using 'is' in the sense of strict identity . . . there are not two things: a flash of lightning and an electrical discharge. There is one thing, a flash of lightning, which is described scientifically as an electrical discharge to the earth from a cloud of ionized water molecules.[8]

The last sentence of this quotation is perhaps to be understood as saying that for

7. Charles Taylor, 'Mind-Body Identity, a Side Issue?' *The Philosophical Review*, LXXVI (1967), p. 202.

8. J. J. C. Smart, 'Sensations and Brain Processes,' *The Philosophical Review*, LXVIII (1959), pp. 141–56 (Chapter 8, pp. 116–27 of this volume). The quoted passages are on pp. 163–165 of the reprinted version in *The Philosophy of Mind*, ed. V. C. Chappell (Englewood Cliffs, N. J., 1962). For another example, see David K. Lewis, 'An Argument for the Identity Theory,' *The Journal of Philosophy*, LXIII (1966), pp. 17–25 (Chapter 10, pp. 150–7 of this volume). Here the assumption is made explicit when Lewis takes events as universals (p. 17 (p. 150 of this volume), footnotes 1 and 2). I do not suggest that Smart and Lewis are confused, only that their way of stating the identity theory tends to obscure the distinction between particular events and kinds of events on which the formulation of my theory depends.

every lightning flash there exists an electrical discharge to the earth from a cloud of ionized water molecules with which it is identical. Here we have a honest ontology of individual events and can make literal sense of identity. We can also see how there could be identities without correlating laws. It is possible, however, to have an ontology of events with the conditions of individuation specified in such a way that any identity implies a correlating law. Kim, for example, suggests that F*a* and G*b* 'describe or refer to the same event' if and only if $a = b$ and the property of being F = the property of being G. The identity of the properties in turn entails that (x) $(Fx \leftrightarrow Gx)$.[9] No wonder Kim says:

If pain is identical with brain state *B*, there must be a concomitance between occurrences of pain and occurrences of brain state *B*. . . . Thus, a necessary condition of the pain-brain state *B* identity is that the two expressions 'being in pain' and 'being in brain state *B*' have the same extension. . . . There is no conceivable observation that would confirm or refute the identity but not the associated correlation.[10]

It may make the situation clearer to give a fourfold classification of theories of the relation between mental and physical events that emphasizes the independence of claims about laws and claims of identity. On the one hand there are those who assert, and those who deny, the existence of psychophysical laws; on the other hand there are those who say mental events are identical with physical and those who deny this. Theories are thus divided into four sorts: *Nomological monism*, which affirms that there are correlating laws and that the events correlated are one (materialists belong in this category); *nomological dualism*, which comprises various forms of parallelism, interactionism, and epiphenomenalism; *anomalous dualism*, which combines ontological dualism with the general failure of laws correlating the mental and the physical (Cartesianism). And finally there is *anomalous monism*, which classifies the position I wish to occupy.[11]

Anomalous monism resembles materialism in its claim that all events are physical, but rejects the thesis, usually considered essential to materialism, that mental phenomena can be given purely physical explanations. Anomalous monism shows an ontological bias only in that it allows the possibility that not all events are mental,

9. Jaegwon Kim, 'On the Psycho-Physical Identity Theory,' *American Philosophical Quarterly*, III (1966), p. 231.
10. Ibid., pp. 227–28. Richard Brandt and Jaegwon Kim propose roughly the same criterion in 'The Logic of the Identity Theory,' *The Journal of Philosophy* LIV (1967), pp. 515–537. They remark that on their conception of event identity, the identity theory 'makes a stronger claim than merely that there is a pervasive phenomenal-physical correlation' (p. 518). I do not discuss the stronger claim.
11. Anomalous monism is more or less explicitly recognized as a possible position by Herbert Feigl, 'The "Mental" and the "Physical,"' in *Concepts, Theories and the Mind-Body Problem*, vol. II, *Minnesola Studies in the Philosophy of Science* (Minneapolis, 1958); Sydney Shoemaker, 'Ziff's Other Minds,' *The Journal of Philosophy*, LXII (1965), p. 589; David Randall Luce, 'Mind-Body Identity and Psycho-Physical Correlation,' *Philosophical Studies*, XVII (1966), pp. 1–7; Charles Taylor, op. cit., p. 207. Something like my position is tentatively accepted by Thomas Nagel, 'Physicalism,' *The Philosophical Review*, LXXIV (1965), pp. 339–356, and briefly endorsed by P. F. Strawson in *Freedom and the Will*, ed. D. F. Pears (London, 1963), pp. 63–67.

while insisting that all events are physical. Such a bland monism, unbuttressed by correlating laws or conceptual economies, does not seem to merit the term 'reductionism'; in any case it is not apt to inspire the nothing-but reflex ('Conceiving the *Art of the Fugue* was nothing but a complex neural event,' and so forth).

Although the position I describe denies there are psychophysical laws, it is consistent with the view that mental characteristics are in some sense dependent, or supervenient, on physical characteristics. Such supervenience might be taken to mean that there cannot be two events alike in all physical respects but differing in some mental respect, or that an object cannot alter in some mental respect without altering in some physical respect. Dependence or supervenience of this kind does not entail reducibility through law or definition: if it did, we could reduce moral properties to descriptive, and this there is good reason to *believe* cannot be done; and we might be able to reduce truth in a formal system to syntactical properties, and this we *know* cannot in general be done.

This last example is in useful analogy with the sort of lawless monism under consideration. Think of the physical vocabulary as the entire vocabulary of some language L with resources adequate to express a certain amount of mathematics, and its own syntax. L¢ is L augmented with the truth predicate 'true-in-L,' which is 'mental.' In L. (and hence L') it is possible to pick out, with a definite description or open sentence, each sentence in the extension of the truth predicate, but if L is consistent there exists no predicate of syntax (of the 'physical' vocabulary), no matter how complex, that applies to all and only the true sentences of L. There can be no 'psychophysical law' in the form of a biconditional, '(*x*) (*x* is true-in-L if and only if *x* is φ)' where 'φ' is replaced by a 'physical' predicate (a predicate of L). Similarly, we can pick out each mental event using the physical vocabulary alone, but no purely physical predicate, no matter how complex, has, as a matter of law, the same extension as a mental predicate.

It should now be evident how anomalous monism reconciles the three original principles. Causality and identity are relations between individual events no matter how described. But laws are linguistic; and so events can instantiate laws, and hence be explained or predicted in the light of laws, only as those events are described in one or another way. The principle of causal interaction deals with events in extension and is therefore blind to the mental-physical dichotomy. The principle of the anomalism of the mental concerns events described as mental, for events are mental only as described. The principle of the nomological character of causality must be read carefully: it says that when events are related as cause and effect, they have descriptions that instantiate a law. It does not say that every true singular statement of causality instantiates a law.[12]

12. The point that substitutivity of identity fails in the context of explanation is made in connection with the present subject by Norman Malcolm, 'Scientific Materialism and the Identity Theory,' *Dialogue*, III (1964–65), pp. 123–124. See also my 'Actions, Reasons and Causes,' *The Journal of Philosophy*, IX (1963), pp. 696–699 and 'The Individuation of Events' in *Essays in Honor of Carl G. Hempel*, ed. N. Rescher, et al. (Dordrecht, 1969).

II

The analogy just bruited, between the place of the mental amid the physical, and the place of the semantical in a world of syntax, should not be strained. Tarski proved that a consistent language cannot (under some natural assumptions) contain an open sentence 'F*x*' true of all and only the true sentences of that language. If our analogy were pressed, then we would expect a proof that there can be no physical open sentence 'P*x*' true of all and only the events having some mental property. In fact, however, nothing I can say about the irreducibility of the mental deserves to be called a proof; and the kind of irreducibility is different. For if anomalous monism is correct, not only can every mental event be uniquely singled out using only physical concepts, but since the number of events that falls under each mental predicate may, for all we know, be finite, there may well exist a physical open sentence coextensive with each mental predicate, though to construct it might involve the tedium of a lengthy and uninstructive alternation. Indeed, even if finitude is not assumed, there seems no compelling reason to deny that there could be coextensive predicates, one mental and one physical.

The thesis is rather that the mental is nomologically irreducible: there may be *true* general statements relating the mental and the physical, statements that have the logical form of a law; but they are not *lawlike* (in a strong sense to be described). If by absurdly remote chance we were to stumble on a nonstochastic true psychophysical generalization, we would have no reason to believe it more than roughly true.

Do we, by declaring that there are no (strict) psychophysical laws, poach on the empirical preserves of science—a form of *hubris* against which philosophers are often warned? Of course, to judge a statement lawlike or illegal is not to decide its truth outright; relative to the acceptance of a general statement on the basis of instances, ruling it lawlike must be a priori. But such relative apriorism does not in itself justify philosophy, for in general the grounds for deciding to trust a statement on the basis of its instances will in turn be governed by theoretical and empirical concerns not to be distinguished from those of science. If the case of supposed laws linking the mental and the physical is different, it can only be because to allow the possibility of such laws would amount to changing the subject. By changing the subject I mean here: deciding not to accept the criterion of the mental in terms of the vocabulary of the propositional attitudes. This short answer cannot prevent further ramifications of the problem, however, for there is no clear line between changing the subject and changing what one says on an old subject, which is to admit, in the present context at least, that there is no clear line between philosophy and science. Where there are no fixed boundaries only the timid never risk trespass.

It will sharpen our appreciation of the anomological character of mental-physical generalizations to consider a related matter, the failure of definitional behaviorism. Why are we willing (as I assume we are) to abandon the attempt to give explicit definitions of mental concepts in terms of behavioral ones? Not, surely, just because all actual tries are conspicuously inadequate. Rather it is because we are persuaded, as we are in the case of so many other forms of definitional reductionism (naturalism in ethics, instrumentalism and operationalism in the sciences, the causal theory of meaning, phenomenalism, and so on—the catalogue of philosophy's defeats), that there is system in the failures. Suppose we try to say, not using any mental concepts, what it is for a man to believe there is life on Mars. One line we could take is this: when a certain sound is produced in the man's presence ('Is there life on Mars?') he produces another ('Yes'). But of course this shows he believes there is life on Mars only if he understands English, his production of the sound was intentional, and was a response to the sounds as meaning something in English; and so on. For each discovered deficiency, we add a new proviso. Yet no matter how we patch and fit the nonmental conditions, we always find the need for an additional condition (provided he *notices, understands*, etc.) that is mental in character.[13]

A striking feature of attempts at definitional reduction is how little seems to hinge on the question of synonymy between definiens and definiendum. Of course, by imagining counterexamples we do discredit claims of synonymy. But the pattern of failure prompts a stronger conclusion: if we were to find an open sentence couched in behavioral terms and exactly coextensive with some mental predicate, nothing could reasonably persuade us that we had found it. We know too much about thought and behavior to trust exact and universal statements linking them. Beliefs and desires issue in behavior only as modified and mediated by further beliefs and desires, attitudes and attendings, without limit. Clearly this holism of the mental realm is a clue both to the autonomy and to the anomalous character of the mental.

These remarks apropos definitional behaviorism provide at best hints of why we should not expect nomological connections between the mental and the physical. The central case invites further consideration.

Lawlike statements are general statements that support counterfactual and subjunctive claims, and are supported by their instances. There is (in my view) no non-question-begging criterion of the lawlike, which is not to say there are no reasons in particular cases for a judgment. Lawlikeness is a matter of degree, which is not to deny that there may be cases beyond debate. And within limits set by the conditions of communication, there is room for much variation between individuals in the pattern of statements to which various degrees of nomologicality are assigned. In all these respects, nomologicality is much like analyticity, as one might expect since both are linked to meaning.

'All emeralds are green' is lawlike in that its instances confirm it, but 'all emeralds are grue' is not, for 'grue' means 'observed before time *t* and green, otherwise blue,' and if our observations were all made before *t* and uniformly revealed green

13. The theme is developed in Roderick Chisholm, *Perceiving* (Ithaca, New York, 1957), chap. 11.

emeralds, this would not be a reason to expect other emeralds to be blue. Nelson Goodman has suggested that this shows that some predicates, 'grue' for example, are unsuited to laws (and thus a criterion of suitable predicates could lead to a criterion of the lawlike). But it seems to me the anomalous character of 'All emeralds are grue' shows only that the predicates 'is an emerald' and 'is grue' are not suited to one another: grueness is not an inductive property of emeralds. Grueness *is* however an inductive property of entities of other sorts, for instance of emerires. (Something is an emerire if it is examined before *t* and is an emerald, and otherwise is a sapphire.) Not only is 'All emerires are grue' entailed by the conjunction of the lawlike statements 'All emeralds are green' and 'All sapphires are blue,' but there is no reason, as far as I can see, to reject the deliverance of intuition, that it is itself lawlike.[14] Nomological statements bring together predicates that we know a priori are made for each other—know; that is, independently of knowing whether the evidence supports a connection between them. 'Blue,' 'red,' and 'green' are made for emeralds, sapphires, and roses; 'grue,' 'bleen,' and 'gred' are made for sapphalds, emerires, and emeroses.

The direction in which the discussion seems headed is this: mental and physical predicates are not made for one another. In point of lawlikeness, psychophysical statements are more like 'All emeralds are grue' than like 'All emeralds are green.'

Before this claim is plausible, it must be seriously modified. The fact that emeralds examined before *t* are grue not only is no reason to believe all emeralds are grue; it is not even a reason (if we know the time) to believe *any* unobserved emeralds are grue. But if an event of a certain mental sort has usually been accompanied by an event of a certain physical sort, this often is a good reason to expect other cases to follow suit roughly in proportion. The generalizations that embody such practical wisdom are assumed to be only roughly true, or they are explicitly stated in probabilistic terms, or they are insulated from counter-example by generous escape clauses. Their importance lies mainly in the support they lend singular causal claims and related explanations of particular events. The support derives from the fact that such a generalization, however crude and vague, may provide good reason to believe that underlying the particular case there is a regularity that could be formulated sharply and without caveat.

In our daily traffic with events and actions that must be foreseen or understood, we perforce make use of the sketchy summary generalization, for we do not know a more accurate law, or if we do, we lack a description of the particular events in which we are interested that would show the relevance of the law. But there is an important distinction to be made within the category of the rude rule of thumb.

14. This view is accepted by Richard C. Jeffrey, 'Goodman's Query,' *The Journal of Philosophy*, LXII (1966), p. 286 ff., John R. Wallace, 'Goodman, Logic, Induction,' same journal and issue, p. 318, and John M. Vickers, 'Characteristics of Projectible Predicates,' *The Journal of Philosophy*, LXIV (1967), p. 285. On pp. 328–329 and 286–287 of these journal issues respectively Goodman disputes the lawlikeness of statements like 'All emerires are grue.' I cannot see, however, that he meets the point of my 'Emeroses by Other Names,' *The Journal of Philosophy*, LXIII (1966), pp. 778–780.

On the one hand, there are generalizations whose positive instances give us reason to believe the generalization itself could be improved by adding further provisos and conditions stated in the same general vocabulary as the original generalization. Such a generalization points to the form and vocabulary of the finished law: we may say that it is a *homonomic* generalization. On the other hand there are generalizations which when instantiated may give us reason to believe there is a precise law at work, but one that can be stated only by shifting to a different vocabulary. We may call such generalizations *heteronomic.*

I suppose most of our practical lore (and science) is heteronomic. This is because a law can hope to be precise, explicit, and as exceptionless as possible only if it draws its concepts from a comprehensive closed theory. This ideal theory may or may not be deterministic, but it is if any true theory is. Within the physical sciences we do find homonomic generalizations, generalizations such that if the evidence supports them, we then have reason to believe they may be sharpened indefinitely by drawing upon further physical concepts: there is a theoretical asymptote of perfect coherence with all the evidence, perfect predictability (under the terms of the system), total explanation (again under the terms of the system). Or perhaps the ultimate theory is probabilistic, and the asymptote is less than perfection; but in that case there will be no better to be had.

Confidence that a statement is homonomic, correctible within its own conceptual domain, demands that it draw its concepts from a theory with strong constitutive elements. Here is the simplest possible illustration; if the lesson carries, it will be obvious that the simplification could be mended.

The measurement of length, weight, temperature, or time depends (among many other things, of course) on the existence in each case of a two-place relation that is transitive and asymmetric: warmer than, later than, heavier than, and so forth. Let us take the relation *longer than* as our example. The law or postulate of transitivity is this:

(L) $\text{L}(x,y)$ and $\text{L}(y,z) \rightarrow \text{L}(x,z)$

Unless this law (or some sophisticated variant) holds, we cannot easily make sense of the concept of length. There will be no way of assigning numbers to register even so much as ranking in length, let alone the more powerful demands of measurement on a ratio scale. And this remark goes not only for any three items directly involved in an intransitivity: it is easy to show (given a few more assumptions essential to measurement of length) that there is no consistent assignment of a ranking to any item unless (L) holds in full generality.

Clearly (L) alone cannot exhaust the import of 'longer than'—otherwise it would not differ from 'warmer than' or 'later than.' We must suppose there is some empirical content, however difficult to formulate in the available vocabulary, that distinguishes 'longer than' from the other two-place transitive predicates of measurement and on the basis of which we may assert that one thing is longer than another. Imagine this empirical content to be partly given by the predicate '$\text{O}(x,y)$'.

So we have this 'meaning postulate':

(M) $\quad \mathrm{O}(x,y) \rightarrow \mathrm{L}(x,y)$

that partly interprets (L). But now (L) and (M) together yield an empirical theory of great strength, for together they entail that there do not exist three objects *a*, *b*, and *c* such that $\mathrm{O}(a,b)$, $\mathrm{O}(b,c)$, and $\mathrm{O}(c,a)$. Yet what is to prevent this happening if '$\mathrm{O}(x,y)$' is a predicate we can ever, with confidence, apply? Suppose we *think* we observe an intransitive triad; what do we say? We could count (L) false, but then we would have no application for the concept of length. We could say (M) gives a wrong test for length; but then it is unclear what we thought was the *content* of the idea of one thing being longer than another. Or we could say that the objects under observation are not, as the theory requires, *rigid* objects. It is a mistake to think we are forced to accept some one of these answers. Concepts such as that of length are sustained in equilibrium by a number of conceptual pressures, and theories of fundamental measurement are distorted if we force the decision, among such principles as (L) and (M): analytic or synthetic. It is better to say the whole set of axioms, laws, or postulates for the measurement of length is partly constitutive of the idea of a system of macroscopic, rigid, physical objects. I suggest that the existence of lawlike statements in physical science depends upon the existence of constitutive (or synthetic a priori) laws like those of the measurement of length within the same conceptual domain.

Just as we cannot intelligibly assign a length to any object unless a comprehensive theory holds of objects of that sort, we cannot intelligibly attribute any propositional attitude to an agent except within the framework of a viable theory of his beliefs, desires, intentions, and decisions.

There is no assigning beliefs to a person one by one on the basis of his verbal behavior, his choices, or other local signs no matter how plain and evident, for we make sense of particular beliefs only as they cohere with other beliefs, with preferences, with intentions, hopes, fears, expectations, and the rest. It is not merely, as with the measurement of length, that each case tests a theory and depends upon it, but that the content of a propositional attitude derives from its place in the pattern.

Crediting people with a large degree of consistency cannot be counted mere charity: it is unavoidable if we are to be in a position to accuse them meaningfully of error and some degree of irrationality. Global confusion, like universal mistake, is unthinkable, not because imagination boggles, but because too much confusion leaves nothing to be confused about and massive error erodes the background of true belief against which alone failure can be construed. To appreciate the limits to the kind and amount of blunder and bad thinking we can intelligibly pin on others is to see once more the inseparability of the question what concepts a person commands and the question what he does with those concepts in the way of belief, desire, and intention. To the extent that we fail to discover a coherent and plausible pattern in the attitudes and actions of others we simply forego the chance of treating them as persons.

The problem is not bypassed but given center stage by appeal to explicit speech behavior. For we could not begin to decode a man's sayings if we could not make out his attitudes towards his sentences, such as holding, wishing, or wanting them to be true. Beginning from these attitudes, we must work out a theory of what he means, thus simultaneously giving content to his attitudes and to his words. In our need to make him make sense, we will try for a theory that finds him consistent, a believer of truths, and a lover of the good (all by our own lights, it goes without saying). Life being what it is, there will be no simple theory that fully meets these demands. Many theories will effect a more or less acceptable compromise, and between these theories there may be no objective grounds for choice.

The heteronomic character of general statements linking the mental and the physical traces back to this central role of translation in the description of all propositional attitudes, and to the indeterminacy of translation.[15] There are no strict psychophysical laws because of the disparate commitments of the mental and physical schemes. It is a feature of physical reality that physical change can be explained by laws that connect it with other changes and conditions physically described. It is a feature of the mental that the attribution of mental phenomena must be responsible to the background of reasons, beliefs, and intentions of the individual. There cannot be tight connections between the realms if each is to retain allegiance to its proper source of evidence. The nomological irreducibility of the mental does not derive merely from the seamless nature of the world of thought, preference and intention, for such interdependence is common to physical theory, and is compatible with there being a single right way of interpreting a man's attitudes without relativization to a scheme of translation. Nor is the irreducibility due simply to the possibility of many equally eligible schemes, for this is compatible with an arbitrary choice of one scheme relative to which assignments of mental traits are made. The point is rather that when we use the concepts of belief, desire and the rest, we must stand prepared, as the evidence accumulates, to adjust our theory in the light of considerations of overall cogency: the constitutive ideal of rationality partly controls each phase in the evolution of what must be an evolving theory. An arbitrary choice of translation scheme would preclude such opportunistic tempering of theory; put differently, a right arbitrary choice of a translation manual would be of a manual acceptable in the light of all possible evidence, and this is a choice we cannot make. We must conclude, I think, that nomological slack between the mental and the physical is essential as long as we conceive of man as a rational animal.

15. The influence of W. V. Quine's doctrine of the indeterminacy of translation, as in chap. 2 of *Word and Object* (Cambridge, Mass., 1960), is, I hope, obvious. In § 45 Quine develops the connection between translation and the propositional attitudes, and remarks that 'Brentano's thesis of the irreducibility of intentional idioms is of a piece with the thesis of indeterminacy of translation' (p. 221).

III

The gist of the foregoing discussion, as well as its conclusion, will be familiar. That there is a categorial difference between the mental and the physical is a commonplace. It may seem odd that I say nothing of the supposed privacy of the mental, or the special authority an agent has with respect to his own propositional attitudes, but this appearance of novelty would fade if we were to investigate in more detail the grounds for accepting a scheme of translation. The step from the categorial difference between the mental and the physical to the impossibility of strict laws relating them is less common, but certainly not new. If there is a surprise, then, it will be to find the lawlessness of the mental serving to help establish the identity of the mental with that paradigm of the lawlike, the physical.

The reasoning is this. We are assuming, under the Principle of the Causal Dependence of the Mental, that some mental events at least are causes or effects of physical events; the argument applies only to these. A second Principle (of the Nomological Character of Causality) says that each true singular causal statement is backed by a strict law connecting events of kinds to which the events mentioned as cause and effect belong. Where there are rough, but homonomic, laws, there are laws drawing on concepts from the same conceptual domain and upon which there is no improving in point of precision and comprehensiveness. We urged in the last section that such laws occur in the physical sciences. Physical theory promises to provide a comprehensive closed system guaranteed to yield a standardized, unique description of every physical event couched in a vocabulary amenable to law.

It is not plausible that mental concepts alone can provide such a framework, simply because the mental does not, by our first principle, constitute a closed system. Too much happens to affect the mental that is not itself a systematic part of the mental. But if we combine this observation with the conclusion that no psychophysical statement is, or can be built into, a strict law, we have the Principle of the Anomalism of the Mental: there are no strict laws at all on the basis of which we can predict and explain mental phenomena.

The demonstration of identity follows easily. Suppose *m*, a mental event, caused *p*, a physical event; then under some description *m* and *p* instantiate a strict law. This law can only be physical, according to the previous paragraph. But if *m* falls under a physical law, it has a physical description; which is to say it is a physical event. An analogous argument works when a physical event causes a mental event. So every mental event that is causally related to a physical event is a physical event. In order to establish anomalous monism in full generality it would be sufficient to show that every mental event is cause or effect of some physical event; I shall not attempt this.

If one event causes another, there is a strict law which those events instantiate when properly described. But it is possible (and typical) to know of the singular causal relation without knowing the law or the relevant descriptions. Knowledge requires reasons, but these are available in the form of rough heteronomic generalizations, which are lawlike in that instances make it reasonable to expect other instances to follow suit without being lawlike in the sense of being indefinitely refinable. Applying these facts to knowledge of identities, we see that it is possible to know that a mental event is identical with some physical event without knowing which one (in the sense of being able to give it a unique physical description that brings it under a relevant law). Even if someone knew the entire physical history of the world, and every mental event were identical with a physical, it would not follow that he could predict or explain a single mental event (so described, of course).

Two features of mental events in their relation to the physical—causal dependence and nomological independence—combine, then, to dissolve what has often seemed a paradox, the efficacy of thought and purpose in the material world, and their freedom from law. When we portray events as perceivings, rememberings, decisions and actions, we necessarily locate them amid physical happenings through the relation of cause and effect; but that same mode of portrayal insulates mental events, as long as we do not change the idiom, from the strict laws that can in principle be called upon to explain and predict physical phenomena.

Mental events as a class cannot be explained by physical science; particular mental events can when we know particular identities. But the explanations of mental events in which we are typically interested relate them to other mental events and conditions. We explain a man's free actions, for example, by appeal to his desires, habits, knowledge and perceptions. Such accounts of intentional behavior operate in a conceptual framework removed from the direct reach of physical law by describing both cause and effect, reason and action, as aspects of a portrait of a human agent. The anomalism of the mental is thus a necessary condition for viewing action as autonomous. I conclude with a second passage from Kant:

> It is an indispensable problem of speculative philosophy to show that its illusion respecting the contradiction rests on this, that we think of man in a different sense and relation when we call him free, and when we regard him as subject to the laws of nature. . . . It must therefore show that not only can both of these very well co-exist, but that both must be thought *as necessarily united* in the same subject. . . .[16]

16. Op. cit, p. 76.

Chapter 40

The irreducibility of consciousness

John R. Searle

I. Emergent properties

SUPPOSE we have a system, *S*, made up of elements *a*, *b*, *c* . . . For example, *S* might be a stone and the elements might be molecules. In general, there will be features of *S* that are not, or not necessarily, features of *a*, *b*, *c* . . . For example, *S* might weigh ten pounds, but the molecules individually do not weigh ten pounds. Let us call such features 'system features.' The shape and the weight of the stone are system features. Some system features can be deduced or figured out or calculated from the features of *a*, *b*, *c* . . . just from the way these are composed and arranged (and sometimes from their relations to the rest of the environment). Examples of these would be shape, weight, and velocity. But some other system features cannot be figured out just from the composition of the elements and environmental relations; they have to be explained in terms of the causal interactions among the elements. Let's call these 'causally emergent system features.' Solidity, liquidity, and transparency are examples of causally emergent system features.

On these definitions, consciousness is a causally emergent property of systems. It is an emergent feature of certain systems of neurons in the same way that solidity and liquidity are emergent features of systems of molecules. The existence of consciousness can be explained by the causal interactions between elements of the brain at the micro level, but consciousness cannot itself be deduced or calculated from the sheer physical structure of the neurons without some additional account of the causal relations between them.

This conception of causal emergence, call it 'emergent1,' has to be distinguished from a much more adventurous conception, call it 'emergent2.' A feature *F* is emergent2 iff *F* is emergent1 and *F* has causal powers that cannot be explained by the causal interactions of *a*, *b*, *c* . . . If consciousness were emergent2, then consciousness could cause things that could not be explained by the causal behavior of the neurons. The naive idea here is that consciousness gets squirted out by the behavior of the neurons in the brain, but once it has been squirted out, it then has a life of its own.

It should be obvious from the previous chapter that on my view consciousness is emergent1, but not emergent2. In fact, I cannot think of anything that is emergent2,

John R. Searle, edited extract from 'Reductionism and the Irreducibility of Consciousness', from *The Rediscovery of the Mind* (Cambridge, MA: MIT Press, 1992).

and it seems unlikely that we will be able to find any features that are emergent2, because the existence of any such features would seem to violate even the weakest principle of the transitivity of causation.

II. Reductionism

Most discussions of reductionism are extremely confusing. Reductionism as an ideal seems to have been a feature of positivist philosophy of science, a philosophy now in many respects discredited. However, discussions of reductionism still survive, and the basic intuition that underlies the concept of reductionism seems to be the idea that certain things might be shown to be *nothing but* certain other sorts of things. Reductionism, then, leads to a peculiar form of the identity relation that we might as well call the 'nothing-but' relation: in general, *A*'s can be reduced to *B*'s, iff *A*'s are nothing but *B*'s.

However, even within the nothing-but relation, people mean so many different things by the notion of 'reduction' that we need to begin by making several distinctions. At the very outset it is important to be clear about what the relata of the relation are. What is its domain supposed to be: objects, properties, theories, or what? I find at least five different senses of 'reduction'—or perhaps I should say five different kinds of reduction—in the theoretical literature, and I want to mention each of them so that we can see which are relevant to our discussion of the mind-body problem.

1. Ontological reduction The most important form of reduction is ontological reduction. It is the form in which objects of certain types can be shown to consist in nothing but objects of other types. For example, chairs are shown to be nothing but collections of molecules. This form is clearly important in the history of science. For example, material objects in general can be shown to be nothing but collections of molecules, genes can be shown to consist in nothing but DNA molecules. It seems to me this form of reduction is what the other forms are aiming at.

2. Property ontological reduction This is a form of ontological reduction, but it concerns properties. For example, heat (of a gas) is nothing but the mean kinetic energy of molecule movements. Property reductions for properties corresponding to theoretical terms, such as 'heat,' 'light,' etc., are often a result of theoretical reductions.

3. Theoretical reduction Theoretical reductions are the favorite of theorists in the literature, but they seem to me rather rare in the actual practice of science, and it is perhaps not surprising that the same half dozen examples are given over and over in the standard text-books. From the point of view of scientific explanation, theoretical reductions are mostly interesting if they enable us to carry out ontological reductions. In any case, theoretical reduction is primarily a relation between theories, where the laws of the reduced theory can (more or less) be deduced from the laws of the reducing theory. This demonstrates that the reduced theory is nothing but a special case of the reducing theory. The classical example that is usually given in textbooks is the reduction of the gas laws to the laws of statistical thermodynamics.

4. Logical or definitional reduction This form of reduction used to be a great favorite among philosophers, but in recent decades it has fallen out of fashion. It is a relation between words and sentences, where words and sentences referring to one type of entity can be translated without any residue into those referring to another type of entity. For example, sentences about the average plumber in Berkeley are reducible to sentences about specific individual plumbers in Berkeley; sentences about numbers, according to one theory, can be translated into, and hence are reducible to, sentences about sets. Since the words and sentences are *logically* or *definitionally* reducible, the corresponding entities referred to by the words and sentences are *ontologically* reducible. For example, numbers are nothing but sets of sets.

5. Causal reduction This is a relation between any two types of things that can have causal powers, where the existence and a fortiori the causal powers of the reduced entity are shown to be entirely explainable in terms of the causal powers of the reducing phenomena. Thus, for example, some objects are solid and this has causal consequences: solid objects are impenetrable by other objects, they are resistant to pressure, etc. But these causal powers can be causally explained by the causal powers of vibratory movements of molecules in lattice structures.

Now when the views I have urged are accused of being reductionist—or sometimes insufficiently reductionist—which of these various senses do the accusers have in mind? I think that theoretical reduction and logical reduction are not intended. Apparently the question is whether the causal reductionism of my view leads—or fails to lead—to ontological reduction. I hold a view of mind/brain relations that is a form of causal reduction, as I have defined the notion: Mental features are caused by neurobiological processes. Does this imply ontological reduction?

In general in the history of science, successful causal reductions tend to lead to ontological reductions. Because where we have a successful causal reduction, we simply redefine the expression that denotes the reduced phenomena in such a way that the phenomena in question can now be identified with their causes. Thus, for example, color terms were once (tacitly) defined in terms of the subjective experience of color perceivers; for example, 'red' was defined ostensively by pointing to examples, and then real red was defined as whatever seemed red to 'normal' observers under 'normal' conditions. But once we have a causal reduction of color phenomena to light reflectances, then, according to many thinkers, it becomes possible to redefine color expressions in terms of light reflectances. We thus carve off and eliminate the subjective experience of color from the 'real' color. Real color has undergone a property ontological reduction to light reflectances. Similar remarks could be made about the reduction of heat to molecular motion, the reduction of solidity to molecular movements in lattice structures, and the reduction of sound to air waves. In each case, the causal reduction leads naturally to an ontological reduction by way of a redefinition of the expression that names the reduced phenomenon. Thus, to continue with the example of 'red,' once we know that the color experiences are caused by a certain sort of photon emission, we then redefine the word in terms of the specific features of the photon emission. 'Red,' according to some theorists, now refers to photon emissions of 600 nanometers. It thus follows trivially that the color red is nothing but photon emissions of 600 nanometers.

The general principle in such cases appears to be this: Once a property is seen to be *emergent1*, we automatically get a causal reduction, and that leads to an ontological reduction, by redefinition if necessary. The general trend in ontological reductions that have a scientific basis is toward greater generality, objectivity, and redefinition in terms of underlying causation.

So far so good. But now we come to an apparently shocking asymmetry. When we come to consciousness, we cannot perform the ontological reduction. Consciousness is a causally emergent property of the behavior of neurons, and so consciousness is causally reducible to the brain processes. But—and this is what seems so shocking—a perfect science of the brain would still not lead to an ontological reduction of consciousness in the way that our present science can reduce heat, solidity, color, or sound. It seems to many people whose opinions I respect that the irreducibility of consciousness is a primary reason why the mind-body problem continues to seem so intractable. Dualists treat the irreducibility of consciousness as incontrovertible proof of the truth of dualism. Materialists insist that consciousness must be reducible to material reality, and that the price of denying the reducibility of consciousness would be the abandonment of our overall scientific world view.

I will briefly discuss two questions: First, I want to show why consciousness is irreducible, and second, I want to show why it does not make any difference at all to our scientific world view that it should be irreducible. It does not force us to property dualism or anything of the sort. It is a trivial consequence of certain more general phenomena.

III. Why consciousness is an irreducible feature of physical reality

There is a standard argument to show that consciousness is not reducible in the way that heat, etc., are. In different ways the argument occurs in the work of Thomas Nagel (1974), Saul Kripke (1971), and Frank Jackson (1982). I think the argument is decisive, though it is frequently misunderstood in ways that treat it as merely epistemic and not ontological. It is sometimes treated as an epistemic argument to the effect that, for example, the sort of third-person, objective knowledge we might possibly have of a bat's neurophysiology would still not include the first-person, subjective experience of what it feels like to be a bat. But for our present purposes, the point of the argument is ontological and not epistemic. It is a point about what real features exist in the world and not, except derivatively, about how we know about those features.

Here is how it goes: Consider what facts in the world make it the case that you are now in a certain conscious state such as pain. What fact in the world corresponds to your true statement, 'I am now in pain'? Naively, there seem to be at least two sorts of facts. First and most important, there is the fact that you are now having certain unpleasant conscious sensations, and you are experiencing these sensations from your subjective, first-person point of view. It is these sensations that are constitutive of your present pain. But the pain is also caused by certain underlying neurophysiological processes consisting in large part of patterns of neuron firing in your thalamus and other regions of your brain. Now suppose we tried to reduce the subjective, conscious, first-person sensation of pain to the objective, third-person patterns of neuron firings. Suppose we tried to say the pain is really 'nothing but' the patterns of neuron firings. Well, if we tried such an ontological reduction, the essential features of the pain would be left out. No description of the third-person, objective, physiological facts would convey the subjective, first-person character of the pain, simply because the first-person features are different from the third-person features. Nagel states this point by contrasting the objectivity of the third-person features with the what-it-is-like features of the subjective states of consciousness. Jackson states the same point by calling attention to the fact that someone who had a complete knowledge of the neurophysiology of a mental phenomenon such as pain would still not know what a pain was if he or she did not know what it felt like. Kripke makes the same point when he says that pains could not be identical with neurophysiological states such as neuron firings in the thalamus and elsewhere, because any such identity would have to be necessary, because both sides of the identity statement are rigid designators, and yet we know that the identity could not be necessary. This fact has obvious epistemic consequences: my knowledge that I am in pain has a different sort of basis than my knowledge that you are in pain. But the antireductionist point of the argument is ontological and not epistemic.

So much for the antireductionist argument. It is ludicrously simple and quite decisive. An enormous amount of ink has been shed trying to answer it, but the answers are all so much wasted ink. But to many people it seems that such an argument paints us into a corner. To them it seems that if we accept that argument, we have abandoned our scientific world view and adopted property dualism. Indeed, they would ask, what is property dualism but the view that there are irreducible mental properties? In fact, doesn't Nagel accept property dualism and Jackson reject physicalism precisely because of this argument? And what is the point of scientific reductionism if it stops at the very door of the mind? So I now turn to the main point of this discussion.

IV. Why the irreducibility of consciousness has no deep consequences

To understand fully why consciousness is irreducible, we have to consider in a little more detail the pattern of reduction that we found for perceivable properties such as heat, sound, color, solidity, liquidity, etc., and we have to show how the attempt to reduce consciousness differs from the other cases. In every case the ontological reduction was based on a prior causal reduction. We discovered that a surface feature of a phenomenon was caused by the behavior of the elements of an underlying microstructure. This is true both in the cases in which the reduced phenomenon was a matter of subjective appearances, such as the 'secondary qualities' of heat or color; and in the cases of the 'primary qualities' such as solidity, in which there was both an element of subjective appearance (solid things feel solid), and also many features independent of subjective appearances (solid things, e.g., are resistant to pressure and impenetrable by other solid objects). But in each case, for both the primary and secondary qualities, the point of the reduction was to carve off the surface features and redefine the original notion in terms of the causes that produce those surface features.

Thus, where the surface feature is a subjective appearance, we redefine the original notion in such a way as to exclude the appearance from its definition. For example, pretheoretically our notion of heat has something to do with perceived temperatures: Other things being equal, hot is what feels hot to us, cold is what feels cold. Similarly with colors: Red is what looks red to normal observers under normal conditions. But when we have a theory of what causes these and other phenomena, we discover that it is molecular movements causing sensations of heat and cold (as well as other phenomena such as increases in pressure), and light reflectances causing visual experiences of certain sorts (as well as other phenomena such as movements of light meters). We then *redefine* heat and color in terms of the underlying causes of both the subjective experiences and the other surface phenomena. And in the redefinition we eliminate any reference to the subjective appearances and other surface effects of the underlying causes. 'Real' heat is now defined in terms of the kinetic energy of the molecular movements, and the subjective feel of heat that we get when we touch a hot object is now treated as just a subjective appearance caused by heat, as an effect of heat. It is no longer part of real heat. A similar distinction is made between real color and the subjective experience of color. The same pattern works for the primary qualities: Solidity is defined in terms of the vibratory movements of molecules in lattice structures, and objective, observer-independent features, such as impenetrability by other objects, are now seen as surface effects of the underlying reality. Such redefinitions are achieved by way of carving off all of the surface features of the phenomenon, whether subjective or objective, and treating them as effects of the real thing.

But now notice: The actual pattern of the facts in the world that correspond to statements about particular forms of heat such as specific temperatures are quite similar to the pattern of facts in the world that correspond to statements about particular forms of consciousness, such as pain. If I now say, 'It's hot in this room,' what are the facts? Well, first there is a set of 'physical' facts involving the movement of molecules, and second there is a set of 'mental' facts involving my subjective experience of heat, as caused by the impact of the moving air molecules on my nervous system. But similarly with pain. If I now say, 'I am in pain,' what are the facts? Well, first there is a set of 'physical' facts involving my thalamus and other regions of the brain, and second there is a set of 'mental' facts involving my subjective experience of pain. So why do we regard heat as reducible and pain as irreducible? The answer is that what interests us about heat is not the subjective appearance but the underlying physical causes. Once we get a causal reduction, we simply redefine the notion to enable us to get an ontological reduction. Once you know all the facts about heat—facts about molecule movements, impact on sensory nerve endings, subjective feelings, etc.—the reduction of heat to molecule movements involves no new *fact* whatever. It is simply a trivial consequence of the redefinition. We don't first discover all the facts and then discover a new fact, the fact that heat is reducible; rather, we simply redefine heat so that the reduction follows from the definition. But this redefinition does not eliminate, and was not intended to eliminate, the subjective experiences of heat (or color, etc.) from the world. They exist the same as ever.

We might not have made the redefinition. Bishop Berkeley, for example, refused to accept such redefinitions. But it is easy to see why it is rational to make such redefinitions and accept their consequences: To get a greater understanding and control of reality, we want to know how it works causally, and we want our concepts to fit nature at its causal joints. We simply redefine phenomena with surface features in terms of the underlying causes. It then looks like a new discovery that heat is *nothing but* mean kinetic energy of molecule movement, and that if all subjective experiences disappeared from the world, real heat would still remain. But this is not a new discovery, it is a trivial consequence of a new definition. Such reductions do not show that heat, solidity, etc., do not really exist in the way that, for example, new knowledge showed that mermaids and unicorns do not exist.

Couldn't we say the same thing about consciousness? In the case of consciousness, we do have the distinction between the 'physical' processes and the subjective 'mental' experiences, so why can't consciousness be redefined in terms of the neuro-physiological processes in the way that we redefined heat in terms of underlying physical processes? Well, of course, if we insisted on making the redefinition, we could. We could simply define, for example, 'pain' as patterns of neuronal activity that cause subjective sensations of pain. And if such a redefinition took place, we would have achieved the same sort of reduction for pain that we have for heat. But of course, the reduction of pain to its physical reality still leaves the subjective experience of pain unreduced, just as the reduction of heat left the subjective experience of heat unreduced. Part of the point of the reductions was to carve off the subjective experiences and exclude them from the definition of the real phenomena, which are now defined in terms of those features that interest us most. But where the phenomena that interest us most are the subjective experiences themselves, there is no way to carve anything off. Part of the point of the reduction in the case of heat was to distinguish between the subjective appearance on the one hand and the underlying physical reality on the other. Indeed, it is a general feature of such reductions that the phenomenon is defined in terms of the 'reality' and not in terms of the 'appearance.' But we can't make that sort of appearance-reality distinction for consciousness because consciousness consists in the appearances themselves. *Where appearance is concerned we cannot make the appearance-reality distinction because the appearance is the reality.*

For our present purposes, we can summarize this point by saying that consciousness is not reducible in the way that other phenomena are reducible, not because the pattern of facts in the real world involves anything special, but because the reduction of other phenomena depended in part on distinguishing between 'objective physical reality,' on the one hand, and mere 'subjective appearance,' on the other; and eliminating the appearance from the phenomena that have been reduced. But in the case of consciousness, its reality is the appearance; hence, the point of the reduction would be lost if we tried to carve off the appearance and simply defined consciousness in terms of the underlying physical reality. In general, the pattern of our reductions rests on rejecting the subjective epistemic basis for the presence of a property as part of the ultimate constituent of that property. We find out about heat or light by feeling and seeing, but we then define the phenomenon in a way that is independent of the epistemology. Consciousness is an exception to this pattern for a trivial reason. The reason, to repeat, is that the reductions that leave out the epistemic bases, the appearances, cannot work for the epistemic bases themselves. In such cases, the appearance is the reality.

But this shows that the irreducibility of consciousness is a trivial consequence of the pragmatics of our definitional practices. A trivial result such as this has only trivial consequences. It has no deep metaphysical consequences for the unity of our overall scientific world view. It does not show that consciousness is not part of the ultimate furniture of reality or cannot be a subject of scientific investigation or cannot be brought into our overall physical conception of the universe; it merely shows that in the way that we have decided to carry out reductions, consciousness, by definition, is excluded from a certain pattern of reduction. Consciousness fails to be reducible, not because of some mysterious feature, but simply because by definition it falls outside the pattern of reduction that we have chosen to use for pragmatic reasons. Pretheoretically, consciousness, like solidity, is a surface feature of certain physical systems. But unlike solidity, consciousness cannot be redefined in terms of an underlying microstructure, and the surface features then treated as mere effects of real consciousness, without losing the point of having the concept of consciousness in the first place.

So far, the argument of this chapter has been conducted, so to speak, from the point of view of the materialist. We can summarize the point I have been making as follows: The contrast between the reducibility of heat, color, solidity, etc., on the one hand, and the irreducibility of conscious states, on the other hand, does not reflect any distinction in the structure of reality, but a distinction in our definitional practices. We could put the same point from the point of view of the property dualist as follows: The apparent contrast between the irreducibility of consciousness and the reducibility of color, heat, solidity, etc., really was *only* apparent. We did not really eliminate the subjectivity of red, for example, when we reduced red to light reflectances; we simply stopped calling the subjective part 'red.' We did not eliminate any subjective phenomena whatever with these 'reductions'; we simply stopped calling them by their old names. Whether we treat the irreducibility from the materialist or from the dualist point of view, we are still left with a universe that contains an irreducibly subjective physical component as a component of physical reality.

To conclude this part of the discussion, I want to make clear what I am saying and what I am not saying. I am not saying that consciousness is not a strange and wonderful phenomenon. I think, on the contrary, that we ought to be amazed by the fact that evolutionary processes produced nervous systems capable of causing and sustaining subjective conscious states. Consciousness is as empirically mysterious to us now as electromagnetism was previously, when people thought the universe must operate entirely on Newtonian principles. But I am saying that once the existence of (subjective, qualitative) consciousness is granted (and no sane person can deny its existence, though many pretend to do so), then there is nothing strange, wonderful, or mysterious about its *irreducibility*. Given its existence, its irreducibility is a trivial consequence of our definitional practices. Its irreducibility has no untoward scientific consequences whatever. Furthermore, when I speak of the irreducibility of consciousness, I am speaking of its *irreducibility according to standard patterns of reduction*. No one can rule out a priori the possibility of a major intellectual revolution that would give us a new—and at present unimaginable—conception of reduction, according to which consciousness would be reducible.

References

Jackson, F. (1982) 'Epiphenomenal Qualia,' *Philosophical Quarterly* 32: 127–136 (see Chapter 43 of this volume).

Kripke, S. A. (1971) 'Naming and Necessity,' in D. Davidson and G. Harman (eds.), *Semantics of Natural Language*. Dordrecht: Reidel, pp. 253–355 and 763–769 (see Chapter 9 of this volume).

Nagel, T. (1974) 'What Is It Like to Be a Bat?' *Philosophical Review* 4 LXXXIII: 435–450 (see Chapter 29 of ths volume).

Chapter 41

The metaphysics of irreducibility

Derk Pereboom and Hilary Kornblith

During the 'sixties and 'seventies, Hilary Putnam, Jerry Fodor, and Richard Boyd, among others, developed a type of materialism that eschews reductionist claims.[1] In this view, explanations, natural kinds, and properties in psychology do not reduce to counterparts in more basic sciences, such as neurophysiology or physics. Nevertheless, all token psychological entities—states, processes, and faculties—are wholly constituted of physical entities, ultimately out of entities over which microphysics quantifies. This view soon became the standard position in philosophy of mind, and reductionism fell out of favor. Recently, however, reductionism has been experiencing a rebirth, and many have suggested that the non-reductive approach was accepted too quickly and too uncritically. In this paper, we attempt to provide a more thorough account of the anti-reductionist position, and, in the process, to defend it against its recent critics.

I. Irreducibility, multiple realizability, and explanation

When Putnam first argued for nonreductive materialism, he cited the phenomenon of multiple realizability as its main justification. Since mental states can be realized by indefinitely many neurophysiological states, and perhaps by many non-neurophysiological states, mental states are not reducible to neurophysiological states. Perhaps because the phenomenon of multiple realizability played such a prominent role in Putnam's presentation of this view, many philosophers identify the claim that mental states are not reducible to neurophysiological states with the claim that mental states are multiply realizable. But this is a mistake. We shall argue that multiple realizability is not the most fundamental feature of irreducibility.

The phenomenon of multiple realizability also played a prominent role in Fodor's general account of anti-reductionism in 'Special Sciences'. Consider a law in some special science:

Derk Pereboom and Hilary Kornblith, 'The Metaphysics of Irreducibility', *Philosophical Studies* 63 (1991).

1. Richard Boyd, 'Materialism Without Reductionism: What Physicalism Does Not Entail,' in Ned Block ed., *Readings in the Philosophy of Psychology*. Volume 1. (Cambridge, Mass.: Harvard University Press, 1980); Jerry Fodor, 'Special Sciences,' in *Readings in the Philosophy of Psychology*, ed. by Ned Block, (Cambridge, Mass.: Harvard University Press, 1980); Hilary Putnam, *Philosophical Papers*, volume 2, (Cambridge: Cambridge University Press, 1975).

S_1x causes S_2x

where S_1 and S_2 are natural kind-predicates in that science. The most appropriate model of reduction requires that every kind that appears in this law be identified with a kind in the reducing science, in virtue of bridge principles. Bridge principles either translate kind-predicates in one science into those of a more basic one, or specify a metaphysical relation, like *being identical to* or *being a necessary and sufficient condition for*, between the kinds of one science and those of the reducing science. But in some cases, the sort of bridge principle required for reducibility will not be available.

If kinds in psychology are multiply realizable in an indefinite number of ways at the neurophysiological level, purported bridge principles for relating psychological to neurophysiological kinds will involve open-ended disjunctions. Such purported bridge principles will have to be of the form:

$P_1 = N_1 \text{ v } N_2 \text{ v } N_3 \ldots$

which says that a certain psychological state, P_1, is identical to an open-ended disjunction of neurophysiological states, N_1 v N_2 v N_3 . . ., or

$P_1 \longleftrightarrow N_1 \text{ v } N_2 \text{ v } N_3 \ldots$

which says that a certain psychological state is necessary and sufficient for an open-ended disjunction of neurophysiological states.[2] Fodor argues that since open-ended disjunctions of kinds in neurophysiology are not natural neurophysiological kinds, psychological kinds cannot be reduced to neurophysiological kinds.

Why are such disjunctions not natural kinds? Fodor's reason is that they are not natural kinds because they cannot appear in laws. They cannot appear in laws because 'laws' involving such disjunctions are not explanatory. Finally, Fodor says that such 'laws' are not explanatory because they do not meet our interests in explanation. Fodor's argument for irreducibility, then, appeals to the fact that purported explanations for psychological phenomena are unsatisfying when couched in terms of open-ended disjunctions. In advancing this claim, Fodor was echoing a point of Putnam's.

There can be little doubt that Putnam and Fodor are right about this. When Mary walks down the street to buy an ice-cream cone, we explain her behavior by appealing to the content of her beliefs and desires: she wanted an ice-cream cone and she believed one could be purchased down the street. Replacing this explanation by one which contains an open-ended disjunction of physical predicates—if Mary is in state P_1 or P_2 or P_3 etc., she will move with trajectory T_1—indeed leaves our interests in explanation unsatisfied.

For many, however, invoking our interests and the satisfaction of our feelings about explanation seems uncomfortably subjective. The reductionist might say that

2. For economy in exposition, we shall focus on reduction in terms of identity, and ignore reduction in terms of necessary and sufficient conditions in the first three sections of this paper.

there exist open-ended disjunctive but nevertheless genuine laws and explanations, even though they might fail to meet certain subjective requirements. If only we were capable of taking in more information at once, the reductionist might say, we wouldn't have any trouble regarding open-ended disjunctive 'laws' as genuine laws. The fact that we fail to find laws satisfying when they contain open-ended disjunctions may simply show a failing on our part, rather than on the part of the laws themselves.

The apparent subjectivity of these anti-reductionist considerations is, however, called into question by an argument for scientific realism. The reductionist wishes to claim that our interests in explanation, which are not met by 'explanations' and 'laws' couched in terms of open-ended disjunctions, are somehow merely parochial; they reflect parochial interests or limitations of scientific investigators. When it is these interests, however, which give rise to and define successful scientific research programs, the claim that these interests are merely parochial loses its plausibility. The success of a scientific research program in prediction and technological application is evidence of the truth of the theories which are instrumental in gaining that success, and of the legitimacy of the interests which give rise to and define that program. More precisely, it is evidence that the interests which define the standards of explanation which are in part constitutive of that research program are not merely parochial, but instead have a purchase on objectivity. Our interests in explanation are not objective merely because they are ours, nor is an explanation a good one merely because it satisfies our interests, whatever they might be. Rather, our interests in explanation make a legitimate claim to objectivity when they are instrumental in giving rise to a successful research program.

One might object that although science should not allow laws containing open-ended disjunctions, metaphysics need not be restricted in this way. Hence: laws containing open-ended disjunctions might well provide metaphysical explanations, and hence reductions of psychological laws. We believe, however, that such an attempt to separate science from metaphysics is misguided. The picture invoked by this objection is of an a priori metaphysics, unguided by science. The more appealing view is that since metaphysics and science both aim to characterize and explain the structure of reality, they should not be viewed as separate enterprises. In this particular case, since the notion of a law is a paradigmatically scientific notion, metaphysics should yield to science for its criteria of lawfulness.

The basis, then, for the claim that psychology is not reducible to neurophysiology is not simply that mental states are multiply realizable at the neurophysiological level, but rather that this multiple realizability shows that attempts at reduction would require laws and explanations of a very peculiar kind; so peculiar, indeed, that they would be unsatisfying as laws and explanations. This dissatisfaction does not rest on merely subjective interests. The legitimacy of our interests depends on the case that can be made for the success of the research program which they partially give rise to and define. We believe that such a case can be made for psychology, and it is there that the argument against reductionism is ultimately founded.

II. Irreducibility and constitutional explanations

More, however, remains to be said about the metaphysical state of affairs that obtains when one causal explanation fails to reduce to another. In order to see this, we must first distinguish between two types of explanation.[3] In addition to the usual causal explanations, we wish to speak of constitutional explanations. When we provide a constitutional explanation for something, we attempt to say what that thing is made of, to specify its constitution. In investigating the issue of reduction, we must look at the different roles constitutional explanations can play.

The notion of reduction at issue in the debate over nonreductive materialism is that of one *type-level* causal explanation reducing to another. That is, whether reductionism in a certain area is true depends on whether an explanation which quantifies over types or kinds at one scientific level reduces to an explanation which quantifies over types or kinds at another. An exploration of the relationships between such type-level causal explanations and constitutional accounts of the kinds and processes referred to in these explanations will serve to elucidate the metaphysies of irreducibility.

Consider the following type-level causal explanation:

Raising the temperature of the gas in a hot air balloon causes it to rise.

Here, a constitutional account of temperature of a gas as mean molecular kinetic energy allows us to deepen this causal explanation, since greater mean molecular kinetic energy is intimately tied, at the type-level, to lower density of the gas in the balloon, which in turn explains the propensity of the balloon to rise.[4] The constitutional account of gas temperature thus invokes properties that illuminate the above type-level causal explanation. In this case, a constitutional account provides us with a *reduction* of a type-level causal explanation because the constitutional account illuminates this explanation. Of course, such illumination is not provided by the constitutional account all by itself, but in conjunction with the system of laws and explanations that govern the specified constitution in its particular scientific domain.

When, however, type-level causal explanations are not reducible to explanations in a more basic science, these causal explanations are not illuminated by constitutional accounts in that more basic science. Consider what Philip Kitcher tells us

3. Here we follow Robert Cummins, *The Nature of Psychological Explanation*, (Cambridge, Mass.: Bradford Books/MIT Press, 1983).

4. This identification is, in fact, an oversimplification, but in ways which do not affect this particular point. For a more precise account of the relationship between temperature and mean molecular kinetic energy, see section IV below.

about the relationship between genetics and molecular biology.[5] In classical genetics, the transmission of genes is accounted for by meiosis, a process in which paired entities 'are separated by a force so that one member of each pair is assigned to a descendent entity'. Kitcher points out that these processes are not a natural kind from the molecular point of view. The power to separate the paired entities is multiply realizable; all that matters is that the bonds between the originally paired entities be *somehow* broken. New bonds are sometimes formed between the constituent molecules of these entities, but many accessory molecules may also be involved. Separation may even result from electromagnetic forces, nuclear forces, or gravity. Moreover, separation may occur due to different varieties of these types of forces.[6] In this example, at the token-level, a constitutional explanation tells us how a token genetic process is realized in molecular material. But since a genetic process-type is multiply realizable at the molecular level, constitutional accounts of various instantiations of this genetic process-type are heterogeneous. Consequently, there is no molecular constitutional explanation which illuminates, rather than obscures, the type-level genetic process. In general, because molecular constitutional accounts of genetic process-types fail to illuminate type-level genetic causal explanations, type-level genetic causal explanations are not reducible to molecular explanations.

This is not to say, however, that *token-level constitutional* accounts are of no interest when there is no reduction in the offing. In all but the special case of microphysical processes, constitutional accounts of token processes will provide illumination. After all, every process is realized in microphysical stuff, and so there is some account to be given of just how it is that the process is so realized. It is one thing to explain how a token process is realized in physical material, but quite another to show that a certain type of process reduces to a physical process. The first is possible for every existing non-microphysical process, the second only for those where there is a constitutional explanation at the type-level.

What is the relationship between the causal powers appealed to in different levels of a constitutional explanation? The answer to this question depends upon whether the constitutional account under discussion provides us with a reduction. In the cases where a constitutional account does provide us with a reduction, the account allows us to identify the types of causal powers of the objects and properties at the two levels of explanation.

For cases in which a constitutional account does not provide a reduction, let us return to the example of the relationship between genetics and molecular biology. A type of gene has certain causal powers, active in any type of genetic process, for example, the power to bring about certain traits in the descendants it produces. These causal powers, we shall argue, are not to be identified with the causal powers

5. Philip Kitcher, '1953 and All That: A Tale of Two Sciences,' *The Philosophical Review* XCIII, No. 3 (July, 1984).
6. Kitcher, pp. 349–50.

of the molecules which wholly constitute the gene. Rather, the relationship is, again, one of token-constitution. The following condition expresses our notion of the token-constitution of causal powers:

> The causal powers of a token of kind Fare constituted of the causal powers of a token of kind G just in case the token of kind F has the causal powers it does in virtue of its being constituted of a token of kind G.

A token gene has the causal powers it does in virtue of the causal powers of the molecules which constitute it; its causal powers do not arise from nowhere. Hence, by our condition, the causal powers of a token gene are constituted from the causal powers of its constituent molecules.

Where there is irreducibility of explanation, there is only token constitution, and no identity of causal powers. In fact, when one type of explanation does not reduce to an explanation at a more basic level, the causal powers at the higher level of explanation are *neither type- nor token-identical to* causal powers at the more basic level. Let us first consider the thesis for type-identity. To the psychological state-type, *desire for ice-cream*, we attribute the causal power to cause ice-cream securing behavior. This type of causal power is not identical to any physical causal power because it is physically multiply realizable. One might challenge the existence of types of psychological causal power that are not identical to physical causal powers by denying that types of entities in irreducible sciences other than microphysics have any causal powers. But this is an unpromising strategy. We naturally attribute causal powers not only to types of psychological states, but to biological types, like genes and bodily organs, and the irreducibility of such types has been successfully argued.

But now, let us examine the token case. Is the token causal power of your present desire for ice-cream, D, identical to the token physical causal power, P, which constitutes it?[7] No. Suppose that P is a token causal power of the molecules, M, that constitute a token brain cell, and that you ingested these molecules while eating your favorite baby cereal on the morning of your first birthday. Suppose also that your mother had the choice of two type-identical boxes of this baby cereal on the previous day, and that she chose the one on the left. If she had instead chosen the box on the right, you would not have had token molecules M (although you would have had molecules M′ of the same type), and because you would lack these token molecules, you would also lack their attendant token molecular causal power P (although M′ would have had a molecular causal power of the same type).

Nevertheless, you clearly would have had the very same token desire for ice-cream with its token psychological causal power D. Hence, a token psychological state and its token psychological causal power can remain the same even when its token molecular constitution, and thus its token molecular causal powers, are

7. Some may reject talk of token causal powers, and prefer instead talk of the (token) instantiations of causal powers. Our argument is no less effective if couched in these terms.

altered.[8] This result can easily be generalized; hence, when one type of explanation does not reduce to another, there is neither type- nor token-identity between causal powers.

Here, in a diversity of causal powers of natural kinds or in explanations, we encounter the most fundamental metaphysical feature of irreducibility. Multiple realizability is indeed a significant feature of irreducibility because it shows that attempts at reduction would require 'laws' involving open-ended disjunctions of heterogeneous kinds. But the deeper metaphysical state of affairs underlying such a situation is the existence of a diversity of causal powers at the two levels of explanation. Multiple realizability is a significant metaphysical feature of irreducibility, but only because it is very powerful evidence of a more fundamental feature, that the causal powers invoked in a lower-level explanation are not identical to those in the explanation which is the target of the attempted reduction.

III. Davidson's anomalous monism

There is an interesting relationship between the view we advocate and Davidson's anomalous monism which, we believe, casts light on both these views.[9] Like us, Davidson rejects any reduction of the psychological to the physical. Unlike us, he also rejects the existence of psychological laws. Finally, and also unlike us, he embraces a token-identity thesis. We believe that the differences between Davidson's position and ours turn on our different accounts of causation: Davidson is committed to a Humean account of causation, while we are committed to a non-Humean account.[10]

As Davidson has pointed out, there can be no exceptionless laws in psychology. The reason for this is quite simple. Psychological events do not constitute the whole of reality. For any psychological process one might name, there is always the possibility that some event from outside the sphere of the psychological might interfere with the normal working of that process. Thus, if it were a law of psychology that creatures in mental state P_1 are caused to go into mental state P_2 when stimulated in way S, it is certainly compatible with this law that a creature in state P_1 who is also stimulated in way S might suffer brain damage in a car accident before this lawful process has the chance to produce mental state P_2. Since extraneous phenomena like car accidents are not governed by psychological laws, the psychological laws there are, if any, could not possibly be exceptionless.[11]

8. Here we follow Boyd and Cummins, rather than Fodor.
9. 'Mental Events,' in *Essays on Actions and Events*, (Oxford: Clarendon Press, 1980), 207–225 (see Chapter 39 of this volume).
10. See 'Causal Relations,' in Davidson, *op. cit.*, 160.
11. Roughly this point is made by Fodor in 'Special Sciences,' p. 129. See also Louise Antony, 'Anomalous Monism and the Problem of Explanatory Force,' *Philosophical Review* XCVIII, No. 2 (April, 1989), p. 176.

We believe that this provides no reason to reject genuine, even if not exceptionless psychological laws, nor the view that they invoke causal powers whose operation is subject to interference. But notice that this is not a position which a Humean about causation can hold. Since Humeans hold that a statement of the form 'A causes B' is true only if A-like events are *always* followed by B-like events, the very idea of a statement which is both a causal law and admits of exceptions is self-contradictory. For a Humean to acknowledge the point above about the limited scope of psychology—that there may be non-psychological events which interfere with psychological processes—forces him to say, as Davidson does, that there are no psychological laws.

Hume's own discussion of causation is devoted to rejecting the robust causal powers we wish to invoke—talk of which is not merely a picturesque way of speaking about exceptionless laws linking events. Once one follows Hume's lead, one is forced to deny the existence of causal laws, not only in psychology, but in any science other than, at most, microphysics. Genetic processes, for example, are subject to interference at the microphysical level, and hence genetic laws will not be exceptionless. Should we conclude that there is no genetic causation? Our best current science would suggest otherwise. Causal claims in genetics and the rest of the special sciences are spared, however, if we assume the existence of real causal powers, talk of which is not merely reducible to talk of exceptionless laws.

The second disagreement we have with Davidson, on the alleged token-identity of mental and physical events, also hinges on the dispute about the Humean view of causation. We hold that token mental states are physically constituted, but not identical to the token physical states which constitute them. How is it that token mental states and their physical constitutions might be distinct? Although we do not claim to possess necessary and sufficient conditions for identity and diversity of token states and their constitutions, we can say that a mental state and its token physical constitution are distinct if the causal powers of the token mental state and the causal power of its physical constitution are distinct. But this kind of appeal to causal powers is not open to a Humean about causation. Because the only causal laws there are for a Humean are exceptionless laws, and because there are no causes which are not backed by exceptionless causal laws, there can be no causal powers at the psychological level of description. The only room there might be for genuine causal powers, on the Humean account, is at the microphysical level, for it is only at this level that we may eliminate the possibility of interfering factors. Such a view would leave us with no clear basis for a distinction between a token mental state and the physical state which constitutes it. Thus, we would thereby be led, as Davidson is, to a token-identity thesis about the relationship between the mental and the physical.

Davidson's position may thus be derived from ours by replacing our commitment to a non-Humean account of causation with a commitment to a Humean account. Alternatively, some of the characteristic and troubling theses of

Davidson's anomalous monism may be avoided by rejecting the Humean view of causation, and by accepting our version of non-reductive materialism.[12]

IV. Species-specific reduction and the charge of dualism

We are now in a position to consider several of the objections to non-reductive materialism.

Kim argues that anti-reductionists assume that even though psychology does not reduce to neurophysiology, there is nevertheless *strong connectibility* between psychological and neurophysiological states.[13] That is,

(S) For each system and any psychological state that it can instantiate, there is a physical condition of that system which is necessary and sufficient for the system to instantiate that psychological state.

So anti-reductionists assume,

$S_1 \rightarrow (P_1 \longleftrightarrow M)$

'which says that for organisms belonging to species S_i (or systems of physical structure S_i) a certain physical state, P_i, exists which is both necessary and sufficient for the given mental property M.'

Kim aims to show that the phenomenon of multiple realizability is easily accommodated within a reductionist framework. Thus he states,

What is important then is that these laws are relative to physical biological structure-types, although for simplicity I will continue to put the matter in terms of species. The substantive theoretical assumption here is the belief that for each psychological state there are physical-biological structure types, at a certain level of description or specification, that generate laws of this form. I think an assumption of this kind is made by most philosophers who speak of multiple realizations of psychological states, and it is a plausible assumption for a physicalist to make. [38][14]

In support of this last point, Kim quotes Ned Block: 'Most functionalists are willing to allow . . . that for each type of pain-feeling organism, there is (perhaps) a single type of physical state that realizes pain in that type of organism.'[38]

This point of Block's fails to support the claim that Kim is making, and for two

12. The importance of a non-Humean account of causation for an adequate defense and elaboration of non-reductive materialism has been pointed out by Boyd, *Materialism Without Reductionism: Non-Humean Causation and the Evidence for Physicalism*, manuscript.

13. Jaegwon Kim, 'The Myth of Nonreductive Materialism,' *Proceedings and Addresses of the American Philosophical Association*, vol. 63, #3 (November, 1989), pp. 31–47. Page numbers in the text are in square brackets.

14. See also Paul Churchland, *Matter and Consciousness*, Revised Edition, (Cambridge, Mass.: MIT Press, 1988), pp. 38–42; Berent Enç, 'In Defense of the Identity Theory,' *Journal of Philosophy*, LXXX, No. 5, (1983).

different kinds of reason. First, even if there is a single type of physical state that normally realizes pain in each type of organism, or in each structure-type, this does not show that pain, *as a type of mental state*, is reducible to physical states. Reduction, in the present debate, must be understood as reduction of types, since the primary object of reductive strategies are explanations and theories, and explanations and theories quantify over types. Furthermore, psychological theories and explanations quantify over types of mental states, like pain, that are instantiated by organisms of many different species and structural types. The suggestion that there are species-specific reductions of pain results in the claim that pains in different species have nothing in common.[15] But this is just a form of eliminationism. If we generalized this view to other mental states, then we would be forced to reject the legitimacy of psychological theories that quantify over mental states which are instantiated in more than one species.

But this is only part of the difficulty here, for Block's comment about pain does not apply to mental states generally. We agree with Block that there are mental states for which, in the normal case, one will likely find a physiological structure for each species which subserves that state. Given the common genetic heritage of members of the same species, it would be astounding if there were not some commonalities of structure across individuals. The closer one gets to the receptors, the more likely one is to find such commonalities. For example, when you and I detect that there is one object occluding another in the center of our visual fields, the mechanism by which we detect the edges of these objects is very much the same. But it is not at all plausible to move from this point about structures close to the sensory receptors to a claim about mental states generally.

For familiar reasons, there is no plausibility to the claim that when you and I believe that Baghdad is in Iraq, there is a single physical structure which underlies that belief in each of us. The further we move away from the sensory receptors; the more unlikely we are to find common physical structures underlying our mental states. The prospects for species-specific reduction here are non-existent. Kim's suggestion then that those who have argued against reduction on the grounds of multiple realizability must grant the existence of species-specific reductions is mistaken. There are good reasons to believe that we will not find single structures subserving particular beliefs, not only across species, but across individuals, and indeed, within individuals across times.

Moreover, the fact that in order to get any species-specific reductions we must limit ourselves to normal cases further undermines the attempt at reduction. When the physical equipment which normal members of species have is damaged and replaced with a prosthesis, the very same mental states are subserved by different physical states. A human being with an artificial eye could detect the edges of objects as well as one with the kind of visual equipment common to the rest of us; we would not want to deny that edge detection occurs in such a person because the

15. Ned Block, 'What is Functionalism?' in Ned Block ed., *op. cit.* (see Chapter 13 of this volume).

physiological laws which cover edge detection in other humans fail to accommodate this particular case. Edge detection is simply not a physiological phenomenon. It is, in the typical case, subserved by a characteristic physiological structure, but it is a higher-level phenomenon governed by higher-level laws. Any attempt to reduce edge detection to the physical mechanisms which standardly (in humans) serve to realize it misses the generalizations which make edge detection the kind of phenomenon it is, namely, a bit of visual information processing.

Admittedly, Kim prefers physical structure-specific, rather than species-specific reduction. But here again, he must answer the question 'What do all of the structure-specific pains have in common?' He would appear to lack resources for a positive answer, and he therefore seems to be committed to eliminating pain as a single type of mental state. Furthermore, since Mary and Jane may have different physical structures realizing their mental states, and since Mary may have different physical structures realizing her mental states at different times, structure-specific reduction has the consequence that there may be nothing that Mary's pain and Jane's pain have in common, and even that there may be nothing that two of Mary's pains have in common. Thus, even if Mary's and Jane's pains, or Mary's pains at different times, are caused by the same types of perceptions, have the same relations to other mental states, cause the same type of behavior, and have the same qualitative characteristics, they would not necessarily be governed by the same laws. Such a proposal certainly eliminates psychological states and psychological explanations as our best psychological theories construe them.

Kim concludes that 'the multiple realizability of the mental has no anti-reductionist implications of great significance; on the contrary, it entails, or at least is consistent with, the local reducibility of psychology . . .' [39] We hope that it is now clear that this view is mistaken. Species-specific correlations are the exception rather than the rule with mental states; they occur only in cases of mental states realized in equipment very close to the sensory receptors. Furthermore, neither species- nor structure-specific reduction is a genuine reduction of *psychology*, for the attempt to reduce mental talk to talk of species- or structure-specific states eliminates those states to which our best current psychological theories are committed.[16]

A related argument against nonreductive materialism, based on an example from physics, has been advanced by Berent Enç, Patricia Churchland and Paul Churchland.[17] Temperature is clearly a natural kind in physics, while, it is claimed, it is both multiply realizable by completely different physical kinds and reducible to these

16. A further reply to Kim is inspired by the version of anti-reductionism according to which part of what determines whether a subject is in a belief state of a certain type is the nature of physical environment in which that subject is embedded. See especially Tyler Burge, 'Individualism and the Mental,' in *Midwest Studies* 1978, (Minneapolis: University of Minnesota Press, 1978), (see Chapter 25 of this volume).

17. Berent Enç, 'In Defense of the Identity Theory,' *Journal of Philosophy*, 1983, pp. 279–298; Patricia Churchland, *Neurophilosophy*, (Cambridge, Mass.: Bradford Books/MIT Press, 1986), pp. 356–8; Paul Churchland, *op. cit.*, pp. 41–42.

various realizations. Thus, by analogy, pain may be a natural kind, and although it is multiply realizable in completely diverse neurophysiological states, it may still be reducible to these realizations. Enç and the Churchlands maintain that according to contemporary physics, temperature in a gas is reducible to the mean molecular kinetic energy of its constituents, while temperature in other media, like a vacuum or a plasma, cannot be realized by mean molecular kinetic energy. Temperature in a vacuum, for instance, is identical to the blackbody distribution of the vacuum's transient radiation. Hence, analogously, the multiple realizability of mental states in thoroughly diverse neurophysiological media is consistent with their reducibility to neurophysiological states.

First, mental states are disanalogous to temperature in a way which undercuts the force of this example. Whereas a particular kind of temperature, such as temperature in gas, can be realized in only one way, belief in a human, for example, can be realized in many ways. Temperature in a gas can only be realized as the kinetic energy of molecules, and is thus not itself multiply realizable, whereas human belief can be realized in many neurophysiological media. Thus, although there is a particular set of laws for gas temperature, couched in terms of mean molecular kinetic energy, human psychological laws cannot analogously be cashed out as neurophysiological laws. Consequently, even if temperature were reducible to its realizations in several domains, mental states in general would not be.

But furthermore, if the various realizations of temperature genuinely had nothing in common, there would be reason to eliminate talk of temperature from our science entirely, rather than maintain the use of the term while simultaneously insisting that it refers to a heterogeneous class. There must be some single property in virtue of which these different realizations all count as temperature, for otherwise they could not qualify as realizations of a single natural kind. Were there nothing these various physical states had in common, the supposed reductions would provide an elimination of temperature. But in fact there is no elimination here. Thermodynamics supplies a characteristic that these different manifestations of temperature do have in common, and it is provided by the following definition:

> Temperature is a quantity which takes the same value in two systems that are brought into thermal contact and are allowed to come to equilibrium.[18]

(Ideally, two systems are brought into thermal contact with each other when they are separated by a *diathermic wall*, a wall which allows exchange of electromagnetic and mechanical forces, but no material exchange.) The systems to which this definition of temperature applies may be homogeneous or heterogeneous pairs of the

18. T. J. Quinn, *Temperature—Monographs in Physical Measurement*, (London: Academic Press, 1983), p. 3, cf. pp. 3–17; Mark W. Zemansky and Richard H. Dittman, *Heat and Thermodynamics*, Sixth Edition, (New York: McGraw-Hill, 1981), pp. 3–10; L. D. Landau and E. M. Lifshitz, *Statistical Physics*, (Oxford: Pergamon Press), pp. 32–4. There are certain precisely circumscribed conditions, which involve cases in which systems do not come to thermal equilibrium in a reasonable amount of time, under which the notion of temperature is ill-defined (Quinn, pp. 13–15).

different media to which Enç and the Churchlands appeal; gasses, liquids, solids, plasmas, and vacuums. Systems of all of these types can be brought into thermal contact and allowed to come to equilibrium. Thus, for example, the temperature of some particular gas and the temperature of some particular vacuum can both be characterized as a quantity which takes the same value when systems made up of the gas and the vacuum are brought into thermal contact and are allowed to come to equilibrium. Hence there is a single characteristic, shared by the various realizations of temperature, to which temperature is reducible. Consequently, Enç and the Churchlands have not produced an example in which a natural kind is realizable by states that have nothing in common, and is yet reducible to these states. Thus they have not provided leverage against the view that the multiple realizability of mental states is powerful evidence for nonreductive materialism.

Finally, Kim claims that nonreductive materialism embraces a dualism about psychological and physical attributes. This claim is misleading. Under no classification is the anti-reductionist's position a kind of dualism. Rather, it is a pluralism at one ontological level, and a monism at the most fundamental level. It is a pluralism in that it holds that there are kinds of entities at many levels of scientific description, and these different levels are not reducible to one another. It is monistic in that it maintains that everything that exists is constituted by microphysical particles.

According to nonreductive materialism, the difference between psychological and physical attributes is no deeper than the differences between biological and physical attributes, or the difference between kind predicates in classical genetics and molecular biology. We would not want to say that because classical genetics does not reduce to molecular biology, there are two fundamental kinds of stuff present here. Similarly, the irreducibility of psychology to neurophysiology does not entail any variety of dualism.

V. The alleged success of some neurophysiological reductions

Patricia Churchland and Paul Churchland suggest that nonreductive materialism is mistaken because many psychological phenomena seem to go begging for neurophysiological explanations.[19] The psychological effect of drugs and brain lesions, sleep, and fainting are good examples. Shouldn't we accept some form of reductionism to accommodate these examples?

No. The right anti-reductionist position is that in each science, there is a *large body* of explanations that do not reduce to explanations in a more basic science. This view is consistent with three points about the relation between psychology and more basic sciences.

19. Paul Churchland, *op. cit.*; Patricia Churchland, *Neurophilosophy*, (Cambridge, Mass: Bradford Books/MIT Press, 1986).

First, nonreductive materialism is consistent with the view that some phenomena in psychology may be best causally explained in terms of kinds and properties in some more basic science. Consider, by analogy, the relation between classical genetics and molecular biology. Even though one is not reducible to the other, certain kinds of mutations in genes may be best explained in virtue of changes in molecular structure. In psychology, when the feeling of pain is caused by a pinprick, a macrophysical event, the pinprick, explains a biological event, tissue damage, and this biological event explains a psychological event, the feeling of pain. The loss of psychological functioning by someone who has undergone a lobotomy is best explained in terms of neurophysiological damage. Hallucinating upon ingesting LSD is also best explained by a mechanism more basic than the psychological.

In general, these instances of cross-science causation occur because entities referred to in a higher-level science are constituted from entities at various more basic levels. In cases where psychological state types tend to be realized in common physiological structures, changes in the entities at the more basic levels may result in changes at the higher levels. Such changes will be lawlike if types of changes at a more basic level result in types of changes at a higher level. The lobotomy example may be a case of such a state of affairs. This does not mean, however, that the kinds in the higher-level science are to be reduced to the physical structures which typically realize them, for those higher-level kinds may be multiply realizable at the lower level. Consequently, there may well be *cross-science laws* that do not reduce to laws in any more basic science. Schematically, there might be laws of the following sort:

N_1x causes P_1x (N_1 is a kind-predicate in neurophysiology, and P_1 is a kind-predicate in psychology)

where this law does not reduce to a purely neurophysiological law because kind P_1 is multiply realizable at the neurophysiological level. The nonreductive materialist can safely admit such cross-science laws, because their widespread incidence fails to undermine the view that large bodies of explanations in the special sciences do not reduce to more basic explanations.

Second, anti-reductionism is compatible with the reducibility of *some kinds* in some special science to kinds in a more basic science. Tiredness might be nothing more than a single type of biological phenomenon (though we doubt it), and perhaps psychological explanations involving tiredness will be illuminated when recast as involving this biological phenomenon. In order for such reductions to be successful, they would clearly have to be more than species-specific. Yet even the reducibility of some psychological kinds to those in a more basic science does not undermine the irreducibility of other, and indeed most psychological kinds, such as beliefs and desires.

Third, anti-reductionism is consistent with the admission that some psychological laws are reducible to neurophysiology. For example

Tiredness typically causes sleep

is plausibly a psychological law. But perhaps both *tiredness* and *sleep* are each types of neurophysiological phenomena, and can be recast as neurophysiological kinds. Furthermore, and more fundamentally, it may be that when 'tiredness' and 'sleep' are replaced with descriptions of these neurophysiological phenomena, the explanation is illuminated, rather than merely obscured. We would be surprised if the Churchlands were correct about this and the neurophysiological understanding to be gained here were anything more than species-specific. But again, even if the Churchlands were right, it would not follow that all or most psychological laws are reducible to neurophysiology. Indeed, type-level explanations for actions by beliefs and desires are typically not illuminated by substitutions of neurophysiological constitutional explanations for psychological terms.

VI. Explanatory exclusion

According to Kim, anti-reductionism falls to what he calls *the problem of explanatory exclusion.*[20] Consider a particular bit of human behavior. According to nonreductive materialism, he maintains, there will be two causal explanations for this event. One is physical in nature, another is psychological. There is a physical explanation of the event in virtue of the causal closure of the physical domain: any physical event that has a cause has a physical cause. At the same time, most of us grant that this event has an explanation in terms of beliefs and desires as well.

But how are we to understand the relationship between these different causes? Kim considers two alternatives. One is that they are separately insufficient but jointly sufficient to cause behavior. Each of the two explanations would then yield *partial causes* of the effect. Kim thinks that not only does this seem absurd, but it also violates the principle of the causal closure of the physical domain. We agree. Such an explanation is absurd, but neither is it a part of non-reductive materialism.

A second possibility is that the effect is *overdetermined.* If the beliefs and desires had not occurred, the physical causes would still have been sufficient to cause the effect, and vice versa. One reason Kim thinks that this is mistaken is that it is absurd to think that there are two independent causal chains leading to the same effect. From what we know about the physiology of limb movement, we must believe that if the pain sensation causes my hand to withdraw, the causal chain from the pain to the limb motion must somehow make use of the causal chain from some appropriate central neurophysiological event to the muscle contraction. We agree.

Kim points out that the problem would be solved if we said that the mental and the physical cause are one and the same. Indeed, he is right about this. Identifying

20. Kim, pp. 43–47. See also Kim, 'Mechanism, Purpose, and Explanatory Exclusion,' *Philosophical Perspectives*, 3 (1989); and 'Explanatory Realism, Causal Realism, and Explanatory Exclusion,' in *Realism and Antirealism* (*Midwest Studies in Philosophy XII*), Peter French et al., eds. (Minneapolis: University of Minnesota Press, 1988).

mental with physical causal powers is one way of vindicating the causal efficacy of the mental.

Yet the anti-reductionist should not give up this easily. Both genetics and microphysics are paradigmatic physical sciences, since the entities and causal powers of each are clearly physical—that is, constituted of physical stuff. But when we explain the child's having blue eyes by means of genetics, we know that at the same time there is a microphysical explanation for the microphysical states that constitute the child's having blue eyes. Consequently, here we also run into the explanatory exclusion problem; for any genetic event, Kim would have to say that there is both a genetic and a microphysical explanation. The existence of the explanatory exclusion problem for sciences whose entities are manifestly constituted of physical stuff should mitigate Kim's worries about explanatory exclusion in the case of psychology and neurophysiology. There is no special problem about explanatory exclusion for psychology. If there is a problem here at all, it is a problem about the relations among the special sciences generally, not one about the relation between the mental and the physical.

We do not mean to argue, however, that we need not be concerned with this problem because it is ubiquitous. Quite the opposite is true. The solution to Kim's problem, however, is easily provided within the account of irreducibility given above. In rejecting a reduction of mental states to the physical states which realize them, we need not choose between saying that the mental causal powers are insufficiently efficacious to produce behavior on their own (they are only partial causes of behavior) and saying that they are wholly independent of the physical states (and thus behavior is overdetermined). Rather, as we have already indicated, mental causal powers are wholly constituted of physical causal powers; they are neither identical to (nor are they necessary and sufficient for) them, nor wholly independent of them. The psychological explanation of an event does not compete with its physical counterpart because the mental causal powers referred to in the psychological explanation are wholly made up of the physical causal powers referred to in the physical explanation. Hence, the claim that a bit of behavior was caused by certain mental states is not an explanation which competes with the physical account which underlies it, any more than the claim that I secured ice-cream with cash competes with the claim that I secured ice-cream with bits of paper and metal. Kim fails to take account of this possibility because he does not recognize that non-reductive materialism is committed both to a constitutional account of mental objects and mental properties, and thereby to a constitutional account of mental causal powers.

VII. Conclusion

We do not believe that the reasons which have been offered of late for rejecting non-reductive materialism should be accepted. The reasons for which reductive accounts were largely abandoned remain good ones, and non-reductive materialism remains the most satisfying and sensible account of the relationship among the special sciences.[21]

21. We wish to thank Lynne Rudder Baker, Stephen Brush, David Christensen, Richard Healey, Jaegwon Kim, George Sher, David Y. Smith, Sydney Shoemaker, and Ken Waters.

Chapter 42

Multiple realization and the metaphysics of reduction

Jaegwon Kim

I. Introduction

It is part of today's conventional wisdom in philosophy of mind that psychological states are 'multiply realizable', and are in fact so realized, in a variety of structures and organisms. We are constantly reminded that any mental state, say pain, is capable of 'realization', 'instantiation', or 'implementation' in widely diverse neural-biological structures in humans, felines, reptiles, mollusks, and perhaps other organisms further removed from us. Sometimes we are asked to contemplate the possibility that extraterrestrial creatures with a biochemistry radically different from the earthlings', or even electro-mechanical devices, can 'realize the same psychology' that characterizes humans. This claim, to be called hereafter 'the Multiple Realization Thesis' ('MR',[1] for short), is widely accepted by philosophers, especially those who are inclined to favor the functionalist line on mentality. I will not here dispute the truth of MR, although what I will say may prompt a reassessment of the considerations that have led to its nearly universal acceptance.

And there is an influential and virtually uncontested view about the philosophical significance of MR. This is the belief that MR refutes psychophysical reductionism once and for all. In particular, the classic psychoneural identity theory of Feigl and Smart, the so-called 'type physicalism', is standardly thought to have been definitively dispatched by MR to the heap of obsolete philosophical theories of mind. At any rate, it is this claim, that MR proves the physical irreducibility of the mental, that will be the starting point of my discussion.

Evidently, the current popularity of antireductionist physicalism is owed, for the most part, to the influence of the MR-based antireductionist argument originally developed by Hilary Putnam and elaborated further by Jerry Fodor[2]—rather more

Jaegwon Kim, 'Multiple Realization and the Metaphysics of Reduction', *Philosophy and Phenomenological Research* 52 (1992).

1. On occasion, 'MR' will refer to the *phenomenon* of multiple realization rather than the *claim* that such a phenomenon exists; there should be no danger of confusion.
2. Jerry Fodor, 'Special Sciences, or the Disunity of Science as a Working Hypothesis' (hereafter, 'Special Sciences'), *Synthese* 28 (1974): 97–115; reprinted in *Representations* (MIT Press: Cambridge, 1981), and as the introductory chapter in Fodor, *The Language of Thought* (New York: Crowell, 1975).

so than to the 'anomalist' argument associated with Donald Davidson.[3] For example, in their elegant paper on nonreductive physicalism,[4] Geoffrey Hellman and Frank Thompson motivate their project in the following way:

'Traditionally, physicalism has taken the form of reductionism—roughly, that all scientific terms can be given explicit definitions in physical terms. Of late there has been growing awareness, however, that reductionism is an unreasonably strong claim.'

But why is reductionism 'unreasonably strong'? In a footnote Hellman and Thompson explain, citing Fodor's 'Special Sciences':

'Doubts have arisen especially in connection with functional explanation in the higher-level sciences (psychology, linguistics, social theory, etc.). Functional predicates may be physically realizable in heterogeneous ways, so as to elude physical definition.'

And Ernest LePore and Barry Loewer tell us this:[5]

'It is practically received wisdom among philosophers of mind that psychological properties (including content properties) are not identical to neurophysiological or other physical properties. The relationship between psychological and neurophysiological properties is that the latter *realize* the former. Furthermore, a single psychological property might (in the sense of conceptual possibility) be realized by a large number, perhaps an infinitely many, of different physical properties and even by non-physical properties.'

They then go on to sketch the reason why MR, on their view, leads to the rejection of mind-body reduction:[6]

'If there are infinitely many physical (and perhaps nonphysical) properties which can realize F then F will not be reducible to a basic physical property. Even if F can only be realized by finitely many basic physical properties it might not be reducible to a basic physical property since the disjunction of these properties might not itself be a basic physical property (i.e., occur in a fundamental physical law). We will understand 'multiple realizability' as involving such irreducibility.'

This antireductionist reading of MR continues to this day; in a recent paper, Ned Block writes:[7]

'Whatever the merits of physiological reductionism, it is not available to the cognitive science point of view assumed here. According to cognitive science, the essence of the mental is computational, and any computational state is 'multiply realizable' by physiological or electronic states that are not identical with one another, and so content cannot be identified with any one of them.'

3. Donald Davidson, 'Mental Events' reprinted in *Essays on Actions and Events* (Oxford: Oxford University Press, 1980) (see Chapter 39 of this volume).
4. 'Physicalism: Ontology, Determination, and Reduction', *Journal of Philosophy* 72 (1975): 551–64. The two quotations below are from p. 551.
5. 'More on Making Mind Matter', *Philosophical Topics* 17 (1989): 175–92. The quotation is from p. 179.
6. 'More on Making Mind Matter', p. 180.
7. In 'Can the Mind Change the World?', *Meaning and Method: Essays in Honor of Hilary Putnam*, ed. George Boolos (Cambridge University Press: Cambridge, 1990), p. 146.

Considerations of these sorts have succeeded in persuading a large majority of philosophers of mind[8] to reject reductionism and type physicalism. The upshot of all this has been impressive: MR has not only ushered in 'non-reductive physicalism' as the new orthodoxy on the mind-body problem, but in the process has put the very word 'reductionism' in disrepute, making reductionisms of all stripes an easy target of disdain and curt dismissals.

I believe a reappraisal of MR is overdue. There is something right and instructive in the antireductionist claim based on MR and the basic argument in its support, but I believe that we have failed to follow out the implications of MR far enough, and have as a result failed to appreciate its full significance. One specific point that I will argue is this: the popular view that psychology constitutes an *autonomous special science*, a doctrine heavily promoted in the wake of the MR-inspired antireductionist dialectic, may in fact be inconsistent with the real implications of MR. Our discussion will show that MR, when combined with certain plausible metaphysical and methodological assumptions, leads to some surprising conclusions about the status of the mental and the nature of psychology as a science. I hope it will become clear that the fate of type physicalism is not among the more interesting consequences of MR.

II. Multiple realization

It was Putnam, in a paper published in 1967,[9] who first injected MR into debates on the mind-body problem. According to him, the classic reductive theories of mind presupposed the following naive picture of how psychological kinds (properties, event and state types, etc.) are correlated with physical kinds:

For each psychological kind *M* there is a unique physical (presumably, neurobiological) kind *P* that is *nomologically coextensive* with it (i.e., as a matter of law, any system instantiates *M* at *t* iff that system instantiates *P* at *t*).

(We may call this 'the Correlation Thesis'.) So take pain: the Correlation Thesis has it that pain as an event kind has a neural substrate, perhaps as yet not fully and precisely identified, that, as a matter of law, always co-occur with it in all pain-capable organisms and structures. Here there is no mention of species or types of

8. They include Richard Boyd, 'Materialism Without Reductionism: What Physicalism Does Not Entail', in Block, *Readings in Philosophy of Psychology*, vol. 1; Block, in 'Introduction: What is Functionalism?' in his anthology just cited, pp. 178–79 (Chapter 13 of this volume); John Post, *The Faces of Existence* (Ithaca: Cornell University Press, 1987); Derk Pereboom and Hilary Kornblith, 'The Metaphysics of Irreducibility' *Philosophical Studies* 63 (1991): 125–45; (Chapter 41 of this volume). One philosopher who is not impressed by the received view of MR is David Lewis: see his 'Review of Putnam' in Block, *Readings in Philosophy of Psychology*, vol. 1.

9. Hilary Putnam, 'Psychological Predicates', in W. H. Capitan and D. D. Merrill, eds., *Art, Mind, and Religion* (Pittsburgh: University of Pittsburgh, 1967); reprinted with a new title, 'The Nature of Mental States', in Ned Block, ed., *Readings in Philosophy of Psychology*, vol. 1 (Cambridge: Harvard University Press, 1980) (Chapter 11 of this volume).

organisms or structures: the neural correlate of pain is invariant across biological species and structure types. In his 1967 paper, Putnam pointed out something that, in retrospect, seems all too obvious:[10]

'Consider what the brain-state theorist has to do to make good his claims. He has to specify a physical-chemical state such that any organism (not just a mammal) is in pain if and only if (a) it possesses a brain of a suitable physical-chemical structure; and (b) its brain is in that physical-chemical state. This means that the physical-chemical state in question must be a possible state of a mammalian brain, a reptilian brain, a mollusc's brain (octopuses are mollusca, and certainly feel pain), etc. At the same time, it must not be a possible brain of any physically possible creature that cannot feel pain.'

Putnam went on to argue that the Correlation Thesis was *empirically false*. Later writers, however, have stressed the multiple realizability of the mental as a *conceptual* point: it is an a priori, conceptual fact about psychological properties that they are 'second-order' physical properties, and that their specification does not include constraints on the manner of their physical implementation.[11] Many proponents of the functionalist account of psychological terms and properties hold such a view.

Thus, on the new, improved picture, the relationship between psychological and physical kinds is something like this: there is no single neural kind N that 'realizes' pain, across all types of organisms or physical systems; rather, there is a multiplicity of neural-physical kinds, N_h, N_r, N_m, . . . such that N_h realizes pain in humans, N_r realizes pain in reptiles, N_m realizes pain in Martians, etc. Perhaps, biological species as standardly understood are too broad to yield unique physical-biological realization bases; the neural basis of pain could perhaps change even in a single organism over time. But the main point is clear: any system capable of psychological states (that is, any system that 'has a psychology') falls under some structure type T such that systems with structure T share the same physical base for each mental state-kind that they are capable of instantiating (we should regard this as relativized with respect to time to allow for the possibility that an individual may fall under different structure types at different times). Thus physical realization bases for mental states must be relativized to species or, better, physical structure-types. We thus have the following thesis:

If anything has mental property M at time t, there is some physical structure type T and physical property P such that it is a system of type T at t and has P at t, and it holds as a matter of law that all systems of type T have M at a time just in case they have P at the time.

We may call this 'the Structure-Restricted Correlation Thesis' (or 'the Restricted Correlation Thesis' for short).

It may have been noticed that neither this nor the correlation thesis speaks of

10. 'The Nature of Mental States', p. 228 (in the Block volume) (see p. 164 of this volume).

11. Thus, Post says, 'Functional and intentional states are defined without regard to their physical or other realizations', *The Faces of Existence*, p. 161. Also compare the earlier quotation from Block.

'realization'.[12] The talk of 'realization' is not metaphysically neutral: the idea that mental properties are 'realized' or 'implemented' by physical properties carries with it a certain ontological picture of mental properties as derivative and dependent. There is the suggestion that when we look at concrete reality there is nothing over and beyond instantiations of physical properties and relations, and that the instantiation on a given occasion of an appropriate physical property in the right contextual (often causal) setting simply *counts as*, or *constitutes*, an instantiation of a mental property on that occasion. An idea like this is evident in the functionalist conception of a mental property as *extrinsically* characterized in terms of its 'causal role', where what fills this role is a physical (or, at any rate, nonmental) property (the latter property will then be said to 'realize' the mental property in question). The same idea can be seen in the related functionalist proposal to construe a mental property as a 'second-order property' consisting in the having of a physical property satisfying certain extrinsic specifications. We will recur to this topic later, however, we should note that someone who accepts either of the two correlation theses need not espouse the 'realization' idiom. That is, it is prima facie a coherent position to think of mental properties as 'first-order properties' in their own right, characterized by their intrinsic natures (e.g., phenomenal feel), which, as it happens, turn out to have nomological correlates in neural properties. (In fact, anyone interested in defending a serious dualist position on the mental should eschew the realization talk altogether and consider mental properties as first-order properties on a par with physical properties.) The main point of MR that is relevant to the antireductionist argument it has generated is just this: *mental properties do not have nomically coextensive physical properties, when the latter are appropriately individuated.* It may be that properties that are candidates for reduction must be thought of as being realized, or implemented, by properties in the prospective reduction base;[13] that is, if we think of certain properties as having their own intrinsic characterizations that are entirely independent of another set of properties, there is no hope of *reducing* the former to the latter. But this point needs to be argued, and will, in any case, not play a role in what follows.

Assume that property *M* is realized by property *P*. How are *M* and *P* related to each other and, in particular, how do they covary with each other? LePore and Loewer say this:[14]

'The usual conception is that *e*'s being *P* realizes *e*'s being *F* iff *e* is *P* and there is a strong connection of some sort between *P* and *F*. We propose to understand this connection as a necessary connection which is *explanatory*. The existence of an explanatory connection

12. As far as I know, the term 'realization' was first used in something like its present sense by Hilary Putnam in 'Minds and Machines', in Sydney Hook, ed., *Dimensions of Mind* (New York: New York University Press, 1960).

13. On this point see Robert Van Gulick, 'Nonreductive Materialism and Intertheoretic Constraints', in *Emergence or Reduction?*, ed. Ansgar Beckermann, Hans Flohr, and Jaegwon Kim (Berlin: De Gruyter, 1992).

14. 'More on Making Mind Matter', p. 179.

between two properties is stronger than the claim that $P \rightarrow F$ is physically necessary since not every physically necessary connection is explanatory.'

Thus, LePore and Loewer require only that the realization base of M be *sufficient* for M, not both necessary and sufficient. This presumably is in response to *MR*: if pain is multiply realized in three ways as above, each of N_h, N_r, and N_{xu} will be sufficient for pain, and none necessary for it. This I believe is not a correct response, however, the correct response is not to weaken the joint necessity and sufficiency of the physical base, but rather to *relativize* it, as in the Restricted Correlation Thesis, with respect to species or structure types. For suppose we are designing a physical system that will instantiate a certain psychology, and let $M_1, \ldots, M_n$ be the psychological properties required by this psychology. The design process must involve the specification of an n-tuple of physical properties, $P_1, \ldots, P_n$, all of them instantiable by the system, such that for each i, P_i constitutes a *necessary and sufficient* condition *in this system* (and others of relevantly similar physical structure), not merely a sufficient one, for the occurrence of M_i. (Each such n-tuple of physical properties can be called a 'physical realization' of the psychology in question.[15]) That is, for each psychological state we must design into the system a nomologically coextensive physical state. We must do this *if we are to control both the occurrence and non-occurrence of the psychological states involved*, and control of this kind is necessary if we are to ensure that the physical device will properly instantiate the psychology. (This is especially clear if we think of building a computer; computer analogies loom large in our thoughts about 'realization'.)

But isn't it possible for multiple realization to occur 'locally' as well? That is, we may want to avail ourselves of the flexibility of allowing a psychological state, or function, to be instantiated by alternative mechanisms within a single system. This means that P_i can be a *disjunction* of physical properties; thus, M_1 is instantiated in the system in question at a time if and only if at least one of the disjuncts of P_i is instantiated at that time. The upshot of all this is that LePore and Loewer's condition that $P \rightarrow M$ holds as a matter of law needs to be upgraded to the condition that, *relative to the species or structure-type in question (and allowing P to be disjunctive)*, $P \leftrightarrow M$ holds as a matter of law.[16]

For simplicity let us suppose that pain is realized in three ways as above, by N_h in humans, N_r in reptiles, and N_m in Martians. The finitude assumption is not essential to any of my arguments: if the list is not finite, we will have an infinite disjunction rather than a finite one (alternatively, we can talk in terms of 'sets' of such properties instead of their disjunctions). If the list is 'open-ended', that's all right, too; it

15. Cf. Hartry Field, 'Mental Representation', in Block, *Readings in Philosophy of Psychology* (Cambridge: Harvard University Press, 1981), vol. 2.

16. What of LePore and Loewer's condition (ii), the requirement that the realization basis 'explain' the realized property? Something like this explanatory relation may well be entailed by the realization relation; however, I do not believe it should be part of the definition of 'realization'; that such an explanatory relation holds should be a consequence of the realization relation, not constitutive of it.

will not affect the metaphysics of the situation. We allowed above the possibility of a realization base of a psychological property itself being disjunctive; to get the discussion going, though, we will assume that these *N*s, the three imagined physical realization bases of pain, are not themselves disjunctive—or, at any rate, that their status as properties is not in dispute. The propriety and significance of 'disjunctive properties' is precisely one of the principal issues we will be dealing with below, and it will make little difference just at what stage this issue is faced.

III. Disjunctive properties and Fodor's argument

An obvious initial response to the MR-based argument against reducibility is 'the disjunction move': Why not take the disjunction, N_h v N_r v N_m, as the single physical substrate of pain? In his 1967 paper, Putnam considers such a move but dismisses it out of hand: 'Granted, in such a case the brain-state theorist can save himself by ad hoc assumptions (e.g., defining the disjunction of two states to be a single 'physical-chemical state'), but this does not have to be taken seriously'.[17] Putnam gives no hint as to why he thinks the disjunction strategy does not merit serious consideration.

If there is something deeply wrong with disjunctions of the sort involved here, that surely isn't obvious; we need to go beyond a sense of unease with such disjunctions and develop an intelligible rationale for banning them. Here is where Fodor steps in, for he appears to have an argument for disallowing disjunctions. As I see it, Fodor's argument in 'Special Sciences' depends crucially on the following two assumptions:

(1) To reduce a special-science theory T_M to physical theory T_P, each 'kind' in T_M (presumably, represented by a basic predicate of T_M) must have a nomologically coextensive 'kind' in T_P;

(2) A disjunction of heterogeneous kinds is not itself a kind.

Point (1) is apparently prompted by the derivational model of intertheoretic reduction due to Ernest Nagel:[18] the reduction of T_2 to T_1 consists in the derivation of laws of T_2 from the laws of T_1, in conjunction with 'bridge' laws or principles connecting T_2-terms with T_1-terms. Although this characterization does not in general require that each T_2-term be correlated with a *coextensive* T_1-term, the natural thought is that the existence of T_1-coextensions for T_2-terms would in effect give us definitions of T_2-terms in T_1-terms, enabling us to rewrite T_2-laws exclusively in the vocabulary of T_1; we could then derive these rewrites of T_2-laws from the laws of T_1 (if they cannot be so derived, we can add them as additional T_1-laws—assuming both theories to be true).

Another thought that again leads us to look for T_1-coextensions for T_2-terms is

17. 'The Nature of Mental States', p. 228 (in the Block volume) (see p. 165 of this volume).
18. *The Structure of Science* (New York: Harcourt, Brace & World, 1961), chap. 11.

this: for genuine reduction, the bridge laws must be construed as *property identities*, not mere *property correlations*—namely, we must be in a position to identify the property expressed by a given T_2-term (say, water-solubility) with a property expressed by a term in the reduction base (say, having a certain molecular structure). This of course requires that each T_2-term have a nomic (or otherwise suitably modalized) coextension in the vocabulary of the reduction base. To put it another way, ontologically significant reduction requires the reduction of higher-level *properties*, and this in turn requires (unless one takes an eliminativist stance) that they be identified with complexes of lower-level properties. Identity of properties of course requires, at a minimum, an appropriately modalized coextensivity.[19]

So assume *M* is a psychological kind, and let us agree that to reduce *M*, or to reduce the psychological theory containing *M*, we need a physical coextension, *P*, for *M*. But why should we suppose that *P* must be a physical 'kind'? And what is a 'kind', anyway? Fodor explains this notion in terms of *law*, saying that a given predicate *P* is a 'kind predicate' of a science just in case the science contains a law with *P* as its antecedent or consequent.[20] There are various problems with Fodor's characterization, but we don't need to take its exact wording seriously; the main idea is that kinds, or kind predicates, of a science are those that figure in the laws of that science.

To return to our question, why should 'bridge laws' connect kinds to kinds, in this special sense of 'kind'? To say that bridge laws are 'laws' and that, by definition, only kind predicates can occur in laws is not much of an answer. For that only invites the further question why 'bridge laws' ought to be 'laws'—what would be lacking in a reductive derivation if bridge laws were replaced by 'bridge principles' which do not necessarily connect kinds to kinds.[21] But what of the consideration that these principles must represent property identities? Does this force on us the requirement that each reduced kind must find a coextensive kind in the reduction base? No; for it isn't obvious why it isn't perfectly proper to reduce kinds by identifying them with properties expressed by non-kind (disjunctive) predicates in the reduction base.

There is the following possible argument for insisting on kinds: if *M* is identified with non-kind *Q* (or *M* is reduced via a biconditional bridge principle '$M \longleftrightarrow Q$', where *Q* is a non-kind), *M* could no longer figure in special science laws; e.g., the

19. My remarks here and the preceding paragraph assume that the higher-level theory requires no 'correction' in relation to the base theory. With appropriate caveats and qualifications, they should apply to models of reduction that allow such corrections, or models that only require the deduction of a suitable analogue, or 'image', in the reduction base—as long as the departures are not so extreme as to warrant talk of replacement or elimination rather than reduction. Cf. Patricia Churchland, *Neurophilosophy* (Cambridge: The MIT Press, 1986), chap. 7.

20. See 'Special Sciences', pp. 132–33 (in *Representations*).

21. Fodor appears to assume that the requirement that bridge laws must connect 'kinds' to 'kinds' is part of the classic positivist conception of reduction. I don't believe there is any warrant for this assumption, however.

law, '$M \rightarrow R$', would in effect reduce to '$Q \rightarrow R$', and therefore loses its status as a law on account of containing Q, a non-kind.

I think this is a plausible response—at least, the beginning of one. As it stands, though, it smacks of circularity: '$Q \rightarrow R$' is not a law because a non-kind, Q, occurs in it, and Q is a non-kind because it cannot occur in a law and '$Q \rightarrow R$', in particular, is not a law. What we need is an *independent* reason for the claim that the sort of Q we are dealing with under MR, namely a badly heterogeneous disjunction, is unsuited for laws.

This means that point (1) really reduces to point (2) above. For, given Fodor's notion of a kind, (2) comes to-this: disjunctions of heterogeneous kinds are unfit for laws. What we now need is an *argument* for this claim; to dismiss such disjunctions as 'wildly disjunctive' or 'heterogeneous and unsystematic' is to label a problem, not to offer a diagnosis of it.[22] In the sections to follow, I hope to take some steps toward such a diagnosis and draw some implications which I believe are significant for the status of mentality.

IV. Jade, jadeite, and nephrite

Let me begin with an analogy that will guide us in our thinking about multiply realizable kinds.

Consider *jade*: we are told that jade, as it turns out, is not a mineral kind, contrary to what was once believed; rather, jade is comprised of two distinct minerals with dissimilar molecular structures, *jadeite* and *nephrite*. Consider the following generalization:

(L) Jade is green

We may have thought, before the discovery of the dual nature of jade, that (L) was a law, a law about jade; and we may have thought, with reason, that (L) had been strongly confirmed by all the millions of jade samples that had been observed to be green (and none that had been observed not to be green). We now know better: (L) is really a conjunction of these two laws:

(L_1) Jadeite is green
(L_2) Nephrite is green

But (L) itself might still be a law as well; is that possible? It has the standard basic form of a law, and it apparently has the power to support counterfactuals: if anything were jade—that is, if anything were a sample of jadeite or of nephrite—then, in either case, it would follow, by law, that it was green. No problem here.

22. See Pereboom and Kornblith, 'The Metaphysics of Irreducibility' in which it is suggested that laws with disjunctive predicates are not 'explanatory'. I think, though, that this suggestion is not fully developed there.

But there is another standard mark of lawlikeness that is often cited, and this is 'projectibility', the ability to be confirmed by observation of 'positive instances'. Any generalized conditional of the form 'All Fs are G' can be confirmed by the *exhaustion* of the class of Fs—that is, by eliminating all of its potential falsifiers. It is in this sense that we can verify such generalizations as 'All the coins in my pockets are copper' and 'Everyone in this room is either first-born or an only child'. Lawlike generalizations, however, are thought to have the following further property: observation of positive instances, Fs that are Gs, can strengthen our credence in the next F's being G. It is this kind of instance-to-instance accretion of confirmation that is supposed to be the hallmark of lawlikeness; it is what explains the possibility of confirming a generalization about an indefinitely large class of items on the basis of a finite number of favorable observations. This rough characterization of projectibility should suffice for our purposes.

Does (L), 'Jade is green', pass the projectibility test? Here we seem to have a problem.[23] For we can imagine this: on re-examining the records of past observations, we find, to our dismay, that all the positive instances of (L), that is, all the millions of observed samples of green jade, turn out to have been samples of jadeite, and none of nephrite! If this should happen, we clearly would not, and should not, continue to think of (L) as well confirmed. All we have is evidence strongly confirming (L_1), and none having anything to do with (L_2). (L) is merely a conjunction of two laws, one well confirmed and the other with its epistemic status wholly up in the air. But all the millions of green jadeite samples *are* positive instances of (L): they satisfy both the antecedent and the consequent of (L). As we have just seen, however, (L) is not confirmed by them, at least not in the standard way we expect. And the reason, I suggest, is that jade is a true disjunctive kind, a disjunction of two heterogeneous nomic kinds which, however, is not itself a nomic kind.[24]

That disjunction is implicated in this failure of projectibility can be seen in the following way: inductive projection of generalizations like (L) with disjunctive antecedents would sanction a cheap, and illegitimate, confirmation procedure. For assume that 'All *F*s are *G*' is a law that has been confirmed by the observation of appropriately numerous positive instances, things that are both *F* and *G*. But these are also positive instances of the generalization 'All things that are *F* or *H* are *G*', for any *H* you please. So, if you in general permit projection of generalizations with a disjunctive antecedent, this latter generalization is also well confirmed. But 'All things that are *F* or *H* are *G*' logically implies 'All *H*s are *G*'. Any statement

23. The points to follow concerning disjunctive predicates were developed about a decade ago; however, I have just come across some related and, in some respects similar, points in David Owens's interesting paper 'Disjunctive Laws', *Analysis* 49 (1989): 197–202. See also William Seager, 'Disjunctive Laws and Supervenience', *Analysis* 51 (1991): 93–98.

24. This can be taken to define one useful sense of kind heterogeneity: two kinds are heterogeneous with respect to each other just in case their disjunction is not a kind.

implied by a well confirmed statement must itself be well confirmed.[25] So 'All *H*s are *G*' is well confirmed—in fact, it is confirmed by the observation of *F*s that are *G*s!

One might protest: 'Look, the very same strategy can be applied to something that is a genuine law. We can think of any nomic kind—say, being an emerald—as a disjunction, being an African emerald or a non-African emerald. This would make "All emeralds are green" a conjunction of two laws, "All African emeralds are green" and "All non-African emeralds are green". But surely this doesn't show there is anything wrong with the lawlikeness of "All emeralds are green"'. Our reply is obvious: the disjunction, 'being an African emerald or non-African emerald', does not denote some heterogeneously disjunctive, nonnomic kind; it denotes a perfectly well-behaved nomic kind, that of being an emerald! There is nothing wrong with disjunctive predicates as such; the trouble arises when the kinds denoted by the disjoined predicates are heterogeneous, 'wildly disjunctive', so that instances falling under them do not show the kind of 'similarity', or unity, that we expect of instances falling under a single kind.

The phenomenon under discussion, therefore, is related to the simple maxim sometimes claimed to underlie inductive inference: 'similar things behave in similar ways', 'same cause, same effect', and so on. The source of the trouble we saw with instantial confirmation of 'All jade is green' is the fact, or belief, that samples of jadeite and sample of nephrite do not exhibit an appropriate 'similarity' with respect to each other to warrant inductive projections from the observed samples of jadeite to unobserved samples of nephrite. But similarity of the required sort presumably holds for African emeralds and non-African emeralds—at least, that is what we believe, and that is what makes the 'disjunctive kind', being an African emerald or a non-African emerald, a single nomic kind. More generally, the phenomenon is related to the point often made about disjunctive properties: disjunctive properties, unlike conjunctive properties, do not guarantee similarity for instances falling under them. And similarity, it is said, is the core of our idea of a property. If that is your idea of a property, you will believe that there are no such things as disjunctive properties (or 'negative properties'). More precisely, though, we should remember that properties are not inherently disjunctive or conjunctive any more than classes are inherently unions or intersections, and that any property can be expressed by a disjunctive predicate. Properties of course can be conjunctions, or disjunctions, *of* other properties. The point about disjunctive properties is best put as a closure condition on properties: the class of properties is not closed under disjunction (presumably, nor under negation). Thus, there may well be

25. Note: this doesn't say that for any *e*, if *e* is 'positive evidence' for *h* and *h* logically implies *j*, then *e* is positive evidence for *j*. About the latter principle there is some dispute; see Carl G. Hempel, 'Studies in the Logic of Confirmation', reprinted in Hempel, *Aspects of Scientific Explanation* (New York: The Free Press, 1965), especially pp. 30–35; Rudolf Carnap, *Logical Foundations of Probability* (Chicago: University of Chicago Press, 1950), pp. 471–76.

properties P and Q such that P *or* Q is also a property, but its being so doesn't follow from the mere fact that P and Q are properties.[26]

V. Jade and pain

Let us now return to pain and its multiple realization bases, N_h, N_r, and N_m. I believe the situation here is instructively parallel to the case of jade in relation to jadeite and nephrite. It seems that we think of jadeite and nephrite as distinct kinds (and of jade not as a kind) because they are different chemical kinds. But why is their being distinct as chemical kinds relevant here? Because many important properties of minerals, we think, are supervenient on, and explainable in terms of, their microstructure, and chemical kinds constitute a microstructural taxonomy that is explanatorily rich and powerful. Microstructure is important, in short, because macrophysical properties of substances are determined by microstructure. These ideas make up our 'metaphysics' of microdetermination for properties of minerals and other substances, a background of partly empirical and partly metaphysical assumptions that regulate our inductive and explanatory practices.

The parallel metaphysical underpinnings for pain, and other mental states in general, are, first, the belief, expressed by the Restricted Correlation Thesis, that pain, or any other mental state, occurs in a system when, and only when, appropriate physical conditions are present in the system, and, second, the corollary belief that significant properties of mental states, in particular nomic relationships amongst them, are due to, and explainable in terms of, the properties and causal-nomic connections among their physical 'substrates'. I will call the conjunction of these two beliefs 'the Physical Realization Thesis'.[27] Whether or not the microexplanation of the sort indicated in the second half of the thesis amounts to a 'reduction' is a question we will take up later. Apart from this question, though, the Physical Realization Thesis is widely accepted by philosophers who talk of 'physical realization', and this includes most functionalists; it is all but explicit in LePore and Loewer, for example, and in Fodor.[28]

Define a property, N, by disjoining N_h, N_r, and N_m; that is, N has a disjunctive definition, N_h v N_r, v N_m. If we assume, with those who endorse the MR-based antireductionist argument, that N_h, N_r, and N_m are a heterogeneous lot, we cannot

26. On issues concerning properties, kinds, similarity, and lawlikeness, see W.V. Quine, 'Natural Kinds' in *Ontological Relativity and Other Essays* (New York: Columbia University Press, 1969); David Lewis, 'New Work for a Theory of Universals', *Australasian Journal of Philosophy* 61 (1983): 347–77: D. M. Armstrong, *Universals* (Boulder, Colorado: Westview Press, 1989).

27. This term is a little misleading since the two subtheses have been stated without the term 'realization' and may be acceptable to those who would reject the 'realization' idiom in connection with the mental. I use the term since we are chiefly addressing philosophers (mainly functionalists) who construe the psychophysical relation in terms of realization, rather than, say, emergence or brute correlation.

28. See 'Special Sciences', and 'Making Mind Matter More', *Philosophical Topics* 17 (1989): 59–79.

make the heterogeneity go away merely by introducing a simpler expression, '*N*'; if there is a problem with certain disjunctive properties, it is not a *linguistic* problem about the form of expressions used to refer to them.

Now, we put the following question to Fodor and like-minded philosophers: If pain is nomically equivalent to *N*, the property claimed to be wildly disjunctive and obviously nonnomic, *why isn't pain itself equally heterogeneous and nonnomic as a kind?* Why isn't pain's relationship to its realization bases, N_h, N_r, and N_m analogous to jade's relationship to jadeite and nephrite? If jade turns out to be nonnomic on account of its dual 'realizations' in distinct microstructures, why doesn't the same fate befall pain? After all, the group of actual and nomologically possible realizations of pain, as they are described by the MR enthusiasts with such imagination, is far more motley than the two chemical kinds comprising jade.

I believe we should insist on answers to these questions from those functionalists who view mental properties as 'second-order' properties, i.e., properties that consist in having a property with a certain functional specification.[29] Thus, pain is said to be a second-order property in that it is the *property of having some property with a certain specification* in terms of its typical causes and effects and its relation to other mental properties; call this 'specification *H*'. The point of MR, on this view, is that there is more than one property that meets specification *H*—in fact, an open-ended set of such properties, it will be said. But pain itself, it is argued, is a more abstract but well-behaved property at a higher level, namely the property of having one of these properties meeting specification *H*. It should be clear why a position like this is vulnerable to the questions that have been raised. For the property of having property *P* is exactly identical with *P*, and the property of having *one* of the properties, $P_1, P_2 \ldots, P_n$, is exactly identical with the disjunctive property, $P_1 \vee P_2 \vee \ldots \vee P_n$. On the assumption that N_h, N_r, and N_m are all the properties satisfying specification *H*, the property of having a property with *H*, namely pain, is none other than the property of having either N_h or N_r or N_m[30]—namely, the *disjunctive* property, $N_h \vee N_r \vee N_m$! We cannot hide the disjunctive character of pain behind the second-order *expression*, 'the property of having a property with specification *H*'. Thus, on the construal of mental properties as second-order properties, mental properties will in general turn out to be disjunctions of their physical realization bases. It is difficult to see how one could have it both ways—that is, to castigate $N_h \vee N_r \vee N_m$ as unacceptably disjunctive while insisting on the integrity of pain as a scientific kind.

Moreover, when we think about making projections over pain, very much the same worry should arise about their propriety as did for jade. Consider a possible law: 'Sharp pains administered at random intervals cause anxiety reactions'. Suppose this generalization has been well confirmed for humans. Should we expect *on that basis* that it will hold also for Martians whose psychology is implemented (we

29. See, e.g., Block, 'Can the Mind Change the World?', p. 155.

30. We might keep in mind the close relationship between disjunction and the existential quantifier standardly noted in logic textbooks.

assume) by a vastly different physical mechanism? Not if we accept the Physical Realization Thesis, fundamental to functionalism, that psychological regularities hold, to the extent that they do, in virtue of the causal-nomological regularities at the physical implementation level. The reason the law is true for humans is due to the way the human brain is 'wired'; the Martians have a brain with a different wiring plan, and we certainly should not expect the regularity to hold for them just because it does for humans.[31] 'Pains cause anxiety reactions' may turn out to possess no more unity as a scientific law than does 'Jade is green'.

Suppose that in spite of all this Fodor insists on defending pain as a nomic kind. It isn't clear that that would be a viable strategy. For he would then owe us an explanation of why the 'wildly disjunctive' *N*, which after all is equivalent to pain, is not a nomic kind. If a predicate is nomically equivalent to a well-behaved predicate, why isn't that enough to show that it, too, is well behaved, and expresses a well-behaved property? To say, as Fodor does,[32] that 'it is a law that . . .' is 'intensional' and does not permit substitution of equivalent expressions ('equivalent' in various appropriate senses) is merely to locate a potential problem, not to resolve it.

Thus, the nomicity of pain may lead to the nomicity of *N*; but this isn't very interesting. For given the Physical Realization Thesis, and the priority of the physical implicit in it, our earlier line of argument, leading from the nonnomicity of *N* to the nonnomicity of pain, is more compelling. We must, I think, take seriously the reasoning leading to the conclusion that pain, and other mental states, might turn out to be nonnomic. If this turns out to be the case, it puts in serious jeopardy Fodor's contention that its physical irreducibility renders psychology an autonomous special science. If pain fails to be nomic, it is not the sort of property in terms of which laws can be formulated; and 'pain' is not a predicate that can enter into a scientific theory that seeks to formulate causal laws and causal explanations. And the same goes for all multiply realizable psychological kinds—which, according to MR, means *all* psychological kinds. There are no scientific theories of jade, and we don't need any; if you insist on having one, you can help yourself with the *conjunction* of the theory of jadeite and the theory of nephrite. In the same way, there will be theories about human pains (instances of N_h), reptilian pains (instances of N_r), and so on; but there will be no unified, integrated theory encompassing all pains in all pain-capable organisms, only a conjunction of pain theories for appropriately individuated biological species and physical structure-types. Scientific psychology, like the theory of jade, gives way to a conjunction of structure-specific theories. If this is right, the correct conclusion to be drawn from the MR-inspired antireductionist argument is not the claim that psychology is an irreducible and autononomous science, but something that contradicts it, namely that it cannot be a science

31. It may be a complicated affair to formulate this argument within certain functionalist schemes; if, for example, mental properties are functionally defined by Ramseyfying a total psychological theory, it will turn out that humans and Martians cannot share any psychological state unless the same total psychology (including the putative law in question) is true (or held to be true) for both.

32. 'Special Sciences', p. 140 (in *Representations*).

with a unified subject matter. This is the picture that is beginning to emerge from MR when combined with the Physical Realization Thesis.

These reflections have been prompted by the analogy with the case of jade; it is a strong and instructive analogy, I think, and suggests the possibility of a general argument. In the following section I will develop a direct argument, with explicit premises and assumptions.

VI. Causal powers and mental kinds

One crucial premise we need for a direct argument is a constraint on concept formation, or kind individuation, in science that has been around for many years; it has lately been resurrected by Fodor in connection with content externalism.[33] A precise statement of the constraint may be difficult and controversial, but its main idea can be put as follows:

[Principle of Causal Individuation of Kinds] Kinds in science are individuated on the basis of causal powers; that is, objects and events fall under a kind, or share in a property, insofar as they have similar causal powers.

I believe this is a plausible principle, and it is, in any case, widely accepted.

We can see that this principle enables us to give a specific interpretation to the claim that N_h, N_r, and N_m are *heterogeneous* as kinds: the claim must mean that they are *heterogeneous as causal powers*—that is, they are diverse as causal powers and enter into diverse causal laws. This must mean, given the Physical Realization Thesis, that pain itself can show no more unity as a causal power than the disjunction, N_h v N_r v N_m. This becomes especially clear if we set forth the following principle, which arguably is implied by the Physical Realization Thesis (but we need not make an issue of this here):

[The Causal Inheritance Principle] If mental property *M* is realized in a system at *t* in virtue of physical realization base *P*, the causal powers of *this instance* of *M* are identical with the causal powers of *P*.[34]

It is important to bear in mind that this principle only concerns the causal powers of *individual instances* of *M*; it does not identify the causal powers of mental property *M in general* with the causal powers of some physical property *P*; such identification is precluded by the multiple physical realizability of *M*.

33. See, e.g., Carl G. Hempel, *Fundamentals of Concept Formation in Empirical Science* (Chicago: University of Chicago Press, 1952); W.V. Quine, 'Natural Kinds'. Fodor gives it an explicit statement in *Psychosemantics* (Cambridge: MIT Press, 1988), chap. 2. A principle like this is often invoked in the current externalism/internalism debate about content; most principal participants in this debate seem to accept it.

34. A principle like this is sometimes put in terms of 'supervenience' and 'supervenience base' rather than 'realization' and 'realization base'. See my 'Epiphenomenal and Supervenient Causation', *Midwest Studies in Philosophy* 9 (1984): 257–70. Fodor appears to accept just such a principle of supervenient causation for mental properties in chap. 2 of his *Psychosemantics*. In 'The Metaphysics of Irreducibility' Pereboom and Kornblith appear to reject it.

Why should we accept this principle? Let us just note that to deny it would be to accept *emergent* causal powers: causal powers that magically emerge at a higher-level and of which there is no accounting in terms of lower-level properties and their causal powers and nomic connections. This leads to the notorious problem of 'downward causation' and the attendant violation of the causal closure of the physical domain.[35] I believe that a serious physicalist would find these consequences intolerable.

It is clear that the Causal Inheritance Principle, in conjunction with the Physical Realization Thesis, has the consequence that mental kinds cannot satisfy the Causal Individuation Principle, and this effectively rules out mental kinds as scientific kinds. The reasoning is simple: instances of *M* that are realized by the same physical base must be grouped under one kind, since *ex hypothesi* the physical base is a causal kind; and instances of *M* with different realization bases must be grouped under distinct kinds, since, again *ex hypothesi*, these realization bases are distinct as causal kinds. Given that mental kinds are realized by diverse physical causal kinds, therefore, it follows that mental kinds are not causal kinds, and hence are disqualified as proper scientific kinds. Each mental kind is sundered into as many kinds as there are physical realization bases for it, and the psychology as a science with disciplinary unity turns out to be an impossible project.

What is the relationship between this argument and the argument adumbrated in our reflections based on the jade analogy? At first blush, the two arguments might seem unrelated: the earlier argument depended chiefly on epistemological considerations, considerations on inductive projectibility of certain predicates, whereas the crucial premise of the second argument is the Causal Kind Individuation Principle, a broadly metaphysical and methodological principle about science. I think, though, that the two arguments are closely related, and the key to seeing the relationship is this: causal powers involve laws, and laws are regularities that are projectible. Thus, if pain (or jade) is not a kind over which inductive projections can be made, it cannot enter into laws, and therefore cannot qualify as a causal kind; and this disqualifies it as a scientific kind. If this is right, the jade-inspired reflections provide a possible rationale for the Causal Individuation Principle. Fleshing out this rough chain of reasoning in precise terms, however, goes beyond what I can attempt in this paper.

VII. The status of psychology: local reductions

Our conclusion at this point, therefore, is this: If MR is true, psychological kinds are not scientific kinds. What does this imply about the status of psychology as a science? Do our considerations show that psychology is a pseudo-science like

35. For more details see my '"Downward Causation" in Emergentism and Nonreductive Physicalism', forthcoming in *Emergence or Reduction?*, ed. Beckermann, Flohr, and Kim, and 'The Nonreductivist's Troubles with Mental Causation', in *Mental Causation*, ed. John Heil and Alfred Mele (Oxford: Clarendon Press, 1993).

astrology and alchemy? Of course not. The crucial difference, from the metaphysical point of view, is that psychology has physical realizations, but alchemy does not. To have a physical realization is to be physically grounded and explainable in terms of the processes at an underlying level. In fact, if each of the psychological kinds posited in a psychological theory has a physical realization for a fixed species, the theory can be 'locally reduced' to the physical theory of that species, in the following sense. Let *S* be the species involved; for each law L_m of psychological theory T_m, $S \rightarrow L_m$ (the proposition that L_m holds for members of *S*) is the '*S*-restricted' version of L_m; and $S \rightarrow T_m$ is the *S*-restricted version of T_m, the set of all *S*-restricted laws of T_m. We can then say that T_m is 'locally reduced' for species *S* to an underlying theory, T_p, just in case $S \rightarrow T_m$ is reduced to T_p. And the latter obtains just in case each *S*-restricted law of T_m, $S \rightarrow L_m$,[36] is derivable from the laws of the reducing theory T_p, taken together with bridge laws. What bridge laws suffice to guarantee the derivation? Obviously, an array of *S*-restricted bridge laws of the form, $S \rightarrow (M_i \leftrightarrow P_i)$, for each mental kind M_i. Just as unrestricted psychophysical bridge laws can underwrite a 'global' or 'uniform' reduction of psychology, species- or structure-restricted bridge laws sanction its 'local' reduction.

If the same psychological theory is true of humans, reptiles, and Martians, the psychological kinds posited by that theory must have realizations in human, reptilian, and Martian physiologies. This implies that the theory is locally reducible in three ways, for humans, reptiles, and Martians. If the dependence of the mental on the physical means anything, it must mean that the regularities posited by this common psychology must have divergent physical explanations for the three species. The very idea of physical realization involves the possibility of physically explaining psychological properties and regularities, and the supposition of multiple such realizations, namely MR, involves a commitment to the possibility of multiple explanatory reductions of psychology.[37] The important moral of MR we need to keep in mind is this: *if psychological properties are multiply realized, so is psychology itself.* If physical realizations of psychological properties are a 'wildly heterogeneous' and 'unsystematic' lot, psychological theory itself must be realized by an equally heterogeneous and unsystematic lot of physical theories.

I am inclined to think that multiple local reductions, rather than global reductions, are the rule, even in areas in which we standardly suppose reductions are possible. I will now deal with a possible objection to the idea of local reduction, at least as it is applied to psychology. The objection goes like this: given what we know about the differences among members of a single species, even species are too wide to yield determinate realization bases for psychological states, and given what we

36. Or an appropriately corrected version thereof (this qualification applies to the bridge laws as well).
37. In 'Special Sciences' and 'Making Mind Matter More' Fodor appears to accept the local reducibility of psychology and other special sciences. But he uses the terminology of local *explanation*, rather than reduction, of psychological regularities in terms of underlying microstructure. I think this is because his preoccupation with Nagelian uniform reduction prevents him from seeing that this is a form of inter-theoretic reduction if anything is.

know about the phenomena of maturation and development, brain injuries, and the like, the physical bases of mentality may change even for a single individual. This throws into serious doubt, continues the objection, the availability of species-restricted bridge laws needed for local reductions.

The point of this objection may well be correct as a matter of empirical fact. Two points can be made in reply, however. First, neurophysiological research goes on because there is a shared, and probably well grounded, belief among the workers that there are not huge individual differences within a species in the way psychological kinds are realized. Conspecifics must show important physical-physiological similarities, and there probably is good reason for thinking that they share physical realization bases to a sufficient degree to make search for species-wide neural substrates for mental states feasible and rewarding. Researchers in this area evidently aim for neurobiological explanations of psychological capacities and processes that are generalizable over all or most ('normal') members of a given species.

Second, even if there are huge individual differences among conspecifics as to how their psychology is realized, that does not touch the metaphysical point: as long as you believe in the Physical Realization Thesis, you must believe that every organism or system with mentality falls under a physical structure-type such that its mental states are realized by determinate physical states of organisms with that structure. It may be that these structures are so finely individuated and so few *actual* individuals fall under them that research into the neural bases of mental states in these structures is no longer worthwhile, theoretically or practically. What we need to recognize here is that the scientific possibility of, say, human psychology is a contingent fact (assuming it is a fact); it depends on the fortunate fact that individual humans do not show huge physiological-biological differences that are psychologically relevant. But if they did, that would not change the metaphysics of the situation one bit; it would remain true that the psychology of each of us was determined by, and locally reducible to, his neurobiology.

Realistically, there are going to be psychological differences among individual humans: it is a commonsense platitude that no two persons are exactly alike—either physically or psychologically. And individual differences may be manifested not only in particular psychological facts but in psychological regularities. If we believe in the Physical Realization Thesis, we must believe that our psychological differences are rooted in, and explainable by, our physical differences, just as we expect our psychological similarities to be so explainable. Humans probably are less alike among themselves than, say, tokens of a Chevrolet model.[38] And psychological laws for humans, at a certain level of specificity, must be expected to be statistical in character, not deterministic—or, if you prefer, 'ceteris paribus laws' rather than

38. Compare J. J. C. Smart's instructive analogy between biological organisms and super-heterodyne radios, in *Philosophy and Scientific Realism* (London: Routledge & Kegan Paul, 1963), pp. 56–57. Smart's conception of the relation between physics and the special sciences, such as biology and psychology, is similar in some respects to the position I am defending here.

'strict laws'. But this is nothing peculiar to psychology; these remarks surely apply to human physiology and anatomy as much as human psychology. In any case, none of this affects the metaphysical point being argued here concerning microdetermination and microreductive explanation.

VIII. Metaphysical implications

But does local reduction have any interesting philosophical significance, especially in regard to the status of mental properties? If a psychological property has been multiply locally reduced, does that mean that the property itself has been reduced? Ned Block has raised just such a point, arguing that species-restricted reductionism (or species-restricted type physicalism) 'sidesteps the main metaphysical question: "What is common to the pains of dogs and people (and all other species) in virtue of which they are pains?"'.[39]

Pereboom and Kornblith elaborate on Block's point as follows:

> '... even if there is a single type of physical state that normally realizes pain in each type of organism, or in each structure type, this does not show that pain, *as a type of mental state*, is reducible to physical states. Reduction, in the present debate, must be understood as reduction of types, since the primary object of reductive strategies is explanations and theories, and explanations and theories quantify over types. ... The suggestion that there are species-specific reductions of pain results in the claim that pains in different species have nothing in common. But this is just a form of eliminativism.'[40]

There are several related but separable issues raised here. But first we should ask: Must all pains have 'something in common' in virtue of which they are pains?

According to the phenomenological conception of pain, all pains do have something in common: they all *hurt*. But as I take it, those who hold this view of pain would reject any reductionist program, independently of the issues presently on hand. Even if there were a species-invariant uniform bridge law correlating pains with a single physical substrate across all species and structures, they would claim that the correlation holds as a brute, unexplainable matter of fact, and that pain as a qualitative event, a 'raw feel', would remain irreducibly distinct from its neural substrate. Many emergentists apparently held a view of this kind.

I presume that Block, and Pereboom and Kornblith, are speaking not from a phenomenological viewpoint of this kind but from a broadly functionalist one. But from a functionalist perspective, it is by no means clear how we should understand

39. 'Introduction: What is Functionalism?' in *Readings in Philosophy of Psychology*, pp. 178–79 (Chapter 13, p. 193 of this volume).

40. In their 'The Metaphysics of Irreducibility'. See also Ronald Endicott, 'Species-Specific Properties and More Narrow Reductive Strategies'. *Erkenntnis* 38 (1993): 303–21. In personal correspondence Earl Conee and Joe Mendola have raised similar points. There is a useful discussion of various metaphysical issues relating to MR in Cynthia Macdonald, *Mind-Body Identity Theories* (London and New York: Routledge, 1989).

the question 'What do all pains have in common in virtue of which they are all pains?' Why should all pains have 'something in common'? As I understand it, at the core of the functionalist program is the attempt to explain the meanings of mental terms *relationally*, in terms of inputs, outputs, and connections with other mental states. And on the view, discussed briefly earlier, that mental properties are second-order properties, pain is the property of having a property with a certain functional specification H (in terms of inputs, outputs, etc.). This yields a short answer to Block's question: what all pains have in common is the pattern of connections as specified by H. The local reductionist is entitled to that answer as much as the functionalist is. Compare two pains, an instance of N_h and one of N_m: what they have in common is that each is an instance of a property that realizes pain—that is, they exhibit the same pattern of input-output-other internal state connections, namely the pattern specified by H.

But some will say: 'But H is only an *extrinsic* characterization; what do these instances of pain have in common that is *intrinsic* to them?' The local reductionist must grant that on his view there is nothing intrinsic that all pains have in common in virtue of which they are pains (assuming that N_h, N_r, and N_m 'have nothing intrinsic in common'). But that is also precisely the consequence of the functionalist view. That, one might say, is the whole point of functionalism: the functionalist, especially one who believes in MR, would not, and should not, look for something common to all pains over and above H (the heart of functionalism, one might say, is the belief that mental states have no 'intrinsic essence').

But there is a further question raised by Block et al.: What happens to properties that have been locally reduced? Are they still with us, distinct and separate from the underlying physical-biological properties? Granted: human pain is reduced to N_h, Martian pain to N_m, and so forth, but what of *pain itself*? It remains unreduced. Are we still stuck with the dualism of mental and physical properties?

I will sketch two possible ways of meeting this challenge. First, recall my earlier remarks about the functionalist conception of mental properties as second-order properties: pain is *the property of having a property with specification H*, and, given that N_h, N_r, and N_m are the properties meeting H, pain turns to be the disjunctive property, N_h v N_r v N_m. If you hold the second-order property view of mental properties, pain has been reduced to, and survives as, this disjunctive physical kind. Quite apart from considerations of local reduction, the very conception of pain you hold commits you to the conclusion that pain is a disjunctive kind, and if you accept any form of respectable physicalism (in particular, the Physical Realization Thesis), it is a disjunctive *physical* kind. And even if you don't accept the view of mental properties as second-order properties, as long as you are comfortable with disjunctive kinds and properties, you can, in the aftermath of local reduction, identify pain with the disjunction of its realization bases. On this approach, then, you have another, more direct, answer to Block's question: what all pains have in common is that they all fall under the disjunctive kind, N_h v N_r v N_m.

If you are averse to disjunctive kinds, there is another more radical, and in some ways more satisfying, approach. The starting point of this approach is the frank acknowledgement that MR leads to the conclusion that pain as a property or kind must go. Local reduction after all is reduction, and to be reduced is to be eliminated as an *independent* entity. You might say: global reduction is different in that it is also *conservative*—if pain is globally reduced to physical property *P*, pain survives as *P*. But it is also true that under local reduction, pain survives as N_h in humans, as N_r in reptiles, and so on. It must be admitted, however, that pain as a kind does not survive multiple local reduction. But is this so bad?

Let us return to jade once again. Is jade a *kind*? We know it is not a mineral kind; but is it any kind of a kind? That of course depends on what we mean by 'kind'. There are certain shared criteria, largely based on observable macroproperties of mineral samples (e.g., hardness, color, etc.), that determine whether something is a sample of jade, or whether the predicate 'is jade' is correctly applicable to it. What all samples of jade have in common is just these observable macrophysical properties that define the applicability of the predicate 'is jade'. In this sense, speakers of English who have 'jade' in their repertoire associate the same *concept* with 'jade'; and we can recognize the existence of the concept of jade and at the same time acknowledge that the concept does not pick out, or answer to, a property or kind in the natural world.

I think we can say something similar about pain and 'pain': there are shared criteria for the application of the predicate 'pain' or 'is in pain', and these criteria may well be for the most part functionalist ones. These criteria generate for us a *concept of pain*, a concept whose clarity and determinacy depend, we may assume, on certain characteristics (such as explicitness, coherence, and completeness) of the criteria governing the application of 'pain'. But the concept of pain, on this construal, need not pick out an objective kind any more than the concept of jade does.

All this presupposes a distinction between concepts and properties (or kinds). Do we have such a distinction? I believe we do. Roughly, concepts are in the same ball park as predicates, meanings (perhaps, something like Fregean *Sinnen*), ideas, and the like; Putnam has suggested that concepts be identified with 'synonymy classes of predicates',[41] and that comes close enough to what I have in mind. Properties and relations, on the other hand, are 'out there in the world'; they are features and characteristics of things and events in the world. They include fundamental physical magnitudes and quantities, like mass, energy, size, and shape, and are part of the causal structure of the world. The property of being water is arguably identical with the property of being H_2O, but evidently the concept of water is distinct from the concept of H_2O (Socrates had the former but not the latter). Most of us would agree that ethical predicates are meaningful, and that we have the concepts of 'good', 'right', etc.; however, it is a debatable issue, and has lately been much debated, whether there are such properties as goodness and rightness.[42] If you find

41. In 'The Nature of Mental States' (Chapter 11 of this volume).

42. I of course have in mind the controversy concerning moral realism; see essays in Geoffrey Sayre-McCord, ed., *Essays on Moral Realism* (Ithaca: Cornell University Press, 1988).

that most of these remarks make sense, you understand the concept-property distinction that I have in mind. Admittedly, this is all a little vague and programmatic, and we clearly need a better articulated theory of properties and concepts; but the distinction is there, supported by an impressively systematic set of intuitions and philosophical requirements.[43]

But is this second approach a form of mental eliminativism? In a sense it is: as I said, on this approach no properties in the world answer to general, species-unrestricted mental concepts. But remember: there still are pains, and we sometimes are in pain, just as there still are samples of jade. We must also keep in mind that the present approach is not, in its ontological implications, a form of the standard mental eliminativism currently on the scene.[44] Without elaborating on what the differences are, let us just note a few important points. First, the present view does not take away species-restricted mental properties, e.g., human pain, Martian pain, canine pain, and the rest, although it takes away 'pain as such'. Second, while the standard eliminativism consigns mentality to the same ontological limbo to which phlogiston, witches, and magnetic effluvia, have been dispatched, the position I have been sketching views it on a par with jade, tables, and adding machines. To see jade as a nonkind is not to question the existence of jade, or the legitimacy and utility of the concept of jade. Tables do not constitute a scientific kind; there are no laws about tables as such, and being a table is not a causal-explanatory kind. But that must be sharply distinguished from the false claim that there are no tables. The same goes for pains. These points suggest the following difference in regard to the status of psychology: the present view allows, and in fact encourages, 'species-specific psychologies', but the standard eliminativism would do away with all things psychological—species-specific psychologies as well as global psychology.

To summarize, then, the two metaphysical schemes I have sketched offer these choices: either we allow disjunctive kinds and construe pain and other mental properties as such kinds, or else we must acknowledge that our general mental terms and concepts do not pick out properties and kinds in the world (we may call this 'mental property irrealism'). I should add that I am not interested in promoting either disjunctive kinds or mental irrealism, a troubling set of choices to most of us. Rather, my main interest has been to follow out the consequences of MR and try to come to terms with them within a reasonable metaphysical scheme.

I have already commented on the status of psychology as a science under MR. As I argued, MR seriously compromises the disciplinary unity and autonomy of psychology as a science. But that does not have to be taken as a negative message. In particular, the claim does not imply that a scientific study of psychological

43. On concepts and properties, see, e.g., Hilary Putnam, 'On Properties', *Mathematics, Matter and Method* (Cambridge: Cambridge University Press, 1975); Mark Wilson, 'Predicate Meets Property', *Philosophical Review* 91 (1982): 549–90, especially, section III.

44. Such as the versions favored by W. V. Quine, Stephen Stich, and Paul Churchland.

phenomena is not possible or useful; on the contrary, MR says that psychological processes have a foundation in the biological and physical processes and regularities, and it opens the possibility of enlightening explanations of psychological processes at a more basic level. It is only that at a deeper level, psychology becomes sundered by being multiply locally reduced. However, species-specific psychologies, e.g., human psychology, Martian psychology, etc., can all flourish as scientific theories. Psychology remains *scientific*, though perhaps not *a science.* If you insist on having a global psychology valid for all species and structures, you can help yourself with that, too; but you must think of it as a *conjunction* of species-restricted psychologies and be careful, above all, with your inductions.[45]

45. This paper is descended from an unpublished paper, 'The Disunity of Psychology as a Working Hypothesis?', which was circulated in the early 1980s. I am indebted to the following persons, among others, for helpful comments: Fred Feldman, Hilary Kornblith, Barry Loewer, Brian McLaughlin, Joe Mendola, Marcelo Sabates, and James Van Cleve.

Questions

1. What is 'multiple realizability'? What evidence might be offered for the claim that mental properties (being in pain, for instance) are multiply realized? Can you think of an alternative to multiple realizability consistent with this evidence?
2. What are the 'special sciences' and what relations do they bear to one another and to physics?
3. Compare Searle's conception of consciousness and its relation to the material world with Chalmers's. Should Searle and Chalmers be seen as allies or competitors?
4. Davidson defends 'token identity', the view that every mental event is identical with some physical event, but denies type identity, the view that mental types are reducible to or identifiable with physical types. What are Davidson's reasons for rejecting type identity? Are they sound? What is at stake here?
5. How does Davidson's conception of the relation mental states or events bear to physical states or events differ from a functionalist's? Or does it? Would it be accurate to describe Davidson as embracing a species of multiple realizability?
6. What are *ceteris paribus* (or 'hedged') laws, and how do they differ from the kinds of 'strict' law we find in physics? Why might you think that we need such laws?
7. Philosophers distinguish *types* and *tokens*. Is the distinction reflected in our ordinary ways of thinking about and describing the world or is it purely a philosophical invention?
8. The prospect of 'downward causation' makes many theorists nervous. Should it? And what is 'downward causation', anyway?
9. Consider a statue of Athena and the lump of bronze from which the statue is formed. The statue and the lump occupy the same region of space. Why might someone want, nevertheless, to deny that the statue *is* the lump? If the statue is not the lump, does this mean that when you count the number of objects in the room, you will need to count *both* the statue and the lump?
10. Kim attacks the position defended by Pereboom and Kornblith. Can you reconstruct Kim's argument? Does the argument have merit? What are its implications for the special (that is 'higher-level') sciences?

Suggested readings

Materialism without reduction—'non-reductive materialism'—has been a hallmark of contemporary philosophy of mind. Davidson advances his distinctive non-reductive scheme—'anomalous monism', according to which mental concepts resist reduction to physical concepts, but material states and events answer to mental ascriptions—in his (1973, 1974), and defends it against critics in his (1987, 1993). Davidson's (1999) brief, but authoritative entry on anomalous monism in the on-line *MIT Encyclopedia of Cognitive Science* is definitely worth a look. McLaughlin (1985) provides a detailed and sympathetic account of Davidson's position; see also McLaughlin (1993). Hannan (1994) sketches an account of the mind and its relation to the body broadly sympathetic to Davidson; see Child (1994) for another book-length discussion; and Heil (2003) for an account of the mind–body relation apparently consistent with anomalous monism. Antony (1989), Campbell (1997), Child (1993), Honderich (1982), Kim (1993*a*), LePore and Loewer (1987), and Stoutland (1976) discuss problems arising from Davidson's view, especially the problem of mental causation: how could 'anomalous' mental properties figure in causal transactions? Campbell's (2001) on-line piece on anomalous monism in the *Field Guide to the Philosophy of Mind* discusses this and other issues

Bickle's on-line discussion of 'inter-theoretic reduction' in the aforementioned *Field Guide* spells out a position advanced in Bickle (1998). Another on-line resource, Stoljar's entry on 'Physicalism' in the *Stanford Encyclopedia of Philosophy*, includes an acute discussion of reduction. Chalmers's (2001) on-line bibliographic entry on the metaphysics of mind incorporates a subsection on 'nonreductive materialism'. Poland (1994) and Post (1991) defend elaborate nonreductive theories. Charles and Lennon's (1992) collection contains papers for and against nonreductive materialist conceptions of the mind. See also Moser and Trout (1995) and Gillett and Loewer (2001). Kim (1993*b*, 1998) develops an important line of criticism against nonreductive theories. McGinn (1991, 1999) takes a very different approach. Van Gulick (1992) takes a sympathetic look at nonreductive theories, Smith (1993) finds them lacking.

Anomalous monism

Antony, L. (1989), 'Anomalous Monism and the Problem of Explanatory Force', *Philosophical Review* 98: 153–87.

Brown, S., ed. (1974), *Philosophy of Psychology*. London: Macmillan.

Campbell, N. (1997), 'The Standard Objection to Anomalous Monism', *Australasian Journal of Philosophy* 75: 373–82.

——(2001), 'Anomalous Monism'. In Nani (2001): <http://host.uniroma3.it/progetti/kant/field/am.htm>.

Child, T. W. (1993), 'Anomalism, Uncodifiability, and Psychophysical Relations', *Philosophical Review* 102: 215–45.

——(1994), *Causality Interpretation, and the Mind.* Oxford: Clarendon Press.

Davidson, D. (1973), 'The Material Mind'. In Suppes et al. 1973: 709–22. Reprinted in Davidson 1980: 245–59.

Davidson, D. (1974), 'Psychology as Philosophy'. In Brown 1974: 41–52. Reprinted in Davidson 1980: 229–39.

——(1980), *Essays on Actions and Events.* Oxford: Clarendon Press.

——(1987), 'Problems in the Explanation of Action'. In Pettit et al. 1987: 35–49.

——(1993), 'Thinking Causes'. In Heil and Mele 1993: 3–17.

——(1999), 'Anomalous Monism'. In Wilson and Keil 1999.

Hannan, B. (1994), *Subjectivity and Reduction: An Introduction to the Mind–Body Problem.* Boulder, CO: Westview Press.

Heil, J. (2003), *From an Ontological Point of View.* Oxford: Clarendon Press.

——and A. R. Mele, eds. (1993), *Mental Causation.* Oxford: Clarendon Press.

Honderich, T. (1982), 'The Argument for Anomalous Monism'. *Analysis* 42: 59–64.

Kim, J. (1993*a*), 'Can Supervenience and 'Non-Strict Laws' Save Anomalous Monism?, In Heil and Mele 1993: 19–26.

LePore, E., and B. Loewer (1987), 'Mind Matters', *Journal of Philosophy* 84: 630–42.

——and B. P. McLaughlin, eds. (1985), *Actions and Events: Perspectives on the Philosophy of Donald Davidson.* Oxford: Basil Blackwell.

McLaughlin, B. P. (1985), 'Anomalous Monism and the Irreducibility of the Mental'. In LePore and McLaughlin 1985: 331–68.

——(1993), 'On Davidson's Response to the Charge of Epiphenomenalism'. In Heil and Mele 1993: 27–40.

Nani, M., ed. (2001), *A Field Guide to the Philosophy of Mind.* <http://host.uniroma3.it/progetti/kant/field/> Rome: University of Rome 3.

Pettit, P., R. Sylvan, and J. Norman, eds. (1987), *Metaphysics and Morality: Essays in Honour of J. J. C. Smart.* Oxford: Basil Blackwell.

Stoutland, F. (1976), 'The Causation of Behavior'. In *Essays on Wittgenstein in Honor of G. H. Von Wright* (*Acta Philosophica Fennica* 28): 286–325.

Suppes, P., L. Henkin, G. Moisil, and A. Joja, eds. (1973), *Proceedings of the Fourth International Congress for Logic, Methodology, and Philosophy of Science.* Amsterdam: North Holland.

Wilson, R. A., and F. Keil, eds. (1999), *MIT Encyclopedia of Cognitive Sciences* <http://cognet.mit.edu/MITECS/login.html> Cambridge, MA: MIT Press.

Reduction

Beckermann, A., H. Flohr, and J. Kim, eds. (1992), *Emergence or Reduction? Essays on the Prospects of Nonreductive Physicalism.* Berlin: De Gruyter.

Bickle, J. (1998), *Psychoneural Reduction: The New Wave.* Cambridge, MA: MIT Press.

——(2001), 'Inter-Theoretic Reduction'. In Nani (2001): <http://host.uniroma3.it/progetti/kant/field/cir.htm>.

Chalmers, D. J. (2001), *Contemporary Philosophy of Mind: An Annotated Bibliography* <http://www.u.arizona.edu/~chalmers/biblio.html> Tucson, AZ: University of Arizona.

Charles, D., and K. Lennon, eds. (1992), *Reduction, Explanation, and Realism.* Oxford: Oxford University Press.

Gillett, C., and B. Loewer, eds. (2001), *Physicalism and Its Discontents.* Cambridge: Cambridge University Press.

Kim, J. (1993*b*), 'The Non-Reductivist's Troubles with Mental Causation'. In Heil and Mele 1993: 189–210. Reprinted in Kim 1993*c*: 336–57.

——(1993*c*), *Supervenience and Mind: Selected Philosophical Essays.* Cambridge: Cambridge University Press.

——(1998), *Mind in a Physical World: An Essay on the Mind-Body Problem and Mental Causation.* Cambridge: MIT Press.

McGinn, C. (1991), *The Problem of Consciousness: Essays Toward a Resolution.* Oxford: Blackwell Publishers.

——(1999), *The Mysterious Flame: Conscious Minds in a Material World.* New York: Basic Books.

Moser, P. K., and J. D. Trout, eds. (1995), *Contemporary Materialism: A Reader.* London: Routledge.

Poland, J. (1994), *Physicalism: The Philosophical Foundations.* Oxford: Clarendon Press.

Post, J. F. (1991), *Metaphysics: A Contemporary Introduction.* New York: Paragon House.

Robinson, H., ed. (1993), *Objections to Physicalism.* Oxford: Clarendon Press.

Smith, A. D. (1993), 'Non-Reductive Physicalism'? In Robinson 1993: 225–50.

Stoljar, D. (2002), 'Physicalism'. In Zalta (2002): <http://plato.stanford.edu/entries/physicalism/>.

van Gulick, R. (1992), 'Nonreductive Materialism and the Nature of Intertheoretical Constraint'. In Beckermann et al. 1992: 157–79.

Zalta, E. N., ed. (2002), *The Stanford Encyclopedia of Philosophy.* <http://plato.stanford.edu/> Stanford, CA: Metaphysics Research Lab, Center for the Study of Language and Information.

Part XI

Is the mind–body problem insoluble?

Introduction

Philosophers and scientists attempting to work out the nature of minds tend to operate on the assumption that the mind–body problem, though challenging, will eventually be tamed. As matters stand at present, it is by no means clear how thoughts or conscious experiences could be at home in—or even in causal contact with—the material world. Qualities of conscious experiences are especially elusive. Empirical advances in the neurosciences have made it easy to think that consciousness is in some way 'vertically' dependent on material goings-on. When it comes to material states and processes, the discovery of dependence relations of this kind typically leads to reduction: macro-properties are reduced to distributions of micro-properties. It is hard to see how this could work in the case of mental properties. Worries about such things push some scientists and philosophers toward dualism: mental states and properties, if not minds themselves, must be distinguished from material states and properties.

The flight to dualism is a reaction to puzzles arising from attempts to locate mental properties in the material world. But dualism introduces new puzzles of its own. How could a material system spawn non-material, mental substances or properties? If mental items do not depend for their existence on material objects and their properties, we face the task of explaining relations among mental and physical objects. What accounts for the apparent fact that the mental and material domains are so tightly *coordinated*? Minds and material bodies appear to interact causally, but mental—material causal interaction seems profoundly mysterious. The thought that mental and physical domains operate in perfect harmony is scarcely less appealing. This leaves two 'eliminativist' options. First, as Stephen Stich and Paul Churchland (Chapters 22, 23) argue, perhaps there are no minds or mental properties. On the other side, we might join George Berkeley, John Foster (Chapter 47) and other idealists, who do away with material bodies and properties: all that exists are minds and their contents; the material world is a mental fabrication.

Insolubility-in-principle

It is hard to see any of these options as especially winning. Perhaps what we need is (as the Monty Python gambit would have it) *something completely different*. But what could this something be? The usual suspects—materialism, dualism, idealism—apparently exhaust the space of possibilities. To be sure, what we can grasp as a possibility depends in some measure on us. Just as early hominids could not have made sense of possibilities envisaged in modern physics, so we, sophisticated as we are, might be in no position to recognize possibilities that would strike neuro-scientists in the distant future as laughably obvious. It could turn out that, although the mind–body problem or the mystery of conscious experience are soluble, they are not capable of solution given conceptual resources available to us at the start of the twenty-first century.

Colin McGinn (Chapter 45) offers another, more dramatic, take on our plight. Our inability to understand ourselves might be no accident. It could turn out that the human mind is constitutionally unable to understand itself. This idea resonates with Gödel's proof of the incompleteness of mathematics. Gödel showed that formal systems rich enough to generate the truths of elementary arithmetic were, if consistent, in principle *incomplete*. (A system is incomplete if there are truths expressible in and implied by the system that cannot be proven true in the system.) The incompleteness of mathematics reflects an established fact about the make-up of formal systems generally. Now, imagine that we finite human beings are, as we surely are, constitutionally limited as to the kinds of thought we could entertain. Imagine, further, that our cognitive limitations were such that we could not so much as entertain the deep truth about our own minds.

Whatever your views on the mind, you will need at least to grant this as a live possibility. Indeed, we should be hard put to establish in advance that the deep truth about anything at all—including the material world—is cognitively available to us. To think that it must be is to exhibit an unwarranted degree of confidence in our finite capacities, what the ancients called *hubris*. It is one thing to adopt a posture of modesty, however, and another matter to suppose that we are, of necessity, cognitively limited when it comes to understanding ourselves. We are not after all in a position analogous to Gödel's; we cannot positively prove that we are cut off from a deep understanding of mental phenomena. Or, is there something about the mind and its capacity for self-understanding that is special in this regard? If you think so, you should be prepared to explain why you think so. You may find ammunition in readings here and in Part XII.

Mary's plight

One source of inspiration might be Frank Jackson's Mary (Chapter 43). Mary, a 'brilliant neuroscientist', has spent her adult life studying the physics, psychophysics, and neurophysiology of color and human color experiences. Mary has, so to speak, 'written the book' on color; she knows *all there is to know* about color. Or, rather, Mary, knows all there is to know about color with one vital exception: she does not know *what it is like* to experience a color. This is something Mary knows nothing about because she has been confined since birth to a wholly black-and-white environment. Mary has never herself had a color experience, and thus (it would seem) has no way to know what it is like , for instance, to experience red.

The argument here is an extension of the familiar idea that conscious experiences must be had to be appreciated. Imagine someone who has never tasted a banana. Could this person know what a banana tasted like—what it was like to taste a banana? This 'subjective' component of conscious experience appears invisible 'from the outside'. Mary is in no position to work out the nature of color experiences—their what-it's-like-ness—from observations of the make-up of subjects undergoing color experiences. This suggests that conscious experiences, or at least qualities of conscious experiences, must fall outside the scope of objective natural science.

Necessity and contingency

Jackson's argument—as well as those of McGinn and Levine (Chapter 44)—depends on a *contingency thesis.*

(CT) It is a contingent fact that creatures with a material constitution like ours undergo conscious experiences with the qualities exhibited by our conscious experiences.

Contingent facts are contrasted with *necessities*. It is true of necessity that the circumference of a circle is π times the circle's diameter or that 2 + 3 = 5. Some philosophers like to put this by saying that such truths hold in 'all possible worlds': there is no possible world in which they are false. Compare this with truths like 'there are nine planets' or 'the Washington Monument is 169.29 meters tall'. These are truths in the actual world, but things could have been otherwise. (In the jargon of possible worlds: there are possible worlds in which there are more or fewer planets, and in which the Washington Monument is greater than or less than 169.29 meters tall.) We can say that such truths are *contingent* truths.

That there are nine planets and that the height of the Washington Monument is 169.29 meters could be said to be 'accidentally true'. Their being true is owing to 'accidental' historical circumstances. Compare contingent truths of this kind—accidental truths—with truths like 'acid turns litmus paper red', or 'objects attract with a force proportional to their mass and inversely proportional to the squares of their distance', or '$E = mc^2$'. *Given the laws of nature*, these statements are not merely accidentally true: they *must* be true.

Does this mean that such truths hold in 'all possible worlds'? Most philosophers regard laws of nature as contingent: the laws could have been otherwise (the laws of nature that hold in the actual world do not hold in some other possible worlds). Worlds in which pigs fly, objects attract in accord with an inverse cube law, or $E \neq mc^2$ are apparently conceivable. These statements, then, are thought to be true only contingently.

How should we understand (CT)? Philosophers who run in these circles interpret the relation between the material constitution of sentient creatures and qualities of conscious experiences as similar to the inverse square law. That is, it is contingently—but not merely accidentally—true that a creature with a particular kind of material constitution has experiences of a particular sort. This relationship is lawful; it holds for any creature in the actual world. But there are worlds in which the relationship does not hold. Locke puts it this way:

> Let us suppose at present, that the different Motions and Figures, Bulk, and Number of such Particles, affecting the several Organs of our Senses, produce in us those different Sensations, which we have from the Colours and Smells of Bodies; *v.g.* that a Violet, by the impulse of such insensible particles of matter of peculiar figures, and bulks, and in different degrees and modifications of their Motions, causes the *Ideas* of the blue Colour, and sweet Scent of that Flower to be produced in our Minds. It being no more impossible, to conceive, that God should annex such *Ideas* to such Motions, with which they have no similitude; than that he should annex the *Idea* of Pain to the motion of a piece of Steel dividing our Flesh, with which that *Idea* hath no resemblance. (Locke 1690: II, viii, 13)

The idea is that God—or Mother Nature—has arranged matters in such a way that pillar boxes and sunsets give rise to visual sensations of a distinctive kind: they *look red*. God could just as easily have arranged matters so that the sensations we had when we apprehend a pillar box or a sunset visually were like those we now have when we eat a spoonful of strawberry ice cream or hear a locomotive whistle. There is no explanation from the nature of things as to why conscious experiences are as they are qualitatively.

The 'explanatory gap'

This point is emphasized by Joseph Levine (Chapter 44) who speaks of an 'explanatory gap' between the way things are in the material world and qualities exhibited by our conscious experiences. Skeptics have sometimes challenged their opponents to provide evidence that conscious experiences are alike across agents: how can I be sure that *my red* is not *your green*? The question takes hold only so long as we assume (CT), only so long as we accept Locke's suggestion that qualities of conscious experiences are only contingently related to their causes and the further suggestion that qualities, generally, could vary independently of the fundamental material properties.

Although it is apparently true that material duplicates will be qualitative duplicates (you could not change an object's qualities without reorganizing its material components in some way), this truth is presumed to be at best a brute fact about our world, a fact to be accepted without further explanation. As you read the selections by Jackson, Levine, and McGinn, you should ask yourself whether this really is so, and, if it is so, what reasons might be offered for thinking it so. The philosopher Wittgenstein is, as we have noted previously, famous for observing that philosophical puzzles can arise from assumptions that strike us as utterly innocent: 'The decisive movement in the conjuring trick has been made, and it was the very one we thought quite innocent' (Wittgenstein 1953: §308). We need, then, to be on our guard before treating assumptions as innocent: in philosophy no assumption is innocent.

Confronting the mind–body problem

Non-philosophers are often frustrated by the endless disagreements characteristic of philosophy. The impression is that philosophers turn tractable problems into impossible riddles. Why not let the sciences get on with it? As we learn more and more about the operation of the brain, we move closer and closer to a solution to the question what minds are and how they are related to bodies.

This is an agreeable picture. No doubt it contains an important element of truth. The trouble is, this conception of science separates science and philosophy in an artificial way. Science is not merely a fact-collecting enterprise. A successful science is not one that produces a large list of truths. A successful science provides us with an *understanding* of some range of phenomena. Take basic physics. Here, facts are important. But more important is the understanding we gain from the discovery of fundamental principles that make it clear to us how things work, why they behave as they do. Scientists ask *what-*

questions, but the deep questions are the *why*-questions. Newton discovered many facts. We remember Newton, not for his empirical discoveries, however, but for his laws.

The formulation of laws governing phenomena is one important way—though not the only way—of making sense of those phenomena. Making sense of phenomena requires equal measures of perspicuous conceptualization and a grip on the empirical data. Descartes hoped to accommodate his dualistic conception of mind to the material world by supposing that minds, although powerless to introduce motion into the material world, could nevertheless affect the *direction* taken by a moving particle. For Descartes motion is conserved. Descartes's world is a *kinematic* world, a world that operates on geometric principles. In such a world, size and shape matter, but there is no room for mass or force.

Newton's world was a re-conceptualized world. Newton's world is *dynamic*; a world in which bodies are acted on by forces. Objects exert forces on one another proportional to their masses. What called for explanation was not motion, per se, but change in velocity. A change in the direction taken by a moving material particle requires the exertion of force. If minds influence the direction taken by particles, then, minds exert force. It is hard to see how they could do this unless minds themselves were material entities.

This is not to suggest that Newton was a materialist, but merely to point out that scientific advance often awaits the re-conceptualization of a particular domain. This is what seems called for in the case of the mind–body problem. Piling up data about the brain might illuminate the relation of minds to bodies, but only if we have a perspicuous way of making sense of that data. It is a good bet that, so long as we look at the matter through the eyes of Descartes, we will be unsuccessful—and for roughly the same reasons Descartes's physics proved unsuccessful. The question is whether we are humanly capable of coming up with a perspicuous conceptualization. McGinn suggests that we are not. Others contend that, when it comes to the mind–body relation, the most we can hope for is a brute correlation between qualitative states of mind and physical goings-on. We can learn that various physical events yield various mental outcomes, but why this should be so is not something capable of further illumination. Our mental and physical concepts are too far apart to be unified under a single theory.

Senseless brutes

I have mentioned appeals to 'brute facts' and 'brute correlations'. But what are these *brutes*? Consider what might be involved in explaining a given phenomenon. One familiar sort of explanation proceeds by division. We explain why things behave as they do, by showing that this is how they ought to behave given the character of their constituent parts. We explain how a mechanical clock operates, for instance, by showing how its parts fit together into a coherent whole. We explain digestion, by showing how components of the digestive tract work in concert to extract nutrition and expel waste. We can push explanation further. We can explain properties of the components of a clock—their rigidity, perhaps, or their elasticity—by looking to *their* components, and we can explain how various digestive organs function by decomposing them into their cellular constituents.

We can continue this way down to the molecular level (where the line between living non-living things begins to blur), and beyond, to the atomic and sub-atomic level. Eventually, however, explanation comes to an end. Molecules behave as they do owing to properties of their constituent atoms, and the atoms owe their properties, hence their behavioral capacities, to their constituents. Sooner or later we reach explanatory bedrock. Atoms behave as they do because their constituents—electrons and quarks, say—are as they are. Once you reach a basic level, however, explanation runs out: things behave as they do because they are as they are, and things with this nature just do behave in this way. Explanation works, not because all explanation is traceable to self-explaining explainers. Explanation works by reducing the complex to the less complex. At the basic level the behavior of objects cannot be further explained. We are comfortable with the fact that explanation 'bottoms out' because we have reduced a large number of complex, largely unrelated, mysteries to a handful of simple mysteries.

Does consciousness—or the relation of consciousness to material goings-on—belong in this select group? Some philosophers think so. The basic laws of nature include the laws of basic physics and one or more additional laws of consciousness. In considering this possibility, you might want to recall a comment made by J. J. C. Smart in defending the mind—brain identity theory.

> States of consciousness . . . seem to be the one sort of thing left outside the physicalist picture, and for various reasons I just cannot believe that this can be so. That everything should be explicable in terms of physics (together of course with descriptions of the ways in which the parts are put together—roughly, biology is to physics as radio-engineering is to electromagnetism) except the occurrence of sensations seems to me frankly unbelievable. Such sensations would be 'nomological danglers', to use Feigl's expression [Feigl 1958: 428]. It is not often realized how odd would be the laws whereby these nomological danglers would dangle. It is sometimes asked, 'Why can't there be psycho-physical laws which are of a novel sort, just as the laws of electricity and magnetism were novelties from the standpoint of Newtonian mechanics?' Certainly we are pretty sure in the future to come across ultimate laws of a novel type, but I expect them to relate simple constituents: for example whatever ultimate particles are then in vogue. I cannot believe that the ultimate laws of nature could relate simple constituents to configurations consisting of billions of neurons (and goodness knows how many billions of billions of ultimate particles) all put together for all the world as though their main purpose was to be a negative feedback mechanism of a complicated sort. Such ultimate laws would be like nothing so far known in science. (Smart, Chapter 8).

To appreciate Smart's point, first consider what a brute physical law might look like. Such a law would pertain to the fundamental features of fundamental particles. Suppose, for instance, that an electron is a fundamental particle. Electrons are negatively charged. In virtue of being negatively charged, electrons repel one another and attract positrons. Can we give a further explanation of the electron's power to repel and attract? Perhaps not. It is a brute fact that negatives repel negatives and attract positives. I am prepared to be told that there is a deeper story here, but you get the idea.

Now consider the idea that the connection between conscious experiences, or the qualities of conscious experiences, and material processes is similarly brute. It is a brute fact that, given a physical process of a particular sort, a conscious experience with a definite character occurs. This alleged brute fact differs from brute facts concerning electrons because it connects something complex—a qualitative experience—with something very complex—a brain process, for instance, involving millions (billions?) of particles. If you accept the idea that conscious states are 'multiply realizable', the situation is much worse. The very same qualitative experience could be the product of many different kinds of particle arrangements.

Perhaps there are such brute facts, but if there are, they are very different from the kinds of brute fact we expect to find in mapping the nature of the material world. Indeed, calling both kinds of fact 'brute' borders on dishonesty. It disguises as just another simple feature of the world what, in other circumstances, could appear miraculous.

Bedrock

A final point. I have spoken of 'reaching bedrock', but is this a realistic prospect? Every time we think we have identified the fundamental ingredients of the material world, we discover that these ingredients in fact include still more fundamental components. Perhaps this will prove to be so for electrons and quarks; perhaps there *is* no fundamental level of reality: no matter how finely you divide things into parts, it is always possible to divide those parts into parts!

This certainly is an abstract possibility (or *is* it? see Heil 2003: chap. 15), but my point about explanation stands. We may someday be able to explain the ultimate explainers in terms of still more ultimate explainers. Explanation bottoms out, however, even if reality does not.

References

Feigl, H. (1958), 'The "Mental" and the "Physical"'. In Feigl et al. 1958: 370–497. Reissued in 1967 as a monograph, *The 'Mental' and the 'Physical'*, Minneapolis: University of Minnesota Press.

——M. Scriven, and G. Maxwell, eds. (1958), *Concepts, Theories, and the Mind–Body Problem* (Minnesota Studies in the Philosophy of Science, vol. 2). Minneapolis: University of Minnesota Press.

Heil, J. (2003), *From an Ontological Point of View*. Oxford: Clarendon Press.

Locke, J. (1690/1978), *An Essay Concerning Human Understanding*, ed., P. H. Nidditch, Oxford: Clarendon Press.

Wittgenstein, L. (1953/1968), *Philosophical Investigations*, trans. G. E. M. Anscombe, Oxford: Basil Blackwell.

Chapter 43
Epiphenomenal qualia
Frank Jackson

It is undeniable that the physical, chemical and biological sciences have provided a great deal of information about the world we live in and about ourselves. I will use the label 'physical information' for this kind of information, and also for information that automatically comes along with it. For example, if a medical scientist tells me enough about the processes that go on in my nervous system, and about how they relate to happenings in the world around me, to what has happened in the past and is likely to happen in the future, to what happens to other similar and dissimilar organisms, and the like, he or she tells me—if I am clever enough to fit it together appropriately—about what is often called the functional role of those states in me (and in organisms in general in similar cases). This information, and its kin, I also label 'physical'.

I do not mean these sketchy remarks to constitute a definition of 'physical information', and of the correlative notions of physical property, process, and so on, but to indicate what I have in mind here. It is well known that there are problems with giving a precise definition of these notions, and so of the thesis of Physicalism that all (correct) information is physical information.[1] But—unlike some—I take the question of definition to cut across the central problems I want to discuss in this paper.

I am what is sometimes known as a 'qualia freak'. I think that there are certain features of the bodily sensations especially, but also of certain perceptual experiences, which no amount of purely physical information includes. Tell me everything physical there is to tell about what is going on in a living brain, the kind of states, their functional role, their relation to what goes on at other times and in other brains, and so on and so forth, and be I as clever as can be in fitting it all together, you won't have told me about the hurtfulness of pains, the itchiness of itches, pangs of jealousy, or about the characteristic experience of tasting a lemon, smelling a rose, hearing a loud noise or seeing the sky.

There are many qualia freaks, and some of them say that their rejection of Physicalism is an unargued intuition.[2] I think that they are being unfair to themselves. They have the following argument. Nothing you could tell of a physical sort

Frank Jackson, 'Epiphenomenal Qualia', *Philosophical Quarterly* 32 (1982).

1. See, e.g., D. H. Mellor, 'Materialism and Phenomenal Qualities', *Aristotelian Society Supp. Vol.* 47 (1973), 107–19; and J. W. Cornman, *Materialism and Sensations* (New Haven and London, 1971).
2. Particularly in discussion, but see, e.g., Keith Campbell, *Metaphysics* (Belmont, 1976), p. 67.

captures the smell of a rose, for instance. Therefore, Physicalism is false. By our lights this is a perfectly good argument. It is obviously not to the point to question its validity, and the premise is intuitively obviously true both to them and to me.

I must, however, admit that it is weak from a polemical point of view. There are, unfortunately for us, many who do not find the premise intuitively obvious. The task then is to present an argument whose premises are obvious to all, or at least to as many as possible. This I try to do in §I with what I will call 'the Knowledge argument'. In §II I contrast the Knowledge argument with the Modal argument and in §III with the 'What is it like to be' argument. In §IV I tackle the question of the causal role of qualia. The major factor in stopping people from admitting qualia is the belief that they would have to be given a causal role with respect to the physical world and especially the brain,[3] and it is hard to do this without sounding like someone who believes in fairies. I seek in §IV to turn this objection by arguing that the view that qualia are epiphenomenal is a perfectly possible one.

I. The Knowledge argument for qualia

People vary considerably in their ability to discriminate colours. Suppose that in an experiment to catalogue this variation Fred is discovered. Fred has better colour vision than anyone else on record; he makes every discrimination that anyone has ever made, and moreover he makes one that we cannot even begin to make. Show him a batch of ripe tomatoes and he sorts them into two roughly equal groups and does so with complete consistency. That is, if you blindfold him, shuffle the tomatoes up, and then remove the blindfold and ask him to sort them out again, he sorts them into exactly the same two groups.

We ask Fred how he does it. He explains that all ripe tomatoes do not look the same colour to him, and in fact that this is true of a great many objects that we classify together as red. He sees two colours where we see one, and he has in consequence developed for his own use two words 'red_1' and 'red_2' to mark the difference. Perhaps he tells us that he has often tried to teach the difference between red_1 and red_2 to his friends but has got nowhere and has concluded that the rest of the world is red_1-red_2 colour-blind—or perhaps he has had partial success with his children, it doesn't matter. In any case he explains to us that it would be quite wrong to think that because 'red' appears in both 'red_1' and 'red_2' that the two colours are shades of the one colour. He only uses the common term 'red' to fit more easily into our restricted usage. To him red_1 and red_2 are as different from each other and all the other colours as yellow is from blue. And his discriminatory behaviour bears this out: he sorts red_1 from red_2 tomatoes with the greatest of ease in a wide variety of viewing circumstances. Moreover, an investigation of the physiological basis of Fred's exceptional ability reveals that Fred's optical system is

3. See, e.g., D. C. Dennett, 'Current Issues in the Philosophy of Mind', *American Philosophical Quarterly*, 15 (1978), 249–61.

able to separate out two groups of wave-lengths in the red spectrum as sharply as we are able to sort out yellow from blue.[4]

I think that we should admit that Fred can see, really see, at least one more colour than we can; red_1 is a different colour from red_2. We are to Fred as a totally red-green colour-blind person is to us. H. G. Wells' story 'The Country of the Blind' is about a sighted person in a totally blind community.[5] This person never manages to convince them that he can see, that he has an extra sense. They ridicule this sense as quite inconceivable, and treat his capacity to avoid falling into ditches, to win fights and so on as precisely that capacity and nothing more. We would be making their mistake if we refused to allow that Fred can see one more colour than we can.

What kind of experience does Fred have when he sees red_1 and red_2? What is the new colour or colours like? We would dearly like to know but do not; and it seems that no amount of physical information about Fred's brain and optical system tells us. We find out perhaps that Fred's cones respond differentially to certain light waves in the red section of the spectrum that make no difference to ours (or perhaps he has an extra cone) and that this leads in Fred to a wider range of those brain states responsible for visual discriminatory behaviour. But none of this tells us what we really want to know about his colour experience. There is something about it we don't know. But we know, we may suppose, everything about Fred's body, his behaviour and dispositions to behaviour and about his internal physiology, and everything about his history and relation to others that can be given in physical accounts of persons. We have all the physical information. Therefore, knowing all this is *not* knowing everything about Fred. It follows that Physicalism leaves something out.

To reinforce this conclusion, imagine that as a result of our investigations into the internal workings of Fred we find out how to make everyone's physiology like Fred's in the relevant respects; or perhaps Fred donates his body to science and on his death we are able to transplant his optical system into someone else—again the fine detail doesn't matter. The important point is that such a happening would create enormous interest. People would say, 'At last we will know what it is like to see the extra colour, at last we will know how Fred has differed from us in the way he has struggled to tell us about for so long'. Then it cannot be that we knew all along all about Fred. But *ex hypothesi* we did know all along everything about Fred that features in the physicalist scheme; hence the physicalist scheme leaves something out.

Put it this way. *After* the operation, we will know *more* about Fred and especially about his colour experiences. But beforehand we had all the physical information we could desire about his body and brain, and indeed everything that has ever featured in physicalist accounts of mind and consciousness. Hence there is more to know than all that. Hence Physicalism is incomplete.

4. Put this, and similar simplifications below, in terms of Land's theory if you prefer. See, e.g., Edwin H. Land, 'Experiments in Color Vision', *Scientific American*, 200 (5 May 1959), 84–99.
5. H. G. Wells, *The Country of the Blind and Other Stories* (London, n.d.).

Fred and the new colour(s) are of course essentially rhetorical devices. The same point can be made with normal people and familiar colours. Mary is a brilliant scientist who is, for whatever reason, forced to investigate the world from a black and white room *via* a black and white television monitor. She specialises in the neurophysiology of vision and acquires, let us suppose, all the physical information there is to obtain about what goes on when we see ripe tomatoes, or the sky, and use terms like 'red', 'blue', and so on. She discovers, for example, *just* which wave-length combinations from the sky stimulate the retina, and exactly how this produces *via* the central nervous system the contraction of the vocal chords and expulsion of air from the lungs that results in the uttering of the sentence 'The sky is blue'. (It can hardly be denied that it is in principle possible to obtain all this physical information from black and white television, otherwise the Open University would *of necessity* need to use colour television.)

What will happen when Mary is released from her black and white room or is given a colour television monitor? Will she *learn* anything or not? It seems just obvious that she will learn something about the world and our visual experience of it. But then it is inescapable that her previous knowledge was incomplete. But she had *all* the physical information. *Ergo* there is more to have than that, and Physicalism is false.

Clearly the same style of Knowledge argument could be deployed for taste, hearing, the bodily sensations and generally speaking for the various mental states which are said to have (as it is variously put) raw feels, phenomenal features or qualia. The conclusion in each case is that the qualia are left out of the physicalist story. And the polemical strength of the Knowledge argument is that it is so hard to deny the central claim that one can have all the physical information without having all the information there is to have.

II. The Modal argument

By the Modal Argument I mean an argument of the following style.[6] Sceptics about other minds are not making a mistake in deductive logic, whatever else may be wrong with their position. No amount of physical information about another *logically entails* that he or she is conscious or feels anything at all. Consequently there is a possible world with organisms exactly like us in every physical respect (and remember that includes functional states, physical history, *et al.*) but which differ from us profoundly in that they have no conscious mental life at all. But then what is it that we have and they lack? Not anything physical *ex hypothesi.* In all physical regards we and they are exactly alike. Consequently there is more to us than the purely physical. Thus Physicalism is false.[7]

6. See, e.g., Keith Campbell, *Body and Mind* (New York, 1970); and Robert Kirk, 'Sentience and Behaviour', *Mind,* 83 (1974), 43–60.

7. I have presented the argument in an inter-world rather than the more usual intra-world fashion to avoid inessential complications to do with supervenience, causal anomalies and the like.

It is sometimes objected that the Modal argument misconceives Physicalism on the ground that that doctrine is advanced as a *contingent* truth.[8] But to say this is only to say that physicalists restrict their claim to *some* possible worlds, including especially ours; and the Modal argument is only directed against this lesser claim. If we in *our* world, let alone beings in any others, have features additional to those of our physical replicas in other possible worlds, then we have non-physical features or qualia.

The trouble rather with the Modal argument is that it rests on a disputable modal intuition. Disputable because it is disputed. Some sincerely deny that there can be physical replicas of us in other possible worlds which nevertheless lack consciousness. Moreover, at least one person who once had the intuition now has doubts.[9]

Head-counting may seem a poor approach to a discussion of the Modal argument. But frequently we can do no better when modal intuitions are in question, and remember our initial goal was to find the argument with the greatest polemical utility.

Of course, *qua* protagonists of the Knowledge argument we may well accept the modal intuition in question; but this will be a *consequence* of our already having an argument to the conclusion that qualia are left out of the physicalist story, not our ground for that conclusion. Moreover, the matter is complicated by the possibility that the connection between matters physical and qualia is like that sometimes held to obtain between aesthetic qualities and natural ones. Two possible worlds which agree in all 'natural' respects (including the experiences of sentient creatures) must agree in all aesthetic qualities also, but it is plausibly held that the aesthetic qualities cannot be reduced to the natural.

III. The 'What is it like to be' argument

In 'What is it like to be a bat?' Thomas Nagel argues that no amount of physical information can tell us what it is like to be a bat, and indeed that we, human beings, cannot imagine what it is like to be a bat.[10] His reason is that what this is like can only be understood from a bat's point of view, which is not our point of view and is

8. See, e.g., W. G. Lycan, 'A New Lilliputian Argument Against Machine Functionalism', *Philosophical Studies*, 35 (1979), 279–87, p. 280; and Don Locke, 'Zombies, Schizophrenics and Purely Physical Objects', *Mind*, 85 (1976), 97–9.

9. See R. Kirk, 'From Physical Explicability to Full-Blooded Materialism', *The Philosophical Quarterly*, 29 (1979), 229–37. See also the arguments against the modal intuition in, e.g., Sydney Shoemaker, 'Functionalism and Qualia', *Philosophical Studies*, 27 (1975), 291–315.

10. *The Philosophical Review*, 83 (1974), 435–50 (Chapter 29 of this volume). Two things need to be said about this article. One is that, despite my dissociations to come, I am much indebted to it. The other is that the emphasis changes through the article, and by the end Nagel is objecting not so much to Physicalism as to all extant theories of mind for ignoring points of view, including those that admit (irreducible) qualia.

not something capturable in physical terms which are essentially terms understandable equally from many points of view.

It is important to distinguish this argument from the Knowledge argument. When I complained that all the physical knowledge about Fred was not enough to tell us what his special colour experience was like, I was not complaining that we weren't finding out what it is like to *be* Fred. I was complaining that there is something *about* his experience, a property of it, of which we were left ignorant. And if and when we come to know what this property is we still will not know what it is like to *be* Fred, but we will know more *about* him. No amount of knowledge about Fred, be it physical or not, amounts to knowledge 'from the inside' concerning Fred. We are not Fred. There is thus a whole set of items of knowledge expressed by forms of words like 'that it is *I myself* who is . . .' which Fred has and we simply cannot have because we are not him.[11]

When Fred sees the colour he alone can see, one thing he knows is the way his experience of it differs from his experience of seeing red and so on, *another* is that he himself is seeing it. Physicalist and qualia freaks alike should acknowledge that no amount of information of whatever kind that *others* have *about* Fred amounts to knowledge of the second. My complaint though concerned the first and was that the special quality of his experience is certainly a fact about it, and one which Physicalism leaves out because no amount of physical information told us what it is.

Nagel speaks as if the problem he is raising is one of extrapolating from knowledge of one experience to another, of imagining what an unfamiliar experience would be like on the basis of familiar ones. In terms of Hume's example, from knowledge of some shades of blue we can work out what it would be like to see other shades of blue. Nagel argues that the trouble with bats *et al.* is that they are too unlike us. It is hard to see an objection to Physicalism here. Physicalism makes no special claims about the imaginative or extrapolative powers of human beings, and it is hard to see why it need do so.[12]

Anyway, our Knowledge argument makes no assumptions on this point. If Physicalism were true, enough physical information about Fred would obviate any need to extrapolate or to perform special feats of imagination or understanding in order to know all about his special colour experience. *The information would already be in our possession.* But it clearly isn't. That was the nub of the argument.

11. Knowledge *de se* in the terms of David Lewis, 'Attitudes *De Dicto* and *De Se*', *The Philosophical Review*, 88 (1979), 513–43.

12. See Laurence Nemirow's comments on 'What is it . . .' in his review of T. Nagel, *Mortal Questions*, in *The Philosophical Review*, 89 (1980), 473–7. I am indebted here in particular to a discussion with David Lewis.

IV. The bogey of epiphenomenalism

Is there any really *good* reason for refusing to countenance the idea that qualia are causally impotent with respect to the physical world? I will argue for the answer no, but in doing this I will say nothing about two views associated with the classical epiphenomenalist position. The first is that mental *states* are inefficacious with respect to the physical world. All I will be concerned to defend is that it is possible to hold that certain *properties* of certain mental states, namely those I've called qualia, are such that their possession or absence makes no difference to the physical world. The second is that the mental is *totally* causally inefficacious. For all I will say it may be that you have to hold that the instantiation of *qualia* makes a difference to *other mental states* though not to anything physical. Indeed general considerations to do with how you could come to be aware of the instantiation of qualia suggest such a position.[13]

Three reasons are standardly given for holding that a quale like the hurtfulness of a pain must be causally efficacious in the physical world, and so, for instance, that its instantiation must sometimes make a difference to what happens in the brain. None, I will argue, has any real force. (I am much indebted to Alec Hyslop and John Lucas for convincing me of this.)

(i) It is supposed to be just obvious that the hurtfulness of pain is partly responsible for the subject seeking to avoid pain, saying 'It hurts' and so on. But, to reverse Hume, anything can fail to cause anything. No matter how often *B* follows *A*, and no matter how initially obvious the causality of the connection seems, the hypothesis that *A* causes *B* can be overturned by an over-arching theory which shows the two as distinct effects of a common underlying causal process.

To the untutored the image on the screen of Lee Marvin's fist moving from left to right immediately followed by the image of John Wayne's head moving in the same general direction looks as causal as anything.[14] And of course throughout countless Westerns images similar to the first are followed by images similar to the second. All this counts for precisely nothing when we know the over-arching theory concerning how the relevant images are both effects of an underlying causal process involving the projector and the film. The epiphenomenalist can say exactly the same about the connection between, for example, hurtfulness and behaviour. It is simply a consequence of the fact that certain happenings in the brain cause both.

(ii) The second objection relates to Darwin's Theory of Evolution. According to natural selection the traits that evolve over time are those conducive to physical survival. We may assume that qualia evolved over time—we have them, the earliest forms of life do not—and so we should expect qualia to be conducive to survival.

13. See my review of K. Campbell, *Body and Mind*, in *Australasian Journal of Philosophy*, 50 (1972), 77–80.

14. Cf. Jean Piaget, 'The Child's Conception of Physical Causality', reprinted in *The Essential Piaget* (London, 1977).

The objection is that they could hardly help us to survive if they do nothing to the physical world.

The appeal of this argument is undeniable, but there is a good reply to it. Polar bears have particularly thick, warm coats. The Theory of Evolution explains this (we suppose) by pointing out that having a thick, warm coat is conducive to survival in the Arctic. But having a thick coat goes along with having a heavy coat, and having a heavy coat is *not* conducive to survival. It slows the animal down.

Does this mean that we have refuted Darwin because we have found an evolved trait—having a heavy coat—which is not conducive to survival? Clearly not. Having a heavy coat is an unavoidable concomitant of having a warm coat (in the context, modern insulation was not available), and the advantages for survival of having a warm coat outweighed the disadvantages of having a heavy one. The point is that all we can extract from Darwin's theory is that we should expect any evolved characteristic to be *either* conducive to survival *or* a by-product of one that is so conducive. The epiphenomenalist holds that qualia fall into the latter category. They are a by-product of certain brain processes that are highly conducive to survival.

(iii) The third objection is based on a point about how we come to know about other minds. We know about other minds by knowing about other behaviour, at least in part. The nature of the inference is a matter of some controversy, but it is not a matter of controversy that it proceeds from behaviour. That is why we think that stones do not feel and dogs do feel. But, runs the objection, how can a person's behaviour provide any reason for believing he has qualia like mine, or indeed any qualia at all, unless this behaviour can be regarded as the *outcome* of the qualia. Man Friday's footprint was evidence of Man Friday because footprints are causal outcomes of feet attached to people. And an epiphenomenalist cannot regard behaviour, or indeed anything physical, as an outcome of qualia.

But consider my reading in *The Times* that Spurs won. This provides excellent evidence that *The Telegraph* has also reported that Spurs won, despite the fact that (I trust) *The Telegraph* does not get the results from *The Times.* They each send their own reporters to the game. *The Telegraph*'s report is in no sense an outcome of *The Times*', but the latter provides good evidence for the former nevertheless.

The reasoning involved can be reconstructed thus. I read in *The Times* that Spurs won. This gives me reason to think that Spurs won because I know that Spurs' winning is the most likely candidate to be what caused the report in *The Times.* But I also know that Spurs' winning would have had many effects, including almost certainly a report in *The Telegraph.*

I am arguing from one effect back to its cause and out again to another effect. The fact that neither effect causes the other is irrelevant. Now the epiphenomenalist allows that qualia are effects of what goes on in the brain. Qualia cause nothing physical but are caused by something physical. Hence the epiphenomenalist can argue from the behaviour of others to the qualia of others by arguing from the behaviour of others back to its causes in the brains of others and out again to their qualia.

You may well feel for one reason or another that this is a more dubious chain of reasoning than its model in the case of newspaper reports. You are right. The problem of other minds is a major philosophical problem, the problem of other newspaper reports is not. But there is no special problem of Epiphenomenalism as opposed to, say, Interactionism here.

There is a very understandable response to the three replies I have just made. 'All right, there is no knockdown refutation of the existence of epiphenomenal qualia. But the fact remains that they are an excrescence. They *do* nothing, they *explain* nothing, they serve merely to soothe the intuitions of dualists, and it is left a total mystery how they fit into the world view of science. In short we do not and cannot understand the how and why of them.'

This is perfectly true; but is no objection to qualia, for it rests on an overly optimistic view of the human animal, and its powers. We are the products of Evolution. We understand and sense what we need to understand and sense in order to survive. Epiphenomenal qualia are totally irrelevant to survival. At no stage of our evolution did natural selection favour those who could make sense of how they are caused and the laws governing them, or in fact why they exist at all. And that is why we can't.

It is not sufficiently appreciated that Physicalism is an extremely optimistic view of our powers. If it is true, we have, in very broad outline admittedly, a grasp of our place in the scheme of things. Certain matters of sheer complexity defeat us—there are an awful lot of neurons—but in principle we have it all. But consider the antecedent probability that everything in the Universe be of a kind that is relevant in some way or other to the survival of *homo sapiens.* It is very low surely. But then one must admit that it is very likely that there is a part of the whole scheme of things, maybe a big part, which no amount of evolution will ever bring us near to knowledge about or understanding. For the simple reason that such knowledge and understanding is irrelevant to survival.

Physicalists typically emphasise that we are a part of nature on their view, which is fair enough. But if we are a part of nature, we are as nature has left us after however many years of evolution it is, and each step in that evolutionary progression has been a matter of chance constrained just by the need to preserve or increase survival value. The wonder is that we understand as much as we do, and there is no wonder that there should be matters which fall quite outside our comprehension. Perhaps exactly how epiphenomenal qualia fit into the scheme of things is one such.

This may seem an unduly pessimistic view of our capacity to articulate a truly comprehensive picture of our world and our place in it. But suppose we discovered living on the bottom of the deepest oceans a sort of sea slug which manifested intelligence. Perhaps survival in the conditions required rational powers. Despite their intelligence, these sea slugs have only a very restricted conception of the world by comparison with ours, the explanation for this being the nature of their immediate environment. Nevertheless they have developed sciences which work surprisingly well in these restricted terms. They also have philosophers, called slugists. Some call themselves tough-minded slugists, others confess to being soft-minded slugists.

The tough-minded slugists hold that the restricted terms (or ones pretty like them which may be introduced as their sciences progress) suffice in principle to describe everything without remainder. These tough-minded slugists admit in moments of weakness to a feeling that their theory leaves something out. They resist this feeling and their opponents, the soft-minded slugists, by pointing out—absolutely correctly—that no slugist has ever succeeded in spelling out how this mysterious residue fits into the highly successful view that their sciences have and are developing of how their world works.

Our sea slugs don't exist, but they might. And there might also exist super beings which stand to us as we stand to the sea slugs. We cannot adopt the perspective of these super beings, because we are not them, but the possibility of such a perspective is, I think, an antidote to excessive optimism.[15]

15. I am indebted to Robert Pargetter for a number of comments and, despite his dissent, to §IV of Paul E. Meehl, 'The Compleat Autocerebroscopist' in *Mind, Matter, and Method*, ed. Paul Feyerabend and Grover Maxwell (Minneapolis, 1966).

Chapter 44

Materialism and qualia: the explanatory gap

Joseph Levine

In 'Naming and Necessity'[1] and 'Identity and Necessity,'[2] Kripke presents a version of the Cartesian argument against materialism. His argument involves two central claims: first, that all identity statements using rigid designators on both sides of the identity sign are, if true at all, true in all possible worlds where the terms refer; second, that psycho-physical identity statements are conceivably false, and therefore, by the first claim, actually false.

My purpose in this paper is to transform Kripke's argument from a metaphysical one into an epistemological one. My general point is this. Kripke relies upon a particular intuition regarding conscious experience to support his second claim. I find this intuition important, not least because of its stubborn resistance to philosophical dissolution. But I don't believe this intuition supports the metaphysical thesis Kripke defends—namely, that pyscho-physical identity statements must be false. Rather, I think it supports a closely related epistemological thesis—namely, that psycho-physical identity statements leave a significant *explanatory gap*, and, as a corollary, that we don't have any way of determining exactly which psycho-physical identity statements are true.[3] One cannot conclude from my version of the argument that materialism is false, which makes my version a weaker attack than Kripke's. Nevertheless, it does, if correct, constitute a problem for materialism, and one that I think better captures the uneasiness many philosophers feel regarding that doctrine.

I will present this epistemological argument by starting with Kripke's own argument and extracting the underlying intuition. For brevity's sake, I am going to assume knowledge of Kripke's general position concerning necessity and the theory of reference, and concentrate only on the argument against materialism. To begin

Joseph Levine, 'Materialism and Qualia: The Explanatory Gap', *Pacific Philosophy Quarterly* 64 (1983).

1. Saul Kripke, 'Naming and Necessity,' reprinted in *Semantics of Natural Language*, second edition, edited by Donald Davidson and Gilbert Harman, D. Reidel Publishing Co., 1972.
2. Saul Kripke, 'Identity and Necessity,' reprinted in *Naming, Necessity, and Natural Kinds*, edited by Stephen Schwartz, Cornell U. Press, 1977 (see Chapter 9 of this volume).
3. My argument in this paper is influenced by Thomas Nagel's in his paper 'What Is It Like To Be a Bat?' (reprinted in *Readings in the Philosophy of Psychology*, volume 1, edited by Ned Block, Harvard U. Press, 1980) (see Chapter 29 of this volume), as readers who are familiar with Nagel's paper will notice as it develops.

with, let us assume that we are dealing with a physicalist type-identity theory. That is, our materialist is committed to statements like:

(1) Pain is the firing of C-fibers.

On Kripke's general theory, if (1) is true at all it is necessarily true. The same of course, is the case with the following statement:

(2) Heat is the motion of molecules.

That is, if (2) is true at all it is necessarily true. So far so good.

The problem arises when we note that, with both (1) and (2), there is a felt contingency about them. That is, it seems conceivable that they be false. If they are necessarily true, however, that means there is no possible world in which they are false. Thus, imagining heat without the motion of molecules, or pain without the firing of C-fibers, must be to imagine a logically impossible world. Yet these suppositions *seem* coherent enough. Kripke responds that the felt contingency of (2) can be satisfactorily explained away, but that this can't be done for (1). Thus, there is an important difference between psycho-physical identities and other theoretical identities, and this difference makes belief in the former implausible.

The difference between the two cases is this. When it seems plausible that (2) is contingent, one can become disabused of this notion by noting that instead of imagining *heat* without the motion of molecules, one is really imagining there being some phenomenon that affects our senses the way heat in fact does, but is not the motion of molecules. The truly contingent statement is not (2) but

(2′) The phenomenon we experience through the sensations of warmth and cold, which is responsible for the expansion and contraction of mercury in thermometers, which causes some gases to rise and others to sink, etc., is the motion of molecules.

However, this sort of explanation will not work for (1). When we imagine a possible world in which a phenomenon is experienced as pain but we have no C-fibers, that is a possible world in which there *is* pain without there being any C-fibers. This is so, argues Kripke, for the simple reason that the experience of pain, the sensation of pain, counts as pain itself. We cannot make the distinction here, as we can with heat, between the way it appears to us and the phenomenon itself. Thus, we have no good account of our intuition that (1) is contingent, unless we give up the truth of (1) altogether.

Now, there are several responses available to the materialist. First of all, the most popular materialist view nowadays is functionalism, which is not committed to even the contingent truth of statements like (1). Rather than identifying types of mental states with types of physical states, functionalists identify the former with types of functional, or what Boyd calls 'configurational' states.[4] Functional states are more abstract than physical states, and are capable of realization in a wide

4. Richard Boyd, 'Materialism Without Reductionism,' reprinted in *Readings in the Philosophy of Psychology*, volume 1.

variety of physical constitutions. In terms of the computer metaphor, which is behind many functionalist views, our mentality is a matter of the way we are 'programmed,' our 'software,' whereas our physiology is a matter of our 'hardware.' On this view, the intuition that pain could exist without C-fibers is explained in terms of the multiple realizability of mental states. This particular dilemma, then, doesn't appear to arise for functionalist materialists.

However, this reply won't work. First of all, a Kripke-style argument can be mounted against functionalist identity statements as well. Ned Block, in 'Troubles with Functionalism,'[5] actually makes the argument. He asks us to imagine any complete functionalist description of pain (embedded, of course, in a relatively complete functionalist psychological theory). Though we have no idea as yet exactly what this description would be, insofar as it is a *functionalist* description, we know roughly what form it would take. Call this functionalist description 'F.' Then functionalism entails the following statement:

(3) To be in pain is to be in state F.

Again, on Kripke's theory of reference, (3) is necessarily true if true at all. Again, it seems imaginable that in some possible world (perhaps even in the actual world) (3) is false. Block attempts to persuade us of this by describing a situation where some object is in F but it is doubtful that it is in pain. For instance, suppose F were satisfied by the entire nation of China—which, given the nature of functional descriptions, is logically possible. Note that all the argument requires is that it should be *possible* that the entire nation of China, while realizing F, not be in pain. This certainly does seem possible.

Furthermore, some adherents of functionalism have moved back toward physicalist reductionism for qualia, largely in response to considerations like those put forward by Block. The idea is this. What Block's example seems to indicate is that functional descriptions are just *too* abstract to capture the essential features of qualitative sensory experiences. The so-called 'inverted spectrum' argument—which involves the hypothesis that two people could share functional descriptions yet experience different visual qualia when viewing the same object—also points up the excessive abstractness of functional descriptions. Now one way some functionalists propose to deal with this problem is to return to a physicalist type-identity theory for sensory qualia, or at least for particular kinds of sensory qualia.[6] The gist of the latter proposal is this. While it's sufficient for being conscious (for having qualia at all) that an entity realize the appropriate functional description, the particular way a qualitative state is experienced is determined by the nature of the physical realization. So if, while looking at a ripe McIntosh apple, I experience

5. Ned Block, 'Troubles with Functionalism,' reprinted in *Readings in the Philosophy of Psychology*, volume 1.

6. Cf. Sydney Shoemaker, 'The Inverted Spectrum,' *The Journal of Philosophy*, volume LXXIX, no. 7, July, 1982.

the visual quality normally associated with looking at ripe McIntosh apples, and my inverted friend experiences the quality normally associated with looking at ripe cucumbers, this has to do with the difference in our physical realizations of the same functional state. Obviously, if we adopt this position Kripke's original argument applies.

So far, then, we see that the move to functionalism doesn't provide materialists with a way to avoid the dilemma Kripke poses: either bite the bullet and deny that (1), or (3), is contingent, or give up materialism. Well, what about biting the bullet? Why not just say that, intuition notwithstanding, statements like (1) and (3) are not contingent? In fact, Kripke himself, by emphasizing the gulf between epistemological possibility and metaphysical possibility, might even seem to give the materialist the ammunition she needs to attack the legitimacy of the appeal to this intuition. For what seems intuitively to be the case is, if anything, merely an epistemological matter. Since epistemological possibility is not sufficient for metaphysical possibility, the fact that what is intuitively contingent turns out to be metaphysically necessary should not bother us terribly. It's to be expected.

In the end, of course, one can just stand pat and say that. This is why I don't think Kripke's argument is entirely successful. However, I do think the intuitive resistance to materialism brought out by Kripke (and Block) should not be shrugged off as *merely* a matter of epistemology. Though clearly an epistemological matter, I think this intuitive resistance to materialism should bother us a lot. But before I can defend this claim, the intuition in question requires some clarification.

First of all, let's return to our list of statements. What I want to do is look more closely at the difference between statement (2) on the one hand, and statements (1) and (3) on the other. One difference between them, already noted, was the fact that the felt contingency of (2) could be explained away while the felt contingency of the others could not. But I want to focus on another difference, one which I think underlies the first one. Statement (2), I want to say, expresses an identity that is *fully explanatory*, with nothing crucial left out. On the other hand, statements (1) and (3) do seem to leave something crucial unexplained, there is a 'gap' in the explanatory import of these statements. It is this explanatory gap, I claim, which is responsible for their vulnerability to Kripke-type objections. Let me explain what I mean by an 'explanatory gap.'

What is explanatory about (2)? (2) states that heat is the motion of molecules. The explanatory force of this statement is captured in statements like (2′) above. (2′) tells us by what mechanism the causal functions we associate with heat are effected. It is explanatory in the sense that our knowledge of chemistry and physics makes intelligible how it is that something like the motion of molecules could play the causal role we associate with heat. Furthermore, antecedent to our discovery of the essential nature of heat, its causal role, captured in statements like (2′), exhausts our notion of it. Once we understand how this causal role is carried out there is nothing more we need to understand.

Now, what is the situation with (1)? What is explained by learning that pain is the firing of C-fibers? Well, one might say that in fact quite a bit is explained. If we believe that part of the concept expressed by the term 'pain' is that of a state which plays a certain causal role in our interaction with the environment (e.g. it warns us of damage, it causes us to attempt to avoid situations we believe will result in it, etc.), (2) explains the mechanisms underlying the performance of these functions. So, for instance, if penetration of the skin by a sharp metallic object excites certain nerve endings, which in turn excite the C-fibers, which then causes various avoidance mechanisms to go into effect, the causal role of pain has been explained.

Of course, the above is precisely the functionalist story. Obviously, there is something right about it. Indeed, we do feel that the causal role of pain is crucial to our concept of it, and that discovering the physical mechanism by which this causal role is effected explains an important facet of what there is to be explained about pain. However, there is more to our concept of pain than its causal role, there is its qualitative character, how it feels; and what is left unexplained by the discovery of C-fiber firing is *why pain should feel the way it does*! For there seems to be nothing about C-fiber firing which makes it naturally 'fit' the phenomenal properties of pain, any more than it would fit some other set of phenomenal properties. Unlike its functional role, the identification of the qualitative side of pain with C-fiber firing (or some property of C-fiber firing) leaves the connection between it and what we identify it with completely mysterious. One might say, it makes the way pain feels into merely a brute fact.

Perhaps my point is easier to see with the example above involving vision. Let's consider again what it is to see green and red. The physical story involves talk about the various wave-lengths detectable by the retina, and the receptors and processors that discriminate among them. Let's call the physical story for seeing red 'R' and the physical story for seeing green 'G.' My claim is this. When we consider the qualitative character of our visual experiences when looking at ripe McIntosh apples, as opposed to looking at ripe cucumbers, the difference is not explained by appeal to G and R. For R doesn't really explain why I have the one kind of qualitative experience—the kind I have when looking at McIntosh apples—and not the other. As evidence for this, note that it seems just as easy to imagine G as it is to imagine R underlying the qualitative experience that is in fact associated with R. The reverse, of course, also seems quite imaginable.

It should be clear from what's been said that it doesn't help if we actually identify qualia with their functional roles. First of all, as I mentioned above, some functionalists resist this and prefer to adopt some form of type-physicalism for qualia. So when seeking the essence of how it feels to be in a certain functional state, they claim we must look to the essence of the physical realization. Secondly, even if we don't take this route, it still seems that we can ask why the kind of state that performs the function performed by pain, whatever its physical basis, should *feel* the way pain does. The analogous question regarding heat doesn't feel compelling. If someone asks why the motion of molecules plays the physical role it does, one can properly reply that an understanding of chemistry and physics is all that is needed to answer that question. If one objects that the phenomenal properties we associate with heat are not explained by identifying it with the motion of molecules, since being the motion of molecules seems compatible with all sorts of phenomenal properties, this just reduces to the problem under discussion. For it is precisely phenomenal properties—how it is for us to be in certain mental (including perceptual) states—which seem to resist physical (including functional) explanations.

Of course, the claim that (1) and (3) leave an explanatory gap in a way that (2) doesn't cannot be made more precise than the notion of explanation itself. Obviously, the D-N model of explanation is not sufficient for my purposes, since (1) and (3) presumably support counter-factuals and could be used, along with other premises, to deduce all sorts of particular facts.[7] What we need is an account of what it is for a phenomenon to be made *intelligible*, along with rules which determine when the demand for further intelligibility is inappropriate. For instance, I presume that the laws of gravity explain, in the sense at issue here, the phenomena of falling bodies. There doesn't seem to be anything 'left out.' Yet I am told that the value of *G*, the gravitational constant, is not derived from any basic laws. It is a given, a primitive, brute fact about the universe. Does this leave us with a feeling that something which ought to be explained is not? Or do we expect that some facts of nature should appear arbitrary in this way? I am inclined to take the latter attitude with respect to *G*. So, one may ask, why does the connection between what it's like to be in a particular functional (or physical) state and the state itself demand explanation, to be made intelligible?

Without a theoretical account of the notion of intelligibility I have in mind, I can't provide a really adequate answer to this question. Yet I think there are ways to at least indicate why it is reasonable to seek such an explanation. First of all, the phenomenon of consciousness arises on the macroscopic level. That is, it is only highly organized physical systems which exhibit mentality. This is of course what one would expect if mentality were a matter of functional organization. Now, it just seems odd that primitive facts of the sort apparently presented by statements like (1) and (3) should arise at this level of organization. Materialism, as I understand it, implies explanatory reductionism of at least this minimal sort: that for every phenomenon not describable in terms of the fundamental physical magnitudes (whatever they turn out to be), there is a mechanism that is describable in terms of the fundamental physical magnitudes such that occurrences of the former are intelligible in terms of occurrences of the latter. While this minimal reductionism does not imply anything about the reducibility of theories like psychology to physics, it does imply that brute facts—of the sort exemplified by the value of *G*—will not arise in the domain of theories like psychology.

7. To elaborate a bit, on the D-N model of explanation, a particular event *e* is explained when it is shown to be deducible from general laws together with whatever description of the particular situation is relevant. Statements (1) and (3) could obviously be employed as premises in a deduction concerning (say) someone's psychological state. Cf. Carl Hempel, 'Aspects of Scientific Explanation,' reprinted in Hempel, *Aspects of Scientific Explanation*, Free Press, 1968.

Furthermore, to return to my original point, the claim that statements (1) and (3) leave an explanatory gap accounts for their apparent contingency, and, more importantly, for the failure to explain away their apparent contingency in the standard way. After all, why is it that we can account for the apparent contingency of (2) in a theoretically and intuitively satisfactory manner, but not for that of (1) and (3)? Even if one believes that we don't have to take this intuitive resistance seriously, it is still legitimate to ask why the problem arises in these particular cases. As I claimed above, I think the difference in this regard between (2) on the one hand, and (1) and (3) on the other, is accounted for by the explanatory gap left by the latter as opposed to the former. Since this is the crucial connection between Kripke's argument and mine, let me belabor this point for a bit.

The idea is this. If there is nothing we can determine about C-fiber firing that explains why having one's C-fibers fire has the qualitative character that it does—or, to put it another way, if what it's particularly like to have one's C-fibers fire is not explained, or made intelligible, by understanding the physical or functional properties of C-fiber firings—it immediately becomes imaginable that there be C-fiber firings without the feeling of pain, and *vice versa*. We don't have the corresponding intuition in the case of heat and the motion of molecules—once we get clear about the right way to characterize what we imagine—because whatever there is to explain about heat is explained by its being the motion of molecules. So, how could it be anything else?

The point I am trying to make was captured by Locke[8] in his discussion of the relation between primary and secondary qualities. He states that the simple ideas which we experience in response to impingements from the external world bear no intelligible relation to the corpuscular processes underlying impingement and response. Rather, the two sets of phenomena—corpuscular processes and simple ideas—are stuck together in an arbitrary manner. The simple ideas go with their respective corpuscular configurations because God chose to so attach them. He could have chosen to do it differently. Now, so long as the two states of affairs seem arbitrarily stuck together in this way, imagination will pry them apart. Thus it is the non-intelligibility of the connection between the feeling of pain and its physical correlate that underlies the apparent contingency of that connection.

Another way to support my contention that psycho-physical (or psycho-functional) identity statements leave an explanatory gap will also serve to establish the corollary I mentioned at the beginning of this paper; namely, that even if some psycho-physical identity statements are true, we can't determine exactly which ones are true. The two claims, that there is an explanatory gap and that such identities are, in a sense, unknowable, are interdependent and mutually supporting. First I will show why there is a significant problem about our ever coming to know that

8. Cf. Locke, *An Essay Concerning Human Understanding*, edited by J. Yolton, Everyman's Library, 1971 (originally published 1690); Bk. II, Ch. VIII, sec. 13, and Bk. IV, Ch. III, secs. 12 and 13.

statements like (1) are true, then I will show how this is connected to the problem of the explanatory gap.

So suppose, as a matter of fact, that having the feeling of pain is identical with being in a particular kind of physical state. Well, which physical state? Suppose we believed it to be the firing of C-fibers because that was the state we found to be correlated with the feeling of pain in ourselves. Now imagine we come across alien life which gives every behavioral and functional sign of sharing our qualitative states. Do they have the feeling of pain we have? Well, if we believed that to have that feeling is to have one's C-fibers fire, and if the aliens don't have firing C-fibers, then we must suppose that they can't have this feeling. But the problem is, even if it is true that creatures with physical constitutions radically different from ours do not share our qualitative states, how do we determine what measure of physical similarity/dissimilarity to use? That is, the fact that the feeling of pain is a kind of physical state, if it is, doesn't itself tell us how thickly or thinly to slice our physical kinds when determining which physical state it is identical to. For all we know, pain is identical to the disjunctive state, the firing of C-fibers *or* the opening of D-valves (the latter disjunct realizing pain (say) in creatures with a hydraulic nervous system).[9]

This objection may seem like the standard argument for functionalism. However, I am actually making a quite different argument. First of all, the same objection can be made against various forms of functionalist identity statements. That is, if we believe that to have the feeling of pain is to be in some functional state, what measure of functional similarity/dissimilarity do we use in judging whether or not some alien creature shares our qualitative states? Now, the more inclusive we make this measure, the more pressure we feel about questions of inverted qualia, and therefore the more reason we have to adopt a physicalist-reductionist position concerning particular kinds of qualia. This just brings us back where we started. That is, if having a radically different physical constitution is sufficient for having different qualia, there must be some fact of the matter about *how* different the physical constitution must be. But what possible evidence could tell between the hypothesis that the qualitative character of our pain is a matter of having firing C-fibers, and the hypothesis that it is a matter of having either firing C-fibers or opening D-valves?[10]

9. This point is similar to an argument of Putnam's in the chapter of *Reason, Truth, and History* (Cambridge U. Press, 1981) entitled 'Mind and Body.' Putnam uses the argument to serve a different purpose from mine, however. The example of the hydraulic nervous system is from David Lewis, 'Mad Pain and Martian Pain,' reprinted in *Readings in the Philosophy of Psychology*, volume 1.

10. Shoemaker, in 'The Inverted Spectrum,' *op. cit.*, explicitly tries to deal with this problem. He proposes a fairly complicated principle according to which disjunctive states like the one mentioned in the text do not qualify for identification with (or realization of) qualitative states. I cannot discuss his principle in detail here. However, the main idea is that we look to the causal role of a quale for its individuation conditions. That is, if the causal effects of pain in human beings are explained by their C-fiber firings *alone*, then the state of having one's C-fibers fire *or* having one's

Now, if there were some intrinsic connection discernible between having one's C-fibers firing (or being in functional state F) and what it's like to be in pain, by which I mean that experiencing the latter was intelligible in terms of the properties of the former, then we could derive our measure of similarity from the nature of the explanation. Whatever properties of the firing of C-fibers (or being in state F) that explained the feel of pain would determine the properties a kind of physical (or functional) state had to have in order to count as feeling like our pain. But without this explanatory gap filled in, facts about the kind or the existence of phenomenal experiences of pain in creatures physically (or functionally) different from us become impossible to determine. This, in turn, entails that the truth or falsity of (1), while perhaps metaphysically factual, is nevertheless epistemologically inaccessible. This seems to be a very undesirable consequence of materialism.

There is only one way in the end that I can see to escape this dilemma and remain a materialist. One must either deny, or dissolve, the intuition which lies at the foundation of the argument. This would involve, I believe, taking more of an eliminationist line with respect to qualia than many materialist philosophers are prepared to take. As I said earlier, this kind of intuition about our qualitative experience seems surprisingly resistant to philosophical attempts to eliminate it. As long as it remains, the mind/body problem will remain.[11]

D-valves open is not a legitimate candidate for the physical realization of pain. Viewed from the standpoint of my argument in this paper, Shoemaker's principle begs the very question at issue; namely, whether the qualitative character of pain is explained by its causal role. For if it isn't, there is no reason to presume that the identity conditions of the physical state causally responsible for pain's functional role would determine the presence or absence of a particular kind of qualitative character. So long as the nature of that qualitative character is not explained by anything peculiar to any particular physical realization of pain, we have no way of knowing whether or not a different physical realization of pain, in a different creature, is associated with the same qualitative character.

11. An earlier version of this paper, under the title 'Qualis, Materialism, and the Explanatory Gap,' was delivered at the APA Eastern Division meetings, 1982. I would like to thank Carolyn McMullen for her comments on that occasion. I would also like to thank Louise Antony, Hilary Putnam, and Susan Wolf for their helpful comments on even earlier versions.

Chapter 45

Can we solve the mind–body problem?

Colin McGinn

How it is that anything so remarkable as a state of consciousness comes about as a result of initiating nerve tissue, is just as unaccountable as the appearance of the Djin, where Aladdin rubbed his lamp in the story . . . (Julian Huxley)

We have been trying for a long time to solve the mind–body problem. It has stubbornly resisted our best efforts. The mystery persists. I think the time has come to admit candidly that we cannot resolve the mystery. But I also think that this very insolubility—or the reason for it—removes the philosophical problem. In this paper I explain why I say these outrageous things.

The specific problem I want to discuss concerns consciousness, the hard nut of the mind–body problem. How is it possible for conscious states to depend upon brain states? How can technicolour phenomenology arise from soggy grey matter? What makes the bodily organ we call the brain so radically different from other bodily organs, say the kidneys—the body parts without a trace of consciousness? How could the aggregation of millions of individually insentient neurons generate subjective awareness? We know that brains are the *de facto* causal basis of consciousness, but we have, it seems, no understanding whatever of how this can be so. It strikes us as miraculous, eerie, even faintly comic. Somehow, we feel, the water of the physical brain is turned into the wine of consciousness, but we draw a total blank on the nature of this conversion. Neural transmissions just seem like the wrong kind of materials with which to bring consciousness into the world, but it appears that in some way they perform this mysterious feat. The mind–body problem is the problem of understanding how the miracle is wrought, thus removing the sense of deep mystery. We want to take the magic out of the link between consciousness and the brain.[1]

Colin McGinn, 'Can We Solve the Mind–Body Problem?', *Mind* 98 (1989).

1. One of the peculiarities of the mind–body problem is the difficulty of formulating it in a rigorous way. We have a sense of the problem that outruns our capacity to articulate it clearly. Thus we quickly find ourselves resorting to invitations to look inward, instead of specifying precisely *what* it is about consciousness that makes it inexplicable in terms of ordinary physical properties. And this can make it seem that the problem is spurious. A creature without consciousness would not properly appreciate the problem (assuming such a creature could appreciate other problems). I

Purported solutions to the problem have tended to assume one of two forms. One form, which we may call constructive, attempts to specify some natural property of the brain (or body) which explains how consciousness can be elicited from it. Thus functionalism, for example, suggests a property—namely, causal role—which is held to be satisfied by both brain states and mental states; this property is supposed to explain how conscious states can come from brain states.[2] The other form, which has been historically dominant, frankly admits that nothing merely natural could do the job, and suggests instead that we invoke supernatural entities or divine interventions. Thus we have Cartesian dualism and Leibnizian pre-established harmony. These 'solutions' at least recognize that something pretty remarkable is needed if the mind–body relation is to be made sense of; they are as extreme as the problem. The approach I favour is naturalistic but not constructive: I do not believe we can ever specify what it is about the brain that is responsible for consciousness, but I am sure that whatever it is it is not inherently miraculous. The problem arises, I want to suggest, because we are cut off by our very cognitive constitution from achieving a conception of that natural property of the brain (or of consciousness) that accounts for the psychophysical link. This is a kind of causal nexus that we are precluded from ever understanding, given the way we have to form our concepts and develop our theories. No wonder we find the problem so difficult!

Before I can hope to make this view plausible, I need to sketch the general conception of cognitive competence that underlies my position. Let me introduce the idea of *cognitive closure.* A type of mind M is cognitively closed with respect to a property P (or theory T) if and only if the concept-forming procedures at M's disposal cannot extend to a grasp of P (or an understanding of T). Conceiving minds come in different kinds, equipped with varying powers and limitations, biases and blindspots, so that properties (or theories) may be accessible to some minds but not to others. What is closed to the mind of a rat may be open to the mind of a monkey, and what is open to us may be closed to the monkey. Representational power is not all or nothing. Minds are biological products like bodies, and like bodies they come in different shapes and sizes, more or less capacious, more or

think an adequate treatment of the mind–body problem should explain why it is so hard to state the problem explicitly. My treatment locates our difficulty in our inadequate conceptions of the nature of the brain and consciousness. In fact, if we knew their natures fully we would already have solved the problem. This should become clear later.

2. I would also classify panpsychism as a constructive solution, since it attempts to explain consciousness in terms of properties of the brain that are as natural as consciousness itself. Attributing specks of proto-consciousness to the constituents of matter is not supernatural in the way postulating immaterial substances or divine interventions is; it is merely extravagant. I shall here be assuming that panpsychism, like all other extant constructive solutions, is inadequate as an answer to the mind—body problem—as (of course) are the supernatural 'solutions'. I am speaking to those who still feel perplexed (almost everyone, I would think, at least in their heart) .

less suited to certain cognitive tasks.[3] This is particularly clear for perceptual faculties, of course: perceptual closure is hardly to be denied. Different species are capable of perceiving different properties of the world, and no species can perceive every property things may instantiate (without artificial instrumentation anyway). But such closure does not reflect adversely on the reality of the properties that lie outside the representational capacities in question; a property is no less real for not being reachable from a certain kind of perceiving and conceiving mind. The invisible parts of the electromagnetic spectrum are just as real as the visible parts, and whether a specific kind of creature can form conceptual representations of these imperceptible parts does not determine whether they exist. Thus cognitive closure with respect to *P* does not imply irrealism about *P*. That *P* is (as we might say) *noumenal* for *M* does not show that *P* does not occur in some naturalistic scientific theory *T*—it shows only that *T* is not cognitively accessible to *M*. Presumably monkey minds and the property of being an electron illustrate this possibility. And the question must arise as to whether human minds are closed with respect to certain true explanatory theories. Nothing, at least, in the concept of reality shows that everything real is open to the human concept-forming faculty—if, that is, we are realists about reality.[4]

Consider a mind constructed according to the principles of classical empiricism, a Humean mind. Hume mistakenly thought that human minds were Humean, but we can at least conceive of such a mind (perhaps dogs and monkeys have Humean minds). A Humean mind is such that perceptual closure determines cognitive closure, since 'ideas' must always be copies of 'impressions'; therefore the concept-forming system cannot transcend what can be perceptually presented to the subject. Such a mind will be closed with respect to unobservables; the properties of atoms, say, will not be representable by a mind constructed in this way. This implies that explanatory theories in which these properties are essentially mentioned will not be accessible to a Humean mind.[5] And hence the observable phenomena that are

3. This kind of view of cognitive capacity is forcefully advocated by Noam Chomsky in *Reflections on Language*, Patheon Books, 1975, and by Jerry Fodor in *The Modularity of Mind*, Cambridge, Mass., MIT Press, 1983. Chomsky distinguishes between 'problems', which human minds are in principle equipped to solve, and 'mysteries', which systematically elude our understanding; and he envisages a study of our cognitive systems that would chart these powers and limitations. I am here engaged in such a study, citing the mind—body problem as falling on the side of the mysteries.

4. See Thomas Nagel's discussion of realism in *The View From Nowhere*, Oxford, Oxford University Press, 1986, ch. VI. He argues there for the possibility of properties we can never grasp. Combining Nagel's realism with Chomsky-Fodor cognitive closure gives a position looking very much like Locke's in the *Essay Concerning Human Understanding*: the idea that our God-given faculties do not equip us to fathom the deep truth about reality. In fact, Locke held precisely this about the relation between mind and brain: only divine revelation could enable us to understand how 'perceptions' are produced in our minds by material objects.

5. Hume, of course, argued, in effect, that no theory essentially employing a notion of objective causal necessitation could be grasped by our minds—and likewise for the notion of objective persistence. We might compare the frustrations of the Humean mind to the conceptual travails of the pure

explained by allusion to unobservables will be inexplicable by a mind thus limited. But notice: the incapacity to explain certain phenomena does not carry with it a lack of recognition of the theoretical problems the phenomena pose. You might be able to appreciate a problem without being able to formulate (even in principle) the solution to that problem (I suppose human children are often in this position, at least for a while). A Humean mind cannot solve the problems that our physics solves, yet it might be able to have an inkling of what needs to be explained. We would expect, then, that a moderately intelligent enquiring Humean mind will feel permanently perplexed and mystified by the physical world, since the correct science is forever beyond its cognitive reach. Indeed, something like this was precisely the view of Locke. He thought that our ideas of matter are quite sharply constrained by our perceptions and so concluded that the true science of matter is eternally beyond us—that we could never remove our perplexities about (say) what solidity ultimately is.[6] But it does not follow for Locke that nature is itself inherently mysterious; the felt mystery comes from our own cognitive limitations, not from any objective eeriness in the world. It looks today as if Locke was wrong about our capacity to fathom the nature of the physical world, but we can still learn from his fundamental thought—the insistence that our cognitive faculties may not be up to solving every problem that confronts us. To put the point more generally: the human mind may not conform to empiricist principles, but it must conform to *some* principles—and it is a substantive claim that these principles permit the solution of every problem we can formulate or sense. Total cognitive openness is not guaranteed for human beings and it should not be expected. Yet what is noumenal for us may not be miraculous in itself. We should therefore be alert to the possibility that a problem that strikes us as deeply intractable, as utterly baffling, may arise from an area of cognitive closure in our ways of representing the world.[7] That is what I now want to argue is the case with our sense of the mysterious nature of the connection between consciousness and the brain. We are biased away from arriving at the correct explanatory theory of the psychophysical nexus. And this makes us prone to an illusion of objective mystery. Appreciating this should remove the philosophical problem: consciousness does not, in reality, arise from the brain in the miraculous way in which the Djin arises from the lamp.

I now need to establish three things: (i) there exists some property of the brain

sound beings discussed in Ch. II of P. F. Strawson's *Individuals*, London, Methuen, 1959; both are types of mind whose constitution puts various concepts beyond them. We can do a lot better than these truncated minds, but we also have our constitutional limitations.

6. See the *Essay*, Book II, ch. IV. Locke compares the project of saying what solidity ultimately is to trying to clear up a blind man's vision by talking to him.

7. Some of the more arcane aspects of cosmology and quantum theory might be thought to lie just within the bounds of human intelligibility. Chomsky suggests that the causation of behaviour might be necessarily mysterious to human investigators: see *Reflections on Language*, p. 156. I myself believe that the mind–body problem exhibits a qualitatively different level of mystery from this case (unless it is taken as an aspect of that problem) .

that accounts naturalistically for consciousness; (ii) we are cognitively closed with respect to that property; but (iii) there is no philosophical (as opposed to scientific) mind–body problem. Most of the work will go into establishing (ii).

Resolutely shunning the supernatural, I think it is undeniable that it must be in virtue of *some* natural property of the brain that organisms are conscious. There just *has* to be some explanation for how brains subserve minds. If we are not to be eliminativists about consciousness, then some theory must exist which accounts for the psychophysical correlations we observe. It is implausible to take these correlations as ultimate and inexplicable facts, as simply brute. And we do not want to acknowledge radical emergence of the conscious with respect to the cerebral: that is too much like accepting miracles *de re*. Brain states cause conscious states, we know, and this causal nexus must proceed through necessary connections of some kind—the kind that would make the nexus intelligible *if* they were understood.[8] Consciousness is like life in this respect. We know that life evolved from inorganic matter, so we expect there to be some explanation of this process. We cannot plausibly take the arrival of life as a primitive brute fact, nor can we accept that life arose by some form of miraculous emergence. Rather, there must be some natural account of how life comes from matter, whether or not we can know it. Eschewing vitalism and the magic touch of God's finger, we rightly insist that it must be in virtue of some natural property of (organized) matter that parcels of it get to be alive. But consciousness itself is just a further biological development, and so it too must be susceptible of some natural explanation—whether or not human beings are capable of arriving at this explanation. Presumably there exist objective natural laws that somehow account for the upsurge of consciousness. Consciousness, in short, must be a natural phenomenon, naturally arising from certain organizations of matter. Let us then say that there exists some property *P*, instantiated by the brain, in virtue of which the brain is the basis of consciousness. Equivalently, there exists some theory *T*, referring to *P*, which fully explains the dependence of conscious states on brain states. If we knew *T*, then we would have a constructive solution to the mind–body problem. The question then is whether we can ever come to know *T* and grasp the nature of *P*.

Let me first observe that it is surely *possible* that we could never arrive at a grasp of *P*; there is, as I said, no guarantee that our cognitive powers permit the solution of every problem we can recognize. Only a misplaced idealism about the natural world could warrant the dogmatic claim that everything is knowable by the human species at this stage of its evolutionary development (consider the same claim made on behalf of the intellect of cro-Magnon man). It *may* be that every property for which we can form a concept is such that *it* could never solve the mind–body problem. We *could* be like five-year old children trying to understand Relativity

8. Cf. Nagel's discussion of emergence in 'Panpsychism', in *Mortal Questions*, Cambridge, Cambridge University Press, 1979. I agree with him that the apparent radical emergence of mind from matter has to be epistemic only, on pain of accepting inexplicable miracles in the world.

Theory. Still, so far this is just a possibility claim: what reason do we have for asserting, positively, that our minds are closed with respect to *P*?

Longstanding historical failure is suggestive, but scarcely conclusive. Maybe, it will be said, the solution is just around the corner, or it has to wait upon the completion of the physical sciences? Perhaps we simply have yet to produce the Einstein-like genius who will restructure the problem in some clever way and then present an astonished world with the solution?[9] However, I think that our deep bafflement about the problem, amounting to a vertiginous sense of ultimate mystery, which resists even articulate formulation, should at least encourage us to explore the idea that there is something terminal about our perplexity. Rather as traditional theologians found themselves conceding cognitive closure with respect to certain of the properties of God, so we should look seriously at the idea that the mind–body problem brings us bang up against the limits of our capacity to understand the world. That is what I shall do now.

There seem to be two possible avenues open to us in our aspiration to identify *P*: we could try to get to *P* by investigating consciousness directly, or we could look to the study of the brain for *P*. Let us consider these in turn, starting with consciousness. Our acquaintance with consciousness could hardly be more direct; phenomenological description thus comes (relatively) easily. 'Introspection' is the name of the faculty through which we catch consciousness in all its vivid nakedness. By virtue of possessing this cognitive faculty we ascribe concepts of consciousness to ourselves; we thus have 'immediate access' to the properties of consciousness. But does the introspective faculty reveal property *P*? Can we tell just by introspecting what the solution to the mind—body problem is? Clearly not. We have direct cognitive access to one term of the mind-brain relation, but we do not have such access to the nature of the link. Introspection does not present conscious states *as* depending upon the brain in some intelligible way. We cannot therefore introspect *P*. Moreover, it seems impossible that we should ever augment our stock of introspectively ascribed concepts with the concept *P*—that is, we could not acquire this concept simply on the basis of sustained and careful introspection. Pure phenomenology will never provide the solution to the mind—body problem. Neither does it seem feasible to try to extract *P* from the concepts of consciousness we now have by some procedure of conceptual analysis—any more than we could solve the life-matter problem simply by reflecting on the concept *life*.[10] *P* has to lie outside the field of the introspectable, and it is not implicitly contained in the concepts we

9. Despite his reputation for pessimism over the mind–body problem, a careful reading of Nagel reveals an optimistic strain in his thought (by the standards of the present paper): see, in particular, the closing remarks of 'What is it Like to be a Bat?', (Chapter 29 of this volume) in *Mortal Questions*. Nagel speculates that we might be able to devise an 'objective phenomenology' that made conscious states more amenable to physical analysis. Unlike me, he does not regard the problem as inherently beyond us.

10. This is perhaps the most remarkably optimistic view of all—the expectation that reflecting on the ordinary concept of pain (say) will reveal the manner of pain's dependence on the brain. If I am not mistaken, this is in effect the view of common-sense functionalists: they think that *P* consists in

bring to bear in our first-person ascriptions. Thus the faculty of introspection, as a concept-forming capacity, is cognitively closed with respect to *P*; which is not surprising in view of its highly limited domain of operation (*most* properties of the world are closed to introspection).

But there is a further point to be made about *P* and consciousness, which concerns our restricted access to the concepts of consciousness themselves. It is a familiar point that the range of concepts of consciousness attainable by a mind *M* is constrained by the specific forms of consciousness possessed by *M*. Crudely, you cannot form concepts of conscious properties unless you yourself instantiate those properties. The man born blind cannot grasp the concept of a visual experience of red, and human beings cannot conceive of the echolocatory experiences of bats.[11] These are cases of cognitive closure within the class of conscious properties. But now this kind of closure will, it seems, affect our hopes of access to *P*. For suppose that we were cognitively open with respect to *P*; suppose, that is, that we had the solution to the problem of how specific forms of consciousness depend upon different kinds of physiological structure. Then, of course, we would understand how the brain of a bat subserves the subjective experiences of bats. Call this type of experience *B*, and call the explanatory property that links *B* to the bat's brain *P*1. By grasping *P*1 it would be perfectly intelligible to us how the bat's brain generates *B*-experiences; we would have an explanatory theory of the causal nexus in question. We would be in possession of the same kind of understanding we would have of our own experiences if we had the correct psychophysical theory of them. But then it seems to follow that grasp of the theory that explains *B*-experiences would *confer* a grasp of the nature of those experiences: for how could we understand that theory without understanding the concept *B* that occurs in it? How could we grasp the *nature* of *B*-experiences without grasping the *character* of those experiences? The true psychophysical theory would seem to provide a route to a grasp of the subjective form of the bat's experiences. But now we face a dilemma, a dilemma which threatens to become a reductio: either we *can* grasp this theory, in which case the property *B* becomes open to us; or we *cannot* grasp the theory, simply because property *B* is *not* open to us. It seems to me that the looming reductio here is compelling: our concepts of consciousness just *are* inherently constrained by our own form of consciousness, so that any theory the understanding of which required us to transcend these constraints would *ipso facto* be inaccessible to us. Similarly, I think, any theory that required us to transcend the finiteness of our cognitive

causal role, and that this can be inferred analytically from the concepts of conscious states. This would make it truly amazing that we should ever have felt there to be a mind–body problem at all, since the solution is already contained in our mental concepts. What optimism! .

11. See Nagel, 'What is it Like to be a Bat?' Notice that the fugitive character of such properties with respect to our concepts has nothing to do with their 'complexity'; like fugitive colour properties, such experiential properties are 'simple'. Note too that such properties provide counter-examples to the claim that (somehow) rationality is a faculty that, once possessed, can be extended to encompass all concepts, so that if *any* concept can be possessed then *every* concept can.

capacities would *ipso facto* be a theory we could not grasp—and this despite the fact that it might be needed to explain something we can see needs explaining. We cannot simply stipulate that our concept-forming abilities are indefinitely plastic and unlimited just because they would have to be to enable us to grasp the truth about the world. We constitutionally lack the concept-forming capacity to encompass all possible types of conscious state, and this obstructs our path to a general solution to the mind–body problem. Even if we could solve it for our own case, we could not solve it for bats and Martians. *P* is, as it were, too close to the different forms of subjectivity for it to be accessible to all such forms, given that one's form of subjectivity restricts one's concepts of subjectivity.[12]

I suspect that most optimists about constructively solving the mind–body problem will prefer to place their bets on the brain side of the relation. Neuroscience is the place to look for property *P*, they will say. My question then is whether there is any conceivable way in which we might come to introduce *P* in the course of our empirical investigations of the brain. New concepts have been introduced in the effort to understand the workings of the brain, certainly: could not *P* then occur in conceivable extensions of this manner of introduction? So far, indeed, the theoretical concepts we ascribe to the brain seem as remote from consciousness as any ordinary physical properties are, but perhaps we might reach *P* by diligent application of essentially the same procedures: so it is tempting to think. I want to suggest, to the contrary, that such procedures are inherently closed with respect to *P*. The fundamental reason for this, I think, is the role of *perception* in shaping our understanding of the brain—the way that our perception of the brain constrains the concepts we can apply to it. A point whose significance it would be hard to overstress here is this: the property of consciousness itself (or specific conscious states) is not an observable or perceptible property of the brain. You can stare into a living conscious brain, your own or someone else's, and see there a wide variety of instantiated properties—its shape, colour, texture, etc.—but you will not thereby *see* what the subject is experiencing, the conscious state itself. Conscious states are simply not potential objects of perception: they depend upon the brain but they cannot be observed by directing the senses onto the brain. In other words, consciousness is noumenal with respect to perception of the brain.[13] I take it this is

12. It might be suggested that we borrow Nagel's idea of 'objective phenomenology' in order to get around this problem. Instead of representing experiences under subjective descriptions, we should describe them in entirely objective terms, thus bringing them within our conceptual ken. My problem with this is that, even allowing that there could be such a form of description, it would not permit us to understand how the subjective aspects of experience depend upon the brain—which is really the problem we are trying to solve. In fact, I doubt that the notion of objective phenomenology is any more coherent than the notion of subjective physiology. Both involve trying to bridge the psychophysical gap by a sort of stipulation. The lesson here is that the gap cannot be bridged just by applying concepts drawn from one side to items that belong on the other side; and this is because neither sort of concept could ever do what is needed.

13. We should distinguish two claims about the imperceptibility of consciousness: (i) consciousness is not perceivable by directing the senses onto the brain; (ii) consciousness is not perceivable by

obvious. So we know there *are* properties of the brain that are necessarily closed to perception of the brain; the question now is whether *P* is likewise closed to perception.

My argument will proceed as follows. I shall first argue that *P* is indeed perceptually closed; then I shall complete the argument to full cognitive closure by insisting that no form of *inference* from what is perceived can lead us to *P*. The argument for perceptual closure starts from the thought that nothing we can imagine perceiving in the brain would ever convince us that we have located the intelligible nexus we seek. No matter what recondite property we could see to be instantiated in the brain we would always be baffled about how it could give rise to consciousness. I hereby invite you to try to conceive of a perceptible property of the brain that might allay the feeling of mystery that attends our contemplation of the brain–mind link: I do not think you will be able to do it. It is like trying to conceive of a perceptible property of a rock that would render it perspicuous that the rock was conscious. In fact, I think it is the very impossibility of this that lies at the root of the felt mind–body problem. But why is this? Basically, I think, it is because the senses are geared to representing a spatial world; they essentially present things in space with spatially defined properties. But it is precisely *such* properties that seem inherently incapable of resolving the mind–body problem: we cannot link consciousness to the brain in virtue of spatial properties of the brain. There the brain is, an object of perception, laid out in space, containing spatially distributed processes; but consciousness defies explanation in such terms. Consciousness does not seem made up out of smaller spatial processes; yet perception of the brain seems limited to revealing such processes.[14] The senses are responsive to certain *kinds* of properties—those that are essentially bound up with space—but these properties are of the wrong sort (the wrong *category*) to constitute *P*. Kant was right, the form of outer sensibility is spatial; but if so, then *P* will be noumenal with respect to the senses, since no spatial property will ever deliver a satisfying answer to the mind–body problem. We simply do not understand the idea that conscious states might intelligibly arise from spatial configurations of the kind disclosed by perception of the world.

I take it this claim will not seem terribly controversial. After all, we do not generally expect that every property referred to in our theories should be a potential object of human perception: consider quantum theory and cosmology.

directing the senses anywhere, even towards the behaviour that 'expresses' conscious states. I believe both theses, but my present point requires only (i). I am assuming, of course, that perception cannot be unrestrictedly theory-laden; or that if it can, the infusions of theory cannot have been originally derived simply by looking at things or tasting them or touching them or . . .

14. Nagel discusses the difficulty of thinking of conscious processes in the spatial terms that apply to the brain in *The View From Nowhere*, pp. 50–1, but he does not draw my despairing conclusion. The case is exactly *unlike* (say) the dependence of liquidity on the properties of molecules, since here we do think of both terms of the relation as spatial in character; so we can simply employ the idea of spatial composition.

Unrestricted perceptual openness is a dogma of empiricism if ever there was one. And there is no compelling reason to suppose that the property needed to explain the mind–brain relation should be in principle perceptible; it might be essentially 'theoretical', an object of thought not sensory experience. Looking harder at nature is not the only (or the best) way of discovering its theoretically significant properties. Perceptual closure does not entail cognitive closure, since we have available the procedure of hypothesis formation, in which *un*observables come to be conceptualized.

I readily agree with these sentiments, but I think there are reasons for believing that no coherent method of concept introduction will ever lead us to *P*. This is because a certain principle of *homogeneity* operates in our introduction of theoretical concepts on the basis of observation. Let me first note that consciousness itself could not be introduced simply on the basis of what we observe about the brain and its physical effects. If our data, arrived at by perception of the brain, do not include anything that brings in conscious states, then the theoretical properties we need to explain these data will not include conscious states either. Inference to the best explanation of purely physical data will never take us outside the realm of the physical, forcing us to introduce concepts of consciousness.[15] Everything physical has a purely physical explanation. So the property of consciousness is cognitively closed with respect to the introduction of concepts by means of inference to the best explanation of perceptual data about the brain.

Now the question is whether *P* could ever be arrived at by this kind of inference. Here we must be careful to guard against a form of magical emergentism with respect to concept formation. Suppose we try out a relatively clear theory of how theoretical concepts are formed: we get them by a sort of analogical extension of what we observe. Thus, for example, we arrive at the concept of a molecule by taking our perceptual representations of macroscopic objects and conceiving of smaller scale objects of the same general kind. This method seems to work well enough for unobservable material objects, but it will not help in arriving at *P*, since analogical extensions of the entities we observe in the brain are precisely as hopeless as the original entities were as solutions to the mind–body problem. We would need a method that left the base of observational properties behind in a much more radical way. But it seems to me that even a more unconstrained conception of inference to the best explanation would still not do what is required: it would no more serve to introduce *P* than it serves to introduce the property of consciousness itself. To explain the observed physical data we need only such theoretical properties as bear upon those data, not the property that explains consciousness, which does not occur in the data. Since we do not need consciousness to explain those data, we do not need the property that explains consciousness. We will never get as far away from the perceptual data in our explanations of those data as we need to

15. Cf. Nagel: 'it will never be legitimate to infer, as a theoretical explanation of physical phenomena alone, a property that includes or implies the consciousness of its subject', 'Panpsychism', p. 183.

get in order to connect up explanatorily with consciousness. This is, indeed, why it seems that consciousness is theoretically epiphenomenal in the task of accounting for physical events. No concept needed to explain the workings of the physical world will suffice to explain how the physical world produces consciousness. So if *P* is perceptually noumenal, then it will be noumenal with respect to perception-based explanatory inferences. Accordingly, I do not think that *P* could be arrived at by empirical studies of the brain alone. Nevertheless, the brain *has* this property, as it has the property of consciousness. Only a magical idea of how we come by concepts could lead one to think that we can reach *P* by first perceiving the brain and then asking what is needed to explain what we perceive.[16] (The mind–body problem tempts us to magic in more ways than one.)

It will help elucidate the position I am driving towards if I contrast it with another view of the source of the perplexity we feel about the mind–brain nexus. I have argued that we cannot know which property of the brain accounts for consciousness, and so we find the mind–brain link unintelligible. But, it may be said, there is another account of our sense of irremediable mystery, which does not require positing properties our minds cannot represent. This alternative view claims that, even if we *now* had a grasp of *P*, we would *still* feel that there is something mysterious about the link, because of a special epistemological feature of the situation. Namely this: our acquaintance with the brain and our acquaintance with consciousness are necessarily mediated by distinct cognitive faculties, namely perception and introspection. Thus the faculty through which we apprehend one term of the relation is necessarily distinct from the faculty through which we apprehend the other. In consequence, it is not possible for us to use one of these faculties to apprehend the nature of the psychophysical nexus. No single faculty will enable us ever to apprehend the fact that consciousness depends upon the brain in virtue of property *P*. Neither perception alone nor introspection alone will ever enable us to witness the dependence. And this, my objector insists, is the real reason we find the link baffling: we cannot make sense of it in terms of the deliverances of a single cognitive faculty. So, even if we now had concepts for the properties of the brain that explain consciousness, we would still feel a residual sense of unintelligibility; we would still take there to be something mysterious going on. The necessity to shift from one faculty to the other produces in us an illusion of inexplicability. We might in fact have the explanation right now but be under the illusion that we do not. The right diagnosis, then, is that we should recognize the peculiarity of the epistemological situation and stop trying to make sense of the psychophysical

16. It is surely a striking fact that the microprocesses that have been discovered in the brain by the usual methods seem no nearer to consciousness than the gross properties of the brain open to casual inspection. Neither do more abstract 'holistic' features of brain function seem to be on the right lines to tell us the nature of consciousness. The deeper science probes into the brain the more remote it seems to get from consciousness. Greater knowledge of the brain thus destroys our illusions about the kinds of properties that might be discovered by travelling along this path. Advanced neurophysiological theory seems only to deepen the miracle.

nexus in the way we make sense of other sorts of nexus. It only *seems* to us that we can never discover a property that will render the nexus intelligible.

I think this line of thought deserves to be taken seriously, but I doubt that it correctly diagnoses our predicament. It is true enough that the problematic nexus is essentially apprehended by distinct faculties, so that it will never reveal its secrets to a single faculty; but I doubt that our intuitive sense of intelligibility is so rigidly governed by the 'single-faculty condition'. Why *should* facts only seem intelligible to us if we can conceive of apprehending them by one (sort of) cognitive faculty? Why not allow that we can recognize intelligible connections between concepts (or properties) even when those concepts (or properties) are necessarily ascribed using different faculties? Is it not suspiciously empiricist to insist that a causal nexus can only be made sense of by us if we can conceive of its being an object of a single faculty of apprehension? Would we think this of a nexus that called for touch and sight to apprehend each term of the relation? Suppose (*per impossibile*) that we were offered *P* on a plate, as a gift from God: would we still shake our heads and wonder how that could resolve the mystery, being still the victims of the illusion of mystery generated by the epistemological duality in question? No, I think this suggestion is not enough to account for the miraculous appearance of the link: it is better to suppose that we are permanently blocked from forming a concept of what accounts for that link.

How strong is the thesis I am urging? Let me distinguish *absolute* from *relative* claims of cognitive closure. A problem is absolutely cognitively closed if no possible mind could resolve it; a problem is relatively closed if minds of some sorts can in principle solve it while minds of other sorts cannot. Most problems we may safely suppose, are only relatively closed: armadillo minds cannot solve problems of elementary arithmetic but human minds can. Should we say that the mind–body problem is only relatively closed or is the closure absolute? This depends on what we allow as a possible concept-forming mind, which is not an easy question. If we allow for minds that form their concepts of the brain and consciousness in ways that are quite independent of perception and introspection, then there may be room for the idea that there are possible minds for which the mind–body problem is soluble, and easily so. But if we suppose that *all* concept formation is tied to perception and introspection, however loosely, then *no* mind will be capable of understanding how it relates to its own body—the insolubility will be absolute. I think we can just about make sense of the former kind of mind, by exploiting our own faculty of a priori reasoning. Our mathematical concepts (say) do not seem tied either to perception or to introspection, so there does seem to be a mode of concept formation that operates without the constraints I identified earlier. The suggestion might then be that a mind that formed all of its concepts in this way—including its concepts of the brain and consciousness—would be free of the biases that prevent *us* from coming up with the right theory of how the two connect. Such a mind would have to be able to think of the brain and consciousness in ways that utterly prescind from the perceptual and the introspective—in somewhat the way we now (it seems) think about numbers. This mind would conceive of the psychophysical link in totally a priori terms. Perhaps this is how we should think of God's mind, and God's understanding of the mind–body relation. At any rate, something pretty radical is going to be needed if we are to devise a mind that can escape the kinds of closure that make the problem insoluble for us—if I am right in my diagnosis of our difficulty. *If* the problem is only relatively insoluble, then the type of mind that can solve it is going to be very different from ours and the kinds of mind we can readily make sense of (there may, of course, be cognitive closure here too). It certainly seems to me to be at least an open question whether the problem is absolutely insoluble; I would not be surprised if it were.[17]

My position is both pessimistic and optimistic at the same time. It is pessimistic about the prospects for arriving at a constructive solution to the mind–body problem, but it is optimistic about our hopes of removing the philosophical perplexity. The central point here is that I do not think we need to do the former in order to achieve the latter. This depends on a rather special understanding of what the philosophical problem consists in. What I want to suggest is that the nature of the psychophysical connection has a full and non-mysterious explanation in a certain science, but that this science is inaccessible to us as a matter of principle. Call this explanatory scientific theory *T*: *T* is as natural and prosaic and devoid of miracle as any theory of nature; it describes the link between consciousness and the brain in a way that is no more remarkable (or alarming) than the way we now describe the link between the liver and bile.[18] According to *T*, there is nothing eerie going on in the world when an event in my visual cortex causes me to have an experience of yellow—however much it seems to *us* that there is. In other words, there is no intrinsic conceptual or metaphysical difficulty about how consciousness depends on the brain. It is not that the correct science is compelled to postulate miracles *de re*; it is rather that the correct science lies in the dark part of the world for us. We confuse our own cognitive limitations with objective eeriness. We are like a Humean mind trying to understand the physical world, or a creature without spatial concepts trying to understand the possibility of motion. This removes the philosophical

17. The kind of limitation I have identified is therefore not the kind that could be remedied simply by a large increase in general intelligence. No matter how large the frontal lobes of our biological descendants may become, they will still be stumped by the mind–body problem, so long as they form their (empirical) concepts on the basis of perception and introspection.

18. Or again, no more miraculous than the theory of evolution. Creationism is an understandable response to the theoretical problem posed by the existence of complex organisms; fortunately, we now have a theory that renders this response unnecessary, and so undermines the theism required by the creationist thesis. In the case of consciousness, the appearance of miracle might also tempt us in a 'creationist' direction, with God required to perform the alchemy necessary to transform matter into experience. Thus the mind–body problem might similarly be used to prove the existence of God (no miracle without a miracle-maker). We cannot, I think, refute this argument in the way we can the original creationist argument, namely by actually producing a non-miraculous explanatory theory, but we can refute it by arguing that such a naturalistic theory must *exist*. (It is a condition of adequacy upon any account of the mind–body relation that it avoid assuming theism.)

problem because it assures us that the entities *themselves* pose no inherent philosophical difficulty. The case is unlike, for example, the problem of how the abstract world of numbers might be intelligibly related to the world of concrete knowing subjects: here the mystery seems intrinsic to the entities, not a mere artefact of our cognitive limitations or biases in trying to understand the relation.[19] It would not be plausible to suggest that there exists a science, whose theoretical concepts we cannot grasp, which completely resolves any sense of mystery that surrounds the question how the abstract becomes an object of knowledge for us. In this case, then, eliminativism seems a live option. The *philosophical* problem about consciousness and the brain arises from a sense that we are compelled to accept that nature contains miracles—as if the merely metallic lamp of the brain could really spirit into existence the Djin of consciousness. But we do not need to accept this: we can rest secure in the knowledge that some (unknowable) property of the brain makes everything fall into place. What creates the philosophical puzzlement is the assumption that the problem must somehow be scientific but that any science *we* can come up with will represent things as utterly miraculous. And the solution is to recognize that the sense of miracle comes from us and not from the world. There is, in reality, nothing mysterious about how the brain generates consciousness. There is no *metaphysical* problem.[20]

So far that deflationary claim has been justified by a general naturalism and certain considerations about cognitive closure and the illusions it can give rise to. Now I want to marshall some reasons for thinking that consciousness is actually a rather simple natural fact; objectively, consciousness is nothing very special. We should now be comfortable with the idea that our own sense of difficulty is a fallible guide to objective complexity: what is hard for us to grasp may not be very fancy in itself. The grain of our thinking is not a mirror held up to the facts of nature.[21] In

19. See Paul Benacerraf, 'Mathematical Truth', *Journal of Philosophy*, 1973, for a statement of this problem about abstract entities. Another problem that seems to me to differ from the mind–body problem is the problem of free will. I do not believe that there is some unknowable property Q which reconciles free will with determinism (or indeterminism); rather, the concept of free will contains internal incoherencies—as the concept of consciousness does not. This is why it is much more reasonable to be an eliminativist about free will than about consciousness.

20. A test of whether a proposed solution to the mind–body problem is adequate is whether it relieves the pressure towards eliminativism. If the data can only be explained by postulating a miracle (i.e. not explained), then we must repudiate the data—this is the principle behind the impulse to deny that conscious states exist. My proposal passes this test because it allows us to resist the postulation of miracles; it interprets the eeriness as merely epistemic, though deeply so. Constructive solutions are not the only way to relieve the pressure.

21. Chomsky suggests that the very faculties of mind that make us good at some cognitive tasks may make us poor at others; see *Reflections on Language*, pp. 155–6. It seems to me possible that what makes us good at the science of the purely physical world is what skews us away from developing a science of consciousness. Our faculties bias us towards understanding matter in motion, but it is precisely this kind of understanding that is inapplicable to the mind–body problem. Perhaps, then, the price of being good at understanding matter is that we cannot understand mind. Certainly our notorious tendency to think of everything in spatial terms does not help us in understanding the mind.

particular, it may be that the extent of our understanding of facts about the mind is not commensurate with some objective estimate of their intrinsic complexity: we may be good at understanding the mind in some of its aspects but hopeless with respect to others, in a way that cuts across objective differences in what the aspects involve. Thus we are adept at understanding action in terms of the folk psychology of belief and desire, and we seem not entirely out of our depth when it comes to devising theories of language. But our understanding of how consciousness develops from the organization of matter is non-existent. But now, think of these various aspects of mind from the point of view of evolutionary biology. Surely language and the propositional attitudes are more complex and advanced evolutionary achievements than the mere possession of consciousness by a physical organism. Thus it seems that we are better at understanding some of the more complex aspects of mind than the simpler ones. Consciousness arises early in evolutionary history and is found right across the animal kingdom. In some respects it seems that the biological engineering required for consciousness is less fancy than that needed for certain kinds of complex motor behaviour. Yet we can come to understand the latter while drawing a total blank with respect to the former. Conscious states seem biologically quite primitive, comparatively speaking. So the theory *T* that explains the occurrence of consciousness in a physical world is very probably less objectively complex (by some standard) than a range of other theories that do not defy our intellects. If only we could know the psychophysical mechanism it might surprise us with its simplicity, its utter naturalness. In the manual that God consulted when he made the earth and all the beasts that dwell thereon the chapter about how to engineer consciousness from matter occurs fairly early on, well before the really difficult later chapters on mammalian reproduction and speech. It is not the *size* of the problem but its *type* that makes the mind–body problem so hard for us. This reflection should make us receptive to the idea that it is something about the tracks of our thought that prevents us from achieving a science that relates consciousness to its physical basis: the enemy lies within the gates.[22]

The position I have reached has implications for a tangle of intuitions it is natural to have regarding the mind–body relation. On the one hand, there are intuitions, pressed from Descartes to Kripke, to the effect that the relation between conscious states and bodily states is fundamentally contingent.[23] It can easily seem to us that there is no necessitation involved in the dependence of the mind on the

22. I get this phrase from Fodor, *The Modularity of Mind*, p. 121. The intended contrast is with kinds of cognitive closure that stem from exogenous factors—as, say, in astronomy. Our problem with *P* is not that it is too distant or too small or too large or too complex; rather, the very structure of our concept-forming apparatus points us away from *P*.

23. Saul Kripke, *Naming and Necessity*, Oxford, Blackwell, 1980 (see Chapter 9 of this volume). Of course, Descartes explicitly argued from (what he took to be) the essential natures of the body and mind to the contingency of their connection. If we abandon the assumption that we know these natures, then agnosticism about the modality of the connection seems the indicated conclusion.

brain. But, on the other hand, it looks absurd to try to dissociate the two entirely, to let the mind float completely free of the body. Disembodiment is a dubious possibility at best, and some kind of necessary supervenience of the mental on the physical has seemed undeniable to many. It is not my aim here to adjudicate this longstanding dispute; I want simply to offer a diagnosis of what is going on when one finds oneself assailed with this flurry of conflicting intuitions. The reason we feel the tug of contingency, pulling consciousness loose from its physical moorings, may be that we do not and cannot grasp the nature of the property that intelligibly links them. The brain has physical properties we can grasp, and variations in these correlate with changes in consciousness, but we cannot draw the veil that conceals the manner of their connection. Not grasping the nature of the connection, it strikes us as deeply contingent; we cannot make the assertion of a necessary connection intelligible to ourselves. There *may* then be a real necessary connection; it is just that it will always strike us as curiously brute and unperspicuous. We may thus, as upholders of intrinsic contingency, be the dupes of our own cognitive blindness. On the other hand, we are scarcely in a position to assert that there *is* a necessary connection between the properties of the brain we can grasp and states of consciousness, since we are so ignorant (and irremediably so) about the character of the connection. For all we know, the connection may be contingent, as access to *P* would reveal if we could have such access. The link between consciousness and property *P* is not, to be sure, contingent—virtually by definition—but we are not in a position to say exactly how *P* is related to the 'ordinary' properties of the brain. It may be necessary or it may be contingent. Thus it is that we tend to vacillate between contingency and necessity; for we lack the conceptual resources to decide the question—or to understand the answer we are inclined to give. The indicated conclusion appears to be that we can never really know whether disembodiment is metaphysically possible, or whether necessary supervenience is the case, or whether spectrum inversion could occur. For these all involve claims about the modal connections between properties of consciousness and the ordinary properties of the body and brain that we can conceptualize; and the real nature of these connections is not accessible to us. Perhaps *P* makes the relation between C-fibre firing and pain necessary or perhaps it does not: we are simply not equipped to know. We are like a Humean mind wondering whether the observed link between the temperature of a gas and its pressure (at a constant volume) is necessary or contingent. To know the answer to that you need to grasp atomic (or molecular) theory, and a Humean mind just is not up to attaining the requisite theoretical understanding. Similarly, we are constitutionally ignorant at precisely the spot where the answer exists.

I predict that many readers of this paper will find its main thesis utterly incredible, even ludicrous. Let me remark that I sympathize with such readers: the thesis is not easily digestible. But I would say this: if the thesis *is* actually true, it will still strike us as hard to believe. For the idea of an explanatory property (or set of properties) that is noumenal for us, yet is essential for the (constructive) solution of a problem we face, offends a kind of natural idealism that tends to dominate our thinking. We find it taxing to conceive of the existence of a real property; under our noses as it were, which we are built not to grasp—a property that is responsible for phenomena that we observe in the most direct way possible. This kind of realism, which brings cognitive closure so close to home, is apt to seem both an affront to our intellects and impossible to get our minds around. We try to think of this unthinkable property and understandably fail in the effort; so we rush to infer that the very supposition of such a property is nonsensical. Realism of the kind I am presupposing thus seems difficult to hold in focus, and any philosophical theory that depends upon it will also seem to rest on something systematically elusive.[24] My response to such misgivings, however, is unconcessive: the limits of our minds are just not the limits of reality. It is deplorably anthropocentric to insist that reality be constrained by what the human mind can conceive. We need to cultivate a vision of reality (a metaphysics) that makes it truly independent of our given cognitive powers, a conception that includes these powers as a proper part. It is just that, in the case of the mind–body problem, the bit of reality that systematically eludes our cognitive grasp is an aspect of our own nature. Indeed, it is an aspect that makes it possible for us to have minds at all and to think about how they are related to our bodies. This particular transcendent tract of reality happens to lie within our own heads. A deep fact about our own nature as a form of embodied consciousness is thus necessarily hidden from us. Yet there is nothing inherently eerie or bizarre about this embodiment. We are much more straightforward than we seem. Our weirdness lies in the eye of the beholder.

The answer to the question that forms my title is therefore 'No and Yes'.[25]

24. This is the kind of realism defended by Nagel in ch. VI of *The View From Nowhere*: to be is not to be conceivable by us. I would say that the mind–body problem provides a demonstration that there *are* such concept-transcending properties—not merely that there *could* be. I would also say that realism of this kind should be accepted precisely because it helps solve the mind–body problem; it is a metaphysical thesis that pulls its weight in coping with a problem that looks hopeless otherwise. There is thus nothing 'epiphenomenal' about such radical realism: the existence of a reality we cannot know can yet have intellectual significance for us.

25. Discussions with the following people have helped me work out the ideas of this paper: Anita Avramides, Jerry Katz, Emie Lepore, Michael Levin, Thomas Nagel, Galen Strawson, Peter Unger. My large debt to Nagel's work should be obvious throughout the paper: I would not have tried to face the mind–body problem down had he not first faced up to it.

Chapter 46

The why of consciousness: a non-issue for materialists

Valerie Gray Hardcastle

In my (albeit limited) experience of these matters, I have discovered that there are two sorts of people engaged in the study of consciousness. There are those who are committed naturalists; they believe that consciousness is part of the physical world, just as kings and queens and sealing wax are. It is completely nonmysterious (though it is poorly understood). They have total and absolute faith that science as it is construed today will someday explain this as it has explained the other so-called mysteries of our age.

Others are not as convinced. They might believe that consciousness is part of the natural world, but surely it is completely mysterious (and maybe not physical after all). Thus far, science has little to say about conscious experience because it has made absolutely no progress in explaining *why* we are conscious at all.

Different sceptics draw different morals from their observation. Some conclude that a scientific theory of consciousness is well-nigh impossible; others believe that it is possible, but do not expect anything of value to be immediately forthcoming; still others remain confused and are not sure what to think. (Perhaps unfairly, I put David Chalmers in the last category, as he remarks, 'Why should physical processing give rise to a rich inner life at all? It seems objectively unreasonable that it should, and yet it does.' (Chalmers, 1995, p. 201.) His intuition that consciousness is too bizarre to be real, yet still exists anyway illustrates the sentiments of the third category quite nicely. Further, as I discuss below, I think his tentative programme of redoing our basic scientific ontology reflects some basic confusions on his part.)

I have also noticed that these two camps have little to say to one another, for their differences are deep and deeply entrenched. I can't say that I expect to change that fact here. I fall into the former camp. I am a committed materialist and believe absolutely and certainly that empirical investigation is the proper approach in explaining consciousness. I also recognize that I have little convincing to say to those opposed to me. There are few useful conversations; there are even fewer converts.

In this brief essay, I hope to make clearer where the points of division lay. In the first section, I highlight the disagreements between Chalmers and me, arguing that

Valerie Gray Hardcastle, 'The Why of Consciousness: A Non-Issue for Materialists', *Journal of Consciousness Studies* 3 (1996).

consciousness is not a brute fact about the world. In section II, I point out the fundamental difference between the materialists and the sceptics, suggesting that this difference is not something that further discussion or argumentation can overcome. In the final section, I outline one view of scientific explanation and conclude that the source of conflict really turns on a difference in the rules each side has adopted in playing the game.

I

In large part, these divergent reactions turn on antecedent views about what counts as explanatory. There are those who are sold on the programme of science. They believe that the way to explain something is to build a model of it that captures at least some of its etiologic history and some of its causal powers. Their approach to explaining consciousness is the same as mine: isolate the causal influences with respect to consciousness and model them (cf. Churchland, 1984; Flanagan, 1992; Hardcastle, 1995; Hardin, 1988).

In contrast, others (e.g. Block, 1995; Chalmers, 1995; McGinn, 1991; Nagel, 1974; Searle, 1992) do not believe that science and its commitment to modelling causal interactions are necessarily the end-all and be-all of explanation. They believe that some things – many things – are explained in terms of physical causes, but qualia may not be. Isolating the causal relations associated with conscious phenomena would simply miss the boat, for there is no way that doing that ever captures the qualitative aspects of awareness. What the naturalists might do is illustrate *when* we are conscious, but that won't explain the *why* of consciousness. The naturalists would not have explained why it is neuronal oscillations (cf. Crick and Koch, 1990), or the activation of episodic memory (cf. Hardcastle, 1995), or an executive processor (cf. Baars, 1988), or whatever, should have a qualitative aspect, and until they do that, they cannot claim to have done anything particularly interesting with consciousness.

To them, I have little to say in defence of naturalism, for I think nothing that I as an already committed naturalist could say would suffice, for we don't agree on the terms of the argument in the first place. Nevertheless, I shall try to say something, if for no other reason than to make the points of disagreement clearer so that informed buyers can chose all the more wisely. Let me sketch in particular the point of conflict between Chalmers and me.

Let us assume a prior and fundamental commitment to materialism. I say that if we are materialists, then we have to believe that consciousness is something physical. Presumably it is something in the brain. If we believe this and we want to know what consciousness is exactly, then we need to isolate the components of the brain or of brain activity that are necessary and sufficient for consciousness. If I understand Chalmers' taxonomy of research programmes correctly, then I am advocating following option five: 'isolate the substrate of experience'. Indeed, it is my contention that pointing out the relevant brain activity conjoined with explaining the structure of experience (his option four) and some functional story about what being conscious buys us biologically (not one of Chalmers' options) would be a complete theory of consciousness. Let us pretend though that I have only completed the first step in this programme and have isolated the substrate of experience. Call this component of the brain C.

Chalmers would reply that though I might have been successful in isolating the causal etiology of consciousness, I have not explained why it is that C should be conscious. Why this? For that matter, why anything? Part of a good explanation, he maintains, is making the identity statement (or whatever) intelligible, plausible, reasonable. I have not done that. Hence, I have not explained the most basic, most puzzling, most difficult question of consciousness. I haven't removed the curiousness of the connection between mind and body. I haven't closed the explanatory gap.

How should I respond? He is, of course, exactly right: scientific theories of consciousness won't explain the weirdness of consciousness to those who find the identity weird. One possible move is to claim that consciousness just being C (or whatever theory you happen to believe) is just a brute fact about the world. That is just the way our universe works. At times, I am sure, it appears that this is what the naturalists are assuming, especially when they dismiss out of hand those overcome by the eeriness of consciousness. This, too, is what Chalmers wants to do with his dual aspect theory: phenomenal qualities are just part and parcel of information. No further explanation needed.

However, this response is too facile. It is true that we accept brute facts about our universe. We believe in things like gravitational attraction and the electromagnetic forces without question. We waste little energy wondering why our universe contains gravity. It just does, and we reason from there. On the other hand, there are other facts about the world that we do not accept as brute. We feel perfectly comfortable expecting an answer to why water is wet. That is not a brute fact. We explain the liquidity of water by appeal to other facts about the world, the molecular structure of water and its concomitant microphysical properties, for example. And these facts are explained in turn by other facts, such as the quantum mechanical structure of the world. Now *these* might be brute facts, but so it goes. (At least this is one popular and rosy view of scientific unity. I shan't defend that here.)

Notice two things. First, the facts we accept as brute are few and basic. Essentially, we accept the most fundamental elements and relations of the universe as given. The rest then depend upon these key ingredients in some fashion. Second, and following from the first observation, it seems highly unlikely that some relatively chauvinistic *biological* fact should ever be brute. For those facts turn on the more fundamental items in the universe. Hence, if one is to claim that consciousness being C is simply a brute fact about the universe, then one is *prima facie* operating with a perverse metaphysics.

Chalmers tries to overcome the latter difficulty by denying that consciousness is biological. However, he has no reason to claim this except that it saves his theory. Considerations of structural coherence and organizational invariance aren't telling because they are generally taken to support material identity. That is, if you find structural isomorphisms between our perceptions and twitches in the brain, then that is taken to be good reason to think that the mind is nothing more than activity in the brain. (What other sort of evidence could you use?) And if you hypothesize that the same 'fine-grained' functional organization supports the same phenomenal experiences, then you are advocating some sort of materialistic functional theory; otherwise the perceptions can diverge even though the functional organization remains the same (cf. Shoemaker, 1975; 1981; see also Lycan, 1987).[1]

The only consideration he brings to bear is the putative 'elegance' of a dual aspect theory. However, when we weigh a suggestion's simplicity and elegance against countervailing data, the data have to win. We already know that not all information has a phenomenal edge to it, insofar as we know quite a bit of our information processing is carried out *un*consciously. Documenting subliminal effects, implicit priming, and repressed but effective memories are all cottage industries in psychology, and have been since Freud.[2] Chalmers is either going to have to deny some of the most robust psychological results we have and claim that no information processing is occurring in those cases, or do a 'bait-and-switch' and claim that, contrary to introspective verbal reports, we are conscious of all of those things (we just don't realize it). Neither option is plausible. Chalmers gives us no counter-examples to the mass of psychological evidence, and denying that first person viewpoints can tell us whether we are conscious denies exactly what Chalmers wants to defend. Hence, we are left with the *prima facie* plausible claim that for all cases of consciousness of which we are aware, consciousness is biological.

In any event, I don't want to make the claim consciousness is brute. So what do I say if I think that consciousness is a biological phenomenon?[3] How do I make my identification of consciousness with some neural activity intelligible to those who find it mysterious? My answer is that I don't. The 'solution' to this vexing difficulty, such as it is, is all a matter of attitude. That is, the problem itself depends on the spirit in which we approach an examination of consciousness.

1. I find it strange (though not inconsistent) that in the first portion of the paper, Chalmers uses the putative imaginability of inverted qualia as an argument against what he calls 'reductionism' (though to me it is simply a good old fashioned identity theory), yet in discussing constraints on possible theories he argues against the possibility of inverted qualia in support of his proto-theory. He should recognize that if the fine-grainedness of his functional organization is fine-grained enough, then we would be discussing the functional organization of neurons (or action potentials, IPSPs, EPSPs, or what have you), which is all one needs to muster a claim for mind-brain identity.
2. I take it that these facts are well known. I summarize quite a bit of this research in Hardcastle (1995). Aside from Freud, other important players include Endel Tulving, George Mandler, Anthony Marcel and Daniel Schacter.
3. Note that claiming that consciousness is biological does not mean that we could not create consciousness artificially. Life is a biological phenomenon too, but that doesn't rule out creating life in test-tubes.

II

Let us return to the example of water being wet. Consider the following exchange. A water-mysterian wonders why water has this peculiar property. She inquires and you give an explanation of the molecular composition of water and a brief story about the connection between micro-chemical properties and macro-phenomena. Ah, she says, I am a materialist, so I am convinced that you have properly correlated water with its underlying molecular composition. I also have no reason to doubt that your story about the macro-effects of chemical properties to be wrong. But I still am not satisfied, for you have left off in your explanation what I find most puzzling. Why *is* water H_2O? Why couldn't it be XYZ? Why couldn't it have some other radically different chemical story behind it? I can imagine a possible world in which water has all the macro-properties that it has now, but is not composed of H_2O.

Of course, people like Kripke have a ready response to the water-mysterians. 'Water = H_2O' is an identity statement. Hence, you can't really imagine possible worlds in which water is not H_2O because you aren't imagining *water* in those cases (or, you aren't *imagining* properly). As Chalmers would claim, it is a *conceptual truth* about water that it is H_2O. But, to the sceptical and unconvinced, to those who insist that they can imagine honest-to-goodness water not being H_2O, what *can* one say? I think nothing. Water-mysterians are antecedently convinced of the mysteriousness of water and no amount of scientific data is going to change that perspective. Either you already believe that science is going to give you a correct identity statement, or you don't and you think that there is always going to be something left over, the wateriness of water.

I doubt there are any such mysterians, so perhaps this is a silly example. Let us now turn to life-mysterians. Consider the following exchange. A life-mysterian wonders why living things have the peculiar property of being alive. She inquires and you give a just-so story about the origin of replicating molecules in primordial soup and wave your hands in the direction of increasing complexity. Ah, she says, I am an evolutionist, so I am convinced that you have properly correlated the history of living things with their underlying molecular composition. I also have no reason to doubt that your story about increasing complexity to be wrong. But I still am not satisfied, for you have left off in your explanation what I find most puzzling, the *aliveness* of life. Why couldn't that be a soul? Why couldn't it have some other radically different evolutionary story behind it, namely, one with God in it? I can imagine a possible world in which living things have all the macro-properties that they have now, but are not comprised of DNA or RNA.

Of course, as Chalmers indicates, we too have a ready response to the life-mysterians. We presume that there is some sort of identity statement for biological life. (Of course, we don't actually have one yet, but for those of us who are not life-mysterians, we feel certain that one is in the offing.) Hence, they can't really imagine possible worlds in which life is not whatever we ultimately discover it to be because they aren't imagining *life* in those cases (or, they aren't *imagining* properly). But, that aside, what *can* we say to those who insist that they can imagine life as requiring an animator? I think nothing. Just getting on with the biological enterprise is perhaps appropriate. Life-mysterians are antecedently convinced of the mysteriousness of life and no amount of scientific data is going to change that perspective. Either you already believe that science is going to give you a correct identity statement, or you don't and you think that there is always going to be something left over, the aliveness of living things.

So what about Chalmers and other consciousness-mysterians? They are no different. They are antecedently convinced of the mysteriousness of consciousness and no amount of scientific data is going to change that perspective. Either you already believe that science is going to give you a correct identity statement, or you don't and you think that there is always going to be something left over, the phenomenal aspects of conscious experience. 'Experience . . . is not *entailed* by the physical.' Chalmers wants to know: 'Why is the performance of these [cognitive] functions *accompanied* by experience?' (p. 203; emphasis mine). Though he does believe that 'experience *arises* one way or another from brain processes,' he thinks that it is a 'conceptual point' that consciousness is not identical to C.

In some sense, of course, I have a ready response to the consciousness-mysterians. Like the water-mysterian and the life-mysterian, consciousness-mysterians need to alter their concepts. To put it bluntly: their failure to appreciate the world as it really is cuts no ice with science. Their ideas are at fault, not the scientific method. Materialists presume that there is some sort of identity statement for consciousness. (Of course, we don't actually have one yet, but for those of us who are not consciousness-mysterians, we feel certain that one is in the offing.) Hence, the sceptics can't really imagine possible worlds in which consciousness is not whatever we ultimately discover it to be because they aren't imagining *consciousness* in those cases (or, they aren't *imagining* properly). But nevertheless, what *can* I say to those who insist that they can imagine consciousness as beyond science's current explanatory capacities? I think nothing, for they can claim that I am conceptually confused as well. Agreeing to disagree is perhaps appropriate.

I suppose we have reached a stand-off of sorts. I say materialism and mechanism entail an identity statement for consciousness, just as we get one for water and we expect one for life. Consciousness is no more mysterious to me than the wetness of water or the aliveness of life. That is to say, I find all of the phenomena interestingly weird, and the identity statements that science produces marvelously curious. But all are on a par. The sceptics do not share my intuitions. So be it. However, I feel no more inclined to try to convince them otherwise than I do trying to convince the religious that souls don't exist. I recognize hopeless projects. Our antecedent intuitions simply diverge too much to engage in a productive dialogue.

III

But perhaps again I am not being fair. The reason water-mysterianism seems implausible is that we are able to embed our understanding of water and H_2O in the sophisticated larger framework of molecular chemistry and sub-atomic physics. We just know an awful lot about how atoms and molecules interact with one another and the corresponding micro- and macro-properties. Life-mysterianism seems implausible to those for whom it seems implausible for similar reasons. We don't know as much about biological history as we do about molecular chemistry, but we do know enough at least to gesture toward a suitable framework in which to embed a decomposition of life. But consciousness might be different. We have far, far to go before we can claim to understand either cognitive or brain processes with any surety. Perhaps there just isn't a suitable larger framework in which to embed an understanding of consciousness; hence, any scientific model we try to construct will appear strained and stilted at best. And perhaps this is what really drives the explanatory gap – we don't yet know what we are talking about when we claim that consciousness is a natural phenomenon.

Suppose this argument is correct (though I am not sure that it is, for reasons I explain below). What follows from it? It can't be that a theory of consciousness is not possible, nor even that consciousness is fundamentally odd. Rather, all we can say is that we have to wait and see what else we learn about the mind and brain before a decomposition and localization of consciousness can be intuitively satisfying. Consciousness might very well be C, but our informed intuitions lag behind.

(An aside: Can we *really* say what would happen if my neural circuits are replaced by silicon isomorphs? Maybe it is reasonable to think that your experiences would not be affected. But, in the same vein, it is reasonable to believe that the world is Euclidean – though it isn't, of course – and it used to be reasonable to burn witches at the stake – though it is no longer. What seems reasonable at first blush often isn't once the parameters of the problem are made sufficiently clear; moreover, our intuitions change as our perspective on the world changes. At present, we simply don't know enough about the explanatory currency of the brain to hypothesize *intelligently* about what will happen if we push on it in various ways. Intuition pumps only work if we have robust and well-founded intuitions in the first place.)

All we can say at this point is that an antecedent commitment to materialism means that an understanding of consciousness will someday be embedded in some larger mind–brain framework. We are just going to have to wait until that time before our intuitions concerning what counts as a satisfactory identification for phenomenal experience will be useful (or even usable).

Nevertheless, though there is a great deal we don't know about the mind and the brain, there is still a lot that we do. Indeed, within the broader framework of currently accepted psychological and neurophysiological theories, we have found striking parallels between our phenomenal experiences and activities in the brain.

Chalmers points to some in his paper, others are more basic. E.g. removing area MT is correlated with phenomenal blindness; ablations in various regions of cortex are correlated with inabilities to perceive shapes, colours, motion, objects; lesions surrounding the hippocampus are correlated with the loss of episodic memory.[4] Or, for less invasive results, consider what happens when various chemicals are added to our brains. We decrease pain, increase sensitivity, induce hallucinations, alter moods, and so on. Data such as these should (someday) allow us to locate conscious experiences both within our information processing stream and within the head.

Perhaps more data, better constructed scientific models, and more agreement among the scientists themselves about the details, would alter the intuitions of the sceptics, but I doubt it. For the difference between someone like Chalmers and me is not in the details; it is in how we understand the project of explaining consciousness itself. It is a difference in how we think of scientific inquiry and what we think explanations of consciousness are supposed to do.

Explanations are social creatures. They are designed for particular audiences asking particular questions within a particular historically determined framework. (See van Fraassen, 1980, for more discussion of this point.) Materialists are trying to explain to each other what consciousness is within current scientific frameworks. Their explanations are designed for them. If you don't antecedently buy into this project, including its biases, history, context, central questions, possible answers, and relevant actors, then a naturalist's explanation probably won't satisfy you. It shouldn't. But that is not the fault of the explanation, nor is it the fault of the materialists. If you don't accept the rules, the game won't make any sense. If you do accept the rules, then the explanations will follow because they are designed for you as a member of the relevant community. (This is not to say that you will *agree* with explanations, just that they will seem to be of the right sort of thing required for an answer.) Who's in and who's out is a matter of antecedent self-selection. I opt in; the sceptics opt out. Because we don't agree on the rules, my explanations don't make sense to them, and their explanations don't make sense to me.

Explanation for the cognitive and biological sciences just *is* a matter of uncovering the appropriate parallels between the phenomena and the physical system. Huntington's chorea is explained by a disruption in the GABA-ergic loop. Equilibrium in neurons is explained in terms of the influx and efflux of ions across the cell membrane. Perceptual binding is explained (maybe) in terms of 40 Hz neuronal oscillations. The withdrawal reflex in *Aplysia* is explained in terms of patterns of activation across the motor system. Echolocation is explained in terms of

4. I note that in each of these cases, there is evidence that such patients still process at least some of the information unconsciously. For example, prosopagnosics claim that they can no longer recognize faces upon visual inspection. However, their galvanic skin response changes in the presence of caretakers or loved ones in a manner consistent with their in fact knowing and recognizing the people. For a review of this literature, see Hardcastle (1995).

deformed tensor networks. So: find the parallels between brain activity and phenomenal experience and you will have found a naturalistic account of consciousness.

Denying the project and devising different criteria for explanation is a perfectly legitimate move to make, of course. There is always room for more. Winning converts though is something else. I wish Chalmers well in that enterprise, for how to do that truly is the gap that remains.

References

Baars, B.J. (1988), *A Cognitive Theory of Consciousness* (Cambridge: Cambridge University Press).

Block, N. (1995), 'On a confusion about a function of consciousness', *Behavioral and Brain Sciences*, **18** (2), pp. 227–47.

Chalmers, D.J. (1995), 'Facing up to the problem of consciousness', *Journal of Consciousness Studies*, **2** (3), pp. 200–19 (Chapter 35 of this volume).

Churchland, P.M. (1984), *Matter and Consciousness* (Cambridge, MA: The MIT Press).

Crick, F. and Koch, C. (1990), 'Toward a Neurobiological Theory of Consciousness', *Seminars in the Neurosciences*, **2**, pp. 263–75.

Flanagan, O. (1992), *Consciousness Reconsidered* (Cambridge, MA: The MIT Press).

Hardcastle, V.G. (1995), *Locating Consciousness* (Amsterdam and Philadelphia: John Benjamins).

Hardin, C.L. (1988), *Color for Philosophers: Unweaving the Rainbow* (New York: Hackett).

Lycan, W.G. (1987), *Consciousness* (Cambridge, MA: The MIT Press).

McGinn, C. (1991), *The Problem of Consciousness* (Oxford: Blackwell).

Nagel, T. (1974), 'What is It Like to be a Bat?' *Philosophical Review*, **83**, pp. 435–50 (Chapter 29 of this volume).

Searle, J. (1992), *The Rediscovery of Mind* (Cambridge, MA: The MIT Press).

Shoemaker, S. (1975), 'Functionalism and Qualia', *Philosophical Studies*, **27**, pp. 291–315.

Shoemaker, S. (1981), 'Absent qualia are not possible—A reply to Block,' *Philosophical Review*, **90**, pp. 581–99.

van Fraassen, B. (1980), *The Scientific Image* (Cambridge, MA: The MIT Press).

Questions

1. What sorts of consideration might lead us to conclude that we could never be in a position to understand the nature of conscious experience and its relation to material goings-on?
2. Imagine someone—a philosopher, no doubt—arguing that an understanding of deep truths about the mind would require a radically different conceptual system. Such a philosopher might point out that Newton's discovery of explanations of the motions of material bodies required that he first invent the Calculus. Are the cases comparable? Do you know of other cases in the history of science in which an advance in understanding required a conceptual revolution?
3. Compare McGinn's argument with the line taken by Nagel in Chapter 29. Should McGinn be read as an extending Nagel's thesis or as making a separate point?
4. What is it to 'know what it is like' to see red or taste an anchovy? Could you ever know what an experience was like without actually having the experience?
5. What would it take to close the 'explanatory gap'?
6. Jackson's Mary is confined to a colorless environment that prevents her from visually experiencing colored objects. Suppose Mary has herself anesthetized and a colleague implants electrodes in Mary's brain. When Mary awakes, she can activate these electrodes by pressing a button. When activated, the electrodes stimulate regions of Mary's visual cortex in just the way a normal perceiver's visual cortex would be stimulated were that perceiver visually experiencing something red. After recovering from the anesthetic, Mary presses the button and the electrodes stimulate her visual cortex. Does Mary now know what it is like to experience red? Would her knowing what it is like under these circumstances create a problem for Jackson's thesis?
7. Some philosophers have argued that Mary, on first experiencing red, does not acquire knowledge of any new facts. Mary knows something she did not know before, but the knowledge in question is the sort you might have in knowing *how* to knot a bow tie or in knowing *how* to bowl a googly, not factual knowledge. Is this so? Would such considerations affect the argument?
8. In Chapter 35, David Chalmers speaks of the 'hard problem' of consciousness. Valerie Gray Hardcastle regards consciousness as a 'non-issue' for materialists. Whom should we believe—and why?
9. Should philosophers get out of the consciousness business and leave it to the psychologists and neuroscientists?
10. The readings thus far have remained largely silent about extrasensory perception, telekinesis, and similar topics. Is this a mistake? Might research into such things provide much-needed additional understanding of the mind and its relation to material bodies?

Suggested readings

Countless discussions of and responses to Jackson's 'knowledge argument' (Chapter 43) have appeared since it was published in 1984. According to Jackson, color-deprived Mary knows all the physical facts, but, lacking certain conscious experiences, fails to know certain facts; therefore, the physical facts are not all the facts. For discussion, see Bigelow and Pargetter (1990), Foss (1989), Gertler (1999), Lewis (1983: 130–2) and Lewis (1988). See also Perry (2001). Jackson's (1986) is a response to Churchland's (1985) attack on the argument. Alter's (2001) entry on the knowledge argument in the on-line *Field Guide to the Philosophy of Mind* includes a useful annotated bibliography, as does Nida-Rümelin's discussion of Jackson in the *Stanford Encyclopedia of Philosophy.* Chalmers's (2001) on-line bibliography provides dozens of entries on the knowledge argument. Ironically, Jackson himself now rejects the argument; see Jackson's (1995) 'Postscript', and (1998).

Although Locke may have been the first to identify the 'explanatory gap', contemporary discussion stems from Levine's Chapter 44; see also Levine (1993). Discussions include Bieri (1995), Block and Stalnaker (1999), Chalmers and Jackson (2001), Ellis and Newton (1998), Hardin (1987, 1992), Levin (1991), Papineau (1998), Price (1996), and Tye (1999). Chalmers's above-mentioned on-line bibliography contains a number of entries on the explanatory gap. Readers unfamiliar with the issues take note: much of what has been written on the issue is technical, difficult, and inconclusive.

The knowledge argument

Alter, T. (2001), 'Knowledge Argument' In Nani (2001): <http://host.uniroma3.it/progetti/kant/field/ka.html>.

Bigelow, J., and Pargetter, R. (1990), 'Acquaintance with Qualia', *Theoria* 61: 129–47.

Chalmers, D. J. (2001), *Contemporary Philosophy of Mind: An Annotated Bibliography* <http://www.u.arizona.edu/~chalmers/biblio.html> Tucson, AZ: University of Arizona.

Churchland, P. M. (1985), 'Reduction, Qualia, and the Direct Introspection of Brain States', *Journal of Philosophy* 82: 8–28.

Foss, J. (1989), 'On the Logic of What It Is Like to be a Conscious Subject', *Australasian Journal of Philosophy* 67: 305–20.

Gertler, B. (1999), 'A Defense of the Knowledge Argument', *Philosophical Studies* 93: 317–36.

Jackson, F. (1986), 'What Mary Didn't Know', *Journal of Philosophy* 83: 291–95.

——(1995), 'Postscript to What Mary Didn't Know'. In Moser and Trout (1995): 184–89.

——(1998), *From Metaphysics to Ethics: A Defense of Conceptual Analysis.* Oxford: Clarendon Press.

Lewis, D. K. (1983), *Philosophical Papers*, vol. 1. New York: Oxford University Press.

——(1988), 'What Experience Teaches', *Proceedings of the Russellian Society* (University of Sydney) 13: 29–57. Reprinted in Lewis 1999: 262–90.

——(1999), *Papers in Metaphysics and Epistemology.* Cambridge: Cambridge University Press.

Moser, P. K., and J. D. Trout, eds. (1995), *Contemporary Materialism: A Reader.* London: Routledge.

Nani, M., ed. (2001), *A Field Guide to the Philosophy of Mind.* <http://host.uniroma3.it/progetti/kant/field/> Rome: University of Rome 3.

Nida-Rümelin, M. (2002), 'Qualia: The Knowledge Argument'. In Zalta (2002): <http://plato.stanford.edu/entries/qualia-knowledge/>.

Perry, J. (2001), *Knowledge, Possibility, and Consciousness.* Cambridge, MA: MIT Press.

Zalta, E. N., ed. (2002), *The Stanford Encyclopedia of Philosophy.* <http://plato.stanford.edu/> Stanford, CA: Metaphysics Research Lab, Center for the Study of Language and Information.

The explanatory gap

Beckermann, A., H. Flohr, and J. Kim, eds. (1992), *Emergence or Reduction? Essays on the Prospects of Nonreductive Physicalism.* Berlin: W. de Gruyter.

Bieri, P. (1995), 'Why is Consciousness Puzzling?' In Metzinger 1995: 45–60.

Block, N. J., and R. Stalnaker (1999), 'Conceptual Analysis, Dualism, and the Explanatory Gap', *Philosophical Review* 108: 1–46.

——O. Flanagan, and G. Güzeldere, eds. (1997), *The Nature of Consciousness: Philosophical Debates.* Cambridge, MA: MIT Press.

Chalmers, D. J., and F. Jackson (2001), 'Conceptual Analysis and Reductive Explanation', *Philosophical Review* 110: 315–60.

Davies, M., and G. Humphreys, eds. (1993), *Consciousness: Psychological and Philosophical Essays.* Oxford: Basil Blackwell.

Ellis, R. D., and N. Newton (1998), 'Three Paradoxes of Phenomenal Consciousness: Bridging the Explanatory Gap', *Journal of Consciousness Studies* 5: 419–42.

Hardin, C. L. (1987), 'Qualia and Materialism: Closing the Explanatory Gap', *Philosophy and Phenomenological Research* 48: 281–98.

——(1992), 'Physiology, Phenomenology, and Spinoza's True Colors'. In Beckermann et al. 1992: 201–19.

Levin, J. (1991), 'Analytic Functionalism and the Reduction of Phenomenal States', *Philosophical Studies* 61: 211–38.

Levine, J. (1993), 'On Leaving out What it's Like'. In Davies and Humphreys 1993: 121–36. Reprinted in Block et al. 1997: 543–55

Metzinger, T., ed. (1995), *Conscious Experience.* Paderborn: Schöningh.

Papineau, D. (1998), 'Mind the Gap', *Philosophical Perspectives* 12: 373–89.

Price, M. C. (1996), 'Should We Expect to Feel as if We Understand Consciousness?' *Journal of Consciousness Studies* 3: 303–12.

Tye, M. (1999), 'Phenomenal Consciousness: The Explanatory Gap as a Cognitive Illusion', *Mind* 108: 705–25.

Part XII

Challenges to contemporary materialism

Introduction

Most of the readings in this volume follow a trend in contemporary philosophy toward materialism, the view that all that exists are material objects, their states, properties, and relations. This is not a very precise characterization. Are fields, for instance, material objects (or are fields states of or relations among material objects)? What of quarks? Quarks are not very like traditional billiard-ball models of material objects. Whatever quarks and fields are, we should count them as material entities. Materialists hold that everything that exists is made up exclusively of these.

Although contemporary philosophy of mind has an important materialist component, only a minority of philosophers of mind would describe themselves as flat-out materialists. Belief that consciousness or intentionality are *grounded* in material states and processes is one thing; belief that mentality is *reducible* to material goings-on is another matter. Jeffrey Poland speaks for many philosophers when he says

> It should be understood that the primacy of physics in ontological matters does not mean that everything is an element of a strictly physical ontology . . . physicalism . . . allows for non-physical objects, properties, and relations. The primacy of the physical ontology is that it grounds a structure that contains everything, not that it includes everything. . . . [W]ith regard to ontological matters, physicalism should not be equated with the identity theory in any of its forms. . . . I prefer the idea of a hierarchically structured system of objects grounded in a physical basis by a relation of *realization* to the idea that all objects are token identical to physical objects. (Poland 1994: 18)

The idea is that, although minds in some way *depend on* material bodies—you could not eliminate the bodies and keep the minds—minds, or mental properties, are nevertheless importantly distinct from material objects and properties. The dependence relation here is mysterious, but philosophers of mind take comfort in what they see as a widespread phenomenon: in general, objects and properties that are investigated by the special sciences (meteorology, biology, anthropology, paleontology, geology, anatomy, and the like) enjoy the same status. If you threw out 'higher-level' mental states or properties solely on the grounds that they depend in a mysterious way on lower-level material phenomena, you would have to toss out all the special sciences as well. In any case, the respect in which higher levels depend on lower levels does not seem so mysterious once you grow accustomed to it.

You need not be impressed by such arguments (indeed I have expressed doubts about them elsewhere in this volume; see the introductions to Parts III, IX, and X). You should know, however, that 'nonreductive materialism' is a dominant view in the philosophy of mind today. Partisans of nonreductive materialism face competition from, on the one hand, unapologetic materialists, and, on the other hand, out-and-out dualists and, at the end of the spectrum furthest from materialism, idealists. I have provided a sampling of these latter possibilities in this final part.

Descartes and Newton

Descartes defended a dualism of substances. Some objects, he thought, are material. These are the extended objects, occupiers of regions of space. Every property of a material object is a 'mode' of extension: a way of being extended. Being square is a way of being extended: the square way. Being tall (or being 2 meters tall) is another way of being extended: the tall (or 2-meter) way. Accelerating at a particular rate is yet another way of being extended. And so on for all the properties of material bodies. (You might wonder whether we can in fact reduce all properties of material bodies to modes of extension. Mass, for instance, does not seem so reducible.) Mental substances, by contrast, are non-extended, 'thinking' entities. All of their properties are modes of thought. A mental substance—a self—might perceive a tower, fear death, feel pain, or believe in God. All these are modes of thought, ways of thinking in Descartes's somewhat liberal characterization of what counts as thinking.

Substance dualism as articulated by Descartes was in trouble right out of the gate. Descartes spent much of his time in correspondence defending the thesis that, although minds and bodies are distinct substances with no properties in common, they could nevertheless causally interact. The case was next to impossible to make out in a period in which causal interaction among material bodies was thought to be the result of material particles colliding in space. This is the 'impact' model of causation. If you think that material bodies are affected only by impact, then causation by a non-material body is a non-starter. (In fact, Descartes's situation was even worse than this. Descartes embraced a 'pipeline' view of causation: nothing can be in an effect that is not present in its cause. How could this work in cases of mental–physical causation in which causes and effects share no properties?)

Newton made life more difficult for those who wanted to see causal relations as grounded in impacts among the basic particles. Newton's particles affect one another *at a distance*. Planets are held in their orbits, not by material tethers but by forces acting instantaneously over empty space. If material bodies can affect one another without touching, why not allow that nonspatial minds could affect material bodies as well?

Philosophers seeking an account of mind–body interaction were reluctant to avail themselves of Newton's relaxed attitude toward action at a distance. This was in part owing to the sense that apparent action at a distance would eventually be explained in some mechanistically satisfying way. And so it has been with the notion that gravity is explicable by the power of material bodies to warp space-time. A planet in orbit around the sun moves in what appears to the planet to be a straight line. It is hard, although perhaps not impossible, to imagine minds controlling material particles indirectly by altering the grain of space-time.

Quantum action at a distance

Although Newtonian action at a distance is a relic of the past, a new and equally puzzling phenomenon has cropped up in the midst of quantum theory. The phenomenon in question was revealed by a theoretical physicist, John Bell (1964; see also Albert 1992). Bell's astonishing result (now called Bell's Theorem), showed that quantum theory implies that, in certain cases of paired particles (paired electrons, for instance), an operation affecting one of the particles affects its partner, although the two are spatially separated and otherwise causally isolated. Action at a distance!

By itself, this result offers no consolation to a Cartesian dualist. An action in one place has a result elsewhere, but the initial action is an occurrence in space and time. More significantly, the action in question involves no transmission of 'information' of the sort that would have to occur in cases of genuine mind–body causation. What Bell's Theorem does is loosen up our thinking and nudge us away from the simple billiard ball model of causation that so often governs the way we picture causal interaction. When this is combined with a certain influential interpretation of quantum theory, dualism can start to seem, not merely, possible, but positively commonsensical!

To understand what all this is about, you need first to understand that quantum theory is an impressive mathematical edifice with an unbeatable track record. It is sometimes said that quantum theory has survived more concentrated attempts at disproof that any other theory in the history of science. Most theories, including Newton's, fail to square with the data in many ways. Scientists explain away these anomalies by appealing to 'interference' of uncontrolled factors, experimental error, and inaccuracies stemming from inadequate instrumentation. When quantum theory has been put to rigorous test, however, it has invariably been on target. To some physicists, including Einstein, many predictions implied by quantum theory were too paradoxical to be taken seriously. (One of these is the Bell result.) As it happens, these seemingly paradoxical predictions have, without exception, been repeatedly borne out in experiment.

What we have in quantum theory is a mathematically winsome explanatory edifice with remarkable predictive power. What we lack is an agreed-upon *interpretation* of the theory: a sense of what the world must be like if the theory is true. As matters now stand, there is scant agreement as to what quantum theory tells us about the world. It is not that there are no interpretations. On the contrary, physicists have put in play at least a half-dozen serious contenders. None of these has achieved anything close to universal acceptance, however. Each turns the quantum world into a seemingly bizarre place. Perhaps the world is one of these bizarre ways. Perhaps some wholly new way of thinking is called for. Or perhaps (shades of McGinn) the human mind is simply unequipped to grasp the fundamental truths of our situation.

I propose to bracket this possibility here. As far as I can tell, we are in no position to ascertain whether we are or are not inherently limited in what we can know about the world and our place in it. (For a contrasting opinion, see Penrose 1989.) Let us at least make an attempt to obtain a better view of the territory.

The quantum world

Before pressing on with quantum theory, one widely misunderstood point must be addressed. It is sometimes suggested that quantum theory governs only the behavior of very small things—like electrons. If quantum theory tells us that these things will behave strangely, that should not concern us. The behavior of very small things 'averages out' in the familiar observable world of medium-sized objects. For the observable world, Newton works well enough; we can leave the paradoxes of quantum theory to those who study minutiae.

Attractive as these sentiments might be, they misrepresent the situation. If quantum theory is true, as it certainly seems to be, it governs you and me, the planet, and the galaxies equally. The theory tells us that a physicist who observes an electron go into a particular quantum state himself goes into that state, and so does everything in the physicist's world. Quantum effects are in this sense 'global'. There is no prospect of insulating the everyday world from the quantum world.

How does this bear on issues in the philosophy of mind? And, in particular, how might it represent a challenge to materialism? Consider one influential interpretation of quantum theory, the so-called Copenhagen interpretation. (The Copenhagen interpretation is so called because of its association with Neils Bohr, the physicist, much of whose work was conducted in Copenhagen.) On this interpretation the observer makes a difference to what is observed. Schrödinger's famous cat provides a colorful illustration of the point. Imagine a box containing a mechanism that, when triggered, will release cyanide gas. The trigger is attached to a device that monitors the radioactive decay of a radium atom. If the atom decays during a particular period of time, the mechanism is triggered and the gas released.

Now we place a cat, Tibbles, in the box and seal it shut. After a period of time we ask: is Tibbles alive or dead? Tibbles, it seems, must be one or the other. (We can assume that the cyanide is instantly lethal.) What quantum theory tells us (on the Copenhagen interpretation), however, is that the system consisting of the radium atom, the triggering mechanism, the cyanide, and Tibbles, are in a 'superposition' of states. In some of these states, the atom has decayed and Tibbles is dead; in others the atom has failed to decay and Tibbles is alive. It is not until the system is *observed* that this superposition of states 'collapses' into a single definite state.

The point is not that, until we open the box, we cannot *know* the state of the system. That, of course, is true, but wholly unremarkable. The point, rather, is that there is no fact of the matter as to what state the system is in until it is observed: our observation of it *makes it the case* that it is in the particular state we observe it to be in. You might try to get around this odd outcome by placing a clock and a camera inside the box. The camera will snap a photo when, and only when, the cyanide is released. Before we open the box, we know that we shall discover that the camera either has or has not snapped a photo. Suppose we open the box and discover that Tibbles is dead, and the camera has snapped a photo showing that the cyanide was released exactly five minutes before we elected to open the box.

Unfortunately, none of this helps. The camera is just an additional part of the quantum system. Until we open the box, the camera and its film, along with everything else in the box, is in a superposition of states. In some of these states the camera's film includes an image of a defunct Tibbles, in some of them it does not. All of these states are equally 'real'. Only when we open the box and observe for ourselves, do the states 'collapse' into a single, definite state.

What you should note is that the world, as depicted by this interpretation of the quantum theory exhibits a perplexing bifurcated character. On the one hand, we have the material systems—the particles, planets, and galaxies—and on the other hand we have conscious observers. The material world, the ultimate quantum system, seems to require for its definiteness a conscious observer! The world is in a superposition of states until it is observed. (Sometimes, for maximum paradoxical effect, this is said to imply that the Big Bang depends for its existence on our having observed subsequent evidence for it!) If any of this is so, quantum theory seems to place minds outside the material world. If minds were themselves parts of the material world, they would be, like the camera in Tibble's box, merely parts of the whole system, hence themselves in a superposition of states.

Philosophers and physicists have had a great deal to say about all this, of course. I do not want to leave you with the impression that 'physics tells us' that the world is, in some peculiar way, mind dependent. You should know, however, that the Copenhagen interpretation of the quantum theory is, and has been, taken very seriously by physicists. In part this is because the alternatives seem equally shocking in their own distinctive ways. (A sensible non-technical discussion of alternative interpretations can be found in Herbert 1985.) In so far as a scientist finds the Copenhagen interpretation compelling, that scientist will be embracing a strongly dualistic conception of reality. Not every argument for dualism is a philosophical argument.

Idealism

John Foster moves us beyond dualism, following Berkeley all the way to idealism. If you think of materialism as the view that everything that exists is a material thing (perhaps excluding numbers, sets, and other 'abstract entities'), idealism is the converse: all that exists is *im*material, mental. Both materialism and idealism have a reductionist flavor. For the materialist, minds and their contents are reduced to material objects and ways material objects are organized. For an idealist, reduction goes the other way: material objects and their properties are reduced to minds and states of mind.

You might think of science as pushing in the direction of materialism. The route to idealism begins with a consideration of thought and language. What *are* the objects we confront as we move about the world? Consider this table. The table has a particular size shape, color, and mass. It is located on the veranda. Notice, however, that perceived qualities of the table are in constant flux. As you rise and move toward the table, your perception of the table's shape undergoes subtle alterations. To see what I mean, imagine holding a sheet of glass in front of you, closing one eye, and tracing the outline of the tabletop as you move relative to it. You will discover that the shape is constantly changing: growing as you approach the table, evolving from a narrow trapezoidal shape, to something more nearly approximating a rectangle.

All of the table's perceived qualities alter in this way with shifts in observation conditions. An idealist will want to know what there could possibly be to the table beyond these shifting 'mind-dependent' impressions. Materialists see a material object lurking 'behind' the appearances. But what an odd object this material table is: it is unobserved and unobservable! It is hard to make sense of such an object.

This style of reasoning is characteristic of idealism. You should note that, for the most part, idealists do not argue simply that materialists are mistaken: what we regard as material objects are, on closer examination, really only states of mind. The claim is much stronger. Talk of material objects is not merely false but positively *meaningless*. This might be put, mildly paradoxically, as follows. Whenever you think you are entertaining thoughts of material objects and their properties, you are in fact thinking of immaterial items. Berkeley was famous for issuing a challenge to materialists: if a materialist could so much as show that materialism was a coherent possibility, he would concede materialism.

Historically, idealism has enjoyed sporadic popularity. It last held sway in the waning years of the nineteenth century, but every generation of philosophers includes its share of idealists. Earlier I noted that materialism is rooted in a scientific approach to the world. The focus of science on observation, however, and the related thought that there could be nothing to the world beyond its observable features, has turned some scientists into idealists. Some of the pioneers of the quantum theory were enthusiastic Berkeleyans. The thought that observers have a role in making the observed what it is does not sound startling if you lean toward the view that all there is to the world are actual and possible observations.

Idealism and materialism apparently lie at opposite ends of the spectrum. Perhaps this is misleading. It might be possible for positions to be so far apart that they turn out, on closer inspection, to be indistinguishable. Wittgenstein makes this point in a discussion of 'solipsism' and 'realism'. (Think of a solipsist as holding, like the idealist, that the observer constitutes the world, and the realist as espousing materialism.)

> Solipsism, when its implications are followed out strictly, coincides with pure realism. The self of solipsism shrinks to a point without extension, and there remains the reality coordinated with it. (1921: §5.641)

You can see the point of these stunningly oracular remarks by imagining a complete description of the contents of the world as offered by an idealist and a materialist. How could these descriptions differ? Wittgenstein's thought is that each provides an identical description, then tacks on a rider: 'and by the way, all this stuff is material' or 'all this stuff is immaterial'.

Dualism redux

Peter Forrest and E. J. Lowe offer considerations favoring more or less traditional forms of dualism. Lowe describes himself as a 'non-Cartesian dualist'. What might he mean by this? Descartes holds that mental and material substances have no properties in common.

Material substances are extended; every property of a material substance is a mode of extension—a way of being extended. Mental substances are non-extended. Mental substances think; every property of a mental substance is a mode of thought.

Lowe rejects this picture, but retains the Cartesian idea that minds and bodies are distinct entities. Like Descartes, Lowe prefers to talk about the self. The self, he holds, is perfectly simple. What could be the parts of a self? You entertain different thoughts, your preferences evolve, and memories come and go. But these are not parts of you in the way arms, legs, hearts, and livers are parts of your body.

The simplicity of the self gives it a kind of metaphysical independence of the body. The body and its parts can be destroyed by being broken down into more fundamental parts and its parts dispersed. But a simple thing cannot be broken down and dispersed (a point emphasized by Descartes). What the self is like—its 'personality', its stock of beliefs, memories, tastes, and talents—might turn out to depend on a body, but that is a different matter.

The simplicity of the self means that selves cannot be identified with the body or a part of the body like the brain. If self (mind) and body are distinct, how are they related? This is always a tricky question for a dualist. Here is one possibility (discussed earlier in the introduction to Part X). Consider a lump of bronze. The lump can change its shape (by being bent, hammered, or melted) while remaining the very same lump. The lump cannot, however, survive our hiving off a portion and replacing it with a like amount of bronze from a distinct lump. The 'identity conditions' on lumps allow for changes in shape, but not for material changes. Now imagine a sculptor forming the lump into a statue of David. The sculptor brings the statue into existence by shaping the lump. In creating the statue, the sculptor does not destroy the lump. After the creative act the statue and the lump both exist. Some philosophers say that the lump composes or makes up the statue. Others describe the statue and lump as coinciding. Still others deny that statues exist; there are only lumps or the particles that make them up. If you are like most people, you probably believe that both the statue and lump exist, although you might be unsure how to describe their relation.

Suppose both statue and lump exist. Now consider their respective parts. The lump's parts will be (let us imagine) particles of bronze. What are the statue's parts. Well, the statue has a head, trunk, arms, legs, hands, feet, fingers, toes, ears, nose. Although each of these bears some intimate relation to portions of the lump, it seems wrong or misleading to describe them as parts of the lump. The lump does not have a finger, or a nose; the statue does. It might seem equally misleading to describe parts of the lump (the 'bronze particles') as parts of the statue. (Compare: in counting the parts of a clock, you count the gears, springs, and casing, but not the particles. A Lego set has 250 parts, not trillions, although trillions of particles might make up all the blocks in the set.)

Now imagine that the mind or self is related to the body in something like the way the statue is related to the lump of bronze that is on the scene when the statue is on the scene. Selves and bodies have very different identity conditions, so there is no prospect of identifying the self with the body. Moreover, the self is simple (or so Lowe contends), altogether lacking in parts. Nevertheless the self and the body (like the statue and the lump) might share certain properties. If the body has a particular mass, so does the self; if the body is in Gundagai, so is the self. The body and the self do not share all their properties. The self possesses only those bodily properties that could be possessed by a simple substance. If having blue eyes, for instance, is something only a composite entity could have, then selves could not have blue eyes (although 'their bodies' could).

Going it alone

Whether you find this brand of dualism plausible will depend on the extent to which you are persuaded by Lowe's arguments. You might have dualist leanings, but be moved by other considerations, perhaps considerations that would lead you to endorse a more traditional brand of substance dualism or maybe some form of 'property dualism', the view that mental and physical properties, though quite different, can be properties of one and the same substance.

Of course, you might regard dualism as a non-starter and prefer some brand of functionalism or materialism. The readings in this part are designed to loosen the grip of materialist sentiments. They are included, not because I believe materialism wrong, but because, in philosophy, it is imperative that we remain explicitly aware of our intellectual commitments. Where philosophical issues arise, no one is entitled to be smug.

References

Albert, D. Z. (1992), *Quantum Mechanics and Experience*. Cambridge, MA: Harvard University Press.

Bell, J. (1964), 'On the Einstein–Podolsky–Rosen Paradox', *Physics* 12: 989—99.

Herbert, N. (1985), *Quantum Reality: Beyond the New Physics*. Garden City: Anchor/Doubleday.

Poland, J. (1994), *Physicalism: The Philosophical Foundations*. Oxford: Clarendon Press.

Penrose, R. (1989), *The Emperor's New Mind: Concerning Computers, Minds, and the Laws of Physics*. New York: Oxford University Press.

Wittgenstein, L. (1921/1961), *Tractatus Logico-Philosophicus*, trans. D. F. Pears and B. F. McGuinness. London: Routledge & Kegan Paul.

Chapter 47

The succinct case for idealism

John Foster

i. The Project

My aim is to establish the truth of phenomenalistic idealism, which takes the physical world to be something logically created by the organization of (i.e. the regularities in and lawlike constraints on) human sense-experience. This position stands in sharp contrast with physical realism, which takes the physical world to be logically independent of the human mind and metaphysically fundamental. Despite his reductive account of the physical world, the idealist is not, of course, committed to saying that there is *no* concrete reality external to, and independent of, the human mind. All he is committed to saying is that, if there is such a reality, it is not itself physical and only contributes to the existence of the physical world via its actual or potential influence on human experience. In fact, idealists normally do envisage some form of external reality to account for the experiential organization. Thus Berkeley, who espouses a form of phenomenalistic idealism in his *Principles*,[1] insists that human sense-experience and the laws which control it are the result of divine volition.

There is no denying that it is physical realism which expresses the view of 'common sense'—the view we all take for granted prior to philosophical reflection. But this is very largely because, prior to reflection, we have a naïve-realist view of sense-perception. Thus we assume our perceptual access to external objects to be direct in a very strong sense—a sense which represents these objects as featuring in the very content of perceptual experience. This view of perception is, it seems to me, clearly mistaken: philosophical reflection (e.g. on the phenomena of illusion and hallucination) reveals that, whatever its precise nature, perceptual contact with an external item is always mediated by the occurrence of some purely internal psychological state which is capable of occurring without such contact being made.[2]

As well as eliminating much of its intuitive appeal, this result may also put pressure on physical realism in a more direct way. It is difficult to think of the external reality as constituting the physical world—i.e. *our* physical world—if we do

John Foster, 'The Succinct Case for Idealism'. In Howard Robinson, ed., *Objections to Physicalism* (Oxford: Clarendon Press, 1993).

1. At least this is how I interpret him. See my 'Berkeley on the Physical World', in J. A. Foster and H. M. Robinson, eds., *Essays on Berkeley* (Oxford, 1985).
2. For a full discussion of this point, see H. Robinson, 'The Argument for Berkeleian Idealism', sect. 4, in Foster and Robinson, eds., *Essays on Berkeley*, and my own *Ayer* (London, 1985), pt. 2, sect. 9.

not have perceptual access to it. But, although naïve realism is false, it is not clear how anything except a direct awareness would qualify as genuine perception at all; after all, without direct awareness, the situation is merely one of there being something in the mind which represents or provides information about the external item. So it may be that we have to construe the physical world as something internal to the mind in order to render it perceptually accessible. In effect, this is how Berkeley argued at the beginning of the *Principles*, when he dismissed realism as involving a 'manifest contradiction'.[3]

I mention this point *en passant*. Whether or not such an antirealist argument can be successfully developed is something I shall not explore further here. My own case against realism, and in favour of idealism, follows a quite different course. Inevitably, in the present context, the case will have to be set out much more briefly, and in simpler terms, than the issues require. I have tried to deal with the full complexities of the topic elsewhere.[4]

ii. The inscrutability of physical content

As well as precluding direct (and arguably *any* form of) perceptual access to the physical world, realism also imposes a severe limit on the scope of our *knowledge* of it. For, within the realist framework, we can at best acquire knowledge of the *structure and organization* of the physical world, not, at least at the fundamental level, of its *content*. Thus while, from our observations, and from the way these support certain kinds of explanatory theory, we may be able to establish the existence of an external space with a certain geometrical structure (one that is three-dimensional, continuous, and approximately Euclidean), we can never find out what, apart from this structure, the space is like in itself: we cannot discover the nature of the thing which has these geometrical properties and forms the medium for physical objects (or if we prefer to construe space not as a concrete thing, but as the abstract system of ways in which physical objects could be geometrically arranged, we cannot discover the nature of the distance-relations which form the building-blocks of these arrangements). Likewise, while, by the same empirical means, we may be able to establish the existence of external objects located in this space, and discover their shape and size, their spatial and spatio-temporal arrangement, their causal powers and sensitivities, and the various ways in which complex objects are composed of simpler ones, we can never discover the ultimate nature of

3. 'For what are the forementioned objects [houses, mountains, rivers, etc.] but the things we perceive by sense, and what do we perceive besides our own ideas or sensations; and is it not plainly repugnant that any one of these or any combination of them should exist unperceived?', *Principles of Human Knowledge*, 1. 4.

4. In *The Case for Idealism* (London, 1982). The relation between the present succinct version and the earlier full one is roughly as follows: sect. ii of this paper corresponds to pt. 2 of the book; sect. iii corresponds to chs. 8–9; sect. iv to chs. 10–11; and sect. 5 to pt. 4. One crucial topic which I treat in detail in the book (pt. 5), but do not discuss here at all, is the nature of time.

their space-filling content. For we can never discover, beyond a knowledge of their spatio-temporal and causal properties, what the simplest objects (the elementary particles) are like in themselves. Of course, we ordinarily take our physical knowledge to be more than merely structural in this way. For, prior to reflection, we think of physical space and its occupants as being, in their intrinsic character, as our sense-experiences (especially our visual experiences) represent them. Thus we think of grass as genuinely pervaded by the intrinsic green which characterizes its standard visual appearance, and we think of the circular shape of a penny as being, in a way which transcends its formal geometrical description, distinctively like the circularity which can feature as a colour-boundary in the visual field. But while such ascriptions of sensible content to the physical world form part of our ordinary view of things, they do not, in the end, have any rational justification. We cannot directly compare our sensory representations with the external items to see if they match, since we only have access to these items through the representations. Nor can we employ an inference to the best explanation to justify the ascriptions, since it is only the theories about structure and organization which play an explanatory role. The only way we could legitimize the ascriptions would be by adopting a 'secondary-quality' account of the facts they purport to record, so that an object's possession of a sensible quality comes to be nothing more than its power to affect human sense-experience. But, in this framework, the ascriptions would cease to have any bearing on the issue of physical content, at least in its fundamental form.

One interesting and surprising consequence of this limitation on the scope of our physical knowledge is that we can envisage the possibility of the physical world's being, in substance and character, purely mental. For, being ignorant of its content, we are free to suppose that the relevant structure and organization are realized in a domain of minds and mental events. For example, we could suppose that physical space is a three-dimensional sensefield (existing in some non-human and non-embodied mind) and that the fundamental physical qualities distributed over its points and regions are *sense*-qualities. Alternatively, we could suppose that the elementary physical particles are minds (again, non-human and non-embodied), and that the spatial position of each particle at a time is fixed by some triple of quality-values which characterize its current psychological condition. In both cases, of course, there would have to be appropriate laws controlling events in the external mental reality (to form the relevant physical laws), and appropriate link-laws connecting these events with events in human minds (to form the relevant psychophysical laws). It must be stressed that mentalistic hypotheses of this sort constitute forms of physical realism, not forms of idealism. For although they offer mentalistic accounts of the physical world, they do so in a way which leaves it as something logically independent of human mentality and metaphysically fundamental. The fact that the envisaged world is composed of minds and mental events has no bearing on either its metaphysical status or its relation to us.

The idea that the physical world might turn out to be composed of psychological elements is a strange one, and might strike us as too bizarre to be taken seriously.

But curiously, apart from the mentalistic hypotheses, we have no way of even forming a conception of what the inscrutable content might be. We cannot form such a conception in *physical* terms; for having evolved to serve the needs of empirical theorizing, our system of physical concepts is not equipped to provide a characterization of factors which are not amenable to empirical tests. Nor is there any third source of descriptive concepts—neither psychological nor physical—on which we can draw. However bizarre they may seem, the mentalistic accounts of what the physical world may be like are, within the framework of realism, the only ones available.

iii. The determinants of physical structure

Another way of responding to the epistemological situation would be to give up physical realism. For, without realism, we could say that what is empirically inscrutable is not the content of the *physical world*, but only that of the external reality (if there is one) which underlies it. In other words, by taking the physical world to be the logical creation of something else (whether something purely human-experiential or something partly external), we could ensure that it only embodies factors which are empirically accessible. For reasons which I shall now (over this and the next section) elaborate, I believe this to be the correct response. In elaborating these reasons, I shall focus on examples in which the external reality is assumed to be mental, since (for reasons already explained) these are the only ones available. And I shall focus in particular on cases in which the external item corresponding to physical space (and according to the realist identical with it) is a sense-field (or an aggregate of sense-fields), since this is the simplest way of envisaging something which is intuitively space-like in its character. I must stress, however, that all this is just for convenience of exposition and that the arguments themselves apply quite generally, whatever the external reality happens to be.

However inaccessible its content, we have so far not challenged the assumption that we can empirically discover the *structure and organization* of the external reality. But we can at least envisage the possibility that the real structure and organization differ from those which are empirically apparent at the human viewpoint. Thus suppose that the external reality consists of a three-dimensional sense-field, with a certain field-time distribution of qualities governed by certain distributional laws.[5] And let R_1 and R_2 be two field-regions of exactly the same shape and size, R_1 containing (or containing those field-processes which underlie events in) Oxford, and R_2 containing (or containing those field-processes which underlie events in) Cambridge. We can then envisage the following possibility. R_1 is positioned within the sense-field where (or in the place which corresponds to where) we ordinarily take Cambridge to be, and R_2 is positioned within the sense-field

5. We need not think of this sense-field as resembling anything which features in our own modes of sensory experience.

where (or in the place which corresponds to where) we ordinarily take Oxford to be. The reason we do not notice this, and would never suspect it from the empirical evidence, is that everything in the external reality is organized, both internally and with respect to effects on human experience, exactly as if the positions of R_1 and R_2 were reversed, i.e. exactly as if they occurred in those field-positions where we ordinarily take their physical correlates to be. Thus, given any type of field-process which would normally continue in a straight line, if such a process comes (in the normal continuous way) to some point on the boundary of R_1, it instantaneously changes its location to the corresponding point on the boundary of R_2, and continues in the corresponding straight line from there. And conversely, if such a process comes (in the normal continuous way) to the boundary of R_2, it undergoes an exactly analogous shift to the boundary of R_1. (For an illustrative example, see Fig. 47.1.) Quite generally, by the standards of how, in the rest of the field, things behave and affect human experience, everything is organized, with respect to the boundaries of R_1 and R_2, as if R_1 had R_2's location, and vice versa. We might put the situation succinctly thus: each of the two regions is *functionally* located where the other is *actually* (sensually) located. In speaking thus of the field's 'functional' geometry, we mean that (non-actual) geometry which its organization suggests—that geometry which the field would need to have, with its organization held constant, for the restoration of organizational (nomological) uniformity.

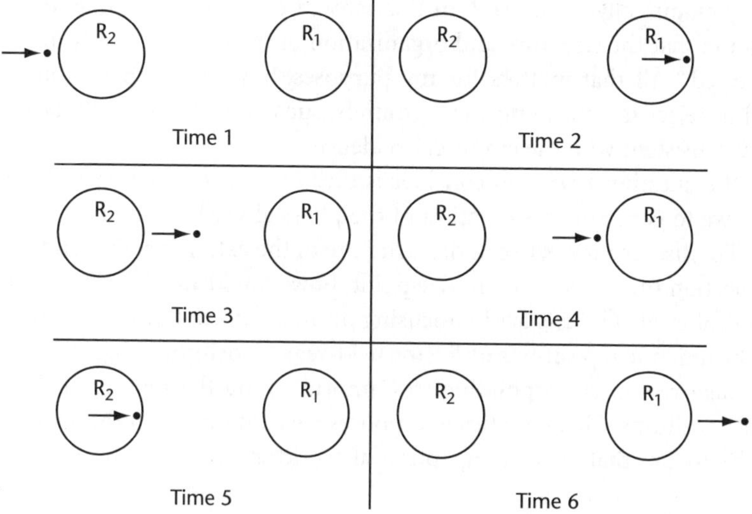

Fig. 47.1 The Oxford–Cambridge case: an illustrative example. *Suppose someone drives from Bath to Norwich, passing in turn through Oxford and Cambridge. Within the external sense-field, the path of the underlying process would be as here illustrated. Notice that whenever the process reaches a boundary of one of the regions, whether from the inside or the outside, there is an immediate jump to the corresponding point on the boundary of the other. As we shall see below, the crucial question is whether the path of the motorist in physical space is correspondingly disjointed*

It is not difficult to find further examples to illustrate the same general point. Thus we could envisage a case in which the external item corresponding to physical space consisted of *two* sense-fields organized as if they were *one*. Or again, though the details of this would be technically complicated, we could envisage a case in which the external item corresponding to physical space was a *two*-dimensional sense-field organized as if it were *three*-dimensional. Nor are we restricted to examples in which the discrepancy between how things really are and how they empirically seem relates to *geometrical* structure. Thus, reverting to the case of a three-dimensional field, we could suppose that there are two sense-qualities Q_1 and Q_2 such that, in respect of some particular region, everything is organized as if Q_1 inside this region were the same as Q_2 outside it, and vice versa. Or again, we could suppose that, over the whole field, two sense-qualities exchange their current distributions and functional roles every hour, so that everything is organized as if each of the qualities in hours 1, 3, 5, 7, . . . was the same as the other quality in hours 2, 4, 6, 8, . . . These last two cases are ones in which the deviance of empirical appearance from external reality relates to qualitative rather than geometrical structure: it concerns the relations of sameness and difference between the forms of qualitative content distributed over the external space.

All these cases, of course, are, by ordinary canons of scientific reasoning, implausible: to postulate any of them would involve attributing a nomological irregularity or complexity to the external reality when the empirical evidence permits a more uniform or simpler interpretation. It is just for this reason that we can speak of the cases as exhibiting a discrepancy between how things externally are and how they empirically seem. And, in this sense, we may even be able to retain the assumption that the structure and organization of the external reality are empirically revealed.[6] All that matters for my purposes, however, is that, even if we are entitled to reject them on empirical grounds, such cases are logically possible and logically consistent with the empirical evidence.

Now the question I want to consider is this. In cases of the sort just envisaged, how are we to construe the situation of the physical world? When we hypothesize this kind of discrepancy between the structure of the external reality and its empirical projection on to the human viewpoint, how should we characterize things at the physical level? Let us start by focusing on the Oxford–Cambridge example, in which the functional positions of R_1 (the field-region corresponding to Oxford) and R_2 (the field-region corresponding to Cambridge) are the reverse of their actual (sensual) positions. There are three responses we could make to this case. The first would be to say that there is no physical world at all—that the organizational

6. In fact I think we cannot. For although we have reason to reject the sorts of case just envisaged, and indeed to reject any case in which the external reality is organized in a way which runs counter to its own structure, I do not think that we have reason to reject the theistic account of the external reality proposed by Berkeley. The issues here, however, are ones which I have no time to discuss in the present paper.

anomaly with respect to the two regions is simply inconsistent with the existence of a physical world. The second would be to accept the existence of a physical world and see its structure as coinciding with that of the external reality. This would involve saying that, contrary to our ordinary beliefs, and to what all the empirical evidence suggests, Oxford really is in Cambridgeshire (coinciding with the field-position of R_1), and Cambridge really is in Oxfordshire (coinciding with the field-position of R_2). The third response would be to accept the existence of a physical world, but say that its structure coincides with how things empirically seem at the human viewpoint. This would involve saying that, despite the positions of R_1 and R_2 in the sense-field, Oxford and Cambridge are where we ordinarily take them to be. Now it seems to me that only the third of these responses has any plausibility. It is just obvious that the envisaged twist in the external organization would not suffice to eliminate the physical world altogether. But granted that we retain our belief in a physical world, we will surely want to model its topology on the functional rather than the actual topology of the sense-field. Thus we will surely want to say that Oxford not only meets all the empirical tests for being to the west of London, but that it actually is so, and that Cambridge not only meets all the empirical tests for being between London and Ely, but that this is its actual position in physical space. The point is that the physical world is, by definition, *our* world in some epistemologically crucial sense. Something can hardly qualify as the topological structure of *our* world, in *that* sense, if it is wholly and (by the laws of nature) necessarily concealed at the human viewpoint. However things may look to God, *our* world must be one to which *we* have empirical access.

Our response to all the other cases of this general sort will, it seems to me, be exactly the same. In each case, we will want to say that the existence of the physical world remains, but that its structure coincides with the structure which is empirically apparent, and reflects the underlying organization, rather than with that which characterizes the external reality. Thus, if we suppose the external reality to comprise two sense-fields which are organized as if they were one, we will conclude that there is only one physical space, reflecting the unitary character of the organization. Likewise, if we suppose that two external qualities exchange their current distributions and functional roles every hour, we will trace the space-time paths of the relevant physical qualities in a way which restores organizational uniformity, rather than in a way which matches the relations of qualitative sameness and difference in the external reality itself. And of course, our intuitions about such cases would be exactly the same without the supposition that the external reality involves a sense-field or anything else of a mentalistic type.

The upshot is that, whatever the nature of the external reality, we must take the structure of the physical world to be logically determined not by the external structure alone, but by this structure together with the way external things are nomologically organized internally and in relation to human experience. This will be so even in the case where, with no discrepancy between how things externally are and how they empirically appear, the external and physical structures coincide. For this coincidence will still logically depend on the fact that the external laws are such as to 'endorse' the external structure and make it empirically manifest at the human viewpoint. Thus, with suitably different laws, we would get a different physical structure—or with a sufficiently radical nomological change, no physical structure (and therefore no physical world) at all.

iv. The argument against ontological realism

Being logically determined by certain pre-physical facts about the external reality, that is, by a combination of the external structure and external organization, the structure of the physical world does not qualify as metaphysically fundamental. Nor, in so far as a crucial part of the external organization concerns the influence of external events on human experience, is it logically independent of the human mind. Already this sounds like an outright rejection of physical realism, which takes the physical world to possess such a status and independence. In fact, however, it would still be possible, at this stage, for the realist to preserve an important aspect of his position. For while conceding that the physical *structure* is derivative and dependent, he could still insist that, at an appropriately basic level of description, the physical *entities* which feature in it, and which qualify as physical by so featuring, are ingredients of the external reality and metaphysically fundamental. In other words, while conceding that realism fails in respect of physical facts and states of affairs, he could still maintain that it succeeds in respect of the (basic) physical ontology.

There are three ways in which this ontological realism could be developed. First, the realist might recognize physical space—or, for some exhaustive mode of division, its components—as metaphysically fundamental, but construe its physical occupants as the logical creation of certain pre-occupant facts about it. Secondly, and conversely, he might recognize physical occupants, or certain categories of occupants, as metaphysically fundamental, but construe physical space as the logical creation of certain prespatial facts about them. Thirdly, he might assign a metaphysically fundamental status to both physical space and its occupants. Now it seems to me that the second of these approaches can be excluded at the outset. The approach requires us to think of the relevant space-occupying physical objects as only *contingently* located in physical space—as things which are logically capable of existing without spatial location. For it represents physical space as something which derives its very existence from the way in which these things are (in respect of their pre-spatial properties and relations) contingently organized. But it is surely clear that we cannot, in this way, think of the spatial location of physical objects as only contingent. For it is part of our basic conception of such objects that physical space is not just their container, but the very form of their existence. Thus our conception of a physical object is as something *existing in* space, something which exists *by and through* its spatial location, something for which spatial location constitutes (if one may put it thus) the *mode of being*. Moreover, and indeed in consequence, it is part of our conception of such objects that, in conjunction with time, the space which contains them forms the framework for their identity. Thus we think of a physical object as deriving its individuality-at-a-time from its spatial position, and as preserving its identity-through-time by following a spatio-temporally continuous path. In short, to suppose that a physical object has the logical capacity to exist without physical space is as absurd as supposing that an event has the logical capacity to exist without time. And here, of course, the point is not just that such an object needs spatial location to qualify as *physical*; it is that, being the (physical) sort of thing it is, the object needs spatial location to exist at all.

This leaves two approaches available to the ontological realist, in each of which he assigns a metaphysically fundamental status to physical space or its components. This assignment avoids the objection to the second approach: there is now no question of having to think of certain physical objects as only contingently located in space. None the less, it is vulnerable to a different, and rather more complex, objection, which I shall now elaborate.

Let us suppose, for the sake of argument, that the external reality (i.e. the external component of the metaphysically fundamental reality) consists of a three-dimensional sense-field (*F*), together with a field-time quality-distribution, distributional laws, and laws linking field-events with human-mental events. Call physical space *P*. The realist's claim, then, is that *P* is the same as *F*, or at least that, for some exhaustive division, the components of *P* are the same as the components of *F*. The point of giving the realist the choice of this second and weaker alternative is to leave room for cases in which the sensual and physical topologies do not coincide. For where this happens, there are bound to be regions in the one which do not correspond to regions in the other. For example, in the case of Oxford and Cambridge outlined earlier, the physical regions of Oxfordshire and Cambridgeshire will not correspond with *regions* (i.e. *uninterrupted* regions) in the field, since each county comprises two portions (namely, its main city and the surrounding area) whose field-correlates are not contiguous.

The first thing we need to recognize is that any genuine space possesses its (real) geometrical structure, or at least the topological aspects of this structure, *essentially*. Thus, given any space, the network of distance-relations between its points, or at least the network of topological relations, is essential to the identities of these points: they could not be the points they are while standing in different relations. In particular, then, we can apply this principle to the case of *physical* space in respect of its *physical* geometry.[7] Thus if we know that the *physical* Oxford-region is in Oxfordshire and that the physical Cambridge-region is in Cambridgeshire, it makes no sense to suppose that the positions of these regions (as portions of physical space) might have been reversed. Likewise, if we know that physical space is

7. For simplicity, I pretend that physical space can be detached from time. Strictly speaking, I should focus throughout on the geometry of P-*time*, or the geometries of the *momentary cross-sections* of P.

three-dimensional, it makes no sense to suppose that the very same set of physical points might have had a two-dimensional arrangement. The point of allowing for a case in which only the *topological* structure of a space is essential to it, is that it may be possible to envisage a 'rubbery' space, in which points can preserve their identities through the kind of stretch-or-bend metrical alterations that rubber allows. What would remain invariant in such a space—both through time and across possible worlds—is topological arrangement: in other words, any (unbroken) line or (whole) region in the original condition of the space would remain a line or region after the permitted alterations.[8]

Now we have already established that the geometrical structure of physical space, and in particular its topological structure, depends not just on the *structure* of the external reality, but on its *structure and nomological organization.* Thus, in the case we are considering, if *A* and *B* are (actually) contiguous regions of *F* (the external sense-field), the nomological organization of *F* will determine whether *A* and *B* are also 'functionally contiguous', and hence determine whether the corresponding regions of *P* (the physical space) are actually contiguous. One way of expressing the point would be to say that, with its structure held constant, the nomological organization of the external reality, internally and in relation to human experience, determines its *physically relevant* geometry (topology). The description 'physically relevant' is designed to preserve neutrality between the realist's position, which takes physical space (or its components) to be metaphysically fundamental, and hence part of the external reality, and the non-realist's view, which rejects this.

The physically relevant geometry (topology) of *F* logically depends on its nomological organization. But this nomological organization, and in particular those aspects which contribute to the physical geometry, characterize *F* only *contingently.* We can envisage exactly the same sense-field existing with a relevantly different organization, yielding a different physical geometry or no physical geometry at all. For example, even if, as things are, the nomological organization endorses the field's actual topology, we can still envisage a possible situation in which, by the standards of uniformity, everything is organized as if two congruent regions were interchanged. It would just be a matter of envisaging appropriately different laws governing the field–time distribution of sense-qualities and the effects of this distribution on human experience.

Putting the various points together, we can now provide a decisive argument against the realist claim. We know that the physically relevant geometry (topology) of *F* logically depends on its nomological organization. And we also know that *F* possesses this nomological organization (including those aspects relevant to the physical geometry) only contingently. From these premisses, it immediately follows that *F* possesses its physically relevant geometry (topology) only contingently. But we also know that, as a genuine space, P possesses its physical geometrical (topo-

8. In fact, for the purposes of my argument, I only need to assume that a space possesses *some* aspect of its geometrical structure essentially.

logical) structure *essentially*. So, standing as they do in different modal relations to the physical (or physically relevant) geometry, *P* and *F* must be numerically distinct. Moreover, since the physical geometry (topology) which is essential to *P* is essential to the identities of its points, we can conclude, more strongly, that the points of *P* are numerically distinct from the points of *F*. And, points being the smallest components of a space, this means that there are no divisions of *P* and *F* relative to which the components of one can be identified with those of the other.

Now as formulated, this argument only explicitly deals with *one* hypothetical case, in which we take the external correlate of physical space to be a three-dimensional sense-field. But of course, exactly the same considerations would apply whatever the nature of the external correlate, and irrespective of whether it was intuitively space-like in its own character. So we can conclude, quite generally, that neither physical space nor its components are metaphysically fundamental: whatever the fundamental external reality, physical points and regions are not ingredients of it.

This means that no form of ontological realism is viable. Since the occupants of physical space are essentially space-occupying, we cannot assign a metaphysically fundamental status to them without assigning a similar status to the space itself. But we cannot assign such a status to physical space, since, in such a case, the dependence of its geometry on the underlying organization would not be reconcilable with the fact that it possessed this geometry, or at least its topological aspects, essentially. In short, once we have accepted that the physical geometry depends on the underlying organization, we cannot recognize any category of physical entities as metaphysically fundamental. All physical entities, along with the physical states of affairs in which they feature, will have to be seen as the logical creation of an underlying reality which is (in both its ontology and its states of affairs) wholly non-physical.

v. From non-realism to idealism

Physical realism is false: the physical world (assuming it exists) is the logical creation of a more fundamental reality which is wholly non-physical. But it does not immediately follow from this that idealism is true. The idealist claims that the physical world is entirely created by the organization of human experience: the external reality is relevant only in so far as it is responsible for this organization. So there is room for a middle position, between realism and idealism, which concedes that the physical world is metaphysically derivative, but insists that the external reality contributes to its creation *directly*, and not just by the way it affects human experience.

However, although there is room for this compromise position, it is hard to find any rationale for it. For on what principles would the external reality directly contribute, and why? We cannot insist on an external reality which is *isomorphic* with the physical reality it sustains; for we have already seen that such isomorphism is not necessary. Thus the structure of the physical world will deviate from the structure of the external reality if the latter (as it were) runs counter to the nomological organization. Nor can we insist on something *approaching* isomorphism; for there could be a *radical* discrepancy between the physical and external structures. Take, for example, the case in which a two-dimensional external sense-field gets a three-dimensional organization; or again, envisage a case in which something like the Oxford–Cambridge set-up is widespread. We cannot even insist that the external reality be as *rich* as the physical reality in its ontology. For there is surely no crucial difference between a case in which the external reality is organized as if its materials were differently structured and a case in which it is organized as if its materials were augmented. Thus we could presumably envisage a case in which the external correlate of physical space is a three-dimensional sense-field with an internal 'hole', but where everything is organized as if, by the standards of uniformity, the hole were filled in.

This last case is particularly interesting. For by envisaging a series of such cases in which the size of the hole is steadily increased—so that more and more of the physical world has no ontological correlate in the external reality—we can gradually approach the situation in which there is no external correlate at all and the organization of human experience is doing all the work. The anti-idealist is obliged to say that, at some stage in this series, the ontological materials become too meagre for the sustainment of a physical world. But it is difficult to see on what rational basis the distinction between sufficient and insufficient materials could be drawn. It is not just the problem of locating the division in the series at a *precise point*: the theorist could perhaps afford to say that, on this matter, our ordinary concept of a physical world leaves us room for manœuvre—that it is irreducibly vague in relation to the underlying quantitative factors on which its application depends. The problem is rather that there seems to be no rationale for imposing a minimum ontological requirement at all. After all, the basic reason for allowing the structure of the physical world to depend on the external organization, not just on the external structure, was to ensure that (as our concept of it surely requires) the physical world turns out to be, in an epistemologically crucial sense, *our* world. But we can secure the world as epistemologically *ours* by making its existence depend solely on the organization of *our experience*—irrespective of the external factors by which that organization is imposed. For, in effect, we make sure that the world is epistemologically ours by making sure that its structure matches what, if we were looking for the best (i.e. the nomologically simplest and most uniform) realist explanation of it, this experiential organization would lead us to postulate.

In fact, once we have abandoned physical realism, the only obstacle to the adoption of a full idealist position is that the latter itself seems vulnerable to two crucial objections. I want to end, therefore, by considering these objections and trying to answer them. But to prepare the way, I need to say a little more about the nature of the idealist view that I am advocating.

The idealist claims that the physical world is logically created by the organization of human sense-experience. This might be taken to imply the possibility of an analytical reduction of the physical to the experiential—the possibility of analysing physical concepts in experiential terms and translating statements about the physical world into statements about experience.[9] If so, the idealist would be in trouble; for it is surely just obvious that such an analysis is not available. No doubt our ordinary physical assertions are, directly or indirectly, responses to our sensory experience; for it is only through such experience that we have any indication of the existence and character of the physical world. But it would surely be just absurd to suggest that such assertions are themselves experiential claims in linguistic disguise—that when we say such things as 'there are apples on the table', or 'the tree has been felled', what we really mean, set out more explicitly, is that our sense-experience is organized in a certain way. In fact, though, the idealist position I want to defend involves a claim of *metaphysical* rather than *analytical* reduction. Thus I am happy to concede that the physical realm is *conceptually* autonomous—that physical concepts cannot be analysed in non-physical terms and that what we say in the physical language cannot be said in any other way. What I want to insist is that physical facts (or states of affairs) are wholly *constituted by* human-experiential facts (or states of affairs)—by which I mean that each physical fact obtains *in virtue of* certain experiential facts, and that its obtaining is *nothing over and above* the obtaining of these facts.[10] In other words, I recognize two metaphysical levels of reality: a derivative level of physical facts, which are *sui generis* and not expressible in any but physical terms; and an underlying and more fundamental level of (non-physical) experiential facts, from which the physical world derives its existence.

As a *metaphysical* reductionist, the idealist need not be worried by the fact that physical concepts cannot be analysed in experiential terms, since this is something he accepts. However, he now seems to be vulnerable at two other points, and it is these that give rise to the two objections.

The first objection arises from the fact that, as well as resisting analysis in experiential terms, our ordinary physical concepts seem to be inherently realist, or at least anti-idealist. Thus our ordinary concept of (say) a table or a tree seems to be, by its very content, of something which exists outside and independently of the human mind; and the same, of course, is true of our concept of any other kind of physical object. So unless we revise such concepts, there seems to be no way of making sense of the claim that facts about physical objects are wholly constituted by facts about human experience. Moreover, it seems that any conceptual revision

9. Or at least, the possibility of providing such a translation within the limits allowed by the possible vagueness or infinite complexity of physical concepts in relation to the experiential factors on which their application depends. I have discussed this point, though in connection with the analytical reduction of *psychological* concepts, in my book *The Immaterial Self* (London, 1991), ch. 2, sect. 3.

10. For more on this notion of constitution, see ibid., ch. 5, sect. 3.

which was sufficiently drastic to avoid this problem would not leave us with concepts which were recognizably *physical* at all.

The answer to this is that the idealist can, in a sense, accommodate this realist, or quasi-realist, aspect of our ordinary physical concepts in his own system. This is because he can draw a distinction between two frameworks of assertion. Thus, on the one hand, there is the *mundane* framework, in which we make ordinary assertions about the physical world, but without claiming anything about their philosophical significance. It is in this framework that, in the course of everyday life, we might find ourselves saying such things as 'there are apples on the table' or 'the tree has been felled'. On the other hand, there is the *philosophical* framework, in which we try to set physical reality in its right philosophical perspective. This is the framework in which the realist and idealist advance their rival accounts. Now the claim that physical objects exist outside and independently of the human mind has quite different interpretations according to the framework in which it is made. Made within the philosophical framework, it is an explicitly anti-idealist claim, entailing the falsity of any position which takes physical facts to be wholly constituted by experiential facts. But made within the mundane framework, it is surely, even for an idealist, trivially true. For, in whatever sense the idealist counts it as true that there is a physical world, and accepts the truth of our ordinary beliefs about it, he must also accept it as true that the human mind causally interacts with this world at the point of the human brain—in the same sort of way that physical objects causally interact with one another. And in the sense in which he counts it as true that the mind and the physical world causally interact, he must also count it as true that the world is something external to human mentality and logically independent of it. But now the idealist can insist that it is only with respect to the *mundane* framework that our ordinary physical concepts represent the items to which they apply as external and human-mind independent. If we take these concepts to be inherently anti-idealist, it is simply because, failing to notice the distinction between the two frameworks, we mistake an uncontroversial claim about the relationship between mind and body at the level of everyday thought for one which advances a view about how things are in the final perspective.

The second objection arises from the fact that, without an *analytical* reduction, there seems to be no way of avoiding a collapse into physical nihilism, which rejects the existence of the physical world altogether. The idealist is claiming that the fundamental reality is wholly non-physical and that the physical world is logically created by the organization of human sense-experience. But it is quite unclear how this creation is supposed to work. Without a reductive analysis of physical concepts, there seems to be no prospect of a deductive route from the experiential facts to the physical, and without a deductive route, there would presumably be no way of establishing the existence of the physical world solely on the basis of the relevant experiential information. So how can the idealist see the experiential facts as genuinely sufficing for the physical? Surely the most he can say, given his view of the fundamental reality, is that the organization of our experience makes it very useful for us to believe in a physical world, but that, strictly speaking, such a belief is false. The organization systematically invites physical interpretation, but the interpretation is in fact mistaken.

To deal with this point, the idealist needs to draw a further distinction—this time between two quite different epistemic perspectives in which the philosophical issue of the physical world can be considered. On the one hand, there is what we might label the *external* perspective. In this, we start with a description of the metaphysically fundamental reality—and, in particular, of the experiential organization—and, without any prior commitment to the existence of a physical world, address ourselves to the question of whether such a reality (such an experiential organization) suffices to create one. On the other hand, there is what we might call the *internal* perspective. In this, we start with our ordinary physical beliefs, held in response to our empirical evidence, and address ourselves to the questions of whether the physical world (whose existence we are now taking for granted) is metaphysically fundamental, and if it is not, what ultimately underlies it. Now it is clear, I think, that, in the external perspective, we could not, without a phenomenalistic analysis of physical concepts, make sense of the claim that the experiential organization suffices for the existence of a physical world. For example, if we were told of a Berkeleian set-up in some *other* universe—a set-up in which the fundamental reality consists of just God and a group of finite minds, and in which God organizes their sense-experience in a way which systematically invites physical interpretation—we could not see this as creating a real physical world: we could only see it as making it seem to the minds in question that such a world exists and making it useful for them to believe that it does. But of course our *actual* perspective is not this, but the *internal* one. We do not start off with an account of the fundamental reality and have to work out from it what physical facts, if any, obtain. Rather, being the minds whose experiential organization invites physical interpretation, we start with the empirically founded assumption that there is a physical world, and only then pursue a philosophical investigation into the question of its relationship with the fundamental reality. In *this* epistemological framework, it seems to me that the idealist's claim is unproblematic. For although there is no way of establishing the existence of the physical world from a knowledge of the experiential organization, I can see no reason for our having to abandon our empirically based belief in its existence in the face of what philosophy reveals about its metaphysical status—the revelation that, if it exists, it is this organization which ultimately creates it. Even though the conceptual autonomy of the physical realm precludes the establishing of physical facts on the basis of experiential, it seems to me that our physical beliefs are sufficiently flexible on the issue of what is metaphysically fundamental to allow us to discover, by philosophical argument, that it is the experiential facts that ultimately make them true.

We should also realize that the issue of whether we end up idealists or nihilists is not, philosophically, unimportant. At first sight, it might seem that it does not much matter whether we say that there is a physical world, but one which is logically created by the experiential organization, or say that there is no physical world, but the experiential organization makes it useful to suppose that there is. In fact, however, the nihilist view would undermine our epistemological situation altogether. For our knowledge of the experiential realm, and *a fortiori* our knowledge that it has the relevant (physical-world-suggesting) organization, depends very heavily on our physical information. This is obvious in the case of one person's knowledge of the experiences of others. But it is also true, in ways I have tried to elaborate elsewhere,[11] that a person's knowledge of his own earlier experiential biography is heavily dependent on his knowledge of his *physical* past. In the end, then, the choice is not between idealism and a nihilism which can preserve the cash value of the physical theory. It is between idealism and a nihilism which leaves us in an epistemic void. No doubt it is partly for this reason that our ordinary beliefs come to have the metaphysical flexibility which I attribute to them.

11. e.g. in *Ayer*, pt. 2, sect. 12.

Chapter 48

Difficulties with physicalism, and a programme for dualists[1]

Peter Forrest

PHYSICALISM is not a precise and articulate theory so much as a programme for metaphysical speculation. It has at its core the *physicalist thesis*, which states that the world, including human beings, can be completely described in physical terms. In addition, the physicalist programme relies only on scientific and causal ways of understanding the world. So it concerns both description and understanding.

There are well-known difficulties with physicalism, which are ultimately based on our experience of ourselves. But because it is a metaphysical programme, and not just an isolated thesis, these difficulties are not, and ought not to be, persuasive until we have a satisfactory rival programme of metaphysical speculation. Now, there are equally well-known difficulties with most versions of dualism. And physicalists complain that these force dualists into a series of *ad hoc* responses. If so, then there is a stalemate. On the one hand, physicalism is charged with empirical inadequacy, because it ignores much of our experience. On the other hand, dualism is charged with theoretical incompetence, because of too frequent a resort to the *ad hoc*. As a result of this stalemate we would be forced to choose between the scientific and manifest images. The purpose of this paper is to argue that things are not so. We can reconcile the manifest and scientific, by defending a non-Cartesian dualist programme.

One-category dualism, as I call the programme which I am advocating, is based on three guiding principles. The first is respect for introspection.[2] The second is respect for what I call the manifest understanding of persons, which I shall discuss below. These two principles entitle the programme to be called dualist in the broad sense. The third principle, the *one-category thesis*, states that an ontological theory which is adequate for the physical world already contains all the concepts and distinctions needed to describe the non-physical, without recourse to the mental as

Peter Forrest, 'Difficulties with Physicalism and a Programme for Dualists'. In Howard Robinson, ed., *Objections to Physicalism* (Oxford: Clarendon Press, 1993).

1. I would like to thank the following for their helpful comments on various versions of this paper: Fred D'Agostino, Robert Elliott, Jim Franklin, David Londey, Jeff Malpas, Erle Robinson, all of the University of New England; David Armstrong; and the editor, Howard Robinson.

2. I stipulate that introspection is not just inner perception (as in body-awareness or the sensation of pain) but includes a wide range of non-inferential beliefs about ourselves.

sui generis. The slogan of one-category dualism is that the mental and physical are different species of the one genus. Its positive heuristic is that we should be careful in describing the ontology of the physical world. For that is far richer than most physicalists think. And it is only because of this unacknowledged ontological richness that the mental need not be thought of as *sui generis.* Within the programme of one-category dualism I shall expound a further speculation, namely the *grand-property hypothesis.* It asserts that there are non-physical qualities[3] of the physical properties of brain-processes.

I shall begin by listing some of the well-known difficulties with physicalism and some of the equally well-known difficulties with dualism. Next I expound a central tenet of my proposed rival programme, namely, that we have what I call a manifest understanding of human beings. Because of the difficulties with dualism, we need a theoretical speculation such as the grand-property hypothesis to support our reliance on manifest understanding. In the last section, I show how this speculation avoids the various difficulties which I have listed.

The position which I shall defend, while contrary to the physicalist thesis, is compatible with the thesis that there are no non-physical contingencies. Everything which the physical description omits could well hold of necessity given the purely physical.[4] However, I think we tend to make rather over-confident claims about what is, or is not, necessary. And in this paper I shall not be relying on those claims. For that reason I merely note the compatibility.[5]

Space does not permit me to go into much detail, or to qualify my assertions or to provide caveats. What I am proposing is therefore very much a programme for dualists rather than a detailed theory.

i

I begin, then, by stating some of the well-known problems for physicalists. For a start there are the *qualia* of sensations. Physicalists may describe a sensation by giving a structural, neurophysiological description of the brain-states of the person having that sensation. Instead of, or in addition to, that structural description, they may characterize a kind of sensation functionally, that is, in causal terms, as likely to cause this, and as likely to be caused by that.[6] The missing-*qualia*

3. By a quality I mean any non-relational property, and not merely one which can be experienced. But the experienceable ones are of greatest interest.
4. As a special case of this, any non-physical being such as God would have to be metaphysically necessary.
5. An argument to show that on the grand-property hypothesis the mental could be taken as supervenient on the physical is to be found in my 'Supervenience: The Grand-Property Hypothesis', *Australasian Journal of Philosophy*, 66 (1988), 1–12.
6. The *this* and the *that* may be stimuli, behaviour, or other mental states. It is not enough to characterize a kind of mental state in terms of stimuli and behaviour.

objection is that even in combination, these two ways of describing sensations fail to acknowledge the occurrence of the *qualia*, that is, the introspectible character of sensations.[7]

I would like, however, to make a concession to the functionalists. The *qualia* are *appropriate* to the functional roles. For example, suppose one of the functional roles of pain is to cause us to avoid the situations which endanger us. Now a state with that functional role could simply fail to have any introspectible character. We could just find ourselves avoiding the situations which put us in that state, rather as compulsive hand-washers just find themselves washing their hands for no reason. However, in addition to the straightforwardly causal account, it can be pointed out that we have good *reason* to avoid the pain-producing situations. What is that reason? It cannot be articulated further than to say that the *qualia*[8] of my pain sensations provide me with all the reason I need for deliberately avoiding pain. In this fashion, pain *qualia* are appropriate to the functional role of pain.

There are well-known difficulties with physicalism concerning representation and intentionality. I shall mention just one of these. Perceptual sensations *represent*, and it is not just that they can represent given a suitable interpretation—anything can represent anything given a suitable interpretation. Rather they carry their interpretation with them: *they are intrinsically meaningful.* For example, there is something about seeing a rock which makes the visual sensation invite interpretation as seeing an object of a certain shape and size.

Next on the agenda of difficulties is the distinction between reasons (for both beliefs and actions) and causes. I have no *a priori* objection to the speculation that reasons are a species of cause. But if they are causes, then they are causes of a special kind. For not every belief which causes another belief is a reason for that other belief. Phenomenologically, the difference between reasons and (other) causes is that my reasons are *my* reasons, whereas (other) causes are things that happen *to me.* Hence there is a connection between reasons and actions, where action is specified as behaviour of which I am the author, as opposed to that which merely happens to me. The difficulty, then, for physicalism is in giving an account of this difference.

An act is free, to some extent I believe, if it is an act done for reasons and not caused (in any other way). So free acts are causally undetermined unless reasons are

7. This objection has been presented by Block, Searle, and Jackson in different ways. See N. Block, 'Troubles with Functionalism', in *Perception and Cognition: Issues in the Foundations of Psychology* (Minnesota Studies in the Philosophy of Science, 9, ed. C. W. Savage; Minneapolis, 1978), 261–325, repr. in id., ed., *Readings in Philosophical Psychology*, 1 (London, 1980), 268–305; J. Searle, 'Analytic Philosophy and Mental Phenomena', in *Midwest Studies in Philosophy*, 5, ed. P. A. French, T. E. Uehling, and T. K. Wettstein (1980), 405–23; and F. Jackson, 'Epiphenomenal Qualia', *Philosophical Quarterly*, 32 (1982), 127–36 (Chapter 43 of this volume). It is also discussed by David Smith, above.
8. It would be natural to talk of the *quality* of the pain sensation. But, because I mean by a quality a non-relational, non-structural property, this begs the question. I use the word *quale* for a property which is experienced without any experience of a relational or structural character to it.

causes. Physicalists can distinguish free acts from other behaviour in a phenomenologically adequate fashion only, I submit, if they can distinguish reasons from (other) causes.

The list of difficulties with physicalism could go on, but I shall conclude by considering the synchronic unity of a person. (Similar difficulties hold for diachronic unity.) Hume complained of the difficulty of finding the self as a further item of introspection. And, indeed, there is no direct evidence for a self separate from and alongside the various mental states which, intuitively, belong to that self. But I am aware of something of a rather different kind. It is the—admittedly fragile and imperfect—unity of the various mental states, with their various *qualia*. And the way in which these mental states are causally connected does not adequately account for this unity. For I can easily imagine the mental states of different people, with different beliefs and desires, being connected causally. Thus, given artificial nerves joining the brains of different people, your belief and my desire might result in a third person acting. Such an 'action' would be unintelligible to any of the three people involved, precisely because they have different beliefs and desires. Yet the appropriate causal connections would be there. So the unity is not entirely due to causal connections. Therefore, in addition to the *qualia* of mental states, we are aware of a non-causal unity.

There are, then, difficulties with physicalism. But there are also difficulties with dualism.[9] First dualists as well as physicalists have problems with unity. We experience the fragile and imperfect unity of the mental life. Again, we experience ourselves not just as unified minds but as psychosomatic unities. Yet again, we may ask what makes two minds *two* minds—what differentiates them? Surely it is the fact that the totality of mental states for the two minds lacks the unity which each mind has. How can the dualist account for these unities? It is tempting to posit a spiritual substance to account for unity. But there is a dilemma here. Either saying that there is a substance is just to repeat that the mental states form a unity, and so is no explanation, or it amounts to positing a substrate (substance in the Lockean sense) which bears the mental states just as all the properties of a material object could be said to be born by a substrate. I have doubts as to whether positing a substrate is much of an explanation of the mere fact that the mental states form a unity of some sort or other, but it certainly goes no way towards explaining the precise kind of unity which we experience the mental as having.

The *problem of origins* occurs for any version of dualism in which suddenly, at some stage in the development of the embryo or foetus, a hitherto non-existent soul or self comes into existence. If having a soul, or whatever the dualist proposes, is an all or nothing affair, then this gradual process of growth leads at one point to the sudden coming into being of a fully formed soul. Notice that this is not the problem of discovering when the mental comes into existence. Why should we be

9. The first four chapters of D. M. Armstrong's *A Materialist Theory of Mind* (London, 1968) still contains, I believe, the best account of the difficulties which the dualist faces, and the problems which I mention are selected from those he lists.

able to discover that? It is a problem of how something discontinuous could depend on something continuous.

Next there is the *problem of interaction*. Suppose, for example, that the intention to whistle causes certain brain processes. What would a psychosomatic interaction law relate? It would have to relate a type of brain process of incredible complexity to a type of mental state characterized in terms of some action. The sheer complexity of the *relata* prevents there being a correlating law which meets the standards of clarity and simplicity required of fundamental laws in scientific explanations. The problem, then, is of giving some account of the interaction which makes it comprehensible.

Finally, intentionality is not just a problem for the physicalist. The Brentano-inspired dualist orthodoxy is that some mental properties are not merely intentional, but irreducibly so. As such they are quite unlike familiar non-relational properties in that they cannot be described or understood without mention of the intentional object, which, if it exists, is typically a physical item. However, because the intentional object need not exist, intentional properties are also quite unlike familiar non-relational properties. According to the objector, the dualist requires some totally new basic category of entity, namely, that of irreducibly intentional properties. And it is a defect in a theory to resort to the *sui generis* in this way.

ii

I now expound the programme of one-category dualism, beginning with the feature which is most obviously dualist. I call it the *manifest understanding* of human beings.[10] First I shall expound it, then I shall consider its application to persons, distinguishing it from folk psychology, and finally I shall reply to two objections to it.

Manifest understanding is that mode of understanding which is non-theoretical, and which requires neither generalization[11] nor articulation. When it occurs there is a single act of knowledge-cum-understanding rather than knowledge followed by understanding. It is not my present concern to discuss the limits of manifest understanding. Rather, I claim that there is much manifest understanding in our day to day way of thinking of persons as beings who perceive, who have memories, who have beliefs, whose behaviour is sometimes a case of action done for reasons, who have virtues and vices, and so on. Poetry, novels, drama, even ordinary conversation, educate us in this way of thinking. As a result, I submit, we have much manifest understanding both of ourselves, and of others.

The paradigm of manifest understanding is our understanding of pain. If someone reports being in pain and also complains about it, that is something we

10. Manifest understanding of the mental requires a realism about *qualia* which is incompatible with the physicalist thesis. I leave it to the reader to supply the details of the argument.

11. That it is not to say that manifest understanding might not be of the general. All I mean is that no process of generalization is required to understand manifestly.

understand. The nature of pain is such that, to put it mildly, it is worthy of complaint. This, I claim, is something which we can understand, indeed can only understand, by experiencing pain. But, you say, could not someone actually seek pain for its own sake (and not for the sake of an associated sexual gratification)? At least, there are reports of those who say they are in pain but it does not bother them. So the connection between pain and our dislike of it (and hence the connection between pain and pain-behaviour) is contingent. I agree. None the less, I submit, we understand the unpleasantness of pain just by knowing it. By contrast, we find the lack of such unpleasantness in need of some further explanation, say in terms of lack of unity in the person.

That knowing certain mental states makes other mental states comprehensible is not itself a theory which helps us understand. Rather it is a claim about understanding. To defend this claim, I note that we sometimes have a 'sense' of having understood. A general scepticism about the reliability of our 'sense' of understanding would undercut even scientific understanding. For what other than this 'sense' of understanding can we rely on when asked to justify the claim that scientific theories enable us to understand? Assuming that we reject such scepticism, we should allow that our 'sense' of having understood is an—admittedly fallible—guide to understanding.

The first three of the difficulties I listed for physicalism are cases in which, I claim, we do have a manifest understanding. The appropriateness of the *qualia* for behaviour, which I pretended was a concession to the functionalist, shows how we have a manifest understanding of that behaviour. Again, reasons are the sort of item which can make beliefs and actions immediately intelligible, without recourse to a scientific theory. (Other) causes are not. As regards representation, there is a similar situation. In some cases, we have only to know the nature of the representing state to understand how it represents.

That there is manifest understanding provides part of the answer to those who object that dualism does not result in a satisfactory alternative to the theoretical understanding of persons provided by physicalism. This partial answer is that manifest understanding is not theoretical. (It is only a partial answer, because it does not, by itself, solve all the problems which we have listed for physicalists and dualists.) In theoretical understanding, we generalize in order to understand. By contrast, manifest understanding requires no generalizations, although it permits them. Thus I can understand my avoidance of pain by considering the nature of my own pain, ignoring that of others.

That not all understanding requires generalization may be argued for by considering our knowledge of others as more than just things which behave in complicated ways. I come to know others only, I submit, by 'putting myself in their shoes'. By an exercise of imagination, I fit mental states to behaviour.[12] However, telepathy apart, I have only my own case to go on. How, then, do I come to realize that

12. See Z. Vendler, *The Matter of Minds* (Oxford, 1984), ch. 1.

another person is in pain? An argument by induction from a single case is far too weak. What is required is something like an inference to the best explanation. More accurately we rely on an interpretation of the behaviour of another based on an imaginative putting of oneself in the other's position. This interpretation is then justified by the understanding it provides. But if generalization were required in order to understand, then that justification would be circular. For we would require knowledge of other minds in order to infer the generalizations which would then enable us to understand. But surely we do know and understand other minds. Hence, I conclude, understanding need not involve generalization.

Another respect in which manifest understanding differs from theoretical understanding is that it is not hypothetical. The generalizations of scientific theories are, typically, hypotheses which, if they fit the facts, provide a way of understanding them. But it is characteristic of manifest understanding that we understand by knowing, without the need for hypothesis.

It is important to distinguish manifest understanding from folk psychology, which is the attempt to assimilate our pre-theoretic thought about persons to *scientific* understanding. But I say that much of this pre-theoretic thought just is manifest understanding, and so is to be contrasted with, rather than assimilated to, scientific understanding. Moreover, folk psychology is conservative in a way in which manifest understanding need not be. Just as new scientific theories can lead to the evolution of scientific understanding, likewise new insights can lead to the evolution of manifest understanding. Hence the objections to folk *psychology*[13] are not automatically reasons for rejecting manifest understanding.

I anticipate two objects to my reliance on manifest understanding. The first is that a way of understanding in which to know is to understand is too easy: the charlatans and obscurantists could go around saying that they too understand things merely by knowing them. I grant that we should exercise the greatest care in our appeal to manifest understanding. For it is an appeal which is easily abused. But, I insist, we should avoid the vice of the puritan, namely prohibiting good things just because they can be abused.

The second objection which I anticipate is based on the claim that there can only be one mode of understanding. I reject that claim. Even the understanding provided by the sciences combines an understanding by means of generalization with a further understanding of these generalizations, obtained by fitting them into suitably elegant or harmonious theories.[14] Yet again, the understanding of a result in mathematics derives, in typical cases, from the ability to prove it. So an independent case can be made for the plurality of modes of understanding.

13. See P. S. Churchland, *Neurophilosophy* (Cambridge, Mass., 1988), 299–310; P. M. Churchland, 'Eliminative Materialism and Propositional Attitudes', *Journal of Philosophy*, 78 (1981), 67–90 repr. in id., *A Neurocomputational Perspective* (Cambridge, Mass., 1989), 1–22 (see Chapter 23 of this volume); and S. Stich, *From Folk Psychology to Cognitive Science: The Case against Belief* (Cambridge, Mass., 1983).

14. See my 'Aesthetic Understanding', *Philosophy and Phenomenological Research*, 51, 3 (Sept. 1991), 525–40.

iii

I shall assume that we accept the thesis that we have considerable manifest understanding of ourselves and each other. If there were no difficulties with dualism there would, therefore, be no need for a dualist *theory*. For manifest understanding is not theoretical. However, we do need theory—or perhaps I should say speculation—in order to meet the difficulties with dualism. Without such a theory we could dismiss the 'sense' of manifest understanding as illusory because it commits us to dualism. To meet these difficulties I recommend the programme of one-category dualism. In accordance with this metaphysical programme, I shall begin by describing an ontology adequate for the physical world. I shall then point out just how little more is required to make it adequate for the mental as well.

Now there are different ways of discussing ontology. But for the sake of exposition, I shall adopt a traditional approach. Let us start, then, with an ontology of properties and relations. Ignoring a few details, an ontologist might claim that the physical world is made up of instantiated properties and relations. Is that adequate? I say not. Even an account of the purely physical needs to take into account, in some way or another, four further categories, namely quantity, quality, becoming, and unity.

First, there is quantity. Most physical properties admit of degrees of intensity. In some cases, this is unproblematic. Thus we might insist that having mass *N* units is just a matter of being made up of *N* disjoint parts each of mass one unit.[15] However, this account cannot be smoothly generalized to those quantities which take vector values. Forces, for example, are characterized by direction as well as strength. Our ontology must be enriched to take into account the fact that properties admit of varying magnitudes, where the degrees may be vector quantities. No doubt there are many metaphysical speculations which would be appropriate here. But one which is especially attractive is that we should include in our ontology various relations of comparative magnitude between physical properties. It is also a plausible speculation that such a relation between properties is internal, in the sense that it is essential to either property that it is related as it is to the other.[16] For example, consider two forces. My intuition is that the forces could not be the forces which they are, if they were not related as they are, both in the proportions of their strengths and in the angle between them. Thus, in many cases, the relations between physical properties are essential to their being the properties they are. Now, I concede that this is speculative. No doubt there are other accounts of magnitudes. However, it is a tenable speculation to extend our ontology of the physical to

15. See D. M. Armstrong, *Universals and Scientific Realism*, 2, *A Theory of Universals* (Cambridge, 1978), ch. 22.

16. See J. Bigelow and R. Pargetter, 'A Theory of Structural Universals', *Australasian Journal of Philosophy*, 67 (1989), esp. 4–5.

include some internal relations, without necessarily accepting the neo-Hegelian thesis that all relations are internal.

Next there is quality. Consider the following attempt to describe the physical world:

There are various properties and relations some of which stand in relations of comparative magnitude to each other, and various combinations of them are instantiated.

Such a description leaves something out, namely the *qualia* of *physical* properties. Those properties of inanimate objects and those relations between them which we experience themselves have *qualia*, and our experience of them acquaints us with those *qualia*. By contrast, purely theoretical properties either lack *qualia* or have *qualia* with which we are not acquainted. My argument for these claims is an appeal to the phenomenology. There is a phenomenological difference between our understanding of those properties and relations which we experience, and those we know of only via a scientific theory. Thus the property of roundness and the relation of adjacency have *qualia* experienceable by humans, whereas simple electromagnetic properties do not. A natural speculation concerning such *qualia* is that they are non-relational properties of the physical properties and relations described by the sciences. In that case they are purely physical, but not described by the physical sciences. This speculation will lead to the grand-property hypothesis when it is generalized to cover the *qualia* of mental states. Readers who are prepared to grant that even the properties of inanimate objects such as rocks have *qualia* not described by the physical sciences, but who give some other account of them, could be led to a rival speculation within the programme of one-category dualism. I ask them to treat the grand-property hypothesis as merely an illustration of how one-category dualism might be developed.

I have just appealed to the phenomenology of perception, but perhaps critics could likewise appeal to the phenomenology. Surely, they might say, the *qualia* are qualities of the things which have the physical properties, not qualities of the physical properties themselves.[17] The phenomenology of perception, I reply, supports the claim that qualities (and in some cases relational properties) are the direct objects of perception, but it tells us nothing at all about what they are properties of. Indeed, if we are prepared to countenance uninstantiated qualities, there is much to be said for the thesis that in a radical illusion what is perceived is an uninstantiated quality. Thus the phenomenology of perception is quite neutral of what the perceived qualities are qualities of, and so is compatible with my suggestion that they are grand-properties.

Then there is becoming. Much could be said of the metaphor—not myth—of passage. But I shall concentrate here on the anisotropy of time. There is a difference between *earlier than* and its converse *later than*, a difference which is not adequately described by pointing to the asymmetry of the relation, or by pointing to processes

17. I am indebted to David Armstrong for pointing out to me just how peculiar my proposal seems initially.

which just happen to proceed in one temporal direction but not the other. Following Grünbaum we may call this an intrinsic difference between *earlier than* and *later than.* Various attempts have been made to characterize this intrinsic difference.[18] Perhaps the commonest is to say that the overall direction of increasing entropy is from earlier to later. I ask readers to judge such attempts themselves. But, for what it is worth, I say that all such attempts rely on accidental accompaniments of the earlier/later distinction, and are not intrinsic.[19] Thus it is not merely conceivable, but physically possible, for entropy to decrease. I submit that we need some further account of the anisotropy of time. As in the case of quantities and qualities, I present what I take to be a tenable speculation. It is that the difference between *earlier than* and *later than* is that at a later time, more is actualized than at an earlier time.[20] Some detail is required to make this speculation comprehensible. Each determinate way the physical world might be corresponds to a 'possible world'. And each of these 'worlds' is given by a physically complete spatio-temporal description. But, I say, what is actual at a given time t is not determinate. So the actual at time t is indeterminate between the members of the subset, W_t, of the set of all possible worlds, where W_t is larger than a singleton.[21] If we reject backward causation, then, all the worlds in W_t agree in their history up to t, but they do not agree in what happens after t. The 'passage of time' consists, I speculate, in the increasing determinacy of what is actual. That is, if time t is later than time s, then the set of worlds W_t is a proper subset of the set W_s.

Finally, there is unity. Consider a description based on the physical sciences, but which completely left out all considerations of unity. In particular consider the following three properties of an electron: *having mass* m_e, *having charge* c_e, and *having spin 1/2*. If we ignore unity, then we cannot distinguish (1) a single particle with a given path in space-time and with all three of those properties, from (2) three particles with the same path, the first having mass m_e, the second having charge c_e, and the third having spin 1/2. For the difference between (1) and (2) is that in (2) the three properties are merely instantiated at the same location, whereas in (1) they form a unity, which cannot, I submit, be adequately analysed in causal terms. To say that there is a substance (in the Aristotelian/scholastic sense) amounts to no more than repeating that the properties do form a unity. An attempt at explanation is made by positing a substrate (substance in the Lockean sense) which bears all the

18. A. Grünbaum, *Philosophical Problems of Space and Time* (Boston Studies in the Philosophy of Science, 12; Dordrecht, 1973).

19. This is, of course, a far from original criticism. Grünbaum's defence against criticisms of this sort is to emphasize epistemological questions. I, however, am not concerned with how convinced we should be that the anisotropy of time is universal. Rather I experience the difference between past and future, and I seek an account of that difference which is adequate to my experience.

20. See my 'Backwards Causation in Defence of Freewill', *Mind*, 94 (1985), 210–17, and my *Quantum Metaphysics* (Oxford, 1988), ch. 8.

21. In the context of special and general relativity what is actual is relative not to a time but to a point in space-time.

properties. What other accounts are there? Perhaps for each individual there is a grand-property, that is, a property of properties, which is peculiar to that individual. Call such a property a grand-haecceity. Then it would serve both to unify the properties of the individual (by being a property of them all) and to individuate otherwise indiscernible objects. Or perhaps no further account provides any understanding and we should take unity as a basic category. In any case it suffices to say that some account has to be given of unity, if we are to have an ontology adequate to the physical world.

In a nutshell that is the Forrest theory of the physical world. It is a world of properties with *qualia*, internally related by comparative magnitude relations, forming unities, and in which the anisotropy of time is due to the anisotropy of increasing actuality. It is not important for my present purpose that this be the only tenable ontology for the physical world, merely that it is one which is not *ad hoc*, and is not significantly inferior to rivals.

iv

We now have all the ontological categories which we need in order to describe the mental. To illustrate this I shall go through the difficulties with physicalism and with dualism.

The *qualia* of sensations may be taken to be non-physical qualities of the physical properties of the brain-processes with which the sensation is correlated. I call this the grand-property hypothesis. We have already speculated that physical properties have qualities. All I am now doing is to posit more qualities than are required to describe the non-sentient. I am not introducing a new genus of items, merely a new species in a genus already required.

Qualia become a little more mysterious when we consider the appropriateness of the *qualia* for the functional role of the physical properties of which they are qualities. The problem here is not that of explaining why the *qualia* are appropriate given that there could be such appropriateness. There is a Darwinian/teleological explanation of *that.* Rather, the problem is that of understanding how there could be appropriateness. A partial solution to this problem is to rely on the manifest understanding of persons. Once you are aware of a given *quale*, then you know that it does provide a reason for acting in a way appropriate to the functional role. But this solution is only partial. For it raises a further ontological problem: what kind of relation is this *providing a reason for?*

The short answer is that *providing a reason for* is not exactly like any physical relation. But merely to give that answer would be an *ad hoc* appeal to the *sui generis.* To avoid the *ad hoc*, I recall the internal relations of comparative magnitude, which were relied on when providing an account of quantity. They were essential to their *relata.* Likewise, *providing a reason for* a certain action is essential to the quality of the mental state which provides a reason for the action. Thus *providing a reason for* is a further species of a genus already introduced in order to describe the physical—namely, relations essential for one or more of their *relata.*

The representative power of sensations is likewise partially understood manifestly, and partially by invoking the category of internal relations. Take the case of the sensation we have when we 'see' an after-image. To be more specific, consider the sensation which occurs when I 'see' an after-image obtained by looking at the setting sun. The sensation itself has the capacity to represent (intrinsically) something red and round. We understand this capacity to represent manifestly, that is, by experiencing it. But to what category does this capacity belong? We should avoid saying it belongs to a *sui generis* category of intentional properties. Instead I treat representation as a species of the genus of internal relations. Thus the quality[22] of the sensation is internally related to what it represents, namely, the quality of the property of being red and round. Furthermore, that there can be the capacity to represent something red and round without there being anything red and round there to be represented is not, *pace* Brentano, a feature peculiar to the mental. (What is peculiar to the mental is the capacity to represent *intrinsically.*) Rather it is a special case of a quite general feature of internal relations. For instance, the property of having mass 250 grams stands in a certain relation to (and could be used to represent—though not intrinsically) the property of having mass 450 grams. And it would do so even if nothing ever had mass 450 grams. The possibility of a non-existent *relatum* is thus a characteristic of internality, not of the mental. And, for what it is worth, I handle it by appealing to uninstantiated properties.

The linked problems of reasons and of freedom require more than the combination of manifest understanding, on the one hand, and an appeal to qualities and internal relations, on the other. But first let us run through that combination. We understand what reasons are, and what freedom is, as a result of our experience of ourselves. I have already assigned *providing a reason for* to the category of a relation internal to various qualities which are its *relata.* But more needs to be said about that relation. Consider the case of pain and pain-behaviour. And suppose the pain-behaviour in question is indeed an action, not just a reflex. Then the pain and the action are related in that the quality of pain provides a reason for the action. In this case the relation of *providing a reason for* is internal to the quality of pain. As regards the associated problem of freedom, the explication of becoming as increasing actuality leaves room for categorical freedom of action, that is, for acts which are done for reasons and which are not determined causally. As I have said, this may conveniently be described using sets of possible determinate worlds. What is actual is indeterminate between these determinate worlds. The physical laws put constraints on the sets of worlds, but within those constraints we are free to ensure that what will be actual at a later time is indeterminate between the members of some

22. If it is indeed a quality. We might analyse the experienceable character of the sensation relationally, namely, as the awareness of an image or sense-datum. For simplicity I ignore this possibility.

smaller set of possible worlds. There is nothing *ad hoc* in this, for increasing actualization is already a feature of the physical world. All I have done is to exploit it.

Finally, there is the unity of a person. I have submitted that an adequate account of the physical world requires that there be unities which cannot be explained in purely causal terms. I rejected the hypothesis that the unity of a person is simply due to a substrate which bears the various properties, because positing a substrate does not account for the kind of unity we experience. Could we handle this difficulty by saying that the substrate has its own peculiar quality? No. For in that case the quality would be just a further property of the person and so an item to be unified rather than a kind of unity. Therefore, if we were otherwise committed to substrates as the best account of the unity of material objects, the failure of this account to generalize to the unity of the mental would be a serious difficulty for the dualist. However, the substrate account was merely one speculation concerning the unity of material objects. Let us compare it with the rival, higher-order haecceity account. Both speculations are subject to the same criticism, namely, that some new entity is posited in an *ad hoc* way just to account for unity. Either that criticism shows that our best policy is to reject both accounts and to take unity as a basic category, or we reject the criticism. In the former case, the special unity of the mental would then be a further species of the basic category of unity but not something *sui generis.* In the latter case, there is little to choose between the two speculations, so dualists are free to choose the one which fits in better with their dualism, namely, the higher-order haecceity account. As in the case of the substrate account, merely positing a higher-order haecceity fails to explain the kind of unity we experience the mental as having. But we may posit a special quality which the higher-order haecceity has without it becoming just another quality to be unified. Thus even if we decide not to treat unity as a basic category, dualists can treat the unity of the mental as a new species of a genus required to handle the unity of material objects.

I now turn to the difficulties for dualists. I have argued that an ontology adequate for the physical world enables us to account for the special unity of the mental, without being *ad hoc.* In addition, the unity of the whole person (non-physical and physical) is ensured by the grand-property hypothesis itself—the non-physical consists of properties of the physical. This handles the difficulties with unity.

On the grand-property hypothesis the *interaction problem* concerns the mysterious correlation between the physical properties of brain-processes and their non-physical qualities. While I do not pretend to have a complete understanding of this correlation, I propose two principles which greatly reduce the mystery. The first of these, the *principle of harmony,* states that none of the pieces of behaviour (including changes of mental state) which tend to happen as a result of the purely physical working of the brain should be incompatible with the acts (including mental acts) which we have reasons to perform. Since the non-physical qualities provide reasons for acts of various kinds, this principle constrains which physical properties of the brain have the non-physical properties in question. This constraint amounts to the requirement that the *qualia* of mental states be appropriate for the functional roles which they play.

The principle of harmony does not exclude Keith Campbell's 'imitation man' who completely lacks all *qualia*.[23] So it provides only a partial understanding of the interaction of the physical and the non-physical. But there is a further principle which leads to a fuller, although still incomplete understanding. It is that sufficiently similar physical properties have similar qualities. Call this the *continuity principle for qualia*. This principle excludes the case in which real people and imitation people are both actual.

Without the continuity principle, the problem of origins would evaporate. For we could say that various mental characteristics suddenly arise in the developing human some time after the physical conditions (i.e. brain development) are appropriate, but we know not when. So the fact that the problem of origins has intuitive appeal justifies my hypothesizing the continuity principle: I am not hypothesizing anything which is antecedently implausible.

Conversely, given the continuity principle there is an obvious argument to show that all *qualia* arise gradually, and hence that the problem of origins has not evaporated. For as the correlated brain-states change by small degrees so, by the continuity principle, should the associated *qualia*. In particular the coming into existence of some *quale* should be gradual. In order to reply to this argument, I first examine the phenomenology. I suggest that the introspectible quality of mental states neither seems to arise gradually nor seems to arise suddenly. The coming into existence of mental states is not introspectible in the way that the mental states themselves are. So we have as much reason to say that they occur gradually, but we are introspectively blind to their occurrence, as to say that they arise suddenly. Hence I could accept the conclusion that the mental arises suddenly. However, introspectible mental states such as having a pain in a toe are correlated not with instantaneous brain-states but with brain-processes. (Frequencies of spiking cannot be instantaneous.) As a consequence, the introspectible qualities do not have precise temporal locations. So we may deny that they come into existence by small degrees without asserting that they come into existence suddenly. This dissolves the problem of origins as usually stated. I leave it to the readers to decide whether various residual puzzles are genuine difficulties for those who reject physicalism.

Conclusion

The well-known difficulties with physicalism become grounds for rejecting it, because there is, I have argued, a viable alternative metaphysical programme, namely one-category dualism, which avoids these difficulties, as well as those of Cartesian dualism. Unlike physicalism, one-category dualism is adequate to experience. Unlike Cartesian dualism, it is theoretically satisfactory. In short, the manifest and scientific images are reconciled.

23. See K. Campbell, *Body and Mind* (London, 1971).

Chapter 49

Non-Cartesian dualism

E. J. Lowe

1. The self as a psychological substance

THE conclusion I draw from the preceding arguments is that a person or subject of mental states must be regarded as a *substance* of which those states are modes, and yet not as a *biological* substance (as the neo-Aristotelian theory would have it). What sort of substance, then? Clearly, a *psychological* substance. That is to say, a person is a substantial individual belonging to a natural kind which is the subject of distinctively psychological laws, and governed by persistence conditions which are likewise distinctively psychological in character. But thus far this is consistent with regarding a person as something like a Cartesian ego or soul, and this is a position from which I wish to distance myself. The distinctive feature of the Cartesian conception of a psychological substance is that such a substance is regarded as possessing *only* mental characteristics, not physical ones. And this is largely why it is vulnerable to certain sceptical arguments to be found in the writings of, *inter alia*, Locke and Kant. The burden of those arguments is that if psychological substances (by which the proponents of the arguments mean *immaterial* 'souls' or 'spirits') are the real subjects of mental states, then for all I know the substance having 'my' thoughts today is not the same as the substance that had 'my' thoughts yesterday: so that, on pain of having to countenance the possibility that my existence is very much more ephemeral than I care to believe, I had better not identify myself with the psychological substance (if any) currently having 'my' thoughts (currently 'doing the thinking in me'). But if *I* am not a psychological substance, it seems gratuitous even to suppose that such substances exist (certainly, their existence cannot be established by the Cartesian *cogito*).

By why should we suppose, with Descartes, that psychological substances must be essentially immaterial? Descartes believed this because he held a conception of substance according to which each distinct kind of substance has only one principal 'attribute', which is peculiar to substances of that kind, and such that all of the states of any individual substance of this kind are modes of this unique and exclusive attribute.[1] In the case of psychological or mental substances, the attribute is Thought; whereas in the case of physical or material substance(s), the attribute is

E. J. Lowe, edited extract from 'Substance and Selfhood', chap. 2 of *Subjects of Experience* (Cambridge: Cambridge University Press, 1996).

1. See René Descartes, *Principles of Philosophy*, I, sect. 53.

Extension. On this view, no psychological substance can possess a mode of Extension, nor any physical substance a mode of Thought. However, I am aware of no good argument, by Descartes or anyone else, in support of his doctrine of unique and exclusive attributes. Accordingly, I am perfectly ready to allow that psychological substances should possess material characteristics (that is, include physical states amongst their modes). It may be that there is no material characteristic which an individual psychological substance possesses *essentially* (in the sense that its persistence conditions preclude its surviving the loss of this characteristic). But this does not of course imply that an individual psychological substance essentially possesses *no* material characteristics (to suppose that it did imply this would be to commit a 'quantifier shift fallacy' of such a blatant kind that I am loath to accuse Descartes himself of it).

How, though, does this repudiation of the Cartesian conception of psychological substance help against the sceptical arguments discussed a moment ago? Well, the main reason why those arguments seem to get any purchase is, I think, that in presupposing that psychological substances would have to be wholly non-physical, they are able to take it for granted that such substances are not possible objects of ordinary sense perception. They are represented as invisible and intangible, and as such at best only perceptible by some mysterious faculty of introspection, and hence only by each such substance in respect of itself. But once it is allowed that psychological substances have physical characteristics and can thus be seen and touched at least as 'directly' as any ordinary physical thing, the suggestion that we might be unable to detect a rapid turnover of these substances becomes as fanciful as the sceptical suggestion that the table on which I am writing might 'in reality' be a succession of different but short-lived tables replacing one another undetectably. Whether one can conclusively refute such scepticism may be an open question; but I see no reason to take it seriously or to allow it to influence our choice of ontological categories.

I believe, then, that a perfectly tenable conception of psychological substance may be developed which permits us to regard such substances as the subjects of mental states: which is just to say that nothing stands in the way of our regarding *persons* precisely as being psychological substances. The detailed development of such a conception is the topic of the remaining sections of this chapter, and for now it must suffice to say that I conceive of psychological substances as the proper subject-matter of the science of psychology, which in turn I conceive to be an autonomous science whose laws are not reducible to those of biology or chemistry or physics. However, it will be appropriate to close the present section with a few remarks on the relationship between psychological and biological substances, that is, between persons and their bodies. (I restrict myself here to the case of persons who—like human persons—have animal bodies.)

With regard to this issue I am, as I indicated at the outset, a *substantial dualist*. Persons are substances, as are their bodies. But they are not identical substances: for they have different persistence conditions, just as do their bodies and the masses of matter constituting those bodies at different times. (I should perhaps emphasize here that where a person's body is a biological substance, as in the case of human persons, the body is to be conceived of as a *living organism*, not as a mere mass of matter or assemblage of physical particles.) Clearly, though, my version of substantial dualism is quite different from Descartes's. Descartes, it seems, conceived a human person to be the product of a 'substantial union' of two distinct substances: a mental but immaterial substance and a material but non-mental substance. How such a union was possible perplexed him and every subsequent philosopher who endeavoured to understand it. The chief stumbling block was, once again, Descartes's doctrine of unique and exclusive attributes. How could something essentially immaterial be 'united' with something essentially material? But psychological substances as I conceive of them are *not* essentially immaterial. Moreover, in my view, human persons are themselves just such psychological substances, not a queer hybrid of two radically alien substances. (I should stress that my criticism of Descartes here pertains solely to his doctrine of 'substantial union' and not to his conception of psychophysical causation, which I consider to be far more defensible.)

So, as for the relationship between a person and his or her body, I do not see that this need be more mysterious in principle than any of the other intersubstantial relationships with which the natural sciences are faced: for instance, the relationship between a biological entity such as a tree and the assemblage of physical particles that constitutes it at any given time. Most decidedly, I do not wish to minimize the scientific and metaphysical difficulties involved here. (I do not, for example, think that it would be correct to say that a person is 'constituted' by his or her body in anything like the sense in which a tree is 'constituted' by an assemblage of physical particles.[2]) None the less, it is my hope that by adopting a broadly Aristotelian conception of substance and by emphasizing not only the autonomy but also the continuity of the special sciences, including psychology and biology, we may see a coherent picture begin to emerge of persons as a wholly distinctive kind of being fully integrated into the natural world: a picture which simultaneously preserves the 'Lockean' insight that the concept of a person is fundamentally a psychological (as opposed to a biological) one, the 'Cartesian' insight that persons are a distinctive kind of substantial particulars in their own right, and the 'Aristotelian' insight that persons are not essentially immaterial beings.

2. The self as a bearer of physical characteristics

Let us recall that we are not required to *deny* that a person or self has physical characteristics, and though we have to regard it as distinct from its body, we are not required to think of the two as separable (except perhaps purely conceptually, or

2. For criticism of this suggestion, see my *Kinds of Being* (Oxford: Basil Blackwell, 1989), pp. 119–20.

purely in imagination). But *what* physical characteristics can we allow the embodied self to possess? All those ascribable to its body? Only some of these? Some or all of these plus others not ascribable to it? We need above all a principled way of distinguishing between those statements of the form 'I am *F*' (where '*F*' is a physical predicate) which are more properly analysed as 'I have a body which is *F*', and those which can be accepted at face value. Here it may help us to consider whether or not the self is a *simple* substance—that is, whether or not it has *parts*. For if not, no statement of the form 'I am *F*' can be taken at face value if being *F* implies having parts. My own view is that the self is indeed a simple substance, and I shall argue for this later.

But does not *every* physical predicate imply divisibility into parts (as Descartes held—this being the basis of one of his main arguments for the immateriality of the self)? No, it does not. For instance, 'has a mass of seventy kilograms' does *not* imply having parts. A self could, thus, strictly and literally have a mass of seventy kilograms without it following logically that it possessed various parts with masses of less than that amount. (After all, an electron has a finite rest mass, but it does not, according to current physical theory, have parts possessing fractions of that rest mass.) Again, 'is six feet tall' does *not*, I consider, imply having parts, *in the relevant sense of 'part'*. The relevant sense of part is this: something is to be counted a 'part' of a substance in this sense only if that thing is itself a substance. We may call such a part a 'substantial part'. Simple substances have no substantial parts. We must, then, distinguish between a substantial part of a thing and a merely *spatial* part of it. A spatial part of an extended object is simply some geometrically defined 'section' of it (not *literally* a section, in the sense of something *cut out* from it, but merely a region of it defined by certain purely geometrical boundaries). Thus, for example, the left-hand third of my desk as it faces me is a *spatial* part of it. It is doubtless the case that there is *also* a substantial part of my desk which at present coincides exactly with that spatial part—namely, the mass of wood contained within that region. But it would be a category mistake to *identify* that mass of wood with the left-hand third of my desk.[3] Now, 'is six feet tall' certainly implies having *spatial* parts, but does not imply having *substantial* parts. Extended things—the claims of Descartes and Leibniz notwithstanding—*can* be simple substances.

So far, then, I can allow that physical statements such as 'I weigh seventy kilograms' and 'I am six feet tall' may be taken at their face value. But a statement such as 'I am composed of organic molecules' *cannot* be so taken, but must be analysed rather as 'I have a body which is composed of organic molecules'. Even so, it is surely evident that if 'I weigh seventy kilograms' is literally true of me, it will be so only in virtue of the fact that I have a body which weighs seventy kilograms. And, indeed, it seems clear that all of the purely physical characteristics which are liter-

3. For further discussion of these issues, see my 'Substance, Identity and Time', *Proceedings of the Aristotelian Society*, supp. vol. 62 (1988), pp. 61–78, and my 'Primitive Substances', *Philosophy and Phenomenological Research* 54 (1994), pp. 531–52.

ally ascribable to the self will be thus ascribable in virtue of their being ascribable to the self's body—we can say that the self's purely physical characteristics 'supervene' upon those of its body.

But what, now, *is* it for the self to 'have' a certain body as 'its' body? Partly, it *is* just a matter of that self having certain physical characteristics which supervene upon those of *that* body rather than any other—though it is clear that this fact must be derivative from some more fundamental relationship. More than that, then, it must clearly also be a matter of the self's perceiving and acting 'through' that body, and this indeed must be the crucial factor which determines *which* body's physical characteristics belong also to a given self. But what *is* it to perceive and act 'through' a certain body rather than any other? As far as agency is concerned, this is a matter of certain parts of that body being directly subject to the agent's (that is, the self's) will: I can, of necessity, move certain parts of *my* body 'at will', and cannot move 'at will' any part of any body that is not part of mine.[4] (Here it may be conceded that someone completely paralysed may still possess a certain body, though only because he *could* once move parts of it 'at will', and still perceives through it; but someone completely paralysed *from birth*—if such a condition is possible—could only be said to 'have' a body in a more attenuated sense.) As far as perception is concerned, apart from the obvious point that one perceives the world from the position at which one's body is located (except under abnormal circumstances, as when one looks through a periscope), it may be remarked that one's own body is perceived in a different manner from others in that one's sensations of it are phenomenologically localized in the parts perceived: when one feels one's foot, one locates that feeling *in the foot*, whereas when one feels a wall, one does not locate that feeling *in the wall*.

Now it is true that in a less interesting sense all action and perception is 'through' a certain body, namely, in the sense that as an empirically ascertainable matter of fact I need my limbs to move and my eyes to see. But *these* facts do not as such serve to qualify my limbs and eyes as especially *mine*, as parts of *my* body. For, of course, I can be fitted with prosthetic devices for locomotion and vision, yet these do not *thereby* become parts of my body (though they *may* do so if they enter into the more intimate relationships discussed a moment ago). What makes my body peculiarly *mine*, then, is not determined merely by the empirically ascertainable dependencies that obtain between its proper functioning and my ability to engage in perception and agency. Thus, for example, even if it should turn out that I need a brain in order to think, it does not follow that this relationship suffices to make that brain peculiarly *mine*. In fact I should say that a certain brain qualifies as mine only derivatively, by virtue of being the brain belonging to *my* body, where the latter qualifies as mine by virtue of having parts related to me in the more intimate ways

4. In another terminology, we may say that movements of certain parts of its own body can necessarily be executed as 'basic' actions by the self. The *locus classicus* for the notion of a 'basic' action is Arthur C. Danto's 'Basic Actions', *American Philosophical Quarterly* 2 (1965), pp. 141–8.

mentioned earlier. As far as these more intimate relationships are concerned, my brain is as alien to me as a stone or a chair.

My thoughts, feelings, intentions, desires and so forth all belong properly to me, not to my body, and are only to be associated with my body in virtue of those intimate relationships which make it peculiarly mine. It is impossible to associate such mental states with a body non-derivatively, that is, without relying upon their ascription to the self or person whose body it is—or so I would claim. No mere examination of brain-function or physical movement can warrant such an association, without a detour through a recognition of the existence of a self or person to whom the body belongs. This recognition, in interpersonal cases, will of course have to issue from empirical evidence—but it will be evidence of embodied selfhood in the first instance, not directly and independently of particular mental goings-on.

3. The self as a simple substance

But what now of my crucial claim that the self is simple, or lacks substantial parts? Well, what substantial parts *could* it have, given that the self is not to be identified with the body? Parts of the body cannot be parts of the self. If the self and the body had exactly the same parts, they would apparently have to be identical substances after all (certainly, standard mereological theory would imply this).[5] Similarly, if it were urged that all and only parts of the brain, say, were parts of the self, this would imply that self and brain were identical. So I conclude that the self can have *none* of the body's parts as parts of itself, unless perhaps the self could have other substantial entities *in addition* to bodily parts as parts of itself. However, no other substantial entity *does* appear to be a tenable candidate for being a substantial part of the self, whether or not in addition to bodily parts. For instance, the self patently does not consist of a plurality of lesser 'selves' acting cooperatively, despite the picturesque 'homuncular' descriptions of mental functioning advanced by some philosophers.[6] Such descriptions are not intelligible if taken literally. (Similarly, we should not take literally overblown talk of 'corporate persons', that is, the idea that

5. See, e.g., Nelson Goodman, *The Structure of Appearance*, 3rd edn (Dordrecht: D. Reidel, 1977), pp. 33ff. Standard mereological theory is possibly wrong on this score, if it is correct (as I believe) to differentiate between a tree, say, and the mass of wood which temporarily composes it—for these may seem to have the same parts, at least during the period in which the one composes the other. However, while the tree and the wood arguably have the same *spatial* parts, it is much more debatable whether they have the same *substantial* parts. For instance, a certain root will be a substantial part of the *tree*, but hardly of the wood composing the tree. (By contrast, a substantial part of the wood composing the tree arguably *is* also a substantial part of the tree.) The issue is a complex one, which I cannot go into in further depth here. But, in any case, I think it independently reasonable to deny that substantial parts of the body are literally parts of the self (and I do not think of the body as in any sense *composing* the self).

6. See, e.g., Daniel C. Dennett, *Brainstorms*, pp. 122–4.

institutions like clubs and firms are genuinely persons in their own right.[7] At neither level—subpersonal nor suprapersonal—does the concept of a person find anything other than metaphorical application.) Nor should we regard the mind's various 'faculties'—will, intellect, appetite, or modern variants thereof, such as linguistic or visual processing 'modules'—as being 'parts' of the self. For in the first place it is a mistake to reify faculties, and in any case they certainly could not qualify as *substantial* parts, which are what are now at issue. Faculties have no possibility of independent existence and should properly be seen as no more than abstractions from the mental lives of persons. For instance, the notion of a will without an intellect, or of a language faculty in the absence of belief and desire, is just nonsense. Finally, it will not do to speak of the self's psychological states and processes themselves—its beliefs, intentions, experiences and so forth—as being 'parts' (much less as being substantial parts) of it: for this would only be at all appropriate on a Humean constructivist view of the self (the 'bundle' theory), which we have rejected. I conclude, therefore, that if the self is a substance, it must indeed be a *simple* substance, entirely lacking substantial parts.

The simplicity of the self goes some way towards explaining its *unity*, including the unity of consciousness that characterizes its normal condition. Where this unity threatens to break down—as in various clinical conditions such as those of so-called multiple personality, schizophrenia, brain-bisection, and so on—we are indeed inclined to speak of a plurality of selves, or of divided selves. In fact I think such talk should again not be taken literally, and that the psychological unity that most fundamentally characterizes the self is not merely to be located at the level of consciousness. A divided consciousness is, I think, in principle consistent with self-identity: what is not is a radical disunity of beliefs and values, manifested in a radical inconsistency of thought and action. (Of course, we all display mild inconsistencies, but no *one* person could intelligibly be interpreted as possessing the incompatibilities of belief and value that typically characterize different persons.) Now, a complex entity can act in disunified ways because the various incompatible or conflicting activities can be referred to different parts of the entity. Thus a corporate entity such as a firm or a club can act inconsistently because its members may act in conflicting ways. But the actions of the self—those that are truly predicable of it (because they are genuinely intentional) and not of the body (such as so-called reflex actions)—cannot in this way be ascribed to different elements or parts within the self. So we see that the simplicity and the unity of the self are indeed intimately related, even though there must clearly be much more to the matter than these brief remarks disclose.

Another consequence of the simplicity of the self is this. If the self is a simple substance, then it appears that there can be no diachronic criterion of identity

7. See, e.g., Roger Scruton, 'Corporate Persons', *Proceedings of the Aristotelian Society*, supp. vol. 63 (1989), pp. 239–66.

which grounds its persistence through time.[8] This is not to say that there may not be some *cause* of its persistence. It may well be, thus, that the continued normal functioning of the brain is a causally necessary condition of the persistence of the self, at least in the case of embodied, human persons. But it would not follow from this that the identity of the self over time is grounded in continuity of brain-function, or indeed anything else. Nor should we think it contrary to the self's status as a substance that its existence may be thus causally dependent upon the functioning of another, distinct substance—the brain or, more generally, the body. No tenable account of substance can insist that a true substance be causally independent of all other substances. For instance, a tree is as substantial an entity as anyone could wish for, yet of course its continued existence depends upon the maintenance of a delicate balance of forces in nature, both within it and between it and its environment. But a tree is a *complex* substance, and accordingly its persistence can be understood as grounded in the preservation of certain relationships between its substantial parts, despite the gradual replacement of those parts through natural processes of metabolism and growth. Not so with a self, any more than with, say, an electron or other 'fundamental' particle. Thus the reason why the self—or any simple substance—cannot be provided with a criterion of diachronic identity is that such a criterion (in the case of a substance or continuant) always makes reference to a substance's constituent parts, of which simple substances have none.[9]

That the diachronic identity of simple substances, including the self, is primitive or ungrounded should not be seen as making their persistence over time somehow mysterious or inscrutable. In the first place, as I have already pointed out, it does not preclude us from recognizing the involvement of various causal factors in their persistence. Secondly, we can still concede, or better insist, that there are certain necessary constraints on the possible history of any simple substance of a given kind, that is to say, limits on the sorts of changes it can intelligibly be said to undergo, or limits arising from empirically discoverable natural laws governing substances of this kind. Thus in the case of the self, a possible history must have a certain internal coherence to be intelligible, not least because perception and action are only possible within a temporal framework that includes both forward and backward-looking mental states (intention and memory). Finally, the persistence of at least some simple substances is, I consider, presumed at the very heart of our understanding of time and change in general, so that we should not expect to be able to give a reductive or exhaustive account of all such persistence.[10] Indeed, since the only simple substances directly known to us without benefit of scientific specu-

8. For more general discussion of persistence and criteria of identity, see my 'Substance, Identity and Time' and also my 'What is a Criterion of Identity?', *Philosophical Quarterly* 39 (1989), pp. 1–21.

9. See further my 'Lewis on Perdurance versus Endurance', *Analysis* 47 (1987), pp. 152–4, my 'The Problems of Intrinsic Change: Rejoinder to Lewis', *Analysis* 48 (1988), pp. 72–7 and, especially, my 'Primitive Substances'.

10. See further my 'Substance, Identity and Time'.

lation and experimentation are precisely *ourselves*, I would urge that the pre-theoretical intelligibility of time and change that is presupposed by all scientific theorizing actually rests upon our acquaintance with ourselves as simple persisting substances. So, although in the *ontological* order of nature it may well be the primitive persistence of fundamental physical particles that underpins objective time-order—makes the world *one* world in time—still, in the *conceptual* order of thought it is the persistence of the self that underpins our very grasp of the notion of objective time-order. If this is indeed so, it would clearly be futile to expect the concept of the self to reveal upon analysis an account of the self's identity over time which did not implicitly presume the very thing in question.

A consequence of the ungroundedness of the self's identity over time is that there is, and can be, no definitive condition that necessarily determines the ceasing-to-be (or, indeed, the coming-to-be) of a self. In the case of complex substances which are governed by criteria of identity the conditions for substantial change (that is, their coming or ceasing-to-be) can be specified fairly exactly, even though these conditions may in some cases be infected by some degree of vagueness. But not so with simple substances—and this is not, with them, a matter of *vagueness* at all (not, at least, in the sense in which 'vagueness' implies the existence of 'fuzzy' boundaries, whose 'fuzziness' may be measured in degrees). This observation certainly seems to apply in the realm of fundamental particle physics, as far as I can judge. Thus if, in a particle interaction, an electron collides with an atomic nucleus and various fission products arise, including a number of electrons, it would seem that there may be no determinate 'fact of the matter' as to whether the original electron is, or is not, identical with a given one of the electrons emerging from the impact event. There is here, it would seem, a genuine indeterminateness (I do not say *vagueness*) of identity.[11] But this should not lead us to view with suspicion the idea that electrons *do* genuinely persist identically through time. Note, too, that known constraints on the possible history of an electron *may* enable us to rule out *some* reidentifications as impossible in a case such as that described—so the indeterminacy is not totally unconstrained, which would be bizarre indeed; but the point is that even when all such constraints are taken into account, there may still be a residual indeterminacy in a given case.

Returning to the self, we see, thus, that while we may well believe that we have good scientific grounds for believing that the functioning of the brain is *causally* necessary for the continued existence of the self, none the less, in the nature of the case, such evidence as we possess for this is bound to be inconclusive (and not just for the reason that all empirical evidence is defeasible), since we lack any proper grasp of what would *constitute* the ceasing-to-be of a self. Lacking that grasp, we

11. A sizeable literature related to this issue has grown out of Gareth Evans's paper 'Can There be Vague Objects?', *Analysis* 38 (1978), p. 208, though this is no place for me to attempt to engage with it. I discuss the electron case more fully and challenge Evans's argument against indeterminate identity in my 'Vague Identity and Quantum Indeterminacy', *Analysis* 54 (1994), pp. 110–14.

cannot really say what empirical evidence would or would not support a claim that a self had ceased to be. This is why the prospects for life after bodily death must inevitably remain imponderable and unamenable to empirical determination.

Against this it may be urged that, since I have allowed that perception and agency are essential to selfhood, I must allow that the cessation of these *would* constitute a terminus for the self's existence. However, it is the *capacity* for perception and agency that is essential, not its perpetual *exercise*. Very well, so can we not say that the demise of this capacity—and certainly its *permanent* demise—would constitute the demise of the self? But this is not really informative. For what would *constitute* the permanent demise of this capacity? Only, as far as I can see, the demise of the self—that is to say, no non-circular answer can be given. It will not do to say that the permanent cessation of brain-function would *constitute* the demise of the capacity for perception and agency. For the most we can really say is that there seems to be an empirical correlation between mental activity and brain-function, at least in the case of human persons. But the capacity for perception and agency does not of its nature *reside* in any sort of cerebral condition. Indeed, there is nothing whatever unintelligible about supposing the existence of a capacity for perception and agency in a being lacking a brain.

4. Physicalism, naturalism and the self

Is physiological psychology, or neuropsychology, a contradiction in terms, then? Not at all, so long as it is seen as telling us empirical facts about the condition of embodied human persons or selves—telling us what sorts of processes as a matter of fact go on in their brains and nervous systems when they think or feel or act. This is not, though, and cannot be, an account of what *constitutes* thought or feeling or agency in a human person. Thought can no more *be* (or be constituted by) a brain-process than a chair can *be* (or be constituted by) a set of prime numbers.[12] Nor should we be tempted into saying such things as that a brain-process may 'realize' an episode of thinking (as more cautious modern physicalists sometimes put it)—for what on earth is this really supposed to *mean*?

In answer to this last question, it will perhaps be said that what it means to say that brain-processes 'realize' thought-episodes is that thought-episodes 'supervene' upon brain-processes, at least in the case of human persons. But this sheds no real illumination either, for the notion of supervenience (however useful it may be in some contexts) is out of its depth here. Suppose we ask what it means to say that thought-episodes supervene upon brain-processes. We shall perhaps be told that what this means is that if *A* and *B* are two human persons who share (type-)-identical brain-states at a given time (that is, whose brain structures are atom-for-atom, neuron-for-neuron indistinguishable at that time, with all of these neurons

12. Cf. P. T. Geach, *Truth, Love and Immortality: An Introduction to McTaggart's Philosophy* (London: Hutchinson, 1979), p. 134.

in identical states of excitation), then of necessity *A* and *B* will be enjoying (type-)identical thought-episodes at that time. (Perhaps not thought-episodes identical in *content*, if we are to accept the conclusions of Putnam and Burge regarding so-called 'Twin-Earth' cases,[13] but none the less ones that are subjectively indistinguishable—whatever that means!) But the empirical status of this sort of claim (and presumably it cannot be paraded as anything more than an empirical claim, since it can have no *a priori* justification) is highly problematic.

Let us first be clear that the thesis must be that thought-episodes supervene *globally* or *holistically* (rather than just piecemeal) upon brain-processes, since it is clear that to the extent that thought is dependent on the brain it can be so only in a holistic way which will not permit us to make any empirically confirmable claims about individual dependencies between particular ('token') thought-episodes and particular ('token') brain-events or processes.[14] So the thesis must be that a person with a brain exactly replicating mine at a level of neuronal organization and excitation will enjoy a mental life (feelings, beliefs, memories and so on) indistinguishable from mine, but not that any partial replication would engender any corresponding partial similarity in mental life. Nothing short of whole-brain replication will do. But what we now need to ask is this: what causal constraints would there be upon the process of bringing two distinct brains into such a state of exact neural replication? It is irrelevant that one might in some sense be able to *imagine* this being done, perhaps instantaneously, by a device that we tendentiously dub a 'brain replicator': you walk in through one door, the operator throws the switch, and then you and your Doppelgänger walk out hand in hand. One might as well say that the trick could be performed by magic. So might pigs fly. But in fact it seems clear that there is simply *no* non-miraculous way in which this feat could be achieved. It would not even suffice, for instance, to take identical twins from the moment of conception and attempt to submit them to exactly similar environmental and social stimuli. For, first of all, the growth of nerve cells involves a good deal of randomness,[15] and secondly, it seems likely that brains, at the relevant level of organization, constitute a class of so-called 'chaotic systems'.[16] Thus it could be that because the twins are subjected to minutely different influences for brief periods during their early development (as is effectively unavoidable), neural connections end up getting laid down in quite different ways in the two brains. The more one reflects on

13. See, especially, Tyler Burge, 'Individualism and the Mental', *Midwest Studies in Philosophy* 4 (1979), pp. 73–121 (Chapter 25 of this volume).
14. This appears to be an inescapable implication of Donald Davidson's well-known thesis of the 'holism of the mental', for which see his *Essays on Actions and Events* (Oxford: Clarendon Press, 1980), p. 217. I do not, for reasons which I have already made plain earlier in this chapter, accept Davidson's own view of the relations between mental and physical events, which is a 'token-token' identity theory. See further my *Kinds of Being*, pp. 113–14, 132–3.
15. See further Gerald M. Edelman, *Neural Darwinism: The Theory of Neuronal Group Selection* (Oxford: Oxford University Press, 1989), pp. 33–7.
16. See, e.g., James P. Crutchfield *et al.*, 'Chaos', *Scientific American* 255 (December 1986), pp. 38–49, and Ary L. Goldberger *et al.*, 'Chaos and Fractals in Human Physiology', *Scientific American* 262 (February 1990), pp. 34–41.

the matter, the more evident it should become that the whole idea of bringing two brains into identical neural states is so completely fanciful that it merits no place in serious philosophical inquiry.[17]

It will not do for the physicalist to protest here that all he is interested in or committed to is the bare conceptual possibility of such whole-brain replication: for even if you can really get your mind around this notion, what are you supposed to *do* with it? Precisely because the notion of such replication is the stuff of pure fantasy utterly beyond the realm of scientific possibility, it cannot be conjoined with any genuine scientific findings from neuropsychology in order to yield a verdict on the truth or falsehood of the supervenience thesis. Nor can we justify such a verdict by consulting our 'intuitions' regarding the upshot of the imagined replication experiment—for we are simply not *entitled* to any 'intuitions' about the matter, and any we do have we probably owe simply to our own prejudices. So my conclusion is that even if the supervenience thesis is coherently statable (and even this may be in question), we can have no possible basis, either empirical or *a priori*, for judging it to be true.

But now it may be objected that this rejection of physicalism even in the comparatively weak form of the supervenience thesis is unacceptably at odds with a 'naturalistic' view of human beings and the mind. The emergence of mind must, it may be said, be recognized as being a result of evolutionary processes working upon the genetic make-up of animal life-forms, through wholly biochemical means. Hence a biological account of mentality is inescapable if one has any pretence to being 'scientific'. There cannot be anything more to thought than can be exhaustively explained in biochemical terms, for otherwise the emergence of mind seems to be an inexplicable freak or accident. But again this is an objection which just reflects a dogmatic prejudice. Indeed, it is thoroughly question-begging and circular. It is just assumed from the outset that any wholly adequate explanation of the *emergence* of mind must be purely biological in character, because it is already presupposed that mind or mentality is a wholly biological characteristic of biological entities—animal life-forms. But the whole burden of my position is precisely that the mind is *not* a biological phenomenon and that mentality is *not* a property of the biological entities which constitute human bodies. That such entities should be apt to embody selves or persons can, indeed, be no accident—but why presume that the evolution of such bodies or organisms is to be explained in exclusively biochemical terms? It is the environment of organisms that determines the evolutionary pressures on them to adapt and change: but the 'environment', in the present instance, cannot necessarily be specified in wholly physical and biochemical terms. All that can be said is that the *proximate* cause of genetic mutation

17. It has also been pointed out that if quantum states of the brain have to be taken into account (as they will be if mental states are at all dependent on them), then exact duplication at the relevant level of organization will be ruled out by quantum mechanical principles: see Roger Penrose, *The Emperor's New Mind: Concerning Computers, Minds, and the Laws of Physics* (Oxford: Oxford University Press, 1989), p. 270.

is biochemical, as are the *proximate* causal factors favouring selection. But these causal factors are themselves effects, and the chain of causation can easily take us beyond the biochemical sphere. After all, we *know* that minds can affect the evolution of organisms, for the intelligent activities of human beings have done so within historical time. So there is nothing miraculous or non-naturalistic in the idea that the evolution of mind and that of body are *mutually interactive*, just as (on my view) individual minds and bodies are themselves mutually interactive. Thus, my answer to the 'evolutionary' objection is that, unless it is presumed, question-beggingly, that only if the mental were biologically based could it affect the environmental selective pressures on organisms, it cannot be held that a non-biological view of the mental such as mine is at odds with evolutionary theory.

But we need not take a purely defensive stance on this issue. It is worth remarking that archaeological evidence points to the occurrence of a fundamental intellectual transition in the human race some 35,000 years ago, not apparently connected with any radical biological or neurological development in the human organism.[18] This was a transition from a primitive condition in which human creativity was limited to the production of the most rudimentary and severely practical tools to a condition recognizably akin to our own, with the flourishing of visual and plastic arts reflective of a sophisticated aesthetic sensibility. The development of this condition, we may reasonably suppose, went hand-in-hand with that of true language, systems of religious thought, and the beginnings of political structures. At the root of these developments, it seems, was the emergence of genuine systems of *representation*, without which the sophisticated level of thought, communication and social structure essential for personal being would be impossible. Now, as I say, it seems likely that these developments were *not* the upshot of any radical change in human brain structure or neural processing capacity, but arose rather through concomitant changes in patterns of social interaction and organization.[19] And indeed we can observe essentially the same phenomenon in microcosm today in the education and socialization of human infants—who, unless they are subjected to appropriate social, cultural and linguistic stimuli at an early age, are doomed never to develop a truly human personality and character. The implication of all this, I suggest, is that selves or persons are not created through biological processes but rather through socio-cultural forces, that is, through the cooperative efforts of other selves or persons. Persons create persons, quite literally.

18. See Randall White, 'Visual Thinking in the Ice Age', *Scientific American* 261 (July 1989), pp. 74–81, and 'Rethinking the Middle/Upper Paleolithic Transition', *Current Anthropology* 23 (1982), pp. 169–92. See also the papers by White and others in Paul Mellars and Chris Stringer (eds.), *The Human Revolution: Behavioural and Biological Perspectives on the Origins of Modern Humans* (Edinburgh: Edinburgh University Press, 1989), especially section 2.

19. This would be consistent with much of the recent work of psychologists, anthropologists and ethologists presented in Richard Byrne and Andrew Whiten (eds.), *Machiavellian Intelligence: Social Expertise and the Evolution of Intellect in Monkeys, Apes, and Humans* (Oxford: Clarendon Press, 1988).

The picture I am sketching of self-creation and the evolution of human personality is not all fanciful or 'unscientific'. On the contrary, what seems utterly fanciful and facile is the biological reductivism which we see promoted so forcefully by many philosophers today.[20] When we reflect on how much we depend for our human condition upon the artificial and social environment that we ourselves have created, it seems quite incredible to suppose that one could hope to explain the human condition as having a basis solely in the organization of the human brain. Indeed, where human brain development and structure *do* differ significantly from those of the higher primates like chimpanzees—for instance, in connection with our respective linguistic capacities—it seems proper to regard the difference as being at least as much a *product* as a *cause* of the different life-styles of human beings and primates. For, of course, the neural structures in these distinctive parts of the human brain develop in human infants only in response to the right sorts of educative and social influences. It is true that a chimpanzee cannot, by being treated from birth like a human child, be made to develop in the way that the latter does, and this seems to betoken some innate biological difference. But we cannot assume that what we possess and the chimpanzees lack is some innate propensity specifically to develop human personality, language-use, aesthetic appreciation, mathematical abilities, and so forth. For it may be that what debars the chimpanzees from taking advantage of our human processes of socialization and personality-creation is not an innate inability to acquire the capacities which these processes confer upon us, but rather just an inability to engage appropriately with these particular processes, geared as they are to specifically human needs and characteristics. After all, a human being could probably never learn to swim if it had to take lessons from dolphins: but this does not show that it is impossible for human beings to acquire a capacity to swim, only that the acquisition process must be one that is geared to human limitations. In like manner, it is not inconceivable that chimpanzees could be inducted into processes of personality-creation, if only processes appropriately tailored to their particular limitations could be discovered.[21] (Whatever one makes of the attempts to teach chimpanzees such as Washoe the genuine use of language, it is clear that they only even began to look successful when they took into account chimpanzees' severely restricted capacities for vocalization, and substituted sign-language for speech.[22]

20. My opposition extends even to the most sophisticated modern proponents of the biological approach, such as Ruth G. Millikan: see her *Language, Thought, and Other Biological Categories* (Cambridge, MA: MIT Press, 1984). However, a detailed critique must await another occasion.

21. I should remark, incidentally, that I by no means wish to deny *mentality* to chimpanzees and other higher primates, though I very much doubt whether any such animal may be said to possess or embody a 'self', as I have defined that term. Thus, inasmuch as mental states necessarily attach to psychological subjects which are not to be identified with biological bodies. I am committed to the view that persons or serves are not the only species of psychological substance, and that—in an older terminology—there are 'animal-souls' which find a place 'below' ourselves in a hierarchy of psychological substances. I hope to discuss this issue more fully elsewhere.

22. See, e.g., Eugene Linden, *Apes, Men and Language* (Harmondsworth: Penguin Books, 1976).

Perhaps the following analogy will help to convey the general sense of my proposal. A potter takes a lump of clay—which has, as such, no specific *propensity* to be formed into any sort of artefact, such as a statue or a vase, though it is *suitable* material for such a purpose, in a way that a bunch of feathers, say, would not be—and he forms it into, let us say, a vase. In creating the vase he has created a new substantial particular, distinct from, though of course embodied in, the lump of clay. In like manner, I suggest, human persons acting cooperatively take the biological 'clay' of their offspring and 'shape' it into new persons. And this 'clay', though of course it has to be *suited* to the 'shaping' processes applied to it, need not be thought of as having a specific *propensity* to receive such a 'shape'. Finally, to complete the analogy, a human person, emerging from this 'shaping' process, is a new substantial particular, distinct from though embodied in the biological entity that is the 'clay'. It is no accident, surely, that it is precisely this metaphor for the creation of persons that we find so often in religious and mythic literature. Note, furthermore, one aspect of the analogy which is particularly apt: what constitutes 'suitable' material for formation into an artefact of any given sort is not purely a function of the inherent properties of that material together with the nature of the sort of artefact in question, but *also* a function of the sorts of creative processes that the artificer is equipped to apply to the material. Clay is a suitable material to make into vases as far as *human* artificers are concerned, but only because human beings have hands with which they can shape the clay. It should also be said, though, that many processes of artefact-creation are facilitated, or sometimes only made possible, through the use of previously created artefacts (for example, the potter's wheel). In like manner, now, what makes *human* biological material 'suitable' for the creation of persons is not just a function of the inherent biological characteristics of that material together with the nature of the psychological capacities which need to be conferred, but also a function of the creative processes available to us given our own particular limitations, although indeed some of these limitations may be progressively transcended through the exploitation of previous products of our own creativity, that is, through exploitation of our growing socio-cultural, linguistic and technological heritage.

I should just stress, in conclusion, that what I have just been developing *is* only an analogy: I do not want to suggest that persons literally *are* artefacts, other than in the liberal sense that they are products of personal creativity. Above all, unlike material artefacts, persons or selves are *simple* substances: parts of their bodies are not parts of *them*, as bits of clay are parts of a vase. Moreover, whereas it is plausible to hold that all of a vase's intrinsic properties supervene upon certain properties of its constituent clay, it is not, as we have seen, reasonable to regard the self's psychological properties as supervening upon any properties of its body, such as neurophysiological properties of its brain. The self is what it is, and not another thing.

Chapter 50

Remarks on the mind–body question

E. Wigner

Introductory comments

FREEMAN Dyson, in a very thoughtful article,[1] points to the everbroadening scope of scientific inquiry. Whether or not the relation of mind to body will enter the realm of scientific inquiry in the near future—and the present writer is prepared to admit that this is an open question—it seems worthwhile to summarize the views to which a dispassionate contemplation of the most obvious facts leads. The present writer has no other qualification to offer his views than has any other physicist and he believes that most of his colleagues would present similar opinions on the subject, if pressed.

Until not many years ago, the 'existence' of a mind or soul would have been passionately denied by most physical scientists. The brilliant successes of mechanistic and, more generally, macroscopic physics and of chemistry overshadowed the obvious fact that thoughts, desires, and emotions are not made of matter, and it was nearly universally accepted among physical scientists that there is nothing besides matter. The epitome of this belief was the conviction that, if we knew the positions and velocities of all atoms at one instant of time, we could compute the fate of the universe for all future. Even today, there are adherents to this view[2] though fewer among the physicists than—ironically enough—among biochemists.

There are several reasons for the return, on the part of most physical scientists, to the spirit of Descartes's '*Cogito ergo sum*,' which recognizes the thought, that is, the mind, as primary. First, the brilliant successes of mechanics not only faded into the past; they were also recognised as partial successes, relating to a narrow range of phenomena, all in the macroscopic domain. When the province of physical theory

E. Wigner, 'Remarks on the Mind–Body Question'. In *Symmetries and Reflections: Scientific Essays of Eugene P. Wigner* (Cambridge, MA: MIT Press, 1967).

1. F. J. Dyson, *Scientific American*, 199, 74 (1958). Several cases are related in this article in which regions of inquiry, which were long considered to be outside the province of science, were drawn into this province and, in fact, became focuses of attention. The best-known example is the interior of the atom, which was considered to be a metaphysical subject before Rutherford's proposal of his nuclear model, in 1911.
2. The book most commonly blamed for this view is E. F. Haeckel's *Welträtsel* (1899). However, the views propounded in this book are less extreme (though more confused) than those of the usual materialistic philosophy.

was extended to encompass microscopic phenomena, through the creation of quantum mechanics, the concept of consciousness came to the fore again: it was not possible to formulate the laws of quantum mechanics in a fully consistent way without reference to the consciousness.[3] All that quantum mechanics purports to provide are probability connections between subsequent impressions (also called 'apperceptions') of the consciousness, and even though the dividing line between the observer, whose consciousness is being affected, and the observed physical object can be shifted towards the one or the other to a considerable degree,[4] it cannot be eliminated. It may be premature to believe that the present philosophy of quantum mechanics will remain a permanent feature of future physical theories; it will remain remarkable, in whatever way our future concepts may develop, that the very study of the external world led to the conclusion that the content of the consciousness is an ultimate reality.

It is perhaps important to point out at this juncture that the question concerning the existence of almost anything (even the whole external world) is not a very relevant question. All of us recognize at once how meaningless the query concerning the existence of the electric field in vacuum would be. All that is relevant is that the concept of the electric field is useful for communicating our ideas and for our own thinking. The statement that it 'exists' means only that: (*a*) it can be measured, hence uniquely defined, and (*b*) that its knowledge is useful for understanding past phenomena and in helping to foresee further events. It can be made part of the *Weltbild*. This observation may well be kept in mind during the ensuing discussion of the quantum mechanical description of the external world.

The language of quantum mechanics

The present and the next sections try to describe the concepts in terms of which quantum mechanics teaches us to store and communicate information, to describe the regularities found in nature. These concepts may be called the language of quantum mechanics. We shall not be interested in the regularities themselves, that is, the contents of the book of quantum mechanics, only in the language. It may be that the following description of the language will prove too brief and too abstract for those who are unfamiliar with the subject, and too tedious for those who are

3. W. Heisenberg expressed this most poignantly [*Daedalus*, 87, 99 (1958)]: 'The laws of nature which we formulate mathematically in quantum theory deal no longer with the particles themselves but with our knowledge of the elementary particles.' And later: 'The conception of objective reality . . . evaporated into the . . . mathematics that represents no longer the behavior of elementary particles but rather our knowledge of this behavior.' The 'our' in this sentence refers to the observer who plays a singular role in the epistemology of quantum mechanics. He will be referred to in the first person and statements made in the first person will always refer to the observer.

4. J. von Neumann, *Mathematische Grundlagen der Quantenmechanik* (Berlin: Julius Springer, 1932), Chapter VI; English translation (Princeton, N.J.: Princeton University Press, 1955).

familiar with it.[5] It should, nevertheless, be helpful. However, the knowledge of the present and of the succeeding section is not necessary for following the later ones, except for parts of the section on the Simplest Answer to the Mind–Body Question.

Given any object, all the possible knowledge concerning that object can be given as its wave function. This is a mathematical concept the exact nature of which need not concern us here—it is composed of a (countable) infinity of numbers. If one knows these numbers, one can foresee the behavior of the object as far as it *can* be foreseen. More precisely, the wave function permits one to foretell with what probabilities the object will make one or another impression on us if we let it interact with us either directly, or indirectly. The object may be a radiation field, and its wave function will tell us with what probability we shall see a flash if we put our eyes at certain points, with what probability it will leave a dark spot on a photographic plate if this is placed at certain positions. In many cases the probability for one definite sensation will be so high that it amounts to a certainty—this is always so if classical mechanics provides a close enough approximation to the quantum laws.

The information given by the wave function is communicable. If someone else somehow determines the wave function of a system, he can tell me about it and, according to the theory, the probabilities for the possible different impressions (or 'sensations') will be equally large, no matter whether he or I interact with the system in a given fashion. In this sense, the wave function 'exists.'

It has been mentioned before that even the complete knowledge of the wave function does not permit one always to foresee with certainty the sensations one may receive by interacting with a system. In some cases, one event (seeing a flash) is just as likely as another (not seeing a flash). However, in most cases the impression (e.g., the knowledge of having or not having seen a flash) obtained in this way permits one to foresee later impressions with an increased certainty. Thus, one may be sure that, if one does not see a flash if one looks in one direction, one surely does see a flash if one subsequently looks in another direction. The property of observations to increase our ability for foreseeing the future follows from the fact that all knowledge of wave functions is based, in the last analysis, on the 'impressions' we receive. In fact, the wave function is only a suitable language for describing the body of knowledge—gained by observations—which is relevant for predicting the future behaviour of the system. For this reason, the interactions which may create one or another sensation in us are also called observations, or measurements. One realises

5. The contents of this section should be part of the standard material in courses on quantum mechanics. They are given here because it may be helpful to recall them even on the part of those who were at one time already familiar with them, because it is not expected that every reader of these lines had the benefit of a course in quantum mechanics, and because the writer is well aware of the fact that most courses in quantum mechanics do not take up the subject here discussed. See also, in addition to references 3 and 4, W. Pauli, *Handbuch der Physik*, Section 2.9, particularly page 148 (Berlin: Julius Springer, 1933). Also F. London and E. Bauer, *La Théorie de l'observation en mécanique quantique* (Paris: Hermann and Co., 1939). The last authors observe (page 41), 'Remarquons le rôle essential que jouela conscience de l'observateur . . .'.

that *all* the information which the laws of physics provide consists of probability connections between subsequent impressions that a system makes on one if one interacts with it repeatedly, i.e., if one makes repeated measurements on it. The wave function is a convenient summary of that part of the past impressions which remains relevant for the probabilities of receiving the different possible impressions when interacting with the system at later times.

An example

It may be worthwhile to illustrate the point of the preceding section on a schematic example. Suppose that all our interactions with the system consist in looking at a certain point in a certain direction at times t_0, $t_0 + 1$, $t_0 + 2$, . . . , and our possible sensations are seeing or not seeing a flash. The relevant law of nature could then be of the form: 'If you see a flash at time t, you will see a flash at time $t + 1$ with a probability ¼, no flash with a probability ¾ if you see no flash, then the next observation will give a flash with the probability ¾, no flash with a probability ¼ there are no further probability connections.' Clearly, this law can be verified or refuted with arbitrary accuracy by a sufficiently long series of observations. The wave function in such a case depends only on the last observation and may be ψ_1 if a flash has been seen at the last interaction, ψ_2 if no flash was noted. In the former case, that is for ψ_1, a calculation of the probabilities of flash and no flash after unit time interval gives the values ¼ and ¾ for ψ_2 these probabilities must turn out to be ¾ and ¼. This agreement of the predictions of the law in quotation marks with the law obtained through the use of the wave function is not surprising. One can either say that the wave function was invented to yield the proper probabilities, or that the law given in quotation marks has been obtained by having carried out a calculation with the wave functions, the use of which we have learned from Schrödinger.

The communicability of the information means, in the present example, that if someone else looks at time t, and tells us whether he saw a flash, we can look at time $t+1$ and observe a flash with the same probabilities as if we had seen or not seen the flash at time t ourselves. In other words, he can tell us what the wave function is: ψ_1 if he did, ψ_2 if he did not see a flash.

The preceding example is a very simple one. In general, there are many types of interactions into which one can enter with the system, leading to different types of observations or measurements. Also, the probabilities of the various possible impressions gained at the next interaction may depend not only on the last, but on the results of many prior observations. The important point is that the impression which one gains at an interaction may, and in general does, modify the probabilities with which one gains the various possible impressions at later interactions. In other words, the impression which one gains at an interaction, called also *the result of an observation*, modifies the wave function of the system. The modified wave function is, furthermore, in general unpredictable before the impression gained at the interaction has entered our consciousness: it is the entering of an impression into our consciousness which alters the wave function because it modifies our appraisal of the probabilities for different impressions which we expect to receive in the future. It is at this point that the consciousness enters the theory unavoidably and unalterably. If one speaks in terms of the wave function, its changes are coupled with the entering of impressions into our consciousness. If one formulates the laws of quantum mechanics in terms of probabilities of impressions, these are *ipso facto* the primary concepts with which one deals.

It is natural to inquire about the situation if one does not make the observation oneself but lets someone else carry it out. What is the wave function if my friend looked at the place where the flash might show at time t? The answer is that the information available about the *object* cannot be described by a wave function. One could attribute a wave function to the joint system: friend plus object, and this joint system would have a wave function also after the interaction, that is, after my friend has looked. I can then enter into interaction with this joint system by asking my friend whether he saw a flash. If his answer gives me the impression that he did, the joint wave function of friend + object will change into one in which they even have separate wave functions (the total wave function is a product) and the wave function of the object is ψ_1. If he says no, the wave function of the object is ψ_2, i.e., the object behaves from then on as if I had observed it and had seen no flash. However, even in this case, in which the observation was carried out by someone else, the typical change in the wave function occurred only when some information (the *yes* or *no* of my friend) entered *my* consciousness. It follows that the quantum description of objects is influenced by impressions entering my consciousness.[6] Solipsism may be logically consistent with present quantum mechanics, monism in the sense of materialism is not. The case against solipsism was given at the end of the first section.

The reasons for materialism

The principal argument against materialism is not that illustrated in the last two sections: that it is incompatible with quantum theory. The principal argument is that thought processes and consciousness are the primary concepts, that our knowledge of the external world is the content of our consciousness and that the consciousness, therefore, cannot be denied. On the contrary, logically, the external world could be denied—though it is not very practical to do so. In the words of Niels Bohr,[7] 'The word consciousness, applied to ourselves as well as to others, is

6. The essential point is not that the states of objects cannot be described by means of position and momentum co-ordinates (because of the uncertainty principle). The point is, rather, that the valid description, by means of the wave function, is influenced by impressions entering our consciousness. See in this connection the remark of London and Bauer, quoted above, and S. Watanabe's article in *Louis de Broglie, Physicien et Penseur* (Paris: Albin Michel, 1952), p. 385.
7. N. Bohr, *Atomic Physics and Human Knowledge*, section on 'Atoms and Human Knowledge,' in particular p. 92 (New York: John Wiley & Sons, 1960).

indispensable when dealing with the human situation.' In view of all this, one may well wonder how materialism, the doctrine[8] that 'life could be explained by sophisticated combinations of physical and chemical laws,' could so long be accepted by the majority of scientists.

The reason is probably that it is an emotional necessity to exalt the problem to which one wants to devote a lifetime. If one admitted anything like the statement that the laws we study in physics and chemistry are limiting laws, similar to the laws of mechanics which exclude the consideration of electric phenomena, or the laws of macroscopic physics which exclude the consideration of 'atoms,' we could not devote ourselves to our study as wholeheartedly as we have to in order to recognise any new regularity in nature. The regularity which we are trying to track down must appear as the all-important regularity—if we are to pursue it with sufficient devotion to be successful. Atoms were also considered to be an unnecessary figment before macroscopic physics was essentially complete—and one can well imagine a master, even a great master, of mechanics to say: 'Light may exist but I do not need it in order to explain the phenomena in which I am interested.' The present biologist uses the same words about mind and consciousness; he uses them as an expression of his disbelief in these concepts. Philosophers do not need these illusions and show much more clarity on the subject. The same is true of most truly great natural scientists, at least in their years of maturity. It is now true of almost all physicists—possibly, but not surely, because of the lesson we learned from quantum mechanics. It is also possible that we learned that the principal problem is no longer the fight with the adversities of nature but the difficulty of understanding ourselves if we want to survive.

Simplest answer to the mind–body question

Let us first specify the question which is outside the province of physics and chemistry but is an obviously meaningful (because operationally defined) question: Given the most complete description of my body (admitting that the concepts used in this description change as physics develops), what are my sensations? Or, perhaps, with what probability will I have one of the several possible sensations? This is clearly a valid and important question which refers to a concept—sensations—which does not exist in present-day physics or chemistry. Whether the question will eventually become a problem of physics or psychology, or another science, will depend on the development of these disciplines.

Naturally, I have direct knowledge only of my own sensations and there is no strict logical reason to believe that others have similar experiences. However, every-

8. The quotation is from William S. Beck, *The Riddle of Life, Essay in Adventures of the Mind* (New York: Alfred A. Knopf, 1960), p. 35. This article is an eloquent statement of the attitude of the open-minded biologists toward the questions discussed in the present note.

body believes that the phenomenon of sensations is widely shared by organisms which we consider to be living. It is very likely that, if certain physico-chemical conditions are satisfied, a consciousness, that is, the property of having sensations, arises. This statement will be referred to as our first thesis. The sensations will be simple and undifferentiated if the physico-chemical substrate is simple; it will have the miraculous variety and colour which the poets try to describe if the substrate is as complex and well organized as a human body.

The physico-chemical conditions and properties of the substrate not only create the consciousness, they also influence its sensations most profoundly. Does, conversely, the consciousness influence the physico-chemical conditions? In other words, does the human body deviate from the laws of physics, as gleaned from the study of inanimate nature? The traditional answer to this question is, 'No': the body influences the mind but the mind does not influence the body.[9] Yet at least two reasons can be given to support the opposite thesis, which will be referred to as the second thesis.

The first and, to this writer, less cogent reason is founded on the quantum theory of measurements, described earlier in sections 2 and 3. In order to present this argument, it is necessary to follow my description of the observation of a 'friend' in somewhat more detail than was done in the example discussed before. Let us assume again that the object has only two states, ψ_1 and ψ_2. If the state is, originally, ψ_1, the state of object plus observer will be, after the interaction, $\psi_1 \times \chi_1$; if the state of the object is ψ_2, the state of object plus observer will be $\psi_2 \times \chi_2$ after the interaction. The wave functions χ_1 and χ_2 give the state of the observer; in the first case he is in a state which responds to the question 'Have you seen a flash?' with 'Yes'; in the second state, with 'No.' There is nothing absurd in this so far.

Let us consider now an initial state of the object which is a linear combination $\alpha\, \psi_1 + \beta\, \psi_2$ of the two states ψ_1 and ψ_2. It then *follows* from the linear nature of the quantum mechanical equations of motion that the state of object plus observer is, after the interaction, $\alpha\, (\psi_1 \times \chi_1) + \beta\, (\psi_2 \times \chi_2)$. If I now ask the observer whether he saw a flash, he will with a probability $|\alpha|^2$ say that he did, and in this case the object will also give to me the responses as if it were in the state ψ_1. If the observer answers 'No'—the probability for this is $|\beta|^2$—the object's responses from then on will correspond to a wave function ψ_2. The probability is zero that the observer will say 'Yes,' but the object gives the response which ψ_2 would give because the wave function $\alpha\, (\psi_1 \times \chi_1) + \beta\, (\psi_2 \times \chi_2)$ of the joint system has no $(\psi_2 \times \chi_1)$ component. Similarly, if the observer denies having seen a flash, the behavior of the object cannot correspond to χ_1 because the joint wave function has no $(\psi_1 \times \chi_2)$ component. All this is quite satisfactory: the theory of measurement, direct or indirect, is

9. This writer does not profess to a knowledge of all, or even of the majority of all, metaphysical theories. It may be significant, nevertheless, that he never found an affirmative answer to the query of the text—not even after having perused the relevant articles in the earlier (more thorough) editions of the *Encyclopaedia Britannica.*

logically consistent so long as I maintain my privileged position as ultimate observer.

However, if after having completed the whole experiment I ask my friend, 'What did you feel about the flash before I asked you?' he will answer, 'I told you already, I did [did not] see a flash,' as the case may be. In other words, the question whether he did or did not see the flash was already decided in his mind, before I asked him.[10] If we accept this, we are driven to the conclusion that the proper wave function immediately after the interaction of friend and object was already either $\psi_1 \times \chi_1$ or $\psi_1 \times \chi_2$ and not the linear combination $\alpha\ (\psi_1 \times \chi_1) + \beta\ (\psi_2 \times \chi_2)$. This is a contradiction, because the state described by the wave function $\alpha\ (\psi_1 \times \chi_1) + \beta\ (\psi_2 \times \chi_2)$ describes a state that has properties which neither $\psi_1 \times \chi_1$ nor $\psi_2 \times \chi_2$ has. If we substitute for 'friend' some simple physical apparatus, such as an atom which may or may not be excited by the light-flash, this difference has observable effects and *there is no doubt that* $\alpha\ (\psi_1 \times \chi_1) + \beta\ (\psi_2 \times \chi_2)$ *describes the properties of the joint system correctly, the assumption that the wave function is either* $\psi_1 \times \chi_1$ or $\psi_2 \times \chi_2$ *does not.* If the atom is replaced by a conscious being, the wave function $\alpha\ (\psi_1 \times \chi_1) + \beta\ (\psi_2 \times \chi_2)$ (which also follows from the linearity of the equations) appears absurd because it implies that my friend was in a state of suspended animation before he answered my question.[11]

It follows that the being with a consciousness must have a different role in quantum mechanics than the inanimate measuring device: the atom considered above. In particular, the quantum mechanical equations of motion cannot be linear if the preceding argument is accepted. This argument implies that 'my friend' has the same types of impressions and sensations as I—in particular, that, after interacting with the object, he is not in that state of suspended animation which corresponds to the wave function $\alpha\ (\psi_1 \times \chi_1) + \beta\ (\psi_2 \times \chi_2)$. It is not necessary to see a contradiction here from the point of view of orthodox quantum mechanics, and there is none if we believe that the alternative is meaningless, whether my friend's consciousness contains either the impression of having seen a flash or of not having

10. F. London and E. Bauer (*op. cit.*, reference 5) on page 42 say, 'Il [l'observateur] dispose d'une faculté caractéristique et bien familière, que nous pouvons appeler la 'faculté d'introspection': il peut se rendre compte de manière immédiate de son propre état.'

11. In an article which will appear soon [*Werner Heisenberg und die Physik unserer Zeit* (Braunschweig: Friedr. Vieweg, 1961)] G. Ludwig discusses the theory of measurements and arrives at the conclusion that quantum mechanical theory cannot have unlimited validity (see, in particular, Section IIIa, also Ve). This conclusion is in agreement with the point of view here represented. However, Ludwig believes that quantum mechanics is valid only in the limiting case of microscopic systems, whereas the view here represented assumes it to be valid for all inanimate objects. At present, there is no clear evidence that quantum mechanics becomes increasingly inaccurate as the size of the system increases, and the dividing line between microscopic and macroscopic systems is surely not very sharp. Thus, the human eye can perceive as few as three quanta, and the properties of macroscopic crystals are grossly affected by a single dislocation. For these reasons, the present writer prefers the point of view represented in the text even though he does not wish to deny the possibility that Ludwig's more narrow limitation of quantum mechanics may be justified ultimately.

seen a flash. However, to deny the existence of the consciousness of a friend to this extent is surely an unnatural attitude, approaching solipsism, and few people, in their hearts, will go along with it.

The preceding argument for the difference in the roles of inanimate observation tools and observers with a consciousness—hence for a violation of physical laws where consciousness plays a role—is entirely cogent so long as one accepts the tenets of orthodox quantum mechanics in all their consequences. Its weakness for providing a specific effect of the consciousness on matter lies in its total reliance on these tenets—a reliance which would be, on the basis of our experiences with the ephemeral nature of physical theories, difficult to justify fully.

The second argument to support the existence of an influence of the consciousness on the physical world is based on the observation that we do not know of any phenomenon in which one subject is influenced by another without exerting an influence thereupon. This appears convincing to this writer. It is true that under the usual conditions of experimental physics or biology, the influence of any consciousness is certainly very small. 'We do not need the assumption that there is such an effect.' It is good to recall, however, that the same may be said of the relation of light to mechanical objects. Mechanical objects influence light—otherwise we could not see them—but experiments to demonstrate the effect of light on the motion of mechanical bodies are difficult. It is unlikely that the effect would have been detected had theoretical considerations not suggested its existence, and its manifestation in the phenomenon of light pressure.

More difficult questions

Even if the two theses of the preceding section are accepted, very little is gained for science as we understand science: as a correlation of a body of phenomena. Actually, the two theses in question are more similar to existence theorems of mathematics than to methods of construction of solutions and we cannot help but feel somewhat helpless as we ask the much more difficult question: how could the two theses be verified experimentally? i.e., how could a body of phenomena be built around them. It seems that there is no solid guide to help in answering this question and one either has to admit to full ignorance or to engage in speculations.

Before turning to the question of the preceding paragraph, let us note in which way the consciousnesses are related to each other and to the physical world. The relations in question again show a remarkable similarity to the relation of light quanta to each other and to the material bodies with which mechanics deals. Light quanta do not influence each other directly[12] but only by influencing material bodies which then influence other light quanta. Even in this indirect way, their

12. This statement is certainly true in an approximation which is much better than is necessary for our purposes.

interaction is appreciable only under exceptional circumstances. Similarly, consciousnesses never seem to interact with each other directly but only via the physical world. Hence, any knowledge about the consciousness of another being must be mediated by the physical world.

At this point, however, the analogy stops. Light quanta can interact directly with virtually any material object but each consciousness is uniquely related to some physico-chemical structure through which alone it receives impressions. There is, apparently, a correlation between each consciousness and the physico-chemical structure of which it is a captive, which has no analogue in the inanimate world. Evidently, there are enormous gradations between consciousnesses, depending on the elaborate or primitive nature of the structure on which they can lean: the sets of impressions which an ant or a microscopic animal or a plant receives surely show much less variety than the sets of impressions which man can receive. However, we can, at present, at best, guess at these impressions. Even our knowledge of the consciousness of other men is derived only through analogy and some innate knowledge which is hardly extended to other species.

It follows that there are only two avenues through which experimentation can proceed to obtain information about our first thesis: observation of infants where we may be able to sense the progress of the awakening of consciousness, and by discovering phenomena postulated by the second thesis, in which the consciousness modifies the usual laws of physics. The first type of observation is constantly carried out by millions of families, but perhaps with too little purposefulness. Only very crude observations of the second type have been undertaken in the past, and all these antedate modern experimental methods. So far as it is known, all of them have been unsuccessful. However, every phenomenon is unexpected and most unlikely until it has been discovered—and some of them remain unreasonable for a long time after they have been discovered. Hence, lack of success in the past need not discourage.

Non-linearity of equations as indication of life

The preceding section gave two proofs—they might better be called indications—for the second thesis, the effect of consciousness on physical phenomena. The first of these was directly connected with an actual process, the quantum mechanical observation, and indicated that the usual description of an indirect observation is probably incorrect if the primary observation is made by a being with consciousness. It may be worthwhile to show a way out of the difficulty which we encountered.

The simplest way out of the difficulty is to accept the conclusion which forced itself on us: to assume that the joint system of friend plus object cannot be described by a wave function after the interaction—the proper description of their state is a mixture.[13] The wave function is $(\psi_1 \times \chi_1)$ with a probability $|\alpha|^2$; it is $(\psi_2 \times \chi_2)$ with a probability $|\beta|^2$. It was pointed out already by Bohm[14] that, if the system is sufficiently complicated, it may be in practice impossible to ascertain a difference between certain mixtures, and some pure states (states which *can* be described by a wave function). In order to exhibit the difference, one would have to subject the system (friend plus object) to very complicated observations which cannot be carried out in practice. This is in contrast to the case in which the flash or the absence of a flash is registered by an atom, the state of which I can obtain precisely by much simpler observations. This way out of the difficulty amounts to the postulate that the equations of motion of quantum mechanics cease to be linear, in fact that they are grossly non-linear if conscious beings enter the picture.[15] We saw that the linearity condition led uniquely to the unacceptable wave function $\alpha\,(\psi_1 \times \chi_1) + \beta\,(\psi_2 \times \chi_2)$ for the joint state. Actually, in the present case, the final state is uncertain even in the sense that it cannot be described by a wave function. The statistical element which, according to the orthodox theory, enters only if I make an observation enters equally if my friend does.

It remains remarkable that there is a continuous transition from the state $\alpha(\psi_1 \times \chi_1) + \beta(\psi_2 \times \chi_2)$ to the mixture of $\psi_1 \times \chi_1$ and $\psi_2 \times \chi_2$ with probabilities $|\alpha|^2$ and $|\beta|^2$, so that every member of the continuous transition has all the statistical properties demanded by the theory of measurements. Each member of the transition, except that which corresponds to orthodox quantum mechanics, is a mixture, and must be described by a statistical matrix. The statistical matrix of the system friend-plus-object is, after their having interacted ($|\alpha|^2 + |\beta|^2 = 1$),

$$\left\|\begin{matrix} |\alpha|^2 & \alpha\beta^* \cos\delta \\ \alpha^*\beta\cos\delta & |\beta|^2 \end{matrix}\right\|$$

in which the first row and column corresponds to the wave function $\psi_1 \times \chi_1$, the second to $\psi_2 \times \chi_2$. The $\delta = 0$ case corresponds to orthodox quantum mechanics; in this case the statistical matrix is singular and the state of friend-plus-object can be described by a wave function, namely, $\alpha(\psi_1 \times \chi_1) + \beta(\psi_2 \times \chi_2)$. For $\delta = \frac{1}{2}\pi$, we have

13. The concept of the mixture was put forward first by L. Landau, *Z. Physik*, 45, 430 (1927). A more elaborate discussion is found in J. von Neumann's book (footnote 4), Chapter IV. A more concise and elementary discussion of the concept of mixture and its characterisation by a statistical (density) matrix is given in L. Landau and E. Lifshitz, *Quantum Mechanics* (London: Pergamon Press, 1958), pp. 35—38.

14. The circumstance that the mixture of the states $(\psi_1 \times \chi_1)$ and $(\psi_2 \times \chi_2)$, with weights $|\alpha|^2$ and $|\beta|^2$, respectively, cannot be distinguished in practice from the state $\alpha(\psi_1 \times \chi_1) + \beta(\psi_2 \times \chi_2)$, if the states χ are of great complexity, has been pointed out already in Section 22.11 of D. Bohm's *Quantum Theory* (New York: Prentice Hall, 1951). The reader will also be interested in Sections 8.27, 8.28 of this treatise.

15. The non-linearity is of a different nature from that postulated by W. Heisenberg in his theory of elementary particles [cf., e.g., H. P. Dürr, W. Heisenberg, H. Mitter, S. Schlieder, K. Yamazaki, *Z. Naturforsch.*, 14, 441 (1954)]. In our case the equations giving the time variation of the state vector (wave function) are postulated to be non-linear.

the simple mixture of $\psi_1 \times \chi_1$ and $\psi_2 \times \chi_2$, with probabilities $| \alpha |^2$ and $|\beta|^2$, respectively. At intermediate δ, we also have mixtures of two states, with probabilities $\frac{1}{2} + (\frac{1}{4} - |\alpha\beta|^2 \sin \delta)^{\frac{1}{2}}$ and $\frac{1}{2} - (\frac{1}{4} - | \alpha\beta |^2 \sin^2\delta)^{\frac{1}{2}}$. The two states are $\alpha(\psi_1 \times \chi_1) + \beta(\psi_2 \times \chi_2)$ and $-\beta^\circ(\psi_1 \times \chi_1) + \alpha^\circ (\psi^2 \times \chi^2)$ for $\delta = 0$ and go over continuously into $\psi_1 \times \chi_1$ and $\psi_2 \times \chi_2$ as δ increases to $\frac{1}{2}\pi$.

The present writer is well aware of the fact that he is not the first one to discuss the questions which form the subject of this article and that the-surmises of his predecessors were either found to be wrong or unprovable, hence, in the long run, uninteresting. He would not be greatly surprised if the present article shared the fate of those of his predecessors. He feels, however, that many of the earlier speculations on the subject, even if they could not be justified, have stimulated and helped our thinking and emotions and have contributed to re-emphasize the ultimate scientific interest in the question, which is, perhaps, the most fundamental question of all.

Acknowledgement

Reprinted by permission from *The Scientist Speculates*, I. J. Good, ed. (London: William Heinemann, Ltd., 1961; New York: Basic Books, Inc., 1962).

Questions

1. Why should anyone prefer idealism to dualism or materialism? Is idealism wholly at odds with the pursuit of a scientific understanding of the world around us?
2. Idealists hold that what we think of as the physical world is actually mind-dependent: tables, trees, and mountains have no existence outside the mind. But how could that be? Aren't we aware of physical objects at a distance from us?
3. According to Peter Forrest, physicalism faces difficulties that can be met by developing a rigorous dualism. What are some of the difficulties and what would a dualist solution to them look like?
4. E. J. Lowe contends that the self is simple. What is his argument?
5. A longstanding problem for dualism is that of explaining the relation minds bear to bodies, and, in particular, how minds and bodies could causally interact. How would Lowe and Forrest address this problem?
6. Lowe defends what he describes as 'non-Cartesian dualism'. How does this brand of dualism differ from the sort of dualism favored by Forrest?
7. Eugene Wigner, a physicist, advocates a distinctive view of the relation minds bear to the material world. To what extent is that view motivated by purely scientific considerations?
8. How far apart are Wigner and John Foster? How would either Wigner or Foster account for the apparent existence of the universe for several billion years prior to the advent of intelligent conscious creatures?
9. Each of the authors in this part raises significant problems for materialism. Do you think these problems are sufficient to lead fair-minded readers with materialist leanings to abandon materialism? If there were good reasons to abandon materialism, what would be the most promising alternative?
10. Is materialism consistent with the existence of a benevolent, all-powerful God? If not, is this a reason to reject materialism? Is one conception of the mind and its relation to the world especially congenial to the existence of God?

Suggested readings

Foster (1982) provides a prolonged argument for idealism of the sort sketched in Chapter 47; see also Robinson (1982). Contemporary idealism owes much to Berkeley; see his (1710) *Principles of Human Knowledge*. If you start looking for contemporary Berkeleyans, you will find them everywhere. There are the physicists who think that the world is in some way mind dependent; there are the pragmatists, like Putnam–see his Dewey Lectures (1994); and there are the 'externalists' (see Part VII) who regard the mind as encompassing its objects.

Plenty of philosophers who would not regard themselves as idealists have reservations about materialism. Robinson (1993) is an excellent collection; see also Moser and Trout (1995) and Gillett and Loewer (2001) for more recent papers for and against materialism.

Nowadays, philosophers who reject materialism tend to espouse some form of dualism. See Foster (1991), Hart (1988), Lowe (1996), O'Leary-Hawthorne and McDonough (1998), Popper (1955), and Popper and Eccles (1977). Chalmers (1996) defends a brand of dualism (sketched in Chapter 35 that in many respects resembles epiphenomenalism. Averill and Keating, (1981) discuss the question whether mind–body interaction would 'violate' laws of nature governing material systems; see also Lowe (1996); Bricke (1975). Herbert (1998) rejects the dualism/materialism dichotomy.

Quantum physics and its relation to minds in general and consciousness in particular can feature philosophers writing badly about physics and physicists doing bad philosophy. Herbert (1985) and Rea (1986) provide non-technical introductions to quantum theory and its several interpretations. More daring readers can look at Bell (1964), which is discussed at length by Albert (1992); see also Maudlin (1994). Chalmers (1996: chap. 10) includes an interesting discussion; see also Byrne and Hall (1999). Goswami (1989), Hodgson (1991), Lockwood (1989, 1996), Penrose (1989), and Stapp (1995) all find, although in very different ways, significance in quantum theory for accounts of mental phenomena.

Chalmers's (2001) on-line bibliography lists many dozen books and articles—under various rubrics—that challenge the materialists. A glance at that bibliography suggests that, although materialists probably outnumber any particular group of anti-materialists, the latter, as a group, outnumber the former. If you add to this list materialists who hedge their materialism in one way or another—non-reductive materialists, for instance (see Part X)—the imbalance shifts dramatically away from the materialists.

Idealism

Berkeley, G. (1710/1998), *A Treatise Concerning the Principles of Human Knowledge*, ed. J. Dancy. Oxford: Oxford University Press.

Foster, J. (1982), *The Case for Idealism*. London: Routledge & Kegan Paul.

Putnam, H. (1994), 'Sense, Nonsense, and the Senses: An Inquiry into the Powers of the Human Mind'. *Journal of Philosophy* 91: 445–517.

Robinson, H. (1982), *Matter and Sense: A Critique of Contemporary Materialism*. Cambridge: Cambridge University Press.

Materialism pro and con

Chalmers, D. J., ed. (2001), *Contemporary Philosophy of Mind: An Annotated Bibliography* (http://www.u.arizona.edu/~chalmers/biblio.html). Tucson, AZ: University of Arizona.

Corbí, J. E., and J. L. Prades (2000), *Minds, Causes, and Mechanisms: A Case against Physicalism.* Oxford: Blackwell Publishers.

Gillett, C., and B. Loewer, eds. (2001), *Physicalism and Its Discontents.* Cambridge: Cambridge University Press.

Moser, P. K., and J. D. Trout, eds. (1995), *Contemporary Materialism: A Reader.* London: Routledge.

Robinson, H., ed. (1993), *Objections to Physicalism.* Oxford: Clarendon Press.

Dualism

Averill, E. W., and B. Keating (1981), 'Does Interactionism Violate a Law of Classical Physics?', *Mind* 90: 102–7.

Bricke, J. (1975), 'Interaction and Physiology', *Mind* 84: 255–9.

Chalmers, D. J. (1996), *The Conscious Mind: In Search of a Fundamental Theory.* New York: Oxford University Press.

Foster, J. (1991), *The Immaterial Self: A Defense of the Cartesian Dualist Conception of the Mind.* London: Routledge.

Hart, W. D. (1988), *The Engines of the Soul.* Cambridge: Cambridge University Press.

Herbert, R. T. (1998), 'Dualism/Materialism', *Philosophical Quarterly* 48: 145–58.

Lowe, E. J. (1992), 'The Problem of Psychophysical Causation', *Australasian Journal of Philosophy* 70: 263–76.

—— (1996), *Subjects of Experience.* Cambridge: Cambridge University Press.

O'Leary-Hawthorne, J. and J. K. McDonough (1998), 'Numbers, Minds, and Bodies: A Fresh Look at Mind–Body Dualism', *Philosophical Perspectives* 12: 349–71.

Popper, K. R. (1955), 'A Note on the Body–Mind Problem'. *Analysis* 15: 131–35.

—— and J. C. Eccles (1977), *The Self and Its Brain.* New York: Springer International.

Quantum theory and the mind

Albert, D. Z. (1992), *Quantum Mechanics and Experience.* Cambridge, MA: Harvard University Press.

Bell, J. S. (1964), 'On the Einstein–Podolsky–Rosen Paradox', *Physics* 12: 989–99.

Byrne, A., and N. Hall (1999), 'Chalmers on Consciousness and Quantum Mechanics', *Philosophy of Science* 66: 370–90.

Goswami, A. (1989), 'The Idealistic Interpretation of Quantum Mechanics', *Physics Essays* 2: 385–400.

Herbert, N. (1985), *Quantum Reality: Beyond the New Physics.* Garden City: Anchor/Doubleday.

Hodgson, D. H. (1991), *The Mind Matters: Consciousness and Choice in A Quantum World.* Oxford: Clarendon Press.

Lockwood, M. (1989), *Mind, Brain, and Quantum: The Compound 'I'.* Oxford: Basil Blackwell.

Lockwood, M. (1996), 'Many-Minds Interpretations of Quantum Mechanics', *British Journal for the Philosophy of Science* 47: 159–88.

Maudlin, T. (1994), *Quantum Non-Locality and Relativity: Metaphysical Intimations of Modern Physics.* Oxford: Blackwell.

Penrose, R. (1989), *The Emperor's New Mind: Concerning Computers, Minds, and the Laws of Physics.* New York: Oxford University Press.

Rea, A. I. M. (1986), *Quantum Physics: Illusion or Reality?* Cambridge: Cambridge University Press.

Stapp, H. P. (1995), 'The Hard Problem: A Quantum Approach', *Journal of Consciousness Studies* 3: 194–210.

Index